"This new edition of Kaczorowska's *EU Law* deserves to be considered one of the most comprehensive textbooks on the market in this fast moving area of law. Remarkably comprehensive, thoroughly detailed, highly readable and totally engaging, it should be considered essential for any academic or practitioner's bookcase and in any law library. I am confident all law students will consider it a valuable resource that is hard to better."

Joanne Sellick, Plymouth University, UK

"This book provides students with a most comprehensive and up to date analysis of all of the key areas of EU Law. It is clearly written, and provides excellent end-of-chapter reading lists and exam-style questions."

Caoimhin MacMaolain, Trinity College Dublin, Ireland

"*EU Law* is fresh, current and erudite. Since the first edition, it has been popular with staff and students alike. Challenging material is presented clearly and the chapters contain a satisfying range of wider arguments and academic opinion."

Chrisoulla Pawlowska, University of Greenwich, UK

OUTLINE CONTENTS

DETAILED CONTENTS

PREFACE

I am happy to have prepared this edition of EU law now, some three years after the coming into force of the Treaty of Lisbon. Unlike the last edition, there has been time for us all to take a backward look to assess the Treaty.

As we know, much of the Treaty of Lisbon is founded on the basis of the previous Treaties, i.e. the TEU and the EC Treaty. In a slightly similar way this book retains the good foundations of its previous editions, but has been substantially developed. This has been achieved by the participation in the preparation of this edition of a group of excellent academic EU lawyers, who have each reviewed every chapter of the book, and provided comments and suggestions ensuring that the appropriate ground is covered to the best advantage of students and lecturers alike. I express my huge appreciation of their assistance. I am delighted that my readers will have the benefit of their wisdom and experience. In addition, of course, I have been assisted by my publishers who suggested that this edition should include end of chapter questions, extended recommended reading lists and the use of diagrams and tables

Now, a few practical matters:

1. The renumbering of the Treaties articles by the ToL raised the matter of how to present case law decided prior to its entry into force. My solution has been to ignore the pre-ToL numbering and instead put in square brackets the current article number. However, on some rare occasions, use of the old number has been unavoidable. In such instances I have placed in square brackets the current numbering immediately after the old.

2. Whenever possible I refer to the EU, rather than to the "EC" or the "Community", but, occasionally, it has been appropriate to retain the historic reference.

3. I refer to the Court of Justice of the European Union (CJEU) as the European Court of Justice (ECJ). This is done to avoid confusion. Indeed, the name CJEU is used in the Treaties first, to refer to all EU courts, including the ECJ, and second, to refer to the ECJ.

4. More than once it has been suggested that I should include in the book a dictionary of "eurojargon". I have decided not to do this, but instead to direct my readers to the official website of the EU which provides "a Plain Language Guide to Eurojargon". This is available at: http://europa.eu/abc/eurojargon/index_en.htm.

5. My last point is that all the so-called "facts" stated in the end of chapter questions are invented. Any similarity to actual facts or circumstances is entirely coincidental.

I am extremely grateful to the team at my publishers who have brought this to publication, in particular, Fiona Briden, Faye Mousley and Damian Mitchell (thanks Damian for organising the cover design – I hope the readers like it!). Finally, I wish to say a huge "thank you" to Mel Dyer of RefineCatch Limited for being so kind, patient, intuitive and efficient in dealing with the printing and presentation of this book.

This book is up to date as at 1 August 2012.

Alina Kaczorowska

VISUAL TOUR OF *EUROPEAN UNION LAW,* THIRD EDITION

PEDAGOGICAL FEATURES

European Union Law offers an array of pedagogical features specifically designed to enhance your teaching and learning experience.

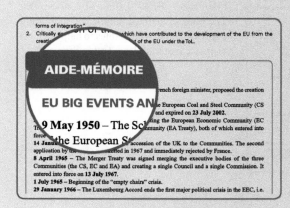

AIDE-MEMOIRES

Visually-stimulating aide-memoires at the end of each chapter help reinforce the key takeaway concepts for students, and provide a useful revision tool.

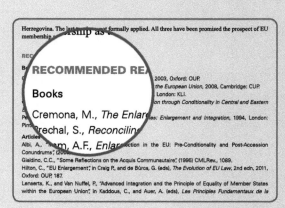

RECOMMENDED READING

Each chapter concludes with a list of important scholarly books and articles relevant to the topic at hand. These key resources guide independent study and provide a useful point of departure for students wishing to develop their studies.

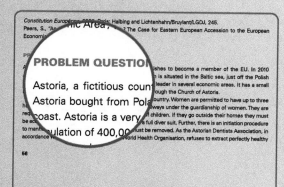

Constitution Européenne 2004, Paris: Halbing and Lichtenhahn/Bruylant/LGDJ, 245.
Peers, S., "An... ...ic Area", ...2 The Case for Eastern European Accession to the European
Economic...

PROBLEM QUESTION

Astoria, a fictitious coun... ...ishes to become a member of the EU. In 2010
Astoria bought from Pol... ...is situated in the Baltic sea, just off the Polish
coast. Astoria is a very... ...leader in several economic areas. It has a small
...ulation of 400,00... ...ough the Church of Astoria.
...country. Women are permitted to have up to three
...ways under the guardianship of women. They are
...children. If they go outside their homes they must
...a full diver suit. Further, there is an initiation procedure
...must be removed. As the Astorian Dentists Association, in
...World Health Organisation, refuses to extract perfectly healthy

56

END OF CHAPTER QUESTIONS

At the end of each chapter you will find assignable problem and essay questions, helping students to think critically and prepare for their assessments.

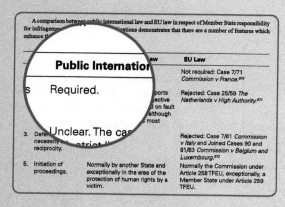

A comparison between public international law and EU law in respect of Member State responsibility for infringeme... ...ations demonstrates that there are a number of features which enhance t...

Public International... aw	**EU Law**
Required.	Not required: Case 7/71 Commission v France.[870]
...ports ...ective ...d on fault ...although ...most	Rejected: Case 25/59 The Netherlands v High Authority.[871]
Unclear. The ca... necessity ...reciprocity.	Rejected: Case 7/61 Commission v Italy and Joined Cases 90 and 91/63 Commission v Belgium and Luxembourg.[972]
5. Initiation of proceedings.	Normally by another State and exceptionally in the area of the protection of human rights by a victim.	Normally the Commission under Article 258 TFEU, exceptionally, a Member State under Article 259 TFEU.

FIGURES, TABLES AND DIAGRAMS

The book contains a number of supporting figures, diagrams and tables to help students visualise material described in the text.

COMPANION WEBSITE

www.routledge.com/cw/kaczorowska

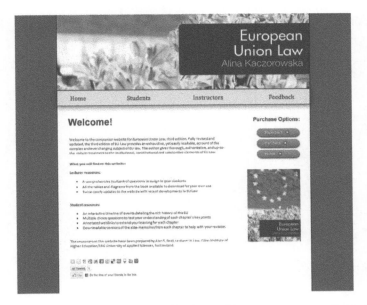

Visit the Companion Website for a whole host of student and instructor resources that both support and enhance the textbook, including:

Lecturer resources

- All the tables and diagrams from the book available to download for your own use
- Twice-yearly updates to the website with recent developments to EU Law

Student resources

- An interactive timeline of events detailing the rich history of the EU
- Multiple choice questions to test your understanding of each chapter's key point
- Annotated weblinks to extend your learning for each chapter
- Downloadable versions of the aide-memoires from each chapter to help with your revision.

TABLE OF CASES

EUROPEAN COURT OF JUSTICE (ALPHABETICAL)

EUROPEAN COURT OF JUSTICE (NUMERICAL)

OPINIONS OF THE EUROPEAN COURT OF JUSTICE

COMMISSION DECISIONS IN COMPETITION CASES (NON-MERGER)

COMMISSION DECISIONS IN MERGER CASES

JUDGMENTS OF THE EUROPEAN COURT OF HUMAN RIGHTS

JUDGMENTS AND OPINIONS OF THE INTERNATIONAL COURT OF JUSTICE AND THE PERMANENT COURT OF INTERNATIONAL JUSTICE

CASES FROM OTHER JURISDICTIONS

France

Germany

Ireland

Italy

USA

TABLE OF LEGISLATION

TREATIES, AGREEMENTS, CONVENTIONS, CHARTERS AND PROTOCOLS

SECONDARY LEGISLATION

Regulations

2003

2006

Directives

(Unless otherwise specified these are of the Council alone)

2006

2007

2008

Decisions

Resolutions Conclusions and Common Understandings of the Council, the Commission and the EP

NATIONAL LEGISLATION

USA

TABLE OF ABBREVIATIONS

AAC – average avoidable cost
AC – Advisory Committee on Restrictive Practices and Dominant Positions
ACP – African, Caribbean and Pacific Countries
AEC – as efficient competitor
AFSJ – Area of Freedom, Security and Justice
A-G – Advocate General
AJDA – Actualité Juridique Droit Administratif
All ER – All England Law Reports
Antitrust L.J – Antitrust Law Journal
AVC – average variable cost
BSE – Bovine Spongiform Encephalopathy
BVerfG – *Bundesverfassungsgericht*, German Federal Constitutional Court
CA – English Court of Appeal
CAP – Common Agricultural Policy
CARDS – Community Assistance for Reconstruction, Development and Stability in the Balkans
CCP – Common Commercial Policy
CCT – Common Customs Tariff
CE – Conseil d'Etat Français
CE marking - *Conformité Européenne*, meaning "European Conformity"
CEE – Charge Having Equivalent Effect to a Customs Duty
CEEP – European Centre of Enterprises with Public Participation
CEPOL – European Police College
CFI – Court of First Instance
CFP – Common Fisheries Policy
CFPR – Centre for Economic Policy Research
CFSP – Common Foreign and Security Policy
CHAP – Complaints Handling – Accueil des Plaignants (welcome to complainants)
Chi. J. Int'l L. – Chicago Journal of International Law
CIVCOM – Committee for Civilian Aspects of Crisis Management
CJEU – Court of Justice of the European Union
CLJ – Cambridge Law Journal
CLP – Current Legal Problems
CLQ – Civil Justice Quarterly
CMLRev – Common Market Law Review
CMLR – Common Market Law Reports

CN – Combined Nomenclature

CoA – Court of Auditors

Colum. J. Eur. L. – Columbia Journal of European Law

COM – Proposed legislation and other Commission communications to the Council and/or the other institutions, and their preparatory papers. Commission documents for the other institutions (legislative proposals, communications, reports, etc.)

Comp. Law – Competition Law Journal

Conn. J. Int'l L – Connecticut Journal of International Law

CoR – Committee of the Regions

COREPER – Committee of Permanent Representatives

COSI – Standing Committee on Internal Security

CS Treaty– European Coal and Steel Community Treaty

CSDP – Common Security and Defence Policy

C-SIS – Central Schengen Information System

CUP – Cambridge University Press

CYELS – Cambridge Yearbook of European Legal Studies

DG – Directorate General

E. Buss. L. Rev – European Business Law Review

EA Treaty – European Atomic Energy Community Treaty

EC – European Community

EC Bull. – Bulletin of the European Communities

ECB – European Central Bank

ECHR – European Convention on Human Rights

ECJ – European Court of Justice

ECLR – European Competition Law Review

ECN – European Competition Network

ECOFIN – Economic and Financial Affairs Council

ECOSOC – United Nations Economic and Social Committee

ECR – European Court Reports

ECSC – European Coal and Steel Community

ECtHR – European Court of Human Rights

EEA – European Economic Area

EEAS – European External Action Service

EEC – European Economic Community

EEIG – European Economic Interest Grouping

EESC – European Economic and Social Committee

EDA – European Defence Agency

EFTA – European Free Trade Association

EGF – European Gendarmerie Force

EHRR – European Human Rights Reports

EIB – European Investment Bank

EJML – European Journal of Migration Law

EJN – European Judicial Network

ELRev – European Law Review

ELJ – European Law Journal

EMCDDA – European Monitoring Centre for Drugs and Drug Addiction

EMS – European Monetary System

EMU – Economic and Monetary Union
EP – European Parliament
EPC – European Political Co-operation
EPL – European Public Law
EPO – European Patent Office
EPP – European Public Procecutor's Office
ERM I – Exchange Rate Mechanism established under the EMS
ERM II – Exchange Rate Mechanism established under the EMU
ERRF – European Rapid Reaction Force
ERTA – European Road Transport Agreement
ESA – EFTA Surveillance Authority
ESCB – European System of Central Banks
ESDI – European Security and Defence Identity
ESDP – Common European Security and Defence Policy
ESIF – European Security and Intelligence Force
ETUC – European Trade Union Confederation
EU – European Union
EU BGs – European Union Battle Groups
EUSC – European Union Satellite Centre
EUISS – European Union Institute for Security Studies
EUMC – European Monitoring Centre for Racism and Xenophobia
EUMS – European Union Military Staff
Euratom – European Atomic Energy Community
EuroCJ – European Competition Law Journal
Eurojust – European Prosecutors Co-operation
Europol – European Police Office
FIN-NET – Financial Dispute Resolution Network
Fordham Intl L.J. – Fordham International Law Journal
FRA – EU Agency for Fundamental Rights
FYR Macedonia – Former Yugoslav Republic of Macedonia
Ga. J. Int'l & Comp. L. – Georgia Journal of International and Comparative Law
GATS – General Agreement on Trade in Services
GATT – General Agreement on Tariffs and Trade
GC – General Council
GDP – Gross Domestic Product
GDR – German Democratic Republic
German L. J. – German Law Journal
GLR – German Law Review
GNI – Gross National Income
GNP – Gross National Product
Harv.L.Rev – Harvard Law Review
HR – High Representative of the Union for Foreign Affairs and Security Policy
Hum.Rts.L.Rev – Human Rights Law Review
ICJ – International Court of Justice
ICJ Rep. – Reports of Judgments, Advisory Opinions and Orders of the International Court of Justice
ICLQ – International and Comparative Law Quarterly

IGC – Intergovernmental Conference
IIA – Inter-Institutional Agreement
ILO – International Labour Organisation
IMI – Internal Market Information System
IMO – International Maritime Organisation
Int'l Rev.L. & Econ – International Review of Law and Economics
IPA – Instrument for Pre-accession Assistance
IPRs – Intellectual Property Rights
ISPA – Instrument for Structural Policies for Pre-Accession
J. Competition L. & Econ. – Journal of Competition Law & Economics
J. Contemp. Health L. & Pol'y – Journal of Contemporary Health Law and Policy
JCMS – Journal of Common Market Studies
JEPP – Journal of European Public Policy
JHA – Justice and Home Affairs
JORF – Journal Officiel de la République Française
JSA – Joint Supervisory Authority for the Schengen Information System
KLI – Kluwer Law International
JV – Joint Venture
LI – Liberal intergovernmentalism
LIEI – Legal Issues of European Integration
LPP – Legal professional privilege
LQR – Law Quarterly Review
LRAIC – long-run average incremental cost
MEP – Member of the European Parliament
MEQR – Measure Having Equivalent Effect to a Quantitative Restriction
MFF – Multiannual Financial Framework
MLG – Multi-Level Governance
MLR – Modern Law Review
MR – Merger Regulation
NAFTA – North American Free Trade Agreement
NATO – North Atlantic Treaty Organisation
NCA – National Competition Authority
NCE – Non-Compulsory Expenditure
NGO – Non-governmental organisation
NHS – National Health Service
NLF – New Legislative Framework
N-SIS – National Schengen Information System
Nw. J. Int'l L. & Bus. – Northwestern Journal of International Law and Business
nyr – not yet reported
OCT – Overseas Countries and Territories
OECD – Organisation for Economic Co-operation and Development
OEEC – Organisation for European Economic Co-operation
OFT – Office of Fair Trading
OHIM – Office for Harmonisation of the Internal Market
OJ – Official Journal of the European Union
OLAF – European Anti-Fraud Office
OMC – Open Method of Co-ordination

OPEC –The Organisation of Petroleum Exporting Countries
OR – Outermost regions
OSCE – Organisation for Security and Co-operation in Europe
OUP – Oxford University Press
Oxford J. Legal Stud. – Oxford Journal of Legal Studies
PCIJ – Permanent Court of International Justice
PJCC – Police and Judicial Co-operation in Criminal Matters
PKK – Kurdish Workers' Party
PLI/Pat – Practising Law Institute
PSC – Political and Security Committee
PSCs – points of single contact
QB – Queen's Bench
QBD – Queen's Bench Division
Q.E. – written question addressed by an MEP to EU institutions
QMV – Qualified Majority Voting
QR – Quantitative restriction
R&D – Research and Development
RBFM – Reglement van het Beamtenfonds voor het Mijnbedrijf, the Regulation
governing the relations between the Dutch social security authority and those
insured by it
REITOX – European Information Network on Drugs and Drug Addiction
RFDA – Revue Française de Droit Administratif
RGM – relevant geographic market
RIAA – Reports of International Arbitral Awards
RIM – Rapid Intervention Mechanism
RIS – Review of International Studies
RPM – relevant product market
RRM – Rapid Reaction Mechanism
RTDE – Revue trimestrielle de droit européen
Rt Hon – Right Honourable
RTM – relevant temporal market
SAPARD – Special Accession Programme for Agriculture and Rural Development
SCE – European Co-operative Society
SEA – Single European Act
SEC – Commission's documents which cannot be classified in any of the other
categories, i.e. a "sweeper up" of all other miscellaneous documents
SFOR – Stabilisation Force in Bosnia and Herzegovina
SGP – Stability and Growth Pact
SIRENE – Supplementary Information Request at the National Entry
SIS – Schengen Information System
SIS-II – second-generation Schengen Information System
SO – Statement of Objections
SSNIP – Small but Significant Non-Transitory Increase in Price
TECS – Europol computer system
TEU –Treaty on European Union
TFEU –Treaty on the Functioning of the European Union
ToA –Treaty of Amsterdam

ToL – Treaty of Lisbon
ToN – Treaty of Nice
TRIPs – Trade Related Aspects of Intellectual Property Rights Agreement
TTBER – Technology Transfer Block Exemption Regulation (Regulation 772/2004)
UKCLR – United Kingdom Competition Law Review
UN – United Nations
UNCTAD – United Nations Conference on Trade and Development
UNESCO – United Nations Educational, Scientific and Cultural Organisation
UNICE – Union of Industrial and Employers' Confederation of Europe
USFTC – United States Federal Trade Commission
VAT – Value Added Tax
WEU – Western European Union
WTO – World Trade Organisation
WW II – World War II
Yale L.J. – Yale Law Journal
YEL – Yearbook of European Law

GLOSSARY OF FOREIGN WORDS

Accueil des plaignants – welcome to complainants

A fortiori – from the stronger, even more so, with even stronger reason

A posteriori – based on observation (i.e. empirical knowledge)

A priori – presupposed, based on deduction or hypothesis rather than experiment, the opposite of a posteriori

Ab initio – from the beginning

Acquis (of the EU) – the entire body of EU law accumulated thus far plus the political, procedural and institutional rules and practices which bind all the Member States together with the European Union

Acte clair – a clear act

Actio popularis – Action to obtain remedy by a person or a group in the name of the general public without being a direct victim or being authorised by a victim to represent him

Ad hoc – for this, for a particular purpose

Ad litem – for the lawsuit

Ad valorem – according to an object's value. Often used in connection with customs duties. Ad valorem duties are levied on products at certain rates per cent on their value

Amicus curiae – "friend of the court", a third party allowed to submit a legal opinion (in the form of an amicus brief) to the court

Bona fides – in (or with) good faith

Contra legem – against the law, interpretation contrary to the meaning of the relevant provision of law

Coup d'état – sudden takeover of the government of a country by elements from within that country (usually by the military), generally carried out by violent or illegal means

Curia Semper Dabit Remedium – court will always give a remedy

Damnum emergens – the loss suffered, as opposed to lucrum cessans

De facto – in fact, actually

De jure – by right, by law, according to law

De minimis – this term comes from the principle de minimis non curat lex – the law does not concern itself with trifles

Effet utile – this refers to the principle of efficiency/effectiveness. In the context of EU law it refers to the manner in which the ECJ interprets EU law. It consists of giving the EU objectives their fullest effect and maximum practical value

En banc – on a bench

Erga omnes – against everybody

Et seq. – and the following

Etc – et cetera – and others of like character; and so on; and so forth

Ex officio – from office, by virtue of the office or position, by right of office

Ex parte – on one side only

Exceptio non adimpleti contractus – the principle according to which performance of an obligation may be withheld by one party if the other party has itself failed to perform the same or a related obligation

Exception prejudicielle - a question concerning the interpretation of a particular provision

Force majeure – greater force

Forum – the place where the court seised with the litigation is located

Homologation – granting of approval by an official authority

Ibid – an abbreviated form of "ibidem" – in the same place, in the same book, on the same page

In abstracto – theoretically, reasoning on general terms without taking account of a factual situation, opposed to in concreto

In camera – in private

Inter alia – among other things

Interim – in the meantime

Ipso facto – by the fact itself, by the mere fact

Jus cogens – compelling law, imperative, peremptory rules of international legal order

Kompetenz-Kompetenz – the power to confer power

Law of the forum – the law of the place where the court seised with the litigation is located

Lex specialis derogat priori – a special statute overrules a general statute

Locus standi – recognised position, right to intervene, right to appear in court

Lucrum cessans – the loss of prospective profits

Nullum crimen sine lege – no crime without a pre-existing law making the act a crime

Nulla poena sine lege – no punishment without a pre-existing prohibitory rule of law

Obiter dictum – a remark in passing. Obiter does not form part of the ratio decidendi of a case and therefore creates no binding precedent, but may be used as persuasive authority in subsequent cases

Passerelle – bridge, gangway, by-pass

Patere legem – comply yourself with the laws that you made for others

Per se – through itself, by himself or itself, in itself, taken alone, inherently, in isolation, without referring to anything else

Prima facie – at first sight, on the face of it, so far as can be judged from the first disclosure

Primus inter pares – first among equals

Prior – the former, earlier

Qua – considered as, in the capacity of

Quaestor – "man who asks questions". In the Roman Republic, a public official who was an accountant and in charge of supervising the financial affairs of the public treasury

Raison d'être – reason for being

Ratio decidendi – the reason for deciding. The principle or principles of law on the basis of which a court decides the case before it

Ratio legis – the underlying principle, reasoning, grounds, scheme

Ratione loci – by reason of location

Ratione materiae – by reason of the matter involved

Ratione personae – by reason of the person concerned

Ratione temporis – by reason of time

Reformatio in pejus - worse improvement, a decision from a court of appeal which places the person bringing an appeal in a less advantageous position than that in which he would have found himself in the absence of an appeal

Res judicata – when a matter has been finally adjudicated upon by a court of competent jurisdiction. It may not be reopened or challenged by the original parties or their successors in interest

Sensu stricto – strictly speaking

Solange – as long as

Stare decisis et non quieta movere – stand by decisions and do not move that which is quiet

Status quo ante – the way things were before

Sui generis – of its own kind, unique

Supra – above

Ubi jus, ibi remedium – where there is a right, there is a remedy

Ultra petita – beyond, in excess of. When a court rules beyond that which was requested by the parties

Ultra vires – beyond the powers

Via – by way of or by means of

Vice versa – the other way round

Vis-à-vis – in relation to

1

THE HISTORY OF EUROPEAN INTEGRATION

CHAPTER OUTLINE

1. This chapter outlines the history of European integration from 1945 to 2012. It explains the main factors contributing to the creation of the first Community in 1951, that is, the European Coal and Steel Community (ECSC), and those relevant to the creation of the other two Communities in 1957, that is, the European Atomic Energy Community (Euratom) and the European Economic Community (EEC). It should be noted that under the Treaty of Maastricht the EEC was renamed to become the European Community (EC), and that under the Treaty of Lisbon (ToL) the EU succeeded to, and replaced the EC.
2. The European Coal and Steel Community Treaty (CS Treaty) was designed to provide a common market for coal and steel. It was concluded for a period of 50 years from its entry into force, and ceased to exist on its expiry on 23 July 2002. The Euratom was designed to create "the conditions necessary for the speedy establishment and growth of nuclear industries". Unlike the EC, which, after a bumpy start, became the main vehicle for European integration, both the ECSC and the Euratom achieved less prominence and became unimportant to the extent that the ECSC was allowed to expire without renewal (the areas of coal and steel are governed by the general principles applicable to the internal market) while the Euratom, continues its controversial and uninspiring existence as a separate Community, i.e. it is legally distinct from the EU.
3. The original EEC Treaty was amended on several occasions. One of the earliest amendments was the Single European Act (SEA), which laid the foundation for the completion of the internal market and created an impetus for further integration. Until the adoption of the SEA, the EEC was, in practice, firmly based on intergovernmentalism – a unanimous vote in the Council being the rule for the adoption of any legislative act, even though the EEC Treaty permitted majority voting. The SEA introduced Qualified Majority Voting (QMV) in the Council in respect of most legislative measures necessary for the creation of the internal market; thus, a Member State could no longer veto legislation of which it disapproved in areas to which QMV applied. The change in the Council voting rules resulted in proliferation of Community legislation, which in turn gave the Commission many more opportunities to effect outcomes through policy implementation. Further, the SEA gave the European Parliament (EP) some legislative powers.
4. The Treaty on European Union (TEU) i.e. the Treaty of Maastricht was designed to create an "ever-closer union among the peoples of Europe" by adding two new areas of intergovernmental co-operation, one on Common Foreign and Security Policy (CFSP) ("Pillar 2") and the other on Co-operation in Justice and Home Affairs (JHA) ("Pillar 3"), to the pre-existing Community structures which themselves became the essential component of Pillar 1. The three Pillars together made up the European Union (EU). However, the degree of integration was considerably less in the areas covered by Pillars 2 and 3 to which the intergovernmental method applied than under Pillar 1 to which the "EU method" applied.
5. Both the TEU and the EC Treaty were further revised by the Treaties of Amsterdam (ToA) and of Nice (ToN).
6. In order to simplify the existing treaties, to provide greater transparency in the EU's decision-making procedures and to further European integration, on 29 October 2004 the 25 Heads of State or Government of the Member States of the EU adopted the Treaty on European Constitution, which

required ratification by all Member States in order to become a binding treaty. Voters in France and the Netherlands rejected the proposed EU constitution. As a result, the European Council Summit held in June 2007 decided to abandon this treaty and instructed the 2007 Intergovernmental Conference (IGC) to prepare a new Reform Treaty (which was subsequently called the Treaty of Lisbon (ToL)).

7. On 13 December 2007 the European Council signed the ToL, which after being challenged in some Member States and initially rejected by the Irish people in a referendum held in July 2008, but subsequently accepted in a second referendum (which took place in October 2009), entered into force on 1 December 2009. The ToL is not an all-encompassing treaty as was the case of the failed Constitutional Treaty. Its sole purpose was to dramatically amend the existing treaties, i.e. the Treaty on European Union (TEU) and the EC Treaty. The latter, under the ToL, was given a new name – the Treaty on the Functioning of the European Union (TFEU). Both these Treaties are of equal legal value. Under the ToL the Charter of Fundamental Rights of the EU became binding and has the same legal value as the TEU and the TFEU. The ToL abolished the Pillar structure but provides special procedures for the CFSP, i.e. in reality the ToL maintaines a separate "Pillar" for the CFSP (see Chapter 7). The ToL finally got rid of the confusing distinction between the EC and the EU as the EU replaced and succeeded to the EC.

8. The two main theories of international relations (IR) which have attempted to explain the political dynamics of European integration, and the nature of the EU political system, are neo-functionalism and liberal intergovermentalism (LI). Neo-functionalism focuses on the concept of "spillover", according to which integration will deepen from economic to political and will culminate in the creation of a supranational entity; emphasises the importance of supranational institutions; and, downplays the role of the Member States. LI posits that Member States are in control of the European integration process in that national preferences determine the speed and extent of delegation of their powers to the EU, and downplays the role of supranational institutions. As neither theory explains the European integration process as a whole, perhaps because the EU is unique, new so called "middle–range theories" have emerged in IR. These, as the name suggests, seek to explain some aspects of European integration rather than deal with it as a whole. Among the new theories the theory of multi-level governance (MLG) seems to gain acceptance. It focuses solely on the governance aspect of the European integration process.

1.1 Introduction

This chapter examines the principal developments in the process of European integration from the end of WWII to August 2012. The EU is a product of that unique process which constantly evolves and has neither a predictable pace nor a final direction. Member States of the EU have differing views on the desirable speed and ultimate depth of integration, but the extent of their commitment to the integration process is often affected by the ever shifting international political and economic environment.

The history of European integration shows constant growth of the scope and strength of the EU's powers (often referred to as "deepening", or "vertical integration") and the geographic expansion of the EU (often referred to as "widening" or "horizontal" integration[1]). This chapter focuses on vertical integration, whilst Chapter 2 deals with horizontal integration. The movement towards "deepening" and "widening" of the EU emphasises its dynamic and evolving nature, which is not surprising bearing in mind that the EU was not created to deal with existing situations but, as Article 1 TEU states, to attain objectives which the Member States have in common. Accordingly, European integration is not an

---

1. On this topic see: E. Berglof, M. Burkart, G. Friebel, and E. Paltseva, "Widening and Deepening: Reforming the European Union", (2008) *American Economic Review* 98/2, 133.

acquired situation, but a process, and not a result, but a means which is used by the Member States to create "ever closer union among the peoples of Europe" (Article 1 TEU) and to promote peace, EU values internally and externally and the well-being of the Union's citizens (Article 3(1) TEU). In order to achieve common objectives the Member States have conferred important competences on the EU, with the result that the EU constitutes a unique regionally integrated political entity. In order to appreciate and understand the nature of the EU it is necessary to examine its history and origin.

1.2 Europe after World War II (WWII)

Some 50 million people lost their lives during WWII, 60 million people of 55 ethnic groups from 27 countries were displaced, 45 million were left homeless, many millions were wounded and only some 670,000 were liberated from Nazi death camps.[2] The psychological devastation of survivors and the physical destruction exceeded anything ever experienced in Europe. After WWII, Europe was in ruins. It was also politically divided as most Central and Eastern European countries were de facto occupied by the Soviet Union.

The rebuilding of Europe not only posed a formidable challenge but was also the catalyst that led to European unity. Many factors contributed to a new perception of post-war Europe; one was the United States' vision of the post-war world and of the reconstruction of Europe;

Three factors determined the policy of the US:

- Politics. With the beginning of the "cold war" the containment of communism came to play an important role in the way the US perceived European reconstruction. During that period no direct fighting took place between the US and the Soviet Union, but they did all they could to keep their existing allies, and to acquire new allies worldwide;

- Economics.The US had emerged from WWII richer and more powerful than ever. As a main supplier for Allied Forces (countries fighting Germany and its allies), its industry and business had boomed. It was the only major belligerent whose own soil, apart from Pearl Harbor, had not been a site of conflict. In 1945–46, the US accounted for half of the gross world products of goods and services, and held two-thirds of the world's gold.[3] Therefore, for the Americans it was necessary to find new markets. Only a prosperous Europe could become a major market for American goods; thus American self-interest contributed to European recovery; and,

- Humanitarianism. There were also humanitarian considerations, which should not be minimised. The chaos facing post-war Europe was an obstacle to any significant progress towards political stability and economic prosperity and to the protection of basic rights. From 1945 to 1947 Europe did not make any significant progress in this direction.

1.3 The Marshall Plan

On 5 June 1947, at a Conference at Harvard University, US Secretary of State George C. Marshall, announced the American plan for European reconstruction. He proposed cash grants to all European nations subject to two conditions:

---

2.   M. Kishlansky, P. Geary and P. O'Brien, *Civilization in the West*, Volume C, 1991, New York: Harper Collins, 920, and W. L. Shirer, *The Rise and Fall of the Third Reich*, 1991, London: Mandarin, 1139.
3.   M. Kishlansky *et al*, *Civilization in the West*, Volume C, 1991, New York: Harper Collins, 920.

- European States were to co-operate in the distribution of American aid; and,

- They had to progressively abolish trade barriers.[4]

All European nations were invited to participate in the Marshall Plan, but Joseph Stalin, the First Secretary of the Russian Communist Party, called the Plan a capitalist plot and forced all countries under his control that had expressed interest in the Plan to withdraw.

As a result of the Marshall Plan US$13.6 billion was transferred to Europe, in addition to US$9.5 billion in earlier loans and US$500 million in private charity.[5] The Marshall Plan was a huge success as it helped to restore Western European trade and production while controlling inflation. By 1951 Western Europe was booming. However, not only the Plan itself but, most importantly, the manner in which it was administered greatly contributed to the unity of Europe. Initially, 16 European countries participated in the Plan: Austria; Belgium; Denmark; France; Greece; Iceland; Ireland; Italy; Luxembourg; the Netherlands; Norway; Portugal; Sweden; Switzerland; Turkey; and, the United Kingdom. West Germany joined the Plan later, and thus through economic co-operation West Germany was reconciled with other European countries.

Under the leadership of France and the United Kingdom, the Committee for European Economic Co-operation was set up, and later replaced by the permanent Organisation for European Economic Co-operation (OEEC), to plan and distribute American aid.

The success of reconstruction through centrally co-ordinated planning and co-operation made clear that the best way for Europe to recover its international prestige was to act as a single entity in world markets. As a result of economic co-operation within the framework of the Marshall Plan, various European organisations began to emerge in order to strengthen inter-governmental integration in political, military and economic matters. One of those organisations was the ECSC, established on the basis of the Schuman Plan.

1.4 The Schuman Plan

Robert Schuman, the French minister for foreign affairs,[6] followed the advice of Winston Churchill, who emphasised in his speeches that France should take Germany back into the community of nations.[7]

Schuman believed that Europe was facing three problems:

- Economic dominance by the US;

- Military dominance by the Soviet Union; and,

- A possible war with rejuvenated Germany.

The Americans supported the idea of political and economic integration in Europe since it would, in the long term, reduce the cost of their obligations and commitments in Europe. Robert Schuman considered that the best way to achieve stability and peace in Europe was to place the production

---

4.   S. Hoffman and Ch. Maier, *The Marshall Plan: A Retrospective*, 1984, Boulder, CO: Westview Press, 6.

5.   J. A. Garraty and R. A. McCaughey, *The American Nation, A History of the United States Since 1865*, 7th edn, 1991, New York: Harper Collins, 826.

6.   P. Gerbet, "La Genèse du Plan Schuman, Dès Origines à la Déclaration du 9 Mai 1950", (1956) *Revue Française de Science Politique*, 525 et seq.

7.   Winston Churchill said: "I am going to say something that will astonish you. The first step in the re-creation of the European family must be a partnership between France and Germany", in M. Charlton, *The Price of Victory*, 1983, London: British Broadcasting Corporation, 38–9.

of steel and coal (then two commodities essential to conduct a conventional war) under the international control of a supranational entity. The creation of a common market for steel and coal meant that interested countries would transfer their powers in those commodities to an independent supranational authority.

On 9 May 1950 Robert Schuman announced his Plan, based on proposals put forward by Jean Monnet, an eminent French economist and the "father of European integration".[8] Although in Schuman's Plan only France and Germany were expressly mentioned, Schuman invited other European States to join, in particular the UK, Italy and the Benelux countries.

The Schuman Plan was enthusiastically accepted by Germany, and Konrad Adenauer, the then chancellor of Germany, saw it as a breakthrough towards the beginning of German statehood and independence. Personally, Adenauer was in favour of closer relations with the West and of the abandonment of traditional German policy, which for centuries had concentrated on the East. The Schuman Plan was advantageous to both Germany and France, as for Germany it offered a way of regaining international respectability, and in the immediate future the opportunity to gain access to the Saarland, and for France, the opportunity to control the German economy and to rebuild French industry.

The Schuman Plan attracted attention in many European countries. As a result, an international conference was held in Paris on 20 June 1950, attended by France; Italy; West Germany; and, the Benelux countries, to consider the Plan. Following from this, a Treaty creating the European Coal and Steel Community was signed on 18 April 1951 in Paris and it entered into force on 23 July 1952.

The Contracting Parties were: Belgium; France; Italy; Luxembourg; the Netherlands; and, West Germany.

The institutional structure of the ECSC was original in that it consisted of:

- The High Authority. This was a supranational body made up of nine representatives appointed by the Member States acting independently in the interests of the ECSC. The High Authority was in charge of the production and distribution of coal and steel, and was entrusted with supranational competencies, including the power to make legally binding "decisions" and "recommendations", directly applicable in Member States. The High Authority initiated policy measures and adopted them by a majority vote. It could impose fines and withhold the transfer of funds to enforce compliance with the CS Treaty. (On supranationality see Chapter 1.7);

- A Special Council of Ministers. It represented the interests of the Member States. Its function was to harmonise the actions of the High Authority and the governments' general economic policy. Its assent was required for important decisions taken by the High Authority;

- The Common Assembly made up of MPs from Member States, with only supervisory and advisory functions; and,

---

8. Jean Monnet (1888–1979) profoundly believed that peace and prosperity in Europe could only be achieved if European States formed a federation, or at least acted as one economic unit. He prepared the Schuman Plan and, in 1952, became the first President of the High Authority of the ECSC. In 1955 he resigned from the office, but instead of retiring, he founded the Action Committee for the United States of Europe, a federalist movement which brought together eminent European politicians and trade union leaders who wanted to advance the idea of European integration. Monnet and his movement were driving forces behind all initiatives in favour of the European Union, including the creation of the Euratom, the internal market, the European Monetary System, the European Council, British membership in the Community and direct elections to the EP. The outstanding achievements of Jean Monnet were recognised by the European Council held in Luxembourg on 2 April 1976, which proclaimed him an "Honorary Citizen of Europe". For a short biography of Jean Monnet see: www. historiasiglo20.org/europe/monnet.htm (accessed 10/10/11).

■ A Court of Justice responsible for ensuring "that in the interpretation and application of this Treaty . . . the law is observed."

The Treaty was concluded for a period of 50 years and expired on 23 July 2002. After its expiry the ECSC ceased to exist. To deal with the consequences of its disappearance a Protocol on the Financial Consequences of the Expiry of the CS Treaty and on the Research Fund for Coal and Steel was attached to the ToN (under the ToL it has become Protocol No. 37 attached to the Treaties). Since the expiry of the ECSC, coal and steel (being goods) are subjected to rules in the Treaties.

It is impossible in a few sentences to explain the reasons for the demise of the ECSC.[9] Probably, the first and the most important reason was that the situation for which it was created had never materialised, i.e. the fear that Germany might regain dominance in steel and coal in Europe, and that due to its dominant position other European States would not have access to steel and coal necessary to rebuild their economies. Even in the 1950s external supplies of steel and coal were not scarce, and German industry did not dominate European markets. Subsequently, both industries were often in crisis due to oversupplies resulting from decreased world consumption. Accordingly, the ECSC, which was established to deal with robust demand and scarce supplies, had to deal with failing demand due to oversupplies. The CS Treaty was not made to deal with that situation and the Member States were not willing to make changes necessary for the ECSC to adjust to new circumstances.

Second, the ECSC had neither created a common market in coal and steel, nor played a central role in the development of national coal and steel industries. Thus, it did not achieve the objectives for which it was established. This was because Member States were not interested in making the ECSC a success. The ECSC rules were not enforced. The Member States persistently protected and subsidised their national industries in breach of the CS Treaty. The mechanisms set out in the CS Treaty aimed at, *inter alia*, eliminating national subsidies; imposing transparency of prices on undertakings; banning cartels;[10] and, adopting crisis management measures allowing the High Authority to impose production quotas, were hardly used until the 1980s. For the first time in 1981, the Member States, unable to deal with a world crisis in the iron and steel industry, agreed to empower the Commission (which took over the tasks of the High Authority under the Merger Treaty) (see Chapter 1.9) to take measures to permanently reduce the production of steel and to reorganise the industry. However, when a new crisis in steel started in the 1990s, the majority of the Heads of State or Government of the Member States, who endorsed neo-liberal free market ideas, refused to empower the Commission to intervene. As a result, in March 1991 the Commission declared that the ECSC would cease to exist in 2002, as provided in the CS Treaty. The Member States had no regrets, as this ended their expensive policy of subsidising industries which were in decline. Further, with the creation of the EEC (see Chapter 1.7) the political interest of the Member States was focused on integrating their entire economies rather than just one sector.

From the point of view of the development of the process of European integration, the ECSC played an important role. It started the process. As John Gillingham stated: "The Schuman Plan . . . ended the competitive bids for heavy industry domination that had wrecked every previous large-scale attempt to reorganise the Continent since 1918, led to *Westintegration* and Franco-German partnership, and resulted in the creation of a new entity, Europe."[11]

---

9.   On this topic see K. J. Alter, "The Theory and Reality of the European Coal and Steel Community", in S. Meunier and K. McNamara (eds), *European Integration and Institutional Change in Historical Perspective*, 2007, Oxford: OUP.

10.   The High Authority had power, however, to authorise mergers aimed at increasing efficiency but not market dominance.

11.   J. Gillingham, *Coal, Steel, and the Rebirth of Europe, 1945–1955: The Germans and French from Ruhr to Economic Community*, 1991, Cambridge: CUP, 364.

Additionally, the CS Treaty was used as a blueprint for the Treaties creating the EEC and the Euratom (see Chapters 1.6 and 1.7) and put into practice the neo-functionalism implicit in the Schuman Plan (see Chapter 1.21.1).

1.5 The Messina Conference

In June 1955 in Messina (Sicily) the foreign ministers of the Member States of the ECSC decided to "pursue the establishment of a United Europe through the development of common institutions, a progressive fusion of national economies, the creation of a common market and harmonisation of social policies".[12] From this materialised two Treaties signed in Rome on 25 March 1957. The first established the European Economic Community (EEC) and the second the European Atomic Energy Community (Euratom). The Treaties came into force on 1 January 1958. Both were concluded for an indeterminate period of time.

1.6 The European Atomic Energy Community (Euratom)

The main objective of the European Atomic Energy Community Treaty (EA Treaty) (as indicated in Article 1 EA) was to create "the conditions necessary for the speedy establishment and growth of nuclear industries".[13] Its tasks were laid down in Article 2 EA and encompass:

- the promotion of research and dissemination of technical information regarding atomic energy;
- the establishment of uniform standards for health and safety;
- the promotion of investment;
- the equitable supply of ores and nuclear fuels;
- the security of nuclear materials;
- the international promotion of peaceful uses of nuclear energy; and,
- the creation of a common market in this area.

The institutional framework set up by the EA Treaty is identical to that of the EEC Treaty.

The Euratom's main success is in the area of safety in that it established and enforces comprehensive safeguard standards for those Member States that choose to use nuclear energy. Thus, it has contributed to the excellent safety record of nuclear plants in the Member States. It has ensured that civil nuclear materials are not misappropriated for military purposes. It has promoted nuclear R&D resulting in modernisation of nuclear technology. It has ensured a regular and equitable supply of ores, source materials and special fissile materials to the Member States.[14] Notwithstanding the above, the nuclear industry remains within the national domain of each Member State, and nuclear research is mainly carried out at national level. The EA Treaty has not evolved in the same way as did the EEC

---

12. Quoted by D. Lasok in D. Lasok, *Law and Institutions of the European Union*, 6th edn, 1994, London, Dublin, Edinburgh: Butterworths, 19.
13. Article 1 EA.
14. See the official website of the Commission on nuclear energy at http://ec.europa.eu/energy/nuclear/euratom/euratom_en.htm (accessed 1/6/12).

Treaty. Its fundamental provisions have remained substantially unamended. As a result, the Euratom suffers many failings:

- Its objective of developing nuclear energy has become obsolete, given that out of 27 Member States 11 never had any nuclear production at all, Italy has abolished it, and Belgium, Germany, Spain and Sweden are working to phase it out;

- It shows a clear "democratic deficit" given the absence of any requirement for the Council to formally consult the European Parliament (EP) on measures adopted under the EA Treaty;

- It does not solve a major concern of EU citizens relating to the impact of the development of the nuclear industry on public health and on the environment. The use of nuclear energy has become particularly unpopular following the Fukushima nuclear disaster triggered by an earthquake and tsunami which occurred in Japan on 11 March 2011. Following that disaster, Germany announced plans to close all its nuclear plants by 2022; and,

- It supports what, in the opinion of many, is an outdated, dangerous and expensive technology.

After the entry into force of the ToL, the Euratom continues its controversial and uninspiring existence as a separate Community, i.e. it is a legal entity distinct from the EU.

1.7 The European Economic Community (EEC)

The European Economic Community became very much the most important Community of the three (the others being the ECSC and the Euratom) and the heart of European integration. The EEC Treaty mainly concerned economic co-operation between Member States, including the establishment of an internal market. Although economic objectives were in the forefront, the Treaty also contained a political agenda. Its Articles 2 and 3 EC laid down the long-term objectives for the Community, that is, the co-ordination of economic and monetary policies leading to an economic and monetary union (EMU) between the Member States.

The EEC's uniqueness and originality lay in its institutions, which have been reformed on many occasions, and are examined in detail in Chapter 3.

The first decade of the Community was exceptional in terms of economic growth, investment and internal integration. Small countries such as Belgium, Luxembourg and the Netherlands realised that their membership allowed them to have an influence, out of proportion with their size, upon international matters and international trade.[15]

It is also important to note that in the first decade of existence of the EEC, the European Court of Justice (ECJ) delivered a number of judgments which laid the constitutional foundations of the EU. In these judgments the ECJ established the principle of supremacy (see Chapter 9); direct effect (see Chapter 10); and, direct applicability of EU law (see Chapter 11), despite the fact that none of these were mentioned in the EEC Treaty. Those audacious judgments, which made of the ECJ a law-maker and a vital integrating player in the EEC and subsequently in the EU, were not counter-attacked by the Member States, which were "infirmed by their incapacity to react with unanimity. . . . The result was that [the Community's and later the EU's] legal system began to evolve along the paths that could not be predicted from the constellation of the Member State preferences at any given time."[16]

---

15.   D. Armstrong, L. Lloyd and J. Redmond, *From Versailles to Maastricht. International Organisation in the Twentieth Century*, 1996, Basingstoke: Macmillan, 154–9.

16.   See A. Stone Sweet, "The European Court of Justice", in P. Craig and G. de Búrca (eds), *The Evolution of EU Law*, 2011, Oxford: OUP, 131.

Since the creation of the European Communities the idea of European integration has been very much alive, but its actual implementation has been beset with difficulties and controversies, the most important being which method of integration should be used in the decision-making procedure of the EU: the "EU method" (before the entry into force of the ToL this method was referred to either as the "Jean Monnet method" or the "Community method"), or the intergovernmental method. Each method presents a different view of the nature of the EU and its governance. Depending upon the method applied, the policy outcome is either control by the EU, under the "EU method" or by the Member States under the intergovernmental method. The "EU method" finds its expression in neo-functionalism and suprantionality. The intergovernmental method is part of the theory of intergovernmentalism (both theories are explained in Chapter 1.21).

The EU method has four main components:

- The Commission has a monopoly on the making of legislative proposals and the power to bring a Member State before the ECJ for any non-implementation of any EU measure;

- The Council of Ministers votes by qualified majority. Any amendment to the Commission's legislative proposal is only possible by a unanimous vote of the Council;

- The EP is a co-legislator *via* the ordinary legislative procedure; and,

- Member States and the EU institutions can take a case to the ECJ.

Under the intergovernmental method the right of the Commission to initiate legislative proposals is either abolished or greatly reduced in that it shares it with Member States. The Council decides by unanimity and thus each Member State can exercise the right of veto. The EP is only consulted and thus has no influence on the adoption or otherwise of a measure.

Under the "EU method", Member States and the Council still have a considerable influence on the policy outcomes but only the intergovernmental method allows a Member State to block the adoption of a measure which it opposes.

The vision of Europe and the shape of European integration depend upon the form of co-operation chosen by the Member States. Supranationality entails important restrictions on national sovereignty and, if successful, leads to the creation of a federal structure. By contrast, intergovernmentalism implies that the competencies of the Member States remain intact unless unanimously agreed. Its ultimate form is a confederation.

1.8 The Luxembourg Accord

The first disagreement among the Member States occurred in 1965. It is known as the "empty chairs" crisis, as France refused to attend Council meetings from July 1965 to January 1966.

The then president of the French Republic, Charles de Gaulle, was in favour of intergovernmentalism and thus against increasing the powers of the Community. The immediate cause of the crisis was the Commission's package of proposals aimed at increasing the competencies of the Commission and of the EP. The Commission's proposal on the adoption of the financing arrangements for the Common Agricultural Policy (CAP) was accepted by France. The two remaining proposals were rejected. The first concerned new methods of financing the Community, aimed at ending national contributions towards the budget and replacing them with a system of "own resources" of the Community (see Chapter 3.6.7.2). This proposal was considered as essential by the Commission to give the institutions more independence from the Member States. The second proposal concerned increasing the involvement of the EP in decision-making procedures in general, and in budgetary matters in particular. It was supported by the EP and by the Netherlands.

The proposals were used by France to express its dissatisfaction in two areas. They were:

- First, that of the role of the Commission, which, under the presidency of Walter Hallstein, was accused by France of exceeding its competence by acting more like a supranational rather than an inter-governmental body; and,

- Second, that of the proposed major change in decision-making within the Council, which consisted of replacing unanimity with qualified majority voting. The EEC Treaty provided that at the beginning of the final stage of the transitional period, which was approaching, the new voting system should apply.

In order to dramatise the situation, France decided not to attend the Council meetings (hence the empty chairs). Under pressure from French farmers, de Gaulle decided to negotiate with other Member States (the Commission was not invited). In January 1966 an informal agreement was reached, known as the Luxembourg Accord, which provided that:

"Where, in the case of a decision which may be taken by majority vote . . . the Council, will endeavour . . . to reach solutions which can be adopted by all the Members of the Council . . . the French delegation considers that where very important interests are at stake the discussion must be continued until unanimous agreement is reached."[17]

Accordingly, the Luxembourg Accord created a *de facto* right of veto for Member States with the result that unanimous voting was the main way of adopting EEC legislation from 1966 until the adoption of the 1986 SEA. The impact of this on the Commission was that it had to be very cautious when making a proposal to ensure that the proposal would not adversely affect the vital interests of any Member State.

The Luxembourg Accord marked a clear confirmation of intergovernmental co-operation and thus constituted a serious blow to supranationality, although the Accord has never been given any legally binding status in EU law.[18] It was the main reason for years of stagnation of the Community, as it prevented progress towards further integration by giving priority to the immediate national interests of the Member States.

1.9 The Merger Treaty

The idea of rationalising the institutional structure of the three Communities was first introduced by the Convention on Certain Institutions Common to the European Communities of 25 March 1957. The Convention provided for the establishment of a single Assembly (the EP), a single Court of Justice, and a single Economic and Social Committee for all three Communities.

Further rationalisation took place in April 1965 when the Treaty (known as the Merger Treaty) establishing a Single Council and a Single Commission of the European Communities was signed. The Treaty came into force on 13 July 1967. Under the Merger Treaty the three Communities shared the same institutions, although they remained legally independent and the competencies of the institutions were subject to the respective Treaties.

---

17. J. Lambert, "The Constitutional Crisis (1965–66)", 4 JCMS, 226.
18. In Case 68/86 *UK v Council* [[1988] ECR 855] para. 38, the ECJ held that decision-making procedures in the Treaty "are not at the disposal of the Member States or of the institutions themselves".

1.10 The 1969 Hague Summit

An important development in shaping future co-operation between Member States, outside the Communities' framework, took place at the proposal of Georges Pompidou, the successor to Charles de Gaulle. A meeting (which became known as The Hague Summit) was convened in The Hague in December 1969, to which Pompidou, more flexible in his approach towards the development of the Community (although as opposed to the construction of a supranational Europe as de Gaulle had been),[19] invited all Heads of State or Government of the Member States.[20] The main decisions taken by The Hague Summit were to:

- enlarge the Communities by admission of the UK, Denmark, Norway and Ireland (see Chapter 2.6.1);

- establish European Political Co-operation (EPC);

- adopt measures leading to Economic and Monetary Union (EMU) between Member States;

- introduce regular meetings of foreign ministers of the Member States;

- reform the CAP financing;

- establish technical co-operation; and,

- put development aid and social policy on the Community agenda.

In the immediate period after The Hague Summit, the international oil crisis and the budgetary crisis within the Community stunted its growth for almost two decades. Nevertheless, during that period certain aspects of the agenda created by the ambitious decisions of The Hague Summit were further developed. Two of the decisions taken at The Hague Summit merit special attention: the establishment of European Political Co-operation and the initiatives aimed at creating EMU, the latter having become a reality under the TEU.

1.10.1 Establishment of European Political Co-operation (EPC)

The Hague Summit decided to examine the best ways of achieving progress in the establishment of a political union. In October 1970 the Davignon Report (named after its author, the political director of the Belgian Foreign Ministry) was adopted by the foreign ministers of the Member States as a basic strategy in this area, and was then approved by the Copenhagen Summit on 23 July 1973.[21] It proposed the harmonisation of foreign policy of the Member States outside the Community framework based upon regular exchanges of their respective views and, when possible, leading to a common position. It therefore recommended traditional intergovernmental co-operation in political matters without any supporting common structures. Some changes to EPC were tabled in a subsequent report, which was adopted by foreign ministers meeting in London on 13 October 1981.[22] The

---

19. H. Simonian, *The Privileged Partnership: Franco-German Relations in the European Community: 1968–1984*, 1985, Oxford: OUP, 35.
20. Meetings of Heads of State or Government of the Member States are referred to as summit meetings. Those meetings were formalised by the Paris Summit in December 1974 as European Council Summits (see Chapter 3.5).
21. (1973) Seventh General Report on the Activities of the European Communities, Brussels, Luxembourg, p 502 et seq.
22. EC Bull. Supp. 3/81, point 14 et seq.

above-mentioned reports and the Solemn Declaration on European Union agreed by the European Council Summit at Stuttgart in 1983 constituted the foundation of EPC.[23] It was incorporated in Title III of the SEA[24] (see Chapter 1.13) and can be viewed as the precursor to the more formalised co-operation in Common Foreign and Security Policy (CFSP) matters under the Treaty of Maastricht, although the CFSP, even under the ToL, remains essentially intergovernmental, rather than supranational (see Chapter 7).

1.11   The Community from 1970 to 1985 – years of stagnation

From 1970 to 1985 the Community was in a state of stagnation. This so-called "Eurosclerosis" can be explained partially by the difficult international situation, but more importantly by lack of desire on the part of the Member States for further integration. Instead of developing an effective strategy for dealing with common problems created by an oil embargo in 1973, each Member State decided to act on its own. As a result, the UK and France signed bilateral agreements with Iran and Saudi Arabia for oil supplies, while the Netherlands was left out in the cold with its supplies completely cut off by the Organisation of Petroleum Exporting Countries.

National interests and national policies prevailed over Community objectives. The stagnation of the Community was exacerbated by three major unsolved issues: budgetary matters; the UK contribution to the Community budget; and, the reform of the CAP. However, there were some positive developments. These included:

- reform of the Community budget;
- creation of "own resources" of the Community, aiming at replacing the system of national contributions;
- the first direct elections in June 1979 to the EP; and,
- formalisation by the Heads of State or Government of the Member States of their meetings as the European Council in December 1974. From that time those meetings were known as European Council summits.

1.12   Relaunch of European integration

The early 1980s witnessed an unexpected emergence of enthusiasm for, optimism about, and commitment to European integration on the part of Member States. Among the factors that contributed to this were:

- the improvement of the international economic situation;
- the commitment of the new French president, François Mitterrand, to the development of the Community, strongly supported by the German chancellor, Helmut Kohl;
- the appointment on 1 January 1985 as president of the European Commission of Jacques Delors, who decided to accelerate the process of integration by submitting concrete projects;

---

23.   EC Bull. 6/83, points 18–29.
24.   Article 30 SEA and Article 1 and 3 SEA Title I.

- the realisation by the Member States that only common action could improve the competitiveness of national economies and increase their share of world exports, especially with regard to the USA, Japan and the newly industrialised countries; and,

- the policy of the two superpowers, the USA and the Soviet Union towards each other. In the early 1980s the aggressive response of the USA to Soviet foreign policy caused European leaders to fear that they might be dragged into a conflict over which they had no control. With the coming to power of Mikhail Gorbachev in 1985 in the Soviet Union, European leaders feared that the fact that the two superpowers were starting talking and accommodating each other might lead to an agreement between the two superpowers, to the detriment of their interests. As a result, they were convinced that there was a need to assert the EC's international position.

This led to the European Council to commissioning and examining a number of proposals for reforming the EEC. One was the Dodge Report which was presented and adopted by the European Council Summit in March 1985.[25] It recommended the introduction of a co-decision procedure designed to give more powers to the EP (see Chapter 5.4); the recognition of the European Council as a Community institution; and, the preparation of a new treaty on the European Union. Another was the White Paper prepared by Lord Cockfield which proposed the establishment of an internal market by the end of 1992. It identified the remaining barriers to trade within the Community, proposed 300 legislative measures necessary to eliminate them, and set out a timetable for their elimination.[26] The European Council Summit in June 1985 welcomed the White Paper and instructed the Council to initiate a precise programme based on it. Further, it decided to convene an Intergovernmental Conference (IGC) to revise the EEC Treaty, despite opposition from the UK, Denmark and Greece. The conference met in Luxembourg and in Brussels during the autumn of 1985. The outcome of the IGC was the Single European Act.

1.13 The Single European Act (SEA)

The SEA was signed on 17 February 1986 by nine Member States and on 28 February 1986 by a further three (Denmark, Italy and Greece), and came into effect on 1 July 1987. It was not very ambitious (which explains its acceptance by the Member States), although it had much potential for expansion. It brought many improvements and developments which are examined below.

1.13.1 The completion of the internal market by 31 December 1992

The SEA defined the internal market as "an area without internal frontiers in which the free movement of goods, persons, services and capital is ensured" (Article 26(2) TFEU). In order to complete the internal market nearly 300 legislative measures designed to eliminate physical, technical and fiscal barriers to the free movement of goods, persons, capital and services were adopted by the Council, two-thirds of them by QMV.

1.13.2 The extension of Community competencies to new areas

The SEA gave new competences to the EEC necessary to achieve the internal market. They concerned Economic and Social Cohesion, Research and Technological Development and the Environment.

---

25.   EC Bull. 3/85, points 3.5.1 et seq.
26.   Lord Cockfield, *The European Union. Creating the Single Market*, 1994, London: Wiley Chancery Law, 28–59.

Further, the SEA expanded the social policy competences of the Community. First, by providing in Article 153 TFEU a legal basis for the adoption of directives to improve health and safety in the working environment, although harmonising measures were restricted to setting minimum requirements in this area and, second, by allowing the Commission to encourage social dialogue under Article 174 TFEU. Both articles in conjunction with the new legislative procedure (that is, the co-operation procedure) under which a measure could be adopted by QMV in the Council, were used to create the social dimension of the Community. In this context it is important to note that at the European Council summit in December 1989 all Member States except the UK endorsed the Charter of the Fundamental Social Rights of Workers. The UK opposed it on the ground that over-regulation of the labour market would discourage the creation of jobs. The rejection by the UK of the Charter led to the adoption by the remaining Member States of a Protocol on Social Policy attached to the TEU.

It must be remembered that in some new areas of competence the Community was already active in practice on the basis of general Treaty provisions, for example, the protection of the environment, research and regional policy, the protection of consumers and social cohesion. Nevertheless, the SEA placed those policies on a formal footing.

Finally, the SEA made, for the first time, a formal reference to the European Monetary System which was created in 1978 and which had the ECU as its unit of currency. This system was the precursor of EMU proposed by the Treaty of Maastricht.

1.13.3 The institutional changes

The institutional improvements, which pushed the Community in a federal direction and increased its democratic legitimacy, were as follows:

- The EP. A new co-operation procedure enhancing the participation of the EP in the decision-making procedures in 10 areas was introduced. The procedure, which has been modified over the years, is set out in Article 294 TFEU. It has been renamed under the ToL and is now referred to as the ordinary legislative procedure. Another new procedure, "the assent procedure" (under the ToL it is called the consent procedure), gave the EP an important new role in that the approval of the EP (by an absolute majority) was thereafter required for the admission of new members to the Community and in respect of conclusion of association agreements with third countries (see Chapters 2.3.2C and 3.6.7.5);

- The European Council. The SEA confirmed the existence of the European Council and affirmed its composition (this is discussed in Chapter 3.5);

- The Council. The SEA extended the areas covered by QMV within the Council. They concerned measures relating to the completion of the internal market with the exception of: fiscal measures; measures relating to the free movement of persons; and, measures relating to the rights and interests of employed persons. As a result, QMV was applied to two-thirds of the measures designed to create an internal market;

- The Commission. The SEA formalised the "comitology" procedure (see Chapter 4.5.2.1). It also provided that, as a rule, the Commission was to exercise implementing powers with regard to measures adopted by the Council. Only in specific cases could the Council exercise directly implementing powers (see Chapter 4.5.2.2).

- The ECJ. The SEA created the Court of First Instance (which under the ToL became the General Court) to ease the workload of the ECJ (this is discussed in Chapter 3.7.6).

1.13.4 The formalisation of the mechanism for European Political Co-operation (EPC)

EPC was initiated by The Hague Summit in 1969. EPC became recognised and incorporated into the structure of the Community in Title III of the SEA, but was not subject to judicial review by the ECJ. Title III SEA declared that Member States would endeavour jointly to formulate and implement a European foreign policy. Accordingly, EPC did not entail the transfer of any legal powers to Community institutions; it essentially formalised a forum for normal inter-state multilateral co-operation. The improvements to EPC effected by the SEA were:

- The distinction between foreign ministers' meetings within EPC and within the Council was abolished;

- An EPC secretariat was set up in Brussels;

- A mechanism was provided to convene emergency meetings of the Political Committee of foreign ministers of the Member States within 48 hours upon a request from at least three Member States;

- The Commission and the EP became associated with EPC; and,

- The Commission and the Presidency of the Council became responsible for ensuring consistency between the external policies of the Community and policies agreed within the framework of EPC.

EPC resulted in adoption of common positions on many issues such as the Middle East, Eastern Europe and South Africa. However, on many occasions vague declarations, after events had taken place, and little direct action, undermined the importance of EPC. The necessity of adopting a new approach to EPC was further highlighted when Member States were faced with the 1990 Gulf Crisis and the deteriorating situation in the former Yugoslavia.

In the 1990 Gulf Crisis, no agreement was reached among Member States on the use of force against Iraq. The position of Member States varied from immediate and unconditional support for the US military action (Prime Minister Margaret Thatcher of the UK was in Colorado with President Bush senior when the crisis arose and promised UK support) to the Irish policy of non-intervention based on neutrality.

In relation to the crisis in the former Yugoslavia, as Dinan stated: "Far from reflecting well on the Community, the Yugoslav War emphasised deep foreign policy differences between Member States and showed the limits of EC international action."[27]

Each international crisis revealed divergences in opinion between Member States and the impossibility of presenting a common front to the outside world. This contributed to the incorporation of a Common Foreign and Security Policy (CFSP) into the Treaty of Maastricht as its Second Pillar (see Chapter 7).

1.13.5 Assessment

The SEA provided a political impetus and the legal framework necessary to create an internal market by 31 December 1992, which, at that date, became, to a great extent, a reality. It order to implement 300 legislative proposals designed to eliminate barriers to the free movement of goods, persons, capital and

---

27. D. Dinan, *Ever Closer Union?* 1994, London: Anne Rienner Publishers, 489.

services, unanimity voting in the Council was replaced by QMV with regard to two thirds of proposals. The SEA also enhanced the role of the EP in the decision-making process and made foreign policy co-ordination a formal part of the EC's activity.[28]

1.14 From the SEA to the Treaty of Maastricht (the Treaty on European Union (TEU))

The Commission stated that "if the programme [the SEA] succeeded, it would fundamentally alter the face of Europe".[29] This was especially true as the SEA contained a hidden agenda, that is, the creation of EMU, a necessary complement to the internal market. However, in order to achieve the objectives set out in the SEA, it was necessary to deal first with persisting internal conflicts. These were dealt with by the adoption of the Delors I Package, a Commission proposal in 1987 for a radical reform of the Community's financial system for the period 1988–93. The Delors I Package introduced budgetary discipline, ended the "British rebate" saga,[30] reformed the CAP and provided for the Commission to put forward new initiatives. The Commission under the Presidency of Jacques Delors was committed to further integration with a view to introducing EMU. Its motto was "one market, one money".

The European Council summit of June 1988 reappointed Jacques Delors as president of the Commission. It also affirmed his vision of the Community by declaring that "in adopting the Single European Act, the Member States of the Community confirmed the objective of progressive realisation of economic and monetary union."[31] The Summit, most importantly, set up a Committee, chaired by Jacques Delors, to examine the measures necessary for the establishment of EMU. The task of this Committee was to prepare concrete stages leading towards monetary union for consideration at the European Council summit in June 1989. Jacques Delors, in his annual speech on 17 January 1989 to the EP, assessed progress in the completion of an internal market and set the agenda for the newly appointed Commission, which was to promote the devolution of more power to the EP by the Member States and the creation of EMU by successive stages. His vision of the Community was clear: it was a "frontier

---

28. For a critical assessment of the SEA see J. H. H. Weiler, "The Transformation of Europe", (1991) 100 Yale L.J. 2403.
29. EC Bull. 6/85, point 18.
30. The terms of EC membership were not favourable to the UK as it gained almost nothing from the CAP. Additionally, the British VAT contribution to the EC budget was very high due to high consumption levels in the UK. From 1 January 1973 to 31 December 1986 the UK's net contribution to the EC Budget was £7,772 million, which represented a net payment of £1.52 million per day of membership (I. Barnes and J. Preston, *The European Community*, 1988, London and New York: Longman, 5 et seq). The main issue was not that the UK contribution was too high, as it was similar to other Member States, but the imbalance between its contribution and its receipts from the EC Budget. This problem was acknowledged from the time of UK accession. However, when Margaret Thatcher became prime minister of the UK, which coincided with the end of the transitional period during which the UK did not pay its full contribution to the EC budget, the renegotiation of the UK financial contribution (which anyway was marginal compared to the UK budget as a whole) became the main preoccupation of the UK government. Thus, during the 1980s the main point on the UK agenda at each European Council summit was to obsessively complain about the injustice of the UK's contribution in an aggressive and perhaps not the most diplomatic manner. This negative attitude of the UK contributed to the growing unpopularity of the UK within the Community and, at the same time, to the growing unpopularity of the Community with the British people. Finally, the European Council summit in Fontainebleau in June 1984 formalised a rebate for the UK from the EC budget as part of a package of EC budget reforms.
31. EC Bull. 6/88, point 1.1.14.

free economic and social area on the way to becoming a political union",[32] although at this stage political union was not his priority. The European Council summit in June 1989 examined the Delors Report[33] without taking particular notice of the changing situation in Europe.[34]

The dismantling of the barbed wire border between Hungary and Austria on 2 May 1989 was the first tear in the "Iron Curtain" and started the sequence of events that led towards the next stage of integration in the 1990s. The old political division between West and East was abolished; the Soviet Union was in a coma; the old order was shattered; and, West and East Germany were on their way to reuniting. In those circumstances, President Mitterrand of France began to put pressure on other Member States to create a political union to counterbalance the implications of German reunification by closely linking Germany to the Community in political matters.[35] The Extraordinary European Council summit held in Dublin on 28 April 1990 formally welcomed East Germany into the Community. In reply Helmut Kohl agreed to political union alongside EMU. The Summit asked foreign ministers to prepare proposals regarding co-operation between Member States in political matters for the European Council summit in June 1990. These were to constitute the basis of a second IGC.[36]

The European Council summit held on 25–26 June 1990 decided to convene the holding of two IGCs on 14 December 1990, one on EMU and the other on political union. The two IGCs were intended to proceed in parallel with ratification of both instruments taking place within the same time frame. In the course of negotiations two approaches emerged:

- The first favoured a "Three Pillars" structure, the so-called Temple, consisting of a main agreement based on the EEC Treaty and two separate arrangements alongside the main framework, one covering co-operation on CFSP and the other Justice and Home Affairs (JHA) matters.

- The second approach was more ambitious and suggested a "tree" model, a single "trunk" having several branches and treating integration in all three areas as a common foundation (the tree) with special arrangements in particular fields (the branches). The second project was strongly federalist and as such judged too controversial by the foreign ministers of the Member States to be submitted for consideration at Maastricht.

The deliberations of the IGCs were based on the first approach with modifications introduced by the Netherlands, which provided for unanimous voting within the CFSP while submitting the implementation of adopted measures to QMV. The IGCs began on 15 December 1990. The European Council summit held on 9 and 10 December 1991 in Maastricht approved the text of the TEU. The final version was signed on 7 February 1992 at Maastricht. It was agreed that the process of ratification should be completed by the end of 1992. Its entry into force was to coincide with the completion of a single market. In practice, the process of ratification of the TEU was fraught with difficulties.

---

32. EC Bull. Supp. 11/89, point 18.
33. J. Delors, *Report on Economic and Monetary Union in the EC*, 1989, Luxembourg: Office for Official Publications of the European Communities.
34. Only a very brief discussion on the changes in the Soviet bloc, EC Bull. 6/89, Presidency Conclusion, point 1.1.16.
35. A united Germany with its 77 million people, that is, 25 per cent of the entire population of the Community at that time, would account for 27 per cent of its GDP.
36. R. Corbett, "The Intergovernmental Conference on Political Union", (1992) 30 JCMS, 274.

The TEU was rejected by Danish voters in a national referendum held on 2 June 1992. However, the European Council summit in December 1992 reassured the Danes, and in a second referendum held on 18 May 1993, 56.8 per cent voted in favour of it.[37] The Treaty was challenged before the German Constitutional Court[38] and the English High Court in *Rees-Mogg*.[39]

1.15 The Treaty of Maastricht and the European Union

The TEU was based on the so-called "Temple" structure, which consisted of the following elements:

1.15.1 The roof of the Temple

The roof of the Temple consisted of common provisions laying down the objectives of the EU. The main purpose of the TEU was to "establish the foundations of an ever closer union among the people of Europe". To attain this purpose, the TEU set the following general objectives for the EU:

- The promotion of economic and social progress and a high level of employment with a view to achieving balanced and sustainable development, through the establishment of an area without internal frontiers, through the strengthening of economic and social cohesion and through the establishment of EMU;

- The establishment of a single currency within the framework of EMU;

- The promotion of an international identity for the EU through implementation of CFSP which might lead to a common defence policy (see Chapter 7.5);

- The establishment of citizenship of the EU (see Chapter 22);

- The development of closer co-operation in the fields of justice and home affairs (JHA) (see Chapter 31);

- The improvement in the effectiveness of the EU institutions mostly by extending the legislative powers of the EP (see Chapter 5.2.2);

- The extension of EU competences to new policies while reinforcing the existing ones (see Chapter 6);

- The affirmation of the commitment of the EU to the protection of fundamental rights (see Chapter 8); and,

- The introduction of the principle of subsidiarity (see Chapter 6.8.1).

1.15.1.1 Pillar 1

Pillar 1, or "The Community Pillar", covered all policies existing under the previous Treaties and introduced fundamental amendments to the EEC Treaty.

---

37. D. Howarth, "The Compromise on Denmark and the Treaty on European Union: A Legal and Practical Analysis", (1994) 31 CMLRev., 765–805.
38. M. Herdegen, "Maastricht and the German Constitutional Court: Constitutional Restraints for an 'Ever Closer Union'", (1994) 31 CMLRev., 235.
39. *R v Secretary of Foreign and Commonwealth Affairs, ex parte Rees-Mogg* [1994] 1 All ER 457, QBD.

The European Economic Community was renamed by the TEU. The name "European Economic Community" was replaced by "European Community" (the EC) in order to underline the fundamental changes in objectives. The most important changes concerning the EC Treaty were:

- The recognition of the principle of subsidiarity, which operates to restrict the Community's involvement in national matters;

- The establishment of European citizenship, which creates new rights for the nationals of Member States (see Chapter 22);

- The redefinition of the objectives of the Community in areas such as health, education, training, industrial policy, telecommunications and energy networks, research and development, consumer protection, trans-European networks, and culture;

- The extension of EC competences in environmental protection and development aid for poor countries;

- The deepening of the Commission's accountability to the EP while extending the EP's participation in decision-making procedures (see Chapter 5.2.2);

- The establishment of EMU depending on the extent to which Member States' economies converge in terms of inflation, interest rates and other criteria laid down in the EC Treaty; and,

- The extension of the ECJ's powers in relation to Member States that refuse to comply with its judgments (see Chapter 14.5).

1.15.1.2   Pillar 2

Pillar 2, or "The Common Foreign and Security Policy Pillar", concerned inter-governmental co-operation on common foreign and security policy (CFSP) (see Chapter 7).

1.15.1.3   Pillar 3

Pillar 3, or "The Justice and Home Affairs Pillar", covered inter-governmental co-operation in the fields of justice and home affairs (JHA) (see Chapter 31). Under the TEU, Pillar 3 consisted of determination of nine areas listed in Article K1 TEU regarded as "matters of common interest" to the Member States. These essentially covered co-operation in criminal justice (and some civil justice matters) and co-operation in asylum, immigration and visa matters. Under Article K9, the so-called "*passerelle*" or "bridge" provision, the Council, acting unanimously on a proposal from the Commission or a Member State, was allowed to transfer items mentioned in Articles K1(1)–(6) from Pillar 3 to Pillar 1. The Council exercised this option. Apart from matters relating to police and judicial co-operation in criminal matters all matters relating to these areas were gradually transferred to the EC Treaty. The ToL completed this process. It abolished the Pillar structure with the consequence that the entirety of Pillar 3 has become Title IV of the TFEU.

1.15.2   The Plinth of the Temple

The base of the Temple (its "plinth") consisted of the final provisions.

The difference between Pillar 1, on the one hand, and Pillars 2 and 3, on the other, was that Pillar 1 was based on the "EU method", while Pillars 2 and 3 were based on the intergovernmental method (see Chapter 1.7). That is, as a matter of principle, unanimity was required for any measure adopted under Pillars 2 and 3.

COMMON PROVISIONS LAYING DOWN THE OBJECTIVES OF THE EU

Pillar 1	Pillar 2	Pillar 3
European Community:	**Foreign policy:**	■ Drug trafficking and weapons smuggling
■ Customs union and Single market	■ Human rights	■ Terrorism
■ Common Agricultural Policy	■ Democracy	■ Trafficking in human beings
■ Common Fisheries Policy	■ Foreign aid	■ Organised Crime
■ EU competition law	**Security policy:**	■ Bribery and fraud
■ Economic and monetary union	■ Common Security and Defence Policy	
■ EU citizenship	■ EU battle groups	
■ Education and Culture	■ Helsinki Headline Goal Force Catalogue	
■ Trans-European Networks	■ Peacekeeping	
■ Consumer protection		
■ Healthcare		
■ Research (e.g. 7th Framework Programme)		
■ Environmental law		
■ Social policy		
■ Asylum policy		
■ Schengen treaty		
■ Immigration policy		
European Coal and Steel Community(until 2002):		
■ Coal and steel industry		
European Atomic Energy Community:		
■ Nuclear power		
EU method	*Intergovernmental method*	*Intergovernmental method*

1.15.3 Assessment

To examine the main features of the TEU is not an easy task. As McAllister said:

"Maastricht is like Janus. It faces both ways: towards intergovernmentalism, and towards some kind of 'federal vocation'. It is as ambiguous as the oracle of Delphi; as the Community itself. It reflects the extent to which the States are, and are not, able to agree."[40]

---

40.   R. McAllister, *From EC to EU, A Historical and Political Survey*, 1997, London: Routledge, 225.

The Treaty of Maastricht was criticised for undermining the unity and the cohesiveness of the EU legal order by introducing many opt-outs (e.g. for the UK and Denmark in respect of the their participation in EMU, and for the UK in respect of the 1989 Social Charter of Rights of Workers); exemptions (e.g. from defence policy provisions for Member States which are neutral or were not full members of the Western European Union (see Chapter 7.6.1); and, for creating two Pillars based on the intergovernmental method of decision-making[41] which excluded any control by the ECJ and the EP of matters covered by these Pillars. Additionally, the Treaty of Maastricht was a lengthy and badly drafted document. However, it brought many important innovations such as: the creation of citizenship of the EU; the establishment of the timetable for the creation of EMU; the introduction of the principle of subsidiarity; the establishment of new competences for the EC; reinforcement of the powers of the EP; and, the creation of new bodies: the Committee of the Regions (see Chapter 3.10.2) and the European Ombudsman (see Chapter 22.9). Further, matters covered by the CFSP and JHA were within the umbrella of the EU and were not entirely disconnected from Pillar I in that the Council was, at the same time, a Community and an EU institution.

1.16 The Treaty of Amsterdam (ToA)

The ToA was signed on 2 October 1997 and came into effect on 1 May 1999. The main features of the ToA were:

- The extension of the objectives of the EU and the EC. In respect of the EU, the objectives included the promotion of economic and social progress; the progressive establishment of the area of freedom, security and justice (AFSJ) (see Chapter 31); furthered development of the concept of EU citizenship; and, the strengthening of existing policies. In respect of the EC, the objectives were not changed, or greatly extended. However, a new obligation was imposed on the EC when adopting legislative measures. They must be assessed in the light of two considerations: the prohibition of discrimination between men and women, and the protection of the environment. Further, the EC gained competence to adopt measures concerning entry to the territory of the EU of non-EU nationals; movement of persons; and, the co-ordination of employment policies;

- The confirmation of the stability pact and the timetable for EMU;

- The suspension of rights of a Member State that violates fundamental rights (see Chapter 2.4);

- The extension of the scope of the principle of non-discrimination to prohibit discrimination based on "sex, racial or ethnic origin, religion or belief, disability, age, and sexual orientation";

- The protection of the processing of personal data and of the free movement of such data in respect of both individuals and Community institutions. This is embodied in Article 16 TFEU;

- The inclusion of a chapter on employment;

- The incorporation of the Social Charter into the EC Treaty. The UK decided to join the Social Protocol. As a result, it was incorporated into the Treaty provisions on social policy, education, training and youth (it is now Title X of the TFEU);

---

41.   D. Curtin, "The Constitutional Structure of the Union: A Europe of Bits and Pieces", (1993) 33 CLMRev., 17.

- The extension of the powers of the EP. The co-decision procedure (under the ToL this procedure is called the ordinary legislative procedure) has been extended to 15 existing Treaty provisions concerning eight areas;

- Involvement of national parliaments in decision-making procedures. The ToA involved national parliaments in the legislative decision-making procedures in the EU in order to give them an opportunity to express their views on matters which might be of particular interest to them. It required the Commission to promptly forward all proposals to national parliaments. Subject to exceptions based on urgency, proposals could not be placed before the Council until six weeks after they were made available to national parliaments. Protocol 13 attached to the ToA set out the above rules (the current position is detailed in Chapter 6.8.2);

- The establishment of the principle of transparency (the current position is examined in Chapter 5.2.3);

- An explanation of the role and application of the principles of subsidiarity and proportionality. This is discussed in Chapter 6.8;

- The introduction of the concept of enhanced co-operation. The concept of enhanced co-operation permits differential integration, that is, in certain projects only some Member States participate. Before the adoption of the ToA, Member States were allowed various opt-outs, for example, participation in EMU or the Schengen system. The ToA formalised this type of arrangement and mainstreamed it to a greater degree. The procedure under the ToA was substantially amended by the ToN, and then by the ToL and accordingly is discussed in Chapter 6.9;

- The introduction of changes in the implementation of the CFSP (the CFSP is examined in Chapter 7); and,

- The incorporation of the Schengen *acquis* into the TEU (see Chapter 31.4).

1.16.1 Assessment

The Treaty of Amsterdam was less ambitious than the Treaty of Maastricht. It failed to introduce the institutional reforms necessary for the accession of new Member States. Nevertheless, it addressed the issue of employment and fundamental rights of EU citizens; eroded the distinction between the Pillars thus giving a clear signal that matters covered by Pillar 2 and 3 might, at an appropriate time, become part of Pillar 1; and confirmed the differentiated integration and co-operation between Member States by introducing the concept of enhanced co-operation.[42]

1.17 The Treaty of Nice (ToN)

The European Council summit held in Nice (December 2000) finally resolved the complicated legacy of the 1997 ToA. Long overdue changes to institutions and decision-making procedures (the most difficult areas to reform), had become of vital importance and urgency in the light of the then future enlargement of the EU. After 350 hours of negotiations in the IGC and five more days of hard bargaining

---

42.   C-D. Ehlermann, "Differentiation, Flexibility, Closer Cooperation: The New Provisions of the Amsterdam Treaty", (1990) 4 ELJ, 246 and J Shaw, "The Treaty of Amsterdam: Challenges of Flexibility and Legitimacy", (1998) 4 ELJ, 63.

within the summit meeting, the 15 Heads of State or Government agreed on the provisional text of the Treaty of Nice. The Treaty entered into force on 1 February 2003.

The most important changes to the ToA introduced by the ToN were:

■ reform of the institutions of the EU, including the redistribution of votes in the Council of the EU. The ToL further reformed the institutions (see Chapter 3);

■ revision of the enhanced co-operation procedure which was further revised by the ToL (see Chapter 6.9); and

■ the establishment of a new mechanism aimed at preventing infringements of fundamental rights (see Chapter 2.4).

1.17.1 Assessment

Irrespective of a vitriolic attack by the EP on the Treaty for being unambitious and shaped by narrow national interests, it is incontestable that the ToN paved the way for future enlargements of the EU. However, important matters were put off until 2004 when a new IGC was convened to deal with them. These were:

■ The status of the Charter of Fundamental Rights of the EU. Should it have binding force? If so, how should this be achieved?

■ Simplification and consolidation of the existing Treaties (the EU, EC and EA Treaties) into one Treaty, to make them clearer and more logical;

■ The clear delimitation of competences between the EU and the Member States. This matter was raised by Chancellor Gerhard Schröeder. Indeed, it was of vital importance for powerful German Länders; and,

■ The role of national parliaments in the European system.

1.18 The constitution that never was

The European Council summit at Laeken held in December 2001 adopted a "Declaration on the Future of the European Union", which committed the European Union to become more democratic, transparent and effective and to pave the way towards a Constitution of the European Union. The task of preparing a form of Constitution was conferred on a novel body – the Convention. The summit appointed Mr Valéry Giscard d'Estaing, the former French President, as chairman of the Convention. Its 105 members represented governments and national parliaments of the Member States and candidate States, the EP and the Commission, i.e. the main parties involved in the debate on the future of the EU. Observer status was granted to 13 representatives of the European Economic and Social Committee, the Committee of the Regions, the European social partners, i.e. bodies representing labour (such as the European Trade Union Confederation), and management (such as the European Confederation of Industries), and the European Ombudsman. The Laeken Declaration posed some 60 questions to be debated and considered by the Convention. These questions focused on the following topics:

■ Better division and definition of competences in the European Union;

■ Simplification of the Union's instruments, and assessment of their influence;

■ Different aspects of the perceived democratic deficit of EU institutions;

■ More democracy, transparency and effectiveness; and,

■ Simplification of the existing treaties.

The opening meeting of the Convention took place on 28 February 2002. A draft of a Treaty establishing a Constitution for Europe was ready in July 2003. Subsequently it served as a basis for the 2003/2004 IGC.[43] The final draft was approved by the European Council summit in June 2004 and signed in Rome on 20 October 2004 by the Heads of State or Government of the 25 Member States and the three then candidate States (Bulgaria, Romania and Croatia). In order for the EU Constitution to enter into force, all Members of the EU had to ratify it either using the parliamentary method, that is, the treaty must be approved by the national parliament of a Member State, or by a referendum, in which case the treaty is submitted directly to citizens who vote for or against it. The method of ratification was left to the Member State. According to the EU Constitution, it was to enter into force on 1 November 2006. The deadline was not met because the peoples of France and the Netherlands rejected the Constitution on 29 May 2005 and 1 June 2005 respectively.[44]

In this context the European Council summit held on 16 and 17 June 2005 decided that the date envisaged for the entry into force of the Constitution was not tenable, but the process of ratification was not abandoned. A year later the European Council summit agreed on "a period of reflection" with a view to deciding the best way forward with regard to institutional reforms. The European Council Summit held in December 2006 decided to continue the period of reflection into 2007. By June 2007, the EU Constitution had been ratified by 18 Member States; others had put ratification on hold.

The European Council summit held in June 2007 decided to abandon the constitutional project; however, as institutional reforms of the kind envisaged by the Constitutional Treaty were necessary, given that the EU, then comprising 27 Member States, could not function properly under the then current rules on governance, the European Council decided to convene an IGC and entrust it with the preparation of a new treaty called the Reform Treaty (see below).

It is submitted that the proposed Constitution was not a "tidying up exercise". It was a very ambitious piece of work that would, for the first time, have clearly defined the division of power between the EU and Member States, and in doing so give the EU greater powers; enhanced the role of the EP; bolstered democratic accountability and transparency by giving national parliaments an important role in the adoption of EU legislation; assigned to the Charter of Fundamental Rights its rightful place, and, "melted" the EU's three Treaties into one.[45]

1.19 The Treaty of Lisbon (ToL): the Treaty on European Union (TEU) and the Treaty on the Functioning of the European Union (TFEU)

On 13 December 2007 the European Council summit held in Lisbon approved the Treaty of Lisbon, which replaced the abandoned Constitutional Treaty. It entered into force on 1 December 2009.

---

43. P. Craig, "Constitutional Process and Reform in the EU: Nice, Laeken, the Convention and the IGC", (2004) 10 EPL, 653.

44. R. Dehousse, "The Unmaking of a Constitution: Lessons from the European Referenda", (2006) 13 *Constellation*, 151.

45. For in depth assessment of the Constitutional Treaty and its comparison with the ToL see: P. Craig, *The Lisbon Treaty, Law, Politics and Treaty Reform*, 2010, Oxford: OUP.

1.19.1 The ratification of the ToL

All Member States (including the Netherlands and France, the two Member States that torpedoed the Constitutional Treaty), except Ireland, decided to effect ratification *via* parliament rather than to expose the ToL to the uncertainty of national referenda. Ireland was the only Member State that, by virtue of its Constitution, had to hold a referendum. On 12 July 2008, the Irish voters rejected the ToL. Subsequently, the Irish Government decided to hold a second referendum after obtaining the following assurances from the European Council held in June 2009:

■ Each Member State would be represented in the Commission of the European Union by one commissioner of its own nationality;

■ Irish neutrality would not be affected by EU law;

■ Sensitive ethical issues such as abortion would be within the exclusive competence of Ireland;

■ Direct taxation would remain within the exclusive competence of Ireland; and,

■ Workers' rights and public services are and would remain valued and protected in Ireland and in the EU.

In the second referendum which took place in October 2009 Irish voters approved the ToL.

In Germany, the ToL was challenged before the German Federal Constitutional Court (BverfG). In July 2009, the Court ruled that the ToL was compatible with the German Constitution. In particular, the Court held that the ToL did not transform the EU into a federal State; that EU citizenship did not replace national citizenship; and, that a Member State, under the ToL, was not required to provide troops for a European army. However, the Court held that a modification of domestic legislation ensuring greater participation of the German parliament in the control and supervision of EU affairs was required. The necessary legislation was subsequently adopted. In this judgment the BverfG confirmed its position on the supremacy of EU law, i.e. that supremacy of EU law derives from the German act conferring power to the EU and not from EU law itself and therefore has maintained its reservations on supremacy of EU law over the German Constitution (see Chapter 9.9.1).[46]

The last hurdle to be jumped before ratification was that the President of the Czech Republic refused to sign the ToL (although the Treaty had been approved by the Czech Parliament, and declared to be in conformity with the Czech Constitution by the Czech Constitutional Court),[47] unless he obtained a guarantee that his country would not be exposed to massive property claims by Germans expelled from the then Czechoslovakia after WWII. In order to accommodate the Czech Republic, Protocol 30 "On the Application of the Charter of Fundamental Rights of the European Union to Poland and to the United Kingdom" was extended to the Czech Republic (see Chapter 8.4.4).

1.19.2 The position of the UK

The UK obtained many opt-outs in key areas. It is allowed (as is Ireland and Denmark) to decide whether to opt in or to opt out of policies relating to the whole of the AFSJ (see Chapter 31). The UK also negotiated for itself and Poland Protocol 30 (which also applies to the Czech Republic, see immediately above) attached to the Treaties that provides that no "court can rule that laws, regulations or administrative practices or action" of the UK/Poland/the Czech Republic are inconsistent with the

---

46.   Decision of 30 June 2009, BVerfGE 123,267.
47.   The full judgment was published in the *Irish Times* on 11 November 2008.

principles set out in the Charter of Fundamental Rights of the EU, and to avoid any doubts, the Protocol emphasises that the Charter creates no new rights enforceable in the UK/Poland/the Czech Republic (see Chapter 8.4.4). Additionally, the UK's previous opt-outs have been confirmed (for example, non-participation in EMU and in the Schengen Agreement). The above, combined with the fact that unanimity of voting in the Council was retained in the CFSP, in direct taxation and in social security matters, made the ToL acceptable to the UK Government. Prime Minister Gordon Brown of the UK said that the ToL had not crossed "red lines" on major concerns for the UK, and therefore there would be no need to call a referendum.

1.19.3 The structure of the ToL

The ToL has only seven articles. The first two contain amendments to the TEU and the EC Treaty (now TFEU), and therefore are very lengthy. Article 3 states that the ToL is concluded for an unlimited time; Article 4 refers to Protocols 1 and 2 attached to the ToL; Article 5 deals with the renumbering of articles, sections and titles of both the TEU and the TFEU; Article 6 concerns the procedure for ratification of the ToL; and, Article 7 confirms that each official language in which the ToL was drafted is authentic and that Italy is the depository of the ToL. Two Protocols, one Annex and the Final Act of the IGC are attached to the ToL. It is to be noted that 37 Protocols, two Annexes and 65 Declarations are attached to the TEU and TFEU and where appropriate to the EA Treaty. Technically, the TEU and the TFEU are part of the ToL and therefore Protocols and Declarations attached to them are also attached to the ToL. However, the ToL specifically provides that the two following Protocols are annexed to it, i.e.:

- Protocol No 1 amending the Protocols annexed to the Treaty on European Union, to the Treaty establishing the European Community and/or to the Treaty establishing the European Atomic Energy Community; and,

- Protocol No 2 amending the Treaty establishing the European Atomic Energy Community.

It can be seen from the above that the ToL is merely a "wrapping" or "introductory" Treaty. Its main purpose is to effect amendments of the TEU and the TFEU Treaty.

The IGC was mandated to base the ToL on the Constitutional Treaty, but with the modifications specified in the mandate. Consequently, elements of that Treaty are present in the ToL. However, unlike the Constitutional Treaty, which proposed the melting of the three existing Treaties into one, the ToL only amended the TEU and the TFEU. It did this in the following ways:

- Article 1(3) TEU provides that the EU shall be based on two Treaties: the Treaty on European Union (as amended) (TEU) and the Treaty on the Functioning of the European Union (which amends the EC Treaty and gives it a new name: the TFEU). Both Treaties are of equal legal value. The TFEU abolishes the Pillar structure which was introduced by the Treaty of Maastricht but special procedures are provided for the CFSP (see Chapter 7). The ToL finally gets rid of the confusing distinction between the EC and the EU. Article 1 TEU specifies that "The Union shall replace and succeed the European Community". As a result of the above changes, only the EU has legal personality and thus is the only entity able to enter into international agreements, including those relating to membership of international organisations.

- The Euratom exists outside the ToL. It is "hanging on the side". Protocol 2 annexed to the ToL contains changes to the EA Treaty and also provides that some provisions of both the TEU and the TFEU apply to the EA Treaty.

1.19.4 Values and objectives of the EU

For any organisation, and the EU is no exception, it is very important to clearly define the objectives that it seeks to achieve and the values on which it is based. In this respect, the ToL defines and provides a better comprehension than the previous treaties of why the Member States are together in the EU and of the values and objectives which are shared by EU citizens.

Article 2 TEU lists the values on which the EU is founded. It states:

"The Union is founded on the values of respect for human dignity, freedom, democracy, equality, the rule of law and respect for human rights, including the rights of persons belonging to minorities. These values are common to the Member States in a society in which pluralism, non-discrimination, tolerance, justice, solidarity and equality between women and men prevail."

Some of the above values were stated in previous Treaties, e.g. the Treaty of Maastricht, others found their origin in the case law of the ECJ and declarations of EU institutions. For example, the Solemn Declaration on European Identity adopted by the European Council summit held in Copenhagen on 14 December 1973[48] states that Member States: "wish to ensure that the cherished values of their legal, political and moral order are respected, and to preserve the rich variety of their national cultures. Sharing as they do the same attitudes to life, based on a determination to build a society which measures up to the needs of the individual, they are determined to defend the principles of representative democracy, of the rule of law, of social justice—which is the ultimate goal of economic progress—and of respect for human rights."

On the basis of Article 2 TEU, the case law of the ECJ and the 1973 Declaration, five founding values can be identified:

- participatory democracy;
- rule of law;
- protection of fundamental rights;
- social justice; and,
- cultural diversity.

The above values, being common to all the Member States, are constitutive to the European identity.

The overreaching objectives of the EU changed with the coming into force of the ToL. Article 3(1) TEU lists as overreaching objectives the promotion of: peace, the EU's values and the well-being of its peoples. The specific objectives of the EU are set in Article 3 TEU as follows:

"2. The Union shall offer its citizens an area of freedom, security and justice without internal frontiers, in which the free movement of persons is ensured in conjunction with appropriate measures with respect to external border controls, asylum, immigration and the prevention and combating of crime.

3. The Union shall establish an internal market. It shall work for the sustainable development of Europe based on balanced economic growth and price stability, a highly competitive social market economy, aiming at full employment and social progress, and a high level of protection and improvement of the quality of the environment. It shall promote scientific and technological advance.

---

48. Available at http://www.ena.lu/declaration_european_identity_copenhagen_14_december_1973 (accessed 7/10/11).

It shall combat social exclusion and discrimination, and shall promote social justice and protection, equality between women and men, solidarity between generations and protection of the rights of the child.

It shall promote economic, social and territorial cohesion, and solidarity among Member States. It shall respect its rich cultural and linguistic diversity, and shall ensure that Europe's cultural heritage is safeguarded and enhanced.

4. The Union shall establish an economic and monetary union whose currency is the euro.

5. In its relations with the wider world, the Union shall uphold and promote its values and interests and contribute to the protection of its citizens. It shall contribute to peace, security, the sustainable development of the Earth, solidarity and mutual respect among peoples, free and fair trade, eradication of poverty and the protection of human rights, in particular the rights of the child, as well as to the strict observance and the development of international law, including respect for the principles of the United Nations Charter."

The above list clearly shows that the ToL assigns a very important place to non-economic objectives, i.e. to social and environmental objectives. Further, it mentions, for the first time, cultural objectives, so that the EU is required to respect "rich cultural and linguistic diversity" and not only safeguard the cultural heritage of Europe, but also develop it. Ambitious international objectives of the EU are contained in Article 3(5) TEU. They are to be pursued in accordance with the principles of international law, including those set out in the UN Charter. The granting by the ToL of international legal personality to the EU allows the EU to play a greater role on the international stage.

1.19.5 The relationship between values and objectives

The values on which the EU is based both characterise the EU's identity and provide the key to achieving its objectives. They apply internally and externally. With regard to internal objectives a measure adopted in breach of fundamental values will be invalid. Further, Article 7 TEU provides a procedure under which the Council may determine the existence of a "clear risk of a serious breach" by a Member State of values on which the EU is based and, if there is no adequate response from the Member State concerned, the European Council may then determine the existence of a serious and persistent breach by a Member State of the values set out in Article 2. The consequence of such a determination is that the Council may decide to suspend certain rights of the Member State concerned, including the voting rights of the representative of that Member State in the Council (see Chapter 2.4). However, in doing this, the Council shall take account of the possible consequences of such a suspension on the rights and obligations of natural and legal persons.

With regard to the external world, the suitability of a candidate State to become a Member State is assessed by reference to the values of the EU. A candidate State must demonstrate that it respects the values. Finally, the founding values are the basis for relations with non-Member States in that international commitments entered into by the EU must not compromise the EU's values. Under Article 3(5) TEU which defines the objectives of the EU with regard to the wider world, the EU is required, throughout the world, to promote the values upon which it is based.

1.19.6 Brief assessment of the ToL

There was much public debate on whether the proposed Constitution was really dead or whether the ToL resurrected it by recycling and relabelling its provisions. In this respect it can be said that the ToL, instead of being an all-encompassing treaty as was the failed Constitutional Treaty, only amended the TEU and the EC Treaty. The ToL avoids any reference suggesting ambition on the part of the EU to become a federation. It does not use the word "constitution". Not only was terminology suggesting a state-like status for the EU abandoned but also any reference to EU paraphernalia such as an anthem, a motto and a flag. Nevertheless, these will continue to be used, at least by the 16 Member States that declared their adherence to them in Declaration 52 attached to the Treaties.

The significance to be given to the ToL depends upon whether it is assessed from the point of view of a Eurosceptic or from that of an advocate of European integration.[49] Nevertheless, both are likely to have been disappointed by the ToL. Each amendment can be criticised by both. For example, for a Eurosceptic the fact that the Member States agreed that QMV will apply to 44 further policies confirmed the increasing loss of national sovereignty. An advocate of European integration, however, will criticise the ToL for extending QMV to many areas which have no impact on achieving a real union (for example, extension in respect of decisions on the methods used for gathering statistics in the eurozone,[50] or concerning the composition of the CoR) while maintaining national vetoes in crucial areas such as direct taxation, defence and the CFSP.

If assessed in simple terms and dispassionately, the ToL effected the reforms necessary in the ever-enlarging EU, i.e. it improved the efficiency of the decision-making process in the EU and made the EU a very democratic entity.

Examples of the improvement of efficiency of the decision-making process in the EU are:

- The ordinary legislative procedure became the main legislative procedure for the adoption of legislative acts and was extended to a further 44 areas;

- Double majority voting in the Council, when it enters into force in 2014, will be more effective than the current weighted voting system (see Chapter 3.4.6);

- The reduction in number of the members of the EP makes it less unwieldy (see Chapter 3.6.2);

- The creation of the post of the High Representative of the Union for Foreign Affairs and Security Policy (HR) who combines the posts of Vice-President of the Commission and of High Representative for Foreign and Security Policy and has to ensure coherence and unity in respect of the EU's external action (see Chapter 7.3.1), as does the establishment of the post of President of the European Council (see Chapter 3.5.5); and,

- The granting of legal personality to the EU.

Examples of the greater democratisation of the EU are:

- The EP gained new powers:
  - legislative (as it became a co-legislator);
  - budgetary (as it gained powers equal to that of the Council over the EU budget); and,
  - political (for example, it elects the President of the Commission) (see Chapter 3.6.7);

- The involvement of national parliaments in the functioning of the EU adds a new dimension to the application of the principle of subsidiarity and reinforces democratic control of the EU activities (see Chapter 6.8.2);

- The social rights of EU citizens are better protected:

---

49. For in depth examination of all aspects of the ToL see J-C. Piris, *The Lisbon Treaty, A Legal and Political Analysis*, 2010, Cambridge: CUP and P. Craig, *Lisbon Treaty, Law, Politics and Treaty Reform*, 2010, Oxford: OUP.

50. A geographic area in the EU consisting of the Member States which have adopted the euro as their currency.

- first through the Charter of Fundamental Rights of the EU, which contains provisions on social rights that must be guaranteed by national courts and by EU courts (see Chapter 8.4); and,
- second through the inclusion of a "social clause" stating that social requirements are to be taken into account in all EU policies;

- The respect for fundamental rights of EU citizens is enhanced through the conferment of a binding legal status on the Charter of Fundamental Rights of the EU and the accession of the EU to the ECHR (see Chapter 8.5);

- Natural and legal persons have wider access to the EU courts under Article 263 TFEU (see Chapter 15.2.7);

- The application of the "EU method" to measures relating to the establishment of the AFSJ ensures judicial (exercised by the EU courts) and political (exercised by the EP and national parliaments) control over the adoption and implementation of such measures (see Chapter 31.1);

- The ToL reinforces the principle of representative democracy; ensures transparency of the EU legislative process; and, the political participation of EU citizens in the process. Article 11(4) TEU contains a new form of popular participation. Under this provision, one million or more of EU citizens, who are nationals of a significant number of Member States, may ask jointly the Commission to prepare a proposal for a legal act necessary to implement the objectives of the Treaties. This "citizens' initiative" has the potential to make a great impact on EU legislation (see Chapter 5.2.2);

- The ToL clarifies the division of competences between the EU and the Member States so that under the ToL it is clearer in which areas a Member State has dominion, in which the EU is empowered to act alone and in which it shares competences with Member States (see Chapter 6); and,

- The ToL provides procedures for Member States wishing to leave the EU (see Chapter 2.5).

1.20 The Treaty on Stability, Co-ordination and Governance in the Economic and Monetary Union (The Fiscal Pact)

The Treaty of Maastricht paved the way for the establishment of EMU. On 1 January 1999, the euro became the common currency and sole legal tender in eleven Member States. Criticism was expressed by many economists relating to EMU's institutional design.[51] The first criticism concerns the extreme independence of the European Central Bank (ECB), the body which is in charge of the monetary policies for the entire eurozone. The ECB is neither accountable to any EU institution nor to the participating Member States. The second criticism is that the institutional design of EMU is incomplete, because in respect of economic policies, there is no EU institution equivalent to the ECB. This means that budgetary and fiscal policies remain within the exclusive domain of each Member State participating in the euro. The global financial crisis of 2008 emphasised the weaknesses of EMU. In particular, the requirements set out in the Treaties relating to budgetary deficits were neither respected nor enforced against Member States running large deficits. That crisis and the subsequent economic downturn resulted in the debt crisis which has affected in particular, Portugal, Ireland, Italy, Greece, and Spain (the so-called PIIGS Member States), and threatened to undermine the economy of all Member States.

---

51. On this topic see: M.O. Hosli, *The Euro: A Concise Introduction to European Monetary Integration*, Boulder, CO: Lynne Rienner, 2005.

On 2 March 2012 the Treaty on Stability, Co-ordination and Governance in the Economic and Monetary Union, commonly known as the Fiscal Pact, was signed by 25 of the 27 EU Member States.[52] The UK and the Czech Republic, which are not members of the eurozone, decided not to become parties to the Fiscal Pact. Even though the Fiscal Pact has been concluded outside the framework of the main EU Treaties, i.e. the TEU and the TFEU, its Article 2(2) states that it must conform with the Treaties and EU law, including procedural rules whenever adoption of secondary legislation is required. The Pact is expected to be incorporated into the framework of the Treaties within five years. The Fiscal Pact is fully applicable to all eurozone Member States which ratify it, and to non-eurozone and future eurozone Member States if they so wish. Its main objective is to remedy the weaknesses of the original rules governing the single currency by improving budgetary discipline; strengthening co-ordination of economic policies of the participating Member States; and, improving the governance of the euro. Under the Pact, a Member State is required to take legislative measures, preferably constitutional, to ensure that its budget is in balance or in surplus as defined by the Pact. If a Member State fails to comply with budgetary and other requirements in that its law is not in conformity with the requirements of the Pact, not only the Commission but also any ratifying Member State may bring proceedings before the ECJ against the defaulting Member State. If the ECJ finds that the Member State concerned is in breach of the Pact and that Member State continues to fail to comply with its judgment, the Court may ultimately impose a fine up to 0.1 per cent of GDP on that State.

The Pact is of particular importance to Member States which are on a bailout programme, i.e. PIIGS, They must ratify the Pact if they wish to be eligible from 1 March 2013 to benefit from any funding from the European Stability Mechanism (a permanent bailout fund with the lending capacity of some €700 bn which became operational in July 2012).

Whether the Fiscal Pact will be sufficient to move the eurozone from crisis into stability, or whether more changes are required to prevent the collapse of the euro, remains to be seen. The Fiscal Pact is expected to enter into force on 1 January 2013 after obtaining twelve ratifications from Member States whose currency is the euro, or on the first day of the month following the deposit of the twelfth instrument of ratification by a Member State whose currency is the euro, whichever is the earlier. If it enters into force, it will constitute a big step towards the creation of a real economic union for the Member States which have ratified it.

1.21 Theories of integration

The theories of European integration attempt to explain the political dynamics of European integration and the nature of the EU political system. Many theories have been developed by political science but none, so far, has fully explained the process of EU integration although each seems to be relevant to explain part of the integration process. The two dominant theories, neo-functionalism and liberal intergovernmentalism (LI), present opposite positions on why States co-operate internationally and establish various regional arrangements to solve problems jointly. Neo-functionalism's vision of the EU system of government is that the EU is a supranational State to which the Member States have transferred their powers and sovereignty. According to intergovernmentalism, the EU is an international organisation.

The two theories have, to some extent, lost their popularity, although they still have their followers. Instead, a new way of thinking of European integration has emerged, the so-called "middle-range

---

52. The text of the Fiscal Pact is available at: http://european-council.europa.eu/media/639235/st00tscg26_en12.pdf (accessed 3/6/12).

theories", which as the name suggests, seek to explain some aspects of European integration rather than deal with it as a whole. Among the middle-range theories, the theory of multi-level governance (MLG) has gained appreciable acceptance. The main theories are briefly examined below.

1.21.1   Neo-functionalism

Neo-functionalism finds its origin in functionalism and, at the same time, constitutes a critique of functionalism. Functionalism is a theory in international relations (IR) formulated by David Mitrany (1888–1975) in the 1930s and 1940s.[53] Functionalists believe that the State, as a form of social organisation, is obsolete and that world problems can only be solved through global integration entailing collective governance, that is, a world-government, and "material interdependence" between States. Such integration is difficult to achieve because it erodes the sovereignty of the State. However, States are willing to work together on relatively small "functional" issues and integrate in limited functional, technical, and/or economic areas. Once they do this, they not only learn how to co-operate but most importantly realise the benefits flowing from integration. This is likely to result in integration achieved in one narrow area spilling over into broader areas, and then into even broader areas so that this eventually leads to global integration.

Neo-functionalism, in particular as developed by Ernst B. Haas and Leon Lindberg,[54] focuses on regional integration and not on global integration.

The main assumptions of neo-functionalism are that:

- Economic integration will lead to political integration;

- The supranational institutions of the EU will, over time, create a supranational agenda which will prevail over the interests of Member States; and,

- The resulting political unity will be reinforced by the formation of supranational interest groups, public (i.e. political elite) and private (e.g. corporations, business, unions, sub-national governments) which will support European integration by putting pressure on governments of the Member States for further integration.

The neo-functional approach is built on the concept of "spillover" effect. According to Lindberg the "spillover effect" refers to "a situation in which a given action, related to a specific goal, creates a situation in which the original goal can be assured only by taking further actions, which in turn create a further condition and a need for more action and so forth".[55]

Neo-functionalists consider that there are three kinds of "spillover":

- Functional, which concerns integration in a specific economic sector or specific issue-area which will spill over into other related areas. An example of this is the creation of the internal market which necessitated the harmonisation of certain aspects of the working environment (such as regulations on health and safety of workers) which was not the original objective of the SEA;

- Political, which refers to a situation where the political elites of the Member States, i.e. their officials and politicians who participate in the decision making processes, as well as private

---

53.   D. Anderson, "David Mitrany (1888–1975): An Appreciation of His Life and Work", (1998) 24 RIS, 579.

54.   C. Strøby Jensen, "Neo-Functionalism", in M. Cini and N. Pérez-Solórzano Borragán (eds), *European Union Politics*, 3rd edn, 2010, Oxford: OUP, 71–85.

55.   L. Lindberg, *The Political Dynamics of European Economic Integration*, 1963, Stanford: Stanford University Press, 8.

interest groups, which always further their own interest, will, with time, develop a perception that their interests are best served by seeking supranational rather than national solutions. Over several years they will develop supranational loyalties and preferences and thus put pressure on national governments to speed up the integration process; and,

■ Cultivated, which refers to a situation in which supranational institutions such as the European Commission, the EP and the ECJ will push the integration process forward. Given that they embody the common interest of the EU they are expected to seek to expand the process of integration. For example, functionalists saw the European Commission as a midwife for the integration process in that in the process of intergovernmental negotiation, which according to Haas is based on the "minimum common denominator", the Commission would act not only as a mediator but also as a political entrepreneur. As a result, the Commission would always seek to "upgrade the common interest" and thus redefine any conflict in such a way as to achieve expansion of the powers of the EU.

Neo-functionalism was criticised on many grounds. First, on empirical grounds because its predictions failed to materialise in so far as the pattern of development of the European Communities and the EU was concerned. Second, on theoretical grounds because it did not take account of the international dimension of European integration; it placed too much emphasis on supranationality, thus neglecting the importance of the nation State; and, it focused on integration of the political elites rather than on the participation of EU citizens in the integration process.

Neo-functionalism was very popular until the 1970s, because it explained well the initial process of European integration. However, with the Luxembourg Accord, and the inertia which characterised the European Communities in the 1970s and the early 1980s, its importance had petered out. After the 1990s, the revival of the European Communities, and creation of the EU, revived the neo-functionalism theory. This revival has, however, been of limited scope in that the "new" neo-functionalists have incorporated into their theories aspects of neo-functionalism which fit their theories. As a result, neo-functionalism is no longer a theory which explains entirely the process of European integration but is relevant to explain some sectorial developments, or some aspects of it. Nevertheless, neo-functionalism remains an important theory to study European integration as it is closely associated with the "EU method" (see Chapter 1.7).

1.21.2 Liberal intergovernmentalism (LI)

Intergovernmentalism is, at the same time, a theory and a method. As a theory it focuses on the nation State as the driving force of European integration (although intergovernmentalists prefer to use the term "co-operation" rather that the term "integration"). The key element of intergovernmentalism is the concept of sovereignty. Its meaning varies but the most basic understanding of it equates "sovereignty" with "independence". Intergovernmentalists submit that Member States are in control of the process of integration and during that process they do not transfer their national sovereignty to European institutions, but instead, when the national interest so requires, they delegate it to them. This entails that European institutions are servants of the Member States and that the Member States when they co-operate are, at most, pooling or sharing sovereignty. Stanley Hoffman, who developed the theory of intergovernmentalism in the mid-1960s, made a distinction between high- and low-level politics. He argued that Member States are likely to seek integration in respect of low-level politics (e.g. in economic matters), but would reject any interference in areas of high politics i.e. in political matters.[56] Since the

---

56. S. Hoffman, *The European Sisyphus. Essays on Europe 1964–1994*, 1995, Oxford: Westview Press.

early 1990s, a new variation of intergovernmentalism, i.e. liberal intergovernmentalism (LI), presented by Andrew Moravcsik has gained recognition. The essence of LI has been explained by its author as follows:

"EU integration can best be understood as a series of national choices made by national leaders. These choices responded to constraints and opportunities stemming from the economic interests of powerful domestic constituents, the relative power of states stemming from asymmetrical interdependence, and the role of institutions in bolstering the credibility of interstate commitments."[57]

In simple terms, Moravcsik posits that:

- States behave rationally and thus will always use the most suitable means to achieve their objectives;

- National preferences in foreign policy result from pressures from domestic social groups which preferences are aggraded through political institutions of a State. Consequently, national goals/preferences are neither fixed nor uniform but vary and are shaped by domestic pressures and interaction;

- The outcome of negotiations between States is essentially determined by their relative bargaining power. In the EU context this means that the largest Member States will always dominate the agenda; and,

- The role of supranational institutions in the European integration process is negligible, because the main European policy making body is the Council. EU institutions are merely a means of locking States into commitments because, without this locking, Member States could easily renege upon their commitments.

It seems that the strongest argument in favour of LI is that under the ToL a Member State may secede from the EU. LI came under intense criticism, for the following reasons: it does not fit the facts on how the process of European integration occurred; its empirical analysis was too selective, as the five case studies chosen by Moravcsik were those that fitted his theory; it did not take account of the fact that major decisions relating to European integration were taken by the European Council rather than occurred on a day-to-day basis; it showed a lack of understanding of policy making by an IGC in that often an IGC has no agenda until the conference has started; it oversimplified the political process in that such a process is not always rational as ideology, belief and symbolism can be of essence; and, it downplays the role of supranational institutions. The main criticism is, however, that LI is difficult to apply to non-economic areas. This failing was acknowledged by Moravcsik.

1.21.3 Multilevel governance (MLG)

This theory focuses on the governance aspect of integration, rather than explaining the process itself. It perceives the EU as a system of multilevel or network governance.[58] This theory, or as some call it,

---

57. A. Moravcsik, *The Choice for Europe: Social Purpose and State Power from Messina to Maastricht*, 1998, London: UCL Press, 18.

58. M. Jachtenfuchs, "Theoretical Perspective on European Governance", (1995) 1 ELJ, 115, and "The Governance Approach to European Integration", (2001) JCMS, 245.

"organising metaphor",[59] emphasises special features of the EU in that the EU is multidimensional; the degree of integration varies depending on the policy area; and, the governance of the EU is composed of multiple coexisting policy models. According to this theory the decision-making process is taken "across multiple territorial levels", and thus instead of focusing on "integration" one should focus on how various authorities, i.e. national, European, regional and local, private and public, participate in the decision-making process in the EU. According to this theory authority has gradually moved from national governments and has been dispersed among various private and public agents. However, there is fluidity between various levels of authority in that authority may move between different levels and varies depending upon the policy area. Marks defined the MLG of the EU as "a set of overreaching, multi-level policy networks [where] . . . the structure of political control is variable, not constant across policy space."[60]

The main criticism of MLG is that it addresses only one aspect of European integration, i.e. governance. A further criticism is that MLG is too static and thus not able to explain the dynamics of European integration.

RECOMMENDED READING

Books

Cini, M. and Pérez-Solórzano Borragán, N. (eds), *European Union Politics*, 3rd edn, 2010, Oxford: OUP.

Corbett, R., *The Treaty of Maastricht*, 1993, London: Longman.

Craig, P., *Lisbon Treaty, Law, Politics and Treaty Reform*, 2010, Oxford: OUP.

Douglas-Scott, S., *Constitutional Law of the European Union*, 2002, London: Pearson Longman, in particular Chapter 1: The European Union in Search of an Identity.

Duff, A. (ed.), *The Treaty of Amsterdam*, 1997, London: Sweet and Maxwell.

Eriksen, E.O., Fossumk, J.E., and Menéndez, A.J. (eds), *Developing a Constitution for Europe*, 2005, London: Routledge.

O'Keefe, D. and Twomey, P. (eds), *Legal Issues of the Maastricht Treaty*, 1992, London: Chancery Law Publishing.

Ott, A. and Vos, E. (eds), *Fifty Years of European Integration*, 2009, Cambridge: CUP.

Piris, J-C., *The Constitution for Europe: A Legal Analysis*, 2006, Cambridge: CUP.

Piris, J-C., *The Lisbon Treaty, A Legal and Political Analysis*, 2010, Cambridge: CUP.

Wiener, A., and Diez, T. (eds), *European Integration Theory*, 2009, 2nd edn, Oxford: OUP.

Articles

Bradley, K., "Institutional Design in the Treaty of Nice", (2001) 38 CMLRev., 1095.

Curtin, D., "The Constitutional Structure of Union: A Europe of Bits and Pieces", (1993) 30 CMLRev.,17.

Ehlermann, C-D., "Differentiation, Flexibility, Closer Cooperation: The New Provisions of the Amsterdam Treaty", (1990) 4 ELJ, 246.

Pescatore, P., "Some Critical Remarks on the SEA", (1987) 24 CMLRev., 9.

Schütze, R., "From Rome to Lisbon: 'Executive Federalism' in the (New) European Union", (2010) 47 CMLRev., 1385.

Shaw, J., "The Treaty of Amsterdam: Challenges of Flexibility and Legitimacy", (1998) 4ELJ , 63.

Sutton, A., "Scrutiny – The IGC 2007: The European Union Comes of Age?" (2008) 14 EPL, 55.

---

59. B. Rosamond, "New Theories of European Integration", in M. Cini and N. Pérez-Solórzano Borragán (eds.), *European Union Politics*, 3rd edn, 2010, Oxford: OUP, 117.
60. Ibid, 116.

Wouters, J., "Institutional and Constitutional Challenges for the European Union: Some Reflections in the Light of the Treaty of Nice", (2001) 26 ELRev., 342.

Ziller, J., "The German Constitutional Court's Friendliness towards European Law: On the Judgment of *Bundesverfassungsgericht* over the Ratification of the Treaty of Lisbon" (2010) 16 EPL, 53.

ESSAY QUESTIONS

1. Critically assess the following statement:

   "The EU is a structurally complex mix of supranationalism, intergovernmentalism and differentiated forms of integration."

2. Critically examine the main factors which have contributed to the development of the EU from the creation of the ECSC to the establishment of the EU under the ToL.

AIDE-MÉMOIRE

EU BIG EVENTS AND BIG DATES

9 May 1950 – The Schuman Plan. R Schuman, the French foreign minister, proposed the creation of the European Steel and Coal Community.

18 April 1951 – Signature of the Treaty creating the European Coal and Steel Community (CS Treaty), which entered into force on **23 July 1952** and expired on **23 July 2002**.

25 March 1957 – Signature of the Treaty creating the European Economic Community (EC Treaty) and the European Atomic Energy Community (EA Treaty), both of which entered into force on **1 January 1958**.

14 January 1963 – France vetoed the accession of the UK to the Communities. The second application by the UK was submitted in 1967 and immediately rejected by France.

8 April 1965 – The Merger Treaty was signed merging the executive bodies of the three Communities (the CS, EC and EA) and creating a single Council and a single Commission. It entered into force on **13 July 1967**.

1 July 1965 – Beginning of the "empty chairs" crisis.

29 January 1966 – The Luxembourg Accord ends the first major political crisis in the EEC, i.e. the "empty chairs" crisis. Under the agreement unanimity voting in the Council was agreed when "vital national interests" of a Member State were at issue.

1 July 1968 – Elimination of all customs duties in respect of industrial products, the creation of the Customs Union among Member States and the establishment of the Common Customs Tariffs for goods from outside the Community (see Chapter 18.2). This was achieved 18 months in advance of the agreed timetable.

1–2 December 1969 – The Hague Summit. The Member States decided to meet regularly at the level of Heads of State or Government. These informal meetings were recognised as a Community institution, that is, the "European Council", by the Paris Summit in December 1974.

24 April 1972 – Creation of the monetary "snake", which constituted the first stage towards the creation of European Monetary Union.

1 January 1973 – Accession of Denmark, Ireland and the UK to the Communities (see Chapter 2.6.1).

7 July 1978 – Creation of the European Monetary System (EMS), replacing the monetary "snake". The Exchange Rate Mechanism (ERM) was launched on **13 March 1979**.

10 June 1979 – First direct elections of members of the EP by citizens of Member States based on universal adult suffrage.

1 January 1981 – Accession of Greece to the Communities (see Chapter 2.6.2).

14 June 1985 – The Schengen I Agreement was signed between Germany, France and the Benelux countries aiming at abolishing the internal borders among them and creating a single external border, where checks for all the Schengen countries were to be carried out in accordance with a common set of rules.

1 January 1986 – Accession of Spain and Portugal to the Communities (see Chapter 2.6.3).

17 and 28 February 1986 – Signature of the Single European Act which entered into force on **1 June 1987.**

19 June 1990 – Signature of the Schengen II Agreement which aimed at eliminating frontier controls between the participating Member States. It entered into force on 26 March 1995.

3 October 1990 – Reunification of Germany (see Chapters 1.14 and 2.6.4).

7 February 1992 – Signature of the Treaty of Maastricht, which entered into force on **31 December 1992** – The official completion of the internal market (see Chapter 17).

1 November 1993, and which created the European Union.

1 January 1995 – Accession of Austria, Finland and Sweden to the EU (see Chapter 2.6.5).

2 October 1997 – Signature of the Treaty of Amsterdam, which entered into force on **1 May 1999.**

1 January 1999 – The Euro became the currency for 11 Member States.

8 December 2000 – The European Council agreed on the Treaty of Nice, which was signed on **26 February 2001** and entered into force on **1 February 2003.**

18 July 2003 – Approval of a draft of a Constitutional Treaty by the European Council summit. The proposed EU Constitution was signed in Rome on **20 October 2004** by the Heads of State or Government of the 25 Member States and the three candidate States. In June 2007, The European Council decided to abandon the Constitutional Treaty. As a result, it never came into force.

1 May 2004 – Accession of 10 Member States to the EU: Cyprus, The Czech Republic, Estonia, Hungary, Latvia, Lithuania, Malta, Poland, Slovakia and Slovenia (see Chapter 2.6.6).

3 October 2005 – Official accession negotiations with Turkey and Croatia commenced (see Chapter 2.6.9E).

1 January 2007 – Accession of Bulgaria and Romania to the EU (see Chapter 2.6.7).

23 June 2007 – The 2007 IG commenced its work on the Reform Treaty (the Treaty of Lisbon – the ToL).

13 December 2007 – The European Council approved the ToL (see Chapter 1.19).

1 December 2009 – Entry into force of the ToL.

2 March 2012 – the signature by 25 Member States of the Treaty on Stability, Co-ordination and Governance in the Economic and Monetary Union, commonly known as the Fiscal Pact.

2

MEMBERSHIP OF THE EU

CONTENTS

CHAPTER OUTLINE

1. Important rights and obligations for the EU and for the Member States derive from membership of the EU. All Member States are equal in that they enjoy the same privileges and must fulfil the same obligations *vis-à-vis* each other and *vis-à-vis* the EU. Under the principle of equality, the EU is required to respect the national identity of Member States and the essential functions of each Member State, in particular those which are intended to ensure the territorial integrity of the State; the maintenance of law and order; and, the safeguarding of national security. Member States are required to co-operate sincerely with EU institutions, and with each other, and in the spirit of solidarity assist each other in extreme circumstances such as natural or man-made disasters, terrorist attacks and armed aggression.

2. Three specific procedures apply to membership of the EU: the admission procedure, the suspension procedure and the withdrawal procedure. Membership of the EU is conditional upon satisfying the so-called "Copenhagen criteria", which were formulated by the European Council meeting in Copenhagen in 1993 and are set out in Article 49 TEU. Membership may be suspended when a Member State disregards the basic values on which the EU is founded. It may be terminated under Article 50

TEU when a Member State expresses its wish to withdraw from the EU. There are no provisions in the Treaties dealing with loss of membership by expulsion. Under public international law the absence of an express provision means that the EU has no power to expel its members.

3. Twenty-seven European States are members of the EU. Accession negotiations with Croatia were concluded on 30 June 2011 and Croatia is scheduled to become a member of the EU on 1 July 2013. Five States: Iceland; the Former Yugoslav Republic of Macedonia; Montenegro; Serbia; and, Turkey, have the status of candidate States. Potential candidate States are: Albania; Bosnia-Herzegovina; and, Kosovo under UNSC Council Resolution 1244. Since the establishment of the Communities, there have been six rounds of enlargement. Each is analysed in this chapter. The enlargement policy regarding States which are official candidates is discussed.

2.1 Introduction

In the preamble to the EEC Treaty the founding Member States were "calling upon the other peoples of Europe who share their ideal to join in their efforts". Thus, from its inception, membership of the Communities was open to other European States. This call of the six founding Member States has been answered on many occasions, with the result that 27 European States are Members of the EU and it is expected that in the near future Croatia and Iceland will join. The impressive geographical expansion, or the "widening" of the EU, also often referred to as "horizontal integration", emphasises the dynamism of European integration. However, as Hilton stated: "Enlarging the European Union (EU) is more than the territorial expansion of EU membership rights and obligations to other European States and peoples. Enlargement also triggers new policy demands on the Union, alters its institutional functioning, and affects its legal corpus."[61] The degree of impact of any enlargement on the EU and on a joining State depends on the scale of enlargement, i.e. the number of joining States, the level of their economic development, and the maturity of their democratic structures.

This chapter examines the challenges of each enlargement as well as the admission procedure. It also briefly comments on rights and obligations of the Member States deriving from their membership of the EU, including the respect for values on which the EU is founded (see Chapter 1.19.4). If a Member State breaches those values, its membership may be suspended. Finally, this chapter outlines the withdrawal procedure applicable when a Member State decides to terminate its membership.

2.2 The principles applicable to Member States of the EU: the principles of equality, sincere co-operation and solidarity

The ToL emphasises that the EU should respect the equality of Member States before the Treaties and their national identities (Article 4(2) TEU). The principle of equality means that in the EU all Member States are equal in that they enjoy the same privileges and have to fulfil the same obligations *vis-à-vis* each other and *vis-à-vis* the EU.[62] Unlike certain international organisations (for example, UNESCO), no special status is granted to any Member State.

Under the principle of equality, EU law applies to all Member States without discrimination. Any difference in treatment is based on objective considerations and proportionate to the objectives that the

---

61. C. Hilton, "EU Enlargement", in P. Craig and G. de Bùrca (eds), *The Evolution of EU Law*, 2nd edn, 2011, 187.
62. See K. Lenaerts and P. Van Nuffel, "Advanced Integration and the Principle of Equality of Member States within the European Union", in C. Kaddous and A. Auer (eds), *Les Principes Fundamentaux de la Constitution Européenne*, 2006, Paris: Halbing and Lichtenhahn/Bruylant/LGDJ, 245.

EU seeks to achieve. However, under EU law the principle of equality does not entail that each Member State has the same voting power. Under the ToL the principle normally applied in international intergovernmental organisations that each member has one vote is an exception. The vast majority of legislative acts are adopted by the Council acting by QMV, which is currently determined on the basis of a "weight" given to each Member State and which from 2014 will be based on a two-fold majority, i.e. one of the Member States and one of populations (see Chapter 3.4.6). However, this change from the norm of "one State one vote" is compensated by the fact that the Council, when it adopts EU legislation by QMV, acts together with the EP, which is directly elected by EU citizens, and therefore democratic control of legislation is ensured.

The EU must respect the national identity of the Member States, including local and regional identity. It is also obliged to respect the essential functions of each Member State, in particular those which are intended to ensure the territorial integrity of the State, the maintenance of law and order, and the safeguarding of national security. Article 4(2) TEU specifies that national security "remains the sole responsibility of each Member State".

Under Article 4(3) TEU, the Member States are required to sincerely co-operate with the EU and with each other. This obligation requires the Member States to take all appropriate measures, whether general or particular, to ensure fulfilment of their obligations arising out of the Treaties or resulting from the acts of the EU institutions and to refrain from taking any measure which could jeopardise the attainment of the EU's objectives. If a Member State fails to fulfil this duty the Commission may commence proceedings against it under Article 258 TFEU (see Chapter 14). One aspect of the duty of sincere co-operation is that each Member State is required to assist others in carrying out tasks which flow from the Treaties.

The ToL expressly recognises the principle of solidarity. Article 222 TFEU imposes a duty on Member States and on the EU to assist a Member State in a situation where it is a victim of a terrorist attack, or of a natural or man-made disaster. Further, the principle of solidarity is emphasised in the area of energy. Under Article 122(1) TFEU, if severe difficulties arise in the supply of certain products, in particular in the area of energy, the Council may, on a proposal from the Commission, acting in the spirit of solidarity, adopt appropriate measures. Another dimension of the principle of solidarity is the "mutual defence clause" inserted in Article 42(7) TEU. It states that if one Member State is a victim of armed aggression on its territory the others are obliged to provide it with help and assistance "by all means in their power", but in accordance with Article 51 of the UN Charter, and subject to any commitments deriving from membership of NATO. Article 42(7) TEU entails that EU members, even if not members of NATO, are obliged to provide aid and assistance to a victim State.

2.3 Admission procedure

The requirements for admission are both substantive and formal. The substantive requirements were defined by the Copenhagen European Council Summit in June 1993 and codified in Article 49 TEU. The formal requirements were changed by the ToL in that under Article 49 TEU the EP and national parliaments are to be notified of any application for EU membership submitted by a candidate State.

2.3.1 Substantive requirements

The Copenhagen Summit set out the following three substantive requirements that a candidate State must satisfy:

- Political requirements – a candidate State must have stable institutions guaranteeing that the values on which the EU is founded are respected;

■ Economic requirements – a candidate State must have a functioning market economy and be able to cope with competitive pressures and market forces within the EU; and,

■ Legal requirements – a candidate State must be able to fulfil the obligations of EU membership, including acceptance of the objectives of political, economic and monetary union. This entails acceptance of the entire body of EU law known as the "*EU acquis*" which before the entry into force of the ToL was referred to as the "*acquis communautaire*".

Article 49 TEU sets out further substantive requirements for admission to the EU, which were not expressly mentioned by the Copenhagen Summit. It requires that a candidate State must be a State within the meaning of public international law, and must be a European State. Further, it confirms the political requirements by stating that a candidate State must respect the values on which the EU is founded. Each of the requirements is considered below.

2.3.1.1 Political requirements

These are defined in Article 2 TEU, which states that:

"The Union is founded on the values of respect for human dignity, freedom, democracy, equality, the rule of law and respect for human rights, including the rights of persons belonging to minorities. These values are common to the Member States in a society in which pluralism, non-discrimination, tolerance, justice, solidarity and equality between women and men prevail."

A liberal-democratic model of government of a candidate State ensuring respect for the civil, political, economic and social rights of its citizens is a vital element of membership of the EU.[63] Therefore, only democratic States which respect human rights can apply for membership. All Member States of the EU, candidate States and potential candidate States must be contracting parties to the ECHR to which, under Article 6(2) TEU, the EU itself will accede in due course (see Chapter 8.5).

2.3.1.2 Economic requirements

The requirements are stated neither in Article 49 TEU nor in any other provision of the Treaties. They derive from the economic nature of the EU. A candidate State is required to have a functioning and competitive market economy, and an adequate legal and administrative framework in the public and private sectors. As the Commission stated in its Report on "Europe and the Challenge of Enlargement": "An applicant country without those characteristics could not be effectively integrated; in fact, membership would be more likely to harm than to benefit the economy of such a country, and would disrupt the working of the Community [EU]."[64]

Notwithstanding the above, the fulfilment of economic requirements has, on occasions, been treated less rigorously than the fulfilment of political requirements in that candidate States have been accepted despite the fact that the level of their economic development was far from the average in the EU.

---

63. See S. Frowein, "The European Community and the Requirement of a Republican Form of Government", (1984) 82 *Michigan Law Review*, 1311 et seq.

64. EC Bull. 3/92, Supp., point 9.

2.3.1.3 Legal requirements

There are two legal requirements.

First, a candidate State must be a State within the meaning of public international law.

A candidate State must be recognised as a State. Reference to the rules of public international law will clarify the legal status of the applying entity. In practice, since the Council must reach a unanimous decision regarding admission of a candidate State, if that State is not recognised by every Member State, its application for admission will be rejected. So far, no irreconcilable problem has arisen in this area, although the candidacy of Cyprus posed delicate problems. Further, the accession of Kosovo may be a challenge, as only 22 of the 27 members of the EU have recognised Kosovo as a State.

The Republic of Cyprus has always been recognised by the international community as one State exercising sovereignty over the entire island of Cyprus although it does not control the Turkish sector. A political settlement between the Greek Cypriots and the Turkish Cypriots was not achieved before the Republic of Cyprus's accession to the EU. As a result, the Republic of Cyprus became a Member of the EU on 1 May 2004, but the Turkish sector, which is recognised only by Turkey as the Turkish Republic of Northern Cyprus, being under military control of Turkey, did not, in fact, join the EU. However, Turkish Cypriots, being citizens of the Republic of Cyprus, are EU citizens, and are entitled to vote in elections to the EP. Reunification of the two communities is subject to on-going negotiations between the President of the Republic of Cyprus and the leader of the Turkish Cypriots. The opening of accession negotiations between the EU and Turkey (see Chapter 2.6.9) will almost certainly force all interested parties to settle peacefully the problem of Cyprus.

Second, a candidate State must accept the EU *acquis*[65] which, according to the EP, constitutes a "criterion of global integration".[66] The term means, in the context of accession, the acceptance by a new Member State, without reservation, and from the commencement of its formal membership, of the body of common rights and obligations, actual and potential, that bind all EU Member States together – in other words, a candidate State must accept all of EU law and its basic political principles and values.[67] Acceptance means more than translation of the *acquis* into national law. It requires that a candidate State has properly implemented the *acquis* through adequate administrative and judicial institutions.[68]

The *acquis* is constantly evolving and comprises:

(a) The normative *acquis*, such as:

- the founding Treaties and their amendments;
- acts enacted by the institutions, such as regulations, directives, decisions, recommendations and opinions (Article 288 TFEU, Article 161 EA);
- other acts whose adoption is provided for by the Treaties (for example, rules of procedure, and so on);
- measures adopted in the area of the external relations of the EU – such as agreements entered into by the EU with one or more third states, with international organisations, or with a national of a third State; and,

---

65. This term is usually used in French (see the English version of the TEU). *Acquis* can be translated into English as "patrimony" (or heritage).

66. In its Resolution on the structure and strategy for the EU with regard to its enlargement adopted on 20 January 1993 the EP emphasised that all candidate States must accept the *acquis communautaire* (now EU *acquis*), including the TEU and the objectives of further integration (A3-0189/92).

67. Upon the fifth enlargement, the EU *acquis* comprised more than 80,000 pages of EU law.

68. Conclusion of the European Council summit held on 9–10 December 1994.

- other agreements the conclusion of which have been necessary to attain the objectives of the Treaties, for example, the Agreement of January 1957 establishing European Schools.

(b)   The political *acquis*, such as declarations, resolutions, principles and guidelines, and so on, adopted by the European Council, or the Council. Also included are common agreements of the Member States regarding the development and strengthening of the EU.

(c)   The judicial *acquis*, that is, the case law of the CJEU, which outlines the essential characteristics of the EU legal order (for example, direct effect, supremacy, unification, co-operation between the ECJ and national courts). It should, however, be noted that in the Acts of Accession there is no reference to specific case law for two reasons:

- The rulings of the ECJ are "acts" of the EU institutions and thus already part of the EU *acquis*; and,
- It is unnecessary, and even dangerous, to "freeze" the case law of the ECJ for new members and, at the same time, allow its further development for older members. Indeed, the ECJ is not bound by its own decisions and it may always change the existing case law in order to promote new and essential objectives of the EU.

The acceptance of the EU *acquis* is a necessary condition for accession as it encompasses rights and obligations attached to the Union and its institutional framework. Candidate States must accept the *acquis* before they join the EU. Only in exceptional circumstances are exemptions, or derogations, granted to candidate States.

2.3.1.4 Geographical requirement

A candidate State must be a European State. This criterion can be explained by the fact that the EU wants to preserve the European identity of the Union.

In the Declaration on European Identity of 14 December 1973, the Heads of State or Government described the essential elements of European identity as "principles of representative democracy, of the rule of law, of social justice – which is the ultimate goal of economic progress – and of respect for human rights".[69] The Commission, in its report on "Europe and the Challenge of Enlargement", stated that:

> "The term 'European' has not been officially defined. It combines geographical, historical and cultural elements . . . and is subject to review. It is neither possible nor opportune to establish now the frontiers of the European Union, whose contours will be shaped over many years to come."[70]

There are 50 recognised States in Europe, including the Vatican City, as well as a number of unrecognised or partially recognised States, including Abkhazia; Kosovo; Transnistria; Sealand; and, South Ossetia.

---

69.   EC Bull. 12/73, point 130.
70.   EC Bull. 3/92, Supp., point 7. It is interesting to note that in 2004, the then EU Commissioner for Enlargement stated: "I am often asked where Europe's ultimate borders lie. My answer is that the map of Europe is defined in the minds of Europeans. Geography sets the frame, but fundamentally it is values that make the borders of Europe. Enlargement is a matter of extending the zone of European values, the most fundamental of which are liberty and solidarity, tolerance and human rights, democracy and the rule of law." Available at http://www.otw. co.at/otw/index.php/e/a/194 (accessed 7/10/11).

Only one non-European State has submitted an application for admission to the EU – Morocco in 1985 – which was rejected in 1987 by the Council as being incompatible with Article 49 TEU because Morocco is not a European State.

2.3.2 Formal requirements

Article 49 TEU sets out the formal conditions for admission. This provision states that:

"Any European State which respects the values referred to in Article 2 and is committed to promoting them may apply to become a member of the Union. The European Parliament and national Parliaments shall be notified of this application. The applicant State shall address its application to the Council, which shall act unanimously after consulting the Commission and after receiving the consent of the European Parliament, which shall act by a majority of its component members. The conditions of eligibility agreed upon by the European Council shall be taken into account.

The conditions of admission and the adjustments to the Treaties on which the Union is founded, which such admission entails, shall be the subject of an agreement between the Member States and the applicant State. This agreement shall be submitted for ratification by all the contracting States in accordance with their respective constitutional requirements."

By virtue of Article 49 TEU a successful candidate State accedes to the EU, and therefore, by implication, to the Euratom.

The following stages in the admission procedure can be identified.

A.   **Submission of a formal application by a candidate State.** The first step in the procedure consists of submitting a formal application for admission, in the form of a letter signed by the minister for foreign affairs of a candidate State, to the Presidency of the Council of the European Union. The application must be notified to the EP and national parliaments. Subsequently, the Council decides whether to initiate negotiations with the applicant State. This can take a considerable time. The Commission becomes involved and, after making investigations, presents a "preliminary opinion", which either recommends the opening of negotiations or advises the Member States to wait until certain requirements are satisfied by the applicant State, or expresses its opposition to the admission. This opinion is not binding but is, nevertheless, of great influence.

The Council may take a position regarding the "preliminary opinion" of the Commission by adopting a "conclusion", which may confirm or ignore the Commission's opinion. In the case of Cyprus and of Malta, the Council confirmed the favourable opinion of the Commission. In relation to Greek accession the Council ignored the negative opinion of the Commission.[71]

B.   **Negotiations.** Negotiations commence with the so-called "screening", which consists of an analytical examination of the EU *acquis*. During that stage, which takes approximately one year, the Commission explains the acquis to the candidate State and, together with that State, evaluates its degree of preparedness. For the purposes of screening and the subsequent negotiations, the *acquis* is broken down into a number of chapters, each covering a specific policy area, e.g. chapter 1 on the free movement of goods, chapter 2 on freedom of movement for workers, and so on. Thus, prior to actual, technical negotiations, the Commission

---

71.   The Council, solely for political reasons (i.e. to support nascent democracy in Greece) decided to accept the Greek application for admission. Opinion on the Greek Application for Membership, EC Bull. 2/76, Supp.

establishes a "screening report" for each chapter of the *acquis*. In respect of each chapter, a candidate State submits its negotiating position, while the Commission prepares a Draft Common Position (DCP) for submission to the Council, which decides whether it can adopt a common position allowing opening of the chapters.

Some negotiations have been lengthy and complex (for example, with Spain, Portugal and Eastern and Central European countries), others swift and smooth (for example, with Austria, Finland, Norway and Sweden).

C.   **End of negotiations.** Once successful negotiations are concluded on all chapters, a draft Accession Treaty that incorporates the result of the negotiations is agreed between the Council and the candidate State. The Draft Accession Treaty is subsequently submitted to the Commission and the EP. The opinion of the Commission is not binding, but in practice, as the Commission is fully involved in negotiations, its opinion is always followed. Since the adoption of the SEA, the EP, within the consent procedure, must give its consent to the accession of a candidate State by majority vote cast by a majority of its members. The Treaty of Accession is usually very short. In the case of the UK it consists of three articles stating that the UK accedes to the three Communities and accepts all Community law. However, the Act of Accession, which is always annexed to the Treaty of Accession, is a voluminous document, often accompanied by protocols, annexes and declarations. Apart from declarations, all these documents are legally binding.

D.   **Ratification of the Treaty of Accession.** The last stage involves the ratification of the Treaty of Accession by the Member States and the candidate State in conformity with respective national constitutional rules. Often, a candidate State submits the final acceptance of its future membership to its people.

The Treaty of Accession enters into force only if all Member States ratify it. In the case of multiple candidatures, non-ratification by any one of the candidates does not affect the accession of others. In the case of Norway, its government notified the EU that, as a result of a negative referendum, it would not ratify the Treaty of Accession. On 1 January 1995 the Council of the EU adopted a decision "adjusting the instruments concerning the accession of new Member States to the European Union",[72] and thus gave legal effect to the withdrawal of Norway from the process of accession.

From the signature of the Treaty of Accession to the actual accession a future Member State is kept informed, and is consulted at all levels and in all areas, and is also involved in the EU decision-making procedures, although it still has no right to vote. Its presence ensures that the existing Member States are fully aware of any difficulties and opposition to new measures, while permitting the new Member State to participate in developments which are taking place within the EU.

2.4 Suspension procedure

Under Article 7(1) TEU, the Council, acting by a majority of four-fifths of its members (excluding the defaulting Member State), on the basis of a reasoned proposal by one-third of the Member States, by

---

72.   [1995] OJ L1/221. A similar decision was taken by the Council when Norway, following a previous negative referendum (53.49 per cent against), failed to join the Communities in 1972.

the EP or by the Commission, and after obtaining consent of the EP, may determine the existence of a "clear risk of a serious breach" by a Member State of values on which the EU is based and which are set out in Article 2 TEU, and subsequently may address a recommendation to the Member State concerned. The defaulting State has the right to present its case before the determination is made. The Council is required to regularly verify that the grounds on which such a determination was made continue to apply.

If there is no adequate response from the Member State concerned, the procedure, set out in Article 7(2) TEU, for suspension of a defaulting Member State's rights deriving from EU membership will be used. Article 7(1) TEU contains an "early warning mechanism".

There are two stages in the procedure under Article 7(2) TEU. The first relates to the determination of the existence of a serious and persistent infringement by a Member State of the fundamental values of the Union. The second relates to a decision either to suspend or not suspend EU membership rights, which may be taken by the European Council once the Council has determined the existence of a serious and persistent breach of Article 2 TEU.

2.4.1 First stage

Under Article 7(2) TEU the European Council (the defaulting Member State is excluded), acting unanimously on a proposal by one-third of the Member States or the Commission, and after obtaining the consent of the EP, may determine the existence of a serious and persistent breach by a Member State of the values on which the EU is founded. Such determination is made after giving an opportunity to the defaulting Member State to present its observations.

2.4.2 Second stage

Once the European Council has made the determination mentioned above, the Council may, acting by a qualified majority, decide to suspend certain rights of the defaulting Member State, including its right to vote in the Council. However, in applying Article 7(2) TEU the Council must take account of the possible consequences of such a suspension on the rights and obligations of natural and legal persons. During suspension, the defaulting Member State is bound to carry out its obligations flowing from the Treaties, and the other Member States are bound to carry out their obligations to the defaulting Member State.

The Council, acting by a qualified majority vote, may decide subsequently to vary or terminate its decision, according to how the situation in the defaulting Member State evolves.

The ToL introduced a possibility for a defaulting Member State to challenge a determination made under Article 7(1) or 7(2) TEU but confined it to procedural aspects of such determination and imposed a strict time limit, in that the Member State concerned is required to bring proceedings before the ECJ within one month from the date of the adoption of an act by the Council or the European Council determining a breach of Article 7(1) or (2) TFEU. Under Article 267 TFEU, the ECJ is required to give a ruling within one month from the date of the commencement of the proceedings.

Article 7 of the TEU does not specify what would happen if a defaulting Member State were to continue violating Article 2 TEU in defiance of a decision adopted under Article 7(2) TEU. It is submitted that in such a situation general principles of public international law will apply to deal with a defaulting Member State.

Neither Article 7(1) nor Article 7(2) TEU has yet been used. However, the EU imposed diplomatic sanctions against Austria in February 2000, to express its condemnation of the election of Jörg Haider (the leader of the extreme right Austrian Freedom Party, known for his racist and xenophobic policies) as a government minister when his party, as a result of the 2000 election, joined a conservative-led

Austrian government. The sanctions consisted of freezing bilateral relations between Austria and 14 other Member States, and the suspension of all contacts at an inter-governmental level between Austria and the EU. The problem was settled when Mr Haider resigned from the Austrian government, although his party did not follow his lead. Article 7 TEU could not have been used because Austria had not actually breached Article 7(1) TEU.

2.5 Withdrawal procedure

The ToL provides for voluntary withdrawal from the EU, which may take place at any time. A Member State that no longer wishes to be a member of the EU must notify the European Council of its desire to leave the EU. Following notification, the procedure set out in Article 50 TEU will be applied, consisting of conducting negotiations between the EU and the Member State concerned with a view to concluding a withdrawal agreement, specifying the arrangements for withdrawal and regulating the future relationship between the EU and the Member State concerned. The Council of the EU will conclude this agreement on behalf of the EU, acting by qualified majority voting (the Member State concerned is not allowed to vote), and after obtaining the consent of the EP.

The Member State concerned will cease to be a member of the EU at the date specified in the withdrawal agreement or, failing any agreement, two years after the notification to the European Council of its intention to withdraw unless the European Council, in agreement with the Member State concerned, unanimously decides to extend this period. Accordingly, the withdrawal may enter into force even if the EU fails to give its consent.

The Member State concerned may always change its mind, or even rejoin the EU following the normal accession procedure set out in Article 49 TEU.

Until now no Member State has expressed a serious desire to leave the EU. The Community has, nevertheless, twice dealt with a situation when a part of an existing territory of a Member State has acquired political sovereignty or autonomy.

The first case concerns Greenland, an integral part of the Kingdom of Denmark at the time of the latter's accession to the Communities. In 1979 the government of Denmark granted home rule to Greenland; as a result Greenland remains under the Danish Crown and its inhabitants are still considered to be Danish citizens. The island enjoys autonomy in all matters except constitutional affairs, foreign relations and defence. In 1985 the people of Greenland decided in a referendum to withdraw from the European Communities, and negotiations were conducted between the Kingdom of Denmark and other Member States. No opposition was expressed to Greenland's withdrawal. Specific provisions for Greenland are set out in Protocol no 34 attached to the Treaties, which regulates the treatment in the EU of fisheries products originating in Greenland.

The second case concerns St Pierre and the Miquelon Islands. Their secession was considered as an internal matter for France, and the Communities merely received notification from the French authorities.

2.6 Current and future membership of the EU

Six EU enlargements, plus one *de facto* enlargement, and one mini-enlargement have taken place, resulting in the EU covering almost all of Western and Central Europe, a substantial part of Eastern Europe, and overseas territories of some Member States which form part of those States, e.g. some Caribbean islands, and French Guyana. On 1 January 2011, the EU had 502.5 million inhabitants, which is more than Russia and the USA put together.

2.6.1   First enlargement

On 1 January 1973 the UK, Denmark and the Republic of Ireland joined the Communities. Following a negative referendum, Norway did not accede. The reasons for accession of these three Member States were different, although the main consideration for Ireland and Denmark was to protect their existing economic links with the UK. Norway held a second referendum on the issue in 1994 and membership was rejected then too.

2.6.1.1   Ireland

In the Republic of Ireland 83 per cent of votes cast were in favour of accession. For Ireland, membership of the EU was very attractive as it provided an opportunity to enter markets in the EU and thus reduce the traditional dependency upon the UK for export trade (70 per cent of exports were to the UK). Furthermore, as an agricultural country, the Republic of Ireland could only gain from being a party to the CAP.

2.6.1.2   Denmark

Denmark, mainly an agricultural country, would clearly benefit from the CAP. Its main commercial partners Germany was already a Member State, while the UK was about to join the EC. The advantages were carefully weighed by the Danes against the disadvantages, which would mainly be the severance of traditional links with other Nordic countries. In the national referendum, which took place after the negative vote in Norway, 63 per cent of Danish votes cast were in favour of accession.

2.6.1.3   The United Kingdom

The most controversial candidate was the UK.[73] However, after the departure from power of France's President de Gaulle, there was no opposition to UK membership. The accession negotiations lasted one year and focused on the following issues:

- The length of the transitional period;

- Agriculture. In the UK food was cheap due to imports from Commonwealth countries. The Heath government had two objectives in this respect: in the short term, to slow down the impact of the CAP by phasing it in as slowly as possible; and in the long term, to obtain compensation for the negative impact of the CAP by a satisfactory budgetary arrangement;

- The UK's contribution to the Community budget. It was agreed that its contribution would be 8.64 per cent of the EC budget in 1973, increasing to 18.92 per cent in 1977, with limits on further increases in 1978 and 1979. There was no agreement regarding 1980 (see Chapter 1.14);

- New commercial arrangements with Commonwealth countries. The African, Caribbean and Pacific (ACP) countries were offered participation in the Yaoundé Convention (which was replaced by the Lomé Conventions and in 2000 by the Cotonou Agreement and more recently by the Economic Partnership Agreements). In addition, the Community General System of Preferences was extended to Commonwealth countries. The question of exports of Caribbean sugar and New Zealand dairy products to the UK required special arrangements; and,

---

73.   The UK's applications had been rejected by France in 1963 and again in 1967.

■ Fisheries. The first enlargement offered an opportunity for the EC to create a Common Fisheries Policy (CFP) based on free and equal access of the Member States to each other's waters; accordingly, UK participation in this policy was negotiated.

The accession negotiations were concluded in January 1972 when the Treaty of Accession of the four applying States was signed. The UK European Communities Act 1972 came into force on 1 January 1973. However, the UK Labour Party opposed the terms of entry and promised in its electoral campaign to "renegotiate" the Treaty of Accession. Indeed, once the Labour Party was in power (1974–79), the question of the UK membership became a main item on the political agenda of the Labour government.[74] In the end a referendum was organised, in which the British people approved UK membership by 67.2 per cent of votes cast.

2.6.2 Second enlargement

The second enlargement concerned Greece, which submitted its application on 12 June 1975. The negotiations were opened on 25 June 1975. On 23 May 1979 the Treaty of Accession and the Act of Accession were signed. Greece became a Member State on 1 January 1981.

Greece was the first Eastern European country to join the EC. Its heritage, resulting from centuries of Ottoman Turkish Empire rule, combined with its Orthodox Christianity, a legacy of the Byzantine Empire, set Greece apart from other Member States. For Greece, with its inefficient agriculture based mainly on small holdings with poor soil and low rainfall, its limited natural resources, weak industry and a fragile democracy as it emerged from years of dictatorship, the attraction of being a Member State was obvious.

2.6.3 Third enlargement

Portugal and Spain joined the EC on 1 January 1986. Portugal applied on 28 March 1977 and Spain applied on 28 July 1977. Both signed the Treaty of Accession on 12 June 1985. The end of military dictatorship in both countries enabled them to submit their applications for accession to the Communities.

The negotiations with Spain were protracted, as its proposed accession posed three major economic problems:

■ Spanish agriculture and its competitiveness, especially against that of France and Italy, made its participation in the CAP very controversial;

■ the Spanish fishing fleet was almost equal in size to that of the entire Community and therefore placed the CFP under strain; and,

■ Spanish industry, especially cotton, woollen textiles, clothing and steel industries, due to low wages, threatened the position of other Member States and posed a challenge to the EC, which already had over-capacity problems in these sectors.

Portugal, a small and relatively poor country, posed no such threats to the economy of existing Member States. Its accession was delayed as a result of applying for membership at the same time as Spain. Furthermore, the negotiations with Spain and Portugal were halted when France decided that, before a

---

74. The matter of "renegotiation" is examined in, Membership of the European Community: Report on Renegotiation, Cmnd. 6003, March 1975.

new enlargement, budgetary matters within the EU should be settled. As a result, it was not until after the European Council summit in 1984, which reached an agreement on contributions to the EU budget, that accession negotiations with Spain and Portugal were resumed.

2.6.4 De facto enlargement: the case of the German Democratic Republic (GDR)

On 3 October 1990, in conformity with the West German Constitution, the former German Democratic Republic (GDR) became an integral part of the Federal Republic of Germany. On that date, by virtue of Article 299 EC, the territorial scope of application of EC Treaties was extended to the former East Germany.[75]

It was not necessary to revise the EC Treaty, as the Federal Republic of Germany, the only legal government of Germany, always considered the GDR as part of its country when signing international treaties. However, Germany, taking into account the importance of the reunification and its impact on the German and EU economies, asked other Member States for approval, which was formally given by the European Council summit on 28 April 1990. Additionally, the summit laid down transitional measures, allowing temporary derogations in the application of EU law to the territory of the GDR in certain areas such as competition policy and protection of the environment.

2.6.5 Fourth enlargement

On 1 January 1995 Austria, Finland and Sweden joined the EU.[76] Norway, although accepted by the EU, did not accede, as a result of a negative referendum (its second such result, having held a previous referendum in 1972).

Austria submitted a formal application on 17 July 1989, Sweden on 1 July 1991, Finland on 18 March 1992 and Norway on 25 November 1992. Formal negotiations commenced on 1 February 1993.

All candidate States were members of the European Free Trade Association (EFTA)[77] and Members of the European Economic Area (EEA).[78] As such, they already had considerable experience of working with the EU institutions and of the interpretation and application of EU law. Also, they had the appropriate "infrastructure", that is, staff, procedures and material support, to deal with negotiations with the EU. These went smoothly and the Treaty of Accession was signed on 24 June 1994. Thereupon, the three joining candidate States had to renounce their EFTA membership and terminate all bilateral agreements between themselves and the EU, and all other international agreements incompatible with membership of the EU.

---

75. See C. W. A. Timmermans, "German Unification and Community Law", (1990) 27 CMLRev., 437–49; C. Tomuschat, "A United Germany within the European Community", (1990) 27 CMLRev., 415–36.
76. On the fourth enlargement see D. Booss and J. Forman, "Enlargement: Legal and Procedural Aspects", (1995) 32 CMLRev, 95–130.
77. The European Free Trade Association, founded in 1959 by the UK, had established a free trade area among its member States. At the time of writing, EFTA members are: Iceland, Liechtenstein, Norway and Switzerland.
78. In 1992 the EFTA countries concluded an agreement with the EU creating the EEA. Under the agreement, the EFTA countries (now reduced to Iceland, Liechtenstein and Norway) accepted the EU internal market *acquis*. These countries also participate in some EU policies and programmes. Switzerland is not part of the EEA but has signed a series of bilateral agreements which define the relationship between the EU and Switzerland. On this topic see T. Pedersen, *European Union and the EFTA Countries: Enlargement and Integration*, 1994, London: Pinter. The book gives a good analysis of the negotiations leading to the creation of the EEA and the movement of Member States of EFTA towards membership of the EU.

2.6.6   Fifth enlargement

The fifth enlargement concerned Central and Eastern European States and Malta and Cyprus. The enlargement was intended to encompass 12 Central and Eastern European States.[79] However, as at 1 May 2004, neither Bulgaria nor Romania were ready to become members of the EU (see Chapter 2.6.7). On that date the following States joined the EU: Cyprus; the Czech Republic; Estonia; Hungary; Latvia; Lithuania; Malta; Poland; Slovakia; and, Slovenia.

The fifth enlargement was the most challenging for the EU and for the candidate States.[80] Apart from the two Mediterranean States, Cyprus and Malta, the applicants were Central and Eastern European States. Some of them were independent States for the first time in their history, for example, Slovakia and Slovenia. All of them were establishing their freedom and independence after the collapse of communism.

The accession process for the eight Central and Eastern European States was long, and even after their accession they were made subject to a lengthy transitional period. The most important restriction concerned the free movement of workers. Older Member States, fearing the influx of poorer, new EU citizens, were given an option to decide when, within seven years after the 2004 accession, to allow workers from new Member States to enter their labour market.

Only the UK, Ireland and Sweden, subject to some conditions relating to access to social benefits, decided to open up their job markets from the day of accession. From the same time Denmark accepted workers from new Member States on condition that they obtain a work permit in Denmark. In respect of participation in the CAP, farmers from new Member States will obtain full-scale support after a 10-year transitional period. However, the new Member States imposed some restrictions on older Member States. Some, fearing a massive loss of ownership of their agricultural land and immovable property to rich nationals from older Member States, were allowed to decree a period during which sales to non-nationals would be subject to restrictions. Generally, the period is seven years, but for Poland it is 12 years.

The biggest problem for the EU related to the reconstruction and adjustment of the economies of the new Member States to the standards required by the Union. Indeed, at the time of enlargement on average the EU's 75 million new citizens earned only 40 per cent of the income enjoyed by people living in the older Member States.[81] The level of GDP for the new EU members varied from 35 per cent of the EU average in the case of Latvia to 74 per cent for Slovenia. During the accession period financial assistance to the new Member States was provided within various EU programmes. In total €3 billion a year was allocated among eight Central and Eastern European countries, whilst Cyprus and Malta received €95 million between them for the period 2000–04.[82] Financial assistance continued to be provided for new Member States. The EU's financial assistance given to the new Member States represents 0.2 per cent of the GDP of the old Member States, rising to 0.3 per cent in 2013.[83]

According to the Commission, the fifth enlargement was very successful and fulfilled the favourable economic expectations of the EU. It increased the security, stability and prosperity of all EU citizens. It increased trade almost threefold between the old Member States and the new Member States in less

---

79.   The author has not adopted the views of the Commission, which considers accession of Bulgaria and Romania in 2007 as being the completion of the fifth enlargement (see Chapter 2.6.7).

80.   On this topic see: T. Grabbe, *The EU's Transformative Power: Europeanization through Conditionality in Central and Eastern Europe*, 2006, Basingstoke: Palgrave Macmillan.

81.   See http://europa/eu.int/abc/12lessons/print_index3_en.htm (accessed 10/12/10).

82.   European Commission, *More Unity and More Diversity, The European Union's Biggest Enlargement*, 2003, Luxembourg: Office for Official Publications of the European Communities.

83.   See the official website of the Commission, in particular its publication entitled "Good to Know about EU Enlargement", available at http://ec.europa.eu/enlargement/pdf/publication/screen_mythfacts_a5_en.pdf (accessed 23/9/11).

than ten years (from 1999 to 2009) and increased trade between the new Member States themselves from less than €15 billion to €77 billion in the same period. It increased employment in the new Member States by 1.5 per cent per annum from their accession to the beginning of the 2008 financial crisis, and provided many opportunities for businesses in the old Member States. The fear of a massive influx of workers from the new Member States did not materialise. In the vast majority of the old Member States, nationals from the new Member States represent less than 1 per cent of the working population, with the exception of Ireland (5 per cent) and the UK (1.2 per cent). The greatest influx of workers from the new Member States took place in 2006 and has since declined.

2.6.7 Sixth enlargement

Bulgaria and Romania signed Treaties of Accession on 25 April 2005. They joined the EU on 1 January 2007. Neither had been ready to accede in 2004 or in 2007 because of difficulties concerning their economies (i.e both being the poorest countries in the EU) and problems of high levels of corruption and organised crime. However, the EU decided that accession would be the best way to encourage future reforms, to ensure that EU funds would be properly administered and measures taken to fight corruption and organised crime.[84] It seems, however, that although Bulgaria and Romania are under specific post-accession monitoring, deep-rooted problems of inefficiency, malpractice and corruption have not been eradicated.[85]

2.6.8 Mini-enlargements outside Europe

These may occur when Member States' territories, located away from Europe, change status from overseas countries or territories (OCT) to that of outmost regions (OR). OCT are not part of the EU. To them only Part IV of the TFEU applies. OR are part of the EU although under Article 349 TFEU the Council may grant derogations from the application of EU law to OR in the light of the structural social and economic situation of OR "which is compounded by their remoteness, insularity, small size, difficult topography and climate, economic dependence on a few products, the permanence and combination of which severely restrain their development". The OR are: Azores; Madeira; Canary Islands; French Overseas Departments; Saint-Barthélemy; and, Saint-Martin.

On 31 March 2011, Mayotte, following a referendum held in March 2009, changed its status from a French OCT to that of being France's 101st department, and the fifth French Overseas Department. It will become an OR of the EU on January 2014.

2.6.9 Candidate countries

It is important to note that pre-accession financial aid was rationalised by Regulation 1085/2006 establishing an Instrument for Pre-Accession Assistance (IPA),[86] which entered into force on 1 January 2007. IPA supersedes the five pre-existing pre-accession programmes: Phare; ISPA; SAPARD; Turkey

---

84. See A. Łazowski, "And Then They Were Twenty Seven . . . A Legal Appraisal of the Sixth Accession Treaty", (2007) 44 CMLRev., 401.
85. See the 2012 Report of Transparency International entitled *Money, Politics, Power: Corruption Risks in Europe*, which states that although both countries enacted anti-corruption laws, "this flurry of legislative activity has not been accompanied by the widespread adoption of ethical norms, actions and behavior," 13. The report is available at http://www.transparency.org/enis/report (accessed 7/5/12).
86. [2006] OJ L210/90.

instrument; and, CARDS (Community Assistance for Reconstruction, Development and Stability in the Balkans). It establishes a coherent, unitary framework for financial assistance for both candidate and potential candidate countries. Under IPA an amount of €11,468 million is intended to be channelled over the period 2007–13 into helping such countries make necessary adjustments with a view to joining the EU.

At the time of writing, there are the following candidate countries: Croatia, the FYR Macedonia, Iceland, Montenegro, Serbia and Turkey.

A. **Croatia.** On 3 October 2005 the EU opened accession negotiations with Croatia, which were completed on 30 June 2011. The anticipated date for the accession of Croatia is 1 July 2013.

B. **The FYR Macedonia.** On 22 March 2004 FYR Macedonia applied to become an official candidate. In December 2005 upon the Commission's recommendation, the European Council approved FYR Macedonia as a candidate State. However, no date has been fixed for opening accession negotiations. The main obstacle is the dispute between the FRY Macedonia and Greece concerning the name of the country. So far, no solution has been reached with Greece.

C. **Iceland.** Iceland applied for membership of the EU on 16 June 2009 and the accession negotiations started on 17 July 2011. Iceland, a member of the EEA and EFTA, as well as an associate member of the Schengen Agreement (see Chapter 31.4.2) since 2000 has a long history of working with the EU. Negotiations are progressing swiftly and it is expected that Iceland will become a Member State in the near future, perhaps at the same time as Croatia.

D. **Montenegro.** Montenegro applied for EU membership on 15 December 2008. On 17 December 2010 the European Council confirmed its status as a candidate State but, at the time of writing, no accession negotiations have been initiated.

D. **Serbia.** On 1 March 2012, the European Council agreed to grant Serbia the status of candidate State. The opening accession negotiations could start in December 2012 if Serbia improves its relations with Kosovo, which it has not recognised as a State, and takes steps to eradicate corruption.

E. **Turkey.** Turkey has been waiting for admission to the EU for many years. Its first application for membership was lodged in April 1987. In December 1989 the Commission issued a negative opinion. It considered that the next step in Turkey's route to Brussels was a customs union with the Community. In January 1996 a customs union was agreed and this remains in force. The main reason for the Commission's negative opinion was Turkey's poor human rights record. However, following a change of government in 1998, Turkey started the process of democratisation which encompasses the improvement of its human rights record.

Turkey was recognised as a candidate State in 1999. On 3 October 2005, the foreign ministers of the EU Member States and the Turkish foreign minister reached agreement regarding the opening of official accession negotiations. This agreement was achieved after Austria, where 80 per cent of voters are against Turkey's accession, backed down from its demand for a "privileged relationship" with Turkey (meaning a second-class membership, rightly rejected by the Turks) as an alternative to membership. On 6 October 2005 the Commission, in its

Communication to the Council and the EP,[87] recommended opening accession negotiations subject to some conditions. The Commission stated that Turkey sufficiently fulfilled the Copenhagen political criteria. It considered, however, that accession could not take place before 2014 and that negotiations should be carried out on the basis of a three-pillar strategy set out in the Communication. Since then negotiations have been opened on 11 chapters out of 33 chapters. However, the pace of negotiations is very slow for many reasons: Turkey's on-going disputes with Cyprus and Greece; the growing support for pro-Islamic parties in Turkey; the deterioration in press freedom; the treatment of the Kurdish minority; and other human rights issues. In the Commission's Communication to the EP and the Council entitled "Enlargement Strategy and Main Challenges 2011-2012" the Commission indicated that it was very impressed by the state of the Turkish economy although it feared that there were signs of "overheating". Human rights violations, in particular of the freedom of expression in media, women's rights and freedom of religion were, however, considered as being matters of concern. Further, the Commission was disappointed that it had not been possible to open a new chapter for negotiations for over a year. The Commission proposed a new, more constructive approach to be applied to solve the impasse in negotiations based on "concrete steps in areas of common interest".

Some EU countries are very supportive of Turkish EU membership, e.g. the UK Prime Minister David Cameron during his visit to Turkey in November 2010 stated that the UK will "fight" for Turkish membership of the EU and that those who oppose it (mainly Germany and Austria) are acting out of protectionism, narrow nationalism and prejudice.[88]

The potential membership of Turkey poses great challenges to the EU. These are:

- demographic (Turkey has 80 million inhabitants);
- cultural (it is a secular country having a mainly Muslim population);
- geopolitical (Turkish accession would entail re-evaluation by the EU of its relations with the Middle East); and,
- Turkey continues to occupy the northern part of Cyprus, with 40,000 Turkish troops stationed on the island, and refuses to recognise Cyprus, a Member State of the EU. Until a solution is found to the Cyprus dispute, Turkey is unlikely to become a Member State.

However, every challenge also being an opportunity, there are many arguments in favour of Turkey's accession. It would:

- help to transform Turkey into a modern, well-functioning democracy, and thus extend peace, stability, prosperity, democracy, human rights and the rule of law not only across Europe but also into Asia;
- strengthen the EU's external security, given that Turkey plays a moderating role in the unstable neighbouring Middle East region;
- strengthen the EU's economy, given that Turkey has a very dynamic and rapidly growing economy;
- ensure the security of energy supplies to the EU. Turkey has at its border the most energy-rich regions on earth, it could therefore provide a corridor for road, rail, air and maritime pipeline connections between the EU and Turkey's southern neighbours;

---

87.   COM(204)656 final.
88.   "Cameron 'Anger' at Slow Pace of Turkish EU Negotiations" available at: http://www.bbc.co.uk/news/uk-politics-10767768 (accessed 4/4/12).

- reward Turkey for its support for NATO;
- create a more multiracial and multi-religious EU;
- reinforce secularism in Turkey (which has been a secular State since 1923); and,
- given that 23 per cent of the Turkish population is under the age of 15, to some extent respond to the problem of the increasingly aging population of the current EU.

2.6.10 Potential candidates

These are the Western Balkan States: Albania (applied on 28 April 2009); Kosovo; and, Bosnia and Herzegovina. The last two have not formally applied. All three have been promised the prospect of EU membership as and when they are ready.

RECOMMENDED READING

Books

Cremona, M., *The Enlargement of the European Union*, 2003, Oxford: OUP.

Grabbe, H., *The EU's Transformative Power: Europeanisation through Conditionality in Central and Eastern Europe*, 2006, Basingstoke: Palgrave Macmillan.

Pedersen, T., *European Union and the EFTA Countries: Enlargement and Integration*, 1994, London: Pinter.

Prechal, S., *Reconciling the Deepening and Widening of the European Union*, 2008, Cambridge: CUP.

Tatham, A.F., *Enlargement of the European Union*, 2009, London: KLI.

Articles

Albi, A., "Ironies in Human Rights Protection in the EU: Pre-Conditionality and Post-Accession Conundrums", (2009) 15 ELJ, 46.

Gialdino, C.C., "Some Reflections on the Acquis Communautaire", (1995) CMLRev., 1089.

Hilton, C., "EU Enlargement", in Craig, P. and de Bùrca, G. (eds), *The Evolution of EU Law*, 2nd edn, 2011, Oxford: OUP, 187.

Lenaerts, K., and Van Nuffel, P., "Advanced Integration and the Principle of Equality of Member States within the European Union", in Kaddous, C. and Auer, A. (eds), *Les Principes Fundamentaux de la Constitution Européenne*, 2006, Paris: Halbing and Lichtenhahn/Bruylant/LGDJ, 245.

Peers, S., "An Even Closer Waiting Room? The Case for Eastern European Accession to the European Economic Area", (1995) 32 CMLRev., 187.

PROBLEM QUESTION

Astoria, a fictitious country located in North Africa, wishes to become a member of the EU. In 2010 Astoria bought from Poland a small island, Wolin, which is situated in the Baltic sea, just off the Polish coast. Astoria is a very prosperous country and a world leader in several economic areas. It has a small population of 400,000 who enjoy freedom of religion through the Church of Astoria.

The Church preserves the traditional customs of the country. Women are permitted to have up to three husbands but men may have only one wife. Men are always under the guardianship of women. They are required to stay at home, cook, clean and take care of children. If they go outside their homes they must be accompanied by an adult female and must wear a full diver suit. Further, there is an initiation procedure to manhood (MP) during which the front teeth must be removed. As the Astorian Dentists Association, in accordance with a recommendation of the World Health Organisation, refuses to extract perfectly healthy front teeth, such teeth are often pulled out by female plumbers with primitive instruments. This procedure leads to mouth infections, lack of appetite, chronic pain and sometimes death. Astorian men claim to be proud of their initiation procedure and, according to the government, reject the idea that MP is a barbaric custom which must cease. The government of Astoria has officially condemned MP but has neither introduced any law prohibiting it nor offered any protection to men who do not wish to undergo MP.

Advise the Astorian government whether its application for membership of the EU is likely to succeed.

ESSAY QUESTION

Critically assess the main requirements for accession to the EU.

AIDE-MÉMOIRE

Requirements for accession to the EU:

Political requirements	Economic requirements	Legal requirements	Geographical requirement	Formal requirements
A candidate State must have stable institutions guaranteeing that the values on which the EU is founded are respected.	A candidate State must have a functioning market economy and be able to cope with competitive pressures and market forces within the EU.	A candidate State must, first, be a State within the meaning of public international law; and, second, accept the EU *acquis*. There are three kinds of *acquis*: normative, political and judicial.	At least part of a candidate State's territory must be in Europe.	These are set out in Article 49 TEU.

ENLARGEMENTS

First Enlargement: On 1 January 1973 Denmark; Ireland; and, the UK joined the Communities.
Second Enlargement: On 1 January 1981 Greece joined the Communities.
Third Enlargement: On 1 January 1986 Portugal and Spain joined the Communities.
De facto enlargement: On 3 October 1990 the former German Democratic Republic (GDR) became an integral part of the Federal Republic of Germany and all three Community Treaties were extended to apply to the former GDR.
Fourth Enlargement: On 1 January 1995 Austria; Finland; and, Sweden joined the EU.
Fifth Enlargement: On 1 May 2004 the following States joined the EU: Cyprus; the Czech

(Continued)

Republic; Estonia; Hungary; Latvia; Lithuania; Malta; Poland; Slovakia; and, Slovenia.

Sixth Enlargement: On 1 January 2007 Bulgaria and Romania joined the EU.

Mini-enlargement outside Europe: On 1 January 2014, Mayotte, as a result of a change of its status in France (from an OCT to a an OR), will become part of the EU.

Anticipated enlargement: Croatia is expected to join the EU on 1 July 2013.

Candidate States: FYR Macedonia; Iceland; Montenegro; Serbia; and, Turkey.

Potential Candidate States: Albania; Bosnia and Herzegovina; and, Kosovo.

3

THE INSTITUTIONAL FRAMEWORK OF THE EU

CONTENTS

CHAPTER OUTLINE

1. This chapter examines the main institutions of the EU. Article 13 TEU lists seven bodies that are entitled to be referred to as "EU institutions". They are: the European Parliament (EP); the European Council; the Council of the European Union (Council), the European Commission (Commission); the Court of Justice of the European Union (CJEU); the European Central Bank (ECB); and, the Court of Auditors (CoA).

2. Each of the seven EU institutions has a specific role to play in the functioning of the EU. The European Council shapes the future of the EU, the Council represents the interests of the Member States; the Commission, the interests of the EU; the EP, the interests of the people of the Member States; the CJEU ensures that in the functioning of the institutional system the law is observed; and the CoA is charged with supervision of the financial aspects of the EU. The ECB defines and implements the monetary policy of the EU.

3. The concept of institutional balance of power is used to describe both the legal principle enshrined in Article 13(2) TEU under which each institution is required to act in accordance with the powers conferred on it by the Treaties, and in conformity with the procedures, conditions and objectives set out in them, and its political dimension, i.e. the power relationships between EU institutions. The division of powers between the EU institutions is complex. In the EU legislative powers lie with the Council and the EP. The EP, from being solely an advisory body, evolved into a directly elected body and, under the ToL, is a co-legislator and jointly with the Council adopts the EU budget. The Commission is the "guardian of the Treaty" and as such supervises and, if necessary, enforces EU law. It also initiates and implements EU legislation. The CJEU (a collective name given to the ECJ, the General Court, formerly known as the CFI, and specialised courts) ensures the observance of law in the implementation of the Treaties by the EU institutions, bodies and agencies and the Member States. Under Article 267 TFEU the ECJ assists national courts in their difficult task of the interpretation of EU law, and thus ensures homogeneity and uniformity in its application in all Member States. The Heads of State or Government of the Member States, the President of the European Council and the President of the Commission form the European Council, which is crucial to the development of the EU as it provides the EU with political impetus on key issues.

3.1 Introduction

The seven main institutions mentioned in Article 13 TEU – the EP, the European Council, the Council, the Commission, the CJEU, the ECB and the CoA – form the basic structure of the institutional system of the EU. The ToL conferred the status of EU institutions on the European Council and the ECB. The European Council which arose from the summit meetings of Heads of State or Government of the Member States was, until the entry into force of the ToL, a body of uncertain institutional status. Under the ToL, the ECB became an EU institution although its independence and special status continues.

To this basic institutional framework the following institutions and bodies must be added:

- two main advisory bodies of the EU: the Economic and Social Committee and the Committee of the Regions which assist the Council and the Commission;

- institutions necessary to carry out tasks peculiar to Economic and Monetary Union which are mainly relevant to the Member States which have adopted the euro as their national currency;

- the European Investment Bank which operates on a non-profit-making basis and grants loans and guarantees finance projects which contribute to the balanced and steady development of the internal market (Article 309 TFEU); and,

- bodies which are within the scope of the Treaties and which assist the Council and the Commission in the accomplishment of their tasks: these are agencies, offices and centres, such as the European Environmental Agency, the European Training Foundation, the European Agency for the Evaluation of Medicinal Products, the Office for Veterinary and Plant Health Inspection and Control, the European Monitoring Centre for Drugs and Drug Addiction, Europol, Eurojust, the EU Agency for Fundamental Rights and the European Chemicals Agency.

The institutional structure of the EU is based on original concepts, new to public international law, but necessary to promote EU values; pursue Union objectives; serve the interests of the Union, its citizens, its Members States; and, ensure the consistency, effectiveness and continuity of its policies and actions (Article 13(1) TEU).

Three principles apply to relations between EU institutions:

- The principle of institutional balance which requires each institution to act in accordance with the powers conferred on it by the Treaties, and in conformity with the procedures, conditions and objectives set out in them (Article 13(2) TEU).[89] As a result, any encroachment of one EU institution on powers attributed to another is prohibited.[90] It is also prohibited for an EU institution to delegate its powers to an external body or to another EU institution if to do so would result in the modification of institutional balance. The principle of institutional balance is static as it is aimed at protecting the prerogatives of each EU institution, although the ECJ used it in a dynamic manner in Case C-70/88 *EP v Council*,[91] in which it recognised the right of the EP to being an action for annulment of EU secondary legislation despite the fact that there was no provision in the EC Treaty to this effect, i.e. there was a gap in the EC Treaty;

- The principle of institutional autonomy, under which each EU institution is empowered to freely organise the manner in which it works. This power is based on the Treaties, which provide that EU institutions are entitled to adopt their own rules of procedure;[92] and,

- The principle of loyal co-operation. Article 13(2) TEU states that: "The institutions shall practice mutual sincere co-operation". The best example of the implementation of the principle of loyal co-operation is when EU institutions enter into inter-institutional agreements. Such agreements between the EP, the Council and the Commission may be of a binding nature (Article 295 TFEU).

Common rules which apply to all institutions concern:

- the seats of the institutions; and,

- the languages of the institutions.

These rules are examined below.

3.1.1   Seats of the institutions

Under Article 341 TFEU the seat of the EU institutions shall be determined by common accord of the Member States. In practice, the determination of the permanent seats of EU institutions has always been subject to fierce competition among the Member States. A Decision of 8 April 1965[93] provided a temporary solution by assigning the seats of the institutions among three different places: Luxembourg, Brussels and Strasbourg. This compromise gave rise to many political, financial and legal difficulties, especially with respect to where the sessions of the EP were to be held.[94] With a view to resolving

---

89.   See J-P. Jacqué, "The Principle of Institutional Balance", (2004) 41 CMLRev., 283.
90.   Case 149/85 *Roger Wybot v Edgar Faure and Others* [1986] ECR 2391.
91.   [1990] ECR I-2041, para. 26.
92.   Case 208/80 *Lord Bruce of Donington v Aspden* [1981] ECR 2205.
93.   [1967] OJ 152/18.
94.   Case 230/81 *Luxembourg v EP* [1983] ECR 255; Case 108/83 *Luxembourg v EP* [1984] ECR 1945; Cases 358/85 and 51/86 *France v EP* [1988] ECR 4821; Cases C-213/88 and C-39/89 *Luxembourg v EP* [1991] ECR I-5643 and Case C-345/95 *France v EP* [1997] ECR I-5215.

matters, an agreement was reached at the European Council summit held at Edinburgh on 12 December 1992,[95] and subsequently adjusted by a European Council Decision adopted at the Brussels summit on 29–30 October 1993,[96] which determined the seats of Community institutions. These pre ToL arrangements were confirmed by Protocol No. 2 attached to the Treaties and the EA Treaty "On the Location of the Seats of the Institutions and Certain Bodies, Offices, Agencies and Departments of the European Union". The Protocol allocates seats as follows:

- The Council has its seat in Brussels; however, during the months of April, June and October the Council meets in Luxembourg;

- The Commission has its seat in Brussels, although certain departments of the Commission, namely the administrative services of the EA, its Statistical Office and the Office for Official Publications, are located in Luxembourg;

- The CJEU, the CoA and the European Investment Bank have their seats in Luxembourg;

- The EP is required to hold 12 periods of monthly plenary sessions, including the budget session, in Strasbourg each year but any additional plenary sessions are to be held in Brussels. The Committee of the EP is required to meet in Brussels. Its secretariat and departments are located in Luxembourg;

- The seat of the ECB is located in Frankfurt; and,

- The seat of the CoR and the EESC is in Brussels.

The European Council in its Decision of 29 October 1993,[97] expressed a preference for the allocation of seats for various bodies and agencies in Member States which did not host any EU institutions. As a result, the European Environmental Agency is located in Copenhagen; the European Agency for Evaluation of Medicinal Products in London; the Agency for Health and Safety at Work in Bilbao; the Office for Harmonization in the Internal Market (Trade Marks, Designs and Models) in Alicante; the Office for Veterinary and Plant Health Inspection and Control in Dublin; the European Monitoring Centre for Drugs and Drug Addiction in Lisbon; Europol and Eurojust in The Hague; the European Police College (CEPOL) in Bramshill, UK; the EU Agency for Fundamental Rights in Vienna; and, the European Chemicals Agency in Helsinki.

3.1.2 Languages

Rules governing the languages of the institutions are determined by the Council, acting unanimously, but without prejudice to the provisions contained in the Rules of Procedure of the ECJ.[98] Regulation 1/1958 as amended[99] provides that the national languages of the Member States are official languages of the EU, all equal in rank and status.

As from 1 January 2007 there are 23 official languages. They are: Bulgarian; Czech; Danish; Dutch; English; Estonian; German; Spanish (its Castilian version); Finnish; French; Greek; Hungarian; Irish; Italian; Latvian; Lithuanian; Maltese; Polish; Portuguese; Romanian; Slovak; Slovene; and, Swedish.

---

95.   [1992] OJ C341/1.
96.   [1993] OJ C323/1.
97.   Decision of the Representatives of the Governments of the Member States on the Location of Seats of Certain Bodies and Departments, [1993] OJ C323/1.
98.   Article 342 TFEU.
99.   [2003] OJ L236/33.

The EU uses three alphabets: Cyrillic; Latin; and, Greek.

All language versions of the Treaties and of EU measures are equally authentic.[100] If there are any discrepancies between different language versions, they should be resolved without giving priority to any particular language.

It should be noted that by virtue of Council Conclusion "On the Official Use of Additional Languages within the Council and Possibly Other Institutions" adopted on 13 June 2005,[101] a Member State may conclude administrative arrangements with the Council and other institutions allowing its citizens to communicate with the Council, or the relevant institution, in languages other than those referred to in Regulation 1/1958 as amended.

The use of 23 official languages in the EU means that all official meetings are conducted in all official languages, which are translated from one to another simultaneously. Also, all official documents are in 23 languages, although French and English are imposed as working languages. All individual acts, that is, those addressed to Member States or to individuals, are written in the language of the relevant Member State. EU acts of general scope of application, for example regulations, are written in the 23 languages.

This use of multiple languages in the everyday running of the EU is necessary to ensure equality between Member States and transparency with regard to the citizens of the EU. In addition, national authorities and courts, which often have to apply EU acts directly to their nationals, must have the relevant text in their own national language. The principles of legal certainty and the protection of individual rights strengthen this requirement. Furthermore, conferring official status on 23 languages permits EU nationals to submit complaints to a particular institution in their own language (see Chapter 22.10).

3.2 The concept of institutional balance of power

Montesquieu's concept of the "separation of powers",[102] under which parliament is responsible for the performance of the legislative functions, government is responsible for executive functions and the courts are responsible for judicial functions, is not appropriate to describe the power relationships between EU institutions, mainly because the EU is a *sui generis* entity: i.e. on the one hand it is not a State or federation and, on the other, it is more than a traditional international organisation.[103] Instead, the concept of institutional balance of power is used to encompass both the legal principle of institutional balance of power enshrined in Article 13(2) TEU (see Chapter 3.1) and its political dimension which refers to power relationships between EU institutions. As Craig stated, the concept of institutional balance "presumes by its very nature a normative and political judgment as to which institutions should be able to partake of legislative

---

100. Article 55 TEU.
101. [2005] OJ C148/1.
102. Montesquieu, *L'Esprit Des Lois*, 1998, Oxford: Voltaire Foundation. He believed that the best government is one elected by the people; that there should be a right balance of power within a government, i.e. the executive, legislative and judicial branches of government should be separated; and, that there should be a system of checks and balances whereby the three branches could exercise controls on each other.
103. Perhaps the best answer as to the identification of the nature of the EU is provided by Douglas-Scott in the following terms: "In the end, it surely matters not whether we call the EU a federal system or not. It exhibits enough federal features to satisfy those who are determined to find it federal, and lacks some which would entitle purists to reject the title ... The EU ... is too sui generis, too complex, too multidimensional, to fit any such categorisation." S. Douglas-Scott, *Constitutional Law of the European Union*, 2002, Harlow: Pearson Longman, 195.

and executive power, and it presumes also a view as to what constitutes the appropriate balance between them".[104]

The power relationships between EU institutions have evolved greatly since the creation of the EEC. This is because of amendments made to the EEC Treaty and the way in which the institutions have actually used the powers and procedures set out in the Treaties; in particular the ECJ, which has always played a great integrationist role (see Chapter 4.7). Until 1975, the institutional balance was essentially bi-polar, as only two institutions had real powers: the Commission and the Council. With the adoption of the Budgetary Treaties in 1970 and 1975, for the first time, the EP acquired some real powers. From that time until the entry into force of the ToL the institutional balance was tri-polar and characterised by a gradual but constant increase in the powers of the EP. The ToL created a more complex hybrid four-polar system, in which four EU institutions have real power in the EU: the EP, the Council, the Commission and the European Council. The four-polar institutional balance includes a hybrid element constituted by the post of the High Representative of the Union for Foreign Affairs and Security (HR) the holder of which wears three hats: she is responsible for conducting and implementing the Union's CFSP; she is an *ex officio* Vice-President of the Commission; and, she chairs the Foreign Affairs Council. The role of the HR within the EU institutional system is complex in terms of the relationship with the EP, the European Council, the Commission and the Council (see Chapter 7.3.1).

Powers exercised by EU institutions can be examined from different perspectives, or as Monar[105] stated, there are different dimensions of power. Monar suggests the following dimensions:

- power relating to the constitutional position of EU institutions;

- power relating to policy initiation;

- power relating to decision-making;

- power relating to implementation of EU legislation and budget as well as control of implementation of EU measures at national level;

- power related to institutional strength; and,

- power linked to public visibility of each institution.

When the institutional changes made by the ToL are examined in the light of the six mentioned dimensions, it appears that the ToL strengthened the powers of the EP and the European Council in almost all dimensions of the institutional balance in the hybrid four-polar institutional system. Accordingly, under the ToL two institutions directly elected by EU citizens, the EP and the European Council, are the most powerful. This assignment of powers enhances the democratic nature of the EU and its legitimacy, but also emphasises that the complex institutional balance created by the ToL requires that all EU institutions and bodies act in accordance with Article 13(2) TEU, i.e. they must co-operate to ensure the consistency, effectiveness and continuity of the Union's policies and actions. As the EP, a supranational institution, and the European Council, an intergovernmental institution, emerge as the two most powerful institutions of the EU, the struggle between intergovernmentalism and

---

104.   P. Craig, "Institutions, Power, and Institutional Balance", in P. Craig and G. de Bùrca (eds), *The Evolution of EU Law*, 2nd edn, 2011, Oxford: OUP, 42.

105.   J. Monar, "The European Union's Institutional Balance of Power after the Treaty of Lisbon", available at http://ec.europa.eu/education/jean-monnet/doc/ecsa10/monarb_en.pdf (accessed 12/4/12).

supranationality (see Chapter 1.7) continues.[106] Having said this, for some commentators, the institutional system of the EU should no longer be examined from the perspective of supranationality and intergovernmentalism as this categorisation "seems increasingly obsolete as supranational and intergovernmental elements are now so intermingled and the distinction at least partially diluted that they are difficult to apply to the institutional reality".[107]

3.3 The European Commission (the Commission)

The Commission represents the interests of the EU. As a "revolutionary" body within the institutional system of the EU, it is also the most controversial institution.[108] It exercises many functions, the most important of which is to "promote the general interest of the Union and take appropriate initiatives to that end" (Article 17 TEU). The Commission is:

- the guardian of the Treaties;

- the initiator of EU legislation;

- the executive arm of the EU; and,

- the representative of the EU in the international arena, except with regard to the CFSP and in other cases provided for in the Treaties.

The Commission employs about 25,000 European civil servants and is divided into departments called Directorates General (DGs). Each DG is responsible for a particular policy area and is headed by a Director General who is accountable to one of the commissioners. Overall co-ordination is provided by the Secretariat General, which also manages the weekly Commission meetings. The Secretariat General is headed by the Secretary General, who is answerable directly to the President of the Commission.

The Commission divides its tasks among its members, and each commissioner is allocated one or more policy areas. Each commissioner has personal advisers who form his or her so-called Cabinet, which liaises between the commissioner and his or her Directorate(s) General. The chief of the Cabinet is usually the same nationality as the commissioner and deputises for him or her as necessary. This chief also meets weekly with other chiefs of Cabinet in order to prepare the agenda for the Commission.

3.3.1 The President of the Commission

The ToL revised rules regarding the election of the President of the Commission and extended his powers over Commissioners.

Under Article 17(7) TEU, the President of the Commission is elected by the EP acting by a majority of its component members, based on a proposal from the European Council, which must be approved by QMV. In the choice of a candidate the European Council is required to take into consideration the result of the elections to the EP. If the candidate selected by the European Council fails to achieve EP approval, the European Council, acting by QMV, is required, within one month of the rejection of the previous candidate, to propose a new candidate.

106. Y. Defuyst, "The European Union's Institutional Balance after the Treaty of Lisbon: 'Community Method' and 'Democratic Deficit' Reassessed", (2008) 39/2 *Georgetown Journal of International Law*, 247.

107. Supra note 105, 22.

108. D. Spence (ed.), *The European Commission*, 3rd edn, 2006, London: Harper.

Under the ToL the EP will not only intensify its scrutiny over the Commission by electing its President but may also influence, to a great extent, the choice of the candidate for the Presidency of the Commission. This may occur if, for example, the largest political group in the EP decides to tie its electoral campaign to a particular person as a candidate for the Presidency of the Commission. In such a situation, it will be very difficult for the European Council not to nominate that person. The link between the elections to the EP and the choice of a candidate for the Presidency of the Commission may also make elections to the EP more personalised and more important for voters. The consequence of this may be that, on the one hand, the Commission will acquire a new source of political legitimacy through the manner in which its President is elected, but on the other hand, if the President is too closely connected to a larger political group in the EP, questions may be raised as to his/her independence and objectivity.

Under Article 17(6) TEU the Commission works under the political guidance of its President who:

- decides matters concerning the internal organisation of the Commission in order to ensure coherence, efficiency and the collegiality of Commission actions;

- divides the tasks of the Commission among its members and is entitled to change the original allocation of tasks in respect of each commissioner in the course of the Commission's term of office. This is subject to an exception in that the HR is, *ex officio*, responsible for External Relations and European Neighbourhood Policy;

- appoints, from amongst the members of the Commission, Vice-Presidents, but not the HR who is a Vice-President *ex officio* and whose appointment is subject to specific rules (see Chapter 7.3.1); and,

- can force a particular commissioner to resign. This possibility changes the relationship between the Commission and the EP. Under this arrangement it is unlikely that the EP will use its motion of censure, unless, based on the principle of collegiate responsibility of the Commission, the EP wants to remove the whole Commission (see Chapter 3.6.7.1). However, the President has no power to force the HR to resign but may make a proposal for her dismissal to the European Council which takes the final decision.

3.3.2 The College of Commissioners

The Commission is made up of one commissioner per Member State; one of them is not only a commissioner but also the HR. Attempts at reducing the number of commissioners have failed. Indeed, the European Council held in July 2009 provided legally binding assurances to the Irish Government prior to the second referendum concerning Ireland's ratification of the ToL that Ireland and other Member States would be represented in the Commission by one commissioner of their nationality. The provisions of the ToL relating to this matter are expected to be amended in the first accession treaty following the ToL.

Commissioners, other than the President of the Commission and the HR (see Chapter 7.3.1), are appointed as follows. The Council, by common accord with the person nominated as President of the Commission, adopts a list of persons intended to be appointed as members of the Commission. The list is established in accordance with a proposal submitted by each Member State. The President, the members of the Commission, and the HR are subject, as a body, to a vote of approval by the EP. After such approval the President and the other members of the Commission are actually appointed by the Council acting by QMV.

3.3.3 Conduct of Commissioners

Commissioners must be chosen on the grounds of their general competence. Article 17(5) TEU specifies that only nationals of the Member States may be appointed as commissioners. Article 17(3) TEU provides that commissioners must act in the general interest of the EU and that their independence must be beyond doubt. In this respect they take a solemn oath before the ECJ. As Article 17(3) TEU provides, their independence requires that they "shall neither seek nor take instructions from any government or from any other body. They shall refrain from any action incompatible with their duties or the performance of their tasks". Under Article 245 TFEU each Member State undertakes to respect the independence of commissioners and not to seek to influence them in the performance of their tasks.

Under Article 245 TFEU commissioners are prohibited during their term from engaging in any other occupation, whether gainful or not, and from any action incompatible with their duties as commissioners. This excludes commissioners from being members of a national parliament or of the EP. However, academic activities, research and teaching are considered to be compatible with the status of commissioner.[109]

The scope of Article 245 TFEU was explained by the ECJ in Case C-432/04 *Commission v Cresson*,[110] in which the ECJ:

- Gave a broad interpretation to the notion of "obligations arising from [a commissioner's office]". It stated that the members of the Commission are required to observe the highest standards of conduct. In particular, they have a duty to ensure that the general interest of the EU takes precedence at all times, not only over national interests, but also over personal interests. Although they have to conduct themselves in a manner which is beyond reproach, a certain degree of gravity of any conduct deviating from those standards is required for that conduct to be censured under Article 245 TFEU. It is for the Court to decide, on a case by case basis, whether the conduct concerned only slightly deviated from those proper standards or whether it reached a degree of gravity which must be censured under Article 245 TFEU.

- Held that the penalty which may be imposed for a breach of the obligations arising from the office of commissioner, may consist of either compulsory retirement or deprivation of the right to a pension or other benefits. The penalty of compulsory retirement applies only where a breach arose, and continued during the term of office. The penalty of deprivation of benefits (pension or other) may be imposed irrespective of whether the breach occurred during or after the term of office, and whether it was discovered or established during or after the term of office.

Commissioners are required to comply with a very strict Code of Conduct[111] under which:

- commissioners are required to act in accordance with the highest standards of public life;

- in order to avoid any conflict of interests, commissioners are subject to a one-year "cooling-off period" after leaving office, during which their prospective jobs may be vetoed by a special ethics committee; and,

- commissioners are required to declare their financial interests and assets (as well as those of their spouse or partner) which might create a conflict of interest in the performance of their duties.

---

109. For more on incompatibility see Q. E. No 2752/94 by F. Herman [1995] OJ C88/38.
110. [2006] ECR I-6387.
111. Com(2011)2904.

3.3.4 Term of office

The term of office of commissioners was extended to five years by the Treaty of Maastricht in order to synchronise it with that of the EP. The mandate is renewable. Any vacancy, however arising, is filled for the remainder of the member's term of office by a new member appointed by common accord of the Member States. However, the Council may, acting unanimously, on a proposal from the President of the Commission, decide not to fill such a vacancy. In the event of any vacancy in the office of President his replacement should be appointed following the usual procedure.[112]

If commissioners no longer fulfil the conditions required for the performance of their duties, or have been guilty of serious misconduct, the ECJ may, on application by the Council acting by a simple majority or by the Commission, compulsorily retire them (Article 247 TFEU). This possibility has been applied only once, and that was in a case of the total incapacity of a commissioner. In the event of any breach of obligations imposed upon commissioners, including those to behave with integrity and discretion even after they have ceased to hold office, sanctions may be imposed by the ECJ consisting of deprivation of pension rights or other benefits (see immediately above). The EP also exercises some disciplinary power, but only over the entire Commission by submitting a motion of censure under Article 243 TFEU (see Chapter 3.6.7.1).

3.3.5 Functioning: the principle of collegiality

The Commission is a collegiate body. This means that no member of the Commission is actually empowered to take any decision on his own and if a member has, in effect, made a decision, it expresses the position of the entire Commission.

The principle of collegiality is based on the equal participation of the commissioners in the adoption of decisions. The immediate consequence of this principle is that decisions should be the subject of collective deliberation and that all the members of the College of Commissioners bear collective responsibility at political level for all decisions adopted. Additionally, this principle means that each decision must be formally approved by the College. Failure to ensure this may render a measure invalid.[113] Apart from the exceptions provided in Articles 10 and 11 of the Commission's Rules of Procedure, the principle of collegiality requires that the Commission seeks a broad consensus among its members, although it may also submit the matter to a formal vote.[114] The President of the Commission is only *primus inter pares*; there is no casting vote.

The principle of collegiality is less formalistic than it appears on the surface, as explained in Case C-191/95 *Commission v Germany*.[115]

THE FACTS WERE:

The Commission decided to issue a reasoned opinion against the government of Germany for failure to provide for appropriate penalties in cases where companies limited by shares failed to disclose their annual accounts, as prescribed in particular by the First Company Directive 68/151/EEC of 9 March 1968 and the Fourth Company Directive 78/660/EEC of

---

112. Article 246 TFEU.
113. Case C-137/92P *Commission v BASF* [1994] ECR I-2555.
114. Under Article 250 TFEU a simple majority of its members is required.
115. [1998] ECR I-5449.

25 July 1978. When Germany did not comply with the opinion, the Commission decided, in conformity with Article 258 TFEU, to bring proceedings before the ECJ against the German Government. Both decisions were challenged by the German Government as not being the subject of collective deliberations by the College of Commissioners.

Held:

The ECJ held that the formal requirement for effective compliance with the principle of collegiality varies according to the nature and legal effect of the act. In the case of acts which have no binding legal effect, it is not necessary for the College "itself formally to decide on the wording of the acts which give effect to those decisions and put them in final form." In such circumstances it is sufficient if the information on which those decisions are based is available to the members of the College. In the present case, the measures in question had no binding legal effect and necessary information was available to the members of the College.

The principle of collegiality also entails that acts adopted by the College of Commissioners, in order to be binding on their addressees, must be authenticated by the signatures of the President of the Commission and of the executive secretary. The objective of authentication is to ensure that the text adopted by the College of Commissioners becomes fixed, so that in the event of a dispute it can be verified that the text adopted corresponds precisely to the text notified or published. In Joined Cases C-286 and 288P *Commission v Solvay*[116] the ECJ held that if an act adopted by the Commission has not been properly authenticated, the CJEU must, of its own motion, raise the issue and annul the act vitiated by that defect. This duty of the courts remains irrespective of whether or not the lack of authentication caused any harm to a party to the dispute.

3.3.6 Competences

The competences of the European Commission are described in Article 17(1) and (2) TFEU. Article 17(1) provides that:

"The Commission shall promote the general interest of the Union and take appropriate initiatives to that end. It shall ensure the application of the Treaties, and of measures adopted by the institutions pursuant to them. It shall oversee the application of Union law under the control of the Court of Justice of the European Union. It shall execute the budget and manage programmes. It shall exercise coordinating, executive and management functions, as laid down in the Treaties. With the exception of the common foreign and security policy, and other cases provided for in the Treaties, it shall ensure the Union's external representation. It shall initiate the Union's annual and multiannual programming with a view to achieving inter institutional agreements."

Article 17(2) confirms the Commission's right to initiate proposals for legislative acts and other acts unless the Treaties provide otherwise (see Chapter 5.3).

The role of the Commission under the CFSP is described in Chapter 7.5.3.

A.   **The European Commission as the "guardian of the Treaty".** The most important function of the Commission is to ensure that the provisions of the Treaties and the acts of the institutions

---

116.   [2000] ECR I-2341.

are complied with by the Member States, any natural or legal person under the jurisdiction of a Member State and all EU institutions, bodies, offices and agencies. In order to fulfil this task the Commission has at its disposal important powers:

- The Commission is empowered to obtain any necessary information from Member States, individuals and undertakings. Member States have a duty to forward information required by the Commission, notify measures and projects of measures they intend to adopt, and provide explanations concerning any question of law or fact which the Commission considers important. This obligation derives either from specific provisions of the Treaties[117] or from measures adopted by the EU institutions,[118] or from Article 4(3) TEU. This article requires Member States to co-operate with the Commission in order to facilitate the achievement of the EU's tasks. The Commission may ask individuals and undertakings to forward information[119] and, under its investigative powers, to verify it. A request for information is often the first step in the Commission's investigation of an alleged infringement of EU law by an undertaking in competition matters (see Chapter 30.2.2);
- The Commission may take preventative actions. The Commission formulates recommendations and delivers opinions intended to ensure effective application of EU law in the future;
- The Commission is empowered to enforce compliance with EU law. The obligation to observe EU law binds Member States, natural and legal persons, and the EU institutions, bodies and agencies. In respect of natural and legal persons, the Commission may impose pecuniary and/or administrative sanctions upon them in matters concerning the control of security under the EA Treaty and in competition issues under the TFEU. With regards to the Member States, under Article 258 TFEU the Commission may bring an action before the ECJ against a Member State which it considers to be in breach of EU law (see Chapter 14.2). If any EU institution, body or agency breaches EU law, the Commission may bring an action under Articles 263 or 265 TFEU; this is mostly applied in respect of the Council (see Chapter 15);
- The Commission may authorise, in certain circumstances, derogations from the provisions of the Treaties. Under the Acts of Accession and in respect of measures adopted by EU institutions in relation to international agreements the Commission is authorised to grant derogations. Under Articles 346, 347 and 114(6) TFEU the Commission is empowered to authorise measures incompatible with the internal market. Such derogations may be authorised in cases where a Member State is faced with serious economic difficulties, internal disturbances and serious international tension, or if its essential interest of national security is in jeopardy; and,
- In the context of EMU, the Commission monitors budgetary discipline in Member States in order to avoid excessive governmental deficits[120] and is empowered to supervise their balance of payments.[121] Powers of the Commission in this area will be extended by the Fiscal Pact (see Chapter 1.20) when, and if, it enters into force.

---

117. For example, Articles 114(5) and 117 TFEU.
118. Especially the final provisions of directives which impose upon the Member States the obligation to notify the Commission of the adoption of implementing measures.
119. For example, Article 337 TFEU.
120. Article 126 TFEU.
121. Articles 143 and 144 TFEU.

B. **The Commission as the initiator of legislative measures.** The general interest of the EU requires that the Commission's main objective is to foster European integration. Consequently, its right to initiate legislative measures in order to further develop the EU is well justified. Article 17(2) TEU confirms the Commission's virtual monopoly on the right to initiate proposals for both legislative and non-legislative acts (for exceptions see Chapter 5.3). However, the Commission's right to initiate legislation and other acts is not exercised lightly and is subject to many safeguards. The role of the Commission as the initiator of legislative measures in examined in depth in Chapter 5.3.

C. **Executive powers of the Commission.** Article 17 TEU states that the Commission shall exercise co-ordinating, executive and management functions, as laid down in the Treaties.

The administration of EU policies necessitates the adoption of numerous binding measures. In addition, the Commission implements the EU budget and administers four special funds: the European Social Fund, the European Development Fund, the European Agricultural Guidance and Guarantee Fund, and the European Regional Development Fund.[122]

By virtue of Article 290 TFEU the Commission exercises delegated powers and under Article 291 implementing powers (see Chapter 4.5.2).

D. **International functions of the Commission.** The international functions of the Commission have been limited as a result of the establishment of the post of HR and the post of President of the European Council. In foreign affairs, with the exception of the CFSP, the Commission shares its tasks with the HR (see Chapter 7.5.3). Under Article 207(3) TFEU, and subject to the procedure outlined in Article 218 TFEU the Commission negotiates international trade agreements in accordance with negotiating directives adopted by the Council. With regard to other international agreements, the Commission will be the negotiator in respect of matters which are not substantially covered by the CFSP. In matters where the principal component is the CFSP, the HR will be negotiator.

3.4 The Council of the European Union (the Council)

Following the entry into force of the Treaty of Maastricht, the Council of Ministers, which was referred to in the Treaties merely as "the Council", adopted Decision 93/591 on 8 November 1993,[123] in which it renamed itself. Since then its official name has been "the Council of the European Union". However, it is generally referred to as "the Council".

The Council, together with the EP, is the main legislative institution of the EU and defines and implements the EU's CFSP, based on the guidelines set by the European Council. It represents the national interests of each Member State and, being an inter-governmental body, its meetings risk degenerating into diplomatic conferences. However, it is also an EU institution, and thus it is required to promote the interests of the EU. This double function led the Council to be called "Janus-faced".[124]

---

122. On this topic see D. Curtin, *Executive Power of the European Union, Law, Practice, and the Living Constitution*, 2009, Oxford: OUP.
123. [1993] OJ L281/18.
124. H. Smit and P. E. Herzog, *The Law of the European Economic Community – A Commentary on the EEC Treaty*, 1976, New York: Matthew Bender, Vol.4, 5–88.

However, the impossible task of promoting simultaneously the two sets of interests, national and EU, is to some extent facilitated by the degree of convergence between the two.

3.4.1 Composition

By virtue of Article 16(2) TEU, "The Council shall consist of a representative of each Member State at ministerial level, who may commit the government of the Member State in question and cast its vote."

This formula, introduced by the TEU, allows Member States with a federal structure to be represented when the Council is examining matters which are within the exclusive competence of regional governments. So, for example, a minister of a *Land* in Germany, or of a region in Belgium, will attend such meetings instead of a minister in the federal government. In such a case, the regional minister is authorised to act on behalf of the Member State and thus commits the federal government both legally and politically.

The Council has no fixed composition and its membership varies according to the matters under discussion. However, there are always as many members as there are Member States. At meetings each minister is accompanied by a civil servant as part of a negotiating team. The Commission is also represented, although its influence depends upon the subject matter under discussion and the competences of the Commission in the area discussed. There are ten different configurations of the Council of the EU:

- General Affairs;
- Foreign Affairs;
- Economic and Financial Affairs;
- Justice and Home Affairs;
- Employment, Social Policy, Health and Consumer Affairs;
- Competitiveness;
- Transport, Telecommunications and Energy;
- Agriculture and Fisheries;
- Environment; and,
- Education, Youth and Culture.

The General Affairs Council is specifically mentioned in Article 16(6) TEU. Its role is to ensure consistency in the work of different Council configurations; to prepare meetings of the European Council; and, to ensure the follow-up of these meetings, acting in co-operation with the Commission and the President of the European Council.

Under the ToL the European Council decides on the list of Council configurations with the exception of the General Affairs Council and the Foreign Affairs Council. However, irrespective of which configuration of the Council adopts a decision, that decision is always a Council decision without any mentioning of the configuration that has adopted it. The Council is a single body.

3.4.2 Competences

The main powers conferred on the Council are defined in Article 16 TEU. This provision states: "The Council shall, jointly with the European Parliament, exercise legislative and budgetary functions. It shall carry out policy-making and co-ordinating functions as laid down in the Treaties."

The Council exercises legislative powers, either together with the EP or alone, and adopts the Union's budget together with the EP. Although the Council has no right to initiate legislative proposals, under Article 241 TFEU it may, acting by a simple majority, request the Commission to prepare any study and to submit to it any appropriate proposal. The Commission is not obliged to act but by virtue of the principle of loyal co-operation must examine any request from the Council, and inform the Council of its reason for non compliance with any such request. The Council has used Article 241 TFEU, as well as its opinions and resolutions, on numerous occasions to put pressure on the Commission to prepare legislative proposals.

One of the tasks of the Council is to co-ordinate certain policies of the Member States. In particular, under Article 121 TFEU the Member States are required to co-ordinate their economic policies within the Council. In order to fulfil this task, the Council, on the recommendation of the Commission, must formulate a draft for broad guidelines on co-ordination of economic policies of the Member States, subject to confirmation by the European Council. On the basis of this, the Council prepares a recommendation for the Member States. This is not the only area in which the Council carries out its co-ordinating function. It also organises co-operation between the Member States in respect of employment policies (Article 148(2) TFEU) the AFSJ (Article 74 TFEU) and in respect of operational police co-operation (Article 87(3) TFEU).

The role of the Council in the area of CFSP is examined in Chapter 7.5.1.

The Council rarely exercises executive powers. Under the ToL, executive powers are exercised by the Commission (Article 291 TFEU) apart from "duly justified cases" and in the cases provided for in Articles 24 and 26 TEU relating to the CFSP. Other cases when the Council retains executive powers are specified in the Treaties, e.g. under Article 43 TFEU with regard to fixing prices for agricultural products and fishing quotas.

Finally, the Council is responsible for the conclusion of international agreements on behalf of the EU with third States or international organisations.

3.4.3 Presidency of the Council

Council meetings are chaired by a representative of the Member State holding the Council Presidency, which changes every six months according to the order established by the European Council under Article 236 TFEU. However, the HR always presides over the Foreign Affairs Council.

Declaration 9 on Article 16(9) of the Treaty on European Union concerning the European Council Decision on the Exercise of the Presidency of the Council, institutionalised team or Trios Presidencies, which were first established by the Council in 2006[125] with a view to ensuring consistency and co-ordination between national Presidencies. Under the team Presidency system the national rotating Presidencies are divided into groups of three. A group is made up on a basis of equal rotation among the Member States, taking into account their diversity and geographical balance within the Union. The team Presidency prepares an 18-month programme which begins with a strategic introduction, describing the main challenges facing the EU, and outlines key focus areas for the Council's work over that period. To ensure future consistency, the subsequent team of Presidencies is consulted. On the basis of the team programme each of the national Presidencies prepares its own six-month programme. Unlike a team programme, a national programme does not need to be approved by the Council. During

---

125. In September 2006, the Council made the following amendment to its Rules of Procedure: "Every 18 months, the three Presidencies due to hold office shall prepare, in close cooperation with the Commission, and after appropriate consultations, a draft programme of Council activities for that period". Point 2 of the Preamble to Council Decision 2006/683/EC/Euratom [2006] OJ L285/47.

any 18-month period, each member of a team holds the presidency for a six-month period in all configurations of the Council, with the exception of the Foreign Affairs configuration which has the HR as its permanent President. Members of the team, other than the one which holds the Presidency, assist the current Presidency in all its responsibilities. Members of the team may decide alternative arrangements among themselves.

The main tasks of the Presidency are as follows:

- The Member State which holds the Presidency chairs the Council meetings, i.e. meetings of all configurations of the Council except the Foreign Affairs Council which is permanently chaired by the HR, and is responsible for preparing and organising the Council's work as efficiently as possible. It convenes Council meetings on its own initiative, or at the request of a Member State or of the Commission; determines the agenda; assists Member States to reach a compromise on EU issues; and, decides on the time of voting. At the meetings of the Council, the Member State that holds the Presidency is represented in two capacities – as a Member State and as President of the Council;

- It presides over bodies, such as COREPER (see below), committees and organs of political co-operation. However, the Chair of the Political and Security Committee is held by a representative of the HR; and,

- It represents the Council in dealings with institutions and bodies of the EU, such as the European Commission, the EP, the CoR and the EESC. In particular, it submits to the EP a work programme at the beginning of the Presidency, reports regularly to the EP and, at the end of the Presidency, presents a detailed report of its achievements, which report is discussed by the EP. It also acts on behalf of the Council in negotiations with the EP in the legislative process. However, in respect of foreign affairs the HR assumes all representative functions.

The Presidency involves a heavy workload for a Member State but, at the same time, gives it an opportunity first, to contribute to the development of the EU and second, to put on the agenda issues of vital national importance which might otherwise never be considered as essential in the context of the EU.

3.4.4 COREPER (the Committee of Permanent Representatives)

Each meeting of the Council is prepared by civil servants acting within a number of committees, the most important being the Committee of Permanent Representatives (COREPER).[126]

This body was initially established on an informal basis to ensure the continuity of the Council's work. It was formally recognised by Article 4 of the Merger Treaty and is now defined in Article 16(7) TEU and Article 240 TFEU. COREPER is made up of permanent representatives of the Member States to the European Union. Each Member State has a permanent delegation in Brussels (similar to an embassy), comprising national civil servants of ambassadorial rank and their deputies. Article 16(7) TFEU sets out the tasks of COREPER. It states that:

"A Committee of the Permanent Representatives of the Governments of the Member States shall be responsible for preparing the work for the Council."

The main objective of COREPER is to prepare proposals, which are negotiated prior to the Council meeting, and thus avoid unnecessary discussion at ministerial level. By so doing, COREPER provides a forum for dialogue between permanent representatives themselves and between them and their

---

126.   Its name is the French acronym.

respective governments. Further, it exercises some political control over the work of the Council in that it provides guidance for, and supervision of, the work of expert groups. Only limited areas are outside the remit of COREPER, e.g. agricultural matters which are dealt with by the Special Committee on Agriculture, and the PSC for the CFSP. The special committees, however, must operate without prejudice to COREPER's competences. There are two configurations of COREPER:

- COREPER I, made up of deputy permanent representatives, which concentrates on technical issues; and,

- COREPER II, comprising the permanent representatives themselves, which focuses on general and political matters.

The Council forwards the matter to be discussed to COREPER I, which may create specialist or *ad hoc* committees, working groups, and so on, in order to examine it. They then refer the matter to COREPER II for further study. The Commission, and often the EP, is also involved in the discussion and negotiation of submitted proposals. The Council's agenda is divided into two parts: so-called "A" items and "B" items. If there is unanimous agreement in COREPER II on the proposal, it is put in Part A of the Council's agenda. Unless the Council opposes the proposal and sends it back to COREPER, it will be adopted by the Council. If there is no agreement in COREPER II, the matter is put in Part B of the Council agenda for resolution.

The timetable for Council meetings is prepared in advance. Regular meetings are usually convened once per month; extraordinary sessions can take place at any time, but the agenda must be forwarded by the Presidency to the Member States at least 14 days in advance.

3.4.5 Sessions

The Council sessions are very frequent and often very long. Members of the Commission have access to the sessions and the right to speak. In the past the deliberations of the Council were held *in camera*. Under the ToL deliberations and votes on draft legislative acts are public. In respect of other activities of the Council its deliberations and votes are still held *in camera* except in respect of:

- deliberations and adoption of non legislative proposals which impose rules which are binding in, or for, the Member States, by means of regulations, directive and decisions;

- debates concerning: the General Affairs Council's 18 month programme; and, priorities of the other Council configurations; and, the Commission's five-year programme, annual work programme and annual policy strategy; and,

- debates on important issues affecting the interest of the EU and its citizens.[127]

3.4.6 Voting

Votes in the Council are personal, although under the Council Rules of Procedure members of the Council may arrange to be represented at a meeting which they are unable to attend. Usually, they are replaced by a permanent representative or a deputy permanent representative of their Member State. However, their replacement has no right to vote. For that reason, under Article 239 TFEU another member of the Council (in addition to casting his or her own vote in accordance with his or her own

---

127.   See The General Secretariat of the Council of the EU, Information Sheet, Openness and Transparency of Council Proceedings, Brussels, July 2011, available at http://ue.eu.int/media/1237859/sn02860-re01.en11-pub.pdf (accessed 3/4/12).

wishes) votes (when requested), on behalf of and in accordance with the instruction of the absentee member. An attending member of the Council cannot act on behalf of more than one other member.

The Treaties provide three modes of voting:

- by simple majority;
- by unanimity; and,
- by qualified majority.

The choice of mode is not left to the Council; this is determined by the legal basis of the act in question. The Treaties normally require qualified majority voting or unanimity.

3.4.6.1 Simple majority

Simple majority voting, which was foreseen as a norm, is now exceptional. Article 238(1) TFEU states that where the Council is required to vote by a simple majority, it shall act by a majority of its component members. The Council votes by simple majority mainly in respect of procedural matters including the adoption of its Rules of Procedure.

3.4.6.2 Unanimity

Unanimous voting requirements, which were assigned a privileged place in the original Treaties, are now infrequent as a result of the revisions of the Treaties. Under the ToL, unanimity is required in relation to direct and indirect taxation, but Member States may decide to settle some tax related issues (such as measures to tackle fraud) by majority voting. National vetoes remain, *inter alia*, with regard to foreign policy, certain aspects of social policy, culture, namely the aspects of Common Commercial Policy which affect cultural and audio-visual issues, constitutional and para-constitutional matters, and the filling of gaps in the Treaties with a view to attaining the objectives of the EU (Article 352 TFEU – see Chapter 6.7).

3.4.6.3 Qualified majority voting (QMV)

Qualified majority voting, which is the most frequently used mode of voting in the Council, was slow to take hold. This was because it took years for the Luxembourg Accord to fade away (see Chapter 1.8). The first change was made by the SEA which, in fact, introduced QMV.

The current mode of voting (i.e. until 2014) is based on a "weight" given to each Member State, designed to ensure fairness in the decision-making process. The system of weighted votes reflects the size of a Member State and its demographic, economic and political "weight" within the EU. It has two objectives: first, to ensure that small Member States are not able to block a particular measure; and, second, to ensure that they have sufficient representation to avoid being systematically outvoted by the larger Member States. The ToL introduced a new system of calculating QMV which will enter into force on 1 November 2014 and will be the only one applicable after 1 April 2017. The change ensures a more equitable and democratic voting system in the EU as it takes greater account of the size of the population of a Member State than the previous system.

3.4.6.3.1 Qualified majority voting until 31 October 2014

Under the ToL QMV is extended to 21 new areas and to 23 areas that under the pre-ToL Treaties required unanimity in the Council. However, the extension of QMV does not necessarily mean that the most important matters from the perspective of the Member States are subject to QMV. Certainly, the abolition of the veto in respect of police and judicial co-operation in criminal matters is the most dramatic, although the UK, Ireland and Denmark have negotiated opt-outs in these areas (see Chapter 31.2).

The number of votes each Member State can cast is as follows:
Germany, France, Italy, the United Kingdom – 29 each
Poland and Spain – 27 each
Romania – 14
The Netherlands – 13
Belgium, Greece, Hungary, Portugal, the Czech Republic – 12 each
Austria, Bulgaria, Sweden – 10 each
Denmark, Finland, Ireland, Lithuania, Slovakia – 7 each
Cyprus, Estonia, Latvia, Luxembourg, Slovenia – 4 each
Malta – 3

The total number of votes capable of being cast is 345.
For adoption, acts of the Council require at least:

- first, 255 votes in favour, out of possible 345 (meaning 73.9 per cent) cast, **by at least a majority of members** (i.e. at least 14 Member States out of 27) where the Treaty requires them to be adopted on a proposal from the Commission;

- 255 votes in favour out of possible 345 (meaning 73.9 per cent) cast, **by at least two-thirds of members** (i.e. at least 18 Member States out of 27) in cases where proposals originate from bodies other than the Commission; and,

- second, that the Member States making up the qualified majority represent at least 62 per cent of the total population of the EU.

With regard to the second criterion, Article 3(3) of Protocol No 36 On Transitional Provisions attached to the Treaties states that: "A member of the European Council or the Council may request that, where an act is adopted by the European Council or the Council by a qualified majority, a check is made to ensure that the Member States comprising the qualified majority represent at least 62 per cent of the total population of the Union. If that proves not to be the case, the act shall not be adopted." This requirement seems optional, but in reality it is compulsory, in that if it is not satisfied, an act cannot be adopted. It is difficult to imagine that a Member State which is unhappy with the result of a vote would not request verification concerning the percentage of population reflecting QMV. This requirement favours larger Member States in terms of population as it prevents a coalition of small Member States from outvoting the larger Member States.

If not all members of the Council participate in a vote,[128] for a proposal to be passed, the same proportion of weighted votes (at least 73.9 per cent) and the same proportion of the population of the Member States (at least 62 per cent) is required.

3.4.6.3.2 The twofold majority QMV system to be used from 1 November 2014 to 31 March 2017 and exclusively from 1 April 2017

From 1 November 2014 the voting system in the Council based on the weighting of votes will be abolished. From that date, the ToL established a twofold majority. Normally (that is, if all members of

---

128. For example if a Member State secures for itself an opt-out or does not participate in enhanced co-operation it will not participate in the vote. However, if a Member State abstains, the calculation will be made according to the usual rules.

the Council participate in the voting) that majority must comprise, for a proposal, which originates from the Commission or from the HR, to pass:

- first, at least 55 per cent of the Member States (that is, in an EU made up of 27 Member States at least 15 of those must be in favour); and,

- second, the total population of the Member States forming the majority must account for at least 65 per cent of the population of the EU.

A blocking minority must include at least four Member States representing more than 35 per cent of the population of the EU. This is to ensure that the UK, Germany and France, which together represent more than 35 per cent of the population of the EU, acting in concert cannot block a proposal.

If a proposal does not originate from the Commission or from the HR, the majority, for a proposal to pass, must comprise at least 72 per cent of the Member States (i.e. at least 20 Member States out of 27) representing at least 65 per cent of the population of the EU.

If not all members of the Council participate in voting, for a proposal to pass it needs, at least, the same proportion of votes (55 per cent or 72 per cent) and the same percentage of the population of the Member States concerned (65 per cent) of the members taking part in the vote.

From 1 November 2014 to 31 March 2017 there will be two alternatives to the twofold majority voting:

- A Member State may, on the ground that the matter under consideration is of particular political sensitivity to that Member State, request that a measure be voted on in accordance with the qualified majority voting system as defined under the Treaty of Nice, i.e. the system in existence from the entry into force of the ToL until 1 November 2014.

- The ToL introduced an "Ioannina"[129]-type compromise as follows: if the minority in the Council is significant in terms of number of Member States but insignificant in terms of ability to block the adoption of a measure, the Council will try to find a satisfactory solution while reserving the option to vote at any time. In order to trigger the Ioannina mechanism the group of Member States wishing to do this must represent either 75 per cent share of population necessary to constitute a blocking minority or three quarters of the number of Member States necessary to constitute a blocking minority. The Ioannina compromise is a deferral, not a veto. Its purpose is to give the Council more time to achieve broader support for a measure.

In order to assess the new voting system in the Council, it is important to note that in fact votes are rarely taken in the Council as almost all matters proceed by way of consensus. This is due to the fact first, that the Council traditionally seeks to achieve broad support for all measures and second, that consensus-building in the Council is greatly facilitated by the extensive preparatory process carried out by COREPER. Accordingly, it may be argued that the new voting system will have no significant impact on the work of the Council. Obviously, an opposite view can be expressed, that is, that the new system will have a great impact on decision-making in the Council, in that the lower threshold

---

129. The Ioannina compromise was an agreement reached by foreign ministers of the Member States at a meeting held in 1994 in Ioannina (Greece) concerning the blocking minority subsequent to the fourth enlargement. It was decided that if members of the Council representing between 23 votes (the blocking minority prior to the fourth enlargement) and 26 votes (the blocking minority subsequent to the fourth enlargement) opposed the taking of a decision by the Council, it would seek to achieve a compromise, within a reasonable time, in that the opposed measure would only be adopted if at least 68 votes out of 87 were cast in favour. The Treaty of Nice did away with the Ioannina agreement.

established for the adoption of a legislative measure, as compared to the current system, will force a Member State unhappy with an intended measure to join the majority of the Member States wishing to proceed with the proposal early in the negotiation process in order to retain some influence on the final outcome. It can also be said that the twofold majority voting system based on the population of a Member State is more democratic than the previous voting system. For example, the UK's voting power based on her share of population of the EU will be 12.3 per cent under the twofold majority system as compared to 8.4 per cent under the weighted votes system. It is also more efficient as it facilitates the formation of majorities and thus speeds the decision-making process.

3.4.6.3.3 The voting system to be used from 1 November 2017

The twofold majority voting system will apply from 1 November 2017. However, a new version of the Ioannina compromise, often referred to as the Ioannina II mechanism, may also be relied upon by a significant number of Member States who oppose the adoption of a measure but on their own are insignificant in terms of ability to block its adoption. Under the Ioannina II mechanism a new threshold for triggering a deferral will apply in that either Member States opposing a proposal will have to have at least 55 per cent of the population necessary to constitute a blocking minority or they will have to represent at least 55 per cent of the Member States necessary to constitute a blocking minority.

3.5 The European Council

The European Council plays a very important role in the institutional system of the EU. Until the entry into force of the ToL its exact institutional status within the EU was always subject to uncertainty.

The European Council originates from informal summit meetings of the Heads of State or Government of the Member States and ministers of foreign affairs started in 1972. In Paris in December 1974 they officially agreed that "summit" meetings should thereafter be held on a regular basis. On 19 June 1983 in Stuttgart, the Heads of State and Government signed the Solemn Declaration on European Union. This specified the composition of the European Council – that is, that it should comprise the Heads of State or Government and the President of the Commission, assisted by the ministers for foreign affairs of the Member States and a member of the Commission – and its main tasks.

Article 2 of the SEA brought the European Council within the framework of the Community but did not define its role or method of voting and did not subject its decisions to the possibility of judicial review by the ECJ. The TEU (before its amendment by the ToL) slightly clarified the European Council's role in Article 4 TEU, by providing that its main task was to give the EU "the necessary impetus for its development and . . . define the general political guidelines thereof".

Under the ToL the European Council became a fully fledged EU institution. Article 13 TEU lists the European Council as one of the institutions of the EU. However, Article 15(1) TEU clearly states that the European Council is not allowed to adopt secondary legislation. Further, the ToL gave the European Council new powers (see Chapter 3.5.1), created a full-time President of the European Council who replaces the six-monthly rotating EU Presidency and provides in Article 262 TFEU that acts of the European Council which produce binding legal effects in relation to third parties are subject to judicial review by the ECJ. Under the ToL the European Council's political role remains unchanged, as is its exclusive competence to decide whether any revision of the Treaties is necessary.

3.5.1 Main tasks

The importance of the European Council stems from the political role it plays in shaping the future of the EU. It exercises the following functions:

- it serves as a platform for the exchange of informal views and for unofficial discussions among the leaders of the Member States;

- it can examine any matter within the competence of the EU as well as any subject of common interest;

- it gives the necessary political impetus for the development of the EU;

- it settles sensitive matters and disputes which the EU institutions are not able to resolve, especially those referred by the Council;

- within the framework of EU foreign action, including the CFSP, it defines principles and general guidelines;

- it decides whether a revision of the Treaties is required under either the ordinary revision procedure or the simplified procedures (see Chapter 4.2.6);

- it decides whether to use the *"passerelle"* clause contained in Article 48(7) TEU (see Chapter 4.2.6);

- it appoints the President of the European Council, selects the High Representative (HR) (see Chapter 7.3.1) and the President of the European Commission;

- it decides on the list of Council configurations with must, in any event, include the General Affairs Council and the Foreign Affairs Council, and on the various configurations of the Presidency of the Council (see Chapter 3.4.1) (Article 236 TFEU); and,

- it determines the existence of a serious and persistent breach by a Member State of the European Union's founding values (see Chapter 2.4) (Article 7(2) TEU).

In the exercise of its supreme political power the European Council can be compared to holding a kind of presidential authority of the EU.

The real problem with the European Council is the continuing perceived democratic deficit in that the EP has very limited control over the activities of the European Council. There is, nevertheless, an argument that the European Council has its own democratic legitimacy, since all the national Heads of State or Government are democratically elected.

All deliberations of the European Council are confidential and there is no record of informal exchanges of views between its members. However, when the European Council wishes to make a statement on matters of international concern or its discussions are aimed at reaching decisions, there is a written record of conclusions, and this is issued, if so authorised, by the Presidency. Declarations and Conclusions of the European Council are adopted by common accord. Under the ToL the European Council can adopt decisions. They are usually implemented by the Council. Any act adopted by the European Council which produces binding legal effect on a third party may be reviewed by the ECJ under Article 263 TFEU (see Chapter 15.2.2).

3.5.2 Composition

Article 15(2) TEU specifies that the European Council should be made up of Heads of State or Government of the Member States, together with the President of the European Council and the President of the Commission. The HR should participate in the work of the European Council. When required, the members of the European Council may be assisted by a minister, and the President of the Commission may be assisted by a member of the Commission.

3.5.3 Functioning

Article 15(1) TEU confirms that the European Council shall meet twice every six months although it can also meet in extraordinary sessions. All meetings are convened by its President.

Under Article 16(6) TEU preparation of European Council meetings is carried out by the General Affairs Council, in liaison with the President of the European Council and with the Commission.

3.5.4 Voting

The European Council normally adopts measures by consensus (Article 15(4) TEU). If, in circumstances specified in the Treaties, a vote is taken by QMV, the President of the European Council and the President of the Commission are not allowed to take part in the vote (Article 235(1) TFEU). There is the same definition of QMV for the European Council as for the Council (see Chapter 3.4.6). For the adoption of Rules of Procedure and other procedural matters the Council votes by a simple majority. When unanimity is required abstentions do not prevent the adoption of a measure.

3.5.5 The President of the European Council

The post of full-time President of the European Council was created by the ToL replacing the six-monthly rotating EU Presidency. The President is elected by the European Council acting by QMV. The term of office is two and a half years, renewable once. This post is permanent and its holder is required to be independent. In this respect Article 15(6) TEU states that the President of the European Council "shall not hold a national office". His main tasks are:

- to prepare the work of the European Council;

- to chair debates of the European Council;

- to try to facilitate consensus within the European Council;

- to ensure continuity of the work of the European Council;

- to deal with foreign policy issues at a Heads of State level but without prejudice to the powers of the HR; and,

- to report to the EP after each of the meetings of the European Council.

The main reason for the creation of the post of President of the European Council was to ensure coherence in the work of the European Council and continuity of its political agenda.

3.6 The European Parliament (EP)

The European Parliament, previously known as the Assembly of the European Communities, renamed itself in 1962 in order to emphasise the role it should play in the Community's policy-making process. Its role has indeed dramatically changed, as each revision of the original Treaties has substantially increased the EP's legislative powers (see Chapter 3.6.7), as follows:

- Initially the EP's powers were purely consultative;

- The SEA recognised the new name and introduced two legislative procedures: the assent and the co-operation procedures;

■ The Treaty of Maastricht introduced the possibility for the EP to request the Commission to prepare a legislative proposal, and added a new procedure to those mentioned above: the co-decision procedure;

■ The ToA extended the scope of application of the co-decision procedure;

■ The ToN further extended the ambit of the co-decision and assent procedures; and,

■ The ToL increased the EP's competences in terms of its legislative and budgetary powers.

The ToL describes the EP as exercising legislative powers "jointly" with the Council. Indeed, under the ordinary legislative procedure (previously known as co-decision procedure), which is the predominant procedure for the adoption of EU legislative acts, the EP is put on an equal level with the Council (see Chapter 5.4). Of particular importance is the application of the ordinary legislative procedure to the adoption of measures relating to the establishment of the AFSJ. This means that the EP is a co-legislator with regard to measures relating to frontier controls; asylum; immigration; judicial co-operation in criminal matters; minimum rules for the definition of and penalties in the areas of serious crime; incentive measures for crime prevention; Eurojust (European Prosecutors Co-operation); police co-operation; Europol; and, civil protection (see Chapter 31).

In budgetary matters, the distinction between Compulsory Expenditure and Non-Compulsory Expenditure was abolished by the ToL. The ordinary legislative procedure applies to both (see Chapter 3.6.7.2).

With regard to international agreements, under a new "consent" procedure (which is a new name given to the assent procedure) the EP's consent is needed for international agreements mentioned in Article 218(6) TFEU. In particular Article 218(6)(v) specifies that the consent of the EP is required for all international agreements in areas which are internally subject to the ordinary legislative procedure or where consent of the EP is needed. This means that if the ordinary legislative procedure applies to adoption of a measure relating to, say, asylum policy, an international agreement on asylum matters with third countries or an international organisation, must obtain the EP's consent.

Under the ordinary procedure for future revision of the Treaties, the EP is entitled to initiate such revision by submitting a proposal to that effect to the European Council. Additionally, the EP's consent is required if the European Council decides to convene a conference of representatives of national governments instead of convening a Convention with a view to revising the Treaties (see Chapter 4.2.6).

The EP exercises political control over some EU institutions, in particular by being involved in the election of the President of the Commission, the members of the Commission and the HR.

The EP, in comparison with other EU institutions in terms of attributed competences and the way it is constituted, has undergone great change since its inception.[130] From 1979 it has been the only directly elected body in the Communities; hence, its claim to be a real parliament. Nevertheless, the EP, unlike national parliaments, is not a real, sovereign parliament as it has no power on its own to initiate and enact legislation or to impose taxes.

3.6.1 Election to the EP

In accordance with Council Decision 76/787 and the annexed Act on direct elections of 20 September 1976[131] adopted by the Council, the members of the EP are elected by direct universal suffrage.

130.　R. Corbett, F. Jacobs and M. Shackleton, *The European Parliament*, 8th edn, 2011, London: Harper.
131.　[1976] OJ L278/1.

Any national of a Member State who is qualified to vote in national elections may stand as a candidate for the EP. In Cases C-145/04 *Spain v UK*[132] and C-300/04 *Eman*,[133] the ECJ held that a Member State has exclusive competence to define the persons who are to be entitled to vote and to stand as a candidate in elections to the EP, but added that in exercising this competence, a Member State must comply with EU law, in particular, with the principle of equal treatment. As a result:

- In Case C-145/04 *Spain v UK*, it was found that the UK was entitled to confer the right to vote at EP elections on qualifying citizens of the Commonwealth residing in Gibraltar, who were neither British nationals nor citizens of the EU.

- In Case C-300/04 *Eman*, it was found that the Netherlands was in breach of the principle of equal treatment. This was because the Dutch Government could not objectively justify the difference in treatment between, on the one hand, Dutch nationals residing in a non-Member State, including those who had transferred their residence from the Netherlands Antilles and Aruba (a Dutch OCT associated with the EU) to a non-Member State and, on the other hand, Dutch nationals who moved from the Netherlands to reside in the Netherlands Antilles and Aruba. The former were entitled to vote and stand as a candidate in elections to the EP; the latter were refused the same entitlement. Thus, in both situations nationals of the Netherlands were living outside the Netherlands, but those living in OCTs were excluded from exercising their right to vote and to stand as candidates in elections to the EP.

Article 22(1) TFEU specifies that citizens of the EU residing in a Member State of which they are not nationals are entitled to vote in, and stand as candidates in elections to the EP in the Member State in which they reside under the same conditions as nationals of that Member State.

Employment by an EU institution is incompatible with membership of the EP, as is the holding of certain offices such as membership of national governments, or membership of national parliaments.

Directive 93/109/EC provided for a uniform electoral procedure[134] but did not introduce a uniform voting system in the Member States. In order to remedy this, Council Decision 2002/772/EC[135] provides that national electoral systems in respect of elections to the EP must meet the condition of proportional representation, which must be ensured either under a party list or a single transferable vote system. However:

- Member States may set a minimum threshold for the allocation of seats. At national level this threshold may not exceed 5 per cent of votes cast; and,

- Subdivision of an electoral area is allowed, provided that this will not generally affect the proportional nature of the voting system.

The first ever elections to the EP were held in 1979. Elections take place every five years.

3.6.2 Composition

The number of parliamentary seats is determined on the basis of the size of population in each Member State but, in the light of the wide differences between large and small Member States, this is not a strict

---

132. [2006] ECR I-7917.
133. Case C-300/04 *M.G. Eman and O.B. Sevinger v College van Burgemeester en Wethouders van Den Haag* [2006] ECR I-8055.
134. [1993] OJ L329/34.
135. [2002] OJ L283/1.

mathematical formula. For example, Luxembourg has only 488,650 inhabitants, while the UK has 61 million. As a result, a compromise was reached which takes into consideration the size of the population in a Member State, while ensuring that the smallest Member States are adequately represented in the EP, and that its overall size does not produce an excessively large and unwieldy body. For that reason, under the ToL the maximum number of seats in the EP is fixed at 750 plus the President of the EP. However, in the EP elections in 2009, as they took place before the entry into force of the ToL, the number of MEPs was limited to 736. The seats are allocated to the Member States according to the principle of "degressive proportionality", for 2009–2014 with a minimum of 5 and a maximum of 99 seats.

The assignment of seats for 2009–2014 is as follows:

Germany	99
France, Italy and the UK	77 each
Spain and Poland	50 each
Romania	33
the Netherlands	25
Greece, Belgium, Portugal, the Czech Republic and Hungary	22 each
Sweden	18
Austria and Bulgaria	17 each
Slovakia, Denmark, Finland	13 each
Ireland and Lithuania	12 each
Latvia	8
Slovenia	7
Estonia, Cyprus and Luxembourg	6 each
Malta	5
Total	736

Members of the EP enjoy certain privileges and immunities, which are listed in Chapter III of Protocol No. 7 on the Privileges and Immunities of the European Union annexed to the Treaties. They are:

- Freedom of movement when they travel to or from the place of meeting of the EP;

- Immunity from any form of inquiry, detention or legal proceedings in respect of opinions expressed or votes cast in the performance of their duties. In Case C-163/10 *Patriciello*,[136] the ECJ held that this immunity may not be granted unless there is an obvious, direct link between the opinion expressed or a vote cast and the performance of the parliamentary duty by the MEP; and,

- During a session of the EP they are, in their home Member State, granted the same immunities as enjoyed by members of their national parliaments, and have immunity from any measures of detention and from legal proceedings in the territory of any other Member State. However, the immunity can be waived by the EP if a member commits a criminal offence. It is interesting to note that the EP has modified its Rules of Procedure following the problem raised by the personal bankruptcy of Bernard Tapie, a member of the EP. In the absence of a uniform electoral procedure at EU level, this matter is governed in each Member State by its national electoral laws.[137]

---

136. Case C-163/10 *Criminal Proceedings against Aldo Patriciello* (NYR, judgment of 6/9/11).
137. On the consequences of the absence of uniform electoral procedure see: Case 294/83 *Parti Ecologiste "Les Verts" v EP* [1986] ECR 1339.

General conditions governing the performance of the duties of MEPs are set out in Decision 2005/684/ EC, Euratom adopted by the EP on 28 September 2005.[138] The decision, which entered into force on 14 July 2009, provides for a uniform salary system and a system for the reimbursement of expenses. Its Article 10 states that the amount of the salary of an MEP shall equal 38 per cent of the basic salary of a judge at the ECJ.

3.6.3 The EP and its political groups

Unlike national parliaments, the EP is not divided into a government and an opposition. MEPs sit in multinational groups based on political affiliation and not in national groups. A political group must have at least 25 members representing between them at least one-quarter of the Member States. Discipline within the political groups is lax, and national delegations and individual MEPs are free to switch allegiances as they wish but they may not belong to more than one group. An MEP who does not belong to any political group is known as a non-attached MEP.

There are seven political groups in the EP:

 Group of the European People's Party (Christian Democrats);

 Group of the Progressive Alliance of Socialists and Democrats in the European Parliament;

 Group of the Alliance of Liberals and Democrats for Europe;

 European Conservatives and Reformists Group;

 Group of the Greens/European Free Alliance;

 Confederal Group of the European United Left - Nordic Green Left; and,

 Europe of Freedom and Democracy Group.

3.6.4 The EP and the European political parties

The ToA recognised the importance of European political parties in Article 191 EC. The revised version of that Article is contained in Article 10(4) TEU which states that "Political parties at European level contribute to forming European political awareness and to expressing the will of citizens of the Union". Under Article 224 TFEU the Council and the EP acting in accordance with the ordinary legislative procedure are allowed to adopt regulations governing political parties at European level, and in particular the rules regarding recognition of political parties at European level and their funding.

The Declaration on Article 10(4) TEU, attached to the ToN, clarified the scope of this article in that it neither involves the transfer of powers from a Member State to the EU, nor affects relevant national constitutional provisions. Funding of political parties at European level from the EU budget must not

---

138.   [2005] OJ L262/1.

be used for direct or indirect funding of national political parties. Furthermore, the funding rules apply on the same terms to all political parties represented in the EP. Regulation 2004/2003 on the funding of political parties at European level[139] sets out rules for obtaining funding for such a party from the EU.

3.6.5 Organisation

From its inception the EP has considered itself a parliament. At that time it was the Assembly of the ECSC and it adopted rules of procedure similar to those of any parliament. Parliamentary status was recognised by the Treaties of Rome and enhanced by the universal suffrage to the EP. Under Article 232 TFEU the EP adopts its own Rules of Procedure. However, the power of the EP is limited by the obligation to respect the allocation of competences between the EU institutions as determined by the Treaties.[140]

The organs of the EP are:

A.   **The President of the EP who is elected by the MEPs.** The President chairs debates, exercises an administrative and disciplinary function similar to those of a leader of any national parliament, and represents the EP in international relations, on ceremonial occasions and in administrative, legal and financial matters. At the beginning of every European Council meeting the President sets out the EP's point of view and its concerns as regards the items on the agenda and other subjects. He also signs the EU budget. He is allowed to delegate his powers to the vice-Presidents. There are 14 vice-Presidents, all elected by the MEPs;

B.   **The *quaestors*, who are elected by the MEPs.** They are responsible for administrative and financial matters directly concerning members of the EP;

C.   **The Bureau of Parliament** made up of the President, vice-Presidents and *quaestors* (who have observer status). It is responsible for the organisation and administration of the EP;

D.   **The Conference of Committee Chairs** which is made up of the President of the EP and the chairperson of each political group. Its main tasks are as follows:

   - It takes decisions on the organisation of the EP's work, and matters relating to legislative planning;
   - It is responsible for matters relating to relations with the other institutions and bodies of the EU, with the national parliaments of Member States, with non-member countries and with non-Union institutions and organisations;
   - It decides on the composition and competences of committees, such as committees of inquiry, joint parliamentary committees, standing delegations and ad hoc delegations (see below); and,
   - It submits proposals to the Bureau of Parliament concerning administrative and budgetary matters relating to the political groups;

E.   **The Secretary General of the EP and the Secretariat of the EP.** Both assist the EP in administrative and organisational matters; and,

F.   **Permanent, temporary, specialised, general and joint committees.** Under its Rules of Procedure, the EP may establish such committees. They may examine particular topics in

---

139.   [2003] OJ L297/1.
140.   This was emphasised by the ECJ in Case 294/83 *Parti Ecologiste "Les Verts" v EP* [1986] ECR 1339.

detail, prepare opinions at the request of the Council and prepare resolutions concerning new initiatives of the EP. Additionally, the EP may set up standing inter-parliamentary delegations.

- **Permanent committees**. There are 20 permanent committees, which meet once or twice per month in Brussels; each of them deals with a specific aspect of EU activities.[141] Their role is to draft, adopt and amend legislation. They also consider proposals from the Council and the Commission. They are of particular importance as they streamline the work of the EP. They prepare reports for debates in the EP, and liaise with the Commission and the Council between parliamentary sessions. They can meet at any time at the request of their chairman, or the President of the EP. The members of committees are elected on the basis of proposals submitted by political groups. Political and geographical factors, and representations by the parliamentary political groups within a committee, are also taken into consideration. In principle, each MEP is a sitting member of one permanent committee, and an advisory member-suppliant of another.

- **Temporary committees**. On a proposal from the Conference of Presidents, the EP may, at any time, create temporary committees, whose powers, composition and term of office are defined when the decision to create them is taken. Their term of office may not exceed 12 months, unless extended by the EP.

- **Committee of Inquiry.** Article 226 TFEU permits the EP to set up a temporary Committee of Inquiry to investigate, without prejudice to the powers conferred by the Treaties on other EU institutions and bodies, alleged contraventions and maladministration in the implementation of EU law, except where the alleged facts are being examined before a court and while the case is still subject to legal proceedings. The request to set up a Committee of Inquiry must specify precisely the subject of the inquiry and include a detailed statement of the grounds for it. A Committee of Inquiry must conclude its work with the submission of a report within not more than 12 months of its creation. The EP may twice decide to extend this period by three months. Therefore, a Committee of Inquiry can sit for a maximum of 18 months.

- **Subcommittees.** Subject to prior authorisation by the Conference of Presidents, a standing or temporary committee may, in the interests of its work, appoint one or more subcommittees, of which it shall at the same time determine the composition and area of responsibility. Subcommittees shall report to the committee that set them up.

- **Joint parliamentary committees.** The EP may set up joint parliamentary committees with the parliaments of States associated with the EU or States with which accession negotiations have been initiated.

- **Standing inter-parliamentary delegations.** Inter-parliamentary delegations may be set up on a proposal from the Conference of Committee Chairs. Their main role is to establish and maintain relations with parliaments of non-Member States. Their competence and the number of their members are determined by the EP.

All EP bodies, particularly the committees, shall co-operate with their counterparts at the Parliamentary Assembly of the Council of Europe in fields of mutual interest, with the aim of improving the efficiency of their work and avoiding duplication of effort.

---

141. There are 17 Internal Affairs Committees and three External Affairs Committees. The External Committee on Foreign Affairs has two subcommittees: one on Human Rights and one on Security and Defence.

3.6.6 Sessions

Article 229 TFEU provides that:

"The European Parliament shall hold an annual session. It shall meet, without requiring to be convened, on the second Tuesday in March.

The European Parliament may meet in extraordinary part-session at the request of a majority of its component Members or at the request of the Council or of the Commission."

In Case 101/63 *Wagner*,[142] the ECJ held that the EP is in session from the opening until the close of the annual session. Each annual session follows immediately the preceding session. Thus, in practice the EP is always in session. Despite this the EP is on holiday in August. The sessions are open to the public.

3.6.7 Competences

Under the original Treaties the EP was only a supervisory and advisory body. The EP's fight for power, strengthened by direct elections, resulted in the acquiring of many important competences. The main functions of the EP are:

- democratic supervision of EU institutions;

- adoption of the EU budget jointly with the Council;

- adoption of EU legislation jointly with the Council;

- participation in the external relations of the EU;

- participation in the revision of Treaties; and,

- protection of fundamental rights within and outside the EU.

3.6.7.1 Democratic supervision of EU institutions

General and permanent democratic supervision is exercised by the EP over the Commission, the Council and other institutions and bodies by various means.

The EP has power to ask the Commission and the Council questions on any topic (Article 230 TFEU) and the HR on matters relating to the CFSP. These questions may take various forms: written, oral without debates, oral with debates, question times, and so on. The possibility of asking questions ensures a follow-up of the legislative and administrative activities of the Commission and the Council, and imposes an obligation to justify them before the EP.

The EP is entitled to examine annual and periodic reports, programmes of action, and so on, submitted by various bodies, including:

- **The Commission.** By virtue of Article 233 TFEU, the Commission must submit an annual report on the activities of the EU to the EP. The Commission has, on its own initiative, decided to annex its annual work programme to these reports. In February each year both are discussed by the EP and commented upon in a resolution on the general policy of the EU. Further, the Commission is required to submit an annual report on the implementation of the budget and only

---

142. Case 101/63 *Wagner v Fohrmann and Krier* [1964] ECR 195.

the EP can adopt a decision on the granting of discharge to the Commission in respect of the implementation of the budget. In addition to general reports, the Commission is required to submit reports on particular topics, e.g. in respect of progress achieved by the EU in social matters under Article 159 TFEU. Under the Framework Agreement on Relations between the EP and the Commission,[143] a number of arrangements are set up to ensure constructive dialogue and flow of information between the EP and the Commission. In particular, under Article 11, the President of the Commission will have regular dialogue with the EP on key horizontal issues and major legislative proposals. This dialogue should also include invitations to the President of the EP to attend meetings of the College of Commissioners;

■ **The Council.** At the beginning of each Presidency the President of the Council presents a work programme for its Presidency to the EP and launches a debate on it with MEPs. At the end of each Presidency a final report is submitted to the EP on the outcomes achieved. Ministers from the Council often participate in debates before the EP and may, at any time, ask the President of the EP for permission to make a statement;

■ **The European Council.** Each summit meeting commences with a declaration by the President of the EP setting out the position of the EP on topics to be discussed by the European Council, notice of which has been forwarded to the EP. At the end of each summit meeting the President of the European Council presents the EP with a report on the outcome of its activities. Also, the European Council is required to submit a written annual report to the EP on progress achieved by the EU. Within the framework of the CFSP the EP may put questions and make recommendations to the Council, and the HR. It also holds a debate twice a year on progress in implementing the CFSP, including CSDP (Article 36 TEU); and,

■ **The ECB.** The president of the ECB is required to submit an annual report to the EP in plenary session.

The EP exercises dismissal and appointment powers. In this respect, the EP elects the President of the Commission,[144] and by a vote of consent approves the Commission as a body. This includes approval of the HR who is *ex officio* the vice-President of the Commission. The extensive interviews of candidates to be Commissioners conducted by the EP in relation to the nomination of the members of the Commission appointed in 2009 demonstrate that the power is far from being theoretical. It appoints an Ombudsman, who deals with complaints by any natural or legal person residing or having its registered office in a Member State with a view to achieving an amicable solution (see Chapter 22.9). Such complaints concern instances of maladministration in the activities of the EU institutions or bodies. The EP must be consulted in respect of the appointment of the President, the Vice-President and the members of the Executive Board of the European Central Bank. Additionally, the EP may force the entire Commission, as a collegiate body, to resign but not its President, nor a particular commissioner. In order to avoid abuse, Article 234 TFEU laid down stringent requirements as to a motion of censure:

■ a time of reflection of at least three days after the motion has been tabled is required;

■ provided that at least 50 per cent of MEPs have voted and that a two-thirds majority of the votes cast is in favour, the motion of censure will be carried; and,

■ the vote must be open.

---

143.   (2010) OJ L304/47.
144.   Articles 17(3) and 7 TEU.

A motion of censure is an exceptional measure; if successful, it may lead to a serious crisis in the EU. Under the ToL the motion of censure is unlikely to be used. This is because the President of the Commission is empowered to force a commissioner to resign. Further, Article 5 of the Framework Agreement on Relations between the EP and the Commission[145] provides that if the EP asks the President of the Commission to withdraw confidence in an individual commissioner, the President shall either require the resignation of that commissioner, or explain his/her refusal to do so before the EP in the following part-session.

Notwithstanding the above, Article 234 TFEU provides a powerful weapon for the EP in the complex political interaction between the four institutions: the EP, the Council, the European Council and the Commission. For example, the use of a motion of censure as mentioned above, although unsuccessful, was one of the main factors leading to the resignation of the Commission presided over by Jacques Santer. On 16 March 1999, for the first time in the history of the EU, the President of the Commission, Jacques Santer, was, together with all commissioners, forced to resign. Under the principle of collegiate responsibility the entire Commission, including its President, was in effect dismissed. Mismanagement, fraud, and the irregularity in awarding of financial contracts committed by some commissioners were confirmed by the "comité de sages" set up jointly by the EP and the Commission following an EP resolution on 14 January 1999 on improving the financial management of the Commission. The resignation occurred shortly after the EP, in fact, failed to pass a motion of censure to dismiss the Commission (293 votes in favour, 232 against and 27 abstentions).

The EP may, at the request of one-quarter of its members, establish a temporary Committee of Inquiry to investigate alleged contraventions or maladministration in the implementation of EU law. Such a body ceases to exist on the submission of its report.

By virtue of Article 24 TFEU every citizen of the EU has the right to petition the EP. This right is expanded in Article 227 TFEU, which provides that any citizen of the EU, and any natural or legal person residing or having its registered office in a Member State, has the right to address, individually or in association with other citizens or persons, a petition to the EP on a matter which comes within the EU's field of activity and which affects him, her or it directly (this topic is discussed in Chapter 22.8).

The EP is a privileged applicant under Article 263 TFEU, and as such automatically has standing to challenge the legality of any reviewable act adopted by EU institutions, bodies and agencies. In practice, the EP has brought many proceedings challenging the legality of acts adopted by the Council. Under Article 265 TFEU the EP is entitled to bring an action against EU institutions or bodies for illegal inaction (see Chapter 15.2.5). Further, the EP may ask the ECJ for an opinion with regard to the compatibility of an envisaged international agreement with the provisions of the Treaties under Article 218(11) TFEU.

3.6.7.2   Adoption of the EU budget jointly with the Council

Until 1969 the Communities were funded through direct financial contributions from the Member States based on their Gross National Income (GNI). In 1969, as a result of an agreement between Member States, the "own resources" were introduced which provides the EU with its own independent source of revenue. The "own resources" of the EU are made up of:

- 1 per cent of all the VAT levied on goods and services in the EU (about 12 per cent of own resources);

---

145.   [2010] OJ L304/47.

- customs duties (from the common customs tariff applied to trade with third countries) (about 11 per cent of own resources);

- agricultural import levies and duties (about 1 per cent of own resources);

- "Gross National Income (GNI) resource". This refers to the contribution made by each Member State based on its share of the EU's total GNI, capped at 1.27 per cent. This accounts for 76 per cent of own resources; and,

- miscellaneous resources such as taxes paid by the staff on their salaries, contributions from third countries to EU programmes and fines imposed for breaches of EU law. This amounts to about 1 per cent of own resources.

The total EU revenue for 2011 amounted to some €126.5 billion, representing around 1 per cent of the 27 Member States GNI which, in turn, is equivalent to about €240 per head of the population. The EU budget is not allowed to be in deficit, i.e. the expenditure must not exceed the revenue The EU budget is mainly spent on EU citizens, directly or indirectly, on helping less developed countries around the world and on humanitarian aid to help non-EU countries afflicted by natural disasters and other crisis situations. Only around six cents in every euro are spent on running the EU, i.e. to cover expenses relating to the staff and building costs.

Before the Budgetary Treaties of 1970 and 1975 were adopted, the EP was only consulted on the Communities' budget. Under the Budgetary Treaties and until the entry into force of the ToL, the EU budget was divided into Compulsory Expenditure, which related to those items resulting from Treaty obligations or secondary legislation, mainly the financing of the CAP, the CFP and the expenditure resulting from international agreements and Non-Compulsory Expenditure, which covered other items such as social and regional policy, research and aid, and so on. The EP had the last word on "Non-compulsory expenditure" and had the right to reject the budget as a whole. Under the ToL, the EP has an equal right to the Council to adopt the entire annual EU budget of the EU. However, before any annual budget is drafted it must accord with the multiannual financial framework (MFF) which is adopted by the Council acting unanimously after obtaining the consent of the EP. The MFF determines:

"the amounts of the annual ceilings on commitment appropriations by category of expenditure and of the annual ceiling on payment appropriations. The categories of expenditure, limited in number, shall correspond to the Union's major sector activity."

The following stages in the budgetary procedure are described in Article 310 TFEU:

- The Commission prepares a preliminary draft, based on estimates of expenditure submitted by each institution, which is placed before the EP and the Council no later than 1 September for the following financial year (from 1 January to 31 December);

- The Council is entitled to make amendments and adopts its reasoned position on the draft budget which is forwarded to the EP for its first reading no later than 1 October;

- The EP has 42 days to accept, or amend the draft budget. Inaction amounts to the acceptance of the draft budget. If the EP approves the Council's position, the draft budget can be adopted. If the EP amends, by a majority of its component members, the draft budget it must be sent to the Council and to the Commission. The Council may, within 10 days, accept the amendments and adopt the draft budget. If the Council refuses to accept the EP's amendments, the President of the EP and the President of the Council must immediately set up a Conciliation Committee;

■ The Conciliation Committee is made up of members of the Council or their representatives and an equal number of MEPs, i.e. a delegation from the Council and a delegation from the EP. The Committee has 21 days to agree on a joint text, which must be approved by QMV of the members or representatives of the Council, and by a majority of the MEPs. The Commission acts as a broker between the two delegations. If the Conciliation Committee fails to agree a joint text, the Commission has to submit a new draft budget. If the joint text has been agreed, the EP and the Council have 14 days to approve or reject it. If the EP adopts the draft budget, it is adopted even if the Council rejects the joint text. Only if both the EP and the Council reject the draft budget is it definitely rejected, with the result that the Commission must prepare a new draft budget.

If, at the beginning of the financial year, the budget has not been adopted, a sum equivalent to no more than 1/12 of the budget appropriations for the preceding financial year may be spent each month. The inconvenience this creates for the institutions is significant, as the previous year's budget continues to operate on a one-twelfth for each month basis. This means that the institutions cannot exceed the previous year's limits, although Article 315 TFEU permits an increase in expenditure on the approval of the Council and the EP.

3.6.7.3 Adoption of EU legislation jointly with the Council

Unlike national parliaments the EP is neither entitled to initiate legislative measures, nor to adopt them on its own accord. It is to be noted however, that by virtue of Article 225 TFEU the EP is entitled to call on the Commission to submit a legislative proposal to the Council on matters on which it considers that the EU is required to act in order to implement the Treaties. The Commission does not have to comply but, if it decides not to proceed, must inform the EP of the reasons. Under the ToL the EP's legislative powers are considerably extended. It, acting jointly with the Council, adopts the vast majority of EU legislation (see Chapter 5.4).

3.6.7.4 Participation in the revision of Treaties

Under the ordinary procedure for future revision of the Treaties (see Chapter 4.2.6.1), the EP is entitled to initiate revision by submitting a proposal to that effect to the European Council. Additionally, the EP's consent is required for a decision of the European Council to convene a conference of representatives of national governments instead of convening a Convention with a view to revising the Treaties (see Chapter 4.2.6.1).

3.6.7.5 Participation in the external relations of the EU

With regard to international agreements, under the consent procedure the EP's consent is needed in respect of all agreements listed in Article 218(6)(a) which includes agreements in areas which are internally subject to the ordinary legislative procedure, i.e. if the ordinary legislative procedure applies to adoption of a measure relating to, say, asylum policy, an international agreement on asylum matters with third countries or an international organisation must obtain the EP's consent.

3.6.7.6 Protection of Fundamental Rights within and outside the EU

The EP plays an important role as a defender and protector of fundamental rights within and outside the EU. In this respect, the EP:

- May initiate a proposal concerning the determination that there is a clear risk of a serious breach by a Member State of the values on which the EU is founded, and the EP's consent is required for the making of such a determination (Article 7(1) TEU). Further, under Article 7(2) TEU, the EP's consent is needed to make a determination of the existence of a serious and persistent breach by a Member State of the values on which the EU is founded (see Chapter 2.4);

- Prepares two annual reports on the fundamental rights situations, one relating to countries outside the EU, and the other in respect of rights enshrined in the Charter of Fundamental Rights (see Chapter 8);

- Conducts debates and adopts resolutions regarding breaches of fundamental rights worldwide. At each of its monthly part-sessions, the EP puts aside time to discuss breaches of fundamental rights, democracy and the rule of law. Often these debates lead to adoption of a resolution condemning governments which are violating fundamental rights;

- When informed by the Council that the EU has suspended an agreement with a third country because that country violates fundamental rights, uses all methods at its disposal to put pressure on that country to rectify the situation; and,

- Established the Sakharov Prize for Freedom of Thought in 1988. The prize is awarded to individuals or organisations who – like Andrei Sakharov – have made a substantial contribution to the struggle for respect of fundamental rights.

3.7 The Court of Justice of the European Union (CJEU)

Under the ToL all EU courts are referred to as the "Court of Justice of the European Union". This collective name covers three courts: the Court of Justice of the European Union which was previously known as the Court of Justice of the European Communities and is colloquially known as the European Court of Justice (the ECJ); the General Court, which was previously known as the Court of First Instance (CFI) and specialised courts which were previously known as "judicial panels". There is only one specialised court in existence, i.e. the European Union Civil Service Tribunal.

The main task of the ECJ and the General Court is to ensure that in the interpretation and application of the Treaties the law is observed (Article 19(1) TEU).

Article 19(3) TEU states that the CJEU shall:

"(a)   rule on actions brought by a Member State, an institution or a natural or legal person;

(b)   give preliminary rulings, at the request of courts or tribunals of the Member States, on the interpretation of Union law or the validity of acts adopted by the institutions;

(c)   rule in other cases provided for in the Treaties."

The overwhelming impact of the ECJ on the development of European integration[146] is discussed in Chapter 4.7.

---

146.   On this topic see: A. Stone Sweet, "The European Court of Justice", in P. Craig and G. de Bùrca (eds), *The Evolution of EU Law*, 2nd edn, 2011, Oxford: OUP, 121.

3.7.1 The ECJ – its composition

Article 19(1) TEU specifies that the ECJ shall consist of one judge from each Member State. This allows the ECJ to have a judge who is an expert in the national law of a Member State, and who speaks the language of that Member State.

The ECJ is assisted by 11 Advocates General (A-Gs). The ToL increased the number of A-Gs from 8 to 11[147] with the result that Poland has acquired a permanent A-G and the number of A-Gs involved in the rotating system has been increased from three to five. Judges and A-Gs are appointed by the Member States by common accord. The ToL introduced a new procedure for appointment of judges and A-Gs. Under Article 255 TFEU, a panel gives an opinion on candidates' suitability to perform the duties of judges and A-Gs before the governments of the Member States make the appointment. The Panel consists of seven persons selected from former members of the ECJ and the General Court, members of national supreme courts and lawyers of recognised competence, one of whom is proposed by the EP. Although the Panel only gives an opinion, which the Member States may choose not to follow, it is difficult in practice to envisage an appointment which goes against the opinion of the Panel, in particular when one of the members of the Panel is nominated by the EP.

The number of A-Gs may be increased by the Council acting unanimously, at the request of the ECJ, especially in order to ease the Court's workload or to accommodate a Member State that considers that it is under-represented in the ECJ. Further, under Article 13 of Protocol No. 3 on the Statute of the CJEU attached to the Treaties, the ECJ may request the EP and the Council, acting in accordance with the ordinary legislative procedure, to appoint assistant rapporteurs, whose independence is beyond doubt and who possess the necessary legal qualifications, to ease the workload of judges in particular when they act as judge-rapporteurs.

Article 253 TFEU provides that the judges and the A-Gs are chosen from persons "whose independence is beyond doubt and who possess the qualifications required for appointment to the highest judicial offices in their respective countries or who are jurisconsults of recognised competence". The inclusion of jurisconsults allows academics, civil service lawyers and jurists, that is, lawyers without professional qualification, to be appointed even though in their own country they would not be eligible for the highest judicial offices.

The originality of the composition of the ECJ is emphasised by the presence of A-Gs, who are members of the Court. By virtue of Article 252 TFEU, the function of an A-G is as follows:

> "It shall be the duty of the Advocate-General, acting with complete impartiality and independence, to make, in open court, reasoned submissions on cases which, in accordance with the Statute of the Court of Justice of the European Union, require his involvement."

Advocates-General are required to be neutral as between the applicant and the defendant. They represent the interests of justice. They review the factual and legal aspects of a case, and must reach a conclusion which constitutes their recommendation of how the ECJ should decide the case. The conclusion is very detailed and often suggests original and new legal approaches to the disputed matter, but is not binding on the ECJ. Even if rejected in a particular case, the opinion of an A-G may be later endorsed in a similar case since it often indicates the direction in which EU law should evolve. Furthermore, the opinion is very useful to help understanding of any case as the judgments of the ECJ are very short. Since 2003 A-Gs give an opinion only if the ECJ considers that a particular case raises a new point of law.

---

147.   See Declaration 38 attached to the Treaties on Article 252 TFEU regarding the number of A-Gs in the CJEU.

The posts of A-G are allocated as follows: one from each of the six largest Member States – Germany, France, Italy, Spain, the UK and Poland – and the remaining five positions rotate in alphabetical order between the 21 smaller Member States.

3.7.2 The ECJ – term of office

Judges and A-Gs are appointed for six years, which term is renewable without any limitation. Usually, they hold the office for two terms. In order to ensure continuity in the work of the ECJ there is a rolling programme of replacement of some of the judges and A-Gs every three years.

Under Protocol No. 7 on the Privileges and Immunities of the European Union, and Protocol No. 3 on the Statute of the ECJ, judges and A-Gs:

- have privileges and immunities similar to other officials of the EU;

- are immune from legal proceedings in respect of acts performed in their official capacity, including words spoken or written, but this immunity may be waived by the ECJ; and,

- in criminal proceedings in any of the Member States, provided immunity is waived, must be tried only by the court competent to judge the members of the highest national judiciary.

Before taking up a post at the ECJ, each judge or A-G must take a solemn oath that they will perform their duties impartially and conscientiously and preserve the secrecy of the deliberations of the Court. The independence of judges or A-Gs requires that they cannot hold any political or administrative post during their term of office, or engage in any occupation incompatible with their mandate, unless an exceptional exemption is granted by the ECJ. They must behave with integrity and discretion both during and after their term of office.

Judges or A-Gs may resign, but should hold their office until their successor is appointed. Usual disciplinary measures apply to both judges and A-Gs. A unanimous opinion of all judges of the ECJ and A-Gs (other than the person concerned) is required in order to decide that one of them no longer fulfils the required conditions or meets the obligations arising from his or her office and thus should be disciplined, dismissed or deprived of his or her right to pension or other benefits. Under Article 6 of Protocol No. 3 when the person concerned is a member of the General Court or of a specialised court, the ECJ is required to consult the relevant court before taking a decision.

3.7.3 The ECJ – organisation

The ECJ remains permanently in session, although hearings do not usually take place during judicial vacations. The duration of judicial vacations is determined by the ECJ in the light of the needs of the Court's business. In case of urgency, the President may convene the ECJ during vacations.

The President of the ECJ is elected for a period of three years (which is renewable) by the judges of the ECJ from among their own number by an absolute majority in a secret ballot. The President:

- directs the judicial business and administration of the Court;

- chairs hearings and deliberations;

- may order interim measures (Article 243 TFEU);

- may suspend the application of a contested act (Article 278 TFEU);

- may suspend enforcement of decisions of the Council or the Commission imposing a pecuniary obligation on persons other than Member States (Article 299 TFEU); and,

■ may grant or refuse (by reasoned order) a request for expedited or accelerated procedure (see Chapter 13.11).

3.7.4 ECJ – functioning

The ECJ may sit as a Full Court, in a Grand Chamber (13 judges) or in chambers of three or five judges. It sits in a Grand Chamber when a Member State or an EU institution, which is a party to the proceedings, so requests, or when the complexity or importance of the matter so requires. The Court sits as a Full Court in exceptional cases listed in the Court's Statute, that is:

■ when the European Ombudsman, or a commissioner or a member of the Court of Auditors must be compulsorily retired or deprived of their right to pension or other benefit; or,

■ when the case under consideration is of exceptional importance in terms of its legal implications for the EU.

The quorum for the Full Court is 15 judges; for chambers of three or five judges the quorum is three judges; and, for the Grand Chamber it is nine. The decisions of the ECJ will be valid only when an uneven number of judges sit in deliberation. For that reason, additional judges have been appointed at times when there was an even number of Member States. The President has no casting vote.

A party to the proceedings cannot apply for a change in composition of the ECJ on the basis that there is a judge who has the nationality of that party, or that there is no judge from the Member State of that party. In order to ensure that there is no conflict of interest, a judge or an A-G is not permitted to take part in a case in which they have previously participated as agent or adviser, or in which they have acted for one of the parties or in any other capacity. Also, the President of the ECJ may, for some special reason, decide that a judge or an A-G should not take part in the disposal of a particular case.

3.7.5 Jurisdiction of the ECJ

There are three categories of proceedings which can be brought before the ECJ: contentious, non-contentious and consultative.

3.7.5.1 Contentious proceedings

The ECJ has jurisdiction in the cases which are the most important from the EU perspective. Accordingly, in contentious matters it has jurisdiction in respect of:

■ actions under Articles 258 and 259 TFEU against a Member State for failure to fulfil its obligation (see Chapter 14);

■ actions (including the imposition of financial penalties) under Article 260 TFEU against a Member State for failing to comply with an earlier judgment of the ECJ (see Chapter 14.5);

■ actions brought in relation to disputes arising from the agreement on the setting-up of the European Economic Area;

■ actions for annulment under Article 263 TFEU brought by a Member State against the EP and/or against the Council (with the exception of measures adopted by the Council in respect of State aid, dumping and implementing powers which fall within the jurisdiction of the General Court) or brought by one EU institution against another;

- actions for failure to act under Article 265 TFEU. The ECJ shares its jurisdiction with the General Court. It has jurisdiction in respect of the same categories of actions as those relating to actions for annulment;

- actions brought under Article 271 TFEU against a Member State for failure to fulfil its obligation under the Statute of the European Investment Bank and the European Central Bank;

- disputes between Member States which relate to the subject matter of the Treaties if the Member States concerned have concluded a special agreement conferring jurisdiction on the ECJ in respect of such a dispute (Article 274 TFEU);

- exceptions set out in the Treaties concerning the CFSP. In those matters the ECJ has jurisdiction only in exceptional circumstances, i.e. it ensures that measures adopted under the CFSP have not encroached on non-CFSP policies of the EU and *vice versa*, i.e. that non-CFSP policies do not impinge on the CFSP (Article 40 TEU), and reviews the legality of sanctions against natural or legal persons imposed under the CFSP (Article 24(1) TEU);

- legality of an act which has determined that that there is a clear risk of a serious breach by a Member State of the EU values or indeed, that there is a serious and persistent breach by a Member State of the values on which the EU is founded but only in respect of procedural stipulations contained in Article 7 TEU. Only the Member State concerned by the determination may make a request and this must be made within one month from the date of such determination (Article 269 TFEU);

- review, in exceptional circumstance, of decisions of the General Court on appeals from the European Union Civil Service Tribunal; and,

- appeals from judgments of the General Court on points of law only.

The ECJ has used its jurisdiction in contentious proceedings in a creative way, and by so doing has shaped inter-institutional relations ensuring that the principle of institutional balance is respected (see Chapter 3.2). It has developed EU administrative law,[148] extended the competences of the Communities, and promoted EU policies. Indeed, in some cases its teleological interpretation of provisions of the Treaties amounted to judicial revision of the Treaties (see Chapter 4.7).

3.7.5.2 Non-contentious proceedings

In non-contentious proceedings, i.e. under the preliminary reference procedure (see Chapter 13), the ECJ rules on questions of EU law which have arisen in a national court or tribunal concerning the interpretation of EU law, or the validity of acts adopted by EU institutions. A final judgment is given by a national court in the light of answers provided by the ECJ in respect of referred questions. Since the abolition of the Pillar structure the ECJ has jurisdiction to give preliminary rulings in the whole of the AFSJ. However, some temporal and substantive restrictions have been imposed (see Chapter 13.4).

Judgments of the ECJ delivered within the preliminary ruling procedure have played a central role in the shaping of the EU legal order and of the relationship between the EU and its Member States.[149] The ECJ has used the procedure to deliver judgments of tremendous political importance which have greatly advanced European integration. Within this procedure the ECJ established constitutional

---

148.   P. Craig, *EU Administrative Law*, 2006, Oxford: OUP.
149.   See A. Annul, *The European Union and its Court of Justice*, 2nd edn, 2006, Oxford: OUP.

principles such as the supremacy of EU law; its direct effect; direct applicability; and, the liability of a Member State for damage caused to individuals by its breach of EU law.[150] Furthermore, judgments delivered within the procedure have been vital to the creation of the internal market and the protection of fundamental rights in the EU (see Chapter 8). The ECJ has used the teleological method of interpretation of provisions of the Treaties (see Chapter 4.7) which in some cases led to accusation being made against it of "judicial activism", i.e. overstepping its judicial powers by pursuing a political agenda. Without its constant support for European integration the EU would not have become what it is today.[151]

3.7.5.3 Consultative proceedings

Unlike its name, the consultative jurisdiction of the ECJ always results in binding decisions. It is not necessary that a dispute exists on the matter brought to the attention of the ECJ, although in practice this is often the case.

The consultative jurisdiction exists in respect of both the EU and the Euratom: Article 218(11) TFEU and Articles 103 and 104 EA. In the case of the EU it arises in the context of international agreements between the EU and a third country, or third countries or international organisations. The Council, the Commission, the EP or a Member State may ask the ECJ for its opinion as to whether the envisaged agreement is compatible with the provisions of the Treaties. If the ECJ considers that the agreement in question is contrary to EU law, the only possibility for that agreement to enter into force, apart from its renegotiation, is to revise the Treaties.

The ECJ has interpreted broadly the concept of an agreement. In its Opinion 1/75,[152] *Re Understanding on a Local Cost Standard*, it held that "any undertaking entered into by entities subject to international law which has binding force, whatever its legal designation" is within the scope of Article 218(1) TFEU. In this Opinion it stated that the purpose of Article 218(1) TFEU is to "forestall complications which would result from legal disputes concerning the compatibility with the Treaty of international agreements binding upon the Community [the EU]".[153] The ECJ may assess both formal and substantive compatibility of an envisaged agreement with the Treaties. In Opinion 2/94 on the Accession of the EU to the ECHR,[154] the ECJ held that in order to deliver its Opinion the purpose of the agreement must be known to the Court. Otherwise, it would not be able to deliver its Opinion.

The procedure in Article 218(1) TFEU can be used prior to the conclusion of an agreement by the Council.[155] Once the agreement becomes binding, the ECJ has no consultative jurisdiction over it, even though a request for an opinion is filed before the conclusion of the agreement. This is because a binding agreement can no longer be regarded as an "envisaged agreement". It is to be noted that the ECJ has no jurisdiction in respect of envisaged agreements concerning CFSP matters.[156]

3.7.6 The General Court (previously known as the Court of First Instance (CFI))

The General Court, formerly known as the Court of First Instance, was created to ease the workload of the ECJ, and enable the ECJ to concentrate on its fundamental tasks without affecting the effectiveness

---

150. See the relevant chapters of this book.
151. K. Alter, *The European Court's Political Power: Selected Essays*, 2009, Oxford: OUP.
152. [1975] ECR 1355, para. 2 of Section A.
153. Ibid, para. 8 of Section A.
154. [1996] ECR I-1759.
155. Opinion 1/04 on *The Exchange of Air Passenger Name Data* [2004] OJ C118/1.
156. M. Cremona, "The Union as a Global Actor: Roles, Models and Identity", (2004) 41 CMLRev., 572.

and the quality of the Community judicial system. The General Court was established by Council Decision 88/591 of 24 October 1988 in accord with the provisions of the SEA.[157]

In accordance with Article 48 of Protocol No. 3 attached to the Treaties, the General Court is made up of 27 judges. They are nominated by the common accord of the Member States, one from each Member State. Judges are appointed for a renewable term of six years and a partial replacement takes place every three years. They are subject to the same rules with regard to nomination, privileges, immunities and disciplinary measures as are judges of the ECJ. However, it is not necessary for judges of the General Court to possess the qualifications required for appointment to the highest judicial offices in their respective countries, but only those for the exercise of high judicial office (Article 254 TFEU).

There are no A-Gs appointed to assist the General Court, but in some cases a judge is called upon to perform a task equivalent to that of an A-G.

The General Court sits in chambers of three judges or five judges and in a Grand Chamber of 13 judges. If an important and complex legal matter is under consideration the General Court may sit in plenary session.

In order to ease the workload of the General Court, under a Council Decision of 26 April 1999 it is permitted to sit "when constituted by a single judge". However, a judge of the General Court may sit as a single judge only in cases which do not raise any difficulties in law or in fact, which are of limited importance, and which do not involve any special circumstances.

The General Court has its own registrar, appointed by its judges, who is in charge of the judicial and practical organisation of the Court. The procedure before the General Court is the same as before the ECJ.

Under Article 256 TFEU the General Court has jurisdiction in respect of:

- actions and proceedings referred to in Articles 263, 265, 268, 270 and 272 TFEU with the exception of those which are within the jurisdiction of specialised courts and those reserved to the ECJ under Protocol No. 3 annexed to the Treaties;

- appeals from specialised courts of which there is currently only one, i.e. the European Union Civil Service Tribunal;

- disputes concerning the application of EU competition law to undertakings;

- actions based on arbitration clauses contained in contracts entered into by, or on behalf of the EU under Article 272 TFEU;

- actions relating to EU trade marks;

- actions brought against decisions of the Community Plant Variety Office or of the European Chemicals Agency; and,

- requests for interim measures under Article 279 TFEU.

3.7.7 Specialised courts

Article 257 TFEU provides for the establishment of specialised courts which are also referred to as judicial panels. Under this provision the EP and the Council may, acting in accordance with the ordinary legislative procedure, establish specialised courts which are to be attached to the General Court. A

---

157. [1988] OJ L319/1.

specialised court may be established on a proposal from the Commission after consultation with the ECJ or at the request of the ECJ after consultation with the Commission.

Members of specialised courts are appointed by the Council acting unanimously, after obtaining an opinion from a panel established under Article 255 TFEU.

The General Court acts in an appellate capacity in respect of decisions delivered by specialised courts. An appeal to the ECJ from the General Court is allowed only in cases where there is a serious risk that the unity or consistency of EU law will be affected.

The first specialised court was established by Council Decision 2004/752/EC/Euratom[158] in respect of cases concerning EU staff. It is called the European Union Civil Service Tribunal. It became operational in December 2005 and is made up of seven judges.

3.8 The Court of Auditors (CoA)

The Court of Auditors calls itself "the financial conscience" of the EU. It was established by the Treaty of Brussels of 22 July 1975, constituted in 1977 and recognised as a Community institution by the Treaty of Maastricht. The ToA enlarged the scope of the Court's audit to Pillars 2 and 3 of the EU and thus the Court became an EU institution. The ToA confirmed the Court's *locus standi* under Article 263 TFEU for the purpose of protecting its prerogatives with regard to other EU institutions. Its role continues unchanged by the ToL.

The CoA has no judicial functions, thus it is not really a court but an independent auditing body, i.e. the EU's financial watchdog.[159] In order to fulfil its tasks the CoA has extensive investigative powers, that is, it can investigate the paperwork of any person or organisation handling EU income or expenditure. However, it has no power to prosecute those responsible for irregularities.[160] In a situation where irregularities are suspected the CoA prepares a written report and, depending upon who is thought to be responsible for them, submits it either to the Commission or to the relevant Member State. If the CoA suspects fraud, corruption, or other illegal activity, it transfers the case to the European Anti-Fraud Office (OLAF).

The CoA is composed of 27 members, one from each Member State. Each member must either have belonged to a national external audit body or be "especially qualified" to carry out the audit. Their independence must be beyond doubt. They are nominated by Member States and appointed by the Council, acting by QMV after consulting the EP, for a six-year renewable term.

The usual limitations and arrangements aimed at ensuring the independence of the members of the CoA, as well as privileges, immunities, disciplinary measures, and so on, apply to them. The members, who sit as a college, elect a President for three years (renewable) to chair the Court's meetings, to ensure that the Court's decisions are properly implemented and to represent the Court in all its external relations. The CoA is independent of other EU institutions and national governments.

The main tasks of the CoA are:

■ to audit all the revenue and expenditure of the EU;

■ to ensure that the financial affairs of the EU are properly managed, especially that all revenue has been received, and all expenditure incurred in a lawful and regular manner;

---

158. [2004] OJ L333/7.

159. I. Harden, F. While, and K. Donelly, "The Court of Auditors and Financial Control and Accountability in the European Communities", (1995) 1 EPL, 599.

160. It is to be noted that the EU has no power to institute criminal proceedings; these would be a matter for national authorities.

- at the end of a fiscal year to produce annual accounts which, together with the replies of the institutions, are published in the Official Journal;

- to prepare special reports and opinions at the request of EU institutions. The CoA must be consulted on any proposal for EU legislation of a financial nature and on proposals for measures relating to the fight against fraud. Its reports and opinions are not legally binding;

- on its own initiative, to draft reports on the financial implications of certain programmes or measures envisaged by the EU; and,

- to assist the EP and the Council in exercising their powers of control over the implementation of the EU budget.

3.9 The European Central Bank (ECB)

This is the central bank for the EU's single currency. It is in charge of the formulation and implementation of the monetary policy of the EU. Under the ToL it became an EU institution (Article 13 TEU and Article 282 TFEU). However, it occupies a special place in the institutional framework of the EU in that being part of the European System of Central Banks (the ESCB which comprises the ECB and the national central banks of all Member States irrespective of whether or not they have adopted the euro) its main objective is to ensure price stability rather than to participate in achieving all of the objectives of the EU. It has, unlike other EU institutions, legal personality. Its activities are not funded from the EU budget but are financed from contributions by national central banks of the Member States. This entails, *inter alia*, that if the ECB is found liable, the ECB itself is liable and must pay compensation to the injured party from its own resources (Article 340(3) TFEU).

3.10 Advisory bodies of the EU: The European Economic and Social Committee (EESC) and the Committee of the Regions (CoR)

These are examined below.

3.10.1 The European Economic and Social Committee (EESC)

The EESC was established by the 1957 Treaty of Rome in order to involve economic and social interest groups in the establishment of the internal market, to provide institutional machinery for briefing the Commission and the Council on social and economic matters and to give to these groups a share in the decision-making processes of the Community.

Under Article 301 TFEU the number of members of the EESC shall not exceed 350. Its members are representatives of various categories of economic and social activity. These include farmers, producers, workers, dealers, craftsmen, professionals, as well as representatives of the general public from all Member States. They are appointed by the Council, acting by QMV after consulting the EP, for a five-year renewable term.

The EESC is divided into three groups:

- "Employers", comprising the representatives of employers' organisations and chambers of commerce;

- "Workers", comprising trade union representatives; and,

■ "Various Interests", made up of representatives of small businesses, farmers, professionals, craftsmen, environmental and consumer groups, and so on.

The members of each group are allocated between six working sections, each in charge of a specific policy area. The EESC is an advisory body entrusted with the task of expressing the opinions of these sections in respect of legislative measures prepared by the Council and the Commission. Its opinions are non-binding.

The EP may consult the EESC if it deems such consultation appropriate. Consultation of the EESC is however compulsory for the Commission with regard to proposals in areas such as the CAP; the right of establishment; the mobility of labour; transport; approximation of laws; social policy; the European Social Fund and vocational training; the guidelines and incentives for employment; the social legislation resulting from agreements between management and labour; measures implementing Article 157 TFEU; and, measures relating to public health (Article 168(4) TFEU). In other areas consultation is optional. The EESC may issue opinions on its own initiative.

The Committee plays a very constructive role within the EU as it represents the citizens of the EU and their interests, and thus constitutes a step towards a people's Union.

3.10.2 The Committee of the Regions (CoR)

Under Article 305 TFEU the number of members of the CoR shall not exceed 350. The CoR consists of representatives of regional and local bodies of the Member States. Their terms of appointment, office, privileges, and so on, are similar to those of the EESC (above). The Treaty of Nice requires members of the Committee of the Regions to be elected members of regional or local authorities, or to be politically answerable to an elected assembly. They are appointed by the Council acting by a qualified majority, after consulting the EP, on the basis of proposals submitted by the Member States.

The CoR was created to allow the regions and local authorities to influence and participate in the EU legislative process.

Under the ToL, the Commission must consult the CoR in many areas, including all areas of compulsory consultation provided for the EESC, i.e. matters involving, *inter alia*, the protection of the environment; the Social Fund; vocational training; cross-border co-operation; and, transport. The Commission, the EP and the Council may also consult the Committee in other areas.

If the EESC is consulted pursuant to Article 304 TFEU (i.e. consultation of the EESC is compulsory), the CoR must be informed by the Commission or by the Council of the request for an opinion. The CoR may issue an opinion on the matter if specific regional interests are involved. The CoR may also provide an opinion on its own initiative but, as is the case of the EESC, its opinions are not binding. If the Council or the Commission fixes a time limit for the submission of an opinion by the CoR or the EESC, this must not be less than one month from the notification of the request. The absence of an opinion will not prevent the Council or the Commission from taking further action.

The CoR gained additional powers under the ToL. The CoR has the right to start proceedings before the ECJ:

■ when it considers that the principle of subsidiarity has been violated by a legislative act for the adoption of which it was "compulsorily" consulted (Article 8 of Protocol No. 2 on the Application of the Principles of Subsidiarity and Proportionality attached to the Treaties); and,

■ to defend its prerogatives (Article 263 TFEU).

3.11 Other institutions, bodies, offices and agencies

The TEU provided for the creation of institutions within the framework of EMU, i.e. the European Central Bank and the European System of Central Banks. Their role has been strengthened by the ToA, the ToN and the ToL.

Among other EU bodies mention should be made of specialised advisory committees created on the ground of Article 242 TFEU. These include, *inter alia*, the Committee of Transport under Article 99 TFEU; the Economic and Finance Committee under Article 134 TFEU; and, the Committee on the European Social Fund under Article 163 TFEU.

Additionally, there is a growing number of EU agencies, each of which has a separate legal personality. They are created by EU secondary legislation to carry out specific technical, scientific or managerial tasks. Examples of agencies are: the European Environmental Agency, the European Training Foundation, the Office for Veterinary and Plant Health Inspection, and so on. Their proliferation, as there are more than 30 agencies in the EU, has been explained by Shapiro, as a response of the Commission to "growing public resentment of Brussels and the Eurocracy (i.e. the EU bureaucracy)".[161] They are supposed to be independent from all political influences but are dependent on the parent institution in that they are required to report to it. Whilst initially agencies were welcomed because of their independence from their parent institutions, i.e. the Commission or the Council, their mushrooming has raised major concerns relating to their accountability and control by other EU institutions than the parent institution. Further, they suffer from the lack of democratic legitimacy. To solve the conflict between independence and accountability without jeopardising the very existence of agencies is a major challenge for the EU.[162] It is to be noted that under Article 32 of the Framework Agreement on Relations between the EP and the Commission,[163] in the context of discussions of the Interinstitutional Working Group on Agencies set up in 2009, the EP and the Commission will aim at establishing a common approach on the role and position of EU agencies including the matter of their supervision.

RECOMMENDED READING

Books

Alter, K., *The European Court's Political Power: Selected Essays*, 2009, Oxford: OUP.

Annul, A., *The European Union and its Court of Justice*, 2nd edn, 2006, Oxford: OUP.

Burrows, N. and Greaves, R., *The Advocate General and EC Law*, 2007, Oxford: OUP.

Coen, D. and Richardson, J. (eds), *Lobbying the European Union: Institutions, Actors, and Issues*, 2009, Oxford: OUP.

Corbett, R., Jacobs, F. and Shackleton, M., *The European Parliament*, 8th edn, 2011, London: Harper.

Curtin, D., *Executive Power of the European Union, Law, Practice, and the Living Constitution*, 2009, Oxford: OUP.

Moury, C. and De Sousa, L. (eds.), *Institutional Challenges in Post-Constitutional Europe: Governing Change*, 2009, Abingdon: Routledge.

Schmitt, H. (ed.), *European Parliament Elections after Eastern Enlargement*, 2010, Abingdon: Routledge.

Spence, D. (ed.), *The European Commission*, 3rd edn, 2006, London: Harper.

---

161. M. Shapiro (1997), "The problems of Independent Agencies in the United States and the European Union", (1997) 4/2 *Journal of European Public Policy*, 276, at 283.

162. On this topic see: B. Rittberger and A. Wonka (eds), "Agency Governance in the EU" (2012) *European Public Policy*, Special Issue as a book.

163. (2010) OJ L304/47.

Articles

Chiti, E., "An Important Part of the EU's Institutional Machinery: Features, Problems and Perspectives of European Agencies" (2009) 46 CMLRev., 1395.

Craig, P., "Institutions, Power, and Institutional Balance", in Craig P. and de Bùrca, G., (eds.) *The Evolution of EU Law*, 2nd edn, 2011, Oxford: OUP, 41.

Defuyst, Y., "The European Union's Institutional Balance after the Treaty of Lisbon: 'Community Method' and 'Democratic Deficit' Reassessed", (2008) 39/2 *Georgetown Journal of International Law*, 247.

Harden, I., While, F., and Donnelly, K., "The Court of Auditors and Financial Control and Accountability in the European Communities", (1995) 1 EPL, 599.

Jacqué, J-P., "The Principle of Institutional Balance", (2004) 41 CMLRev., 283.

Kraemer H., "The European Union Civil Service Tribunal: A New Community Court Examined After Four Years of Operation", (2009) 46 CMLRev., 1873.

Lang, J. T., "Checks and Balances in the European Union: The Institutional Structure and the 'Community Method' ", (2006) 12 EPL, 127.

Moberg, A., "The Nice Treaty and Voting Rules in the Council", (2002) 40 JCMS, 259.

Stone Sweet, A., "The European Court of Justice", in Craig P., and de Bùrca, G., (eds.), *The Evolution of EU Law*, 2nd edn, 2011, Oxford: OUP, 121.

PROBLEM QUESTION

The President of the Commission consults you, a lawyer with expertise in EU law, on the following matter.

The Commission wishes to bring proceedings against a former Commissioner, Mrs Smith, alleging that she showed favouritism to her close acquaintance, Mr Johnson who was her dentist. When Mrs Smith took office she wanted to employ Mr Jonhson, then aged 66, as her personal adviser. When this proved impossible because first, her Cabinet was already in place and all posts of personal adviser filled, and second, he was at that time 66 and thus too old to be appointed temporarily, she used her influence to employ him as a visiting scientist, although in fact he worked exclusively as her personal adviser. Further, soon after Mr Johnson's monthly allowance as a visiting scientist was reduced in order to take account of a pension which was paid to him in his country, Mrs Smith's Cabinet made a series of 13 mission orders payable to Mr Johnson, totalling €6,900. The Commission established that the missions were fictitious. Also, when Mr Johnson's position as a visiting scientist was reclassified, his monthly allowance was increased by approximately €1,000. When Mr Johnson's contract as a visiting scientist expired he was offered another such contract, so that in total he was employed as a visiting scientist for 28 months although the Commission's rules provided for a maximum duration of 24 months for such contracts. He did not, however, stay until the end of his contract, as he requested termination of the contract on medical grounds, and this was agreed. Notwithstanding that, Mrs Smith used her influence again to offer him a post as her special adviser. He rejected that offer and died shortly afterwards.

Advise the President of the Commission.

ESSAY QUESTION

Critically assess the results of the struggle of the EP to expand its institutional powers, in particular in respect of the EU budget, EU legislation and appointments to the highest posts in the EU.

AIDE-MÉMOIRE

THE INSTITUTIONAL FRAMEWORK OF THE EU

PRESIDENT OF THE EUROPEAN COUNCIL
- PREPARES WORK OF THE EUROPEAN COUNCIL;
- ENSURES CONTINUITY OF THE WORK OF THE EUROPEAN COUNCIL

THE EUROPEAN COUNCIL
- IT IS THE ULTIMATE POLITICAL DECISION-MAKER IN THE EU;
- IT GIVES THE NECESSARY IMPETUS FOR THE DEVELOPMENT OF THE EU

THE COUNCIL

REPRESENTS THE NATIONAL INTERESTS OF THE MEMBER STATES

- JOINTLY WITH THE EP ADOPTS EU LEGISLATION AND THE EU BUDGET;
- FRAMES THE CFSP AND TAKES THE NECESSARY DECISIONS FOR DEFINING AND IMPLEMENTING IT; AND,
- CONCLUDES INTERNATIONAL AGREEMENTS

THE INSTITUTIONAL BALANCE IS BASED ON A FOUR POLAR HYBRID SYSTEM (THE HYBRID ELEMENT IS CONSTITUTED BY THE HR)

THE EP

REPRESENTS THE INTERSTS OF EU CITIZENS

- JOINTLY WITH THE COUNCIL ADOPTS EU LEGISLATION AND THE EU BUDGET;
- EXERCISES DEMOCRATIC SUPERVISION OF ALL EU INSTITUTIONS; AND,
- PARTICIPATES IN THE CONDUCT OF EXTERNAL RELATIONS

THE EUROPEAN COMMISSION
REPRESENTS THE INTERESTS OF THE EU
- IT IS THE GUARDIAN OF THE TREATIES;
- INITIATES LEGISLATIVE MEASURES; AND,
- EXERCISES EXECUTIVE POWERS

ADVISORY BODY: THE EESC

ADVISORY BODY: THE CoR

EU INSTITUTIONS EXERCISING CONTROL OVER EU ACTIVITIES

JUDICIAL CONTROL

THE COURT OF JUSTICE OF THE EUROPEAN UNION (CJEU). THIS COLLECTIVE NAME COVERS THE ECJ +THE GENERAL COURT +SPECIALISED COURTS. THE CJEU ENSURES THAT IN THE INTERPRETATION AND APPLICATION OF THE TREATIES LAW IS OBSERVED

FINANCIAL CONTROL

THE COURT OF AUDITORS (CoA)

IT IS THE FINANCIAL WATCHDOG OF THE EU

IT ENSURES THAT THE FINANCIAL AFFAIRS OF THE EU ARE PROPERLY MANAGED

MONETARY CONTROL (EUROZONE)

THE EUROPEAN CENTRAL BANK

THIS IS THE CENTRAL BANK FOR THE EU'S SINGLE CURRENCY

IT FORMULATES AND IMPLEMENTS THE MONETARY POLICY OF THE EU

EU INSTITUTIONS

EU BODIES

QMV IN THE COUNCIL

QMV until 31 October 2014

QMV is determined according to a weighting of votes. Each Member State has a certain number of votes according to its size, and its economic, political and demographic weight.

An act will be adopted if:

The Council acts on a proposal from the Commission or the HR	The Council acts on a proposal from bodies other than the Commission or the HR
States: at least a simple majority of States vote in favour (in the EU of 27 Member States 255 votes must be cast in favour=at least 14 Member States must vote in favour) **Population**: votes in favour represent at least 62% of the EU's population	**States**: at least two-thirds of States vote in favour (in the EU of 27 Member States 255 votes must be cast in favour=at least 18 Member States must vote in favour) **Population**: votes in favour represent at least 62% of the EU's population

QMV from 1 November 2014 to 31 March 2017
There Will Be Two Options

QMV as defined after 1 April 2017 will normally apply (see below)	QMV as defined before 31 October 2014 may apply at the request of a Member State in respect of a proposal of particular political sensitivity for that State (see above)

A mechanism of deferral called the "Ioannina I" compromise will be introduced. If Member States which are against a proposal are significant in number but still insignificant to block its adoption (at least three-quarters of the Member States necessary to constitute **a blocking minority** or at least representing 75% of the population of the EU necessary to constitute **a blocking minority**) all Member States must seek a solution whilst reserving the option to vote at any time.

QMV after 1 APRIL 2017

QMV will require a double majority:
States: at least 55% of EU States must vote in favour
Population: votes in favour must represent 65% of the EU's population

Blocking Minority: must include at least 4 Member States representing more than 35% of the EU's population

(Continued)

A deferral mechanism called the "Ioannina II" compromise will be introduced. If a number of Member States opposing a proposal represent 55% of the population necessary to constitute **a blocking minority** or they represent at least 55% of the Member States necessary to constitute **a blocking minority**, all the Member States must seek a solution whilst reserving the option to vote at any time.

Special note about the three Councils

The European Council	The Council of the European Union	The Council of Europe
Is made up of Heads of State or Government of all EU countries, the President of the European Council and the President of the European Commission. It meets, four times a year, in Brussels. Its meetings are called "summits". It is the highest-level policy-making body in the EU. It gives the necessary political impetus for the development of the EU and reviews progress in attainment of EU objectives.	Adopts, jointly with the EP, the majority of EU legislation and the EU budget. It has no fixed composition. Its membership varies according to the matter under consideration. It consists of representatives of each Member State at ministerial level authorised to commit the government of that State. It is generally referred to as "the Council".	Is an inter-governmental organisation created in 1949 which has a membership of 47 European States. It is not an EU institution at all! It is best known for its fundamental rights activities including the preparation of the ECHR and supervision of its application.

DO NOT CONFUSE THE THREE COUNCILS!

4

SOURCES OF EU LAW

CHAPTER OUTLINE

The EU legal system is structured and hierarchical. The sources of EU law and their hierarchy are as follows:

1. Primary sources. These are:

- The founding Treaties: the EEC and the EA Treaties as amended by subsequent Treaties. After the entry into force of the ToL, the EU is founded on the TEU and the TFEU;

- Protocols and Annexes attached to these Treaties which form an integral part of them;

- Acts of accession of new Member States;

■ Acts adopted by the Council, or the Council and the EP for the adoption of which approval by the Member States in accordance with their respective constitutional requirements is necessary (e.g. see Articles 311 and 223(1) TFEU); and,

■ The Charter of Fundamental Rights of the European Union (Article 6(1) TEU) (see Chapter 8).

The primary sources are at the pinnacle of the hierarchy of EU law.

2. General principles of EU law. These refer mainly to a body of unwritten principles which underpin the EU legal order. In the hierarchy of sources, general principles are either part of primary sources or inferior to primary sources, but above all other sources. This depends on their origin. Many principles are expressly mentioned in the Treaties and in the Charter of Fundamental Rights of the EU and are therefore clearly primary sources. The ECJ has recourse to general principles in order to supplement other sources of EU law.

3. External sources. These derive from international agreements concluded between the EU and third States or international organisations. The EU has legal personality and as such is empowered to enter into international agreements. By virtue of Article 216(2) TFEU such international agreements are binding on the EU and the Member States and form an integral part of EU law. In the hierarchy of sources they rank below primary sources and general principles of EU law but above secondary sources.

4. Secondary sources. These are legislative and non-legislative binding acts which the relevant EU institutions are empowered to adopt. Three types – regulations, directives and decisions – are binding; the remainder – recommendations and opinions – have no binding legal force. Secondary sources which are binding rank in importance below primary sources, general principles of EU law and law stemming from international agreements. The ToL establishes a hierarchy of secondary sources in that a distinction is made between those binding acts which are adopted on the basis of the Treaties, and which are referred to in Article 289 TFEU as legislative acts, and those binding acts which are adopted on the basis of secondary acts, i.e. on the basis of legislative acts. These non-legislative acts are either delegated or implementing acts.

5. EU acts not expressly mentioned in Article 288 TFEU. Some are binding, some are of a non-binding nature. If binding, their ranking depends on their object and material content.

6. Case law of the ECJ. There is no doctrine of precedent under EU law. However, for many reasons, the most important being legal certainty, the ECJ is reluctant to depart from the principles laid down in earlier cases. Thus, previous case law is important as it provides guidelines for subsequent cases which raise the same or similar issues, but previous judicial decisions are not regarded as a complete statement of law and are not binding on national courts or on the ECJ. Thus, they cannot be formally regarded as a source of EU law. However, as the ECJ has established constitutional principles and important concepts of EU law in its judgments, which have subsequently become sources of EU law, its case law is indeed an important source of EU law.

With regard to soft law, it can be described as "rules of conduct which in principle have no legally binding force but which nevertheless may have practical effect". A new approach of the EU to soft law under which it becomes a hybrid between traditional soft law and hard law is a key element of the Open Method of Co-ordination (OMC).

4.1 Introduction

The ECJ in Case 6/64 *Costa v ENEL* held that "By contrast with ordinary international treaties, the EEC Treaty has created its own legal system which, on the entry into force of the Treaty, became an integral part of the legal systems of the Member States and which their courts are bound to apply."[164] Accordingly, the ECJ recognised the EU law system as unique, autonomous and distinct from international law and from national legal systems of the Member States. The EU legal system, as any organised legal system, has its own sources of law, written and unwritten, and its own hierarchy of sources otherwise it would not be possible to classify it as a legal system.

Any organised legal system which is made up of various legal sources needs to establish a relationship of inferiority and superiority between them to ensure that inferior sources are compatible with superior sources. The EU legal system is no exception. It is hierarchical in nature. However, the Treaties, apart from establishing the hierarchy of secondary sources by drawing a clear distinction in Articles 289, 290 and 291 TFEU between legislative, delegated and implementing acts, do not establish any hierarchy of sources. It was the ECJ which defined the various sources of EU law as well as a hierarchical relationship between them. Based on the Treaties and the case law of the ECJ the following hierarchy of sources of EU law can be established:

- First, primary sources. These are: contained in the founding Treaties as amended; Protocols and Annexes attached to them; Acts of accession of new Member States; and, acts adopted by the Council, or the Council and the EP for the adoption of which approval by the Member States in accordance with their respective constitutional requirements is necessary (e.g. Articles 311 and 223(1) TFEU). Further, under Article 6(1) TEU the Charter of Fundamental Rights of the European Union is regarded as a primary source of EU law;

- Second, general principles of EU law. Some of these have been codified in the Treaties and the Charter of Fundamental Rights and are, therefore, part of primary sources;

- Third, external sources which derive from international agreements concluded between the EU and third countries or international organisations;

- Fourth, secondary sources, which are listed in Article 288 TFEU, i.e. regulations, directives and decisions. The ToL makes a distinction between legislative acts adopted by EU institutions on the basis of Treaties and non-legislative acts which are adopted on the basis of legislative acts, i.e. delegated and implementing acts. Legislative acts are superior to non-legislative acts;

- Fifth, some atypical acts, i.e. which do not take the form of regulations, directives or decisions, may have binding effect. Some of them are mentioned in the Treaties, others have their origin in the practice of EU institutions; and,

- Sixth, the case law of the ECJ merits special attention. It is not regarded as a formal source of EU law but, in practice, the ECJ, in order to ensure coherence and consistency of its case law, relies on earlier cases to decide subsequent cases which raise the same or similar issues. Further, as the ECJ in its judgments established the constitutional principles of EU law, ensured respect for fundamental rights by EU institutions and the Member States, and created EU administrative law, its case law is indeed an important source of EU law. This is, in particular, in the light of the fact that often the case law of the ECJ has been codified by the Member States either as an amendment to Treaties or as secondary legislation.

With regard to soft law, it has no legally binding force but may nevertheless produce practical effect. When used within the OMC it facilitates convergence of Member States' differing policies and may lead to creation of hard law.

---

164.   Case 6/64 *Flaminio Costa v E.N.E.L.* [1964] ECR 585.

4.2 Primary sources of EU law

The primary sources of EU law are examined below.

4.2.1 The founding treaties and their amendments

The two founding treaties are:

- The Treaty of Rome of 25 March 1957 establishing the European Economic Community (EEC); it entered into force on 1 January 1958.

- The Treaty of Rome of 25 March 1957 establishing the European Atomic Energy Community (Euratom); it entered into force on 1 January 1958.

Both founding treaties were concluded for an unlimited period and have been amended many times. The last amendments to the founding treaties took place in December 2009 when the ToL entered into force. The purpose of this Treaty was to amend the Treaty on European Union (TEU) and the EC Treaty which was renamed to become the Treaty on the Functioning of the European Union (TFEU). As a result, the ToL itself is not designed to have a lasting existence of its own. It does not constitute a third treaty. It contains only seven articles, however, the first two are very long as they contain amendments to the TEU and the TFEU (see Chapter 1.19). The Euratom exists outside the ToL. It is "hanging on the side". Protocol 2 annexed to the ToL contains changes to the EA Treaty and also provides that some provisions of both the TEU and the TFEU apply to the EA Treaty.

The founding Treaties, as amended (now contained in the TEU and the TFEU), are considered to be "the constitutional Treaties". The idea that the founding Treaties establishing the three Communities are different from classical international treaties was recognised by the ECJ in Case 26/62 *Van Gend en Loos*,[165] in which the Court held that "this Treaty is more than an agreement which merely creates mutual obligations between the Contracting States" and that "the Community constitutes a new legal order of international law", which creates rights and obligations not only for the Member States but more importantly for their nationals "which become part of their legal heritage".

The EU is now founded on the TEU and the TFEU. Article 1 TEU states that "The Union shall be founded on the present Treaty and on the Treaty on the Functioning of the European Union (hereinafter referred to as "the Treaties"). Those two Treaties shall have the same legal value." The equality between the TEU and TFEU means that neither is subordinate to the other. Indeed, the separation of the two Treaties is formal rather than substantive in that both Treaties constitute one text and no hierarchy as to their importance is established. The fusion of the EU and the European Community as well as the suppression of the pillar structure has resulted in the disappearance of any frontiers between the two Treaties although special rules still apply to the CFSP (see Chapter 7). The EU courts have jurisdiction to interpret both Treaties, with exceptions concerning matters covered by the CFSP. Despite the fact that neither Treaty prevails the TEU, which contains provisions on principles; values; fundamental rights; objectives of the EU; and, provisions on the institutional framework of the EU, is essential to the interpretation of both Treaties, in particular the TFEU which contains detailed provisions on the functioning of the EU. The same legal standing as that of the Treaties is granted to the Charter of Fundamental Rights of the European Union in the light of which all provisions of both Treaties are to be interpreted subject to Protocol 30 (see Chapter 8.4).

---

165. *NV Algemene Transport- en Expeditie Onderneming van Gend & Loos v Netherlands Inland Revenue Administration* [1963] ECR 3.

4.2.2 Protocols and Annexes to the Treaties

In accordance with Article 2(2) of the Vienna Convention of 23 May 1969 on the Law of Treaties, Protocols and Annexes to the founding Treaties, or to Treaties amending the founding Treaties, have the same legal effect as the Treaties themselves. This is repeated in Article 51 TEU, which states that "The Protocols and Annexes to the Treaties shall form an integral part thereof."

The ECJ has confirmed many times the binding force of Protocols and Annexes.[166] The Protocols could have been incorporated into the Treaties. However, their existence saves the Treaties themselves from being too lengthy.

4.2.3 Declarations annexed to the Treaties

Sixty-five Declarations have been annexed to the Treaties. Declarations are of various kinds: they may be made by the Conference which adopted the Treaty, by Member States, or by a Member State or EU institutions expressing their intention or views on a particular point. Declarations annexed to the Treaties are not legally binding as, unlike the Annexes and Protocols, they have not been incorporated into the Treaties by express provisions. In fact they are annexed to the Final Acts of the Conferences adopting them, and not directly to the Treaties. Under Article 31 SEA, and Article L TEU, declarations annexed to those two Treaties were expressly excluded from the jurisdiction of the ECJ. Accordingly, the ECJ had no power to interpret them.

It is submitted that the specific nature of EU law prevents declarations from acquiring any legal effect, or giving rise to an obligation: first, they cannot be classified as EU acts; second, they are not incorporated into the Treaties; and third, they cannot restrict, exclude or modify the legal effect of the Treaties. In C-354/04P *Gestoras*,[167] the ECJ refused to give any legal effect to a declaration. In Case C-49/02 *Heidelberger*,[168] the ECJ held that declarations cannot be used to interpret a provision of secondary legislation, unless a specific reference is made in the wording of the relevant provision.[169]

It should be noted that the ECJ has compulsory jurisdiction to resolve any dispute between Member States falling within the scope of the Treaties and to provide clarifications on a particular point of law. Accordingly, the ECJ is the final arbiter on the rights and obligations of a Member State and would, if required, define them irrespective of the content of any declaration made by a Member State.

4.2.4 Acts of accession

Acts of accession are legally binding. They are similar, from the point of view of the legal effect they produce, to the Treaties.

4.2.5 Other primary sources

In some circumstances the Treaties provide that acts adopted by the Council or by the Council and the EP will not enter into force until approved by the Member States in accordance with their respective constitutional requirements. Examples of such acts are decisions relating to the system of own resources

---

166. Case 149/85 *Wybot* [1986] ECR 2391; Case 314/85 *Foto-Frost* [1987] ECR 4199; Case 260/86 *Commission v Belgium* [1988] ECR 955.
167. Case C-354/04P *Gestoras Pro Amnistía and Others v Council* [2007] ECR I-1579.
168. Case C-354/04P *Heidelberger Bauchemie GmbH* [2004] ECR I-6129.
169. Case C-292/89 *The Queen v Immigration Appeal Tribunal, ex parte Gustaff Desiderius Antonissen* [1991] ECR I-745; and Case C-329/95 *Administrative proceedings brought by VAG Sverige AB* [1997] ECR I-2675.

of the EU (Article 311 TFEU) and decisions concerning election to the EP by direct universal suffrage (Article 223(1) TFEU). Bearing in mind that national parliaments are involved in the process of adoption of these acts they are considered to be primary sources of EU law. The consequence of classifying them as primary sources of EU law is that the ECJ has no jurisdiction to assess their validity although it is empowered to interpret them. What occurs when provisions of such acts are within the scope of the relevant act, but contrary to the Treaties, has not yet been answered by the ECJ. Hopefully, there will be no need to find the answer given that they are drafted with the idea that any contradiction between their content and the Treaties shall be avoided and further they are subject to scrutiny by the EU institutions and national parliaments.

4.2.6 Revision of Treaties: Article 48 TEU

The ToL set out two revision procedures: the "ordinary revision procedure" and the "simplified revision procedure".

4.2.6.1 The ordinary revision procedure (Article 48(1)–(5) TEU)

There are two versions of the ordinary revision procedure. Under Article 48(1)–(5) TEU both versions start with the submission of a proposal for amendments to the Treaties by any Member State, the EP, or the Commission, to the Council. The next step is for the Council to submit the proposal to the European Council and to notify it to national parliaments. If the European Council decides that the proposed amendments are worthy of consideration it has two options. It may either convene a Convention or may decide that the proposed amendments do not justify the establishment of a Convention and can be dealt with by a Conference of representatives of the governments of the Member States.

■ In the first version of the ordinary revision procedure, the European Council adopts, by a simple majority, a decision, after consulting the EP and the Commission, to convene a Convention to examine the proposal. The Convention is made up of representatives of the national parliaments, of the Heads of State or Government of the Member States, of the European Parliament and of the Commission. The European Central Bank is consulted in the case of institutional changes in the monetary area. The Convention is convened by the President of the European Council to prepare draft amendments to the Treaties. The Convention is required to adopt by consensus a recommendation to a Conference of representatives of the governments of the Member States which will make any final amendments to the amendments agreed by the Convention.

The Convention system has been used on two occasions: to draft the Charter of Fundamental Rights and to prepare the Constitutional Treaty. The main advantages of convening a Convention are that this ensures wide input into the revision process and makes it transparent.

■ In the second version of the ordinary revision procedure, i.e. when amendments are regarded by the European Council as not being sufficiently important to convene a Convention, the European Council may decide by a simple majority, after obtaining the consent of the EP, to convene a Conference of representatives of the governments of the Member States and to give them instructions as to the required amendments.

In both versions the amendments enter into force if ratified by all the Member States in accordance with their respective constitutional requirements. Article 48(5) TEU states that if two years after the signature of a treaty amending the Treaties, four-fifths of the Member States have ratified it but one or more Member States have difficulties in proceeding with ratification, the matter should be referred to the European Council. However, the ToL does not specify how the European Council will then deal with the matter.

4.2.6.2 Simplified revision procedures (Article 48(6) and (7) TEU)

Article 48(6) and (7) TEU sets out two new simplified procedures for revision of the Treaties which are often referred to as "self-amending" or "*passerelle*" provisions which translates into English as "bridging" provisions. "*Passerelle*" provisions are ones which allow the reduction of procedural requirements, or the making of adjustments or amendments to the Treaties, without the necessity to have recourse to formal Treaties revision procedures as described in Article 48(1)–(5) TEU (above).

■ The first is described in Article 48(6) TEU. A Member State, the EP or the Commission may submit to the European Council a proposal for revising all or some of the provisions of Part III of the TFEU on the internal policies of the EU. The European Council may decide to make such an amendment after consulting the EP and the Commission and, if relevant, the ECB. However, the amendment must be approved by the Member States in accordance with their respective constitutions. Consequently, voting in national parliaments or, if required under national law, referenda, will be necessary for any amendment to become binding. Further, the amendment must not increase the competences of the EU.

■ The second is described in Article 48(7) TEU. It allows Member States to abolish vetoes in all areas in which unanimity is required if the European Council agrees unanimously to do this. The only exception concerns defence matters. Further, the European Council may, acting unanimously, allow the Council to apply the ordinary legislative procedure, instead of a special legislative procedure provided for the adoption of legislative acts in the relevant area. In addition to the requirement of unanimity in the European Council, national parliaments must be notified and must give their approval. If any of them opposes the European Council decision within six months of the date of such notification, the decision must not be adopted. Further, a decision under Article 48(7) TEU may be adopted after obtaining the consent of the EP, based on a majority of its component members. Article 48(7) TEU contains a general "*passerelle*" provision on the basis of which special "*passerelle*"-type procedures may be used in respect of specific areas, e.g. under Article 312(2) TFEU the European Council may, unanimously, adopt a decision authorising the Council to act by QMV when adopting a multiannual financial framework. "*Passerelle*" provisions, because they can significantly alter the provisions of the Treaties, are controversial in a situation where national parliaments have no right to veto the proposed change, e.g. Article 153(2) TFEU under which the Council may change the requirements for adoption of decisions in certain areas of social policy from special legislative procedures to the ordinary legislative procedure.

4.2.7 Ranking of primary sources in the hierarchy of sources of EU law

Primary sources come first in the hierarchy of sources of EU law – all other sources are subordinate.

The superiority of the primary sources over other sources of EU law is strengthened by the prohibition of any revision of the Treaties, either by an act or a practice of the EU institutions or the Member States, outside the procedures set out in the Treaties. In Case 43/75 *Defrenne*,[170] the ECJ

---

170. Case 43/75 *Gabrielle Defrenne v Sabena* [1976] ECR 455.

rejected the possibility of revision of the Treaties based on Article 39 of the 1969 Vienna Convention on the Law of Treaties, which provides that a revision of a particular treaty may result from a common accord of all contracting parties. The Court held that a modification of the Treaty can take place, without prejudice to other specific provisions contained in the Treaty, only on the grounds of Article 48 TEU. Accordingly, the Member States are not permitted to act by a common agreement to revise the Treaties outside the existing procedures and therefore exclude the EU institutions from participating in these procedures.[171]

It is important to note that the ECJ has no power to rule on validity of primary sources but has jurisdiction to interpret them. The validity of primary sources is determined by reference to, and in accordance with, international law.

4.3 General principles of EU law

In "judicial legislation" a special place is given to the general principles of EU law. These are unwritten rules of law which a judge of the ECJ has to find and apply, but not create. General principles have a triple role to play. They are applied to:

- avoid denial of justice;

- fill what would otherwise be gaps in EU law; and,

- strengthen the coherence of EU law.

Article 340(2) TFEU expressly allows judges of the ECJ to apply general principles common to the laws of the Member States to determine non-contractual liability of the EU. However, the ECJ has not limited the application of the general principles to this area, but has applied them to all aspects of EU law.

In formulating general principles the ECJ draws inspiration from many sources including the following major sources:

- public international law and its general principles inherent in all organised legal systems;

- national laws of the Member States by identifying general principles common to the laws of the Member States;

- EU law by inferring the general principles from the nature of the EU; and,

- international conventions on the protection of fundamental rights.

These sources are examined below.

4.3.1 Public international law and its general principles inherent in all organised legal systems

The creation of a new international legal order by the Community did not preclude the ECJ from making reference to the general principles of public international law. Indeed, the ECJ has endorsed some of them, e.g. the principle of compatibility of successive conventional obligations;[172] the right

---

171. The conclusion of agreements with third countries which would alter the provisions of the Treaties is included: see Opinion 1/91 [EEA Agreement I] [1991] ECR I-6079 and Opinion 1/92 [EEA Agreement II] [1992] ECR I-2821.

172. Case 10/61 *Commission v Italy* [1962] ECR 1.

of nationals to enter and remain in the territory of their own country;[173] the rule of customary international law concerning the termination and the suspension of a treaty by reason of a fundamental change of circumstances;[174] and rejected others as contrary to this new legal order. For example, the principle of reciprocity, especially under its form of the *exceptio non adimpleti contractus* (the principle according to which performance of an obligation may be withheld if the other party has itself failed to perform the same or a related obligation) was considered by the ECJ as incompatible with the EU legal order.[175]

4.3.1.1 The principle of legal certainty

The most important principle of public international law recognised by the ECJ is the principle of legal certainty which is in itself vague. In the context of EU legislation it means that the law must be certain, that is, clear and precise,[176] and its legal implications foreseeable, especially in its application to financial matters.[177] Further, all EU acts aimed at producing legal effects must be adopted on a proper legal basis.[178] At national level it means that national legislation implementing EU law must be worded in such a way as to be clearly understandable to those concerned as to the content of their rights and obligations.[179] The ECJ has given a concrete scope of application to the principle of legal certainty in order to escape its tautological nature and to clarify its content. As a result, under the principle of legal certainty, the following have been established by the ECJ:

- the principle of non-retroactivity of administrative acts;[180]

- the principle of good faith which requires that EU institutions in administrative and contractual matters act in conformity with that principle;[181]

- the principle of *patere legem*[182] (under this principle an authority which has made law for others must itself comply with that law);

- the principle of vested or acquired rights;[183] and,

- the principle of legitimate expectations which means that "those who act in good faith on the basis of law as it is or seems to be should not be frustrated in their expectations". This principle has given rise to many cases in the context of commercial activities of individuals and undertakings.[184]

---

173. Case 41/74 *Yvonne van Duyn v Home Office* [1974] ECR 1337.

174. Case C-162/96 *A. Racke GmbH & Co. v Hauptzollamt Main* [1998] ECR I-3655.

175. Joined Cases 90 and 91/63 *Commission v Belgium and Luxembourg* [1964] ECR 625.

176. Case C-110/03 *Belgium v Commission* [2005] ECR I-2801.

177. Case 325/85 *Ireland v Commission* [1987] ECR 5041.

178. Case C-325/91 *France v Commission* [1993] ECR I-3283.

179. Case 257/86 *Commission v Italy* [1988] ECR 3249; Case C-376/02 *Stichting "Goed Wonen" v Staatssecretaris van Financiën* [2005] ECR I-3445.

180. Case 234/83 *Gesamthochschule Duisburg v Hauptzollamt München – Mitte* [1985] ECR 327.

181. Joined Cases 43/59, 45/59 and 48/59 *Eva von Lachmüller and Others v Commission* [1960] ECR 463.

182. Case 38/70 *Deutsche Tradax GmbH v Einfuhr- und Vorratsstelle für Getreide und Futtermittel* [1971] ECR 145; Case 68/86 *UK v Council* [1988] ECR 855.

183. Case 100/78 *Claudino Rossi v Caisse de Compensation pour Allocations Familiales des Régions de Charleroi et Namu* [1979] ECR 831; Case 159/82 *Angelique Verli-Wallace v Commission* [1983] ECR 2711.

184. On this topic see: S. Schønber, *Legitimate Expectations in Administrative Law*, 2000, Oxford: OUP.

4.3.1.2 Procedural rights

Another category of general principles taken from public international law concerns the procedural rights necessary to safeguard the protection of substantive rights, such as the right to defence and especially to a fair hearing in administrative proceedings,[185] including the right to be heard before the Commission in competition cases in the stage of the preliminary enquiry[186] and before the CJEU[187] and the refusal to recognise the possibility of an extraordinary appeal without any written text.[188]

4.3.2 General principles common to the laws of the Member States

It is not necessary that a general principle is recognised by the legal systems of all Member States. It is sufficient if a given principle is common to several national legal systems, although "non-negligible divergences" constitute an obstacle to its recognition.[189] Advocate General Slynn in Case 155/79 *AM* explained the manner in which the ECJ discovers unwritten principles of EU law by citing H. Kutscher, a former judge of the ECJ. He explained:

> ".. when the Court interprets or supplements Community law on a comparative law basis it is not obliged to take the minimum which the national solutions have in common, or their arithmetic mean or the solution produced by a majority of the legal systems as the basis of its decision. The Court has to weigh up and evaluate the particular problem and search for the 'best' and 'most appropriate' solution. The best possible solution is the one which meets the specific objectives and basic principles of the [EU] . . . in the most satisfactory way." [190]

As can be seen from the above, the discovery of general principles common to the Member States is based on a comparative study of national laws of the Member States but avoids any mechanical or mathematical approach leading to the lowest common denominator. To the contrary, the spirit of national laws, their evolution and general features are taken into consideration by the ECJ. The general tendency, or sometimes lack of general tendency, may also inspire the judges.

In the process of discovering of general principles, the ECJ is entitled to choose the most appropriate from the point of view of the objectives of EU law, but subject to the principle in *Hoechst*[191] that the substance of fundamental rights is left untouched. It has, for example, recognised a principle which is rejected by all Member States but one[192] and rejected a principle common to national laws of all Member States but incompatible with the requirements of EU law.[193] Once the ECJ incorporates a national principle into EU law, it becomes an independent, autonomous principle which may have a different meaning from one known to national laws. Among the principles common to the national laws of the Member States the ECJ has discovered and adopted the following:

---

185. Case 7/69 *Commission v Italy* [1970] ECR 111; Case 17/74 *Transocean Marine Paint Association v Commission* [1974] ECR 1063, Case 85/76 *Hoffmann-La Roche v Commission* [1979] ECR 461; Case 53/85 *AKZO Chemie BV and AKZO Chemie UK Ltd v Commission* [1986] ECR 1965.
186. Case 374/87 *Orkem v Commission* [1989] ECR 3283.
187. Joined Cases 42 and 49/59 *SNUPAT v High Authority* [1961] ECR 53.
188. Case 12/68 *X v Audit Board of the European Communities* [1970] ECR 291.
189. Joined Cases 46/87 and 227/88 *Hoechst AG v Commission* [1989] ECR I-2859.
190. Case 155/79 *AM and S v Commission* [1982] ECR 1575 at 1649.
191. Joined Cases 46/87 and 227/88 *Hoechst AG v Commission* [1989] ECR I-2859.
192. Case 9/69 *Claude Sayag and S.A. Zurich v Jean-Pierre Ledu and Others* [1969] ECR 329.
193. Case 26/67 *Danvin* [1968] ECR 315.

■ the principle of equality before economic regulation;[194]

■ the principle of the hierarchy of legal measures which allows distinguishing between legislative acts and measures necessary to their implementation;[195]

■ the principle of the prohibition of unjust enrichment;[196]

■ the principle of non-contractual liability of the EU institutions, bodies, offices and agencies;[197]

■ the principle of confidentiality of written communications between lawyer and client,[198] but it applies only in the context of an independent lawyer, not in the relationship of an in-house lawyer;[199]

■ the principle of access to the legal process;[200]

■ the principle of the protection of business secrets of an undertaking;[201] and,

■ the principle of the retroactive application of a more lenient penalty in favour of natural and legal persons who have earlier incurred a more severe penalty.[202]

4.3.3 General principles inferred from the nature of the EU

The ECJ has inferred from the specific nature of the Communities/EU and from the objectives and the context of the Treaties a certain number of principles. Some of them are well rooted in EU law, others are more dubious. In this respect the ECJ in Case C-353/92 *Greece v Council*[203] rejected the principle of EU preference which had been acknowledged as a general principle of EU law in previous decisions.[204] This rejection demonstrates that the list of general principles is not exhaustive or definitive.

General principles inferred from the nature of the EU can be divided into two categories. The first concerns institutional and constitutional law of the EU; the second relates to principles which are inherent to the creation of the internal market.

4.3.3.1 General principles reflecting institutional and constitutional law of the EU

These principles are:

■ The principles of direct effect, direct applicability, supremacy of EU law, effectiveness of EU law and the principle of the liability of Member States in damages for breaches of EU law *vis-à-vis* individuals. They derive from the objectives of the Treaties and have been developed

---

194. Case 8/57 *Groupement des Hauts Fourneaux et Aciéries Belges v High Authority* [1957–58] ECR 245.

195. Case 25/70 *Einfuhr- und Vorratsstelle für Getreide und Futtermittel v Köster et Berodt & Co* [1970] ECR 1161.

196. Case 26/67 *Henri Danvin v Commission* [1968] ECR 315. Also, see Chapter 16.8.

197. Joined Cases 83 and 94/76, 4, 15 and 40/77 *Bayerische HNL Vermehrungsbetriebe GmbH & Co. KG and Others v Council and Commission* [1978] ECR 1209.

198. Case 155/79 *AM & S v Commission* [1982] ECR 1575.

199. Case C-550/07 *Akzo Nobel Chemicals* [2009] ECR I-8301, see Chapter 30.2.2.2.

200. Case 222/84 *Marguerite Johnston v Chief Constable of the Royal Ulster Constabulary* [1986] ECR 1651.

201. Case 53/85 *AKZO Chemie BV and AKZO Chemie UK Ltd v Commission* [1986] ECR 1965; Case C-36/92P *SEP NV v Commission* [1994] ECR 1911.

202. Joined Cases 387/02, 391/02 and 403/02 *Criminal Proceedings against Berlusconi and Others* [2005] ECR I-3565.

203. Case C-353/92 *Greece v Council* [1994] ECR I-3411.

204. Case 5/67 *W. Beus GmbH & Co. v Hauptzollamt München* [1968] ECR 83.

by the ECJ to promote effective enforcement of EU law within the national legal systems of the Member States;

■ The principle of solidarity.[205] Solidarity is required in the internal and external relations of the Member States. The Treaty of Maastricht developed the principle of solidarity and recognised it as binding. Instances where the principle of solidarity is of particular relevance have been detailed by the ToL. Under Article 222 TFEU in all situations where a Member State is the object of a terrorist attack or victim of a natural or man-made disaster other Member States and the EU are required to assist and help the Member State concerned. Under Article 42(7) TEU when a Member State is the victim of armed aggression on its territory, the other Member States have the duty to aid and assist the Member State concerned by all means in their power in accordance with Article 51 of the UN Charter and subject to their international commitments. Apart from the exceptional situations described above, the principle of solidarity means that all Member States should contribute to the harmonious development of the Union and thus the principle of solidarity strengthens economic and social cohesion within the EU and the commitment of all Member States to the foreign policy of the EU;

■ The principle of loyal co-operation between EU institutions and Member States, and between Member States themselves based on Article 4(3) TEU (see Chapter 2.2);

■ The principle of subsidiarity (see Chapter 6.8.1);

■ The principle of conferral (see Chapter 6.2);

■ The principle of effective judicial protection of citizens of the EU (see Chapter 12.6);

■ The principle of equality. This is a principle of fundamental importance to the EU.[206] It entails not only the equality between Member States (see Chapter 2.2) but also equality in the treatment of EU citizens. Article 9 TEU states: "In all its activities, the Union shall observe the principle of the equality of its citizens, who shall receive equal attention from its institutions, bodies, offices and agencies". The Treaties prohibit all forms of discrimination (direct and indirect) based on nationality.[207] This is recognised by Article 18 TFEU. Article 19 TFEU extends the principle of non-discrimination to prohibit discrimination based on sex, racial or ethnic origin, religion or belief, disability, age[208] and sexual orientation. Article 2 TEU provides that equality between women and men constitutes a fundamental value on which the Union is founded; and,

■ The principle of proportionality. This was known only to German law but has become a general principle of EU law since it responds to the needs of the EU legal order.

The principle of proportionality can be described as an instrument for the balancing of conflicting interests to decide which are to be given priority. Accordingly, the first step in the application of the principle of proportionality is to identify the relevant interests, e.g. public, private, national, EU, etc., and to give them some value or weight.

There are at least two, and sometimes three, tests, or stages, in a proportionality inquiry. At the least the principle of proportionality requires that a measure, whether adopted by a Member State or an EU

---

205. Case 39/72 *Commission v Italy* [1973] ECR 101.

206. See M. Bell, *Anti-Discrimination Law and the EU*, 2002, Oxford: OUP, and M. Bell and L. Waddington, "Reflecting on Inequalities in European Equality Law", (2003) 28 ELR, 349.

207. Case 155/80 *Summary Proceedings against Sergius Oebel* [1981] ECR 1993.

208. Case C-144/04 *Werner Mangold v Rüdiger Helm* [2005] ECR I-9981.

institution, must be subject to two tests: the test of suitability which assesses, usually in abstract, whether the means chosen are appropriate to achieve a particular end, and the necessity test which requires assessment of whether a less restrictive measure is available to achieve the same objective as that which was chosen by a Member State or an EU institution. The measure which is least onerous, and which causes least hardship or impediment, must be selected. A third test is often added.[209] This assesses whether a measure has imposed an excessive burden on the individual.

The content and scope of the principle of proportionality has been subject to considerable debate.[210] Under German Constitutional law the principle of proportionality is considered as a tool in the balancing of conflicting interests, without giving priority to any of them. The ECJ has been accused of bias in applying the proportionality test in that its balancing of interests is not value-neutral as it interprets the principle with a view to promoting European integration. According to Tridimas, the ECJ has different standards of scrutiny depending on whether it is assessing the proportionality of EU measures (i.e. the horizontal dimension of proportionality) or of national measures.(i.e. the vertical dimension of proportionality). His view is that, with regard to an EU measure, it will be annulled only if the Court finds that the measure is manifestly inappropriate to achieve the objective sought. With regard to a national measure, the level of scrutiny is very high in that a national measure will be in breach of EU law if the Court finds that the national legislator has not chosen the least restrictive available alternative.[211] He also argues that proportionality *sensu stricto* has been applied only when the ECJ has found it suitable to promote the desired outcome, i.e. to protect fundamental rights (which are understood as fundamental human rights and fundamental freedoms guaranteed by the Treaties) in the vertical dimension. Harbo[212] challenges the distinction between horizontal and vertical dimensions. He posits that the decisive factors in the assessment of a measure by the ECJ in the light of the requirements of the principle of proportionality are whether a measure concerns fundamental rights, and whether it is a legislative or an administrative measure, irrespective of its national or EU origin.

In the debate on the application of the principle of proportionality it is obvious that the ECJ interprets the principle of proportionality in different ways depending upon the areas of law and the substance of conflicting interests at stake. In areas where EU institutions enjoy a large measure of discretion, which involves political, economic and social choices on their part, and in which they are called upon to undertake complex assessments (such as measures taken under the CAP or measures relating to the protection of public health), the Court will tend not to interfere unless there is blatant and obvious infringement of the principle, that is, if a measure is manifestly inappropriate as to the objective pursued (see Chapter 16.7.2).

4.3.3.2   General principles reflecting the neo-liberal philosophy of the internal market

The principles of the free movement of goods, people, services and capital; the principle of the homogeneity of the internal market; the principles relating to competition law; and so on, are closely related to the proper functioning of the internal market.

---

209.   This test is referred to as the proportionality *sensu stricto* test, i.e. in a narrow or strict sense.

210.   T. Tridimas, *The General Principles of EU Law*, 2007, Oxford: OUP; N. Emiliou, *The Principle of Proportionality in European Law – A Comparative Study*, 1996, London/The Hague: Kluwer; T-I. Harbo, "The Function of the Proportionality Principle in EU Law", (2010) ELJ, 158; and G. de Bùrca, "The Principle of Proportionality and its Application in EC Law", (1993) YEL, 105.

211.   T. Tridimas, ibid., Chapters 3 and 5.

212.   T-I. Harbo, "The Function of the Proportionality Principle in EU Law", (2010) ELJ, 158.

4.3.4   Protection of fundamental rights

The protection of fundamental rights is examined in Chapter 8. It is important to note that before the entry into force of the ToL, the ECJ had found sources of inspiration for establishing the extent of protection of fundamental rights under EU law in constitutional traditions common to the Member States;[213] the ECHR; other international conventions which the Member States have ratified;[214] and, the Charter of Fundamental Rights of the EU. With the entry into force of the ToL, the Charter of Fundamental Rights became a primary source of EU law. However, the existence of the Charter does not mean that the ECJ will be prevented from recognising the existence of fundamental rights additional to those set out in the Charter. Indeed, Article 6(3) TEU states:

"Fundamental rights, as guaranteed by the European Convention for the Protection of Human Rights and Fundamental Freedoms and as they result from the constitutional traditions common to the Member States, shall constitute general principles of the Union's law."

On the basis of Article 6(3) TEU, if appropriate, the ECJ may refer to these principles in order to complement the fundamental rights protected in the Charter.

4.3.5   Ranking of general principles of EU law

In the hierarchy of sources, general principles are either part of primary sources or inferior to them but above all other sources. This depends on their origin. Some general principles are expressly mentioned in the Treaties and some are contained in the Charter of Fundamental Rights of the EU, and are therefore primary sources of EU law. It is to be noted that many general principles of EU law, because of their importance in the EU legal system, have, with time, been incorporated into the Treaties, and thus from unwritten principles they became written principles, and from being inferior to primary sources, became part of the highest ranking sources of EU law.

4.4   External sources which derive from international commitments of the EU

By virtue of Article 216(2) TFEU international agreements entered into by the EU with third countries or international organisations are binding upon the EU institutions and the Member States. This provision conflicts with the general principle of public international law according to which only contracting parties to an international agreement are bound by it.

In Case 181/73 *Haegeman v Belgium*,[215] the ECJ held that the provisions of international agreements to which the EU is a contracting party, from their entry into force, form an integral part of the EU legal order. Advocate General Rozes stated in Case 270/80 *Polydor*[216] that an act by which the Council expresses the willingness of the Community to be bound by an international agreement, if such an act is adopted, neither modifies the nature, nor legal effects of an international agreement but has only "instrumental" character.

---

213.   Case 11/70 *Internationale Handelsgesellschaft mbH v Einfuhr- und Vorratsstelle für Getreide und Futtermittel* [1970] ECR 1125.

214.   Such as the International Covenant on Civil and Political Rights in Case C-249/96 *Lisa Jacqueline Grant v South-West Trains Ltd* [1998] ECR I-621; The European Social Charter and the ILO Convention no. 111 concerning discrimination in respect of employment and occupation in Case 149/77 *Defrenne v Sabena* [1978] ECR 1365.

215.   [1974] ECR 449.

216.   Case 270/80 *Polydor Limited v Harlequin Records Shops Limited* [1982] ECR 329.

If an international agreement to which the EU is a contracting party provides for the establishment of a body empowered to supervise or monitor its proper functioning, or its uniform application in all contracting States, then any decisions adopted by such a body also form an integral part of the EU legal order.[217] The same applies to "recommendations" of such bodies because of their "direct link" with an international agreement.[218]

The ECJ accepts the supremacy of international agreements concluded between the EU and third States or international organisations because their conformity with the Treaties can be verified either prior to or after their conclusion. With regard to prior verification, under Article 218(11) TFEU, a Member State, the EP, the Council or the Commission may ask the ECJ for an opinion as to the compatibility of an envisaged agreement with the Treaties. If the ECJ's opinion is adverse, the envisaged agreement will not enter into force unless it is amended or the Treaties are revised (see Chapter 3.7.5.3). Once an international agreement has been concluded, its validity can be challenged under Articles 263 and 267 TFEU.[219]

4.4.1 Ranking of international agreements concluded by the EU with third countries in the hierarchy of sources of EU law

In the hierarchy of sources of EU law, international agreements concluded between the EU and third countries or international organisations are situated below primary sources and general principles of EU law, but above secondary sources.

In Case 40/72 *Schröeder*,[220] the ECJ held that international agreements and all acts of the EU institutions adopted in relation to their conclusion prevail over secondary sources of EU law. As a result, all unilateral measures such as regulations, directives and decisions must be interpreted in conformity with international agreements. Any conflicting secondary legislation may be annulled by the ECJ by virtue of Article 263 TFEU.[221] Also any breach of an international agreement by EU institutions may give rise to liability for damages under Article 340(2) TFEU.[222]

4.5 Secondary sources of EU law

Under the Treaties, Member States have conferred important legislative powers on the EU institutions which enable them to implement the provisions of the Treaties and thus give full effect to EU law and policies.

The ToL is the first Treaty which makes a reference to legislative acts adopted by EU institutions. Previously, the founding Treaties carefully avoided any mention of "law-making powers" or "legislation" in relation to EU institutions. However, the ECJ did not hesitate to refer expressly to "legislative powers of the Community" in Case 106/77 *Simmenthal*[223] and the "legislative scheme of the Treaty" in Case 25/70 *Köster*.[224]

---

217. Case 87/75 *Conceria Daniele Bresciani v Amministrazione Italiana delle Finanze* [1976] ECR 129; Case C-192/89 *S. Z. Sevince v Staatssecretaris van Justitie* [1990] ECR I-3461; Case C-69/89 *Nakajima All Precision Co. Ltd v Council* [1991] ECR I-2069.

218. Case C-188/91 *Deutsche Shell AG v Hauptzollamt Hamburg-Harburg* [1993] ECR I-363.

219. Opinion 1/75 *Local Cost Standard* [1975] ECR 1355.

220. Case 40/72 *Schröeder KG v Germany* [1973] ECR 125.

221. Case C-188/88 *NMB v Commission* [1992] ECR I-1689.

222. Case 181/73 *Haegeman v Belgium* [1974] ECR 449.

223. In Case 106/77 *Amministrazione delle Finanze dello Stato v Simmenthal SpA* [1978] ECR 629, para.18.

224. Case 25/70 *Einfuhr- und Vorratsstelle für Getreide und Futtermittel v Köster et Berodt & Co* [1970] ECR 1161, para. 6.

The ToL rationalised, simplified and provided for the hierarchy of secondary sources. It retained regulations, directives and decisions as legally binding instruments for legislative acts and for non-legislative acts. In this respect Article 288 TFEU states that the EU institutions "shall adopt regulations, directives, decisions, recommendations and opinions". However, the same provision expressly states that recommendations and opinions have no binding force, and thus they are neither legal acts nor considered as sources of EU law.

Article 289(3) TFEU states that "legal acts adopted by legislative procedure shall constitute legislative acts". As a result, acts adopted in accordance with the ordinary legislative procedure and special legislative procedures are to be regarded as legislative acts. Legislative acts are to be distinguished from non-legislative acts which are of two kinds:

- Delegated acts. Under Article 290(1) TFEU "A legislative act may delegate to the Commission the power to adopt non-legislative acts of general application to supplement or amend certain non-essential elements of the legislative act"; and,

- Implementing acts. These are described in Article 290(2) TFEU as follows: "Where uniform conditions for implementing legally binding Union acts are needed, those acts shall confer implementing powers on the Commission, or, in duly justified specific cases and in the cases provided for in Articles 24 and 26 of the Treaty on European Union, on the Council".

The ToL therefore established a hierarchy of secondary sources of EU law in that a distinction is made between those binding acts which are adopted on the basis of the Treaties, and which are referred to in Article 289 TFEU as legislative acts and those binding acts which are adopted on the basis of secondary acts, i.e. on the basis of legislative acts. These non-legislative acts are either delegated or implementing acts. They are inferior to legislative acts.

Legislative and non-legislative acts may take the form of regulations, directives or decisions. There is no hierarchy between them. As a result, a regulation may modify a directive if this is allowed by the relevant provision of the Treaty.

4.5.1 Legislative acts

Article 289 TFEU specifies that legislative acts are those which are adopted by the ordinary or special legislative procedure. Article 289(4) TFEU, however, provides an important clarification. Some acts which are adopted on the basis of the Treaties in accordance with special rules provided for in the Treaties are to be regarded as legislative acts despite the fact that they have not been adopted in accordance with the ordinary or special legislative procedures.

The ToL introduced a rigid classification of legislative acts in that once they are adopted in accordance with the ordinary legislative procedure, or a special legislative procedure, they are deemed to be legislative acts irrespective of their content. This entails that if the content of a legislative act is purely administrative in nature it will still be regarded as a legislative act. Conversely, if the content of an administrative act is of general application it will not be regarded as a legislative act. This rigidity may cause problems in that some provisions of the Treaties, e.g. Article 103 and Article 109 TFEU, provide for adoption of acts which are normally of a legislative nature although for their adoption no reference to the ordinary legislative procedure or any special legislative procedure is made in the relevant article. One consequence of this rigidity is that if an act is not considered as a legislative act, although its content is legislative in nature, no delegated acts can be adopted on its basis. This will result in a potential "gap". Ultimately it will be the task of the ECJ to decide how to fill the gap.

Classification of a particular act, that is, whether it should be considered as a regulation, directive or decision, depends upon its content, not its nomenclature, and the ECJ has often reclassified an act.[225] The choice of a particular form – regulation, directive or decision – for a specific act is determined by reference to the provision of the Treaties which constitutes its legal basis (see Chapter 4.5.3.2). In Case 20/59 *Italy v High Authority*,[226] the ECJ held that if the form is expressly provided in a provision of the Treaty, the competent authority has no choice but to enact it accordingly. The question whether a less prescriptive measure can be adopted than that required by a particular provision (for example, instead of adopting a regulation the Council adopts a directive even though a particular provision provides for the former) must be answered in the negative. If there is no indication as to what kind of measure should be adopted, or a particular provision leaves the choice open,[227] the EU institution invested with power to adopt the measure must decide which is most appropriate to achieve the objective prescribed by the provision in question[228] and act in accordance with the principle of proportionality.[229] This choice is, nevertheless, subject to judicial review by the ECJ under Article 263 TFEU (see Chapter 15.2.3).

4.5.1.1 Regulations

Regulations are the most important form of EU acts. They ensure uniformity of solutions on a specific point of law throughout the EU. They apply *erga omnes* (in relation to everyone) and simultaneously in all Member States. Article 288 TFEU defines regulations in the following terms:

> "A regulation shall have general application. It shall be binding in its entirety and directly applicable in all Member States."

A regulation is comparable to a statutory law in England. Its main features are discussed below.

A. **A regulation has general application.** The ECJ in Case 101/76 *Koninklijke*[230] explained this feature of a regulation by stating that it applies "to objectively determine situations and produces legal effects with regard to persons described in a generalised and abstract manner". Regulations are expressed in general, abstract terms, and the mere fact that it is possible to determine the number, or even identity, of the persons affected by a measure does not call into question its nature as a regulation, provided that the class of those potentially within its scope of application is not closed at the time of its adoption[231] (see Chapter 15.2.7.6).

B. **A regulation is binding in its entirety.** This means that its incomplete[232] or selective[233] implementation is prohibited under EU law. Also, its modification or adjunction, or the introduction of any national legislation capable of affecting its content or scope of application, is contrary to EU law.[234]

---

225. Joined Cases 16/62 and 17/62 *Confédération Nationale des Producteurs de Fruits et Légumes and Others v Council* [1962] ECR 471, Case 25/62 *Plaumann and Co. v Commission* [1963] ECR 95.
226. [1960] ECR 325.
227. For example, Article 103 TFEU or Article 46 TFEU, which provide for regulations or directives, or Article 177 TFEU which refers only to "measures" in general.
228. Joined Cases 8–11/66 *Société anonyme Cimenteries C.B.R. Cementsbedrijven N.V. and others v Commission* [1967] ECR 75.
229. Article 296(1) TFEU.
230. Case 101/76 *Koninklijke Scholten Honing v Council and Commission* [1977] ECR 797, para. 21.
231. Case 231/82 *Spijker Kwasten BV v Commission* [1983] ECR 2559.
232. Case 39/72 *Commission v Italy* [1973] ECR 101.
233. Case 18/72 *NV Granaria Graaninkoopmaatschappij v Produktschap voor Veevoeder* [1972] ECR 1163.
234. Case 40/69 *Hauptzollamt Hamburg-Oberelbe v Firma Paul G. Bollmann* [1970] ECR 69.

The above well-established principles acquire special importance in the case of an incomplete regulation. EU regulations are incomplete if they require Member States to adopt necessary measures to ensure their full application. Sometimes this requirement is expressly stated in a regulation itself, as for example the obligation to adopt laws, regulations or administrative provisions in order to ensure its efficient application.[235] Sometimes a reference is made to Article 4(3) TEU which provides that Member States shall take all necessary measures to fulfil their obligations arising from the Treaties. National measures are subordinated to the provisions contained in a regulation and must neither alter them nor hinder their uniform application throughout the EU.[236]

In circumstances described in Article 291 TFEU, the Commission is required to adopt implementing measures.

C. **Regulations are directly applicable in all Member States.** This means that they become part of the national law of the Member States at the date of their entry into force. Member States which embrace the dualist model of reception of international law into domestic law (see Chapter 11.1) must not take measures transforming regulations into their national legal systems either by enacting them or adopting separate national measures. In any event, a Member States is prohibited from taking any national implementing measures that conceal the nature of an EU regulation.[237]

4.5.1.2 Directives

Directives are defined in Article 288 TFEU in the following terms:

"A directive shall be binding, as to the result to be achieved, upon each Member State to which it is addressed, but shall leave to the national authorities the choice of form and methods."

Directives are used to harmonise national legislations, regulations and administrative provisions. They respect the autonomy of national institutional and procedural systems while imposing upon Member States the obligation to achieve a necessary result.

There are three main features of directives.

A. **Unlike regulations, directives have no general application unless they are addressed to all Member States.** Directives are binding only on their addressees, that is, a particular Member State, or some Member States, or all of them. They have general scope of application when they are addressed to all Member States. In Case 70/83 *Kloppenburg*,[238] the ECJ classified EC directives addressed to all Member States as acts having general application. In such a situation, they require that a certain result must be obtained throughout the EU within a specific time limit.

B. **Article 4(3) TFEU imposes on an addressee Member State an obligation to achieve the objective of a directive but leaves the choice of measures, procedures, methods, and so**

---

235. Case C-52/95 *Commission v France* [1995] ECR I-4443; Case 128/78 *Commission v United Kingdom [Re Tachographs]* [1979] ECR 419.
236. Case C-290/91 *Johannes Peter v Hauptzollamt Regensburg* [1993] ECR I-2981.
237. Case 34/73 *Variola v Amministrazione delle Finanze* [1973] ECR 981.
238. Case 70/83 *Gerda Kloppenburg v Finanzamt Leer* [1984] ECR 1075.

on, necessary to achieve that result to its discretion. In order to achieve the prescribed result directives are often very precise and detailed. For that reason, directives often leave little or no choice as to their implementation. Accordingly, in many cases, directives must be implemented into national law as they stand.

In Case 38/77 *Enka*,[239] the ECJ held that it follows from Article 288 TFEU that discretion left to the Member States as to the choice of form and methods is subject to the achievement of the result that the Council or the Commission intended to obtain. Thus, if necessary, an addressee Member State may be left without any margin of discretion as to the manner of implementation of a directive.[240]

The essential objective of directives is to achieve the prescribed results. This means that the national law of the Member State must be in conformity with the prescribed results once the time limit for the implementation of a directive expires. For that reason sometimes no changes are necessary at the national level, if under national law the prescribed result has already been achieved. Nevertheless, in the majority of cases an addressee Member State has to implement a directive into national law. The ECJ held that it is not necessary to copy the text of a directive into a national text. This seems, however, to be the best way to avoid any disputes.[241] Partial or selective implementation of a directive is contrary to EU law. Also, its implementation cannot be limited to a certain territory of a Member State. In Case C-157/89 *Commission v Italy*,[242] the ECJ held that a Member State cannot invoke the autonomy of some of its regions in order to avoid implementation of some provisions of a directive.

The choice of methods and forms of implementation of directives has been restricted by the ECJ. The Court held that they must ensure legal certainty and transparency.[243] In Case 102/79 *Commission v Belgium*,[244] the ECJ held that a simple administrative practice, or an internal circular, is not sufficient to ensure legal certainty,[245] since such methods are easily modified by national administrations and lack adequate publicity.

In the UK EU directives are usually implemented by statutory instruments under the 1972 European Community Act but sometimes by an act of Parliament.

C. **It is clear from the wording of Article 288 TFEU that an addressee Member State is responsible for the implementation of directives into national law.** Usually directives provide for a specific time limit within which they must be brought into effect in the territories of the Member States. It is very important to note that directives enter into force at the date specified by them, or if no date is specified, then 20 days after publication, but they produce their full legal effect after the expiry of a fixed time limit which varies depending upon the subject-matter of the directive. In most cases the time limit is no more than two years.

---

239. *Enka BV v Inspecteur der Invoerrechten en Accijnzen Arnhem* [1977] ECR 2203.
240. This position has been confirmed in other cases: Case 102/79 *Commission v Belgium* [1980] ECR 1473; Case 150/88 *Kommanditgesellschaft in Firma Eau de Cologne & Parfümerie-Fabrik, Glockengasse n. 4711 v Provide Srl* [1989] ECR 3891; Case C-29/90 *Commission v Greece* [1992] ECR 1971.
241. Case 252/85 *Commission v France* [1988] ECR 2243; Case C-360/87 *Commission v Italy* [1991] ECR I-791; Case C-190/90 *Commission v The Netherlands* [1992] ECR I-3265; Case C-217/97 *Commission v Germany* [1999] ECR I-5087.
242. [1991] ECR I-57, also Case C-33/90 *Commission v Italy* [1991] ECR I-5987.
243. Case C-131/88 *Commission v Germany* [1991] ECR I-825; Case C-58/89 *Commission v Germany* [1991] ECR I-4983.
244. [1980] ECR 1473; see also Case C-360/88 *Commission v Belgium* [1989] ECR 3803.
245. Case C-58/89 *Commission v Germany* [1991] ECR I-4983.

Before the expiry of the time limit some obligations may arise for a Member State (see Chapter 11.4), but not for individuals, as the ECJ held in Case 80/86 *Kolpinghuis*.[246] However, once the time limit has expired, the situation changes dramatically.[247] In Case 270/81 *Felicitas*,[248] the ECJ held that the general principle is that in all cases when a directive is correctly implemented into national law, it produces legal effects with regards to individuals through the implementing measures adopted by the Member State concerned. An individual is entitled to base a claim before a national court upon a directive when the directive has been incompletely or incorrectly implemented by a Member State. It is important to note that directives do not have horizontal direct effect (but see exceptions in Chapter 10.8.5). Non-implementation of a directive within a prescribed time limit produces the following results:

● It becomes directly applicable upon the expiry of the time limit;[249]
● If its provisions are directly effective, an individual may rely on them in proceedings before a national court upon the expiry of the time limit;
● The Commission may bring an action under Article 258 TFEU against the Member State concerned for breach of EU law (see Chapter 14.2). It is to be noted that the Commission may also bring proceedings when, during the transposition period, a Member State has adopted national measures liable seriously to compromise the result prescribed by the directive;[250] and,
● An individual may, upon the expiry of the time limit, sue a defaulting Member State for damages, provided certain conditions are satisfied[251] (see Chapter 12.2).

It is important to note that all directives, in their final provisions, impose on the Member State concerned an obligation to provide a list of measures which have been taken in order to implement them. This facilitates the task of the Commission regarding the determination of conformity of national law with EU law in the area covered by the relevant directive. When a Member State does not notify the Commission, or provides an incomplete notification, it is in breach of Article 4(3) TEU even if it has taken all necessary measures. In either circumstance, the Commission is empowered to bring an action before the ECJ by virtue of Article 258 TFEU (see Chapter 14.2).

4.5.1.3 Decisions

Decisions have no general scope of application unless addressed to all Member States. They may be addressed to all or to a particular Member State, or to any legal or natural person or they may have no addressees. The effect of a decision is specified in Article 288 TFEU, which states that:

"A decision shall be binding in its entirety. A decision which specifies those to whom it is addressed shall be binding only on them."

---

246.   Case 80/86 *Criminal proceedings against Kolpinghuis Nijmegen BV* [1987] ECR 3969.
247.   On direct applicability and direct effect of directives see Chapters 10 and 11.
248.   Case 270/81 *Felicitas Rickmers-Linie KG & Co. v Finanzamt für Verkehrsteuern, Hambourg* [1982] ECR 2771.
249.   Case 148/78 *Criminal Proceedings against Tullio Ratti* [1979] ECR 1629.
250.   Case C-422/05 *Commission v Belgium* [2007] ECR I-4749.
251.   Joined Cases C-6/90 and C-9/90 *Andrea Francovich and Danila Bonifaci and Others v Italy* [1991] ECR I-5357.

This definition covers both decisions which are addressed to specified parties and decisions which have no particular addressees. With regard to a decision specifying its addressee the ECJ in Case 54/65 *Châtillon*[252] described it as:

"A measure emanating from the competent authority, intended to produce legal effects and constituting the culmination of procedure within that authority, whereby the latter gives its final ruling in a form from which its nature can be identified."

Decisions which are addressed to particular persons are similar to administrative acts issued by national authorities. In most cases, decisions are issued by the Commission in competition matters, or by the Council if a Member State fails to fulfil EU obligations.

Decisions which have addressees are binding in their entirety, which means that they may prescribe not only a particular result to be achieved but also the form and methods necessary to achieve it. This distinguishes them from directives, which are merely binding as to the result to be achieved. A decision may be very detailed.

Decisions are directly effective *vis-à-vis* their addressees only; but in certain cases, that is, if a person (natural or legal) proves that he/she/it has *locus standi* under Article 263 TFEU, that person may bring annulment proceedings under this article as well as claim damages under Article 340(2) TFEU.[253]

Decisions which are not addressed to any particular addressee are, e.g. decisions adopted in the framework of trade policy such as action programmes.

It is submitted that decisions adopted within the CFSP cannot be equated with decisions referred to in Article 288 TFEU (see Chapter 7.5.1).

4.5.2 Binding non-legislative secondary acts

There is a difference between a delegated act and an implementing act in that:

■ Separate Treaty provisions are applicable to each of them and each has its own definition on the basis of which it is clear that they are mutually exclusive, i.e. the same act cannot be at the same time a delegated and an implementing act;

■ The scope of each act is different. With regard to a delegated act it is of general application to supplement or amend certain non-essential elements of a legislative act. As to an implementing act its adoption is required because there is a need for uniform conditions for the implementation of a legally binding act;

■ Different powers are exercised by the Commission when it adopts a delegated act and when it adopts an implementing act. The delegation of powers is always discretionary and the institution which has delegated its powers can always revoke the delegation. The Commission, when exercising its delegated powers is allowed not only to amend a legislative act but also "supplement" it. This clearly involves the exercise of "quasi-legislative" powers by the Commission. As to an implementing act it is purely executive. Normally, Member States are required to implement legally binding acts of the EU but in the circumstances described in Article 291(2) TFEU, i.e. "where uniform conditions for implementing legally binding Union acts are needed, those acts shall confer implementing powers on the Commission", the Commission is required to act, i.e. its intervention is compulsory;

---

252. Case 54/65 *Compagnie des Forges de Châtillon, Commentry & Neuves-Maisons v High Authority* [1966] ECR 185, p. 195.
253. See Chapters 15 and 16.

- Under Article 291 TFEU implementing acts may be either of individual or general scope of application depending upon the circumstances. This is not the case with delegated acts which are always of a general scope and thus the Commission is not allowed to adopt a delegated act relating to a measure of an individual nature; and,

- In respect of delegated acts, the exercise of the delegated power by the Commission is controlled by the legislator, i.e. the EU institution which has adopted the basic legislative act which is to be amended or supplemented by the Commission. The legislator can revoke the delegation or oppose the entry into force of the delegated act. So far as implementing acts are concerned, the power of control is exercised by the Member States.

In order to distinguish implementing acts from legislative acts and delegated acts, the word "implementing" must be inserted in the title of implementing acts and the word "delegated" in the title of delegated acts. Whether the distinction in the title of the act will be sufficient to avoid confusion so far as EU citizens are concerned remains to be seen. The use of the same nomenclature, i.e. regulations, directives and decision for acts which can be of a legislative or non legislative nature and in respect of implementing and delegated acts, challenges the principle of transparency. However, it can also be said that the introduction of different nomenclature for different acts would make the system of secondary acts of the EU very complex.

4.5.2.1 Delegated acts

The main justification for the Council and the EP choosing to delegate to the Commission the power to adopt non-legislative acts is that this eases the workload of the Council and the EP. Had the Council and the EP been required to deal with the technical details of all its numerous legislative acts, and subsequent modifications of those acts, they would have been engulfed, and incapable of exercising their substantial and vital tasks. Further, delegated acts are easier to amend or supplement than legislative acts (e.g. it takes on average 14–18 months to amend a directive under the ordinary legislative procedure). However, the efficiency of a decision-making process should not be compromised by lack of supervision by the Council and the EP over the manner in which the Commission actually exercises the delegated powers. This double consideration was addressed by the ToL, which, first, abolished the controversial "comitology system",[254] and second, introduced Article 290 TFEU which ensures the right balance between the need for efficiency and the necessity to properly scrutinise the Commission's use of delegated powers. Article 290 TFEU defines the scope, content and practical arrangements for the exercise of delegated powers by the Commission. It establishes the following requirements relating to the exercise of delegated powers by the Commission:

- The act which expressly provides for the exercise of delegated powers by the Commission must be of general application;

---

254. In order to ensure that the Commission exercises delegated powers in accordance with the Council's instructions, a system of procedural mechanisms, the so-called "comitology", was established by the Member States. It consisted of numerous committees, each comprising national civil servants and presided over by a non-voting Commission representative. The Commission was required to consult the relevant committee before adopting the act. Comitology was recognised by the SEA in Article 202 EC and legitimised by the ECJ in Case 25/70 *Einfuhr- und Vorratsstelle für Getreide und Futtermittel v Köster et Berodt & Co* ([1970] ECR 1161) Comitology became one of the hallmarks of EU administration and was criticised for lack of transparency, complexity and most importantly (as for many years the EP had no supervisory powers over committees) lack of democratic scrutiny.

■ The Commission is allowed to amend or supplement certain non-essential elements of a legislative act. Article 290(1) TFEU states that essential elements of legislative acts can never be subject to delegation;

■ An EU institution which delegates its power to the Commission must define the objective, content, scope and duration of the delegation of power. As a result, the delegation must be clear, precise and detailed. Although Article 290 TFEU does not specify any time limit as to the duration of the delegation the possibility of revocation of the delegation entails that when the Commission is not acting appropriately the delegating institution may revoke the powers it has delegated; and,

■ Article 290(2) TFEU specifies two methods of control that the delegating institution may use: first it may revoke the delegation and second it may oppose the entry into force of the delegated act. The right to revoke is an extreme measure and will rarely be exercised. The most likely cause is when new circumstances undermine the basis of the delegation of power. The second method of scrutiny of delegated acts takes place once the delegated act is notified to the legislator, i.e. the EP and the Council if the basic legislative act was adopted in accordance with the ordinary procedure. Article 290(2)(b) TFEU states that the delegated act may enter into force only if no objection has been made by the EP or the Council within a period set by the legislative act. The consequence of an objection is that the delegated act will not enter into force. This entails that the Commission may adopt a new act, amend the existing act, submit a proposal for a new legislative act, or do nothing. In order to revoke an act or to oppose its entry into force the EP must act by a majority of its component members and the Council by QMV.

The Council, the Commission and the EP reached a Common Understanding on how to implement Article 290 TFEU.[255] The basic features are as follows:

■ The Commission commits itself to carry out the preparatory work by systematically consulting experts from the relevant national authority of each of the Member States which will be responsible for implementation of the delegated act. The Commission will ensure that the national experts have sufficient time to make worthwhile contributions;

■ Each delegated act is to be accompanied by an Explanatory Memorandum providing information about the preparatory work;

■ In principle, the legislator will have two months from submission of the draft delegated act within which to either revoke the delegation or express its objections; and,

■ When a delegated act is opposed it cannot enter into force. In the light of the objections, which may be on any grounds whatsoever, the Commission will decide whether to adopt a new draft act, amend the existing draft act, do nothing or prepare a legislative proposal if the objections were based on its having overstepped the powers delegated to it.

4.5.2.2 Implementing acts

Implementing acts are purely executive acts. Article 291(2) TFEU specifies that the Commission or, in special circumstances, the Council may exercise implementing powers only when the basic legislative

---

255. Council 8753/11 of 10/4/11. Available at http://register.consilium.europa.en/pdf/en/11/st08/st08753.en11.pdf (accessed 5/5/12).

act so provides and only "where uniform conditions for implementing legally binding Union acts are needed".

In the light of Article 291 TFEU, the matter of the circumstances in which adoption of an implementing act is required is vital. Obviously, legislative acts themselves, i.e. EU regulations, directives and decisions do not require implementing measures given that they are either directly applicable (i.e. regulations and decisions) or require a Member State to take the necessary measures to ensure that the objective laid down in a directive is achieved within a specific time-limit. However, particular provisions of EU regulations, directives and decisions may require the Commission to adopt implementing measures to ensure uniformity (i.e. to avoid them being implemented differently in different Member States). Additionally, a delegated act may require implementing measures. However, the Commission is not allowed to use its implementing powers to amend or supplement a delegated act as this is expressly prohibited under Article 290 TFEU. As a result, the Commission can give itself the power to implement a delegated act only "where uniform conditions for implementing legally binding Union acts are needed". When exercising implementing powers the intervention of the Commission is compulsory, not optional.

The power of control over the manner in which the Commission exercises its implementing powers is granted to Member States. Under Article 291(3) TFEU, the EP and the Council adopted Regulation 182/2011 laying down the Rules and General Principles Concerning Mechanisms for Control by Member States of the Commission's Exercise of Implementing Powers.[256] Under the Regulation, the system of control is based on committees made up of representatives of Member States and chaired by a representative from the Commission. The committees operate under two procedures:

A. **The examination procedure.** This applies to:
- implementing measures of general scope;
- other implementing measures relating to:
  - programmes with substantial budgetary implications;
  - the CAP and the CFP;
  - taxation;
  - the environment, security and safety, the protection of the health or safety of humans, animals and plants; and,
  - the CCP.

The examination committee, to which the Commission submits a draft implementing act, can approve, or reject that draft act by QMV (the same voting rules as in the Council apply) or deliver no opinion. If the examination committee rejects the draft, the Commission has two options, either submit to the examination committee an amended draft act within two months of the delivery of the negative opinion or submit the existing draft, within one month of delivery of the negative opinion, to an appeal committee. If the examination committee delivers no opinion the Commission can adopt the draft act subject to exceptions. The exceptions are specified in Article 5(4)(a), (b) and (c) of the Regulation (they concern measures relating to taxation; financial services; protection of the health or safety of humans, animals and plants; measures opposed by a simple majority of the examination committee; and, measures adoption of which is prohibited by the relevant legislative act in a situation where no opinion is delivered) and Article 5(5). In cases covered by Article 5(4)(a), (b) and (c) of the Regulation

---

256. [2011] OJ L55/13.

the Commission has the same options as it has if the examination committee rejects the draft act, i.e. either to submit to the examination committee an amended draft within two months of the date on which an opinion was due, or to submit the existing draft to an appeal committee within one month of the date on which an opinion was due. Article 5 sets out special rules applicable to the CCP (i.e. in respect of anti-dumping and countervailing duties). If no opinion is delivered within the specified time-limit by the examination committee, and a simple majority of its members opposes the measure, the Commission must consult with the Member States and subsequently submit the draft act to the appeal committee which will deliver a final decision. The appeal committee is made up of senior representatives of the Member States and delivers its opinion by majority. If the appeal committee delivers a positive opinion the Commission can adopt the measure. If the appeal committee delivers a negative opinion, the Commission cannot adopt the measure. If the appeal committee delivers no opinion, the Commission can adopt the act subject to an exception relating to the CCP in that in that area if no opinion is delivered the Commission cannot adopt the act.

B. **The advisory procedure.** This applies to all areas not covered by the examination procedure, but, in duly justified cases, it may also apply to areas to which the examination procedure is normally applicable. The advisory committee adopts its opinion by a simple majority. The Commission must take "utmost account" of the opinion but it is not required to follow it. In other words, the opinion is not binding on the Commission.

In addition to the two main procedures, Regulation 182/2011 provides for two fast tracking procedures:

- Under Article 7 of the Regulation, the Commission is allowed to adopt implementing acts in exceptional cases, i.e. where a delay in adopting an implementing act may cause a significant disruption of the markets in the area of agriculture or put at risk the financial interests of the EU. An adopted implementing act must be submitted to the appeal committee immediately after its adoption. If the appeal committee rejects the adopted implementing act the Commission must repeal it immediately.

- Under Article 8 of the Regulation, the Commission may, in duly justified cases, adopt an immediately applicable implementing act. However, the adopted act cannot remain in force for longer than six months. The Commission must submit it to the relevant committee within 14 days of its adoption. The measure will be repealed if the relevant committee delivers a negative opinion by QMV.

The system under Regulation 182/2011 ensures that national interests are protected and duly taken account of when the Commission adopts implementing acts. In this respect, it is important to note that often technical details have great impact on the relevant sector of the national economy, and by allowing a Member State to have its say on the matter confidence in the implementation process is enhanced. However, Regulation 182/2011 gives the EP a very limited role to control the Commission's use of implementing powers. The EP may only indicate, by adopting a non-binding resolution, at any time, that it considers a draft implementing act exceeds the powers conferred on the Commission by the relevant legislative act. The Commission is then required to review the draft act in the light of the EP's resolution but is not obliged to take any further action. The Council is given the same opportunity as the EP, but, of course, *via* committees, it, *de facto*, controls the exercise of the Commission's implementing powers.

4.5.3 Requirements relating to the adoption of secondary acts

In order to be valid secondary acts must conform to certain requirements. These are examined below.

4.5.3.1 Statement of reason(s)

With regard to legislative acts, Article 296 TFEU provides that measures must "state the reasons on which they are based and shall refer to any proposals, initiatives, recommendations, requests or opinions required by the Treaties".

The objective of this requirement was explained by the ECJ in Case 24/62 *Germany v Commission*[257] as permitting:

- the parties concerned by any particular measure to defend their rights;
- the EU courts to exercise their supervisory functions; and,
- all Member States and all EU citizens to ascertain the circumstances in which EU institutions apply the provisions of the Treaties.

Every measure must indicate the detailed reasons for its enactment.[258] These must be clear and unequivocal,[259] taking into account the context and the other rules applicable to the subject-matter. They must also be precise if the adoption of a measure is subject to the assessment of an economic situation by an EU institution.[260]

A less detailed statement of reasons is accepted if an applicant who wishes to challenge the validity of a measure under Article 263 TFEU has contributed to, or participated in the procedure leading to the adoption of that measure,[261] or if the measure derives from a constant practice of EU institutions,[262] but if there has been any change in that practice more detailed explanations as to the legal basis of the challenged measure and objectives which it aims to achieve are required.

The EU courts must raise, of their own motion, the absence of or insufficiency of "reasons for enactment" of EU acts challenged before them.[263] Such absence or insufficiency may result in the annulment of a measure by the EU court.

With regard to non-legislative acts, i.e. implementing acts and delegated acts, these must refer to the legislative acts on the basis of which they have been adopted.

4.5.3.2 Legal basis

The choice of a legal basis for non-legislative acts poses no problem as they must be based on a relevant legislative act. However, in respect of legislative measures the determination of their legal basis is not easy, especially in the context of the involvement of the EP in the legislative procedures

---

257. [1963] ECR 63.
258. For example, Case C-27/90 *SITPA v Oniflhor* [1991] ECR I-133; Case C-69/89 *Nakajima All Precision Co Ltd v Council* [1991] ECR I-2069; Case C-353/92 *Greece v Council* [1994] ECR I-3411.
259. Case 1/69 *Italy v Commission* [1969] ECR 277.
260. Case 24/62 *Germany v Commission* [1963] ECR 143.
261. Case 13/72 *The Netherlands v Commission* [1973] ECR 27; Case 1252/79 *SpA Acciaierie e Ferriere Lucchini v Commission* [1980] ECR 3753.
262. Case 73/74 *Groupement des Fabricants de Papiers Peints de Belgique and Others v Commission* [1975] ECR 1491; Case 102/87 *France v Commission* [1988] ECR 4067.
263. Case T-471/93 *Tiercé Ladbroke SA v Commission* [1995] ECR II-2537.

of the EU. There are, however, three main principles which assist the relevant institutions in choosing the appropriate legal basis for a legislative act (i.e. the relevant provision of the Treaties). These are:

■ The choice must be based on objective criteria which are amenable to judicial review by the CJEU.[264] This ensures legal certainty;

■ If an EU measure pursues a twofold purpose or has a twofold component and if one of them is identifiable as the main or predominant purpose or component, whereas the other is merely incidental, the act must be based on a single legal basis, namely that required by the main or predominant purpose or component.[265] This is referred to as the theory of "principal and accessory". The fact that under one provision of the Treaty the EP would have greater involvement in the adoption of a measure than under another provision, e.g. one provision requires recourse to the ordinary legislative procedure whilst the other provides for the use of the consultation procedure, is irrelevant in the determination of which of the two provisions is predominant. The choice of the legal basis must rest on objective factors, in particular, the aim and the content of the measure, not on political considerations;[266] and,

■ Exceptionally, if an EU measure simultaneously pursues several objectives which are inseparably linked and are of equal importance, that is, without one being secondary and indirect in relation to the other, the measure may be based on dual (or even) several legal bases.[267] This is subject to an exception. Adoption of a measure on several/dual legal bases is precluded if the legal bases involved are incompatible, i.e. the procedures laid down in each legal basis are irreconcilable, or where the use of two, or more, legal bases is liable to undermine the rights of the EP.[268] In such a situation, the legal basis which gives the EP greater participation in the adoption of a measure will prevail, e.g. a legal basis which provides for the use of the ordinary legislative procedure will prevail over a legal basis which excludes the participation of the EP in the adoption of the measure[269] or only provides for consultation of the EP. This approach enhances the principle of democracy in that it ensures that the EP, which is directly elected by EU citizens, and through which they participate in the decision making process in the EU, has the greatest possible involvement in the adoption of a measure.

4.5.3.3 Publication of a measure

In Case 98/78 *Racke*,[270] the ECJ held that the fundamental principles of the EU legal order require that an act emanating from public authorities cannot produce legal effect unless it comes to the knowledge of its addressees.

---

264. Case C-269/97 *Commission v Council* [2000] ECR I-2257; Case C-300/89 *Commission v Council* ("*Titanium dioxide*") [1991] ECR I-2867; Case C-336/00 *Austria v Martin Huber* [2002] ECR I-7699; Case C-176/03 *Commission v Council* [2005] ECR I-7879.
265. Case C-42/97 *Parliament v Council* [1999] ECR I-869; Case T-99/05 *Spain v Commission* [2007] ECR II-40.
266. Case C-269/97 *Commission v EP and Council* [2000] ECR I-2257, para. 44.
267. Case C-336/00 *Austria v Martin Huber* [2002] ECR I-7699; Case C-281/01 *Commission v Council* [2002] ECR I-2049; *Opinion 2/00 [Re Cartegena Protocol]* [2001] ECR 1-9713; Case C-178/03 *Commission v EP and Council* [2006] ECR I-107.
268. Case C-300/89 *Commission v Council* ("*Titanium Dioxide*") [1991] ECR I-2867; and Joined Cases C-164/97 and C-165/97 *Parliament v Council* [1999] ECR I-1139.
269. Case C-178/03 *Commission v EP and Council* [2006] ECR I-107.
270. Case 98/78 *A. Racke v Hauptzollamt Mainz* [1979] ECR 69.

Depending upon the form of a measure, it must be either published in the Official Journal of the European Union or notified to its addressee.[271] Article 297 TFEU provides that all legislative acts must be published in the OJ whilst non-legislative acts adopted in the form of a regulation, a directive or a decision are to be published in the OJ if they take the form of:

- regulations or directives addressed to all Member States; or,

- decisions which do not specify to whom they are addressed.

Under Article 297 TFEU measures not required to be published in the OJ must be notified to their addressees:

- to natural or legal persons residing within the EU, by registered letter or delivery with acknowledgment;[272]

- to natural or legal persons residing outside the EU, through diplomatic channels, that is, ambassadors accredited to the EU institutions; and,

- to Member States, through their permanent representatives in Brussels.

4.5.3.4   Date of entry into force of a measure

The date of entry into force of a particular measure may be specified in the measure itself. If a measure is notified, it enters into force on the day of its notification, unless otherwise provided for in the measure; and if published, and in the absence of any specification, it is deemed by virtue of Article 297 TFEU to become operative 20 days after its publication. This applies to both legislative and non-legislative acts.

The ECJ held in Case 98/78 *Racke*[273] that the day of publication does not mean the day on which the OJ is available in the territory of each Member State but the day when it is available at the seat of the Office for Official Publications of the EU at Luxembourg. Unless proved to the contrary, this is, for evidential purposes, taken to be the day the OJ containing the text of the act in question was published.

In relation to an act which requires publication, a specific date is usually fixed for its entry into force. This is done to avoid the risk of its immediate entry into force, without any transitional period, undermining the principles of legal certainty and legitimate expectation.[274] In Case 17/67 *Firma Max Neumann*,[275] the ECJ held that only in a case of extreme necessity may an act enter into force immediately, that is, on the day of its publication in the OJ. The institutions concerned must have serious reasons to believe that delay between the date of the publication of an act and its entry into force would cause prejudice to the EU, and that its immediate entry into force is necessary to prevent speculation or a legal void.

---

271.   Case 185/73 *Hauptzollamt Bielefield v Offene Handelsgesellschaft in Firma H. C. König* [1974] ECR 607.
272.   Decision 22/60 of the High Authority of 7/09/1960, [1960] OJ B/1248.
273.   Case 98/78 *A. Racke v Hauptzollamt Mainz* [1979] ECR 69.
274.   Case 74/74 *CNTA SA v Commission* [1975] ECR 533.
275.   Case 17/67 *Firma Max Neumann v Hauptzollamt Hof/Saale* [1967] ECR 441.

4.5.3.5 Retroactivity

The ECJ rejected retroactive application of secondary legislation, apart from in exceptional cases when the objective to be achieved by a measure requires this. In such cases the legitimate expectations of the persons concerned by that measure must be respected.[276]

The ECJ confirmed the right of an EU institution to withdraw or to abrogate a measure, but in doing so laid down certain conditions. When a measure creates individual rights, withdrawal is permitted: within a reasonable time (approximately six months); solely for reasons of illegality;[277] and public and private interests must be duly taken into account.[278] When a measure does not afford rights to individuals, it may be withdrawn within a reasonable time (according to the ECJ this seems to be between two and three years).[279]

4.5.4 Ranking of secondary sources in the hierarchy of sources of EU law

Secondary sources of EU law are, in the hierarchy of sources, classified after primary sources, general principles of EU law, and international agreements concluded between the EU and third States or international organisations. Secondary legislative acts are superior to non-legislative binding acts, i.e. delegated acts and implementing acts.

4.6 EU acts not expressly mentioned in Article 288 TFEU

There are sources of EU law, not mentioned in Article 288 TFEU, which are strictly speaking not secondary sources but some of which, nevertheless, may produce binding legal effects.[280] In this category two kinds of act can be distinguished. First, acts which are mentioned in the Treaties; and second, acts which are not mentioned in the Treaties.

4.6.1 Acts which are mentioned in the Treaties

The Treaties expressly mention the following acts:

■ Those which despite their name, are of different legal nature from those listed in Article 288 TFEU, e.g. directives adopted by the Council on the basis of Article 218(2) TFEU, which are addressed to the Commission or to the HR to give instructions in connection with negotiating international agreements to be concluded between the EU and third countries or between the EU and international organisations;

---

276. Case 98/78 *Racke* [1979] ECR 69; Case 14/81 *Alpha Steel Ltd. v Commission* [1982] ECR 749; Case C-248/89 *Cargill BV v Commission* [1991] ECR I-2987 and Case C-365/89 *Cargill BV v Produktschap voor Margarine, Vetten en Olien* [1991] ECR I-3045.

277. Joined Cases T-79, 84–86, 91–92, 94, 96, 98, 102 and 104/89 *BASF and Others v Commission* [1992] ECR II-315.

278. Joined Cases 42 and 49/59 *SNUPAT v High Authority* [1961] ECR 53; Joined Cases 53 and 54/63 *Lemmerz-Werke and Others v High Authority* [1963] ECR 239; Case 15/85 *Consorzio Cooperative d'Abruzzo v Commission* [1987] ECR 1005.

279. Case 14/61 *Koninklijke Nederlandsche Hoogovens en Staalfabrieken N.V. v High Authority* [1962] ECR 253.

280. See European Parliament, Report Kirk-Reay, Doc. 148/78 of 30.5.1978.

■ Inter-institutional agreements. Under Article 295 TFEU the EP, the Council and the Commission are allowed to make arrangements for co-operation with each other, in particular by concluding inter-institutional agreements which may be of a binding nature;

■ With regard to the CFSP, the European Council shall adopt general guidelines and decisions whilst the Council shall adopt decisions (Articles 22, 25(a) and 26 TEU) (see Chapter 7.5.1). Whether decisions adopted in the context of the CFSP have the same legal nature as decisions adopted by virtue of Article 288 TFEU is debatable. It is submitted that the specificity of the CFSP suggests that decisions adopted within the framework of the CFSP are of a different legal nature than those referred to in Article 288 TFEU. In this respect, it can be said that Article 24(1) TEU specifically states that "the adoption of legislative acts shall be excluded" in matters relating to the CFSP. In the light of the fact that under the Treaties only three types of act can be adopted: legislative, delegated and implementing, it is clear that by excluding the possibility of adopting legislative acts in CFSP matters the Treaties also exclude the possibility of adopting delegated or implementing acts in CFSP matters within the meaning of Articles 290 and 291 TFEU. This is because delegated and implementing acts can only be adopted on the basis of a legislative act as they do not exist independently of legislative acts. Obviously, under the CFSP the European Council and the Council are empowered to adopt binding decisions, but such decisions cannot be based on legislative acts because those institutions have no power to adopt legislative acts in CFSP matters. Further, a decision within the meaning of Article 22 TEU does not fit the description of a delegated act, or an implementing act, and on the ground of Article 24 TEU it cannot be a legislative act;

■ Internal rules of procedure which regulate the composition, functioning and procedures of each EU institution. They are binding on the institution concerned. The rules of procedure of the EU courts are special in that they are binding on both the courts and the parties to the proceedings; and,

■ Recommendations and opinions that one EU institution addresses to another, some of them are binding, some are not.

4.6.2 Acts not mentioned by the Treaties

These are: resolutions, deliberations, conclusions, communications and common declarations of two or more EU institutions adopted by various EU institutions. The EP has expressed its concern at the increasing number of atypical acts (i.e. those which take a form not mentioned in the Treaties) adopted by EU institutions outside the EC Treaty.[281] The ToL responded by, first, simplifying the nomenclature of secondary sources of EU law and second by stating in Article 296(3) TFEU that "When considering draft legislative acts, the European Parliament and the Council shall refrain from adopting acts not provided for by the relevant legislative procedure in the area in question".

In principle acts not mentioned by the Treaties are part of "soft law", i.e. they are not legally binding (see Chapter 4.8), but the ECJ will determine on a case-by-case basis whether they are intended to produce binding legal effects. The ECJ has, on rare occasions, held that where the institution concerned has expressed its intention to be bound by them, such acts may produce legal effects.[282]

---

281.   See Report Burger, EP Doc. Session 215/68–69 of 12.03.1969.
282.   E.g. Proceedings of 20 March 1970 in Case 22/70 *Commission v Council [ERTA]* [1971] ECR 263, or in Case C-25/94 *Commission v Council* [1996] ECR I-1469, an arrangement between the Council and the Commission

4.7 The contribution of the ECJ to the creation of sources of EU law

The special position of the ECJ as a law-maker requires some explanation.

The ECJ as an EU institution enjoys a special status given that:

■ Until the establishment of the General Court (formerly known as the CFI), the ECJ was the one and only judicial institution in the Community. Its authority is similar to that of national supreme courts, such as the Supreme Court of the United Kingdom, or the *Cour de Cassation* in France. There is no control over and no appeal against its decisions. The creation of the General Court has not changed the position of the ECJ. However, the latter constitutes an appellate court on points of law from the decisions of the General Court; and,

■ The ECJ's mission is not only to apply the law expressly laid down by, or under, the Treaties but, more importantly, to promote continuous development of EU law, to supplement its provisions, and to fill gaps in the Treaties. Bingham J in *Samex SpA* described this as a "creative process of supplying flesh to a sparse and loosely constructed skeleton".[283]

4.7.1 Methods of interpretation in EU law

The ECJ, in order to carry out its tasks, relies on a variety of methods of interpretation and a number of interpretive devices. The interpretation of EU law is based on Article 31 of the 1969 Vienna Convention on the Law of Treaties, which provides that interpretation should be based on the ordinary meaning of the terms of a treaty in the context and in the light of its object and purpose. However, the ECJ has given priority to interpretation "in the general context" (the systematic method) "and in the light of its object and purpose" (the teleological method) over the literal interpretation of the Treaties.[284]

In Case 283/81 *CILFIT*,[285] the ECJ emphasised the particular difficulties in the interpretation and application of EU law. EU legislation is drafted in several languages and each version is authentic. Thus, the comparison of different versions is sometimes necessary. Furthermore, EU law uses terminology and refers to legal concepts which are peculiar to it. The EU meaning of legal concepts often differs from the meaning under national laws of the Member States. In *CILFIT* the ECJ summarised the complexity of the interpretation of EU law in the following terms:

> "every provision of the Community law [EU law] must be placed in its context and interpreted in the light of the provisions of Community law [EU law] as a whole, regard being had to the objectives thereof and to its state of evolution at the date on which the provision in question is to be applied."[286]

In addition to the above, the ECJ relies on other methods of interpretation depending upon the case and the degree to which the provision to be interpreted is ambiguous, obscure or imprecise.

The most characteristic features of interpretation of EU law by the ECJ are:

---

which clearly stated that the two institutions intended to enter into a binding commitment towards each other or a Communication issued by the Commission in Case C-57/95 *France v Commission* [1997] ECR I-1627).

283.   *Customs and Excise Commissioners v Samex SpA* [1983] 3 CMLR 194.

284.   The method used by the ECJ has been described as being "meta-teleological", see M. Lasser, *Judicial Deliberations: A Comparative Analysis of Judicial Transparency and Legitimacy*, 2004, Oxford: Oxford University Press; H. Rasmussen, *On Law and Policy of the European Court of Justice: A Comparative Study in Judicial Policy Making*, 1986, Dordrecht: Martinus Nijhoff; and M. Maduro, *We, the Court*, 1998, Oxford: Hart Publishing.

285.   Case 283/81 *Srl CILFIT and Lanificio di Gavardo SpA v Ministry of Health* [1982] ECR 3415.

286.   Ibid, para. 20.

- The wide eclecticism of the methods used to interpret EU law combined with the willingness to draw from each of them the maximum effectiveness;
- The consideration given to the originality and autonomy of EU law *vis-à-vis* international law and national laws of the Member States;
- The consideration given to the need to maintain the coherence of the EU legal system; and,
- The consideration given to the need to ensure the unity and homogeneity of EU law.

These considerations and methods require and, at the same time, allow the ECJ to become a law-maker. Whether this "judicial legislation" should be criticised or considered as an asset is a different matter.[287] The ECJ's use of the concept of effectiveness provides a good example. In public international law the concept of effectiveness is applied by an international judge when confronted with two possible interpretations of a legal provision, one which confers some meaning on it, and the other which renders it devoid of any significance. The judge gives priority to the former. The ECJ not only sets aside an interpretation which renders a provision devoid of its effectiveness, but more importantly rejects any interpretation which results in limiting or weakening the effectiveness of that provision.[288]

In interpreting EU law, the ECJ takes into consideration the evolving nature of the EU and thus interprets EU law in the light of new needs which did not exist at the time of ratification of the founding Treaties.

Such constitutional principles as supremacy of EU law, direct applicability, direct effect of EU law and a Member State's liability for damage caused to individuals have been established by the ECJ.

None of the constitutional principles mentioned above were contained or provided for in the founding EEC Treaty entered into in 1957 by Belgium; France; Germany; Italy; Luxembourg; and, the Netherlands, or in the subsequent amendments to that Treaty. They were progressively inferred by the ECJ, and each of them provided an integrationist impetus that appeared, at different times, to be lacking on the part of different Member States. Their impact on legal, political and internal market European integration has been overwhelming.[289]

Resulting from what many perceived to be the ECJ's apparent political activism, it was accused of "running wild" and of contravening one of the basic principles of liberal democracy, that is, that of judicial neutrality and independence.[290] Democracy requires that law is created by democratically accountable politicians, not judges. The Court itself made little effort to justify its activism and few seem to have cared that, since its inception, the "Supreme Court" of the new Europe has, in addition to pursuing its primary purpose, been pursuing a virtually political agenda.[291] Commentators have stated various reasons why the ECJ's judicial activism has been acceptable to the Member States. According to Shapiro, the main reason was that Member States governments were incapable of reacting with unanimity to the most audacious judgments of the ECJ. As a result, those judgments would stick, develop and consolidate, especially when supported by the Commission and private actors who have benefited from European integration.[292] Douglas-Scott suggests first, that the Member States did not

287. See R. Lecourt, *L'Europe des Juges*, 1976, Bruxelles, Bruylant; I. Ward, *A Critical Introduction to European Law*, 2nd edn, 2003, London: Butterworths, 97–101.
288. Case C-437/97 *Evangelischer Krankenhausverein Wien v Abgabenberufungskommission Wien and Wein & Co. HandelsgesmbH v Oberösterreichische Landesregierung* [2000] ECR I-1157.
289. On this topic see A. Stone Sweet, "The European Court of Justice", in P. Craig and G. de Bùrca (eds), *The Evolution of EU Law*, 2nd edn, 2011, Oxford: OUP, 121.
290. I. Ward, *A Critical Introduction to European Law*, 2nd edn, 2003, London: Butterworths, 97–101.
291. Ibid, 99.
292. M Shapiro, "The European Court of Justice" in P. Craig and G. de Bùrca (eds), *The Evolution of EU Law*, 1999, Oxford: OUP, 329–31.

feel threatened bearing in mind that they possess a lot of control over the integration process, second, the audacious judgments, with some exceptions, "have initially been of too low a visibility to create an immediate practical effect or to serve as a target for the media or any popular dialogue" and third, the Member States were interested in ensuring that all Member States comply with EU law.[293]

For some, the Court's activism has been necessary and desirable; for others it has been inexcusable. It is certainly true, however, that without the ECJ having been active in promoting legal and political integration the EU would not be the great power which it is today. In the submission of the author, it is fascinating that whilst the political elite of Europe, during the last half of the twentieth century, failed to develop any unified vision as to how Europe would look at the beginning of the twenty-first century, the judges of the ECJ followed a constant course for 50 years which in many ways made Europe what it is today.

4.7.2 Precedent in EU law

Under EU law there is no doctrine of precedent. The previous case law of the ECJ is neither binding on the General Court, nor on national courts, nor on itself. The EU legal system follows civil law systems in its approach to precedent. However, there are a number of arguments in favour of the recognition of the binding nature of previous judgments of the ECJ. These are set out below:

- The ECJ, having a major role to play in the development of the EU legal order (which according to its judgment in Case 26/62 *Van Gend*[294] "constitutes a new legal order of international law"), will depart from its previous case law only in exceptional circumstances, and after considering all legal implications;

- The ECJ has gradually built coherent, stable and consistent case law that can serve as a yardstick for other European courts, national courts, litigants and their counsel and the ECJ is unlikely to frustrate their expectations, without mature reflection;

- The principle of legal certainty which requires that law must be reasonably predictable, so that citizens may arrange their affairs in full knowledge of the legal consequences, and the principle of equality, which requires that like situations must be treated in like manner, necessitate that some recognition is given to the binding nature of previous law. Thus previous judgments of the ECJ, which have formulated general propositions about law, are expected to be followed because of the need for legal certainty and equality;

- It can be said that the ECJ's judgment in Case 283/81 *CILFIT*,[295] in which the Court stated that national courts of final instance are not obliged to refer a question relating to the interpretation of EC law to the ECJ if they consider that, in the light of the previous case law, the answer is obvious, constitutes an implicit recognition of the binding nature of previous decisions of the ECJ;

- By departing from its previous case law, the ECJ would, to some extent, undermine its own authority;

- The ECJ, while delivering a new judgment, makes reference in the text of that judgment to previous relevant cases which raise the same or similar issues;

293. S. Douglas-Scott, *Constitutional Law of the European Union*, 2002, Harlow: Pearson /Longman, 216–17.
294. [1963] ECR 3.
295. Case 283/81 *Srl CILFIT and Lanificio di Gavardo SpA v Ministry of Health*, [1982] ECR 3415.

■ The doctrine of precedent is not as rigid as it may appear in that if it seems that a previous case was wrongly decided, the courts will use every effort to distinguish the circumstances of the current case from those of the previous case, so allowing themselves not to follow the previous case. Further, in countries where the doctrine of *stare decisis* is recognised,[296] supreme courts are allowed to deviate from the existing case law if circumstances so require. In the UK the House of Lords (now the Supreme Court) made a declaration in 1966 stating that its decisions, although binding upon all lower courts, are not binding on itself; and,

■ The acceptance of the binding nature of ECJ judgments may even be acceptable to civil law countries. Although civil law countries have no doctrine of *stare decisis*, most of them accept the doctrine of *jurisprudence constant* (consistent case law), according to which a long series of previous decisions applying a particular rule of law carries great weight and may be determinative in subsequent cases.[297]

It is submitted that although the case law of the ECJ is not formally recognised as a source of EU law, it is, in fact, an important source of law. The ECJ in its case law has established constitutional principles and important concepts of EU law, which have subsequently become sources of EU law. However, its case law is not cast in stone. In exceptional circumstances, the ECJ has departed from its earlier case law. It was in Case C-10/89 *HAG II*[298] that the ECJ, for the first time, overturned its previous judgment delivered 16 years earlier in Case *HAG I*[299] and stated that the previous judgment was wrongly decided. Subsequently, the ECJ has given judgments conflicting with its earlier judgments.[300]

4.8 "Soft law" and the open method of co-ordination (OMC)

Article 288 TFEU expressly provides that recommendations and opinions have no binding force. They are adopted in areas in which the EU has no legislative powers, or when a transitional period is necessary in order to achieve a certain stage at which EU institutions will be empowered to adopt binding measures. In Case 322/88 *Grimaldi*,[301] the ECJ held that recommendations are not devoid of all legal effect. National judges are obliged to take them into consideration in the interpretation of EU law. In opinions, EU institutions express their views on a given question.

Recommendations and opinions are part of "soft law", and can be described as EU measures which have no binding legal force or whose binding legal force is less than absolute.[302] These are not only recommendations, opinions, but also codes of conduct, guidelines, action plans, notices, strategies,

---

296. The legal term *stare decisis et non quieta movere* means "stand by decisions and do not move that which is quiet".
297. See R. Youngs, *English, French and German Comparative Law*, 1998, London: Cavendish, 50 et seq.
298. Case C-10/89 *CNL SUCAL v HAG GF (HAG II)* [1990] ECR I-3711.
299. Case 192/73 *Van Zuylen v HAG (HAG I)* [1974] ECR 731.
300. For example: Cases 115 and 116/81 *Rezguia Adoui v Belgian State and City of Liège; Dominique Cornuaille v Belgian State* [1982] ECR 1665 in relation to Case 41/74 *Van Duyn v Home Office* [1974] ECR 1337; Case 302/87 *EP v Council (Comitology)* [1988] ECR 5615 in relation to Case C-70/88 *EP v Council (Chernobyl)* [1990] ECR I-2041. See also Joined Cases C-267 and 268/91 *Criminal proceedings against Bernard Keck and Daniel Mithouard* [1993] ECR I-6097 (Chapter 20.5).
301. Case 322/88 *Salvatore Grimaldi v Fonds des Maladies Professionnelles* [1989] ECR 4407.
302. According to F. Snyder, soft law can be defined as "rules of conduct which in principle have no legally binding force but which nevertheless may have practical effect": "Soft Law and Institutional Practice in the European Community", in S. Martin (ed.), *The Construction of Europe*, 1994, The Hague: Kluwer, 198.

communications, etc. Soft law as opposed to "hard law" (i.e. binding rules) is seen as an attractive option for achieving specific objectives without being too heavy handed.

Soft law mechanisms (such as guidelines, benchmarking and sharing best practice) has become an integral part of the open method of co-operation (OMC) which was endorsed by the 2000 Lisbon Council as being appropriate to help the Member States to develop national policies with a view to achieving the ambitious Lisbon Agenda. According to the European Council OMC involves:

- "Fixing guidelines for the Union combined with specific timetables for achieving the goals which they set in the short, medium and long terms;
- Establishing, where appropriate, quantitative and qualitative indicators and benchmarks against the best in the world and tailored to the needs of different Member States and sectors as a means of comparing best practice;
- Translating these European guidelines into national and regional policies by setting specific targets and adopting measures, taking into account national and regional differences;
- Periodic monitoring, evaluation and peer review organised as mutual learning processes."[303]

The OMC mainly applies to areas in which the EU co-ordinates policies of Member States, under Article 5 TFEU, employment and economic policies of the Member States, under Article 6 TFEU, social protection, social inclusion, education, youth and training. It may also be used in other areas bearing in mind that the participation of the Member States in the OMC is voluntary. In those areas EU measures never take the form of regulations, directives, or decisions, but may take the form of guidelines, or common objectives. Such measures may have varying binding effect, e.g. Member States may be required to achieve some objectives, but no sanctions are imposed if the objectives are not met. However, peer pressure and naming and shaming mechanisms entail that a Member State will try to comply.

The OMC is an integral part of new modes of governance in the EU,[304] which have been used by the EU to respond to various regulatory shortcomings, such as limited decision-making capacity in the EU, concerns of the Member States to retain their competence in the areas of economic and social policies not essential to the creation of the internal market, and the encroachment on Member States' competences by the teleological interpretation of the Treaties by the ECJ.[305]

The OMC builds on the usual soft law process used in policy making and the experimentation with new forms of governance in the EU, i.e. new methods of economic governance in which the use of the "EU method" (see Chapter 1.7) is impossible, either because the EU has a weak competence or no competence at all but in which some level of EU regulation is necessary.

The OMC can be described as a strategy to achieve common objectives by the Member States, while respecting their diversities. The OMC is characterised by the combined use of modes of governance such as targets, deadlines, benchmarking, peer reviewing and evaluation, the adoption of which result in the establishment or adjustment of soft law instruments such as recommendations, common objectives, etc. The OMC differs depending on the policy areas in that there may be shorter or longer

---

303. Presidency Conclusions, p. 37. Available at http:// www.europarl.europa.eu/summits/lis1_en.htm#d (accessed 21/6/12).

304. They include a variety of policy-making instruments such as the use of framework directives, soft law, co-regulation, partnership models, voluntary agreements and the social dialogue. On this topic see: A. Héritier, "New Modes of Governance in Europe: Policy Making without Legislating?", in A. Héritier (ed.), *Common Goals: Reinventing European and International Governance*, 2002, Boulder, CO: Rowman and Littlefield, 185.

305. On this topic see: E. Szyszczak, "Experimental Governance: The Open Method of Co-ordination", (2006) 12 ELJ, 486, at 487; J. Scott and D. Trubek, "Mind the Gap: Law and New Governance in the European Union", (2002) 8/2 ELJ, 1.

periods for achievements of objectives, guidelines may be set by EU institutions or by the Member States, the enforcement may be harder or softer.

At first glance it may seem that the OMC is similar to the traditional EU "soft law". However, the similarity is illusory. The OMC is different from traditional soft law in the following ways:

1. The OMC focuses on inter-governmental co-operation whereby the Council and the Commission determine the development and the content of the OMC and the ECJ has no input. Under traditional "soft law", the approach is supra-national as the ECJ and the Commission determine its content. Due to recognition of "soft law" by the ECJ it has been included into the *EU acquis*;

2. Under the OMC, policy formulation and monitoring takes place at the highest political level (the Council and the European Council) whilst the monitoring of traditional, "soft law" is done through the peer review process at an administrative level, often on an *ad hoc* basis;

3. Traditional soft law is used at random in relation to any chosen particular policy area. The OMC is used systematically in relation to all policy areas with a view to achieving a common objective. It links not only national policies with each other and different EU policies one to the other but also national policies with EU policies. Borras and Jacobsson pointed out that the OMC provides: "The possibility for truly bottom-up political dynamics, which differ from the top-down structures of the previous law-making";[306]

4. The OMC is not confined to States but seeks the participation of all stakeholders, private and public. This is not the case of traditional soft law as it does not seek the participation of social partners; and,

5. The OMC emphasises the mutual learning process through co-operation, exchange of knowledge and experiences. Traditional soft law has no such objective.

The effectiveness of the OMC is disputed. Those in favour argue that the OMC respects subsidiarity (see Chapter 6.8), accommodates diversity between Member States; involves lower cost than hard law; helps to avoid political deadlock; is open to stakeholders participation; is flexible and easy to revise; and, creates a regulatory climate for convergence of Member States deferring policies which may lead to the creation of hard law. Its opponents argue that it leads to uneven integration; low effectiveness bearing in mind that compliance is weak, as it rests on peer pressure and naming and shaming; and, that the OMC is an exercise in futility because, in fact, Member States repackage existing national policies to demonstrate their apparent compliance with EU objectives.[307]

RECOMMENDED READING

Books
Bell, M., *Anti-Discrimination Law and the EU*, 2002, Oxford: OUP.

Bernitz, U., Nergelius, J. and Cardner, C., *General Principles of EC Law in a Process of Development*, 2008, London: KLI.

---

306. "The Open Method of Co-operation and New Governance Patterns in the EU", (2004) 11/2 *Journal of European Public Policy*, 185, at 189.

307. On this topic see: S. Kröger, "The Open Method of Coordination: Underconceptualisation, Overdetermination, De-politicisation and Beyond", in S. K. Kröger (ed.), *What We Have Learnt: Advances, Pitfalls and Remaining Questions in OMC Research*, (2009) 13/1 European Integration Online Papers, Special Issue, 1.

Douglas-Scott, S., *Constitutional Law of the European Union*, 2002, Harlow: Pearson /Longman.

Everson, M. and Eisner J., *The Making of a European Constitution: Judges and Law Beyond Constitutive Power*, 2007, London: Routledge Cavendish.

Maduro, M., *We, the Court*, 1998, Oxford: Hart.

Senden, L., *Soft Law in European Community*, 2004, Oxford: Hart.

Tridimas, T., *The General Principles of EU Law*, 2007, Oxford: OUP.

Ward, I., *A Critical Introduction to European Law,* 2nd edn, 2003, London: Butterworths.

Articles

Bast, J., "New Categories of Acts after the Lisbon Reform: Dynamics of Parliamentarization in EU Law", (2012) 49 CMLRev., 885.

Bell, M., and Waddington, L., "Reflecting on Inequalities in European Equality Law", (2003) 28 ELR, 349.

Harbo, T-I., "The Function of the Proportionality Principle in EU Law", (2010) ELJ, 158.

Hofmann, H., "Legislation, Delegation and Implementation under the Treaty of Lisbon: Typology Meets Reality", (2009) 15 ELJ, 482.

Scott, J., and Trubek, D., "Mind the Gap: Law and New Governance in the European Union", (2002) 8/2 ELJ, 1.

Stone Sweet, A., "The European Court of Justice", in Craig, P. and de Bùrca, G. (eds.), *The Evolution of EU Law*, 2nd edn, 2011, Oxford: OUP, 121.

Szyszczak, E., "Experimental Governance: The Open Method of Co-ordination", (2006) 12 ELJ, 486

PROBLEM QUESTION

You are asked by an A-G to prepare a memorandum on whether the ECJ should recognise the principle of non-fault liability of the EU for both legislative and administrative acts adopted by the EU in a situation where such acts have caused damage to individuals. The following arguments should be considered.

The argument against the recognition of the above principle is that no such principle is recognised by the vast majority of legal systems of the Member States. Indeed, even in Member States where the principle of non-fault liability is recognised, its application is confined to exceptional circumstances, and apart from France, limited solely to administrative acts. Under French law the recognition of non-fault liability for legislative acts is justified by the fact that the French Conseil d'État (Council of State – the highest administrative court in France) has no jurisdiction to review the constitutionality of national legislation. Further, damages can be awarded subject to strict conditions requiring that the damage suffered is unusual, special, serious and direct, that the challenged legislation is not pursuing the common good and that the legislature has not ruled out compensation as a matter of principle. It results from the above that the principle of non-fault liability for legislative acts adopted by EU institutions should not be recognised in EU law because first, it is not a "general principle common to the laws of the Member States" and second, under EU law, contrary to French law, the CJEU have jurisdiction to review EU acts in the light of the Treaties and fundamental principles of EU law, and therefore EU law provides for the possibility of the liability of the EU to be put in issue if those higher-ranking norms are infringed.

The argument in favour of the recognition of the principle of non-fault liability for acts adopted by EU institutions where such acts have caused damage to individuals is that no mechanical approach is taken to the selection of general principles of EU law. Therefore it is of no importance how many Member States share the relevant principle. What is important is that the principle is appropriate to the needs and specific features of the EU legal system. Accordingly, the principle of non-fault liability of the EU for both legislative and administrative acts adopted by EU institutions responds to the particular requirements of the EU legal order for the following reasons:

- It serves the interests of justice as it would offset the severity of the conditions relating to the establishment of non-contractual liability of the EU for unlawful acts.
- It meets the requirements of good governance as it would force the relevant EU institutions to be very careful when exercising their discretion to adopt legislative acts, which would be lawful but which may cause particularly serious damage to citizens of the EU.

ESSAY QUESTION

Critically assess whether the Commission's use of delegated and implementing powers is properly supervised.

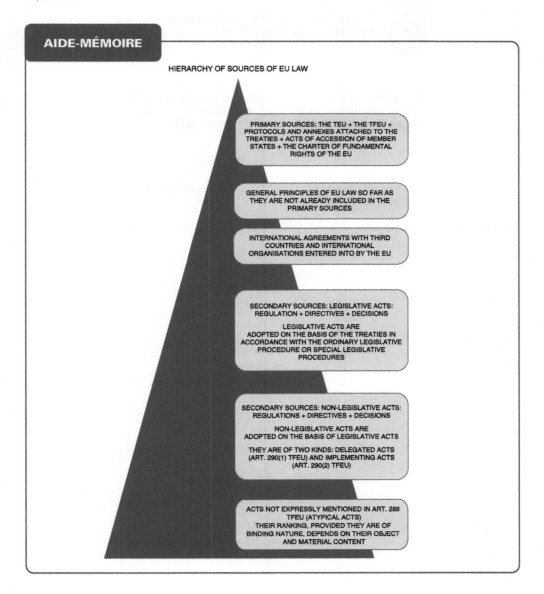

AIDE-MÉMOIRE

HIERARCHY OF SOURCES OF EU LAW

PRIMARY SOURCES: THE TEU + THE TFEU + PROTOCOLS AND ANNEXES ATTACHED TO THE TREATIES + ACTS OF ACCESSION OF MEMBER STATES + THE CHARTER OF FUNDAMENTAL RIGHTS OF THE EU

GENERAL PRINCIPLES OF EU LAW SO FAR AS THEY ARE NOT ALREADY INCLUDED IN THE PRIMARY SOURCES

INTERNATIONAL AGREEMENTS WITH THIRD COUNTRIES AND INTERNATIONAL ORGANISATIONS ENTERED INTO BY THE EU

SECONDARY SOURCES: LEGISLATIVE ACTS: REGULATION + DIRECTIVES + DECISIONS

LEGISLATIVE ACTS ARE ADOPTED ON THE BASIS OF THE TREATIES IN ACCORDANCE WITH THE ORDINARY LEGISLATIVE PROCEDURE OR SPECIAL LEGISLATIVE PROCEDURES

SECONDARY SOURCES: NON-LEGISLATIVE ACTS: REGULATIONS + DIRECTIVES + DECISIONS

NON-LEGISLATIVE ACTS ARE ADOPTED ON THE BASIS OF LEGISLATIVE ACTS

THEY ARE OF TWO KINDS: DELEGATED ACTS (ART. 290(1) TFEU) AND IMPLEMENTING ACTS (ART. 290(2) TFEU)

ACTS NOT EXPRESSLY MENTIONED IN ART. 288 TFEU (ATYPICAL ACTS) THEIR RANKING, PROVIDED THEY ARE OF BINDING NATURE, DEPENDS ON THEIR OBJECT AND MATERIAL CONTENT

DELEGATED ACTS - CONTROL PROCEDURE

- A legislative act must define objectives, content, scope, duration and conditions of delegation

- Preparatory work must be carried out by the Commission in consultation with "national experts"

- Draft measure of a delegated act must be submitted to the EU legislator

- The legislator (normally the Council and the EP) may (usually within 2 months)

Revoke the delegation (the EP by absolute majority and the Council by QMV)	Express objections (the EP by absolute majority and the Council by QMV)
The act cannot be adopted	The act cannot be adopted

IMPLEMENTING ACTS – CONTROL PROCEDURES UNDER REGULATION 182/2011

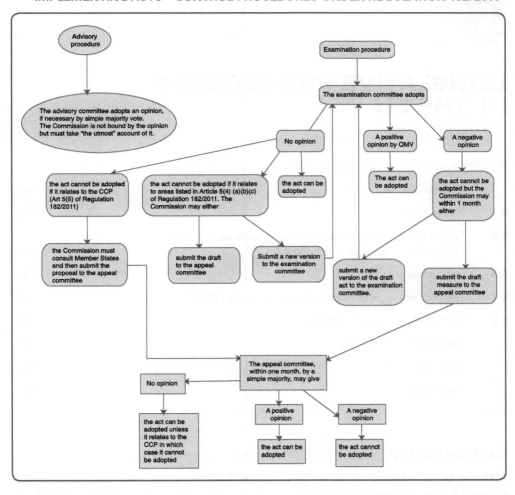

5

LEGISLATIVE PROCEDURES
IN THE EU

CHAPTER OUTLINE

1. One of the main objectives of the ToL was to reform the EU legislative procedures, i.e. to simplify and make them more transparent and democratic. The ToL achieved this to a considerable extent and in many ways:

- It simplified the law making process by establishing the ordinary legislative procedure (which was previously known as the co-decision procedure) as a standard procedure for adopting legislative acts. This procedure ensures that the EP is put on an equal footing with the Council with the result that no act can be adopted without both bodies' agreement. The remaining procedures are called "special procedures". Two of them involve the EP, i.e. the consent procedure (which was previously known as the assent procedure) and the consultation procedure;

- It reinforced the principle of representative democracy by extending the application of the ordinary legislative procedure to approximately 40 new areas of EU policies. As a result the ordinary legislative procedure (under which the EP, the only body in the EU directly elected by EU citizens, legislates jointly with the Council) applies to approximately 83 areas of EU policy. Additionally, under the *"passerelle"* provisions (i.e. bridging provisions which allow switching from special legislative procedures to the ordinary procedure, without the necessity to use the

IGC mechanism requiring ratification by all Member States) there is the opportunity for the EP's prerogatives to be further extended. It is to be noted that the EP as well as being now involved in the ordinary legislative procedure was formerly, and remains, involved in special procedures under which it is either consulted or gives its consent to legislative proposals. The principle of representative democracy has been reinforced not only by the above, but also by the fact that under the ToL national parliaments, which are directly elected by EU citizens in their own States, are very much involved in the EU legislative process and have the power to block the adoption of legislative proposals through the use of the "yellow and orange cards" procedure (see Chapter 6.8.2);

- ▪ It has reinforced participatory democracy by:
  - ● Imposing a duty on all EU institutions to give EU citizens and their representative associations the opportunity to make known, and publicly exchange, their views;
  - ● Requiring the Commission to conduct broad consultations with parties concerned to ensure that the EU's actions are coherent and transparent; and,
  - ● Giving EU citizens an opportunity to submit proposals direct to the Commission for adoption of legal acts necessary to implement the Treaties. Regulation 211/2011 on the citizens' initiative, which entered into force on 1 April 2012, sets out the procedure and conditions for implementing this right; and,
- ▪ It has enhanced the importance of the principle of transparency by requiring the EP to meet in public and the Council to "open" its deliberations and votes on draft legislative acts to the public.

2. Legislative proposals are normally initiated by the Commission, although in exceptional cases this initiative is shared with the HR in respect of non-CFSP foreign policies, the implementation of the "solidarity clause" (Article 222(3) TFEU), and the imposition of economic sanctions under Article 215(1) TFEU. Further, in respect of measures concerning judicial and police co-operation in criminal matters, not only the Commission, but also Member States forming at least one quarter of all the Member States, have the right to initiate proposals (Article 76 TFEU).

The Council (under Article 241 TFEU) and the EP (under Article 225 TFEU) are entitled to ask the Commission to prepare any proposals considered desirable for attainment of the objectives of the Treaty. Under Article 11(4) TEU, which has been implemented by Regulation 211/2011, EU citizens, under the conditions set out in the Regulation, can ask the Commission to prepare a proposal for a legal act necessary to implement any provision of the Treaties. However, neither the EP, nor the Council, nor EU citizens can force the Commission to act in this respect.

Under the Smart Regulation programme and in conformity with Article 11(2) and (3) TEU the Commission's approach to legislative proposals involves the widest possible consultation with all interested parties and the economic, social and financial assessment of the impact of legislative proposals.

The legal basis of a proposal, that is, the relevant article of the EU Treaty, determines which EU institutions are involved in its adoption and under which procedure that occurs.

3. Under Article 294 TFEU the ordinary legislative procedure has become the standard procedure for the adoption of EU legislative acts. It involves the triparty participation of the Commission, the Council and the EP.

4. Some special legislative procedures involve the participation of the EP, others allow the Commission and the Council to act jointly, or the Council or the Commission to act alone. Two special procedures in which the EP is involved are:

- ▪ The consultation procedure under which the Council is required to consult the EP but is not bound by the EP's opinion; and,

■ The consent procedure under which the Council has to obtain the EP's assent before adopting a legislative act. The EP can accept or reject a legislative proposal but cannot amend it.

5.1 Introduction

The pre-ToL legislative procedures were criticised for being complex, bureaucratic, secretive and difficult to understand. They also exacerbated the EC's democratic deficit. The ToL responded to this criticism. First, it simplified the legislative procedures; second it introduced many innovations aimed at reducing or even eliminating democratic deficit in the EU's legislative process; and, third, it made that process more transparent, Notwithstanding this, the EU legislative process is still complex, and differs greatly from that by which legislation is passed by national parliaments.

5.2 Simplification, democratisation and transparency of the EU legislative process under the ToL

This section examines how the ToL simplified the EU legislative process and made it more democratic and transparent.

5.2.1 Simplification of the EU legislative process

This was achieved by establishing the ordinary legislative procedure as the standard procedure for adopting legislative acts. The procedure ensures that the EP is put on an equal footing with the Council with the result that no act can be adopted without both bodies' agreement. The word "ordinary" emphasises that this procedure has become the predominant way of adopting EU legislation. The remaining procedures are called "special procedures". Two of them involve the EP, i.e. the consent procedure (which was previously known as the assent procedure) and the consultation procedure. Other examples of special procedures are those involving:

■ the Council and the Commission (e.g. Article 31 TFEU on adoption of measures relating to the Common Customs Tariff); and,

■ only the Commission in the adoption of legislative measures (e.g. Article 106(3) TFEU concerning measures relating to undertakings with a special position).

5.2.2 Enhancement of democratic representation by the ToL

With regard to the enhancement of democratic representation, the principle of democracy finds its most important expression in representative institutions. Under the ToL, the EP, whose members are directly elected by EU citizens, has seen its prerogatives enlarged. The ordinary procedure applies to virtually all areas in which the Council takes decisions by QMV. This represents approximately 40 new areas, including agriculture; fisheries; structural funds and vital policies covered by the AFSJ, such as frontier controls; immigration; judicial co-operation in criminal matters; minimum rules for the definition of, and the penalties in, areas of serious crime; incentives for crime prevention; Eurojust; police co-operation; Europol; and, civil protection. As a result, under the ToL the ordinary procedure applies to approximately 83 areas. Further, the ToL contains so called *"passerelle"* or bridging clauses which allow switching from special legislative procedures to the ordinary legislative procedure without the necessity to use the IGC mechanism requiring ratification by all Member Sates. There are two types of "*passerelle*" provisions:

■ A general "*passerelle*" provision contained in Article 48(7) TEU which allows the European Council, acting unanimously, after obtaining the consent of the EP (which shall be given by a majority of its component members) to authorise the application of the ordinary procedure for any area or case, provided that no national parliament opposes the proposed switch within six months of being notified of the European Council initiative; and,

■ Specific "*passerelle*" provisions. The following "*passerelle*" provisions contemplate the possibility of switching from the special procedure to the ordinary procedure:

● Under Article 81 TFEU the Council, acting unanimously, may propose a change from the special procedure to the ordinary procedure for the adoption of measures in the area of judicial co-operation in civil matters concerning family law with cross-border implications. The proposal must be notified to national parliaments and any of them may oppose the change within six months.

● No right of veto is given to national parliaments when the change of procedures concerns: certain fields of social policy (Article 153(2) TFEU); certain areas of environmental policy (Article 192(2) TFEU); and certain policies concerning the AFSJ. In all these cases the Council must act unanimously.

The EP is involved in special procedures in which it is either consulted or gives its consent. The ToL enhances the principle of representative democracy by involving national parliaments in the EU legislative process. Their role is described in Article 12 TEU and certainly the most valuable contribution of national parliaments is the possibility of using the "yellow and orange cards" procedure (see Chapter 6.8.2) to ensure that legislative proposals adopted by the Commission are compatible with the principle of subsidiarity. It is also important to note that the members of the European Council and the Council, who represent national governments at the EU level, are directly elected by EU citizens and democratically accountable either to their national parliaments, or to their citizens.

As to participatory democracy, Article 11(2) TEU imposes on EU institutions an obligation to give citizens and their representative associations the opportunity to make known, and publicly exchange, their views in all areas of Union action.[308] Article 11(3) TEU requires the Commission to conduct broad consultations with parties concerned in order to ensure that the Union's actions are coherent and transparent. The best method for ensuring broad consultation on vital EU legislative initiatives is to use referenda. Although this has been suggested for some time it has never been used. However, Article 11(4) TEU provides for a new form of popular participation. Under this provision no fewer than one million EU citizens, who are between them nationals of a significant number of Member States, can ask the Commission to prepare a proposal for a legal act necessary to implement the Treaties. Regulation 211/2011 on the citizens' initiative of 16 February 2011,[309] which entered into force on 1 April 2012, sets out the procedure and conditions for implementing the citizens' initiative.[310]

Under the Regulation a "significant number" of Member States is defined as being at least one quarter of the total number of EU Member States. With regard to the minimum number of supporters

---

308. V. Cuesta Lopez, "The Lisbon Treaty's Provisions on Democratic Principles: A Legal Framework for Participatory Democracy", (2010) 16 EPL, 123.

309. [2011] OJ L65/1.

310. Editorial, "Direct Democracy and the European Union . . . Is that a Threat or a Promise?" (2008) 45 CMLRev., 929.

required in each Member State, that number is equal to the number of the members of the EP in the relevant Member State, multiplied by 750. The organiser of a citizens' initiative must register the initiative with the Commission, and will have 12 months to collect the required one million signatures. The organiser is described as a committee of at least seven EU citizens who are resident in seven different Member States. The organiser will be required to submit information on funding of, and support for any proposed initiative. In order to prevent potential abuses the Regulation contains provisions relating to the verification of statements of support. The Commission will have three months to examine the initiative and decide how to deal with it.

The citizens' initiative has the potential to make a great impact on EU legislation but its use must respect the principle of equality enshrined in Article 9 TEU so that legislative initiatives exercised by a strong and well-organised group will not frustrate the will of the majority of EU citizens.

5.2.3 The principle of transparency

The fundamental importance of the principle of transparency, which emerged in the EU in the last decade of the twentieth century, was recognised by the ToA, and is confirmed in Article 1 TEU which states that: "This Treaty marks a new stage in the process of creating an ever closer union among the peoples of Europe, in which decisions are taken as openly as possible [i.e. transparently] and as closely as possible to the citizen". In general, the application of the principle of transparency takes two forms, the right of access to documents of the EU institutions and the public nature of the legislative process.

With regard to access to documents, Article 1 TEU is further detailed in Article 15 TFEU. The main innovation of the ToL is that new general rules on access to documents of all EU institutions will be adopted to ensure that all EU institutions conduct their work as openly as possible "in order to promote good governance and ensure the participation of civil society" and that all persons, natural and legal, not only EU citizens, will have the right to consult documents which are in possession of all EU institutions. Regulation 1049/2001,[311] which needs to be amended, is the main legislation which contains rules on principles, conditions and limits on the right of access to documents of the EP, the Council and the Commission. Also, Article 42 of the Charter of Fundamental Rights confirms the right of access to EP, Council and Commission documents. The case law of the CJEU on the interpretation of Regulation 1049/2001 was summarised by the General Court in Case T-190/10 *Egan and Hackett*,[312] as follows:

> "the exceptions to access to documents must be interpreted and applied strictly so as not to frustrate application of the general principle that the public should be given the widest possible access to documents held by the institutions. . . . Furthermore, the principle of proportionality requires that derogations remain within the limits of what is appropriate and necessary for achieving the aim in view."

Although most EU institutions, agencies and bodies have adopted rules similar to those contained in Regulation 1049/2001, there are some exceptions, in that the ECJ has never adopted rules relating to access to its documents. However, Article 15(3) TEU specifies that for the ECJ, the ECB, and the European Investment Bank, rules on access will be confined to areas in which they "exercise their administrative tasks" although those bodies may, at their own initiative, give access to other documents. Article 15(3) TFEU requires that each institution, body and agency adopts its own rules of procedure

---

311.   [2001] OJ L 145/43.
312.   Case T-190/10 *Egan and Hackett v EP*. Judgment of 28/3/12 (NYR), para. 88.

regarding access to its documents which are in conformity with those to be set out in the revised version of Regulation 1049/2001. Article 15(3) TFEU also requires that the EP and the Council ensure the publication of documents relating to the legislative procedures. Accordingly, it seems that both institutions must ensure the greatest possible access to such documents.

The ToL's innovation on the public nature of the legislative process is that under Article 15(2) TEU the EP is required to meet in public whilst the Council under Article 15(2) and Article 16(8) TEU is required to meet in public only when it deliberates and votes on a draft legislative act. Regarding other activities of the Council, its deliberations and votes are still held *in camera,* except in respect of:

- deliberations on and adoption of non-legislative proposals which impose rules which are binding in, or for, the Member States, by means of regulations, directives and decisions;

- debates concerning the General Affairs Council's 18-month programme, and priorities of the other Council configurations, and on the Commission's five-year programme, annual work programme and annual policy strategy; and,

- debates on important issues affecting the interest of the EU and its citizens.[313]

It should be noted that Article 296 TFEU enhances the principle of transparency and democracy, as it requires that legal acts must "state the reasons on which they are based and shall refer to any proposals, initiatives, recommendations, requests or opinions required by the Treaties". This requirement ensures that EU citizens are able to identify the reasons for which an act has been adopted. As Von Bogdandy stated, the requirement of stating reasons in legal acts is hardly known in national legal orders.[314]

5.3 Legislative proposals

While the legislative process is usually initiated by the Commission, this may also be done jointly by the Commission and the HR in respect of non-CFSP foreign matters; the implementation of the "solidarity" clause (Article 222(3) TFEU); and, the imposition of economic sanctions under Article 215(1) TFEU.

In respect of measures concerning judicial and police co-operation in criminal matters not only the Commission but also a quarter of the Member States acting together have the right to initiate proposals (Article 76 TFEU).

It should be noted that the Council (under Article 241 TFEU) and the EP (under Article 225 TFEU) are entitled to ask the Commission to prepare any proposals considered desirable for the attainment of the objectives of the Treaties. The Commission is not obliged to agree to the request. However, with regard to the EP, under Article 16 of the Framework Agreement on Relations between the EP and the Commission,[315] the Commission has committed itself to report on the concrete follow-up of any request from the EP within three months of its submission. If the Commission decides to make a legislative proposal, it shall do it at the latest after one year of the request, or shall include it in its next year's Work Programme. If the Commission refuses to submit a proposal it must give the EP detailed explanations of its rejection of the request.

---

313. See the General Secretariat of the Council of the EU, Information Sheet, "Openness and Transparency of Council Proceedings", Brussels, July 2011, available at http://ue.eu.int/media/1237859/sn02860-re01.en11-pub.pdf (accessed 3/4/12).

314. A. von Bogdandy, "Founding Principles", in A. von Bogdandy and J. Bast, *Principles of European Constitutional Law,* 2nd edn, 2010, Oxford: Hart Publishing, 51.

315. [2010] L304/47.

Regulation 211/2011, which implements Article 11(4) TEU, gives EU citizens the right to ask the Commission to prepare a legislative proposal in respect of a matter within the competence of the Commission if that matter, according to those citizens, requires EU legislation for the purpose of implementing the Treaties. However, the Commission is not obliged to propose legislation as a result of the initiative.[316]

Once the Commission decides that a legislative act is needed in any particular area, the appropriate Directorate General formulates a broad outline of an envisaged proposal for approval by the relevant commissioner who, all being well, submits it to the College of Commissioners (that is, the commissioners acting together). If the College agrees that the proposal is worth pursuing and the timing is right, it is then subject to further consideration as outlined below.

Under the Better Regulation programme[317] launched in 2002 (and revised in November 2006[318]), addressed to all EU institutions and to the Member States, and the Inter-Institutional Agreement (IIA) on Better Lawmaking signed by the EP, the Council and the Commission in 2003,[319] the Commission adopted a new approach to legislative proposals.[320] The main objectives of the Better Regulation programme were:

- simplification of EU legislation;

- reduction of administrative burdens and costs resulting from EU law for EU citizens, businesses, Member States and other organisations;

- introduction of impact assessments of legislative proposals; and,

- broader consultation with those potentially affected before proposing legislation.

The success of the Better Regulation programme[321] prompted the Commission to adopt an even more ambitious approach to EU policy-making, by transforming "Better Regulation" into "Smart Regulation". The Commission's Communication, "Smart Regulation: Ensuring that European Laws Benefit People and Businesses",[322] outlines the main elements of the "Smart Regulation" programme. This programme significantly improves all vital elements of the "Better Regulation" programme, whilst providing for greater involvement of end-users (i.e. EU citizens, businesses and other organisations) in the decision-making process. End-users are well informed of all major Commission's initiatives through publicly available "roadmaps" and other documents and have sufficient time to make their contributions (a minimum consultation period is fixed at eight weeks). Arrangements are made to ensure that due consideration is given to their contributions. The aims of "Smart Regulations" are to improve the quality of EU legislation and to increase its relevance to end-users.

If a proposal complies with the impact assessment and other above-mentioned requirements, it is submitted to the College of Commissioners, which decides by a simple majority vote whether or not it should proceed. If the decision is in the affirmative, the proposal is translated into all official languages of the EU, submitted to the Council, the EP and national parliaments, and published

---

316. On citizens' initiative, see: M. Setälä and T. Schiller (eds), *Citizens' Initiatives in Europe: Procedures and Consequences of Agenda-Setting by Citizens (Challenges to Democracy in the 21st Century)*, 2012, Basingstoke: Palgrave Macmillan.

317. See the official website of the Commission on better regulation available at http://ec.europa.eu/governance/better_regulation/index_en.htm (accessed 7/10/12).

318. COM(2006) 689 final.

319. [2003] OJ C321/1.

320. See: A. Meuwese and P. Popelier, "Legal Implications of Better Regulation: A Special Issue" (2011) 17/3 EPL, 455.

321. IP/10/1296 of 8/10/10.

322. Ibid.

in the OJ. However, if a proposal concerns areas in which the Commission is empowered to legislate alone, it is translated and published in the OJ. There is no need to send it to any other institution or to national parliaments.

Upon receipt of a proposal, the Council normally sends it to COREPER, or in rare cases to a specialised committee (for example, the Special Committee on Agriculture or, the Political Committee), for further study. All items on the Council's agenda, apart from those prepared by specialised committees, are examined by COREPER, unless the Council (by unanimity) or COREPER (by simple majority) decides otherwise (see Chapter 3.4.4).

When the Commission forwards a proposal to the EP, it is first examined by an MEP working in one of the parliamentary committees, who prepares a report. Subsequently, the relevant parliamentary committee considers the report, and may amend or change it. The report is then submitted to the EP, which in plenary session takes a vote on the report, rejecting or adopting it. By so doing, the EP gives its opinion on the proposal.

In conformity with Article 4 of Protocol No. 2 attached to the ToL, the Commission must forward directly to national parliaments all legislative proposals and all amended proposals at the same time as they are sent to the EP and the Council. Similarly, the EP is required to send its legislative proposals and its amended proposals to national parliaments. As to the Council, it must send to national parliaments legislative proposals and amended proposals originating from a group of Member States, the Court of Justice, the European Central Bank or the European Investment Bank.

Under Article 293(3) TFEU, the Commission may decide to alter or withdraw any proposal for a legislative act as well as for any binding non-legislative act as long as the Council has not acted. This means, for example, that in respect of the ordinary legislative procedure, the Commission is empowered to withdraw a legislative proposal on which the EP has already stated its position at first reading (see below). If this occurs, under Article 39 of the Framework Agreement on Relations between the EP and the Commission, the latter must provide detailed explanations to the EP before withdrawing such a proposal. The Commission may have good reasons for withdrawal – for example, a proposal may no longer be relevant due to change of circumstances, or the Commission may decide that amendments made by the EP at first reading will not be acceptable to the Council[323] and thus there be no chance that a proposal, as amended, would became a legislative act. The matter of whether the Commission may withdraw a proposal upon which the Council has already stated its position seems to be in the affirmative bearing in mind that the Commission has the power to initiate legislative proposals and therefore it should be allowed to withdraw one if it considers that, for various reasons, it is no longer appropriate, However, under the Article 294 TFEU procedure this option is not available to the Commission. The terms of Article 294 TFEU are clear as to the options open to the EP and to the Council at second reading, and the legal implications of each of them (see below).

The legal basis adopted by the Commission will determine which procedure is to be used. Under the ToL, it is usually the ordinary legislative procedure.

5.4 The ordinary legislative procedure: Article 294 TFEU

Within the ordinary procedure the EP stands on an equal footing with the Council, as the procedure involves joint decision-making between them. Under the ToL the ordinary procedure applies to 83 areas

---

323. In this respect the position of the Council may be known to the Commission due to the fact that it is normally invited to participate in meetings of the Council, see Article 5(2) of the Council's Rules of Procedure [2009] OJ L325/35.

of EU policies. The ordinary procedure, which was introduced by the Treaty of Maastricht under the name of co-decision procedure, was very complex.[324] The ToA simplified it and the ToL, without making any substantive changes, renamed it. The procedure is still very complex. It involves co-operation between the Commission, the Council and the EP. For that reason in 2007 the three institutions adopted a Joint Declaration on Practical Arrangements for the Co-decision Procedure which remains in force and applies to the ordinary legislative procedure.[325] Further, the Framework Agreement on Relations between the EP and the Commission[326] improves the planning and co-ordination of the two institutions relating to legislative procedures. Innovations relating to Article 294 TFEU procedure are explained below.

Under the ordinary procedure national parliaments act as "watchdogs", i.e. decide whether a draft legislative act accords with the requirements of the principle of subsidiarity. The CoR and the ESC must be consulted, if the Treaties so provide, and may also submit opinions if they consider appropriate.

The ordinary procedure may be extended to new areas under the *"passerelle"* provisions (see Chapter 4.2.6) and may also be suspended under the "emergency brake" procedure. In respect of certain matters concerning the creation of the AFSJ (see Chapter 31) and social security (Article 48 TFEU), a member of the Council may oppose the use of the ordinary procedure if it considers that proposed draft legislation would affect fundamental aspects of the legal system of the Member State he represents. In such a situation the procedure is suspended and the matter is referred to the European Council which, within four months, may either refer the matter back to the Council and thus terminate the suspension of the ordinary procedure or take no action or request the Commission to prepare a new proposal. If the European Council takes no action the legislation originally proposed is deemed not to have been adopted.

The ordinary legislative procedure is described in Article 294 TFEU. Its various stages can be summarised as follows:

5.4.1 Proposal

The Commission forwards a proposal to the EP, the Council and national parliaments.

5.4.2 First reading

A. First, the EP acting by simple majority delivers its opinion which:

- may approve the proposal without amendments; or,
- may contain amendments.

B. Then, the Commission may:

- incorporate any EP amendments into its original proposal if it is of the view that they improve the proposal or are likely to facilitate agreements between the EP and the Council, and then resubmit the amended proposal to the Council; or,
- retain the original proposal without incorporating any amendments.

C. Then, the Council may by QMV:

- accept the Commission's proposal and, provided that the EP did not make any amendments, it can adopt the act; or,

---

324. A. Dashwood, "Community Legislative Procedures in the Era of the Treaty on European Union", (1994) 19 ELRev., 343.

325. [2007] OJ C145/5. The Declaration replaced the previous one adopted in 1999.

326. [2010] OJ L304/47,

- accept the Commission's proposal with amendments proposed by the EP having been incorporated into the proposal by the Commission. The act can then be adopted; or,
- adopt a common position:
  - rejecting any or all amendments made by the EP. In this situation the Council forwards the common position to the EP together with a statement of reasons; or,
  - rejecting the Commission's proposal, which proposal was not amended by the EP, because the Council wants to make changes to it.

5.4.3 Common position

If the Council has adopted a common position, the Commission sends a communication to the EP explaining why it supports or opposes the common position, together with the text of the common position. If relevant, the Commission comments on the Council's views on the EP's amendments.

5.4.4 Second reading

A.   **The EP.** It has three months (which may be extended by one month) to express its opinion on the Council's common position. Within that time the EP may:

- make amendments (including repeating those rejected by the Council at the first reading) by an absolute majority of its component members. The amended text is forwarded to the Council and the Commission; or

- approve the Council's common position (by simple majority). The act can be adopted; or

- take no action. The act can be adopted; or

- reject the Council's common position by an absolute majority. The act is deemed not to have been adopted. The procedure ends.

B.   **The Commission.** It must deliver an opinion on any of the EP's amendments. Under Article 37 of the Framework Agreement on Relations between the EP and the Commission, the Commission must take the utmost account of EP amendments adopted at second reading. If it decides to reject them, i.e. to give a negative opinion for important reasons, after consideration by the College of Commissioners, it must explain its decision before the Parliament, and in any event in its Opinion. If the Commission gives a negative opinion on at least one amendment, the Council will have to act by unanimity if it wishes to accept the EP's overall position.

C.   **The Council.** It has three months (which may be extended by one month) following the receipt of the EP's amendments to:

- approve them either by QMV or, if the Commission has delivered a negative opinion, by unanimity. The act can be adopted;

- reject the EP's amendments to its common position. In this situation the President of the Council and the President of the EP will set up a Conciliation Committee within six weeks of the rejection of the amendments by the Council (this may be extended by two weeks).

5.4.5 The conciliation stage

A Conciliation Committee is made up of an equal number of representatives of the EP (the EP delegation) and of the Council (the Council delegation) and the Commissioner in charge of the dossier who acts as a broker between the two delegations. Its purpose is to produce a joint text – a compromise between the position of the Council and the EP on disputed points – within six weeks (which may be extended by two weeks) from the setting-up of the Conciliation Committee. A joint text must be approved by both delegations as follows:

■ The Council delegation, by QMV or unanimity depending upon the subject matter of the proposal; and,

■ The EP delegation, by simple majority.

If the Conciliation Committee fails to produce a joint text, the procedure ends. The act is deemed not to have been adopted.

5.4.6 Third reading

If the Conciliation Committee agrees on a joint text, it must be adopted within six weeks (which may be extended to eight weeks) by both the EP and the Council:

■ the EP must adopt the joint text by a majority of the votes cast; and,

■ the Council must adopt the joint text by QMV.

If either institution fails to adopt the joint text within the prescribed time limit, the act is deemed not to have been adopted. The procedure ends.

5.5 Special legislative procedures

Some special legislative procedures involve the participation of the EP; others allow the Commission and Council to act jointly, or the Council or the Commission to act alone. Special procedures which involve the EP are the consent procedure and the consultation procedure.

5.5.1 The consent procedure

Under the consent procedure, introduced by the SEA, the Council acts on a proposal of the Commission after receiving consent from the EP. The EP can only vote on the entire proposal, without the possibility of making any amendments. Usually, the Council is required to act by unanimity, but QMV is sufficient for the conclusion of international agreements referred to in Article 218(8) TFEU. The EP acts by a majority of the votes cast, except for a decision upon an application for membership of the EU where an absolute majority is required.

Examples of provisions which require adoption of legislative acts in accordance with the consent procedure are:

■ Article 7(2) TEU, concerning sanctions imposed on a Member State for a serious and persistent breach of fundamental human rights;

■ Article 49 TEU, concerning the accession of new members to the EU;

■ Article 223(1) TFEU, concerning proposals on a uniform procedure for elections to the EP;

■ Article 218 TFEU concerning the conclusion of association agreements, an agreement on EU accession to the ECHR; agreements establishing a specific institutional framework by organising co-operation procedures; agreements having important budgetary implications for the EU; and, other specific international agreements to which either the ordinary legislative procedure applies or the consent of the EP is required;

■ Article 311 TFEU, under which the EP must give its consent to the adoption of implementing measures for the EU's own resources system by the Council; and,

■ Article 25 TEU, under which the Council is required to obtain the consent of the EP in respect of the adoption of measures aimed at strengthening the rights of EU citizens or adding new rights.

It is to be noted that some provisions of the Treaties, i.e. Articles 223(2), 226(3) and 228(4) TFEU give the EP the right to initiate legislative acts but consent of the Council, or both the Council and the Commission, is needed for the adoption of any such act.

5.5.2 The consultation procedure

Under the EEC Treaty, the consultation procedure was the only legislative procedure involving the participation of the EP. It requires the Council to obtain the opinion of the EP.

This procedure starts with the submission of a formal proposal by the Commission to the Council. The latter must ask the EP for its opinion on the proposal. The Council is not obliged to follow the opinion delivered by the EP but must receive it. The EP has a duty to co-operate loyally with other EU institutions, and especially to deliver its opinion within a reasonable time in order to allow the Council to adopt a measure within the required time frame.[327]

What occurs when the EP fails to deliver its opinion was explained by the ECJ in Case 138/79 *Roquette*.[328]

THE FACTS WERE:

The Council adopted Regulation 1293/79 on the basis of Article 43(2) EC [replaced by Article 20 TFEU], which required the consultation of the EP, but without receiving an opinion from the EP. The Council argued that it requested the opinion but the EP did not reply and thus, by its own conduct, and knowing the urgency of the matter, the EP made it impossible for the Council to comply with the consultation requirement.

Held:

The ECJ held that when the Treaty provides for the consultation of the EP, this requirement must be strictly complied with, since "due consultation of the Parliament in the cases provided for by the Treaty . . . constitutes an essential formality disregard of which means that the measure concerned is void."

---

327. Case C-65/93 *EP v Council* [1995] ECR I-643. See also, R. Kardasheva, "The Power to Delay: The European Parliament's Influence in the Consultation Procedure", (2009) 47 JCMS, 385.
328. Case 138/79 *SA Roquette Frères v Council* [1980] ECR 3333.

> **Comment**
>
> *The arguments of the Council would have been accepted if it had exhausted all existing procedural possibilities provided by EU law to force the EP to deliver its opinion, which was not the case in Roquette.*

If the Council or the Commission amends its initial proposal substantially, the EP must be consulted a second time, unless the modification matches the amendments suggested by the EP.[329]

Article 40 of the Framework Agreement on Relations between the EP and the Commission imposes a duty on the Commission to ensure that the EP has a reasonable time to consider any proposal by the Commission and that the Council will not reach a political agreement without taking account of the EP's opinion. Additionally, under Article 40, the Commission undertakes, if appropriate, to withdraw a legislative proposal which has been rejected by the EP. Nevertheless, if the Commission decides to maintain such a proposal, for important reasons, and after consideration by the College of Commissioners, it must explain its position before the EP.

5.5.3 The Council's power to legislate alone

Procedures where the Council can legislate without the participation of the EP are relics of the early days of the Communities and apply to very limited areas.

Under these procedures the Council can adopt legislation proposed by the Commission, or acting on its own initiative, without the participation of any other institution. Examples of these procedures are:

- Article 26 TFEU in respect of fixing common customs duties;

- Article 108(2) TFEU in respect of compatibility of grants of aid by the Member States with EU competition law; and,

- some aspects of the CCP (Article 207(3) TFEU).

5.5.4 The Commission's own powers of legislation

The Commission has independent, but limited, power to legislate without the participation of any other EU institution. This power is operable only in cases where specific articles of the Treaty so authorise.

Under the ToL the Commission is empowered to enact legislative measures in limited areas, that is, concerning monopolies and concessions granted to companies by Member States (Article 106(3) TFEU) and concerning the right of workers to remain in a Member State after having been employed there (Article 45(3)(d) TFEU). It appears that the Commission has rarely used this free-standing power to adopt legislative measures.[330]

---

329. Case 41/69 *ACF Chemiefarma NV v Commission* [1970] ECR 661; Case C-65/90 *EP v Council* [1992] ECR I-4593; Joined Cases C-13/92 to C-16/92 *Driessen en Zonen and Others v Minister van Verkeer en Waterstaat* [1993] ECR I-4751; and Case C-408/95 *Eurotunnel SA and Others v SeaFrance* [1997] ECR I-6315.

330. So far, only two directives have been adopted using this procedure: one on transparency between Member States and companies (Dir. 80/723 [1980] OJ L195/35) and the other on competition in the telecommunications sector (Dir. 88/301 [1988] OJ L131/73).

RECOMMENDED READING

Books

O'Brennan, J. and Raunio, T. (eds), *National Parliaments within the Enlarged European Union. From 'Victims' of Integration to Competitive Actors?*, 2009, Abingdon: Routledge.

Setälä, M., and Schiller, T. (eds), *Citizens' Initiatives in Europe: Procedures and Consequences of Agenda-Setting by Citizens (Challenges to Democracy in the 21st Century)*, 2012, Basingstoke: Palgrave Macmillan.

Sieberson, S.C., *Dividing Lines between the European Union and Its Member States*, 2008, Cambridge: CUP.

Articles

Alemanno, A., "The Better Regulation Initiative at the Judicial Gate: A Trojan Horse within the Commission's Walls or the Way Forward?" (2009) 15 ELJ, 382.

Cuesta Lopez, V., "The Lisbon Treaty's Provisions on Democratic Principles: A Legal Framework for Participatory Democracy" (2010) 16 EPL, 123.

Heliskoski, J., and Leino, P., "Darkness at the Break of Noon" (2006) 43 CMLRev, 735.

Kardasheva, R., "The Power to Delay: The European Parliament's Influence in the Consultation Procedure", (2009) 47 JCMS, 385.

Meuwese, A., and Popelier, P., "Legal Implications of Better Regulation: A Special Issue" (2011) 17/3 EPL, 455.

Von Bogdandy, A., "Founding Principles", in A. von Bogdandy and J. Bast, *Principles of European Constitutional Law*, 2nd edn, 2010, Oxford: Hart Publishing, 51.

ESSAY QUESTIONS

1. Discuss perceived deficiencies in the EU ordinary legislative procedure and make proposals for reform.
2. Critically discuss how the Commission ensures that its legislative proposals are fit for purpose and relevant to EU citizens.

AIDE-MÉMOIRE

The ordinary legislative procedure

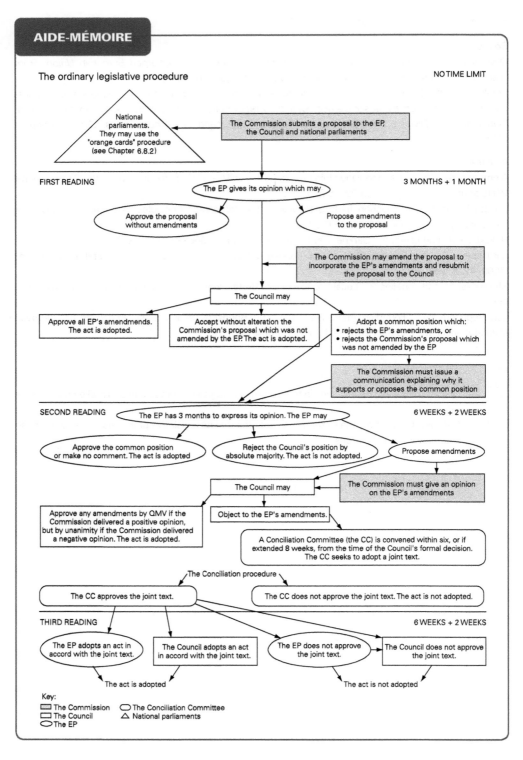

National parliaments. They may use the "orange cards" procedure (see Chapter 6.8.2)

NO TIME LIMIT

The Commission submits a proposal to the EP, the Council and national parliaments

FIRST READING

3 MONTHS + 1 MONTH

The EP gives its opinion which may

Approve the proposal without amendments

Propose amendments to the proposal

The Commission may amend the proposal to incorporate the EP's amendments and resubmit the proposal to the Council

The Council may

Approve all EP's amendmends. The act is adopted.

Accept without alteration the Commission's proposal which was not amended by the EP. The act is adopted.

Adopt a common position which:
• rejects the EP's amendments, or
• rejects the Commission's proposal which was not amended by the EP

The Commission must issue a communication explaining why it supports or opposes the common position

SECOND READING

6 WEEKS + 2 WEEKS

The EP has 3 months to express its opinion. The EP may

Approve the common position or make no comment. The act is adopted

Reject the Council's position by absolute majority. The act is not adopted.

Propose amendments

The Commission must give an opinion on the EP's amendments

The Council may

Approve any amendments by QMV if the Commission delivered a positive opinion, but by unanimity if the Commission delivered a negative opinion. The act is adopted.

Object to the EP's amendments.

A Conciliation Committee (the CC) is convened within six, or if extended 8 weeks, from the time of the Council's formal decision. The CC seeks to adopt a joint text.

The Conciliation procedure

The CC approves the joint text.

The CC does not approve the joint text. The act is not adopted.

THIRD READING

6 WEEKS + 2 WEEKS

The EP adopts an act in accord with the joint text.

The Council adopts an act in accord with the joint text.

The EP does not approve the joint text.

The Council does not approve the joint text.

The act is adopted

The act is not adopted

Key:
▢ The Commission   ◯ The Conciliation Committee
▢ The Council   △ National parliaments
◯ The EP

6

COMPETENCES OF THE EU

CONTENTS

CHAPTER OUTLINE

1. The ToL clarified the distribution of power between the EU and the Member States. This was an important element in the democratisation of the EU and a clear response to the Member States' complaints about "creeping competences drift" in favour of the EU.

2. The principle of conferral is contained in Article 5(2) TEU which provides that the EU can "act only within the limits of the competences conferred upon it by the Member States in the Treaties to attain the objectives set out therein. Competences not conferred upon the Union in the Treaties remain with the Member States". The principle of conferral guarantees that the EU cannot extend its competence at the expense of the Member States without their prior consent.

3. Article 3 TFEU provides a list of exclusive competences of the EU. It also codifies the pre-ToL case law of the ECJ on the doctrine of implied powers with regard to exclusive external competences of the EU in Article 3(2) TFEU.

4. Article 4 TFEU provides a non-exhaustive list of competences shared between the EU and the Member States. Areas of competences conferred on the EU not mentioned in Article 4 are within the shared competences if they are neither mentioned in Article 6 TFEU (which lists supporting, co-ordinating or supplementing competences of the EU) nor in Article 3 TFEU (which lists the exclusive competences of the EU). For the exercise of shared competences two principles are vital:

■ the principle of subsidiarity under which in the areas of shared competences the EU can only intervene if certain objectives set out by the Treaties cannot be attained by the Member States and only if the EU can attain them with greater efficiency than the Member States; and,

■ the principle of proportionality according to which the EU's action, its content and form shall not exceed what is necessary to achieve the objectives of the Treaties.

Protocol No. 2 on the Application of the Principles of Subsidiarity and Proportionality attached to the Treaties established not only the conditions for the application of these principles but also a system for monitoring the application of the principle of subsidiarity. Under the Protocol, national parliaments were granted extensive powers to monitor the application of the principle of subsidiarity through the "yellow and orange cards" procedure.

5. Supporting, co-ordinating and supplementing competences refer to areas in which the Member States have not conferred competences on the EU but have decided to act through it. In these areas the EU supports, co-ordinates, encourages or supplements measures taken at national level. Article 6 TFEU provides a list of areas in which the Member States have exclusive competence but the EU can support, co-ordinate or supplement the action of the Member States. It is important to note that in these areas the EU can adopt binding measures but in no circumstances is it allowed to harmonise, totally or partially, national laws of the Member States. Special rules are applicable to four areas, i.e. economic, employment and social policies and the CFSP.

6. Article 352 TFEU can be used to achieve the objectives of the Treaties as listed in Article 3 TEU but not the objectives of the CFSP. It is to be used when the EU has neither express nor implied powers (i.e. when there is a gap in the Treaties), but needs to adopt measures in order to achieve an objective specified by the Treaties. The role of Article 352 TFEU has been marginalised by the facts that for the adoption of a measure under that article the Council is required to obtain the EP's consent (previously under Article 308 EC the Council was required to consult the EP) and that its use is subject to the "yellow and orange cards" procedure available to national parliaments.

7. The ToL reformed the enhanced co-operation procedure to make it more attractive to the Member States, mainly by providing that when an enhanced procedure is in progress, the Council acting unanimously may adopt a decision, stipulating that it will act by QMV where the Treaty stipulates that the Council shall act unanimously. The only constraint imposed on the Council is that it must consult the EP. However, a restriction is imposed as to initial authorisation in that the EP has to consent to this.

6.1 Introduction

The term "competence" refers to the responsibility for decision making in a particular policy area.

Since the inception of the EC important competences have been transferred to the EC/EU by Member States, which has had the effect of shrinking their individual spheres of competence, thus imposing limitations on their sovereignty. Since the establishment of the Community, its areas of competence have considerably expanded. This growth of Community competences, in particular in the circumstances where they were acquired through the teleological interpretation of the EC Treaty by the ECJ, combined with the fact that the division of competences between the EC and the Member States was not clearly defined in the EC Treaty, became one of the most crucial issues in a debate about the future of the EU. In this debate the position of the parties concerned can be summarised as follows:

- The Member States feared that the system of delimitation of powers under the EC Treaty, based on the objectives to be achieved and means of achieving those objectives, made it very difficult to decide whether the Community, when adopting an act, acted within its competence or exceeded its powers, and by this encroached on national sovereignty. This fear was understandable in the light of the past record of the EC.[331] The lack of clear boundaries between national and Community action reinforced the feeling of encroachment by the EC;

- EU citizens feared that the EC would acquire more and more powers without adequate democratic oversight; and,

- The EC feared that an irrevocable fixing of the Community competences would stall the dynamics of European integration, given that the Community may, as a result, not be free to respond to new challenges in ways which would allow its objectives to be fulfilled.

The issue of division of competences became part of a fundamental reform of the EU. The Declaration on the Future of Europe, issued by the Nice European Council and attached to the Treaty of Nice, had called upon the 2004 IGC to address the issues of "how to establish and monitor a more precise delimitation of powers between the European Union and the Member States, reflecting the principle of subsidiarity".[332] In 2004 the IGC made proposals which were incorporated into the failed Constitutional Treaty, but subsequently, with some amendments, found their place in the ToL. They are as follows:

- The ToL codifies and describes the division of competences between the Union and the Member States (Article 2 TFEU). It clearly identifies policy areas in which the EU exercises exclusive, shared and supportive competences;

- The importance of the principle of conferral is emphasised in the Treaties as well as in Protocols and Declarations attached to them. Under this principle the EU exercises only the competences which Member States have conferred upon it with the result that competences not conferred upon it remain with the Member States;

- For the first time, the Treaties expressly provide for the possibility of reducing the competences of the Union, if appropriate. In this respect Article 48(2) TEU specifies that proposals for the revision of the treaties "may, *inter alia*, serve either to increase or to reduce the competences conferred on the Union in the Treaties". Although it has always been possible for the Member States to reduce competences of the EU, until the ToL this had never been specified so clearly. In fact, any revision of the Treaties had been in favour of the development of the EU *acquis* and thus in favour of the extension of competences of the EC and the EU;

---

331. On this topic see: M.A. Pollack, "Creeping Competence: The Expanding Agenda of the European Community", (1994) 14/2 *Journal of Public Law*, 95; and S. Weatherill, "Competence Creep and Competence Control", (2004) 23 YEL, 15.
332. Declaration on the Future of Europe, para. 5(1).

- With regard to areas of shared competences, Protocol No. 25 on the Exercise of Shared Competences attached to the Treaties envisages a situation where an EU institution decides to cease exercising its competence in a particular area. Such a situation occurs in particular when an EU institution decides to repeal a legislative act in order to comply with the principles of subsidiarity and proportionality. The Protocol states that the Council may, at the initiative of one or several of its members and in accordance with Article 241 TFEU, request the Commission to submit proposals for repealing a legislative act. In the area covered by the repealed legislative act Member States would regain their competence;

- National parliaments have been given an important role in monitoring the application of the principles of subsidiarity (see Chapter 6.8.2);

- The ToL established special rules with regard to four areas: economic, employment and social policies which are to be co-ordinated by Member States and the CFSP;

- The use of the "flexibility clause" contained in Article 352 TFEU has been marginalised (see Chapter 6.7); and,

- Under Article 47 TEU, the EU was granted legal personality. The EU, being the successor of the EC, has absorbed its legal personality. Since the entry into force of the ToL there is only one legally recognised organisation, the EU, with a single legal personality. However, the granting of legal personality to the EU does not have any implications on the allocation of competences between the EU and the Member States. Declaration No. 24 attached to the Treaties confirmed that "the fact that the European Union has a legal personality will not in any way authorise the Union to legislate or to act beyond the competences conferred upon it by the Member States in the Treaties".

Under the ToL, the EU did not acquire any new exclusive competences although it gained new shared and supporting, co-ordinating or supplementing competences. It is to be noted that prior to the entry into force of the ToL, the EU had already legislated in the majority of "new" areas on other legal bases. As a result, the ToL rather confirmed the pre-existing competences of the EU than extended them. Entirely new competences, i.e. areas in which the EU had not acted or had no ability to act prior to the entry into force of the ToL, relate to: space policy; administrative co-operation aimed at improving the capacity of Member States, at their request, to implement EU law effectively; sport; crime prevention; establishment of a European Public Prosecutor; measures facilitating co-ordination and co-operation among Member States in respect of diplomatic and consular protection of EU citizens; and, the solidarity clause contained in Article 222 TFEU.

6.2 The principle of conferral

The principle under which the EU may only exercise competences conferred on it by the Treaties to attain objectives set out therein is known as the principle of conferral, and often referred to as the principle of attributed powers. It is defined in Article 5(2) TEU in the following terms:

"Under the principle of conferral, the Union shall act only within the limits of the competences conferred upon it by the Member States in the Treaties to attain the objectives set out therein. Competences not conferred upon the Union in the Treaties remain with the Member States."

The implications of the principle of conferral are stated in Article 4 TEU. It provides that "competences not conferred upon the Union in the Treaties remain within the Member States" and that the Union "shall respect essential State functions, including ensuring the territorial integrity of the State, maintaining law and order and safeguarding national security. In particular, national security remains the sole responsibility of each Member State".

The principle of conferral entails that only the Member States can create new competences for the EU or reduce them, not EU institutions. For that purpose Member States must use the revision procedures set out in the Treaties.[333] The principle also emphasises that the EU does not have general law-making capacity as opposed to a sovereign State. For example, under the British doctrine of Parliamentary sovereignty, the British Parliament "has under the English constitution, the right to make or unmake any law whatever. Its legislative powers are inherent, not conferred by any person or body".[334] Accordingly, the EU does not have what is called in German "*Kompetenz-Kompetenz*", i.e. the power to confer powers on itself. One implication of the doctrine of "*Kompetenz-Kompetenz*" is the dilemma as to whether the ECJ has jurisdiction to determine conclusively the limits of the legislative powers of the EU. Constitutional courts of some Member States, in particular Germany (see Chapter 9.9.1), claim that the determination of limits of EU legislative power are not only a matter for the ECJ, but also for national constitutional courts. Those courts claim to be mandated by national constitutions to monitor whether the EU has acted within the powers conferred by the Treaties. This is not the view of the ECJ.[335]

The principle of conferral regulates the matter of when the EU is able to act. It concerns the vertical division of power, i.e. between the EU and its Member States, and must be distinguished from the horizontal division of power which relates to the division of powers between EU institutions.

The consequence of the principle of conferral is that all acts of the EU must be based on a legal basis set out in the Treaties. The legal basis indicates the scope of competence of the EU, the institutions which are authorised to act, the procedure to be used, and the form which the act should take, i.e. a regulation, directive or decision. The choice of a legal basis is not at the discretion of the relevant institutions, it depends on objective factors which are the purpose and intended content of the act. The ECJ monitors whether EU institutions have selected the proper legal basis of an EU act (see Chapter 4.5.3.2).

In respect of the vertical division of power, if no legal basis exists for an act, the act will be invalid even if it benefits a private party.[336] In Case C-370/7 *Commission v Council*,[337] the ECJ held that:

> "The legal basis of [an EU] act must also be indicated in the light of the principle of conferred powers enshrined in [Article 5(2) TEU], according to which the [EU] must act within the powers conferred on it and of the objectives assigned to it by the Treaty in both the internal action and the international action of the [EU]. In that connection, the appropriate legal basis has constitutional significance, since, having only conferred powers, the [EU] must tie that decision to a Treaty provision which empowers it to approve such a measure."

With regard to horizontal division of powers, the wrong choice of legal basis may affect the institutional balance and, undermine the principle of democracy (see Chapter 3.2) given that the provision which is the legal basis of an act will determine the applicable decision-making procedure, i.e. the extent to which each EU institution participates in the adoption of a measure. If an incorrect legal basis provides for the use of a different decision-making procedure from that which should have

---

333. Case 43/75 *Defrenne v Sabena* [1976] ECR 455.
334. R. Schütze, *European Constitutional Law*, 2012, Cambridge: CUP, 153.
335. See G. Beck, "The Problem of Kompetenz-Kompetenz: A Conflict between Right and Right in which There is no Praetor", (2005) 30 ELRev., 42.
336. Case 111/63 *Lemmerz-Werke v High Authority* [1965] ECR 677, 591.
337. [2009] ECR I-8917, paras. 46 and 47.

been chosen, this may ultimately have implications on the determination of the content of a measure[338] (see Chapter 4.5.3.2).

The principle of conferral sits uneasily with the teleological interpretation of the Treaties by the ECJ (see Chapter 4.7.1), bearing in mind that the ECJ has, by means of the teleological interpretation of the Treaties, created "creeping competence drift". It is unlikely that the coming into force of the ToL has ended the "creeping competence drift". This is because of the ECJ's assumption that, first, the Treaties do not recognise any "reserved areas", being areas of exclusive competences of the Member States, where the fundamental freedoms are concerned, i.e. the four freedoms which constitute the basis of the internal market: the free movement of persons, good, services and capital. Second, the ECJ has been the main driving force in furthering European integration. It "constitutionalised" the EC Treaty, i.e. it transformed the EC from an international organisation into an entity no longer governed by international law, but instead by principles of its own "constitutional charter".[339] The principles of supremacy, direct effect, etc. were neither mentioned in the EEC Treaty, nor in any of its amendments, but were established by the ECJ. Nowadays they constitute the foundation of EU law. It is unlikely, and even contrary to the mission of the ECJ, to confine itself to the literal interpretation of the Treaties. Third, the question of whether a teleological interpretation of the Treaties can be taken to mean that the EU has powers beyond those explicitly established in the Treaty has been answered in the affirmative by the ECJ in that it has established the doctrine of implied powers. Under the doctrine when a provision of the Treaties confers a specific task on the EU, that provision must be regarded as impliedly conferring on it powers to carry out that task.[340]

Additionally, prior to the entry into force of the ToL, Articles 114 and 352 TFEU contributed to the creation of the "creeping competence drift" by giving the EU institutions open-ended powers. Under Article 114 the EU has the general power to harmonise national laws in order to create the internal market. Article 352 TFEU is even more general as it contains a "flexibility clause" under which the Council has power to legislate in all areas of EU law with the exception of the CFSP, when this is necessary to attain objectives of the Treaties (see Chapter 6.7). However, under the ToL both Articles have less potential to contribute to "creeping competence drift".

It is important to note that the ToL created a powerful tool for the Member States against irregular exercise of Union competences in that it revised the definition of the principle of subsidiarity and involved national parliaments in monitoring compliance of the EU with the principle of subsidiarity (see Chapter 6.8.2).

6.2.1 "Reserved areas" of Member States and the requirements of the internal market

It has been long established by the case law of the ECJ that the exercise of exclusive competences by Member States may be subject to requirements of EU law. In Case C-438/05 *Viking*[341] the ECJ held that:

> "even if, in the areas which fall outside the scope of the [EU's] competence, the Member States are still free, in principle, to lay down the conditions governing the existence and exercise of the rights in

---

338. See Opinion of A-G Maduro in Case 133/06 *EP v Council* [2008] ECR I-3189, para. 32.
339. See F. Snyder, "The Unfinished Constitution of the European Union: Principles, Processes and Culture", in J.H.H. Weiler and M. Wind (eds), *European Constitutionalism Beyond the State*, 2003, Cambridge: CUP, 62.
340. Joined Cases 281, 283, 284, 285 and 287/85 *Germany v Commission* [1987] ECR 3203, para. 28.
341. Case C-438/05 *International Transport Workers' Federation and Finnish Seamen's Union v Viking Line ABP and OÜ Viking Line Eesti* [2007] ECR I-10779, para. 40.

question, the fact remains that, when exercising that competence, the Member States must nevertheless comply with [EU] law."

In this case, the ECJ brought within the scope of the Treaties some aspects of employment law, i.e., the right to strike and the right to impose lock-outs, notwithstanding the fact that Article 153(5) TFEU expressly excludes both rights from the scope of the Treaties. Similarly, in Case C-135/08 *Rottmann*,[342] the ECJ held that although the determination of conditions governing the acquisition and loss of nationality are within the exclusive competence of each Member State, the withdrawal of naturalisation by a Member State, as it would entail the loss of EU citizenship, and therefore the loss of important rights attached to the status of EU citizenship, was within the scope of the Treaties and could only be effected if the requirements of the principle of proportionality were satisfied. In Case C-348/96 *Calfa*,[343] the ECJ held that despite the fact that criminal legislation was within the exclusive competence of each of the Member States, EU law sets certain limitations to their powers in that "such legislation may not restrict the fundamental freedoms guaranteed by [EU law]". In Case C-34/09 *Zambrano*[344] the ECJ created the doctrine of the "substance of rights" which further blurs the distinction between a "purely" internal situation and a situation which is within the scope of the Treaties (see Chapter 22.3.1).

The impact of EU law on the exercise of exclusive competences by the Member States raises the question as to the circumstances in which a Member State must take due account of EU law. In one of the earliest cases, the ECJ held that European integration leads to encroachment on national sovereignty in all cases where it is necessary "to prevent the effectiveness of the Treaty from being considerably weakened and its purpose from being compromised".[345] However, in Case C-376/98 *Germany v EP and Council (Tobacco Advertising)*,[346] the ECJ took a restrictive approach in that it held that if any impact on EU law (in that case EU competition law) was sufficient to bring national rules within the scope of EU competence, EU legislative competence would be unlimited. By doing this, the ECJ set a threshold of appreciable effect or impact on national law of EU law as triggering the application of EU law. Notwithstanding this, in *Viking*, a case decided after the *Tobacco Advertising* case, the ECJ held that the potential effect on national rules of the free movement rules was sufficient to engage EU competence. The *Viking* approach erodes the principle of conferral but, at the same time, emphasises the difficult matter of vertical division of competences. Literal interpretation of Article 5(2) TEU entails that any encroachment of the EU on exclusive competences of the Member States, irrespective of whether the impact of national law on the effectiveness of EU law is slight, or appreciable, is prohibited. However, if such interpretation is accepted, then the principle of effectiveness would be undermined, in particular when national rules restrict the fundamental freedoms and rights guaranteed under EU law.

---

342. Case C-135/08 *Janko Rottmann v Freistaat Bayern* [2010] ECR I-149.
343. Case C-348/96 *Criminal Proceedings against Donatella Calfa* [1999] ECR I-11, para. 17.
344. Case C-34/09 *Gerardo Ruiz Zambrano v Office National de l'Emploi (ONEM)* (Judgment of 8/3/11 (NYR)). See also: A. Tryfonidou, "Redefining the Outer Boundaries of EU Law: The *Zambrano, McCarthy* and *Dereci* Trilogy", (2012) 18 EPL, 493.
345. Case 30/59 *De Gezamenlijke Steenkolenmijnen in Limburg v High Authority of the European Coal and Steel Community* [1961] ECR 1, 24.
346. [2000] ECR I-8419.

6.2.2 The doctrine of implied powers

The ECJ has endorsed the doctrine of implied powers[347] in Case 8/55 *Fédération Charbonnière*.[348] The ECJ mainly applied it in relation to external competences of the EU, although the doctrine also has an internal dimension.

The internal dimension of the doctrine of implied powers relates to the powers of the EU institutions with regard to Member States. In Joined Cases 281, 283–5 and 287/85 *Germany and Others v Commission*,[349] the ECJ held that when the Commission is under an obligation to carry out a specific task assigned to it by the Treaty, the Treaty implicitly confers on the Commission the necessary powers to carry out that task. However, in Case T-240/04 *France v Commission*,[350] the General Court held that only exceptionally are implied internal powers recognised and in order to be so recognised they must be necessary to ensure the practical effect of the provisions of the Treaty or of the basic regulation at issue.

With regard to the external competences of the EU, the pre-ToL scarcity of Treaty provisions enabling the EU to act externally resulted in the establishment and development of the doctrine of implied powers by the ECJ. In Case 22/70 *ERTA*[351] the EC held that the external competences of the Community derive not only from express provisions of the Treaty, "but may equally flow from other provisions of the Treaty and from measures adopted, within the framework of those provisions, by the Community institutions".

The case law of the ECJ relating to conditions under which the EU could rely on the doctrine of external implied powers and the determination of the nature of those powers, i.e. whether exclusive to the EU, or shared with the Member States, was codified in Article 3(2) and Article 216 TFEU. The codification does not reflect the nuances of the pre-ToL case law, but nevertheless constitutes a point of departure in the determining of whether the EU has powers to act externally, and identifies the nature of the competence.

6.3 Exclusive competences of the EU

If the EU enjoys exclusive competence in a particular area, Member States are prevented from acting unilaterally or collectively in that area, irrespective of whether or not the EU has already acted, except when the EU has explicitly authorised them to adopt legally binding acts or measures implementing acts adopted by EU institutions (Article 2(1) TFEU). The principle of subsidiarity does not apply to areas in which the EU enjoys exclusive competences but the principle of proportionality does. Article 3 TFEU identifies areas which are within the exclusive competence of the EU.

Under Article 3(1) TFEU the EU has exclusive competences in the following areas:

- the Customs Union;

- those competition rules that govern the internal market;

- monetary policy with regard to Member States that have adopted the euro;

---

347. The doctrine of implied powers was recognised by the International Court of Justice in its *Advisory Opinion on Reparation for Injuries Suffered in the Service of the United Nations* [1949] ICJ Reports, 569.
348. Case 8/55 *Fédération Charbonnière de Belgique v High Authority* [1954–56] ECR 292.
349. [1987] ECR 3203.
350. [2009] ECR II-4133, para. 37.
351. Case 22/70 *Commission v Council (ERTA)* [1971] ECR 263, para. 16.

- the conservation of marine biological resources under the Common Fisheries Policy; and,

- the Common Commercial Policy.

In addition, under Article 3(2) TFEU, the EU has exclusive external competence with regard to the conclusion of an international agreement:

- when its conclusion is provided for in a legislative act of the Union; or

- when its conclusion is necessary to enable the EU to exercise an internal competence; or

- in so far as its conclusion may affect common rules or alter their scope.

The above three situations set out in Article 3(2) TFEU in which the EU has exclusive external competence, which is not based on express provisions of the Treaties, are explained below.

6.3.1 Exclusivity arising out of internal legislative acts of the EU

The first possibility set out in Article 3(2) TFEU concerns a situation where there is an express empowerment for the EU to conclude an international agreement contained in a legislative act of the EU. This possibility matches the ECJ's standpoint in Opinion 1/94 in which it held that "whenever the [EU] has included in its internal legislative acts provisions relating to the treatment of nationals of non-member countries or expressly conferred on its institutions powers to negotiate with non-member countries, it acquires exclusive external competence in the spheres covered by those acts".[352] For the ECJ, the acquisition of exclusivity was automatic. The aforementioned possibility listed in Article 3(2) TFEU acknowledges that when an internal legislative act expressly confers an external power on the EU, this power will be exclusive by nature. This raises the issue of whether exclusivity arising from an express internal empowerment would apply irrespective of whether internally the competence in question is shared, or complementary. It is submitted that if an internal EU act specifies that only the EU can have the competence to act externally, there should be no problem unless the agreement in question goes beyond the stipulations provided in the Treaties.

6.3.2 Exclusivity arising out of the necessity to effectuate the internal competence of the EU

The second possibility set out in Article 3(2) TFEU concerns a situation where conclusion of an international agreement is necessary to enable the EU to exercise its internal competence. It is clear that the "necessity" criterion will determine whether the EU's external competence is exclusive or not, and that if necessity is established, the EU will enjoy exclusivity irrespective of whether internally the competence in question is shared or complementary. In the understanding of the second possibility *Opinion 1/76 (Re Rhine Navigation Case)*[353] is very instructive. This is because first, it concerns a situation where the EU could not exercise its internal competence without first exercising its external competence, second the issue of necessity was discussed by the ECJ and third, the ECJ held that, contrary to its position in the *ERTA* case, exclusive external competence was not dependent on the actual exercise of internal powers.

---

352. *Opinion 1/94 WTO* [1994] ECR I-5267, para. 95.
353. [1977] ECR 741.

With regard to the first point, the EU could not exercise its internal competence to regulate the navigation of vessels on the Rhine-Moselle waterway system because not only were Member States, i.e. the Benelux countries, Germany and France, but also Switzerland, a non-Member State, the main users of the waterway, and therefore it was necessary to include a non-Member State in the arrangement. Accordingly, no internal measure was appropriate because only an international agreement could properly deal with the rationalisation of the use of vessels on these rivers.

So far as the second point is concerned, all the States involved were contracting parties to two previous Conventions on the matter. As a result, amendments to those Conventions were negotiated and agreed by all States concerned including Switzerland. The ECJ accepted that the participation of the six Member States was necessary to secure the required amendments because of special circumstances. In this respect the ECJ held: "The participation of these States [i.e. the six Member States] in the Agreement must be considered as being solely for this purpose [i.e. for the purpose of amending the Convention] and not as necessary for the attainment of other features of the system."[354] In the Opinion, the ECJ took a very restrictive view of what was necessary and accepted the right of the Member States to participate in amendments because of the special circumstances, but not their participation in other aspects relating to the Rhine-Moselle waterway system.

With regard to the third point, in subsequent Opinions[355] the ECJ emphasised the peculiarity of the situation which arose in Opinion 1/76 in that normally, under the doctrine of implied powers, the exercise of an exclusive external competence by the EU depends upon its prior exercise of the relevant internal competence.

It is submitted that the second possibility set out in Article 3(2) TFEU concerns very rare cases where internal competence may be effectively exercised only at the same time as, or subsequent to, the exercise of external competence. This, to some extent, alleviates the fear that the EU will have exclusive external competences in the areas in which internally it does not enjoy exclusivity.

6.3.3 Exclusivity arising from the exercise of EU internal competences

The third possibility set out in Article 3(2) TFEU concerns a situation where the EU enjoys exclusivity because the conclusion of an international agreement may affect common rules or alter their scope. In the *ERTA* case the ECJ did not hesitate to state that external implied powers of the EU were exclusive in nature. The pre-ToL case law shows that in order to decide whether the EU had exclusive competence, the ECJ proceeded as follows:

- First, it had to determine whether the EU had competence in the relevant area, and if so, whether the competence was explicit or implied; and,

- Second, if the ECJ found that the EU had implied competence, it determined its nature, i.e. whether the relevant competence was exclusive or shared between the EU and the Member States. This determination of the nature of a competence was decided on a case-by-case basis. In *Opinion 1/03 Lugano Convention*,[356] the ECJ held that account must be taken of:

  - whether the relevant area is covered by the EU rules and also by the provisions of the intended agreement. However, the scope of the rules in question was not in itself decisive;

---

354. Ibid, para. 7.
355. See *Opinion 1/94 WTO* [1994] ECR I-5267, para. 85; and *Opinion 1/03 Lugano Convention* [2006] ECR I-1145, para. 115.
356. *Opinion 1/03* [2006] ECR I-1145.

- the nature and content of those rules and those provisions with a view to ensuring that the agreement is not capable of undermining the uniform and consistent application of the EU rules and the proper functioning of the system which they establish; and,
- the current state of EU law in the area in question as well as its future development, in so far as that is foreseeable at the time of the judgment.[357]

Opinion 1/03 shows how the ECJ is likely to proceed to determine whether an envisaged agreement affects or alters the scope of common rules although it does not provide specific rules for the determination of whether EU legislation is part of common rules.

6.3.4 The relationship between Article 3(2) TFEU and Article 216(1) TFEU

Article 216(1) TFEU states:

"The Union may conclude an agreement with one or more third countries or international organisations where the Treaties so provide or where the conclusion of an agreement is necessary in order to achieve, within the framework of the Union's policies, one of the objectives referred to in the Treaties, or is provided for in a legally binding Union act or is likely to affect common rules or alter their scope."

The relationship between Article 216(1) TFEU and Article 3(2) TFEU is not clear and thus has been subject to differing views. Cremona argues that Article 3(2) TFEU "conflates the two separate questions of the existence of implied external competence and the exclusivity of that competence",[358] with the result that implied shared competence could disappear. Craig states that because of the significant overlap between the two Articles it is unlikely that their interpretation by the ECJ would differ. This would mean that in all situations mentioned in Article 216(1) TFEU, the EU will enjoy exclusive external competence. According to him:

"if an agreement is made pursuant to Article 216 TFEU on the ground that it is necessary to achieve a Union objective within the framework of a Union policy, this will probably be interpreted as exclusive EU competence for the purpose of Article 3(2) on the ground that the agreement is necessary to enable the EU to exercise its internal competence, more specifically because Article 7 TFEU and other Treaty provisions mandate that such objectives should be taken into account in the development of EU policy." [359]

Is the above interpretation of the relationship between Article 216(1) TFEU and Article 3(2) TFEU correct? This question will certainly be answered by the ECJ at some stage. Meanwhile it is submitted that:

- First, each Article concerns a different matter, i.e. Article 216(1) TFEU concerns situations in which the EU has competence, either exclusive or shared or supportive, co-ordinating or supplementing, to make an international agreement, whilst Article 3(2) concerns the exclusivity of that competence;
- Second, Articles 216(1) and 3(2) do not mirror each other. The major difference between them is that only Article 216(1) TFEU refers to a situation "where the conclusion of an agreement is necessary in order to achieve, within the framework of the Union's policies, one of the objectives

---

357. *Opinion 2/91 (Re ILO Convention 170)* [1993] ECR I-1061.
358. P. Craig, *Lisbon Treaty*, 2010, Oxford: OUP, 167.
359. Ibid, 400.

referred to in the Treaties". It cannot be said that it matches the situation described in Article 3(2) TFEU which gives the EU exclusive competence in a situation where the conclusion of an international agreement "is necessary to enable the EU to exercise an internal competence", a situation which is rare and which refers to exceptional circumstances such as those described in Opinion 1/76;

■ Third, one of the main objectives of the reform of EU law was to clearly determine the competences of the EU and of the Member States. Surely, the Member States were not prepared, when ratifying the ToL, to allow the EU to expand its exclusive competences beyond situations described in Article 3(2) TFEU, and thus Article 3(2) TFEU is the only authority on the exclusivity of EU external competences. By contrast, Article 216(1) TFEU embodies the pre-ToL law on the existence of the EU's implied competences. However, as clearly established in the pre-ToL case law, existence of implied external competence is not tantamount to exclusivity; and,

■ Fourth, the above interpretation is in conformity with the ECJ's statement in Opinion 1/3 in which it held that internal competence can give rise to exclusive competence only if exercised, and that the situation that arose in Opinion 1/76[360] was exceptional because the internal competence could be effectively exercised only at the same time as external competence. Article 3(2) TFEU covers the exceptional situation, but in all other cases the adoption of internal rules is necessary in order to achieve an objective of the EU. Once such rules are adopted, the third situation described in Article 3(2) TFEU will be of relevance in that the EU will have exclusive competence for the conclusion of an international agreement only "insofar as its conclusion may affect common rules or alters their scope".

6.4 Competences shared between the EU and the Member States

Most competences conferred on the EU are shared between the EU and the Member States. Under the principle of subsidiarity, in the areas of shared competences the EU can only intervene if certain objectives set out by the Treaties cannot be attained by the Member States and only if the EU can attain them with greater efficiency than the Member States. Further, any EU action in those areas must respect the principle of proportionality, i.e. such action "shall not exceed what is necessary to achieve the objectives of the Treaties".[361] Protocol No. 2 on the Application of the Principles of Subsidiarity and Proportionality attached to the Treaties establishes not only the conditions for the application of these principles but also a system for monitoring their application. Under the Protocol, national parliaments are granted extensive powers to police the application of the principle of subsidiarity.

Article 2(2) TFEU states that in areas of shared competences Member States are allowed to act within the limitations imposed by the Treaty provisions as long as the EU is inactive or ceases to be active. These limitations mean that a Member State cannot adopt measures contrary to the EU's principles and values, for example, in breach of the principle of non-discrimination on the ground of nationality,[362] or in breach of the principle of loyal co-operation as embodied in Article 4(3) TEU. Further, Article 2(2) TFEU clearly envisages a situation where the Union has decided to cease exercising its competence in a particular area in which case Member States will regain that area.

---

360. *Opinion 1/76 [Re Rhine Navigation Case]* [1977] ECR 741, para. 89.
361. Article 25 TFEU.
362. Case 61/77 *Commission v Ireland* [1978] ECR 417.

In the areas of shared competences the concept of pre-emption is of relevance.[363] This means that when the EU has acted in an area of shared competences Member States are prevented from taking any binding measures in that area. However, the nature of the exclusivity of the EU in this circumstance is different from that under Article 3(2) TFEU (see Chapter 6.3) because the EU may cease to exercise its competence in the area of shared competences with the result that the competence in question will revert to the Member States. This is in contrast to a situation where the EU has exclusive competence in that even if the EU ceases to exercise its powers or has never taken any measures, the area is still within the EU's exclusive powers and can never be claimed back by the Member States.

Further, it is important to determine the extent of the EU action in respect of the particular area because even in the pre-empted area there may be room for action for the Member States. This depends on the manner in which the EU has intervened in the particular area.

If an area is fully harmonised, then it has been pre-empted. However, even in such a situation a Member State may maintain national provisions by virtue of Article 114(4) TFEU if it establishes before the Commission the necessity of its action on the grounds listed in Article 36 TFEU or relating to the protection of the environment or the working environment. However, Article 114(4) TFEU only applies in exceptional situations and any derogation based on it is subject to the discretion and supervision of the Commission.

If there is partial harmonisation then it is necessary to determine whether the Member States are still authorised to act or whether there is a gap in EU rules. In the first circumstance, a Member State is allowed to adopt national rules under the condition that such rules do not undermine EU harmonising measures.[364] In the second instance, only the EU can fill gaps in EU law.

In some areas the competence of the EU is limited to the adoption of minimum rules, e.g. in the area of protection of environment or in the area of social policy, and therefore Member States may always adopt more generous rules.

The pre-emptive effect of Article 2(2) TFEU prompted Member States to attach Protocol No. 25 on Shared Competence to the Treaties. This Protocol provides that when the EU has taken measures in a particular area "the scope of this exercise of competence only covers those elements governed by the Union act in question and therefore does not cover the whole area". Nevertheless, whether it would be possible for the EU to pre-empt the entire area of shared competence depends on the relevant provisions of the Treaties.

Some areas of shared competences are listed in Article 4 TFEU, others are those which are neither mentioned in Article 6 TFEU (which lists supporting, co-ordinating or supplementing competences of the EU) nor in Article 3 TFEU (which lists exclusive competences of the EU).

Article 4 TFEU provides the following non exhaustive list of areas falling within shared competences:

- the internal market;

- social policy with regard to specific aspects defined in the Treaty;

- economic and social cohesion;

- agriculture and fisheries, excluding the conservation of marine biological resources;

---

363. E. Cross, "Pre-emption of Member State Law in the European Community: A Framework for Analysis", (1992) 29 CMLRev., 447; R. Schütze, "Supremacy without Pre-emption? The Very Slowly Emergent Doctrine of Community Pre-emption", (2006) 43 CMLRev.,1023; and A. Arena, "The Doctrine of Union Preemption in the EU Internal Market: Between Sein and Sollen", (2011) 17 Colum. J. Eur. L, 477.

364. Case 65/75 *Ricardo Tasca* [1976] ECR 291.

- environmental matters;

- consumer protection;

- transport;

- trans-European networks;

- energy;

- the AFSJ; and,

- common safety concerns in public health matters, for aspects defined in the TFEU.

Article 4(3) and (4) TFEU provides that in the areas of research, technological development, and space and in the areas of development co-operation and humanitarian aid, the exercise of shared competences "shall not result in Member States being prevented from exercising theirs". This means that in those five areas the EU and the Member States share not only the competence, but also the exercise of that competence.

6.5 Supporting, co-ordinating and supplementing competences of the EU

These refer to areas in which the Member States have not conferred competences on the EU but have decided to act through it. In these areas the EU supports, co-ordinates, encourages or complements measures taken at national level.[365] Article 6 TFEU provides the following list of areas in which the Member States have exclusive competence but the EU can support or co-ordinate or supplement the action of the Member States:

- protection and improvement of human health;

- industry;

- culture;

- tourism;

- education, vocational training, youth and sport;

- civil protection; and,

- administrative co-operation.

Under Article 2(5) TFEU in the above areas the EU may adopt incentive measures or other specific measures and make recommendations, but is prohibited from taking harmonising measures relating to national laws of Member States (Article 2(5) TFEU). The real meaning of Article 2(5) TFEU is that, depending upon the area, the EU is empowered to take measures, including binding measures, in order to achieve the objectives specified for the relevant area. Whether any binding measures can be adopted by the EU depends on whether the relevant article of the Treaty so provides. For example, in respect of tourism, Article 195(2) TFEU states that the EU can use the

---

365. R. Schütze, "Co-operative Federalism Constitutionalized: The Emergence of Complementary Competences in the EC Legal Order", (2006) 31 ELRev., 167.

ordinary legislative procedure to establish specific measures necessary to achieve the objective of promoting the competitiveness of Union undertakings in the area of tourism. However, under no circumstances is the EU allowed to harmonise, partially or totally, national laws and regulations of the Member States. Obviously, any dispute between the Member States and the EU on whether a specific binding EU measure constitutes harmonisation of national laws will ultimately be decided by the ECJ.

Article 2(3) TFEU sets out specific rules with regard to economic, employment and social policies, and the Common Foreign and Security Policy (CFSP).

Under Article 5 TFEU the EU is required to define "broad guidelines" in respect of economic and employment policy. In these two areas the competence of the EU is to align national polices with a view to preventing Member States from disrupting each other's policies. With regard to social policy, the EU has discretion to decide whether to take any initiatives aimed at co-ordinating Member States' social policies.

The special treatment given to these three above areas is explained by political considerations. On the one hand, their exclusion from the areas of shared competences was resisted by many Member States which feared that the EU would pre-empt their action in these vital areas and, on the other hand, the position of other Member States which felt that the EU should have more extensive powers in these areas than it normally enjoys under supportive, co-ordinating and supplementary competences. As a result, these three areas in terms of EU competences are situated between shared and supporting, co-ordinating or supplementing competences.

The CFSP is not included in Title I of the TFEU. The peculiarity of the CFSP necessitated the establishment of special rules as to the determination and the exercise of the competences by the EU and its Member States. These are set out in Article 24 TEU (see Chapter 7.5.4).

6.6 Article 114 TFEU – the harmonisation clause

In the context of the establishment of the internal market, Article 95(1) EC [Article 114 TFEU] served as a legal basis for numerous EC measures. This provision was rather vague as it stated that the Council, after consulting the EP, and acting by QMV, may adopt measures having as their object the improvement of the conditions for the establishment and functioning of the internal market. Not surprisingly, Member States have often considered that the choice of Article 95(1) EC as a legal basis for a particular measure was inappropriate.

In 2002, the ECJ elucidated the meaning of Article 95(1) EC [Article 114 TFEU]. It held that this article is not a "catch-all-provision" allowing the Council to legislate as it wishes.[366] A measure adopted on the basis of Article 95 EC [Article 114 TFEU] "must genuinely have as its object the improvement of the conditions for the establishment and functioning of the internal market". Article 95(1) EC [Article 114 TFEU] does not confer general legislative powers on EU institutions, but a specific power to adopt measures intended to improve the functioning of the internal market. Consequently, the choice of Article 95 EC [Article 114 TFEU] cannot be justified by the fact that there is a mere finding of disparity between national rules, nor by the fact that there is an abstract risk of obstacles to the freedom of movement, nor by the fact that there is a risk of distortion of competition.[367] Otherwise a judicial review of compliance with the requirement of EU law for a proper legal basis might be rendered nugatory. The

---

366. Case C-491/01 *R and Secretary of State for Health, ex parte: British American Tobacco (Investments) Ltd and Others* [2002] ECR I-11453.
367. Case C-376/98 *Germany v EP and Council* [2000] ECR I-8419.

ECJ emphasised that Article 95(1) EC [Article 114 TFEU] can only be used as a legal basis to prevent future obstacles to trade resulting from disparity of national laws, and the emergence of such obstacles must be likely.[368]

Under the TFEU, further clarifications are provided in that:

- Article 114(2) TFEU excludes from the scope of Article 114 TFEU measures relating to fiscal provisions, the free movement of persons and the rights and interests of employed persons; and,

- Article 114(1) TFEU states that the ordinary legislative procedure is to be used for the adoption of measures which have as their object the establishment and functioning of the internal market and that when using it the EP and the Council must consult the EESC. Consequently, an abuse of Article 114 TFEU is less likely to occur under the TFEU than was the case under the EC Treaty given the involvement of the EP and the EESC.

6.7 Article 352 TFEU – the "flexibility clause"

Other than by means of revising the Treaties, the possibility of modifying the extent of the competences of the EU is provided for in Article 352 TFEU. Its main function is to serve as a legal basis for any EU action which might become necessary to respond to "unforeseen circumstances", i.e. new challenges and developments. It substantially revises its predecessor – Article 308 EC. Its use has been restricted not only by procedural requirements set out in that Article, but also by some Member States which have established procedures requiring the approval of their parliaments of any new draft measure, or any measure which substantially amends or renews an existing measure, based on Article 352 TFEU.

6.7.1 The pre-ToL use of the "flexibility clause"

To ensure that the objectives of the internal market were met, Article 308 EC allowed the Council, acting unanimously, on a proposal from the Commission, and after consulting the EP, to take measures it considered necessary, in a situation where the Community had no explicit or implied powers to act. In the 1970s and 1980s Article 308 EC was used to extend the competences of the Community without actually revising the EC Treaty. On the basis of Article 308 EC the Council adopted legislation in important areas not covered, at that time, by the EC Treaty, e.g. environmental protection, regional aid, and research and technology. The Council leant, probably too frequently, upon Article 308 EC for two reasons:

- First, the Paris Summit held in October 1972 decided that in order to establish an economic and monetary union, as well as promote the social dimension of the Community, all provisions of the EC Treaty, including Article 308 EC, should be widely used. As a result, in the 1970s but mainly in the 1980s, the Council used Article 308 EC extensively and systematically. By 15 March 1992 677 measures, both internal and external, had been adopted on the basis of this article; and,

- Second, the Council could only adopt a measure on the ground of Article 308 EC if acting unanimously. This requirement ensured that no measure contrary to the interests of any Member

---

368. Case C-350/92 *Spain v Council* [1995] ECR I-1985; Case C-377/98 *The Netherlands v EP and Council* [2001] ECR I-7079; Joined Cases C-434/02 *Arnold André GmbH v Landrat des Kreises Herford* [2004] ECR I-11825 and C-210/03 *Swedish Match AB and Swedish Match UK Ltd v Secretary of State for Health* [2004] ECR I-11893; Case C-380/03 *Germany v EP and Council* [2006] ECR I-11573.

State had any realistic chance of adoption. Thus, all extensions of competences under Article 308 EC were acceptable to all Member States.

The Commission was not happy about the extensive use of Article 308 EC by the Council because the use of this Article, in effect, involved revision of the EC Treaty outside the revision procedure specified in the EC Treaty. Further, revision of the EC Treaty by the Council undermined the democratic process within each Member State because the new competences had been given to the EC by the executive of each Member State, rather than by its legislative body or according to constitutional procedures used in a Member State. This democratic deficit was not compensated for by the fact that the EP was involved in the adoption of a measure, bearing in mind that the EP was only consulted under Article 308 EC. Resulting from the above, the ECJ imposed two conditions to be met in order to use Article 308 EC as the legal basis of a Community act.

■ In Case 45/86 *Commission v Council (Re General Tariff Preferences)*,[369] the ECJ held that a measure could only be adopted under Article 308 EC if there was no other appropriate provision in the EC Treaty which would provide a legal basis for Community action. It could, however, have been used where powers existed elsewhere in the Treaty but were insufficient to attain the relevant Community objective;[370] and,

■ In *Opinion 2/94 (Re ECHR)*,[371] the ECJ held that Article 308 EC could not serve as justification for widening the scope of the EC's powers beyond the general framework set up by the Treaty provisions in general, and those provisions which referred to the EC's tasks and activities in particular. In this Opinion the issue was whether Article 308 EC could be used as a possible legal basis for the accession of the EC to the European Convention of Human Rights. The ECJ held that Article 308 EC "cannot be used as a basis for the adoption of provisions whose effect would, in substance, be to amend the Treaty without following the procedure which it provides for that purpose."[372]

As can be seen from the above, the ECJ restored Article 308 EC to its initial role, that is, subject to the two above conditions, it could be used for filling gaps in the EC Treaty, but it could not be used for extending the areas of competence of the Community.

6.7.2 The "flexibility" clause under the ToL: Article 352 TFEU

The fear that Article 352 TFEU would be used as a back-door means to amend the Treaties prompted some Member States to provide safeguards to ensure that the EU will be unable to grant itself new competences not covered by the Treaties without approval of national parliaments. In the UK, section 8 of the 2011 European Union Act, which Act implements the ToL, specifies that a Minister of the Crown may not vote in favour of, or otherwise support, a draft decision based on Article 352 TFEU unless the draft decision is approved by Act of Parliament. In urgent cases, a Minister of the Crown must move a motion to this effect, which must be approved without amendment by each House of Parliament. There is an exemption from the above requirements in section 8(6) in respect of a measure which only extends or renews an existing measure without changing its substance. Arrangements

---

369.   [1987] ECR 1493.
370.   Case 45/86 *Commission v Council (Re General Tariff Preferences)* [1987] ECR 1493.
371.   [1996] ECR I-1759.
372.   Ibid, para. 30.

similar to those introduced by section 8 of the 2011 UK European Union Act were made in Germany, following the BVerfG's judgment of 30 June 2009[373] concerning the compatibility of the ToL with the German Constitution, in which the Court held that "the undetermined nature of future cases of [Article 352's] application" entails that the German government may not support its use without seeking specific, prior statutory authorisation from the legislature, pursuant to Article 23 of the German Constitution.

In any event, the ToL reduced the importance of the "flexibility clause" contained in Article 352 TFEU by making the following amendments to Article 308 EC:

- Article 352 TFEU can be used to achieve the objectives of the Treaties as listed in Article 3 TEU but does not apply to the CFSP;

- For the adoption of a measure under Article 352 TFEU the Council is required to obtain the EP's consent, whereas under Article 308 EC the Council was merely required to consult the EP;

- Under Article 352 TFEU, the Commission is required to "draw national Parliaments' attention to proposals based on this Article", so allowing them to use the "yellow and orange cards" procedure; and,

- Article 352(3) TFEU specifies that "measures based on this Article shall not entail harmonisation of Member States' laws or regulations in cases where the Treaties exclude such harmonisation".

Declarations 41 and 42 on Article 352 TFEU, attached to the Treaties, further explain the potential use of Article 352 TFEU. Declaration 41 excludes any action based on Article 352 TFEU in respect of the objectives of the Union set out in Article 3(1) TEU, i.e. concerning external action of the EU to promote peace, its values and the well-being of its peoples. This is because any such action will be within the scope of the CFSP to which Article 352 does not apply. Declaration 42 states that Article 352 TFEU, being an integral part of an institutional system based on the principle of conferral, cannot be used to adopt measures whose effect would, in substance, amend the Treaties outside the procedures provided for that purpose. Declaration 42 reiterates the position taken by the ECJ in Opinion 2/94. Its main aim is to confirm the desire of the Member States to prevent any extension of the EU's competences.

6.8 The exercise of competences by the EU: the principles of subsidiarity and proportionality and the role of national parliaments in the implementation of the principle of subsidiarity

The exercise of competences by the EU is subject to compliance with the requirements of the principles of subsidiarity and proportionality. It must be noted, however, that the principle of subsidiarity does not apply to exclusive competences of the EU although the principle of proportionality does. The ToL gives national parliaments an important role in the implementation of the principle of subsidiarity. This power of control of national parliaments is however limited, first because it applies only to draft legislative acts and does not cover draft delegated or implementing acts and second, it does not extend to the implementation of the principle of proportionality.

---

373. Decision of 30 June 2009, BVerfG 123, 267, para. 328.

6.8.1 The principle of subsidiarity

The principle of subsidiarity has a long history. It derives from the Catholic doctrine of Thomas Aquinas and has been used by the Roman Catholic Church.[374]

In the context of social organisation, the principle of subsidiarity means that decisions affecting individuals should always be taken at the lowest practical level, as closely as possible to the individuals concerned, and that in those areas where individuals are the most competent to decide for themselves their initiatives should not be impeded by any authorities.

The principle of subsidiarity has its constitutional and political dimension in federations. It allocates powers between federal and local authorities in order to strike a balance between the needs of the federation and the protection of the interests of members of the federation, and thus decides which functions should be performed at the federal level, which should be shared between federal and local levels and which should be within the exclusive competence of the latter.

Subsidiarity is an elusive concept. It is submitted that its best definition is the following: "It is a principle for allocating power upwards as well as downwards, but it incorporates a presumption in favour of allocation downwards in case of doubt."[375] It is not tantamount to decentralisation and it admits degrees of exercise of powers. It entails that decisions should always be taken at the lowest practical level, thus leaving the EU to concentrate on the essential and vital objectives.

The principle of subsidiarity maintains the integrity of the EU while allowing the participation of national authorities in decision-making procedures provided they can exercise their functions satisfactorily. Subsidiarity maintains the balance of power between the EU and the Member States, and imposes the burden of proof upon the EU institutions. Under the ToL the control of subsidiarity by national parliaments enhances the democratic legitimacy of the EU.

6.8.1.1 The development of the principle of subsidiarity: from the SEA to the ToL

The principle of subsidiarity was implicit in Article 235 of the EC Treaty concerning the extension of competences of the Community. The SEA introduced it explicitly in relation to the protection of the environment. As a general principle of EU law it was, for the first time, expressly mentioned in the Treaty of Maastricht, i.e. in its Preamble, Articles A and B and in Article 5 EC. Its meaning, however, given its elusive nature and its political and legal connotations, was highly disputed. In order to clarify its meaning under EC law, the Edinburgh European Council (December 1992), adopted guidelines regarding the practical and procedural implications deriving from the principle of subsidiarity for EC institutions. Given the obvious link between the principle of subsidiarity and the principle of proportionality, the guidelines summarised and explained the procedural and practical steps necessary for implementation of both principles by the Community institutions.

The guidelines discussed above were incorporated into a Protocol on the Application of the Principles of Subsidiarity and Proportionality, which Protocol was annexed to the ToA. In the light of the fact that protocols annexed to a Treaty form an integral part of that Treaty, the Protocol conferred

---

374. According to Pope Pius XI: "It is an injustice, a grave evil and disturbance of right order for a larger and higher association to arrogate to itself functions which can be performed efficiently by smaller and lower societies." Cited by J. Steiner, "Subsidiarity under the Maastricht Treaty", in D. O'Keefe and P. Twomey (eds), *Legal Issues of the Treaty of Maastricht*, 1994, London: Chancery Law Publishing, 50. See also P. Carozza, "Subsidiarity as a Structural Principle of International Human Rights Law", (2003) 97(1) *American Journal of International Law*, 38–79.

375. The CEPR Annual Report, 1993, "Making Sense of Subsidiarity: How Much Centralization for Europe?", (1993) 4 *Monitoring European Integration*, 4.

binding character on the principles of subsidiarity and proportionality and thus they have become subject to judicial review. The Protocol was complemented by the 1993 Inter-Institutional Agreement on Procedures for Implementing the Principle of Subsidiarity[376] between the Council, the EP and the Commission, requiring these institutions to respect the principle of subsidiarity and to take concrete steps to implement it.

6.8.1.2 Principle of subsidiarity under the ToL

The ToL recognises the importance of the proper application of the principle of subsidiarity and thus of drawing a clear demarcation line between the competences of a Member State and those of the EU. It ensures respect for the principle of subsidiarity in the following ways:

- It identifies areas that are within the exclusive competence of the EU on the one hand, and of its Member States, on the other;

- It provides procedures for ensuring the proper application of the principle of subsidiarity by EU institutions; and,

- It provides the following definition of the principle of subsidiarity in Article 5(3) TEU.

"Under the principle of subsidiarity, in areas which do not fall within its exclusive competence, the Union shall act only if and insofar as the objectives of the intended action cannot be sufficiently achieved by the Member States, either at central level or at regional and local level, but can rather, by reason of the scale or effects of the proposed action, be better achieved at Union level."

It can be said that, on the basis of the above definition, the following criteria should be satisfied in order for the EU to take action in an area where it shares competences with the Member States:

- The sufficiency criterion, that is, an action must be necessary in the sense that neither individuals alone nor Member States alone will achieve the objectives of the action;

- The benefit criterion, that is, an action must bring added value over and above that which could be achieved by individuals or a Member State;

- The close to the citizen criterion, which requires that decisions must be taken as closely as possible to the citizen; and,

- The autonomy criterion, which requires that an action should secure greater freedom for the individual.

6.8.1.3 The application of the principle of subsidiarity by the EU institutions

Under Article 1 of Protocol 2 on the Application of the Principles of Subsidiarity and Proportionality each EU institution is required to ensure "constant respect" for both principles. This is to be achieved as follows.

A.   **The European Commission.** In order to satisfy the requirements of subsidiarity the Commission must:

---

376.   [1993] OJ C329/132.

- Carry out wide consultations, where appropriate at regional and local level in respect of a proposed legislative act. Within the "smart regulation" approach (see Chapter 5.3) the importance of consulting all stakeholders including social partners as well as giving them an appropriate length of time to respond has been enhanced. If, in cases of exceptional urgency, the Commission fails to carry out such consultations it must give reasons for its decision in its proposal;

- In the preamble to any legislation, where the EU does not have exclusive competence, the Commission has to justify the proposed legislation in the light of subsidiarity and proportionality. This justification forms part of the measure's legal basis. The Commission must show that it is more appropriate to act at EU level than at national level, using qualitative and if possible quantitative indicators;

- In accordance with the OMC, in secondary legislation the Commission gives preference to directives rather than regulations. Similarly, non-binding measures, such as recommendations, opinions and non-compulsory codes of conduct, are used when appropriate rather than binding measures. Further, the Commission relies on techniques of minimum standards and the principle of mutual recognition when appropriate. The principle of subsidiarity entails that co-operation between Member States should be encouraged by the Commission, which often supports, completes or supervises joint initiatives of the Member States; and,

- The Commission is required to submit an annual report to the European Council, the EP, the Council and national parliaments on the application of Article 5 TEU. This annual report must also be forwarded to the EESC and the CoR.

B.   **The Council.** The Council must examine each proposal submitted by the Commission, and its own amendments to such proposals, in the light of the principle of subsidiarity.

C.   **The EP.** The EP, being a co-legislator in most areas, is very much involved in the application of the principle of subsidiarity. The Inter-institutional Agreement on Procedures for Implementing the Principle of Subsidiarity provides that the EP must take into account the principle of subsidiarity and, in the light of Article 5 TEU, justify any amendment which substantially changes a proposal submitted by the Commission.

D.   **The ECJ.** The principle of subsidiarity is not only a socio-political concept but also a fundamental principle of EU law. No special procedure has been established to bring an issue of subsidiarity before the ECJ, although a proposal that this should occur was made by the EP.[377]

The issue of subsidiarity is most likely to arise in two types of proceedings before the CJEU:

- Under Article 267 TFEU, which enables national courts or tribunals, when they are faced with a question of interpretation or validity of EU law, the resolution of which is necessary for them to give judgment, to refer that question to the ECJ under the preliminary ruling procedure (see Chapter 13); and,

- Under Article 263 TFEU, which concerns judicial review of acts of EU institutions, bodies, offices and agencies, an applicant may challenge an act itself by claiming that it was adopted in violation of the requirements laid down in Article 5 TEU. Article 8 of Protocol No. 2 extends the list of potential applicants under Article 263 to include the CoR in respect of legislative acts for the adoption of which the TFEU provides that it be consulted. However, national parliaments

---

377.   A. G. Toth, "Is Subsidiarity Justiciable?" (1994) 19 ELRev., 268, especially at 273.

have no *locus standi* under Article 263 TFEU but a Member State may bring an action on behalf of its national parliament.

The pre-ToL case law shows that the ECJ had never annulled any EC/EU legislation on the ground that it was adopted in breach of subsidiarity. The ECJ's position was stated in Case C-84/94 *(Re Working Time Directive),*[378] in which it held that judicial review of the application of the principle of subsidiarity must be limited to examining whether the challenged legislation "has been vitiated by manifest error or misuse of powers, or whether the institution concerned has manifestly exceeded the limits of its discretion". In a judgment delivered by the Grand Chamber of the ECJ, in Joined Cases C-154/04 and C-155/04 *Alliance for Natural Health,*[379] the Court confirmed that only in extreme circumstances will the Court find that the principle of subsidiarity has been breached.

This approach is understandable in that the principle is, in reality, of a political nature. The ECJ in its pre-ToL case law was reluctant to clearly state what subsidiarity really means in terms of the allocation of competences between the Community and the Member States. The ECJ's reluctance could be explained by the fact that the concept of exclusive competences of the Community was created by the ECJ itself as that concept had no legal basis in the original EC Treaty. In *Alliance for Natural Health* the ECJ held that:

> "the principle of subsidiarity does not call into question the powers conferred on the Community by the Treaty, as interpreted by the Court of Justice."[380]

This is a reminder that the principle of subsidiarity is concerned with how power is exercised by the EU and not with the question of what powers are conferred on it. However, when the legitimacy of the decision-making process in the EU is challenged on the ground of subsidiarity, this necessarily involves the delicate task of defining areas of shared and exclusive competences. This is because subsidiarity does not apply to areas within the exclusive competence of the EU.

It is submitted that the attitude of the ECJ towards the principle of subsidiarity may change under the ToL, the reason being that the ToL clearly defines the areas of exclusive competence of the EU. Therefore, the threat that the principle of subsidiarity will have a radical impact on judicial determination of the exclusive competences of the EU has been removed. Further, the establishment of a list of areas of shared competences under the ToL facilitates the consideration by the ECJ of whether a particular legislative action on the part of the EU is necessary or the best one. Finally, the enhanced role of national parliaments and the CoR in the monitoring of the proper application of the principle of subsidiarity is conducive to making subsidiarity more intrusive as a general legal principle.

6.8.2 The control of subsidiarity by national parliaments

Under Protocol No. 1 on the Role of National Parliaments in the European Union, all EU draft legislative acts must be forwarded to national parliaments. Within eight weeks of receipt of a draft legislative act or of any amendment to it, national parliaments may issue a reasoned opinion stating why what has been received does not comply with the principle of subsidiarity and indicate their opposition by voting against the proposal. During that period, save in exceptional circumstances, EU institutions must abstain from adopting any measures based on the draft act.

---

378. Case C-84/94 *United Kingdom v Council (Re Working Time Directive)* [1996] ECR I-5755, para. 58.
379. *Joined Cases C-154/04 and C-155/04 R on the Application of Alliance for Natural Health and Others v Secretary of State for Health and National Assembly for Wales* [2005] ECR I-6451.
380. Ibid, para. 102.

It is, however, Protocol No. 2 on the Application of the Principles of Subsidiarity and Proportionality which specifies the extent of control of national parliaments over the application of the principle of subsidiarity by EU institutions. It establishes a new procedure, known as the "yellow and orange cards", which gives national parliaments the opportunity to monitor the proper application of the principle of subsidiarity.

Under Protocol No. 2, each national parliament has been allocated two votes. If the parliament consists of two chambers or houses, each of them holds one of these votes. In an EU of 27 Member States, the total number of votes available is 54. If at least one third of those votes (18 votes) indicate that the principle of subsidiarity has not been complied with, the Commission, or the institution which initiated the proposed act, must review the proposal and decide whether it wishes to withdraw, amend or maintain it. A reason must be given to justify the decision.

In respect of a proposed legislative act concerning the AFSJ originating from the Commission or a group of Member States, lower thresholds apply. The review procedure is triggered if at least one quarter of the votes of the national parliaments disagree with the proposal. This is the "yellow cards" procedure.

The "orange cards" procedure applies only to the ordinary legislative procedure (see Chapter 5.4). If at least a simple majority of votes (currently 28) cast by national parliaments indicate objections to a proposal, the Commission must review the proposal. If the Commission decides to maintain its proposal, it must issue a reasoned opinion stating why it considers that the proposal complies with the principle of subsidiarity. This reasoned opinion, together with reasoned opinions from the national parliaments, is then forwarded to the legislator (that is, the Council and the EP jointly), which decides the fate of the proposal. This means that if the Council by a majority of 55 per cent of its members and if the EP by a simple majority of the votes cast reject the proposal, it will not be given further consideration.

If an act is adopted despite it being challenged by national parliaments, a Member State may bring an action for infringement of the principle of subsidiarity under Article 263 TFEU on behalf of its national parliament (Article 8 of Protocol No. 2). However, this may lead to a potentially embarrassing situation if the government of a Member State has agreed on a measure but its national parliament finds the measure to be in breach of the principle of subsidiarity. Nevertheless, this is a matter to be settled by the domestic law, i.e. to decide whether the national parliament can force the government to act on its behalf, and further, whether in proceedings under Article 263 TFEU the government will be allowed to present its views, or only act as an agent of its parliament.

It should be noted that national parliaments are not entitled to monitor the application of the principle of subsidiarity with regard to draft delegated and implementing acts, although such acts are legally binding within the EU legal order (see Chapter 4.5.2).

6.8.3 The principle of proportionality

Article 5 TEU states that:

> "Under the principle of proportionality, the content and form of Union action shall not exceed what is necessary to achieve the objectives of the Treaties."

The principle of proportionality was recognised by the ECJ in Case C8/55 *Fédération Charbonnière*[381] and has since become a general principle of EU law (see Chapter 4.3.2).

---

381.   Case C8/55 *Fédération Charbonnière de Belgique v High Authority* [1954–56] ECR 245.

Unlike the principle of subsidiarity, the principle of proportionality applies to all measures adopted by the EU irrespective of whether they are taken under exclusive, shared, supporting, co-ordinating or supplementing competences. The difference between the principle of subsidiarity and the principle of proportionality is that the principle of subsidiarity determines whether the EU is empowered to exercise the competence in question whilst the principle of proportionality determines whether measures adopted by the EU are suitable for the purpose of achieving the desired objective and whether they do not go beyond what is necessary to achieve it.

Article 5 of Protocol No. 2 imposes an obligation on the Commission to justify any legislative act with regard to both principles. The justification must be detailed enough to facilitate the appraisal of the compliance of the draft act with both principles. In respect of the principle of proportionality, the Commission is required to include assessment of the financial impact of the draft act and, in the case of a directive, of its implications for the rules to be put in place by Member States, including, where necessary, the regional legislation. The financial or administrative burden that the draft act would entail must be "minimised and commensurate with the objective to be achieved".

The principle of proportionality, being by nature open-textured, entailing value judgments, and institutional choices in particular in politically sensitive areas of national competence, has been applied by the Union courts in differing manner depending upon the area under consideration and substantive interests at stake. This has been criticised as undermining the principle of legal certainty and transparency. Under Article 5 TEU the principle of proportionality is used to control the exercise of the Union's legislative powers, an area which is not likely to attract a high level of scrutiny by the ECJ (see Chapter 4.3.2). As the ECJ held in Case C-491/01 *British American Tobacco*,[382] the EU legislature should be allowed broad discretion to determine appropriate measures where the objective pursued "entails political, economic and social choices on its part, and in which it is called upon to undertake complex assessments. Consequently, the legality of a measure adopted in that sphere can be affected only if the measure is manifestly inappropriate having regard to the objective which the competent institution is seeking to pursue."

On rare occasions, the ECJ invalidated EU legislation when the institution concerned adopted measures manifestly inappropriate having regard to the objective pursued. For example, in *ABNA*[383] the ECJ annulled a provision of an EU directive as being disproportionate. According to that provision, manufacturers of compound animal feed, at the customer's request, were obliged to indicate the quantitative composition of the feed. The manufacturers argued that the disclosure of the formulas for the composition of their products would put them at risk of such formulas being used by their competitors and thus would have deleterious effect on their investments, research and innovation. The ECJ agreed.

6.9 Exercise of the EU's competences by a limited number of Member States: the enhanced co-operation procedure

The possibility for some Member States to establish closer co-operation between themselves, through the EU institutions and procedures, was introduced by the ToA, and is known as "enhanced co-operation". The IGC, revising the ToA, decided that the conditions triggering enhanced co-operation needed

---

382. Case C-491/01 *The Queen v Secretary of State for Health, ex parte British American Tobacco (Investments) Ltd and Imperial Tobacco Ltd* para. 123. See also Case C-58/08 *R on the Application of Vodafone Ltd and Others v Secretary of State for Business, Enterprise and Regulatory Reform* [2010] ECR I-4999, para. 68.

383. Joined Cases C-453/03, C-11/04, C-12/04 and C-194/04 *ABNA v Secretary of State for Health and Others* [2005] ECR I-10423.

substantial amendment. The ToA limited the use of enhanced co-operation to matters dealt with in Pillar 1 and in Pillar 3 (matters concerning police and judicial co-operation in criminal matters), imposed strict conditions for its use, and gave the right of veto to every Member State, even if that Member State did not wish to participate. Under the ToA the procedure was never used. The ToN profoundly revised the enhanced co-operation procedure in order to make it more attractive to Member States. The ToL further reformed it. Provisions relevant to enhanced co-operation are contained in Title IV of the TEU and Title III of Part Six of the TFEU. The procedure was used for the first time under Council Regulation 1259/2010 of 20 December 2010, in the area of law applicable to divorce and legal separation.[384]

Enhanced co-operation is a mixed blessing. On the one hand, it introduces flexibility into the workings of the EU, as it allows co-operation among groups of Member States, as against amongst all Member States, on some projects, and on the other hand, it threatens the coherence of the EU. The danger is that enhanced co-operation allows for differential integration, i.e. instead of all Member States moving towards the achievement of the EU's objectives at the same speed, some of them are allowed to move faster, and consequently some of them may never catch up. Further drawbacks are those of complexity and fragmentation of the EU's legal order.[385] Having said this in a Union of diverse members, diverse approaches may be seen as appropriate.

6.9.1 The main features of the enhanced co-operation procedure

These are:

- The ToL provides for the possibility of instituting enhanced co-operation in all areas of competences of the EU including the CFSP, and within the CFSP, the CSDP apart from areas in which the EU enjoys exclusive competences;

- Article 20 TEU provides that the enhanced co-operation procedure should further the objectives of the Union, protect its interests and reinforce its integration process whilst Article 326 TFEU states that the procedure must not undermine the internal market or the EU's economic, social and territorial cohesion; must not constitute a barrier to, or discrimination in, trade between the Member States and must not distort competition between them. Under Article 327 TFEU any enhanced co-operation must respect the competences, rights and obligations of non-participating Member States;

- Article 20(1) TEU specifies that enhanced co-operation may be undertaken only as a last resort, that is, when it has been established within the Council that the objectives of such co-operation cannot be achieved within a reasonable period by applying the relevant provisions of the Treaties;

- Article 328 TFEU requires that when enhanced co-operation is being established, it shall be open to all Member States, at any time, provided that any Member State that wishes to participate complies with decisions taken within the established enhanced co-operation framework. The Commission and the participating Member States shall ensure that as many non-participating Member States as possible are encouraged to take part;

- Article 20(4) TFEU provides that acts adopted within the framework of enhanced co-operation do not form part of the EU *acquis*;

---

384. [2011] OJ L343/10.
385. N. Walker, "Flexibility within a Metaconstitutional Framework", in G. de Búrca and J. Scott (eds), *Constitutional Changes in the EU: From Uniformity to Flexibility*, 2000, Oxford: Hart Publishing, 10.

■ Acts adopted within the framework of enhanced co-operation shall be applied by the participating Member States and their implementation shall not be impeded by non-participating Member States;

■ In respect of enhanced co-operation which is in progress and which does not have military or defence implications, the Council acting unanimously may adopt a decision, stipulating that it will act by QMV where the Treaty stipulates that the Council shall act unanimously (Article 333 TFEU). The only constraint imposed on the Council is that it must consult the EP;

■ Once enhanced co-operation has been established, only participating Member States are entitled to vote in the Council on matters relating to that particular co-operation although all Members of the Council may take part in deliberations;

■ Under Article 332 TFEU expenditure resulting from enhanced co-operation, other than administrative costs, shall be borne by the participating Member States, unless the Council acting unanimously, after consulting the EP, decides otherwise; and,

■ Article 334 TFEU requires that the Council and the Commission ensure the consistency of activities decided upon within the framework of enhanced co-operation with other policies and activities of the EU.

The ToL's main innovation so far as enhanced co-operation is concerned was that it provides differing rules for the establishment of, and participation in, enhanced co-operation in progress, depending on the policy areas. It establishes the general procedure in Article 329(1) TFEU and specific procedures in respect of three areas: the CFSP, the AFSJ and the CSDP.

6.9.2 General procedure for enhanced co-operation

Interested Member States (at the minimum, nine) are required to address a request to the Commission specifying the scope and objectives of their intended enhanced co-operation. The Commission may then either submit a proposal for approval to the Council or may refuse to do this in which case a reason for refusal must be given. If the Commission decides to submit the proposal, the Council acting by QMV may, after obtaining the consent of the EP, grant authorisation to proceed.

With regard to any enhanced co-operation which is in progress, an interested Member State is required to notify the Commission of its intention to join. The Commission within four months of the date of receipt of the notification may, either confirm the participation of the Member State concerned, or decline the request in which case it should indicate arrangements to be adopted which would satisfy the conditions for participation, and set a deadline for re-examining the request. On the expiry of that deadline, the Commission must re-examine the request. If the Commission still considers that the conditions for participation have not been fulfilled by the Member State concerned, it must forward the request to the Council which will take a final decision (Article 331(1) TFEU).

6.9.3 Enhanced co-operation in the CFSP

Under Article 329(2) TFEU, Member States (at a minimum, nine) must submit a request directly to the Council for authorisation to commence enhanced co-operation. The Council, after receiving an opinion from the HR on whether enhanced co-operation is consistent with the EU's CFSP and from the Commission on its compatibility with other Union policies, acting unanimously, may give authorisation to proceed. The EP is only informed of the request.

An interested Member State is required to notify its intention to join any enhanced co-operation which is in progress to the Council, the HR and the Commission. However, only the opinion of the HR will be taken into account by the Council when it decides, by unanimity, on that Member State's participation. However, if the Council refuses the request it must indicate the arrangements to be adopted to fulfil the conditions for participation and set a deadline for re-examining the request.

6.9.4 Enhanced co-operation in the AFSJ

At least nine Member States may establish enhanced co-operation based:

- on draft directives concerning police and judicial co-operation in criminal matters (Article 82(3) TFEU); or,

- on directives establishing minimum rules concerning the definition of criminal offences and sanctions in the areas of particularly serious crimes with a cross-border dimension resulting from the nature or impact of such offences or from a special need to combat them on a common basis (Article 83(3) TFEU).

The interested States are only required to notify the establishment of enhanced co-operation to the EP, the Council and the Commission. No authorisation from the Council is needed. The relaxed rules, as compared with other enhanced co-operation, are justified by the fact that the adoption of a draft directive has been either suspended or blocked at the initiative of a Member State which has pulled the "emergency brake", i.e. decided that the adoption of the proposed measure would affect fundamental aspects of its criminal justice system (see Chapter 31.5.2).

6.9.5 Enhanced co-operation in the CSDP

In the CSDP there are three types of enhanced co-operation. One is called the "permanent structured co-operation". It can be established under Article 42 TEU by "those Member States whose military capabilities fulfil higher criteria and which have made more binding commitments to one another in this area with a view to the most demanding missions". There is no minimum threshold in terms of the number of participating States (Article 46 TEU). Another concerns the participation of Member States in missions outside the EU for peace-keeping; conflict prevention; and, strengthening international security in accordance with the principles of the UN Charter (Article 46 TEU). The third concerns co-operation within the framework of the European Defence Agency. Co-operation between Member States wishing to be part of the European Defence Agency will be defined by the Council which will adopt, acting by QMV, a decision defining the Agency's statute, seat and operational rules (Article 45(2) TEU) (see Chapter 7.6).

RECOMMENDED READING

Books

Birkinshaw, P.J. and Varney, M., *The European Union Legal Order after Lisbon*, 2010, London: KLI.

Corrias, L., *The Passivity of Law: Competence and Constitution in the European Court of Justice*, 2011, Amsterdam: Springer.

Konstadinides, T., *Division of Powers in European Union Law: The Delimitation of Internal Competences between the EU and the Member States*, 2009, London: KLI.

Articles

Arena, A., "The Doctrine of Union Preemption in the EU Internal Market: Between Sein and Sollen", (2011) 17 Colum. J. Eur. L, 477.

Craig, P., "Competence: Clarity, Conferral, Containment and Consideration", (2004) 29 ELRev., 323.

Emiliou, N., "Opening Pandora's Box: The Legal Basis of Union Measures before the Court of Justice" (1994) 19 ELR, 488.

Harbo, T-I., "The Function of the Proportionality Principle in EU Law", (2010) 16 ELJ, 158.

Schütze, R., "Co-operative Federalism Constitutionalized: The Emergence of Complementary Competences in the EC Legal Order", (2006) 31 ELRev., 167.

Schütze, R., "On Federal Ground: The European Union as an (Inter)national Phenomenon", (2009) 46 CMLRev., 1069.

Schütze, R., "Supremacy without Pre-emption? The Very Slow Emergent Doctrine of Pre-emption", (2006) 43 CMLRev., 1023.

Slater, D., "The Scope of EC Harmonizing Powers Revisited", (2003) 4 *German Law Journal*, 137.

Van Ooik, R., "The European Court of Justice and the Division of Competence in the European Union", in Obradovoc, D., and Lavranos, N. (eds), *Interface between EU Law and National Law*, 2007, Groningen: Europa Law Publishing, 11.

Von Bogdandy, A., and Bast, J., "The Federal Order of Competence", in Von Bogdandy, A., and Bast, J. (eds), *Principle of European Constitutional Law*, 2nd edn, 2010, Oxford: Hart Publishing, 275.

Weatherill, S., "Competence Creep and Competence Control", (2004) 23 YEL, 15.

PROBLEM QUESTION

Greece submitted to the International Maritime Organisation (IMO) a proposal for monitoring the compliance of ships and port facilities with the requirements of Chapter XI-2 of the International Convention for the Safety of Life at Sea and the International Ship and Port Facility Security Code. The EU is not a member of the IMO, but since the entry into force of Regulation 725/2004 on enhancing ship and port facility security, has enjoyed exclusive competences in the area of maritime transport. This exclusive competence of the EU in the area of maritime transport is confirmed in Articles 91 and 100(2) TFEU.

The Commission intends to start proceedings against Greece for breach of Article 4(3) TEU, and Articles 91 and 100(2) TFEU. Greece's arguments in defence are first that, it submitted only a proposal, i.e. a non-binding measure, to the IMO, and second, on the basis of a gentleman's agreement adopted by the Council of the European Union in 1993, it was allowed to submit proposals to the IMO.

Advise Greece whether it has infringed Article 4(3) TEU, and Articles 91 and 100(2) TFEU.

ESSAY QUESTION

Explain the main features of the enhanced co-operation procedure and critically assess its impact on the harmonious and uniform development of the EU.

AIDE-MÉMOIRE

Competences of the EU are exercised under the principal of conferral, i.e the EU can exercise competences conferred on it by the Treaties. Competences not conferred on the EU remain with the Member States. Under Article 2(2) TFEU there is the possibility to give a shared competence back to the Member States when, and if, the EU decides to cease exercising it.

The TOL distinguishes three main types of competences

EXCLUSIVE	SHARED	SUPPORTIVE
Only the EU has competence to legislate in areas of its exclusive competence. The principle of proportionality applies but not the principle of subsidiarity	In the areas of shared competences both the EU and the Member States can legislate. The principle of subsidiarity and proportionality apply. Under Protocol 2 national parliaments control the application of the principle of subsidiarity through the "yellow and orange cards" procedure	In the areas of supportive competences Member States have exclusive competence but the EU can provide support and co-ordination (but not harmonisation)

COMPETENCES	POLICY AREAS
EXCLUSIVE THE EXHAUSTIVE LIST OF EXCLUSIVE COMPETENCES IS CONTAINED IN ARTICLE 3 TFEU	• THE CUSTOMS UNION • COMPETITION RULES NECESSARY FOR THE FUNCTIONING OF THE INTERNAL MARKET • MONETARY POLICY FOR MEMBER STATES WHICH HAVE ADOPTED THE EURO • CONSERVATION OF MARINE BIOLOGICAL RESOURCES UNDER THE COMMON FISHERIES POLICY • THE COMMON COMMERCIAL POLICY • CONCLUSION OF AN INTERNATIONAL AGREEMENT COVERED BY AN EXCLUSIVE INTERNAL COMPETENCE (THE ERTA CASE)
SHARED SOME ARE IDENTIFIED IN ARTICLE 4 TFEU, THE REMAINDER ARE DETERMINED ON THE BASIS OF ELIMINATION, I.E. A COMPETENCE IS SHARED IF IT IS NEITHER MENTIONED UNDER EXCLUSIVE NOR UNDER SUPPORTIVE COMPETENCE	• THE INTERNAL MARKET • SOCIAL POLICY FOR ASPECTS DEFINED IN THE TFEU • ECONOMIC, SOCIAL AND TERRITORIAL COHESION • AGRICULTURE AND FISHERIES, EXCLUDING CONSERVATION OF MARINE BIOLOGICAL RESOURCES • ENVIRONMENT • CONSUMER PROTECTION • TRANSPORT • TRANS-EUROPEAN NETWORKS • ENERGY • THE AFSJ • COMMON SAFETY CONCERNS IN PUBLIC HEALTH MATTERS IN RESPECT OF THE ASPECTS DEFINED IN THE TFEU • THE AREAS OF RESEARCH, TECHNOLOGICAL DEVELOPMENT AND SPACE BUT THE EU'S EXERCISE OF THAT COMPETENCE "SHALL NOT RESULT IN MEMBER STATES BEING PREVENTED FROM EXERCISING THEIRS" • THE AREAS OF DEVELOPMENT CO-OPERATION AND HUMANITARIAN AID BUT THE EU'S EXERCISE OF THAT COMPETENCE "SHALL NOT RESULT IN MEMBER STATES BEING PREVENTED FROM EXERCISING THEIRS"
SUPPORTIVE THE EXHAUSTIVE LIST OF SUPPORTIVE COMPETENCES IS CONTAINED IN ARTICE 6 TFEU	• PROTECTION AND IMPROVEMENT OF HUMAN HEALTH • INDUSTRY • CULTURE • TOURISM • EDUCATIONAL, VOCATIONAL TRAINING, YOUTH AND SPORT • CIVIL PROTECTION • ADMINISTRATIVE CO-OPERATION

NOTE: SPECIAL RULES APPLY TO ECONOMIC, EMPLOYMENT, SOCIAL POLICIES AND THE CFSP

RULES RELATING TO THE ESTABLISHMENT OF ENHANCED CO-OPERATION

	GENERAL ENHANCED CO-OPERATION	ENHANCED CO-OPERATION IN THE AREA OF FSJ IN CRIMINAL MATTERS	ENHANCED CO-OPERATION IN THE CFSP	ENHANCED CO-OPERATION IN THE CSDP (PERMANENT STRUCTURED CO-OPERATION)
AUTHORISING EU INSTITUTION	THE COUNCIL	NOT REQUIRED	THE COUNCIL	THE COUNCIL
TYPE OF VOTE IN THE COUNCIL	QMV	N/A	UNANIMITY	QMV
MINIMUM NUMBER OF MEMBER STATES REQUIRED TO ESTABLISH ENHANCED CO-OPERATION	9	9	9	NO MINIMUM IS SET
TYPE OF PROCEDURE USED BY THE EP	CONSENT	THE EP MUST BE INFORMED	THE EP MUST BE INFORMED	N/A
PARTICIPATION OF THE COMMISSION	THE COMMISSION MAKES A PROPOSAL	THE COMMISSION MUST BE INFORMED	THE COMMISSION GIVES ITS OPINION	N/A
PARTICIPATION OF OTHER EU INSTITUTIONS OR BODIES	N/A	N/A	THE HR MUST GIVE HER OPINION	THE HR MUST GIVE HER OPINION

7

THE COMMON FOREIGN AND SECURITY POLICY (CFSP): A COMPONENT OF EU FOREIGN ACTION

CHAPTER OUTLINE

1. Under the ToL the intrinsic dualism of the EU's foreign action remains in that external action under the TFEU is conducted in accordance with the "EU method" and the CFSP is "subject to specific rules and procedures" (Article 24 TEU), i.e. the intergovernmental method. However, the ToL established new institutional arrangements and mechanisms aimed at enhancing the coherence and efficiency of EU external action.

2. The main innovations introduced by the ToL aimed at improving the coherence of EU foreign policy were:

■ The creation of the post of the High Representative of the Union for Foreign Affairs and Security Policy (HR);

■ The establishment of the European External Action Service (EEAS);

■ The ability for the European Council to make determinations of "strategic interests and objectives" for all EU external action; and,

■ The creation of the post of the President of the European Council who exercises external representative responsibilities.

3. The ToL refers to the EU's external action as comprising all its policies towards the wider world and sets out the principles and objectives applicable to all areas of EU foreign action whether provided for in the TFEU or the TEU. The principles are those which have inspired the creation, development and enlargement of the EU. The objectives are listed in Article 21(2) TEU.

4. The European Council and the Council are the main decision making bodies within the CFSP. The main role of the European Council is to "identify the Union's strategic interests, determine the objectives of and define general guidelines" for the CFSP as well as to decide on EU strategy when facing international crises. The Council "shall frame the common foreign and security policy and take the decisions necessary for defining and implementing it on the basis of the general guidelines and strategic lines defined by the European Council". However, neither the European Council nor the Council are empowered to adopt legislative acts in respect of any CFSP matters. The European Council acts by unanimity, so does the Council, subject to exceptions concerning mainly decisions implementing the European Council guidelines and the potential use of the "*passerelle* clause". The Commission, resulting from the HR being *ex officio* Vice-President of the Commission, is fully associated with the CFSP. It is the HR, not the Commission, who has the right to initiate proposals in the CFSP areas. The EP is consulted and kept informed. The ECJ has no jurisdiction under the CFSP but it is required to ensure that the CFSP does not encroach on other EU policies and *vice versa*, and has jurisdiction to review the legality of sanctions imposed against natural and legal persons under the CFSP. As to the Member States they are required to implement measures adopted by the Council, co-operate with each other and "actively and unreservedly in a spirit of loyalty and mutual solidarity" support the CFSP.

5. With regard to the Common Security and Defence Policy (CSDP) the ToL:

■ Extended and enhanced the objectives of the CSDP;

■ Introduced a "mutual defence clause" and a "solidarity clause";

■ Established new procedures to finance "urgent initiatives" under the CFSP, and in particular preparatory activities for CSDP missions, i.e. measures ensuring rapid access to the EU budget and the creation of a "start-up fund";

■ Provided for the possibility of the Council to entrust the implementation of a CSDP operational task to a "coalition of willing and able States";

■ Established the European Defence Agency (EDA);

■ Increased flexibility as to the establishment and subsequent development of the "permanent structured co-operation"; and,

■ Expanded the Petersberg tasks (see Chapter 7.6.1) to include joint disarmament operations, military advice and assistance tasks, conflict prevention and post-conflict stabilisation.

6. Resulting from the ToL the CFSP has the potential to have a stronger political profile and an increased capacity to act consistently on the international stage. The main mechanism for ensuring this is the creation of the post of HR who has the necessary power under the Treaties, a substantial budget and a diplomatic corps, i.e. the EEAS, and who is empowered to speak on behalf of the EU, even in front of the UN Security Council.

7.1 Introduction

The EU is often described as an economic giant but a political dwarf.[386] Its economic weight in the international arena has not been matched by an equal gravitas in international politics. This dichotomy can be explained by historical reasons. From its inception the Community was a "civilian power",[387] that is, an organisation implicitly rejecting power politics and concentrating on the economic aspects of European integration.[388] In reality, it lacked military capacity to conduct a defence policy. This aspect of European affairs was developed mainly within the framework of NATO. The collapse of Communism, the reunification of Germany and the American policy of burden-shedding in military matters have changed perspectives on Europe's future foreign and defence policy. However, the realistic objective of the CFSP for the EU was and remains more to agree on a common position in international policy (that is, to speak with one voice) than to achieve a unified foreign policy conducted by supranational bodies, with the EU raised to the status of a superpower. This is because Member States are not currently willing, and may never be willing, to give up their exclusive power to conduct national and foreign policies as they wish. In particular, Member States which have a substantive military capability do not wish to lose the power and influence which that capability affords them in the international arena.

7.2 Dualism of EU foreign action

Prior to the entry into force of the ToL, only the Communities were expressly recognised as having international legal personality. However, it was generally agreed that the EU had implicitly acquired international legal personality.[389] This situation was highly unsatisfactory, as it created confusion outside the EU and diminished its external role. Under the ToL the EU absorbed the legal personality of the EC. Article 47 TEU states that only the EU has international legal personality. This means that the Union can enter into international agreements with third countries and international organisations, be held liable for breaches of international law, and seek redress at the international level against other subjects of international law which have infringed its rights.

Prior to the entry into force of the ToL, the external action of the EU was conducted in Pillar 1 in accordance with the "EU method" and in Pillars 2 and 3 in accordance with the intergovernmental method (see Chapter 1.7). Although the ToL abolished the Pillar structure the distinction between the EU method and the intergovernmental method remains.[390] Article 24 TEU states that the CFSP and its vital component, the Common Security and Defence Policy (CSDP), is "subject to specific rules and

---

386. K. Neumann, "European Security after Iraq: Challenges and Options", in K. Von Wogau (ed.) *The Path to European Defence*, 2004, Antwerp: Maklu Publishers, 69.

387. H. Bull, "Civilian Power Europe?" (1982) *Journal of Common Market Studies*, 149.

388. P. Tsakaloyannis, "From Civilian Power to Military Integration", in J. Lodge (ed.), *The EC and the Challenge of the Future*, 1989, London: Pinter, 243.

389. P. de Schoutheete and S. Andoura, "The Legal Personality of the European Union", (2007) LX *Studia Diplomatica*, 1–9.

390. J. Wouters, D. Coppens and B. De Meester, "The European Union's External Relations after the Lisbon Treaty", in S. Griller and J. Ziller (eds.), *The Lisbon Treaty: EU Constitutionalism without a Constitutional Treaty?* 2008, Vienna and New York: Springer, 143–203.

procedures", i.e. the intergovernmental method. This results in provisions relating to the EU foreign policy being found in both the TFEU and the TEU. With regard to the TFEU, some foreign policies are expressly covered by its provisions, e.g. trade; development assistance; other forms of co-operation with third States; humanitarian aid; neighbouring policy; enlargement; and, diplomatic and consular protection of EU citizens when in a non EU country where their own State has no representation, others are based on the doctrine of implied powers (see Chapter 6.2.2). Under this doctrine, which was loosely codified in Article 216(1) TFEU every internal policy of the EU may potentially have an external dimension, including the AFSJ (see Chapter 31). The TEU contains mainly rules concerning the CFSP including the CSDP.

One of the main objectives of the reform leading to the adoption of the ToL was to enhance the coherence of the EU's foreign policy, i.e. to make the EU's external action more efficient and effective despite the division between intergovernmental CFSP and other areas of EU foreign action. The option of applying the "EU method" to the CFSP was non-existent. For example, the British Government clearly stated its position in its 2007 White Paper entitled "The Reform Treaty: The British Approach to the European Union Intergovernmental Conference" that a condition of signing of the ToL was "the maintenance of the UK's independent foreign and defence policy".[391] In those circumstances the ToL represented a step towards greater coherence both in terms of the location in the EU's Treaty architecture of provisions relating to the external action of the EU and in terms of establishing new institutional arrangements and mechanisms with a view to maximising EU influence and presence on the global stage.

With regard to the ToL's architecture, a new Chapter I of Title V on "General Provisions on the Union's External Action" was inserted into the TEU which sets out principles and objectives applicable to all provisions relating to EU external action irrespective of whether those provisions are located in the TFEU or the TEU. However, the splitting of provisions on the EU's external action into those governed by the "EU method" (which are located in the TFEU) and those to which the intergovernmental method applies (which are contained in the TEU) has not been complete. Some provisions of the TFEU are relevant to the CFSP (e.g. those relating to enhanced co-operation; those concerning the new "solidarity clause" (see Chapter 2.2); and, the provisions on the imposition of economic or diplomatic sanctions on natural and legal persons) and *vice versa*.

With regard to institutional innovations the most important is the establishment of the post of a High Representative of the Union for Foreign Affairs and Security Policy (hereafter the HR) who ensures the uniform external representation of the EU, i.e. the HR is the single face and voice of the EU on the world political stage.

7.3 Innovations introduced by the ToL aimed at improving the coherence of EU foreign action

The main innovations were: the creation of the post of the HR; the establishment of the European External Action Service (EEAS); and, the ability for the European Council to make determinations of "strategic interests and objectives" for all EU external action. However, the complexity of the nature of EU's external representation remains bearing in mind that the President of the European Council has external representative responsibilities in respect of the CFSP (see Chapter 3.5.5).

---

391. The Reform Treaty: The British Approach to the European Union Intergovernmental Conference, July 2007, CM 7174, 7.

7.3.1 Creation of the post of the HR

The procedure for appointment of the HR is as follows: the European Council acting by a qualified majority, with the agreement of the President of the Commission, appoints the HR. Subsequently, the HR, the President of the Commission and the Commissioners must be approved by the EP by a vote of consent. The first HR, Baroness Catherine Ashton, was appointed in accord with this procedure in November 2009 for a five year term.

The holder of the post wears three hats:

■ She is the Vice-President of the Commission and, as a member of the Commission, responsible for External Relations. The position of the HR in the Commission is very strong in that the HR is the only Vice-President and the only Commissioner who is appointed *ex officio* (although subject to the approval of the President of the Commission) and the only Commissioner who cannot be forced by the President of the Commission to resign. However, the EP has the right to apply a motion of censure on the entire Commission, including the HR (see Chapter 3.6.7). Further, the European Council, with the approval of the President of the Commission, may end the HR's term of office. It is to be noted that the HR is bound by Commission procedures to the extent that this is consistent with the tasks carried out by her within the CFSP. Under Article 18(4) TEU, the HR as a Commissioner, is "responsible within the Commission for responsibilities incumbent upon it in external relations and for co-ordinating other aspects of the Union's external action".

■ She replaced the High Representative for the Common Foreign and Security Policy, a post created under the ToA which was assigned to the Secretary General of the Council. The post of Secretary General of the Council became a separate post from that of HR.

Within the framework of the CFSP, the HR:

● ensures unity, consistency and effectiveness of EU action relating to the CFSP acting in co-operation with the Council and the Commission;
● assists the Council in all matters relating to the CFSP;
● if requested, acts on behalf of the Council in conducting political dialogue with third parties;
● ensures the implementation of CFSP decisions together with the Council and the Member States;
● refers any question, initiative or proposal on the CFSP to the Council;
● represents the EU externally in all CFSP matters including before the UN Security Council;
● regularly consults the EP;
● has the right to propose the appointment of EU Special Representatives, who are accountable to her, with a mandate in relation to particular policy issues (Article 33 TEU);
● is responsible for facilitating the harmonisation of Member States' views on the CFSP; and,
● fulfils many other tasks which are set out in the aide-mémoire to this chapter.

■ She is the President of the Foreign Affairs Council. In this capacity, the HR has the right to make proposals to the Council and the right to convene extraordinary meetings of the Foreign Affairs Council at either her own initiative or that of a Member State. Views differ as to whether it is a good idea to submit proposals to a body which one chairs.

By merging three posts, the ToL ensured uniform external representation as well as greater coherence and unity in the conduct of EU foreign policy.[392] However, some Member States fear that too much power has been vested in one post. In this respect it can be said that with regard to the CFSP the HR only supervises the implementation of measures adopted by the European Council and the Council acting unanimously, This is clearly stated in Declaration 14 attached to the Treaties which provides that the provisions of the CFSP, including those relating to the new post of HR:

> "will not affect the existing legal basis, responsibility and powers of each Member State in relation to the formulation and conduct of its foreign policy, its national diplomatic service, relations with third countries and participation in international organizations, including a Member State's membership of the Security Council of the UN."

Declarations 13 and 14 emphasise that the ToL will not give any new powers to the Commission or the EP, and that defence and security matters are within the exclusive competence of each Member State.

If the Member States do not all agree on a common policy with regard to a particular international issue, the HR will have no reason to exercise her power of implementation. However, if there is agreement between the Member States to present a common front on a particular issue, the voice of the HR (being the voice of 27 countries) will carry enormous weight.

7.3.2 Establishment of the EEAS

In order to assist the HR is performing her tasks a new body, the European External Action Service (EEAS) was created by the ToL. This body, accountable to the HR, is made up of officials from the relevant departments of the General Secretariat of the Council and of the Commission as well as diplomats from the Member States. Council Decision 2010/427/EU of 26 July 2010[393] outlined the organisation, structure and functioning of the EEAS. The Decision describes the EEAS as a functional autonomous body of the EU separate from the Commission and the Council and endows it with its own independent budget. The EEAS was formally launched on 1 December 2010 and is expected to have a staff of about 5,400. It is in fact the foreign ministry of the EU. Its main task is not only to assist the HR, but also to assist the President of the European Council, the President of the Commission and Commissioners in the area of external relations and to work in close co-operation with the diplomatic services of Member States. The EEAS maintains diplomatic relations with almost all countries in the world and oversees the implementation of the EU's aid and humanitarian budget. Internally, it is divided into directorates-general. Externally, it has more than 130 delegations in non-Member States and international organisations which have functions similar to those of an embassy.

The creation of the EEAS was as controversial as the creation of the post of HR, in that it suggested that it is, in fact, the beginning of a European foreign service and will constitute a threat to the national foreign services of the Member States. A further controversy concerns the relationship between the Commission and the EEAS in that the Commission remains in control of the EU's Trade, Aid, Development, Energy and Enlargement policies whilst Neighbourhood and International Development policies are to be shared between the Commission and the EEAS. It has been argued that rivalry between the Commission and the EEAS relating to different strands of EU external action will cause friction and

---

392. C. Kaddous, "Role and position of the High Representative of the Union for Foreign Affairs and Security Policy under the Lisbon Treaty", in S. Griller and J. Ziller (eds), *The Lisbon Treaty: EU Constitutionalism without a Constitutional Treaty?* 2008, Vienna and New York: Springer, 205–21.

393. [2010] OJ L201/30.

undermine the coherence of EU foreign action. In this respect, it must be noted that the HR, being a Commissioner, should ensure appropriate co-ordination between the EEAS and the Commission. Finally, the EP, which controls the EEAS mainly *via* the budgetary procedure, wants to play a more prominent role in controlling the EEAS, in particular it wishes to acquire the right to participate in the appointments of senior EEAS officials.

7.3.3 The power of the European Council to make determinations under Article 22 TEU

Under Article 22 TEU the European Council has the ability to make determinations of "strategic interests and objectives" for all EU external action. Such determinations "shall concern the relations of the Union with a specific country or region or may be thematic in approach. They shall define their duration, and the means to be made available by the Union and the Member States" (Article 22(1) TEU). The determinations will be made by the European Council on a recommendation from the Council to which the HR, for the CFSP, and the Commission, for non-CFSP foreign policy, may submit joint proposals.

7.3.4 The powers of the President of the European Council in EU external action

One of the main tasks of the President of the European Council, a new position created by the ToL, is to "provide impetus" for the work of the European Council, to ensure "the preparation and continuity" of its work and to facilitate cohesion and consensus within the European Council. Thus he has a great influence on the work of the European Council in all areas of EU activity including its external action which are defined in Article 22 TEU. The President of the European Council is also entitled to convene extraordinary meetings to deal with new international developments. Further, without prejudice to the powers of the HR, the President of the European Council ensures the external representation of the EU on issues concerning the CFSP.

7.4 The principles and objectives of EU foreign action

Article 21 TEU sets out the principles which will guide the EU's external action. These principles, inspired by the EU's creation, development and enlargement, are: democracy, respect for the rule of law, the protection of fundamental rights, respect for human dignity, observance of the principles of equality and solidarity, and respect for the principles of the UN Charter and international law.

Article 21(2) TEU lists the EU's objectives in its external relations. It states:

"The Union shall define and pursue common policies and actions, and shall work for a high degree of cooperation in all fields of international relations, in order to:

(a)   safeguard its values, fundamental interests, security, independence and integrity;

(b)   consolidate and support democracy, the rule of law, human rights and the principles of international law;

(c)   preserve peace, prevent conflicts and strengthen international security, in accordance with the purposes and principles of the United Nations Charter, with the principles of the Helsinki Final Act and with the aims of the Charter of Paris, including those relating to external borders;

(d)   foster the sustainable economic, social and environmental development of developing countries, with the primary aim of eradicating poverty;

(e)   encourage the integration of all countries into the world economy, including through the progressive abolition of restrictions on international trade;

(f)   help develop international measures to preserve and improve the quality of the environment and the sustainable management of global natural resources, in order to ensure sustainable development;

(g)   assist populations, countries and regions confronting natural or man-made disasters; and

(h)   promote an international system based on stronger multilateral cooperation and good global governance."

7.5   The Common Foreign and Security Policy (CFSP)

Specific provisions on CFSP are contained in Chapter 2 TEU. Section 1 of Chapter 2 deals with the CFSP (Articles 23–41 TEU), whilst section 2 applies to CSDP, the vital component the CFSP (Articles 42–47 TEU). The objectives for the CFSP are the same as those set out for all foreign EU action. Under Article 25 TEU they are to be pursued through:

"(a)   the general guidelines;

 (b)   decisions defining:

   (i)   actions to be undertaken by the Union;

   (ii) positions to be taken by the Union;

   (iii) arrangements for the implementation of the decisions referred to in points (i) and (ii); and by

(c)   strengthening systematic cooperation between Member States in the conduct of policy."

7.5.1   The powers of the decision-making bodies under the CFSP

The main decision-making bodies within the CFSP are the European Council and the Council in its formation of the Foreign Affairs Council. The European Council "shall identify the Union's strategic interests, determine the objectives of and define general guidelines for the common foreign and security policy, including for matters with defence implications". At extraordinary meetings convened to deal with emergency situations, the European Council will have power to define the Union's strategy in respect of such situations (Article 26(1) TEU).

Under Article 26(2) TEU the Council "shall frame the common foreign and security policy and take the decisions necessary for defining and implementing it on the basis of the general guidelines and strategic lines defined by the European Council".

Under Article 31(1) TEU, neither the European Council nor the Council is empowered to adopt legislative acts in respect of CFSP matters.

Both the European Council and the Council act by unanimity except where the treaty specifically provides otherwise (Article 31 TEU). The main exceptions, under which the Council may act by QMV, are contained in Article 31(2) TEU and concern the following four types of decision:

■   those which define an action or position on the basis of a decision of the European Council relating to the Union's strategic interests and objectives, as referred to in Article 22(1) TEU. In this situation the Council will implement any decision reached unanimously by the European Council;

■   those which define an action or position on the basis of a proposal made by the High Representative "following a specific request from the European Council, made on its own initiative or that of the

High Representative". In this situation the Council will act on the basis of a request unanimously agreed by the European Council;

■ those which implement a decision defining a Union action or position. The Council will vote by QMV in respect of a decision unanimously taken by the European Council; and,

■ those concerning the appointment of a special representative in accordance with Article 33 TEU. As above, the Council will implement a decision taken unanimously by the European Council.

In the above four situations the rule that decisions under the CFSP are taken unanimously is not challenged. The ToL only confirms the principle previously established under Pillar 2 that the Council is entitled to adopt implementing measures by QMV. Under Article 238(4) TFEU abstentions do not prevent a decision from being adopted by unanimity.

The list of exceptions set out in Article 31(2) TEU is not complete. There are the following additional exceptions which concern:

■ decisions relating to a "start-up fund" (Article 41(3) TEU);

■ decisions relating to the statute, seat and operational rules of the European Defence Agency (Article 45 TEU);

■ some decisions regarding Permanent Structured Co-Operation (see Chapter 6.9.5); and,

■ decisions relating to procedural matters.

Further, Article 31(3) TEU contains a "*passerelle*" provision under which QMV may apply to matters not expressly mentioned under Article 31(2). However, only the European Council acting unanimously may decide to make use of the "*passerelle*" provision. Therefore, the "*passerelle*" provision is unlikely to be used. In the UK, the government is required to obtain approval of both Houses of Parliament before agreeing on the use of the "*passerelle*" provision.

Even in respect of exceptions set out in Article 31(2) TEU a Member State may object to the Council's voting by QMV. Article 31(2) TEU contains "an emergency brake" procedure under which when a Member State considers that for vital and stated reasons of national policy the use of QMV is inappropriate, the vote will not be taken. The HR will intervene and will try to act as a broker, and if she fails, the matter will be referred to the European Council for a decision by unanimity.

A Member State may exercise "constructive abstention", i.e. may abstain from voting in respect of the adoption of a particular decision which requires unanimity and thus not hinder its adoption. The purpose of the use of constructive abstention is to alleviate the rigid principle of unanimity in the CFSP. It is a choice of a Member State whether to use a veto or whether to abstain. When abstaining in a vote a Member State may qualify its abstention by making a formal declaration. If this occurs, a Member State is not obliged to apply the decision but must not act in a manner which will conflict with EU action taken pursuant to that decision. However, the rule of "constructive abstention" does not apply if the number of Member States abstaining in such a manner represents more than one third of the Member States comprising at least one third of the population of the EU, so the consequence here is that the decision is not adopted (Article 31(1) TEU).

7.5.2 The role of the Political and Security Committee (PSC)

The PSC is vital to the CFSP and the CSDP. The PSC is made up of permanent representatives of the Member States at ambassadorial level. The PSC meets two, or three times a week. Under the CFSP, the

PSC contributes to defining EU external policies and responds to international crises by delivering opinions to the Council at the request of the Council, the HR or, on its own initiative. It also affects implementation of agreed policies, without prejudice to the powers of the HR.

7.5.3 Role of the Commission, the EP and the ECJ in the CFSP

The Commission is fully associated with the CFSP. The Commission and the HR may submit jointly proposals to the European Council concerning non-CFSP areas (Article 22 TEU). However, under the ToL the Commission has lost its right of initiative in respect of the CFSP in favour of the HR.

The EP is a consultative body under the CFSP. The HR is required to inform, and regularly consult with, the EP on the "main aspects and basic choices" of the CFSP and the CSDP and to ensure that the views of the EP are taken into account. The EP is entitled to ask the Council questions and to make recommendations to it and to the HR. It also holds twice a year an annual debate on progress in implementing the CFSP and CSDP (Article 36 TEU). As a result, democratic control by the EU of the CFSP is still weak as it consists mainly of consultations with the EP.

The ECJ has no jurisdiction in respect of matters covered by the CFSP. However, it has jurisdiction to ensure that the CFSP does not encroach on other EU policies and *vice versa*, i.e. that non-CFSP policies do not impinge on the CFSP (Article 40 TEU). Further, under Article 275 TFEU, the ECJ has jurisdiction to review the legality of sanctions against natural or legal persons imposed under the CFSP (Article 24(1) TEU).

7.5.4 Commitments of Member States under the CFSP

The ToL strengthened the commitment of Member States to the achievement of the objectives of the CFSP. Article 24(3) TEU stresses that "The Member States shall work together to enhance and develop their mutual political solidarity. They shall refrain from any action which is contrary to the interests of the Union or likely to impair its effectiveness as a cohesive force in international relations".

The main commitment of the Member States within the CFSP is to implement measures adopted by the Council.

Member States have obligations towards each other to consult and exchange information, especially when only some of them are members of particular international organisations or attend particular international conferences where decisions that potentially affect all of them may be taken.

Member States also have obligations with regard to the Union. In this respect, the Member States must support the CFSP "actively and unreservedly in a spirit of loyalty and mutual solidarity" (Article 24(3) TEU). If a Member State is a member of an international organisation where decisions that potentially affect the Union may be taken, that Member State must defend the interests of the EU (Article 34(2) TEU). In the case of the Permanent Members of the UN Security Council, this must be achieved without compromising their responsibilities deriving from the UN Charter. Also, diplomatic and consular missions of Member States and EU delegations to third countries and to international organisations must co-operate in ensuring that actions taken by the EU are complied with and implemented. Furthermore, they are required to exchange information, carry out joint assessments and contribute to the implementation of Article 20(2)(c) TFEU and Article 23 TEU, that is, to ensure diplomatic and consular protection of EU citizens in countries where their governments are not represented (see Chapter 22.6).

7.6 The Common Security and Defence Policy (CSDP)

It is important to emphasise the connection between the CSDP and other EU policies, in particular those relating to the creation of the AFSJ. Many structures and mechanisms set up under one policy support, develop and enhance another. Consistency and efficiency require that whatever security, emergency or other serious problems arise in an area, the EU must tackle them using the full spectrum of its capabilities and resources. Article 21(3) TEU imposes an obligation on the Council and the Commission, assisted by the HR, to co-operate in order to ensure such consistency.

The CSDP, which is a vital component of the CFSP, has its own objectives in addition to those set out in respect of all EU external action. Article 42(2) TEU provides that "The common security and defence policy shall include the progressive framing of a common Union defence policy. This will lead to a common defence, when the European Council, acting unanimously, so decides." The main innovations of the ToL concerning the CSDP were:

- The inclusion of a form of mutual defence clause. If one Member State becomes a victim of armed aggression all other Member States are bound to aid and assist that victim State by all means in their power. However, such assistance must:
  - be in conformity with Article 51 of the UN Charter which contains an exception to the prohibition of the use of force in international relations on the ground of self-defence;
  - respect commitments of Member States which are members of NATO, which remains the basis of their collective defence and the forum for their implementation; and,
  - be consistent with "the specific character of the security and defence policy of certain Member States" (Article 42(7) TEU);
- The inclusion of a "solidarity clause" contained in Article 222 TFEU. The clause does not specifically apply to the CSDP but is relevant in all situations where a Member State is the object of a terrorist attack or victim of a natural or man-made disaster. In those circumstances the EU and its Member States are required to assist the State concerned with all relevant means including military;
- The establishment of new procedures to finance "urgent initiatives" under the CFSP, and in particular preparatory activities for CSDP missions. Timely and appropriate levels of financing of such missions, as they are performed using capabilities provided by the Member States, are vital for their success. In order to ensure "rapid access" to the EU budget for missions financed by the EU, the Council will adopt a decision establishing the appropriate procedures. For missions which will not be financed from the Union budget, a new "start-up fund" will be established to which Member States will contribute. The details relating to the establishment, financing (in particular the amounts to be contributed to the fund) and functioning of the "start-up fund" will be provided by a Council decision. The "start-up fund" is seen by many as the first step towards the establishment of a common defence budget for the EU. Under Article 41(3) TEU, the HR is authorised to use the "start-up fund";
- The possibility for the Council to entrust the implementation of a CSDP operational task to a group of Member States which are "willing and have the necessary capacity" to accomplish it. The HR is to be associated with any such "coalition of the able and willing" among the Member States in terms of working out details concerning the management of the tasks in question;

- The establishment of the European Defence Agency (EDA) (which in fact was created in 2004!)[394] with a view to progressively improving the military capabilities of the Member States. Individual Member States will decide whether to join the EDA. The tasks of the EDA are set out in Article 45 TEU;

- The establishment of "permanent structured co-operation" which constitutes a specific form of enhanced co-operation in the areas covered by the CSDP; and,

- The expansion of the "Petersberg tasks" (see Chapter 7.6.1) to include joint disarmament operations, military advice and assistance tasks, conflict prevention and post-conflict stabilisation (Article 43 TEU).

The CSDP has two dimensions: the defence dimension and the security dimension. They are examined below.

7.6.1 The defence dimension

When the Maastricht Treaty was negotiated the Member States agreed to include "the eventual framing of a common defence policy, which might lead to a common defence" in the scope of that Treaty. Under Pillar 2 of the TEU, the Western European Union (WEU) was made responsible for ensuring a common defence policy.

The WEU was founded on 6 May 1955 on the basis of the Brussels Treaty of 1948, which provided for collective defence and co-operation in economic, social and cultural matters. The WEU was only intended to strengthen security co-operation among its Contracting States and for that reason activities other than defence were subsequently transferred to the Council of Europe. As a result of the creation of NATO, the WEU lost its importance at European level. The EU re-energised the WEU for many reasons, *inter alia*, because not all Member States were members of NATO and because of the desire of the US to reduce its military commitments in Europe.

In June 1992, at a meeting near Bonn, the foreign ministers and defence ministers of the WEU countries had defined the future objectives of the WEU. These were called "Petersberg tasks" (named after the Hotel Petersberg where the meeting took place) and consisted of:

- conflict prevention tasks;

- humanitarian and rescue tasks;

- peacekeeping tasks; and,

- tasks of combat forces in crisis management including peacemaking.

The ToA incorporated the Petersberg tasks into Title V of the TEU. Thus, all Member States whether or not members of WEU could participate in carrying out the Petersberg tasks.

In 1996, at a meeting in Berlin, NATO foreign ministers decided to build up the European Security and Defence Identity (ESDI) within the NATO structures rather than within the EU. This led to the establishment of close links with the WEU, which, under various agreements, was allowed to use NATO assets and capacities in its own military operations executed on behalf of the EU.

The Balkan War in 1995, and in particular NATO's intervention in Kosovo, changed the course of the EU defence policy. British Prime Minister Tony Blair and French President Jacques Chirac, for

---

394.　Under a Joint Action adopted by the Council on 12 July 2004 [2004] O J L45/17.

different reasons, recognised the necessity of setting up a new, genuine European defence strategy. In December 1998 at St Malo they issued a Declaration stating that:

"the Union must have the capacity for autonomous action, backed by credible military forces, the means to decide to use them, and a readiness to do so, in order to respond to international crises."[395]

The Cologne European Council (June 1999) endorsed the above Franco-British declaration and stated that the EU should have the ability to fulfil Petersberg tasks without prejudice to actions by NATO. The Cologne European Council outlined the ESDP [now the CSDP] and thus rejected the ESDI. The Council stated that the integration of the WEU into the EU, despite the previous arrangement, had to be abandoned as the Petersberg tasks would in future be carried out within the framework of the EU. As a result, the performance of the Petersberg tasks became part of the ESDP, and is now part of the CSDP. They are listed in Article 43(1) TEU.[396]

The CSDP has three components: military, civilian and conflict prevention.

7.6.1.1 The military component

The content of this component was defined by the Helsinki European Council (December 1999). The Council agreed that:

■ By 2003 Member States must, between them and co-operating on a voluntary basis in operations directed by the EU, be able to deploy within 60 days and to sustain for at least one year military forces of up to 50,000–60,000 persons in order to carry out the Petersberg tasks. This was the main objective of the military component and it was called a "Headline Goal";

■ New political and military bodies and structures should be established to ensure the necessary political and strategic direction of the above operations;

■ New arrangements should be made in order to ensure full consultation, co-operation and transparency between the EU and NATO; and,

■ Appropriate arrangements should be put in place for non-European NATO members and other interested States to contribute to EU military crisis management.

Once the ambitious agenda of the Helsinki European Council was largely achieved, the European Council of June 2004 decided to further develop the EU's military crisis management capability by setting new "Headline Goal 2010". Under this document, the Member States made a commitment that by the year 2010, at the latest, they would be capable of responding "with rapid and decisive action applying a fully coherent approach to the whole spectrum of crisis management operations" and would redress shortfalls identified in the previous Headline Goal.[397]

The so-called "Headline Goal" has materialised as the European Rapid Reaction Force (ERRF).[398] The formal agreement creating the ERRF was signed on 22 November 2004, and the ERRF was

---

395. Available at http://www.fco.gov.uk/resources/en/news/2002/02/joint-declaration-on-eu-new01795 (accessed 7/8/12).

396. See G. L. Graf von Kielmansegg, "The Meaning of Petersberg: Some Considerations on the Legal Scope of ESDP operations", (2007) 44 CMLRev., 629.

397. The Headline Goal 2010 together with the Council Declaration of 8 December 2008 on the Enhancement of the Capacities of the European Security and Defence Policy can be found at http://www.consilium.europa.eu/showPage.aspx?id=1349&lang=EN (accessed 7/8/12).

398. On this topic see: F. Naert, *International Law Aspects of the EU's Security and Defence Policy, with a Particular Focus on the Law of Armed Conflict*, 2010, Antwerp: Intersentia, ch. 3.

programmed to be fully operational by 2005. Informally, the ERRF, consisting of fewer than 50,000 soldiers, was put at the disposal of the EU much earlier. The first mission of the ERRF, known as "Operation Concordia", was launched on 31 March 2003 in the Former Yugoslav Republic of Macedonia and consisted of peacekeeping and other tasks necessary to control civil unrest in the FYR Macedonia. That mission was successfully accomplished and indeed, the list of completed and ongoing military EU operations is impressive.[399]

The ERRF is neither an EU army nor a standing army. Troops or units assigned by national armies to be part of the ERRF remain with their national armies, unless they are deployed by the EU. The commitment of national forces to any particular EU operation remains a sovereign decision of the Member State concerned.

Part of the military component, but this also can be part of the civilian component (see Chapter 7.6.1.2), is the European Union Battle Groups (EU BGs), which became operational on 1 January 2007. Each group comprises 1,500 combat soldiers. Larger Member States have their own battle groups while smaller Member States have created common groups. There are 18 groups which rotate every six months; two are always ready for immediate deployment. The EU BGs are at the disposal of the EU, can be deployed within five to ten days to deal with emergency situations when the UN or NATO cannot intervene quickly enough, and are sustainable for at least 30 days. They are intended to carry out the Petersberg tasks, in particular to undertake rapid response operations either for stand-alone operations or for the initial stage of larger operations. However, EU BGs have never been deployed. One of the main reasons is that for them to be deployed the unanimous approval of all 27 Member States is required.

In the context of the military component of the CSDP, it is appropriate to mention the Eurocorps which was born out of a Franco-German initiative and became operational in 1994.[400] It comprises one French and one German division, plus contingents from Belgium, Spain and Luxembourg, the so called "framework nations". In addition to the five "framework nations", a further seven countries, Austria, Greece, Italy, Poland, Romania, Turkey, and the USA, "the sending nations" have pledged troops or contribute operational staff. Eurocorps has approximately 60,000 soldiers of which about 1,000 are stationed at its headquarters, in Strasbourg. Eurocorps is not subordinate to any military organisation, although it has been certified by both the EU and NATO as satisfying the criteria for rapid reaction corps. Eurocorps is an army that could be placed at the disposal of any organisation, including NATO and the EU, and even a nation State, to perform humanitarian, peacekeeping and peace restoring missions. Eurocorps can also be employed in high-intensity combat operations. It participated in peacekeeping missions in Bosnia-Herzegovina, in Kosovo and in Afghanistan.

The issue of co-operation between the EU and non-European States which are members of NATO poses no major problem. Appropriate co-operation arrangements have been put in place.

7.6.1.2 The civilian component

This was developed by the Feira European Council of June 1999 and the Göteborg European Council of June 2001. It includes:

- ▪ Police co-operation: the possibility of providing up to 5,000 policemen, including 1,000 within 30 days, for various policing tasks ranging from restoring order to the training of local police forces;

---

399. It can be found at http://www.consilium.europa.eu/showPage.aspx?id=268&lang=en (accessed 10/4/12).

400. Jokingly its establishment was regarded either as "a French plot to winkle Germany out of NATO or a German plot to seduce France into NATO". See: G. Steil, "The Eurocorps and Future European Security Architecture", (1993) 2/2 European Security, 214–15.

- Strengthening the rule of law: the possibility of providing up to 200 judges, prosecutors and other experts in this area;

- Civilian administration: the possibility of providing personnel to deal with various civilian aspects of crisis management such as help to guarantee free elections, or to reform the judicial, taxation or any other system of a requesting state, or to re-establish viable local administration; and,

- Civil protection to operate in emergency situations: the possibility of providing within three to seven hours two or three assessment teams consisting of ten experts and of providing intervention teams consisting of 2,000 people.

All objectives of the civilian component have been achieved, the most important being the creation of the European Security and Intelligence Force (ESIF) consisting of up to 5,000 police to support peacekeeping missions, the Committee for Civilian Aspects of Crisis Management (CIVCOM) in charge of gathering information, making recommendations and giving its opinion to the Political and Security Committee on civilian aspects of crisis management, and the police unit attached to the Council Secretariat and the Joint Situation Centre.

The European Gendarmerie Force (EGF),[401] which became fully operational on 20 July 2006, constitutes an important element of the civilian component. The EGF was created on the initiative of five Member States – France, Italy, The Netherlands, Portugal and Spain – with a view to handling crises that require management by police forces. The EGF is primarily at the disposal of the EU, but can also be deployed at the request of other international organisations, including NATO and the UN. It is based in Vicenza (Italy) in the "Generale Chinotto" barracks.

7.6.1.3   The conflict prevention component

The Göteborg European Council (June 2001) adopted the EU Programme for the Prevention of Violent Conflict. The HR plays an important role in this third component by ensuring consistency and effectiveness of all actions of the EU in respect of the regions concerned. If practicable, the EU must take measures with a view to enhancing the stability of a region and to creating a favourable political environment in it. In February 2001 the Commission set up a Rapid Reaction Mechanism (RRM) aimed at providing rapid financing for crisis management. The mechanism is used where there is a threat to public order or public security, or other similar circumstances which may destabilise a country.

7.6.2   The security dimension

The security dimension of the CSDP is based on the European Security Strategy agreed by the Brussels European Council in December 2003. It provides guidelines in respect of the EU's international security strategy, sets out the main priorities and determines the main threats to the EU's security such as terrorism, proliferation of weapons of mass destruction, regional conflicts, organised crime, and so on. The strategy was a response to the 9/11 terrorist attacks on targets in the USA, and to the conflict in Iraq.

7.7   Assessment of the CFSP including the CSDP

The CFSP is based on the intergovernmental method. As a result any measure adopted within the CFSP is subject to judicial review by the ECJ only in very limited circumstances and the involvement of the

---

401.   The agreement to create the EGF was signed on 17 September 2004.

EP is modest. Progress in the development of the CFSP has been hindered by the requirement of unanimity in the European Council and in the Council. The ToL holds enormous potential for the achievement of greater coherence in the external action of the EU. In particular, creation of the post of HR, the holder of which has the necessary power, a substantial budget and a diplomatic corps, i.e. the EEAS, and who is empowered to speak on behalf of the EU, even before the UN Security Council, constitutes a step forward. It is submitted, however, that by allocating to the President of the European Council external representative functions on matters concerning the CFSP, and in the light of the fact that the President of the European Commission it unlikely to abandon the EU's foreign policy entirely to the HR, the main objective of the reform consisting of achieving a more coherent and effective EU external action may be jeopardised.[402] In any event, the Member States retain real power in all CFSP matters and it will depend on their political will as to whether or not the potential in these matters offered by the ToL is realised.

The military intervention of the US, the UK and their allies in Iraq launched on 20 March 2003, despite the lack of authorisation from the UN Security Council, showed deep divisions between the Member States of the EU. However, when the EU speaks with one voice, it is a powerful voice. The EU can impose economic and diplomatic sanctions, and within the CSDP, may intervene militarily against brutal regimes, although this is not the primary task of the military dimension of the EU.

The political weight of the EU, its credibility as the promoter of fundamental rights and provider of humanitarian assistance, whether in emergency situations or on a long-term basis, was firmly established by creation of the CSDP. By the end of July 20|2 the EU had completed a total of seven civilian and five military missions and remained involved in 11 civilian missions and three military missions across Europe, Africa, the Middle East and Asia.[403]

---

402. See the Dehaene Report, "On the Impact of the Treaty of Lisbon on the Development of the Institutional Balance of the European Union" (2008) 2073(INI) submitted to the EP, in particular its para. 61, which sets out guidelines for a successful relationship between the HR, the President of the European Council and the President of the Commission, which would appear to have been followed by the parties concerned. It states that:

   "–   the President of the European Council represents the Union at the level of Heads of State or Government in matters concerning the CFSP, but does not have the power to conduct political negotiations in the name of the Union, which is the task of the Vice-President of the Commission (High Representative); he/she may also be called upon to fulfill a specific role of representation of the European Council at certain international events;

   –   the President of the Commission represents the Union at the highest level in relation to all aspects of the external relations of the Union, except for matters concerning CFSP, or any specific sectoral policies falling within the scope of the external action of the Union (foreign trade etc.); the Vice-President of the Commission (High Representative) or the competent/mandated Commissioner may also assume this role under the authority of the Commission;

   –   the Vice-President of the Commission (High Representative) represents the Union at ministerial level or in international organisations concerning the Union's overall external action; he/she also carries out the functions of external representation as President of the Foreign Affairs Council."

   .   The Report is available at: http://www.europarl.europa.eu/sides/getDoc.do?type=REPORT&reference=A6-2009-0142&language=EN (accessed 10/8/12).

403.   For details see: http/// www.consilium.europa.eu/eeas/security-defence/eu-operations.aspx?lang=en (accessed 3/7/12).

RECOMMENDED READING

Books

Cardwell, P.J., *EU External Relations and Systems of Governance: The CFSP, Euro-Mediterranean Partnership and Migration*, 2009, Abingdon: Routledge.

De Vasconcelos, Á. (ed.), *What Ambitions for European Defence in 2020?*, 2009, Paris: European Union Institute for Security Studies.

Finn, L. (ed.), *The EU as a Foreign and Security Policy Actor*, 2009, Dordrecht: Republic of Letters Publishing.

Keukeleire, S., and McNaughton, J., *The Foreign Policy of the European Union*, 2008, Basingstoke: Palgrave.

Naert, F., *International Law Aspects of the EU's Security and Defence Policy, with a Particular Focus on the Law of Armed Conflict*, 2010, Antwerp: Intersentia.

Orbie, J. (ed.), *Europe's Global Role: External Policies of the European Union*, 2008, Farnham: Ashgate.

Articles

Kaddous, C., "Role and Position of the High Representative of the Union for Foreign Affairs and Security Policy under the Lisbon Treaty", in Stefan Griller, S., and Jacques Ziller, J. (eds), *The Lisbon Treaty: EU Constitutionalism without a Constitutional Treaty?*, 2008, Vienna and New York: Springer, 205.

Neframi, E., "The Duty of Loyalty: Rethinking its Scope through its Application in the Field of EU External Relations" (2010) 47 CMLRev., 323.

Von Kielmansegg, Graf, G.L., "The Meaning of Petersberg: Some Considerations on the Legal Scope of ESDP Operations" (2007) 44 CMLRev., 629.

Wouters, J. Coppens D., and De Meester, B., "The European Union's External Relations after the Lisbon Treaty," in Griller, S., and Ziller, J. (eds.), *The Lisbon Treaty: EU Constitutionalism without a Constitutional Treaty?*, 2008, Vienna and New York: Springer, 143.

ESSAY QUESTIONS

1. Critically examine the main changes made to the CFSP by the ToL.
2. To what extent do you agree with the statement, "the Commission, the EP and the ECJ should play a more prominent role in the EU's Common Foreign and Security Policy"?

AIDE-MÉMOIRE

SPECIFIC TASKS PERFORMED BY THE HR		
As the Vice-President of the Commission, she:	**As the HR for the CFSP, including the CSDP, she:**	**As the President of the Foreign Affairs Council, she:**
▪ is responsible for all tasks the Commission exercises in external relations (Article 18(4) TEU); and, ▪ co-ordinates the Commission's external actions (Article 18(4) TEU).	▪ implements the CFSP (Articles 24(1), 27(2) and 32 TEU); ▪ ensures, acting together with the Council, that the Member States support EU foreign policy and implement the CFSP (Article 24(3) TEU); ▪ ensures unity, consistency and effectiveness of EU action relating to the CFSP acting in co-operation with the Council and the Commission (Article 26(2) TEU); ▪ represents the EU externally on CFSP matters, including before the UN Security Council (Article 27(2) TEU); ▪ conducts political dialogue with third parties, if requested (Article 27(2) TEU); ▪ refers any question, initiative or proposal on the CFSP to the Council (Articles 30(1) and 42(4) TEU); ▪ acts as a go between when a Member State decides to use the "emergency brake" procedure, i.e. it objects to the use of QMV by the Council (Article 31(2) TEU); ▪ proposes the appointment of a special representative who will carry out his or her mandate under the authority of the HR (Article 33 TEU); ▪ organises the co-ordination of Member States' actions in international organisations and at international conferences (Article 34(1) TEU);	▪ makes proposals to the FA Council (Article 27(1) TEU); ▪ assists the FA Council (Article 21(1) TEU); ▪ convenes extraordinary meetings of the FA Council (Article 30(2) TEU); and, ▪ chairs meetings of the FA Council (Article 27(1) TEU).

(Continued)

(Continued)

SPECIFIC TASKS PERFORMED BY THE HR		
As the Vice-President of the Commission, she:	**As the HR for the CFSP, including the CSDP, she:**	**As the President of the Foreign Affairs Council, she:**
	▪ consults and informs the EP on CFSP matters and ensures that the views of the EP are taken into account (Article 36 TEU); ▪ requests opinions from the Political and Security Committee (Article 38 TEU); ▪ submits proposals on the new "start-up fund", and uses the fund under the authority of the Council (Article 41(3) TEU); ▪ ensures co-ordination of the civilian and military aspects of CSDP missions, acting under the authority of the Council and in constant contact with the Political and Security Committee (Article 43(2) TEU); ▪ agrees with a "coalition of willing and able" Member States to which the Council entrusts a CSDP operational task on the management of that task (Article 44(1) TEU); ▪ provides an opinion on the establishment of "permanent structured co-operation" under the CSDP (Article 46(2) TEU) and keeps the Council and the EP informed as to its development; ▪ provides an opinion on whether a Member State should join a "permanent structured co-operation" in progress (Article 46(3) TEU); ▪ makes recommendations to the Council for the opening of negotiations with a third State or an international organisation with a view to signing an agreement which has CFSP implications (Article 218(3) TFEU), and for the suspension of an existing agreement falling under the CFSP (Article 218(9) TFEU); ▪ proposes CSDP missions (Article 42(4) TEU); and, ▪ has responsibility, jointly with the Council, over the Political and Security Committee when the Committee directs CSDP crisis management operations (Article 38 TEU).	

8

PROTECTION OF FUNDAMENTAL RIGHTS IN THE EU

CONTENTS

CHAPTER OUTLINE

1. The ToL not only confirms previously acknowledged fundamental rights as general principles of EU law, but also recognises them as basic values on which the EU is founded (Article 2 TEU). It reiterates and extends previous commitments of the EU to the protection of fundamental rights; makes the Charter of Fundamental Rights of the European Union a binding instrument; provides for the accession of the EU to the ECHR; and, establishes the promotion of fundamental rights as one of the objective of its external action (Article 3(5) TEU).

2. Three stages in the development of the protection of fundamental rights by the ECJ can be identified. Initially, the ECJ refused to recognise fundamental rights as relevant to Community law. Subsequently, it recognised them as forming part of the general principles of EU law. Finally, it determined the extent to which the Member States are bound by fundamental rights of the EU, this being when they implement secondary EU legislation and when they derogate from or seek to restrict EU rights.

3. The recognition of fundamental rights as general principles of EC law gained political acceptance, first by EC institutions, which in 1977 issued a Joint Declaration on Fundamental Rights, and second, by the Member States, all of which endorsed the ECJ's approach to the protection of fundamental rights in the amendments to the EEC Treaty. With time, however, the political agenda of EU institutions and some Member States became more ambitious. It focused on two methods of introducing and enhancing the protection of fundamental rights: first, *via* the adoption of a separate EU bill of rights, which materialised with the adoption of the Charter of Fundamental Rights of the European Union, and second, *via* accession of the EU to the ECHR. This was achieved by the ToL.

4. The Charter of Fundamental Rights of the European Union was adopted to increase the visibility of the protection of fundamental rights within the EU. It sets out civil; cultural; economic; political; and, social rights. Under the ToL the Charter has the same legal value as the TEU and TFEU. Thus the Charter became a primary source of EU law. Its 50 articles contain "rights, freedoms and principles".

The Charter sets out its scope of application in "horizontal" articles, i.e. Articles 51–54. Article 51(1) states that the Charter is addressed to the institutions, bodies and agencies of the EU and the Member States "only when they are implementing EU law". Article 51(1) also provides that, in its application, the principle of subsidiarity must be respected. Article 6(1) TEU and Article 51(2) of the Charter confirm that the Charter neither extends the scope of application of EU law, nor creates any new competences for the EU, nor any new tasks for the Union. A consequence of this is that the EU will not be able to legislate to vindicate a right set out in the Charter unless the power to do so is set out in the Treaties themselves.

The Charter makes a distinction between rights and principles. This distinction can be explained by the fact that the Charter covers a wide range of rights and, in particular, in respect of some social or economic rights their recognition as free-standing judicially enforceable rights would not be acceptable for some Member States. Thus, the "rights" referred to in the Charter as principles express aspirations and objectives to be pursued by the Union and its Member States and do not constitute free-standing rights. Charter principles, contrary to Charter rights, do not give rise to direct claims for positive action by the EU or Member States. They may be implemented through legislative or executive acts adopted by EU institutions (or by the Member State when they implement EU law) and are judicially cognizable only when courts interpret such acts and rule on their legality.

5. The UK and Poland feared that the Charter and its interpretation by the ECJ might spread to unrelated areas of national law, despite this being clearly precluded by Article 51(1) of the Charter as it requires a link between national law and EU law for the application of the Charter. They feared that the Charter, drafted in opaque language, might create "new rights" which are not provided for by national or international sources. They secured the adoption of Protocol 30 on the application of the Charter in their respective countries, and in December 2009 this was extended by the European Council to the Czech Republic. The ECJ in Case C-411/10 *NS* confirmed that the Protocol does not constitute an opt-out for the UK, Poland and the Czech Republic from the Charter itself.

6. Article 6(2) TEU provides that the EU shall accede to the ECHR. The terms of accession are specified in the Draft Agreement on the Accession of the European Union to the European Convention on Human Rights.

8.1 Introduction

The extent and the quality of protection of fundamental rights in the EU changed dramatically with the entry into force of the ToL. Under Article 2 TEU, which lists the values on which the Union is founded, respect for fundamental rights, including the rights of persons belonging to minorities, is recognised as one of them. The great innovations of the ToL in respect of the protection of fundamental rights were as follows:

- Under Article 6(1) TEU, the Charter of Fundamental Rights of the European Union became legally binding and has the same legal value as the TFEU and TEU;

■ Under Article 6(2) TEU the EU will become a contracting party to the ECHR; and,

■ Under Article 3(5) TEU the promotion of fundamental rights constitutes one of the objectives of EU external action.

Additionally, the EU confirms its previous commitments to the protection of fundamental rights, *inter alia*, in Article 6(3) which states that fundamental rights, as guaranteed by the ECHR and as they result from the constitutional traditions common to the Member States, constitute general principles of Union law.

The above innovations mark the move of the EU towards the creation of a Union of fundamental rights, a move which emphasises that appropriate protection of fundamental rights in the EU will contribute to the solidification of the achievements of integration rather than threaten its objectives.

8.2 The development of the protection of fundamental rights by the ECJ

Three stages in the development of the protection of fundamental rights by the ECJ can be identified. They are examined below.

8.2.1 Stage I

At their inception the Communities focused on economic objectives. This, and the existence of the ECHR explain why the matter of protection of fundamental rights was initially neglected.[404]

The ECJ was, nevertheless, confronted with fundamental rights issues quite early in its life. The cases which arose before the ECJ concerned alleged contradictions between obligations imposed by the High Authority and the rights granted to undertakings under their national constitutional law. These cases posed a dilemma for the ECJ. First, the rights and freedoms contained in national constitutions were superior to any other sources of law, and their observance was imposed on any relevant public authorities of the various Member States in their dealings with the public. However, to permit national constitutional laws to prevail over Community law would have compromised the uniform application of Community law. Second, the founding Treaties neither contained any reference to fundamental rights nor imposed on Community institutions any requirements to observe those rights. The initial approach of the ECJ was provided in Case 1/58 *Stork*,[405] in which it refused to allow the examination of Community law in terms of its compliance with fundamental rights contained in national constitutions. The ECJ justified its decision on the ground that its task was to apply Community law, not the national laws of Member States.

8.2.2 Stage II

The criticism expressed by Member States, together with the establishment of the principle of supremacy of Community law led the ECJ to alter its position in an *obiter* statement in Case 29/69 *Stauder*[406] in which it held that fundamental rights constituted general principles of Community law and as such were protected by the ECJ. This position was further elaborated in Case 11/70 *Internationale*

---

404. See M. Zuleeg, "Fundamental Rights and the Law of the European Communities" (1971) 8 CMLRev., 446.
405. Case 1/58 *Friedrich Stork & Cie v High Authority* [1959] ECR 17, also Joined Cases 36, 37, 38–59 and 40/59 *Präsident Ruhrkolen-Verkaufsgesellschaft mbH and Others v High Authority* [1960] ECR 423 where the ECJ refused to invalidate EU law on the grounds of national law, even where contained in the national constitution.
406. Case 29/69 *Erich Stauder v City of Ulm-Sozialamt* [1969] ECR 419.

Handelsgesellschaft[407] in which the ECJ confirmed that the principle of supremacy entails that Community law prevails over any national law, including national constitutional law protecting fundamental rights, but recognised that fundamental rights "inspired by the constitutional traditions common to the Member States, must be ensured within the framework of the structure and objectives of the Community."[408]

There are the following three implications of Case 11/70 *Internationale Handelsgesellschaft.*

- First, the ECJ found a positive base for incorporating fundamental rights into Community law, i.e. the constitutional traditions common to the Member States;

- Second, the ECJ by incorporating the protection of fundamental rights, which is a central feature of modern national constitutional law, into Community law strengthened the authority of Community law against potential challenges before national courts based on domestic constitutional rights; and,

- Third, the ECJ incorporated into the legal system of Community law not only rights which are set out in the ECHR, i.e. political and civil rights, but also those which are more mundane such as the right to economic liberty.

In Case 11/70 *Internationale Handelsgesellschaft,* the applicant alleged that its right to freedom of action and economic liberty was breached by EEC regulations concerning forfeiture of an export licence deposit for maize meal. The claimant failed to export the quantities of maize for which he had obtained a licence, because it was more profitable to sell maize meal to a domestic buyer than to export. Under EEC regulations, failure to export, unless justified by *force majeure,* resulted in the forfeiture of a deposited sum. Even under the German Constitution the right at issue was not clearly written, but derived from a highly controversial interpretation of Article 2(1) of the Constitution, which states that everyone has the right to free development of their personality.[409] It must be remembered that the judgment was delivered in 1970, a time when it was controversial whether these types of economic interest could be classified as judicially enforceable constitutional rights in most Member States. However, the ECJ did not examine whether in Member States other than Germany these types of economic interests enjoyed constitutional protection, i.e. whether they were common to the constitutional tradition of the Member States. One reason for the broad interpretation of fundamental rights by the ECJ was to show to national courts that the protection of fundamental rights under Community law is the same as under national constitutional law and thus to assure national constitutional courts, that their scrutiny of EU law in terms of its compliance with national constitutions was not necessary. Another implication of this was that there should be no reservation on the part of those courts from accepting the principle of supremacy as understood by the ECJ (see Chapter 9.2). However, the judgment of the ECJ was not sufficient for the German Federal Constitutional Tribunal (BVerfG), which had referred the case of *Internationale Handelsgesellschaft* to the ECJ for a preliminary ruling. Whilst the ECJ had held that the EEC regulations did not breach the rights of the claimant, the BVerfG, once the case returned to it, held that the principle of proportionality enshrined in German Constitutional law was violated by

---

407. Case 11/70 *Internationale Handelsgesellschaft mbH v Einfuhr- und Vorratsstelle für Getreide und Futtermittel* [1970] ECR 1125, para. 3.
408. Ibid, para. 4.
409. M. Kumm, "Internationale Handelsgesellschaft, Nold and the New Human Rights Paradigm", in L. Azoulai and M. Maduro (eds), *The Past and Future of EU Law: The Classics of EU Law Revisited on the 50th Anniversary of the Treaties of Rome,* 2010, Oxford: Hart Publishing, 106.

the deposit system established by EEC regulations.[410] This was the beginning of an uneasy and complex relationship between the BVerfG and the ECJ (this is discussed in Chapter 9.9.1) and illustrates the difficulties facing the ECJ when it embarked on the judicial development of fundamental rights.

In Case 4/73 *Nold*[411] the ECJ found an additional source from which fundamental rights protected by the Community legal order derive, i.e. international conventions for the protection of fundamental rights, especially the ECHR, to which all Member States are contracting parties. It held:

"international treaties for the protection of human rights on which the Member States have collaborated or of which they are signatories, can supply guidelines which should be followed within the framework of Community law."[412]

The ECJ has, however, emphasised that the protection of fundamental rights is not absolute, and, "far from constituting unfettered prerogatives, [it] must be viewed in the light of the social function",[413] and thus it is legitimate that "these rights should, if necessary, be subject to certain limits justified by the overall objectives pursued by the Community, on condition that the substance of these rights is left untouched".

It can be said that the recognition of fundamental rights by the ECJ was necessary because of:

■ the extension of the competences of the EC;

■ the emergence of the principle of supremacy of EC law which entails that EC law prevails over all national law, including constitutional provisions guaranteeing fundamental rights. Some Member States, in particular Germany and Italy could not accept the supremacy of EC law without any guarantees of protection of fundamental rights on the part of the EC; and,

■ the necessity of ensuring that the protection of fundamental rights would not jeopardise the achievement of objectives set out in the Treaties. The establishment of an EC standard of protection of fundamental rights by the ECJ, which was inspired by the constitutional traditions of the Member States[414] and international human rights treaties to which Member States are contracting parties,[415] allowed the ECJ to examine Community acts in the light of their compatibility with fundamental rights but subject to restrictions justified by objectives pursued by the Community. These restrictions, as the ECJ held in Case 44/79 *Hauer*,[416] must not however, constitute a disproportionate and intolerable interference with fundamental rights.

The ECJ has recognised numerous fundamental rights as general principles of EU law (see Chapter 4.3.4). However, the ECJ in Case C-249/96 *Grant*[417] explained the limitations on the power to act in the field of human rights as follows: "Although respect for the fundamental rights which form an integral part of those general principles of law is a condition of the legality of Community acts, those rights cannot in themselves have the effect of extending the scope of the Treaty provisions beyond the

410. *Internationale Handelsgesellschaft* [1974] 2 CMLR 540.
411. Case 4/73 *J. Nold, Kohlen- und Baustoffgroßhandlung v Commission* [1974] ECR 491.
412. Ibid, para. 13.
413. Case 265/87 *Hermann Schräder HS Kraftfutter GmbH & Co. KG v Hermann Schräder HS Kraftfutter GmbH & Co. KG* [1989] ECR 2237, para. 15.
414. Case 11/70 *Internationale Handelsgesellschaft* [1970] ECR 1125.
415. Such as the International Covenant on Civil and Political Rights in Case C-249/96 *Lisa Jacqueline Grant v South-West Trains Ltd* [1998] ECR I-621; the European Social Charter and the ILO Convention no. 111 concerning discrimination in respect of employment and occupation in Case 149/77 *Defrenne v Sabena* [1978] ECR 1365.
416. Case 44/79 *Liselotte Hauer v Land Rheinland-Pfalz* [1979] ECR 3727.
417. Case C-249/96 *Lisa Jacqueline Grant v South-West Trains Ltd* [1998] ECR I-621, para. 45.

competences of the Community". As a result the EU can protect human rights within the limits of powers conferred on it by the Treaties. Accordingly, review by the ECJ of the Member States' compliance with the human rights standard is only possible when the matter is within the scope of EU law. In Case C-299/95 *Kremzow*[418] the applicant claimed that his right to free movement was infringed when he was unlawfully imprisoned for murder. The ECJ held that there was no connection between his situation and EU law on the free movement of persons. As a result, the ECJ had no jurisdiction to review national measures in the light of their compatibility with the human rights standard as the circumstances of the case fell outside the scope of EC law. This approach was confirmed by Article 51(2) of the Charter of Fundamental Rights of the European Union (see Chapter 8.4.3).

8.2.3 Stage III

In the third stage of the development of fundamental rights by the ECJ, the Court decided that the duty to protect them recognised in EU law applies not only to EU institutions but also to the Member States when acting within the scope of EU law. This development is controversial for the following reasons:

- First, the case law of the ECJ on this matter has not yet been fully developed, in that the ECJ has not yet set out the criteria for determining to what extent fundamental rights of the EU are binding on the Member States when they are acting within the scope of EU law;

- Second, some Member States are reluctant to accept the ECJ is the final authority on the standards of human rights protection to be applied to them; and,

- Third, the ECJ's teleological interpretation of the Treaties has blurred the line between situations which are within or outside the scope of EU law. In particular, the case law on EU citizenship and fundamental freedoms illustrates this point (see Chapter 22.3.1).

This matter of the extent to which Member States are bound by EU fundamental rights is of great importance bearing in mind the expanding competences of the EU resulting in the potential areas in which the Member States might be bound by the Union's fundamental rights being very broad. Further, it also raises the question of how far integration through fundamental rights should go. According to Kühling, the case law of the ECJ shows that "the ECJ is neither employing the approach of utilising fundamental rights to review all actions by Member States, nor is it absolutely refusing to conduct such an examination".[419] The position of the ECJ is in between the two approaches. Its case law shows that in two situations fundamental rights of the EU have a binding effect on the Member States. They are:

- Where Member States implement secondary EU legislation. In Case 5/88 *Wachauf* [420] the ECJ held that the protection of fundamental rights is imposed not only on EU institutions, especially when they adopt binding measures, but also on the Member States in their application of such measures. Thus, national authorities in applying EU law must ensure "as far as possible" that fundamental rights are protected;[421] and,

---

418. Case C-299/95 *Fridrich Kremzow v Austria* [1997] ECR I-2629.

419. J. Kühling, "Fundamental Rights", in A. von Bogdandy and J. Bast, *Principles of European Constitutional Law*, 2nd edn, 2010, Oxford: Hart Publishing, 497.

420. Case 5/88 *Hubert Wachauf v Bundesamt für Ernährung und Forstwirtschaft* [1989] ECR 2609.

421. C-351/92 *Graff* [1994] ECR I-3361.

■ Where Member States derogate from EU law or seek to restrict EU rights on the grounds of public policy, public interest or other grounds. In Case C-260/89 *ERT*[422] the ECJ held that when a Member State justifies national rules which are likely to obstruct the exercise of the free movement of services: "such justification, provided for by Community law, must be interpreted in the light of the general principles of law and in particular of fundamental rights".

In the above case, ERT, a Greek radio and television company enjoyed exclusive rights relating to broadcasting programmes. ERT sought an injunction in a domestic court against the respondent, who had set up a TV station and begun to broadcast programmes in violation of ERT's exclusive statutory rights. Greece justified the granting of monopoly rights to ERT on Treaty provisions (Articles 59(1) and 90(1) EC), i.e. on derogations expressly set out in the Treaty. The ECJ held that justifications based on the Treaty could only be accepted if compatible with the fundamental rights of the EU. In subsequent cases, the ECJ has scrutinised the compliance of national measures with fundamental rights, not only in respect of Treaty-based derogations, but also with regard to "mandatory requirements", i.e. justifications which derive from the case law of the ECJ and concern indirectly discriminatory national measures or non-discriminatory measures liable to hinder or make less attractive the exercise of the relevant freedom. The entry into force of the Charter of Fundamental Rights has intensified the broad review powers of the ECJ regarding the compatibility of actions of the Member States with fundamental rights.

8.2.4 Assessment

For the ECJ the protection of fundamental rights, initially ignored and rejected on the basis that it was not part of Community law,[423] has become of crucial importance. In Case C-402/05P *Kadi*[424] the ECJ annulled certain EC Regulations implementing UN Security Council binding resolutions on the ground that they were in breach of fundamental rights protected by the EU legal order, i.e. the right to defence, in particular the right to be heard, the right to an effective legal remedy and the right to property. It held that the provisions of the UN Charter themselves could not prevail over fundamental rights which were part of EU law (see Chapter 9.5).[425] The implications of the *Kadi* judgment so far as they relate to this chapter are:

■ First, that an EU regulation which violates fundamental rights is within the ECJ's scrutiny even if it implements a UNSC resolution binding on the Member States in a situation where the Member States have no discretion as to its implementation. The review of the validity of any EU act in the light of fundamental rights, as the ECJ stated in *Kadi* "must be considered to be the expression, in a Community based on the rule of law, of a constitutional guarantee stemming from the EC Treaty as an autonomous legal system which is not to be prejudiced by an international agreement";[426]

■ Second, that no obligation under the UN Charter should be given effect within the EU legal order if it undermines the foundations of the EU. The clear implication of the *Kadi* judgment is that as

---

422. Case C-260/89 *Elliniki Radiophonia Tiléorassi AE (ERT) and Panellinia Omospondia Syllogon Prossopikou v Dimotiki Etairia Pliroforissis and Sotirios Kouvelas and Nicolaos Avdellas and Others* [1991] ECRI-2925, para. 43.
423. Cases 36, 37 38 and 40/59 *Geitling v High Authority* [1960] ECR 423.
424. [2008] ECR I-6351.
425. On this topic see: T. Tridimas, "Terrorism and the ECJ: Empowerment and Democracy in the EC Legal Order", (2009) 34 ELRev., 102.
426. [2008] ECR I-6351, para. 316.

long as the UN does not itself guarantee effective judicial protection, the ECJ will enforce fundamental rights law rather than a binding UN resolution; and,

■ Third, that the position taken by the ECJ in *Kadi* put pressure on the UN Security Council to change its policy towards fundamental rights and thus contributed to the strengthening of fundamental rights at international level. Accordingly, the judgment should not be regarded as undermining the UN but as encouraging co-operation between international organisations which pursue the objective of protecting and promoting fundamental rights.

The firm stand of the ECJ on the protection of fundamental rights is enhanced in its judgment in Case C-411/10 *NS*[427] (for facts, see Chapter 8.4.3.1). In this case the ECJ confirmed that: Member States have a non-negotiable obligation to protect fundamental rights even in most sensitive areas, such as immigration; this obligation derives from the Charter of Fundamental Rights rather than from any EU secondary legislation; and, the absolute trust that all Member States will observe human rights is no longer taken for granted. In this case one of the matters under consideration was whether a Member State may establish a conclusive presumption that when it transfers an asylum seeker to another Member State which, under the relevant Regulation, is responsible for examining the asylum application, the receiving Member State will observe the fundamental rights. It was very clear from the judgment of the ECtHR in *MSS v Belgium and Greece*[428] that the receiving Member State, Greece, could not comply with its fundamental rights obligations deriving from EU law. The ECJ held that a conclusive presumption that all Member States are always safe for asylum-seekers breaches the Charter. Accordingly, in the name of the protection of fundamental rights, the ECJ has signed a death warrant to the concept of absolute mutual trust that every Member State will observe fundamental rights. However, a rebuttable presumption is acceptable under EU law. The ECJ made a distinction between a situation where a responsible Member State "merely" breaches EU legislation and where it breaches the Charter. In the first situation a Member State where an asylum-seeker is present may proceed with the transfer. In the second situation the transfer is not allowed. In practice, however, it may not be easy to establish whether the responsible Member State "merely" breaches EU legislation, which breach does not amount to a breach of the Charter, or whether it breaches the Charter.

8.3 Political acceptance of fundamental rights: from the Treaty of Maastricht to the ToL

The recognition of fundamental rights as general principles of EU law prompted the Council, the Commission and the European Parliament to sign a Joint Declaration on 5 April 1977 which expressed their commitment to the protection of fundamental rights.[429] Although the Declaration was solely a political statement, it suggested a new approach, that is, the need for the Community to incorporate the ECHR into EC law. This initiative was blocked by the Member States at the Maastricht Conference and, finally, in Opinion 2/94 the ECJ held that the EC had no competence to accede to the ECHR without revising the Treaty.[430]

Notwithstanding the above, the Member States did endorse the approach of the ECJ to the protection of fundamental rights. For the first time the Treaty of Maastricht recognised fundamental rights as

---

427. Case C-411/10 *NS v Secretary of State for the Home Department* (judgment of 21/12/11 (NYR)).
428. *MSS v Belgium and Greece*, Application no. 30696/09, Council of Europe: European Court of Human Rights, 21 January 2011, available at: http://www.unhcr.org/refworld/docid/4d39bc7f2.html (accessed 23/6/12).
429. [1977] OJ C/103/1; see Forman, "The Joint Declaration on Fundamental Rights", (1977) ELRev., 210.
430. [1996] ECR I-1759.

guaranteed by the ECHR and, resulting from the constitutional traditions common to the Member States, as fundamental principles of EU law. Further, the Treaty of Maastricht incorporated three provisions relating to the protection of fundamental rights. These provisions:

- Provided that matters of common interest in Co-operation in the Fields of Justice and Home Affairs shall be dealt with in accordance with the requirements of the ECHR and the 1951 Convention on the Status of Refugees (Article 78(1) TFEU);

- Provided that Community policy in the field of development co-operation "shall contribute to the general objective of developing and consolidating democracy and the rule of law, and that of respecting human rights and fundamental freedoms" (Article 208 TFEU); and,

- Introduced the possibility of suspending certain rights of a Member State when the Council determines the existence of "serious and persistent violation" of fundamental rights by that Member State (Articles 7(2) and (3) TEU).

The ToN added a new paragraph to Article 7 TEU allowing the Council to determine the existence of a "clear risk of a serious breach" of fundamental rights by a Member State and to address appropriate recommendations to that prospectively defaulting Member State (Article 7(1) TEU) (see Chapter 2.4).

With time, the political agenda of EU institutions and some Member States was more ambitious. It focused on two methods of introducing and enhancing protection of fundamental rights under EU law: first, *via* the adoption of a separate EU bill of rights and second, *via* accession of the EU to the ECHR. Both were achieved by the ToL.

8.4 The Charter of Fundamental Rights of the European Union

The origin and main features of the Charter are examined below.

8.4.1 The Charter's origin and impact on EU law prior to the entry into force of the ToL

The idea of creating an EU Charter of Fundamental Rights was put forward by the German EU Presidency in early 1999. This idea was approved by the Cologne Council of June 1999 which mandated the drafting of a Charter to the Convention. The composition of that Convention and its tasks were established by the Tampere European Council (December 1999). This was to be "a task of revelation rather than creation, of compilation rather than innovation".[431] The Convention was made up of 15 personal representatives of the Heads of State or Government of the Member States, 16 members of the European Parliament, and 30 members of national parliaments. The Convention commenced its work in November 1999, electing as its chairman the former President of the Federal Republic of Germany, Roman Herzog. It completed its work on 20 October 2000 and sent its draft Charter to the European Council together with non-binding Explanations for each article of the draft Charter.

At the Nice European Council (December 2000), the Council, the EP and the Commission jointly made a solemn Declaration to respect the Charter. The Nice European Council welcomed this Declaration of commitment by these three institutions but decided to consider the question of the Charter's legal status during the general debate on the future of the European Union, which was initiated

---

431. See the Commission Communication on the Charter of Fundamental Rights of the European Union, para. 7, COM(2000) 559.

on 1 January 2001. During that process, the Charter was revised in parallel with the drafting of a Constitutional Treaty. The revised version was then incorporated as Part Two of the draft Constitutional Treaty. The revision was necessary to respond to concerns of the UK. During the negotiations leading to the adoption of the ToL further amendments were made to "horizontal" provisions of the Charter (i.e. Articles 51 to 54 of the Charter which clarify its scope and applicability) and to its Explanations. This resulted in the Charter (as amended) being "solemnly proclaimed" for the second time by the EP, the Commission and the Council on 12 December 2007.[432]

Until the entry into force of the ToL the Charter was not binding, but even as a non-binding document, had substantial impact on EU law. This is in the light of the fact that the three institutions which proclaimed the Charter had committed themselves to respect it. In particular, the Commission decided that any proposed legislative or regulatory act adopted by it should be subject to a compatibility check with the Charter.[433] Since the establishment of the Fundamental Rights Agency (FRA)[434] the Commission has referred its legislative proposals to the Agency for examination of their compatibility with the Charter. The EP did not hesitate to challenge EU legislative acts before the ECJ on the ground of their incompatibility with fundamental rights, including those confirmed by the Charter,[435] and the ECJ referred to the Charter in numerous judgments.[436]

8.4.2 The substantive provisions of the Charter

Under Article 6(1) TEU the Charter of Fundamental Rights, as amended in 2007, is a binding document and has the same legal value as the Treaties. Thus the Charter has become a primary source of EU law.

The Charter confirms that fundamental rights are indivisible, interrelated and interdependent. It contains civil; cultural; economic; political; and, social rights.[437] Its catalogue of rights is more extensive than that contained in the ECHR which lists only civil and political rights. Each of 50 "rights, freedoms and principles" contained in six Titles is drawn from the ECHR; the European Social Charter; the Community Charter of Social Rights of Workers; common constitutional traditions of the Member States; judgments of the ECJ and ECtHR; and, international human rights conventions of the UN, the Council of Europe and the ILO to which all Member States are contracting parties. Its Titles and the matters dealt with under them are as follows:

Title I: Dignity, affirms the protection of the dignity of the person; the right to life; the right to the integrity of the person; freedom from torture and inhuman or degrading treatment or punishment; and, the prohibition of slavery and forced labour;

---

432. The text of the amended Charter and its revised Explanations can be found in [2007] OJ C303/1 and C/303/17.

433. The Commission Communication on Compliance with the Charter of Fundamental Rights in Commission legislative proposals: Methodology for Systematic and Rigorous Monitoring, COM (2005) 172.

434. The FRA was established on 1 March 2007 by Regulation 168/2007 [2007] OJ L53/1. Its main tasks are, *inter alia*: provision of advice and assistance to the EU's institutions and to the Member States when implementing EU law, with a view to supporting them when they take measures or formulate policies within their respective competences having fundamental rights implications; academic research; and close co-operation with Member States, civil society and international organisations active in the area of the protection of human rights.

435. See Case C-540/03 *EP v Council* [2006] ECR I-5769.

436. For the first time the ECJ made reference to the Charter in Case C-540/03 *EP v Council* [2006] ECR I-5769. Subsequently, the ECJ has frequently referred to the Charter, e.g. Case C-303/05 *Advocaten voor de Wereld VZW v Leden van de Ministerraad* [2007] ECR I-3635.

437. On the Charter see: Lord Goldsmith, "A Charter of Rights, Freedoms and Principles", (2001) 38 CMLRev. 1201; and K. Lenaerts and E. de Smijter, "A Bill of Rights for the European Union", (2001) 38 CMLRev., 273.

Title II: Freedoms, guarantees the right to liberty and security; respect for private and family life; protection of personal data; the right to marry and found a family; freedom of thought, conscience and religion; freedom of expression and information; freedom of assembly and association; freedom of the arts and sciences; the right to education; freedom to choose an occupation and the right to engage in work; freedom to conduct a business; the right to property; the right to asylum; and, protection in the event of removal, expulsion or extradition;

Title III: Equality, guarantees equality before the law; non-discrimination; cultural, religious and linguistic diversity; equality between men and women; the rights of the child; the rights of the elderly; and, social and occupational integration of persons with disabilities to ensure their independence and participation in the life of the community;

Title IV: Solidarity, provides for workers' rights to information and consultation within the undertaking; collective bargaining and action; access to placement services; protection in the event of unjustified dismissal; fair and just working conditions; prohibition of child labour; protection of young people at work; the right to family and professional life; social security and social assistance; the right of access to health care; the right to access to services of general economic interest; and the right to environmental and consumer protection;

Title V: Citizens' rights, guarantees the right of EU citizens to vote and stand as candidates at elections to the EP and at municipal elections if they reside in a host Member State; the right to good administration; the right of access to documents and to the Ombudsman; the right to petition the EP; freedom of movement and residence; and, the right to diplomatic and consular protection; and,

Title VI: Justice, assures the right to an effective remedy and a fair trial; the presumption of innocence and the right of defence; respect for the principles of legality and proportionality of criminal offences and penalties; and, the right not to be tried or punished twice in criminal proceedings for the same criminal offence.

On 19 December 2010 the Commission adopted a strategy to ensure the effective implementation of the Charter. The Commission stated that it would ensure that all EU legislative acts are in accord with the Charter at each stage of the legislative process, i.e. from the early preparatory work in the Commission to their application by Member States. Further the Commission would provide information to EU citizens on the relevance of the Charter, in particular through the Commission's new e-Justice portal[438] and will publish an Annual Report on the Charter's application to monitor the progress achieved.[439]

8.4.3 "Horizontal" provisions of the Charter

The Charter sets out its scope of application in "horizontal" articles. Article 51(1) states that the Charter is addressed to the institutions, bodies and agencies of the EU and the Member States "only when they are implementing EU law". Thus, the Charter does not apply to purely domestic law. A link between a national situation and EU law must be established for the Charter to be applicable. Article 51(1) also provides that in the application of the Charter the principle of subsidiarity must be respected. Article 6(1) TEU and Article 51(2) of the Charter confirm that the Charter neither extends the scope of application of EU law, nor creates any new competences for the EU, nor any new tasks for the Union. A consequence of the situation confirmed by Article 6(1) TEU and Article 51(2) of the Charter is that the EU will not be able to legislate to vindicate a right set out in the Charter unless the power to do so is set out in the Treaties themselves.

---

438.   Available at https://e-justice.europa.eu/home.do?action=home (accessed 2/1/12).

439.   IP/10/1348.

Article 52 on the scope of guaranteed rights provides that any limitations imposed on the exercise of the rights and freedoms contained in the Charter must be provided by law, and respect the essence of those rights and freedoms. Subject to the principle of proportionality any limitation may be imposed, but only if it is necessary and genuinely meets objectives of general interest recognised by the EU, or the need to protect the rights and freedoms of others.

Article 52 of the Charter provides some guidance on how to interpret the rights set out in the Charter. In particular it states that where Charter rights correspond to ECHR rights, the meaning and scope of the rights shall be the same as those laid down by the ECHR. As to rights resulting from constitutional traditions common to the Member States, Article 52(4) provides that those rights are to be interpreted in harmony with those traditions. Article 52(6) provides that full account is to be taken of national laws and practices when Charter articles make reference to national law. Article 52(7) requires courts of the Union and the Member States to give "due regard" to the Explanatory Memorandum accompanying the Charter. Article 52(5) explains the difference between "rights" and "principles".

Articles 53 and 54 provide that nothing in the Charter shall be interpreted as restricting fundamental rights, and that the Charter shall not be interpreted as providing a right to engage in activity which aims to destroy or limit the rights set out in the Charter.

Horizontal provisions of the Charter have been drafted in opaque language. This raises uncertainties. Particularly controversial issues are:

- the meaning of the word "implementing" in Article 51(1) of the Charter;

- the legal implications of a distinction between "rights, freedoms and principles";

- the issue of whether the Charter creates new rights or whether it merely confirms existing rights; and,

- the issue of whether the Charter can produce horizontal direct effect (see Chapter 10.4).

The main controversies surrounding the interpretation and application of the Charter are examined below

8.4.3.1 The meaning of the word "implementing" in Article 51(1) of the Charter

Article 51(1) states that "the provisions of this Charter are addressed to the institutions, bodies, offices and agencies of the Union . . . and to the Member States only when they are implementing Union Law." The literal interpretation of Article 51(1) of the Charter clearly excludes the ERT situation from the scrutiny of the ECJ (see Chapter 8.2.3). This entails that the Charter applies only when a Member State acts as agent of the EU in the areas of shared administration, or when it implements EU directives, and in some exceptional circumstances where an EU regulation or decision requires a Member State to take implementing measures.[440] However, the Explanatory Memorandum to the Charter, to which a Member State is required to give due regard, states that on the basis of the case law of the ECJ, "the requirement to respect fundamental rights defined in a Union context is only binding on the Member States when they act in the scope of Union law", i.e. this explanation includes the ERT situation into the scope of the Charter. The post-ToL case law of the ECJ confirms its pre-ToL case law on the meaning of the word

---

440.   A. Arnull, "From Charter to Constitution and Beyond: Fundamental Rights in the New Europe", (2003) *Public Law*, 780–81.

"implementing".[441] This is exemplified by the judgment of the ECJ in Case C-279/09 *DEB*.[442] In this case the ECJ assessed German legislation relating to the conditions for granting legal aid to legal persons, which were more restrictive than those relating to natural persons, in the light of Article 47 of the Charter, in particular its paragraph 3 which specifies that legal aid is to be made available to those who lack sufficient resources in so far as such aid is necessary to ensure effective access to justice. The German legislation did not implement any EU law. The connection between the German legislation and EU law was that the claimant DEB, a German undertaking engaged in supplying energy in Germany, alleged that it had suffered a loss as a result of the delayed transposition in Germany of Directives 98/30/EC and 2003/55/EC, which were intended to facilitate non-discriminatory access to the national gas networks. In Case C–64/03 *Commission* v *Germany*,[443] the ECJ found that indeed, Germany had failed its obligation to transpose these Directives within the prescribed time limit. DEB claimed that because of the failure of Germany to transpose the Directives in time it had no access to the gas network which resulted in its losing important contracts leading to its inability to carry on its commercial activities and to successfully pursue proceedings against Germany. DEB also claimed that the effect of refusal of legal aid deprived it of any possibility of seeking to establish the liability of the German State for infringement of EU law. The ECJ held that the principle of effective legal protection set out in Article 47 of the Charter must be interpreted as meaning that it is not impossible for legal persons to rely on that principle to obtain legal aid. The ECJ left to the referring court the task of assessing whether the conditions for granting legal aid constituted a limitation on the right of access to the court which undermined the very core of that right. However, the ECJ set out various factors in the light of which the referring court should make the assessment. These factors, which are used in the case law of the ECtHR and which the ECJ has accepted as applicable under EU law, are, *inter alia*, the subject-matter of the litigation; the probability of a successful outcome of the case for the applicant; the capacity of the litigant to represent himself; the interests at stake; and, the complexity of the applicable law and procedures. According to the ECJ also factors specific to legal persons should be taken into consideration, such as whether such a person is profit-making or non-profit-making; the financial capacity of the applicants partners or shareholders; and, the ability of those partners or shareholders to obtain the sums necessary to institute legal proceedings.[444]

The meaning of the word "implementing" was further examined by the ECJ in Case C-411/10 *NS*.[445]

THE FACTS WERE:

Regulation 343/2003, known as the "Dublin II Regulation," provides the criteria and mechanisms for determining the Member State responsible for dealing with an asylum application submitted by a national of a third country. The principal rule is that the Member State responsible for examining an asylum application is that through which the asylum-seeker entered the EU.

NS, an Afghan national, applied for asylum in the UK although he first entered the EU through Greece. Under the Regulation Greece was responsible for examining his application.

---

441.   Case C-442/00 *Caballero v Fondo de Garantia Salarial (Fogasa)* [2002] ECR I-11915, paras 29 and 30.
442.   Case C-279/09 *DEB Deutsche Energiehandels- und Beratungsgesellschaft mbH v Germany* [2010] ECR I-13849.
443.   [2004] ECR I–3551.
444.   Ibid, paras 61 and 62.
445.   Case C-411/10 *NS v Secretary of State for the Home Department* (judgment of 21/12/11 (NYR)).

NS did not make any asylum application in Greece, but was arrested there and subsequently sent to Turkey, where he was detained in appalling conditions for two months. He escaped from Turkey, travelled to the UK and on arrival there lodged an application for asylum. In accordance with the Regulation, the UK authorities submitted a request to Greece to examine NS's application. Greece did not respond within the relevant time limit which, under the Regulation, meant that it assumed responsibility for examining the asylum application. In those circumstances, the UK Secretary of State decided to transfer NS from the UK to Greece. The decision was challenged by NS before the High Court of Justice (England and Wales). NS claimed that his transfer to Greece would lead to a breach of his fundamental rights in the light of the then situation in Greece, which was described by the UNHCR as a "humanitarian crisis". On this ground NS requested the Secretary of State to exercise her discretion under Article 3(2) of the Regulation, i.e. to accept responsibility for examining his asylum application instead of Greece.

The High Court referred a number of questions to the ECJ within the preliminary ruling procedure. The High Court asked, inter alia, whether a decision adopted by a Member State, on the basis of the Dublin II Regulation, to examine a claim for asylum which is not its responsibility under the criteria set out in Regulation, falls within the scope of EU law for the purposes of Article 6 TEU and/or Article 51 of the Charter.

Held:

The ECJ held that a decision adopted by a Member State to transfer an asylum seeker to a Member State which is responsible for examining an asylum application under the Regulation implements EU law for the purposes of Article 6 TEU and/or Article 51 of the Charter of Fundamental Rights.

Comment:

The judgment elucidates the matter of whether a decision which is discretionary (i.e. under Article 3(2) of the Regulation a Member State has discretion to decide whether or not to examine an asylum application instead of the Member State which under the Regulation is primarily responsible for such examination) "implements" the Regulation within the meaning of Article 51 of the Charter. The ECJ answered in the affirmative. This answer is logical, bearing in mind that it would be difficult to argue that a decision once adopted under Article 3(2) of the Regulation does not implement the Regulation. Such a decision forms part of the system established under the Regulation and produces the legal consequences specified in the Regulation. For example, a Member State must inform other interested Member States of its decision. Further, the interpretation given by the ECJ to the term "implementing" in the commentated case is in line with its previous case law, in particular, Case C-540/03 EP v Council.[446]

8.4.3.2 The legal implications of a distinction between "rights, freedoms and principles"

The Charter sets out freedoms, rights and principles. The determination of the meaning of "freedoms" poses no difficulties. Title II of the Charter, which contains a list of "freedoms" actually uses the word "rights" in the majority of its articles, e.g. Article 6 refers to the right to liberty and security, Article 7 refers to the right to respect for private and family life, Article 11 refers to the right to freedom of

---

446.   [2006] ECR I-5769, para. 104.

expression. However, it is uncertain whether the freedom of the arts and sciences in Article 13 contains a right or a principle. It seems that "freedoms", although a separate category under the Charter, refer either to rights or principles.

The distinction between rights and principles is confusing. The reason for its introduction was that the Charter covers a broad range of rights, and some Member States were unwilling to recognise some of them, in particular those relating to social and economic rights, as free standing rights. Views differ as to the meaning of "principles". According to Lord Goldsmith QC, who was the UK representative on the Convention which drafted the 2000 version of the Charter, "rights" refer to "individually justiciable classic rights" which are mainly civil and political rights, whilst principles express "aspirations and objectives for what Government should do". On the legal plane the difference is that principles are not justiciable in the same way as classical rights as they "only give rise to rights to the extent that they are implemented by national law or, in those areas where there is such competence, by Community law".[447] Whether the distinction made by Lord Goldsmith is correct will, at same stage, be clarified by the ECJ but in the light of the Explanatory Memorandum it seems that some economic rights are justiciable (see below).

The Charter and its Explanatory Memorandum provide some clarification as to the meaning of "principles". Article 52(5) of the Charter explains that principles set out in the Charter "may be implemented by legislative and executive acts" of the EU and the Member States when implementing EU law. They "shall be judicially cognizable only in the interpretation of such acts and in the ruling on their legality". On the basis of Article 52(5) of the Charter it can be said that this provision confirms that principles, alone, cannot give rise to directly enforceable rights but they may impact on the interpretation of the nature and scope of rights afforded by the EU or national implementing legislation and even on their validity. With regard to validity of EU law, or national law implementing EU law, a declaration of invalidity made by the ECJ in respect of EU law, or by a national court dealing with national law implementing EU law, may affect directly enforceable rights, i.e. if the relevant law is invalid so are any "rights" which it had sought to create.

The Explanatory Memorandum provides some examples of principles: Article 25 on the "rights" of the elderly, Article 26 on the integration of persons with disabilities and Article 37 on environmental protection. However, the Explanatory Memorandum states that some articles may contain elements of rights and principles, e.g. Article 23 on equality between men and women, Article 33 on family and professional life and Article 34 on social security and social assistance. As a result, some social and economic rights may not be mere principles but may confer justiciable rights on individuals.

It is submitted that in the context of the Charter the main difference between rights and principles is that with regard to a Charter principle, an individual cannot rely on it to force the EU or a Member State to take a positive action is the absence of Union's (or the Member State when implementing Union law) legislation or executive acts. Under Article 52(5) of the Charter, principles may be implemented through legislative or executive acts adopted either by the EU or by the Member States when they implement EU law, and are judicially cognisable only when such acts are interpreted or reviewed. In contrast, Charter rights are judicially enforceable. Thus, an individual can rely on a Charter right, to force the EU or a Member State to take a positive action in the absence of any legislative of executive acts on the part of the EU (or the Member State) to protect the right concerned. Usually, an individual will rely on a Charter right when the EU, or a Member State when implementing EU law, has not adequately protected that right.

---

447. Paper by the Rt Hon Lord Goldsmith QC presented to the Henrich Böll Stiftung 2001, "A Charter of Rights, Freedoms and Principles" para. 35, available at http://www.gruene-akademie.de/download/europa_goldsmith.pdf (accessed 14/3/12).

8.4.3.3 The issue of whether the Charter contains new rights or whether it merely confirms existing rights

The Charter in its preamble "reaffirms" that it contains existing rights rather than creates new rights. The Explanatory Memorandum identifies a source for each of the Charter rights based on the constitutional traditions and international treaties to which Member States are contracting parties, including the ECHR; the Social Charter of the Union; and, the case law of the ECtHR and the ECJ. Consequently, if the original source of a right is binding on a Member State, the simple restatement of that right in the Charter cannot deprive the underlying right of its binding legal status.

From the point of view of the UK, the right of collective bargaining and action embodied in Article 28 of the Charter gives rise to the concern that the Charter creates a new free-standing right. This Article states:

> "Workers and employers, or their respective organizations, have, in accordance with Union law and national laws and practices, the right to negotiate and conclude collective agreements at the appropriate levels and, in cases of conflicts of interest, to take collective action to defend their interests, including strike action."

Under UK law there is no specific right to strike. Consequently, the issue arises whether Article 28 introduces into UK law a new, free-standing right to strike. In this respect the Explanatory Memorandum relating to Article 28 provides that this provision is based on Article 6 of the European Social Charter which provides for a right to collective bargaining, points 12–14 of the Community Charter of the Fundamental Social Rights of Workers which concern collective action, and Article 11 ECHR which was interpreted by the ECtHR as encompassing the right to collective action.[448] However, Article 11 ECHR contains rights which are not absolute and thus may be limited by national law.

It is submitted that in any event the right to strike has been recognised under EU law. In Case C-438/05 *Viking*[449] and Case C-341/05[450] the ECJ held that the right to take collective action, recognised by international conventions, is also recognised under EU law as it forms an integral part of the general principles of EU law. However, this right is not absolute but subject to restrictions and limitations, and as such needs to be reconciled with other fundamental rights and principles protected under the Treaties in the light of the principle of proportionality. Accordingly, it seems that as such it is justiciable in the UK on the ground that it constitutes a general principle of EU law (see below).

8.4.4 Protocol 30 on the application of the Charter to Poland, the UK and the Czech Republic

Despite the assurances contained in Article 6(1) TEU and Article 51(2) of the Charter and in other "horizontal provisions" of the Charter, some Member States, in particular the UK and Poland, feared that the Charter and its interpretation by the ECJ might spread to unrelated areas of national law. For that reason, during the negotiations leading to the adoption of the ToL, the UK and Poland secured the adoption of Protocol 30 on the application of the Charter in their particular country. The European

---

448. *Schmidt and Dahlström v Sweden* (application No 5589/72) judgment of Feb 1976, Series A, No 21 at para. 36.

449. Case C-438/05 *International Transport Workers' Federation and Finnish Seamen's Union v Viking Line ABP and OÜ Viking Line Eesti* [2007] ECR I-10779.

450. C-341/05 *Laval und Partneri Ltd v Svenska Byggnadsarbetareförbundet and Others* [2007] ECR I-11767.

Council held in December 2009[451] agreed to a demand made by the President of the Czech Republic to extend the application of Protocol 30 to the Czech Republic.

Protocol 30 contains two provisions:

■ Article 1(1) states that the Charter does not extend the ability of the ECJ or any court or tribunal in the UK, Poland or the Czech Republic "to find the laws, regulations or administrative provisions, practices or action" of the UK, or Poland or the Czech Republic inconsistent with the Charter.

■ Article 1(2) provides that (in order to dissipate any doubt) nothing in Title IV of the Charter, which concerns the "solidarity" rights, creates justiciable rights applicable in the UK, Poland or the Czech Republic except in so far as such rights are provided for by the laws and practices of the Member State concerned.

■ Article 2 states that to the extent that a provision of the Charter refers to national laws and practices, it shall apply to the UK, Poland and the Czech Republic only to the extent that the rights or principles it contains are recognised by the law and practices of the UK, Poland or the Czech Republic.

In respect of Article 1(2) of Protocol 30 it can be said that this provision confirms the distinction between the rights and principles which is recognised by Article 52(5) and its Explanatory Memorandum. It clarifies any doubts as to Title IV in that it confirms that Title IV sets out only principles, not justiciable rights. On the basis of Article 1(2) it is unlikely that any Article set out in Title IV will be found to contain justiciable rights in respect of the UK, Poland or the Czech Republic because such a finding would be inconsistent with the express wording of Article 1(2) of Protocol 30.

With regard to Article 2 of Protocol 30, it confirms what Article 52(6) of the Charter states, i.e. that "full account" of national laws and practice should be taken into account where there is reference to them in the Charter.

The Protocol raises an issue as to whether it constitutes an opt-out from the Charter so far as the UK, Poland and the Czech Republic are concerned.[452] In Case C-411/10 *NS*[453] (for facts see Chapter 8.4.3.1), the ECJ provided some clarifications as to the binding force and scope of Protocol 30. First, the ECJ confirmed that Protocol 30 does not constitute an opt-out of the Charter. Second, the ECJ held that Article 1(1) of the Protocol adds nothing to the Charter. It reaffirms the content of Article 51 of the Charter which seeks to prevent any extension of areas of application of the Charter. Third, with regard to Article 1(2) of the Protocol the ECJ confirmed that it may have effect in cases dealing with "solidarity" rights, i.e. social rights. As Case C-411/10 *NS* did not concern social rights its application was irrelevant. A-G Trstenjak in her Opinion was more explicit. She stated that Article 1(2) of the Protocol reaffirmed Article 51(1) of the Charter in that the Charter does not create justiciable rights and entitlements between private individuals. However, it "appears to rule out new EU rights and entitlements being derived from Articles 27 to 38 of the Charter of Fundamental Rights, on which those entitled could rely

451.   Council of the European Union (1 December 2009), Brussels European Council 29/30 October 2009: Presidency Conclusions, 15265/1/09 REV 1, available at http://www.consilium.europa.eu/uedocs/cms_data/docs/pressdata/en/ec/110889.pdf (accessed 14/3/10).

452.   M. Dougan, "The Treaty of Lisbon 2007: Winning Minds, Not Hearts", (2008) 45 CMLRev., p. 617, at 665–71 and C. Barnard, "The 'Opt-out' for the UK and Poland from the Charter of Fundamental Rights: Triumph of Rhetoric over Reality?" in S. Griller and J. Ziller (eds), *The Lisbon Treaty, EU Constitutionalism without a Constitutional Treaty?* 2008, Springer, 257.

453.   Judgment of 21/12/11 (NYR).

against the United Kingdom or against Poland".[454] With regard to Article 2 of the Charter it is only relevant with regard to social rights.

On the authority of Case C-411/10 *NS* it appears that the interpretation of the Charter in respect of the UK, Poland and the Czech Republic may differ as compared with other Member States in cases dealing with social rights. However, this will depend upon whether the ECJ decides that the Charter rights and the general principles of EU law are the same; if so, there is no difference between the Charter and the general principles. Consequently, the Protocol will be meaningless. This is because the Protocol confirms in its preamble that it is without prejudice to other obligations devolving upon Poland and the UK (as well as the Czech Republic) under the TFEU, the TEU and Union law generally. Therefore, Article 6(3) TEU ensures that on the basis of general principles of EU law any EU or UK, or Polish or Czech implementing legislation can be challenged on the ground of infringements of fundamental rights. Those principles exist independently from the Charter with the consequence that when the ECJ decides that a Charter right constitutes a general principle of EU law, any protection afforded under the Protocol will be removed. However, if the ECJ decides that the general principles of EU law are not identical to the rights contained in the Charter, the Protocol will be of relevance in that national courts and the ECJ will be prevented from assessing national law in terms of its compatibility with the Charter. It is also submitted that even if the Charter rights and the general principles of EU law are somehow found to be different from each other, the ECJ will probably develop its case law in the direction of ensuring their convergence.

8.5 Accession of the EU to the European Convention on Human Rights (ECHR)

Article 6(2) TEU states that the EU shall accede to the ECHR. Protocol 8 "Relating to Article 6(2) of the Treaty on European Union on the Accession of the Union to the European Convention on the Protection of Human Rights and Fundamental Freedoms" provides that any agreement relating to the accession must make provision for preserving the specific characteristics of the Union and EU law and ensure that the accession neither affects the competences of the Union nor the powers of its institutions nor the situation of Member States in relation to their commitments under the ECHR (in particular in respect of Protocols attached to the ECHR to some of which only some Member States are contracting parties), nor the obligation of the Member States to submit to the ECJ a dispute concerning interpretation or application of the Treaties.

The accession agreement, as any international agreement, will be concluded in conformity with the requirements set out in Article 218 TFEU. However, Article 218(8) TFEU specifically mentions that an agreement on accession of the EU to the ECHR must be subject to unanimity in the Council and will enter into force after being approved by the Member States in accordance with their respective constitutional requirements. Pursuant to Article 218(6)(a)(ii) TFEU, the Council is required to obtain the consent of the EP for conclusion of the agreement on the EU's accession.

Under Article 218(2) TFEU the Council authorises the opening of negotiations on the recommendation of the Commission, adopts a negotiating directive, authorises the signing of the agreement and concludes it. Under Article 218(10) TFEU the EP must be kept fully informed at all stages of the negotiations. At the time of writing, a Draft Agreement on the Accession of the European Union to the European Convention on Human Rights has been made public.[455] The main features of the draft are:

---

454.   Ibid, para. 173.
455.   CDDH–UE(2011) 16 fin.

- The ECtHR will have jurisdiction to assess acts, measures and omissions of the EU in the light of the ECHR;

- The EU will initially be a contracting party to the ECHR and only to two of its Protocols guaranteeing substantive rights, i.e. Protocol 1 which guarantees the right to property and the right to education; and, Protocol 6 which abolishes the death penalty in peacetime. However, under the draft agreement the EU will have the option of acceding to further Protocols;

- It establishes a new co-respondent mechanism under which the EU may become a co-respondent when proceedings are brought against one or more Member States of the EU, and allows a Member State or Member States of the EU to become co-respondent(s) when the application is directed against the EU. The circumstances under which the co-respondent mechanism will be applied are specified in the Draft Agreement. When the EU is a co-respondent, but the ECJ has not yet assessed the compatibility of EU law with the ECHR, the ECJ will be given a limited time to make such assessment. Obviously, the accelerated procedure will be used by the ECJ (see Chapter 13.11);

- It provides for the possibility of a contracting State to the ECHR to start proceedings against the EU, and *vice versa*, but excludes it with regard to a Member State of the EU. This is because Article 344 TFEU bars a Member State from submitting any dispute concerning the interpretation or application of the Treaties to any method of settlement other than by the ECJ;

- A judge will be elected with regard to the EU. He/she will have the same rights and duties as other judges and therefore he/she will be involved in all cases, not only in cases brought against the EU;

- The EU will have voting rights in the Committee of Ministers of the Council of Europe. However, in respect of supervision and the execution of judgments and friendly settlements in cases involving the EU a special voting procedure will apply to ensure that EU Member States (which form a majority within 47 contracting States to the Council of Europe) will not be able to overrule the non-EU States; and,

- The EU will contribute to the budget of the Council of Europe.

The relationship between the ECJ and the ECtHR as defined in the Draft Agreement, does not jeopardise the autonomy of the ECJ.[456] The ECJ will be treated by the ECtHR as any "domestic court", akin to constitutional or supreme courts of a contracting State to the ECHR, over which the ECtHR exercises "external restraint".

It is to be noted that the rights set forth in the Charter of Fundamental Rights are broader than those in the ECHR not only in terms of wording but more importantly in terms of the types of rights protected. Whilst the ECHR is concerned with the protection of civil and political rights, the catalogue of rights recognised by the Charter is much broader as it encompasses not only civil and political rights but also economic; cultural; social; and, citizens' rights.[457] With the accession of the EU to the ECHR, the ECJ will remain the final authority with regard to the interpretation of Charter provisions which do not overlap with the ECHR and its Protocols 1 and 6. Further, under Article 52(3) of the Charter, the Union

---

456. T. Lock, "Walking on a Tightrope: The Draft ECHR Accession Agreement and the Autonomy of the EU Legal Order", (2011) 48 CMLRev., 1025.

457. P. Lemmens, "The Relation between the Charter of the EU and the ECHR: Substantive Aspects", (2001), 8 *Maastricht Journal of European and Comparative Law*, 49.

is not prevented from widening the protection guaranteed under the ECHR. This matter of whether the scope of protection under the Charter of Fundamental Rights, in particular the rights set out in its Article 1, concerning human dignity, Article 18, concerning the right to asylum, and Article 47, concerning the right to an effective remedy, is wider than the protection conferred by Article 3 of the ECHR, was examined in Case C-411/10 *NS*.[458] The ECJ held that the circumstances of this case did not lead to differing application of the ECHR and the Charter although it was clear that the ECJ had employed its own standard of protection. However, A-G Trstenjak in her Opinion stated that in the areas where the provisions of the Charter overlap with the provisions of the ECHR, high importance should be attached to the case law of the ECtHR but "it would . . . be wrong to regard the case-law of the European Court of Human Rights as a source of interpretation with full validity in connection with the application of the Charter."[459] Indeed, as long as the EU is not a contracting party to the ECHR, the Charter remains the main source of fundamental rights in the EU, and its interpretation by the ECJ is binding on the Member States. This can be illustrated as follows:

After the accession of the EU to the ECHR

The ECtHR will be the final court with regard to the interpretation of the rights set out in the Charter of Fundamental Rights of the EU which overlap with the rights contained in the ECHR and its Protocols 1 and 6. Below is the logo of the ECHR.

EUROPEAN COURT OF HUMAN RIGHTS
COUR EUROPEÈNNE DES DROITS DE L'HOMME

The ECJ will be the final court with regard to the interpretation of the provisions of the Charter of Fundamental Rights of the EU which are not part of the ECHR and its Protocols 1 and 6. Below is the logo of the ECJ.

Court of Justice of the European Union

The matter of whether the EU should accede to the ECHR was highly debated. It is submitted that the main advantages are as follows:

1. The accession of the EU to the ECHR will ensure that there is one standard of protection of fundamental rights Europe-wide with regard to rights covered by the ECHR and its Protocols 1 and 6. Accordingly, EU citizens, national courts, Member States, EU institutions, and EU courts will know that the human rights standards established by the ECtHR are to be followed bearing in mind that the ECJ will surrender its autonomy in the interpretation of EU law in the

---

458.   Judgment of 21/12/11 (NYR).
459.   Ibid, para. 146.

areas covered by the ECHR to another international body, i.e. the ECtHR. Indeed, in the past, both courts did not always speak with one voice. This is because both scrutinise the same fundamental rights issue from different perspectives. Both employ the teleological interpretation. However, the objectives of the ECHR do not necessarily coincide with the objectives of the EU. The main objective of the ECHR is to protect civil and political rights guaranteed under the ECHR. The objectives of the EU are set out in Article 3 TEU (see Chapter 1.19.4). Accordingly, for the ECJ the protection of fundamental rights is not the only yardstick, as it is for the ECtHR, in the interpretation of the Treaties. Different objectives pursued by the ECHR and the EU have resulted in certain divergences in the interpretation of the ECHR by the ECJ, bearing in mind that EU law restricts certain rights on the grounds of the overriding interests of the EU.[460] In particular, in respect of enforcement of EU competition law, the ECJ and the ECtHR have divergent views on the application of Article 6 and Article 8 of the ECHR with regard to the right not to incriminate oneself, the scope of legal privilege, and the extent of the right to inviolability of premises and other places including private homes (this is discussed in detail in Chapter 30.2.8). This is not the only area in which, on rare occasions, the ECJ and the ECtHR disagree on the interpretation of the ECHR. With regard to Article 10 of the ECHR, in Case C-159/90 *Grogan*,[461] the ECJ did not find Ireland in breach of Article 10 of the ECHR for the imposition of a ban on students distributing information on availability of abortion in the UK. However, the ECtHR found that Article 10 was breached in essentially the same factual situation.[462] In the Case C-260/89 *ERT*[463] the ECJ left to the referring court to assess whether monopoly rights on broadcasting conferred on ERT under Greek law constituted a breach of Article 10 of the ECHR (for facts see Chapter 8.2.3). The ECtHR ruled that conferral of such monopoly rights constituted a violation of Article 10 of the ECHR.[464]

The examples mentioned above are rare and constitute an exception rather than the rule. The ECtHR in the *Bosphorus* case[465] clearly indicated that scrutiny by the ECtHR of ECJ judgments will occur only exceptionally. In this case, the ECtHR held that the standard of protection of fundamental rights within the EU was satisfactory in terms of substantive guarantees and procedural mechanisms controlling their observance. It also declined to re-examine the issue of violation of the ECHR on the ground that it had already been examined by the ECJ in a reference for a preliminary ruling from the Irish Supreme Court. This conclusion was reached after the ECtHR reviewed the system of protection of fundamental rights in the EU, and the examination of the *Bosphorus* case contained in the Opinion of the A-G and by the ECJ. The ECtHR was satisfied that the EU protects fundamental rights in a manner which can be regarded as at least equivalent to that established under the ECHR.[466]

---

460. R. A. Lawson, "Confusion or Conflict? Diverging Interpretations of the European Convention on Human Rights in Strasbourg and Luxembourg", in R. A. Lawson and M. de Blois (eds), *The Dynamics of the Protection of Human Rights in Europe – Essays in Honour of Henry G. Schermers*, Volume III, 1994, Dordrecht: Martinus Nijhoff Publishers, 219 and P. Mahoney, "The Charter of Fundamental Rights of the European Union and the European Convention from the Perspective of the European Convention" (2002) 23 HRLJ 300.

461. Case C-159/90 *Society for the Protection of Unborn Children v Grogan* [1991] ECR I-4685.

462. *Open Door Counselling Ltd and Dublin Well Women Centre Ltd and Others v Ireland* (1993) 15 EHRR, 244.

463. [1991] ECR I-2925.

464. *Informationsverein Lentia v Austria* (1993) 17 EHRR 93.

465. (2006) 42 EHRR, 1. See also *DH & Others v Czech Republic* (2008) 47 EHRR, 3, para. 187.

466. Ibid, in para. 155 of the judgment the ECtHR stated that "equivalent" meant the same as "comparable" and that any requirement that the organisation's protection be "identical" rather than "comparable" could run counter to

Nevertheless, the accession of the EU to the ECHR will prevent the possibility of inconsistencies and ensure that differing standards of protection of rights covered by the ECHR and its Protocols 1 and 6 will not occur;

2. Member States will not be held accountable for breaches of fundamental rights committed by EU institutions. In *Matthews v UK*,[467] the ECtHR found the UK in breach of Article 3 of Protocol 1 to the ECHR by denying the applicant, a Gibraltar national, the right to vote in direct elections to the EP. The exclusion was based on the EC Act on Direct Elections of 1976 which was annexed to Council Decision 76/787,[468] and which had status equivalent to a Community Treaty and as such could not be challenged before the ECJ because the ECJ has no jurisdiction to review EU treaties. Similarly, in *Cantoni v France*,[469] although the ECtHR found no violation of Article 7 of the ECHR it held that the fact that Article L. 511 of the French Public Health Code was based almost word for word on Directive 65/65 did not exclude that Article from the ambit of Article 7 of the ECHR;

3. The EU will participate in the judicial system established by the ECHR in that it will be able to defend itself when a case concerns directly or indirectly the EU and will have its own judge in the ECtHR who will provide the necessary expertise on EU law;

4. The accession will prevent private litigants from *forum shopping*, i.e. the opportunity to choose the court, the ECJ or the ECtHR, which, in their view, will have a more favourable approach to their claim; and,

5. The EU will be, both liable for any violation of the ECHR, and required to comply with judgments of the ECHR.

It is submitted that the accession of the EU to the ECHR constitutes the best way of enhancing the legal protection of fundamental rights in the EU legal order and is a sign of self-confidence and maturity on the part of the EU, as it shows the world the EU's readiness for its institutions to be monitored, on fundamental rights issues within the scope of the ECHR and its Protocols 1 and 6, by an outside body.

RECOMMENDED READING

Books

Andreangeli, A., *EU Competition Enforcement and Human Rights*, 2008, Cheltenham: Edward Elgar Publishing Ltd.

Di Federico, G. (ed.), *The EU Charter of Fundamental Rights: From Declaration to Binding Instrument (Ius Gentium: Comparative Perspectives on Law and Justice)*, 2010, Dordrecht: Springer.

---

the interests of international co-operation. Similarly in *Kokkelvisserij v Nederlands* the ECtHR considered that the protection of fundamental rights under EU law was equivalent to that under the ECHR, see a case note by Van de Heyning in (2009) CMLRev., 2117; see also L. Besselink, "The European Union and the European Convention on Human Rights: From Sovereign Immunity in Bosphorus to Full Scrutiny Under the Reform Treaty?", in: I. Boerefijn and J. Goldschmidt (eds), *Changing Perceptions of Sovereignty and Human Rights, Essays in Honour of Cees Flinterman*, 2008, Antwerp: Intersentia, 295 at 305.

467. [1999] 28 EHRR 361.
468. [1976] OJ L278/1.
469. (1996) ECHR (Ser. V) 1996, 1614.

Hervey, T. and Kenner, J. (eds), *Economic and Social Rights Under the EU Charter of Fundamental Rights*, 2nd edn, 2006, London: Hart.

Peers, S., and Ward, A. (eds), *The EU Charter of Fundamental Rights*, 2004, Oxford: Hart Publishing.

Articles

Albi, A., "Ironies in Human Rights Protection in the EU: Pre-Accession Conditionality and Post-Accession Conundrums", (2009) 15 ELJ, 46.

Costello, C., "The Bosphorus Ruling of the European Court of Human Rights: Fundamental Rights and Blurred Boundaries in Europe", (2006) 6 HumRts L Rev, 87.

De Búrca, G., "The Evolution of EU Human Rights Law", in Craig, P., and De Búrca, G. (eds), *The Evolution of EU Law*, 2nd edn, 2011, Oxford: OUP, 465.

Greer, S. and Williams, A., "Human Rights in the Council of Europe and the EU: Towards 'Individual', 'Constitutional' or 'Institutional' Justice?", (2009) 15 ELJ, 462.

Harpaz, G., "The European Court of Justice and its Relations with the European Court of Human Rights: The Quest for Enhanced Reliance, Coherence and Legitimacy", (2009) 46 CMLRev., 105.

Kühling, J., "Fundamental Rights", in von Bogdandy, A., and Bast, J., *Principles of European Constitutional Law*, 2010, 2nd edn, Oxford: Hart Publishing.

Kumm, M., "Internationale Handelsgesellschaft, Nold and the New Human Rights Paradigm", in Azoulai, L., and Maduro, M. (eds), *The Past and Future of EU Law: The Classics of EU Law Revisited on the 50th Anniversary of the Treaties of Rome*, 2010, Oxford: Hart Publishing, 106.

Lawson, R.A., "Confusion or Conflict? Diverging Interpretations of the European Convention on Human Rights in Strasbourg and Luxembourg", in Lawson, R.A., and de Blois, M. (eds), *The Dynamics of the Protection of Human Rights in Europe – Essays in Honour of Henry G. Schermers*, Volume III, 1994, Dordrecht: Martinus Nijhoff Publishers, 219.

Lock, T., "Walking on a Tightrope: The Draft ECHR Accession Agreement and the Autonomy of the EU Legal Order", (2011) 48 CMLRev., 1025.

Mahoney, P., "The Charter of Fundamental Rights of the European Union and the European Convention from the Perspective of the European Convention", (2002) 23 HRLJ, 300.

Sirpis, P. and Novitz, T., "Economic and Social Rights in Conflict: Political and Judicial Approaches to Their Reconciliation", (2008) 33 ELRev., 411.

Spaventa, E., "The Horizontal Application of Fundamental Rights as General Principles of EU Law", in Arnull, A., Barnard, C., Dougan, M., and Spaventa, E. (eds), *A Constitutional Order of States? Essays in Honour of Alan Dashwood*, 2011, Oxford: Hart Publishing.

Van den Berghe, F., "The EU and Issues of Human Rights Protection: Some Solutions to More Acute Problems?", (2010) 16 ELJ, 112.

Von Bernstorff, J., and von Bogdandy, A., "The EU Fundamental Rights Agency within the European and International Human Rights Architecture: The Legal Framework and Some Unsettled Issues in a New Field of Administrative Law", (2009) 46 CMLRev., 1035.

Wouters, J., "The EU Charter of Fundamental Rights – Some Reflections on its External Dimension", (2001) 1 *Maastricht Journal of European and Comparative Law*, 3.

PROBLEM QUESTION

John, a British national who is a beneficiary of a grant received from the CAP's funds, is unhappy with EU Regulations governing the financing of the CAP which require the publication of information on natural persons who receive aid from the CAP's funds. The information, which is made available to the public through a website operated by the British Agricultural Office, includes names, municipality of residence and, where available, postcode of beneficiaries and sums awarded to them. John objects to the publication of his personal details as contrary to EU law.

Advise John.

ESSAY QUESTION

Critically assess the following statement "The provisions of the Charter of Fundamental Rights of the EU on the interpretation and application of that Charter, (i.e. the provisions commonly referred to as horizontal provisions) lack clarity."

AIDE-MÉMOIRE

THE PROTECTION OF FUNDAMENTAL RIGHTS IN THE EU IS BASED ON

THE CHARTER OF FUNDAMENTAL RIGHTS OF THE EUROPEAN UNION. THE CHARTER IS BINDING AND HAS THE SAME LEGAL VALUE AS THE TFEU AND THE TEU. ITS PROVISIONS ARE ADDRESSED TO THE INSTITUTIONS, BODIES AND AGENCIES OF THE EU AND THE MEMBER STATES WHEN THEY ARE IMPLEMENTING EU LAW. THE CHARTER ONLY CONFIRMS THE EXISTING RIGHTS AND DOES NOT CREATE NEW RIGHTS. ITS BENEFICIARIES ARE EU CITIZENS AND ALL PERSONS RESIDING WITHIN THE TERRITORY OF THE EU. EACH OF THE 50 ARTICLES OF THE CHARTER'S "RIGHTS, FREEDOMS AND PRINCIPLES" ARE CONTAINED IN SIX TITLES AS FOLLOWS:	THE ECHR THE EU WILL ACCEDE TO THE ECHR (ART. 6 (2) TEU). AS A RESULT THE ECtHR WILL BE THE FINAL AUTHORITY ON THE INTERPRETATION OF THE RIGHTS SET OUT IN THE CHARTER WHICH OVERLAP WITH THE RIGHTS CONTAINED IN THE ECHR AND ITS PROTOCOLS 1 & 6.	THE GENERAL PRINCIPLES OF EU LAW WHICH INCLUDE FUNDAMENTAL RIGHTS AS GUARANTEED BY THE ECHR AND AS THEY RESULT FROM THE CONSTITUTIONAL TRADITIONS COMMON TO THE MEMBER STATES (ART. 6(3) TEU)

DIGNITY	FREEDOMS	EQUALITY	SOLIDARITY	CITIZENS' RIGHTS	JUSTICE
THIS CONCERNS • HUMAN DIGNITY; • THE RIGHT TO LIFE; • THE RIGHT TO INTEGRITY OF PERSON; • FREEDOM FROM TORTURE AND INHUMAN OR DEGRADING TREATMENT OR PUNISHMENT; AND, • PROHIBITION OF SLAVERY	THIS CONCERNS • RIGHT TO LIBERTY AND SECURITY; • RESPECT FOR PRIVATE AND FAMILY LIFE; • FREEDOM OF THOUGHT, CONSCIENCE AND RELIGION; • FREEDOM OF EXPRESSION AND INFORMATION; • FREEDOM OF ASSEMBLY AND ASSOCIATION; • FREEDOM OF ARTS AND SCIENCE; • THE RIGHT TO EDUCATION; • FREEDOM TO CHOOSE AN OCCUPATION AND RIGHT TO ENGAGE IN WORK; • FREEDOM TO CONDUCT BUSINESS; • RIGHT TO PROPERTY; • RIGHT TO ASYLUM; AND, • PROTECTION IN THE EVENT OF REMOVAL, EXPULSION OR EXTRADITION	THIS CONCERNS • NON DISCRIMINATION; • CULTURAL AND LINGUISTIC DIVERSITY; • EQUALITY BETWEEN MEN AND WOMEN; • THE RIGHTS OF THE CHILD; • THE RIGHTS OF THE ELDERLY; AND, • INTEGRATION OF PERSONS WITH DISABILITIES	THIS CONCERNS • WORKERS' RIGHT TO INFORMATION AND CONSULTATION WITHIN THE UNDERTAKING; • RIGHT OF COLLECTIVE BARGAINING AND ACTION; • RIGHT OF ACCESS TO PLACEMENT SERVICES; • PROTECTION IN THE EVENT OF UNFAIR DISMISSAL; • FAIR AND JUST WORKING CONDITIONS; • PROHIBITION OF CHILD LABOUR AND PROTECTION OF YOUNG WORKERS; • PROTECTION OF FAMILY AND PROFESSIONAL LIFE; • ENTITLEMENT TO SOCIAL SECURITY AND SOCIAL ASSISTANCE; • ACCESS TO AND BENEFIT OF HEALTH CARE; • ENVIRONMENTAL PROTECTION; AND, • CONSUMER PROTECTION	THIS CONCERNS • RIGHT TO VOTE AND STAND AS CANDIDATES AT ELECTIONS TO THE EP; • RIGHT TO VOTE AND STAND AS CANDIDATE AT MUNICIPAL ELECTIONS AT THE PLACE OF RESIDENCE; • RIGHT TO GOOD ADMINISTRATION; • RIGHT TO ACCESS A DOCUMENT; • RIGHT TO REFER TO THE EU OMBUDSMAN; • FREEDOM OF MOVEMENT AND RESIDENCE; AND, • RIGHT TO DIPLOMATIC AND CONSULAR PROTECTION OUTSIDE THE EU	THIS CONCERNS • RIGHT TO AN EFFECTIVE REMEDY AND TO FAIR TRIAL; • RIGHT TO BE PRESUMED INNOCENT UNTIL PROVEN GUILTY AND RIGHT TO DEFENCE; • RESPECT for PRINCIPLES OF LEGALITY AND PROPORTIONALITY OF CRIMINAL OFFENCES AND PENALTIES; AND, • RIGHT NOT TO BE TRIED OR PUNISHED TWICE IN CRIMINAL PROCEEDINGS FOR THE SAME OFFENCE

9

SUPREMACY OF EU LAW

CONTENTS

CHAPTER OUTLINE

1. The founding Treaties and their amendments are silent on the issue of priority between national laws and EU law. However, the ToL, without directly mentioning the principle of supremacy, in Declaration 17 confirmed that in accordance with the case law of the ECJ "the Treaties and the law adopted by the Union have primacy over the law of Member States". Indeed, the ECJ in Case 6/64 *Costa v ENEL* had no hesitation in declaring that EU law must take priority over, and supersede any national provision which clashes with EU law.

2. Supremacy, at least as asserted by the ECJ, is over both ordinary national law and national constitutional law of Member States, even when national constitutional law relates to the protection of fundamental rights or to the internal structure of the Member State. It applies when there is a conflict between EU law and national law and when both appear to be capable of being applied to the same factual situation. However, as there is no ECJ case law on measures adopted under the CFSP and given that the ECJ, as a matter of principle, has no jurisdiction in respect of such measures, it is uncertain whether the principle of supremacy applies to them.

3. Supremacy from the principle of supremacy that a national court is bound to enforce EU law and give full effect to it, if necessary refusing, on its own motion, to apply any conflicting provision of national legislation in a situation where the issue of EU law has been pleaded by the parties to the proceedings. In such a situation when faced with a national provision which clashes with EU law, a national court should not wait for annulment or repeal of inconsistent national law by domestic legislatures or constitutional organs. However, the duty of national courts to raise points of EU law of their own motion is subject to the principle of national procedural autonomy although the ECJ has established some exceptions.

4. In Joined Cases C-402/05 P and C-415/05 P *Kadi*, the ECJ held that although EU courts have no jurisdiction to review the legality of measures adopted by the UNSC, in fact, it did review them. In this case, the ECJ held that EU law prevails over binding measures adopted by the UNSC if such measures are in breach of fundamental rights protected under EU law.

5. The principle of supremacy has limitations arising from EU law itself: first, the EU can only act within the limits of its competences; second, under Article 4(2) TEU the EU must respect the national identity of the Member State; third, the principle of supremacy must take account of the general principles of EU law, in particular the principles of legal certainty and legitimate expectations; and, fourth, international agreements entered into prior to the accession of a Member State to the EU prevail over EU law.

6. The principle of supremacy necessarily limits the sovereign rights of the Member States. Some Member States continue to struggle to accept the absolute nature of the principle of supremacy of EU law as enunciated by the ECJ.

9.1 Introduction

There is no mention of the supremacy of Community law [EU law][470] in the founding Treaties and its amendments thereof. However, the ToL, without any express provision having been inserted into the Treaties to this effect, in Declaration 17 confirms the case law of the ECJ on the principle of supremacy. Declaration 17 quotes an Opinion of the Council Legal Service on the Primacy of EC Law of 22 June 2007 which states that: "The fact that the principle of primacy will not be included in the future treaty shall not in any way change the existence of the principle and the existing case-law of the Court of Justice." Accordingly, it appears that Declaration 17 does not make any changes as to the existence and meaning of the principle of supremacy, it simply confirms the current position of the ECJ on this matter.

---

470. The terms "supremacy" and "primacy" are used interchangeably in the English language; see B. de Witte, "Direct Effect, Primacy, and the Nature of the Legal Order", in P. Craig, and G. de Bùrca (eds), *The Evolution of EU Law*, 2nd edn, 2011, Oxford: OUP, p. 323. The ECJ uses the term "primacy"; Article I-6 of the failed Constitutional Treaty and Declaration 17 attached to the Treaties use the term "primacy". In France there is no confusion between the terms, as "primacy" (*primauté*) is used consistently. Some commentators argue that there is a difference between the two: on this topic see: M. Avbelj, "Supremacy or Primacy of EU law – (Why) Does it Matter", (2011) 17/6 ELJ, p. 744. In this book, the word supremacy is used.

The supremacy of EU law, according to the ECJ, is based on the fact that, contrary to ordinary international treaties, the founding Treaties have created their own legal system. In Case 6/64 *Costa v ENEL*[471] the ECJ held that: "The Treaty has created its own legal system which on the entry into force of the Treaty, became an integral part of the legal systems of the Member States". According to the ECJ the supremacy results from the peculiar nature of the EU and not from concessions made by constitutional laws of the Member States. For that reason, the supremacy of EU law does not depend on which theory each Member State applies in order to determine the relationship between national and international law.

From the perspective of the ECJ the supremacy of EU law is unconditional and absolute. All EU law prevails over all national laws within the scope of EU law. This means that national laws, including national constitutional law, when in conflict with EU law, will yield to all sources of EU law, i.e.:

- The provisions of the Treaties, and Protocols and Annexes attached to them;

- The Charter of Fundamental Rights of the EU;

- Secondary legislation (that is, regulations,[472] directives,[473] and decisions[474]). However, as the ECJ has no jurisdiction over matters relating to the CFSP, with the exceptions set out in Article 275 TFEU (see Chapter 7.5.3) and in the absence of pre-ToL case law on this matter, it is uncertain whether the principle of supremacy applies to measures adopted under the CFSP;

- The general principles of EU law;[475] and,

- International agreements concluded between the EU and third countries[476] or international organisations.

This absolute effect of the principle of supremacy means that "even the most minor piece of technical [EU] legislation ranks above the most cherished constitutional norm".[477]

The principle of supremacy is addressed to all authorities of a Member State. It entails that the legislator is prevented from enacting legislation contrary to EU law, and must amend and repeal conflicting legislation. The government must not adopt administrative or other measures incompatible with EU law, and is prevented from entering into international agreements with third States when such agreements are incompatible with EU law. The principle of supremacy imposes on national courts a duty first, to avoid a conflict between national law and EU law by interpreting national law in conformity with EU law "so far as possible" but not *contra legem* (see Chapter 10.8.2), and second requires that any conflicting national law is to be set aside, and, when relevant, substituted by directly effective EU provisions (see Chapter 9.6). It is important to note that national courts are required to set aside a national provision which clashes with an EU provision, but there is no requirement to nullify it. The national provision remains valid and applicable to aspects of national law which do not clash with EU law. In Joined Cases C-10/97 to C-22/97 *IN.CO.GE.'90*[478] the Commission argued that any national

---

471. [1964] ECR 585.

472. Case 43/71 *Politi SAS v Ministry for Finance of the Italian Republic* [1971] ECR 1039; Case 84/71 *SpA Marimex v Ministero delle Finanze* [1972] ECR 89.

473. Case 158/80 *Rewe-Handelsgesellschaft Nord mbH and Rewe-Markt Steffen v Hauptzollamt Kiel* [1981] ECR 1805; Case 8/81 *Ursula Becker v Finanzamt Münster-Innenstadt* [1982] ECR 53.

474. Case 130/78 *Salumificio de Cornuda v Amministrazione delle Finanze dello Stato* [1979] ECR 867.

475. Case 5/88 *Hubert Wachauf v Bundesamt für Ernährung und Forstwirtschaft* [1989] ECR 2609.

476. Case 38/75 *Douaneagent der NV Nederlandse Spoorwegen v Inspecteur der Invoerrechten en Accijnzen* [1975] ECR 1439; Cases 267–269/81 *Amministrazione delle Finanze dello Stato v SPI and SAMI* [1983] ECR 801.

477. Cited by B. de Witte, supra note 470.

478. Joined Cases C-10/97 to C-22/97 *Ministero Delle Finanze v IN.CO.GE.'90 Srl and Others* [1998] ECR I-6307.

provision inconsistent with EU law should be treated as non-existent and void. The Court disagreed. It held that:

- in situations not covered by EU law national courts can uphold the validity of national law which clashes with EU law; and,

- in a situation where EU law is applicable, national courts must disapply inconsistent national law whilst ensuring that any rights conferred by EU law are enforced under the domestic procedure.[479]

The principle of supremacy is also binding on administrative bodies of a Member State.[480]

9.2 The establishment of the doctrine of supremacy of EU law by the ECJ

The issue of priority between EU law and national law of the Member States arose before national courts in the early years of the Community. National courts referred to the ECJ for clarifications, under the procedure laid down in Article 267 TFEU. The ECJ took it upon itself to firmly establish the principle of supremacy of Community law as a necessary condition for the existence of the Community itself and its peculiar nature in the international legal order.

Two years after the 1962 judgment in *Van Gend*[481] (see Chapter 10.1), the ECJ was ready to spell out the full implications of its judgment in that case and to enunciate the principle of supremacy of EC law over the national laws of the Member States. This it did in Case 6/64 *Costa v ENEL*.[482]

THE FACTS WERE:

Costa was a shareholder of a private undertaking nationalised by the Italian Government on 6 September 1962. When subsequently assets of many private undertakings (including that in which Costa held shares) were transferred to ENEL, a company which was created by the Italian Government for the purposes of the nationalisation, Costa, who was also a lawyer, refused to pay an electricity bill for £1 sent by ENEL and was accordingly sued by ENEL. He argued, inter alia, that the nationalisation legislation was contrary to various provisions of the EC Treaty. The Milanese Giudice Conciliatore referred the matter to the ECJ under Article 267 TFEU. The Italian Government claimed that the referral was "absolutely inadmissible" since a national court, which is obliged to apply national law, cannot avail itself of Article 267 TFEU. In the meantime the Italian Constitutional Council decided in favour of national legislation.

Held:

The ECJ held that membership of the Community entailed a permanent limitation of the sovereign rights of the Member States to the extent that national law enacted subsequent to the accession of a Member State to the Community could not be given effect if and so far

---

479. See also Case 34/67 *Firma Gebrüder Lück v Hauptzollamt Köln-Rheinau* [1968] ECR 245.

480. Case 103/88 *Fratelli Costanzo v Comune di Milano* [1989] ECR 1839 and Case 224/97 *Erich Ciola v Land Vorarlberg* [1999] ECR I-2517. On this topic see: M. Claes, *The National Courts: Mandate in the European Constitution*, 2006 Oxford: Hart Publishing, ch. 10.

481. *NV Algemene Transport- en Expeditie Onderneming van Gend & Loos v Netherlands Inland Revenue Administration* [1963] ECR 3.

482. [1964] ECR 585.

> as it was contrary to Community law. The ECJ held "the law stemming from the Treaty, an independent source of law, could not, because of its special and original nature, be overridden by domestic legal provisions, however framed, without being deprived of its character as Community law and without the legal basis of the Community itself being called into question."[483]
>
> **Comment:**
>
> To justify the supremacy of EC law, the ECJ based its reasoning on the following three arguments:
>
> First, the direct applicability and direct effect of Community law would be meaningless (see Chapters 10 and 11) if Member States were permitted, by subsequent legislation, to unilaterally nullify the effects of EC law by means of a legislative measure which would prevail over Community law. Furthermore, the ECJ stated that the precedence of Community law is confirmed by what is now Article 288 TFEU, whereby a regulation "shall be binding" and "directly applicable in all Member States". The Court held that "This provision, which is subject to no reservation, would be quite meaningless if a State can unilaterally nullify its effects by means of a legislative measure which could prevail over Community law."
>
> Second, by transferring certain competences to the Community institutions the Member States have limited their sovereignty. The ECJ held that: "By creating the Community of unlimited duration . . . and more particularly real powers stemming from a limitation of sovereignty or a transfer of powers from the Member States to the Community, the Member States have limited their sovereign rights, albeit within limited fields, and have thus created a body of law which binds both their nationals and themselves." Accordingly, in areas in which the Member States have transferred their powers to the Community they no longer have power to legislate.
>
> Third, there is the need to maintain the uniformity of application of Community law. This ensures homogeneity of the Community legal order. In this respect the ECJ held that: "The executive force of Community law cannot vary from one Member State to another in deference to subsequent domestic laws, without jeopardising the attainment of the objectives of the Treaty set out in Article 3(2) EC [repealed] and giving rise to the discrimination prohibited by [Article 18 TFEU]."

The position of the ECJ has not changed since its decision in *Costa*. If anything, the ECJ has become increasingly radical in confirming the obvious implications of the supremacy of EU law with regard to the Member States.[484] Whatever the reaction of the Member States and no matter how long it takes to gain full recognition of this principle by the Member States, for the EU supremacy is a necessary requirement of its existence.

It is correct to say that in order to achieve the objectives of the founding Treaties, to uniformly apply EU law throughout the EU, to ensure the proper functioning of the internal market, and for the EU to become a fully integrated structure, the supremacy of EU law must be respected by the Member States. Otherwise, the EU will cease to exist as we currently understand it.[485]

---

483. Ibid, at 594.
484. See Chapter 14.2.2.3.
485. As the ECJ explained in Case 14/68 *Walt Wilhelm and Others v Bundeskartellamt* [1969] ECR 1.

9.3 Supremacy of EU law over national law including constitutional law of the Member States

The ECJ confirmed that a provision of national constitutional law cannot be invoked in order to exclude the application of EU law given that this is contrary to the EU public order, and, further, this position of the ECJ remains unchanged when fundamental rights enshrined in the Constitution of a Member State are at issue.

These matters were dealt with in Case 11/70 *Internationale Handelsgesellschaft*.[486]

THE FACTS WERE:

EC regulations set up a system of export licences, guaranteed by a deposit, for certain agricultural products. The system required that products be exported during the validity of a licence; otherwise the deposit would be forfeited. The plaintiff lost a deposit of DM17,000 and argued that the system, introduced by EC regulations and run by the West German National Cereals Intervention Agency, was in breach of the fundamental human rights provisions contained in the German Constitution, in particular its right to freedom of action and economic liberty and the principle of proportionality. The Frankfurt Administrative Court referred to the ECJ under Article 267 TFEU to determine the validity of one of the two regulations in question.

Held:

The ECJ confirmed the supremacy of Community law over national constitutional law in the following terms: "the law stemming from the Treaty, an independent source of law, cannot because of its very nature be overridden by rules of national law, however framed, without being deprived of its character as Community law and without the legal basis of the Community itself being called in question. Therefore, the validity of a Community measure or its effect within a Member State cannot be affected by allegations that it runs counter to either fundamental rights as formulated by the constitution of that Member State or the principles of a national constitutional structure."[487]

In this case, the ECJ declared the regulations in question as valid and the system of deposit as an appropriate method of attaining the objectives relating to the common organisation of the agricultural markets.

Comment:

In Case 11/70 Internationale Handelsgesellschaft, *the ECJ held that fundamental rights, taking into account their importance, cannot be disregarded by the EU. Respect for them forms an integral part of the general principles of EU law and the protection of such rights must be ensured within the framework of the structure and objectives of the EU (see Chapter 8.2.2). Thus, the ECJ responded to the challenges to the principle of supremacy based on the protection of fundamental rights. Further, Declaration 17, attached to the Treaties, although a non-binding instrument, affirms the recognition by the Member States of primacy of EU law over national law at every level, including constitutional law of the Member States taking into account that the position of the ECJ on the supremacy of EU law is clear and unambiguous.*

---

486.   [1970] ECR 1125.
487.   Ibid, para. 3.

If there is a conflict between EU law and national law enacted prior to a Member State's accession to the EU, it must be resolved in favour of EU law. All pre-dating national law is deemed to be abrogated, or at least devoid of legal effect, in so far as it is contrary to EU law. For reasons of legal certainty an express repeal of conflicting pre-existing national law is desirable, and in some circumstances required under EU law.[488]

Where there is conflict between EU law and national law enacted subsequent to the accession of a Member State to the EU, the former prevails. This was established in Case 6/64 *Costa v ENEL*.[489]

9.4 Supremacy of EU law and international agreements entered into by a Member State

A distinction must be made between international agreements entered into by a Member State prior to, and subsequent to its accession to the EU.

9.4.1 Agreements concluded prior to accession to the EU

International agreements concluded before accession of a Member State to the EU prevail over EU law. Article 351(1) and (2) TFEU endorses this principle. It provides that:

"The rights and obligations arising from agreements concluded before 1 January 1958 or, for acceding States, before the date of their accession, between one or more Member States on the one hand, and one or more third countries on the other, shall not be affected by the provisions of this Treaty.

To the extent that such agreements are not compatible with the Treaties, the Member State or States concerned shall take all appropriate steps to eliminate the incompatibility established. Member States shall, where necessary, assist each other to this end and shall, where appropriate, adopt a common attitude."

The scope of Article 351 TFEU was examined by the ECJ in Case C-466/98 *Commission v UK*.[490]

THE FACTS WERE:

This case concerned "open sky" agreements concluded between many EU Member States and the USA. The UK Government concluded the first agreement with the USA in 1946. This was the Bermuda I Agreement, which was amended in 1977 by the Bermuda II Agreement. In 1992, the USA Government offered the UK (and other Member States) the possibility of concluding a bilateral "open sky" agreement revising the Bermuda II Agreement. In 1995, the UK signed such an agreement ignoring the Commission's letter of formal notice stating that negotiation and conclusion of agreements in the area of air transport was within the exclusive competence of the Commission.

According to the UK, as the rights and obligations conferred in the Bermuda I Agreement were not substantially changed by the Bermuda II Agreement, the Bermuda II Agreement,

---

488.   Case 167/73 *Commission v France* [1974] ECR 359.
489.   [1964] ECR 585.
490.   [2002] ECR I-9427.

although concluded four years after accession of the UK to the Communities, constituted a continuation of the Bermuda I Agreement and therefore could not be considered as a new agreement. It was therefore within the scope of Article 351(1) TFEU. This was not the opinion of the Commission.

Held:

The ECJ found that the Bermuda II Agreement was a new agreement, mainly on the basis that its preamble expressly stated that the Bermuda II Agreement was replacing the Bermuda I Agreement in order to respond to the development of traffic rights between the USA and the UK. This necessity to adjust the Bermuda I Agreement to new circumstances demonstrated that the Bermuda II Agreement was a new agreement creating new rights and obligations between the contracting parties and as such was outside the scope of Article 351 (1) TFEU.

Article 351 TFEU protects pre-accession agreements with third States from challenges based on their incompatibility with EU law while seeking to prevent Member States from relying on previous international agreements in order to escape their obligations imposed by the Treaties. In Case 10/61 *Commission v Italy*,[491] the ECJ held that Italy could not invoke GATT (a pre-accession agreement) provisions on customs duties to escape the obligations of the EC Treaty relating to intercommunity exchanges[492] because Article 351 TFEU only guarantees rights held by third countries under pre-accession agreements. Also, Article 351 TFEU imposes an important limitation on a Member State's obligations arising out of an international agreement concluded prior to its accession, in that the EU as such cannot be bound by such an agreement with regard to third countries.[493]

In practice, the principle contained in Article 351 TFEU poses difficult problems for national judges in the case of a conflict between international agreements and EU law. This problem is best illustrated by the contradictions between the Conventions of the International Labour Organisation and the EC Directive relating to the night work of women.[494]

International agreements concluded between Member States before their accession to the EU, but which remain in force subsequent to the accession, are usually subject to special provisions of the Treaties.[495]

9.4.2 Agreements concluded subsequent to accession

In accordance with the principles of public international law, subsequent international agreements should not affect earlier agreements. Accordingly, international agreements concluded by Member States after their accession to the EU will be disregarded if incompatible with EU law.

---

491. [1962] ECR 1.
492. Also, in Case C-144/89 *Commission v UK* [1991] ECR I-3533 the ECJ held that the provisions on the CFP could not be replaced by conventional rules emanating from an international convention entered into by the UK prior to the accession to the Communities with regard to other Member States.
493. Case 812/79 *Attorney General v Juan C. Burgoa* [1980] ECR 2787.
494. Case C-345/89 *Criminal Proceedings against Alfred Stoeckel* [1991] ECR I-4047; Case C-158/91 *Criminal Proceedings against Jean-Claude Levy* [1993] ECR I-4287; Case C-13/93 *ONEM v Madeleine Minne* [1994] ECR I-371.
495. For example, Article 350 TFEU concerning the customs union between Belgium and Luxembourg as well as the Benelux Union.

9.5 Supremacy of EU law and binding resolutions of the UN Security Council (UNSC)

The background to the issue of validity of UNSC resolutions under EU law is that the UNSC itself and its Sanctions Committee (which was set up to ensure that Members of the UN were implementing UNSC resolutions) identified some terrorist organisations and persons involved in terrorist activities and placed them on a particular UN list (that is, the affected persons list). Members of the UN were required to ensure that funds controlled by those individuals or entities (for example, Osama bin Laden, al-Qaeda, and the Taliban) were frozen. The Member States of the EU decided to take collective action pursuant to the UNSC resolutions. Accordingly, the Council adopted a number of Common Positions under Pillar 2 and Pillar 3, on the basis of some of which further implementing measures (for example, regulations) were adopted. To these regulations a list of persons, entities and bodies affected by the freezing of funds was attached. The list was regularly updated by the UNSC Sanctions Committee and the Commission was empowered to amend or supplement that list accordingly.

The Council placed on the above-mentioned list not only persons and entities identified by the UNSC, but also others identified on the basis of information from Member States. A number of individuals and entities whose names were put on the list brought proceedings to annul the Council's and Commission's implementation of the UNSC resolutions on the ground that their fundamental rights had been breached in various ways, in particular, the right to a fair hearing.

The General Court, in dealing with cases concerning the affected person, made a distinction between a situation where the applicant was placed on the affected persons list by the UNSC or the UNSC Sanctions Committee and a situation where inclusion of a person or entity on the list was decided completely autonomously by the Council on the basis of information supplied by one or more Member States.

■ In the first situation, the General Court decided that it had no jurisdiction to review the legality of the relevant UNSC resolution directly or indirectly, although it had jurisdiction to determine whether those resolutions were in conformity with *jus cogens*.[496] Its conclusion was that given the procedural guarantees contained in UNSC resolutions, fundamental rights were sufficiently protected when assessed in the light of *jus cogens*.[497] Accordingly, the General Court upheld the validity of the relevant EU regulations.

■ In the second situation involving the exercise of the Community's own powers, entailing a discretionary appreciation by the Community of who should be on the list, the Community institutions were bound to comply with the requirements of fundamental rights. The General Court found that the contested Community legislation did not contain a sufficient statement of reasons and that it was adopted in the course of a procedure during which the applicant's right to a fair hearing was not observed. As a result, the General Court annulled the relevant Community acts in so far as they concerned the applicants.[498]

---

496. *Jus cogens* are imperative, peremptory rules of international legal order. They are superior to any other rules of international law. They are so fundamental that they bind all States and do not allow any exception. A peremptory rule is defined in Article 53 of the 1969 Vienna Convention on the Law of Treaties as: "a norm accepted and recognised by the international community of States as a whole as a norm from which no derogation is permitted and which can be modified only by a subsequent norm of general international law having the same character."

497. Case T-306/01 *Yusuf and Al Barakaat International Foundation v Council and Commission* [2005] ECR II-3533 and Case T-315/01 *Kadi v Council and Commission* [2005] ECR II-3649, see Posch, A., "The Kadi Case: Rethinking the Relationship between EU Law and International Law?" (2009) 15 Colum.J.Eur.L, 1.

498. Case T-228/02 *Organisation des Modjahedines du Peuple d'Iran v Council* [2006] ECR II-4665; Case T-47/03 *Jose Maria Sison v Council* [2007] ECR II-73 and Case T-327/03 *Stichting Al-Aqsa v Council* [2007] ECR II-79.

On appeal, the ECJ confirmed the judgments of the General Court in respect of the annulment of measures involving the exercise of the Community's own powers, but refused to uphold those judgments in so far as the validity of EU measures implementing resolutions adopted by the UNSC under Chapter VII of the UN Charter was concerned (i.e. resolutions which under Article 103 of the UN Charter are binding on all members of the UN and prevail over any conflicting international agreements).

In Joined Cases C-402/05 P and C-415/05 P *Kadi*[499] the ECJ decided that the EU was not bound by the UN Charter and secondary UN law in circumstances where secondary UN law was adopted in breach of fundamental principles of EU law, i.e. in breach of fundamental rights, in particular, the right to a fair trial. The ECJ held that neither the ECJ nor the General Court has jurisdiction to review the lawfulness of resolutions adopted by the UNSC "even if that review were to be limited to the examination of that resolution with *jus cogens* "[500] and that no judgment of the EU courts can challenge the primacy of obligations deriving from the UN Charter, even if that judgment finds EU measures implementing a UNSC resolution as being contrary to the higher rule of law of the EU legal system. However, the ECJ has jurisdiction to review the validity of any EU act, including that giving effect to a binding UN resolution, in the light of fundamental principles of EU law. The ECJ emphasised that such a review:

"must be considered to be the expression, in a Community based on the rule of law, of a constitutional guarantee stemming from the EC Treaty as an autonomous legal system which is not to be prejudiced by an international agreement."[501]

The ECJ found that the UN resolution, which left no discretion to the Member States as to its implementation, "patently" violated the right of defence, in particular the right to be heard, and the right to effective judicial review of those rights in respect of the persons concerned. As a result, the ECJ annulled the challenged measure (i.e. Regulation 881/2002).

Two conclusions follow from the *Kadi* case. The first conclusion is that the protection of fundamental rights in the EU is of the highest importance in that the EU will give preference to the protection of fundamental rights even if this means a breach of the UN Charter. As the ECJ stated: "It is . . . clear from the case-law that respect for human rights is a condition of the lawfulness of Community acts and that measures incompatible with respect for human rights are not acceptable in the Community."[502] The second conclusion is that the EU legal system is autonomous with regard to international legal order, i.e. EU law prevails over binding measures adopted by the UNSC if such measures are in breach of fundamental principles of EU law.

9.6 Application of the principle of supremacy by national courts

Supremacy of EU law creates problems for national courts, in particular in a situation where according to national law only a superior court, or a constitutional court, has power to declare national law to be unconstitutional. This issue was examined in Case 106/77 *Simmenthal*.[503]

---

499. Joined Cases C-402/05 P and C-415/05 P *Kadi and Al Barakaat International Foundation v Council and Commission* [2008] ECR I-6351. The position taken by the ECJ has been confirmed in many cases, e.g. Joined Cases C-399/06P and Case C-403/06 P *Faraj Hassan and Chafiq Ayadi v Council and the Commission* [2009] ECR I-11393.

500. Para. 287.

501. Para. 316.

502. Para. 284.

503. *Case 106/77 Amministrazione delle Finanze v Simmenthal SpA* [1978] ECR 629.

THE FACTS WERE:

Simmenthal imported a consignment of beef from France to Italy. He was asked to pay for veterinary and public health inspections carried out at the frontier. He paid, but sued in the Italian court for reimbursement of the money paid out, arguing that the fees charged were contrary to Community law. After reference to the ECJ, which held that the inspections were contrary to Article 35 TFEU as being equivalent in effect to a quantitative restriction on imports and that the fees were consequently unlawful under Article 30 TFEU being charges equivalent to customs duties, the Italian court ordered the Italian Ministry to repay the fees. The ministry refused to repay, claiming that the national statute of 1970 under which Simmenthal was liable to pay fees was still preventing any reimbursement and could only be set aside by the Italian Constitutional court. The matter was referred once again to the ECJ under Article 267 TFEU.

Held:

The ECJ held that:

- *In the event of incompatibility of a subsequent legislative measure of a Member State with Community law, every national judge must apply Community law in its entirety and must set aside any provision of national law, prior or subsequent, which conflicts with Community law.*
- *National courts should not request or await the prior setting aside of an incompatible national provision by legislation or other constitutional means, but of their own motion, if necessary, refuse the application of conflicting national law and instead apply Community law.*

In Case C-213/89 *Factortame (No. 1)*[504] the ECJ went further. In this case a UK Act of Parliament was incompatible with directly effective rights deriving from the EC Treaty. The ECJ held that the effectiveness of EU law entails that an English court seised with a dispute governed by EU law was required to grant interim relief in a situation where under English law the English courts had neither the power to suspend, by way of interim relief, the operation of a statute pending the preliminary ruling of the ECJ, nor to grant interim relief against the Crown, i.e. against the government. This is a far reaching consequence of the supremacy of EU law in that national courts, in order to give full effect to EU law, must create new remedies when national rules do not provide effective protection for individuals who seek damages or other remedies for breaches of their EU rights by a Member State (see Chapter 12.6). As B de Witte stated, the principle of supremacy requires more than just "setting aside" of a conflicting national provision.[505]

Similarly, administrative authorities are required to set aside any national provision incompatible with EU law.[506] In relation to sanctions, especially of a penal nature, imposed under national law but incompatible with EU law, those sanctions are considered as being devoid of any legal effect.[507]

---

504. Case C-213/89 *R v Secretary of State for Transport, ex parte Factortame Ltd and Others* [1990] ECR I-2433. See also Case C-314/08 *Krzysztof Filipiak v Dyrektor Izby Skarbowej w Poznaniu* [2009] ECR I-11049, and Joined Cases C-188/10 and C-189/10 *Aziz Melki and Sélim Abdeli* [2010] ECR I-5667.

505. Supra note 470, 342–43.

506. Case 103/88 *Fratelli Costanzo SpA v Comune di Milano* [1989] ECR 1861.

507. Case 88/77 *Minister for Fisheries v C.A. Schonenberg and Others* [1978] ECR 473; Case 269/80 *R v Robert Tymen* [1981] ECR 3079; Joined Cases C-338/04, C-359/04 and C-360/04 *Criminal Proceedings against Massimiliano Placanica* [2007] ECR I-1891.

The principle of supremacy entails the following consequences for national courts:

■ In a dispute before a national court which involves a conflict between EU law and national law, a national court is required to interpret national law in conformity with EU law irrespective of whether or not a provision of EU law is directly effective[508] and irrespective of whether the proceedings are between an individual and a Member State or its emanation, or between individuals.[509] However, the duty imposed on national courts to interpret national law in conformity with EU law has its limitation in that national judges are required to interpret national rules conflicting with provisions of EU law only "as far as possible" (see Chapter 10.8.2). It is only when a dispute cannot be resolved *via* the consistent interpretation that a national court considers the issue of direct effect of the relevant EU provision[510] (see Chapter 10);

■ If a claimant relies on EU law to "exclude", i.e. set aside a national provision which is contrary to a provision of EU law, and if his claim is successful, the national court must disapply the inconsistent national provision. However, as explained above, the setting aside of a national provision may result in creation of a new remedy in cases where individuals are seeking damages or other remedies for breaches of EU law by a Member State. With regard to directives, when a Member State has exceeded the limits of the discretion set out in a directive in exercising its choice as to the form and methods for implementing it, individuals may rely on its provisions irrespective of whether these provisions are directly effective to achieve the setting aside of a conflicting national provision. This was confirmed by the ECJ in Case C-287/98 *Linster*;[511] and,

■ If a claimant successfully relies on EU law to "substitute" a provision of EU law for a relevant national provision, the national court will replace the inconsistent national provision by the relevant provision of EU law, but only if that provision of EU law is directly effective. Indeed, if a provision of EU law is not clear, precise and unconditional (i.e. has no direct effect), how can it replace the existing national law? (On this topic see Chapter 10.2.)

If it is not possible to resolve a dispute as above, an individual is not without a remedy. He has the right to claim compensation under the principle of State liability (see Chapter 12).

9.6.1 *Ex officio* application of EU law

The ECJ has refused to acknowledge the logical consequences of its judgment in *Simmenthal* in that it has not imposed on national courts a general duty to apply EU law *ex officio*, i.e. when parties to the proceedings did not raise points of EU law. Instead, the ECJ has relied on the principle of autonomy of national procedural law (see below) to determine, on a case-by-case basis whether, in the circumstances of each case, a national court is required to apply EU law on its own motion. Under this approach the respect for autonomy of procedural law of each Member State is subject to the principle of equivalence (i.e. that national procedural rules applicable to a claim under EU law must not be less favourable than those governing similar domestic actions), and the principle of effectiveness (i.e. that national procedural rules must not render practically impossible or excessively difficult the exercise of rights conferred by EU law) (see Chapter 12.6).

---

508. Case C-397-403/01 *Pfeiffer and Others v Deutsches Rotes Kreuz, Kreisverband Waldshut eV* [2004] ECR I-8835.
509. Case C-2/97 *Società Italiana Petroli SpA (IP) v Borsana Srl* [1998] ECR I-8597.
510. Case C-262/97 *Rijksdienst voor Pensioenen v Robert Engelbrecht* [2000] ECR I-7321; Case 249/85 *Albako v BALM* [1987] ECR 2345.
511. Case C-287/98 *Luxembourg v Berthe Linster and Others* [2000] ECR I-6917.

It emerges from the case law of the ECJ that a national court is obliged to apply EU law *ex officio*:

■ When national public policy rules require *ex officio* application of national law, EU law equivalent to the national law must be applied *ex officio*. For example, in Joined Cases C-222/05 to C-225/05 *Van der Weerd*,[512] national rules at issue related to public policy concerned the powers of administrative bodies and the court itself and provisions relating to admissibility. The provisions of EU law relevant to the dispute, i.e. Directive 85/511, were not of a similar importance in the EU legal order and therefore the national procedural rules did not breach the principle of equivalence. As a result, the national court had no obligation to apply on its own motion the relevant EU law. Obviously, in each Member State the requirements of public policy may be defined differently with the consequence that in some Member States where the concept of public policy is defined in broader terms than those in *Van der Weerd* a national court may be required to apply Directive 85/511 *ex officio*. This approach challenges the uniformity in the application of EU law;

■ In Case C-126/97 *Eco Swiss*[513] and in Joined Cases C-295/04 to C-298/04 *Manfredi*[514] the ECJ ruled that Articles 101 and 102 TFEU are matters of public policy and must be automatically applied by the national court. The implication of these rulings is that the EU has developed the concept of EU public policy although its content has not been clearly defined by the ECJ. Further, the ECJ has not, so far, specified the extent of the duty to apply EU law *ex officio* in that it is not clear whether a national court must only raise, *ex officio*, the point of EU law or whether it is required to broaden the dispute which is before the court and/or supplement the facts; and,

■ With regard to a number of provisions of EU directives[515] relating to the protection of consumers, the ECJ held that national courts have a duty to apply some of them *ex officio*. Under Directive 93/13 the duty to protect consumers from unfair contractual terms goes very far. National courts are required to investigate the legal and factual elements necessary to determine whether a contractual term is unfair when those elements are not immediately available to it and despite any national procedural rule to the contrary.[516]

The case law of the ECJ is very liberal with regard to the application of EU law *ex officio* by national courts in that in many cases it has accepted that no such obligation exists under EU law. In Joined Case C-430 and 431/93 *Van Schijndel*,[517] the ECJ decided that in the particular circumstances of that case (i.e. in civil proceedings in which a judge was allowed to act on his own motion only in exceptional cases where the public interest required his intervention), EU law did not require the national court to

---

512. Joined Cases C-222/05 to C-225/05 *J. van der Weerd and Others v Minister van Landbouw, Natuur en Voedselkwaliteit* [2007] ECR I-4233.

513. Case C-126/97 *Eco Swiss China Time Ltd v Benetton International NV* [1999] ECR I-3055.

514. Joined Cases C-295/04 to C-298/04 *Vincenzo Manfredi and Others v Lloyd Adriatico Assicurazioni SpA and Others* [2006] ECR I-6619.

515. On Directive 93/13 on unfair terms in consumer contracts see: Joined Case C-240-244/98 *Océno Grupo Editorial SA* [2000] ECR I-4941 and Case C-137/08 *VB Pénzügyi Lízing Zrt v Ferenc Schneider* [2010] ECR I-847; on Article 11(2) of Directive 87/102 concerning the right of a consumer to pursue remedies against a grantor of credit, see Case C-429/05 *Rampion and Godard v Franfinance SA and K par K SAS* [2007] ECR I-817; on Article 4 of Directive 85/577 concerning the duty of a trader to give notice of the consumer's right of cancellation of a contract negotiated away from business premises see Case C-227/08 *Eva Martín Martín v EDP Editores SL* [2009] ECR I-11939. On the protection of consumers see: V. Trstenjak and E. Beysen, "European Consumer Protection Law: Curia Semper Dabit Remedium", (2011) 48 CMLRev., 95.

516. Ibid, Case C-137/08 *VB Pénzügyi Lízing Zrt v Ferenc Schneider* [2010] ECR I-847.

517. Joined Cases C-430 and 431/93 *Jeroen van Schijndel and Johannes Nicolaas Cornelis van Veen v Stichting Pensioenfonds voor Fysiotherapeuten* [1995] ECR I-4705.

raise of its own motion an issue concerning EU law. In Case C-455/06 *Heemskerk*[518] the ECJ held that the referring court had no duty to raise, *ex officio*, the relevant EU law in a situation where to do this would be in breach of a national procedural rule which prohibited *reformatio in pejus*, i.e. a rule stating that the person bringing an appeal must not be placed in a less advantageous position than that in which he would have found himself in the absence of an appeal. This was despite the fact that the *ex officio* application of EU law would have corrected a misapplication of EU law by the relevant national authorities and would have resulted in the recovery of an export refund granted from EU funds which seemed to have been paid unduly to the claimant. Accordingly, the ECJ refused to condemn a national procedural rule, even though the *ex officio* application of EU law would have ensured the protection of the financial interests of the EU.

The ECJ's approach, based on the principle of autonomy of national procedural law, to the *ex officio* application of EU law undermines the principle of supremacy of EU law, which should ensure that EU law prevails irrespective of whether or not the parties to proceedings have raised the issue of EU law before national authorities. It also jeopardises the uniform application of EU law in that, relying on national procedural rules, which differ from one Member State to another, national courts will reach differing decisions depending on whether they are allowed to, or willing to, apply EU law on their own motion. Finally, the test of lawfulness of national law which, on the one hand, seeks to ensure respect for procedural autonomy of national rules and, on the other, the effective protection of rights conferred under EU law, is very complex and allows many justifications (e.g. the protection of the right of defence, the requirement of the principle of legal certainty, and the necessity to properly conduct procedure) for avoiding the application of EU law.

9.7 The limits of the doctrine of supremacy of EU law

The principle of supremacy has its limitations. They derive from the EU itself. These are:

- ■ The principle of conferral according to which the EU can only act within the limits of its competences (see Chapter 6.2);

- ■ The duty of the EU to respect the national identities of the Member States (Article 4(2) TEU). Some academic commentators argue that Article 4(2) TEU provides a justification for overcoming the idea of absolute supremacy of EU law as understood by the ECJ;[519]

- ■ The general principles of EU law, in particular the principle of legal certainty and legitimate expectations; and,

- ■ Under Article 351(1) and (2) TFEU, international agreements entered into prior to the accession of a Member State to the EU prevail over EU law (see Chapter 9.4.1).

9.7.1 The principle of legal certainty and the principle of *res judicata*

In Case C-234/04 *Kapferer*[520] the ECJ held that under EU law there is no obligation for a national court to review, and possibly set aside, a judgment which has became final and thus has acquired the status of

---

518.   C-455/06 *Heemskerk BVFirma Schaap v Productschap Vee en Vlees* [2008] ECR I-8763.

519.   On this topic see: Von Bogdandy, A., and Schill, S., "Overcoming Absolute Primacy: Respect for National Identity under the Lisbon Treaty", (2011) 48 CMLRev., 1417.

520.   C-234/04 *Kapferer v Schlank and Schick GmbH* [2006] ECR I-2585.

res judicata, but is contrary to a subsequent judgment of the ECJ. This is a consequence of the requirements of the principle of legal certainty. The judgment in *Kapferer* clarified the previous judgment of the ECJ in Case C-453/00 *Kühne*,[521] in which the referring court asked the ECJ the question whether and in what circumstances an administrative decision which has become final can be reopened where it becomes apparent from a judgment of the ECJ subsequent to the final decision that the decision was based on incorrect interpretation of EU law. The ECJ held that the administrative body concerned was, by virtue of Article 4(3) TFEU, under a duty to review its decision in order to take account of the interpretation of the relevant provision of EU law given in the meantime by the ECJ. This was because:

- national law conferred on an administrative body competence to reopen a decision in question, which has become final;

- the administrative decision became final only as a result of a judgment of a national court against whose decisions there is no judicial remedy;

- judgment was based on an interpretation of EU law which, in the light of a subsequent judgment of the ECJ, was incorrect and which was adopted without a question being referred to the ECJ for a preliminary ruling in accordance with the conditions provided for in Article 234 EC; and,

- the person concerned complained to the administrative body immediately after becoming aware of that judgment of the ECJ.

The ECJ distinguished its decision in *Kapferer* from its decision in *Kühne*. The Court explained that the situation in *Kapferer* was different from that in *Kühne*, because the judgment in *Kapferer* had become *res judicata* and the four conditions set out in *Kühne* were not satisfied, whereas they were in *Kühne*.

The judgment in *Kapferer*, which imposes an important limitation on the scope of the principle of supremacy of EU law, is well justified for the following reasons:

- The principle of *res judicata* is of great importance to national legal systems as it ensures both the stability of law and legal relations, and the sound administration of justice;

- Prior to the entry into force of the ToL, the Member States clearly stated their position as to the importance of the principle of *res judicata* in Article 68(3) EC (repealed). This Article allowed the Council, the Commission or a Member State to request a preliminary ruling on matters dealt with under Title IV of the EC Treaty, and stated that such a ruling should not apply to judgments of national courts which had become *res judicata*. Thus, it would be incongruous for the ECJ to take a totally opposed stand to that clearly expressed by the Member States; and,

- Despite the fact that the principle of *res judicata* overrides the principle of supremacy of EU law, in practice individuals have not been left without a remedy in a situation where a judgment, which had become *res judicata* and was subsequently found to be contrary to EU law, was rendered against them. In *Kühne* the ECJ emphasised that proceedings resulting in a judicial decision, which has acquired the status of *res judicata*, and proceedings seeking to establish the liability of a Member State are fundamentally different one from another in terms of purpose and

---

521. [2004] ECR I-837. In Joined Cases C-392/04 and C-422/04 *i-21* and *Arcor v Germany* [2006] ECR I-8559, the ECJ confirmed that an administrative body responsible for the adoption of an administrative decision incompatible with EU law is under an obligation to review and possibly to reopen that decision if the four conditions set out in *Kühne & Heitz* are fulfilled.

of parties involved. Indeed, the main objective of proceedings seeking to establish Member State liability for infringement of EU law is for the individuals concerned to obtain compensation for damage caused to them by a mistaken judicial decision and not to revise a judgment delivered by a court adjudicating at last instance. Consequently, the principle of *res judicata* does not call into question the principle of Member State liability (see Chapter 12).

In Case C-119/05 *Lucchini*,[522] however, the ECJ imposed an important restriction on the primacy of the principle of *res judicata* over the principle of supremacy of EU law. In this case the ECJ held that in a situation where a Member State granted aid to an undertaking in breach of a Commission decision declaring all the aid applied for to be incompatible with the internal market, a judgment delivered by a national court which confirmed entitlement to the grant of the aid (and which made no reference to EU law or the relevant Commission decision) should be set aside as contrary to EU law. This was notwithstanding the fact that under national law the national judgment had become *res judicata*. The ECJ justified this on the following grounds:

- First, that the national court had no jurisdiction to decide whether the State aid applied for by the claimant was compatible with the internal market. By virtue of Article 108 TFEU the Commission has exclusive competence to decide on such matters, and its decisions are subject to judicial review under Article 263 TFEU;

- Second, national courts have no jurisdiction to declare an EU act invalid. In this case the relevant act was the decision of the Commission, on the basis of which national implementing measures were taken. This matter is within the exclusive competence of the ECJ (see Chapter 13.8); and,

- Third, neither the Italian court of first instance, nor the Italian appellate court had referred to the applicable provisions of EU law or to the Commission's decision.

On the basis of the above the ECJ could have stated that, irrespective of the fact that the national judgment had became *res judicata*, that judgment had no effect on the matter of recovery of State aid as it neither concerned the validity of the aid nor its compatibility with the requirements of the internal market. Instead, the ECJ chose to rely on the principle of supremacy of EU law. The Court held that according to well-established EU law, national courts must give full effect to the provisions of EU law and, if necessary, on their own motion, set aside any provision of national law, including, in this case, the relevant provision of the Italian Civil Code containing the principle of *res judicata*.

The implication of this case is that the principle of *res judicata* will be disregarded if a national judgment, which has become *res judicata*, validates an encroachment by national authorities on an exclusive competence of EU law. However, this is not the only case where the principle of *res judicata* will not be applied. It is clear from the judgment of the ECJ in Case C-2/08 *Fallimento*,[523] that on rare occasions the principle of supremacy will prevail over the principle of *res judicata*. This will, however, occur only exceptionally and be decided by the ECJ on a case-by-case basis.

---

522. Case C-119/05 *Ministero dell'Industria, del Commercio e dell'Artigianato v Lucchini SpA, formerly Lucchini Siderurgica SpA* [2007] ECR I-6199.

523. Case C-2/08 *Amministrazione dell'Economia e delle Finanze and Agenzia delle Entrate v Fallimento Olimpiclub Srl* [2009] ECR I-7501. In this case the ECJ held that the effectiveness of EU law would be undermined if the principle of *res judicata* would lead to a situation where EU law would continue to be misapplied as a result of a national court being prevented from reopening a judgment based on an erroneous interpretation of EU law which had acquired the force of *res judicata*.

9.7.2 The principle of legal certainty and a national provision declared incompatible with EU law during a transitional period between the annulment of that provision and its amendment by a Member State

The matter of a temporary suspension of the application of the principle of supremacy of EU law was considered by the ECJ in Case C-409/06 *Winner Wetten*.[524]

THE FACTS WERE:

The referring German court was uncertain how to deal with national legislation governing a State monopoly on sport betting which was incompatible with both EU law and the German Constitution during a transitional period between the annulment of that legislation by the German Federal Constitutional Tribunal (BVerfG) and its amendment by the German legislature in a situation where the BVerfG had maintained its applicability for a transitional period. In other words, the issue was whether it was acceptable under EU law to temporarily suspend the application of the principle of supremacy of EU law, and thus allow Member States to maintain national law incompatible with EU law for a transitional period only in order to avoid an unacceptable legal vacuum that would exist if the incompatible provisions were not to be applied.

Held:

The ECJ gave the referring court an unequivocal answer. The national legislation could not continue to apply during a transitional period because there were no overriding considerations justifying its maintenance. However, when such overriding considerations exist (i.e. where the disapplication of national rules would create a legal vacuum threatening the public or private interests) the possibility of temporary suspension of the application of the principle of supremacy can occur under conditions to be defined by the ECJ itself.

Comment:

The main submission of Member States was that under EU law, the ECJ has, on some occasions, maintained the application of secondary legislation which it had found unlawful in order to avoid a legal vacuum, and thus, by analogy, the same possibility should be given to Member States. This was a clever argument which forced the ECJ to hint that it may accept such a possibility in the future. This was contrary to the Opinion of the A-G who categorically excluded such suspension of the application of the principle of supremacy. However, the ECJ emphasised that conditions for such exceptional suspension could be determined solely by it.

9.7.3 Other circumstances in which the principle of legal certainty limits the application of the principle of supremacy

There are other circumstances in which the principle of legal certainty prevails over the principle of supremacy. For example, the ECJ can impose a restriction on retroactive effect of preliminary rulings (see Chapter 13.9) or tolerate an unlawfully levied charge on an individual in a situation where its

---

524. Case C-409/06 *Winner Wetten GmbH v Bürgermeisterin der Stadt Bergheim* [2010] ECR I-8015.

imposition resulted from an excusable error on the part of national authorities and a long period had elapsed between the imposition and the claim by the individual during which both the national authorities and the individual concerned were aware that the charges were unlawful.[525]

9.8 The principle of supremacy of EU law in the UK

The European experience regarding the principle of supremacy of EU law shows that Member States may not be keen on this principle, and an example of this is the UK where for many years the British judiciary had difficulty in reconciling the irreconcilable, i.e. in reconciling the principle of supremacy of EU law with Dicey's model[526] of Parliamentary sovereignty according to which:

- British courts may not question the validity of Parliamentary legislation.

- There are no limits to the legislative power of Parliament subject to the exception that Parliament cannot limit its own powers for the future. This means that no legislation enacted by Parliament is irreversible and that a later Act of Parliament impliedly repeals an earlier Act in so far as they are inconsistent.

The breakthrough came in *Factortame (No.2)*,[527] (for facts see Chapter 12.5) in which the UK Law Lords accorded supremacy to EU law. In this respect, Lord Bridge said:

"If the supremacy, within the European Community, of Community law over national law of Member States was not always inherent in the EEC Treaty it was certainly well-established in the jurisprudence of the European Court of Justice long before the United Kingdom joined the Community. Thus, whatever limitation of its sovereignty Parliament accepted when it enacted the European Communities Act 1972 it was entirely voluntary. Under the terms of the Act of 1972 it has always been clear that it was the duty of a United Kingdom court, when delivering final judgment, to override any rule of national law found to be in conflict with any directly enforceable rule of Community law."[528]

In *Factortame (No. 2)* and *R v Secretary of State for Employment, ex parte Equal Opportunities Commission*, the House of Lords (now the UK Supreme Court)[529] established that an "implied supremacy clause" is inserted in any UK Act of Parliament enacted since 1972 to the effect that any inconsistence between the act and EU law is resolved in favour of EU law unless Parliament expressly and unequivocally indicates that it intends to derogate from EU law.[530] The "implied supremacy clause" was further explained in *Thoburn (Metric Martyrs)* in which Laws J made a distinction between constitutional statutes, a superior category of statutes which govern constitutional rights of citizens, and "ordinary statutes". Examples of "constitutional" statutes are Magna Carta, the Human Rights Act 1998 and the European Communities Act 1972 (ECA). Laws J classified the ECA as being of a constitutional nature on the ground that: "It incorporated the whole corpus of substantive Community rights and obligations,

---

525. C-188/95 *Fantask* [1997] ECR I-6783.

526. A. V. Dicey, *Introduction to the Study of the Law of the Constitution*, 8th edn, 1915, London: Macmillan; reprinted Indianapolis, IN: Liberty Fund, 1982, at 3–4 (Introduction).

527. [1991] 1 AC 603.

528. Ibid, at 658.

529. [1995] 1AC 645.

530. P. Craig, "Britain in the European Union", in J. Jowell and D. Oliver (eds), *The Changing Constitution*, 6th edn, 2011, Oxford: OUP, ch. 4.

and gave overriding domestic effect to the judicial and administrative machinery of Community law. It may be there has never been a statute having such profound effects on so many dimensions of our daily lives. The ECA is, by force of the common law, a constitutional statute."[531] The doctrine of implied repeal does not apply to constitutional statutes. They can only be repealed in express terms. Laws J also stated that the acceptance of supremacy of EU law is based on the common law in the light of any domestic statutes.

The debate as to whether the supremacy of EU law flows from the political choice made by the UK Parliament in 1972, or whether it derives from EU law seems to be settled by clause 18, the so called "sovereignty" clause, of the UK European Union Act 2011 (EUA) which states that:

"Directly applicable or directly effective EU law (that is, the rights, powers, liabilities, obligations, restrictions, remedies and procedures referred to in section 2(1) of the European Communities Act 1972) falls to be recognised and available in law in the United Kingdom only by virtue of that Act or where it is required to be recognised and available in law by virtue of any other Act."[532]

To ensure that the EU will not encroach on national competences the EUA introduced a system of control by UK Parliament and by its citizens *via* referenda. The system far exceeds any equivalent regime of control in other Member States. Indeed, the range of situations in which a referendum is required to be held is very broad and may prove disruptive to the working of the EU in that the EU will have to wait for a referendum to be organised by the UK and perhaps face a real crisis if the outcome is negative on matters which have no real importance to an average citizen. For example, a referendum would need to be held, to change the voting in the Council from unanimity to QMV, when the Council intends to make changes to the list of military products exempt from internal market provisions pursuant to Article 346 TFEU. The cost of organising a referendum combined with the fact that many matters subject to referenda are of no real relevance to UK citizens and thus will be decided by a small fraction of the population holding strong views may well prove counterproductive.[533]

9.9 The principle of supremacy in Member States other than the UK

Only two of the original six Member States, Luxembourg and the Netherlands,[534] accepted the reasoning of the ECJ and recognised the supremacy of EU law based on the peculiar nature of the EU legal order.[535] It is outside the scope of this book to deal in detail with the acceptance or otherwise of the principle of supremacy of EU law by Member States other than the UK. In general, Member States are willing to accept the principle of supremacy of EU law over their ordinary national law. The problem lies in the relationship between national constitutional law and EU law. This is examined below with regard to two Member States, one being an original Member State (Germany), and the other being a "new" Member State which acceded to the EU in 2004 (Poland).

---

531. *Thoburn v Sunderland City Council* [2002] 4 All ER 156, 185.

532. On this topic see: P. Craig, "The European Union Act 2011: Locks, Limits and Legality", (2011) 48 CMLRev., 1915.

533. On this topic see: M. Gordon and M. Dougan, "The United Kingdom's European Union Act 2011: 'Who Won the Bloody War Anyway?'" (2012) ELR, 3.

534. Decision *Metten v Minister van Financiën* of 7 July 1996, NJB-katern (1995) 426.

535. See M. Thill, "La Primauté et l'Effet Direct du Droit Communautaire dans la Jurisprudence Luxembourgeoise", [1990] RFDA, 978.

9.9.1 Germany

The recognition of the supremacy of EU law is the main challenge for the BVerfG. It has attributed to itself three different review functions with regard to EU law.[536] The exercise of those functions encroaches on the competences of the ECJ, which is the final supreme judicial authority on EU law.

First, the BVerfG , decided in 1974 *Solange I* (in German, Solange means "as long as"),[537] that it had competence to review whether EU law is compatible with fundamental rights enshrined in the German Constitution. The BVerfG held that as long as there is a hypothetical conflict between EU law and the guarantees of fundamental rights in the German Constitution, the rights as embodied in the German Constitution would override EU law. In a subsequent judgment in 1986 in (*Solange II*)[538] the BVerfG qualified its judgment in *Solange I* by stating that the ECJ had demonstrated that EU law ensures efficient protection of fundamental rights equal to the protection guaranteed by the German Constitution and therefore the BVerfG will not exercise its jurisdiction as specified in *Solange I* as long as the ECJ maintained high standards for protection of fundamental rights. Subsequently, the BVerfG in the *Bananas* case[539] limited the review of EU law on the basis of fundamental rights even more strictly. As Payandeh states, the BVerfG "has retreated from reviewing whether single EU acts comply with the German Constitutional fundamental rights guarantees and restricts itself to the review of whether EU law and institutions provide for an adequate level of rights protection in general".[540] Under this restrictive approach a clash between the BVerfG and the ECJ is unlikely. Such an event will be even more unlikely once the EU has acceded to the ECHR. After this occurs, both the BVerfG and the ECJ will be subject to scrutiny by the ECtHR in the areas covered by the ECHR and its Protocols 1 and 6 (see Chapter 8.5).

Second, in *Brunner and Others v The European Union Treaty*[541] the BVerfG had to deal with a case in which the constitutionality of the Treaty of Maastricht was challenged. The BVerfG rendered a long judgment in which it held that the supremacy of EU law was conditional. The BVerfG ruled that it was empowered to ensure that Union institutions and bodies were acting within the limits of powers granted to them under the EC Treaty and thus did not jeopardise the constitutional rights of German inhabitants. Accordingly, the BVerfG reserved to itself ultimate jurisdiction to review the validity of EU acts and to declare any EU *ultra vires* act inapplicable in Germany. However, in its judgment in *Honeywell*[542] in which the issue was whether the judgment of the ECJ in *Mangold* (see Chapter 10.5) constituted an *ultra vires* act and therefore was not applicable in Germany, the BVerfG held that this was not the case and took a very strict approach to the *ultra vires* review significantly mitigating the possibility that it will ever declare an act of an EU institution to be *ultra vires*.

Third, the BVerfG in its 2009 judgment on the Treaty of Lisbon[543] held that it had competence to review whether EU legal acts were compatible with the constitutional identity of the German Constitution. In this judgment the BVerfG stated that supremacy of EU law derives from the German

---

536. See M. Payandeh, "Constitutional Review of EU law After Honeywell: Contextualizing the Relationship between the German Constitutional Court and the EU Court of Justice", (2011) 48 CMLRev., 9.

537. *Internationale Handelsgesellschaft mbH v Einfuhr- und Vorratstelle für Getreide und Futtermittel* [1974] 2 CMLR, 540.

538. *Re Wünsche Handelsgesellschaft* [1987] 3 CMLR, 225.

539. Bundesverfassungsgericht, 7 June 2000, 2 BvL 1/97, available in English at http://www.bverfg.de/entscheidungen/ls20000607_2bvl000197en.html (accessed 28/6/12).

540. Supra note 536, 14.

541. [1994] 1 CMLR 57.

542. Decision of 6 July 2010, 2BvB 2661/06 NYR.

543. Decision of 30 June 2009, BVerfGE 123, 267. Available in English at: http://www.bverfg.de/entscheidungen/es20090630_2bve000208en.html (accessed 28/6/12). See also D. Doukas, "The Verdict of the German Federal Constitutional Court on the Lisbon Treaty: Not Guilty, but Don't do it Again!", (2009) ELRev., 866.

act conferring powers to the EU, and not from EU law. It also stated that it will intensify its control over EU acts to ensure that they comply not only with common European human rights standards, but also with the principle of conferral (see Chapter 6.2). The third review function established in the above judgment concerns the transfer of sovereign powers from the German State to the EU and establishes an additional base for the review of actions of EU institutions, bodies and agencies. This jurisdiction of the BVerfG was exercised in the *Bailout* judgment of 7 September 2011[544] regarding financial contributions of Germany to aid Greece, and to the euro rescue plan adopted by the EU in 2010. The BVerfG held that the contributions were legal and did not violate the German Parliament's prerogative to have final control over the German budget. However, it also imposed restrictions in that the German Parliament will remain the final authority as to the participation of Germany in any future bailouts.

These three above review functions have the potential to create conflict between Germany and the EU. However, such conflict is unlikely to occur as both the ECJ and the BVerfG will try to avoid it as far as possible. In the *Honeywell* case the BVerfG stated that its review function must be exercised with openness towards EU law which entails the following:

- first, the BVerfG will refer to the ECJ within the preliminary rulings procedure under Article 267 TFEU any alleged *ultra vires* act of EU for interpretation or the assessment of validity;

- second, only the BVerfG will have power to declare an EU act to be *ultra vires* within Germany; and,

- third, the BVerfG will exercise its jurisdiction only if any apparent transgression of EU competence is sufficiently serious, i.e. it is obvious and has impact on the allocation of competences between the EU and its Member States.

It is important to note that despite the existence of the three review mechanisms the BVerfG has, in fact, never declared any EU act inapplicable in Germany.

9.9.2 Poland

The position of the Polish Constitutional Tribunal is clear. EU law prevails over all national law except the Polish Constitution.[545] The Polish courts have competence to decide whether the EU has complied with the principle of conferral, proportionality and subsidiarity. Where EU law violates any of those principles EU law will be *ultra vires* and thus may not prevail over national law. If there is an unavoidable conflict between EU law and the Polish Constitution, i.e. a conflict which cannot be resolved even by interpretation in favour of EU law, it will be resolved by either the making of an amendment to the Polish Constitution or the withdrawal of Poland from the EU. This approach was tested when the Polish Constitutional Tribunal[546] found that national law implementing the Framework Directive on the European Arrest Warrant was incompatible with the Polish Constitution (which prohibits the extradition of Polish citizens) and that the time limit for implementation of the Directive had elapsed. The Polish

---

544. Summary of the judgment is available in English at http://www.juradmin.eu/en/reflets/pdf/Reflets%202011%20No%202.pdf (accessed 30/6/12).

545. Judgment of the Polish Constitutional Tribunal of 11/05/2005 available at http://www.trybunal.gov.pl/OTK/teksty/otkpdf/2005/K_18_04.pdf (accessed 12/12/09).

546. W. Sadurski, 'Solange Chapter 3': Constitutional Courts in Central Europe – Democracy – European Union, EUI Working Paper, Law, No. 2006/40.

Constitutional Tribunal was willing to delay annulment of the contested law in order to give time for the Polish legislature to make necessary amendments to the Polish Constitution.[547]

RECOMMENDED READING

Books

Alter, K., *Establishing the Supremacy of European Law: The Making of an International Rule of Law in Europe*, 2nd edn, 2003, Oxford: OUP.

Barents, R., *The Autonomy of Community Law*, 2003, The Hague: KLI.

Articles

Briza, P., "Lucchini SpA – Is There Anything Left of the *Res Judicata* Principle?" (2008) 27(1) CJQ, 40 (Comment on Case C-119/05 *Ministero dell'Industria del Commercio e dell'Artigianato v Lucchini SpA*).

Craig, P. "The European Union Act 2011: Locks, Limits and Legality", (2011) 48 CMLRev., 1915.

De Witte, B., "Direct Effect, Primacy, and the Nature of the Legal Order", in Craig, P., and de Bùrca, G. (eds), *The Evolution of EU Law*, 2nd edn, 2011, Oxford: OUP, 323.

Łazowski, A., "Half Full and Half Empty Glass: The Application of EU Law in Poland (2004–2010)", (2011) 48 CMLRev., 503.

Payandeh, M., "Constitutional Review of EU Law After Honeywell: Contextualizing the Relationship between the German Constitutional Court and the EU Court of Justice", (2011) 48 CMLRev., 9.

Schmid, C., "All Bark and No Bite: Notes on the Federal Constitutional Court's 'Banana Decision'", (2001) 7 ELJ, 95.

Trstenjak, V., and Beysen, E., "European Consumer Protection Law: Curia Semper Dabit Remedium", (2011) 48 CMLRev., 95.

Von Bogdandy, A., and Schill, S., "Overcoming Absolute Primacy: Respect for National Identity under the Lisbon Treaty", (2011) 48 CMLRev., 1417.

Ward, A., "Do Unto Others as You Would Have Them Do Unto You: *Willy Kempter* and the Duty to Raise EC Law in National Litigation", (2008) 33 ELRev., 739.

PROBLEM QUESTION

A Council Regulation of 2009 on the common organisation of the internal market in poultry meat set out a system of payments, known as "refunds", under which refunds were to be paid to EU producers exporting poultry meat products to non-Member States. The amounts to be "refunded" depended upon the customs tariff classification of the exported products.

Melex Ltd ("Melex"), a Dutch company, exported poultry meat products to non Member States and was initially granted refunds, but subsequently those products were reclassified so that they fell within a class in respect of which "refunds" were not payable. As a result, a request for reimbursement of sums paid to Melex was made by the Dutch authorities. Melex unsuccessfully appealed to the Dutch appellate body against the reimbursement request. The appellate body did not refer any question of interpretation of tariff classification to the ECJ for a preliminary ruling. Melex reimbursed the sums received.

Three years later the ECJ delivered a judgment in which it gave an interpretation of the relevant provision of the 1995 Regulation in line with that submitted by Melex to the Dutch appellate body.

---

547. Polish Constitutional Tribunal, 27 April 2005, No P 1/05; noted by D. Laczykiewicz (2006) 43 CMLRev., 1181. Łazowski, A., "Half Full and Half Empty Glass: The Application of EU Law in Poland (2004–2010)", (2011) 48 CMLRev., 503.

Melex is considering seeking a review of the customs classification of its poultry meat products and, as a consequence, recovery of the refunds which it had reimbursed.

Advise the managing director of Melex what, if any issues may arise under EU law, how they might be addressed and what remedies are available to Melex.

ESSAY QUESTION

Critically discuss the implications for the national courts of the Member States, including national constitutional courts, of the absolute nature of the principle of supremacy of EU law.

SUPREMACY OF EU LAW

This means that EU law takes priority over, and supersedes any national law which clashes with EU law (Case 6/64 *Costa* v *ENEL* and Declaration 17 attached to the Treaties which confirms the position of the ECJ on supremacy of EU law).

CLASH BETWEEN NATIONAL LAW AND EU LAW

In the event of a conflict between EU law and national law, the conflicting domestic provisions must be set aside. A national court must not request or await the prior setting aside of an incompatible national provision by legislation, or other constitutional means but must do this on its own motion (Case 106/77 *Simmenthal*). However:

- A Member State is not required to nullify conflicting national law, which may continue to apply to situations outside the scope of EU law (Joined Cases C-10/97 to C-22/97 *Ministero Delle Finanze*).

- There is no general duty imposed on national courts to apply EU law *ex officio* (i.e. when the parties to the proceedings have not raised points of EU law) (Case C-312/93 *Petebroeck* and in Joined Cases C-430–431/93 *Van Schijndel*) but there are some exceptions.

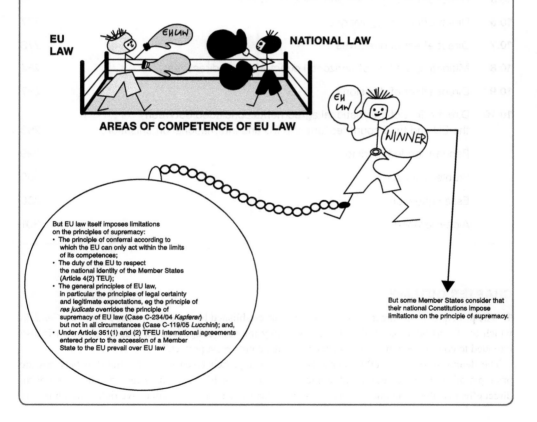

EU LAW

NATIONAL LAW

AREAS OF COMPETENCE OF EU LAW

But EU law itself imposes limitations on the principles of supremacy:
- The principle of conferral according to which the EU can only act within the limits of its competences;
- The duty of the EU to respect the national identity of the Member States (Article 4(2) TEU);
- The general principles of EU law, in particular the principles of legal certainty and legitimate expectations, eg the principle of *res judicats* overrides the principle of supremacy of EU law (Case C-234/04 *Kapferer*) but not in all circumstances (Case C-119/05 *Lucchini*); and,
- Under Article 351(1) and (2) TFEU international agreements entered prior to the accession of a Member State to the EU prevail over EU law

But some Member States consider that their national Constitutions impose limitations on the principle of supremacy.

10

DIRECT EFFECT OF EU LAW

CHAPTER OUTLINE

1. The principle of the direct effect of EU law was established by the ECJ in Case 26/62 *Van Gend*, in which the Court held that: "[EU law] . . . not only imposes obligations on individuals but it is also intended to confer upon them rights which national courts must protect."

The definition of direct effect depends upon the approach taken to the relationship between the principle of direct effect and the principle of supremacy of EU law. Under the "primacy" approach, direct effect is "the technique which allows individuals to enforce their subjective rights, which is only available in the internal legal order in an instrument that comes from outside that order, against another (State or private) actor". Under the "dual" approach, direct effect is to be understood as "the capacity of a provision of EU law to produce independent legal effects within the national legal system". The ECJ has not given preference to either approach. The definition of direct effect consistently used by the ECJ is that a provision of EU law has direct effect when it has the capacity to confer rights on individuals which they may invoke and rely upon in proceedings before national courts. However, the meaning of "rights" has evolved in that it encompasses not only the creation of a legal right but also the possibility of relying on directly effective provisions of EU law for other purposes, e.g. to review legality of national measures.

The importance of the principle of direct effect lies in the fact that it allows individuals to enforce their rights deriving from EU law in the circumstances where a Member State has not adopted implementing measures when it is required to do so, or when it has incorrectly implemented EU law, or when it has implemented it correctly, but applied it incorrectly.

2. In order to produce direct effect, a provision of EU law must be clear, precise, unconditional, and, if relevant, the time-limit for its implementation into national law must have expired (the direct effect test).

3. EU law makes a distinction between horizontal and vertical direct effect. Vertical direct effect refers to a situation where an individual is allowed to rely on a provision of EU law in national proceedings against a Member State or its emanations. Horizontal direct effect concerns a situation where an individual is allowed to rely on a provision of EU law in national proceedings against another individual. In practice, this distinction is very important since it considerably limits the scope and the effectiveness of EU law in the case of a provision which may have only vertical direct effect.

4. Provisions of the Treaties and of regulations may have both horizontal and vertical direct effect.

5. The Charter of Fundamental Rights of the EU may be vertically directly effective, but cannot have horizontal direct effect except in two situations:

- when a Charter right has the same content as a provision of the Treaties, which has been recognised as capable of being horizontally directly effective (Article 52(2) of the Charter); and,

- when a Charter right embodies a general principle of EU law, which has been recognised as capable of being horizontally directly effective.

6. In the light of the judgments of the ECJ in Case C-144/04 *Mangold* and in Case C-555/07 *Kücükdeveci,* general principles of EU law can have direct horizontal effect, but it is still unclear in what circumstances this may occur.

7. Subject to the direct effect test, provisions of directives can only have vertical direct effect, and only after the time limit for their implementation has expired. A Member State which has failed to transpose a directive within the prescribed time limit cannot rely on an unimplemented directive in proceedings against individuals. Individuals can rely on a directive, irrespective of whether its provisions have direct effect, to determine whether the national authority, in exercising its choice as to the form and methods for implementing the directive, has kept within the limits of its discretion set out in the directive.

In order to alleviate the negative consequences of the denial of horizontal direct effect of directives, the ECJ has developed the following four approaches:

- It has extended the concept of a Member State by introducing the autonomous EU concept of a public body;

■ It has imposed the duty on national courts to interpret national law in conformity with EU law. This is referred to as indirect effect. It is important to note that the duty of consistent interpretation of national law with EU law applies to all EU law, not only to EU directives, and irrespective of whether the parties to the proceedings are individuals or public bodies. However, national courts have neither the duty to interpret national law *contra legem* nor to interpret it in such a way as to ignore the general principles of EU law, in particular the principles of legal certainty and non-retroactivity in criminal matters;

■ It has allowed individuals to rely on a directive in proceedings against a State or its emanations despite the fact that such an action affects the rights of individuals who are not part of the vertical relationship, i.e. a relation between a State and the claimant. This is referred to as "triangular" horizontal effect; and,

■ It has allowed individuals to rely on the principle of State liability (see Chapter 12).

The ECJ has allowed individuals, on some rare occasions, to rely on directives in proceedings against other individuals, but has not explained the reason of its judgments.

8. A decision addressed to a Member State can only produce vertical direct effect. A decision addressed to a natural or a legal person can produce both vertical and horizontal direct effect.

9. The test for direct effect of provisions of international agreements concluded between the EU and third countries or international organisations, is stricter than that concerning other sources of EU law in that the ECJ will not only apply the usual direct effect test, but also take into account the spirit, general scheme and terms of the agreement. Provisions of international agreements can have vertical direct effect. However, it is uncertain whether they can have horizontal direct effect as there is no judicial authority on this point.

10.1 Introduction

In the decentralised system of enforcement of EU law, i.e. in the situation where national courts and administrative authorities are required to apply EU law, the principle of direct effect as well as other general principles of EU law, in particular the principle of supremacy, are vital to ensure not only the effectiveness of EU law but also that rights of individuals deriving from EU law are adequately protected under national law (see Chapter 12.6).

The above was one of the reasons why the ECJ established the principle of direct effect. It is not mentioned in the Treaties. It was "discovered" by the ECJ, although not invented by it. Under public international law, some provisions of international treaties may confer rights on, or impose obligations on individuals. This possibility was recognised for the first time by the Permanent Court of International Justice (PCIJ) in the case *Concerning Competences of the Courts of Danzig*[548] in which it was held that an exception to the principle of individuals not being subject to public international law arises if the intention of the contracting parties was to adopt a Treaty which creates rights and obligations for them capable of being enforced by municipal courts. The PCIJ emphasised that this intention must be express and not inferred from the Treaty since this kind of international Treaty constitutes an exception to a general principle. Such Treaties are classified under public international law as "self-executing". They automatically become part of the national law of the contracting parties and are directly enforceable in national courts.

---

548. Advisory Opinion of 3 February 1928, Series B, No. 15, esp. 17.

The *Danzig* exception that an international Treaty can confer rights on individuals enforceable in municipal courts has become a principle of EU law. In Case 26/62 *Van Gend*,[549] the ECJ held that EU law is directly effective and thus creates rights and obligations for EU citizens enforceable before national courts.

THE FACTS WERE:

In 1960 Van Gend imported urea-formaldehyde, a chemical product, into the Netherlands from Germany. In December 1959 the Netherlands enacted legislation which modified the Benelux tariff system, and which brought into effect the Brussels Convention on Nomenclature unifying the classification of goods for customs purposes. Under the new nomenclature Van Gend's product was reclassified. This resulted in an increase in the duty payable on urea-formaldehyde to 8 per cent on an ad valorem basis, as compared to 3 per cent payable previously under Dutch law. On 14 January 1958 the EEC Treaty came into force. Its Article 12 [repealed] provided that:

"Member States shall refrain from introducing between themselves any new customs duties on imports or exports or any charge having equivalent effect, and from increasing those which they already apply in their trade with each other."

Van Gend challenged the increase in the duty payable as contrary to Article 12 of the EEC Treaty [repealed]. When his claim was rejected by the customs inspector, he appealed to the Dutch Customs Court in Amsterdam. Under Article 267 TFEU the Customs Court submitted two questions to the ECJ:

- first, whether Article 12 of the EEC Treaty [repealed] could create rights for individuals as claimed by Van Gend; and,
- second, provided the answer to the first question was in the affirmative, whether the modification in the Belelux tariff system was prohibited by Article 12 of the EEC Treaty [repealed].

The Governments of Belgium, Germany and the Netherlands submitted memoranda to the ECJ claiming that first, Article 12 of the EEC Treaty [repealed] created obligations for Member States and not rights for individuals and second, that if a breach of Community law occurred, the proceedings should solely be based on Articles 258 and 259 TFEU (see Chapter 14).

Held:

The Court stated that Article 12 of the EEC Treaty (repealed) had direct effect and accordingly, Van Gend could rely on it in proceedings before a national court.

Comment:

The impact of the decision in Van Gend on European integration has been enormous for the following reasons.

First, the EEC Treaty did not specify what legal effects it was to produce in national legal systems. In Van Gend the ECJ specified those effects in that EU law has become a source

---

549.   Case 26/62, *NV Algemene Transport- en Expeditie Onderneming van Gend & Loos v Netherlands Inland Revenue Administration* [1963] ECR 1.

of directly enforceable rights and obligations for individuals and public authorities when the criteria for direct effect are satisfied. The ECJ set out those criteria. A provision of EU law is directly effective if it is clear, precise and unconditional. In Van Gend the obligation of Article 12 of the EEC Treaty addressed to the Member States was a negative obligation in that they were required to abstain from introducing new customs duties, any charge having equivalent effect, and from increasing those which they already apply in their trade with each other. Accordingly no implementation measures were necessary. And thus Article 12 of the EEC Treaty was unconditional. This provision, however, did not expressly confer rights on individuals. The ECJ responded to this by stating that rights created under Community law for individuals not only arise "where they are expressly granted by the Treaty, but also by reason of obligations which the Treaty imposes in a clearly defined way upon individuals as well as upon the Member States and upon the institutions of the Community".[550] There was no doubt as to the clarity and precision of Article 12 of the EEC Treaty.

Second, individuals have become subjects of EU law which creates for them rights and obligations enforceable before national courts. The principle of direct effect therefore increases the legal protection of individuals by ensuring that they have access to national courts and remedies in matters governed by EU law.

Third, the ECJ used the teleological interpretation of the Treaty to "discover" the principle of direct effect and thus rejected the approach of the PCIJ in Danzig based on the intention of the contracting parties. The objective of the EEC Treaty was to create an internal market of direct concern to individuals. In order to achieve this objective it was necessary to ensure that EU law is recognised and enforced efficiently and uniformly in all Member States. The principle of direct effect was an effective way to ensure this. As the ECJ emphasised: "The vigilance of individuals concerned to protect their rights amounts to an effective supervision in addition to the supervision entrusted by [Articles 258 and 259 TFEU] to the diligence of the Commission and of the Member States."[551]

The ECJ justified the establishment of the principle of direct effect on the peculiar nature of the EEC Treaty which was "more than an agreement which created mutual obligations between the contracting States" as it established the Community which "constitutes a new legal order of international law . . . the subjects of which comprise not only Member States but also their nationals".[552] A further justification was based on an argument drawn from Article 267 TFEU (under which national courts may request from the ECJ a preliminary ruling on the interpretation and validity of EU law), that the Member States "have acknowledged that Community law has an authority which can be invoked by their nationals before those courts and tribunals".[553]

10.2   The principle of direct effect, its meaning and development

There is no generally accepted definition of the principle of direct effect. It is narrowly defined under the "primacy" approach and has a broad meaning under the "dual" approach. Further, since the

---

550.   Ibid, p. 12.
551.   Ibid.
552.   Ibid, p. 12.
553.   Ibid.

judgment of the ECJ in *Van Gend* it has evolved in terms of its scope of application and the effects that it may produce.

10.2.1 The relationship between the principle of direct effect and the principle of supremacy: the primacy and dual approaches

There are two approaches to the relationship between the principle of direct effect and the principle of supremacy. Under the primacy approach the principle of supremacy is dominant and ensures unity between national law and EU law.[554] Under the dual approach each system is separate and the connecting factor between them is the principle of direct effect.

According to the primacy approach, the importance of the principle of direct effect is underplayed whilst the principle of supremacy has overwhelming effects within the national legal systems. In the view of Lenaerts and Corthaut, direct effect is "the technique which allows individuals to enforce their subjective rights, which is only available in the internal legal order in an instrument that comes from outside that order (i.e. from EU law), against another (State or private) actor. It is a highly powerful tool."[555] The emphasis is on "subjective rights", which are to be understood as individual rights.[556] When individuals seek to enforce their objective rights they rely on the "invocability" of EU law, i.e. they rely on the principle of supremacy to exclude the application of the inconsistent national provision and thus it is irrelevant whether or not the provision in question is directly effective. However, the principle of direct effect regains its importance when an individual relies on EU law to "substitute" a relevant provision of EU law for a national provision. The substititionary effect is understood as "the direct and immediate application of Union law so as to create new rights and obligations derived from the Treaties which do not already exist within the national legal system".[557] The national court will replace the inconsistent national provision by the relevant provision of EU law, but only if such a provision of EU law is directly effective. Indeed, if a provision of EU law is not clear, precise and unconditional (that is, not directly effective), how can it replace the existing national law?

The essence of the dual approach is that the principle of supremacy is regarded as a kind of remedy to be applied by domestic courts when they are dealing with disputes involving a conflict between EU law and national law. A provision of EU law can only be relied upon by an individual in national proceedings when it passes the test of direct effect. Accordingly, "under this model, direct effect encompasses any and every situation in which Union norms produce independent effects within the national legal systems. In other words, direct effect enjoys a monopoly over rendering Union norms justiciable before a national court. Its threshold criteria act as triggers, and thus a necessary precondition for the principle of supremacy."[558] The duty of national courts to interpret national law in conformity with EU law derives from their obligation of loyal co-operation to give full effect to EU law and not from the principle of supremacy.

---

554. M. Dougan, "When Worlds Collide! Competing Visions of the Relationship between Direct Effect and Supremacy" (2007) 44 CMLRev., 931.

555. K. Lenaerts and T. Corthaut, "Of Birds and Hedges: The Role of Primacy in Invoking Norms of EU Law", (2006) 31 ELRev., 310 and Tridimas, "Black, White and Shades of Grey: Horizontality of Directives Revisited", (2002) 21 YEL, 327.

556. The distinction between subjective and objective rights is unknown in common law, but it is recognised in civil law tradition. Legal rules which have a general and abstract character, and are not designed for any particular person are objective rights. See N.M. Koranov, *General Theory of Law*, 1909, Boston: Boston Book Company, reprinted 2000, 168.

557. *Wyatt and Dashwood's European Union Law*, 6th edn, 2011, Oxford: Hart Publishing. 279.

558. Ibid.

Muir summarises the main differences between the two approaches as follows:[559]

■ First, although all academic commentators agree on the criteria for direct effect, they disagree as to the circumstances in which the criteria must be satisfied. Under the primacy approach, those criteria must be met when an individual seeks to enforce his/her subjective rights. Under the dual approach, the criteria for direct effect must be satisfied in any type of litigation involving individuals, even in the case of indirect judicial review, that is, in a situation where the validity of national law is raised as an incidental question in national proceedings between individuals in the context of EU directives;

■ Second, with regard to EU law which is not directly effective, under the primacy approach, the principle of supremacy requires that incompatible national law is set aside by a national court, even in an incidental judicial review case. Under the dual approach, national law remains valid until a Member State replaces it with the consequence that an individual will have to rely on the principle of State liability (see Chapter 12) as he/she will have no claim under national law based on direct effect of EU law; and,

■ Third, the distinction between vertical and horizontal direct effect will produce different results depending upon the approach selected. This is particularly important with regard to horizontal direct effect of EU directives. Under the primacy approach an individual will not be able to seek to enforce his subjective rights. In the incidental review cases, however, a national court will have to set aside a national provision that is incompatible with EU law. The dual approach will neither allow the enforcement of a subjective right nor the setting aside of a national provision in incidental review cases.

In practice, in most cases the approach applied is of no relevance as the same result will be achieved under both. However, in some situations the different approaches will result in different outcomes in litigation between individuals (see Chapter 10.8.5). The ECJ has not given preference to either of the above approaches. Its case law is unclear (see Chapter 10.8.5). For example, for the advocates of the primacy approach the outcome of the ECJ's judgment in Case C-555/07 *Kücükdeveci*[560] is a natural consequence of the principle of supremacy, i.e. a national provision conflicting with a general principle of EU law (in this case the principle of non-discrimination based on age) must be set aside, and this has nothing to do with the recognition of horizontal direct effect of the said general principle. For the advocates of the dual approach, in *Kücükdeveci*, the ECJ has recognised that general principles of EU law can produce horizontal direct effect (on this point see the discussion in Chapter 10.5).

10.2.2 The evolving nature of the principle of direct effect

The ECJ's definition of the principle of direct effect is that a provision of EU law can, subject to the direct effect test (see Chapter 10.2.5), create rights for individuals, who can invoke and rely on them in proceedings before a national court. This definition, although often used by the ECJ and academic commentators, has been criticised as imprecise and artificial.[561] It has been noted by many academic commentators that "direct effect" is broader than just the creation of rights in that a directly effective

---

559. E. Muir, "Of Ages in – and Edges of – EU Law", (2011) 48 CMLRev., 42–44.
560. Case C-555/07 *Seda Kücükdeveci v Swedex GmbH & Co. KG* [2010] ECR I-365.
561. S. Prechal, *Directives in EC Law*, 2nd edn, 2005, Oxford: OUP, 99 et seq.

provision of EU law may be relied upon by individuals for many purposes.[562] Prechal[563] gives the following example concerning Directive 76/207. In Case C-271/91 *Marsall II*,[564] the claimant relied on that directive to claim compensation for discriminatory dismissal, i.e. she relied on her right to equal treatment. In Case C-345/89 *Stoeckel*,[565] the defendant successfully relied on the same directive in criminal proceedings brought against him for employing women at night, which was prohibited under national law, while no such prohibition existed against employing male employees. In these circumstances it is difficult to maintain that the directive created a substantive right for the employer. Further, individuals can rely on direct effect with a view to challenging the legality of national implementing measures, or even the lack of them, in particular with regard to EU directives. If this occurs, direct effect is used as the standard for reviewing the legality of national measures.[566] The definition proposed by Prechal with regard to "the creation of a right" is that the principle of direct effect should be defined as "the possibility for an individual to invoke provisions of EU law in order to protect his interests",[567] i.e. the right should be understood as a kind of "procedural" right to invoke EU law. Another issue which has been debated is that the "invocability" of direct effect should be assessed from the point of view of a national court rather than that of individuals. National courts, at the end of the day, have to decide whether a provision of EU law is "sufficiently operational in itself to be applied"[568] and in some circumstances must apply it irrespective of whether the parties to a dispute have relied on it.[569] In the light of the above and the fact that when a provision of EU law is directly effective, it can be relied upon, not only before national courts, but also before national administrations, including municipal authorities,[570] Prechal proposes the following definition of direct effect:

> "Direct effect is the obligation of a court or another authority to apply the relevant provision of [EU] law, either as a norm which governs the case or a standard for legal review."[571]

A definition of the principle of direct effect proposed by the advocates of the dual approach is that direct effect should be understood as "the capacity of Union law to produce independent legal effects within the national legal system".[572] A provision of EU law has this capacity when it satisfies the conditions for direct effect (see Chapter 10.2.5). Under this definition the principle of direct effect has an even wider scope than under the definition proposed by Prechal as it covers any EU provision which may produce independent legal effects in a national legal system. This will include, for example, Article 267 TFEU which certainly produces independent legal effects in national legal systems, i.e. allows, or even compels national courts, to make requests for a preliminary ruling but confers no rights whatsoever on individuals, given that they cannot force a court or tribunal within the meaning of Article 267 TFEU to refer a matter of interpretation or validity of EU law to the ECJ (see Chapter 13.6.1).

---

562. T. Downes and C. Hilson, "Making Sense of Rights: Community Rights in EU Law", (1999) 24 ELRev., 121.
563. S. Prechal, *Directives in EC Law*, 2nd edn, 2005, Oxford: OUP, 99 and 100.
564. Case C-271/91 *M. Helen Marshall v Southampton and South-West Hampshire Area Health Authority* [1993] ECR I-4367.
565. Case C-345/89 *Criminal Proceedings against Alfred Stoeckel* [1991] ECR I-4047.
566. Supra note 563, 234–37.
567. Ibid, 100.
568. Opinion of A-G Van Gerven in Case C-128/92 *H. J. Banks & Company Limited v British Coal Corporation* [1994] ECR I-1209, para. 27.
569. Supra note 563, 240.
570. Case 103/88 *Fratelli Costanzo SpA v Comune di Milano* [1989] ECR 1839.
571. Supra note 563, 241.
572. *Wyatt and Dashwood's European Union Law*, 6th edn, 2011, Oxford: Hart Publishing, 244 and 248–51.

The above shows that the principle of direct effect has evolved and that its focus is no longer on the creation of rights of individuals as it may be used for various purposes by claimants. Further, the case law has clearly established that the ECJ has relaxed the criteria for direct effect and that assessment of them must be made in the context of each case (see Chapter 10.2.5).

The most important consequence deriving from the principle of direct effect is that it gives individuals the opportunity to directly enforce EU law before national courts, and thus to protect their interests. Further, the principle of direct effect makes EU law accessible to individuals without their having to rely on a State to implement EU law into national law, when it is required to do so but has not taken implementing measures, or when it incorrectly implements EU law, or when it implements it correctly, but applies it incorrectly. Further, the principle of direct effect reinforces the effectiveness of EU law in that when individuals have a particular interest to protect they are likely to seek to enforce EU law before national courts, and thus force national authorities to comply with EU law.

10.2.3 The meaning of the term "individuals" and the circumstances in which they can rely on the principle of direct effect

Individual means not only any natural or legal person[573] but also any legal entity, whether private or public[574] who or which may be "concerned" by the relevant provision.[575]

Three categories of persons may rely on direct effect of a relevant provision of EU law:

■ Its direct beneficiaries. In almost all cases based upon direct effect brought before the ECJ a claimant has claimed a right conferred upon him/her by EU law and thus his/her direct interest in the application of the relevant provision was self-evident;

■ Indirect beneficiaries. In Case C-345/89 *Stoeckel,*[576] an employer successfully relied on Directive 76/207 whose direct beneficiaries were employees; and,

■ Those who have a direct interest in the application of the relevant provision of EU law although they do not come within the *ratione personae* scope of the relevant provision, i.e. they are neither direct nor indirect beneficiaries of the provision in question. For example, in Joined Cases C-87/90, C-88/90 and C-89/90 *Verholen*[577] the ECJ stated that an individual may rely on Directive 79/7 before a national court if he bears (i.e. suffers) the effects of a discriminatory national provision regarding his spouse, who was not a party to the national proceedings, provided that his spouse comes within the scope of the directive.

10.2.4 Direct effect: vertical and horizontal

Vertical direct effect refers to a situation where an individual is allowed to rely on a provision of EU law in national proceedings against a Member State or its emanations.

---

573. Case 138/86 *Direct Cosmetics Ltd and Laughtons Photographs Ltd v Commissioners of Customs and Excise* [1988] ECR 3937.

574. See for example, Joined Cases C-487/01 and C-7/02 *Gemeente Leusden and Holin Groep BV cs v Staatssecretaris van Financiën* [2004] ECR I-5337.

575. On this topic see S. Prechal, *Directives in EC Law*, 2nd edn, 2005, Oxford: OUP, 238.

576. [1991] ECR I-4047.

577. Joined Cases C-87/90, C-88/90 and C-89/90 *A. Verholen and Others v Sociale Verzekeringsbank Amsterdam* [1991] ECR I-*3757.*

Horizontal direct effect concerns a situation where an individual is allowed to rely on a provision of EU law in national proceedings against another individual.

If a provision of EU law is only vertically directly effective, an individual is barred from commencing proceedings based on that provision against another individual before a national court. This may produce unfair results, as explained in Chapter 10.8.1.

10.2.5 Criteria for direct effect

The criteria for direct effect that emerged from decisions of the ECJ, rendered mostly under Article 267 TFEU, are simple. A provision of EU law, in order to produce direct effect, must be:

- sufficiently clear and precise;[578]

- unconditional in that it is capable of judicial application without any need for adoption of further implementing measures, either at national or EU level;[579] and,

- if relevant, the deadline for implementation of the relevant EU provision into national law must have expired. This mainly concerns directives.

The ECJ has interpreted the first two criteria broadly:

- First, it held that lack of clarity or precision did not hinder a provision from producing direct effect if that provision may be clarified or defined in more precise terms by means of interpretation by the EU courts or a national judge;[580]

- Second, a condition attached to a provision which suspends the application of that provision does not nullify its direct effect but merely delays it, until the realisation of the condition or the expiry of the time limit;[581] and,

- Third, a provision is considered as unconditional, despite the requirement for adoption of some implementing measures on the part of a Member State or an EU institution, if neither a Member State nor an EU institution has discretion to adopt those measures. In Case 57/65 *Lütticke*,[582] the ECJ held that in order to implement Article 110(3) TFEU, the Member States had no discretionary powers, and thus the provision was directly effective. In Case 8/81 *Becker*,[583] the ECJ held that if implementation measures concern solely procedural matters, the provision in question is still considered as unconditional and as such may be enforced before national courts.

What is important in the determination of whether the criteria for direct effect are satisfied is the context of each case, in particular what the party to the proceedings seeks to achieve. If he seeks to ascertain the

---

578. Case 148/78 *Criminal Proceedings against Tullio Ratti* [1979] ECR 1629; Case 8/81 *Ursula Becker v Finanzamt Münster-Innenstadt* [1982] ECR 53. The phrase "clear and precise" was examined in depth in Case C-236/92 *Comitato di Coordinamento per la Difesa della Cava v Regione Lombardia* [1994] ECR I-483.

579. Case 203/80 *Criminal Proceedings against Guerrino Casati* [1981] ECR 2595; and Case 43/75 *Defrenne Sabena* [1976] ECR 455.

580. Case 27/67 *Firma Fink -Frucht GmbH v Hauptzollamt München-Landsbergerstrasse* [1968] ECR 223; Case 43/75 *Defrenne v Sabena* [1976] ECR 455; Case C-262/88 *Douglas Harvey Barber v Guardian Royal Exchange Assurance Group* [1990] ECR I-1889.

581. Case 2/74 *Jean Reyners v Belgium* [1974] ECR 631; Case 59/75 *Pubblico Ministero v Flavia Manghera and Others* [1976] ECR 91.

582. Case 57/65 *Alfons Lütticke GmbH v Hauptzollamt Sarrelouis* [1966] ECR 205.

583. Case 8/81 *Ursula Becker v Finanzamt Münster-Innenstadt* [1982] ECR 53.

existence of a "subjective" right, or relies on direct effect as a defence in criminal proceedings the threshold for precision, clarity and unconditionality will be much higher than when a party is seeking an annulment of a national measure on the bases of its incompatibility with EU law.[584]

10.3 Direct effect of the Treaties

The ECJ in *Van Gend* (see Chapter 10.1) established that Article 12 of the EEC Treaty [repealed] was vertically directly effective. The question of whether other provisions of the Treaty could have vertical direct effect was answered by the ECJ in Case 57/65 *Lütticke*.[585]

THE FACTS WERE:

Lütticke imported whole milk powder from Luxembourg on which the German customs authorities levied duty and a turnover tax. Lütticke claimed that the imported product should be exempt from turnover tax as domestic natural milk and whole milk powder were exempt under the Turnover Tax Law. The Finanzgericht des Saarlands referred to the ECJ under Article 267 TFEU the question whether Article 110 TFEU, which prohibits the imposition of such taxes, has direct effect and so confers rights upon individuals which a national court must protect.

Held:

The ECJ held that Article 110 TFEU does produce such direct effect and consequently creates individual rights which must be enforced by national courts. Therefore, all doubts as to the existence or not of vertical direct effect of Treaty provisions were dispelled.

The question of whether Treaty provisions can have horizontal direct effect was decided by the ECJ in Case 43/75 *Defrenne*.[586]

THE FACTS WERE:

Miss Defrenne, who was employed as an air hostess by the Belgian airline company SABENA (a private company), claimed for losses she sustained in terms of the lower pay she received compared with male cabin stewards doing the same work. The Belgian Labour Court referred to the ECJ, within the preliminary ruling procedure, the question of whether she could rely on Article 157 TFEU, which prohibits all discrimination between men and women workers, and thus requires that they receive equal pay for performing the same task in the same establishment or service. The wording of Article 157 TFEU clearly indicated that further measures were necessary to implement this article.

---

584. See Opinion of A-G Léger in Case C-287/98 *Grand Duchy of Luxemburg v Berthe Linster, Aloyse Linster and Yvonne Linster* [2000] ECR I-6917, para. 82.
585. *Alfons Lütticke v Hauptzollampt Saarlouis* [1966] ECR 205.
586. Case 43/75 *Defrenne v Sabena* [1976] ECR 455.

> **Held:**
>
> *The ECJ held that in Miss Defrenne's case it was easy to apply Article 157 TFEU as the facts clearly showed that she was discriminated against. It stated that: "the prohibition of discrimination between men and women applies not only to the action of public authorities, but also extends to all agreements which are intended to regulate paid labour collectively, as contracts between individuals".[587]*

The case law of the ECJ has gradually identified those provisions of the Treaties which have both vertical and horizontal effect, those which have only direct vertical effect and those which do not produce direct effect.[588]

10.4 Direct effect of the Charter of Fundamental Rights of the EU

Article 51(1) of the Charter provides that its provisions are addressed to EU institutions, bodies and agencies and the Member States when they implement EU law. This indicates that (except as mentioned below) the Charter can only produce vertical direct effect as it is not addressed to individuals but clearly imposes obligations on EU institutions and the Member States. However this is subject to the following exceptions:

- Article 52(2) of the Charter states that "rights recognised by the Charter for which provision is made in the Treaties shall be exercised under the conditions and within the limits defined by those Treaties". Accordingly, if a provision of the Treaties is directly effective, a Charter right based on that provision will also be directly effective. There are some problems with Article 52(2). First, it does not identify all the Charter rights based on the Treaties. Second, there are instances where a Charter right is broader than that existing under the relevant provision of the Treaties. The Charter's Explanatory Memorandum provides little guidance on how to solve this problem although it acknowledges its existence. It gives an example where Charter rights are more expansive than Treaty rights. It concerns Article 21(1) of the Charter which prohibits discrimination on grounds of sex, race, colour, ethnic or social origin, genetic features, language, religion or belief, disability, age, or sexual orientation, and Article 19 TFEU which prohibits discrimination based on sex, racial or ethnic origin, religion or belief, disability, age, or sexual orientation. The Explanatory Memorandum states that there is no contradiction or incompatibility between Article 21(1) of the Charter and Article 19 TFEU, although it is obvious that the grounds listed in Article 21(1) are much broader than those set out in Article 19 TFEU. It seems that, in the light of the fact that the Charter does not create new rights, grounds which are not mentioned in Article 19 TFEU but are listed in Article 21(1) of the Charter are not covered by Article 52(2) of the Charter;[589] and,

- If a right enshrined in the Charter is embodied in a general principle of EU law, which principle is horizontally directly effective, individuals will be able to rely on it (see below).

---

587.   Ibid, para. 39.

588.   A. Dashwood, "Viking and Laval: Issues of Horizontal Direct Effect", (2007–08) 10 CYELS, 525.

589.   K. Lenaerts and E. de Smijter, "A 'Bill of Rights' for the European Union", (2001) 28 CMLRev., 284–85.

10.5   Direct effect of general principles of EU law

General principles which are embodied in the Treaties can produce both vertical and horizontal direct effect. For example, the principle of non-discrimination on the ground of gender contained in Article 157 TFEU can produce both vertical and horizontal direct effect as illustrated in the *Defrenne* case.

General principles embodied in the Charter, provided they pass the test for direct effect, can produce vertical direct effect. As to other general principles, the view is that they may have vertical direct effect.[590] However, until the judgment in Case C-144/04 *Mangold*,[591] there was no indication in the case law of the ECJ that a general principle can produce horizontal direct effect.

THE FACTS WERE:

In 2003 Mr Mangold, a German national aged 56, entered into an employment contract with Mr Helm, a lawyer practising in Germany. Mr Mangold's employment was to be for six months only. This was in accordance with a special provision of German law which had been enacted with a view to facilitating employment of employees older than 52 and which specifically provided for six-month fixed-term contracts. A few weeks after commencing employment, Mr Mangold brought proceedings against his employer before a German Labour Court, claiming that the national law was contrary to Directive 1999/70 (which gives effect to the framework agreement on fixed-term work entered into by ETUC, UNICE and CEEP) and Directive 2000/78 (which establishes a general framework for combating discrimination on the grounds of religion or belief, disability, age or sexual orientation as regards employment and occupation, with a view to putting into effect in the Member States the principle of equal treatment). Accordingly, he argued that the clause fixing the term of his employment was void.

Neither directive makes a specific reference to the prohibition of discrimination based on age. Further, at the time of the proceedings the transitional period for the implementation of Directive 2000/78 had not expired.

Held:

The ECJ held that the principle of non-discrimination, being a general principle of EU law, the source of which could be found in recitals 1 and 4 of the preamble to the directive and in various international instruments and in the constitutional traditions common to the Member States, allowed Mr Mangold to challenge the German legislation. This was because that legislation did not take account of other factors (such as an earlier contract of employment of indefinite duration concluded with the same employer), but imposed the conclusion of fixed-term contracts of employment once the worker had reached the age of 52. The ECJ considered that observance of the general principle of equal treatment, in particular in respect of age, could not depend on the expiry of the period for the transposition of a directive which directive intended to lay down a general framework for combating discrimination on the grounds of age.

---

590.   See, for example, Case C-520/03 *José Vicente Olaso Valero v Fondo de Garantía Salarial (Fogasa)* [2004] ECR I-12065; Case C-442/00 *Rodríguez Caballero v Fondo de Garantía Salarial (Fogasa)* [2002] ECR I-11915; Case C-183/04 *Emeka NE v Ipourgos Ikonomikon* [2006] ECR I-8167.

591.   Case C-144/04 *Werner Mangold v Rüdiger Helm* [2005] ECR I-9981.

Comment:

Four issues were particularly controversial. First, at the time of commencement of the main proceedings the transposition period for the implementation of Directive 2000/78 had not expired. Accordingly, on the authority of Case 148/78 Ratti, Mr Mangold could not rely on its provisions. Second it has been well established under EU law that directives have no horizontal direct effect and thus Mr Mangold in any event could not rely on Directive 2000/78. Third, it was unclear whether Mr Mangold could continue national proceedings on the basis of the relevant provision of the directive or rely on the principle of non discrimination based on age or both. Fourth, the ECJ did not mention the issue of horizontal direct effect.

The above judgment was very controversial. Its exact meaning was unclear. In this circumstance, in Case C-555/07 *Kücükdeveci*,[592] a national court, within the preliminary rulings procedure, asked the ECJ to elucidate its judgment in *Mangold*.

THE FACTS WERE:

Ms Kücükdeveci had been employed by Swedex GmbH & Co. KG since 1996, at which time she was 18 years old. Her employer dismissed her in 2006. She challenged the dismissal on the ground that the calculation of the period of notice applicable to her, dismissal was contrary to Directive 2000/78. Under German law, only periods of employment completed after the age of 25 were taken into account in calculating the notice period. At the time of proceedings Directive 2000/78 was in force in Germany.

Held:

The ECJ held that the principle of non-discrimination on grounds of age as given expression by Council Directive 2000/78 must be interpreted as precluding national legislation (such as that at issue in the main proceedings) which provides that periods of employment completed by an employee before reaching the age of 25 are not to be taken into account in calculating the notice period for dismissal.

Comment:

The answer of the ECJ to the referring court in respect of the implications of its judgment in Mangold was as follows:

"It must be recalled here that, . . ., Directive 2000/78 merely gives expression to, but does not lay down, the principle of equal treatment in employment and occupation, and that the principle of non-discrimination on grounds of age is a general principle of European Union law in that it constitutes a specific application of the general principle of equal treatment."[593]

The above paragraph may be interpreted in many ways. However, the following points seem obvious from the judgment:

> *The ECJ did not relax its position of refusing to accept that EU directives can have direct horizontal effect;*

---

592.   Case C-555/07 *Seda Kücükdeveci v Swedex GmbH & Co. KG* [2010] ECR I-365.
593.   Ibid, para. 50.

> The ECJ confirmed that the principle of non-discrimination on the ground of age constitutes a general principle of EU law and that Directive 2000/78 makes this principle real and more specific;
>
> The ECJ examined the matter in the main proceedings by reference to the principle of non-discrimination based on age rather than to Directive 2000/78, but emphasised that the existence of the Directive was essential as it specified the content of the general principle; and,
>
> The ECJ allowed the claimant to rely on EU law in a horizontal dispute, i.e. a dispute involving another individual within the realm of EU law. However, it did not clearly explain why and in what circumstances.

The above judgments have initiated heated debate.[594] Some academic commentators submit that in those judgments the ECJ clearly established that general principles of EU law, provided they pass the test for direct effect, can produce both horizontal and vertical direct effect.[595] Muir submits that the *Kücükdeveci* effect should be subjected to three cumulative conditions: first, there must exist a well-circumscribed general principle of EU law; second, the principle in question must be substantiated through secondary legislation; and, third, there must be a relationship between the principle and the directive, i.e. the sole purpose of the directive is to give effect to the general principle.[596]

It is submitted that to recognise that general principles of EU law may have direct horizontal effect entails far reaching consequences for the EU system of allocation of competences and for institutional equilibrium within the EU.[597] Additionally, such recognition would mean, on the one hand, that the protection of the fundamental rights of those who are discriminated against will be reinforced and, on the other, that individuals will have responsibilities for discharging the EU non-discrimination obligation of which other individuals are beneficiaries.[598] In this respect, many commentators emphasise the detrimental effect on individuals of "horizontalisation" of general principles, as this will undermine the principle of legal certainty and the principles of legitimate expectations. Indeed, general principles of EU law normally bestow rights on individuals, not enforceable obligations. For example, in *Mangold* and in *Kücükdeveci*, the employer, who was found liable, had complied with national law, i.e. he had done nothing wrong.

De Witte doubts the appropriateness of using general principles of EU law, i.e. judge-made norms, which are often vague, in horizontal disputes. In this respect he stated: "In the constitutional law of many countries, general principles and even written fundamental rights are not directly enforceable by courts against private parties but require implementation or specification by the legislator."[599] One may argue, however, that when secondary legislation constitutes an expression of the relevant principle, that

---

594. M. Schmidt, "The Principle of Non-discrimination in Respect of Age: Dimensions of the ECJ's Mangold Judgment", (2006) 7 GLR, 505; C. Tobler, "Putting Mangold in Perspective: In Response to Editorial Comments, Horizontal Direct Effect – A Law of Diminishing Coherence", (2007) 44 CMLRev. 1177.

595. *Wyatt and Dashwood's European Union Law*, 6th edn, 2011, Oxford: Hart Publishing, 255.

596. E. Muir, "Of Ages in – And Edges of – EU Law", (2011) 48 CMLRev., 60.

597. See Opinion of A-G Colomer in Joined Cases C-55 and 56/07 *Michaeler and Others v Amt für sozialen Arbeitsschutz and Autonome Provinz Bozen* [2008] ECR I-3235 paras 21-22.

598. F. Fontanelli, "General Principles of the EU and a Glimpse of Solidarity in the Aftermath of Mangold and Kücükdeveci", (2011) EPL, 225.

599. B. de Witte, "Direct Effect, Primacy and the Nature of the Legal Order", in P. Craig and G. de Búrca (eds.), *The Evolution of EU Law*, 2nd edn, 2011, Oxford: OUP, 339.

principle is sufficiently substantiated. Accordingly, the existence of secondary legislation should be a precondition for the application of a general principle to which secondary legislation gives expression. With regard to EU directives, which are, as submitted in Chapter 11.4 directly applicable, i.e. they form part of national law from the time of their entry into force, and not from the time of the expiry of the transitional period, their theoretical application during the transitional period is sufficient for a general principle to apply.

A further question is whether general principles of EU law can have direct horizontal effect only in areas in which a Member State is required to take, or has taken, measures implementing secondary legislation. In Case C-555/07 *Kücükdeveci*, the ECJ stated that "The need to ensure the full effectiveness of the principle of non-discrimination on grounds of age, as given expression in Directive 2000/78, means that the national court, faced with a national provision falling within the scope of European Union law which it considers to be incompatible with that principle, and which cannot be interpreted in conformity with that principle, must decline to apply that provision."[600] This statement suggests that general principles of EU law may produce direct horizontal effect in respect of any national provision falling within the scope of EU law. This approach is consistent with the view expressed by A-G Shapston in Case C-427/06 *Bartsch*,[601] but may have far-reaching implications.[602]

It is submitted that it is necessary to remember that direct effect of EU law is not automatic and therefore, a general principle of EU law, in order to be directly effective, must pass the usual test for direct effect.

10.6 Direct effect of regulations

Provisions of regulations can have both vertical and horizontal direct effect. Whether or not a particular provision has direct effect is a matter for the proper construction of that provision in the light of the criteria for direct effect set out by the ECJ. The vertical direct effect of regulations was recognised in Case 93/71 *Leonesio*.[603]

THE FACTS WERE:

Under Council Regulation 2195/69 relating to a scheme to reduce dairy herds and over-production of dairy products, payments to farmers who slaughtered their dairy cows were required to be made within two months of slaughtering. The Italian Government delayed implementation of the scheme until the introduction of necessary budgetary provisions (part of the cost was paid by national authorities). Leonesio slaughtered her dairy cows and did not receive payment within the two-month period. Leonesio brought an action before a national court against the Italian Ministry of Agriculture for payments which referred the matter to the ECJ.

---

600. Case C-555/07 *Seda Kücükdeveci v Swedex GmbH & Co. KG* [2010] ECR I-365, para. 53.
601. Case C-427/06 *Birgit Bartsch v Bosch und Siemens Hausgeräte (BSH) Altersfürsorge GmbH* [2008] ECR I-7245, para. 69, i.e. where "some specific substantive rule of [EU] law is applicable to the situation".
602. Editorial Comments, "The Scope of Application of the General Principles of Union Law: An Ever Expanding Union?", (2010) 47 CMLRev., 1589.
603. Case 93/71 *Leonesio v Italian Ministry of Agriculture* [1972] ECR 287. Similar conclusions were reached by the ECJ in Case 43/71 *Politi SAS v Ministry for Finance of the Italian Republic* [1973] ECR 1039.

> *Held:*
>
> *The ECJ held that the regulation "because of its nature and its purpose within the system of sources of [EU] law . . . has direct effect and is, as such, capable of creating individual rights which national courts must protect."[604]*

Horizontal direct effect of regulations was confirmed by the ECJ in Case C-253/00 *Muñoz.*[605] However, Member States are not prevented from adopting implementing measures unless they alter, obstruct or obscure the direct effect of, or the nature of, a regulation.[606] Further, a regulation itself, may expressly state that a Member State is required to take implementing measures[607] (see Chapter 4.5.1.1).

10.7 Direct effect of directives

Four main arguments were invoked against direct effect of directives:

- First, Article 288 TFEU provides that only regulations are directly applicable. On this basis it was argued that directives can neither be directly applicable nor directly effective;

- Second, Article 288 TFEU clearly states that directives are addressed only to the Member States and leaves to them the form, methods and procedures necessary to attain the objectives pursued by the relevant directive. Therefore, directives cannot create rights for individuals since they are not addressees of directives. According to this argument individual rights can only be conferred by national measures implementing directives;

- Third, the difference between regulations and directives would disappear if the latter could have direct effect. Such equality between them, from a legal point of view, would be incompatible with the Treaties given that they expressly provide that only directives are appropriate to harmonise specific areas of EU law; and,

- Fourth, until the entry into force of the Treaty of Maastricht there was no requirement under EU law to publish directives in the Official Journal. Thus, the argument was that it would be against the principle of legal certainty to give direct effect to directives.

The ECJ's arguments in favour of conferring on directives the ability to have direct effect were as follows:

- The refusal to confer on directives the ability to have direct effect is incompatible with Article 288 TFEU, which states that directives have binding force. Consequently, individuals should invoke them in appropriate circumstances.

---

604. Ibid, para. 5.
605. Case C-253/00 *Antonio Muñoz Cia SA v Frumar Ltd* [2002] ECR I-7289 and Joined Cases C-4/10 and C-27/10 *Bureau National Interprofessionnel du Cognac* (judgment of 14/7/11 (NYR)), para. 40.
606. See Case 50/76 *Amsterdam Bulb BV v Produktschap voor Siergewassen* [1977] ECR 137.
607. Case C-52/95 *Commission v France* [1995] ECR I-4443; Case 128/78 *Commission v United Kingdom (Re Tachographs)* [1979] ECR 419.

■ The principle of effectiveness, which has been applied by the ECJ in order to promote effective enforcement of EU law within the legal systems of the Member States,[608] requires recognition of the direct effect of directives, which entails their application by national courts; and,

■ It is inferred from Article 288 TFEU, which makes no distinction between various legislative acts adopted by EU institutions in the circumstances where a national court decides to refer a question relating to interpretation or validity of those acts to the ECJ, that no distinction should be made between directives and other secondary legislation in terms of their ability to produce direct effect. Consequently, Article 267 TFEU implies that individuals should be allowed to rely on provisions of directives in proceedings before national courts.

Based on the above arguments, the ECJ has recognised that directives can have direct effect.

The ECJ first invoked the possibility that directives may produce direct effect in Case 9/70 *Franz Grad*.[609] In this case the question concerned direct effect of a Council decision, but the ECJ stated that other measures mentioned in Article 288 TFEU may produce direct effect, *inter alia*, directives.

In Case 33/70 *SACE*,[610] the ECJ was asked to give its ruling on the combined effect of directly effective provisions of the EC Treaty and of the directive implementing them. The Court's judgment indicated the possibility of a directive having direct effect.

The first decision of the ECJ in which direct effect of a directive was expressly recognised was Case 41/74 *Van Duyn*.[611]

THE FACTS WERE:

Miss Van Duyn, a Dutch national, arrived at Gatwick Airport on 9 May 1973. She intended to work as a secretary at the British headquarters of the Church of Scientology of California. The British immigration authorities refused her leave to enter on the grounds of public policy. Although it was not unlawful to work for the Church of Scientology, the UK Government warned foreigners that the effects of the Church's activities were harmful to the mental health of those involved. Miss Van Duyn challenged the decision of the immigration authorities on two grounds:

■ *Article 45 TFEU which grants workers the right of free movement between Member States subject to its paragraph 3, which imposes limitations on grounds of public policy, public security or public health; and,*

■ *Article 27(2) of Directive 2004/38, (it was then Article 3(1) of Directive 64/221) which further implements Article 45(3) TFEU and which provides that measures taken by Member States regarding public policy must be based exclusively on the personal conduct of the individual concerned.*

Miss Van Duyn claimed that Article 27(2) of Directive 2004/38 was directly effective and that the refusal to allow her to enter the UK was not based on her conduct but on the general policy of the British Government towards the Church of Scientology.

---

608. See R. Ward, "National Sanctions in EC Law: A Moving Boundary in the Division of Competence", (1995) 1 ELJ, 205.

609. Case 9/70 *Franz Grad v Finanzamt Traunstein* [1970] ECR 825. On direct effect of EU decisions see Chapter 10.9.

610. Case 33/70 *SpA SACE v Finance Minister of the Italian Republic* [1970] ECR 1213.

611. Case 41/74 *Yvonne van Duyn v Home Office* [1974] ECR 1337.

> The English High Court asked the ECJ whether both Article 45 TFEU and Article 27(2) of Directive 2004/38 were directly effective.
>
> *Held:*
>
> The ECJ held that both produced direct effect. In particular, the ECJ held that given the nature, general scheme and wording of Article 27(2) of Directive 2004/38 its effectiveness would be greater if individuals were entitled to invoke it in national courts. Therefore, based on the principle of effectiveness, the ECJ decided that Article 27(2) of Directive 2004/38 was directly effective.

The case law of the ECJ regarding directives has further elucidated the concept of direct effect. Seven main points of guidance have appeared:

1. The general principle is that directives should be correctly implemented into national law, so that individuals can rely on their provisions before national courts through the national implementing measures.[612] As a result, there should be no need to verify whether a provision of a directive satisfies the three criteria for direct effect, that is, it must be clear, precise and unconditional. In this way, an individual should have the benefit of rights conferred by directives in the manner envisaged by Article 288 TFEU. Therefore, the question of direct effect should not arise since the correct transposition of provisions of directives means that they are part of national law.

   The question of whether a directive has been correctly implemented into national law concerns, in reality, the conformity of national law with EU law, and not the question of direct effect. Thus, any relevant provision of a directive implemented into national law can be invoked in any dispute (including a dispute between individuals) in order to verify whether national authorities have implemented it in accordance with requirements specified in the directive.[613] Furthermore, implementing measures may be called into question in the process of interpretation of national law in conformity with EU law. In this respect, in Case 14/83 *Von Colson and Kamann*[614] the ECJ held that national courts in applying national law, and especially its provisions implementing directives, have a duty to interpret national law in the light of the text and objectives of the directive in question in order to achieve the results envisaged in the directive. This case established the doctrine of indirect effect (see Chapter 10.8.2).

2. The circumstances in which an individual may rely on direct effect of a directive are:

   - when a directive has not been transposed into national law at all and the deadline for its transposition has expired;
   - when a directive has been incorrectly implemented by a Member State; and,

---

612. Case 270/81 *Felicitas Rickmers-Linie KG & Co. v Finanzamt für Verkehrsteuern, Hambourg* [1982] ECR 2771.

613. Case 51/76 *Verbond van Nederlandse Ondernemingen v Inspecteur der Invoerrechten en Accijnzen* [1977] ECR 113, at para. 24.

614. Case 14/83 *Sabine von Colson and Elisabeth Kamann v Land Nordrhein-Westfalen* [1984] ECR 1891; also Case 31/87 *Gebroeders Beentjes BV v The Netherlands* [1988] ECR 4635; Joined Cases C-397 to C-403/01 *Bernhard Pfeiffer and Others v Deutsches Rotes Kreuz, Kreisverband Waldshut eV* [2004] ECR I-8835.

- when a directive has been correctly implemented but not correctly applied by national authorities.[615]

3.   In order to curtail non-implementation of directives by Member States within the specific time limit, usually laid down in the directives, the ECJ held in Case 148/78 *Ratti*[616] that, provided the provisions of a directive are sufficiently precise and unconditional, their non-implementation within the prescribed period does not affect their direct effect.

THE FACTS WERE:

Ratti was selling solvents and varnishes. He fixed labels to certain dangerous substances in conformity with Directives 73/173 and 77/728, but contrary to Italian legislation of 1963. He was prosecuted by Italian authorities for breach of Italian legislation. Directive 73/173 had not been implemented in Italy, although the time limit prescribed for its implementation had elapsed on 8 December 1974. Also Directive 77/728 had not been transposed into Italian law but the time limit for its implementation had not then yet expired. The Milan Court asked the ECJ under Article 267 TFEU which set of rules should be applied, national law or Directives 73/173 and 77/728.

Held:

The ECJ held that if the provisions of a directive are sufficiently precise and unconditional, although that directive is not implemented within the prescribed period, an individual may rely upon them.

4.   A Member State which has failed to transpose a directive within the prescribed time limit cannot rely on it in proceedings against individuals.[617]

5.   An individual is allowed to rely on a directive, irrespective of whether it is directly effective, against a Member State, in order to determine whether the national legislature, in exercising its choice as to the form and methods for implementing the directive, has kept within the limits of its discretion set out in the directive.

For the first time, in Case 51/76 *VNO*[618] the ECJ decided that individuals could rely on provisions of a directive in proceedings before national courts in order to determine whether the national authorities, in exercising their choice as to the form and methods for implementing the relevant directive, had kept within the limits of their discretion set out by that directive. Thus, the Court focused on the level of discretion available to Member States under the directive. The Court based its reasoning on the principle of effectiveness of EU law and the requirements of Article 288 TFEU. This reasoning was confirmed in Case C-287/98 *Linster.*[619]

---

615.   Case C-62/00 *Marks and Spencer plc v Commissioners of Customs & Excise* [2002] ECR I-6325.

616.   Case 148/78 *Publico Ministero v Ratti* [1979] ECR 1629.

617.   Case 80/86 *Criminal proceedings against Kolpinghuis Nijmegen BV* [1987] ECR 3969; Joined Cases C-397 to C-403/01 *Pfeiffer* [2004] ECR I-8835.

618.   Case 51/76 *Verbond van Nederlandse Ondernemingen* [1977] ECR 113; see also Case C-72/95 *Aannemersbedrijf P.K. Kraaijeveld BV e.a. v Gedeputeerde Staten van Zuid-Holland* [1996] ECR I-5403; and Case C-435/97 *WWF and Others v Autonome Provinz Bozen and Others* [1999] ECR I-5613.

619.   Case C-287/98 *Luxemburg v Berthe Linster and Others* [2000] ECR I-6917.

In a situation where the prescribed time limit for implementation of a directive has expired, an individual can rely on its provisions in proceedings before a national court against a Member State to challenge national implementing measures. It is the task of the national court to determine whether the disputed national measure falls outside the margin of discretion which the directive leaves to the Member State.

6   Directives cannot have horizontal direct effect. In Case 152/84 *Marshall I,*[621] the ECJ held, for the first time, that directives can have only vertical direct effect.

---

620.   [1985] OJ L 175/40.
621.   Case 152/84 *Marshall v Southampton and South West Hampshire Area Health Authority (AHA) (Teaching)* [1986] ECR 723.

Held:

The ECJ held that the AHA was a public body and that individuals could rely on directives against a Member State regardless of whether it acted as a public authority or as an employer. However, the ECJ rejected the idea that directives can have horizontal direct effect. It stated:

"With regard to the argument that a directive may not be relied upon against an individual, it must be emphasized that according to [Article 288 TFEU] the binding nature of a directive, which constitutes the basis for the possibility of relying on the directive before a national court, exists only in relation to 'each Member State to which it is addressed'. It follows that a directive may not of itself impose obligations on an individual and that a provision of a directive may not be relied upon as such against such a person."[622]

The ECJ, has consistently confirmed its ruling in *Marshall I* despite contrary opinions of As-G.[623] In Case C-91/92 *Faccini Dori*, the ECJ held:

"The effect of extending that case law [on vertical direct effect] to the sphere of relations between individuals would be to recognise a power in the [EU] to enact obligations for individuals with immediate effect, whereas it has competence to do so only where it is empowered to adopt regulations."[624]

The above is a very valid reason, but the main argument against attributing direct horizontal effect to directives is that direct effect is intended to force a Member State to comply with its EU law obligations in order to ensure that individuals derive benefits from EU law. For that reason directives should not apply to their detriment. That is why the principle of horizontal direct effect does not apply to relations between individuals.

As A-G Ruiz-Jarabo Colomer stated in his Opinion in Joined Cases C-152/07 to C-154/07 *Arcor*:[625]

"The doctrine of direct effect operates on a vertical, one-way plane (from an individual to the State), in that traffic in the opposite direction (reverse vertical relationships) and perpendicular routes which would enable a directive to be relied on between individuals (horizontal direct effect) are both prohibited."

Notwithstanding this, in some exceptional cases the ECJ has allowed directives to have horizontal direct effect (see Chapter 10.8.5).

---

622. Ibid, para. 48.
623. Opinions of A-G Van Gerven in Case C-271/91 *M. Helen Marshall v Southampton and South-West Hampshire Area Health Authority* [1993] ECR I-4367 at 4381; Jacobs in Case C-316/93 *Nicole Vaneetveld v Le Foyer SA and Others* [1994] ECR I-763 at 765; Lenz in Case C-91/92 *Paola Faccini Dori v Recreb Srl* [1994] ECR I-3325.
624. Case C-91/92 *Paola Faccini Dori v Recreb Srl* [1994] ECR I-3325, para. 24, confirmed many times: Case C-472/93 *Luigi Spano and others v Fiat Geotech SpA and Fiat Hitachi Excavators SpA* [1995] ECR I-4321; Joined Cases 387/02, 391/02 and 403/02 *Criminal Proceedings against Berlusconi and Others* [2005] ECR I-3565; Case C-80/06 *Carp Snc di L. Moleri e V. Corsi v Ecorad Srl* [2007] ECR I-4473.
625. Joined Cases C-152/07 to C-154/07 *Arcor AG & Co. KG* (C-152/07), *Communication Services TELE2 GmbH* (C-153/07), *Firma 01051 Telekom GmbH* (C-154/07) *v Germany* [2008] ECR I-5959, para. 98.

7.   If a provision of a directive embodies a provision of the Treaties,[626] which is directly horizontally effective or a general principle of EU law, which can produce this effect, then, obviously, an individual will not enforce his rights under the directive but under the relevant provision of the Treaties or under the relevant general principle of EU law. With regard to the reliance on general principles of EU law, this raises many questions (see Chapter 10.5). In particular, it is still unclear whether cases such as *Mangold* and *Kücükdeveci* are to be understood as meaning that a pre-condition for the existence of direct effect of a general principle of EU law is that such a principle must be given expression in secondary legislation, in particular in EU directives.

10.8   Mitigating the lack of horizontal direct effect of directives

The refusal to give horizontal direct effect to directives means that even if the conditions for direct effect are satisfied, an individual cannot rely on direct effect to take proceedings against another individual. As a result, individuals cannot enforce their rights because the other party involved is an individual.[627] This is obviously an unjust and unfair situation since, for example, if individuals are employed in the public sector, they may bring proceedings against their employer based on the direct effect of a directive, but if those individuals work in the private sector, they have no remedy based on direct effect of a directive against their employer.[628] Thus, if a Member State fails to properly implement a directive, those who have a legitimate claim under the directive can only enforce their rights against a public body or its emanations, not against another individual. However, such persons are not left without any remedy. They can bring proceedings against a Member State for damages resulting from incorrect implementation of a directive (see Chapter 12).

In order to overcome the practical implications deriving from refusal to confer horizontal direct effect on directives, the ECJ has developed four approaches, and is possibly developing an additional approach. These are:

A.   Under the first approach, the ECJ has extended the meaning of a State to include its emanations;

B.   Under the second approach, the ECJ has imposed a duty on national courts to interpret national law in conformity with EU law. The result of this duty is the creation of what is known as indirect effect;

C.   Under the third approach, the ECJ allows an individual to bring proceedings against a State in a situation where such an action affects the rights of individuals who are not part of the vertical relationship.[629] This is referred to as "triangular" horizontal effect;

D.   Under the fourth approach, an individual may use the principle of State liability to claim compensation in a situation where he has suffered losses because a Member State failed to

---

626.   Case C-381/99 *Susanna Brunnhofer v Bank der österreichischen Postsparkasse AG* [2001] ECR I-4961.

627.   On this question see S. Prechal, "Remedies after Marshall", (1990) CML Rev., p 451.

628.   For example, in Case 152/84 *Marshall I* the claimant succeeded in her equal pay claim against a public heath authority based on Directive 76/207/EEC, whilst in *Duke v GEC Reliance Ltd* [1988] 1 All ER 626, the claimant failed in a similar claim brought against a private company.

629.   Case C-201/02 *The Queen on the Application of Delena Wells v Secretary of State for Transport, Local Government and the Regions* [2004] ECR I-723 and Joined Cases C-152/07 to C-154/07 *Arcor*, supra note 625.

implement the relevant EU directive correctly within the specified time-limit, or implemented it incorrectly, or implemented it correctly but applied it incorrectly (see Chapter 12); and,

E.   With regard to the possible fifth approach it is uncertain whether there is a fifth emerging way in which the ECJ attempts to remedy the lack of horizontal direct effect of directives. Case law on this topic is confusing. It is submitted, however, that the ECJ has allowed individuals, on some rare occasions, to rely on directives in proceedings against another private party.[630] Only time will tell whether or not the ECJ maintains the thrust of these judgments.

10.8.1   The first approach: the extended interpretation given by the ECJ to the meaning of a State

On the basis of the vertical direct effect of directives, individuals have directly enforceable rights on which they may rely in an action against a Member State in proceedings before national courts. Bearing in mind that any action against a Member State is in fact taken against a body of the relevant Member State, the question arises as to what bodies are considered as belonging to a Member State. In Case 152/84 *Marshall I*[631] (for facts see Chapter 10.7) the ECJ held that Mrs Marshall's employer, the AHA, was a public body regardless of the capacity in which it was acting, that is, as public authority or employer. It emphasised that:

> "The argument submitted by the United Kingdom that the possibility of relying on provisions of the directive against the respondent *qua* organ of the State would give rise to an arbitrary and unfair distinction between the rights of State employees and those of private employees, does not justify any other conclusion. Such a distinction may easily be avoided if the Member State concerned has correctly implemented the directive into national law."[632]

In order to maximise the effect of directives, the ECJ introduced an autonomous meaning of a public body in Case C-188/89 *Foster*.[633] It is a body:

> "whatever its legal form, which has been made responsible pursuant to a measure adopted by a public authority, for providing a public service under the control of that authority and had for that purpose special powers beyond those which resulted from the normal rules applicable in relations between individuals".

It results from the above definition that for EU law purposes the term "public body" includes not only public bodies *sensu stricto* but also various emanations of a State. Three criteria must be satisfied in order to consider an entity as a public body. These are:

- It must be made responsible for providing a public service;

- It must provide that service under the control of the Member State; and,

- It must have special powers to provide that service, beyond those normally applicable in relations between individuals.

---

630.   See I. Ward, *A Critical Introduction to European Law*, 2nd edn, 2003, London: LexisNexisButterworths, 78–80.

631.   Case 152/84 *Marshall v Southampton and South West Hampshire Area Health Authority (AHA) (Teaching) (No.1)* [1986] ECR 723.

632.   Ibid, para. 51.

633.   Case C-188/89 *Foster and Others v British Gas plc* [1990] ECR I-3313.

The three criteria set out in *Foster* are not easy to apply, in particular criteria 2 and 3. The ECJ has not specified the degree of special power/control by the State necessary to satisfy the *Foster* test. It has broadly interpreted both criteria[634] with the result that an individual can rely on a directive against a body which has no control over the implementation of a directive but under EU law will be, nevertheless, held responsible for the default of the Member State. The consequence of this approach was noted by A-G Jacobs in his Opinion in Case C-316/93 *Vaneetveld*.[635] With regard to commercial undertakings which some degree of participation or control of a Member State against whom a directive can be enforced as opposed to its direct competitors in the private sector against whom the same directive cannot be enforced by individuals. His conclusion was that the recognition of direct horizontal effects of a directive is a better solution than the expansion of the concept of a public body in terms of ensuring legal certainty.

The matter of whether all three criteria set out in *Foster* must be applied cumulatively has been answered in the affirmative by the ECJ.[636] This is exemplified in Case C-157/02 *Asfinag*.[637]

THE FACTS WERE:

Asfinag, an Austrian undertaking, which under a licence concluded with the Austrian Government was responsible for the construction, operation, maintenance and financing of Austrian motorways and expressways and was allowed to impose tolls and user charges in order to finance itself, argued that it was not a public body within the meaning of EU law.

Held:

The ECJ held that Asfinag was a public body.

Comment:

The ECJ based its reasoning on the facts that the Austrian State:

- *was the sole shareholder of Asfinag;*
- *had the right to check all measures taken by the company and its subsidiaries;*
- *could require any information at any time;*

---

634. The following bodies have been regarded as emanations of a Member State: tax authorities – Case 8/81 *Becker* [1982] ECR 53; police authorities – Case 222/84 *Johnston* [1986] ECR 1651; health boards – Case 152/84 *Marshall* [1986] ECR 723; local government bodies – Case 103/88 *Fratelli Constanzo* [1989] ECR 1839; professional bodies established by statutory instruments – Joined Cases 266–7/87 *The Royal Pharmaceutical Society of Great Britain* [1989] ECR 1295; and a body set up by the German Government to promote German agriculture and the German food industry, but which carried out its activity through a private company whose organs were set up in accordance with private law rules and financed by compulsory contributions paid by undertakings in the German agriculture and food sector – Case C-325/00 *Commission v Germany* [2002] ECR I-9977.

635. Case C-316/93 *Nicole Vaneetveld v Le Foyer SA and Le Foyer SA v Fédération des Mutualités Socialistes et Syndicales de la Province de Liège* [1994] ECR I-763, para. 31.

636. It is interesting to note that in Joined Cases C-253/96 to C-256/96 *Helmut Kampelmann and Others v Landschaftsverband Westfalen-Lippe* ([1997] ECR I-6907, para. 47) the ECJ appeared to hesitate as to whether the 3 criteria should apply cumulatively. In these cases the ECJ seemed to reduce the test to two criteria, i.e. criterion 1 and either criterion 2 or criterion 3. However, this approach was subsequently abandoned.

637. Case C-157/02 *Rieser Internationale Transporte GmbH v Asfinag* [2004] ECR I-1477. See also Joined Cases C-250/09 and C-268/09 *Vasil Ivanov Georgiev v Tehnicheski Universitet – Sofia, Filial Plovdiv* [2010] ECR I-11869, para. 70.

> ◾ *imposed objectives in terms of the organisation of traffic, safety and construction;*
> ◾ *approved the annual budgets of Asfinag; and,*
> ◾ *fixed the amount of the tolls to be levied.*
>
> *Accordingly, Asfinag satisfied all three criteria set out in Foster. The Austrian State was the sole shareholder and exercised direct control over it. Further, Asfinag provided public services and had special powers as it was allowed to impose tolls and user charges in order to finance itself.*

The full cumulative test was applied by the Court of Appeal of England and Wales in *Doughty*.[638] The Court ruled that Rolls Royce, a nationalised body responsible for providing defence equipment to the government, did not satisfy all the criteria in *Foster*. The Court found that Rolls Royce was "under State control" as it was 100 per cent owned by the State, but made a distinction between services provided for the public and services provided to the State, and thereby ruled that the first condition set out in *Foster* was not satisfied. Also, Rolls Royce had no special powers. As a result, Mrs Doughty, an employee of Rolls Royce, in a very similar situation to Mrs Marshall, could not invoke Directive 76/207 and was barred from commencing proceedings against her employer.[639]

10.8.2 The second approach: interpretation of national law in conformity with EU law by national courts: indirect effect

National judges are required to interpret national law in conformity with EU law. This principle constitutes a logical consequence of the supremacy of EU law and applies in relation to all EU law irrespective of whether a provision of EU law is directly effective. National law, whether enacted before or after the entry into force of the Treaties in the relevant Member State, must conform to EU law. In Case 14/83 *Von Colson and Kamann*,[640] the ECJ emphasised that national judges are obliged to interpret national law in the light of the text and objectives of EU law, which in this particular case was a directive. This solution is based on two premises:

■ First, on Article 4(3) TEU, which imposes upon the Member States a duty of loyal and active co-operation. Article 4(3) TFEU provides that Member States must take all appropriate measures, whether general or particular, to fulfil their obligations arising out of the Treaties and resulting from measures adopted by EU institutions. They must facilitate accomplishment of the tasks of EU institutions. This means that the Member States must adopt implementing measures in respect of the Treaties and acts of EU institutions; and,

■ Second, in Case 30/70 *Scheer*,[641] the ECJ held that under Article 4(3) TFEU the Member States have a duty to do whatever possible to ensure the effectiveness of the provisions of EU law. According to the ECJ Article 4(3) TFEU applies to all national bodies, including national courts,

---

638. *Doughty v Rolls Royce* [1992] 1 CMLR 1045.
639. On the implications of the broad interpretation of the concept of a State see A-G Jacobs' Opinion in Case C-316/93 *Nicole Vaneetveld v Le Foyer SA and Le Foyer SA v Fédération des Mutualités Socialistes et Syndicales de la Province de Liège* [1994] ECR I-763, para. 31.
640. Case 14/83 *Sabine von Colson and Elisabeth Kamann v Land Nordrhein-Westfalen* [1984] ECR 1891.
641. Case 30/70 *Otto Scheer v Einfuhr- und Vorratsstelle für Getreide und Futtermittel* [1970] ECR 1197.

which have a duty to ensure that national law conforms to EU law, and thus the requirement of the principle of effectiveness is satisfied, that is, rights vested in individuals by EU law must be protected by national courts. The combined effect of Article 288 TFEU, Article 4(3) TEU and the principle of effectiveness secures adequate enforcement of any obligations imposed on individuals.

The possibility of obliging national courts to interpret national law in conformity with EU law was mentioned for the first time in Case 111/75 *Mazzalai*,[642] in which the ECJ approved the conclusion of A-G Darmon, who said that the interpretation of a directive in the light of EU law may be useful for national judges in order to ensure that their interpretation conforms to the requirements of EU law. However, it was two decisions of the ECJ, Case 14/83 *Von Colson and Kamann*[643] and Case 79/83 *Harz*,[644] that provided a new solution to the problem of mitigating the effect of the vertical/horizontal public/private dichotomy of directives.

THE FACTS WERE:

Von Colson and Harz, both females, argued that they were discriminated against on grounds of gender when applying for a job: Von Colson in the public service when she applied for the post of prison social worker, and Harz in the private sector when she applied to join a training programme with a commercial company. Under German law implementing Council Directive 76/207, although it was accepted that Von Colson and Harz had been discriminated against unlawfully, they were entitled to receive only nominal damages, that is, reimbursement of their travel expenses. They claimed that such implementation was contrary to Article 6 of Directive 76/207, which provides that:

"Member States shall introduce into their national legal systems such measures as are necessary to enable all persons who consider themselves wronged by failure to apply to them the principle of equal treatment . . . to pursue their claims by judicial process after possible recourse to other competent authorities."

Both applicants argued that the remedy under German law was inadequate and that they should be offered the post or receive substantial damages. Under Article 267 TFEU the German labour court referred to the ECJ the following questions: whether Article 6 of Directive 76/207 was directly effective, and whether under that Directive Member States were required to provide for particular sanctions or other legal consequences in cases of discrimination on grounds of sex against a person seeking employment.

Held:

The ECJ held that:

- *national law must be interpreted in such a way as to achieve the result required by the directive regardless of whether the defendant was a Member State or a private party;*
- *sanctions for discrimination were left to national law. The Court stated that, on the one hand, the employer is not obliged to offer a contract of employment to an applicant being discriminated against on the ground of gender but, on the other hand, the principle of*

---

642. Case 111/75 *Impresa Costruzioni comm. Quirino Mazzalai v Ferrovia del Renon* [1976] ECR 657, para. 10.
643. Case 14/83 *Sabine von Colson and Elisabeth Kamann v Land Nordrhein-Westfalen* [1984] ECR 1891.
644. Case 79/83 *Dorit Harz v Deutsche Tradax GmbH* [1984] ECR 1921.

effectiveness requires that compensation must, in any event, be adequate to the damage sustained and must amount to more than purely nominal compensation. The German Labour Court subsequently found that it had power to award damages to both plaintiffs not exceeding six months gross salary.

Comment:

In both cases the interpretation of national law in conformity with the Directive provided an efficient remedy to the applicants tantamount to conferring on Article 6 of Directive 76/207 horizontal direct effect.

A further issue that arose in the case law was whether interpretation in conformity with EU law was restricted to national law implementing measures or extended to all national law. The answer was provided by the ECJ in Case C-106/89 *Marleasing*.[645]

THE FACTS WERE:

Under the Spanish Civil Code a company could be nullified on the grounds of "lack of cause". Marleasing claimed that the defendant company was established in order to defraud its creditors, that the founders' contract was a sham and since the contract of association was void for "lack of cause", it, as one of the creditors, could recover its debt personally from those behind the scheme. The defendants argued that under Article 11 of the EC First Company Directive 68/151, which provided an exhaustive list of the grounds on which the nullity of a company may be declared, lack of cause was not mentioned. Directive 68/151 had not been implemented in Spain, although the prescribed time limit for its implementation had elapsed. The Spanish court asked the ECJ, within the preliminary ruling procedure, whether Article 11 of Directive 68/151 was directly effective, and whether it prevented a declaration of nullity on grounds other than those listed in that provision.

Held:

The ECJ **held:**

- *that directives could not produce horizontal direct effect, thus the defendant could not rely on Article 11 in proceedings against another individual. Also Article 11 of Directive 68/151 exhaustively listed the grounds of nullity and did not include the grounds on which Marleasing relied; and,*
- *that based on its judgment in* Von Colson *the Spanish court was obliged "so far as was possible" to interpret national law, whether it pre-dated or post-dated the directive, in the light of EU law.*

Comment:

The obligation of interpretation of national law "so far as possible" in conformity with EU law meant that the Spanish court had to interpret Spanish law in such a way as to disregard provisions of the Spanish Civil Code which predated Directive 68/151, so the duty of interpretation extended to all national law.

---

645. Case C-106/89 *Marleasing SA v La Comercial Internacional de Alimentacion SA* [1990] ECR I-4135.

10.8.2.1 Limitations imposed on the Marleasing doctrine

Marleasing was a very controversial case. On the one hand, the judgment states that the obligation to interpret national law in conformity with EU law is demanded only "as far as possible". On the other hand, the judgment in *Marleasing* did not require a national judge to interpret a national provision in the light of the directive. It simply struck down a conflicting national provision which was never intended to implement the directive.[646] This seems, in fact, to apply the concept of direct effect under a different name. The ECJ did, however, elucidate the meaning of *Marleasing* in Case C-334/92 *Wagner Miret*.[647]

THE FACTS WERE:

Wagner Miret was employed as a senior manager in a Spanish company that became insolvent. Under Directive 80/987 Member States were required to set up a fund to compensate employees should their employer became insolvent. Spain had established such a fund, but it did not apply to senior management staff.

Held:

The ECJ held that:

- *Directive 80/987 was not precise enough to produce direct effect, and that Spanish law clearly limited access to the fund, and that*
- *Spanish law could not be interpreted in such a way as to include senior management staff within the group of people to be compensated from that fund as that law clearly excluded higher management staff from claiming from the fund payment of amounts owing by way of salary.*

Comment:

The ECJ accepted that a national court has no duty to interpret national law contra legem, i.e. a national court is not required to interpret national law in a way which is contrary to the express terms of the relevant national legislation.

In Joined Cases C-397–403/01 *Pfeiffer*,[648] the ECJ held that when domestic provisions which have been specifically enacted for the purpose of transposing a directive and are intended to confer rights on individuals are incompatible with that directive, a national court must presume that the Member State had the intention of fulfilling the obligations arising from the directive and is therefore bound to interpret national law, so far as possible, in the light of the wording and the purpose of the directive concerned, in order to achieve the result sought by the directive. The national court must take into consideration the whole body of rules of national law, not only the provisions of national law implementing the directive, and must select, from the interpretative methods recognised by national

---

646. See also Case C-472/93 *Luigi Spano and others v Fiat Geotech SpA and Others* [1995] ECR I-4321 and Case C-449/93 *Rockfon A/S v Specialarbejderforbundet i Danmark* [1995] ECR I-4291.

647. Case C-334/92 *Wagner Miret v Fondo de Garantia Salarial* [1993] ECR I-6911.

648. Joined Cases C-397-403/01 *Pfeiffer and Others v Deutsches Rotes Kreuz, Kreisverband Waldshut eV* [2004] ECR I-8835.

law, the one which allows it to construe the challenged provision of national law in such a way as to ensure that the directive is fully effective. As a result, the national court must do whatever lies within its jurisdiction to ensure that the objective of the directive is achieved.

However, the duty to interpret national law in conformity with EU law is not absolute so as to require interpretation of national law *contra legem*, but only "so far as possible". In this context a question arises as to the meaning of the words "so far as possible", that is, as to the limit of a national court's obligation to interpret national law in the light of the wording and the purpose of the directive in order to achieve the results prescribed in Article 288 TFEU. It is submitted that the limits can be identified as follows.

First, in *Wagner Miret* the ECJ accepted that the contested directive could not be interpreted so as to include the applicant within its scope of application. In subsequent cases the ECJ confirmed that national courts are not required to interpret national law *contra legem*.[649]

Second, the duty to interpret national law in conformity with EU law is limited by the general principles of EU law, in particular the principles of legal certainty and non-retroactivity in criminal matters. In Case 80/86 *Kolpinghuis Nijmegen*,[650] the ECJ established that the uniform interpretation of EU law must be qualified in criminal proceedings, if the effect of interpreting national legislation in the light of a directive would be to impose criminal liability on individuals in circumstances where such liability would not arise under the national legislation taken alone. In this case, the ECJ held that the obligation for a national judge to make reference to the terms of the directive, when he interprets relevant provisions of national law, is limited by general principles of EU law, and especially by the principle of legal certainty and non-retroactivity.

In Joined Cases C-74/95 and C-129/95 *Criminal Proceedings against X*[651] an Italian judge, within the preliminary rulings procedure under Article 267 TFEU, asked the ECJ to interpret some provisions of Directive 90/270 on the minimum safety and health requirements for work with display screens. The Italian court did not exclude the possibility that the interpretation provided by the ECJ might, in due course, have determined or aggravated the liability of individuals who were in breach of that directive, although Italian law, which implemented its provisions, did not provide for any penal sanctions. The ECJ held that:

"the obligation on the national court to refer to the content of the directive when interpreting the relevant rules of its national law is not unlimited, particularly where such interpretation would have the effect, on the basis of the directive and independently of legislation adopted for its interpretation, of determining or aggravating the liability in criminal law of persons who act in contravention of its provisions."[652]

The ECJ explained that the principle of legal certainty in relation to crime and punishment precludes bringing criminal proceedings in respect of conduct not clearly defined as culpable by law. In support of its decision the ECJ referred to the general principles of law which result from the common constitutional tradition of the Member States and Article 7 of the ECHR. However, the duty of consistent

---

649. Case C-192/94 *El Corte Inglés SA v Cristina Blázquez Rivero* [1996] ECR I-1281; Case C-111/97 *EvoBus Austria GmbH v Niederösterreichische Verkehrsorganisations GmbH (Növog)* [1998] ECR I-5411; Case C-81/98 *Alcatel Austria AG and Others, Siemens AG Österreich and Sag-Schrack Anlagentechnik AG v Bundesministerium für Wissenschaft und Verkehr* [1999] ECR I-7671 and Case C-105/03 *Criminal Proceedings against Maria Pupino* [2005] ECR I-5285.

650. Case 80/86 *Criminal Proceedings against Kolpinghuis Nijmegen BV* [1987] ECR 3969.

651. [1996] ECR I-6609.

652. Ibid, para. 24. See also Joined Cases 387/02, 391/02 and 403/02 *Criminal Proceedings against Berlusconi and Others* [2005] ECR I-3565.

interpretation applies to rules of criminal procedure. In Case C-105/03 *Pupino*,[653] the ECJ held that national courts are bound to interpret national rules relating to the conduct of criminal proceedings and the means of taking evidence in conformity with EU law. This distinction between rules of criminal proceedings and substantive criminal law, although confirmed by the ECJ in subsequent cases,[654] has been criticised on two grounds: first, that in some cases it is difficult to make a distinction between substantive and procedural rules; and, second, the interpretation of rules of procedure and evidence can have important detrimental effects on determining or aggravating criminal liability of the accused person.[655]

The matter of whether the duty imposed on national courts to interpret national law in conformity with EU law is negated in a situation where, as a result of consistent interpretation, civil liability, which would not otherwise have existed, will be imposed on an individual remains unclear. A debate arose on this matter in the light of judgments of the ECJ relating to criminal law cases[656] and tax law cases. In Case C-321/05 *Kofoed*,[657] which concerned tax law, the ECJ stated that "the requirement of a directive compliant interpretation cannot reach the point where a directive, by itself and without national implementing legislation, may create obligations for individuals or determine or aggravate the liability in criminal law of persons who act in contravention of its provisions". The reference to the possibility of the "creation of an obligation" may suggest that when the outcome of consistent interpretation would be the imposition of civil liabilities or obligations on a private party such interpretation would not be permitted. Although the matter is unclear it is submitted that the application of criminal and tax law in terms of their negative consequences for individuals cannot be compared with consequences deriving from civil or administrative law. Accordingly, the position taken by the A-G in Case C-456/98 *Centrostel*[658] seems preferable. He stated:

> "I am of the opinion that the Court's case-law establishes two rules: (1) a directive cannot of itself impose obligations on individuals in the absence of proper implementation in national law; (2) the national courts must nevertheless interpret national law, as far as possible, in the light of the wording and purpose of relevant directives. While that process of interpretation cannot, of itself and independently of a national law implementing the directive, have the effect of determining or aggravating criminal liability, it may well lead to the imposition upon an individual of civil liability or a civil obligation which would not otherwise have existed."

Third, national courts have no duty to interpret national law in conformity with EU law before the expiry of the transposition period of a directive. In Case C-212/04 *Adeneler*,[659] the ECJ held that:

> "where a directive is transposed belatedly, the general obligation owed by national courts to interpret domestic law in conformity with the directive exists only once the period for its transposition has expired".

---

653. Case C-105/03 *Criminal Proceedings against Maria Pupino* [2005] ECR I-5285.
654. Case C-404/07 *György Katz v István Roland Sós* [2008] ECR I-7607.
655. E. Spaventa, "Opening Pandora's Box: Some Reflections on the Constitutional Effects pf the Decision in Pupino", (2006) 3 *European Constitutional Law Review*, 5.
656. Case C-168/95 *Criminal Proceedings against Luciano Arcaro* [1996] ECR I-4705.
657. Case C-321/05 *Hans Markus Kofoed v Skatteministeriet* [2007] ECR I-5795, para. 46.
658. Case C-456/98 *Centrostel v Adipol* [2000] ECR I-6007, para. 35.
659. Case C-112/04 *Konstantinos Adeneler and Others v Ellinikos Organismos Galaktos (ELOG)* [2006] ECR I-6057, para. 115.

10.8.3 The third approach under which the ECJ allows an individual to bring proceedings against a State in a situation where such proceedings affect the rights of individuals who are not part of the vertical relationship – "triangular" horizontal effect

In Case C-201/02 *Wells*,[660] the ECJ held, for the first time, that "adverse repercussions on the rights of third parties, even if the repercussions are certain, do not justify preventing an individual from invoking the provisions of a directive against the Member State concerned". In *Wells*, the claimant was allowed to rely on Directive 85/337 to force a Member State to carry out an environmental impact assessment, as provided for in the directive, resulting in a temporary (or, depending on the results of that assessment, even permanent) cessation of the working of a quarry, located near the claimant's dwelling-house. In *Wells*, the ECJ held that the obligation in question was not imposed on the quarry owners but on the Member State. Accordingly, the argument submitted by the UK, that to allow the claimant to rely on the Directive would amount to giving "inverse direct effect" to the relevant provisions of the Directive in relation to the quarry owners, was rejected. The ECJ confirmed that directives can produce "triangular" horizontal effect in Joined Cases C-152/07 to C-154/07 *Arcor*.[661]

THE FACTS WERE:

The cases related to the liberalisation of telecommunications markets based on EU directives, which in Germany were implemented on 1 August 1996 by the German Law on Telecommunications. Before the liberalisation Deutsche Telekom enjoyed a legal monopoly in Germany in the retail provision of fixed-line telecommunications services. Following liberalisation, Deutsche Telekom had to compete with alternative operators with regard to local network access services. Abusive practices of Deutsche Telekom with regard to its competitors had been condemned by a Commission decision and this condemnation was confirmed by the General Court in Case T-271/08 Deutsche Telekom.[662]

The claimants, Arcor AG and others, all operators of public telecommunications networks in Germany offering their customers a carrier selection service through interconnection to the local network of Deutsche Telekom, brought proceedings before a national court challenging the decision of the German Federal Agency for Electricity, Gas, Telecommunications, Post and Rail Networks ("the regulatory authority") which approved a connection charge of €0.004 per minute in respect of call charges for the provision of calls originating in Deutsche Telekom's national telephone network. The decision had been adopted on 29 April 2003 by the regulatory authority and was justified on the ground that revenues from end users accruing to Deutsche Telekom, an undertaking in a dominant position, did not cover all the costs of activating the local loop[663] with the result that in the absence of a connection charge there would have been a deficit.

---

660. Case C-201/01 *The Queen on the application of Delena Wells v Secretary of State for Transport, Local Government and the Regions* [2004] ECR I-723, see also Case C-201/94 *The Queen v The Medicines Control Agency, ex parte Smith & Nephew Pharmaceuticals Ltd and Primecrown Ltd v The Medicines Control Agency* [1996] ECR I-5819, para. 57.

661. Joined Cases C-152/07 to C-154/07 *Arcor AG & Co. KG (C-152/07), Communication Services TELE2 GmbH (C-153/07) and Firma 01051 Telekom GmbH (C-154/07) v Germany* [2008] ECR I-5959.

662. Case T-271/08 *Deutsche Telekom AG v Commission* [2008] ECR II-477.

663. The term "local loop" refers to the physical circuit connecting the network termination point at a subscriber's premises to the main distribution frame or equivalent facility in the fixed public telephone network.

As a result of the Commission decision finding Deutsche Telekom AG in breach of Article 102 TFEU,[664] the German regulatory authority, by decision of 23 September 2003, had revoked the decision of 29 April 2003, on the ground that Deutsche Telekom no longer had any connection cost deficit, since an increase in the price paid by end-users for provision of the local loop had been approved in the interim. However, as the decision had no retrospective effect, the claimants had brought proceedings challenging the retrospective connection charges before the relevant German court which had upheld their claims. Germany and Deutsche Telekom brought an appeal against this decision. The referring court asked the ECJ, inter alia, the question whether in circumstances where proceedings adversely affect a third party (i.e. Deutsche Telekom, which was not a party to the proceedings) the claimants (Arcor AG and others) were allowed to rely on a directive against a Member State (i.e. the German regulatory authority).

Held:

The ECJ held that the claimants could rely on the relevant directives. It stated that:

"It is clear that Deutsche Telekom is a third party in relation to the dispute before the referring court and is capable only of suffering adverse repercussions because it levied the connection charge at issue in the main proceedings and because, if that charge were removed, it would have to increase its own subscribers' rates. Such a removal of benefits cannot be regarded as an obligation falling on a third party pursuant to the directives relied on before the referring court by the appellants in the main proceedings."[665]

Comment:

The ECJ clearly established that the relevant provisions of directives satisfied the test for direct effect and that Deutsche Telekom, a third party in relation to the dispute before the referring court, would suffer adverse financial consequences and probably would have to increase its own subscribers' rates. However, it is also clear that in those circumstances the loss of unlawful benefits cannot be equated to the creation of a new obligation on a third party, i.e. Deutsche Telekom. Indeed, Deutsche Telekom would not suffer genuine damage by being prevented from imposing unlawful charges.

10.8.4 The fourth approach: the reliance on the principle of State liability

Under this approach, an individual may rely on the principle of State liability to claim compensation in a situation where he has suffered losses through the Member State's failure to implement the relevant EU directive correctly within the specified time-limit (see Chapter 12).

---

664. Decision 2003/707/EC (Case COMP/C-1/37.451, 37.578, 37.579 – *Deutsche Telekom AG* ([2003] OJ L 263/9) fining Deutsche Telekom €12 600 000 for abusing its dominant position by operating abusive pricing in the form of a "margin squeeze" by charging its competitors (*inter alia*, the claimants in the commented cases) prices for wholesale access that were higher than its prices for retail access to the local network. The decision of the Commission was confirmed by the General Court in Case T-271/03 *Deutsche Telekom AG v Commission* [2008] ECR II-477.

665. Ibid, para. 38.

10.8.5 The fifth approach: exceptional circumstances under which directives may have horizontal direct effect

In some circumstances, the ECJ have allowed individuals to rely on EU directives in horizontal disputes. One exception can be called "a procedural" direct horizontal effect and was established in Case C-443/98 *Unilever*.[666]

THE FACTS WERE:

Directive 83/189 (the Technical Standard Directive), which lays down the procedure for the provision of information in the field of technical standards and regulations,[667] was adopted in order to remove technical obstacles to the free movement of goods. Under the Directive Member States are required to notify the Commission of any national draft technical regulations within the scope of the Directive, the reason being that other Member States and the Commission then have an opportunity to assess the compatibility of any relevant draft technical regulation with Article 34 TFEU. Under the Directive, subsequent to notification, the notifying Member State is required to suspend the enactment procedure of a relevant draft regulation for an initial period of three months, which period may be extended in various ways. One of them is provided for in Article 9(3) of Directive 83/189, according to which the suspension period mentioned above may be extended by 12 months following the date of notification if the Commission expresses its intention to propose an EU measure in the area covered by the proposed national draft technical regulation.

Italy prepared a draft regulation concerning labelling indicating the geographical origin of various kinds of olive oil and notified it to the Commission. Following this, the Commission published in the OJ a notice indicating that the three months period of suspension applied to the Italian draft law. Before the end of the suspension period the Commission informed the Italian Government that it intended to legislate in the area covered by the draft law and therefore required Italy to suspend for one year enactment of its draft law. Despite this the Italian Parliament continued the enactment procedure. In response the Commission stated that should Italy enact the draft law, the Commission would start proceedings against Italy under Article 258 TFEU and would declare the new Italian law unenforceable against individuals. Despite this, Italy enacted its draft legislation. Four months later the Commission adopted Regulation 2815/98 concerning marketing standards for olive oil[668] which, in particular, laid down rules governing the designation of origin of virgin and extra virgin olive oils on their labels or packaging.

After the entry into force of the new Italian legislation, but before the adoption of Regulation 2815/98, Unilever, an Italian company, delivered to a warehouse of Central Food, also an Italian company, 648 litres of extra virgin olive oil. Central Food refused to pay for these goods on the ground that the olive oil was not labelled in accordance with the new Italian law. Unilever started proceedings against Central Food for payment of sums due under the contract, arguing that the legislation did not apply as it was in breach of Directive 83/189 and

---

666. Case C-443/98 *Unilever Italia SpA v Central Food SpA* [2000] ECR I-7535.
667. [1983] OJ L 109/8.
668. [1998] OJ L 349/56.

that Unilever's products were labelled in conformity with the preceding (and still in force) legislation. The Italian Pretore di Milano referred the matter to the ECJ.

Held:

The ECJ held that the Italian court was required, in civil proceedings between individuals concerning contractual rights and obligations, to refuse to apply the new Italian legislation. Consequently, the ECJ, by allowing Unilever to rely on Article 9(3) of Directive 83/189, attributed to this provision horizontal direct effect.

Comment:

The ECJ explained that the principle that directives cannot produce horizontal direct effect did not apply where a national technical regulation was adopted in breach of Articles 8[669] and 9 of Directive 83/189 and thus affected by a substantial procedural defect. This was because, as the ECJ held:

"Directive 83/189 does not in any way define the substantive scope of the legal rule on the basis of which the national court must decide the case before it. It creates neither rights nor obligations for individuals."

It flows from the above that the above-described exception, which can be called "procedural direct horizontal effect", applies in a situation where a directive is of a procedural nature, that is, it neither creates new law, nor any rights nor any obligations for individuals. The result in *Unilever* was that the preceding Italian law was applicable to the dispute as the new Italian law was rendered inapplicable by the ECJ. The judgment may seem unfair in relation to Central Food, but the company had a very powerful remedy at its disposal: the use of the principle of State liability. Italy was in blatant breach of EU law, and the breach was sufficiently serious to guarantee an award of damages to Central Food if it suffered loss (see Chapter 12).

It is submitted that on the authority of Case C-226/97 *Lemmens*,[670] that the ECJ will limit the exception set out in *Unilever* to a situation where the failure of national authorities to notify national implementing measures is liable to hinder the objectives of the internal market. In *Lemmens*, the claimant, a Dutch national, challenged his criminal conviction for drink-driving on the ground that the Dutch legislation on breath-analyser apparatus had not been notified to the Commission under the Technical Standard Directive. His conviction was based on evidence obtained by means of such apparatus. The ECJ held that the claimant could not rely on the Directive because:

"While failure to notify technical regulations [national implementing measures], which constitutes a procedural defect in their adoption, renders such regulations inapplicable inasmuch as they hinder the use or marketing of a product which is not in conformity therewith, it does not have the effect of rendering unlawful any use of a product which is in conformity with regulations which have not been notified." [671]

In *Lemmens* the failure to notify was not liable to hinder the free movement of goods in the internal market whilst in *Unilever* it did have such effect.

---

669.   See Case C-194/94 *CIA Security v Signalson and Securitel* [1996] ECR I-2201.

670.   Case C-226/97 *Criminal Proceedings against Johannes Martinus Lemmens* [1998] ECR I-3711.

671.   Ibid, para. 35.

Advocates of the dual approach (see Chapter 10.2.1) treat this case as an exception but without being able to explain the motives behind the judgment of the ECJ. However, under the primacy approach there is no inconsistency between this judgment and the denial of direct horizontal effect to EU directives. This is because an individual is not relying on horizontal direct effect of the directives but on the principle of supremacy according to which any national provision which is inconsistent with EU law must be set aside by a national court. The adverse effect that this produces on individuals is of no relevance.

The explanation that Directive 83/189 did not create any new laws, rights or obligations on individuals cannot apply to other cases in which the ECJ has allowed individuals to rely on EU directives in horizontal disputes. In. Case C-129/94 *Bernáldez*[672] criminal proceedings were instituted against Mr Bernaldez who had caused an accident while driving intoxicated. Under Spanish law, the insurance company was not required to compensate for damage to property and personal injuries caused to third parties if the driver was intoxicated, but an obligation to that effect was imposed by EU directives on motor insurers. In the light of the fact that the referring court could not interpret Spanish law in conformity with EU law because it was clearly incompatible with EU law, and that according to *Marleasing* a *contra legem* interpretation was not required, the ECJ allowed the application of an unimplemented directive (but the time-limit for its implementation had expired) to a horizontal relationship, i.e. between the insurer and the insured person. Similarly, in Case C- 215/97 *Bellone*[673] in proceedings between private parties, a commercial agent and its principal, a private company, in which the agent claimed various indemnities after the principal terminated the contract of agency, the ECJ allowed the application of Directive 86/653 relating to self-employed commercial agents. The directive excluded the application of Italian law under which the agent had no claim because the contract was void as it had not been entered on the register of commercial agents and representatives at the same time as the contract was concluded. Under Italian law registration was compulsory but under the EU directive there was no obligation to register an agency contract.[674]

The number of cases in which the ECJ has allowed individuals to rely on a directive in proceedings against other individuals is limited.[675] Nevertheless, those judgments introduce uncertainty and have neither been explained satisfactorily by academic commentators, nor by the ECJ, nor the A-Gs.[676]

10.9 Direct effect of decisions

Under Article 288 TFEU, two kinds of decision can be adopted by EU institutions, i.e. those which identify their addressees and those which have no addressees. It states that a decision which specifies those to whom it is addressed shall be binding only on them. It is submitted that both kinds of decision may create rights and obligations for individuals or Member States and may produce direct effect. As a result, irrespective of whether a decision identifies its addressee or not, it may be directly effective if it satisfies the criteria for direct effect.

---

672. Case C-129/94 *Criminal proceedings against Rafael Ruiz Bernáldez* [1996] ECR I-1829.

673. Case C- 215/97 *Bellone v Yokohama SpA* [1998] 215/97.

674. For similar cases see Case C-441/93 *Panagis Pafitis and Others v Trapeza Kentrikis Ellados A.E. and Others* [1996] ECR I-1347; C-456/98 *Centrosteel Srl v Adipol GmbH* [2000] ECR I-6007 and Case C-381/98 *Ingmar GB Ltd v Eaton Leonard Technologies Inc* [2000] ECR I-9305.

675. See also Case C-441/93 *Panagis Pafitis and Others v Trapeza Kentrikis Ellados A.E. and Others* [1996] ECR I-1347 and Case C-77/97 *Österreichische Unilever GmbH v Smithkline Beecham Markenartikel GmbH* [1999] ECR I-431.

676. See M. Hedemann-Robinson, *Enforcement of European Union Environmental Law: Legal Issues and Challenges*, 2007, Abingdon: Routledge-Cavendish, 213–61.

In Case 9/70 *Franz Grad*[677] the ECJ recognised that the combined effect of a Treaty provision, a directive and a decision may have direct effect and therefore create rights for individuals enforceable before national courts.

In Case C-156/91 *Hansa Fleisch*,[678] the above approach was confirmed in relation to a decision standing alone. Additionally, decisions adopted by a body created by an international treaty concluded between the EU and third countries may produce direct effect.[679]

A decision addressed to a legal or natural person may produce horizontal direct effect. For example, a decision adopted by the Commission regarding an undertaking which is in breach of competition law may be relied on by another undertaking, which is a victim of anti-competitive practice by the former. Under Article 299 TFEU, decisions which impose pecuniary obligations on persons other than States are enforceable in accordance with the national procedures of the Member State of the addressee. However, a decision addressed to a Member State can only produce vertical direct effect. The justification for the rejection of horizontal direct effect is the same as in the case of directives.[680]

10.10 Direct effect of international agreements concluded between the EU and third countries, and the EU and international organisations

The ECJ has the same approach towards international agreements concluded between the EU and third countries as monist countries, i.e. such agreements upon their ratification by the EU form part of EU law. In order to determine whether a provision of an international agreement can produce direct effect, the ECJ will proceed as follows:[681]

▪ First, in conformity with the principles of public international law, it is for the contracting parties to decide what effect the provisions of the agreement are to have in the internal legal order of the contracting parties. If the agreement is silent on this point then it is the task of the ECJ to determine whether the provision in question is directly effective; and,

▪ Second, the ECJ will take into account the spirit, general scheme and terms of the agreement but not the nature of the legal measure approving the international agreement at the EU level to decide whether the relevant provision is directly effective. The best summary of the ECJ's approach is given in the conclusion of A-G M Darmon in Case 12/86 *Demirel*.[682] He emphasised that a provision of an agreement concluded between the EU and third countries may be considered as producing direct effect when, in relation to its terms, object and nature, it contains a clear and precise obligation which is not subordinated to the intervention of any subsequent act. This means, for example, that a provision of an international agreement, which may be drafted in terms identical to a provision of EU law (which is recognised as capable of producing direct

---

677. *Franz Grad v Finanzamt Traunstein* [1970] ECR 825.

678. Case C-156/91 *Hansa Fleisch Ernst Mundt GmbH & Co. KG v Landrat des Kreises Schleswig-Flensburg* [1992] ECR I-5567.

679. For example, a decision adopted by the Association Council EEC-Turkey: Case C-192/89 *S. Z. Sevince v Staatssecretaris van Justitie* [1990] ECR I-3461; Case C-237/91 *Kazim Kus v S. Z. Sevince v Staatssecretaris van Justitie* [1992] ECR I-6781; Case C-171/95 *Recep Tetik v Land Berlin* [1997] ECR I-329.

680. Case C-80/06 *Carp Snc di L. Moleri e V. Corsi v Ecorad Srl* [2007] ECR I-4473.

681. Case 104/81 *Hauptzollamt Mainz v C.A. Kupferberg & Cie KG* [1982] ECR 3641; Case C-149/96 *Portugal v Council* [1999] ECR I-8395: Joined Cases C-120/06 P and C-121/06 P *FIAMM and FIAMM Technologies v Council and Commission* [2008] ECR I-6513 and Case C-160/09 *Ioannis Katsivardas – Nikolaos Tsitsikas OE v Ipourgos Ikonomikon* [2010] ECR I-4591.

682. Case 12/86 *Meryem Demirel v Stadt Schwäbisch Gmünd* [1987] ECR 3719.

effect), may not be regarded as directly effective since the object and nature of the agreement will determine whether the relevant provision of the agreement can produce direct effect. Consequently, the test for direct effect of international agreements to which the EU is a party is stricter than the normal test of direct effect for other sources of EU law, in that, for such international agreements, the alleged direct effect must be consistent with the system and context of the treaty, as well as satisfying the other standard conditions for direct effect.[683]

The form in which an international agreement is introduced into EU law, that is, whether by a decision or by a regulation adopted by the Council, is not taken into consideration by the ECJ in determining whether any of its provisions produce direct effect.

With regard to horizontal direct effect of international agreements, it is rare that an international agreement is concluded with the intention of conferring rights and duties on natural or legal persons. It seems that this is the main reason why there is no case law on this topic, although in Case 270/80 *Polydor*[684] the question of whether an international agreement can produce horizontal direct effect was asked of the ECJ but not answered.

RECOMMENDED READING

Books

Prechal, S., *Directives in EC Law*, 2nd edn, 2005, Oxford: OUP.

Vereecken, M. and Nijenhuis, A. (eds), *Settlement Finality in the European Union: The EU Directive and its Implementation in Selected Jurisdictions*, 2005, The Hague: KLI.

Articles

Betlem, G., "The Doctrine of Consistent Interpretation – Managing Legal Uncertainty", (2002) 22 Oxford J. Legal Stud., 397.

Dashwood, A., "From *Van Duyn* to *Mangold via Marshall*: Reducing Direct Effect to Absurdity?" (2006–07) 9 CYELS, 81.

Dashwood, A., "*Viking* and *Laval*: Issues of Horizontal Direct Effect" (2007-08) 10 CYELS, 525.

Fontanelli, F., "General principles of the EU and a Glimpse of Solidarity in the Aftermath of Mangold and Kücükdeveci", (2011) EPL, 225.

De Witte, B., "Direct Effect, Primacy and the Nature of the Legal Order", in Craig, P. and de Búrca, G. (eds), *The Evolution of EU Law*, 2nd edn, 2011, Oxford: OUP, 339.

Kaddous, C., "Effects of International Agreements in the EU Legal Order", in Cremona, M. and de Witte, B. (eds), *EU Foreign Relations Law – Constitutional Fundamentals*, 2008, Oxford: Hart Publishing, 291.

Král, R., "Questioning the Limits of Invocability of EU Directives in Triangular Situations", (2010) 16 EPL, 239.

Lenaerts, K., and Corthaut, T., "Of Birds and Hedges: The Role of Primacy in Invoking Norms of EU Law", (2006) 31 ELRev., 310.

Lohse, E. J., "Fundamental Freedoms and Private Actors – towards an 'Indirect Horizontal Effect'", (2007) 13/1 EPL,159.

---

683. See Case C-308/06 *The Queen on the application of: International Association of Independent Tanker Owners (Intertanko), International Association of Dry Cargo Shipowners (Intercargo), Greek Shipping Co-operation Committee, Lloyd's Register, International Salvage Union v Secretary of State for Transport* [2008] ECR I-4057, and C. Timmermans, "The International Lawyer and the EU", in C. Wickremasinghe (ed.), *The International Lawyer as Practitioner*, 2000, London: British Institute of International and Comparative Law, 95.

684. Case 270/80 *Polydor Ltd v Harlequin Records Shops* [1982] ECR 329.

Muir, E., "Of Ages in – And Edges of – EU Law", (2011) 48 CMLRev., 60.

Prescatore, P., "The Doctrine of Direct Effect: An Infant Disease of Community Law", (1983) 8 ELRev., 155.

Tridimas, T., "Black, White, and Shades of Grey: Horizontality of Directives Revisited", (2002) 21 YEL, 327.

Tridmans, T., "Horizontal Effect of Directives: A Missed Opportunity", (1994) 19 ELRev., 621.

PROBLEM QUESTION

John, a national of Estonia, intends to learn English. Recently, in a café near his place of work, he was approached by a representative of Interdiffusion Ltd, a private company established in Estonia, which provides English language correspondence courses. There, he signed a contract to participate in such a course. Three days later, John changed his mind and sent a letter to Interdiffusion cancelling his subscription to the course. In response, Interdiffussion informed John that under Estonian law he must comply with the contract and pay the sums due. Under Article 5 of Directive 85/577/EC a consumer has a right to cancel a contract negotiated away from the business premises of the trader within seven days of its conclusion. Article 5 of Directive 85/577/EC has been found clear, precise and unconditional by the ECJ in a case decided three months ago. However, Directive 85/577/EC has not been implemented into Estonian law although the time limit for its implementation expired three years ago.

Advise John.

How, if at all, would your advice differ if Interdiffusion was a branch of the Estonian Ministry of Education?

ESSAY QUESTION

Critically assess whether the refusal of the ECJ to recognise that provisions of EU directives can have direct horizontal effect is justified.

Source of EU law	Whether that source of EU law may have vertical direct effect	Whether that source of EU law may have horizontal direct effect
Treaties	Yes	Yes
Charter of Fundamental Rights	Yes	NO, unless – a Charter right has the same content as a provision of the Treaties, which has been recognised as capable of being horizontally directly effective (Article 52(2) of the Charter); – a Charter right embodies a general principle of EU law, which has been recognised as capable of being horizontally directly effective.
General principles of EU law (neither enshrined in the Treaties, nor the Charter of Fundamental Rights)	Yes	Yes, but it is still unclear in what circumstances this may occur
Regulations	Yes	Yes
Directives	Yes	NO but there are some exceptions, i.e. procedural direct horizontal effect and some other rare cases
Decision addressed to: – individuals – Member States	 Yes Yes	 Yes NO
International agreements	Yes NOTE: The test for direct effect of provisions of international agreements is more stringent than for other sources of EU law.	Uncertain. There is no case law on this point

11

DIRECT APPLICABILITY OF EU LAW

CHAPTER OUTLINE

1. Public international law leaves each State to decide on the relationship between its national law and international law. In respect of this relationship there are two main theories: dualism and monism. The EU has espoused the monist approach to the relationship between EU law (a species of international law) and national laws of the Member States by establishing the principle of direct effect, the principle of supremacy and the principle of direct applicability of EU law.

2. Under the principle of direct applicability EU law becomes part of national laws of the Member States without the need for it to be transformed into national law by the use of the appropriate constitutional machinery such as an act of parliament, that is, there is no need (as there is in dualist countries like the UK in relation to international treaties) to pass an Act of Parliament to give effect to it. This entails that EU law, being part of national law of a Member State, can be enforced by individuals before national courts and administrative authorities of that Member State. However, there is a controversy as to whether all EU law is directly applicable.

3. The founding Treaties, their amendments, protocols and conventions attached to them and the Charter of Fundamental Rights in the EU are all directly applicable.

4. With regard to secondary sources, regulations and decisions are directly applicable, but in respect of directives views diverge. Some argue that they are directly applicable, others disagree. This controversy is examined in the light of the judgment of the ECJ in *Wallonie* and in Case C-422/05 *Commission v Belgium*.

5. In respect of international agreements concluded between the EU and third countries or international organisations, a distinction must be made between international agreements which become part of EU law without any need for adoption of EU legislation, and international agreements which require adoption of implementing measures by the appropriate EU institutions or by the Member States. While the first mentioned international agreements are directly applicable, the direct applicability of the second mentioned agreements depends on the type of secondary legislation which is adopted to give effect to such agreements, that is, is it a regulation, a directive or a decision?

11.1 Introduction

Public international law leaves each State to decide on the relationship between its municipal law and international law. In respect of this relationship, two main theories: dualism and monism have influenced national constitutional law with regard to the application of international law by municipal courts and other domestic bodies. There are many variations of dualism and monism[685] but the basic theoretical postulations of each theory can be summarized as follows.

Monism, which is mainly embraced by civil law countries, considers both international law and municipal law to be part of the same legal order, and emphasises the supremacy of international law within the municipal sphere. The doctrine of incorporation is associated with monism. According to that doctrine rules of international law form part of municipal law without any express act of adoption, i.e. any positive act on the part of the State. This entails that rules of customary international law will not require any implementing legislation in order to become part of municipal law of the State concerned. With regard to international treaties they automatically become law within a contracting State, i.e. such treaties are directly applicable in that they become an integral part of the municipal law upon completion of the ratification procedure by a Contracting State. Consequently, from ratification an international treaty is part of municipal law and enforceable by individuals. However, a provision of international law is applied by municipal courts as such and not as a provision of municipal law.

Dualism, which is mainly adhered to by common law countries, regards international law and municipal law as independent systems, separate from each other and having differing spheres of application. The doctrine of transformation reflects the dualist view according to which international law has no binding effect in municipal law unless it is expressly and specifically transformed into municipal law by the use of the appropriate constitutional machinery such as an act of parliament. This entails that an international treaty duly ratified produces legal effect only at the international level, that is, it is only binding on the contracting States. In order to be applied by national courts it is necessary, by a second step, to pass enabling legislation, so that it can take effect at the national level. However, once an international provision is implemented into national law, it is applied by national courts as any other municipal provision, not as an international one. It is to be noted that dualist States accept the doctrine of incorporation with regard to customary international law. They consider rules of customary international law to be automatically part of domestic law as long as they are not inconsistent with Acts of Parliament or authoritative judicial decisions, or established usage.[686]

---

685. See P-M Dupuy, "International Law and Domestic (Municipal) Law", The Max Planck Encyclopedia of Public International Law, 2011; online edition [www.mpepil.com] (accessed 3/9/12).

686. See Lord Denning in *Trendtex Trading Corporation v Central Bank of Nigeria* [1977] QB 529, at 554.

The EU has embraced the monism theory by establishing the principle of direct applicability, direct effect and supremacy of EU law.

Under the principle of direct applicability national transformation measures with regard to EU law are prohibited unless the relevant EU legislation expressly requires otherwise. The principle of direct applicability has its origin in the special nature of EU law. In Case 6/64 *Costa v ENEL*[687] the ECJ stated that the EEC Treaty had, by contrast with ordinary international treaties, "created its own legal system which, on the entry into force of the Treaty, became an integral part of the legal systems of the Member States and which their courts are bound to apply."

Additionally, Article 288 TFEU provides that regulations are directly applicable in all Member States. In Case 106/77 *Simmenthal*,[688] the ECJ held that direct applicability means that rules of EU law must be fully and uniformly applied in all Member States from the date of their entry into force and for so long as they continue to be in force. However, there is a controversy as to whether other sources of EU law are directly applicable (see below).

With regard to the principle of direct effect, it ensures that EU law, when it passes the test for direct effect, is enforceable by individuals before national courts and national administrative bodies without their having to rely on a Member State to implement EU law into national law, when it is required to do so but has not taken implementing measures, or when it incorrectly implements EU law, or when it implements it correctly, but applies it incorrectly (see Chapter 10).

The principle of supremacy gives EU law a special status in Member States. This entails first, that EU law takes precedence when there is a conflict between EU law and national law and second, that no future national legislation will have priority over legislation incorporating the Treaties and EU acts (see Chapter 9).

The preference for the monist theory derives from the nature of the EU as only monism is compatible with the idea of European integration. Indeed, EU law cannot tolerate national divergences as to Member States relations *vis-à-vis* EU law, since the dualist system jeopardises the attainment of the objectives of the Treaties and is contrary to the spirit and objectives of EU law. Member States may preserve the dualist system in relation to international law, but this choice is excluded in relations between EU law and national law.

It is important to note that the doctrine of direct applicability is distinct from the doctrine of direct effect (see above). In the early years of the Community the terms "direct applicability" and "direct effect" were not always used correctly, that is, they were often mistaken for each other and some authors challenged the distinction between them.[689] The correct view is that each doctrine is distinct and has a different meaning under EU law.[690]

11.2 Direct applicability of the Treaties

The EEC Treaty contained no provision relating to its direct applicability. It was left to each Member State to follow its national constitutional procedure necessary for the ratification of the Treaty. Subsequent treaties, amending the EEC Treaty, have, however, included a provision, e.g. Article 357

---

687. [1964] ECR 585.
688. Case 106/77 *Amministrazione delle Finanze dello Stato v Simmenthal SpA* [1978] ECR 629, para. 14.
689. D. Wyatt, "Directly Applicable Provisions of EEC Law", (1975) 125 New Law Journal, 485, at 576 and 577.
690. J. P. Warner, "The Relationship between European Community Law and the National Laws of Member States", (1977) 93 Law Quarterly Review, 8; J. Winter, "Direct Effect and Direct Applicability: Two Distinct and Different Concepts in Community Law", (1972) 9 CMLRev., 425.

TFEU, stating that the relevant treaty shall be ratified by a Member State in accordance with its respective constitutional requirements and enter into force on a specific date if all the instruments of ratification have been deposited with a particular government designated as the depository, or, on the first day of the month following the deposit of the instrument of ratification by the last signatory State to take this step.

Under Article 2(1)(b) of the Vienna Convention on the Law of Treaties the term ratification is described as referring to ". . . the international act . . . whereby a State establishes on the international plane its consent to be bound by a treaty". Accordingly, ratification is a procedure which brings a treaty into force at the international level. In the case of EU treaties, ratification involves the deposit of the instruments of ratification with a designated depository. It is important to note that "ratification must not be confused with the approval of the legislature or other State organ whose approval may be constitutionally necessary as a condition precedent to the making of the international act".[691]

The EU is only concerned with the necessary constitutional requirements relating to the ratification of a treaty, and not whether a necessary approval of the legislature, or other organ of a Member State has been obtained so that the relevant treaty has a binding effect in municipal law. Upon ratification, EU Treaties automatically become law in a Member State from the perspective of EU law. Implementing legislation is not required, but it is for each Member State to decide whether it is necessary to make the relevant EU treaty applicable within the national legal system by means of an Act of Parliament or other similar act.

11.3 Direct applicability of regulations

The direct applicability of regulations is expressly recognised in Article 288 TFEU. In the UK their direct applicability is recognised by section 2(1) of the European Communities Act 1972. Not only are any implementing measures unnecessary, they are regarded as obstructing the direct applicability of EU regulations. In Case 34/73 *Variola*[692] the ECJ was asked whether provisions of a regulation can be implemented into Italian law by internal measures reproducing the contents of that regulation in such a way as not to affect its substance. The ECJ held that:

"By virtue of the obligations arising from the Treaty and assumed on ratification, Member States are under a duty not to obstruct the direct applicability inherent in regulations and other rules of Community law."

The Constitutional Court of Italy recognised the above statement of the ECJ in the *Frontini* case.[693] It held that it derived from the logic of the Community system that regulations, being directly applicable legislative acts, should not be subject to national implementing measures capable of modifying them, imposing conditions as to their entry into force, substituting them, derogating from them or abrogating them, even partially.

In monist countries direct applicability of regulations is self-evident. In France, in case *Syndicat des Hautes Graves de Bordeaux*[694] the French *Conseil d'Etat* (highest administrative court) in its Decision of 22 December 1978 held that regulations, by virtue of Article 288 TFEU, become from their

---

691.   I. Sinclair, *The Vienna Convention on the Law of Treaties*, 1984, Manchester: Manchester University Press, 41.

692.   Case 34/73 *Fratelli Variola S.p.A. v Amministrazione italiana delle Finanze* [1973] ECR 981, para.10.

693.   [1974] 2 CMLR 372.

694.   R.526, RTDE, 1979.717. Concl. Genevois.

publication an integral part of national law of the Member States. The French Constitutional Court confirmed this.[695]

11.4 Direct applicability of directives

Directives are addressed to the Member States i.e. to one of them, some of them, or all of them. Article 288 TFEU provides that Member States are under an obligation to achieve the objectives set out in EU directives. Procedures and methods necessary to attain these objectives are left to the discretion of the Member States.

Whether directives are directly applicable is a matter of controversy. For English scholars directives are not directly applicable since they require implementing measures.[696] Others, especially from monist Member States, argue that Member States only have powers to implement directives, which is quite different from the incorporation of international treaties into municipal law.[697] They make a distinction between the competence of execution and the competence of reception. Member States exercise the former in relation to directives but not the latter. Those scholars refuse to accept that until directives are transposed into municipal law, they do not exist from a legal point of view. In this respect, Judge P. Pescatore said that a directive cannot be considered as "a judicial non-entity from an internal viewpoint".[698]

The question of direct applicability of directives was considerably clarified by the ECJ in Case C-129/96 *Inter-Environnement Wallonie*[699]

THE FACTS WERE:

Inter-Environnement Wallonie ASBL, a non-profit-making organisation, applied to the Belgian Conseil d'Etat for the annulment of a Walloon Regional Council Decree which expressly purported to implement Directive 75/442 on hazardous waste, as amended by Directive 91/689, and which was issued during the period prescribed for the transposition of Directive 91/689. The applicant argued that the Decree was contrary to the directive as it did not include within its definition of waste a substance or object which directly or indirectly forms an integral part of an industrial production process. The Belgian Conseil d'Etat asked the ECJ, inter alia, whether Articles 4(3) and 288 TFEU preclude Member States from adopting national legislation contrary to a non-implemented directive before the period for its transposition has expired.

Held:

The ECJ confirmed three important points:

- *First, the Court held that directives enter into force at the date of their notification to their addressees and not at the end of the transposition period laid down in the directive itself;*

695. Decisions of 30 December 1977, RTDE, 1979, 142, note G. Isaac and J. Molinier.

696. See for example J. Tillotson, *European Community Law*, 2nd edn, 1996, London: Cavendish, 69.

697. For example R. Kovar, "La Contribution de la Cour de Justice à l'Edification de l'Ordre Juridique Communautaire", (1993) 4/1 *Recueil de l'Académie de Droit Européen*, p 57 et seq.

698. P. Pescatore, "L'Effet des Directives Communautaires: une Tentative de Démythification", 1980 Recueil Dalloz-Sirey, Chr., 171.

699. C-129/96 *Inter-Environnement Wallonie ASBL v Région Wallonne* [1997] ECR I-7411; the judgment in the *Wallonie* case was confirmed by the ECJ in Case C-157/02 *Rieser Internationale Transporte GmbH v Autobahnen- und Schnellstraßen-Finanzierungs-AG (Asfinag)* [2004] ECR I-1477.

> ■ Second, the ECJ confirmed that although a directive enters into force upon its notification to a Member State concerned, it only becomes legally effective from the expiry of the implementation period; and,
>
> ■ Third, prior to the judgment in this case it had been well established that before the expiry of the transposition period, no obligations or rights arise from a directive for a Member State or for individuals.[700] For that reason, it had been widely assumed that until the transposition of directives into national law, or the expiry of the transposition period, they did not exist from a legal point of view, and thus were not considered as directly applicable. The judgment of the ECJ in the above case challenged those assumptions. The ECJ held that by virtue of Article 4(3) and 288 TFEU Member States have an obligation to refrain from adopting and bringing measures into force during a directive's transposition period if such measures are likely to seriously compromise the result required by the directive.

The principle established by the ECJ in *Wallonie* was applied by the French Conseil d'Etat in Case No 269814 *M. Sueur et autre* of 29 October 2004.[701] In this case two EU directives, which were both in force, but for one of which the transposition period had not yet expired (the new directive), set out rules which were incompatible with each other. The French Conseil d'Etat decided that during the period when both the directives were simultaneously in force, a Member State could either:

■ adopt measures compatible with the older directive, subject to the requirement that such measures would not seriously undermine the achievement of the objectives of the new directive; or

■ adopt measures which were incompatible with the older directive but aimed at achieving the result required by the new directive.

The limitation imposed upon the legislative freedom of a Member State during the transposition period can be explained only if directives are directly applicable. In this respect the Commission stated in the *Wallonie* case that, on the basis of Articles 4(3) and 288 TFEU, a Member State has a kind of standstill obligation, which means that during the implementation period no national measures should be adopted (whether or not they intend to implement the directive) which "increase the disparity between the national and [EU] rules". Consequently, the Member States must, during that period, refrain from jeopardising the achievement of one or more of the objectives of the directive. Indeed, if such measures were to be adopted it would create legal uncertainty for individuals.

The standstill obligation is legally enforceable. For the first time, in Case C-422/05 *Commission v Belgium*[702] the ECJ declared a Member State in breach of Articles 4(3) TEU and Article 288 TFEU for adopting national measures almost at the end of a transitional period (three months before its expiry) which were liable to seriously compromise the result prescribed by the directive in question.

It is submitted that the fact that a Member State can be declared in breach of its obligations under EU law for adopting national measures incompatible with the requirements of a relevant directive during the period allowed for its transposition, demonstrates that directives are in general terms directly applicable from the time of their notification to the Member State concerned. Further, the obligation imposed on a Member State during the transposition period to abstain from adopting national measures which have (as the Commission emphasised in this case) "a lasting negative impact on the conditions

---

700. Case 148/78 *Criminal Proceedings against Tullio Ratti* [1979] ECR 1629.
701. See (2004) Europe, No. 12, para. 391,11.
702. [2007] ECR I-4749.

for the transposition and application of the Directive" intensifies as the time for transposition of a directive draws near. The above case confirms that directives not only have legal existence during the transposition period but may give rise to binding obligations with regard to the Member States. The above judgment of the ECJ shows that the role played by directives in the framework of the EU legal system is more important than, at first glance, Article 288 TFEU may suggest.

The issue whether individuals can rely on a directive before the expiry of the transposition period to challenge national rules, whether intended to implement the directive or not, which conflict with the requirements laid down in provisions of the directive has been answered in the affirmative by the ECJ. In particular, they can have legitimate claims against their Member States in a situation where it is obvious, as it was in Case C-422/05 *Commission v Belgium*, that it would be highly unlikely for a Member State to meet the deadline for transposition of the directive as it had introduced national rules fundamentally contrary to the requirements of the directive almost at the end of the transposition period.

It is important to note that in Case C-491/01 *British American Tobacco*[703] the ECJ accepted a request for a preliminary ruling from the High Court (England and Wales) challenging the validity of a directive in a situation where the main proceedings were commenced before the expiry of a transition period for implementation of that directive and in the absence of any national implementing measures.

Following from all the above, it can be said that directives are directly applicable from the moment of their notification to the Member State concerned and as such form an integral part of national law before the expiry of the time limit prescribed for their implementation.

11.5 Direct applicability of decisions

Decisions are directly applicable, irrespective of whether they are addressed to a Member State or to a natural or to a legal person. The same principle applies to decisions which have no identified addressees.

11.6 Direct applicability of international agreements concluded between the EU and third countries, and between the EU and international organisations

By virtue of Article 216(2) TFEU international agreements concluded between the EU and third countries, or international organisations, are binding on EU institutions, and on Member States.

International agreements normally specify the conditions for their entry into force. Some international agreements become part of EU law without any need for EU legislation; others require adoption of implementing measures by the appropriate EU institutions and, in some instances, by the Member States.

For an international agreement that does not require adoption of any implementing measures, the EU act which authorises its conclusion and the expression of the EU's consent to be bound by it has the effect of incorporating the agreement into EU law. It is directly applicable. In practice, a decision or a regulation adopted by the Council reproducing in its annexe the text of an agreement, is often published in the OJ.

With regard to an international agreement that requires adoption of implementing measures, it is for the Commission to ensure that the appropriate secondary legislation is adopted in good time so that EU

---

703.   C-491/01 *R v Secretary of State for Health, ex parte: British American Tobacco (Investments) Ltd and Others*
       [2002] ECR I-11453.

obligations stemming from an international agreement are fulfilled. In some cases, implementing measures may be required not only at EU level but also, in conformity with the principle of subsidiarity, at national level. If an international agreement is implemented by means of a regulation or a decision, it is directly applicable. However, if the EU adopts a directive, the controversy as to its direct applicability persists.

If national implementing measures are required to give effect to an international agreement, that agreement will become part of national law of the relevant Member State in accordance with the terms specified in the implementing legislation.

RECOMMENDED READING

Book

Falkner, G., Treib, O., Hartlapp, M. and Leiber, S., *Complying with Europe: EU Harmonization and Soft Law in the Member States*, 2005, New York: CUP.

Article

Winter, J., "Direct Effect and Direct Applicability: Two Distinct and Different Concepts in Community Law", (1972) 9 CMLRev., 425.

PROBLEM QUESTION

On 1 December 2011 France enacted legislation regulating night flights of certain types of civil subsonic jet aircraft. According to the Commission, the French legislation is in breach of an EU directive related to noise in EU airports. The directive's transposition period expired on 1 February 2012. On 15 January 2012, the Commission started proceedings against France for a breach of EU law before the ECJ.

Advise the Commission on the admissibility of its action against France.

ESSAY QUESTION

Explain why application of the principle of direct applicability to EU directives raises controversy.

DIRECT APPLICABILITY OF EU LAW

The principle of direct applicability of EU law regulates the relationship between EU law and national law of the Member States in terms of how EU law is put into effect in the domestic legal systems of Member States.

In the EU context, direct applicability means that directly applicable rules of EU law must be fully and uniformly applied in all Member States from the date of their entry into force and for so long as they continue to be in force. There is no need for their implementation, i.e. there is no need (in dualist countries like the UK) to pass an Act of Parliament to give effect to them, apart from EU directives which normally require implementing measures. For that reason there is a controversy as to whether EU directives are directly applicable.

Directly applicable EU law	EU law the direct applicability of which is controversial
▪ The Treaties, Protocols and Annexes attached to them and the Charter of Fundamental Rights. ▪ Regulations ▪ Decisions ▪ International agreements concluded between the EU and third countries, and between the EU and international organisations, that do not require the adoption of legislative measures at EU or national level.	EU directives – there is no doubt that a directive, during the period between its entry into force and the end of the transposition period normally specified in that directive, has legal existence. During that period it may give rise to obligations for the Member State concerned (Case C-129/96 *Inter-Environnement Wallonie* and Case C-422/05 *Commission v Belgium*) and its validity may be challenged (Case C-491/01 *British American Tobacco*).

Note: Direct applicability of international agreements, which require the adoption of secondary legislation at EU level, depends on the type of secondary legislation, i.e. whether it is a regulation, a directive, or a decision (see above).

12

MEMBER STATE LIABILITY FOR DAMAGE CAUSED TO INDIVIDUALS BY A BREACH OF EU LAW FOR WHICH IT IS RESPONSIBLE

CONTENTS

CHAPTER OUTLINE

1. The principle of Member State liability was established in Joined Cases C-6 and 9/90 *Francovich* in which the ECJ stated that "a principle of State liability for damage to individuals caused by a breach of Community law for which it [a Member State] is responsible is inherent in the scheme of the Treaty".

2. In subsequent cases the ECJ clarified the conditions which must exist for a Member State to incur liability. These are:

- the rule of law which has been infringed must confer rights on individuals;

- the breach must be sufficiently serious to merit an award of damages; and,

- there must be a direct causal link between the Member State's breach of EU law and the loss suffered by the applicant.

3. A Member State is liable regardless of the organ of the Member State whose act or omission infringed EU law. Accordingly, a Member State may be liable for damage caused to an individual by a manifest infringement of EU law attributable to a supreme court of that Member State. It can also be held accountable for wrongful acts of its organs or its officials when they act beyond their capacity, but to all appearances as competent officials or organs.

4. The application by national courts of the conditions for liability is illustrated in the *Factortame* cases, the most important cases in terms of the impact of EU law on UK law.

5. The scope of the principle of national procedural autonomy, and its limits, are of great practical importance in respect of all claims based on EU law which are adjudicated by national courts. This matter is of even greater importance with regard to claims concerning Member State liability for damage caused to individuals, given that the principle of national procedural autonomy entails that any claim for reparation must be made in accordance with the domestic rules on liability. However, the principle of Member State liability has eroded the principle of procedural autonomy to the point where it requires a Member State to create a new remedy in damages, if an equivalent remedy does not already exist under national law.

12.1 Introduction

The principle that a Member State should be liable in damages to individuals who have suffered loss as a result of that Member State's infringement of EU law is today one of the cornerstones of EU law. The main justifications for its introduction into EU law, mentioned by the ECJ in Joined Cases C-6/90 and C-9/90 *Francovich*,[704] were the peculiarity of the EU legal system, the necessity of ensuring the effectiveness of EU law, and the requirements of Article 4(3) TFEU.

First, with regard to the peculiarity of the EU legal system, the ECJ stated in *Francovich* that the EC Treaty created a new legal order, which imposes obligations and confers rights on both the Member States and individuals. Rights conferred on individuals are part of their legal heritage. The ECJ emphasised that "Those rights arise not only where they are expressly granted by the Treaty but also by virtue of obligations which the Treaty imposes in a clearly defined manner both on individuals and on the Member States and the Community [Union] institutions."[705] The ECJ expressly referred to its judgments in Case 26/62 *Van Gend*,[706] in which it established the principle of direct effect and in Case 6/64 *Costa v ENEL*[707] in which it established the principle of supremacy of EU law. According to the ECJ, EU law, being special, has the ability to create rights for individuals, including the right to obtain compensation for loss they suffer as a result of a Member State's violation of their EU rights.

The second justification was that the rights created for individuals by EU law must be given effect. The ECJ held that the full effectiveness of EU law would be impaired, and the protection of the rights granted by EU law would be weaker if individuals were unable to obtain redress when their rights are infringed by a breach of EU law for which a Member State can be held responsible.[708]

The third justification was based on Article 4(3) TEU which requires the Member States to take all necessary measures to fulfill their obligations deriving from EU law. This according to the ECJ includes

---

704. Joined Cases C-6/90 and C-9/90 *Francovich v Italian State and Bonifaci v Italian State* [1991] ECR I-5357.
705. Ibid, para. 31.
706. [1963] ECR 1.
707. [1964] ECR 585.
708. Supra note 704, para. 33.

an obligation to ensure that individuals have appropriate remedies under national law in a situation where their rights are violated by a Member State.

The above justifications were challenged by some commentators.[709] They pointed out that there was no express provision of the Treaty establishing the principle of State liability, and thus its appearance in EU law was as unjustified as those of the principle of direct effect and the principle of supremacy. The effectiveness justification was challenged on the basis that the Treaty provides for a mechanism ensuring the effectiveness of EU law, i.e. Articles 258 and 259 TFEU, which allows the ECJ to declare a Member State in breach of EU law. The argument based on Article 4(3) TEU was good, but provided a very weak legal base for the establishment of the principle of State liability.

In order to respond to the criticism based on effectiveness of EU law it is necessary to understand the context in which the ECJ established the principle of State liability and its implications. In the late 1980s many Member States delayed the implementation of directives which were mainly used to complete the internal market. At that time there was no effective penalty for non-implementation of directives. Penalties for defaulting Member States were only introduced in 1993 by the Treaty of Maastricht in Article 260(2) TFEU. Non-implementation of directives not only hindered European integration but also resulted in discrimination against nationals of non-complying Member States, as they could not enforce their rights deriving from directives. Indeed, the duty imposed on national courts to interpret national law in conformity with EU law, i.e. the indirect effect of EU law (see Chapter 10.8.2), was of no assistance to individuals in a situation where a Member State did not implement the relevant directive in that national courts had nothing to interpret. Also the reliance on the principle of direct effect has its limitations bearing in mind that only provisions of EU law which pass the direct effect test can be relied upon by individuals in national proceedings. Accordingly, when neither was available an individual was often left without remedy to enforce his right deriving from EU law.[710] The ECJ by establishing the principle of State liability not only put pressure on the Member States to implement directives correctly and timely, but also closed the gap between individuals' rights and individuals' remedies. The principle of State liability enhances judicial protection of individuals' rights in that any provision of EU law, whether directly effective or not, can serve as a basis for an action in damages against a Member State when the conditions laid down for liability in damages are satisfied in respect of the particular case (see Chapter 12.3). Further, the establishment of the principle of State liability may not be as revolutionary as it may appear at the first glance. It constitutes a continuation of the ECJ's prior cases relating to repayment of charges imposed in breach of EU law (see Chapter 19.7). A-G Mischo in his Opinion in *Francovich* stated that there was no crucial difference between an action for reimbursement and an action for damages.[711]

There has been no harmonisation of substantive or procedural law governing remedies for enforcement of EU law before national courts, other than some sectorial legislation[712] and some measures relating to the AFSJ.[713] The decentralised system of enforcement of EU law entails that EU law is enforced by national courts in accordance with fundamental principles established by the ECJ, unless the Treaties specify otherwise. In Case 60/75 *Russo*,[714] the ECJ held that a Member State should

---

709. See S. Douglas-Scott, *Constitutional Law of the European Union*, 2002, Harlow: Longman, 32 and 102.

710. D. Curtin, "Directives: The Effectiveness of Judicial Protection of Individual Rights", (1990) 27 CMLRev., 709.

711. Supra note 704, para. 41.

712. For example in respect of public procurement (Directive 2007/66/EC [2007] OJ L335/31), environmental law (Directive 2004/95 [2004] OJ L301/42) and its amendments and IPRs (Directive 2004/48 [2004] OJ L195/16).

713. E.g. Article 81 TFEU which concerns the adoption of measures concerning judicial co-operation in civil matters with a view to eliminating obstacles to the cross-border functioning of civil proceedings, and Articles 82–86 TFEU concerning harmonisation of criminal law measures (see Chapter 31.5).

714. Case 60/75 *Russo v Aima* [1976] ECR 45.

pay compensation for damage caused by its own breach of EU law, but referred to national law to lay down the necessary conditions applicable to liability in damages, i.e. the Court recognised the principle of national procedural autonomy. All Member States acknowledge the principle that the State is liable under national law for unlawful acts of a public authority, provided that the damage is caused by the public authority in the exercise of its functions.[715] However, the nature and effectiveness of available remedies vary greatly from one Member State to another. The establishment of the principle of supremacy and direct effect emphasised the problems with national remedies and procedural rules. In Case C-213/89 *Factortame (No 1)*[716] it was apparent that the claimants could not obtain interim relief under English law, and in Case106/77 *Simmenthal*[717] that a national court was obliged under national procedural rules to wait for a superior court to invalidate national legislation conflicting with EU law. In order to mitigate this problem, and to enhance the effective judicial protection of fundamental rights of EU citizens, the ECJ imposed limitations on the principle of national procedural autonomy based on the right of access to a court, the principle of equivalence and the principle of effectiveness. This resulted in an obligation being imposed on a Member State to create a new remedy in damages, if an equivalent remedy does not already exist under national law.

12.2 The establishment of the principle of Member State liability

In Joined Cases C-6/90 and C-9/90 *Francovich*[718] the ECJ established the principle of State liability.

THE FACTS WERE:

As a result of the bankruptcy of his employer, Francovich lost 6,000,000 lira. In due course he sued that employer but could not enforce judgment as the employer had become insolvent. He decided to commence proceedings, under Directive 80/987, which was not implemented in Italy although the prescribed time limit had already elapsed, against the Italian State for sums due, or for compensation in lieu. Directive 80/987 on protection of employees in the event of the insolvency of their employers required that the Member State set up a scheme under which employees of insolvent companies would receive at least some of their outstanding wages. In Case 22/87 Commission v Italy *the ECJ had held that Italy was in breach of EU law for non-implementation of Directive 80/987. The Italian court made reference to the ECJ under Article 267 TFEU to determine whether the provision of the Directive in relation to payment of wages was directly effective, and whether the Italian State was liable for damages arising from its failure to implement the Directive.*

Held:

The ECJ held that the provision in question was not sufficiently clear to be directly effective, but made the following statement in relation to the second question: "the principle whereby a State must be liable for loss and damage caused to individuals as a result

---

715. D. Curtin, "Directives: The Effectiveness of Judicial Protection of Individual Rights", (1990) 27 CMLRev., 709, at 732.

716. Case C-213/89 *R v Secretary of State for Transport, ex parte Factortame Ltd and Others* [1990] ECR I-2433.

717. Case 106/77 *Amministrazione delle Finanze v Simmenthal SpA* [1978] ECR 629.

718. Joined Cases C-6/90 and C-9/90 *Andrea Francovich, Danila Bonifaci and Others v Italy* [1991] ECR I-5357.

of breaches of Community law for which the State can be held responsible is inherent in the system of the Treaty".[719]

Comment:

In this case the ECJ upheld the claim against the Italian Government and established three conditions necessary to give rise to liability in the case of total failure of a Member State to implement a directive. They are as follows:

1. *The result required by the directive must include the conferring of rights for the benefit of individuals;*

2. *The content of those rights must be clearly identifiable by reference to the directive; and,*

3. *There must be a causal link between the breach of the Member State's obligation and the damage suffered by the individual.*

The three above-mentioned conditions have been further clarified in subsequent cases.[720]

12.3 Development of the principle of Member State liability

In *Francovich* the ECJ left many matters relating to the scope of the remedy in damages unclear. In particular: whether an entitlement to compensation for damage existed in respect of breaches of EU law other than non-implementations of directives; whether any such entitlement be conditional on fault on the part of the organ of the Member State responsible for the breach; whether any such entitlement would apply when constitutional law breached EU law bearing in mind that many Member States did not recognise such liability; whether it applied only to directly effective EU law; and whether it applied to all organs of a State, including its legislator and judiciary.[721] Some of these matters were clarified in Joined Cases C-46/93 and C-48/93 *Brasserie du Pêcheur and Factortame (No. 3)*;[722] others in the subsequent case law of the ECJ.

THE FACTS WERE:

Case C-46/93 Brasserie du Pêcheur

A French brewer, Brasserie du Pêcheur, brought proceedings in a German court against Germany for losses it had suffered as a result of a ban imposed by the German authorities on beer which did not comply with the purity standards imposed by the German Biersteuergesetz (Law on Beer Duty). Brasserie was forced to cease exporting beer to Germany. In Case

---

719. Ibid, para. 35.

720. W. Van Gerven, "Remedies for Infringements of Fundamental Rights", (2004) EPL, 261–84.

721. On this topic see J. Steiner, "From Direct Effect to Francovich: Shifting Means of Enforcement of Community Law", (1993) 18 ELRev., 3.

722. Joined Cases C-46/93 and C-48/93 *Brasserie du Pêcheur SA v Bundesrepublik Deutschland, and The Queen v Secretary of State for Transport, ex parte Factortame Ltd and Others* [1996] ECR I-1029.

178/84 Commission v Germany[723] *the ECJ had already ruled that such a ban was incompatible with Article 34 TFEU.*

Case C-48/93 Factortame (No. 3)

The UK Government had enacted the Merchant Shipping Act 1988, which made the registration of fishing vessels dependent upon conditions as to their owner's nationality, residence and domicile, so depriving Factortame, a Spanish owned company, of its right to fish within the UK's quota under the terms of the Common Fisheries Policy. Factortame brought an action before the English High Court seeking damages for losses it had suffered as a result of the enactment of the Merchant Shipping Act 1988. In previous judgments (Case C-221/89 Factortame (No. 2)[724] *and Case C-246/89* Commission v United Kingdom[725]*) the ECJ had held such legislation contrary to EU law.*

Held:

The ECJ held that Member States would be liable for breaches of EU law in certain circumstances. These are:

1. *The rule of law which has been breached must be one which is intended to confer rights on individuals;*

2. *The breach must be sufficiently serious to merit an award of damages. To be held liable a Member State must have "manifestly and gravely" disregarded the limits of its discretion. To assess whether this condition is satisfied, national courts should take into consideration a number of factors such as: "the clarity and precision of the rule breached, the measure of discretion left by that rule to the national or Community authorities, whether the infringement and the damage caused was intentional or involuntary, whether any error of law was excusable or inexcusable, the fact that the position taken by a Community institution may have contributed towards the omission, and the adoption or retention of national measures or practices contrary to Community law";[726] and,*

3. *There must be a direct causal link between the Member State's default and the loss suffered by the claimant.*

Comment:

The ECJ further established/confirmed:

- *A Member State's liability for its breaches of EU law, whether legislative, executive, or administrative. A Member State is liable regardless of the organ whose act or omission has breached EU law;*

- *That it is irrelevant whether the provision of EU law breached by a Member State is directly effective or not. The ECJ emphasised that direct effect constitutes a minimum guarantee, and thus State liability is a necessary corollary of the principle of effectiveness of EU law; and,*

---

723. [1987] ECR 1227.
724. [1991] ECR I-3905.
725. [1991] ECR I-4585.
726. Case C-46/93 *Brasserie du Pêcheur SA v Germany* [1996] ECR I-1029, para. 56.

> ■ That *"reparation for loss or damage cannot be made conditional upon fault (whether intentional or negligent) going beyond that of a sufficiently serious breach of Community law".*[727] *The imposition of such a supplementary condition would undermine the right to reparation.*
>
> An additional justification for the establishment of the principle of State liability was based on Article 340(2) TFEU which governs the liability of the EU for unlawful EU acts or omissions. The ECJ decided to abolish the disparity between the conditions governing liability of EU institutions based on Article 340(2) TFEU, and the conditions under which a Member State may incur liability for damage caused to individuals in like circumstances. In this respect the ECJ stated: *"The protection of the rights of individuals derived from [EU] law cannot vary on whether a national authority or [an EU] institution is responsible for the damage."*[728]

In subsequent cases the ECJ clarified the scope of the principle of State liability as follows:

1. The apparent disparity between the second condition laid down in *Francovich* and the second condition set out in *Brasserie* and *Factortame* was explained by the ECJ when it held that both are "in substance . . . the same since the condition that there should be a sufficiently serious breach, although not expressed in *Francovich*, was nevertheless evident from the circumstances of the case". Notwithstanding the ECJ's explanation, it can be argued that in *Brasserie* the ECJ introduced a new condition i.e. the notion of a threshold level of seriousness below which the breach is not sufficiently serious, although it has caused damage to the claimant, to merit compensation. This is not explicit in the second condition set out in *Francovich*;[729]

2. In Case C-470/03 *Lehtinen*,[730] the ECJ endorsed the principle of public international law according to which a Member State can be held accountable for wrongful acts of its organs or its officials when they act beyond their capacity but to all appearances as competent officials or organs.[731] In this case the ECJ held that a Member State can be liable in a situation where a public official makes what are in fact personal statements, but which give the persons to whom they are addressed the impression that they express an official position taken by the Member State. The Court emphasised that the decisive factor for statements of an official to be attributed to the Member State is whether the persons to whom those statements are addressed can reasonably suppose, in the given context, that they are positions taken by the official with the authority of his office. When a Member State is found liable in such a situation, EU law does not preclude an official from being held liable in addition to the Member State, but does not require this;

3. The ECJ has placed the onus upon national courts to uphold rights flowing from EU law under national rules governing public liability in tort. It has imposed upon those courts the duty to verify whether or not the conditions governing state liability for a breach of EU law are

---

727. Case C-46/93 *Brasserie du Pêcheur SA* [1996] ECR I-1029, paras. 75–80. See also Case C-429/09 *Günter Fuß v Stadt Halle (No.2)* [2010] ECR I-12167, para. 67.

728. Case C-46/93 *Brasserie du Pêcheur v Germany* [1996] ECR I-1029, para. 51.

729. Joined Cases C-178/94, C-179/94, C-188/94, C-189/94 and C-190/94 *Dillenkofer and Others v Germany* [1996] ECR I-4845, para. 23.

730. C-470/03 *AGM COS.MET Srl v Suomen Valtio, Tarmo Lehtinen* [2007] ECR I-2749.

731. See *The Jessie* (1921) RIAA 57 and *The Wonderer* (1921) RIAA 68.

fulfilled. National courts must ensure that the protection of EU rights is given equal status and is not less favourable than the protection afforded to similar rights arising under domestic law (i.e. it must respect the principle of equivalence). National procedural rules must not impose any procedure that makes it more difficult, or even impossible, for an individual to rely upon those rights (i.e. they must respect the principle of effectiveness) (see Chapter 12.6);

4.   In a Member State with a federal structure the reparation of damage is not necessarily ensured by the central government of that Member State, but may instead be provided by the government of the relevant member of the federal structure;[732]

5.   In Member States in which some legislative and administrative tasks are devolved to territorial bodies possessing a certain degree of autonomy, or to any other public body legally distinct from the Member State, reparation of damage caused by such a body to individuals may be made by that body;[733] and,

6.   In Case C-445/06 *Danske*[734] the ECJ held that an obligation to pay compensation does not arise if the injured party has wilfully or negligently failed to avert the damage by not utilising an available legal remedy. However, it qualified this by stating that: "It would . . . be contrary to the principle of effectiveness to oblige injured parties to have recourse systematically to all the legal remedies available to them even if that would give rise to excessive difficulties or could not reasonably be required of them."

12.3.1   The first condition for Member State liability – the breached provision must confer rights on individuals

According to the case law[735] of the ECJ, the purpose of the legal rule infringed must be to grant rights to the individual, the content of which can be identified with sufficient precision on the basis of the relevant provision of EU law.

To be unconditional and sufficiently precise in the above context requires that the words of a provision relied upon by the claimant are sufficiently clear to identify the persons entitled to benefit from that right, and to ascertain whether the claimant is such a person, the extent and content of that right and the identity of the legal body charged with protecting that right.[736]

12.3.2   The second condition for Member State liability – the breach of EU law must be sufficiently serious to merit an award of damages

The most difficult criterion set out for the determination of Member State liability is that relating to "a sufficiently serious breach" of EU law. In respect of what is to be regarded as a sufficiently serious breach, the ECJ held that "where a Member State was not called upon to make any legislative choices and possessed only considerably reduced, or even no discretion, the mere infringement of Community [EU] law may be sufficient to establish a sufficiently serious breach".[737] Thus, the condition requiring a

---

732.   Case C-302/97 *Konle v Austria* [1999] ECR I-3099.
733.   Case C-424/97 *Salomone Haim v Kassenzahnärztliche Vereinigung Nordrhein (Haim II)* [2000] ECR I-5123.
734.   Case C-445/06 *Danske Slagterier v Germany* [2009] ECR I-2119, para. 62.
735.   E.g. Case C-429/09 *Günter Fuß v Stadt Halle (No.2)* [2010] ECR I-12167, paras 49 and 50.
736.   Case C-6/90 *Francovich* [1991] ECR I-5357.
737.   Case C-5/94 *R v Minister of Agriculture, Fisheries and Food ex parte Hedley Lomas (Ireland) Ltd* [1996] ECR, I-2553, para. 28. See also Case C-319/96 *Brinkmann Tabakfabriken GmbH v Skatteministeriet* [1998] ECR I-5255.

sufficiently serious breach of EU law implies manifest and grave disregard by the Member State for the limits set on its discretion. What exactly "sufficiently serious" or "manifest and grave" means can only be gleaned from looking at the subsequent decisions of the ECJ.

One of them is Case 392/93 *British Telecommunications*,[738] which concerned failure to properly implement Article 8(1) of Directive 90/531. In this case the ECJ found that:

■ The Member State concerned had a wide discretion of power in the field in which it was acting;

■ The wording of the provisions of the original directive was imprecise and as a result was capable of being interpreted in the manner implemented;

■ Implementation had been carried out after taking legal advice as to the meaning of the directive;

■ There was no ECJ case law on the subject; and,

■ There was no objection from the Commission to the interpretation applied.

In the light of the above, there was not a sufficiently serious breach of EU law.

In Case C-5/94 *Hedley Lomas*,[739] which concerned the UK authorities' refusal, in breach of a directive, to grant an export licence, the ECJ stated that "where the Member State was not called upon to make any legislative choices and possessed only considerably reduced, or even no discretion, the mere infringement of Community law may be sufficient to establish a sufficiently serious breach". Accordingly, the UK was found in breach of EU law.

In Joined Cases C-178, 179 and 189/94 *Dillenkofer*,[740] the ECJ held that non-implementation of a directive within the prescribed time limit constitutes, *per se*, a serious breach of EU law, and consequently gives rise to a right of reparation for individuals suffering injury.

In Case C-140/97 *Rechberger*,[741] Austria incorrectly implemented Article 7 of Directive 90/314, which, the ECJ held, left no discretion to a Member State in its implementation. Thus, Austria "manifestly and gravely" disregarded the limits of its discretion and therefore was held liable.

In Case C-429/09 *Fuß (No. 2)*,[742] the ECJ held that a decision adopted by national authority which was made in manifest breach of its previous case law on the same point of law amounted to a sufficiently serious breach within the meaning of the second condition.

In recent cases, the ECJ stated that the focus on a Member State's discretion as the main factor in determining whether there has been a sufficiently serious breach of EU law, although still important, was not decisive. In Case C-278/05 *Robins*,[743] the ECJ held that a national court while determining whether the second condition for liability has been satisfied must take account of all factors relevant to the case. These factors are:

■ the clarity and precision of the provision of EU law allegedly breached by the Member State;

■ the measure of discretion enjoyed by that Member State;

■ whether the infringement or damage caused was intentional or voluntary;

738.   Case 392/93 *R v HM Treasury ex parte British Telecommunications plc* [1996] ECR I-1631.

739.   Case C-5/94 *R v Minister of Agriculture, Fisheries and Food ex parte Hedley Lomas (Ireland) Ltd* [1996] ECR I-2553 and Case C-429/09 *Günter Fuß v Stadt Halle (No. 2)* (judgment of 25/11/10 (NYR)).

740.   Joined Cases C-178, 179 and 189/94 *Dillenkofer and Others v Germany* [1996] ECR I-4845.

741.   Case C-140/97 *Rechberger and Others v Austria* [1999] ECR I-3499.

742.   Case C-429/09 *Günter Fuß v Stadt Hall* [2010] ECR I-12167, para. 52.

743.   Case C-278/05 *Carol Marilyn Robins and Others v Secretary of State for Work and Pensions* [2007] ECR I-1053.

■ whether any error of law was excusable; and,

■ whether the position taken by EU institutions may have contributed towards the adoption or maintenance of national measures or practice contrary to EU law.

In *Robins,* the claimant challenged national measures implementing Article 8 of Directive 80/987/EEC on the protection of workers in the event of the employer's insolvency. The ECJ found that:

■ Under Article 8 of the Directive a Member State enjoys considerable discretion for the purposes of determining the level of protection of entitlement to pension benefits;

■ Article 8 of the Directive lacked the necessary clarity and precision; and,

■ The Commission contributed towards the adoption of incorrect national measures. Indeed, the Commission stated in its report[744] that it "appears" that the UK correctly implemented the Directive. The ECJ agreed with the Opinion of the A-G that the use of the word "appears" in the Commission's report should not be construed to the disadvantage of the UK in the determination of whether the UK's implementing measures addressed adequately the requirements of Article 8.

In the above circumstances it was highly unlikely that a referring court would find that the claimant had satisfied the second condition.[745]

12.3.3 The third condition for Member State liability – there must be a direct causal link between the breach of EU law and the loss suffered by an individual

In Joined Cases C-46/93 and C-48/93 *Brasserie du Pêcheur and Factortame (No. 3),*[746] the ECJ held that it is for the national courts to determine whether there is a direct causal link between the breach of the obligation resting on the Member State and the damage sustained by the injured parties. This is largely a question of fact. Thus national procedural rules are relevant as to the establishment of the causal link, the quantification of loss and the type of damage which can be recoverable. Nevertheless, national procedural rules must respect the principles of equivalence and effectiveness[747] (see Chapter 12.6).

12.4 Breach of EU law by a Supreme Court of a Member State

In Case C-224/01 *Köbler*[748] the ECJ, for the first time, had to decide whether the principle of Member State liability is applicable in a situation where the infringement of EU law is attributable to a supreme court of a Member State.

---

744. COM(95) 164 final of 15/6/1995.
745. See Case C-452/06 *The Queen, on the application of Synthon BV v Licensing Authority of the Department of Health* [2008] ECR I-7681.
746. [1996] ECR I-1029, para. 65.
747. C. Kremer, "Liability for Breach of European Community Law: An Analysis of the New Remedy in the Light of English and German Law", (2003) YEL 203.
748. C-224/01 *Gerhard Köbler v Austria* [2003] ECR I-10239.

THE FACTS WERE:

Under Austrian Salary Law a university professor, on completion of 15 years' service as a professor at Austrian universities, was eligible for a special length-of-service increment to be taken into account in the calculation of his retirement pension.

Since 1986 Mr Köbler had been employed, under a public law contract with the Austrian State, as an ordinary professor in Innsbruck (Austria). Before 1986 Mr Köbler taught at universities in various Member States. When in 1996 Mr Köbler applied to the competent Austrian authorities for the special length-of-service increment, his request was refused on the ground that he had not completed 15 years' exclusively at Austrian universities.

Mr Köbler challenged the above decision before the Austrian Supreme Administrative Court as contrary to Article 45 TFEU and Regulation 1612/68. The Court decided to ask the ECJ for a preliminary ruling. Subsequent to the judgment of the ECJ in Case C-15/96 Schöning-Kougebetopoulou[749] delivered on 15 January 1998, the Austrian Supreme Administrative Court was asked by the Registrar of the ECJ whether it deemed it necessary to maintain its request for a preliminary ruling. The Supreme Administrative Court requested the parties to the national proceedings to give their views on the matter, emphasising that, at first glance, the legal issue submitted for a preliminary ruling had been resolved in the light of the judgment of the ECJ in Case C-15/96 Schöning-Kougebetopoulou, in a way favourable to Mr Köbler. On 24 June 1998, the Austrian Supreme Administrative Court withdrew its request for a preliminary ruling and, by a judgment of the same day, dismissed Mr Köbler's application on the ground that the special length-of-service increment was a loyalty bonus and as such could be objectively justified under the provisions on the free movement of workers by a pressing public-interest reason!

In response Mr Köbler brought proceedings before the Regional Civil Court in Vienna against the Republic of Austria for reparation of the loss he allegedly suffered as a result of non-payment to him of the special length-of-service increment. He claimed that the judgment of the Austrian Supreme Administrative Court of 24 June 1998 was in breach of directly applicable EU law as it had disregarded the judgment of the ECJ in Case C-15/96 Schöning-Kougebetopoulou. In these circumstances the Austrian Regional Civil Court decided to refer the matter to the ECJ for a preliminary ruling on a number of questions.

Held:

The ECJ confirmed that the principle of Member State liability applies to judicial decisions of a national court adjudicating at last instance.

The ECJ examined the conditions necessary to establish the liability of a Member State:

- In respect of the first condition, which requires that the legal rule infringed must confer rights on individuals, the ECJ, without any hesitation, decided that Article 45 TFEU and Article 7(1) of Regulation 1612/68 were intended to confer rights on individuals.

- From the context of the case it appears that the second condition which requires that the breach in question must be sufficiently serious was also satisfied, taking into account that:

---

749.   Case C-15/96 *Kalliopé Schöning-Kougebetopoulou v Freie und Hansestadt Hamburg* [1998] ECR I-47.

■ *The Austrian Supreme Administrative Court in its order for reference of 22 October 1997 had stated that: ". . . the special length-of service increment for ordinary university professors is in the nature of neither a loyalty bonus nor a reward, but is rather a component of salary under the system of career advancement" but had come to the opposite conclusion when delivering its judgment of 24 June 1998.*

■ *The Austrian Supreme Administrative Court had misinterpreted the judgment of the ECJ in Case C-15/96 Schöning-Kougebetopoulou in which the ECJ held that a national measure which makes a worker's remuneration dependent on his length of service, but excludes any possibility for comparable periods of employment completed in the public service of another Member State to be taken into account, was in breach of EU law.*

■ *In the light of the above and given that the ECJ did not rule on the issue of whether or not such a national measure could be justified under EU law in Schöning-Kougebetopoulou, the Austrian Supreme Administrative Court should have maintained its request for a preliminary ruling as the requirements set out in Case 283/81 CILFIT were not fulfilled.*

So, on the substantive issue, the ECJ held in effect that the Austrian Supreme Administrative Court had prima facie *breached EU law (contrary to the ECJ's decision in Schöning-Kougebetopoulou) by not treating Mr Köbler's work experience in universities in other EU Member States as reckonable for the purpose of the 15-year increment to be used when calculating his pension. On the procedural issue of whether a preliminary reference should have been made to the ECJ by the Austrian Supreme Administrative Court, the ECJ held that the Court should have made such a reference in order to determine whether there was any possible justification (that is, any exception/derogation) under EU law for the Austrian policy.*

Despite all the above, the ECJ found that the breach of EU law by the Austrian Supreme Administrative Court was not sufficiently serious to give rise to liability on the part of the Austrian State. This conclusion of the ECJ was contrary to the opinion expressed by the A-G, who felt that the Austrian Supreme Administrative Court made an inexcusable error when it dismissed the application of Mr Köbler.

Comment:

It is submitted that the ECJ, when it failed to qualify the breach as being sufficiently serious, also failed in one of its main functions, that is, to protect the rights of individuals conferred upon them by EU law. It is interesting to note that in the above judgment the ECJ emphasised the role of the judiciaries of the Member States in the protection of rights derived by individuals from EU law. In particular, the ECJ stated that:

". . . [where] an infringement of those rights by a final decision of such a court (a court of a Member State adjudicating at last instance) cannot thereafter normally be corrected, individuals cannot be deprived of the possibility of rendering the State liable in order in that way to obtain legal protection of their rights"[750].

It is not clear why this reasoning did not operate to entitle Mr Köbler to damages.

Two arguments submitted to the ECJ against the extension of the principle of Member State liability to national courts adjudicating at last instance in a situation where incorrect decisions taken by such courts have caused damage to individuals were particularly

---

750.   C-224/01 *Gerhard Köbler v Austria* [2003] ECR I-10239, para. 34.

interesting: one, based on the principle of res judicata is discussed in Chapter 9.7; the other, based on the independence of the judiciary, is examined below.

In its judgment the ECJ noted that there is a basic difference between Member State responsibility and the personal liability of the judges, and because of this difference, State liability for judicial decisions, taken by national judges adjudicating at last instance, contrary to EU law, "does not appear to entail any particular risk that the independence of a court adjudicating at last instance will be called into question".This point is not well explained.

It is submitted that better explanations could have been given to support the imposition of Member State liability on national courts deciding in the last instance. These are that:

- *The objective of ensuring the independence and authority of the judiciary has not been considered as hindering the introduction, in most Member States, of proceedings aimed at redressing the malfunctioning of civil or administrative courts, even if such courts are the highest courts in a Member State;*

- *In respect of miscarriages of justice in penal proceedings, most Member States have set up special procedures allowing for the revision of final judgments. Consequently, Member States should not introduce double standards, one where national law in concerned, and one where EU law is concerned; and,*

- *The situation already exists in many Member States whereby the duty of judges of supreme courts of a Member State to be impartial is not undermined despite the fact that if their decisions relating to the interpretation and to the application of the ECHR are wrong, then their government may pay compensation to such citizens as have suffered as a result of those wrong decisions.*

The judgment in *Köbler* was further clarified in Case C-173/03 *Traghetti*.[751]

THE FACTS WERE:

In 1981 TDM, an Italian maritime transport undertaking, brought proceedings before an Italian court against its competitor, Tirrenia di Navigazione (Tirrenia), seeking compensation for damage that Tirrenia caused it between 1976 and 1980 as a result of charging fares below the cost price on the maritime cabotage market between mainland Italy and the islands of Sardinia and Sicily. According to TDM, the conduct of Tirrenia constituted unfair competition and abuse of a dominant position in breach of Article 102 TFEU. The charging of low fares was made possible by subsidies granted to Tirrenia by the Italian authorities, which subsidies, according to TDM, were in breach of Articles 110 and 112 TFEU.

TDM's claim was dismissed by all Italian courts, as was its request submitted to national courts for a preliminary ruling under Article 267 TFEU. When, in the last resort, the Italian Supreme Court (the Italian Corte Supreme di Cassazione) dismissed the claim, TDM (in fact, its administrator as TDM was put into liquidation during the national proceedings) brought proceedings against the Italian State before the Tribunale di Genova seeking reparation for

---

751. C-173/03 *Traghetti del Mediterranes SpA (TDM) v Italy* [2006] ECR I-5177.

damage caused to it by the judgment of the Italian Supreme Court, in particular by the Italian Supreme Court's erroneous interpretation of EU law and its refusal to make a reference for a preliminary ruling under Article 267 TFEU. The Tribunale di Genova decided to refer to the ECJ as it was uncertain about the effect of Köbler on Italian legislation, which limited liability of the Supreme Court as follows:

1. *It excluded liability in connection with the interpretation of provisions of law or assessment of facts or evidence in the exercise of judicial functions by the Supreme Court;*

2. *It limited liability to cases of intentional fault or serious misconduct.*

Held:

The ECJ held that the exclusion of liability was contrary to EU law.

Comment:

The Court emphasised that the exclusion of liability would amount to depriving the principle of Member State liability of all practical effect and lead to a situation where individuals would have no judicial protection if a national court adjudicating in the last instance committed a manifest error whilst interpreting provisions of law or assessing facts and evidence.

The ECJ stated that the limitation of liability solely to cases of intentional fault and serious misconduct would be in breach of EU law if it leads to exclusion of liability in cases where a manifest infringement of the applicable law has been committed. In this respect it referred to its judgment in Köbler in which it indicated that liability for an infringement of EU law resulting from a judgment of a supreme court occurs only in exceptional cases where the court has manifestly infringed EU law. The following factors should be taken into account in deciding whether or not a supreme court of a Member State has manifestly infringed EU law:

- *the degree of clarity and precision of the rule infringed;*

- *whether the error of law was excusable or inexcusable;*

- *the position taken, where applicable, by a Community institution on the disputed matter; and,*

- *non-compliance by that court with the obligation to make a reference for a preliminary ruling.*

The ECJ concluded that while a Member State is allowed to impose conditions as to liability for infringement of EU law by its supreme court, under no circumstances may such conditions be stricter than those for a manifest infringement of EU law as defined in Köbler. Accordingly, a condition based on a concept of intentional fault or serious misconduct that goes beyond manifest disregard of EU law is contrary to EU law as it would call into question the right to reparation founded on the EU legal order. This position was confirmed by the ECJ in Case C-379/10 Commission v Italy.[752]

---

752. Judgment of 24/11/11(NYR).

It is to be noted that in Case C-154/08 *Commission v Spain*[753] (for facts, see Chapter 14.2.2.3) the ECJ, for the first time, found that a Member State was in breach of EU law when its supreme court incorrectly interpreted provisions of EU law having failed to make a request for a preliminary ruling to the ECJ, as it ought to have done, on the interpretation of the relevant provisions.

12.5 The application of the principle of State liability in the UK – the *Factortame case*

The leading case on this topic is *Factortame (No. 4)*,[754] in which the House of Lords (now the Supreme Court) applied the three conditions for liability and found the UK liable. This case is one of the numerous Factortame cases concerning the UK Merchant Shipping Act 1988, which made the registration of fishing vessels in the UK dependent upon conditions as to the nationality, residence and domicile of their owners.

THE FACTS WERE:

According to the UK Merchant Shipping Act 1988 a vessel could be registered as British if it was British owned, and it was British owned if both the legal owners and not less than 75 per cent of the beneficial owners were qualified persons or qualified companies. Being regarded as a "qualified person" was conditional upon being a British citizen resident and domiciled in the UK, and in order to be a "qualified company" at least 75 per cent of its directors had to be "qualified persons"; at least 75 per cent of its shares had to be owned by "qualified persons"; it had to be incorporated in the UK; and, its principal place of business had to be in the UK.

Factortame, being a Spanish-owned company, could not register, and, not being registered, was prevented from fishing within the UK's quota under the terms of the CFP. Factortame sought an interim order from the national court, which would result in the suspension of operation of the relevant provisions of the Act. In proceedings before the English courts, the House of Lords held that the applicants would suffer irreparable damage if the interim relief which they sought was not granted. Notwithstanding this, the House of Lords found that English courts had no jurisdiction to grant such relief, as the remedy was barred by statute. The House of Lords referred to the ECJ a question of whether, regardless of the position of English law, EU law required in the type of situation involved in this case, the setting aside of the statute thus granting interim relief to the claimants. The ECJ answered in the affirmative (Factortame (No. 1)).[755] In Factortame (No. 2)[756] the ECJ held UK legislation as contrary to EU law; this was confirmed in Case C-246/89 Commission v UK.[757]

After the preliminary rulings delivered by the ECJ in Joined Cases C-46/93 and C-48/93 Brasserie Du Pêcheur and Factortame (No. 3),[758] the question for the domestic courts was

---

753. [2009] ECR I-9735.
754. *R v Secretary of State for Transport, ex parte Factortame Ltd and Others (No. 4)* [1999] 3 CMLR 597.
755. Case C-213/89 *R v Secretary for Transport, ex parte Factortame Ltd (No. 1)* [1990] ECR I-2433.
756. Case C-221/89 *R v Secretary for Transport, ex parte Factortame Ltd (No. 2)* [1991] ECR I-3905.
757. [1991] ECR I-4585.
758. Joined Cases C-48/93 *Brasserie Du Pêcheur SA v Federal Republic of Germany and R v Secretary of State for Transport, ex parte Factortame Ltd and Others (No. 3)* [1996] ECR I-1029.

to determine whether the UK's breaches of EU law were sufficiently serious as to entitle the claimants to compensation.

The UK Divisional Court held that the UK's breach of EU law was sufficiently serious to give rise to liability in damages to individuals, who suffered loss as a consequence of that breach. The Court of Appeal upheld the decision of the Divisional Court in Factortame (No. 4).[759] The Secretary of State appealed to the House of Lords. He argued that:

- The UK had a wide measure of discretion in dealing with a serious economic problem. Therefore, it could not be said that when exercising its discretion, the UK manifestly and gravely disregarded its powers; and,

- No liability could be imposed on the UK even if there was a breach of EU law, since the breach was excusable for a number of reasons: first, the law in this area was unclear until the ECJ had given judgments; second, the conduct of the UK could be objectively justified on substantial grounds taking into account that, on the one hand, under the common fisheries policy the quotas allocated to Member States were to be protected by them and, on the other hand, under international law it is a state's prerogative to decide who should be entitled to register a vessel and fly its flag.

Held:

The House of Lords held:[760]

With regard to the condition of nationality, that the legislation was in breach of Article 18 TFEU and that this breach was sufficiently serious to give rise to liability in damages to individuals who suffered loss as a consequence.

The judgment of the House of Lords is not surprising. In Factortame (No. 3) the ECJ had already dealt with the arguments invoked in Factortame (No. 4) by the Secretary of State. In this respect Lord Slynn said:

"It was obvious that what was done by the Government was not done inadvertently. It was done after anxious consideration and after taking legal advice. . . . The shortness of the transitional period, the fact that there was no way in domestic law of challenging the statute, and that the respondents were obliged not merely to avoid being removed from the old register but to apply to be put on the new register all emphasised the determination of the Government to press ahead with the scheme despite the strong opposition of the Commission and the doubts of its officials.

Therefore, it seems clear that the deliberate adoption of legislation which was clearly discriminatory on the ground of nationality was a manifest breach of fundamental Treaty obligations."[761]

Lord Hope emphasised that if in the present case damages were not to be held to be recoverable, it would be hard to envisage any case, short of one involving bad faith, where damages would be recoverable.

---

759. *R v Secretary of State for Transport, ex parte Factortame Ltd (No. 4)* [1998] EULR 456.

760. *Regina v Secretary of State for Transport, Ex Parte Factortame Ltd and Others (Factortame No. 4)* [2000] 1 AC 524.

761. Ibid, 542.

All Law Lords agreed that the breach of EU law by the UK was sufficiently serious to entitle the respondents to compensation for damage directly caused by that breach.

2. *In respect of the domicile condition, the House of Lords agreed that it should be treated in the same way as nationality. Thus, that condition was also considered breached and the breach as being sufficiently serious.*

3. *In relation to the residence condition, Lord Slynn held that, on the one hand, the condition was excusable taking into account the aim of the legislation which was to protect the livelihood of British fishing communities, but, on the other hand, it was not, taking into account that this condition was applied not only to fishermen but also to shareholders and directors of companies owning fishing vessels. Consequently, the condition of residence could not be justified where the discrimination was so obvious. Further, the British Government all along took the view that the residence condition in itself was not sufficient to achieve its objective and so, taken separately, could not be justified.*

Comment:

The Factortame *cases made a great impact on the law of the UK for three reasons:*

- *The UK expressly recognised the principle of supremacy of EU law;*

- *For the first time since 1688, that is, prior to the Bill of Rights, the British judiciary was able to overturn the will of the legislature, even though it has knowledge of its express wish; and,*

- *The UK courts, including the House of Lords, for the first time ever applied the conditions for Member State liability.*

The *Factortame* saga can be illustrated as follows:

Factortame (No. 1)	Factortame (No. 2)	Factortame (No. 3)	Factortame (No. 4)	Factortame (No. 5)
Main issue: compatibility of the 1988 Act with EU law and granting of interim relief to Factortame.	Main issue: the compatibility of the 1988 Act with EU law.	Main issue: clarifications of the conditions for State liability.	Main issue: the right to damages.	Main issue: limitation period.

(Continued)

(Continued)

Factortame (No. 1)	Factortame (No. 2)	Factortame (No. 3)	Factortame (No. 4)	Factortame (No. 5)
The Divisional Court (DC) (now the Administrative Court): referred to the ECJ the compatibility matter and granted interim relief (10/3/1989). The Court of Appeal: reversed the DC's grant of interim relief (22/3/1989). The House of Lords (now Supreme Court): upheld the Court of Appeal's reversal and requested a preliminary ruling from the ECJ on interim relief (18/5 1989). The ECJ: confirmed the duty of a national court to grant interim relief (10/6/1990). The House of Lords: Granted interim relief to Factortame (11/10/1990).	The ECJ: found the 1988 Act in breach of EU law (25/6/1991).	The DC: requested a preliminary ruling from the ECJ (18/11/1992). The ECJ set out the conditions for State liability (5/4/1996).	The DC: ruled that the conditions for State liability were satisfied so Factortame should be compensated (31/7/1997). The Court of Appeal rejected the appeal of the UK government (8/4/1998). The House of Lords: rejected the appeal of UK government and ruled in favour of Factortame (28/10/1999). The matter was settled. In March 2000, Factortame and others received £55 million including interest of approx. £26 million.	The Technology and Construction Court held that the Limitation Act 1955 applied to claims under the Merchant Shipping Act 1988. Accordingly, any claims were admissible if lodged by 10/7/1996 (this did not concern Factortame and those who joined the original claim lodged in December 1988). Rejected the Factortame claim for damages for injury to feelings, and aggravated damages.

12.6 National procedural autonomy and the principle of Member State liability

State liability is one of three actions which are based directly on EU law and which have been developed by the ECJ. The other two are: the action for interim relief in respect of putative violations of individuals' EU rights (see Chapter 13.10); and, the action for recovery of charges levied in violation of EU law (see Chapter 19.7). All these actions are pursued through national courts which, on the basis of the principle of national autonomy, apply national remedies and procedural rules.

In the absence of uniform EU procedural rules it is for the domestic legal system of each Member State to designate the courts and tribunals having jurisdiction in respect of claims based on EU law and to lay down the procedural rules governing those actions for safeguarding rights which individuals derive from EU law.[762] This is known as the principle of national procedural autonomy, which was recognised by the ECJ in Case 33/76 *Rewe-Zentralfinanz.*[763]

Procedural rules are very important as they concern such matters as causation, remoteness of damage, interim relief, limitation periods, quantum of damages, burden of proof, evidence, *locus standi*, and so on. Leaving such important matters to be decided by national procedural rules which, on the one hand, are different in different Member States, and on the other hand, do not take into account the peculiarity of EU law, could undermine the extent of the protection of the rights conferred by EU law on individuals, prejudice legal certainty and justice, and call into question the authority of EU law.

The ECJ has been very aware of the above implications of the principle of procedural autonomy on the uniform application and effectiveness of EU law. The Court's call for the adoption of legislation harmonising the most important aspects of procedural law not having been answered by the EU legislature.[764] As a result, the Court has developed its own way of dealing with this matter.

On the basis of Article 4(3) TEU, which requires Member States to take all necessary measures to achieve the objectives set out in the Treaties and to abstain from adopting any measures which may jeopardise their achievement, the ECJ has gradually limited the scope of the principle of procedural autonomy. The limitations are imposed by the right of access to a court, the principle of equivalence and the principle of effectiveness.

12.6.1 The right of access to a court

The right of access to a court was recognised by the ECJ in Case 222/84 *Johnson*[765] as a general principle of EU law. It is enshrined in Article 47(2) of the Charter of Fundamental Rights, which corresponds to Article 6(1) ECHR. Article 47(2) of the Charter states: "Everyone is entitled to a fair and public hearing within a reasonable time by an independent and impartial tribunal previously established by law. Everyone shall have the possibility of being advised, defended and represented."

In cases decided before the entry into force of the ToL[766] (see Chapter 15.2.7.4) it was clear that in some circumstances an individual had no access to judicial process. The ToL's response was provided in Article 19(1) TEU which imposes on Member States a duty to ensure that individuals have "remedies sufficient to ensure effective legal protection in the fields covered by Union law".

12.6.2 The principle of equivalence

The principle of equivalence requires that under national procedural rules claims based on EU law must not be treated less favourably than those relating to similar domestic claims.[767] The main difficulty in the application of the principle of equivalence is the identification by a national court of whether there is an action under national law sufficiently similar to that which is available under EU law. In this respect, the ECJ indicated that the similarity must be assessed broadly as account is to be taken of the

---

762.   C.N. Kakouris, "Do the Member States Possess Judicial Procedural 'Autonomy'?" (1997) 34 CMLRev., 1389–1412.

763.   Case 33/76 *Rewe-Zentralfinanz eG et Rewe-Zentral AG v Landwirtschaftskammer für das Saarland* [1976] ECR 1989.

764.   See A. Arnull, *The European Union and its Court of Justice*, 1999, Oxford: OUP, 151. However, in the Area of Freedom, Security and Justice, the EU has been developing a body of EU procedural rules in civil and criminal matters. See Chapter 31.5.

765.   Case 222/84 *Marguerite Johnston v Chief Constable of the Royal Ulster Constabulary* [1986] ECR 1651.

766.   For example, Case C-50/00 *UPA v Council* [2002] ECR I-6677.

767.   Supra note 763.

objective or purpose of the actions in question determined in the light of their "essential characteristics".[768] Once similarity is established a national court must determine whether an action based on EU law is treated less favourably under national procedural rules than a similar action based on national law. For that purpose, a national court must take into account "the role played by that provision in the procedure as a whole, as well as the operation and any special features of that procedure before the different national courts".[769]

In Case C-118/08 *Transportes Urbanos*[770] the ECJ held that differing procedural rules concerning an action to establish State liability depending on whether the action is based on a breach of EU law or on a breach of a national constitutional provision were in breach of the principle of equivalence. In this case, under Spanish procedural rules a claimant in an action to establish State liability based on a breach of EU law was required to exhaust all remedies, whether administrative or judicial, against the administrative measure which had caused him harm and which had been adopted pursuant to legislation contrary to EU law. No such requirement was imposed on a claimant in actions to establish State liability based on a breach of a provision of the Spanish Constitution. The principle of equivalence could only be breached if both actions were similar to each other. In dealing with this point the ECJ compared both actions in terms of their purpose and essential characteristics and came to the conclusion that they were indeed similar. Accordingly, the Spanish procedural rules were in breach of the principle of equivalence.

If there is no comparable action under national law, the principle of equivalence does not apply[771] with the result that the contested national rule applies subject to the principle of proportionality.[772] For example, in Case C-336/94 *Dafeki,*[773] German provisions under which certificates of civil status were accorded different values depending on whether they were German or foreign did not apply to a migrant EU worker seeking to obtain early retirement benefit. The claimant was not entitled to the benefit because according to her original birth certificate she was born on 3 December 1933 but she had a valid claim under a rectified birth certificate issued in accordance with Greek procedures, which stated that she was born on 20 February 1929. The ECJ held that the German authorities were required to accept her rectified birth certificate unless its accuracy was seriously undermined by concrete evidence relating to the claimant.

The ECJ usually leaves it to national judges to determine whether the principle of equivalence has been complied with on the ground that they have direct knowledge of the relevant national procedural rules. However, EU law does not require a Member State to apply the most favourable rules to actions based on EU law,[774] it merely provides that comparable actions should be treated in the same way.

12.6.3 The principle of effectiveness

The principle of effectiveness requires that the application of domestic rules and procedures must not render the protection of individuals' EU rights practically impossible or excessively difficult.[775] A national procedural rule which is in breach of the principle of effectiveness must be set aside. For

---

768.   Case C-261/95 *Palmisani v INPS* [1997] ECR I-4025, para. 27.

769.   Case C-326/96 *B.S. Levez v T.H. Jennings (Harlow Pools) Ltd* [1998] ECR I-7835, para. 44.

770.   C-118/08 *Transportes Urbanos y Servicios Generales SA v Administración del Estado* [2010] ECR I-635.

771.   Case C-261/95 *Palmisani v INPS* [1997] ECR I-4025.

772.   Case C-336/94 *Eftalia Dafeki v Landesversicherungsanstalt Württemberg* [1997] ECR I-6761.

773.   Ibid.

774.   Case C-231/96 *Edis v Ministero delle Finanze* [1998] ECR I-4951.

775.   Case 45/76 *Comet BV v Produktschap voor Siergewassen* [1976] ECR 2043.

example, in Case 106/77 *Simmenthal*,[776] a national court was required to set aside national law incompatible with EU law without requesting or waiting for the legislature or other branches of government to set aside the incompatible national provision by legislation or other constitutional means. Many conditions for the establishment of State liability imposed by national rules have been set aside as incompatible with the principle of effectiveness, e.g. a condition making reparation dependent on proof of intentional fault, serious misconduct, negligence[777] or misfeasance in public office[778] and a condition excluding loss of profit as a head of damage.[779]

The ECJ has stated that in order to decide whether a national procedural provision renders the exercise of rights conferred upon individuals impossible or excessively difficult, reference must be made to the role of that provision in the procedure, its progress and its special features. In that context, it is necessary to take into consideration, where relevant, the principles which form the basis of the national legal system, such as the protection of the rights of the defence, the principle of legal certainty and the proper conduct of proceedings.[780] The ECJ assesses, on a case-by-case basis, whether the requirements of the principle of effectiveness are respected and thus places each case in its own factual and legal context as a whole. This contextual approach was not always applied by the ECJ. In particular between the mid-1980s and 1993, the ECJ was in its most interventionist period so far as the application of the principle of effectiveness was concerned.[781] The increasing intrusion of the ECJ into the autonomy of procedural rules was particularly evident in the following cases:

- In Case 14/83 *Von Colson and Kamann*,[782] on the basis of the principle of effectiveness a national court was required to ensure that compensation was adequate to the injury sustained and amounted to more than purely nominal compensation, and further that the penalty for a breach of EU law was adequate and proportional so as to deter breach of obligations imposed in the context of the Equal Treatment Directive;

- In Case C-271/91 *Marshall II*,[783] a national court was required to award the claimant full and adequate compensation and thus disregard any national rule setting a maximum limit on the recoverable quantum of damage for sex discrimination;

- In Case C-213/89 *Factortame (No. 2)*,[784] a national court was required to grant interim relief to the claimants, although under national rules it had no jurisdiction to do so as this remedy was barred by statute;

- In Joined Cases C-6/90 and C-9/90 *Francovich* the ECJ created a specific damages action based on EU law;

---

776. [1978] ECR 629.
777. Case C-173/03 *Traghetti del Mediterranes SpA (TDM) v Italy* [2006] ECR I-5177.
778. Joined Cases C-46/93 and C-48/93 *Brasserie du Pêcheur SA v Germany and R v Secretary of State for Transport, ex parte Factortame Ltd and Others (Factortame (No. 3))* [1996] ECR I-1029.
779. Case C-470/03 *AGM-COS.MET v Suomen valtio and Tarmo Lehtinen* [2007] ECR I-2749.
780. Case C-312/93 *Peterbroeck v Belgium* [1995] ECR I-4599; Joined Cases C-430/93 and C-431/93 *Jeroen van Schijndel and Johannes Nicolaas Cornelis van Veen v Stichting Pensioenfonds voor Fysiotherapeuten* [1995] ECR I-4705; Case C-129/00 *Commission v Italy* [2003] ECR I-14637; Case C-222/05 *Van der Weerd v Jeroen van Schijndel and Johannes Nicolaas Cornelis van Veen v Stichting Pensioenfonds voor Fysiotherapeuten* [2007] ECR I-4233.
781. On this topic see: M. Dougan, "The Vicissitudes of Life at Coalface: Remedies and Procedures for Enforcing Union Law before National Courts", in P. Craig and G. de Bùrca (eds), *The Evolution of EU Law*, 2nd edn, 2011, Oxford: OUP, 407.
782. Case 14/83 *Sabine von Colson and Elisabeth Kamann v Land Nordrhein-Westfalen* [1984] ECR 1891.
783. C-271/91 *Marshall v Southampton and South West Area Health Authority II* [1993] ECR I-4367.
784. C-213/89 *R v Secretary of State for Transport, ex parte Factortame Ltd and Others (No. 2)* [1990] ECR I-2433.

■ In Case C-177/88 *Dekker*,[785] a national court was required to disregard a national procedural rule which made the employer's liability for breach of the principle of equal treatment subject to proof of fault attributable to the employer; and,

■ In Case C-208/90 *Emmott*,[786] probably the most controversial case of all the above, in which the ECJ held that a Member State could not rely on a national limitation period, which was reasonable, in an action against it based on a directive for as long as it had not properly implemented that directive into national law. The possible implications of this case might have been far reaching in that the ruling might have entailed that when a Member State implemented a directive incorrectly, but acted in good faith, it could have nevertheless found itself liable with regard to numerous retrospective claims (but see below the subsequent case law on this topic).

The interventionist approach was criticised on many accounts, mainly that the ECJ was acting as a legislator and that its application of the principle of effectiveness undermined the principle of legal certainty and the coherence of national legal systems. Further Member States were not pleased with the financial consequences of the ECJ's interventionist approach.[787]

From 1993 onwards, the ECJ has changed the manner in which it applies the principle of effectiveness. Whether the reason behind a new approach was that the ECJ wanted to respond to the above criticism, or whether it decided that it had almost accomplished its task of properly safeguarding rights which individuals derive from EU law, is a matter of conjecture. This, however, does not mean that the ECJ will refuse to intervene when appropriate. For example, in Case C-432/05 *Unibet*,[788] the ECJ imposed, for the first time, on a Member State an obligation to create a specific damages action if an equivalent action was unknown in national law. Thus, the statement in Case 158/80 *Rewe* that there was no obligation imposed on the Member States to create new remedies has been qualified by the development of the principle of State liability.

The post-1993 approach is well exemplified in Case C-445/06 *Danske*,[789] in which the ECJ provided three important clarifications as to the limitation period imposed under national law in respect of actions for compensation based on State liability and thus qualified its judgment in *Emmott*.

■ The first issue was whether the limitation period begins to run only upon the directive in question being fully and correctly transposed into national law, or whether, in accordance with German law, when the first injurious effects occur and further injurious effects are foreseeable. The ECJ held that the rule in *Emmott* applies to exceptional circumstances, i.e. when the time-limit has already expired prior to the establishment of a situation incompatible with EU law and thus the time-limit is set in such a manner as to deprive the injured parties of any opportunity whatsoever to rely on their rights before national courts. Therefore, in was in the light of the circumstances in *Emmott* that the ECJ stated that, until such time as a directive has been properly transposed, a defaulting Member State may not rely on an individual's delay in initiating proceedings. In *Danske* the situation was different in that the existence of the time-limit did not produce a result

---

785. Case C-177/88 *Elisabeth Johanna Pacifica Dekker v Stichting Vormingscentrum voor Jong Volwassenen (VJV-Centrum) Plus* [1990] ECR I-3941.

786. Case C-208/90 *Theresa Emmott v Minister for Social Welfare and Attorney General* [1991] ECR I-4269.

787. See R. Caranta, "Judicial Protection against Member States: A New *Jus Commune* Takes Shape", (1995) 32 CMLRev., 703.

788. Case C-432/05 *Unibet (London) Ltd and Unibet (International) Ltd v Justitiekanslern* [2007] ECR I-2271.

789. Case C-445/06 *Danske Slagterier v Germany* [2009] ECR I-2119.

similar to that in *Emmott* and therefore there was no breach of the principle of effectiveness. Accordingly, the ECJ held that EU law does not preclude the commencement of the limitation period being fixed at the time when the first injurious effects have been produced, even if that date is prior to the correct transposition of the relevant directive;

▓ The second issue was whether the three-year limitation period imposed under German law was in conformity with the principle of effectiveness. The ECJ decided that, in principle, such a time-limit is not liable to make it in practice impossible or excessively difficult to exercise the rights conferred by EU law and therefore is compatible with the principle of effectiveness. However, the ECJ added that in order to serve their purpose of ensuring legal certainty, limitation periods must be fixed in advance;[790] and,

▓ The third issue was whether the limitation period can be interrupted or suspended by proceedings brought by the Commission under Article 258 TFEU against the Member State concerned in a situation where there is no effective legal remedy in the State in question to compel it to transpose a directive. The ECJ decided that the limitation period for claims seeking to establish State liability in relation to loss and damage arising from the inadequate transposition of a directive is not interrupted or suspended where the Commission brings infringement proceedings under Article 258 TFEU against the State concerned.

It follows from the above that due to the requirements of EU law, procedural rules for obtaining compensation have, to a great extent, been modified/amended/disregarded to ensure that an appropriate remedy is available to an individual whose EU rights have been infringed by a Member State. The equivalence and effectiveness principles have been used to achieve some consistency in the remedies available at national level. In some exceptional cases the principle of effectiveness has led to the creation of a wholly new remedy.

It is important to add that the duty imposed on national courts to interpret national law in conformity with EU law means that national judges are obliged to creatively construe domestic procedural rules in order to give effect to EU law and, thus, to contribute to reformulation of the parameters of national remedial regimes.

National courts are still struggling to give the appropriate form and substance to an action for damages based on State liability against a Member State or its emanations, in particular given that damages principles, as opposed to remedies, are still underdeveloped at the EU level. On the one hand, more clarification is needed from the ECJ as to the ambit of the remedy in damages, and on the other, national law needs to find ways, acceptable to EU law, to incorporate this remedy into national procedural law.

RECOMMENDED READING

Books

Hofstötter, B., *Non-Compliance of National Courts: Remedies in European Community Law and Beyond*, 2005, The Hague: Asser Press.

Lenaerts, K., Arts, D., and Maselis, I., *Procedural Law of the European Union*, 3rd edn, 2012, London: Sweet & Maxwell.

Ward, A., *Individual Rights and Private Party Judicial Review in the EU*, 2nd edn, 2007, Oxford: OUP.

---

790.   Case C-62/00 *Marks & Spencer plc v Commissioners of Customs & Excise* [2002] ECR I-6325.

Articles

Beutler, B., "State Liability for Breaches of Community Law by National Courts: Is the Requirement of a Manifest Infringement of the Applicable Law an Insurmountable Obstacle?" (2009) 46 CMLRev., 773.

Dougan, D., "The Vicissitudes of Life at the Coalface: Remedies and Procedures for Enforcing Union Law before National Courts", in Craig, P. and de Bùrca, G. (eds) *The Evolution of EU Law*, 2nd edn, 2011, Oxford: OUP, 407.

Granger, M.-P. F., "National Applications of Francovich and the Construction of a European Administrative *Ius Commune*", (2007) 32 ELRev., 157.

Kremer, C., "Liability for Breach of European Community Law: An Analysis of the New Remedy in the Light of English and German Law", (2003) YEL, 203.

Meltzer, D. J., "Member State Liability in Europe and the United States", (2006) 4 Int'l J. Const. L, 39.

Prechal, S., "Community Law in National Courts: The Lesson from Van Schijndel", (1998) 35 CMLRev., 681.

Van Gerven, W., "Of Rights, Remedies and Procedures", (2000) 37 CMLRev., 501.

PROBLEM QUESTION

Jessica, a former employee of ASW Limited, an English company placed in insolvent liquidation in April 2010, was a member of occupational supplementary pension schemes sponsored by that company. Due to the insolvency of ASW those pension schemes were terminated in July 2010.

Actuarial valuations carried out on behalf of ASW's pension schemes trustees indicated that the assets held in the pension schemes were insufficient to cover all the benefits of all members, and as a result, the benefits of ASW employees, who were not yet in receipt of a pension, were to be reduced. The reduction for Jessica is dramatic, as she will receive only 20 per cent of her previously expected benefits.

Article 8 of Directive 80/987/EEC, which has been implemented in the UK, requires a Member State to ensure that the necessary measures are taken to protect the interests of employees, and of persons having already left the employer's undertaking or business at the date of the onset of the employer's insolvency. This being in respect of rights conferring on them immediate or prospective entitlement to old-age benefits, including survivors' benefits, under supplementary company or inter-company pension schemes outside the national statutory social security schemes.

As the English state pension system pays pensioners, on average, as little as 37 per cent of their final salary, the expected supplementary pensions under the ASW pension schemes represented, according to Jessica, the greater part of her expected financial provision for her old age.

The ECJ in a case decided two months ago held that Directive 80/987/EEC does not impose a duty on a Member State to guarantee in full the accrued rights of employees. The ECJ emphasised that the directive leaves considerable latitude as to the means to be adopted to ensure protection. A Member State may therefore impose, for example, an obligation on employers to insure or provide for the setting-up of a guarantee institution. Further, the ECJ held that Article 8 of the Directive lacked the necessary clarity and precision with regard to the level of protection required.

Jessica considers that the UK legislation did not provide her with the level of protection prescribed by Article 8 of the Directive, and wishes to bring an action against the UK Government for compensation for the loss suffered. Advise Jessica.

ESSAY QUESTION

Critically discuss whether the principles of equivalence and effectiveness are sufficient to ensure adequate protection of the rights of individuals to obtain damages or other remedies before national courts for their losses resulting from a Member State's breach of EU law.

AIDE-MÉMOIRE

The principle of State liability
A Member State may be held liable for damage caused to individuals (Joined Cases C-6/90 and C-9/90 *Francovich and Bonifaci v Italian State*).

The claimant
Any individual

The defendant
The Member State is liable regardless of the organ (legislative, executive, administrative or judicial Case C-224/01 *Köbler*) whose act or omission allegedly infringed EU law.

The claim must satisfy the following three substantive conditions:

The rule of law, which has been breached, must be one which is intended to confer rights on individuals
A national judge must ascertain, from the wording of the relevant EU provision, the identity of the persons entitled to benefit from the right in question, whether the claimant is such a beneficiary, the extent and content of the right and the identity of the legal body charged with protecting that right. It is not necessary for the relevant EU provision to have direct effect.

The breach must be sufficiently serious to merit an award of damages
The establishment of the existence of a sufficiently serious breach will be based on the following factors:
- clarity and precision of the provision of EU law allegedly breached by the Member State;
- the measure of discretion enjoyed by the Member State;
- whether the breach or damage caused was intentional or voluntary;
- whether any error of law was excusable; and,
- whether the position taken by EU institutions may have contributed towards the adoption or maintenance of national measures or practice contrary to EU law.

There must be a direct causal link between the Member State's default and the loss suffered by the applicant
Under the principle of national procedural autonomy the existence of a causal link is to be determined by reference to national procedural rules (Case 33/76 *Rewe-Zentralfinanz*) but subject to the principal of effectiveness and the principle of equivalence.

The claim is enforced under national procedural law.

In the absence of EU rules, national remedies and procedural rules apply (i.e. the principle of national procedural autonomy) subject to the following limitations:
- A claimant must have access to a court;
- The principle of equivalence or non-discrimination, which requires that under national procedural rules claims based on EU law must not be treated less favourably than similar domestic claims, must be respected;
- The principle of effectiveness, which requires that the application of domestic rules and procedures must not render the protection of individuals' EU rights practically impossible or excessively difficult, must be respected;
- The requirement that, if an equivalent remedy does not exist under national law, a new damages remedy must be created by a Member State (Joined Cases C-6/90 and C-9/90 *Francovich and Bonifaci v Italian State*)

AIDE-MÉMOIRE

Case name	Contribution to the establishment and the content of the principle of State liability
Joined Cases C-6/90 and C-9/90 *Francovich and Bonifaci*	In this case the ECJ established the principle that a Member State should be liable in damages to individuals who have suffered loss as a result of that Member State's infringement of EU law. It also specified the conditions for liability which were revised in Joined Cases C-46/93 and C-48/93 *Brasserie du Pêcheur and Factortame (No. 3)* (see below). Justifications for the establishment of the principle of State liability: the peculiarity of the EU legal system; the necessity of ensuring the effectiveness of EU law; the requirements of Article 4(3) TFEU; and, the necessity to force Member States to comply with EU law, in particular to implement directives necessary to complete the internal market.
Joined Cases C-46/93 and C-48/93 *Brasserie du Pêcheur and Factortame (No. 3)*	The ECJ clarified the conditions for liability. These are: **1. The rule of law which has been breached must be one which is intended to confer rights on individuals.** **2. The breach must be sufficiently serious to merit an award of damages.** This is assessed in the light of the following factors: "the clarity and precision of the rule breached, the measure of discretion left by that rule to the national or Community authorities, whether the infringement and the damage caused was intentional or involuntary, whether any error of law was excusable or inexcusable, the fact that the position taken by a Community institution may have contributed towards the omission, and the adoption or retention of national measures or practices contrary to Community law". **3. There must be a direct causal link between the Member State's default and the loss suffered by the claimant.**
Joined Cases C-178, 179 and 189/94 *Dillenkofer*	The ECJ held that non-implementation of a directive within the prescribed time limit constitutes, *per se,* a serious breach of EU law, and consequently gives rise to a right of reparation for individuals suffering injury.
Case C-5/94 *Hedley Lomas*	A State may be liable if its administrative practice violates EU law.
Case C-445/06 *Danske*	The ECJ held that an obligation to pay compensation does not arise if the injured party has wilfully or negligently failed to avert the damage by not utilising an available legal remedy. However, it qualified this by stating that: "It would...., be contrary to the principle of effectiveness to oblige injured parties to have recourse systematically to all the legal remedies available to them even if that would give rise to excessive difficulties or could not reasonably be required of them."
Case C-470/03 *Lehtinen*	The ECJ endorsed the principle of public international law according to which a Member State can be held accountable for wrongful acts of its organs or its officials when they act beyond their capacity but to all appearances as competent officials or organs.
Case C-224/01 *Köbler*	A Member State may incur liability for violation of EU law by judgments of its supreme court. If this occurs the applicant can obtain only financial compensation as the revision of the relevant judgment is not required under EU law.
Case C-154/08 *Commission v Spain*	The ECJ, for the first time, found that a Member State was in breach of EU law when its supreme court incorrectly interpreted provisions of EU law having failed to make a request for a preliminary ruling to the ECJ, as it ought to have done, on the interpretation of the relevant provisions of EU law.

13

PRELIMINARY RULINGS:
ARTICLE 267 TFEU

CHAPTER OUTLINE

1. Article 267 TFEU states that the Court of Justice of the European Union (CJEU) is empowered to give preliminary rulings on the interpretation of the Treaties and the validity and interpretation of acts of the EU institutions, bodies, offices and agencies. Article 256(3) TFEU specifies that not only the ECJ but also the General Court shall have jurisdiction to give preliminary rulings in the areas determined by the Statute of the CJEU. However, at the time of writing, the ECJ has not made any arrangements to share its jurisdiction with the General Court and consequently, the ECJ alone is empowered to give preliminary rulings.

2. The ToL extended the ECJ's jurisdiction to give preliminary rulings to the whole of the AFSJ but subject to a temporal limitation with regard to some measures in the field of police and judicial co-operation in criminal matters. In the AFSJ the ECJ may use the urgent preliminary ruling procedure to deal speedily with referrals in extremely urgent cases, e.g. when a person whose legal situation is to be assessed by the referring court on the basis of the answer from the ECJ is in custody or deprived of liberty.

3. The ECJ is precluded from giving preliminary rulings on the validity of primary sources (as opposed to their interpretation); on the validity of its own judgments; on interpretation and validity of matters excluded by Article 276 TFEU; on CFSP matters with the exceptions stated in Article 23(1) TEU; and, on the validity of EU acts when they fall within the exception established in Case C-188/92 *TWD*. Although the ECJ has no jurisdiction to rule on validity and interpretation of national law and compatibility of national law with EU law it has pushed the limits of Article 267 TFEU by giving preliminary rulings on interpretation of national law dealing with "purely" internal situations when its provisions reproduce or make reference to the contents of EU provisions. The justification of the ECJ is that concepts and provisions taken from EU law should be interpreted uniformly irrespective of the circumstances in which they are to apply.

4. The ECJ has taken a functional approach to the determination of a body which is allowed to make a reference under Article 267 TFEU as opposed to a literal approach under which only bodies actually called a "court" or "tribunal" under national law would be regarded as a "court or tribunal" under Article 267 TFEU. The criteria for determination of whether a body is a "court or tribunal" within the meaning of Article 267 TFEU were summarised in Case C-54/96 *Dorsch Consult* and for that reason are often referred to as *Dorsch Consult* criteria. Under those criteria a body must:

- be established by law;
- be permanent;
- have compulsory jurisdiction over the dispute;
- use adversarial procedure;
- apply rules of law;
- be independent; and,
- be called upon to give a decision of a judicial nature.

5. In the context of preliminary rulings on the interpretation of EU law a distinction is made between discretionary and mandatory referrals. This is based on Article 267 TFEU which states in its second para. that courts and tribunals "may" make a request for a preliminary ruling and para. 3 which states that courts and tribunals against whose decisions there is no judicial remedy under national law "shall" refer. The case law shows that the 2nd para. refers to lower courts which have an unfettered discretion to decide whether and when to refer to the ECJ. Mandatory referrals are provided for in para.3 of Article 267 TFEU, which imposes an obligation on national courts or tribunals adjudicating at last instance (this comprises not only final appellate courts in each Member State, but also all courts which decide a case in the last instance) to refer, but this is subject to the doctrine of *acte clair* (Case 283/81 *CILFIT*).

6. With regard to preliminary rulings on the validity of acts of EU institutions, all national courts and tribunals must refer to the ECJ if in doubt as to the validity of the relevant act.

7. The ECJ has rarely refused to give a preliminary ruling. This may, however, occur when a referred question has no relevance to the main dispute, or when a referring court has not provided sufficient factual and legal background in its reference. It is uncertain whether the ECJ still requires that there must be a genuine dispute between the parties to national proceedings for it to accept a referral.

8. A preliminary ruling on the interpretation of EU law is binding on the referring court and has retroactive effect unless the ECJ decides otherwise. A preliminary ruling on the validity of EU law entails that if the ECJ declares an act invalid all national courts and tribunals, not only the referring court, have to set aside that act. Although the ECJ has no power to replace an invalid act it has authorised itself to replace invalidated provisions by appropriate alternatives while the adoption of required measures by the institution concerned is awaited.

9. There is an ongoing debate whether the preliminary rulings procedure needs to be reformed in the light of many factors such as the expansion of competences of the EU under the ToL; the generous definition of "court and tribunal" under Article 267 TFEU; the growth in scope and volume of EU secondary acts; and, the geographical expansion of the EU; all of which may cause delays in the delivery of preliminary rulings and even affect their quality. So far, however, the ECJ has resisted any attempt to limit access of national courts and tribunals to the ECJ within the preliminary rulings procedure. In March 2011, the ECJ submitted a proposal to the EP and Council for amendments to the Statute of the CJEU and its Rules of Procedure. It deals mainly with improving the functionality of the General Court whilst leaving the preliminary rulings procedure unchanged.

13.1 Introduction

Article 267 TFEU states:

"The Court of Justice of the European Union shall have jurisdiction to give preliminary rulings concerning:

(a) the interpretation of the Treaties;

(b) the validity and interpretation of acts of the institutions, bodies, offices or agencies of the Union.

Where such a question is raised before any court or tribunal of a Member State, that court or tribunal may, if it considers that a decision on the question is necessary to enable it to give judgment, request the Court to give a ruling thereon.

Where any such question is raised in a case pending before a court or tribunal of a Member State against whose decisions there is no judicial remedy under national law, that court or tribunal shall bring the matter before the Court.

If such a question is raised in a case pending before a court or tribunal of a Member State with regard to a person in custody, the Court of Justice of the European Union shall act with the minimum of delay."

Article 267 TFEU states that the CJEU shall have jurisdiction to give preliminary rulings, and Article 256 TFEU states that the General Court may deliver preliminary rulings in areas to be specified by the Statute of the CJEU. At the time of writing, no such specification has been made and it seems unlikely that the ECJ will relinquish its exclusive jurisdiction to give preliminary rulings.[791] However,

---

791. See the Information Note on References from National Courts for a Preliminary Ruling issued by the ECJ [2009] OJ C297/1, para. 3.

if the situation changes in the future, the ECJ will, by virtue of Article 258(3) TFEU, have power to review a preliminary judgment of the General Court in a situation where there will be a serious risk of the unity or consistency of EU law being affected by such a judgment. Further, if the General Court were to have jurisdiction to give preliminary rulings, under Article 258(3) TFEU, it would be entitled to refer a request for a preliminary ruling to the ECJ in respect of cases which would require a decision of principle likely to affect the unity or consistency of EU law (see Chapter 13.11).

Article 256 TFEU constitutes one of the possible options to reform the preliminary ruling procedure. Some argue that the increased workload of the ECJ due to the expansion of competences of the EU under the ToL, the generous definition of "court and tribunal" under Article 267 TFEU and the geographical expansion of the EU, will have implications on the length and even the quality of preliminary rulings (this is discussed in depth in Chapter 13.11). However, this is not the view of the ECJ.

Under Article 267 TFEU, the ECJ has jurisdiction both to interpret EU law and to assess the validity of EU acts adopted by EU institutions, bodies, agencies or offices. As a result, it exercises two different functions, although both contribute to define the scope of application of EU law. The interpretation of EU law under Article 267 TFEU has become the main activity of the ECJ. In respect of the validity of EU acts national courts have no jurisdiction to declare them invalid. Only the ECJ can make a declaration of invalidity. National courts must refer to the ECJ whenever there is a reasonable doubt as to the validity of an EU act at issue.

The preliminary ruling procedure has been used by the ECJ as a platform to deepen European integration (see Chapter 4.7.1). The fundamental principles of EU law, such as the principle of direct effect, the principle of supremacy of EU law, and the principle of liability of a Member State for damage caused to individuals by its breach of EU law, have been enunciated within the framework of the preliminary ruling procedure. Furthermore, the procedure has also contributed to the legal protection of individuals. It allows them, *via* national courts, to have access to the ECJ.

13.2 The evolving nature of co-operation between the ECJ and national courts within the preliminary ruling procedure

The preliminary ruling procedure constitutes the main form of co-operation between national courts and the ECJ. This co-operation is necessary to ensure uniformity in the interpretation and application of EU law, bearing in mind that the Treaties do not establish any relationship of superiority or subordination between the ECJ and national courts. The relationship is effectively one of partnership. In the absence of a system allowing the making of appeals to the ECJ from judgments of national courts, the preliminary rulings procedure constitutes a means of ensuring there are not 27 differing interpretations of a particular provision of EU law.[792] Without the procedure this could easily occur as national courts apply EU law independently from one another, and are always more or less influenced by their own legal system. Obviously, it is always possible for the Commission to start proceedings against a Member State for breaches of EU law under Article 258 TFEU (see Chapter 14.2) but the use of this procedure is at the discretion of the Commission; occurs after an alleged breach has been committed; and, may prejudice rather than foster harmonious relations between the EU and its Member States (see Chapter 14.2.3).

The preliminary ruling procedure has evolved in parallel with evolution of the EU. The relationship of co-operation remains at the heart of the procedure, but it cannot be denied that there is a slow

---

792. Case 166/73 *Rheinmühlen-Düsseldorf v Einfuhr- und Vorratsstelle für Getreide und Futtermittel* [1974] ECR 33.

movement from co-operation to co-ordination, i.e. the ECJ, from being a partner, has become a master and from having a bilateral relationship with national courts to having a multilateral relationship with them in that preliminary rulings which are addressed to the referring courts are, in fact, followed, by all national courts, i.e. they are treated as precedent.[793]

Many factors have influenced the change in the relationship between the ECJ and national courts.

First, in Joined Cases 28–30/62 *Da Costa*[794] the ECJ held that if a matter before a national court has previously been interpreted by the ECJ even though it may not be identical (but the point of law is the same), there is no need for national courts to refer to the ECJ. The implication of this approach is that, in fact, the ECJ has established a doctrine of precedent. This approach was enhanced when the ECJ endorsed the doctrine of *acte clair* which exempts national courts from making referrals not only when the ECJ has already made a preliminary ruling on a particular point of EU law, but also in a situation where the correct application of EU law is so obvious as to leave no scope for reasonable doubt (see Chapter 13.6.2.2). As a result, not only a referring court but, in fact, all national courts follow the ruling and the case law of the ECJ subject to safeguards set out by the doctrine of *acte clair*. No blame can be put on the ECJ for adopting this position bearing in mind that it would be a waste of time and resources of the ECJ to continuously answer questions already clear and decided by it. At the same time, reliance on the doctrine of *acte clair* means that national courts apply EU law, as interpreted by the ECJ, without any need for referrals and thus have been "enrolled" by the ECJ as enforcers of EU law.[795] The role of national courts as enforcers of EU law has been strengthened by the reform of EU competition law (see Chapter 30.1). In this area the Treaties delegated enforcement power to national courts. They are required to apply EU competition law to cases which are within the scope of Articles 101 and 102 TFEU. Thus national courts have become part of the judicial system of the EU.

Second, the principle of supremacy of EU law facilitates the acceptance of the case law of the ECJ as precedent. National courts are bound under Article 4(3) TEU to give priority to EU law if there is a conflict between national law and EU law (see Chapter 9.6). For them, the possibility of relying on cases already decided by the ECJ is very attractive. Instead of making a referral on a question already decided by the ECJ they can apply the existing case law and thus speedily dispose of the case under consideration.

Third, the relationship between the ECJ and national courts has been influenced by the judgment in Case C-224/01 *Köbler*[796] (see Chapter 12.4). On the basis of this case, when a supreme court of a Member States fails to seek a ruling from the ECJ and gets EU law wrong, an aggrieved party may have an indirect route to the ECJ,[797] i.e. he/she may make an indirect appeal to the ECJ in respect of a case decided by a supreme court. This is well illustrated in *Köbler*.

---

793. T. de la Mare and C. Donnelly, "Preliminary Rulings and EU Legal Integration: Evolution and Stasis", 376–78 and A. Stone Sweet, "The European Court of Justice", 122, both in P. Craig and G. de Bùrca (eds), *The Evolution of EU Law*, 2nd edn, 2011, Oxford: OUP.

794. Joined Cases 28-30/62 *Da Costa en Schaake NV, Jacob Meijer NV, Hoechst-Holland NV v Netherlands Inland Revenue Administration* [1963] ECR 31.

795. Supra note 793.

796. Case C-224/01 *Gerhard Köbler v Austria* [2003] ECR I-10239.

797. P. J. Wattel, "Köbler, Cilfit and Welthgrove: We Can't go on Meeting like This", (2004) 41 CMLRev., 177 at 190; T. de la Mare and C. Donnelly, "Preliminary Rulings and EU Legal Integration: Evolution and Stasis", supra note 793, at 376–378; and A. A. S. Zuckerman, "Appeals to the High Court against House of Lords Decisions on the Interpretation of Community Law – Damages for Judicial Error", (2004) 23 CJQ, 8.

13.3 The subject-matter jurisdiction of the ECJ under Article 267 TFEU

Under Article 267(1) TFEU national courts may request the ECJ to give preliminary rulings on the following matters.

13.3.1 Interpretation of primary sources of EU law

These include the Treaties, the Charter of Fundamental Rights of the EU as it has the same legal status as the Treaties (see Chapter 4.2), Protocols and Annexes to the Treaties; and acts of accession to the Communities and the EU.[798]

General principles of EU law can form the subject-matter of referrals. Many principles are expressly mentioned in the Treaties and in the Charter of Fundamental Rights and are therefore clearly primary sources. Some are implemented by EU legislative acts. When neither of the above applies there is no reason why a national court should not refer the matter of their interpretation to the ECJ.

13.3.2 Interpretation and validity of acts of EU institutions

Article 267(1)(a) TFEU states that the ECJ has jurisdiction to give preliminary rulings in respect of the validity and interpretation of acts of the EU institutions, bodies, offices or agencies. In Case 9/70 *Franz Grad*,[799] the ECJ held that all acts adopted by EU institutions, without distinction, are capable of being referred under Article 267 TFEU. This comprises not only acts expressly mentioned in Article 288 TFEU, or in the Treaties, but also such acts as resolutions of the Council.[800]

The jurisdiction of the ECJ is neither limited to acts which produce direct effect nor to those which have binding effect. Indeed, national courts may refer questions concerning EU law which is not directly effective. This is so because determining the exact meaning of national law which they have to apply, and which implements EU directives or decisions addressed to a Member State, may pose difficult interpretation problems,[801] or may give rise to doubts as to its validity.[802] Further, the ECJ has jurisdiction to interpret non-binding acts such as recommendations[803] and opinions.

13.3.3 Interpretation of judgments of the ECJ

Judgments of the ECJ delivered within the preliminary rulings procedure can be the subject matter of a referral, either by the referring court[804] or by any other court or tribunal.[805] The ECJ has always refused to regard its preliminary rulings on the interpretation of EU law as irrevocable. Accordingly, the ECJ may modify its interpretation of EU law and thus national courts are entitled to bring the same, or a similar matter (although based on different facts or supported by new legal arguments[806]), before the

---

798. Case 812/79 *Attorney General v Juan C. Burgoa* [1980] ECR 2787.
799. Case 9/70 *Franz Grad v Finanzamt Traunstein* [1970] ECR 825.
800. Case 59/75 *Pubblico Ministero v Flavia Manghera and Others* [1976] ECR 91.
801. Case 111/75 *Impresa Costruzioni comm. Quirino Mazzalai v Ferrovia del Renon* [1976] ECR 657.
802. Case 5/77 *Carlo Tedeschi v Denkavit Commerciale S.R.L* [1977] ECR 1555.
803. Case 113/75 *Giordano Frecassetti v Amministrazione delle Finanze dello Stato* [1976] ECR 983; Case C-322/88 *Salvatore Grimaldi v Fonds des Maladies Professionnelles* [1989] ECR 4407.
804. Case 244/80 *Foglia v Novello II* [1981] ECR 3045.
805. Case C-135/77 *Robert Bosch GmbH v Hauptzollamt Hildesheim* [1978] ECR 855.
806. In Case 22/78 *ICAC* [1979] ECR 1168 the ECJ upheld its previous ruling on the ground that the new referral did not demonstrate any new factual or legal circumstances which would lead to a different interpretation.

ECJ by way of a subsequent reference for a preliminary ruling. For that reason a new referral (or a referral concerning the same or similar question) cannot easily be dismissed. For example, in Case 28/67 *Molkerei-Zentrale*,[807] the ECJ examined at length new arguments invoked against its previous interpretation.

If the referred question is identical to one already decided, the ECJ may accept the preliminary question, but refer to the previous ruling and deal with the referral by means of a reasoned order. Further, under the Rules of Procedure, the ECJ is entitled to dispose of a referral from national courts by means of a reasoned order, where the answer to a preliminary question can clearly be deduced from the existing case law.

National courts may also refer questions regarding interpretation of ECJ judgments delivered within the context of other procedures, e.g. a judgment delivered under Article 258 TFEU (see Chapter 14).[808]

13.3.4 Interpretation and validity of international agreements concluded between the EU and third countries

In Case 181/73 *Haegemann*,[809] the ECJ held that international agreements concluded by the EU are to be considered as acts adopted by the EU institutions within the meaning of Article 267 TFEU. The treatment of international agreements as EU acts is very important since this approach ensures uniformity in their interpretation and application throughout the EU. There are some arguments challenging this approach. First, it can be argued that Article 267 TFEU was intended to apply to unilateral acts rather than to bilateral acts such as international agreements and second, that the ECJ does not interpret the act of the Council relating to the conclusion of a specific agreement, which is an act of an EU institution, but the agreement itself.[810]

When the EU is not a contracting party to an international agreement the ECJ, in principle, has no jurisdiction under Article 267 TFEU.[811] This is subject to an exception. Indeed, so far as international agreements concluded by a Member State and a third country are concerned, the ECJ has made a distinction between a situation where an agreement has become binding on the EU because the EU has, subsequent to its conclusion, assumed full powers in the area covered by the agreement, and a situation where there has been no full transfer of powers from a Member State to the EU in the area concerned. In the former situation, the ECJ is empowered to interpret the agreement,[812] but in the latter, is has no jurisdiction under Article 267 TFEU.[813]

---

807. Case 28/67 *Firma Molkerei-Zentrale Westfalen/Lippe GmbH v Hauptzollamt Paderborn* [1968] ECR 143.

808. Joined Cases 314/81–316/81 and 83/82 *Procureur de la Republic v Waterkeyn and Others* [1982] ECR 4337.

809. Case 181/73 *R. & V. Haegemann v Belgium* [1974] ECR 449, which concerned an association agreement between the EEC and Greece. The *Haegemann* jurisprudence has been confirmed in many cases, for example in Case 52/77 *Leonce Cayrol v Giovanni Rivoira & Figli* [1977] ECR 2261 concerning the association agreement between the EEC and Spain, and Case 65/77 *Razanatsimba* [1977] ECR 2229 concerning the Lomé Convention.

810. See Opinion of A-G Trabucchi in Case 87/75 *Conceria Daniele Bresciani v Amministrazione Italiana delle Finanze* [1976] ECR 129.

811. Case 130/73 *Magdalena Vandeweghe and Others v Berufsgenossenschaft für die chemische Industrie* [1973] ECR 1329.

812. Joined Cases 21/72 to 24/72 *International Fruit Company NV and others v Produktschap voor Groenten en Fruit* [1972] ECR 1219; and Case C-308/06 *The Queen, on the application of International Association of Independent Tanker Owners (Intertanko) and Others v Secretary of State for Transport* [2008] ECR I-4057.

813. Case C-301/08 *Bogiatzi v Deutscher Luftpool, and Others* [2009] ECR I-10185.

It is important to mention that national courts or tribunals of third countries, that are contracting parties to an agreement, are neither allowed to refer to the ECJ under Article 267 TFEU, nor are they bound by its judgments.[814]

The jurisdiction of the ECJ to give preliminary rulings extends to decisions adopted by bodies created by international agreements with a view to ensuring proper application of their provisions.[815]

13.3.5 Interpretation of national provisions based on EU law and purely internal situations

Under Article 267 TFEU, the role of the ECJ is to interpret EU law, not national law. Therefore, matters of interpretation and the validity of national law are outside the ECJ's jurisdiction.[816] However, the ECJ will accept references in respect of purely internal matters in a situation where a provision of national law is based on or makes a reference to EU law. This was held by the ECJ in Joined Cases C-297/88 and C-197/89 *Dzodzi*.[817] Important limitations on the *Dzodzi* approach were imposed in Case C-346/93 *Kleinwort Benson*,[818] in which the ECJ held that with regard to wholly internal situations it would accept referrals only if two conditions were satisfied:

- The reference by national law to the provision of EU law must be "direct and unconditional"; and,

- The application of the relevant provision of EU law must be "absolutely and unconditionally" binding on the national court.

However, the above conditions have not been observed by the ECJ in subsequent cases despite repeated requests from A-Gs.[819] Accordingly, the ECJ accepts requests for a preliminary ruling also where national law makes indirect and implied references to EU law. The justification of the ECJ is that its preliminary rulings are necessary to forestall future differences of interpretation of, provisions or concepts taken from EU law which should be uniformly interpreted irrespective of the circumstances in which they are to apply.[820]

It is important to note that subsequent to the judgment in Case C-448/98 *Guimont*[821] (for facts and comments on *Guimont* see Chapter 20.7), the ECJ is willing to accept referrals concerning purely internal situations in the context not only of the free movement of goods, but also in relation to the free movement of capital and services where the referred case raises the issue of reverse discrimination, if

---

814. See Opinion 1/09 on the Creation of European and Community Patents Court (8/3/11 (NYR)).

815. Case C-192/89 *S. Z. Sevince v Staatssecretaris van Justitie* [1990] ECR I-3461 and Case C-188/91 *Deutsche Shell AG v Hauptzollamt Hamburg-Harburg* [1993] ECR I-363.

816. For example Case 75/63 *Mrs M.K.H. Hoekstra (née Unger) v Bestuur der Bedrijfsvereniging voor Detailhandel en Ambachten* [1964] ECR 177; and Case C-347/89 *Freistaat Bayern v Eurim-Pharm GmbH* [1991] ECR I-1747.

817. Case C-197/89 *Massam Dzodzi v Belgium* [1990] ECR I-3763, see also Case C-231/89 *Krystyna Gmurzynska-Bscher v Oberfinanzdirektion Köln* [1990] ECR I-4003.

818. Case C-346/93 *Kleinwort Benson Ltd v City of Glasgow District Council* [1995] ECR I-615.

819. E.g. in Case C-306/99 *BIAO v Finanzamt für Großunternehmen in Hamburg* [2003] ECR I-1, A-G Jacobs called upon the ECJ to "affirm the criteria which is laid down in *Kleinwort Benson*".

820. Case C-130/95 *Bernd Giloy v Hauptzollamt Frankfurt am Main-Ost* [1997] ECR I-4291 and Case C-126/10 *Foggia – Sociedade Gestora de Participações Sociais SA v Secretário de Estado dos Assuntos Fiscais* (judgment of 10/11/11 (NYR)).

821. Case C-448/98 *Criminal Proceedings against Jean-Pierre Guimont* [2000] ECR I-10663.

its reply "might be useful" to the referring court.[822] The *Guimont* variation of the *Dzodzi* approach has been criticised as increasing the risk of wasting the resources of litigants, of national courts and of the ECJ itself, given that in many cases the ECJ will deliver a purely theoretical ruling.[823]

It is submitted that the ECJ will refuse to interpret national law in a situation where EU law cannot be applied, either directly or indirectly, to the circumstances of the case.[824]

13.3.6 Matters excluded from referral

The ECJ will refuse to give preliminary rulings on the following:

- The validity of primary sources, taking into account that their constitutional nature, cannot be determined by the ECJ;

- Validity of judgments of the ECJ;[825]

- The matters specified in Chapter 13.4;

- Provisions relating to the CFSP and acts adopted on the basis of those provisions. This exclusion is subject to two exceptions set out in Article 24(1) TEU, in that the ECJ has jurisdiction:

  - to decide whether measures adopted under the CFSP have encroached on other policies of the EU and vice versa, i.e. whether measures adopted in non-CFSP policies have impinged on CFSP matters; and,

  - to review the legality of decisions providing for restrictive measures against natural or legal persons adopted by the Council on the basis of Chapter 2 of Title V TEU.

  In respect of both exceptions proceedings for annulment of the above measures under Article 263 TFEU will be the appropriate way to challenge them, although if there are national implementing measures, it seems obvious that a national court or tribunal will be entitled to make a referral to the ECJ concerning issues covered by those exceptions; and,

- Validity of EU acts when they fall within the exception established in Case C-188/92 *TWD*[826] (see Chapter 13.8.2).

---

822. With regard to Article 30 TFEU, the ECJ held that when national authorities impose charges on goods crossing internal/regional borders the situation is within the scope of EU law, i.e. this may be a breach of Article 30 TFEU, and consequently any referral relating to such situations will be accepted (see Case C-363/*93 René Lancry SA and Others v Direction Générale des Douanes and Others* [1994] ECR I-3957 and Case C-72/03 *Carbonati Apuani Srl v Comune di Carrara* [2004] ECR I-8027). The *Guimont* approach has been applied to the free movement of capital (Case C-515/99 *Hans Reisch and Others v Bürgermeister der Landeshauptstadt Salzburg* [2002] ECR I-2157) and to freedom to provide services (Case C-6/01 *Anomar and Others v Estado Português* [2003] ECR I-8621).

823. See C Ritter, "Purely Internal Situations, Reverse Discrimination, Guimont, Dzodzi and Article 234", (2006) 31/5 ELRev., 690.

824. In Case C-310/10 *Ministerul Justitiei si Libertatilor Cetatenesti v Stefan Agafitei and Others* (judgment of 7/7/11).

825. Case 69/85 *Wünsche v Germany* [1986] ECR 947.

826. Case C-188/92 *TWD Textilwerke Deggendorf GmbH v Germany* [1994] ECR I-833. See also Case C-441/05 *Roquette Frères v Ministre de l'Agriculture, de l'Alimentation, de la Pêche et de la Ruralité* [2007] ECR I-1993.

13.4 Extension of the preliminary ruling procedure to the AFSJ

Under the ToL, the ECJ gained jurisdiction to give preliminary rulings in respect of the whole of the AFSJ subject to some temporary restrictions. These are dealt with next.

Under Article 10 of Protocol No. 36 on Transitional Provisions of the Treaty of Lisbon, in the area of police and judicial co-operation in criminal matters, the ECJ has no jurisdiction to give preliminary rulings in respect of measures adopted before the entry into force of the ToL for a period of five years following the entry into force of the ToL. However, if any particular measure, adopted before the entry into force of the ToL, is amended before the expiry of that period then that measure will be within the jurisdiction of the Court from the time of amendment. The temporal restriction does not apply to Member States which, prior to entry into force of the ToL, made a Declaration under Article 35(1) TEU (since repealed) allowing their courts to make requests for a preliminary ruling in this area. An additional limitation is contained in Article 276 TFEU under which the ECJ has no jurisdiction to give preliminary rulings on the validity or proportionality of operations carried out by the police or other law enforcement services of a Member State or the exercise of the responsibilities incumbent upon Member States in respect of the maintenance of law and order and the safeguarding of internal security. This is less controversial than it looks, given that the ECJ has never had jurisdiction to review internal situations. However, nothing will prevent the ECJ from giving a preliminary ruling on the compatibility of certain acts of national authorities with EU law or the interpretation of the relevant EU acts.

13.4.1 The urgent preliminary ruling procedure

Preliminary rulings concerning the resolution of legal issues relating to the AFSJ, pose a special problem for the ECJ in terms of the duration of preliminary ruling proceedings. In 2012, the average duration of such proceedings was 16.4 months.[827] For cases concerning the AFSJ the ECJ must respond quickly in order to comply with Article 6 ECHR and to ensure that the interests of justice are met. In addition, national courts are often required, either under EU law or under national law, to deliver a judgment within a short time limit or to give priority treatment to cases involving asylum, immigration, and/or matrimonial matters and matters of parental responsibility, European arrest warrants, and so on. In order to respond to those concerns, an urgent preliminary ruling procedure was established. It is governed by Article 23a of Protocol 3 and Article 104b of the Rules of Procedure of the ECJ. This procedure is additional to the expedited procedure (see Chapter 13.11).

Council Decision 2008/79/EC[828] amending Protocol No 3 on the Statute of the Court of Justice authorised the ECJ to introduce the urgent procedure enabling the Court to deal expeditiously and appropriately with requests for preliminary rulings in matters relating to the AFSJ. The procedure entered into force on 1 March 2008. It is difficult to list all cases in which the procedure will be used but Article 267(4) TFEU provides one example, i.e. the urgent preliminary ruling procedure is to be used in a situation where a case pending before a court or tribunal of a Member State concerns a person in custody or deprived of liberty and the answer to the question raised in the referral is decisive as to the assessment of that person's legal situation. Other examples are proceedings relating to parental authority or custody of children.[829]

---

827. The 2011 Annual Report of the CJEU, p. 10, available at http://curia.europa.eu/jcms/jcms/Jo2_7000 (accessed 26/6/12).

828. [2008] OJ L24/42.

829. See Case C-195/08 *PPU Inga Rinau* [2008] ECR I-5271) in which the ECJ, for the first time, rendered a judgment under the urgent procedure. The referral was made in proceedings between Mrs Rinau and Mr Rinau regarding the return to Germany of their daughter Luisa, who had been retained in Lithuania by Mrs Rinau. The ECJ was

The main features of the urgent preliminary ruling procedure are:

- In the written stage of the procedure only the parties to the main proceedings, the Member State of the court which has made the reference, the European Commission, and the Council and the EP (if either or both of them adopted the challenged measure) are entitled to make written submissions. These must be in the language of the case and made within a very short period of time of receipt of notice of the referral. Further in some cases the written procedure may be omitted. In the oral stage of the proceedings, other interested parties, in particular Member States other than that of the referring court, can make oral observations on the questions referred by the national court and on the written observations submitted by the authorised parties;

- A special Chamber within the ECJ screens and processes referrals made under the urgent procedure. If a preliminary ruling is dealt with under the urgent procedure, the Chamber will give its ruling shortly after the hearing, and after hearing the A-G;

- The procedure is, for the most part, carried out electronically. As far as possible, all procedural documents are allowed to be submitted and served by fax or e-mail; and,

- The ECJ may, on its own motion, decide to deal with a referral under the urgent procedure.

From 2008 until the end of 2011, 20 requests were made for the use of the urgent procedure of which 12 were approved. In 2011, the average duration of such proceedings was 2.5 months.[830]

13.5 National courts and tribunals that can refer to the ECJ under Article 267 TFEU

Article 267 TFEU specifies that only courts and tribunals may ask for preliminary rulings. This prevents the parties to a dispute referring directly to the ECJ. If a contract concluded between private parties specifies that any dispute on a point of EU law shall be referred to the ECJ, it will decline jurisdiction. Private parties cannot impose jurisdiction upon the ECJ.[831]

In most cases the question of whether a particular body is a court or a tribunal is self-evident although in some circumstances even a court recognised as such under national law may not be regarded as a court within the meaning of Article 267 TFEU (see Case C-96/04 *Standesamt Stadt Niebüll*[832] below). Uniformity in the application of EU law requires that the definition of a court or a tribunal for the purposes of Article 267 TFEU is independent of national concepts and has an autonomous, EU meaning. The case law of the ECJ has gradually determined the criteria for identifying a body which is a "court or a tribunal". It emerges from the case law, which was summarised by the ECJ in Case C-54/96 *Dorsch Consult*[833] (and therefore often referred to as the *Dorsch Consult* criteria) that the following criteria are relevant in determining whether a body making a reference is a court or tribunal for the purposes of Article 267 TFEU:

---

asked to interpret Council Regulation 2201/2003 on jurisdiction and the recognition and enforcement of judgments in matrimonial matters and on matters of parental responsibility. The referral was received at the ECJ on 14 May 2008 and the judgment was rendered less than two months later.

830. The 2011 Annual Report of the CJEU, 10. Available at http://curia.europa.eu/jcms/jcms/Jo2_7000 (accessed 26/6/12).
831. Case 44/65 *Hessische Knappschaft v Maison Singer and Sons* [1965] ECR 965; Case 93/78 *Lothar Mattheus v Doego Fruchtimport und Tiefkühlkost eG* [1978] ECR 2203.
832. Case C-96/04 *Criminal Proceedings against Standesamt Stadt Niebüll* [2006] ECR I-3561.
833. Case C-54/96 *Dorsch Consult Ingenieurgesellschaft mbH v Bundesbaugesellschaft Berlin mbH* [1997] ECR I-4961.

- Whether the body is established by law, i.e. it must not be established by private parties;

- Whether it is permanent, i.e. it must not exercise a judicial function only on an occasional basis;

- Whether its jurisdiction is compulsory, i.e. there must be no alternative remedies available to the parties;

- Whether its procedure is adversarial;

- Whether it applies rules of law rather than principles of fairness;

- Whether it is independent. The criterion of independence encompasses three requirements:

  - first, the body in question must act as a third party in relation to the parties to the dispute;
  - second, members of the body must enjoy the safeguards which ordinarily apply to judiciary in relation to removal from office and re-assignment, This is to ensure stability in the composition of the body and to prevent any external intervention or pressures from influencing the outcome of a dispute; and,
  - third, members of the body must have no interest in the outcome of the proceedings apart from the strict application of the rule of law;[834] and,

- Whether it is called upon to give a decision of a judicial nature.

The above criteria confirm that the ECJ has taken the so called "functional" approach to the determination of the meaning of "court or tribunal" under Article 267 TFEU, as opposed to the "literal" approach which would limit the possibility of making a reference to bodies actually called "court" or "tribunal" under national law. The functional approach is a mixed blessing. There are certainly two main advantages of the functional approach. First, more referrals reach the ECJ than would be the case under the literal approach with the result that EU law is more likely to be applied correctly and consistently in the Member States. Second, the functional approach may result in costs and time savings for the litigants. This may occur when appeals from bodies within the meaning of Article 267 TFEU are allowed to bodies regarded as "courts or tribunals" under national law in a situation where the sole purpose of an appeal would be to obtain a request for a preliminary ruling. Notwithstanding the advantages, the main drawback of the functional approach is that the ECJ may be overburdened with requests for preliminary rulings (see Chapter 13.11).

Under the functional approach the ECJ decided:

- In Case 61/65 *Vaassen-Göbbels*,[835] that a Dutch social security arbitration tribunal could refer since:

  - its members and the Chairman were appointed by the Dutch Minister for Social Affairs and Public Health who also laid down the rules of procedure;
  - it was a permanent body which settled disputes under Article 89 of the RBFM;[836]
  - the procedure was adversarial;

---

834. See Case C-506/04 *Graham J. Wilson v Ordre des avocats du barreau de Luxembourg* [2006] ECR I-8613.

835. Case 61/65 *G. Vaassen-Göbbels (a widow) v Management of the Beambtenfonds voor het Mijnbedrijf* [1966] ECR 261.

836. Reglement van het Beamtenfonds voor het Mijnbedrijf, the Regulation governing the relations between the social security authority and those insured by it.

- the jurisdiction of the social security arbitration tribunal was compulsory in all disputes involving the social security authority and the insurer; and,
- it was bound to apply rules of law and not equity.

■ In Case C-24/92 *Corbiau*,[837] that the director of taxation (Directeur des Contributions) in Luxembourg was not a court or tribunal and could not refer to the ECJ. This was because he was not independent as there was an institutional link between the Luxembourg tax authorities (which made the decision challenged by Corbiau) and the director of those authorities.

■ In Case 138/80 *Borker*,[838] that the Paris Conseil de l'Ordre des Avocats à la Cour de Paris (Paris Bar Council) was not a court or tribunal within the meaning of Article 267 TFEU because that body was not exercising any judicial function. In fact the body "made a request for a declaration relating to a dispute between a member of the Bar and the Courts or tribunals of another Member State".

■ In Case 246/80 *Broekmeulen*,[839] that the Appeals Committee for General Medicine, which was established by the Royal Netherlands Society for the Promotion of Medicine (and not considered as a court or tribunal under Dutch law), was a court or a tribunal for the following reasons:

- the national authorities appointed the chairman and one-third of the members of the Appeals Committee, so constituting a significant degree of involvement of The Netherlands public authorities in its composition;
- the procedure was adversarial;
- there was no appeal from the Appeals Committee to the courts; and,
- any general practitioner, whether Dutch or from another Member State, intending to establish himself/herself in The Netherlands, was compelled to have his/her status recognised by the Society. In the case of refusal the Appeals Committee was competent in the last resort to decide the question of his/her registration as a doctor.

■ In Case C-53/03 *Syfait*[840] that the Greek Competition Authority was not a court or tribunal as it was not an independent body because:

- the lawfulness of its decisions was, subject to some limitations, reviewed by the Minister for Development;
- its members, although independent in the exercise of their duties, could be dismissed or their appointment could be terminated without any special safeguards; and,
- it was not called upon to give a decision of a judicial nature.

■ In Case C-96/04 *Standesamt Stadt Niebüll*,[841] that a German local court (Amtsgericht) was not a court or tribunal within the meaning of Article 267 TFEU.

---

837. Case C-24/92 *Pierre Corbiau v Administration des Contributions* [1993] ECR I-1277.
838. Case 138/80 *Jules Borker* [1980] ECR 1975, para. 4.
839. Case 246/80 *C. Broekmeulen v Huisarts Registratie Commissie* [1981] ECR 2311.
840. C-53/03 *Synetairismos Farmakopoion Aitolias & Akarnanias (Syfait) and Others v GlaxoSmithKline plc and Others* [2005] ECR I-4609.
841. Case C-96/04 *Standesamt Stadt Niebüll* [2006] ECR I-3561.

THE FACTS WERE:

The German Registry Office brought proceedings before a local court in order to transfer the right to determine a child's surname to one of his parents. The child in question, Leonhard Matthias, was born in Denmark to a married couple Dorothee Paul and Stefan Grunkin, both German nationals. Under Danish law the child was given the double-barrelled surname composed of his father's and mother's surnames. The German authorities refused to recognise the child's surname on the ground that under German law a child is not allowed to bear a double-barrelled surname. The child's parents challenged that refusal before the German courts. Their action was dismissed at final instance by the German Constitutional Court. In the meantime the parents divorced, but refused to change their child's surname as required by German law. The Registrar's Office in Niebüll brought the matter before the local court, which decided to refer to the ECJ questions on the compatibility of the German law with Articles 18 and 21 TFEU.

Held:

The ECJ held that:

■ The referring court, although it was a court under German law, was not a court or tribunal within the meaning of Article 267 TFEU on the ground that the court was exercising administrative authority, without at the same time being called on to decide a dispute.

Comment:

There was no dispute before the local court leading to a decision of a judicial nature as the dispute between the parents and the German administrative authorities was settled at the last instance by the German Constitutional Court, and there was no dispute between the parents as they both refused to change their child's surname. This case emphasises the importance of the functional criterion in the determination of the concept of "court or tribunal" in that an entity which is entitled to refer to the ECJ must exercise a judicial function, i.e. must be required to give a decision of a judicial nature. Similarly, in Case C-497/08 Amiraike Berlin GmbH,[842] the ECJ refused a referral from the Amtsgericht Charlottenburg, a German court recognised as such under German law, when it was exercising administrative functions consisting of the appointment of the liquidator of a company, without any dispute being raised before it and thus without being called to give a decision of a judicial nature.

■ In Case 14/86 *Pretore di Salò*,[843] an Italian Pretore, a magistrate who initially acts as a public prosecutor and then as an examining magistrate, and thus exercises not only a judicial function but also other tasks, was found to be a court or tribunal for the purposes of Article 267 TFEU. The ECJ accepted the referral on the ground that the request emanated from a body that acted in the general framework of its task of judging, independently and in accordance with the law,

---

842. [2010] ECR I-101, see also Case C-78/99 *Salzmann* [2001] ECR I-4421 in which an Austrian district court acting as a land registry, i.e. carrying out an administrative function, was not regarded as a court or tribunal within the meaning of Article 267 TFEU.

843. Case 14/86 *Pretore di Salò v Persons Unknown* [1987] ECR 2545.

despite the fact that certain functions performed by that body were not strictly speaking of a judicial nature.[844]

■ In Joined Case C-74/95 and C-129/95 *Criminal Procedures against X*,[845] the ECJ refused to accept a referral from an Italian public prosecutor. Advocate General Ruiz Jarabo Colomer stressed that the main task of the Procura della Repubblica (the Italian Public Prosecutor) is to submit evidence during the trial and thus it is a party to the proceedings. Further, it does not exercise judicial functions and as such should not be regarded as a court or a tribunal under Article 267 TFEU.

13.5.1 The distinction between private and public arbitration

The ECJ makes a distinction between private and public arbitration.

With regard to private arbitration, the ECJ has been consistent in rejecting referrals from private arbitrators. In Case 102/81 *Nordsee*[846] the ECJ explained that a private arbitrator will not be recognised as a court or tribunal within the meaning of Article 267 TFEU when first, the parties to a private contract freely selected arbitration as a way of resolving any dispute between them, and second, public authorities were involved neither in the choice of arbitration by the parties, nor were they "called to intervene automatically in proceedings before the arbitrator". The ECJ emphasised that if private arbitration raises questions concerning EU law, national courts may have jurisdiction to examine those questions:

■ in the framework of assistance they provide for arbitral tribunals, especially in the context of certain judicial measures which are not available to the arbitrator; or

■ when determining and interpreting the law applicable to the contract under consideration; or

■ within the framework of control which they exercise in relation to arbitration awards.[847]

If public authorities are involved in arbitration, the situation is very different from that concerning private arbitration. For example, in Case 109/88 *HKFD*,[848] a Danish Industrial Arbitration Board was recognised as a court or tribunal within the meaning of Article 267 TFEU because its jurisdiction was imposed upon the parties if they could not agree on the application of a collective agreement; its composition and procedure were governed by Danish law; and, its award was final.

13.6 Preliminary rulings on the interpretation of EU law: the distinction between discretionary and compulsory reference by courts and tribunals to the ECJ

There are two possible approaches to ensuring uniformity in the application of EU law:

■ The first, consisting of compulsory referrals to the ECJ each time a national court or tribunal has difficulties with the interpretation of EU law. This would be inconvenient in terms of the duration of proceedings and the heavy workload imposed upon the ECJ.

---

844. Confirmed in Case 318/85 *Regina Greis Unterweger* [1986] ECR 955; Case C-393/92 *Municipality of Almelo and others v NV Energiebedrijf Ijsselmij* [1994] ECR I-1477.
845. Joined Cases C-74/95 and C-129/95 *Criminal Procedures against X* [1996] ECR I-6609.
846. Case 102/81 *Nordsee Deutsche Hochseefischerei GmbH v Reederei Mond* [1982] ECR 1095, para. 12.
847. Case C-393/92 *Municipality of Almelo and others v NV Energiebedrijf Ijsselmij* [1994] ECR I-1477 and Case C-126/97 *Eco Swiss China Time v Benetton International* [1999] ECR I-3055.
848. 109/88 *Handels-og Kontorfunktionaererernes Forbund I Danmark (HKFD) v Dansk Arbejdsgiverforening* [1989] ECR 3199.

■ The second, consisting of granting an unlimited discretion to national courts and tribunals (whatever their position in the hierarchy of the national judicial system) as to whether or not to refer to the ECJ. However, to grant such discretion to national courts and tribunals would jeopardise the homogeneity of EU law.

EU law rejected both of these approaches with Article 267 TFEU representing a compromise between them. Accordingly, national courts or tribunals against whose decisions there is no judicial remedy under national law "shall bring" a question of interpretation of EU law before the ECJ, while other national courts or tribunals have unfettered discretion in matters of referrals.

The idea behind this compromise is that, on the one hand, in the case of obviously wrong decisions of lower courts on a point of EU law, an appeal to a superior court will rectify that mistake. On the other, the obligation to refer imposed on the courts of last resort will prevent a body of national law, that is, not in accordance with EU law, from being established in a Member State.[849]

13.6.1 Discretion of national courts and tribunals to refer: Article 267(2) TFEU

Lower courts within the meaning of Article 267(2) TFEU have an unfettered discretion to refer to the ECJ. Article 267 TFEU recognises the exclusive jurisdiction of national courts to decide whether and when to refer.

A national judge has the sole discretion as to whether to refer. The ECJ has emphasised many times that national courts have the best knowledge of the case and that, taking into account their responsibility for rendering correct judgments, they, alone, are competent to assess the relevance of the question of EU law raised in the dispute and the necessity of obtaining a preliminary ruling.[850] Neither the parties to the dispute, nor their legal representatives, nor any other public authorities, which under certain national legal systems may interfere in the proceedings, can force a national court to refer. Further, a national judge may decide to refer even if the parties to the dispute have not raised the issue,[851] or not to refer even if so requested by one of them,[852] or by both as in Joined Cases C-320/94 and C-328/94 *Reti Televise Italiana*.[853] In Case C-85/95 *J Reisdorf*,[854] the ECJ held that parties may not challenge as irrelevant to the dispute a question referred by a national judge to the ECJ.

National procedural rules cannot impose restrictions on the court's discretion to make a referral. In Joined Cases 146/73 and 166/73 *Rheinmühlen*,[855] the ECJ emphasised that "a rule of national law whereby a court is bound on points of law by the rulings of a superior court cannot on this ground alone deprive the inferior courts of their power, provided for under Article [267 TFEU],

---

849. Case C-393/98 *Ministério Público and Antonio Gomes Valente v Fazenda Pública* [2001] ECR I-1327; Case C-99/00 *Criminal Proceedings against Kenny Roland Lyckeskog* [2002] ECR I-4839; Case C-495/03 *Intermodal Transports BV v Staatssecretaris van Financiën* [2005] ECR I-8151.

850. For example in Case 53/79 *ONPTS v Damiani* [1980] ECR 273; Case 26/62 *Van Gend en Loos* [1963] ECR 3.

851. Case 126/80 *Maria Salonia v Giorgio Poidomani and Franca Baglieri, née Giglio* [1981] ECR 1563.

852. Case C-152/94 *Geert Van Buynder* [1995] ECR I-3981.

853. Joined Cases C-320/94 and C-328/94 *Reti Televisive Italiane SpA and Others v Ministero delle Poste e Telecomunicazioni* [1996] ECR I-6471.

854. Case C-85/95 *John Reisdorf v Finanzamt Köln-West* [1996] ECR I-6257.

855. Joined Cases 146/73 and 166/73 *Rheinmühlen-Düsseldorf v Einfuhr- und Vorratsstelle für Getreide und Futtermittel* [1974] ECR 139, para. 3; see also Case C-312/93 *Peterbroeck, Van Campenhout & Cie SCS v Belgium* [1995] ECR I-4599; Case C-173/09 *Georgi Ivanov Elchinov v Natsionalna Zdravnoosiguritelna Kasa* [2010] ECR I-8889.

to refer questions to the Court for a preliminary ruling".[856] However, it is outside the jurisdiction of the ECJ to verify whether the decision to refer was taken in conformity with national procedural rules.[857]

National courts may refer a question at any stage of the proceedings. The ECJ, in Case 70/77 *Simmenthal*,[858] held that the proper administration of justice requires that a question should not be referred prematurely. However, it is outside the jurisdiction of the ECJ to specify at which particular point of the proceedings the national courts should ask for preliminary rulings.[859] In order to facilitate the tasks of national courts and tribunals, the ECJ issued an Information Note on References from National Courts for a Preliminary Ruling.[860]

From the perspective of the ECJ, it has stated on many occasions that where the questions submitted concern the interpretation of EU law, the Court is in principle bound to give a ruling.[861] Once the ECJ is seised by the referring court, it has jurisdiction to give a ruling until the withdrawal of the reference by the referring court.[862] In Case C-194/94 *CIA*,[863] the ECJ rejected the submission of the original parties that a modification of national law applicable to the dispute, subsequent to the referral, rendered the preliminary ruling unnecessary. The ECJ held that this question should be assessed by the referring court, which was solely competent to decide whether or not a preliminary ruling was still required in order to enable it to give judgment. In Case 31/68 *Chanel*,[864] the ECJ held that, when in a matter of which it is seised it is informed by the referring court, or the superior court, that an appeal has been lodged in the national court against the national decision, proceedings in the case before the ECJ should be postponed until the decision of the referring court is confirmed by a superior court, or overturned, in which case the ECJ must set aside the proceedings under Article 267 TFEU.

It emerges from the case law that the ECJ's acceptance or rejection of a request for a preliminary ruling will depend on:

- the relevance of the referred question to the dispute at issue;

- whether the referring court has properly determined the factual and legal context of the dispute; and,

- whether the question referred is general or hypothetical.

It is uncertain whether the requirement that there must be a genuine dispute between the parties to the main proceedings is still relevant (see below).

---

856. See also Case C-210/06 *Cartesio Oktató és Szolgáltató bt* [2008] ECR I-9641.

857. Case 65/81 *Francesco Reina and Letizia Reina v Landeskreditbank Baden-Württemberg* [1982] ECR 33; Case C-10/92 *Maurizio Balocchi v Ministero delle Finanze dello Stato* [1993] ECR I-5105, affirmed in Case C-39/94 *SFEI and Others v La Poste and Others* [1996] ECR I-3547.

858. Case 70/77 *Simmenthal SpA v Amministrazione delle Finanze* [1978] ECR 1453.

859. Joined Cases 36 and 71/80 *Irish Creamery Milk Suppliers Association* [1981] ECR 735; Case 72/83 *Campus Oil Limited and others v Minister for Industry and Energy and Others* [1984] ECR 2727.

860. [2009] OJ C297/1.

861. Case C-326/00 *IKA v Vasillos Ioannidis* [2003] ECR I-1703; Case C-145/03 *Heirs of Annette Keller v INSS and Ingesa* [2005] ECR I-2529; Case C-419/04 *Conseil Général de la Vienne v Directeur Général des Douanes et Droits Indirect* [2006] ECR I-5645.

862. Case 106/77 *Amministrazione delle Finanze dello Stato v Simmenthal SpA* [1978] ECR 629.

863. Case C-194/94 *CIA Security International SA, Signalson SA et Secutitel SA*, [1996] ECR I-2201.

864. Case 31/68 *SA Chanel v Cepeha Handelsmaatschappij NV* [1970] ECR 403. Ord.

13.6.1.1 Existence of a genuine dispute

In Case 104/79 *Foglia v Novello*,[865] the ECJ refused to give a preliminary ruling on the ground that there was no genuine dispute between the parties to national proceedings.

THE FACTS WERE:

Foglia, an Italian wine merchant, entered into a contract with Novello, an Italian national, for the delivery of liqueur wine to a person residing in France. The parties inserted an express clause providing that Novello would not pay any unlawfully levied taxes. The French authorities imposed a tax on the importation of the wine to France, which Foglia paid, although his contract with a shipper also provided that he should not be liable for any charges imposed in breach of the free movement of goods. Foglia brought proceedings against Novello, who refused to reimburse the French tax levied on Foglia.

Held:

The ECJ declined to exercise jurisdiction on the ground that there was no real dispute in the case. It held that:

"It . . . appears that the parties to the main action are concerned to obtain a ruling that the French tax system is invalid for liqueur wine by the expedient of proceedings before an Italian court between two private individuals who are in agreement as to the result to be obtained and who have inserted a clause in their contract in order to induce the Italian court to give a ruling on the point. The artificial nature of this expedient is underlined by the fact that Foglia did not exercise its rights under French law to institute proceedings over the consumption tax although it undoubtedly has an interest in doing so in view of the clause in the contract by which it was bound and moreover by the fact that Foglia paid the duty without protest."[866]

Comment:

Both parties had the same interest in the outcome of the dispute. This was to obtain a ruling on the invalidity or otherwise of the French legislation, since under their contracts they were not liable to pay for any unlawful charges imposed by France. Their action was a collusive and artificial device aimed at obtaining a ruling and not a genuine dispute which the ECJ could settle.

When the Italian court subsequently asked the ECJ to provide clarification of its preliminary judgment in Case 104/79 *Foglia v Novello*, the ECJ accepted the second reference but once again declined, on the same grounds,[867] to give a preliminary ruling.

The ruling in *Foglia v Novello* was much criticised[868] and seems to have been overruled. In Case C-412/93 *Leclerc-Siplec*[869] the ECJ accepted a referral when parties to the main proceedings "organised"

865. Case 104/79 *Foglia v Novello* [1980] ECR 745.
866. Ibid, para. 10.
867. Case 244/80 *Foglia v Novello II* [1981] ECR 3045.
868. See E. Bebr, "The Possible Implications of Foglia v Novello II", (1982) 19 CMLRev. , 421; D. Wyatt, "Foglia (No. 2): The Court Denies it Has Jurisdiction to Give Advisory Opinions", (1982) 7 ELRev., 186.
869. C-412/93 *Leclerc-Siplec v TF1 and M6* [1995] ECR I-179.

proceedings before a national court leading to the reference for a preliminary ruling (as was the case in *Foglia*), i.e there was no real dispute as they agreed that national law was contrary to EU law, and the only purpose of the proceedings was to obtain a preliminary ruling on incompatibility of national law with EU law. The only difference between the situation in Case C-412/93 *Leclerc-Siplec* and that in *Foglia v Novello* was that the parties in *Leclerc-Siplec* challenged the compatibility of French law with EU law before a French court whilst in *Foglia v Novello* the parties challenged the compatibility of French law with EU law before an Italian court. However, in Case C-150/88 *Provide*[870] the ECJ accepted a referral from a German court, despite the fact that the compatibility of Italian law with EU law was at issue. Thus, it seems that the scope of *Foglio and Novello* is very limited, if not overruled by subsequent cases. This is even more evident in the light of the ECJ's ruling in Case C-144/04 *Mangold*[871] (see Chapter 10.5), in which Mr Mangold, who worked for Mr Helm, a practising lawyer in Germany, brought proceedings against his employer on the ground that his employment contract was contrary to Directive 2000/78 which prohibits discrimination based on age. The German government argued that the dispute was fictitious or contrived in the light of the fact that in the past Mr Helm had publicly argued a case identical to Mr Mangold's, to the effect that the challenged German law was in breach of the EU directive. Despite this, the ECJ accepted the referral. Finally, in most recent preliminary rulings the ECJ has not mentioned the existence of a genuine dispute as a ground for inadmissibility of a referral. For example in Case C-310/10 *Agafiței*,[872] the ECJ held:

> "The Court may refuse to rule on a question referred for a preliminary ruling by a national court only where it is quite obvious that the interpretation of European Union law that is sought bears no relation to the actual facts of the main action or its purpose, where the problem is hypothetical, or where the Court does not have before it the factual or legal material necessary to enable it to give a useful answer to the questions submitted to it."

13.6.1.2   Relevance of a referred question to the main dispute

The relevance of a referred question to the actual dispute was for the first time clearly assessed in Case 126/80 *Salonia*.[873] In this case, the ECJ held that a request for a preliminary ruling may be rejected if the question referred is not relevant to the actual case. However, that was not so in this case.

Subsequently, the ECJ declined its jurisdiction to answer a question which had no connection with the subject matter of the main action,[874] or as the ECJ held in Case C-18/93 *Corsica Ferries*,[875] which "does not respond to the objective need to resolve the main action", or to assess the validity of EU acts which do not apply to a particular dispute.[876]

The above approach is mitigated by the ability of the ECJ to reformulate the question referred by a national court,[877] or to take into consideration a provision of EU law which the national court did not

---

870. Case C-150/88 *Kommanditgesellschaft in Firma Eau de Cologne & Parfümerie-Fabrik, Glockengasse n. 4711 v Provide Srl* [1989] ECR 3891.
871. C-144/04 *Mangold v Helm* [2005] ECR I-9981.
872. Case C-310/10 *Ministerul Justisiei si Libertatilor Cetatenesti v Stefan Agafitei* (judgment of 7/7/11(NYR)), para. 27.
873. Case 126/80 *Maria Salonia v Giorgio Poidomani and Franca Baglieri, née Giglio* [1981] ECR 1563.
874. Case C-343/90 *Manuel José Lourenço Dias v Director da Alfândega do Porto* [1992] ECR I-4673; Cases C-332, 333 and 335/92 *Eurico Italia Srl, Viazzo Srl and F & P SpA v Ente Nazionale Risi* [1994] ECR I-711.
875. Case C-18/93 *Corsica Ferries Italia Srl v Corpo dei Piloti del Porto di Genova* [1994] ECR I-1783, para. 14.
876. Case C-297/93 *Rita Grau-Hupka v Stadtgemeinde Bremen* [1994] ECR I-5535.
877. Case 35/85 *Procureur de la République v Gérard Tissier* [1986] ECR 1207; Case C-315/92 *Verband Sozialer Wettbewerb eV v Clinique Laboratoires SNC and Estée Lauder Cosmetics GmbH* [1994] ECR I-317.

mention in its referral.[878] Furthermore, in Case C-67/96 *Albany*[879] and in Joined Cases C-115/97 to C-117/97 and Case C-357/97 *Brentjevis*[880] the ECJ stated that there is a presumption that a referred question is relevant to the main dispute.

13.6.1.3 Determination of the factual and legal context of the dispute

A request for a preliminary ruling should state:

▪ All the relevant facts with clarity and precision;

▪ The legal context of the dispute; and,

▪ The reasons which compelled the judge to ask for a referral and the arguments submitted by the parties to the dispute.[881]

The ECJ has underlined that a well-drafted referral contributes to a better comprehension of the factual and legal context of the dispute and thus assists the Member States and the EU institutions in the preparation of their observations, and the ECJ in giving a useful reply.

In early cases the ECJ held that it was not its task to verify the facts and the qualification of the legal nature of the referred question.[882] In later cases the ECJ declined to exercise its jurisdiction for lack of relevant information.[883] More recent cases demonstrate that the insufficient contextualisation of a dispute will lead to the rejection of referrals as being manifestly inadmissible.[884]

The strict requirement of contextualisation of a dispute is of lesser importance in areas in which the facts are not that essential, for example, if the referred question concerns the validity of EU acts. In Case C-295/94 *Hüpeden*[885] and Case C-296/94 *Pietsch*[886] a national court formulated the referred question in very lucid but very brief terms – is provision X of Regulation Y valid? The ECJ accepted the referral. In Case C-316/93 *Vaneetveld*,[887] the ECJ held that, despite insufficient information submitted by the national court on the legal and factual context of the dispute (which was less essential in this case as the subject-matter concerned technical points), it was able to formulate a useful reply.

It is interesting to note that the facts of a case, as described by a national court, have been accepted by the ECJ even though they may be inexact or even erroneous. This occurred in Case C-352/95

---

878. Case C-151/93 *Voogd Vleesimport en Export BV* [1994] ECR I-4915.

879. Case C-67/96 *Albany International BV v Stichting Bedrijfspensioenfonds Textielindustrie* [1999] ECR I-5751.

880. Joined Cases C-115/97 to C-117/97 *Brentjens' Handelsonderneming BV v Stichting Bedrijfspensioenfonds voor de Handel in Bouwmaterialen* [1999] ECR I-6025.

881. See para. 21–24 of the 2009 Information Note, supra note 860.

882. Case 20/64 *SARL Albatros v SOPECO* [1965] ECR 29; Case 5/77 *Carlo Tedeschi v Denkavit Commerciale S.R.L* [1977] ECR 1555.

883. Joined Cases C-320–322/90 *Telemarsicabruzzo Spa and others v Circostel, Ministero delle Poste e Telecommunicazioni and Ministero della Difesa* [1993] ECR I-393.

884. For example, the ECJ issued an order of manifest inadmissibility of referrals for lack of information in Case C-378/93 *La Pyramide SARL* [1994] ECR I-3999; Case C-458/93 *Mostafa Saddik* [1995] ECR I-511; Case C-167/94 *Criminal Proceedings against Juan Carlos Grau Gomis and Others* [1995] ECR I-1023; Case C-307/95 *Max Mara Fashion Group S. r. l v Ufficio del Registro di Reggio Emilia* [1995] ECR I-5083; Case C-101/96 *Italia Testa* [1996] ECR I-3081; Case C-191/96 *M Modesti* [1996] ECR I-3937; Case C-196/96 *Lahlou Hassa* [1996] ECR I-3945; Case C-158/99 *Corticeira Amorim-Algarve Ltd*, order of 2/7/1999 (unpublished).

885. C-295/94 *Hüpeden & Co. KG v Hauptzollamt Hamburg-Jonas* [1996] ECR I-3375.

886. Case C-296/94 *Bernhard Pietsch v Hauptzollamt Hamburg-Waltershof* [1996] ECR I-3409.

887. Case C-316/93 *Nicole Vaneetveld v Le Foyer SA and Le Foyer SA v FMSS* [1994] ECR I-763.

Phytheron[888] and in Case C-223/95 *Moksel.*[889] The explanation of the ECJ is that the separation of functions between national courts and the ECJ within the framework of Article 267 TFEU requires that it is the task of a national court to determine the particular factual circumstances of each case, and the ECJ has jurisdiction solely to give a ruling on the interpretation and the validity of EU law on the basis of the facts submitted by the national court.

13.6.1.4 Hypothetical or general questions

In Case 93/78 *Mattheus*,[890] the ECJ declined to exercise its jurisdiction because the referred question concerned not the interpretation of EU law in force, but the opinion of the Court on the enactment of future laws. The ECJ has also refused to answer general or hypothetical questions.[891]

13.6.2 Mandatory referral by national courts of last resort: Article 267(3) TFEU

The ECJ has clarified the exact meaning of Article 267(3) TFEU, which states that if a question of interpretation of EU law "is raised in a case pending before a court or tribunal of a Member State, against whose decision there is no judicial remedy under national law, the court or tribunal shall bring the matter before the Court".

13.6.2.1 Definition of "courts or tribunals" against whose decision there is no judicial remedy

The ECJ decided that the concept of courts "against whose decision there is no judicial remedy under national law" (that is, under national law there is no right of appeal against their decisions) comprises not only final appellate courts in each Member State, but also all courts which decide a case in the last instance. In Case 6/64 *Costa v ENEL*,[892] the Giudice Conciliatore in Milan was the court of last instance because of the small sum of money involved in the dispute, that is, £1 which Costa refused to pay. This demonstrates that any court or tribunal against whose decision in a given case there is no judicial remedy falls within the scope of Article 267(3) TFEU, although in other cases an appeal would be possible against decisions of that court and tribunal.

The uncertainty as to whether a national court, against whose decision an appeal is possible, but only on leave to appeal being granted by a higher court or the lower court itself, is a "final court", within the meaning of Article 267 TFEU, was answered in Case C-99/00 *Kenny Roland Lyckeskog.*[893] In this case the Swedish Court of Appeal was uncertain whether it was a court of last resort in a situation where an appeal against its judgments was possible in three situations only: first, only in "special circumstances", second, when a judgment of it raised an issue of importance such that the Supreme Court's decision would be necessary in order to provide guidance for other Swedish courts, and third, when there had been manifest negligence or serious error in its decision. It was clear from the facts of the case that leave to appeal was unlikely to be granted. The ECJ held that the fact that the Swedish Supreme Court examines appeals only in special circumstances did not transform the Court of Appeal into a court of

888. Case C-352/95 *Phytheron International SA v Jean Bourdon SA* [1997] ECR I-1729.
889. Case C-223/95 *A. Moksel AG v Hauptzollamt Hamburg-Jonas* [1997] ECR I-2379.
890. Case 93/78 *Lothar Mattheus v Doego Fruchtimport und Tiefkühlkost eG* [1978] ECR I-2203.
891. Case C-467/04 *Criminal Proceedings against Gasparini and Others* [2006] ECR I-9199.
892. [1964] ECR 614.
893. Case C-99/00 *Criminal Proceedings against Kenny Roland Lyckeskog* [2002] ECR I-4839.

last resort. The ECJ held that the Swedish Supreme Court when it considers the admissibility of an appeal concerning EU law will be under an obligation to refer under Article 267 TFEU either at the admissibility stage or at a later stage. The judgment in *Lyckeskog* was confirmed in Case C-210/06 *Cartesio*,[894] in which the ECJ held that the Regional Court of Appeal in Hungary, whose decisions were subject to "extraordinary" appeals to the Hungarian Supreme Court, was not a court of final resort given that appeals from its judgments were available even if only in limited circumstances. Accordingly, any lower court cannot be regarded as the final court unless the lower court itself decides whether to grant leave and its decision is final.

13.6.2.2 Conditions relating to mandatory reference by national courts of last resort

At first glance, it seems that the terms of Article 267(3) TFEU are imperative and that they impose an obligation upon the courts of last instance to ask for a preliminary ruling each time the interpretation of EU law is at issue. This impression is, however, not correct, in that the ECJ has, over the years, come to recognise three exceptions.

In Joined Cases 28–30/62 *Da Costa*,[895] the ECJ held that Article 267(3) TFEU "unreservedly" requires the courts of last resort to refer, but recognised the first exception, i.e. that it is not necessary to refer if the ECJ has already interpreted the same question in an earlier case since "the authority of an interpretation under Article 234 [Article 267 TFEU] already given by the Court may deprive the obligation [to refer] from its purpose and thus empty it of its substance". Such is the case especially when the question raised is materially identical to a question which has already been the subject of a preliminary ruling. Even so, the ECJ may still accept such a reference, as exemplified in *Da Costa* where the question asked was identical to that raised in Case 26/62 *Van Gend*.[896]

The second exception was recognised in Case 83/78 *Pigs Marketing Board*[897] in which the ECJ held that the court should assess the relevance of the question raised before it in the light of the necessity to obtain a preliminary ruling.

The above two exceptions were restated and a third exception was developed in Case 283/81 *CILFIT*[898] in which the extent of the discretion of courts of last resort was fully explained.

THE FACTS WERE:

The Italian Ministry of Health imposed a fixed health inspection levy on imports of wool coming from other Member States. An Italian importer of wool challenged the levy. The Italian court considered that the case law on this matter was reasonably clear, but as a court of final instance, it was uncertain whether or not it should refer the question of the legality of this levy to the ECJ. The Italian court asked the ECJ whether it was obliged to refer under Article 267 TFEU when EU law was sufficiently clear and precise and there were no doubts as to its interpretation.

---

894. Case C-210/06 *Cartesio Oktató és Szolgáltató bt* [2008] ECR I-9641.
895. Joined Cases 28-30/62 *Da Costa en Schaake NV, Jacob Meijer NV, Hoechst-Holland NV v Netherlands Inland Revenue Administration* [1963] ECR 31.
896. [1963] ECR 3.
897. Case 83/78 *Pigs Marketing Board v Raymond Redmond* [1978] ECR 2347.
898. Case 283/81 *Srl CILFIT and Lanificio di Gavardo SpA v Ministry of Health* [1982] ECR 3415.

Held:

The ECJ held that:

■ *The courts of last resort, like any other courts or tribunals, have the discretion to assess whether a referral is necessary to enable them to give judgment. They are not obliged to refer if a question concerning the interpretation of EU law raised before them is not relevant to the dispute, that is, if it can in no way affect the outcome of the case.*

■ *The principle set out in* Da Costa *applies. Accordingly, if the ECJ has already dealt with a point of law at issue, even though the questions are not strictly identical, the court of last resort is not obliged to refer.*

■ *There is no obligation to refer if "the correct application of Community law [EU law] may be so obvious as to leave no scope for any reasonable doubt as to the manner in which the question raised is to be resolved. However, before it comes to the conclusion that such is the case, the national court or tribunal must be convinced that the matter is equally obvious to the courts of the other Member States and to the Court of Justice (ECJ)."*[899]

In *CILFIT* the ECJ endorsed the French doctrine of *acte clair.* According to that doctrine, the court before which the *exception prejudicielle* (a question concerning the interpretation of a particular provision) is raised, must refer it to a competent court in order to resolve that question, but only if there is real difficulty concerning its interpretation, or if there is a serious doubt in this respect. Having said this, if the provision in question is clear, and if its meaning is obvious, the court should apply it immediately.

It stems from *CILFIT* that it is not necessary for a court of last resort to refer to the ECJ:

■ If the question of EU law is irrelevant to the dispute;

■ If the question of EU law has already been interpreted by the ECJ even though it may not be identical. However, this does not mean that national courts, whatever their position in the hierarchy of national courts, are prevented from referring an identical or a similar question to the ECJ. In *CILFIT* the ECJ clearly stated that all courts remain entirely at liberty to refer a matter before them if they consider it appropriate to do so; and,

■ If the correct application of EU law is so obvious as to leave no scope for reasonable doubt. This follows from the French doctrine of *acte clair.* However, the ECJ added that before a national court concludes that such is the case, it must be convinced that the question is equally obvious to courts in other Member States and to the ECJ itself. Furthermore, the ECJ added three requirements, which a national court must take into consideration, when deciding whether the matter is clear and free of doubts. These are:

● It must assess whether the matter is equally obvious to the courts of the other Member States in the light of the characteristic features of EU law and especially the difficulties that its interpretation raises, that is, that it is drafted in several languages and all versions are equally authentic;

---

899.   Ibid, para. 16.

- It must be aware that EU law uses peculiar terminology and has legal concepts which have different meanings in different Member States; and,
- It must bear in mind that every provision of EU law must be placed in its context and interpreted in the light of the provisions of EU law as a whole, its objectives, and the state of its evolution at the date on which that provision is to be applied.

With regard to courts within the scope of Article 267(2) TFEU the ruling in *CILFIT* assists them in deciding whether to refer, while under Article 267(3) TFEU it imposes a duty on courts of last resort to refer to the ECJ if there are any reasonable doubts as to the meaning of a provision of EU law.

13.6.2.3   Mechanisms ensuring that courts and tribunals of final resort refer to the ECJ when the conditions set out in CILFIT are not satisfied

The endorsement by the ECJ of the doctrine of *acte clair* has sensibly extended the discretion of the courts of last resort. It has also increased the risk of conflicting decisions being rendered by the highest courts in each Member State. On many occasions national courts have decided not to refer to the ECJ on the basis of this doctrine and have imposed their own interpretation of EU law, and have thus prevented the ECJ from expressing its views.[900] There are, however, two mechanisms under EU law ensuring that courts of final resort refer to the ECJ when the conditions set out in *CILFIT* are not satisfied.

First, the ECJ in its judgment in Case C-224/01 *Köbler*[901] (for facts see Chapter 12.4) clearly established that a Member State may be liable for loss or damage caused to an individual if its courts of final instance fail to refer a case to the ECJ for a preliminary ruling. This certainly curbs the tendency of such courts to abuse the doctrine of *acte clair*.[902] In *Köbler* the acknowledgment of the principle of State liability for judicial decisions of a national court adjudicating at last instance came as no surprise. This is so given previous judgments of the ECJ, in particular in Joined Cases C-46 and 48/93 *Brasserie du Pêcheur and Factortame*,[903] and in Case C-392/93 *British Telecommunications*.[904]

In *Köbler* the ECJ made a very important clarification as to State liability for loss or damage caused to an individual by a decision of a national court adjudicating at last instance. It held that non-compliance by the court in question with its obligation to make a reference for a preliminary ruling under the third paragraph of Article 267 TFEU constituted one of the decisive factors in determining whether or not the breach of EU law was sufficiently serious as to justify the award of damages to the applicants. In this respect, A-G Léger in his Opinion went further. He emphasised the role that this obligation plays in the

---

900. For example, in *R v Secretary of State for the Home Department (ex parte Sandhu)* ([1982] 2 CMLR 553) the House of Lords refused to refer to the ECJ, although the question whether a divorced Indian husband of a British national, who was threatened with deportation from the UK, was entitled to stay in the UK on the basis of Directive 68/360 was far from being clear and free of doubts at that time. See A. Arnull, "The Use and Abuse of Art.177EC", (1989) 52 MLR 622.

901. Case C-224/01 *Gerhard Köbler v Austria* [2003] ECR I-10239.

902. See H. Scott and N. W. Barber, "State Liability under Francovich for Decisions of National Courts", (2004) 120 LQR 403; and A. A. S. Zuckerman, "Appeals to the High Court against House of Lords Decisions on the Interpretation of Community Law – Damages for Judicial Error", (2004) 23 CJQ, 8.

903. Joined Cases C-46 and 48/93 *Brasserie du Pêcheur SA v Bundesrepublik Deutschland and The Queen v Secretary of State for Transport, ex parte Factortame Ltd and Others* [1996] ECR I-1029.

904. Case C-392/93 *The Queen v H.M. Treasury, ex parte British Telecommunications plc* [1996] ECR I-1631; see also Case C-302/97 *Klaus Konle v Austria* [1999] ECR I-3099 and Case C-424/97 *Salomone Haim v Kassenzahnärztliche Vereinigung Nordrhein* [2000] ECR I-5123.

exercise of the right to obtain a judicial determination in the light of Article 6(1) of the ECHR. According to him:

> "the obligation to make a reference for a preliminary ruling tends to form part of the analysis of the 'right to challenge a measure before the courts' (or the 'right to obtain a judicial determination'). According to the settled case-law of the European Court of Human Rights, although [t]he right to have a preliminary question referred to . . . the Court of Justice is not absolute . . ., it is not completely impossible that, in certain circumstances, refusal by a domestic court trying a case at final instance might infringe the principle of fair trial, as set forth in Article 6(1) of the Convention, in particular where such refusal appears arbitrary."[905]

Although the ECJ did not refer to Article 6(1) of the ECHR in the context of the duty of a national court to make a reference for a preliminary ruling as explained in *CILFIT*, the Court did, nevertheless, in this case reinforce this obligation in respect of a supreme court deciding a case at last instance. However, with the accession of the EU to the ECHR, the argument of A-G Léger regains its full strength.

Second, a close link between Article 267(3) TFEU and Article 258 TFEU (see Chapter 14.2) entails that when a national court or tribunal of last resort erroneously interprets EU law the Commission may start proceedings under Article 258 TFEU against the Member State concerned for a breach of EU law. The best example is provided by the ECJ's judgment in Case C-154/08 *Commission v Spain*[906] (this is examined in depth in Chapter 14.2.2.3), in which the ECJ held that Spain was in breach of EU law when its supreme court made an error of law by incorrectly interpreting the Sixth VAT Directive (the supreme court had no doubt as to the correct interpretation of the Directive and thus did not make a referral to the ECJ for a preliminary ruling). It is clear from this case that national law, including a national constitution, cannot shield a Member State from incurring liability when its supreme court commits errors in interpreting EU law.

13.7 Effects of preliminary rulings on the interpretation of EU law

Three issues arise with regard to the effects of preliminary rulings concerning the interpretation of EU law: first the legal effect of a preliminary ruling with regard to the referring court, second, the temporal effect of a preliminary ruling and third the implications of retroactive effect of a preliminary ruling on the finality of a decisions of a national administrative body or a national court.

13.7.1 Effects of a preliminary ruling with regard to the referring court

The Treaties are silent on the legal effect of preliminary rulings concerning the interpretation of EU law. In Joined Cases 28–30/62 *Da Costa*,[907] the ECJ defined the legal effects of preliminary rulings. It stated that the referring court is bound by the interpretation given by the ECJ, both in reply to the question and when the referring court decides an identical question.

The *ratio legis* (the underlying principle) of proceedings under Article 267 TFEU requires that the preliminary ruling is taken into consideration by the referring court. However, this obligation is limited. Only if the ruling permits the referring court to resolve the dispute at issue is such a ruling binding on

---

905.   Case C-224/01 *Gerhard Köbler v Austria* [2003] ECR I-10239, para. 147.
906.   [2009] ECR I-187.
907.   [1963] ECR 31.

it. In any event, the referring court may refer the same question in a second referral as happened in *Foglia v Novello (No 2)*.[908]

It may occur, however, that a referring court ignores a preliminary ruling of the ECJ.[909] The most famous example is the case of *Arsenal Football Club v Matthew Reed*.[910] In this case Arsenal Football Club brought proceedings against Mr Reed for infringement of its trade mark. Mr Reed was selling and offering for sale unofficial merchandise (i.e. not manufactured by Arsenal or with its authority) such as scarves, bearing official Arsenal logos outside the club's grounds. He had been selling Arsenal souvenirs for 30 years at his stalls outside the club's grounds. His stalls normally bore notices stating that the products were not official, but when he could obtain official merchandise an appropriate notice was also displayed, and such merchandise was sold at a higher price. Mr Reed argued that there was no infringement of the trade mark and that his products were perceived as a badge of support, loyalty or affiliation by those to whom they were directed, and not as indicating trade origin. Laddie J. asked the ECJ to interpret Article 5(1)(a) of Directive 89/104 relating to trade marks (see Chapter 21.6.2). The ECJ held[911] that where a third party used, in the course of trade, a sign which was identical to a validly registered trademark on goods which were identical to those for which it was registered, the trade mark proprietor was entitled, in circumstances such as those in the instant case, to rely on Article 5(1)(a) of the Directive to prevent that use, and that it was immaterial that, in the context of that use, the sign was perceived as a badge of support for or loyalty or affiliation to the trademark proprietor. Laddie J. disagreed with the judgment of the ECJ and gave judgment for Reed on the ground that the ECJ exceeded its jurisdiction by making findings of facts which were inconsistent with those made by him. This judgment was overruled by the Court of Appeal,[912] which held that the ECJ did not disregard the facts presented by Laddie J., but the factual finding made by the ECJ that the use of the trade mark by Mr Reed was likely to jeopardise the guarantee of origin of the trade mark, which constituted the essential function of the trade mark rights owned by Arsenal, was inevitable in the circumstances of the case. It is clear from the above case, that Laddie J. was wrong, and that instead of ignoring the preliminary ruling from the ECJ, he should have made a second referral containing relevant arguments concerning his disagreement with the preliminary ruling. The example of the UK Supreme Court in respect of referrals to the ECJ is relevant here. The Court will not make a referral in a situation where an answer to a question on EU law is "clear beyond the bounds of reasonable argument".[913] This includes a situation where a preliminary ruling has been delivered. If the answer from the ECJ does not meet this standard, the Court will refer again.[914]

13.7.2 Temporal effects of a preliminary ruling

Preliminary rulings have retroactive effect, that is, they apply from the entry into force of the provision in question. In Case 61/79 *Denkavit* [915] the ECJ held that:

> "the rule as . . . interpreted may, and must, be applied by the courts even to legal relationships arising and established before the judgment ruling on the request for interpretation."

---

908. Case 244/80 [1981] ECR 3045.
909. D. W. K. Anderson and M. Demetriou, *References to the European Court*, 2nd edn, 2002, London: Sweet & Maxwell, 327–30. The authors examine situations in which national courts have disregarded preliminary rulings of the ECJ.
910. *Arsenal Football Club v Matthew Reed* [2003] 2 CMLR 25.
911. Case C-206/01 *Arsenal Football Club v Matthew Reed* [2002] ECR I-10273.
912. [2003] 2 CMLR 25.
913. *R (Countryside Alliance) v Attorney General* [2007] UKHL 52.
914. *O'Byrne v Aventis Pasteur* [2008] UKHL 34.
915. Case 61/79 *Amministrazione delle Finanze dello Stato v Denkavit italiana Srl* [1980] ECR 1205, para. 16.

The retroactive effect of a preliminary ruling, that is, from the entry into force of the provision in question, has two main drawbacks. First, national rules on the limitation period differ from one Member State to another and, consequently, the outcome of a preliminary ruling may have different implications for litigants in different Member States. Second, a preliminary ruling may have a serious impact on the public finances of Member States in a situation where reimbursement of unlawful amounts paid by claimants, or likely to be paid by a Member State, resulting from its unlawful conduct may cause serious economic repercussions for that Member State.[916] However, this exception to the principle of retroactivity suffers important limitations:

- Only the ECJ may decide not to apply a judgment retroactively and any temporal limitation must be confined to the case in which the particular ruling is given.

- Only in exceptional circumstances will the ECJ deny its judgment retroactive effect, bearing in mind that to do this would be contrary to the principle of legal certainty. Two conditions must be satisfied before the ECJ decides not to give retroactive effect to its judgment:
  - those concerned should have acted in good faith; and,
  - there should be a risk of serious practical difficulties if the effects of a judgment are not limited in time.[917]

For example, in Case 309/85 *Barra*[918] the ECJ refused to restrict the temporal effect of its earlier ruling in Case 293/83 *Gravier*.[919] As a result, illegal fees charged by the Belgian authorities for vocational training courses for nationals from other Member States were reimbursed to those persons who were entitled to claim reimbursement before the delivery of the ruling in *Gravier*, i.e. irrespective of whether they had started legal proceedings before the delivery of the judgment in *Gravier*. However, the ECJ decided to impose temporal restrictions with regard to its rulings in Case 24/86 *Blaizot*[920] and Case 43/75 *Defrenne*.[921] This meant that the rulings applied only to those persons who had commenced proceedings before a national court prior to the rulings, and for everyone else the rulings applied only from the date they were given. In *Blaizot* the ECJ held that university education was within the scope of the Treaty if it constituted vocational training. As a result, illegal fees charged for university courses by Belgium were reimbursed only to students who had already brought proceedings before Belgian courts and could not be charged to future students. In *Defrenne* claims for backdated pay could only be made by those who had already started legal proceedings or submitted an equivalent claim prior to the date of the ruling. The differences in salary between male stewards and female air hostesses were to be abolished prospectively.

---

916.   For example Case 43/75 *Defrenne v Sabena* [1976] ECR 455; Case 61/79 *Amministrazione delle Finanze dello Stato v Denkavit Italiana Srl* [1980] ECR 1205; Case 24/86 *Vincent Blaizot v University of Liège and Others* [1988] ECR 379; Case C-57/93 *Anna Adriaantje Vroege v NCIV Instituut voor Volkshuisvesting BV and Stichting Pensioenfonds NCIV* [1994] ECR I-4541; Cases C-197/94 and C-252/94 *Société Bautiaa* [1996] ECR I-505; Case C-262/88 *Douglas Harvey Barber v Guardian Royal Exchange Assurance Group* [1990] ECR I-1889; Case C-184/04 *Uudenkaupungin Kaupunki* [2006] ECR I-3039.

917.   Case C-402/03 *Skov Æg v Bilka Lavprisvarehus A/S and Bilka Lavprisvarehus A/S v Jette Mikkelsen and Michael Due Nielsen* [2006] ECR I-199; Case C-184/04 *Uudenkaupungin Kaupunki* [2006] ECR I-3039.

918.   [1988] ECR 355.

919.   [1985] ECR 593.

920.   [1988] ECR 379.

921.   [1976] ECR 455.

13.7.3 The implications of retroactive effect of preliminary rulings on the finality of decisions of a national administrative body or a national court. The principle of *res judicata* and its limitations

It emerges from the case law of the ECJ (see Chapter 9.7.1) that:

■ A judicial decision which has become final after all rights of appeal have been exhausted, or after the expiry of the time limit provided for appeal proceedings, can no longer be challenged.[922] This is subject to the exception set out in Case C-119/05 *Lucchini*,[923] and in circumstances determined on a case by case basis by the ECJ.[924] In *Lucchini* the ECJ held that a national judgment which had became *res judicata* but encroached on exclusive competences of the Commission exercised under Article 108 TFEU, was in breach of EU law and could no longer enjoy the status of *res judicata*.

■ An administrative decision which has satisfied the requirements set out in Case C-453/00 *Kühne* (see Chapter 9.7.1), becomes *res judicata*, that is, can no longer be called into question.[925]

It is to be noted that although a national court or an administrative body which has rendered a decision, which in the light of a subsequent judgment of the ECJ, was in breach of EU law, is not (subject to the above exceptions) required to reopen national proceedings in order to comply with EU law, individuals have not been left without a remedy. They may rely on a preliminary ruling of the ECJ in national proceedings to establish Member State liability for infringement of EU law and thus obtain compensation for damage caused to them by a mistaken judicial or administrative decision which under national law has become *res judicata*.

13.8 Preliminary rulings on the validity of EU acts

The question of the validity of acts adopted by EU institutions, bodies, offices and agencies may be referred to the ECJ. However, the ECJ can neither rule on the validity of the primary sources, e.g. the Treaties and the Charter of Fundamental Rights (taking into account their constitutional nature), nor on matters covered by Articles 275 and 276 TFEU. Further, the ECJ will refuse to give preliminary rulings concerning the validity of its own judgments.[926]

13.8.1 Requirements in referrals on validity of EU acts

Lower courts have discretion as to whether to refer to the ECJ in a situation where the validity of an EU measure is contested. Normally, they will make a reference for a preliminary ruling if they have serious doubts as to the validity of the relevant EU measure.

---

922. Case C-234/04 *Kapferer v Schlank and Schick GmbH* [2006] ECR I-2585.
923. Case C-119/05 *Ministero dell'Industria, del Commercio e dell'Artigianato v Lucchini SpA, formerly Lucchini Siderurgica SpA*. [2007] ECR I-6199.
924. Case C-2/08 *Amministrazione dell'Economia e delle Finanze and Agenzia delle Entrate v Fallimento Olimpiclub Srl, in liquidation* [2009] ECR I-7501.
925. Case C-453/00 *Kühne & Heitz NV v Productschap voor Pluimvee en Eieren* [2004] ECR I-837. This was confirmed in Joined Cases C-392/04 and C-422/04 *i-21 Germany GmbH and Arcor AG & Co.KG v Germany* [2006] ECR I-8559.
926. Case 69/85 *Wünsche Handelsgesellschaft GmbH & Co v Germany* [1986] ECR 947.

With regard to courts against whose decisions there is no judicial remedy under national law, in Case C-344/04 *International Air Transport*[927] the ECJ confirmed that such a court is required to refer only where it considers that one or more arguments for invalidity of the EU act which have been put forward by the parties or otherwise raised by its own motion are well founded. Consequently, they have discretion and will refer only if the case raises any real doubt as to the validity of the relevant EU Act.

The leading case on referrals to the ECJ on the validity of EU acts is Case 314/85 *Foto-Frost*.[928]

THE FACTS WERE:

Foto-Frost applied to a German municipal court to declare a decision adopted by the Commission invalid on the grounds that the decision was in breach of requirements set out in a Council regulation which delegated authority to the Commission to adopt decisions. The German court requested a preliminary ruling as to whether it could review the validity of the decision in question.

Held:

The ECJ held that "national courts have no jurisdiction themselves to declare the acts of [EU] institutions invalid". The ECJ justified its decision on the following grounds:

- *For the uniformity of EU law it is especially important that there are no divergences between Member States as to the validity of EU acts, since this would jeopardise the very unity of the [EU] legal order as well as detract from the fundamental requirement of legal certainty.*

- *The coherence of the system requires that where the validity of EU measures is challenged before national courts, the jurisdiction to declare a measure invalid must be reserved to the ECJ. The ECJ drew a comparison between its exclusive jurisdiction under Article 263 TFEU and its jurisdiction to give preliminary rulings on the validity of EU acts under Article 267 TFEU.*

Comment:

This case confirmed that the ECJ has exclusive jurisdiction to declare an EU act invalid. Accordingly, whilst national courts may consider the validity of EU acts and may declare them valid, they must, if they have doubts as to their validity, make reference under Article 267 TFEU.[929]

In Case C-491/01 *British American Tobacco*,[930] the ECJ accepted a referral from the High Court of England and Wales challenging validity of a directive the deadline for transposition of which had not expired at the time of commencement of the main proceedings and also, when at that time, there were

---

927. Case C-344/04 *The Queen, on the application of International Air Transport Association and European Low Fares Airline Association v Department for Transport* [2006] ECR I-403.
928. Case 314/85 *Foto-Frost v Hauptzollamt Lübeck-Ost* [1987] ECR 4199.
929. Joined Cases C-304/04 and C-305/04 *Jacob Meijer and Eagle International Freight BV v Inspecteur van de Balastingdienst-Douanedistrict Arnhem* [2005] ECR I-6251.
930. Case C-491/01 *R V Secretary of State, ex parte British American Tobacco* [2002] ECR I-11453.

no national measures adopted to transpose it into national law. This approach is consistent with the theory that EU directives are directly applicable (see Chapter 11.4).

In Case C-461/03 *Schul*,[931] the ECJ had an opportunity to extend the principles set out in the *CILFIT* judgment to referrals concerning the validity of EU measures but refused to change its position set out in *Foto-Frost*. It justified the refusal on the following grounds:

- Even if, at first glance, it may appear that provisions of EU law, which have been declared invalid by the ECJ, are comparable to the challenged provisions, the latter may, in fact, have a different legal and factual context;

- The possibility of a national court ruling on the invalidity of an EU measure would be liable to jeopardise the essential unity of the EU legal order and undermine the fundamental requirement of legal certainty. Indeed, national courts in various Member States may have differing opinions as to the validity of a given measure; and,

- The coherence of the system of judicial protection instituted by the Treaties would be undermined given that Article 267 TFEU constitutes, as do Articles 263 and 277 TFEU, a means of reviewing the legality of EU measures. The Treaties entrusted such review to the ECJ, not to national courts.

13.8.2 Circumstances in which the ECJ will refuse to give a preliminary ruling on validity of EU acts

Article 267 TFEU provides an opportunity for a non-privileged applicant who cannot satisfy the requirements for standing under Article 263 TFEU, and thus cannot challenge the validity of EU acts directly before the General Court to challenge EU acts or national measures implementing an EU act (see Chapter 15.2.7). For that reason, the ECJ has refused to accept referrals in which the party to the proceedings before the referring court seeks annulment of either an EU act or a national implementing measure based on that act in a situation where that party would have had standing to seek annulment of an EU act but failed to do this within a very strict time-limit imposed by Article 230(6) TFEU. This is exemplified in Case C-188/92 *TWD*.[932]

THE FACTS WERE:

TWD, a German company, was a beneficiary of aid granted by the relevant German authority. The Commission found that the aid was unlawful and required Germany to recover it. The German authorities forwarded a copy of the Commission decision to TWD and informed it that it could challenge the decision of the Commission before the ECJ under Article 263 TFEU. When the German authorities adopted a decision requiring TWD to repay the aid, TWD brought an action before the German court challenging the decision of the German authorities, partially on the ground that the Commission's decision on which it was based was unlawful. By the time the action was brought before the German court, the time

---

931. Case C-461/03 *Gaston Schul Douane-expediteur BV v Minister van Landbouw, Natuur en Voedselkwaliteit* [2005] ECR I-10513.

932. Case C-188/92 *TWD Textilwerke Deggendorf GmbH v Bundesrepublik Deutschland* [1994] ECR I-833. See also Case C-441/05 *Roquette Frères* [2007] ECR I-1993.

limit for challenging the Commission's decision before the ECJ had elapsed. The German court referred two matters to the ECJ, first it asked whether an indirect challenge of an EU act was possible under Article 267 TFEU and second whether the Commission decision was invalid.

Held:

The ECJ held that indirect challenge was not possible because TWD was informed of the Commission's decision by the German authorities and could "without doubt" have challenged it in Article 263 TFEU proceedings.

In subsequent cases the ECJ has clarified its judgment in *TWD*. The ECJ will refuse to give a preliminary ruling on the validity of EU acts in the following circumstances:

- first, if the act to be challenged is a decision addressed to the claimant. He must challenge it under Article 263 TFEU. Even if he challenges it before a national court (and does so within the time-limit prescribed by Article 263 TFEU), the ECJ will refuse to give a preliminary ruling;[933] and,

- second, if there is no doubt that the claimant would have had standing under Article 263 TFEU but failed to seek the annulment of an EU act within the time-limit specified in that Article (see Chapter 15.2.9). There is a doubt where applicants wish to challenge EU directives or other acts of general application.[934] Nevertheless, in many instances, the complex case law of standing for individuals under Article 263 TFEU makes it very difficult to establish "without doubt" that the claimant has standing under Article 263 TFEU. Accordingly, if in doubt the claimant should start proceedings under Article 263 TFEU in order to ensure that his claim would not be time-barred.

13.9 Effects of preliminary rulings on the validity of EU acts

The peculiarity of the legal effects of preliminary rulings on the validity of EU acts derives from their close connection with the effects of actions for annulment under Article 264 TFEU, and from the distinction between a preliminary ruling confirming the validity of the act concerned, and a preliminary ruling declaring that act invalid.

If the ruling of the ECJ confirms the validity of an EU act, the referring court, as well as all other courts and tribunals within the meaning of Article 267 TFEU, may apply the act, but if they believe that it is invalid, refer again to the ECJ under Article 267 TFEU.

If the ECJ declares the challenged act invalid, the situation is more complex. In Case 66/80 *International Chemical Company*,[935] the ECJ held that although the preliminary ruling declaring an act invalid was addressed to the referring national court, it constituted, at the same time, sufficient justification for all other national judges to consider the act in question invalid in respect of judgments they might render. However, the ECJ added that its declaration in respect of the invalidity of an act should not prevent national courts from referring again a question already decided by the ECJ if there are problems regarding the scope or possible legal implications of the act previously declared invalid.

---

933. Case C-178/95 *Wiljo NV v Belgische Staat* [1997] ECR I-585.
934. E.g. Case 408/95 *Eurotunnel SA and Others v SeaFrance* [1997] ECR I-6315.
935. Case 66/80 *SpA International Chemical Corporation v Amministrazione delle Finanze dello Stato* [1981] ECR 1191.

The extent of the ECJ's liberal approach in this area is illustrated in Case 32/77 *Giuliani*,[936] in which the ECJ agreed to answer the question whether it continued to maintain its position in respect of an act previously declared invalid. The Court's willingness to deal with the issue is justified by the fact that an EU act declared invalid under Article 267 TFEU nevertheless remains in force. Only the institution, body, office or agency that adopted the act in question is empowered to annul or modify it. It is also liable to compensate for any damage caused by the act. In addition, only national authorities are entitled to nullify a national provision which was adopted in order to implement or to apply an invalid act.[937]

It is important to note that the ECJ may declare only part of an act invalid.[938] The analogy with the effects of a successful action for annulment under Article 264 TFEU is obvious (see Chapter 15.2.10). For that reason, the ECJ decided that it is empowered to specify the consequences deriving from the invalidity of an act. These are as follows:

■ First, the ECJ held that it has jurisdiction to limit the temporal effect of preliminary rulings. In principle, all preliminary rulings have retroactive effect, including those confirming, or denying the validity of EU acts.[939] The ECJ has applied, by analogy, Article 264 TFEU in the context of Article 267 TFEU. In Case 112/83 *Produits de Maïs*,[940] the ECJ held that the maintenance of the coherence of the EU legal order provides sufficient justification for the application of Article 264 TFEU in the context of Article 267 TFEU. Initially, the ECJ decided that if a regulation was invalid with effect from the date of its judgment to this effect, but only as to the future, the referring court was barred from drawing any consequences from the ECJ's declaration of invalidity of the act, even for the parties to the main proceedings in which the question of validity arose.[941]

This above approach was strongly criticised by national courts which considered that the ECJ had encroached upon their jurisdiction, since under Article 267 TFEU national courts have to apply EU law to the main proceedings.[942] The justification provided by the ECJ was based on the principle of legal certainty. The strong opposition of national courts was, however, taken into account by the ECJ in Case C-228/92 *Roquette*,[943] in which it held that the exceptional prospective effect of a preliminary ruling should not deprive those who had commenced proceedings before the date of the ECJ's judgment confirming invalidity of an act, or who had made an equivalent claim, of the right to rely on that invalidity in the main proceedings. For that reason, in many cases the ECJ has applied the solution it adopted in *Defrenne*, that is, temporal limitations are not imposed upon the parties to the main action nor on those who had instituted legal proceedings or made an equivalent claim prior to the date of the judgment.[944]

■ Second, the ECJ has authorised itself to replace invalidated provisions by appropriate alternatives while the adoption of required measures by the institution concerned is awaited.[945]

---

936.   Case 32/77 *Antonio Giuliani v Landesversicherungsanstalt Schwaben* [1977] ECR 1863.
937.   Case 23/75 *Rey Soda v Cassa Conguaglio Zucchero* [1975] ECR 1279.
938.   Case 130/79 *Express Dairy Foods Limited v Intervention Board for Agricultural Produce* [1980] ECR 1887.
939.   Joined Cases 117/76 and 16/77 *Rückdeschel and Others v Hauptzollamt Itzehoe* [1977] ECR 1753.
940.   Case 112/83 *Société des Produits de Maïs SA v Administration des Douanes et Droits Indirects* [1985] ECR 719.
941.   Case 4/79 *Providence Agricole de Champagne* [1980] ECR 2823.
942.   For example, the judgment of 26 June 1985 of the French Conseil d'Etat in *ONIC v Société Maïseries de Beauce*, AJDA, 1985, 615, concl. Genevois, and the judgment of 21 April 1989 of the Italian Constitutional Court in *Fragd*, RDI, 1989, 103.
943.   Case C-228/92 *Roquette Frères SA v Hauptzollamt Geldern* [1994] ECR I-1445.
944.   Case 41/84 *Pietro Pinna v Caisse d'Allocations Familiales de la Savoie* [1986] ECR 1.
945.   Case 300/86 *Luc Van Landschoot and Mera NV v FEFAC and Others* [1988] ECR 3443.

- Third, the ECJ has reserved to the EU institution, body, office or agency concerned the exclusive right to draw conclusions from the invalidity of its act and take the necessary measures to remedy the situation.[946]

13.10   Interim relief

In the context of validity of EU acts the matter of interim measures arises with particular intensity. This matter may also have some importance in relation to the interpretation of EU law. Indeed, sometimes for a party to the proceedings the question of interim relief is vital if his rights under EU law are to have any substance.

Under Article 267 TFEU, an interim measure may be ordered by the EU courts or a national court for the period between seizure of the court and its final decision. In Cases C-143/88 and C-92/89 *Zuckerfabrik*[947] the ECJ held that a national court should suspend the application of a national measure implementing an EU act if certain stringent conditions are satisfied. These are as follows:

- a preliminary ruling on the issue of validity has been sought from the ECJ;

- there is a serious doubt as to the validity of the EU act;

- the matter is urgent;

- there must be a risk to the applicant of serious and irreparable harm, that is, damages would not be an adequate remedy; and,

- the interests of the EU have been duly taken into account by the national court concerned.

In Case C-213/89 *Factortame (No. 1)*,[948] the ECJ held that if a rule of national law prevents the court from granting interim relief, that rule should be set aside. In that case this led to the interim suspension of the operation of a statute, a remedy which until then was not available to national courts.

In Case C-465/93 *Atlanta*,[949] the ECJ first, restated and clarified the conditions under which a national court may grant interim relief and, second, ruled that national courts may grant not only negative (that is suspensatory) but also positive (that is creating a new legal position) interim measures. In this case the issue was whether or not a national court is allowed, in certain circumstances, to grant interim relief from the application of an EU act.

THE FACTS WERE:

Council Regulation 404/93 provided for a revised system of import quotas for bananas from non-traditional African, Caribbean and Pacific (ACP) countries. Following from this, the German Federal Food Office (BEF) granted Atlanta, a German company, such revised/ reduced quotas. Atlanta challenged the regulation and asked for interim relief. The German court asked the ECJ whether it could, while awaiting a preliminary ruling, temporarily resolve

---

946.   Case 124/76 *S. A. Moulins et Huileries de Pont-a-Mousson v Office National Interprofessionnel des Cereales, and Societe Cooperative "Providence Agricole de la Champagne" v Office National Interprofessionnel des Cereales* [1977] ECR 1795.

947.   Cases C-143/88 and C-92/89 *Zuckerfabrik Südderdithmarschen v Hauptzollamt Itzehoe* [1991] ECR I-415.

948.   Case C-213/89 *R v Secretary of State for Transport, ex parte Factortame (No. 1)* [1990] ECR I-2433.

949.   Case C-465/93 *Atlanta Fruchthandelsgesellschaft v BEF* [1995] ECR I-3761.

the disputed legal position by an interim order, and, if so, under what conditions and whether a distinction should be made between an interim order designed to preserve an existing legal position and one which was intended to create a new legal position.

Held:

The ECJ held that it has jurisdiction under Article 267 TFEU to order any necessary interim measures. It held that:

"The interim legal protection which the national courts must afford to individuals under Community law must be the same, whether they seek suspension of enforcement of a national administrative measure adopted on the basis of a Community regulation or the grant of interim measures settling or regulating the disputed legal positions or relationships for their benefit."[950]

Comment:

In this case the ECJ added the following conditions to those laid down in Zuckerfabrik:

- *The national court must justify why it considers that the ECJ should find the measure invalid;*

- *The national court must take into consideration the extent of the discretion allowed to EU institutions with regard to the adoption of the challenged measure;*

- *The national court must assess the EU interest in the light of the impact of suspension on the EU legal regime, that is, it must consider, on the one hand, the cumulative effect which would arise if a large number of courts were also to adopt interim measures for similar reasons and, on the other, those special features of the applicant's situation which distinguish the applicant from other operators concerned;*

- *If the grant of interim relief represents a financial risk for the EU, the national court must require the applicant to provide adequate guarantees, such as the deposit of money or other security; and,*

- *The national court must take into account any previous Article 263 TFEU judgments concerning the disputed legislation.*

13.11 Is reform of the preliminary rulings procedure necessary?

Many academic commentators[951] and some A-Gs (see below) believe that the preliminary rulings procedure is in need of urgent reform. In particular, they consider that the extension of competences of the EU under the ToL and the enlargement of the EU, will result in the ECJ being overburdened with referrals. The likely consequences of this are unacceptable delays in dealing with preliminary rulings by the ECJ and an adverse impact on their quality.

---

950. Ibid, para. 28.
951. See T. de la Mare and C. Donelly, "Preliminary Rulings and EU Law Legal Integration: Evolution and Stasis", in P. Craig and G. de Búrca (eds), *The Evolution of EU Law*, 2nd edn, 2011, Oxford: OUP, 387–95.

On the topic of delay, in 2011 the average duration of preliminary ruling proceedings was 16.4 months, which can be considered reasonable.[952] It is important to note that under the ToL, if needed, the ECJ has at its disposal various procedures allowing it to deal with cases speedily. These are:

- The simplified procedure. If a question referred is identical to a question already answered by the ECJ, or an answer to it admits no reasonable doubt, or may be easily inferred from existing case law, the ECJ may deliver its judgment by reasoned order;

- The expedited procedure. This is used for very urgent cases. This procedure allows such cases to be prioritised and entails avoidance of various procedural stages;

- The urgent preliminary rulings procedure which applies only to preliminary rulings in the AFSJ (see Chapter 13.4.1); and,

- A procedure established under Article 20 of the Statute of the CJEU under which cases may be determined without an Opinion of an A-G where they do not raise any new point of law. In 2010 about 52 per cent of cases were decided on this basis.[953]

The above shows that the ECJ can use various procedures when the time factor is of great relevance to the resolution of the case. Notwithstanding this, in some cases preliminary rulings have been used as tactical devices to gain time during which an activity regarded as illegal under national law could continue until the delivery of the judgment. The best example is provided by the UK Sunday trading cases[954] in which the referral to the ECJ permitted the defendant companies to trade on Sundays while awaiting the preliminary rulings. Over a number of years the defendants who were in breach of the UK Shops Act argued that the Act was contrary to provisions of EU law on the free movement of goods (see Chapter 20.5). It seems that in such cases it should be the duty of the referring court to emphasise the need for the ECJ to deliver its preliminary ruling speedily.

So far as the quality of preliminary rulings is concerned, in *O'Byrne v Aventis Pasteur*,[955] the UK Supreme Court found that the preliminary ruling given by the ECJ in Case C-127/04 *O'Byrne*[956] was not sufficiently clear and decided to ask for further clarifications in a second referral. For the claimant, as the Supreme Court stated, this was an unfortunate situation because "he has been trying for over seven years to litigate the question of whether he is entitled to any compensation".[957] There are other examples of dissatisfaction of national courts with responses from the ECJ.[958] Obviously, complaints do not mean that the quality of the ECJ's judgments have been impaired. In general national courts receive well drafted and well reasoned responses to preliminary questions. Where there are instances of obscurity or ambiguity a referring court may always make a second referral.

In fairness to the ECJ it should be said that under Article 267 TFEU it is not easy to draw a line between the interpretation and the actual application of EU law. Under Article 267 TFEU the ECJ has

---

952. See Annual Report 2011, Curia, Court of Justice of the European Union, supra note 827.
953. Ibid.
954. One of them was Case 145/88 *Torfaen Borough Council v B & Q plc* [1989] ECR 3851. Also see A. Arnull, "What Shall We Do on Sunday?", 16 ELRev., 112.
955. [2008] UKHL 34.
956. Case C-127/04 *Declan O'Byrne v Sanofi Pasteur MSD Ltd, formerly Aventis Pasteur MSD Ltd* [2006] ECR I-1313.
957. Supra note 955, para. 21.
958. The UK Court of Appeal in *Test Claimants in the FII Litigation v HMRC* [2010] EWCA Civ. 103 had doubts as to the meaning of the ECJ response and decided to make a second referral in the same case. Also see: M. Bobek, "Learning to Talk: Preliminary Rulings, the Courts of the New Member States and the Court of Justice", [2008] 45 CMLRev., 1640.

jurisdiction to interpret EU law *in abstracto* and objectively. However, the necessity to assist national courts in rendering a judgment in a particular case requires that ECJ judges give their decision within the context of the law and facts of the case. Accordingly, the boundary between interpretation and application is fluid and varies depending upon the degree of precision of the question asked by national courts, the complexity of the factual and legal context of the dispute, and so on. For that reason, the ECJ is in a difficult position because:

- On the one hand, if its rulings are in fact not preliminary rulings but rulings on the merits (which has occurred on numerous occasions), the ECJ, instead of interpreting EU law, is applying it, and thus encroaching upon the jurisdiction of national courts and undermining the division of competences between national courts and the ECJ. This is contrary to the spirit and the terms of Article 267 TFEU.

- On the other hand, if the preliminary ruling is too general, or the interpretation of a provision of EU law is too abstract, the national judge would have a large measure of discretion, so that the preliminary ruling may, instead of clarifying a particular question, obscure it even more. This situation calls into question the main objective of Article 267 TFEU, that is, to ensure uniformity of application of EU law throughout the EU.

It is not easy for the ECJ to reach a decision which is neither too precise nor too general, and indeed, some decisions of the ECJ under Article 267 TFEU have left no doubts as to the outcome of the case.[959]

Many proposals have been made as to how to reform the preliminary rulings procedure.[960] The TFEU itself in Article 256(3) provides for the possibility of transfer of the jurisdiction with regard to preliminary rulings in "specific areas" to the General Court. This possibility, however, does not seem very attractive.[961] This is because, first, Article 256(3) TFEU is unclear, in particular when it states that the General Court "may" refer cases to the ECJ when a "decision of principle" is involved. Second, under Article 256(3) TFEU the ECJ may review General Court preliminary rulings "exceptionally". This review is, on the one hand, necessary to ensure the consistency, efficiency and unity of EU law, but, on the other, undermines the authority of such rulings by introducing uncertainty for a referring court as to whether the preliminary ruling is the final statement from the Union's courts on a particular point of EU law.

Some proposals came from within the ECJ, i.e. from its A-Gs. For example, A-G Cruz Villalón in Case C-173/09 *Elchinov*[962] argued that the developments in EU law require the reassessment of the ruling in *Rheinmühlen I*[963] under which national courts have discretion to refer at any stage of the

---

959. Case 33/65 *Adrianus Dekker v Bundesversicherungsanstalt für Angestellte* [1965] ECR 905; Case 82/71 *Ministère Public de la Italian Republic v Sail* [1972] ECR 119; Case C-213/89 *R v Secretary of State for Transport ex parte Factortame (1)* [1990] ECR I-2433; Case 222/84 *Marguerite Johnston v Chief Constable of the Royal Ulster Constabulary* [1986] ECR 1651; Case C-292/93 *British Telecom* [1996] ECR I-1631; and Case C-224/01 *Köbler v Austria* [2003] ECR I-10239.

960. J. Komárek, "In the Court(s) We Trust?: On the Need for Hierarchy and Differentiation in the Preliminary Rulings Procedure" (2007) 32 ELRev., 467; H. Rasmussen, "Remedying the Crumbling EC Judicial System", (2000) 37 CMLRev., 1071.

961. L. Heffernan, "The Community Courts post-Nice: A European Certiorari Revisited" (2003) 52 ICLQ 907. More enthusiastic about the possibility of conferral of the preliminary rulings procedure to the General Court is T. Tridimas, in his article entitled "Knocking on Heaven's Door: Fragmentation, Efficiency and Defiance in the Preliminary Reference Procedure" (2003) 450 CMLRev., 9.

962. Case C-173/09 *Georgi Ivanov Elchinov v Natsionalna Zdravnoosiguritelna Kasa* [2010] ECR I-8889.

963. Case 166/73 *Rheinmühlen-Düsseldorf v Einfuhr- und Vorratsstelle für Getreide und Futtermittel (Rheinmühlen I)*

proceedings and despite any national procedural rule to the contrary. In *Elchinov* the referring court, under national procedural rules, was bound by a ruling of a higher court, and thus prevented from making a reference to the ECJ although it had doubts as to the compatibility of the ruling of the higher court with EU law.

The A-G contended that, in the light of the ECJ's judgments:

■ in Case C-224/01 *Köbler*[964] which established the financial liability of Member States for judicial acts, even in those States where actions against courts for compensation were previously unknown (see Chapter 12.4);

■ in Case C-129/00 *Commission v Italy*[965] in which the Commission, for the first time, brought an action against a Member State for failure to fulfill its obligations in a situation where a supreme court of a Member State was in breach of EU law (see Chapter 14.2.2.3);

■ in Case C-453/00 *Kühne*[966] and in Case C-234/04 *Kapferer*[967] which confirmed the primacy of the principle of *res judicata* over the principle of supremacy of EU law although there are some exceptions (see Chapter 9.7.1);

individuals have adequate legal remedies under EU law and thus the unfettered discretion of national courts to refer under Article 267 TFEU should be limited to ensure that the ECJ is not overburdened with requests made by national courts. The ECJ ignored the submissions made by the A-G.

The ECJ has resisted any attempt at modifying its jurisdiction under Article 267 TFEU. Its position is clearly stated in a draft proposal for amendments to the Statute of the CJEU (the Statute of the three courts of the EU) and the Rules of Procedure of the ECJ submitted in March 2011 to the EP and the Council.[968] The proposal states that the situation in the ECJ is satisfactory as evidenced by the fact that the ECJ reduced the average duration of preliminary rulings from 25.5 months in 2003 to 16 months in 2010. However, the ECJ acknowledged that in order to improve the efficiency and productivity of EU courts, whilst maintaining the quality of judgments, some changes are necessary. The main proposed change that would affect the preliminary rulings procedures (as well as other procedures) is the termination of the automatic participation of the Presidents of Chambers of five judges in all cases before the Grand Chamber. This would ease the heavy workload imposed on the Presidents of those Chambers whilst allowing increased participation of other judges in cases assigned to the Grand Chamber. Another proposed change concerns the creation of the post of Vice-President of the ECJ who would assist the President in carrying out his duties, and participate in every case assigned to the Grand Chamber. A proposed change, which does not affect the preliminary rulings procedure, relates to the increase of the number of judges of the General Court to 39 (see Chapter 3.7.6). No increase is suggested with regard to the number of judges of the ECJ.

It is submitted that the position of the ECJ on the need for reform of the preliminary ruling procedure, despite differing views expressed by many commentators, does not deserve any criticism. After all, the

---

([1974] ECR 33). In Case C-205/08 *Umweltanwalt von Kärnten v Kärntner Landesregierung* ([2009] ECR I-11525) A-G Ruiz-Jarabo Colomer argued that the meaning of a "court or tribunal" is too flexible and invited the ECJ to take a stricter approach in that only "bodies forming part of the judicial power of every State" with some exceptions should be allowed to refer under Article 267 TFEU. The ECJ ignored the invitation.

964.   Case C-224/01 *Köbler v Austria* [2003] ECR I-10239.

965.   [2003] ECR I-14637.

966.   Case C-453/00 *Kühne & Heitz NV v Produktschap voor Pluimvee en Eieren* [2004] ECR I-837.

967.   Case C-234/04 *Rosmarie Kapferer v Schlank & Schick GmbH* [2006] ECR I-2585.

968.   The text of the proposal is available at http://curia.europa.eu/jcmc/jcms/Jo2_7031 (accessed 25/6/12).

preliminary rulings procedure has been working satisfactorily, and has ensured wide open access to the ECJ of courts and tribunals within the meaning of Article 267 TFEU. It remains to be seen whether this view is shared by the EP, the Council and the Member States.

RECOMMENDED READING

Books

Broberg, M. and Fenger, N., *Preliminary References to the European Court of Justice*, 2010, Oxford: OUP.

Obradovic, D., and Lavranos, N. (eds.), *Interface between EU Law and National Law: Proceedings of the Annual Colloquium of the G. K. van Hogendorp Centre for European Constitutional Studies*, 2007, Groningen: European Law Publishing.

Sinaniotis, D., *Interim Protection of Individuals before the European and National Courts*, 2006, The Hague: KLI.

Articles

Anagnostaras, G., "Preliminary Problems and Jurisdiction Uncertainties: The Admissibility of Questions Referred by Bodies Performing Quasi-Judicial Functions", (2005) 30 ELRev., 878.

Bobek, M., "Learning to Talk: Preliminary Rulings, the Courts of the New Member States and the Court of Justice", [2008] 45 CMLRev., 1640.

Broberg, M., "*Acte Clair* revisited: Adapting the *Acte Clair* Criteria to the Demands of the Times", (2008) 45 CMLRev., 1383.

Broberg, M., "Preliminary References by Public Administrative Bodies: When Are Public Administrative Bodies Competent to Make Preliminary References to the European Court of Justice?", (2009) 15 EPL, 207.

De la Mare, T., and Donelly, C., "Preliminary Rulings and EU Law Legal Integration: Evolution and Stasis", in P. Craig and G. de Búrca (eds), *The Evolution of EU Law*, 2nd edn, 2011, Oxford: OUP, 363.

Komárek, J., "In the Court(s) We Trust?: On the Need for Hierarchy and Differentiation in the Preliminary Ruling Procedure", (2007) 32/4 ELRev., 467.

Ritter, C., "Purely Internal Situations, Reverse Discrimination, Guimont, Dzodzi and Article 234", (2006) 31 ELRev., 690.

Waldhoff, C., "Recent Developments Relating to the Retroactive Effect of Decisions of the ECJ", (2009) 46 CMLRev., 173.

PROBLEM QUESTION

Claudia, a German national, is unhappy with a decision of the Spanish Immigration Adjudicator and in dispute with him regarding his refusal to refer a matter of interpretation of EU law relevant to her dispute to the ECJ. The Spanish Immigration Adjudicator is a body established on the basis of Spanish legislation to deal with disputes concerning rights of foreigners to enter and remain in Spain. It is a permanent body which makes its determinations in accordance with Spanish law and procedures. Its proceedings are adversarial. The Adjudicator is appointed for a period of one year by the Spanish Minister of the Interior and may be removed at any time. Decisions delivered by the Adjudicator are subject to appeal to the Minister of the Interior.

Advise Claudia.

ESSAY QUESTION

Critically assess whether there is a need to reform the preliminary rulings procedure.

AIDE-MÉMOIRE

Source of law	Admissibility of referrals on the interpretation of that source of law	Admissibility of referrals on the validity of that source of law
Primary sources of EU law	Yes, but not on matters specified in Chapter 13.2 and relating to the CFSP except those specified in Art. 24(1) TEU.	NO
General Principles of EU law	Yes	Yes
Acts of EU institutions, bodies, agencies or offices	Yes	Yes, but subject to the exception established in Case C-188/92 *TWD*.
Judgments of the ECJ	Yes	NO
International agreements concluded between the EU and third countries, and international agreements concluded by a Member State prior to its accession to the EU in an area which subsequent to its accession falls within the exclusive competence of the EU	Yes	Yes
National law of a Member State	No but the ECJ has made some exceptions.	NO

THE CRITERIA FOR ESTABLISHING WHETHER A NATIONAL BODY MEETS THE DEFINITION OF A "COURT OR TRIBUNAL" WITHIN THE MEANING OF ARTICLE 267 TFEU.

THE BODY MUST

1. BE ESTABLISHED BY LAW, I.E. MUST NOT BE ESTABLISHED BY PRIVATE PARTIES

2. BE PERMANENT, I.E. IT MUST NOT EXERCISE A JUDICIAL FUNCTION ONLY ON AN OCCASIONAL BASIS

3. HAVE COMPULSORY JURISDCITION, I.E. THERE MUST BE NO ALTERNATIVE REMEDIES AVAILABLE TO THE PARTIES

4. USE ADVERSARIAL PROCEDURE

5. APPLY RULES OF LAW RATHER THAN PRINCIPLES OF FAIRNESS

6. BE INDEPENDENT

The criterion of independence encompasses three elements:

- the body in question must act as a third party in relation to the parties to the dispute;

- members of the body must enjoy the safequards which ordinarily apply to the judiciary in relation to removal from office and re-assignment; and,

- members of the body must have no interest in the outcome of the proceedings apart from the strict application of the rule of law.

7. BE CALLED UPON TO GIVE A DECISION OF A JUDICIAL NATURE

14

ENFORCEMENT OF EU LAW – ACTIONS AGAINST MEMBER STATES

CHAPTER OUTLINE

1. The EU can enforce compliance with its rules through effective sanctions against a Member State in breach of its obligations deriving from EU law. The effectiveness of its enforcement mechanisms confers a unique status on EU law in that it far exceeds that of public international law.

2. The most important and most frequently used enforcement action is provided for and defined in Article 258 TFEU. It allows the Commission to bring proceedings against a Member State for failure to fulfil an obligation under the Treaties. The Commission, as the "guardian of the Treaties", has a wide discretion and can set aside the proceedings at any stage, or continue them even if a defaulting Member State has terminated the breach but did so after the expiry of the time limit fixed in the reasoned opinion.

3. The procedure itself reflects the philosophy of Article 258 TFEU, that is, that the action should not be brought unless there is no other possibility of enforcing EU law. The use of non-contentious means in the proceedings under Article 258 TFEU constitutes one of its dominant features. Two stages can be identified in the procedure:

- The informal stage during which the Commission invites the Member State concerned to provide explanations, comments and relevant information with a view to discussing and settling the matter. If this fails, the Commission may proceed to the formal stage; and,

- The formal stage consists of an administrative phase and a judicial phase. During the administrative phase the Commission continues the dialogue with the Member State concerned, and if necessary issues a letter of formal notice, which defines the subject-matter of the dispute and sets a reasonable period in which the alleged failure must be corrected. If, after the expiry of that period, the Member State persists in its failure, the Commission may issue a reasoned opinion, setting out the legal arguments supporting its view that the Member State has failed its obligations arising out of the Treaties, and fixing a new time limit within which the alleged breach must be remedied. If the Member State concerned still persists in its failure, the Commission may commence a judicial phase by bringing proceedings against the defaulting Member State before the ECJ.

4. The ECJ will dismiss an application under Article 258 TFEU if the Commission has not complied with the procedural requirements imposed by that provision. As to defences other than procedural, they are rarely successful. This is mainly because the ECJ has, on the one hand, rejected defences recognised under public international law, such as reciprocity and necessity, as being unsuitable to the EU legal order, and, on the other, restrictively interpreted circumstances likely to exonerate a defaulting Member State.

5. Actions under Article 259 TFEU, where one Member State decides to bring proceedings before the ECJ against another Member State, are rare. This is because the political implications of such an action may damage friendly relations between the Member States involved. Consequently, Member States prefer that the Commission acts against the defaulting State under Article 258 TFEU.

6. A judgment of the ECJ declaring a failure of a Member State to fulfil a Treaty obligation is declaratory in nature. The defaulting Member State is required to take all necessary measures to comply with that judgment within the shortest possible period.

7. The Commission may request that the ECJ impose pecuniary sanctions on the defaulting Member State in the following situations:

- If a Member State fails to comply with a judgment of the ECJ declaring that Member State in breach of EU law, the Commission may bring proceedings for the imposition of pecuniary sanctions. To that effect the Commission may start new proceedings under Article 258 TFEU. However, the ToL removes the requirement that the Commission submits to the defaulting Member State a "reasoned opinion". This considerably speeds up the new proceedings.

- Under Article 260(2) TFEU the Commission may, in its application to the ECJ which asks for a finding of failure, when a Member State has failed to notify to it measures transposing a directive adopted under a legislative procedure, request the ECJ to impose a pecuniary penalty. In such a situation the Commission is not required to wait until a Member State concerned fails to comply with a judgment of the ECJ to propose a pecuniary penalty.

The Commission is required to propose the amount of penalty, but the ECJ is not bound by it. The amount of penalty – which may take the form of a lump sum, a daily payment or both – depends on the seriousness of the breach, the duration and the need to ensure that the penalty is a deterrent to further infringements. However, when the Commission asks for the imposition of a pecuniary penalty in its application for a finding of a failure to notify to it measures transposing a directive, and the ECJ finds that there has been an infringement, the ECJ may impose the financial penalty proposed by the Commission but the amount of such penalty should not exceed that specified by the Commission. The Member State concerned has an obligation to pay on the date set by the ECJ in its judgment.

14.1 Introduction

The availability of an action for failure to fulfil an obligation arising from the Treaties, which may be brought against a defaulting Member State, enhances the originality of the EU legal order. The fact that the EU can enforce compliance with its rules through effective sanctions against a Member State which is in breach of its obligation confers a unique status on EU law.[969]

A comparison between public international law and EU law in respect of Member State responsibility for infringement of its international obligations demonstrates that there are a number of features which enhance the originality of EU law:

		Public International Law	EU Law
1.	Existence of loss suffered by a victim State.	Required.	Not required: Case 7/71 *Commission v France.*[970]
2.	Existence of fault on the part of a defaulting State.	Unclear. The case law supports both strict liability (the objective theory) and liability based on fault (the subjective theory), although the objective theory is most widely accepted.	Rejected: Case 25/59 *The Netherlands v High Authority.*[971]
3.	Defences such as necessity and reciprocity.	Accepted.	Rejected: Case 7/61 *Commission v Italy* and Joined Cases 90 and 91/63 *Commission v Belgium and Luxembourg.*[972]
4.	Initiation of proceedings.	Normally by another State and exceptionally in the area of the protection of human rights by a victim.	Normally the Commission under Article 258 TFEU, exceptionally, a Member State under Article 259 TFEU.
5.	Jurisdiction of the ICJ and the ECJ.	The ICJ: only if both States which are parties to the proceedings agree.	Under Articles 258 & 259 TFEU the ECJ has exclusive, mandatory and unreserved jurisdiction in all types of actions for failure by a Member State to fulfil an obligation. Under Article 344 TFEU the ECJ has exclusive jurisdiction to settle disputes between Member States concerning the interpretation or application of the Treaties.[973]

(Continued)

---

969. On Article 258 TFEU procedure see: M. Smith, *Centralised Enforcement, Legitimacy and Good Governance in the EU,* 2010, Abingdon: Routledge.
970. [1971] ECR 1003.
971. [1960] ECR 355.
972. In Case 7/61 *Commission v Italy* ([1961] ECR 317) the ECJ rejected the defence based on necessity and in Joined Cases 90 and 91/63 *Commission v Belgium and Luxembourg* ([1964] ECR 625) the defence based on reciprocity.
973. See Case C-459/03 *Commission v Ireland* [2006] ECR I-4635.

(Continued)

	Public International Law	**EU Law**
6. Effect of a judgment finding a State in breach of its obligation.	A judgment of the ICJ is binding on the defaulting States.	The judgment of the ECJ is binding on the defaulting Member State, but as it often determines the exact scope of an obligation at issue, it is followed by other Member States on which the same obligation is imposed.[974]
7. Sanctions for non-compliance with a judgment finding a State in breach of its obligations.	At the request of the ICJ the UNSC may impose sanctions on the defaulting State. This has never occurred.	Pecuniary sanctions may be imposed on a Member State which refuses to comply with a judgment of the ECJ (see Chapter 14.5).

The jurisdiction of the ECJ in respect of actions for failure to fulfil obligations was extended under the ToL. The ECJ, in addition to the pre-ToL jurisdiction over Community law, gained jurisdiction over the AFSJ. However, in respect of measures concerning police and judicial co-operation in criminal matters (i.e. Framework decisions) adopted prior to the entry into force of the ToL, Protocol 9 on Transitional Provisions attached to the Treaties establishes special rules. It shields these measures from the jurisdiction of the ECJ and from enforcement action of the Commission under Article 258 TFEU until 1 December 2014. If any such measure is amended before the expiry of that period then that measure will be within the powers of EU institutions from the time of amendment. The ECJ has no jurisdiction with regard to CFSP matters apart from the exceptions set out in Article 24(1) TEU.

It is to be noted that some provisions of the Treaties provide for simplified proceedings against a Member State which has failed to fulfil its obligations deriving from the Treaties. The common point of these procedures is the possibility for the Commission or a Member State to bring the matter directly before the ECJ in a much shorter period of time than under Article 258 or 259 TFEU. Usually the administrative stage takes a different, simplified form, and the Commission is not bound to deliver a reasoned opinion. Those procedures are described, *inter alia*, in Articles 108(2), 114(9) and 348 TFEU and include the Rapid Intervention Mechanism examined in Chapter 20.9.

14.2 Action against a Member State by the Commission under Article 258 TFEU

Article 258 TFEU states:

"If the Commission considers that a Member State has failed to fulfil an obligation under the Treaties, it shall deliver a reasoned opinion on the matter after giving the State concerned the opportunity to submit its observations.

If the State concerned does not comply with the opinion within the period laid down by the Commission, the latter may bring the matter before the Court of Justice of the European Union."

---

974. Case 7/71 *Commission v France* [1971] ECR 1003.

The case law of the ECJ has clarified terms used in Article 258 TFEU, in particular it has defined:

- the notion of "failure of a Member State to fulfil an obligation under the Treaties"; and,

- the concept of a Member State as a defendant.

Article 258 TFEU sets out a procedure to be followed by the Commission, which gives the Member State an opportunity, on the one hand, of remedying the breach before the action is brought before the ECJ, and on the other hand, of presenting its defence to the Commission's complaint. If the Commission still considers that a Member State is in breach of its obligation, it may institute proceedings before the ECJ. At the judicial stage, it is extremely difficult for a Member State to justify its failure to comply with EU law. Various imaginative defences have been pleaded, and the great majority of them have been summarily rejected by the ECJ.

The above topics are dealt with below.

14.2.1 Definition of a failure of a Member State to fulfil an obligation under the Treaties

Failure to fulfil an obligation under the Treaties entails that there is an obligation imposed by the Treaties. The obligation must be well determined, that is, Article 258 TFEU requires that a Member State must be in breach of a pre-existing, specific and precise obligation.[975] However, recent case law shows that the Commission is allowed to bring proceedings not only for specific violations of EU law but also for "general and persistent infringements" of EU law. In Case C-494/01 *Commission v Ireland,*[976] the Commission brought proceedings against Ireland not only on the ground of incorrect application of the Directive on Waste in some specifically identified situations, but also on the ground that there were breaches of a general nature in implementing the directive, namely, systematic deficient administrative practices over a long period. The ECJ held that:

> "nothing prevents the Commission from seeking in parallel a finding that provisions of a directive have not been complied with by reason of the conduct of a Member State's authorities with regard to particular specific identified situations and a finding that those provisions have not been complied with because its authorities have adopted a general practice contrary thereto, with the particular situations illustrate where appropriate."[977]

So far, the ECJ has not indicated what type of infringement will fall into this category and what kind of evidence the Commission will be required to submit. However, in Case C-88/07 *Commission v Spain,*[978] the ECJ confirmed that a general and persistent infringement can be found in respect of a general administrative practice of long duration. In this case, the general administrative practice consisted of withdrawing from the Spanish market a number of herbal products lawfully produced and/or marketed in another Member State on the ground that they were not included in a national register (created by national law) and were thus deemed to be a medicinal product marketed without the requisite authorisation. The ECJ held that the general administrative practice constituted a general and persistent infringement of Articles 34 TFEU and 36 TFEU, and of the relevant EU decision which requires a Member State to communicate to the Commission any national measure which derogates

---

975. Case 7/71 *Commission v France* [1971] ECR 1003.
976. [2005] ECR I-3331.
977. Ibid, para. 27.
978. [2009] ECR I-1353.

from the free movement of goods. The consequence of this new approach is that the Commission is allowed to submit new examples of infringements of the EU obligation in question to the ECJ as this merely constitutes additional evidence supporting the claim of general and persistent infringement and not new pleas.[979] Further, a defaulting Member State will have to remedy not only the specifically identified breaches of EU law but also change its administrative practices.

Article 258 TFEU refers to "an obligation". The term is widely interpreted. It comprises obligations imposed:

- by the Treaties, Protocols, Annexes and all other primary sources;

- by EU secondary legislation – regulations,[980] decisions[981] and directives;[982]

- by binding acts, not expressly mentioned in Article 289 TFEU,[983] adopted by EU institutions; and,

- by international agreements concluded between the EU and third countries which by virtue of Article 216(2) TFEU "are binding upon institutions of the Union and on Member States".[984] In Case C-239/03 *Commission v France*,[985] the ECJ confirmed that Member States are obliged to comply with obligations arising from mixed agreements, that is, agreements concluded jointly by the EU and its Member States with non-Member States in the areas in which the EU and the Member States share competences. The ECJ ruled that mixed agreements have the same status as purely EU agreements in so far as their provisions are within the scope of EU competences.[986]

Non-compliance by a Member State with a ruling of the ECJ under Article 258 TFEU constitutes a breach of EU law by that Member State. It will be dealt with under Article 260 TFEU.

A failure by a Member State to fulfil an obligation is assessed in the light of the nature and scope of that obligation[987] and may result from an action, or from an omission, or a failure to act.[988] In Case 301/81 *Commission v Belgium*,[989] the ECJ held that in order to show a failure to fulfil an obligation it is not necessary to prove opposition, or inertia, on the part of a Member State.

Failure under Article 258 TFEU may arise in the following situations:

A. It may consist of some action taken by a Member State, such as the application of national law incompatible with EU law, the adoption of a legislative act contrary to EU law,[990] or an express refusal to fulfil an obligation imposed by EU law. In Case C-459/03 *Commission v Ireland*,[991] the ECJ found Ireland in breach of Article 258 TFEU, when Ireland brought proceedings against the UK before an arbitration tribunal established in accordance with the

---

979.   P. Wenneras, "A New Dawn for Commission Enforcement under Articles 226 and 227 EC. General and Persistent Infringements, Lump Sums and Penalty Payments", (2006) CMLRev., 31.
980.   Case 33/69 *Commission v Italy* [1970] ECR 93; Case 8/70 *Commission v Italy* [1970] ECR 961.
981.   Cases 6 and 11/69 *Commission v France* [1969] ECR 523.
982.   The majority of proceedings under Article 258 TFEU concern EU directives.
983.   Case 141/78 *France v UK* [1979] ECR 2923.
984.   Case 104/81 *Kaupferberg Hauptzollamt Mainz v C.A. Kupferberg & Cie KG a.A.* [1982] ECR 3641;
       Cases 194 and 241/85 *Commission v Greece* [1988] ECR 1037; Case C-228/91 *Commission v Italy* [1993] ECR I-2701.
985.   [2004] ECR I-9325.
986.   See, to that effect, Case 12/86 *Meryem Demirel v Stadt Schwäbisch Gmünd* [1987] ECR 3719 and Case C-13/00 *Commission v Ireland* [2002] ECR I-2943.
987.   Case 31/69 *Commission v Italy* [1970] ECR 25.
988.   Case C-265/95 *Commission v France* [1997] ECR I-6959.
989.   [1983] ECR 467.
990.   Case C-157/89 *Commission v Italy* [1991] ECR I-57.
991.   [2006] ECR I-4635.

dispute settlement procedure set out under the UN Convention on the Law of the Sea, without having first informed and consulted the relevant EU institutions. The Court ruled that the provisions of the Convention invoked by Ireland were part of EU law, as a result of transfer of these matters to the EU, and consequently the ECJ had exclusive jurisdiction to deal with any disputes relating to their interpretation or application.

B. It may arise from a failure to act. In many cases under Article 258 TFEU the Commission has initiated proceedings against a Member State for non-implementation of EU directives within the prescribed time limit. The ToL strengthened the Commission's powers to force Member States to implement EU directives in that under Article 260(3) TFEU the Commission may propose the imposition of pecuniary penalties in the initial infringement proceedings, i.e. in the application to the ECJ in which it asks for a finding of a failure.

In Case C-32/05 *Commission v Ireland,*[992] the ECJ imposed a limit on the discretion of Member States relating to transposition of directives. A Member State may choose any form or method when implementing EU directives or may decide that national law does not require any legislative or regulatory measures. However, it must ensure that when the relevant directive seeks to create rights for individuals, their legal situation must be sufficiently clear and precise so that the persons concerned "are put in a position to know the full extent of their rights and, where appropriate, to be able to rely on them before national courts".[993] This entails that arguments of a Member State that implementing measures are not required when national courts, in the light of general principles of constitutional and administrative law, interpret national law in conformity with EU law will not suffice to convince the ECJ that a Member State has fulfilled its obligation.[994] However, in Case 300/95 *Commission v UK,*[995] the ECJ imposed a heavy burden on the Commission to prove an infringement when the UK argued that it had complied with EU law in a situation where its courts had to interpret national law implementing an EU directive *contra legem* to achieve the objective of the Directive.

THE FACTS WERE:

The Commission argued that the United Kingdom was in violation of Article 7 of Council Directive 85/374 on product liability, as it implemented the Directive without transposing its text verbatim. *The UK Government argued that it had correctly implemented the Directive given that it is left to the discretion of the Member State to decide as to the form and methods of implementation of directives. What counts is that the objectives of the directive are attained. According to the UK the objectives were attained. The Commission considered that this was not the case, since the British courts had to interpret Article 7 of Directive 85/374* contra legem *in order to achieve the objectives of that directive.*

Held:

The ECJ rejected the application submitted by the Commission. The ECJ held that in order to assess the scope of national legislative or administrative provisions, the Commission must

---

992. [2006] ECR I-11323.
993. Ibid, para. 34.
994. Case C-58/02 *Commission v Spain* [2004] ECR I-621.
995. [1997] ECR I-2649.

take into account the way that national courts interpret those provisions in practice, i.e. it must prove that the national courts, in practice, interpret the provision in question in a manner inconsistent with EU law.

The ECJ reminded the Commission that in order to establish the failure of a Member State to fulfil its obligations, the Commission could not base its application under Article 258 TFEU on a supposition or a simple allegation.[996]

Comment:

It is submitted that the ECJ's dicta, which confers on national courts the role of being a guardian of EU law, is contrary to the principle of legal certainty, especially when national courts have to interpret a provision of national law implementing EU law contra legem in order to attain the objective required by a directive. It is also submitted that in subsequent cases the ECJ clearly stated that persons concerned must have an actual possibility to be aware of their rights deriving from the directive. This will not be the case when national law is clearly inconsistent with EU law to the point that national judges are required to interpret it contra legem.

C.   It may arise from an administrative practice contrary to EU law. Such a practice must be, to some degree, of a consistent and general nature in order to amount to a failure to fulfil obligations for the purposes of Article 258 TFEU.[997] Such a practice can give rise to Article 258 TFEU proceedings, even if the applicable national law itself complies with EU law.[998]

D.   It may arise from failure to comply with Article 4(3) TEU which states:

"Pursuant to the principle of sincere cooperation, the Union and the Member States shall, in full mutual respect, assist each other in carrying out tasks which flow from the Treaties.

The Member States shall take any appropriate measure, general or particular, to ensure fulfilment of the obligations arising out of the Treaties or resulting from the acts of the institutions of the Union.

The Member States shall facilitate the achievement of the Union's tasks and refrain from any measure which could jeopardise the attainment of the Union's objectives."

Article 4(3) first indent expressly recognises the principle of mutual sincere co-operation. Indents 2 and 3 Article 4(3) represent the revised version of Article 10 EC, which has been successfully used by the Commission as a legal basis in actions for failure to fulfil obligations.

In Case C-137/91 *Commission v Greece (Re Electronic Cash Registers)*[999] the ECJ explained the autonomous function of Article 4(3) TEU indents 2 and 3.

---

996.   Case C-62/89 *Commission v France* [1990] ECR I-925; Case C-159/94 *Commission v France* [1997] ECR I-5815; Case C-431/02 *Commission v UK* (judgment of 12/10/2004, unpublished); Case C-441/02 *Commission v Germany* [2006] ECR I-3449.

997.   Case C-387/99 *Commission v Germany* [2004] ECR I-3751; Case C-494/01 *Commission v Ireland* [2005] ECR I-3331; Case C-287/03 *Commission v Belgium* [2005] ECR I-3761.

998.   Case C-278/03 *Commission v Italy* [2005] ECR I-3747; Case C-441/02 *Commission v Germany* [2006] ECR I-3449.

999.   [1992] ECR I-4023.

THE FACTS WERE:

Greek law enacted in 1988 required the use of electronic cash registers by certain retailers. However, the approval of such registers was conducted by Greece's national authorities, which refused to certify any register containing less than 35 per cent "add-on value" from Greece. Other Member States complained to the Commission that this policy was contrary to the free movement of goods. During the investigation the Commission sent two faxes to the Greek Permanent Representation in Brussels asking for more information. None came. The Commission considered that lack of response constituted an infringement of Article 4(3) indents 2 and 3. In those circumstances, the Commission issued a formal notice under Article 258 TFEU against Greece, but the latter did not respond. Finally, the Commission delivered its reasoned opinion. No reply was received by the Commission, which then decided to bring proceedings before the ECJ.

The Government of Greece challenged the Commission proceedings. It claimed that it gave the Commission all necessary information concerning the legislation in question at a meeting in Athens in September 1990 and a year later sent the Commission the text of a new Act. According to the Greek Government there was no reason for providing additional information required by the Commission as the latter was fully aware of the situation before the action under Article 258 TFEU was brought. The Commission argued that the Greek Government provided the required information two years after it was requested and that at that stage the time limit fixed by the reasoned opinion had elapsed.

Held:

The ECJ held that Greece had violated Article 4(3) TEU indents 2 and 3. The ECJ stated that "the failure to reply to the Commission's questions within a reasonable period made the task which it has to perform more difficult and therefore amounts to a violation of the obligation of co-operation laid down in Article [4(3) indents 2 and 3]".

It emerges from the case law of the ECJ that Article 4(3) TEU indents 2 and 3 imposes a positive duty on Member States to co-operate with the Commission in its investigations into alleged violations of EU law. Failure to do so is in itself sufficient to give rise to liability of a Member State under Article 258 TFEU,[1000] regardless of whether a Member State refuses, or simply ignores the request of the Commission for information,[1001] or omits to forward necessary indications allowing the Commission to exercise its role of "guardian of the Treaties",[1002] or otherwise violates its obligation of loyal co-operation.[1003]

1000. See also Case C-33/90 *Commission v Italy* [1991] ECR I-5987; Case C-65/91 *Commission v Greece* [1992] ECR I-5245.
1001. Case 272/86 *Commission v Greece* [1988] ECR 4875; Case C-375/92 *Commission v Spain* [1994] ECR I-923.
1002. For example, Case C-40/92 *Commission v UK* [1994] ECR I-989.
1003. For example, in Case C-459/03 *Commission v Ireland* [2006] ECR I-4635, Ireland was in breach of Article 10 EC [Article 4(3) TFEU] for bringing proceedings against the UK under the dispute settlement procedure laid down in the UN Convention on the Law of the Sea, without informing and consulting the relevant Community institutions, and for ignoring the Commission's request to suspend these proceedings.

14.2.2 Member States as defendants

Proceedings under Article 258 are brought against the defaulting Member State. A failure, within the meaning of Article 258 TFEU, arises regardless of the national body which is at the origin of the action or inaction.

14.2.2.1 Constitutionally independent branches of the Member State

In Case 77/69 *Commission v Belgium*,[1004] the ECJ held that a Member State is liable for a failure attributable to its constitutionally independent body. In this case, the Belgian government[1005] tried to plead in its defence the independence of the Belgian parliament, which could not be forced by the government to adopt a required legislative act. The ECJ answered that:

> "the liability of a Member State under Article [258 TFEU] arises whatever the agency of the State whose action or inaction is the cause of the failure to fulfil its obligations, even in the case of a constitutionally independent institution."[1006]

In Cases 227–230/85 *Commission v Belgium*,[1007] the ECJ emphasised that the national division of competences between central and regional authorities which, especially in the context of a federal State, may result in a large measure of autonomy being conferred on the local or regional authorities, would not constitute a sufficient defence for a Member State. This is even if the local or regional authorities are solely empowered to implement necessary local legislation, and have failed to do so.

14.2.2.2 Private or semi-public bodies

A failure to fulfil an obligation under the Treaty by any private or semi-public body, which is controlled by a Member State, is imputable to that Member State.

In Case 249/81 *Commission v Ireland (Re Buy Irish Campaign)*,[1008] Ireland was held liable for financing through the Irish Goods Council (a government-sponsored body) a campaign to "Buy Irish" which promoted Irish products to the disadvantage of imports, although the Irish Goods Council could not adopt binding measures and the campaign was a failure.

14.2.2.3 A Member State's judiciary

It results from the case law of the ECJ that a Member State is liable under Article 258 TFEU if the failure is imputable to its court or tribunal.

In Case C-129/00 *Commission v Italy*,[1009] the Commission complained that the Italian Supreme Court (*Corte Suprema di Cassazione*) was mainly responsible for erroneous interpretation of EU law, which interpretation had been followed by a substantial proportion of Italian courts. The ECJ declared that Italy was in breach of EU law by failing to amend the relevant legislation, which was construed and applied by the Italian courts including its Supreme Court, in a manner inconsistent with EU law. A-G

1004. [1970] ECR 237; also Case 8/70 *Commission v Italy* [1970] ECR 961.
1005. The term "government" means the executive.
1006. 77/69 *Commission v Belgium* [1970] ECR 237, para. 15.
1007. [1988] ECR 1; see also Case C-57/89 *Commission v Germany* [1991] ECR I-883; Case C-47/99 *Commission v Luxembourg* [1999] ECR I-8999.
1008. [1982] ECR 4005.
1009. [2003] ECR I-14637.

Geelhoed in his Opinion delivered in this case emphasised the relevance of the judgment of the ECJ in Case C-224/01 *Köbler*[1010] to the procedure under Article 258 TFEU (see Chapter 12.4). He suggested the application of the following criteria to decide whether or not judicial decisions of national courts incompatible with EU law amount to a failure on the part of a Member State to fulfil its obligations under the Treaties. They are as follows:

- Whether judgments incompatible with EU law delivered by national courts adjudicating at last instance are regarded by inferior courts as a judicial authority in the national legal order;

- Whether judicial decisions contrary to EU law are important in numerical terms and in terms of their judicial authority, that is, for example are not isolated or numerically insignificant judicial decisions and have been confirmed by supreme courts in appeal proceedings; and,

- How substantial is the impact of judicial decisions incompatible with EU law on the achievement of the objectives sought by EU law which have been infringed by national decisions incompatible with it. In particular, whether judicial decisions incompatible with EU law have produced harmful effects in respect of economic operators who have to carry out their economic activities in more difficult conditions than their competitors or other persons who are in a similar situation in other Member States.

The Commission's reluctance to initiate proceedings against a Member State for breach of EU law by its highest courts is now history.[1011] In Case C-154/08 *Commission v Spain*,[1012] the Commission brought proceedings against Spain for the infringement of EU law by its Supreme Court which erroneously interpreted the Sixth VAT Directive, Directive 77/388/EEC. The Spanish Supreme Court had no doubt as to the interpretation of the directive and thus did not make a request for a preliminary ruling to the ECJ. The three criteria stated above were satisfied, in that the judgment of the Spanish Supreme Court was followed by the Spanish national tax administration and other Spanish courts, and had considerable impact on economic operators in Spain. The Spanish Government argued that, as the independence of the Spanish Supreme Court was protected by the Spanish Constitution, it could not remedy the breach. The ECJ swiftly rejected this line of defence by stating that, in accordance with its earlier case law, in particular Case C-129/00 *Commission v Italy*,[1013] a Member State may be held responsible for action or inaction of any of its agencies including a constitutionally independent institution such as its supreme court. For the first time ever, the ECJ declared that a Member State was in breach of EU law as a result of a Supreme Court judgment. Neither in *Köbler*, nor in Case C-129/00 *Commission v Italy* (above), nor in Case C-173/03 *Traghetti*[1014] had the ECJ made any direct statements condemning the highest national courts for their failure to comply with EU law. Therefore the importance of the judgment in Case C-154/08 *Commission v Spain* is that the ECJ condemned the ruling of the supreme court of a Member State itself and not the conduct of the national administration based on an erroneous ruling of a supreme court as occurred in Case C-129/00 *Commission v Italy*. The implication of Case C-154/08 *Commission v Spain* is that the Commission may bring proceedings against a Member State once a national court of last instance closes a case and gets it wrong. The above judgment should be applauded but one wonders

---

1010. C-224/01 *Gerhard Köbler v Austria* [2003] ECR I-10239.
1011. The Commission initiated proceedings against the French Cour de Cassation and the German Bundesfinanzhof (the highest court in financial matters), but both cases were settled. See question EQ No. 1907/85 [1986] OJ C137/7.
1012. [2009] ECR I-187.
1013. [2003] ECR I-14637.
1014. Case C-173/03 *Traghetti del Mediterranes SpA (TDM) v Italy* [2006] ECR I-5177.

to what extent the initiation of proceedings under Article 258 TFEU against a supreme court of a Member State, which would inevitably undermine the authority of the court in question, may damage the spirit of co-operation between the ECJ and national courts.

It is important to note that in Case C-154/08 *Commission v Spain*, the ECJ seems to have approved the criteria set out by A-G Geelhoed in *Köbler* (see above) when it stated that isolated or numerically insignificant judicial decisions incompatible with EU law, which have not been confirmed by supreme courts in appeal proceedings, may not necessarily amount to a failure on the part of a Member State to fulfil its obligations under the Treaties.

14.2.2.4 Private individuals

A Member State may be responsible for actions of its nationals, if it is in a position to prevent or terminate such actions. In Case C-265/95 *Commission v France*[1015] the ECJ found France liable for not taking all measures necessary to prevent its citizens from obstructing the free movement of fruits and vegetables within the internal market (see Chapter 20.2.4).

14.2.3 The procedure which the Commission must observe in the pursuance of its tasks under Article 258 TFEU

The Commission becomes aware of infringements of EU law by Member States in many ways, e.g. from complaints from individuals, from the Commission's own investigations, from complaints from other EU institutions, e.g. the EU Ombudsman, the EP, and from the media.

In order to properly manage infringement proceedings the Commission has introduced many innovations,[1016] in particular in respect of the pre-infringement procedure, i.e. in respect of the informal phase of proceedings. The first innovation was the introduction of the Complaints Handling – *Accueil des Plaignants*[1017] (CHAP) system.

Since 2009 the Commission has been using the *CHAP* complaints handlings registration system for complaints and enquiries from individuals alleging breaches of EU law by Member States. The system ensures proper and timely assignment of complaints to the relevant department of the Commission which then provides systematic feedback to the complainants on the handling of their complaints. In 2010, 4035 complaints were registered in CHAP, 52.5% were closed on the basis of comprehensive responses from the Commission, 14% were closed on the ground of lack of competence by the EU, 17% were under examination *via* EU Pilot (see below), and 9% were transformed into infringement proceedings.

The second innovation relates to the introduction of a problem-solving system involving the Member States. This is called EU Pilot. It is a system which allows the Commission to transfer complaints from individuals, as well as its own findings of alleged infringements, to the competent authorities of the Member State concerned for discussion with a view to achieving a speedy and satisfactory solution. In 2010, 81% of responses supplied by the Member States were considered by the Commission as acceptable. Only about 160 cases were considered as requiring further steps by the Commission under Article 258 TFEU. Overall in 2010 the Commission was involved in approximately 2010 infringement cases, 88% of which were satisfactorily resolved without reaching the ECJ. As can be seen from the above, the taking of proceedings before the ECJ is only a minor part of the Commission's mission as "Guardian of the Treaties".

1015. [1997] ECR I-6959.
1016. See Commission's 28th Annual Report on Monitoring the Application of EU Law, COM(2011) 588 final.
1017. The French words " Accueil des Plaignants" mean in English "welcome complainants."

The Commission has also modified its infringement database (NIF). Currently NIF contains pre-infringement and infringement cases. In the future it will only contain cases which the Commission decides to pursue in the formal stage which starts with the letter of formal notice (below). This will enhance the transparency of the Commission's handling of infringement cases.

The Commission is the master of proceedings under Article 258 TFEU. It enjoys a broad discretion and may decide to start or not to start proceedings, and may terminate them at any stage. The ECJ has no jurisdiction to consider whether the Commission's exercise of that discretion is appropriate.[1018] The wide discretion is justified by the fact that under Article 258 TFEU it has no obligation to act. In Case 48/65 *Lütticke*[1019] the ECJ held that neither the Commission's formal letter of notice, nor its reasoned opinion, have binding legal effect. Accordingly, neither can be challenged under Article 263 TFEU. Indeed, the Article 258 TFEU procedure is not intended to redress grievances of individuals. It is objective in nature as its purpose is to objectively assess a Member State's compliance with EU law.[1020] However, if a complaint that originates from an individual is not pursued by the Commission, such individual may complain to the EU Ombudsman (see Chapter 22.9).

In the past, investigations by the EU Ombudsman into the handling of complaints by the Commission, and its disapproval of the Commission's procedure relating to the management of complaints in terms of lack of transparency and lack of response to complainants,[1021] led to substantive improvement of the quality of the infringement procedure, and more generally changes to all administrative procedures of EU institutions. Indeed, the Ombudsman was the main force behind the adoption in 2001 of the European Code of Good Administrative Behaviour which all EU institutions and bodies, their administrations and their officials should respect in their relations with the public. Furthermore, under pressure from the EU Ombudsman the Commission's handling of the infringement procedures has changed over time and ultimately resulted in the adoption of pre-infringement tools such as CHAP and EU Pilot, and modifications to its NIF. Finally, under the ToL the principle of transparency ensures a wide access to documents in the possession of the Commission including those relating to the Article 258 TFEU procedure.[1022]

In the informal stage the Commission enjoys a double discretion:

- first, it decides whether or not a Member State is in breach of an obligation; and,

- second, it assesses various aspects of the situation in question, especially by placing it in the political context, in order to determine whether to commence proceedings against the defaulting Member State.

In many cases the Commission may decide not to act when faced with sensitive political issues. For example, the UK was in breach of EU law for more than 20 years by not introducing national legislation required by the ECJ subsequent to its ruling in *Van Duyn*.[1023] A-G Roemer in Case 7/71 *Commission v*

1018. Case C-236/99 *Commission v Belgium* [2000] ECR I-5657; Case C-383/00 *Commission v Germany* [2002] ECR I-4219.

1019. [1966] ECR 19.

1020. Case 416/85 *Commission v UK* [1988] ECR I-3127; Case C-255/05 *Commission v Italy* [2004] ECR I-5767.

1021. In 1997 the EU Ombudsman started its own-initiative inquiry into the handling of complaints by the Commission under Article 258 TFEU. See the 1997 Annual Report of the Ombudsman available at http://www.ombudsman.europa.eu/activities/annualreports.faces (accessed 8/7/12). On this topic see: C. Harlow and R. Rawlings, "Accountability and Law Enforcement: The Centralized EU Infringement Procedure", (2006) 31 ELRev., 447.

1022. See Joined Cases C-514, 528 and 532/07P *Sweden and API v Commission* [2010] ECR I-8533.

1023. The violation was finally rectified by the Immigration (European Economic Area) Order 1994, SI 1994/1895.

France[1024] suggested that in certain circumstances the Commission should abstain from initiating proceedings under Article 258 TFEU, i.e.

- when there is a possibility of reaching a settlement;

- when the effect of the breach of EU law is minor;

- when proceedings by the Commission would be likely to create a major political crisis in the defaulting Member State, especially in the context of a minor violation of EU law by that Member State; and,

- when there is a possibility that the provision in question will be modified or annulled in the near future.

14.2.3.1 The informal phase

At the informal stage the Commission invites the Member State concerned to provide some explanations and the Member State is reminded that it has an obligation to co-operate under Article 4(3) TEU indents 2 and 3.[1025] The request for information takes the form of a "letter pre-258 proceedings". It fixes a time limit for reply. Usually the Commission and representatives of the Member State discuss the matter. Sometimes the negotiations between them take a considerable time; sometimes the matter will be settled immediately. The length of time spent during the informal phase is of some importance, especially when the Commission decides to take formal proceedings against the defaulting Member State. Usually the longer the period of time spent on the informal proceedings, the more easily the ECJ will accept a short deadline for compliance imposed by the Commission in the formal proceedings.

The existence of informal proceedings emphasises the non-punitive nature of Article 258 TFEU. The objective of the provision is to terminate the violation of EU law, and not to exacerbate the dispute. However, if no settlement is possible, the Commission will start the formal phase which comprises an administrative and a judicial stage.

14.2.3.2 The administrative stage (pre-litigation procedure)

The pre-litigation procedure fulfils two main objectives: it gives the Member State concerned the opportunity to comply with its obligations under EU law, and to avail itself of its right to defend itself against charges formulated by the Commission.[1026] During the pre-litigation procedure the Commission is required to perform two acts, that is, sending the letter of formal notice and preparing the reasoned opinion.

14.2.3.3 Letter of formal notice

In Case 51/83 *Commission v Italy*,[1027] the ECJ held that the letter of formal notice constitutes an essential formal requirement under Article 258 TFEU and its omission would result in the inadmissibility of an action under this Article.

1024. [1971] ECR 1003.
1025. Case 147/77 *Commission v Italy* [1978] ECR 1307.
1026. Case 293/85 *Commission v Belgium* [1988] ECR 305; Case C-439/99 *Commission v Italy* [2002] ECR I-305; Case C-431/02 *Commission v UK* (judgment of 12/10/2004, unpublished).
1027. [1984] ECR 2793.

The letter of formal notice determines the scope of the case which cannot later be widened, even at the stage of the reasoned opinion.[1028] It invites an allegedly defaulting Member State to submit its observation on the disputed matters, and guarantees the right of defence of the Member State, although the Member State is not obliged to reply. Usually the Commission gives a defaulting Member State two months to reply, but in urgent matters this time limit may be shortened.

The procedure may be terminated if the Commission is convinced that, in the light of the explanations provided by the Member State, there is no violation of EU law, or if the failure is corrected immediately. Otherwise, after the expiry of the time limit fixed in the letter of formal notice, the Commission will normally issue a reasoned opinion.

14.2.3.4 Reasoned opinion

The main difference between the letter of formal notice and the reasoned opinion is that the former "is intended to define the subject-matter of the dispute and to indicate to the Member State . . . the factors enabling it to prepare its defence",[1029] while in the reasoned opinion the Commission must establish the legal arguments in respect of the alleged failure of a Member State to fulfil its obligation under the Treaties.[1030]

The reasoned opinion must contain a cogent and detailed exposition of the reasons which led the Commission to the conclusion that the Member State has failed to fulfil its obligation under the Treaties.[1031]

The reasoned opinion invites the defaulting Member State to cease the infringement. It also fixes a time limit for the Member State concerned to comply – usually two months, but in urgent cases this period may be shortened. The time limit cannot be changed by the ECJ,[1032] although it will be taken into account when the ECJ determines whether the Commission gave a "reasonable time" to comply with the reasoned opinion. In Case 74/82 *Commission v Ireland*,[1033] the ECJ viewed with disapproval the period of five days given in the reasoned opinion to Ireland to amend its legislation, which had been in force for more than forty years. There was no urgency requiring the fixing of such a short period, but the action was not dismissed. The ECJ took into consideration the fact that the Commission issued its reasoned opinion on 9 November 1981 and referred to the ECJ on 19 February 1982, which means that the Irish had two and a half months to deal with the matter, and took the view that in the light of this a period of five days was not unreasonable. Thus, as the Court noted, the Commission's regrettable behaviour did not affect the admissibility of the action.

If the Member State concerned complies with the reasoned opinion within the prescribed time limit, the Commission is barred from bringing proceedings before the ECJ.[1034] Otherwise, the Commission may commence the next step in the proceedings under Article 258 TFEU, that is, bring the matter before the ECJ.

With regard to the formal stage of the procedure, in Case 7/71 *Commission v France*,[1035] the ECJ held that proceedings under Article 258 TFEU are not confined to a pre-established time limit "since,

---

1028. Case 51/83 *Commission v Italy* [1984] ECR 2793.
1029. Case 51/83 *Commission v Italy* [1984] ECR 2793.
1030. In Case 7/61 *Commission v Italy (Re Pigmeat case)* [1961] ECR 317 the ECJ held that "the opinion referred to in Article [226] of the Treaty [Article 258 TFEU] must . . . contain a sufficient statement of reasons to satisfy the law".
1031. Case C-207/96 *Commission v Italy* [1997] ECR I-6869; Case C-439/99 *Commission v Italy* [2002] ECR I-305.
1032. Case 28/81 *Commission v Italy* [1981] ECR 2577; Case 29/81 *Commission v Italy* [1981] 2585.
1033. [1984] ECR 317.
1034. Case C-200/88 *Commission v Greece* [1990] ECR I-4299.
1035. [1971] ECR 1003, p. 1016, para. 5.

by reason of its nature and its purpose, this procedure involves a power on the part of the Commission to consider the most appropriate means and time-limits for the purposes of putting an end to any violation of the Treaty". This aspect of the Commission's discretion is enhanced by the possibility of bringing proceedings against a defaulting Member State, even when the latter has complied with the reasoned opinion but after the expiry of the time limit specified in it.

The issue of whether a Member State has failed to fulfil its obligation is determined by reference to the situation prevailing in that Member State at the end of the time limit set out in the reasoned opinion and not by reference to the time when proceedings were brought before the ECJ.[1036] As a result, the Commission may bring proceedings many years after the expiry of the time limit fixed in the reasoned opinion, and irrespective of whether or not the alleged infringement has been brought to an end.[1037] In Case 7/61 *Commission v Italy*,[1038] the ECJ recognised that the Commission may many years later, have an interest in determining whether a violation of EU law has occurred. In Case 39/72 *Commission v Italy*[1039] the ECJ held that its ruling in such a case may be useful, especially in order to establish the basis of a Member State's liability with regard to other Member States; the EU; and, individuals concerned. If the Commission decides to bring proceedings many years after the expiry of a deadline specified in a reasoned opinion it does not have to show an interest to bring those proceedings or to state reasons why it is bringing an action for failure to fulfil obligations. This is because the subject-matter of the action, as it is to be found in the application, corresponds to the subject-matter of the dispute as stated in the letter of formal notice and in the reasoned opinion.[1040] The case law shows that excessive delay in bringing proceedings before the ECJ can only make the Commission's action inadmissible if the excessive delay makes it "more difficult for the Member State in question to refute the Commission's arguments thereby infringing its rights of the defence".[1041]

14.2.4 The procedure before the ECJ

The judicial stage commences with the Commission lodging an application to the ECJ asking for a declaration that a Member State has failed to fulfil its obligation arising from EU law. The application must state the subject matter of the dispute and set out its legal and factual context. The ECJ fully investigates the merits of the case, and the Member State may, in its defence, invoke arguments not previously invoked.[1042] The ECJ decides the matter taking into consideration the situation as it was at the expiry of the time limit fixed in the reasoned opinion.[1043] It must not take account of any subsequent changes.[1044] Obviously in some cases, changes in national legislation between the expiry of the period of compliance fixed by the reasoned opinion and the lodging of an application with the ECJ may be so

---

1036. Case C-143/02 *Commission v Italy* [2003] ECR I-2877; Case C-446/01 *Commission v Spain* [2003] ECR I-6053.
1037. Case C-519/03 *Commission v Luxembourg* [2005] ECR I-3067 and Case C-562/07 *Commission v Spain* [2009] ECR I-9553.
1038. [1961] ECR 317.
1039. [1973] ECR 101.
1040. Case C-333/99 *Commission v France* [2001] ECR I-1025; Case C-474/99 *Commission v Spain* [2002] ECR I-5293; and Case C-33/04 *Commission v Luxembourg* [2005] ECR I-3067.
1041. Case C-333/99 *Commission v France* [2001] ECR I-102.
1042. Contrary to the opinion of the Commission, the ECJ confirmed in Case C-414/97 *Commission v Spain* [1999] ECR I-5585 that the Member State's right to defence entails that new arguments may be invoked before the ECJ.
1043. Case C-200/88 *Commission v Greece* [1990] ECR I-4299; Case C-133/94 *Commission v Belgium* [1996] ECR I-2323; Case C-310/03 *Commission v Luxembourg* [2004] ECR I-1969; Case C-312/03 *Commission v Belgium* [2004] ECR I-1975.
1044. Case C-211/02 *Commission v Luxembourg* [2003] ECR I-2429.

fundamental as to render any judgment by the ECJ otiose. This occurred in Case C-177/03 *Commission v France*,[1045] in which the ECJ emphasised that:

"In such situations, it may be preferable for the Commission not to bring an action but to issue a new reasoned opinion precisely identifying the complaints which it intends pursuing, having regard to the changed circumstances."

The ECJ may, in the light of the legal arguments submitted by both parties during the proceedings under Article 258 TFEU, give an interlocutory ruling, inviting the Commission and the Member State concerned to find a solution ensuring the effective application of EU law, but as with any interlocutory decision, the proceedings can be reopened if necessary.[1046] Additionally the Commission is entitled to request interim measures.

14.2.5 Defences

Defences can be divided into substantive and procedural. With regard to substantive defences, few have succeeded bearing in mind that some defences recognised under public international law have been rejected by the ECJ. Probably the best defence for a defaulting Member State is to deny the existence of the obligation. However, even the fact that the time limit prescribed in a directive for its implementation has not yet expired may not be invoked in some circumstances. In Case C-422/05 *Commission v Belgium*,[1047] the ECJ declared, for the first time, that a Member State may be in breach of Articles 4(3) TEU indents 2 and 3 and Article 288 TFEU for adopting national measures almost at the end of a transitional period (three months before its expiry) which were liable to seriously compromise the result prescribed by the directive in question (see Chapter 11.4). The severity with which the ECJ assesses substantive defences has led the Member States to rely more often on procedural defences rather than substantive defences.

14.2.5.1 Successful defences based on the procedural requirements of Article 258 TFEU

The ECJ will first assess whether the Commission has complied with the procedural requirements imposed by Article 258 TFEU. This is necessary to ensure that a defaulting Member State's rights to defence are protected. The ECJ will dismiss an application under Article 258 TFEU in the following circumstances:

A. **If the time limit fixed by the Commission either in the letter of formal notice or in the reasoned opinion is not reasonable.** In Case 293/85 *Commission v Belgium [Re University Fees]*,[1048] which concerned the compliance of Belgium with the ECJ ruling in *Gravier*, Belgium was given only eight days to reply to the letter of formal notice and 15 days to comply with the reasoned opinion. The ECJ held that these time limits were insufficient for Belgium given the complexity of the matter.[1049]

1045. [2004] ECR I-11671, para. 21.
1046. Case 170/78 *Commission v UK* [1980] ECR 415; Case 149/79 *Commission v Belgium* [1980] ECR 3881.
1047. [2007] ECR I-4749.
1048. [1988] ECR 305.
1049. In Case 293/83 *Gravier v City of Liege* [1989] ECR 593, the ECJ held that the fees (so called "minerval") imposed upon EU nationals studying in Belgium were discriminatory and in breach of Article 56 TFEU, which ensures the free movement of services throughout the EU. The *Gravier* case is discussed in Chapter 22.3.4.1.

The ECJ will take into account many factors in deciding whether or not the time limit fixed by the Commission may be considered as reasonable. In Case 85/85 *Commission v Belgium*,[1050] the ECJ held that a period of 15 days was reasonable in the light of the considerable length of time taken by the informal proceedings.

B. **If the complaints and legal arguments in the application under Article 258 TFEU are not identical to those invoked in the letter of formal notice and the reasoned opinion.**[1051] The case law of the ECJ demonstrates that historically the Court rigorously applied the requirement that the letter of formal notice and the reasoned opinion must contain identical complaints and legal argument..This was done, on the one hand, to protect the defaulting Member State against new complaints and legal arguments of the Commission and, on the other hand, to counterbalance the discretion which the Commission enjoys under Article 258 TFEU.[1052] However, the ECJ changed its position in the mid 1990s.[1053] In Case C-433/03 *Commission v Germany*,[1054] the ECJ stated that it is not necessary that the statement of the subject matter of proceedings set out in the reasoned opinion matches exactly that contained in the application under Article 258 TFEU lodged with the ECJ. What counts is that the subject matter of the proceedings has not been extended or altered in either document.[1055] In Case C-433/03 *Commission v Germany*, the Commission added to the strength of its application by referring to the then recent case law relevant to the proceedings. The ECJ agreed that this addition did not change the substance of the complaint and accordingly rejected Germany's argument that the Commission should have sent Germany a further reasoned opinion setting out the more recent changes in the case law before starting the infringement proceedings before the ECJ.

C. **If the Commission fails to identify the subject matter of the dispute with sufficient precision in its application.** The Commission is required to set out in its application to the ECJ the subject matter of the proceedings, a summary of legal arguments and the factual context of the case with sufficient clarity and precision to enable the Member State to prepare its defence and the Court to give a ruling. Accordingly it is necessary for the Commission to set out the essential points of law and facts on which the case is based "coherently and intelligibly in the application itself and for the heads of claim to be set out unambiguously so that the Court does not rule *ultra petita* or indeed fail to rule on an objection".[1056]

In Case C-141/10 *Commission v the Netherlands*,[1057] the Dutch government successfully claimed that the Commission had failed to satisfy the above requirements.

1050. [1986] ECR 1149, see also Case 74/82 *Commission v Ireland* [1984] ECR 317 already examined in this chapter.
1051. For example, Case C-210/91 *Commission v Greece* [1992] ECR I-6735; Case C-157/91 *Commission v The Netherlands* [1992] ECR I-5899; Case C-296/92 *Commission v Italy* [1994] ECR I-1.
1052. Case C-191/95 *Commission v Germany* [1998] ECR I-5449, Case C-365/97 *Commission v Italy* [1999] ECR I-7773.
1053. Case C-375/95 *Commission v Greece* [1997] ECR I-5981; Case C-105/02 *Commission v Germany* [2006] ECR I-9659.
1054. [2005] ECR I-6985.
1055. Case C-279/94 *Commission v Italy* [1997] ECR I-4743; Case C-52/00 *Commission v France* [2002] ECR I-3827; Case C-139/00 *Commission v Spain* [2002] ECR I-6407. and Case C-340/10 *Commission v Cyprus* (judgment of 15/3/12 (NYR)).
1056. E.g. Case C-178/00 *Italy v Commission* [2003] ECR I-303, para. 6; Case C-296/01 *Commission v France* [2003] ECR I-13909, para. 121, and Case C-195/04 *Commission v Finland* [2007] ECR I-3351, para. 22.
1057. Judgment of 19/4/12 (NYR).

THE FACTS WERE:

The Commission brought proceedings against the Netherlands for breaches of Regulation 1408/71 on the Application of Social Security Schemes to Employed Persons, to Self-Employed Persons and to Members of their Families, and of Articles 45 to 48 TFEU with regard to EU migrant workers who are employed on drilling platforms in the Netherlands. The Dutch government argued that the Commission did not identify with sufficient precision provisions of national law, or practices in the Netherlands, which were in breach of EU law; did not explain how national law and practices put workers living on drilling platforms at a disadvantage as compared to other workers in the Netherlands; and, failed to identify provisions of the Dutch social security legislation that, allegedly, had a discriminatory effect on those workers.

Held:

The ECJ dismissed the action as inadmissible.

Comment:

The ECJ expressed its astonishment at the lack of precision in the Commission's application. Indeed, the application stated that the failure consisted, without giving any legal or factual clarifications, of refusal of the Netherlands to grant "some social security benefits" to workers employed on drilling platforms. With regard to Article 45 TFEU, the ECJ held that it had insufficient information to apprehend exactly the scope of the infringement of that provision alleged by the Commission and consequently, decide whether such a breach existed in this case.

14.2.5.2 Successful substantive defences

The ECJ accepted the following defences:

A. **Unlawful obligation.** The strongest defence is for the Member State concerned to bring an action for annulment under Article 263 TFEU of the challenged measure. The ECJ has permitted a defaulting Member State to call into question the validity of an EU act in Article 258 TFEU proceedings. It seems quite strange that a defaulting Member State may challenge the validity of EU acts in proceedings under Article 258 TFEU in view of the fact that Member States have privileged *locus standi* under Article 263 TFEU to challenge the validity of any EU act. Indeed, initially the court insisted on use being made of Article 263 TFEU by a Member State.[1058] There is no clear justification for the change of attitude of the ECJ, but it seems that the reason may be provided by Article 277 TFEU which allows the challenging of EU legislation indirectly, through the medium of attacking implementing measures adopted on the basis of that legislation, and thus, at least theoretically, an escape from the strict deadline of Article 263 TFEU (see Chapter 15.3.1.2). However, with regard to Article 258 TFEU proceedings the ECJ has limited the opportunity of a Member State to rely on the unlawfulness of an EU act to two situations:

1058. For example, Case 20/59 *Italy v High Authority* [1960] ECR 325.

■ The first was discussed by the ECJ in Case 226/87 *Commission v Greece*,[1059] in which the ECJ stated that a Member State may call into question the legality of a decision if such a decision is affected by evident and serious vices which render it "non-existent".[1060] With regard to regulations, in Case 116/82 *Commission v Germany*[1061] the ECJ accepted that illegality of a regulation may be invoked as a defence to proceedings under Article 258 TFEU; and,

■ The second was established in Case 6/69 *Commission v France*,[1062] in which the French Government successfully proved that the decision in question was adopted in an area in which the Member State had exclusive competence.

B. **Force majeure.** Another possibility for a Member State is to invoke the defence of *force majeure*, although this defence has never been successfully pleaded. The reason is that the ECJ has always interpreted this concept strictly. The definition of *force majeure* was provided in Case 296/86 *McNicoll* [1063] in proceedings under Article 263 TFEU, and has been transposed to proceedings under Article 258 TFEU.[1064] In that case the ECJ held that:

> "whilst the concept of *force majeure* does not presuppose an absolute impossibility of performance, it nevertheless requires that non-performance of the act in question be due to circumstances beyond the control of persons pleading *force majeure*, that the circumstances be abnormal and unforeseeable and that the consequences could not have been avoided through the exercise of all due care." [1065]

As a result, what are considered under national law as exonerating circumstances, such as unforeseeable and irresistible political events – namely the dissolution of a national parliament, political difficulties, governmental crises, delays in the legislative procedure, social and economic disorders, and so on – were rejected by the ECJ.[1066] Consequently, it is very difficult for a Member State to successfully plead this defence although in Case 101/84 *Commission v Italy [The Traffic Statistics Case]*[1067] the Government of Italy was close to succeeding.

THE FACTS WERE:

The Italian Government argued that following a bomb attack by the Red Brigade (a terrorist organisation) on the Ministry of Transport's data-processing centre, which destroyed its register, it was impossible to comply with EC Directive 78/546 which required the Member State to forward statistical data in respect of the carriage of goods by road.

1059. Case 20/59 *Italy v High Authority* [1960] ECR 325.
1060. Case 15/85 *Consorzio Cooperative d' Abruzzo v Commission* (1987) ECR 1005.
1061. [1986] ECR 2519, also Case C-258/89 *Commission v Spain* [1991] ECR I-3977.
1062. [1969] ECR 523.
1063. Case 296/86 *McNicoll v Ministry of Agriculture* [1988] ECR 1491.
1064. Case 145/85 *Denkavit België NV v Belgium* [1987] ECR 565; Case C-105/02 *Commision v Germany* [2006] ECR I-9659.
1065. Case 296/86 *McNicoll v Ministry of Agriculture* [1988] ECR 1491, para. 11.
1066. See K. D. Magliveras, "Force Majeure in Community Law", [1990] 15 ELRev., 460.
1067. [1985] ECR 2629.

> *Held:*
>
> *The ECJ held that the delay of four-and-a-half years between the terrorist attack and the implementation of the directive was too long to exonerate Italy. In this respect the ECJ held that:*
>
> "... although it is true that the bomb attack, which took place before 18 January 1979, may have constituted a case of *force majeure* and created insurmountable difficulties, its effect could only have lasted a certain time, namely the time which would in fact be necessary for an administration showing a normal degree of diligence to replace the equipment destroyed and to collect and prepare the data."[1068]

C. **Uncertainty as to the exact meaning of the obligation.** Under Article 258 TFEU the Commission must determine with precision, or at least sufficiently from a legal point of view, the obligation which a Member State has failed to fulfil.[1069] This requirement has been used by the Member States as a defence under Article 258 TFEU.

Initially, the ECJ recognised this defence only if the uncertainty as to the exact meaning of the obligation related to its essential aspect.[1070] Gradually, however, the ECJ has accepted that even in proceedings under Article 258 TFEU Member States are entitled to elucidation by the ECJ as to the exact scope of the obligations they are supposed to fulfil, especially in the event of divergent interpretations.[1071] The extent of the ECJ's acceptance of this defence is still difficult to determine. In this respect, in Case C-133/94 *Commission v Belgium*[1072] the Government of Belgium pleaded, *inter alia,* the obscurity and ambiguity of a provision concerning the concept of "chemical installation" under Council Directive 85/337/EEC on environmental impact assessments. The Commission implicitly agreed with Belgium, as the Commission subsequently decided to define the precise meaning of that concept. Notwithstanding this, the ECJ held Belgium in breach of Article 258 TFEU.

14.2.5.3 Unsuccessful substantive defences

The ingeniousness of the Member States in constructing defences to Article 258 TFEU proceedings is astonishing. Over the years they have attempted to plead almost every justification imaginable for their failure to fulfil their obligations under the Treaties.

The following are examples of the most popular unsuccessful defences.

A. **Defence based on reciprocity.** This defence is recognised under public international law but rejected by EU law as contrary to the spirit and objectives of the EU legal order.[1073] A Member

---

1068. Ibid, para. 16.
1069. Case 20/59 *Italy v High Authority* [1960] ECR 325.
1070. Case 26/69 *Commission v France* [1970] ECR 565; Case 70/72 *Commission v Germany* [1973] ECR 813.
1071. Case 7/71 *Commission v France* [1971] ECR 1003.
1072. [1996] ECR I-2323.
1073. G. Conway, "Breaches of EC Law and the International Responsibility of Member States", (2002) 13 *European Journal of International Law*, 679; B. Simma and D. Pulkowski, "Of Planets and the Universe: Self-Contained Regimes in International Law", (2006) 17(3) *European Journal of International Law*, 483–529.

State cannot withhold its own performance even if either an EU institution or another Member State has failed to perform its obligations.[1074]

The position of the ECJ is fully justified because under the Treaties unlawful actions or omissions of either Member States or EU institutions are investigated and properly dealt with.[1075] Further, the ECJ has the mandatory and exclusive jurisdiction to deal with disputes relating to the interpretation and application of EU law. The ECJ alone decides whether a Member State has complied with obligations arising out of EU law. Accordingly, there is neither the need, nor any justification, for permitting Member States to "take the law into their own hands".

The rejection of defences based on reciprocity entails that:

1. Any unilateral action of a Member State aimed at correcting the effect of a violation of EU law by another Member State is prohibited.

    If a Member State considers that another Member State has failed to fulfil its obligations under EU law, that Member State may bring an action under Article 259 TFEU against the defaulting Member State, or ask the Commission to act under Article 258 TFEU.

    In Case 232/78 *Commission v France (Re Restrictions on Imports of Lamb)*[1076] the ECJ held that:

    > "A Member State cannot under any circumstances unilaterally adopt, on its own authority, corrective measure or measures to protect trade designed to prevent any failure on the part of another Member State to comply with the rules laid down by the Treaty."

This statement was repeated almost word for word by the ECJ in Case C-14/96 *Denuit*,[1077] in which a Belgian judge asked the ECJ whether Belgium was entitled to take unilateral measures against Member States which were in breach of Council Directive 89/552 establishing a single audiovisual area in the EU, especially to oppose the retransmissions to the territory of Belgium of programmes broadcast by the national broadcasting body of another Member State which did not comply with certain provisions of the Directive.[1078]

2. A Member State cannot invoke in its defence that another Member State is also in breach of the same obligation, even though the Commission has not initiated proceedings against that other Member State.[1079]

3. Neither a Member State which is an alleged victim of violation of EU law by another Member State, nor any other Member State is allowed to plead that violation in its defence.[1080]

1074. Cases 90 and 91/63 *Commission v Luxembourg and Belgium (Re Import of Powdered Milk Products)* [1964] ECR 625.
1075. Case C-359/93 *Commission v The Netherlands* [1995] ECR I-157.
1076. [1979] ECR 2729, para. 9.
1077. Case C-14/96 *Criminal Proceedings against Paul Denuit* [1997] ECR I-2785.
1078. See also: Joined Cases 142–143/80 *Amministrazione delle Finanze dello Stato v Essevi SpA and Carlo Salengo* [1981] ECR 1413; Case C-11/95 *Commission v Belgium* [1966] ECR I-4115; Case C-118/03 *Commission v Germany* (unpublished).
1079. Case 232/78 *Commission v France [Re Restrictions on Imports of Lamb]* [1979] ECR 2729.
1080. Case 52/75 *Commission v Italy* [1976] ECR 277.

4. A Member State cannot rely in its defence under Article 258 TFEU on the fact that an EU institution has acted unlawfully or failed to act when it was under a duty to act. Articles 263 and 265 TFEU provide in such a case an appropriate procedure for the very purpose of rectifying those problems[1081] (see Chapter 15). In Case C-359/93 *Commission v The Netherlands*,[1082] the ECJ held that this defence would also be rejected if an EU institution fails to comply with its obligations under the Treaty subsequent to a failure by a Member State.

B. **Defence based on necessity.** This defence, rejected by the ECJ, is recognised under public international law, which sets out stringent criteria for such a defence to be accepted, i.e. there must be exceptional circumstances of extreme urgency, the *status quo ante* (the situation which previously existed) must be re-established as soon as possible, and the State concerned must act in good faith.[1083]

In Case 7/61 *Commission v Italy [The Pigmeat case]*,[1084] Italy banned all imports of pork into Italy from other Member States in order to avert an economic crisis. The ECJ held that with respect to emergency situations the appropriate remedy was laid down in Article 226 (now repealed) and, for reasons similar to those under the principle of reciprocity, declared the unilateral action by Italy to be in breach of EU law.

C. **Defence based on the peculiarity of national systems, especially their constitutional, administrative and institutional organisation.** This defence was rejected by the ECJ in Case 77/69 *Commission v Belgium*.[1085]

THE FACTS WERE:

The Government of Belgium argued that its attempts to pass necessary amendments to legislation relating to the tax on wood were fettered by the Belgian parliament, a body which the government had no power to compel to act. A draft to amend a discriminatory tax scheme on wood was submitted to the Belgian parliament, but had fallen with the dissolution of parliament.

Held:

The ECJ held that the Member State was liable under Article 258 TFEU whenever an agent of the Member State, including a constitutionally independent institution, fails to fulfil its obligation arising from EU law.

Similarly in Case 1/86 *Commission v Belgium (Re Failure to Implement Directives)*,[1086] the ECJ rejected the justification submitted by the Belgian Government which stated that it was

---

1081.   Cases 90 and 91/63 *Commission v Belgium and Luxembourg* [1964] ECR 625.
1082.   [1995] ECR I-157.
1083.   The defence of necessity was successfully invoked by the UK when it bombed the *Torrey Canyon*, a ship flying the Liberian flag, which was grounded outside the British territorial waters, as it represented a threat of an ecological disaster, but this defence failed in the *Rainbow Warrior* case [1990] 82 ILR 499.
1084.   [1961] ECR 317.
1085.   [1970] ECR 237.
1086.   [1987] ECR 2797.

constitutionally unable to compel some of its regions to comply with a judgment of the ECJ requiring the implementation of a number of EU directives within the prescribed time limit.

D. **Defence based on political and economic difficulties experienced by a Member State, or specific local conditions.** Political difficulties cannot be pleaded in order to justify a failure to comply with obligations resulting from EU law. In Case 8/70 *Commission v Italy*,[1087] a defence based on a ministerial crisis in Italy was rejected. Indeed, in the light of the political turbulence in Italy after WWII, the acceptance of this defence would have paralysed the operation of EU law in that country.

Interesting arguments relating to political difficulties were submitted by the UK in Case 128/78 *Commission v UK (Re Tachographs)*.[1088]

THE FACTS WERE:

The Commission brought an action against the UK for failure to comply with Regulation 1463/70 relating to the introduction of tachographs in commercial vehicles. By this regulation tachographs were made compulsory, and had to replace the use of individual record books. They were strongly opposed by the trade unions in the UK (where they were described as "the spy in the cab"). The Government of the UK suggested that the installation and use of tachographs should be on a voluntary basis. It argued that the resistance from the trade unions would lead to political difficulty, would result in strikes in the transport sector and thus seriously damage the whole economy of the UK.

Held:

The ECJ held that Regulation 1463/70 was, as is any other regulation, binding in its entirety on the Member States, and thus its incomplete or selective application would breach EU law. In addition, the ECJ stated that it was inadmissible for a Member State to disapply those provisions of the regulation which it considered contrary to national interests. Practical difficulties in the implementation of an EU measure cannot permit a Member State to unilaterally opt out of fulfilling its obligations, since the EU institutional system ensures that due consideration is given to national interests in the light of the principles of the internal market and the legitimate interests of the other Member States. As a result, the ECJ rejected the possibility of political difficulties as a justification for non-compliance with Regulation 1463/70.

Defences based on economic difficulties,[1089] or threats of social troubles, or specific local conditions[1090] were rejected by the ECJ. In Case C-45/91 *Commission v Greece*,[1091] the Greek

---

1087. [1970] ECR 961.

1088. [1979] ECR 419.

1089. Case 70/86 *Commission v Greece* [1987] ECR 3545.

1090. Case C-56/90 *Commission v United Kingdom (Re Bathing Water Directive)* [1993] ECR I-4109; Case 339/87 *Commission v The Netherlands (Re Protection of Wild Birds)* [1990] ECR I-851.

1091. [1992] ECR I-2509.

Government tried to justify its failure to implement the directive on the safe disposal of toxic waste, on the ground of "opposition by the local population". This argument was rejected and the ECJ repeated that a Member State cannot rely on an internal situation to justify its failure to fulfil its obligations under the Treaties. However, in Case C-265/95 *Commission v France [Re French Farmers]*,[1092] the ECJ indicated that a defence based on social unrest may be accepted if a Member State "can show that action on its part would have consequences for public order with which it could not cope by using the means at its disposal". So far, no Member State has proved this.

E. **Defences based on the minimal effect of the violation of EU law.** There is no *de minimis* rule under Article 258 TFEU. The scale, or the frequency of the infringement cannot justify the failure of a Member State to fulfil its obligations under the Treaties. In Case C-105/91 *Commission v Greece*,[1093] the Greek Government admitted that its scheme on taxation of foreign vehicles was unlawful and discriminatory, but argued that the Greek vehicles which were eligible for tax concessions represented no more than 10 per cent of the internal demand, and thus there was no manifest discrimination. This argument was rejected.

It should, however, be remembered that in some areas of EU law, in particular in EU competition law, the *de minimis* rule is accepted (see Chapter 26.4.3).

F. **Defence based on direct effect of EU law.** This defence was invoked in Case 167/73 *Commission v France*.[1094] It failed as the ECJ held that it was likely to confuse EU citizens and create legal uncertainty. It is, however, an interesting defence given that, on the one hand, the supremacy of EU law ensures that in the case of a conflict between EU law and national law the former will prevail and, on the other hand, an individual may rely on directly effective provisions of EU law in proceedings brought before a national court.

In Case 29/84 *Commission v Germany (Re Nursing Directive)*[1095] the ECJ held that a defence based on direct effect of EU law might be accepted provided three conditions were satisfied: administrative practice must fully ensure the application of EU law; there must be no legal uncertainty concerning the legal situation which the directive regulates; and, individuals concerned must be aware of their rights. In this case those conditions were not satisfied. The defence is unlikely to succeed bearing in mind the stringent conditions set out by the ECJ. Further, in Case C-253/95 *Commission v Germany*,[1096] the ECJ stated that direct effect can be invoked only in special circumstances, in particular when a Member State has not taken the necessary implementing measures as required under the directive, or if it has adopted implementing measures, but they have not conformed to the directive. The ECJ emphasised that direct effect constitutes a minimum guarantee in that it ensures the right of persons affected by incorrect implementation of EU directives to rely on direct effect against the defaulting Member State, and thus is insufficient in itself to ensure the full and complete application of EU law.

1092. [1997] ECR I-6959, para. 56.
1093. [1997] ECR I-6959, para. 56.
1094. [1992] ECR I-5871.
1095. [1974] ECR 359.
1096. [1985] ECR 1661.

14.3 Action against a Member State by another Member State under Article 259 TFEU

For the Member States an alternative to proceedings under Article 258 TFEU is provided in Art 259 TFEU which states that:

> "A Member State which considers that another Member State has failed to fulfil an obligation under the Treaties may bring the matter before the Court of Justice of the European Union.
>
> Before a Member State brings an action against another Member State for an alleged infringement of an obligation under the Treaties, it shall bring the matter before the Commission.
>
> The Commission shall deliver a reasoned opinion after each of the States concerned has been given the opportunity to submit its own case and its observations on the other party's case both orally and in writing.
>
> If the Commission has not delivered an opinion within three months of the date on which the matter was brought before it, the absence of such opinion shall not prevent the matter from being brought before the Court."

Article 259 TFEU recognises the autonomous right of any Member State to act against another Member State that has failed to fulfil its obligations arising from EU law.

A Member State is not required to justify its interest to act and thus may bring an action against the defaulting Member State if it believes that the general interests of the EU necessitate such action, or if it considers that the illegal conduct of another Member State affects its own vital interests.

The Commission is very much involved in the proceedings:

- First, before a Member State brings an action against another Member State, the Commission must be informed; and,

- Second, the Commission must proceed in exactly the same manner as under Article 258 TFEU, that is, it investigates the matter, gives both parties an opportunity to submit their arguments orally and in writing, and finally delivers a reasoned opinion within three months of the date on which the matter was brought before it.

The involvement of the Commission serves two purposes:

- The Commission acts during the three months period as an intermediary between the Member States concerned; it attempts to settle the case and find an acceptable solution. The period is a "cooling off" period during which the Commission endeavours to resolve the matter in the light of the EU interest; and,

- It emphasises the Commission's privileged role as the "Guardian" of the Treaties and the exceptional nature of an action by one Member State against another.

The case law on Article 259 TFEU confirms the benefit of the Commission's involvement. Actions under this Article are extremely rare and seldom reach the ECJ. The ECJ has delivered only a handful of judgments under Article 259 TFEU, e.g. Case 141/78 *France v UK (Re Fishing Mesh)*[1097] and Case C-388/95 *Belgium v Spain*.[1098] At the time of writing, Case C-364/10 *Hungary v Slovak Republic* is pending before the ECJ. The fact that the case reached the ECJ is explained by its high political profile, and the willingness of Hungary to exacerbate the dispute. In this case a decision was taken at the highest governmental level of Slovakia to prohibit the President of Hungary from attending a ceremony

---

1097. [1979] ECR 2923.
1098. [2000] ECR I-3123.

inaugurating a statue of Saint Stephen in a small town of Slovakia on 20 August 2009. This date is particularly important for both Member States. For Hungary, it is a national holiday commemorating Saint Stephen, the founder and first king of Hungary. For Slovakia, it is the anniversary of the evening before which on 21 August 1968, Warsaw Pact troops, including Hungarian troops, invaded Czechoslovakia (at that time Slovakia was part of Czechoslovakia). The President of Hungary was refused entry into the territory of Slovakia for security reasons. The Hungarian government brought proceedings against Slovakia on the ground that the refusal of Slovakia to give access to its territory to the President of Hungary breached Article 3(2) TEU, and Article 21(1) TFEU as implemented by Directive 2004/38 (see Chapter 22.4), i.e. the right to free movement granted to EU citizens. A-G Bot delivered his Opinion[1099] on 6 March 2012. According to him, the dispute concerned the treatment of Heads of State, a matter within the sphere of diplomatic relations, and thus within the exclusive competence of the Member States. For that reason, accordingly, EU law does not apply to the dispute.

Normally, disputes between Member States concerning the application of the Treaties are, for political reasons, dealt with under Article 258 TFEU. This solution is advantageous to the Member States for three reasons:

■ The Member State concerned avoids unnecessary confrontations with another Member State while achieving the objectives sought, that is, compelling the defaulting Member State to comply with EU law;

■ The Commission bears the burden of proof and conducts the investigations; and,

■ The Member State concerned may participate in the Article 258 TFEU proceedings. Under Article 40 of the Statute of the CJEU, a Member State, or any EU institutions, may intervene to support or reject an application of the Commission in the case brought before the ECJ.[1100]

14.4 Effect of a ruling confirming failure of a Member State to fulfil its EU obligations

There is no express provision in the Treaties regarding the legal effect of ECJ rulings under Article 258 TFEU. However, it results from Article 260(1) TFEU that they are declaratory in nature.

Article 260(1) TFEU states that:

"If the Court of Justice of the European Union finds that a Member State has failed to fulfil an obligation under the Treaties, the State shall be required to take the necessary measures to comply with the judgment of the Court."

Article 260(1) TFEU makes clear that the defaulting Member State must comply with the judgment, including paying, or contributing to, the applicant's costs if so ordered. Further, if the Commission, in its application for finding a failure of a Member State to notify national measures implementing a directive adopted in accordance with legislative procedures, has asked the ECJ to impose pecuniary

---

1099. The Opinion is available at http://curia.europa.eu/jcms/jcms/j_6 (accessed 8/7/12).

1100. In such a case the ECJ grants or refuses leave to intervene in support of the order sought by the Commission or the Member State concerned. For example in Case C-80/92 *Commission v Belgium* [1994] ECR I-1019, the ECJ granted the UK leave to intervene in support of the form of order sought by the Commission; in Case C-246/89 *Commission v UK (Re Nationality of Fishermen)* [1991] ECR 1-4585 the ECJ granted leave to Spain to intervene in support of the form of order sought by the Commission and to Ireland to intervene in support of the form of order sought by the UK. However, private parties are not permitted to intervene.

penalties, and if the ECJ has found an infringement and agreed to impose the proposed penalties, the payment obligation takes effect on the date set by the Court in its judgment.

If the application is successful, the defendant is required to take all necessary measures in order to remedy the failure and its consequences, both past and future.[1101] Furthermore, national courts and national authorities of the defaulting Member State are required to disapply any national law declared incompatible with EU law and to take all appropriate measures to ensure the effective application of EU law.[1102]

For individuals there are important consequences flowing from a ruling under Article 258 TFEU. In Joined Cases 314–316/81 and 83/82 *Waterkeyn*[1103] the ECJ held that:

"if the Court finds in proceedings under [Articles 258 to 260 TFEU] . . . that a Member State's legislation is incompatible with the obligations which it has under the Treaty the courts of that State are bound by virtue of [Article 258 TFEU] to draw the necessary inferences from the judgment of the Court. However, it should be understood that the rights accruing to individuals derive, not from that judgment, but from the actual provisions of [EU] law having direct effect in the internal legal order."

Another possible important consequence of an Article 258 TFEU ruling is that individuals who have suffered loss resulting from the infringement of EU law by the relevant Member State may, in national proceedings, rely on the ECJ's judgment confirming that infringement. Such a ruling of the ECJ often provides sufficient evidence for national courts to decide whether the second condition relating to a Member State's liability, that is, requiring a sufficiently serious breach of EU law, has been satisfied (see Chapter 12.3.2).

The Treaties do not specify a time limit for compliance with a judgment rendered under Article 258 TFEU. However, the ECJ has imposed strict conditions in this respect. In Case 69/86 *Commission v Italy*[1104] the ECJ held that: "it is beyond dispute that the action required to give effect to a judgment must be set in motion immediately and be completed in the shortest possible period."

The ECJ is not a federal court and thus is not empowered to annul national law incompatible with EU law,[1105] or to compel a defaulting Member State to comply with the Court's judgment by granting an injunction, or to order a Member State to take specific measures.[1106] The ECJ may, however, impose pecuniary penalties.

14.5 Pecuniary sanctions under Article 260(2) and (3) TFEU

Non-compliance with judgments rendered under Article 258 TFEU became a serious problem in the late 1980s. At that time, when the Commission started to pursue defaulting Member States more vigorously than previously, it discovered that Member States were very reluctant to co-operate with the Commission on many matters. Until the entry into force of the Treaty of Maastricht the excessive delays and flagrant refusals on the part of defaulting Member States to comply with judgments of the ECJ were

---

1101. Case 70/72 *Commission v Germany* [1973] ECR 813.
1102. Case 48/71 *Commission v Italy* [1972] ECR 527.
1103. Joined Cases 314–316/81 and 83/82 *Procureur de la République v Waterkeyn* [1982] ECR 4337, p. 4350.
1104. [1987] ECR 773, para.8. See also Case 169/87 *Commission v France* [1988] ECR 4093 and Case C-334/94 *Commission v France* [1996] ECR I-1307, which probably set a record – more than 20 years of non-compliance! (That is, between the judgment of the ECJ in the original infringement proceedings given on 4 April 1974 and the subsequent proceedings based on Article 258 TFEU).
1105. For example Case 6/60 *Jean-E Humblet v Belgium* [1960] ECR 559.
1106. Case C-104/02 *Commission v Germany* [2005] ECR I-2689.

not subject to any penalties. Despite this, the Commission, as the Guardian of the Treaties, was bound to take the necessary steps to compel the defaulting Member State to remedy the breach.[1107] These steps consisted of commencing second proceedings based on Article 258 TFEU for breach of Article 260 TFEU.[1108] In those circumstances, a more radical approach was necessary. The Treaty of Maastricht introduced the possibility for the ECJ to impose pecuniary penalties on Member States which refused to comply with its judgments. Under the ToL, Article 260(2) and (3) TFEU further reformed the system of imposition of pecuniary penalties.

Article 260(2) and (3) TFEU states that:

"1.   If the Court of Justice of the European Union finds that a Member State has failed to fulfil an obligation under the Treaties, the State shall be required to take the necessary measures to comply with the judgment of the Court.

2.   If the Commission considers that the Member State concerned has not taken the necessary measures to comply with the judgment of the Court, it may bring the case before the Court after giving that State the opportunity to submit its observations. It shall specify the amount of the lump sum or penalty payment to be paid by the Member State concerned which it considers appropriate in the circumstances.

   If the Court finds that the Member State concerned has not complied with its judgment it may impose a lump sum or penalty payment on it.

   This procedure shall be without prejudice to Article 259.

3.   When the Commission brings a case before the Court pursuant to Article 258 on the grounds that the Member State concerned has failed to fulfil its obligation to notify measures transposing a directive adopted under a legislative procedure, it may, when it deems appropriate, specify the amount of the lump sum or penalty payment to be paid by the Member State concerned which it considers appropriate in the circumstances.

   If the Court finds that there is an infringement it may impose a lump sum or penalty payment on the Member State concerned not exceeding the amount specified by the Commission. The payment obligation shall take effect on the date set by the Court in its judgment."

The ToL shortened the stages leading to such imposition as follows:

- When the Commission brings proceedings for the imposition of pecuniary sanctions following non-compliance of a Member State with an earlier judgment of the ECJ finding that Member State in breach of EU law, the Commission is not required to submit to the defaulting Member State a "reasoned opinion" as was the case before the entry into force of the ToL. The removal of the reasoned opinion requirement speeded up the procedure and avoids unnecessary repetition of the Commission's work given that the failure has already been declared in the original proceedings on the same legal basis. However, Article 260(2) ensures that the Member State concerned has the opportunity to submit its observation before the Commission commences Article 260(2) proceedings.

- Under Article 260(3) TFEU the Commission may, in its application to the ECJ which asks for a finding of failure, when a Member State has failed to notify to it measures transposing a directive adopted under a legislative procedure, request the ECJ to impose a pecuniary penalty. In such a situation the Commission is not required to wait until the Member State concerned fails to

1107.   Case 281/83 *Commission v Italy* [1985] ECR 3397.
1108.   Case 48/71 *Commission v Italy* [1972] ECR 527.

comply with a judgment of the ECJ to propose a pecuniary penalty. This possibility should be welcome as it:

● concerns a failure which is obvious and therefore there is no need for the Commission to wait until the defaulting Member State fails again to comply with the initial judgment of the ECJ before any pecuniary penalty can be imposed;
● puts more pressure on the Member States to implement EU directives; and,
● ensures that the amount of pecuniary penalty imposed by the ECJ will not be higher than that proposed by the Commission.

Shortly after the ToL came into effect, the Commission adopted a Communication on the "Implementation of Article 260(3) TFEU" [1109] in which it stated that:

■ With regard to the infringement procedure pursuant to Article 228(2) TFEU the 2005 Commission Communication remains applicable[1110] (see below);

■ With regard to the infringement procedure pursuant to Article 228(3) TFEU the Commission will normally ask for the imposition of a periodic penalty payment as it considers that such penalty is the more appropriate to secure the implementation of directives. However, in some circumstances the Commission will also ask for the imposition of a lump sum;

■ In cases before the ECJ where the Commission has only sought the imposition of a penalty it will withdraw its action if the Member State notifies the transposition measures required to end the infringement. However, in cases where the Commission has also asked for the imposition of a lump sum it will not withdraw its action despite the fact that the required notification has been made by the Member State concerned; and,

■ The determination of the amount of the penalty payment and of the lump sum will be made in accordance with the method outlined in the 2005 Commission's Communication.

In the 2005 Communication,[1111] the Commission specified its policy under Article 260 TFEU and defined the method of calculating pecuniary sanctions. The communication was the response of the Commission to the judgment of the ECJ in Case C-304/02 *Commission v France* (see below). The communication provides that the Commission in all cases under Article 260 TFEU will ask the ECJ to impose both a daily penalty payment and a lump sum on a defaulting Member State, and sets out the following detailed mode of calculation of penalties applicable to all types of non-compliance with an original judgment.

With regard to the determination of the amount of the daily penalty:

■ It is based on the "basic uniform lump sum" of €600 per day of delay.

■ The basic lump sum is adjusted by two co-efficient multiplicands: one takes account of the gravity of the infringement and the other of the period of non-compliance. For example, the Commission considers as very serious the breach of the principle of non-discrimination, and as serious the infringement of provisions ensuring the four freedoms.[1112] The first multiplicand is within the scale from 1 to 20, and the second from 1 to 3 calculated at a rate of 0.10 per cent per month from the date of delivery of the Article 258 TFEU judgment.

1109.   SEC(2010) 1371 final.
1110.   SEC(2005) 1658.
1111.   Ibid.
1112.   Agence Europe No. 6742, 6.6. 1996.

- In order to make the penalty a real deterrent to non-compliance with the judgment, the Commission established a special invariable factor "n" for each Member State, which takes into consideration the financial capacity of the defaulting Member State, which is calculated on the basis of the GNP of each Member State, combined with the weighting of voting rights in the Council.

To calculate the amount of a daily penalty payment the co-efficient for seriousness and for duration are multiplied by the "n" factor of the relevant Member State. As to a lump sum, a minimum amount has been set for each Member State.

Prior to the adoption of the 2005 Communication two cases decided under Article 260 TFEU attracted attention: first, Case C-387/97 *Commission v Greece*,[1113] because in that case, for the first time ever, the ECJ ordered a Member State to pay daily penalty payments for non-compliance with its initial judgment[1114] and second, Case C-304/02 *Commission v France*[1115] in which the ECJ ordered France to pay both a lump sum penalty and a daily penalty payment not merely one or the other.

The ECJ is not bound by the figure suggested by the Commission. It may increase or reduce the figure or may decide not to impose any penalty at all as only it is entitled, in each case, to decide what is just, proportionate and equitable.[1116] The ToL introduced one limitation on the ECJ's powers in that under Article 260(2) TFEU proceedings the ECJ, on finding the infringement, may impose a lump sum or penalty payment not exceeding the amount specified by the Commission.

In Case C-304/02 *Commission v France*[1117] the ECJ ordered France to pay both a penalty payment and a lump sum. The ECJ imposed a penalty payment of €57,761,250 for each period of six months of non-compliance with the initial judgment (i.e. in Case C-64/88 *Commission v France*) starting from delivery of the judgment in Case C-304/02 *Commission v France* and continuing until the day on which the breach of obligations in the initial judgment was brought to an end. Additionally, France was required to pay a lump sum of €20,000,000 for France's persistent non-compliance with the initial judgment.

With regard to the implementation of the judgment in Case C-304/02 *Commission v France*, the General Court in Case T-139/06 *France v Commission*[1118] clarified the Commission's powers relating to enforcement of ECJ judgments pursuant to Article 228(2) TFEU. In Case C-304/02 *Commission v France*, France was ordered to pay immediately the lump sum of €20,000,000. However, payments of any penalty payment were subject to the six-monthly finding by the Commission of the absence of full compliance with that judgment. According to the Commission, six months after the delivery of judgment in Case C-340/02 France had not brought the infringement to an end. As a result, on 2 March 2006, the Commission adopted a decision requesting a payment of the periodic payment of €57,761,250. France sought to annul the Commission's decision before the General Court. The General Court held that under the judgment delivered by the ECJ in Case C-340/02 the Commission had power to make the finding of non-compliance autonomously, without any need to bring fresh proceedings before the ECJ, and was therefore entitled to order France to pay a penalty payment of €57,761,250 to the EU own resources

---

1113. [2000] ECR I-5047.

1114. Case C-45/91 *Commission v Greece* [1992] ECR I-2509.

1115. [2005] ECR I-6263.

1116. For example, in Case C-119/04 *Commission v Italy* ([2006] ECR I-6885) the ECJ did not impose any penalty because Italy provided evidence that it had complied with the initial judgment albeit after the date on which the Commission had issued its reasoned opinion.

1117. [2005] ECR I-6263.

1118. Judgment of 19/10/11 (NYR).

account. The Commission decided in November 2006 that France had, by then, complied with the judgment in Case C-304/02.

14.5.1 Conclusion

The efficiency and transparency of management of cases under Article 258 TFEU has greatly improved with the introduction of CHAP, EU Pilot and the reform of NIF. In particular, CHAP responds to the criticism that complaints from individuals were ignored by the Commission, and ensures that complainants have systematic feedback on their complaint. Judging by the fact that 81 per cent of cases were settled by the Commission in 2010, EU Pilot is a success.[1119] The possibility for the Commission to request financial sanctions against a Member State for failure to notify national measures implementing a directive has enhanced compliance by the Member States. According to the Commission, in most cases, the sending of a letter of formal notice suffices to bring an infringement to an end.[1120] The principle of transparency has also been given due consideration. First, with regard to the general public, summary information of all infringement proceedings is available on the Commission's website and access to documents relating to infringement proceedings has been widened. Second, under the revised Framework Agreement on the Relations between the EP and the Commission,[1121] the EP may request the Commission to provide information relating to a specific case, subject to the confidentiality rules. Third, the rules on the application of financial sanctions on the Member States were clarified by the Commission in its 2010 Communication.[1122]

The infringement procedure, a unique feature of EU law, has undergone substantial reform and continues to improve in terms of efficiency, transparency and accountability. The imposition of both a penalty payment and a lump sum sends a clear message to Member States which persist in ignoring the Court's judgments, i.e. the price for non compliance may be very high. Its deterrent effect is obvious. According to the Commission in 2010 the number of ongoing infringement proceedings decreased by 30 per cent as compared with the previous year.[1123]

RECOMMENDED READING

Books

Borzsak, L., *The Impact of Environmental Concerns on the Public Enforcement Mechanism under EU Law*, 2011, The Netherlands: KLI.

Smith, M., *Centralised Enforcement, Legitimacy and Good Governance in the EU*, 2010, Abingdon: Routledge.

Tallberg, J., *European Governance and Supranational Institutions: Making States Comply*, 2003, London: Routledge.

Articles

Conway, G., "Breaches of EC Law and the International Responsibility of Member States", (2002) 13, *European Journal of International Law*, 679.

1119. See 2010 Commission Report on the Monitoring the Application of EU Law, COM(2011) 588 final.
1120. Ibid.
1121. [2010] OJ L 304/47.
1122. SEC(2010) 1371 final.
1123. Ibid.

Evans, A. C., "The Enforcement Procedure of Article 169 EEC: Commission Discretion", (1979) 4 ELRev., 442.

Harlow, C., and Rawlings, R., "Accountability and Law Enforcement: The Centralised EU Infringement Procedure", (2006) ELRev., 452.

Kilbey, I., "Financial Penalties under Article 228(2) EC: Excessive complexity?", (2007) 44 CMLRev., 743.

Magliveras, K. D., "Force Majeure in Community Law", (1990)15 ELRev., 460.

Prete, L, and Smulders, B., "The Coming of Age of Infringement Proceedings", (2010) 47 CMLRev., 9.

Schrauwen, A., "Fishery, Waste Management and Persistent and General Failure to Fulfil Control Obligations: The Role of Lump Sum and Penalty Payments in Enforcement Actions under Community Law", (2006) 18 JEL, 289.

Wenneras, P., "New Dawn for Commission Enforcement under Articles 226 and 227 EC. General and Persistent Infringements, Lump Sums and Penalty Payments", (2006) CMLRev., 31.

Wenneras, P., "Sanctions against Member States under Article 260 TFEU: Alive, but not Kicking?" (2012) 49 CMLRev., 145.

PROBLEM QUESTION

The Commission wishes to bring proceedings against Spain before the ECJ. This is because the Commission considers that Spain is in breach of Article 43 TFEU guaranteeing the freedom of establishment by enacting legislation subjecting the opening of shopping centres in Catalonia to prior authorisation which is given only after establishing that the opening of a shopping centre will have no impact on existing small traders.

Spain advances the following arguments:

1. The legislation in question was enacted by the Autonomous Community of Catalonia (ACC). Under the Spanish Constitution, the Spanish government has no power to compel the ACC to repeal the legislation;

2. In the reasoned opinion the Commission has given Spain 10 days to repeal the legislation in question. This time-limit cannot be regarded as reasonable;

3. Very similar legislation is in force in France. The Commission has not brought any proceedings against France; and,

4. The legislation was introduced to avoid social unrest. Small traders in Catalonia have threatened to destroy governmental buildings if no action has been taken to protect them from competition from large shopping centres.

Advise the Commission whether the arguments submitted by Spain are likely to be accepted by the ECJ.

ESSAY QUESTION

Critically assess whether the system for imposition of financial penalties on Member States, which refuse to comply with judgments of the ECJ finding them in breach of their obligations deriving from the Treaties, contributes to the effective enforcement of EU law.

AIDE-MÉMOIRE

PROCEDURE UNDER ARTICLE 258 TFEU

Applicant: The Commission

Must establish

Failure: any shortcoming relating to fulfilment of obligations arising from the Treaties. It may result from an action, or from an omission, or a failure to act of the Member State concerned.

Must follow the procedure

Procedure:

1. Informal phase: pre-258 proceedings letter.
2. Formal phase:
   - Administrative stage (pre-litigation procedure):
     - Letter of Formal Notice (Case 51/83 *Commission v Italy*);
     - Reasoned Opinion (Case 7/61 *Commission v Italy [Re Pigmeat case]*).
   - Judicial stage: the Commission brings proceedings before the ECJ.

Defendant: a Member State

Member State = any national body including parliament (Case 77/69 *Commission v Belgium*); the judiciary (Case C-129/00 *Commission v Italy* and Case C-154/08 *Commission v Spain*); any private or semi-private body which the Member State controls (Case 249/81 *Commission v Ireland Re Buy Irish Campaign*); and, private individuals if the Member State was in a position to prevent, or terminate their conduct which had breached EU law (Case C-265/95 *Commission v France*)

Defences:

Procedural defences:
- The time limit fixed by the Commission either in the letter of formal notice or in the reasoned opinion is not reasonable (293/85 *Commission v Belgium [Re University Fees]*);
- The complaints and legal arguments in the application under Article 258 TFEU are not identical to those invoked in the letter of formal notice and the reasoned opinion (Case C-433/03 *Commission v Germany*);
- The Commission has failed to identify the subject matter of the dispute with sufficient precision (Case C-141/10 *Commission v the Netherlands*).

Substantive defences:
Successful or potentially successful defences:
- Unlawful obligation (Case 226/87 *Commission v Greece* and Case 6/69 *Commission v France*);
- Force majeure (Case 101/84 *Commission v Italy*);
- Uncertainty as to the meaning of the obligation (Case C-133/94 *Commission v Belgium*).

Unsuccessful:
- Reciprocity (Cases 90 and 91/63 *Commission v Luxembourg and Belgium [Re Import of Powdered Milk Products]*);
- Necessity (Case 7/61 *Commission v Italy [Pigmeat case]*);
- Peculiarity of a national system (Case 77/69 *Commission v Belgium*);
- Difficulty existing in the EU legal order (Case C-263/96 *Commission v Belgium*);
- Political difficulties (Case 8/70 *Commission v Italy*);
- Economic difficulties (Case 70/86 *Commission v Greece*);
- Minimal effect of the violation (Case C-105/91 *Commission v Greece*);
- Administrative practices (Case 167/73 *Commission v France [Re French Merchant Seamen]*);
- Direct effect of EU law (Case 167/73 *Commission v France*).

(Continued)

(Continued)

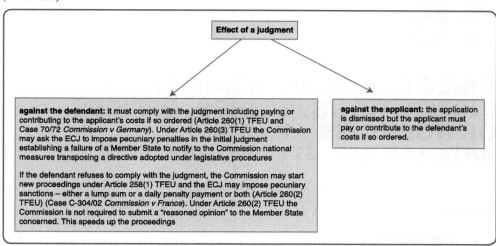

Effect of a judgment

against the defendant: it must comply with the judgment including paying or contributing to the applicant's costs if so ordered (Article 260(1) TFEU and Case 70/72 *Commission v Germany*). Under Article 260(3) TFEU the Commission may ask the ECJ to impose pecuniary penalties in the initial judgment establishing a failure of a Member State to notify to the Commission national measures transposing a directive adopted under legislative procedures

If the defendant refuses to comply with the judgment, the Commission may start new proceedings under Article 258(1) TFEU and the ECJ may impose pecuniary sanctions – either a lump sum or a daily penalty payment or both (Article 260(2) TFEU) (Case C-304/02 *Commission v France*). Under Article 260(2) TFEU the Commission is not required to submit a "reasoned opinion" to the Member State concerned. This speeds up the proceedings

against the applicant: the application is dismissed but the applicant must pay or contribute to the defendant's costs if so ordered.

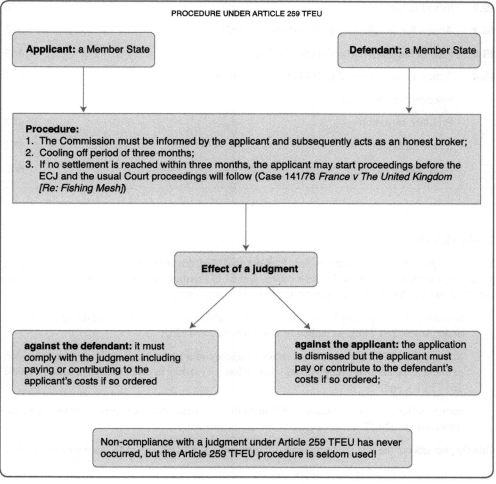

PROCEDURE UNDER ARTICLE 259 TFEU

Applicant: a Member State

Defendant: a Member State

Procedure:
1. The Commission must be informed by the applicant and subsequently acts as an honest broker;
2. Cooling off period of three months;
3. If no settlement is reached within three months, the applicant may start proceedings before the ECJ and the usual Court proceedings will follow (Case 141/78 *France v The United Kingdom [Re: Fishing Mesh]*)

Effect of a judgment

against the defendant: it must comply with the judgment including paying or contributing to the applicant's costs if so ordered

against the applicant: the application is dismissed but the applicant must pay or contribute to the defendant's costs if so ordered;

Non-compliance with a judgment under Article 259 TFEU has never occurred, but the Article 259 TFEU procedure is seldom used!

15

DIRECT ACTIONS AGAINST EU INSTITUTIONS, BODIES, OFFICES OR AGENCIES – PART I
ARTICLES 263, 277 AND 265 TFEU

CONTENTS

CHAPTER OUTLINE

1. This chapter outlines the various forms of the so-called direct action, which involves bringing proceedings directly before the Union's courts against EU institutions, bodies, offices or agencies. Direct actions can be divided into three categories. They may seek:

- to annul an act adopted by EU institutions, bodies, offices or agencies either by doing this directly under Article 263 TFEU or indirectly under Article 277 TFEU;

- to compel an EU institution, body, office or agency to adopt a measure, or to take a decision defining its position in circumstances where it has a legal duty to take a particular action (Article 265 TFEU); and,

- compensation for damage caused by EU institutions, bodies, offices or agencies or their servants under Article 340(2).

This chapter sets out the first two categories of direct actions, whilst Chapter 16 deals with the third.

2. Article 263 TFEU sets out the conditions for admissibility of an action for annulment. They are:

A.   Any act adopted by an EU institution, body, office or agency which produces binding legal effect in relation to third parties, irrespective of its form and name, can be reviewed under Article 263 TFEU.

B.   There are three categories of applicants under Article 263 TFEU:

■ privileged applicants: the Council, the EP, the Commission and the Member States. They can bring an action for annulment against all reviewable acts and are not required to justify their interest to act;

■ semi-privileged applicants, such as the CoA, ECB and CoR can only bring an action for annulment of acts which encroach on their prerogatives; and,

■ non-privileged applicants: natural and legal persons. A prerequisite for starting an action under Article 263 TFEU is that such persons must show an interest in seeking the annulment of the contested act. Prior to the entry into force of the ToL non-privileged applicants were rarely successful, apart from a situation where they were direct addressees of a decision, i.e. a classic judicial review situation. Otherwise they had to satisfy the admissibility threshold by establishing that they were directly and individually concerned by a decision addressed to "another person", or that an act in the form of a regulation or a directive, i.e. an act of general application, was in fact a decision addressed to them. The ToL facilitated access to the Union's courts for non-privileged applicants in that it makes a distinction between challenges concerning regulatory acts and non-regulatory acts. On the authority of Case T-262/10 *Microban,* regulatory acts are all acts of general application, apart from legislative acts, which do not require any implementing measures. To challenge a regulatory act non-privileged applicants have to prove only that they are directly concerned by the act. This is fairly easy to establish (see below). However, in respect of non-regulatory acts non-privileged applicants must show that they are directly and individually concerned by the act.

To be directly concerned applicants must show that the contested measure affects their legal position and that the measure leaves no discretion to its addressee as to its implementation.

With regard to individual concern, the *Plaumann* test applies under which the applicant must show that he is affected by the contested measure by reason of certain attributes which are peculiar to him or by reason of circumstances which differentiate him from all other persons. The ECJ has interpreted the test very strictly with the result that it is very difficult for a non-privileged applicant to satisfy it. However, the ECJ has relaxed its strict approach in some special circumstances.

C.   An act must be challenged within two months of its publication/notification, as thereafter it becomes immune from annulment. The time limit applies to all applicants, is rigorously enforced, and the only excuses accepted by the CJEU are *force majeure* or exceptional circumstances.

D.   Article 263(2) TFEU sets out the grounds for annulment of EU acts. They are:

■ lack of competence;

■ infringement of an essential procedural requirement;

- infringement of the Treaties or any rule of law relating to their application; and,

- misuse of powers.

E.   If an action for annulment is successful, the EU courts, by virtue of Article 264 TFEU, will declare the contested act void. The declaration applies *erga omnes* and the institution which adopted it is, under Article 266 TFEU, required to take all necessary measures to comply with the judgment. In exceptional circumstances the EU courts may declare all or some provisions of the annulled act to be operative until a competent institution adopts an act which will replace the one struck down by the Court.

3. Article 277 TFEU which deals with the plea of illegality can only be invoked as an ancillary plea, that is, as a means by which applicants, in support of an action challenging implementing measures addressed to them or to a third person, plead the illegality of the general measure upon which the implementing measures are based. For that reason the plea is referred to as an indirect action, that is, it challenges indirectly the validity of a measure on the basis of which a subsequent measure has been taken. A plea of illegality is not explicitly time-barred but cannot be used to circumvent the requirements of Article 263 TFEU.

4. The purpose of an action for failure to act under Article 265 TFEU is to compel the relevant EU institution, body, office or agency to act in circumstances where it has a legal duty to do this.

A.   Potential defendants are EU institutions, bodies, offices and agencies.

B.   There are three categories of applicants:

- privileged applicants: EU institutions (but not the EU courts) and Member States;

- semi-privileged applicants: the ECB, the CoA and the CoR. They have *locus standi* to raise an action for failure to act in respect of areas within their respective fields of competence; and,

- non-privileged applicants: any natural or legal person. They have *locus standi* under Article 265 TFEU but only if the relevant EU institution, body, office or agency has failed to adopt a measure which they are legally entitled to claim. They have to satisfy the same requirements for *locus standi* as under Article 263 TFEU. However, they cannot rely on Article 265 TFEU to circumvent the time limit set out in Article 263(5) TFEU.

C.   The procedure comprises two stages:

- The administrative stage. During this the applicant must call upon the relevant institution to act. Thereafter, the institution has two months to act in accordance with the request, or to define its position, that is, to issue a statement of its views on a particular matter, or its proposal for action, or, in the case of refusal of the request, the reason for not taking a particular action. When an EU institution, has defined its position, but the applicant is dissatisfied with it, he may rely on Article 263 TFEU to challenge the position taken by the relevant institution but cannot take any further action under Article 265 TFEU.

- The judicial stage. If the EU institution, body, office or agency that has been called upon to act fails to define its position within two months of being so requested, the applicant has a further two months within which it may bring an action before the CJEU for failure to act.

D.   By virtue of Article 266 TFEU the effect of a successful action under Article 265 TFEU is that the defaulting institution will be required to take the necessary measures to remedy its failure in conformity with the judgment of the Union's court. If it does not do this, a repeat action may be brought under Article 265 TFEU.

15.1 Introduction

By virtue of Article 5(2) TEU all EU institutions are required to act within the limits of the powers conferred upon them by the Treaties. EU law provides a number of mechanisms with a view to ensuring that EU institutions, bodies, offices and agencies function properly and do not exceed their powers. In this respect Union courts exercise jurisdiction similar to that exercised by the administrative courts in the Member States.

The EU recognises the following actions against EU institutions, bodies, offices and agencies:

■ actions under Article 263 TFEU for annulment of EU acts;

■ actions under Article 265 TFEU for failure to act against EU institutions, bodies, offices or agencies;

■ the so-called plea of illegality, defined in Article 277 TFEU; and,

■ actions for damages caused by EU institutions to the applicant involving non-contractual liability of the former under Articles 268 and 340(2) TFEU. These are examined in Chapter 16.

The ToN limited the ECJ's jurisdiction in respect of actions brought under Articles 263 and 265 TFEU to the most important cases, that is, those brought by privileged and semi-privileged applicants. Accordingly, actions brought by non-privileged applicants, i.e. by natural and legal persons are adjudicated by the General Court.

The important feature of the above actions is that natural and legal persons are allowed to bring them before the Union courts. Under the ToL access to the courts was widened although there are still uncertainties as to the extent to which the new rules improve individuals' access to justice within the EU. For that reason, for individuals considering attacking EU acts under Article 263 TFEU, an action in a national court may be more appropriate provided implementing measures have been adopted at national level. If action is to be taken in a national court, a natural or legal person should bring an action for judicial review of national measures implementing the contested EU act, as the contested act itself is immune from challenge in this way. Bearing in mind that only the ECJ is entitled to declare an EU act as invalid, a national court will refer the issue of validity of an EU act, where this is in doubt, to the ECJ under Article 267 TFEU. Meanwhile a national court will suspend the operation of a national measure based on the contested EU act. The final result may be a declaration of invalidity of the EU act by the ECJ, and thus a natural or legal person may achieve the objective of successfully challenging the legality of an EU act in an indirect manner (see Chapter 13.9).

With the entry into force of the ToL, the Union courts' jurisdiction under Article 263 TFEU was extended as follows:

■ In respect of the AFSJ, the Union courts have jurisdiction over all acts adopted by EU institutions, bodies, offices and agencies. This is subject to two limitations:

● A temporal limitation, in that in the field of police and judicial co-operation in criminal matters in respect of measures which were adopted before the entry into force of the ToL the Union courts' jurisdiction will commence five years after the entry into force of the ToL.

However, if any particular measure (adopted before the entry into force of the ToL) is amended before the expiry of that period then that measure will be within the jurisdiction of the Court from the time of amendment.

- A pre-ToL limitation, in that the ECJ has no jurisdiction to review the validity and proportionality of operations carried out by police and other enforcement agencies with a view to maintaining law and order and the safeguarding of the internal security of a Member State (see Chapter 31.1).

- Under Article 269 TFEU, the ECJ has jurisdiction to assess the lawfulness of procedural aspects of a determination made by the European Council or the Council that a clear risk has been identified of serious infringement by a Member State of values on which the EU is founded. Proceedings may be brought by the Member State against whom the determination has been made within one month from the date of that determination. The ECJ must give its ruling within one month from the date of request.

- Member States are empowered to bring an action for annulment of an EU act which according to their national parliament, or one of its parliament's chambers, does not comply with the principle of subsidiarity. Although such an action is brought by a Member State it may also be simply "notified" by a Member State, as the actual applicant is the national parliament or a chamber of that parliament. Further, the CoR can bring an action for annulment based on the infringement of the principle of subsidiarity, but only in respect of acts on which it is required to be consulted.

- With regard to the CFSP the ECJ has no jurisdiction. However, this is subject to two exceptions:

  - Under Article 40 TEU, the ECJ has jurisdiction to ensure that the implementation of the CFSP does not impinge on non-CFSP policies of the EU and *vice versa*, i.e. that measures adopted in non-CFSP matters do not encroach on CFSP matters.

  - The ECJ has jurisdiction to review the legality of decisions providing for restrictive measures against natural or legal persons adopted by the Council on the basis of Chapter 2 of Title 5 of the TEU (see Chapter 9.5).

15.2 Action for annulment under Article 263 TFEU

Article 263 TFEU provides:

"The Court of Justice of the European Union shall review the legality of legislative acts, of acts of the Council, of the Commission and of the European Central Bank, other than recommendations and opinions, and of acts of the European Parliament and of the European Council intended to produce legal effects *vis-à-vis* third parties. It shall also review the legality of acts of bodies, offices or agencies of the Union intended to produce legal effects *vis-à-vis* third parties.

It shall for this purpose have jurisdiction in actions brought by a Member State, the European Parliament, the Council or the Commission on grounds of lack of competence, infringement of an essential procedural requirement, infringement of the Treaties or of any rule of law relating to their application, or misuse of powers.

The Court shall have jurisdiction under the same conditions in actions brought by the Court of Auditors, by the European Central Bank and by the Committee of the Regions for the purpose of protecting their prerogatives.

Any natural or legal person may, under the conditions laid down in the first and second paragraphs, institute proceedings against an act addressed to that person or which is of direct and individual concern to them, and against a regulatory act which is of direct concern to them and does not entail implementing measures.

Acts setting up bodies, offices and agencies of the Union may lay down specific conditions and arrangements concerning actions brought by natural or legal persons against acts of these bodies, offices or agencies intended to produce legal effects in relation to them.

The proceedings provided for in this Article shall be instituted within two months of the publication of the measure, or of its notification to the plaintiff, or, in the absence thereof, of the day on which it came to the knowledge of the latter, as the case may be."

An action for annulment is similar to what is known under the law of England and Wales (and also recognised in Scottish law) as an application for judicial review.

The requirements imposed by Article 263 TFEU are examined below. They concern:

- acts which can be reviewed;

- applicants permitted to act on the basis of Article 263 TFEU;

- the grounds for annulment; and,

- the time limit for bringing an action for annulment.

15.2.1 Reviewable acts

Article 263 TFEU specifies the following legislative and other acts as reviewable:

- Acts of the Council, the Commission and of the European Central Bank other than recommendations and opinions, which intend to produce legal effects with regard to third parties;

- Acts adopted jointly by the EP and the European Council intended to produce legal effects with regard to third parties; and,

- Acts of bodies, offices or agencies of the EU intended to produce legal effects *vis-à-vis* third parties.

The simplicity of the above list is illusive. Its effect is that in fact, any act, whatever its nature and form, which produces binding legal effects is reviewable under Article 263 TFEU.

15.2.2 Author of the act

The principle that only acts adopted by the EU institutions, bodies, offices or agencies are reviewable is self-evident but poses many challenges in practice. These are examined below.

15.2.2.1 Acts adopted by Member States

Acts adopted by a particular Member State or Member States are outside the scope of Article 263 TFEU. This includes the Treaties, Protocols and Annexes attached to them and the Charter of Fundamental Rights. Further, national measures impacting on EU law are dealt with through the preliminary reference procedure under Article 267 TFEU. In practice, however, it is not always easy to determine whether a particular act should be considered as adopted by an EU institution or a Member State. For example, in Case C-97/91 *Oleificio Borelli*[1124] the ECJ held that it had no jurisdiction to rule

---

1124.   Case C-97/91 *Oleificio Borelli SpA v Commission* [1992] ECR I-6313.

on lawfulness of an opinion unfavourable to the applicant adopted by the relevant national authorities, which opinion led up to the Commission's decision refusing to grant aid to the applicant. Thus, a national measure is not reviewable under Article 263 TFEU despite the measure having been adopted pursuant to an EU act.

Sometimes Member States act within the Council, but outside its competence as an EU institution. The question of how to determine whether an act, irrespective of its form and name, adopted by the Council is an act of the Council or an act adopted by the Member States meeting within the framework of the Council (that is, as an international conference) was resolved in Case 22/70 *Commission v Council [ERTA]*.[1125] In this case the ECJ had to decide, *inter alia*, whether deliberations concerning the European Road Transport Agreement (ERTA) were reviewable under Article 263 TFEU. The ECJ held that the "status" of an act depends on the determination of who, at the relevant time, had competence to negotiate and conclude it. The legal effect of the deliberations varies depending upon whether they are considered as an act within the competence of the EU, or as an expression of policy co-ordination between the Member States in a specific area. The ECJ decided that the deliberations in this case belonged to the former category, as the EU had competence to negotiate and conclude the ERTA. Accordingly, they were reviewable under Article 263 TFEU. However, in Joined Cases C-181/91 and C-248/91 *EP v Council and Commission*,[1126] the ECJ held inadmissible for the purposes of Article 263 TFEU an act adopted on the proposal of the Commission by "the Member States meeting within the Council" granting emergency aid to Bangladesh. This was because the EU had no exclusive competence in the area of humanitarian aid.

15.2.2.2 Acts adopted by the European Council

Under the ToL, the European Council became a fully fledged EU institution authorised to adopt binding acts. As a result, those of its acts which are intended to produce binding effects with regard to third parties are reviewable under Article 263 TFEU.

15.2.2.3 Acts adopted by the EP

Until the entry into force of the Treaty of Maastricht acts adopted by the EP were not formally reviewable. In practice, however, the ECJ, had, in a number of decisions, recognised that acts of the EP were reviewable:

- In Case 230/81 *Luxembourg v EP*[1127] deliberations of the EP concerning the change of its seat were challenged by Luxembourg. The ECJ held the action admissible on the grounds that the deliberations concerned all three Communities and based its decision on Article 38 CS which permits a challenge to acts of the Parliament.

- In Case 294/83 *Les Verts*,[1128] the ECJ could not make reference to Article 38 CS (as it had in Case 230/81 *Luxembourg v EP)* because the applicant was a legal person and as such its action for annulment was ruled out under both the CS and the EC Treaties. Despite this, the ECJ recognised the reviewability of acts emanating from the EP and explained that since the EC was a Community based on the rule of law, neither the Member States, nor Community institutions, could escape the control of the conformity of their acts with the basic constitutional charter, that is the EC

1125.   [1971] ECR 263 (see Chapter 6.2.2).
1126.   [1993] ECR I-3685.
1127.   [1983] ECR 255.
1128.   Case 294/83 *"Les Verts" v EP* [1986] ECR 1339.

Treaty. This full recognition of acts of the EP as reviewable constituted an example of judicial revision of the Treaty. This revision was well justified, taking into account the evolution of the EP from an advisory and supervisory body to a body increasingly involved in the decision-making procedures. It was also arguably necessary in the light of the principle of effectiveness to ensure the control of the legality of the EP's acts, in particular those intended to produce legal effect with regard to a third party, although a formal amendment to the EC Treaty might have been the better way to achieve this.

The case law of the ECJ shows that reviewable acts of the EP comprise not only acts adopted by the EP as an institution, but also by its organs, such as its Bureau for the allocation of funds amongst political parties,[1129] and the Declaration of the President of the European Parliament regarding the adoption of the EU budget.[1130]

Acts which are not considered as reviewable under Article 263 TFEU include: an act establishing a parliamentary commission of inquiry;[1131] the waiver of immunity;[1132] and, acts emanating from the EP's political parties or political groups.[1133]

15.2.2.4   Acts adopted by bodies, offices or agencies of the EU

The ToL, for the first time, expressly recognised that not only acts adopted by EU institutions but also those adopted by EU bodies, offices or agencies, provided they produce binding legal effects with regard to third parties, are reviewable under Article 263 TFEU. However, before the entry into force of the ToL, the Union's courts recognised the possibility of challenging the validity of acts emanating from bodies, offices or agencies of the EU. The Courts accepted for review, *inter alia*, acts adopted by the EIB;[1134] the European Investment Fund; the Board of Appeal of the Community Trade Mark Office under Article 63 of Council Regulation 40/94;[1135] and the European Agency for Reconstruction.[1136] Further, in Joined Cases C-193 and 194/87 *Maurissen*[1137] the ECJ accepted an action for annulment brought by a legal person against the CoA.

15.2.2.5   International agreements concluded between the EU and third countries

There is a distinction between international agreements themselves, and acts adopted by EU institutions regarding the conclusion or application of such agreements. In the first case, the ECJ has no jurisdiction under Article 263 TFEU because international agreements are not acts of EU institutions; they are international treaties within the meaning of public international law.[1138] However, in the second case, the ECJ is empowered to annul, for example, a decision of the Commission concerning the conclusion of an agreement with a third country,[1139] or a decision regarding the application of an international

---

1129. [1986] ECR 1339.
1130. Case 34/86 *Council v Parliament* [1986] ECR 2155; Case C-284–90 *Council v Parliament* [1992] ECR I-2328.
1131. Case 78/85 *Groupe des Droites Européennes v EP* [1986] ECR 1754 (Ord.).
1132. Case 149/85 *Roger Wybot v Edgar Faure and Others* [1986] ECR 2391.
1133. Case C-201/89 *Jean-Marie Le Pen and the Front National v Detlef Puhl and Others* [1990] ECR I-1183.
1134. Case T-460/93 *Tete v EIB* [1993] ECR II-1257.
1135. [1994] OJ L11/1.
1136. Case T-411/06 *Sogelma v European Agency for Reconstruction* [2008] ECR II-2771.
1137. Cases C-193 and 194/87 *Maurissen v CoA* [1990] ECR I-95.
1138. Case C-122/95 *Germany v Council* [1998] ECR 973.
1139. Case C-327/91 *France v Commission* [1994] ECR I-3641.

agreement,[1140] because those acts emanate from EU institutions and as such are reviewable under Article 263 TFEU.

15.2.3 Nature of the act

In Case 22/70 *ERTA*,[1141] the ECJ held that not only acts listed in Article 288 TFEU can be challenged under Article 263 TFEU but also any act which has binding legal effects, whatever its nature and form. The ToL confirms this development as Article 263 TFEU states that all acts adopted by EU institutions, bodies, offices or agencies which produce legal effects with regard to third parties are reviewable. According to the case law of the ECJ, an act produces binding legal effects when it adversely affects the interest of a third party by bringing about a distinct change in that party's legal position.[1142]

The content and scope of application of an act are the decisive factors as to the determination of its nature, not its form and name. The case law of the ECJ clarified this point in relation to borderline cases. For example, the following acts are considered as reviewable under Article 263 TFEU:

- deliberations of the Council in ERTA;[1143]

- a communication of the Commission which by means of interpretation of a directive introduces new obligations;[1144]

- a Code of Conduct adopted with a view to co-ordinating management of structural funds, but published in the section "Communication and information" of the Official Journal;[1145]

- a letter from the Commission;[1146]

- a decision orally communicated to the applicant;[1147]

- an official declaration made by the Commissioner in charge of competition matters declaring the EU Merger rules inapplicable to the acquisition of Dan Air by British Airways;[1148]

- a letter from the Commission stating reasons for rejecting a complaint under competition law;[1149] and,

- a letter from the Director General of the Directorate General for Agriculture of the Commission informing a Member State of the reduction of advanced funds in respect of the financing of rural developments from the European Guidance and Guarantee Fund.[1150]

The ECJ has held that the following acts are not reviewable under Article 263 TFEU:

1140. Case 30/88 *Greece v Commission* [1989] ECR 374.
1141. Case 22/70 *Commission v Council [ERTA]* [1971] ECR 263.
1142. Case 60/81 *IBM* [1981] ECR 2639; Case C-521/06 P *Athinaïki Techniki v Commission* [2008] ECR I-5829 and Case C-322/09 P *NDSHT v Commission* [2010] ECR I-0000.
1143. [1971] ECR 263.
1144. Case C-325/91 *France v Commission* [1993] ECR I-3283.
1145. Case C-303/90 *France and Belgium v Commission* [1991] ECR I-5315.
1146. Case 1/57 *Usines à Tubes de la Sarre v High Authority* [1957–1958] ECR 105.
1147. Cases 316/82 and 40/83 *Kohler v CoA* [1984] ECR 641; Case T-3/93 *Air France v Commission* [1994] ECR II-121.
1148. Case T-3/93 *Air France v Commission* [1994] ECR II-121.
1149. Case T-37/92 *BEUC and NCC v Commission* [1994] ECR II-285.
1150. Case C-249/02 *Portugal v Commission* [2004] ECR I-10717.

■ All acts which only confirm an existing situation, since they do not modify the legal position of the applicant;[1151]

■ All acts which set up a global policy of the EU in a specific subject area, that is, establishing programmes of the EU, since they envisage future measures and thus do not change the current legal situation of the applicant;[1152]

■ All internal measures adopted by any EU institution which produce legal effects only with regard to that institution, such as instructions, internal rules, circulars, and so on.[1153] However, these may be challenged indirectly, provided they produce binding legal effect, if an individual decision was based on such internal measures;[1154]

■ All preparatory acts of EU institutions, because to be challengeable an act must be a final statement of an institution's position, not merely an interim position.[1155] In Case 60/81 *IBM*[1156] the Commission decision to commence proceedings against IBM, and a statement of objections to its marketing practices as being incompatible with Articles 101 and 102 TFEU (which was annexed to the decision), was considered as a step in the proceedings. The idea behind the exclusion of these acts from the scope of Article 263 TFEU is that work of EU institutions would be paralysed if preparatory acts were reviewable. However, an action for annulment of such acts is allowed if they produce binding effects or if they constitute a final position in ancillary proceedings, which would result in the adoption of a final decision. The distinction is difficult to apply in practice, especially in cases concerning competition law, State aid and anti-dumping measures – for example, a decision to forward documents to a complaining undertaking,[1157] a decision to deny access to a file in an anti-dumping case,[1158] a decision to refuse to initiate proceedings under Article 106(2) TFEU[1159] or Article 108(2) TFEU concerning State aid,[1160] or an injunction issued by the Commission requiring a Member State to provide information in proceedings relating to allegedly unlawful aid.[1161] All were regarded as reviewable, but a letter refusing to protect confidentiality of documents forwarded to the Commission by the applicant was not considered as a reviewable act;[1162]

■ A decision of the Commission to refuse to initiate proceedings against a Member State which is allegedly in breach of EU law under Article 258 TFEU. In Case 48/65 *Lütticke*,[1163] the ECJ held that a part of the procedure prior to bringing the Member State before the ECJ constitutes a stage

---

1151. Joined Cases 42 and 49/59 *SNUPAT* [1961] ECR 53; Case T-106/05 *Evropaiki Dinamiki v Commission* [2006] ECR II-82.

1152. Case 9/73 *Carl Schlüter v Hauptzollamt Lörrach* [1973] ECR 1135; Case C-142/95P *Associazione Agricoltori della Provincia di Rivigo and Others v Commission* [1996] ECR I-6669.

1153. Case C-322/91 *TAO v Commission* [1992] ECR 1–6373 (Ord).

1154. Joined Cases 32 and 33/58 *SNUPAT v High Authority* [1959] ECR 127.

1155. Case T-175/96 *Berthu v Commission* [1997] ECR II-811; Case T-376/04 *Polyelectrolyte Producers Group v Council and Commission* [2005] ECR II-3007 (Ord.).

1156. Case 60/81 *IBM v Commission* [1981] ECR 2639.

1157. Case 53/85 *AKZO Chemie BV and AKZO Chemie UK Ltd v Commission* [1986] ECR 1965; Case T-46/92 *Scottish Football Association v Commission* [1994] ECR II-1039.

1158. Case C-170/89 *BEUC v Commission* [1991] ECR I-5709.

1159. Case C-313/90 *CIRFS and Others v Commission* [1993] ECR I-1125.

1160. Case C-312/91 *Spain v Commission* [1992] ECR I-4117; Case C-47/91 *Italy v Commission* [1992] ECR I-4145.

1161. Joined Cases C-463/10 P and C-475/10 P *Deutsche Post AG v Commission* (judgment of 13/10/11 (NYR)).

1162. Cases T-90/96 and T-136/96 *Automobiles Peugeot SA v Commission* [1997] ECR II-663.

1163. Case 48/65 *Alfons Lütticke GmbH v Commission* [1966] ECR 19.

which is designed to invite the Member State to fulfil its obligations arising out of the Treaties. At this stage of Article 258 TFEU proceedings, the Commission states its position by issuing an opinion. Such an opinion cannot produce binding legal effects. This position of the ECJ has been confirmed in many cases;[1164] and,

■ A decision of the Commission to bring a civil action before courts in the USA against certain manufacturers of tobacco products in the USA for their alleged involvement in smuggling cigarettes into the EU and thus causing the EU a loss of customs and tax revenue which are part of "own resources" of the EU.[1165] The ECJ held that the decision did not produce binding legal effects as it did not change the legal position of the likely defendants in proceedings in the USA.

15.2.4   Applicants under Article 263 TFEU

Article 263 TFEU establishes three categories of applicants:

■ Privileged applicants, who may bring an action for annulment against all reviewable acts and are not required to justify their interest to act;

■ Semi-privileged applicants, such as the CoA, the ECB and the CoR which may only challenge acts in order to defend their prerogatives; and,

■ Non-privileged applicants, who, apart from a situation where they are addressees of a decision, must establish that they are directly and individually concerned by a non-regulatory act and directly concerned by a regulatory act which does not entail any implementing measures.

15.2.5   Privileged applicants

Under Article 263 TFEU the Council, the EP, the Commission and the Member States are privileged applicants. They may challenge any reviewable acts and they have unrestricted *locus standi*.

In relation to the Commission its privileged status is justified on the basis that the Commission is the Guardian of the Treaties, as specifically provided in Article 17(1) TEU.

The granting of this privileged status on the Council is a logical consequence of its position within the institutional framework of the EU.

The Member States as contracting parties to the Treaties are particularly interested in defending their rights against unlawful measures adopted by EU institutions, bodies, offices or agencies. A Member State under its unrestricted *locus standi* may challenge an act addressed to another Member State[1166] or even an act which was adopted with its consent.[1167] The only condition for privileged applicants is that they must challenge an act within the time limit set out in Article 263(5) TFEU.

The EP was initially denied *locus standi*, but became a semi-privileged applicant under the Treaty of Maastricht and finally acquired the status of a privileged applicant under the ToN. The current status

---

1164. Case C-87/89 *Sonito v Commission* [1990] ECR I-1981; Case C-247/90 *Emrich v Commission* [1990] ECR I-3913; Case T-479 and 559/93 *Bernardi v Commission* [1994] ECR II-1115.

1165. Case C-131/03P *R.J. Reynolds Tobacco Holdings, Inc. and Others v Commission* [2006] ECR II-7795.

1166. Case 6/54 *The Netherlands v High Authority* [1954–1956] ECR 103.

1167. Case 166/78 *Italy v Council* [1979] ECR 2575; Italy had voted in favour of the measure in the Council.

of the EP is well justified given that it has become a co-legislator and the fact that it is the only directly elected body of the EU.

It is submitted that the omission of the European Council from the list of privileged applicants is justified on the basis that it is difficult to imagine a situation where it would wish to bring an action under Article 263 TFEU. However, Craig argues that there may be instances in which the European Council might so wish, in particular in respect of matters relating to the CFSP over which the ECJ has jurisdiction.[1168] If this occurs, the ECJ may resort to the same approach as it took in relation to the EP, i.e. it may allow the European Council *locus standi* to protect its prerogatives.

15.2.6 Semi-privileged applicants

These are the CoA, the ECB and the CoR. These institutions have *locus standi* for the purpose of protecting their prerogatives. It is submitted that all other EU bodies, agencies and offices, as they are not mentioned in Article 263 TFEU as semi-privileged applicants, will have to establish *locus standi* in accordance with the criteria set out for non-privileged applicants in a situation where they wish to protect their prerogatives.

15.2.7 Non-privileged applicants

Non-privileged applicants under Article 263 TFEU are natural or legal persons. Unless they are addressees of a decision, they have many hurdles to jump to establish *locus standi* under Article 263 TFEU.

15.2.7.1 Interest to act

Applicants under Article 263 TFEU must first justify their interest in seeing the contested measure annulled. Such an interest must be present and actual, not merely hypothetical. In Case T-141/03 *Sniace*,[1169] the General Court held that this requirement constitutes a prerequisite for any action for annulment. This prerequisite is usually not mentioned in the case law, given that in 99 per cent of cases the interest of an applicant to bring an action for annulment is self-evident.

Non-privileged applicants are required to show that an EU act has affected their rights protected under the EU law "at present". As a result, an interest regarding a future legal situation which might happen, which is uncertain, or subject to changes in circumstances in law or in fact, is outside the scope of Article 263 TFEU.[1170] Further, applicants are required to prove that the contested measure has had a detrimental effect on their personal situation.[1171] Accordingly, applicants cannot challenge a decision which is favourable to their interests.[1172]

The ECJ has been very liberal in the assessment of the interest to act under Article 263 TFEU. The ECJ considered admissible an application where the contested decision had already been complied

---

1168. P. Craig, *The Lisbon Treaty*, 2010, Oxford: OUP, 127–28.

1169. Case T-141/03 *Sniace SA v Commission* [2005] ECR II-1197, see also Case T-167/01 *Schmitz-Gotha Fahrzeugwerke GmbH v Commission* [2003] ECR II-1873 (Ord).

1170. E.g. see Case T-138/89 *NBV v Commission* [1992] ECR II-2181.

1171. See Case 77/77 *Benzine en Petroleum Handelsmaatschappij BV v Commission* [1978] ECR 1513.

1172. Ibid.

with by its addressee at the time when the action for annulment was brought,[1173] and where the contested measure had already been annulled.[1174] In Case T-121/08 *PC-Ware*[1175] the General Court held that an applicant is allowed to bring an action for annulment if the annulment sought would have the effect of preventing future repetition of the alleged illegality. In this case the applicant brought proceedings against a decision of the Commission rejecting its tender submitted within the context of a public procurement procedure, although the contract for which it applied had already been partially performed by a successful tenderer. The General Court held that the applicant had interest in bringing proceedings under Article 263 TFEU in respect of a frame-work contract, which was likely to serve as a model for similar future procurement contracts, when the annulment sought would have the effect of preventing the unlawfulness alleged by the applicant from recurring in the future. However, very strict requirements as to the admissibility of applications in relation to the nature of the act and to the situation of the applicant with regard to the act have more than balanced the favourable approach of the Union courts to the concept of the interest to act.

15.2.7.2 Locus standi of professional organisations or associations

An association has *locus standi* in the following situations:

- ■ Where the relevant EU act has granted it procedural rights to that effect, e.g. the Merger Regulation.[1176]

- ■ Where it represents its members which themselves are either directly concerned by a regulatory act which does not entail any implementing measures or directly and individually concerned by a non-regulatory act.[1177] In such a situation the association substitutes itself for one or more of the members whom it represents.

- ■ Where the relevant EU act affects an association's own interests so as to distinguish it individually.[1178] This occurs when the participation of the association in the preparation of the challenged acts was substantial.[1179]

Accordingly, professional associations which wish to defend the general interest of their members, but do not fall within any of the above situations, have no *locus standi* under Article 263 TFEU.[1180]

1173. Case T-46/92 *Scottish Football Association v Commission* [1994] ECR II-1039; Cases T-480 and 483/93 *Antillean Rice NV and Others v Commission* [1995] ECR II-2305.

1174. Case 76/79 *Karl Könecke Fleischwarenfabrik GmbH & Co. KG v Commission* [1980] ECR 665.

1175. Case T-121/08 *PC-Ware Information Technologies v Commission* [2010] ECR II-1541.

1176. Case T-12/93 *Comité Central d'Entreprise de la SA Vittel and Comité d'Etablissement de Pierval v Commission* [1995] ECR II-1247.

1177. Joined Cases C-182/03 and C-217/03 *Belgium and Forum 187 ASBL v Commission* [2006] ECR I-5479.

1178. Cases 67/85, 68/85 and 70/85 *Kwekerij Gebroeders van der Kooy BV and Others v Commission* [1988] ECR 219; and Case C-313/90 *CIRFS and Others v Commission* [1993] ECR I-1125.

1179. Case C-313/90 *Comité International de la Rayonne et des Fibres Synthétiques and Others v Commission* [1993] ECR I-1125; Joined Cases T-227/01 to T-229/01, T-265/01, T-266/01 and T-270/01 *Territorio Histórico de Álava – Diputación Foral de Álava and Others v Commission* [2009] ECR II-3029; Joined Cases T-481–484/93 *Vereniging van Exporteurs in Levende Varkens and Others v Commission* [1995] ECR II-2941.

1180. Joined Cases 16/62 and 17/62 *Confédération Nationale des Producteurs de Fruits et Légumes and Others v Council* [1962] ECR 471 and Case 282/85 *DEFI v Commission* [1986] ECR 2469.

15.2.7.3   Locus standi of public interest groups

Groups which attempt to act in the public interests, such as Greenpeace,[1181] have no *locus standi* under Article 263 TFEU. The reason being that had they had this standing, an *actio popularis* would have been introduced which is contrary to the philosophy of Article 263 TFEU.

15.2.7.4   The distinction between regulatory and non-regulatory acts

Non-privileged applicants can always challenge a decision addressed to them. This is a classic judicial review situation and thus needs no further explanation.

Prior to entry into force of the ToL, non-privileged applicants could satisfy the admissibility threshold by establishing that they were directly and individually concerned by a decision addressed to "another person" or that an act in the form of a regulation or a directive, i.e. an act of general application, was in fact a decision addressed to them. To establish individual concern was extremely difficult in respect of acts of general application because a non-privileged applicant had to show that the effect of such an act was so peculiar to him, and to him alone, that he was individually distinguished from everybody else by the act.

The ToL facilitates access to the Union courts for non-privileged applicants in that it makes a distinction between challenges concerning regulatory and non-regulatory acts. In respect of regulatory acts which do not entail any implementing measures non-privileged applicants need only to prove that they are directly concerned by the act. This is fairly easy to establish. However, in respect of non-regulatory acts the pre-ToL requirements for *locus standi* remain.

Neither Article 263 TFEU nor the Treaties provide any definition of the concept of a "regulatory act". However, the General Court in Case T-262/10 *Microban*[1182] elucidated the meaning of both a "regulatory act" and the concept of direct concern with regard to challenges to regulatory acts.

THE FACTS WERE:

The applicants, Microban International Ltd and Microban (Europe) Ltd, manufactured and sold antimicrobial and antibacterial additives designed to provide antimicrobial and antibacterial protection in a wide range of products. They sought the annulment of Commission Decision 2010/169/EU in which the Commission decided not to include in the list of additives authorised by Commission Directive 90/128/EEC relating to plastic materials and articles intended to come into contact with foodstuffs,[1183] an additive called triclosan, which may be used in the manufacture of plastic materials and articles intended to come into contact with foodstuffs.

The story started in March 1998 when Ciba Inc asked the Commission to include triclosan in the list of authorised additives under Directive 90/128/EEC. In 2008, the Commission decided, on the basis of positive opinions from first, the EC Scientific Committee on Food, and second, its successor the European Food Safety Agency, to include triclosan on the

---

1181.   Case C-321/95 *Stichting Greenpeace Council (Greenpeace International) and Others v Commission* [1998] ECR I-1651.

1182.   Case T-262/10 *Microban International Ltd and Microban (Europe) Ltd v Commission* (Judgment of 25/10/12 (NYR)).

1183.   [1990] OJ L 75/19.

"provisional" list of additives provided for by Article 4a(3) of Commission Directive 2002/72/EC relating to plastic materials and articles intended to come into contact with foodstuffs.[1184] Additives on that provisional list, as opposed to those on "the positive list," may continue to be used subject to national law for as long as they are included on the provisional list. In April 2009, Ciba Inc withdrew its application for authorisation of the use of triclosan. In March 2010, the Commission, on the basis that there was no valid application for the use of triclosan, adopted the contested decision under which triclosan was removed from the provisional list, and at the same time, not included in the positive list.

Held:

The General Court annulled the contested decision.

Comment:

The Commission argued, first, that the contested decision was not a regulatory act and second, that it was not of individual concern to the applicants.

With regard to the first point, the General Court stated that the Commission Decision was a regulatory act. The Court held:

"the meaning of 'regulatory act' for the purposes of the fourth paragraph of Article 263 TFEU must be understood as covering all acts of general application apart from legislative acts".[1185]

The Commission's decision satisfied all the criteria for a regulatory act. It was adopted by the Commission in the exercise of implementing powers conferred on it by the relevant EU regulation and it was an act of general application as it applied to all natural and legal persons engaged in the production/marketing of triclosan and products containing this substance. It did not require any further implementing measures.

With regard to the second point, the General Court stated that the concept of direct concern has the same meaning regardless of whether an applicant challenges a regulatory act or a non-regulatory act. The Court stated that "it must be observed that, according to case-law, by allowing a natural or legal person to institute proceedings against regulatory acts of direct concern to them which do not entail implementing measures, the fourth paragraph of Article 263 TFEU pursues an objective of opening up the conditions for bringing direct actions . . . Accordingly, the concept of direct concern, as recently introduced in that provision cannot, in any event, be subject to a more restrictive interpretation than the notion of direct concern as it appeared in the fourth paragraph of [Article 263 (4) TFEU]."[1186] This shows that the pre-ToL case law on direct concern still stands. The General Court held that the applicants were directly concerned because, first the contested decision directly affected their legal situation and, second, the contested decision was addressed to the Member States which had no discretion it its implementation and were not required to take any implementing measures. Its implementation was automatic and derived from EU rules.

1184. [2002] OJ L220/18.

1185. Supra note 1182, para. 21. See also Order of the General Court of 6 September 2011 in Case T-18/10 R *Inuit Tapiriit Kanatami and Others v Parliament and Council* [2010] ECR 11-75, summ.pub, para. 56, in which the General Court provided the same definition of a regulatory act as in the *Microban* case (para. 56) and provided a definition of a measure of general application (para. 63).

1186. Supra note 1182, para. 32.

It is submitted that the above interpretation of "regulatory acts", i.e. there are any acts other than those adopted in accordance with either the ordinary legislative procedure or special legislative procedures, which do not require implementing measures, will ensure the right to effective judicial remedy under Article 263 TFEU for applicants finding themselves in a situation similar to that which occurred in Case T-177/01 *Jégo-Quéré v Commission*.[1187] In that case the General Court decided to relax the test of individual concern in order to ensure effective judicial protection for the applicant. It held that the applicant was individually concerned, although it had failed the usual test for individual concern, by a measure of general application which did not necessitate any implementing measures at national level. The applicant could not initiate proceedings before the national courts, despite the fact that the measure in question (by restricting his rights or by imposing obligations on him) affected his legal position in a manner which was both definite and immediate. Indeed, the only way in which the applicant could gain access to a national court was to knowingly infringe the contested measure. In that case, the General Court emphasised that individuals should not be required to breach the law in order to have access to justice. The General Court followed, with slight modifications, the revolutionary Opinion delivered by A-G Jacobs in Case C-50/00P *UPA*.[1188] In *UPA* the association of Spanish farmers appealed to the ECJ against an order of the General Court which dismissed its application for judicial review of a Council regulation reforming the common organisation of the market in olive oil on the ground that UPA was not individually concerned. UPA argued that the regulation, being directly applicable in the Member States, did not require any implementing measures with the result that UPA could not challenge its validity before national courts *via* the preliminary ruling procedure. Accordingly, had the ECJ rejected its application, UPA would have been left without legal remedy and thus would have been denied effective judicial protection.

A-G Jacobs stated that, at least for two reasons, it was unacceptable that an individual could not challenge, in most cases, a measure which had adversely affected him if such a measure was of a general application. First, Article 263(4) TFEU must comply with the principle of effective judicial protection. Accordingly, when such protection was not provided by national courts, EU courts were required to provide it. Second, the most appropriate procedure for challenging the validity of EU acts and, at the same time, less liable to cause legal uncertainty, was that prescribed by Article 263 TFEU, not the preliminary ruling procedure. He added that "the Court's restrictive attitude towards individual applicants is anomalous in the light of its case-law on other aspects of judicial review and recent developments in the administrative laws of the Member States".[1189]

The A-G provided a new interpretation of the concept of individual concern as follows: "a person is to be regarded as individually concerned by [an EU] measure where, by reason of his particular circumstances, the measure has, or is liable to have, a substantial adverse effect on his interests". Accordingly, the A-G suggested that the more a measure affects an individual the easier it should be for him to challenge it.

Three months after the General Court's judgment in *Jégo-Quéré*, the ECJ in *UPA* rejected the A-G's Opinion and consequently, the judgment of the General Court in *Jégo-Quéré*. The ECJ, contrary to the Opinion of the A-G, did not accept that the appellant had no legal remedies, i.e. was suffering a denial of justice under EU law. It stated that the Treaty established a complete system of legal remedies and therefore the applicant could have challenged the measure either *via* the preliminary ruling procedure or using the plea of illegality (see Chapter 15.3). If neither was available for the applicant, it was for the

---

1187.   Case T-177/01 *Jégo-Quéré & Cie SA v Commission* [2002] ECR II-2365.
1188.   Case C-50/00P *Unión de Pequeños Agricultores (UPA) v Council* [2002] ECR I-6677.
1189.   Ibid, para. 37.

Member State to ensure the effectiveness of the appellant's right to judicial protection.[1190] In paragraph 41 of the judgment, the ECJ stated that: "it is for the Member States to establish a system of legal remedies and procedures which ensure respect for the right to effective judicial protection."

This solution was subsequently enshrined in Article 19(1) TEU. As a result, it is the responsibility of Member States, not the EU, to ensure that their citizens have the right to effective legal remedies. If a Member State fails to do this, the Commission may commence Article 258 TFEU proceedings, and an applicant may start proceedings against the defaulting Member State before a national court based on the principle of State liability. However, the proposal of A-G Jacobs and the judgment of the General Court in *Jégo-Quéré*, had contributed to the removal of the individual concern requirement in respect of regulatory acts under Article 230 TFEU. Applicants are no longer required to establish individual concern when challenging such acts. Under the current version of Article 263 TFEU, the applicant in *Jégo-Quéré* would have gained access to the Union's court given that the contested measure was a regulatory act, i.e. a Commission regulation. However, the applicant in the *UPA* case would not have succeeded because the contested regulation was a legislative act and would remain so under the ToL.

15.2.7.5 Challenges of both regulatory and non-regulatory acts by non-privileged applicants under Article 263 TFEU: the concept of direct concern

In respect of both those regulatory acts which do not require any implementing measures, and non-regulatory acts, a non-privileged applicant is required to establish that he is directly concerned by the relevant act.

In order to establish direct concern, applicants must show that the relevant measure directly affects their legal situation and that the addressee of that measure has no discretion in implementing it, i.e. such implementation must be purely automatic and resulting from EU rules without the application of other intermediate rules.[1191]

The best way to illustrate this point is to examine Case 123/77 *UNICME*.[1192]

THE FACTS WERE:

Under a Council regulation, only holders of an import licence issued by the Italian Government were allowed to import Japanese motorcycles. The applicants, Italian importers of such motorcycles and their trade association, UNICME, challenged the regulation.

Held:

The ECJ held that the applicants were not directly concerned because the Italian Government had discretion as to the grant of import licences. As a result, they were concerned not by the regulation, but by the subsequent refusal of import licences by the Italian authorities.

1190. The reasons for the ECJ's rejection of A-G Jacobs proposal are examined by C. Kombos, "A Paradox in the Making, Detecting Something Positive in 'UPA' under the 'Ten Kate' Effect", (2009) 15 ELJ, 520.

1191. Case C-404/96 P *Glencore Grain v Commission* [1998] ECR I-2435; Case C-486/01 P *National Front v EP* [2004] ECR I-6289; Case C-15/06 P *Regione Siciliana v Commission* [2007] ECR I-2591.

1192. Case 123/77 *UNICME and Others v Council* [1978] ECR 845.

If a Member State has no discretion as to the application of an EU measure, applicants can claim that they are directly concerned. For example, in Joined Cases 41–44/70 *International Fruit*[1193] the granting of import licences for dessert apples, which was based on an EU rule, was modified by a Commission regulation. The latter imposed on the Member States specific rules for dealing with such licences. As a result, national authorities had no discretion in the matter.

If a Member State first decides how to deal with a particular issue and then asks the Commission to confirm that decision, as occurred in Joined Cases 106 and 107/63 *Toepfer*,[1194] the applicant is directly concerned (once the decision of the national authority has been confirmed by the Commission) because a Member State must follow a confirmation by the Commission.

One exception to the above rule was established in Case 11/82 *Piraïki Patraïki*,[1195] in which the ECJ held that an applicant satisfies the requirement relating to direct concern in a situation where the likelihood of the addressee of the relevant measure not giving effect to it is purely theoretical and the addressee's intention to act in conformity with it is not in doubt.

THE FACTS WERE:

The Commission gave permission to the French Government to impose quotas on imports of yarn from Greece. Although the French authorities had discretion as to whether or not to impose quotas, in the light of previous restrictions imposed on such imports and of a request to use the quotas submitted to the Commission by the French Government, which was granted, it was highly unlikely, or as the ECJ held "purely theoretical," that the French authorities would not exercise their discretion to impose quotas.

Held:

The ECJ held that the possibility that a Member State might decide not to make use of the authorisation obtained from the Commission was entirely theoretical, since there could be no doubt as to the intention of the Member State to act in accordance with the authorisation. Accordingly, the link between the applicant and an EU act was not severed by a mere possibility that a Member State may not take authorised measures, which in this case was highly unlikely. Therefore the applicants were directly concerned by the measure.

It is to be noted that the ECJ has always refused to recognise that a region of a Member State can claim to be directly concerned by an EU measure. In Case C-15/06P *Regione Siciliana*[1196] the General Court decided that Sicily, a region of Italy which possesses legal personality under national law, was directly concerned by a Commission decision withholding assistance granted to Italy to build a dam in Sicily and requesting reimbursement of sums already paid in the light of delays and irregularities in the implementation of aid. Both the General Court and the ECJ agreed that the region of Sicily was individually concerned given the financial implications of the request for reimbursement, but the ECJ

1193. Joined Cases 41–44/70 *International Fruit Co v Commission* [1971] ECR 411.

1194. Joined Cases 106 and 107/63 *Alfred Toepfer and Getreide-Import Gesellschaft v Commission* [1965] ECR 405.

1195. Case 11/82 *SA Piraiki-Patraiki and Others v Commission* [1985] ECR 207, see also Case 62/70 *Werner A Bock v Commission* [1971] ECR 897; Case 29/75 *Kaufhof AG v Commission* [1976] ECR 431; Case T-85/94 *Commission v Branco* [1995] ECR II-45.

1196. Case C-15/06P *Regione Siciliana v Commission* [2007] ECR I-2591.

agreed with the Commission that the region was not directly concerned because the aid was granted to Italy, not to the region, and the Italian Government enjoyed discretion: first as to whether to grant assistance to the region and second, as to the repayment of the sums due from the State budget. An argument put forward by the region based on lack of effective judicial protection was given short shrift. Indeed, the Italian Government, as a privileged applicant and direct beneficiary of aid, could have brought proceedings for annulment of the contested decision under Article 263 TFEU.

15.2.7.6 Challenges of non-regulatory acts by non-privileged applicants: the concept of individual concern

Article 263 TFEU requires that an applicant who wishes to challenge a non-regulatory act must prove that he is both directly and individually concerned by that act. Obviously, there is no problem if such an act is specifically addressed to him. Prior to the entry into force of the ToL, an applicant had to prove that a decision addressed to "another person" or that an act in the form of a regulation or a directive, i.e. an act of general application, was in fact a decision addressed to him. Under the ToL the reference is to "any act". As a result, the applicant needs only to establish that the act in question, whether in the form of a regulation, directive or a decision addressed to a third party, is of direct and individual concern to him.

A.   **The concept of individual concern.** The most confusing and complicated matter under Article 263 TFEU is the issue of individual concern, mostly because of inconsistency in the decisions of the EU courts in this area. Individual concern was defined by the ECJ in Case 25/62 *Plaumann*.[1197]

THE FACTS WERE:

Plaumann was an importer of clementines, established in Germany. Under the Common Customs tariff he paid 13 per cent customs duty, as did any importer of clementines from outside the EU. The Government of Germany asked the Commission for authorisation under Article 25(3) EC Treaty (repealed) to suspend this duty. The Commission refused and issued a decision in this respect. Plaumann challenged this decision.

Held:

The ECJ held that Plaumann was not individually and directly concerned by the Commission's decision, although he was affected, as any importer of clementines, by the decision. His commercial activities were such that they could, at any time, be practised by any person, and thus he did not distinguish himself from others in relation to the challenged decision. The ECJ stated that individual concern can be established if persons other than the addressees of the decision demonstrate "that the decision affects them by reason of certain attributes which are peculiar to them or by reason of circumstances in which they are differentiated from all other persons".[1198]

1197.   Case 25/62 *Plaumann & Co. v Commission* [1963] ECR 95.
1198.   Ibid, at 107.

In the above case the applicant was considered as being a member of an "open class", that is, anyone may, at any time, practice the commercial activity in question and potentially join the group of producers of particular goods.

In Joined Cases 106 and 107/63 *Toepfer*[1199] the ECJ explained the circumstances in which an applicant will be regarded as belonging to a "fixed" group and therefore individually concerned within the meaning of Article 263(4) TFEU.

THE FACTS WERE:

On 1 October 1962, being the day on which the German authorities mistakenly reduced the levy on imports of maize from France to Germany, Toepfer applied for a licence to import maize from France to Germany. The German intervention agency realised the mistake and refused to grant licences from 2 October 1962. Three days later the Commission confirmed this ban on the grant of licences and authorised the German authority to reimpose the full levy. Toepfer challenged the Commission's decision on the grounds that he was individually and directly concerned.

Held:

The ECJ held that the applicant was individually concerned because the number and identity of those individually concerned "had become fixed and ascertainable before the contested decision was made". They were a "closed group": the decision affected their interests and position in a way significantly different from other importers who might wish to apply for a licence after the adoption of the decision by the German authorities but during the remaining period of the ban. Therefore, only those who applied on 1 October were individually concerned since from 2–4 October applications were refused and on 4 October the Commission issued its decision. As a result, Toepfer was within the closed group who applied on 1 October; the larger group, that is, those who applied between 2–4 October was open since they were refused licences and could reapply thereafter without loss to them as the levy would be the same after 2 October.

Similarly, in Case 62/70 *Bock*,[1200] the ECJ held that Bock was individually concerned by a decision adopted by the Commission because when he applied for a licence to import Chinese mushrooms, the German authorities refused to grant it and asked the Commission to confirm their decision, which the Commission did. The decision was issued to deal with Bock's application. Accordingly, he belonged to an ascertainable and fixed group of importers at the time of the adoption of that decision.

The fact that the identities of the economic operators to whom a measure applies were known to the Commission at the time a measure was adopted is not on its own sufficient to establish individual concern. What is required is that the measure affects applicants in a

---

1199. Joined Cases 106 and 107/63 *Alfred Toepfer and Getreide-Import Gesellschaft v Commission* [1965] ECR 405.

1200. Case 62/70 *Bock v Commission* [1971] ECR 897.

special way, that is, distinguishes them from all other persons by reason of certain attributes which are peculiar to them or by reason of their peculiar circumstances.[1201]

The ECJ restrictively interprets "certain peculiar attributes" or "circumstances which differentiate" a person from others. As a result, the ECJ refused to recognise that a person was individually concerned in the following situations:

- in the *Plaumann* case, where the decision concerned specific activities, that is, importing of clementines;

- where the number of the affected persons was limited;[1202]

- where an undertaking was the only one concerned by a measure in a particular Member State;[1203]

- where an undertaking operated in a determined zone and the regulation expressly applied to that geographically delimited zone;[1204]

- where an undertaking was a direct competitor of another undertaking to which the decision was addressed;[1205]

- where the number of undertakings concerned was limited to three undertakings in a Member State, and potential competitors would not be in a position to enter the market for at least two years;[1206] and,

- where an undertaking was the largest importer of the relevant product in two Member States.[1207]

The ECJ's unrealistic approach to the concept of individual concern based on the assumption that as long as any person at any time may practice a particular activity, or become a member of a particular class of producers, has been subject to criticism within the ECJ, as exemplified by the Opinion of A-G Jacobs in *UPA* (see Chapter 15.2.7.4), and by academic commentators.[1208] Many explanations have been provided for the refusal of the ECJ to relax its strict interpretation of the concept of individual concern. Probably, the most widely accepted is that the ECJ wishes to further EU integration. A less restrictive approach would have been disruptive to the functioning of the EU in that too many challenges would have been lodged against EU measures which result from many compromises and many years of negotiations

1201. Joined Cases C-15/91 and C-108/91 *Josef Buckl & Söhne OHG and Others v* Commission [1992] ECR I-6061; Case C-309/89 *Codorníu SA v Council* [1994] ECR I-1853; Case T-476/93 *FRSEA and FNSEA v Council* [1993] ECR II-1187; and Case T-472/93 *Campo Ebro Industrial SA v Council* [1995] ECR II-421.
1202. In *Plaumann* there were 30 importers of clementines. A similar situation arose in Case T-11/99 *Firma Léon Van Parys NV v Commission* [1999] ECR II-1355.
1203. Case 231/82 *Spijker Kwasten BV v Commission* [1983] ECR 259; Case 97/85 *Union Deutsche Lebensmittelwerke GmbH and Others v Commission* [1987] ECR 2265.
1204. Case 30/67 *Industria Molitoria Imolese and Others v Council* [1968] ECR 115.
1205. Case 10 and 18/68 *Società "Eridania" Zuccherifici Nazionali and Others v Commission* [1969] ECR 459.
1206. Case 101/76 *KSH NV v Council and Commission* [1977] ECR 797.
1207. Case C-209/94 *Buralux SA v Commission* [1996] ECR I-615.
1208. See, e.g. A. Ward, "Amsterdam and Amendment to Article 230: An Opportunity Lost or Simply Deferred", in A. Dashwood and A. Johnston, *The Future of the Judicial System of the European Union*, 2001, Oxford: Hart Publishing, 37.

between EU institutions and the Member States.[1209] Nevertheless, the ECJ has decided to relax its very strict interpretation of the concept of individual concern in some circumstances as discussed below.

B. **Relaxation of the restrictive interpretation of requirements relating to individual concern in cases where the applicant participates in the procedure that leads to the adoption of the challenged act: anti-dumping, competition, and State aid cases.**

Some procedures leading to the adoption of a measure grant specific procedural rights to certain persons, such as the right to lodge a complaint; the right to have the complaint examined; the right to obtain information; and the right to submit a view on a particular matter. For that reason it is less difficult for those persons to distinguish themselves from others who did not participate in the adoption of the relevant measure. However, it is only when an applicant has specific procedural rights guaranteed by the legal basis of an act that his participation in the procedure leading to the adoption of that act will confer on him individual concern. In Case T-114/99 *CSR Pampryl*,[1210] the General Court held: "in the absence of expressly guaranteed procedural rights, it would be contrary to the wording and spirit of [Article 263 TFEU] to allow any individual, where he has participated in the preparation of a legislative measure, subsequently to bring an action against that measure".

Accordingly, when an applicant submits a complaint to the Commission and subsequently exchanges correspondence with the Commission this will not be sufficient to give him *locus standi* under Article 263 TFEU in a situation where there is no specific procedure provided for an individual to be associated with the adoption of the contested measure and when it is clear that the applicant is neither an actual nor potential addressee of that measure.[1211]

The main areas of EU law in which persons can benefit from specific procedural guarantees are competition law, and State aids.[1212] In anti-dumping cases, however, the participation in the procedure is only an element to be taken into account in the determination of whether an applicant has distinguished himself from other undertakings.

In competition cases an undertaking, which has lodged a complaint against a competitor under Article 17(2) of Regulation 1/2003 (see Chapter 30.2.1) alleging that the competitor is in breach of Article 101 or 102 will be individually concerned by a decision addressed by the Commission to the competitor confirming that there was no breach of competition rules on its part.[1213] This is not because a complaining undertaking is in a relationship of competition with the competitor, but because it initiated the proceedings which resulted in the adoption of the measure.

1209. H. Rasmussen, "Why is Article 173 [now Article 260 TFEU] against Private Plaintiffs?", (1980) 35 ELRev., 112.
1210. Case T-114/99 *CSR Pampryl v Commission* [1999] ECR II-3331, para. 50.
1211. Case T-585/93 *Stichting Greenpeace Council (Greenpeace International) and Others v Commission* [1995] ECR II-2205.
1212. For procedural rights guaranteed in other areas of EU law see: e.g. Case T-13/99 *Pfizer Animal Health SA v Council* [2002] ECR II-3305.
1213. Case 26/76 *Metro SB-Großmärkte GmbH & Co. KG v Commission* [1977] ECR 1875; Joined Cases 142 and 156/84 *BAT and R. J. Reynolds Industries Inc. v Commission* [1986] ECR 1899.

Similarly, a decision of the Commission, upon receiving a complaint, to refuse the opening of proceedings under Article 108(2) TFEU concerning aid granted to an undertaking by a Member State, may be challenged by the undertaking which made the complaint[1214] provided that the complaining undertaking's position in the market has been significantly affected by the contested measure.[1215]

Anti-dumping[1216] cases are special in terms of establishing *locus standi* under Article 263 TFEU because applicants have to challenge EU regulations (i.e. an act of general application). Under Regulation 384/96 on Protection against Dumped Imports from Countries not Members of the EU[1217] the procedure for possible imposition of anti-dumping duty normally commences when an undertaking lodges a complaint to the Commission. If the Commission considers the complaint justified it will open an investigation by publishing a Notice to this effect in the OJ. At this stage all interested parties are invited to submit their views and to be heard. Subsequently, the Commission will either terminate its investigation or impose anti-dumping duties. Such duties are determined on the basis of the Commission's investigation of production prices of the product at issue; export prices; and, exceptionally, import prices of individually identified undertakings. As can be seen the procedure provides for some specific procedural guarantees for undertakings and any finding of the existence of dumping is based on prices charged by undertakings operating on the relevant market. For that reason, the case law of the ECJ distinguishes four situations in which an undertaking will be regarded as individually concerned by the imposition of anti-dumping duties, irrespective of whether or not the applicant had participated in the procedure[1218] although its participation will constitute an element to be taken into account in the establishment of individual concern. For example, in Case 264/82 *Timex*[1219] the applicant challenged a regulation which was adopted because of Timex's complaints concerning cheap mechanical watches coming from the Soviet Union. The regulation imposed an anti-dumping duty taking into account information forwarded by Timex. However, Timex then claimed that the new duty was too low. The ECJ held that because the regulation was based on Timex's situation, Timex was individually concerned. It is to be noted that Timex's situation, irrespective of its participation in the procedure leading to the adoption of the challenged act, was within the scope of the second situation described below.

Those individually concerned for the purposes of Article 263 TFEU are as follows:

1. Producers and exporters of the product on which the anti-dumping duty was imposed on the basis of data relating to their activities provided that they can show that they were identified in the challenged act or were concerned by the preliminary investigations;[1220]

1214. Case 169/84 *Cofaz SA and Others v Commission* [1986] ECR 391, Case C-198/91 *William Cook plc v Commission* [1993] ECR I-2487, Case C-225/91 *Matra SA v Commission* [1993] ECR I-3203.
1215. Case T-117/04 *Vereniging Werkgroep Commerciële Jachthavens Zuidelijke Randmeren and Others v Commission* [2006] ECR II-3861.
1216. In the context of the internal market, dumping occurs when a non-EU undertaking sells its products below domestic market prices, which are at the same time below the real cost of the products. This strategy is used to penetrate the market and eliminate competitors.
1217. [1996] OJ L56/1. This is the basic regulation which has been amended many times.
1218. Case T-162/09 *Adolf Würth GmbH & Co. KG and Arnold Fasteners (Shenyang) Co. Ltd v Council* (judgment of 9/4/12 (NYR)), para. 34.
1219. Case 264/82 *Timex Corporation v Council* [1985] ECR 861.
1220. E.g. Joined Cases 239/82 and 275/82 *Allied Corporation and others v Commission* [1984] ECR 1005 and Case C-156/87 *Gestetner Holdings v Council and Commission* [1990] ECR I-781.

2. Importers whose resale prices were taken into account for the construction of export prices and are therefore concerned by the findings relating to the existence of dumping;[1221]

3. Importers associated with exporters in non-member countries on whose products anti-dumping duties are imposed particularly where the export price has been calculated on the basis of importers selling prices on the internal market;[1222]

4. Unrelated importers (i.e. importers not mentioned in 1–3 above), but only in exceptional circumstances, i.e. where a regulation seriously affected that importer's business activities. This occurred in Case C-358/89 *Extramet*.[1223] In this case Extramet, a French company which imported calcium metal from outside the EU, and then processed it for use in the metallurgical industry, sought annulment of a Council regulation imposing an anti-dumping duty on imports of calcium metal. The regulation was adopted as a result of a complaint from Péchiney, the sole producer of calcium metal in the EU who also processed it. Péchiney was Extramet's main competitor and after the anti-dumping duty had been introduced, refused to supply calcium metal to Extramet.

    The ECJ took account of the economic situation of Extramet (i.e. it was the largest importer of the product on which the anti-dumping duty was imposed and the end-user of that product; had difficulty in obtaining supplies from alternative sources; and, its business depended on imports of the product) and the fact the Commission did not investigate the conduct of Péchiney which according to Extramet amounted to anti-competitive conduct prohibited under Article 102 TFEU. The ECJ held that Extramet differentiated itself from other undertakings so it had established individual concern.[1224] The situation that occurred in Extramet is unlikely to be repeated bearing in mind the restrictive interpretation of "exceptional circumstances".[1225] So far only Extramet was successful in relying on this exception.

C. **Relaxation of the restrictive interpretation of requirements relating to individual concern in cases where the relevant EU institution has a duty to take account of the consequences of the intended act on the position of the applicant.** The restrictive interpretation of requirements relating to individual concern has been relaxed in cases where the relevant EU institution has a duty, i.e. provisions of EU law impose an obligation on that institution, to take account of the consequences of the intended act on the position of individuals.

The above is exemplified in Case C-152/88 *Sofrimport*.[1226]

THE FACTS WERE:

In conformity with a regulation Sofrimport shipped apples from Chile. This regulation was amended to the effect that it suspended import licences for Chilean apples. When the amended regulation came into force, apples being imported by Sofrimport were in transit.

1221. Case 118/77 *Import Standard Office (ISO)* [1979] ECR 1277 and Joined Cases C-133/87 and C-150/87 *Nashua Corporation and Others v Commission* [1990] ECR I-71.
1222. Joined Cases 277/85 and 300/85 *Canon v Council* [1988] ECR 5731 and *Case C-156/87 Gestetner Holdings v Council and Commission* [1990] ECR I-781.
1223. Case C-358/89 *Extramet Industrie SA v Council* [1991] ECR I-2501.
1224. See A. Arnull, "Challenging EC Anti-dumping Regulations, The Problem of Admissibility", ECLR, 1992, 73.
1225. See e.g. Case T-598/97 *British Shoe Corporation Footwear Supplies Ltd and Others v Council* [2002] ECR II-1155.
1226. Case C-152/88 *Sofrimport SARL v Commission* [1990] ECR I-2477.

The French authorities refused to issue an import licence to Sofrimport and the latter challenged the regulation.

Held:

The ECJ held that an earlier regulation imposed a duty upon the EU authorities to take into consideration the case of goods in transit when adopting a new regulation, and consequently importers with goods in transit constituted a fixed and ascertainable group and could be considered as individually concerned.

Similar circumstances occurred in Joined Cases T-480/93 and T-483/93 *Antillean Rice*.[1227] In these cases the applicants' shipment of rice was in transit when the contested decision was adopted by the Commission. In addition, as a result of a meeting between The Netherlands' permanent representative's office and the Commission, in which the applicants had participated, the Commission was aware of the particular situation. These factors differentiated the applicants from other existing and future exporters of rice. Consequently, they were considered as being individually concerned.

It can be seen from the above that when a provision of EU law imposes a duty on the Commission to take account of the peculiar situation of the applicant,[1228] such a situation will be regarded as constituting "specific circumstances" within the meaning of the case law of the ECJ.

D.   **Applicants who differentiate themselves from others by being holders of intellectual property rights or other acquired rights.** The restrictive interpretation of the requirement of individual concern has been relaxed in respect of applicants who differentiate themselves from others by being holders of intellectual property rights in a situation where an act of general application "expropriates" the intellectual property right from the applicants, i.e. it prevents an applicant from using his intellectual property rights in the course of his business.

The leading case on the above is Case C-309/89 *Codorníu*.[1229]

THE FACTS WERE:

Codorníu, a Spanish producer of quality sparkling wines, had been the holder of a graphic trade mark since 1924 for one of its wines designated as "Gran Cremant de Codorníu". In certain regions of France and Luxembourg the word "cremant" was also used for a particular quality of wine. The producers in those countries asked the EU to adopt a regulation which would reserve the word "cremant" only for their sparkling wine. Council Regulation 2045/89 restricted the use of the word "cremant" to wines originating in France and Luxembourg in

---

1227. Joined Cases T-480/93 and T-483/93 *Antillean Rice Mills NV and Others v Commission* [1995] ECR II-2305.

1228. See also Case 11/82 *Piraïki Patraïki and Others v Commission* [1985] ECR 207 (Chapter 15.2.7.5); Case 62/70 *Bock v Commission* [1971] ECR 897; Case 29/75 *Kaufhof AG v Commission* [1976] ECR 431; Case T-85/94 *Branco v Commission* [1995] ECR II-45.

1229. Case C-309/89 *Codorníu SA v Council* [1994] ECR I-1853.

order to protect the traditional description used in those areas. Codorníu challenged the regulation.

Held:

The ECJ held that Codorníu was differentiated from other producers of wine since it had registered and used the word "cremant" since 1924. Although Regulation 2045/89 was a "true" regulation, it did not prevent it from being of individual concern to Codorníu, which was badly affected by the regulation. Also, the restriction of the word "cremant" to wine originating from a certain region of France and Luxembourg could not be objectively justified and, in addition, was contrary to Article 18 TFEU which prohibits discrimination based on nationality.

Comment:

The ECJ recognised that the protection of intellectual property rights may confer on the holder of those rights locus standi *under Article 263 TFEU in specific circumstances.*

The meaning of "specific circumstances" was explained, *inter alia*, in Case T-30/07 *Denka.*[1230]

THE FACTS WERE:

The applicant, Denka International BV ("Denka"), a manufacturer of dichlorvos, an insecticide, for which it held a patent and which it sold under the trade mark "Denkarepon," brought an action for partial annulment of Commission Directive 2006/92/EC[1231] of 9 November 2006 which amended annexes to Council Directives 76/895/EEC, 86/362/EEC and 90/642/EEC as regards maximum residue levels for captan, dichlorvos, ethion and folpet. This directive modified the maximum residue level for dichlorvos from the previously applicable 2 mg/kg to a new residue level of 0.01 mg/kg. The change of the maximum level for dichlorvos resulted in the applicant being unable to sell dichlorvos because the new maximum residue level was so low that it made unlikely any demand for the product. Denka claimed, inter alia, that it was in a situation similar to that of the applicant in the Codorníu case. It submitted that it was individually concerned by the contested directive by reason of being a holder of a patent and a trade mark for dichlorvos and that the use of the trademark had been greatly affected by the directive.

Held:

The General Court held that the existence of legal protection for a trademark is not, in itself, capable of distinguishing the applicant from all other manufacturers and distributors of dichlorvos.[1232] The Court explained why the situation of Denka differed from that of the applicant in Case C-309/89 Codorníu. In Codorníu, the contested regulation reserved the description "crémant" to an identified class of producers, even though the applicant had registered that same designation as a trade mark and had used it over a long period before

---

1230. Case T-30/07 *Denka International BV v Commission* [2008] ECR II-101 (Ord).
1231. [2006] OJ L 311/31.
1232. Case T-196/03 *European Federation for Cosmetic Ingredients v EP and Council* (Ord) [2004] ECR II-4263.

the adoption of the contested regulation. For that reason, as the General Court stated, Codorníu *was:*

"... clearly distinguished from all other economic operators. Rather than the enjoyment in the abstract of an intellectual right, it was the specificity of the designation which that right protected and which the contested measure had, in a way, expropriated from the applicant that gave rise to the solution adopted in Codorníu v Council."

Comment:

In Denka, the contested directive neither aimed to reserve a specific intellectual right to certain operators to the detriment of the applicant, nor affected the substance of a specific trademark used by the applicant. Therefore, Denka was not in a situation comparable to that of an undertaking such as Codorníu, which exploited a trade mark for sparkling wines, but rather in a situation comparable to that of champagne producers. Indeed, as the Commission submitted, the contested directive had not prevented Denka from using its trademark "Denkarepon" with regard to its products. Obviously, the judgment of the General Court would have been different had Denka been able to register its products under the trademark "Dichlorvos" and had so done!

It can be submitted that *Codorníu* is not different from other cases in which the applicants were recognised as individually concerned by an EU measure. This is because what had distinguished *Codorníu* from others who were not able to establish individual concern was that it had acquired intellectual property rights prior to the adoption of the relevant measure and thus was in the same situation as *Toepfer.*[1233] Accordingly, when a contested measure adversely alters rights which were acquired by an applicant prior to its adoption, it does not matter whether those rights concern intellectual property rights, or rights of a proprietary nature[1234] or any other rights.

E.   **Relaxation of the restrictive interpretation in cases where political interests of the EU are at issue.** The restrictive interpretation of the requirement of individual concern has been relaxed where political interests of the EU are at issue.

One of the rare cases where the ECJ was prepared to relax its strict interpretation of the concept of individual concern was Case 294/83 *Les Verts*,[1235] in which the French Ecology Party challenged a decision of the EP's Bureau relating to financing of the electoral campaign preceding the 1984 EP elections.

The ECJ held that the French Ecology Party was individually concerned because:

"A political grouping which, unlike its rivals, is not represented in the European Parliament but which is able to put up candidates in the direct elections to the Parliament must, in order to avoid inequality in the protection afforded by the Court to groupings competing in the same elections, be regarded as being both directly and individually concerned."

1233. Joined Cases 106/63 and 107/63 *Toepfer and Getreide-Import Gesellschaft v Commission* [1965] ECR 405.
1234. Case C-125/06P *Commission v Infront WM AG* [2008] ECR I-2271.
1235. Case 294/83 *Parti Ecologiste "Les Verts" v EP* [1986] ECR 1339, para. 4 of the summary.

The French Ecology Party failed the *Plaumann* test because it could neither be differentiated by reason of its peculiar attributes, as it was one of a potentially very wide group of political parties, nor by reason of circumstances as it had not decided whether to field candidates in the election The ECJ's judgment can, however, be explained by political considerations, namely to ensure the widest possible participation of political parties in elections to the EP, and thus enhance the democratic legitimacy of the EU.

15.2.8   Grounds for annulment

Article 263(2) TFEU sets out the grounds for annulment of EU acts. These are:

- lack of competence;

- infringement of an essential procedural requirement;

- infringement of the Treaties or any rule of law relating to their application; and,

- misuse of powers.

The Union courts must apply the first two grounds *ex officio* in any event,[1236] but the last two only if invoked by the applicant. It is very important to claim all possible, and perhaps all conceivable grounds, because introduction of new grounds after expiry of the time limit is not permitted. Further, the Union courts are empowered to specify and further crystallise the grounds invoked by the applicant.[1237]

15.2.8.1   Lack of competence

This ground is similar to substantive *ultra vires* in British administrative law, which occurs when the administration acts beyond its powers. EU institutions, bodies, offices or agencies have only the powers conferred upon them by the Treaties.

It was expected that this ground would be invoked often, especially by the Member States in respect of the encroachment of EU law upon the national competences of the Member States. This has not materialised. As a result, this ground is rarely used, mostly because the applicants prefer to base their claims on the infringement of the Treaties.[1238] Lack of competence is mainly relied upon in cases challenging the legal basis of EU acts.[1239]

15.2.8.2   Infringement of an essential procedural requirement

Infringement of an essential procedural requirement is analogous to procedural *ultra vires*. It occurs when an EU institution, body, office or agency fails to comply with a mandatory procedural requirement in the adoption of a measure, for example if the Council fails to consult the EP when the Treaties require mandatory consultation of the EP prior to the adoption of a measure. The ECJ has annulled acts which provided for optional consultation of the EP where the Council did not give enough time to the EP to

---

1236. Case 1/54 *France v High Authority* [1954–56] ECR 1.
1237. Case 4/73 *J. Nold, Kohlen- und Baustoffgroßhandlung v Commission* [1974] ECR 491.
1238. For example, see Joined Cases 3–18/58, 25/58 and 26/58 *Barbara Erzbergbau AG and others v High Authority* [1960] ECR 173.
1239. Case C-350/92 *Spain v Council* [1995] ECR I-1995; Case C-84/94 *UK v Council (Working Time Directive)* [1996] ECR I-5758; Case C-249/02 *Portugal v Commission* [2004] ECR I-10717.

issue its opinion,[1240] or when the EP was not reconsulted when an act of the Council substantially altered an original proposal submitted to the EP.[1241] When an EU institution fails to comply with its own internal Rules of Procedure, the ECJ will annul the act in question.[1242]

Failure to provide reasons for an act as required by Article 296 TFEU is most often invoked under this ground.[1243]

15.2.8.3 Infringement of the Treaties or any rule of law relating to their application

This is the most often invoked ground. It encompasses not only infringements of the provisions of the Treaties but of all sources of EU law, including the Charter of Fundamental Rights,[1244] the general principles of EU law[1245] and infringements of international agreements concluded between the EU and third countries.[1246]

15.2.8.4 Misuse of powers

The ECJ has adopted the same definition of misuse of powers as under French administrative law (*detournment de pouvoir*).[1247] Misuse of powers is analogous to the English doctrine of improper purpose. In order to rely on this ground, the applicant must prove that an EU institution, body, office or agency has used its powers for objectives other than those provided for by the Treaties. Thus, a legitimate power must have been used for an illegal end, or in an illegal way.

This ground is often invoked, but rarely successful because of the burden of proof it imposes on the applicant, who must prove, first, the actual subjective intention of an EU institution when it acted, and second, that an act was adopted with the exclusive purpose of achieving objectives other than prescribed by the Treaties, or evading a procedure specifically provided by the Treaties for dealing with the circumstances of the case.[1248] The second element is particularly difficult to establish given the multiplicity of objectives which an EU institution may legitimately pursue when adopting an act. Misuse of powers, however, was successfully invoked in the context of a dispute between the EU and its staff when the EU servant proved that an EU institution acted in bad faith.[1249]

1240. Case 138/79 *SA Roquette Frères v Council* [1980] ECR 3333.

1241. Case 41/69 *ACF Chemiefarma NV v Commission* [1970] ECR 661 and Case C-388/92 *EP v Council* [1994] ECR I-2067.

1242. Case C-137/92P *Commission v BASF* [1994] ECR I-2555.

1243. Case 24/62 *Germany v Commission (Brennwein)* [1963] ECR 63; Case T-102/03 *CIS v Commission* [2005] ECR II-2357.

1244. See Joined Cases C-92/09 and C-93/09 *Volker und Markus Schecke GbR (C-92/09), Hartmut Eifert (C-93/09) v Land Hessen* [2010] ECR I-11063.

1245. Case 62/70 *Bock v Commission* [1971] ECR 897; Case 17/74 *Transocean Marine Paint Association v Commission* [1974] ECR 1063; Case C-212/91 *Angelopharm GmbH v Freie Hansestadt Hamburg* [1994] ECR I-171; Case 25/70 *Einfuhr- und Vorratsstelle für Getreide und Futtermittel v Köster et Berodt & Co* [1970] ECR 1161.

1246. Joined Cases 21–24/72 *International Fruit Company NV and others v Produktschap voor Groenten en Fruit* [1972] ECR 1219.

1247. Case 2/57 *Compagnie des Hauts Fourneaux de Chasse v High Authority* [1957–58] ECR 199.

1248. Case C-331/88 *The Queen v Minister of Agriculture, Fisheries and Food and Secretary of State for Health, ex parte: Fedesa and Others* [1990] ECR I-4023.

1249. In Joined Cases 18 and 35/65 *Gutmann v Commission* [1966] ECR 61, a Community official was allegedly transferred to Brussels in the interest of the service, but in fact it was a disciplinary transfer; Case 105/75 *Franco Giuffrida v Council* [1976] ECR 1395.

15.2.9   Time limit for an action for annulment under Article 263 TFEU

The time limit is two months and begins to run from the date of publication of an act in the Official Journal, or from its notification to the applicant.[1250] If the act was published, by virtue of Article 81 of the Rules of Procedure of the ECJ,[1251] the time limit is extended by 14 days. Additionally, if an applicant is at a distance from the Union courts, the time is further extended by a single period of ten days.[1252] Therefore, the time limit for an applicant from the UK is two months, plus 14 days, plus ten days, provided the contested act was published in the OJ.[1253]

In the absence of publication or notification the time limit starts to run on the day when the act comes to the knowledge of the applicant, in the sense that it knows the essential content of the challenged act including the grounds on which it has been adopted.[1254] This is subject to an exception; if the party knows about the existence of the relevant act concerning it but has no precise knowledge of its content, that is, of its essential aspects, it is for that party to request from the relevant institution the full text of that act within a reasonable period.[1255] The General Court considered the period of 15 days as being reasonable in Joined Cases T-432/93, T-433/93 and T-434/93 *Socurte*[1256] and of three weeks in Case T-465/93 *Murgia Messapica*,[1257] but the ECJ rejected a delay of two months in Case C-102/92 *Ferriere Acciaierie Sarde*.[1258] However, there could be cases where a much longer period would be considered reasonable as the test is what is reasonable in all the circumstances.

The time limit is rigorously enforced by the EU courts. Once it elapses, the application is deemed inadmissible[1259] and the act becomes immune from annulment. This is justified by the principles of legal certainty and equality in the administration of justice.[1260]

In Joined Cases 25 and 26/65 *Simet*[1261] the ECJ accepted an exception, based on *force majeure*, to the strict observance of the time limit. In Case T-218/01 *Rémy*,[1262] the General Court emphasised that apart from *force majeure*, only exceptional circumstances make an action admissible by derogation from the time limit set out in Article 263 TFEU. An example of this is when the conduct of the relevant EU institution gives rise to pardonable confusion in the mind of a party acting in good faith and exercising all the diligence required of a normally prudent person. Both points were illustrated in Case T-12/90 *Bayer*.[1263]

1250. In Case 76/79 *Karl Könecke Fleischwarenfabrik GmbH & Co. KG v Commission* [1980] ECR 665, the ECJ held that the time limit starts to run the day after the notification takes place.

1251. [2011] OJ L162/17.

1252. Ibid.

1253. This period includes official holidays, Saturdays and Sundays, and is not suspended during judicial vacations of the EU courts. If the period ends on Saturday, Sunday or an official holiday, it is extended until the end of the first following working day: Art. 80(1)(d)(e) and Art. 80(2) of the Rules of Procedure of the ECJ [2011] OJ L162/17.

1254. Case T-468/93 *Frinil-Frio Naval e Industrial SA v Commission* [1994] ECR II-33.

1255. Joined Cases T-485/93, T-491/93, T-494/93 and T-61/98 *Société Louis Dreyfus et Cie v Commission* [2000] ECR II-3659.

1256. Joined Cases T-432/93, T-433/93 and T-434/93 *Socurte and Others v Commission* [1995] ECR II-503.

1257. Case T-465/93 *Murgia Messapica v Commission* [1994] ECR II-361.

1258. Case C-102/92 *Ferriere Acciaierie Sarde SpA v Commission* [1993] ECR I-801.

1259. For example, Case 108/79 *Salvatore Belfiore v Commission* [1980] ECR 1769.

1260. Case 209/83 *Ferriera Valsabbia SpA v Commission* [1984] ECR 3089.

1261. Joined Cases 25 and 26/65 *Simet and Others v High Authority* [1967] ECR 113. See also Case T-106/05 *Evropaiki Dinamiki v Commission* [2006] ECR II-82 (Ord.).

1262. Case T-218/01 *Laboratoire Monique Rémy SAS v Commission* [2002] ECR II-2139 (Ord.).

1263. Case T-12/90 *Bayer AG v EC Commission* [1991] ECR II-219, upheld by the ECJ in Case C-195/91P *Bayer* [1994] ECR I-5619.

THE FACTS WERE:

The Commission sent notification to the applicant company fining it for a number of infringements of Article 101 TFEU. The company brought an action under Article 263 TFEU to have the Commission's decision judicially reviewed. In response, the Commission argued that the application was inadmissible as it was time-barred under both Article 263 TFEU and the ECJ's rules of procedure.

The applicant argued that the action was not time-barred, and relied on three separate contentions to support this argument. First, it was submitted that the Commission was guilty of a number of irregularities in the notification. In particular, the Commission notified the decision to the company's registered office and not to the company's legal department with which it had conducted all previous correspondence. Second, the company claimed that its internal organisational breakdown was an excusable error. Finally, the company pleaded force majeure in order to justify the delay in submitting the application under Article 263 TFEU.

Held:

The General Court rejected all three arguments. The Court held that in the notification the Commission complied with the necessary formalities contained in its rules of procedure as it sent the decision by registered letter with postal acknowledgment of receipt. The letter duly arrived at Bayer's registered office. Both the arguments relating to excusable error and force majeure were also rejected. The Court held that the delay had been caused by fault on the part of the applicants. Bayer could not claim that it committed any excusable error. In this respect, the fact that the Commission sent a letter to the applicant's registered office, whereas it had previously addressed all its communications directly to the applicant's legal department, could not constitute an exceptional circumstance since this is a normal procedure. The inadequate functioning of the applicant's internal organisation was the reason why the letter was not forwarded to the legal department. This circumstance could not be considered as unforeseeable, and force majeure, since in order to establish the existence of force majeure, there must "be abnormal difficulties, independent of the will of the person concerned and apparently inevitable, even if all due care is taken."[1264]

It is to be noted that in Case C-229/05P *Ocalan*[1265] the applicant, Mr Serif Vanly, who missed the deadline for lodging an application at the Registry of the General Court, argued that the formalistic approach to the time limit should be relaxed in a situation where a case concerns serious breaches of fundamental rights. This was rejected by the ECJ.

15.2.10 Effect of annulment of an EU Act

The effect of annulment is described in Article 264 TFEU, which provides:

"1. If the action is well founded, the Court of Justice of the European Union shall declare the act concerned to be void.

1264. Case T-12/90 *Bayer AG v EC Commission* [1991] ECR II-219, para. 44.
1265. Case C-229/05P *Osman Ocalan, on behalf of the Kurdistan Workers' Party (PKK) and Serif Vanly, on behalf of the Kurdistan National Congress (KNK) v Council* [2007] ECR I-439.

2.   However, the Court shall, if it considers this necessary, state which of the effects of the act which it has declared void shall be considered as definitive."

The effect of annulment is that, subject to Article 264(2) TFEU, an act is void. The judgment of the EU courts applies *erga omnes*,[1266] that is, it can be relied upon by everybody, not only the parties to the proceedings.

A successfully challenged act, subject to Article 264(2) TFEU, is void immediately, that is, from the day on which the court renders its decision. This means that the act in question is devoid of past, present and future legal effects.

In respect of judgments rendered by the General Court the act is void from the expiry of the time limit for appeal, or from the time the appeal was rejected.

A decision of annulment has retroactive effect. However, under Article 264(2) TFEU the Union courts may declare some, or all of, provisions to be operative. Use of the declaratory power of the courts may be justified for a number of reasons, such as the need for legal certainty,[1267] respect for legitimate expectation, or the need to suspend the effects of annulment until a competent institution adopts an act which will replace the one struck down.[1268]

Under Article 266 TFEU a decision of annulment imposes upon the EU institution whose act has been declared void an obligation "to take the necessary measures to comply with the judgment of the Court of Justice of the European Union". If that institution refuses to comply with the decision of the Union court, the aggravated party may bring an action under Article 265 TFEU, and, if appropriate, commence an action for damages under Article 340(2) TFEU.

In Case C-310/97P *Assidomän Kraft*[1269] the ECJ provided important clarifications concerning the effect of its own judgment annulling a decision adopted by the Commission.

THE FACTS WERE:

This case closed the saga of the Wood Pulp Cartel cases,[1270] in which the Commission found more than forty suppliers of wood pulp in violation of EU competition law, despite the fact that most of the relevant undertakings were not resident within the EU. Fines were imposed on 36 of the undertakings for violation of Article 101(1) TFEU. Among those fined were nine Swedish undertakings, which paid their fines. Subsequently, 26 of the undertakings appealed to the ECJ against the decision. They challenged the Commission's finding that they breached competition law through concertation of prices for their products by means of a system of quarterly price announcements. However, the nine Swedish undertakings that had already paid fines, including AssiDomän, decided not to participate in the annulment proceedings. The ECJ annulled the decision of the Commission that the undertakings concerned infringed Article 101(1) TFEU through concertation of prices for their products on the grounds that the Commission had not provided a firm, precise and consistent body of evidence in this respect. As a result, the ECJ annulled

---

1266. Case 3/54 *Assider v High Authority* [1954–56] ECR 63.

1267. Case C-21/94 *EP v Council* [1995] ECR I-1827.

1268. Case C-65/90 *EP v Council* [1992] ECR 4616; Case 275/87 *Commission v Council* [1989] ECR 259.

1269. C-310/97P *Commission v Assidomän Kraft Products AB and Others* [1999] ECR I-5363.

1270. Joined Cases C-89/85, C-104/85, C-114/85, C-116/85, C-117/85, C-125/85, C-126/85, C-127/85, C-128/85 and C-129/85 *A. Ahlström Osakeyhtiö and Others v Commission (Re Wood Pulp Cartel)* [1993] ECR I-1307.

or reduced the fines to €20,000 imposed on the undertakings which had instituted proceedings.

AssiDomän, Kraft Products and other undertakings, which did not join in the annulment proceedings, asked the Commission to refund to each of them the fines that they had paid to the extent that they exceeded the sum of €20,000. The Commission refused to refund these fines on the grounds that it had already complied with the ECJ order by reducing the fines in respect of the undertakings participating in the proceedings, and that the decision of the ECJ had no necessary impact on the fines imposed upon the Swedish undertakings. The undertakings concerned challenged that decision, first before the General Court and, subsequently before the ECJ.

Held:

The ECJ held that the Swedish undertakings were not entitled to have the fines reduced. The court justified its judgment on two grounds: first, the ECJ cannot rule ultra petita, that is, the scope of the annulment which it pronounces may not go further than that sought by the applicant and thus unchallenged aspects concerning other addressees did not form part of the matter to be tried by the ECJ. Second, although the authority erga omnes exerted by an annulling judgment attaches to both the operative part and the ratio decidendi of the judgment, it cannot entail annulment of an act not challenged before the ECJ but alleged to be vitiated by the same illegality. Consequently, Article 266 TFEU cannot be interpreted as requiring the institution concerned to re-examine identical or similar decisions allegedly affected by the same irregularity addressed to addressees other than the applicant.

Comment:

The judgment of the ECJ is fully justified in so far as the Commission's decision is regarded as a bundle of individual decisions against each participating undertaking, and not as a single decision addressed to all of them. This solution was confirmed in Joined Cases C-238/99P et seq. Limburgse Vinyl[1271] in which a number of undertakings successfully challenged the Commission's decision on the ground that it had not been signed by the appropriate persons. The ECJ held that the challenged decision was binding on those undertakings who had not appealed, but it was void in respect of the undertakings that lodged the appeal.

Although the solution consisting of considering the Commission's decision as a bundle of separate decisions addressed to each participating undertaking penalised the undertakings which decided not to appeal, it is, at the same time, fair. Undertakings may decide not to challenge a Commission decision in competition matters for a number of reasons, the most important being that the appeal procedure involves considerable investment in terms of time and money. Hindsight is very useful but the fact is that if an undertaking has chosen to economise by not spending time and money on an appeal and the judgment of the court in similar matters arrives after the limitation period has expired, it will be too late to jump on the bandwagon. Conversely, if the outcome turns out to be against the appellant, the decision not to participate will have been well justified.

1271. Joined Cases C-238/99P et seq. *Limburgse Vinyl Maatschappij NV and Others (Re PVC Cartel (No. II)) v Commission* [2002] ECR I-8375.

15.3 Plea of illegality under Article 277 TFEU

Article 277 TFEU provides:

> "Notwithstanding the expiry of the period laid down in Article 263, sixth paragraph, any party may, in proceedings in which an act of general application adopted by an institution, body, office or agency of the Union is at issue, plead the grounds specified in Article 263, second paragraph, in order to invoke before the Court of Justice of the European Union the inapplicability of that act."

The procedure under Article 277 TFEU complements the procedure under Article 263 TFEU. The plea of illegality can only be invoked as an ancillary plea, that is, as a means by which applicants, in support of an action that challenges implementing measures addressed to them or to a third person (in which latter case applicants must show that they are directly and individually concerned so far as non-regulatory acts are concerned and directly concerned with regard to regulatory acts which do not entail implementing measures), plead the illegality of the general measure upon which the implementing measures are based. For that reason, it is referred to as an indirect action, that is, it challenges indirectly the validity of a measure on the basis of which a subsequent measure has been adopted. In practice, the plea of illegality is mostly used to challenge individual decisions based on EU regulations whose validity is called into question.[1272]

Unlike actions under Article 263 TFEU, the plea of illegality is not time-barred[1273] (but see below regarding the link the ECJ has made with Article 263 TFEU by saying Article 277 cannot be used to circumvent requirements of Article 263 TFEU).

The grounds for an action under Article 277 TFEU are the same as for an action for annulment under Article 263 TFEU, that is, lack of competence; infringement of an essential procedural requirement; infringement of the Treaty or any rule of law relating to its application; and, misuse of powers.

The main feature of the plea of illegality is that, subject to certain conditions, it allows avoidance of the stringent requirements imposed under Article 263 TFEU for access to the Union courts in terms of *locus standi* and the time limit. The ECJ held in Joined Cases 87, 130/77, 22/83, 9 and 10/84 *Salerno*[1274] that:

> "The sole purpose of art [277 TFEU] is to protect parties against the application of an unlawful regulation where the regulation itself can no longer be challenged owing to the expiry of the period laid down in art [263 TFEU]. However, in allowing a party to plead the inapplicability of a regulation, art [277 TFEU] does not create an independent right of action; such a plea may only be raised indirectly in proceedings against an implementing measure, the validity of the regulation being challenged in so far as it constitutes the legal basis of that measure."

Thus, the plea of illegality constitutes an alternative way of judicially reviewing EU acts, and so permits any person to raise indirectly the question of the validity of an EU act. This point is well illustrated by Case 92/78 *Simmenthal*.[1275]

1272. Joined Cases 275/80 and 24/81 *Krupp Stahl AG v Commission* [1981] ECR 2489.
1273. Joined Cases 25 and 26/65 *Simet v High Authority* [1967] ECR 113; Case C-289/99P *Schiocchet SARL v Commission* [2000] ECR I-10279.
1274. Joined Cases 87, 130/77, 22/83, 9 and 10/84 *Vittorio Salerno and Others v Commission and Council* [1985] ECR 2523, para. 36.
1275. Case 92/78 *SpA Simmenthal v Commission* [1979] ECR 777.

15.3.1 Requirements imposed by Article 277 TFEU

Article 277 TFEU imposes some requirements relating to the type of acts that can be challenged and relating to persons who can claim *locus standi*. These are examined below.

15.3.1.1 Reviewable acts

Article 277 TFEU provides that any act of general application adopted by an EU institution, body, office or agency may be challenged. The pre-ToL version of Article 277 TFEU limited the reviewable acts to regulations adopted jointly by the EP and the Council, and regulations of the Council, of the Commission, or of the ECB. However, even before the entry into force of the ToL the ECJ had interpreted this provision broadly. As a result, an applicant was allowed to rely on the plea of illegality not only against regulations adopted by the above-mentioned institutions, but also against any act of general application capable of producing legal effects similar to those produced by regulations.

15.3.1.2 Applicants

Article 277 TFEU cannot be used to circumvent the requirements of Article 263 TFEU. For that reason, the addressees of individual acts who have not challenged them within the time limit prescribed by Article 263(5) TFEU are not permitted to rely on the plea of illegality.[1276] With regard to individuals, on the authority of Case C-188/92 *TWD*[1277] (see Chapter 13.8.2), if there is no doubt that the claimant would have had standing under Article 263 TFEU, but failed to seek the annulment of an EU act within the time-limit specified in Article 263 TFEU, he would not have had standing under Article 277 TFEU. There is no doubt where applicants challenge EU directives or other acts of general application[1278] and when they were not officially informed of the decision in sufficient time to allow them to challenge it under Article 263 TFEU.[1279]

The Commission and some A-Gs have suggested that Article 277 TFEU should not be construed as giving *locus standi* to Member States to challenge acts of general application, as opposed to decisions addressed to them which they are not allowed to challenge under Article 277 TFEU, once the time limit set out in Article 263 TFEU has expired.[1280] The reason for this suggestion being that Member States are privileged applicants under Article 263 TFEU[1281] and therefore should not be allowed to rely on Article 277 TFEU, as such reliance might encourage them to ignore certain apparently illegal regulations and thus not challenge them within the time limit imposed by Article 263 TFEU. However, in Case C-442/04 *Spain v Council*,[1282] the ECJ held that as Article 277 TFEU states that "any party" may bring Article 277 TFEU proceedings there are no limitations in respect of applicants. Consequently, Member States may rely on Article 277 TFEU to challenge measures of general application. The main reason for the broad

---

1276. In Case 156/77 *Commission v Belgium* ([1978] ECR 1881) the ECJ held that Article 277 TFEU can never be relied upon by a Member State when it is an addressee of a decision, given that the purpose of Article 277 TFEU is to allow the challenge of a regulation not of a decision (para. 22).

1277. Case C-188/92 *TWD Textilwerke Deggendorf GmbH v Bundesrepublik Deutschland* [1994] ECR I-833. See also Case C-441/05 *Roquette Frères* [2007] ECR I-1993.

1278. E.g. Case 408/95 *Eurotunnel SA and Others v SeaFrance* [1997] ECR I-6315.

1279. Case C-241/95 *R v Intervention Board for Agricultural Produce, ex parte Accrington Beef Co. Ltd and Others* [1996] ECR I-6699, para. 14-16.

1280. See Case C-11/00 *Commission v ECB* [2003] ECR I-7147, para. 74.

1281. See G. Bebr, "Judicial Remedy of Private Parties Against Normative Acts of the EEC: the Role of the Exception of Illegality", (1966) 4 CMLRev., 7.

1282. [2008] ECR I-3517; see also, Case C-11/00 *Commission v ECB* [2003] ECR I-7147.

interpretation of the words "any party" by the ECJ is that in most cases defects in general acts are discovered after some time, once the act has been applied by a Member State. This usually occurs after the expiry of the time limit set out in Article 263 TFEU. Also, a Member State may invoke the plea of illegality within the framework of enforcement proceedings under Article 258 TFEU.[1283]

EU institutions, unlike Member States and individuals, are not required to prove their interest when invoking pleas of illegality.

15.3.2   Exclusive jurisdiction of the EU courts under Article 277 TFEU

The EU courts have exclusive jurisdiction over pleas of illegality.[1284] National courts have no jurisdiction to deal with a plea of illegality. There is, however, an indirect possibility based on Article 267 TFEU for an applicant to rely on a plea of illegality in national proceedings when challenging national measures are introduced to implement an EU act.[1285] As national courts have no jurisdiction to declare an EU act void, and provided they have reasons to believe that the EU act is invalid, they will under Article 267 TFEU ask the ECJ to determine the validity of such an act. However, the possibility to refer to the ECJ is subject to conditions established in Case C-188/92 *TWD*[1286] (see above and see Chapter 13.8.2).

15.3.3   Effect of a successful action under Article 277 TFEU

If the applicant is successful, the general act, which may be called a parent act, is rendered inapplicable only to that applicant's case. The implementing measure is annulled in respect of the applicant, but the parent act is still in force since it cannot be declared void as it is immune from direct challenge under Article 263 TFEU by lapse of time. In practice, the institution which adopted the parent act will amend or repeal that act under Article 266(1) TFEU, as it is under a legal obligation to comply with a judgment of the ECJ.

15.4   Action under Article 265 TFEU for failure to act

When an EU institution, body, office or agency has a positive obligation to act, that is, it must adopt certain measures required by the Treaties but fails to do so, Article 265 TFEU confers jurisdiction upon the CJEU to compel such an institution to act.

Article 265 TFEU states:

"Should the European Parliament, the European Council, the Council, the Commission or the European Central Bank, in infringement of the Treaties, fail to act, the Member States and the other institutions of the Union may bring an action before the Court of Justice of the European Union to have the infringement established. This Article shall apply, under the same conditions, to bodies, offices and agencies of the Union which fail to act.

1283. Case 116/82 *Commission v Germany* [1986] ECR 2519.

1284. Joined Cases 31/62 and 33/62 *Milchwerke* [1962] ECR 501; Joined Cases 31 and 33/62 *Wöhrmann* [1962] ECR 501.

1285. Case 216/82 *Universität Hamburg v Hauptzollamt Hamburg-Kehrwieder* [1983] ECR 2771.

1286. Case C-188/92 *TWD Textilwerke Deggendorf GmbH v Bundesrepublik Deutschland* [1994] ECR I-833, confirmed in Case C-178/95 *Wiljo NV v Belgium* [1997] ECR I-585.

The action shall be admissible only if the institution, body, office or agency concerned has first been called upon to act. If, within two months of being so called upon, the institution, body, office or agency concerned has not defined its position, the action may be brought within a further period of two months.

Any natural or legal person may, under the conditions laid down in the preceding paragraphs, complain to the Court that an institution, body, office or agency of the Union has failed to address to that person any act other than a recommendation or an opinion."

The action under Article 265 TFEU is similar to the historic English writ of *mandamus* or, in Scotland, to the petition for an order requiring the specific performance of a statutory duty.

An action for failure to act is separate and different from an action for annulment, and has its own specific requirements

15.4.1 Defaulting institution

Under the ToL an action for failure to act may be brought against any EU institution, body, office or agency.

15.4.2 Applicants

There are three categories of applicants: privileged; semi-privileged; and, non-privileged.

A. **Privileged applicants.** Article 265 TFEU provides that Member States and the institutions of the EU are privileged applicants. They may bring an action before the ECJ to establish that a defendant institution has failed to act. They may require that the defendant institution adopts any act: regulations, directives, decisions and even a proposal concerning the EU budget,[1287] provided that EU law imposes a duty to act. The EP, which was initially excluded from bringing an action for annulment under Article 263 TFEU, has always been included in the list of privileged applicants under Article 265 TFEU;

B. **Semi-privileged applicants.** The ECB, the CoA and the CoR are semi-privileged applicants. They have *locus standi* to raise an action for failure to act in respect of areas within their respective fields of competence; and,

C. **Non-privileged applicants.** Non-privileged applicants are natural and legal persons complaining that "an institution, body, office or agency has failed to address to that person any act other than a recommendation or an opinion". The literal interpretation of these words implies that applicants may only challenge a failure of an institution to adopt an act addressed to them, that is, an individual decision. This would have limited their *locus standi* under Article 265 TFEU even more than under Article 263 TFEU. Fortunately, the ECJ has interpreted Article 265 TFEU broadly by treating actions for failure to act as the same as actions for annulment in respect of *locus standi* of non-privileged applicants. This was clearly confirmed in Case 246/81 *Lord Bethell*.[1288]

1287. Case 302/87 *EP v Council* [1988] ECR 5637.
1288. Case 246/81 *Lord Bethell v Commission* [1982] ECR 2277.

THE FACTS WERE:

Lord Bethell, a member of the EP and chairman of the Freedom of the Skies Committee, complained to the Commission about anti-competitive practices of a number of European airlines in relation to passenger fares. He argued that the Commission was under a duty to submit proposals under Article 102 TFEU to curtail those practices. Unsatisfied with the answer from the Commission, he brought an action for failure to act against the Commission under Article 265 TFEU, claiming that the Commission's reply amounted in fact to a failure to act, and alternatively under Article 263 TFEU arguing that the answer should be annulled.

Held:

The ECJ held that the application of Lord Bethell would be admissible only if the Commission "having been duly called upon . . . has failed to adopt in relation to him a measure which he was legally entitled to claim by virtue of the rules of Community law".[1289] Lord Bethell, although indirectly concerned by the measure as a user of the airlines and chairman of the Freedom of the Skies Committee which represented users, was, nevertheless, not in the legal position of a potential addressee of a decision, which the Commission had a duty to adopt with regard to him. His application under Article 263 TFEU was rejected for the same reason. The analogy between locus standi *of non-privileged applicants under Articles 263 and 265 TFEU was thus confirmed by the ECJ.*

The similarity between Articles 263 and 265 TFEU entails that an application under Article 265 TFEU is admissible if the applicants are addressees of a prospective measure or if they are directly and individually concerned by a non-regulatory measure which an EU institution has failed to adopt,[1290] or if they are directly concerned by a regulatory measure which does not entail implementing measures. However, as an action for failure to act has its own peculiarity, an applicant for this remedy is entitled to require an institution to adopt a preparatory act which, although not reviewable under Article 263 TFEU, constitutes an essential step in the process leading to the adoption of an act which produces legal effects.[1291]

15.4.3 Procedure under Article 265 TFEU

The procedure under Article 265 TFEU comprises two stages: an administrative stage and a judicial stage. The latter takes place before the Union courts. The procedure is examined below.

15.4.3.1 Administrative stage

An action for failure to act may be brought before the Union courts only if the institution, body, office or agency concerned has been called upon to act by the applicant, who has notified it of the complaint, and indicated precisely what measures he wishes that institution to take.[1292]

1289.   Ibid, para. 13.

1290.   See Joined Cases 97/86, 99/86, 193/86 and 215/86 *Asteris E.A. v Commission* [1988] ECR 2118; Case T-166/98 *Cantina Sociale Di Doliniova Soc. Coop. Rl and Others v Commission* [2004] ECR II-3991.

1291.   Case 302/87 *EP v Council* [1988] ECR 5615 and Case T- 28/90 *Asia Motor France SA and Others v Commission* [1992] ECR II-2285.

1292.   Joined Cases 114–117/79 *Fournier and Others v Commission* [1980] ECR 1529.

There is no specific time limit for the submission of a complaint, but in Case 59/70 *The Netherlands v Commission*[1293] the ECJ held that the right to notify the Commission of its omission, or failure to act, should not be delayed indefinitely and that the complaint should be lodged within a "reasonable time". This decision was rendered in relation to the CS Treaty, but it seems that it can be transposed to the ToL.

Once the institution concerned is notified of the complaint, it has two months to define its position. The main problem is to determine what is meant by the phrase "define its position". The ECJ has gradually clarified this phrase.

The Court held that the institution defined its position if it had adopted any act, apart from a reply asking the applicant to wait (which could not be considered as an answer),[1294] or referring to a position previously taken. By way of example, when the Commission sends a letter refusing to start proceedings against a competitor undertaking, it defines its position.[1295] When an institution adopts a different act from that which was requested by the applicant,[1296] it also defines its position.

Refusal to act by an institution concerned is not necessarily tantamount to a failure to act. The institution concerned must be legally bound under EU law to act.[1297] If it has discretion in this respect, an action for failure to act is not admissible. This point is illustrated by Case 48/65 *Lütticke GmbH*.[1298]

THE FACTS WERE:

Lütticke argued that a German tax on the importation of milk powder was contrary to Article 110 TFEU. It asked the Commission to take enforcement action against Germany under Article 258 TFEU. The Commission replied that the tax was not contrary to EU law, and, as a result, it did not intend to take action under Article 258 TFEU.

Held:

The ECJ held that first, by refusing to act, the Commission defined its position, and second, under Article 258 TFEU the Commission enjoyed a large measure of discretion whether or not to start proceedings. Thus, the applicant could not force the Commission to act since he was not legally entitled to a particular measure. The Commission had no duty to act in respect of his request.

Once the institution concerned defines its position, proceedings under Article 265 TFEU are terminated. If an applicant is legally entitled to a specific measure and unhappy about the answer it obtained from a particular institution, it may then bring proceedings against that institution under Article 263 TFEU to annul the decision adopted in this case.

It is interesting to note that unsuccessful applicants under Article 265 TFEU, i.e. those in respect of whom the ECJ decides that the institution in question did define its position, have often asked the ECJ to transform their action under Article 265 TFEU into an action under Article 263 TFEU. The ECJ has

---

1293. [1971] ECR 639.

1294. Joined Cases 42 and 49/59 *SNUPAT v High Authority* [1961] ECR 53.

1295. Case 125/78 *GEMMA v Commission* [1979] ECR 3173.

1296. Case C-107/91 *ENU v Commission* [1993] ECR I-599; Case C-25/91 *Pesqueras Echebastar SA v Commission* [1993] ECR I-1719.

1297. Case T-28/90 *Asia Motor France SA and Others v Commission* [1992] ECR II-2285; Case T-32/93 *Ladbroke Racing Ltd v Commission* [1994] ECR II-1015.

1298. Case 48/65 *Alfons Lütticke GmbH v Commission* [1966] ECR 19.

always refused. Its refusal may have serious consequences for the applicant if by the time of receipt of that refusal the time limit of two months provided under Article 265 TFEU has expired, since this would mean that the time limit for bringing an action under Article 263 has also expired.[1299]

15.4.3.2 Judicial stage

If the institution concerned does not define its position within two months, the applicant has another two months to bring proceedings before the CJEU. The applicant is required to submit an application limited to the points it raised in its original complaint to the institution concerned.[1300] The time limit is strictly enforced by the CJEU.[1301]

If after the commencement of an action under Article 265 TFEU, but before the judgment, the institution in question defines its position, the application is considered as admissible but "without object".[1302] This solution seems unfair to the applicant, especially if it envisages bringing an action under Article 340(2) TFEU against the institution concerned. The ECJ justified its position by stating that in such circumstances a judgment under Article 265 TFEU would have no effect with respect to the defaulting institution.

The consequence of a successful action under Article 265 TFEU is that the ECJ declares the failure to act of the institution concerned, which under Article 266 TFEU "shall . . . take the necessary measures to comply with the judgment of the Court of Justice of the European Union" within a reasonable period of time.[1303]

RECOMMENDED READING

Books

Gordon, R., *EC Law in Judicial Review*, 2007, Oxford: OUP.

Hofmann, H., Rowe, G. C., and Türk, A. H., *Administrative Law and Policy of the European Union*, 2011, Oxford: OUP.

Lenaerts, K., Arts, D., and Maselis, I., *Procedural Law of the European Union*, 2nd edn, 2006, London: Sweet & Maxwell.

Türk, A. H., *Judicial Review in EU Law*, 2009, Cheltenham: Edward Elgar Publishing.

Ward, A., *Judicial Review and the Rights of Private Parties in EU Law*, 2nd edn, 2007, Oxford: OUP.

Articles

Arnull, A., "Private Applicants and the Action for Annulment since *Codorniu*", (2001) 38 CMLRev., 7.

Balthasar, S., "Locus Standi Rules for Challenges to Regulatory Acts by Private Applicants: the New Article 263(4) TFEU", (2010) 35 ELRev., 542.

Barav, A., "Exception of Illegality in Community Law: A Critical Analysis", (1974) 11 CMLRev., 366.

Barents, "The Court of Justice after the Treaty of Lisbon", (2010) 47 CMLRev., 709.

1299. Case T-28/90 *Asia Motor France SA and Others v Commission* [1992] ECR II-2285.
1300. Joined Cases 24 and 34/58 *Chambre Syndicale de la Sidérurgie de l'Est de la France and Others v High Authority* [1960] ECR 281; Cases 41 and 50/59 *Hamborner Bergbau AG, Friedrich Thyssen Bergbau AG v High Authority* [1960] ECR 493.
1301. Cases 5–11/62 and 13–15/62 *San Michele and Others v High Authority* [1962] ECR 449; Case C-25/91 *Pesqueras Echebastar SA v Commission* [1993] ECR I-1719.
1302. Case 302/87 *EP v Council* [1988] ECR 5615, in which the Council submitted the project of the EU budget after the EP submitted its application under Article 265 TFEU.
1303. Case 13/83 *EP v Council* [1985] ECR 1513.

Capdevila, C.M., "The Action for Annulment, The Preliminary Reference on Validity and the Plea of Illegality: Complementary or Alternative Means?", (2006) 25 YEL, 451.

Corthaut, T., and Vanneste, F., "Waves between Strasbourg and Luxembourg. The Right of Access to Court to Contest the Validity of Legislative and Administrative Measures", (2006) 25 YEL, 475.

Kombos, C., "A Paradox in the Making, Detecting Something Positive in 'UPA' under the 'Ten Kate' Effect", (2009) 15 ELJ, 520.

Tridimas, T., and Poll, S., "Locus Standi of Individuals under Article 240(4): The Return of Euridice?" In Arnull, A., Eeckhout, P., and Tridimas, T. (eds), *Continuity and Changes in EU Law, Essays in Honour of Sir Francis Jacobs*, 2008, Oxford: OUP, Chapter 5.

Voght, M., "Indirect Judicial Protection in EU Law: The Case of the Plea of Illegality", (2006) 31 ELRev., 364.

Ward, A. "Locus Standi under Article 230(4) of the EC Treaty: Crafting a Coherent Test for a 'Wobbly Polity'", (2003) 22 YEL, 45.

PROBLEM QUESTION

Hans is one of four producers of margarine in Germany. He, and the three other producers, wish to bring proceedings for annulment of Commission Decision 11/11 adopted one month ago and addressed to Germany regarding measures for the promotion of sales of butter in Berlin. The Commission adopted Decision 11/11 on the basis of Council Regulation 1079/10 which authorises the Commission to take measures to expand the markets for milk products.

Under Decision 11/11 Germany was required to take 900 tons of butter from public stocks, package it in 250 gram packets, and stamp the packets with the words "Free EU butter". Subsequently, those packets have been marketed in larger packages containing one packet of "Free EU butter" and one packet of open-market butter of the same weight as "Free EU butter". The packages have been sold at a price equal to the price normally chargeable for 250 grams of open-market butter. As a result of Decision 11/11, the sale of margarine in Berlin has dramatically fallen and if the promotion of butter continues Hans will have to dismiss half of his workforce. According to Hans, Decision 11/11 is in breach of the principle of freedom to carry on business, the principle of protection of legitimate expectations, the principle of proportionality and the principle of fair competition.

Advise Hans as to whether he is likely to succeed if he brings proceedings against the Commission under Article 263 TFEU.

ESSAY QUESTION

Critically assess whether the ToL adequately responded to demands for relaxation of *locus standi* requirements for non-privileged applicants under Article 263 TFEU.

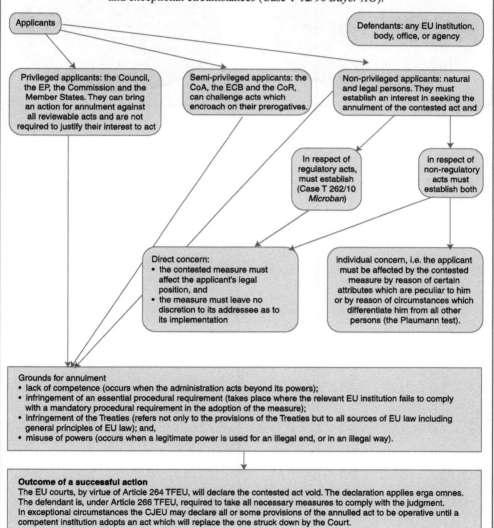

AIDE-MÉMOIRE

Actions for annulment under Article 263 TFEU

Reviewable act: any act adopted by an EU institution, body, office or agency which produces binding legal effect in relation to third parties, irrespective of its form and name

Time limit for starting proceedings

The proceedings must be commenced within **two months** of the publication of the act, or its notification to the applicant, or, in the absence thereof, of the day on which it came to the applicant's knowledge. This is strictly enforced: the only exceptions are based on force majeure and exceptional circumstances (Case T-12/90 *Bayer AG*).

Applicants

Defendants: any EU institution, body, office, or agency

Privileged applicants: the Council, the EP, the Commission and the Member States. They can bring an action for annulment against all reviewable acts and are not required to justify their interest to act

Semi-privileged applicants: the CoA, the ECB and the CoR, can challenge acts which encroach on their prerogatives.

Non-privileged applicants: natural and legal persons. They must establish an interest in seeking the annulment of the contested act and

In respect of regulatory acts, must establish (Case T 262/10 *Microban*)

in respect of non-regulatory acts must establish both

Direct concern:
- the contested measure must affect the applicant's legal position, and
- the measure must leave no discretion to its addressee as to its implementation

individual concern, i.e. the applicant must be affected by the contested measure by reason of certain attributes which are peculiar to him or by reason of circumstances which differentiate him from all other persons (the Plaumann test).

Grounds for annulment
- lack of competence (occurs when the administration acts beyond its powers);
- infringement of an essential procedural requirement (takes place where the relevant EU institution fails to comply with a mandatory procedural requirement in the adoption of the measure);
- infringement of the Treaties (refers not only to the provisions of the Treaties but to all sources of EU law including general principles of EU law); and,
- misuse of powers (occurs when a legitimate power is used for an illegal end, or in an illegal way).

Outcome of a successful action
The EU courts, by virtue of Article 264 TFEU, will declare the contested act void. The declaration applies erga omnes. The defendant is, under Article 266 TFEU, required to take all necessary measures to comply with the judgment. In exceptional circumstances the CJEU may declare all or some provisions of the annulled act to be operative until a competent institution adopts an act which will replace the one struck down by the Court.

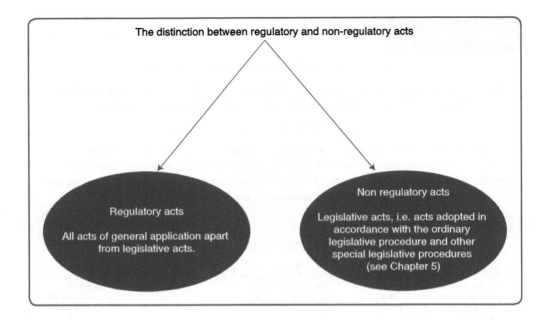

The distinction between regulatory and non-regulatory acts

Regulatory acts

All acts of general application apart from legislative acts.

Non regulatory acts

Legislative acts, i.e. acts adopted in accordance with the ordinary legislative procedure and other special legislative procedures (see Chapter 5)

Plea of illegality under Article 277 TFEU

Can only be invoked as an ancillary plea, that is, to challenge a measure implementing an EU act (for example, a decision which implements a regulation), not the act itself. Any act of general application adopted by an EU institution, body, office or agency is reviewable under Article 277 TFEU.

Time limit for starting proceedings

No time limit, but the plea of illegality cannot be used to circumvent the requirements of Article 263 TFEU (Case 156/77 *Commission v Belgium*).

> **Applicants**
> Any party other than one who had locus standi to bring a direct action under Article 263 TFEU but neglected to do so within the time prescribed under Article 263(5) TFEU (Case C-188/92 *TWD Textilwerke*)

> **Defendants:**
> Any EU institution, body, agency or office

> **Grounds for annulment (THE SAME AS UNDER ART. 263 TFEU)**
> • lack of competence (occurs when the administration acts beyond its powers);
> • infringement of an essential procedural requirement (takes place where the relevant EU institution fails to comply with a mandatory procedural requirement in the adoption of the measure);
> • infringement of the Treaties (refers not only to the provisions of the Treaties but to all sources of EU law including general principles of EU law); and,
> • misuse of powers (occurs when a legitimate power is used for an illegal end, or in an illegal way)

> **Outcome of a successful action**
> The implementing measure is annulled in respect of the applicant but the act itself is still in force.

Action Under Article 265 TFEU For Failure To Act

"Failure" exists only if an EU institution, body, office or agency has a duty to act deriving from EU law.

Time limit for starting proceedings

- To request the defaulting institution to act: no specific time limit but the request must be made within a reasonable time (Case 59/70 *The Netherlands v Commission*);

- To start judicial proceedings: two months from the expiry of the two-month period during which the defendant was called upon to act (Joined Cases 5-11/62 and 13-15/62 *San Michele*), but failed to do so.

(Continued)

(Continued)

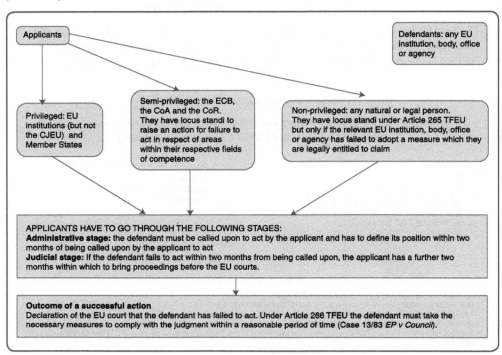

16

DIRECT ACTIONS AGAINST EU INSTITUTIONS, BODIES, OFFICES OR AGENCIES – PART II
ACTION FOR DAMAGES: NON-CONTRACTUAL LIABILITY OF THE EUROPEAN UNION UNDER ARTICLE 340(2) TFEU

CONTENTS

CHAPTER OUTLINE

1. Article 340(2) TFEU deals with non-contractual liability of the EU, which must make good any damage caused by its institutions and by its servants in the performance of their duties. In Case 5/71 *Schöppenstedt* the ECJ held that an action in damages is autonomous and thus an applicant is not required to proceed first under Articles 263 or 265 TFEU.

2. Applicants under Article 340(2) and (3) TFEU are any natural and legal person (including associations, but they are subject to the conditions set out in Case T-304/01 *Abad Pérez*) and Member States.

3. Defendants are any EU institution, but not the ECJ. In addition, an action may be brought against the EIB, the ECB and any body, office, or agency created on the basis of the Treaties which acts on behalf of the EU.

4. In Case C-352/98 *Bergaderm,* the ECJ held that the EU incurs non-contractual liability under the same conditions as a Member State. These are:

- the rule of law which has been breached must be one which is intended to confer rights on individuals;

- the breach must be sufficiently serious to merit an award of damages; and,

- there must be a direct causal link between the infringement of the rule and the damage suffered by the claimant. All three conditions must be satisfied.

5. In Case C-47/07 *Masdar*, the ECJ decided that a claim based on unjust enrichment may be brought under Article 340(2) TFEU. The only requirement that the applicant must satisfy is the proof of enrichment of the defendant for which there is no valid legal basis and the impoverishment of the applicant which is linked to that enrichment.

6. In Joined Cases C-120/06 P and C-121/06 P *FIAMM*, the ECJ rejected the possibility that the EU may be held liable for lawful acts that may cause damage to the applicant.

16.1 Introduction

Article 340 TFEU deals with liability of the EU. Article 340(1) TFEU governs contractual liability of the EU and provides that such liability shall be governed by the law applicable to the contract. The EU's contracts will normally contain a choice of law clause. Under Article 272 TFEU the Union courts have jurisdiction to give judgment pursuant to any arbitration clause contained in a contract concluded by or on behalf of the EU irrespective of, whether the contract is governed by public or private law. Article 340(2) and 340(3) TFEU deals with non-contractual liability of the EU. It states:

"(2)   In the case of non-contractual liability, the Union shall, in accordance with the general principles common to the laws of the Member States, make good any damage caused by its institutions or by its servants in the performance of their duties.

(3)   Notwithstanding the second paragraph, the European Central Bank shall, in accordance with the general principles common to the laws of the Member States, make good any damage caused by it or by its servants in the performance of their duties".

The exclusive jurisdiction of the Union courts over disputes relating to non-contractual liability of the EU is based on Article 268 TFEU which provides:

"The Court of Justice of the European Union shall have jurisdiction in disputes relating to compensation for damage provided for in the second and third paragraphs of Article 340."

The General Court has jurisdiction in actions for damages brought by individuals while the ECJ exercises jurisdiction in such actions commenced by Member States. So far no such actions have been commenced by any Member State.

Non-contractual liability of the EU is the corollary of the transfer of certain powers to the EU institutions by Member States, which requires that individuals are protected against unlawful conduct of the EU. Article 340(3) TFEU reiterates the pre-ToL case law of the ECJ under which the Court allowed proceedings against the ECB. If the ECB is found liable, bearing in mind that it is an independent EU institution financed by contributions from national central banks of the Member States, the ECB itself is liable (not the EU) and must pay compensation to the injured party from its own resources.

It is important to note that in Case 169/73 *Compagnie Continentale*[1304] the ECJ held that when it is a provision of the Treaties which causes damage to the applicant, there will be no liability on the part of any EU institution unless otherwise specified by the Treaties. This is because the Treaties are agreements concluded between Member States, i.e. the author of the act is not the EU but the Member States.

16.2 The autonomous nature of an action under Article 340(2) TFEU

In the majority of cases an action for damages is based on the illegality of EU acts. As a result of alleged illegality being at issue, an action for damages under Article 340(2) TFEU may be an effective way of getting round the time limit of two months imposed by Articles 263 and 265 TFEU, with the additional benefit for natural and legal persons of the possible receipt of compensation.

In Case 5/71 *Schöppenstedt*[1305] the ECJ held that an action for damages under Article 340(2) TFEU is autonomous as it has a special role to play within the system of remedies. The difference between an action for annulment under Article 263 TFEU (see Chapter 15.2) and an action for damages is that the latter is intended not to annul a particular measure, but to make good damage caused by an EU institution in the exercise of its functions.

The autonomous nature of an action under Article 340(2) TFEU is subject to an exception known as "an abuse of process". If an action for damages would have the same effects and purpose as an action for annulment, but the applicant did not institute the latter within the prescribed time limit, the former will be inadmissible.[1306] In Case T-86/03 *Holcim*, the General Court explained that the exception based on "abuse of process" is "applicable only where the alleged damage flows exclusively from an individual administrative measure which has become definitive, which the party concerned could have challenged by means of annulment".[1307] Accordingly, if an application under Article 340(2) TFEU is intended, in fact, to nullify an individual decision which has become definitive (that is, immune from annulment due to the expiry of the time limit provided for in Article 263(5) TFEU), it will be rejected.[1308]

Unlike a judgment under Article 263 TFEU which is valid *erga omnes,*[1309] a judgment under Article 340(2) TFEU produces binding legal effects solely in relation to the applicant.

An action for damages is also independent from an action for failure to act under Article 265 TFEU.[1310]

1304. Case 169/73 *Compagnie Continentale France v Council* [1975] ECR 117; Case T-113/96 *Édouard Dubois et Fils v Council and Commission* [1998] ECR II-125, confirmed by the ECJ in Case C-95/98P *Édouard Dubois et Fils* [1999] ECR I-9835.
1305. Case 5/71 *Aktien-Zuckerfabrik Schöppenstedt v Council* [1971] ECR 975.
1306. Case T-166/98 *Cantina Sociale di Dolianova Soc. coop, ri and Others v Commission* [2004] EC II-3991.
1307. Case T-86/03 *Holcim (France) SA v Commission* (Ord) [2005] ECR II-1539, paras 49-51.
1308. Case 175/84 *Krohn & Co. Import-Export v Commission* [1986] ECR 753; Case T-514/93 *Cobrecaf SA and Others v Commission* [1995] ECR II-621; Case T-547/93 *Orlando Lopes v ECJ* [1996] ECR II-185; Case T-47/02 *Manfred Danzer v Council* [2006] ECR II-1779.
1309. See also Case T-489/93 *Unifrut Hellas EPE v Commission* [1994] ECR II-1201.
1310. Case 4/69 *Alfons Lütticke GmbH v Commission* [1971] ECR 325.

16.3 Parties to proceedings under Article 340(2) TFEU

Applicants: any natural and legal person, as well as a Member State, may bring an action under Article 340(2) TFEU provided it is for loss resulting from unlawful conduct of EU institutions, or from a wrongful act of its servants in the performance of their duties.

Associations have standing under Article 340(2) TFEU if either:

- they can establish a particular interest of their own, distinct from that of their individual members; or

- right to compensation has been assigned to them by their members.[1311]

Defendants: an action may be brought against an EU institution or institutions, EU bodies, agencies and offices.[1312] In most cases, the defendant is either the Commission, or the Council, or both, in respect of an allegedly wrongful act adopted by the Council acting on a proposal submitted by the Commission. Actions against the EP are rare, but its activities may also cause damage to a natural or a legal person.[1313] Under the ToL more actions against the EP are expected in the light of the facts that the EP has become a co-legislator in respect of acts adopted in accordance with the ordinary legislative procedure and that it often participates in special legislative procedures. Prior to the entry into force of the ToL the ECJ interpreted the notion of "an institution" broadly. This interpretation went beyond the list established in Article 7 TEU in that it permitted the bringing of actions against the EIB,[1314] the ECB and the EU Ombudsman.[1315] However, the ECJ rejected the bringing of an action against the European Council.[1316] The situation changed under the ToL. The European Council, being an EU institution, is within the scope of Article 340(2) TFEU.

While in theory an action against the ECJ is possible, in practice the ECJ cannot be a judge and a party in the same proceedings. However, the General Court may be held liable under Article 340(2) TFEU for failure to adjudicate within a reasonable time.[1317] Actions brought by staff against the ECJ or the General Court arising from contracts of employment are dealt with under Article 270 TFEU by the EU Civil Service Tribunal (see Chapter 3.7.7).

The procedure under Article 340(2) TFEU is within the exclusive competence of the Union courts and therefore, national courts are prohibited from intervening in that procedure. In Case C-275/00 *First and Franex*,[1318] a Belgian court by interlocutory order commissioned an expert report concerning the assessment of the alleged damage caused by the way in which the Commission dealt with the dioxin crisis in the EU, with a view to using that report against the Commission in Article 340(2) proceedings. The ECJ held it has "exclusive jurisdiction to prescribe, with regard to one of the institutions of the [EU], any interim measure or measure of inquiry, such as commissioning an expert report whose purpose is to establish the role of that institution in the events which allegedly caused damage, for the purposes of an action which may be brought against the [EU] to establish its non-contractual liability".[1319]

1311. Case T-304/01 *Julia Abad Pérez and Others v Council and Commission* [2006] ECR II-4857.
1312. Case 63 and 69/72 *Wilhelm Werhahn Hansamühle and Others v Council* [1973] ECR 1229.
1313. T-203/96 *Embassy Limousine and Services v EP* [1998] ECR II-4239.
1314. Case 370/89 *SGEEM and Others v European Investment Bank* [1992] ECR I-6211.
1315. Case T-209/00 *Lamberts v Ombudsman* [2002] ECR II-2203, confirmed by the ECJ in Case C-234/02P *European Ombudsman v Lamberts* [2004] ECR I-2803.
1316. Case T-346/03 *Grégoire Krikorian and Others v EP and Others* [2003] ECR II-6037, confirmed by the ECJ in Case C-18/04P (unpublished).
1317. Case C-385/07 P *Der Grüne Punkt – Duales System Deutschland GmbH v Commission* [2009] ECR I-6155 and Case C-583/08 *Christos Gogos v Commission* [2010] ECR I-4469.
1318. Case C-275/00 *EC v First NV and Franex NV* [2002] ECR I-10943.
1319. Ibid, para. 46.

16.4 Time limit

The admissibility of an action for damages is subject to a time limit. Under Article 46 of the Statute of the CJEU the commencement of proceedings under Article 340(2) TFEU "shall be barred after a period of five years from the occurrence of the event giving rise thereto". This unclear provision has been explained by the ECJ as meaning that an applicant may bring an action under Article 340(2) TFEU within five years from the day the damage materialised.[1320]

It is logical to require that the limitation period cannot begin to run before all the requirements governing the obligation to make good the damage are satisfied. However, the fact that an applicant considers that it has not yet got all necessary evidence to prove, to the requisite legal standard, that all conditions set out in Article 340(2) TFEU are satisfied cannot prevent the limitation period from running. Only the Union courts can decide whether or not the conditions for liability are satisfied.[1321] The ECJ in Case C-51/05P *Dolianova*[1322] stated that the determination of the moment at which time starts to run is made on the basis of objective criteria, in that time starts to run from the moment at which the unlawful act had actually and objectively caused damage to the applicant in the form of an adverse impact on his assets, and not from the time of the occurrence of the event, or the fact giving rise to the damage.[1323] The running of time is interrupted by:

- proceedings brought by the applicant before the Union courts; or,

- a preliminary request addressed by the applicant to the relevant institution, but only if followed by an application under Articles 263 or 265 TFEU within the time limit set out in those provisions.[1324]

Neither commencement of proceedings before a national court,[1325] nor an exchange of communications between the applicant and the relevant EU institution, interrupts the running of time.[1326]

16.5 Distinction between liability of the EU and liability of its servants

The EU must make good any damage caused by its institutions and by its servants in the performance of their duties. Liability of the EU for acts of its servants is based on the concept of fault (*faute personnelle*), i.e. the wrongful act or omission of EU servants acting in the course of their duty.

In Case 9/69 *Sayag*[1327] the ECJ held that the EU is liable only for those acts of its servants, which by virtue of the internal and direct relationship, constitute the necessary extension of the tasks conferred on the EU institutions. In this case, the ECJ interpreted the concept of "an act performed in the course of duties" narrowly. Mr Sayag, who was an employee of the Euratom, was instructed to take Mr Leduc and other persons to visit Euratom's installations in Mol, Belgium. He decided to

---

1320. Case T-174/00 *Biret International v Council* [2002] ECR II-17. See M. Broberg, "The Calculation of the Period of Limitation in Claims against the European Community for Non-contractual Liability", (2001) 26 ELRev., 275–90.
1321. Case C-282/05P *Holcim (Deutschland) AG v Commission* [2007] ECR I-2941.
1322. Case C-51/05P *Cantina Sociale di Dolianova Soc. coop, ri and Others v Commission* [2008] ECR I-5341.
1323. Case 256/80 *Birra Würher SpA and Others v Council and Commission* [1982] ECR 85; Case 145/83 *Stanley George Adams v Commission* [1985] ECR 3539.
1324. Case T-174/00 *Biret International SA v Council* [2002] ECR II-17. See also Case T-106/98 *Fratelli Murri v Commission* [1999] ECR II-2553.
1325. Case C-136/01 *Autosalone Ispra dei Fratelli Rossi v European Atomic Energy Commission* [2002] ECR I-6565.
1326. Case T-166/98 *Cantina Sociale di Dolianova Soc.Coop.RI. and Others v Commission* [2004] ECR II-3991.
1327. Case 9/69 *Claude Sayag v Jean-Pierre Leduc and Others* [1969] ECR 329.

drive them in his private car and obtained a travel order from the Euratom on the basis of which his travel expenses were reimbursed by the Community. While travelling his car was involved in an accident in which his passengers were injured. When they brought an action for damages against Mr Sayag before a Belgian court, Mr Sayag argued that he was acting in the performance of his duties and thus the action should be brought against the Euratom. The Belgian court referred this matter to the ECJ which ruled that the Community was not responsible for an accident caused by a servant and that the existence of a travel order did not bring the driving of a private car within the performance of a servant's duties. It held that only in the case of *force majeure* or in exceptional circumstances would the use of a private car have been considered as part of the servant's performance of his duties. The remedy of a person suffering damage in such a situation is to commence action against the servant before a national court, which has jurisdiction *ratione loci*, and liability will be determined under the law of the *forum*. Conversely, if a wrongful act or omission was committed by an employee acting in the course of his duties, the victim should commence proceedings against the EU before the General Court, and liability would be determined according to EU law. If there is joint liability of a servant and the relevant EU institution, then the EU, after compensating the victim, may bring an action against the servant in order to recover all or part of any compensation paid to the victim.

16.6 Distinction between liability of the EU and liability of the Member States

National authorities apply and implement EU measures. When the conduct of the national authority causes damage to individuals, the question arises: who is liable, the Member State, or the EU? The best solution for applicants would be to permit them to claim compensation for their loss at their option, either before national courts or before the Union courts. Unfortunately, this option is rejected by EU law because:

- first, an EU judge does not have jurisdiction to decide cases against the Member States in tort, nor does a national judge have power to decide such cases against the EU; and,

- second, the division of competences between the EU and the Member States in general, and in relation to a disputed matter in particular, prohibits encroachment on each other's sphere of competence.

Following from the above, three situations can be distinguished. These are examined below.

16.6.1 Liability for wrongful or negligent implementation or application by national authorities of lawful EU acts

In this case, an action for damages should be brought against national authorities before national courts according to national procedure, and the conditions of liability should be determined by national administrative law. In Case 101/78 *Granaria*,[1328] the ECJ held that the question of compensation for loss incurred by individuals caused by a national body or by agents of the Member States, resulting from either their infringement of EU law or an act or omission contrary to national law while applying EU law, is not covered by Article 340(2) TFEU.

1328. Case 101/78 *Granaria BV v Hoofdproduktschap voor Akkerbouwprodukten* [1979] ECR 623.

16.6.2 Liability of national authorities in the case of correct application or implementation of unlawful EU acts

When national authorities have correctly applied or implemented an EU measure, there is no fault on the part of the Member State concerned. As a result, the EU is liable for damage resulting from an unlawful act. However, national courts have jurisdiction, exceptionally in respect of actions concerning monetary compensation. This exception was explained by the ECJ in Case 96/71 *Haegeman*.[1329]

THE FACTS WERE:

Haegeman, a Belgian company, which imported wine from Greece (at that time Greece was not a Member State), was required to pay a countervailing charge imposed by a Council regulation. Belgian authorities collected monies which went to the EU's funds. The applicant alleged that the relevant regulation was unlawful and that it had suffered damage as a result of its existence.

Held:

The ECJ held that for the applicant the proper forum was in a national court, as the monies were collected by national authorities and thus the applicant was in a direct relationship with them, not with the Council. If the applicant sought to challenge the relevant regulation, national courts could refer the matter under Article 267 TFEU, since only the ECJ has jurisdiction to declare an EU act void.

If a measure is declared void by the EU courts, a national court will award compensation for the total damages suffered by the successful claimant. The sum awarded will be paid from national funds but national authorities can obtain reimbursement from EU funds.[1330]

The exclusive jurisdiction of national courts in actions for monetary compensation suffers some exceptions. The applicant can bring an action directly before the CJEU in the following circumstances:

- On the authority of Case 175/84 *Krohn*,[1331] in a situation where the wrongful act is entirely attributable to an EU institution which has directly, exclusively and effectively exercised the power of decision without any involvement of national authorities, i.e. national authorities had no discretion whatsoever in the matter;

- If it is impossible for national courts to order payments in the absence of EU provisions authorising national authorities to pay the claimed amount;[1332] and,

- If an action before national courts would, for procedural or other reasons, not result in the payment of the alleged damages.[1333]

1329. Case 96/71 *R. & V. Haegeman v Commission* [1972] ECR 1005.
1330. J. A. Usher, *Legal Aspects of Agriculture in the European Community*, 1988, Oxford: OUP, 104–106, 150–51.
1331. Case 175/84 *Krohn & Co. Import-Export v Commission* [1986] ECR 753.
1332. For example, Joined Cases 64 and 113/76, 167 and 239/78, 27, 28 and 45/79 *Dumortier Frères SA v Council* [1979] ECR 3091; Case 5/71 *Aktien-Zuckerfabrik Schöppenstedt v Council* [1971] ECR 975; Case T-166/98 *Cantina Sociale di Dolinova Soc. Coop. Rl and Others v Commission* [2004] ECR II-3991.
1333. Case 281/82 *Unifrex v Commission* [1984] ECR 1969; Case 81/86 *De Boer Buizen BV v Council and Commission* [1987] ECR 3677; Case T-167/94 *Detlef Nölle v Council and Commission* [1995] ECR II-2589; Case

It should be noted that in all actions, which do not involve claims for payments of money, the CJEU has jurisdiction.[1334]

16.6.3 Joint liability of the EU and a Member State

In Joined Cases 5, 7 and 13 to 24/66 *Kampffmeyer*,[1335] the ECJ held that if there is joint liability of the EU and a Member State for an unlawful act, the applicant must first bring an action before a national court. Subsequently, the national court must refer the case under Article 267 TFEU to the ECJ, which, if it finds the measure unlawful, will annul the contested act. After annulment, the national court will assess the liability of the Member State and award damages corresponding to the damage caused by the national authorities. The next step for the applicant will be to bring an action before the General Court to determine the liability of the EU, and obtain an award of damages.[1336]

It is submitted that the solution adopted in relation to the division of responsibility between the EU and the Member State is too complex, time-consuming and confusing. Further, in cases where neither national courts nor the Union courts have jurisdiction to decide a particular case, a denial of justice may result.[1337] However, under Article 19(1) TEU Member States are required to provide remedies sufficient to ensure effective legal protection of individuals in fields covered by EU law. Therefore, they will be responsible, in the last resort, to ensure that individuals are adequately compensated in cases where the EU refuses to do this.

16.7 Conditions for liability under Article 340(2) TFEU

Article 340(2) TFEU contains general guidance on non-contractual liability of the EU, and leaves the ECJ to determine specific rules in this area. Article 340(2) TFEU is unique as it requires the ECJ to establish the conditions of liability based on "general principles of the laws of the Member States". This means that general principles of law of the Member States regarding liability of public authorities are relevant. Furthermore, it is not necessary that a particular rule is recognised in all Member States since this would lead to a lowest common denominator and thus ensure the minimum protection for victims of wrongful conduct of EU institutions, bodies, agencies and offices.

The ECJ's approach is selective and based on a comparative study of national legal systems in the light of the specific requirements of EU law. This approach leaves the ECJ a considerable margin of appreciation in the selection of general principles appropriate to the peculiar needs of the EU. This is necessary taking into account the wide variety of types of actions for damages based on Article 340(2) TFEU. On the one hand, the ECJ exercises its jurisdiction in relation to non-contractual liability in the context of disputes involving the economic policies of the EU and thus must take into account the legal and financial implications of its judgments when awarding damages to an applicant or determining unlawful conduct on the part of the EU institutions. On the other hand, the ECJ must often resolve the delicate question of delimitation of competences between the EU and the Member States.

T-195/00 *Travelex Global and Financial Services Ltd and Interpayment Services Ltd v Commission* [2003] ECR II-1677.

1334. Case 126/76 *Firma Gebriider Dietz v the Commission* [1977] ECR 2431; Case C-282/90 *Industrie- en Handelsonderneming Vreugdenhil BV v Commission* [1992] ECR I-1937; Case C-104/89 and C-37/90 *Mulder and Others v Council and Commission* [1992] ECR I-3026.

1335. Joined Cases 5, 7, and 13 – 24/66 *Firma E. Kampffmeyer and Others v Commission* [1967] ECR 245.

1336. On this topic see W. Wills, "Concurrent Liability of the Community and a Member State", (1992) 17 ELR, 204–06.

1337. The best illustration is provided by Case C-55/90 *James Joseph Cato v Commission* [1992] ECR I-2533.

Initially the ECJ developed the following two differing regimes according to the particular type of EU liability under Art 340(2) TFEU:

- Liability relating to a failure of administration. Failure of administration comprises all defects in the organisation and functioning of the service such as "negligence in the management",[1338] inappropriate supervision,[1339] breach of the principle of confidentiality of information obtained by the Commission,[1340] forwarding of erroneous information by EU institutions,[1341] and breach of the provisions relating to hygiene and security at work.[1342] The EU is liable in damages in cases of inexcusable errors or manifest and grave lack of diligence.

  Under this regime, an applicant had to establish the wrongful conduct of the institution; the existence of damage; and a causal link between the two.

- Liability relating to adoption of legislative acts. EU institutions were especially protected against actions in damages caused by legislative acts for the very simple reason that all legislative acts entail that their authors enjoy a large margin of discretion. Indeed, it is not important whether a legislative act concerns economic policies *sensu stricto* or other areas such as transport, social policy and so on; what is important is that an institution has discretion, and must exercise it in the interests of the EU. It must make choices in devising EU policies in the areas of competence of the EU in order to attain the objectives which are essential for integration of national policies and especially to harmonise national laws in specific areas.[1343] This is regardless of the fact that the relevant legislative measures may adversely affect individual interests. The threat of numerous applications for damages should not be allowed to hinder the EU in its policy making. For that reason the ECJ in Case 5/71 *Schöppenstedt*[1344] set out very restrictive requirements for establishing EU liability. It held:

  > "When legislative action involving measures of economic policy is concerned, the Community does not incur non-contractual liability for damage suffered by individuals as a consequence of that action, by virtue of the provisions contained in Article [340], second paragraph, of Treaty [TFEU], unless a sufficiently flagrant violation of a superior rule of law for the protection of the individual has occurred."[1345]

This was referred to under EU law as the "Schöppenstedt formula". The formula required proof of three conditions with regard to legislative acts adopted by the EU, i.e. the applicant was required to show that the EU had committed a sufficiently serious breach of a superior rule of law which was intended to protect the rights of individuals. In addition, an applicant had to establish unlawful conduct on the part of the EU; the existence of damage; and, a causal link between the conduct and the damage. It can be seen from the above that when applicants were seeking to establish EU liability for failure of administration, their task was less onerous than in

---

1338. Case 9/56 *Meroni & Co., Industrie Metallurgiche, SpA v High Authority* [1957–1958] ECR 133.
1339. Joined Cases 19/60, 21/60, 2/61 and 3/61 *Société Fives Lille Cail and Others v High Authority* [1961] ECR 281.
1340. Case 145/83 *Adams v Commision* [1985] ECR 3539.
1341. Joined Cases 19, 20, 25 and 30/69 *Richez-Parise and Others v Commission* [1970] ECR 325; Case 169/73 *Compagnie Continentale France v Council* [1975] ECR 117.
1342. Case 308/87 *Alfredo Grifoni v Euratom* [1990] ECR I-1203.
1343. Case C-63/89 *Les Assurances du Crédit SA and Compagnie Belge d'Assurance Crédit SA v Council* [1991] ECR I-1799.
1344. Case 5/71 *Aktien-Zuckerfabrik Schöppenstedt v Council* [1971] ECR 975, para. 11.
1345. Ibid.

cases where applicants were seeking to establish liability of the EU for wrongful acts having legal effect.[1346]

In Case C-352/98 *Bergaderm*[1347] the ECJ merged the two regimes relating to non-contractual liability of the EU, i.e. that concerning general liability relating to a failure of administration; and that specifically regarding the liability of the EU for legislative acts. The Court also synchronised the rules of liability of the EU and the liability of Member States.[1348] Accordingly, the EU incurs liability under the same conditions as a Member State. These are:

1.   The rule of law which has been breached must be one which is intended to confer rights on individuals;

2.   The breach must be sufficiently serious to merit an award of damages; and,

3.   There must be a direct causal link between the EU's default and the loss suffered by the claimant.

All three conditions must be satisfied. If one of them is unfulfilled, the application is dismissed in its entirety without the necessity for the CJEU to examine the remaining conditions.[1349]

It is to be noted that despite the ECJ's express statements that the conditions for EU non-contractual liability are the same as those under which a Member State may incur liability for damage caused to individuals by a breach of EU law,[1350] the General Court has persistently referred to the "old" test, i.e. contained in the Schöppenstedt formula. Only in Case T-18/99 *Cordis*[1351] did the General Court apply the "new" test established by the ECJ in *Bergaderm*. The difference between the "old" test and the "new" test may not be dramatic but nevertheless, the "new" test is potentially more generous to applicants.[1352] Furthermore, the use of the "old" test by the General Court is confusing for litigants.

16.7.1   The rule of law which has been breached must be one which is intended to confer rights on individuals

A breach by EU institutions of any rule of EU law which is intended to protect the interests of individuals will satisfy the first condition. It is not, however, necessary that the rule has as its exclusive object the protection of individuals. It is sufficient that it has an effect on the protection of individuals in general. In Joined Cases 5, 7 and 13–24/66 *Kampffmeyer*,[1353] the ECJ held that the failure of the Commission to investigate fully the protective measures concerning the imposition of a levy on maize had infringed a

---

1346.   Case T-203/96 *Embassy Limousines and Services v EP* [1998] ECR II-4239.

1347.   C-352/98 *Laboratoires Pharmaceutique Bergaderm SA v Commission* [2000] ECR I-5291. On the assessment of the judgment in *Bergaderm* see T. Tridimas, "Liability for Breach of Community Law: Growing Up and Mellowing Down", (2001) CMLRev., 301.

1348.   Some academic commentators argue that a perfect convergence is not possible given the differences between them in that the EU institutions must enjoy a wide discretion as they have to make choices of economic policies and thus the ECJ will find EU institutions liable only in exceptional cases. See C. Hilson, "The Role of Discretion in EC law on Non-contractual Liability", (2005) 42 CMLRev., 677.

1349.   Case C-146/91 *KYDEP v Council and Commission* [1998] ECR II-4073.

1350.   See Case C-352/98 *Laboratoires Pharmaceutique Bergaderm SA v Commission* [2000] ECR I-5291, para. 41 and Case C-312/00P *Commission v Camar Srl and Tico Srl* [2000] ECR II-2193, para. 53.

1351.   Case T-18/99 *Cordis Obst und Gemüse Großhandel GmbH v Commission* [2001] ECR II-913, para. 45.

1352.   On this topic see C. Hilson, "The Role of Discretion in EC law on Non-contractual Liability", (2005) 42 CMLRev., 677.

1353.   Joined Cases 5, 7 and 13-246/66 *Firma E. Kampffmeyer and others v Commission* [1967] ECR 245.

rule of law which was of a general nature as it referred to the free trade in maize and the support of the maize market, but was, nevertheless, for the protection of individuals.

The first condition excludes rules which do not protect any individual interests. Such rules may concern the non respect of requirements relating to decision-making procedures, for example, non-consultation of the EP in the adoption of a measure which was required by that procedure, or absence of a proposal from the Commission. In Case C-282/90 *Vreugdenhil*[1354] the ECJ held that the principle of the division of competences between EU institutions has as its objective the maintenance of institutional balance (see Chapter 3.2) and not the protection of individuals. Accordingly, a failure to observe this principle cannot be sufficient on its own to render the EU liable. The implications of this judgment are that lack of competence is not a serious illegality, and that the principle of the division of competences between the EU institutions has no relevance to the protection of individuals. Some commentators criticise this approach on the ground that normally lack of competence constitutes a fundamental flaw and is closely connected to the protection of rights of individuals.[1355] A-G Bot in his Opinion in Case C-221/10P *Artegodan*[1356] stated that to accept that the principle of division of competences (in this case the principle of the division of competences between the EU and its Member States) is not a superior rule of law protecting individuals "amounts to a presumption that the choice thus made by the legislature of the Union has no regard for guarantees of individuals' rights, or for how those rights may be affected. I reject such a presumption because, since it impacts on what was decided, the identity of the author of an act must be considered as being directly at the origin of a possible violation of the rights of individuals. I would add that the consequences to be drawn, including as regards compensation, from the lack of competence of the author of an act must be weighed all the more carefully in an international organisation governed by the principle of allocation of powers."

The answer from the ECJ in Case C-221/10 P *Artegodan*[1357] was ambiguous. On the one hand, the ECJ confirmed that the infringement of the principle of the division of competences is not intended to protect individuals and therefore on its own cannot cause the EU to incur non-contractual liability. On the other, the Court stated that such infringement "when it is accompanied by an infringement of a substantive provision which has such an intention, is capable of giving rise to that liability".[1358] Accordingly, the ECJ refused to recognise the principle of division of competences as a superior rule of law intended to confer rights on individuals, and thus refused to endorse the suggestion of the A-G that such a principle may have relevance to the protection of individuals. However, the ECJ held in this case the General Court had made an error of law, i.e. as it had not taken account of the fact that the infringement of the principle of division of competences between the EU and its Member States was accompanied by an infringement of a substantive provision of EU law, which intended to protect rights of individuals.

Whether a rule of EU law is intended to protect the interests of individuals is determined on a case-by-case basis. Thus, the assumption that any rule of EU law automatically protects interests of individuals, or general interest of individuals, is incorrect. This is exemplified by Case T-415/03 *Cofradia*.[1359] In this case, the Council, in accordance with Regulation 3760/92, which provides for the conclusion of agreements between Member States relating to fishing quota swaps, had authorised the

---

1354. Case C-282/90 *Industrie- en Handelsonderneming Vreugdenhil BV v Commission* [1992] ECR I-1937.
1355. M. De Guillenchmidt and J. C. Bonichot, *Les Petites Affiches*, 1992, No 112, 11, cited by A-G Bot in his Opinion in Case C-221/10P *Artegodan GmbH v European Commission and Germany* (judgment of 19/4/12) para. 41.
1356. Ibid, para. 44.
1357. Case C-221/10P *Artegodan GmbH v European Commission and Germany* (judgment of 19/4/12 (NYR)).
1358. Ibid, para. 82.
1359. Case T-415/03 *Cofradía de Pescadores de "San Pedro" de Bermeo and Others v Council* [2005] ECR II-4355.

transfer to France of part of the anchovy quota allocated to Portugal under the Act of Accession of Spain and Portugal to the EU. This resulted in reduction of the effective fishing possibilities for Spanish fishermen. Spanish owners of fishing vessels and Spanish fishermen's associations brought proceedings under Article 340(2) TFEU. The General Court found that the Council's conduct was unlawful as it breached the Act of Accession and the principle of relative stability of each Member State's fishing activities for each of the fish stocks concerned which is enshrined in the relevant EU Regulations concerning the CFP. However, the Court ruled that the principle of relative stability did not confer any rights on individuals (i.e. any guarantee that they could catch a fixed quota of fish). It concerns only relations between Member States, i.e. the maintenance of a right to a fixed quota of catches for each Member State. In respect of the provision of the Act of Accession relating to allocation of the quota for anchovy in the Bay of Biscay, which was breached by the Council, the Court held that this provision was made for the sole benefit of the Member States. Further, as this provision made no reference to the situation of anchovy fishermen in the Bay of Biscay, the Council was not obliged to take account of the particular situation of those fishermen when it authorised a transfer of the quota for anchovy. As a result, the applicants did not satisfy the first condition relating to non-contractual liability of the EU.

16.7.2 The breach must be sufficiently serious to merit an award of damages

With regard to the existence of a sufficiently serious breach of EU law, the Union's courts when assessing the seriousness of the breach refer to the same factors as those applicable to non-contractual liability of a Member State (see Chapter 12.3.2). Accordingly, the Union's courts will take account of the following:

- the clarity and precision of the EU rule breached;

- whether the infringement was intentional or accidental;

- whether any error of law was excusable;

- the degree of discretion enjoyed by the EU institution concerned;

- the "complexity of the situations to be regulated"; and,

- the difficulties in the application or interpretation of the relevant text.

With regard to the margin of discretion enjoyed by EU institutions, even when an EU institution has little or no discretion, a finding of liability is not automatic as other factors, similar to those applicable to non-contractual liability of a Member State for the infringement of EU law, are taken into consideration by the CJEU.

In respect of competition cases, claims based on non-contractual liability of the Commission will often, or perhaps always, be dismissed on the basis of the complexity/difficulties in applying the relevant provisions of EU law. In Case T-28/03 *Holcim (Deutschland)*[1360] the General Court refused to hold the Commission liable despite the fact that the Court recognised that the Commission's discretion, while adopting a decision finding Holcim in breach of Article 101(1) TFEU, was reduced. The refusal was on the ground that the case was extremely complex as it involved investigation into almost the entire European cement industry and the Commission had great difficulties in applying Article 101(1) TFEU given the numerous factual elements of the case. On appeal, the ECJ held that the matter of

---

1360. Case T-28/03 *Holcim (Deutschland) AG v Commission* [2005] ECR II-1357.

complexity was a factual matter and thus it was for the General Court alone to determine it.[1361] Similarly, in Case T-212/03 *My Travel*,[1362] manifest and grave defects in the Commission's economic assessment of the proposed concentration, which resulted in the concentration being declared incompatible with the internal market, which in turn caused losses to My Travel, did not amount to a sufficiently serious breach. This was because the General Court took account of the complexity of the situation to be regulated, difficulties in the application of merger rules in terms of time constraints imposed on the Commission and the margin of discretion available to the Commission.

When the Commission cannot rely on the complexity of a situation a finding of liability is more likely. For example, in Case T-351/03 *Schneider*,[1363] the General Court decided that the Commission, in the context of assessing the compatibility of the proposed concentration with the internal market, breached Schneider's rights of defence, i.e. it formulated the statement of objections in such a way that the applicant was not objectively capable of resolving the specific problems identified by the Commission which were essential to the decision of incompatibility adopted by the Commission. The General Court rejected the Commission's arguments based on the difficulties relating to the complex nature of market analysis and the rigid time constraints imposed by the Merger regulation. It held that the drafting of the statement of objections "did not involve any particular technical difficulty or call for any additional specific examination that could not be carried out for reason of time and the absence of which cannot be attributed to a fortuitous or accidental drafting problem that could be compensated for by a reading of the statement of objections as a whole".[1364] The assessment of the General Court was confirmed by the ECJ.[1365]

It results from the above that in competition matters, in particular in the area of merger control, whilst the General Court has acknowledged that, in principle, deficiencies in the economic assessment can constitute a sufficiently serious breach of EU law,[1366] factors such as the complexity of the matter under consideration, will make it difficult, if not impossible, for an applicant to succeed under Article 340(2) TFEU. However, with regard to procedural deficiencies, the threshold for triggering EU liability is much lower.

With regard to irregularity in administering EU matters giving rise to liability, this is assessed by comparison with the conduct in similar circumstances of a normal prudent and diligent administration.[1367]

It should be said that the change of approach of the CJEU to non-contractual liability of the EU initiated by the ECJ in *Bergaderm* has not eliminated the requirement that only grave illegality will permit applicants to successfully claim damages under Article 340(2) TFEU.

16.7.3 There must be a direct causal link between the infringement of the rule by the EU and the damage suffered by the claimant

This condition requires the existence of actual damage and a link between the damage and the infringement.

1361. Case C-282/05 *Holcim (Deutschland) AG* [2007] ECR I-2941. Such matters may be discussed in the context of appeal proceedings only where the applicant alleges that the General Court has distorted the facts. This was not alleged in this case.

1362. Case T-212/03 *MyTravel Group plc v Commission* [2008] ECR II-1967.

1363. Case T-351/03 *Schneider Electric SA v Commission* [2007] ECR II-2237.

1364. Ibid, para. 155.

1365. Case C-440/07 *Commission v Schneider Electric SA* [2009] ECR I-6413.

1366. Case T-212/03 *My Travel plc v Commission* [2008] ECR II-1967.

1367. Case T-225/99 *Comafrica and Dole Fresh Fruit v Commission* [2001] ECR II-1975; Case T-88/09 *Idromacchine and Others v Commission* (judgment of 8/11/11 (NYR)).

16.7.3.1 Damage

The damage suffered must be actual and certain,[1368] regardless of whether it is present or future.[1369] It must not be purely hypothetical[1370] or speculative.[1371] In Case C-243/05P *Agraz*,[1372] the ECJ ruled that uncertainty regarding the exact quantification of damage would not preclude a finding that the damage alleged by the applicant was sufficiently certain. Thus, in a situation where the damage alleged is real and actual but there is uncertainty as to its exact extent, the condition relating to certainty of damage is satisfied.

Compensation may be obtained for all damage suffered, i.e. for *damnum emergens* (the actual loss) and *lucrum cessans* (the income/profit which would have been earned/made). A-G Capatori said in Case 238/78 *Ireks-Arkady*[1373] that damage "covers both a material loss . . . a reduction in a person's assets, and also the loss of an increase in those assets which would have occurred if the harmful act had not taken place".

Thus, compensation for loss is intended to provide, so far as possible, restitution for the victim.[1374] This includes the possibility for an applicant to request not only monetary compensation but also injunctions. In Case T-279/03 *Galileo*,[1375] the applicants, belonging to the Galileo group of companies, sought, *inter alia*, an injunction prohibiting the Commission from using the word "Galileo". The Commission argued that under Article 340(2) TFEU the right to compensation does not include the right to seek injunctions. The General Court decided otherwise. It held that Union courts are empowered to impose on the EU "any form of reparation that accords with the general principles of non-contractual liability common to the laws of the Member States, including, if it accords with those principles, compensation in kind, if necessary in the form of an injunction to do or not to do something".[1376] Accordingly, the applicants were entitled to seek an injunction.

As to the actual amount of damages, this is generally negotiated between the parties. However, if they cannot reach agreement, the CJEU will determine the amount.[1377] It is for applicants to produce the evidence with regard to the facts and the extent of the loss which they claim to have suffered.[1378]

A.   **Duty to mitigate loss.** There is a duty to mitigate loss. In Joined Cases C-104/89 and 37/90 *Mulder*[1379] the ECJ reduced the damages which might otherwise have been awarded by the

---

1368. Case 51/81 *De Franceschi SpA Monfalcone v Council and Commission* [1982] ECR 117; Case T-478/93 *Wafer Zoo v Commission* [1995] ECR II-1479; Case C-243/05P *Agraz SA and Others v Commission* [2006] ECR I-10833.

1369. Case 33/59 *Compagnie des Hauts Fourneaux de Chasse v High Authority* [1962] ECR 381; Case 51/81 *De Franceschi SpA Monfalcone v Council and Commission* [1982] ECR 117.

1370. Case 54/65 *Compagnie des Forges de Châtillon, Commentry & Neuves-Maisons v High Authority* [1966] ECR 185; Case 4/65 *Société Anonyme Métallurgique Hainaut-Sambre v High Authority* [1965] ECR 1099.

1371. Joined Cases 54–60/76 *Compagnie Industrielle et Agricole du Comté de Loheac and Others v Council and Commission* [1977] 645; Case 74/74 *CNTA v Commission* [1975] ECR 533.

1372. Case C-243/05P *Agraz SA and Others v Commission* [2006] ECR I-10833.

1373. Case 238/78 *Ireks-Arkady GMbH, Kulmbach v Council and Commission* [1979] ECR 2955, 2998.

1374. Case C-308/87 *Alfredo Grifoni v Euratom* [1994] ECR I-341; Case C-295/03P *Alessandrini Srl and Others v Commission* [2005] ECR I-5673.

1375. Case T-279/03 *Galileo International Technology and Others v Commission* [2006] ECR II-1291.

1376. Ibid, para. 63, see also Case T-19/07 *Systran SA and Systran Luxembourg SA v Commission* [2010] ECR II-6083.

1377. Joined Cases C-104/89 and C-37/90 *Mulder and Others v Council and Commission* [2000] ECR I-203; and Joined Cases T-79/96, T-260/97 and T-117/98 *Camar and Tico v Commission and Council* [2000] ECR II-2193.

1378. Case 26/74 *Société Roquette Frères v Commission* [1976] ECR 677; Case T-184/95 *Dorsch Consult Ingenieurgesellschaft mbH v Council and Commission* [1998] ECR II-667.

1379. Joined Cases C-104/89 and C-37/90 *J. M. Mulder and Others v Council and Commission* [1992] ECR I-3061.

amount of profit which the producers could have reasonably earned from alternative activities. Although the ECJ made no suggestion as to alternative activities the word "reasonably" implies that fundamentally different activities from their usual business were not considered as alternatives.

B.   **Contributory negligence.** EU law recognises contributory negligence. If applicants have contributed through their own negligence to the damage, the amount of damages will be reduced proportionally. This was the situation in Case 145/83 *Adams*[1380] in which the ECJ awarded only half of the amount claimed by Adams on the ground that Adams contributed through his negligence to the resulting damage.

THE FACTS WERE:

Adams was employed by the Swiss-based multinational Hoffmann-La Roche. He forwarded confidential information to the Commission concerning breaches of Article 102 TFEU by his employer, who, as a result, was heavily fined. During the proceedings Hoffmann-La Roche asked the Commission to disclose the name of the informant. The Commission refused, but forwarded to Hoffmann-La Roche certain documents which enabled them to identify Adams as the source of the leaked information. The forwarding of the relevant information was contrary to the duty of confidentiality contained in Articles 17(3) and 7 TEU. In the meantime Adams moved to Italy where he set up his own business. Hoffmann-La Roche used its international connections to destroy that business. The Commission failed to inform Adams that his former employer was planning to persecute him. On his return to Switzerland Adams was arrested by the Swiss police for economic espionage and held in solitary confinement. His wife committed suicide. Adams brought proceedings before the ECJ against the Commission for loss of earnings and loss of reputation as a result of his conviction and imprisonment.

Held:

The ECJ held that the Commission was liable for the breach of duty of confidentiality, as it allowed Adams to be identified as an informer, and awarded Adams £200,000 in damages for his mental anguish and lost earnings, and £176,000 for costs, half of what he had demanded. The reason for the reduction was Adams' contributory negligence. The ECJ held that Adams contributed to the resulting damage by failing to warn the Commission that he could be identified from the confidential documents, and by failing to enquire about progress of the proceedings, especially before returning to Switzerland.[1381]

16.7.3.2   The existence of a causal connection

The requirement of causality means that the damage must be a direct consequence of the infringement.[1382] The burden of proof is on the applicant.[1383]

1380.   Case 145/83 *Adams v Commission* [1985] ECR 3539.
1381.   N.M. Hunnings, "The Stanley Adams Affair or the Biter Bit", (1987) 24 CMLRev., 65.
1382.   Case 18/60 *Louis Worms v High Authority* [1962] ECR 195.
1383.   Case 40/75 *Société des Produits Bertrand SA v Commission* [1976] ECR 1.

In Joined Cases 64/76 and 113/76, 239/78, 27, 28 and 45/79 P *Dumortier Frères*[1384] the ECJ held that there is no obligation to compensate all prejudicial consequences, however remote, resulting from the unlawful legislative act.

> ## THE FACTS WERE:
>
> *A regulation which abolished production refunds for maize grits but not for maize starch, both used in brewing and baking and thus in direct competition with each other, was successfully challenged by the producers of maize grits. As a result of this successful action brought under Article 263 TFEU, the producers of maize grits brought an action under Article 340(2) TFEU. They claimed compensation in relation to loss of refunds prior to the adoption of the regulation, lost sales and the closure of factories by two producers and the bankruptcy of a third.*
>
> ### Held:
>
> *The ECJ held that the regulation was contrary to the principle of non-discrimination and equality, affected a limited and clearly defined group (that is, the producers of maize grits) and the damage exceeded the bounds of the inherent economic risks in this sector of business.*
>
> *The ECJ awarded damages only in relation to the loss of refunds. The reduction in sales was not considered as resulting from the abolition of refunds since the producers had increased the price of maize grits and had thus passed the loss to their purchasers. The closing of factories and the bankruptcy were not a sufficiently direct result of the withdrawal of refunds. Damage that is too remote will not give rise to the right of reparation.*

The Union's courts will assess, on a case-by-case basis, whether the damage suffered by an applicant is a sufficiently direct consequence of an unlawful act or conduct on the part of the EU institution concerned.[1385] The case law shows that the damage must be directly attributable to conduct of the institution concerned as opposed to the applicant's own choice or decision[1386] and that the causal link must not be interrupted by negligence of the applicant.[1387]

16.8   Unjust enrichment actions under Article 340(2) TFEU

In Case C-47/07 P *Masdar*[1388] the ECJ ruled that a claim based on unjust enrichment can be brought under Article 340(2) TFEU. The ECJ stated that although a claim based on unjust enrichment does not fall under the rules governing non-contractual liability in the strict sense, it nevertheless cannot deny legal redress to persons who have suffered a loss which has increased the wealth of another

---

1384.   Joined Cases 64/76 and 113/76, 239/78, 27, 28 and 45/79 P *Dumortier Frères SA and Others v Council* [1979] ECR 3091.

1385.   Case C-446/04 *Test Claimants in the FII Group Litigation v Commissioners of Inland Revenue* [2006] ECR I-11753 and Case C-440/07P *Commission v Schneider Electric SA* [2009] ECR I-6413.

1386.   Case T-113/04 *Atlantic Container Line AB and Others v Commission* [2007] ECR II-171.

1387.   Case C-282/05P *Holcim (Deutschland) AG v Commission* [2007] ECR I-2941.

1388.   Case C-47/07 P *Masdar (UK) Ltd v Commission* [2008] ECR I-9761.

person, solely on the ground that there is no express provision under the Treaties for pursuing that type of action.

The conditions for liability set out under Article 340(2) TFEU do not apply to an action for unjust enrichment. The only requirement that a claimant must satisfy is the proof of enrichment of the defendant for which there is no valid legal basis and the impoverishment of the applicant which is linked to that enrichment.

The ECJ decided to create the new action under Article 340(2) TFEU for the following reasons:

- an action for unjust enrichment is recognised by national laws of the Member States; and,

- any denial of access to the CJEU in a situation where the EU has been unjustly enriched to the detriment of an applicant would be contrary to the principle of effective judicial protection laid down in the case law of the ECJ and enshrined in Article 47 of the Charter of Fundamental Rights.

16.9 Rejection by the ECJ of non-contractual liability of the EU for damage caused by lawful EU acts

For a number of years there have been doubts as to whether the EU can be held liable under Article 340(2) TFEU for lawful acts in a situation where such acts have caused damage to individuals. In Case T-69/00 *FIAMM*,[1389] the General Court decided that, in some exceptional circumstances, such liability may arise. The exceptional circumstances referred to are that the damage must be unusual (i.e. it must exceed the limits of the economic risks inherent in the sector concerned) and special in nature, i.e. the EU measure must affect a limited and clearly defined group in a disproportionate manner by comparison with other operators. However, in the above mentioned case the General Court decided that the first requirement was not satisfied. On appeal, the ECJ rejected the possibility that the EU can be held liable for lawful acts adopted by an EU institution.

The main justification provided by the ECJ for the rejection of the principle of non-fault liability of the EU for legislative acts was that no such principle is recognised by the vast majority of legal systems of the Member States. The Commission pointed out that even in Member States where the principle of non-fault liability is recognised, its application is confined to exceptional circumstances, and apart from France, limited solely to administrative acts. Under French law the recognition of non-fault liability for legislative acts is justified by the fact that the French *Conseil d'État* (Council of State – the highest administrative court in France) has no jurisdiction to review the constitutionality of national legislation and is subject to strict conditions requiring that the damage must be unusual, special, serious and direct, that the challenged legislature is not pursuing the common good and that the legislature has not ruled out compensation as a matter of principle. According to the Commission and the Council the principle of non-fault liability for legislative acts adopted by EU institutions should not be incorporated into EU law because first, it is not a "general principle common to the laws of the Member States", and second, under EU law, unlike French law, the EU courts have jurisdiction to review EU acts in the light of the Treaties and fundamental principles of EU law and therefore EU law provides for the possibility of the liability of the EU to be put in issue if those higher-ranking norms are infringed.

Are the above justifications convincing? The A-G, in his Opinion in *FIAMM*, submitted excellent arguments in favour of the recognition of the principle of non-fault liability in EU law, namely, that it is well established that no mechanical approach is taken to the selection of general principles of EU law.

1389. Case T-69/00 *FIAMM v Council and Commission* [2005] ECR II-5393.

Therefore it is of no importance how many Member States adhere to a particular principle. What is important is that the principle in question is appropriate to the needs and specific features of the EU legal system. According to the A-G non-fault liability of the EU for both legislative and administrative acts adopted by EU institutions would respond to the particular requirements of the EU legal order for the following reasons:

- The interests of justice would be served as it would offset the severity of the conditions relating to the establishment of non-contractual liability of the EU for unlawful acts; and,

- It would meet the requirements of good governance as it would force the relevant EU institutions to be very careful when exercising their discretion to adopt legislative acts, which would be lawful but which might cause particularly serious damage to citizens of the EU.

The above are, certainly, very convincing arguments.

RECOMMENDED READING

Books

Biondi, A., and Farley, M., *The Right to Damages in European Law*, 2009, London: KLI.

Hofmann, H., Rowe, G. C., and Türk, A. H., *Administrative Law and Policy of the European Union*, 2011, Oxford: OUP.

Lenaerts, K., Arts, D., and Maselis, I., *Procedural Law of the European Union*, 2nd edn, 2006, London: Sweet & Maxwell.

Wakefield, J., *Judicial Protection through the Use of Article 288(2) EC*, 2002, The Hague: KLI.

Articles

Gutman, K., "The Evolution of the Action for Damages against the European Union and Its Place in the System of Judicial Protection", (2011) 48 CMLRev., 695.

Hartley, T.C., "Concurrent Liability in EEC Law: A Critical Review of Cases", (1977) 2 ELRev., 249.

Hilson, C., "The Role of Discretion in EC Law on Non-Contractual Liability", (2005) 42 CMLRev., 677.

Toth, A.G., "The Concept of Damage and Causality as Elements of Non-Contractual Liability", in Schermers, H.G., Heukels, T., and Mead, P. (eds), *Non-Contractual Liability of the European Communities*, 1988, The Hague: Martinus Nijhoff Publishers, ch. 3.

Tridimas, T., "Liability for Breach of Community Law: Growing Up and Mellowing Down", (2001) 38 CMLRev., 301.

Wils, W., "Concurrent Liability of the Community and a Member State", (1992) 17 ELRev., 191.

Wakefield, J., "Retrench and Reform: The Action for Damages", (2009) 28 YEL, 390.

PROBLEM QUESTION

From 2009, Expertex Ltd was carrying out a number of management advice projects within an EU programme called Lighthouse. While carrying out a Lighthouse project in Germany, Expertex identified several financial problems concerning the general implementation of that programme in Germany. The government of Germany sent a report to the Commission to this effect. In response, an official from the Commission in charge of the Lighthouse programme sent a fax to the programme co-ordinators in Germany, Poland, Hungary and Romania informing them that Expertex had not satisfied its financial commitments in Germany, and therefore should not be considered as a reliable partner. The official also asked the addressees of the fax to pass his message on to any person concerned. As a result, Expertex was never again chosen for any project within the framework of Lighthouse.

In 2011, Mr James, the manager of Expertex, learnt about the fax sent by the Commission official and met officials from the Commission who admitted that a mistake had been made. Immediately after the meeting, the Commission sent a fax to the programme co-ordinators of all the relevant governments "rectifying" the previous fax, and recommending that any exclusion of Expertex from the experts list should be removed. Mr James, nevertheless, remains convinced that Expertex has been unjustly excluded from projects carried out within the framework of Lighthouse, bearing in mind that despite many applications submitted to the Commission his company has never, subsequent to the German contract, been awarded any contract within the Lighthouse programme, or any other EU programme. Accordingly, he recently contacted the Commission again whereupon the Commission replied stating that Expertex is not on its exclusion list.

Mr James is still dissatisfied with the conduct of the Commission. He claims that the Commission is guilty of a manifest lack of care in respect of the rectification of its mistake. He intends to bring an action against the Commission under Article 340(2) TFEU seeking compensation.

Advise Mr James whether his intended action is likely to be successful.

ESSAY QUESTION

Critically assess the following statement made by A-G Mackenzie-Stuard in 1975 in which he compared the rules on non-contractual liability of the EU with a colonial-era map of Africa. He said: "The coast is shown; we see the deltas of great rivers, but where they lead and where they have their sources are as yet uncharted."[1390]

1390. Lord Mackenzie-Stuard, "The Non-contractual Liability of the EEC", (1975) 12 CMLRev., 495 at 514.

AIDE-MÉMOIRE

Action for damages: non-contractual liability of the EU under Article 340(2) TFEU
The EU must make good any damage caused by its institutions and by its servants in the performance of their duties (Case 9/69 *Sayag*).

Applicants: any natural and legal person (including associations, but they are subject to the conditions set out in Case T-304/01 *Abad Pérez*) and Member States.

Defendants: any EU institution (but not the ECJ) and any EU body, office or agency.

The claim must meet the conditions set out by the ECJ in Case C-352/98 *Bergaderm* in which the ECJ held that the EU incurs non-contractual liability under the same conditions as a Member State. These are:

• the rule of law which has been breached must be one which is intended to confer rights on individuals;
• the breach must be sufficiently serious to merit an award of damages; and,
• there must be a direct causal link between the infringement of the rule and the damage suffered by the claimant.

All three conditions must be satisfied.

The claim must be brought within five years from the day the damage materialised, (not the time of the occurrence of the event or fact giving rise to damage (Case 256/80 *Birra Wührer*)). The limitation period may be suspended by:
• Proceedings brought by the applicant before the Union courts, or
• A preliminary request addressed by the applicant to the relevant institution, but only if followed by an application under Article 263 or 265 TFEU and within the time limit set out in those provisions (Case C-282/05P *Holcim*).

Outcome of a successful action
Damages are awarded to the applicant.

Miscellaneous Matters

1. *Claims based on unjust enrichment*

    They may be brought under Article 340(2) TFEU. The only requirement is that the applicant proves enrichment of the defendant without any valid legal basis and his impoverishment deriving from the enrichment of the defendant (Case C-47/07 *Mosdar*).

2. *No Liability of the EU for lawful acts*

    The ECJ rejected the possibility that the EU may be required to compensate for damage caused by its institutions in the absence of unlawful conduct on their part (Joined Cases C-120/06P and C-121/06P *FIAMM*).

17

AN INTRODUCTION TO THE INTERNAL MARKET OF THE EU

CONTENTS _____

17.1 Introduction

Any type of arrangement in which countries agree to coordinate their trade, fiscal, and/or monetary policies is described as economic integration. Depending on the degree of involvement of the participating economies the following different forms of economic integration can be distinguished:

▪ **A free trade area.** This consists of the removal of all customs duties and quotas on goods passing between the participating States. Each participating State retains the power to regulate its trading relations with non-participating States, i.e. it can unilaterally determine its external customs duties and impose quotas on imports coming from outside the area. For example, the North American Free Trade Agreement (NAFTA) created a free trade area between the US, Canada and Mexico.

▪ **A customs union.** This occurs when participating States, in addition to agreeing to eliminate customs duties and quotas between themselves, set a common external tariff on imports coming from the rest of the world. An example of a customs union is Mercosur, a customs union between Brazil, Argentina, Uruguay, Paraguay and Venezuela. The EU became a customs union in 1968.

▪ **A common market or internal market.** This occurs when the participating States establish, in addition to a customs union, a free flow of the factors of production, i.e. goods, labour, services and capital. The best example is the EU which officially created an internal market on 31 December 1992.

▪ **An economic union.** This entails complete integration of the economies of the participating States, including unification of their fiscal, monetary and social policies. The closest to the achievement of an economic union is the Benelux Economic Union. The EU has not yet reached this stage of development.[1391]

The creation of a common market was the main objective of the Treaty of Rome which established the European Economic Community (EEC) in 1958 between the six founding Member States. From that time until the adoption of the Single European Act (SEA) in 1986 the only significant step towards the creation of a common market was the completion of a customs union on 1 July 1968 between the same six founding Member States.

The SEA gave new impetus to the achievement of the common market (see Chapter 1.13). The SEA replaced the term "common market" by "internal market"[1392] and defined it as: "an area without internal frontiers in which the free movement of goods, persons, services and capital is ensured in accordance with the provisions of the Treaty" (Article 26(2) TFEU).

During the period leading to completion of the internal market (which was officially completed on 31 December 1992), the EU adopted a new approach to technical harmonisation and standards, as opposed to the pre-SEA approach consisting of harmonisation of national laws through detailed technical specifications. The new approach was defined by a Council Resolution of 7 May 1985.[1393] It was modernised by a new regulatory framework (known as New Legislative Framework (NLF)), which has three components:

- Regulation 765/08 setting out the requirements for accreditation and market surveillance relating to the marketing of products;[1394]

- Decision 768/2008/EC of the European Parliament and of the Council of 9 July 2008 on a common framework for the marketing of products;[1395] and,

- Regulation 764/08 laying down procedures relating to the application of certain national technical rules to products lawfully marketed in another Member State[1396] (see Chapter 17.2.3).

The main objective of the NFL is to remove the remaining barriers to free movement of goods and to boost trade between the Member States. Regulation 765/2008 requires each Member State to establish a market surveillance system for all products covered by EU harmonising legislation except for those which are specifically excluded, e.g. food and animals. This is to protect consumers and professionals from unsafe products. Further, the Regulation requires a Member State to establish one accreditation body responsible for accrediting all "conformity assessment bodies", i.e. bodies carrying out testing and inspection of manufacturing products and processes for the purpose of certifying conformity with specified requirements (such as an EU directive or an international standard) operating within its territory. This is to ensure that the services provided by assessment bodies are of high quality. Finally,

---

1391. See the Report submitted by the President of the European Council to the European Council on 26 June 2012 entitled "Towards a Genuine Economic and Monetary Union" , available at http://ec.europa.eu/economy_finance/ focuson/crisis/documents/131201_en.pdf (accessed 19/7/12). On the basis of this report, the European Council invited the President of the European Council, to prepare a specific and time-bound road map for the achievement of a genuine Economic and Monetary Union for those Member States which have the euro as their currency.

1392. For the meaning of the term "internal market" see L. W. Gormley, "Competition and Free Movement: Is the Internal Market the Same as a Common Market?", (2002) E. Bus. L. Rev, 517, and K. J. M. Mortelmans, "The Common Market, the Internal Market and the Single Market, What's in a Market?", (1998) CMLRev., 101.

1393. [1985] OJ C136/1.

1394. [2008] OJ L218/30.

1395. [2008] OJ L218/82.

1396. [2008] OJ L218/21

under the Regulation, the CE marking system has been clarified and strengthened. A Member State must ensure that the CE mark is correctly applied, i.e. it is to be affixed to a product only when its use is specifically required by EU legislation and can only be used by the manufacturer of the product. The CE marking is protected by a trade mark. Accordingly, a Member State may impose penalties for its misuse.

Decision No 768/2008 is a "toolkit" to be used in drafting future EU directives and revising the existing directives relating to the marketing of products in the EU.[1397]

With regard to non-harmonised areas, i.e. not covered by EU legislation, which concern such goods as certain foodstuffs, furniture, bicycles, Regulation 764/2008 enhances the application of the principle of mutual recognition (see Chapter 17.2.3). Under the Regulation a Member State is required to set up a product contact point which provides, free of charge, information relating to the marketing of the product concerned in that Member State. When national authorities intend to refuse a product lawfully marketed in another Member State access to the national market, they are required to provide the trader concerned with detailed reasons for the refusal and inform him of remedies available under national law to challenge the refusal.

An important element in ensuring the free movement of goods is the work of EU standardisation bodies: the European Committee for Standardisation; the European Committee for Electrotechnical Standardisation; and, the European Telecommunications Standards Institute.

With regard to areas other than the free movement of goods, the Commission, in order to unlock the potential of the internal market, in its 2012 Single Market Act[1398] put forward 12 key priority measures with a view to generating sustainable economic growth, fighting unemployment and achieving Europe 2020 targets.[1399] Among the key priority measures are: adoption of legislation improving access to finance for more than 20 million European small and medium-sized enterprises; modernisation of legislation on the recognition of professional qualification to facilitate the free movement of EU citizens (see Chapter 24.8); and revision of legislation on European product standardisation and its extension to the free movement of services. The Commission intends to deliver those priorities by the end of 2012. The next stage in the Commission's work is to prepare a plan of action relating to the development of the internal market beyond 2012.

As can be seen from the above although the internal market was officially completed on 31 December 1992, in practice, its creation is an ongoing process. Important gaps remain in some areas. Administrative obstacles and lack of enforcement continue to hinder the free movement of factors of production. Additionally, the world-wide economic and financial crises from 2007 onward have brought new challenges. The Commission has been taking new initiatives aimed at stimulating growth of the internal market as evidenced by the adoption of the 2012 Single Market Act.

17.2 The three key principles essential to the establishment and development of the internal market

The ECJ has relied on three principles to create, maintain and develop the internal market, as follows.

1397. For details see the Commission website http://ec.europa.eu/enterprise/policies/single-market-goods/regulatory-policies-common-rules-for-products/new-legislative-framework (accessed 18/7/12).

1398. COM/2011/0206 final.

1399. For details of those targets see: http://ec.europa.eu/internal_market/smact/docs/20120206_new_growth_en.pdf (accessed 18/7/12).

17.2.1 The principle of non-discrimination

A general principle of non-discrimination based on nationality is embodied in Article 18 TFEU. It requires goods, persons, services and capital to enjoy the same treatment in a host Member State as that given by that State to its nationals, domestic goods, services, and capital. The main benefit of "national treatment" is that it does not interfere with national regulatory autonomy. Consequently, Member States are free to regulate the way that goods are produced, services are provided and its nationals are treated on their territory. Any discrimination based on nationality can only be justified on the grounds provided by the Treaties and must be necessary and proportionate to the objectives that a national measure seeks to achieve.

The principle of non-discrimination requires not only that the same rules are applicable to similar situations but also, conversely, that different situations are treated differently. The case law of the ECJ shows that all forms of indirect discrimination which, by applying distinguishing criteria other than nationality (such as residence), have in practice the same discriminatory result, are prohibited. However, indirect discrimination may be justified on grounds mentioned in the Treaties as well as grounds not mentioned in the Treaties but established by the case law of the ECJ (see below).

17.2.2 Beyond discrimination – unlawful non-discriminatory obstacles to the free movement

For the ECJ, the principle of non-discrimination was a starting point in eliminating obstacles to the four freedoms. The Court has not only condemned any discrimination, either direct or indirect, but has gone beyond this and held that non-discriminatory obstacles to the exercise of any of the four freedoms are contrary to provisions of the Treaties. Accordingly, all measures even if they are non-discriminatory which substantially prevent/restrict, or create obstacles to, the free movement are prohibited. However, in respect of the free movement of goods, the access to the market test, which encompasses the non-discriminatory approach, is applied in a limited manner (see Chapter 20.6).

National rules which are not discriminatory but nevertheless restrict access to the market of a Member State can be justified only if they are based on objective considerations, which are independent of nationality and are proportionate to the aim legitimately pursued by the national law.[1400] It is to be noted that the concept of objective justification was developed by the ECJ itself, in the absence of any explicit provision in the Treaties.

The advantage of the market access approach is that it contributes to the creation of the internal market by removing unjustified restrictions. The disadvantage is that it is very intrusive into national regulatory autonomy because it requires that a national rule, although non-discriminatory, must be removed unless it can be justified. This poses a challenge to national legislation enacted by democratically elected bodies in the Member States given that almost any national rules may have some negative effect on the internal market even if that was not the intention of the rule and the effect is slight.

1400. Case C-15/96 *Kalliopé Schöning-Kougebetopoulou v Freie und Hansestadt Hamburg* [1998] ECR I-47; Case C-224/01 *Köbler v Austria* [2003] ECR I-10239; Case C-464/02 *Commission v Denmark* [2005] ECR I-7929; Case C-109/04 *Karl Robert Kranemann v Land Nordrhein-Westfalen* [2005] ECR I-2421; Case C-208/05 *ITC Innovative Technology Center GmbH v Bundesagentur für Arbeit* [2007] ECR I-181.

17.2.3 The principle of mutual recognition

The principle of mutual recognition was introduced by the ECJ in the *Cassis de Dijon* case[1401] in the context of the free movement of goods (see Chapter 20.3.2). Under the *Cassis de Dijon* approach the principle means that a product lawfully produced and marketed in one Member State must be accepted in other Member States even if it does not match technical or other specifications of those Member States. The principle of mutual recognition is not absolute as Member States are allowed to exclude such a product from their national market on the grounds of derogations set out in the Treaties and on the basis of mandatory requirements aimed at protecting vital public interests (see Chapter 21).

The Commission had identified the main problems with the application of the principle,[1402] clarified its meaning and incorporated it as a main tool of the internal market strategy 2003–2006. Based on the Commission's experience with the application of the principle of mutual recognition, the EP and Council adopted Regulation 764/2008[1403] which sets out procedures for relevant national authorities and traders aimed at minimising the possibility of technical rules creating obstacles to the free movement of goods.

The principle of mutual recognition has gradually been applied to other freedoms than the free movement of goods, namely the free movement of services and the recognition of the qualifications of EU citizens (see Chapter 24.8).[1404]

The main advantage of the application of the principle of mutual recognition it that it guarantees the achievement of the objectives of the internal market without the need to harmonise Member States' national legislation and thus maintains the diversity of products and services within the internal market.

17.3 The "SOLVIT" network

"SOLVIT", an online network,[1405] assists EU citizens and undertakings to find out-of-court solutions to problems relating to any aspect of the internal market. Each Member State has its "SOLVIT centre" which attempts to find a solution within a 10-week deadline, free of charge. The suggested solution is not binding but in many cases solves problems regarding the misapplication of internal market law by public authorities of the Member State concerned. SOLVIT and other networks, for example, FIN-NET, which aims at solving problems in the cross-border financial services sector, enhance the ways in which the EU seeks to remove obstacles erected by Member States to the realisation of the internal market.

1401. Case 120/78 *Rewe-Zentral AG v Bundesmonopolverwaltung für Branntwein* (known as the *Cassis de Dijon* case) [1979] ECR 649.

1402. On this topic see: M. P. Maduro, "So Close and Yet so Far: The Paradoxes of Mutual Recognition", (2007) 14 JEPP, 814.

1403. [2008] OJ L218/21.

1404. It is to be noted that the principle of mutual recognition is not a homogeneous concept under EU law in that with regard to measures relating to the AFSJ it takes a different form from that it takes in the context of the internal market. In the AFSJ, it ensures the free movement of judicial decisions and thus on the basis of the principle of mutual recognition individuals are subjected to disadvantageous or even coercive measures of a host Member State (e.g. arrest warrant) which interfere with their fundamental rights. On this topic see: M. Möstl, "Preconditions and Limits of Mutual Recognition", (2010) 47 CMLRev., 405.

1405. The website of SOLVIT is: http://europa.eu.int/solvit/site/index_en.htm (accessed 18/7/12).

RECOMMENDED READING

Books

Barnard, C., *The Substantive Law of the EU. The Four Freedoms*, 3rd edn, 2010, Oxford: OUP.

Davies, G., *European Union Internal Market Law*, 2006, London: Routledge Cavendish.

Davies, M., *Nationality Discrimination in the European Internal Market*, 2003, The Hague: KLI.

Shuibhne, N. (ed.), *Regulating the Internal Market*, 2006, Cheltenham: Edward Elgar.

Syrpis, P. (ed.), *The Judiciary, the Legislature and the EU Internal Market*, 2012, Cambridge: CUP.

Tryfonidou, A., *Reverse Discrimination in EC Law*, 2009, London: KLI.

Articles

Dougan, M., "Minimum Harmonization and the Internal Market", (2000) 37 CMLRev, 853.

Ehlermann, C.-D., "The Internal Market Following the Single European Act", (1987) 24 CMLRev., 361.

Mortelmans, K. J. M., "The Common Market, the Internal Market and the Single Market, What's in a Market?" (1998) CMLRev., 101.

Möstl, M., "Preconditions and Limits of Mutual Recognition", (2010) 47 CMLRev., 405.

Weatherill, S., "New Strategy for Managing the EC's Internal Market", (2000) 53 CLP, 595.

18

ABOLITION OF CUSTOMS DUTIES AND CHARGES HAVING EQUIVALENT EFFECT TO CUSTOMS DUTIES (CEEs)

CHAPTER OUTLINE

1. Article 28 TFEU provides for the establishment of a customs union between the Member States covering all trade in goods. Goods are not defined in the Treaties but the ECJ has defined them as all products which have a monetary value and which may be the object of commercial transactions.

2. Any customs union has two dimensions: internal, which involves the creation of a single customs territory between the participating States in which there are no customs duties, quotas or similar restrictions on goods passing between the participating States, and external, which requires that the same customs duties and trade regulations apply to goods coming from non-participating States. The external aspects of the customs union within the EU are based on the Common Customs Tariff and the Common Commercial Policy. The internal aspects of the customs union are covered by Articles 28–30 TFEU.

3. Article 30 TFEU prohibits a Member State from maintaining customs duties on goods imported from another Member State, or on its exports, or on goods from third countries which have been released by a Member State for free circulation in the EU, or from introducing any charges having equivalent effect to customs duties (CEEs).

4. The concept of a CEE is an autonomous EU legal concept. It has been defined by the ECJ as covering any pecuniary charge, however small and whatever its designation and mode of application, which is imposed unilaterally on goods by reason of the fact that they cross a frontier, including a regional and internal frontier, even if it is not discriminatory, protectionist or imposed for the benefit of the Member State.

5. The prohibition set out in Article 30 TFEU is absolute. However, the ECJ held that a charge which might appear to be a CEE escapes the prohibition, i.e. falls outside the scope of Article 30 TFEU, in the following situations:

- When it constitutes a payment for a service actually rendered to the importer or exporter. However, such a service must genuinely benefit the importer; must provide a specific benefit to him, rather than be imposed for reasons of the general interest; and, the sum charged for the service must be proportionate to the cost of the service.

- When it constitutes a payment for a service which is required under EU law or under international law. In such a situation a Member State is allowed to charge for that service provided the amount charged does not exceed the real cost of providing the service.

- When it is in fact a tax, i.e. when it relates to a general system of internal dues applied systematically and in accordance with the same criteria to domestic products and imported products alike (see Chapter 19). It this situation its lawfulness or otherwise is assessed in the light of Article 110 TFEU.

18.1 Introduction – the definition of goods

Article 28 TFEU provides that the customs union between the Member States covers all trade in goods. The ECJ has defined "goods" as all products which have a monetary value and which may be the object of commercial transactions.[1406] This definition includes:

- Waste. In Case C-2/90 *Commission v Belgium*,[1407] the ECJ refused to make a distinction between recyclable waste which has commercial value and non-recyclable waste which has no intrinsic value. Accordingly, there are now in free circulation between Member States not only goods which have commercial value but also goods which are capable of generating costs for undertakings;[1408]

- Consumer goods including medical products;[1409]

- Gold and silver collectors' coins provided they are not currently in circulation as legal tender;[1410]

- Goods and materials supplied in the context of the provision of services;[1411]

1406. Case C-97/98 *Peter Jägerskiöld v Torolf Gustafsson* [1999] ECR I-7319, para. 33.
1407. [1992] ECR I-4431.
1408. Case C-277/02 *EU-Wood-Trading GmbH v Sonderabfall-Management-Gesellschaft Rheinland-Pfalz mbH* [2004] ECR I-11957.
1409. Case 215/87 *Heinz Schumacher v Hauptzollamt Frankfurt am Main-Ost* [1989] ECR 617.
1410. Case 7/78 *R v Thompson* [1978] ECR 2247.
1411. Case 45/87 *Commission v Ireland (Re: Dundalk Water Supply)* [1988] ECR 4929.

- Electricity and gas;[1412] and,

- Goods originating in non-Member States which have completed customs formalities at the external frontier of the EU and are in free circulation between Member States.

Unlawful goods are outside the scope of the Treaties.[1413]

When goods are ancillary to a main activity, they are covered by provisions of the Treaties other than those relating to the free movement of goods. Accordingly, advertisement materials, lottery tickets which are sold in one Member State for a lottery organised in another Member State[1414] and the supply of goods such as car body parts, oils, and so on, for repair of vehicles[1415] in another Member State do not fall within the definition of "goods". They are covered by the provisions of the Treaties relating to the free movement of services. Further, shares, bonds and other securities which can be valued in money and form the subject of commercial transactions are dealt with under the rules relating to the free movement of capital rather than the free movement of goods.

18.2   Customs union, its external and internal aspects

Any customs union has two dimensions: internal and external. Internally, the participating States are required to create a single customs territory in which there are no customs duties, quotas or other restrictions imposed on goods passing between them. Externally, the participating States are required to impose the same customs duties and trade regulations on goods coming from non-participating States.

Article 28(1) TFEU regulates both external and internal aspects of the customs union. It states that:

"The Union shall comprise a customs union which shall cover all trade in goods and which shall involve the prohibition between Member States of customs duties on imports and exports and of all charges having equivalent effect, and the adoption of a common customs tariff in their relations with third countries."

The external aspects of the customs union within the EU are based on the Common Customs Tariff and the Common Commercial Policy. The internal aspects of the customs union are covered by Articles 28–30 TFEU.

18.3   Meaning of customs duties and charges having equivalent effect
to customs duties (CEEs)

A customs duty is a charge levied on imports and exceptionally on exports by the customs authorities of a State. Duties are usually based on the value of a product. The actual rates of duties are normally specified by the relevant national law. A customs duty has two functions: first, it raises revenue for the State, and second, it protects domestic producers from more efficient foreign competitors who can

---

1412. Case C-159/94 *Commission v France* [1997] ECR I-5815.
1413. Case C-137/09 *Marc Michel Josemans v Burgemeester van Maastricht* [2010] ECR I-13019 (judgment of 16/10/10 (NYR)) (see Chapter 24.6).
1414. Case C-275/92 *Her Majesty's Customs and Excise v Gerhart Schindler and Jörg Schindler* [1994] ECR I-1039; Case C-6/01 *Anomar and Others v Estado Português* [2003] ECR I-8621.
1415. Case C-55/93 *Criminal Proceedings against Johannes Gerrit Cornelis van Schaik* [1994] ECR I-4837.

manufacture the relevant product cheaper than domestic producers, or from those who manufacture the product at similar costs, but as a result of customs duties, have to sell them at a higher price than rival domestic producers. The prohibition of the imposition of customs duties in the EU is a pre-condition for the free movement of goods, as it ensures that a Member State will not protect its industry at the expense of competitors from other Member States. One of the rare cases where the ECJ dealt with customs duties is Case 26/62 *Van Gend*,[1416] in which the ECJ established that Article 12 of the EEC Treaty (repealed) had direct effect and thus the trader could rely on it before a national court (see Chapter 10.1) .

Article 30 TFEU prohibits not only customs duties but also any CEE. The prohibition of CEEs prevents Member States trying to get around Article 30 by relabelling or disguising what are in fact customs charges.

There is no definition of "charges having equivalent effect to customs duties" in the Treaties. In Case 24/68 *Commission v Italy [Re Statistical Levy]*,[1417] the ECJ defined a CEE as:

"any pecuniary charge, however small and whatever its designation and mode of application, which is imposed unilaterally on goods by reason of the fact that they cross a frontier and which is not a custom duty in the strict sense . . ., even if it is not imposed for the benefit of the State, is not discriminatory or protective in effect and if the product on which the charge is imposed is not in competition with any domestic product."

The case law shows that a CEE has the following characteristics:

1. It must be a pecuniary charge.[1418] Other obstacles are within the scope of the provisions relating to non-tariff barriers on the free movement of goods.

2. Its amount is irrelevant. Even a small charge[1419] or a charge below the direct and indirect costs of services provided by the customs authorities[1420] is prohibited by Article 30 TFEU.

3. It may result not only from a measure imposed by a Member State or other public authority but also from an agreement concluded between individuals as exemplified in Case 16/94 *Dubois*.[1421]

THE FACTS WERE:

Dubois and General Cargo, who were forwarding agents, refused to pay a "transit charge" imposed on them by GE, the owner of an international road station near Paris where the customs authorities held offices. GE imposed the charge for vehicles completing customs clearance on their station in order to offset the costs of having the customs authorities on their premises. Dubois and General Cargo argued that a "transit charge" was in breach of Article 30 TFEU.

1416. Case 26/62 *NV Algemene Transport- en Expeditie Onderneming van Gend & Loos v Netherlands Inland Revenue Administration* [1963] ECR 1.
1417. [1969] ECR 193, para. 9.
1418. Case 46/76 *Bauhuis v Netherlands* [1977] ECR 5.
1419. Case 24/68 *Commission v Italy (Re Statistical Levy)* [1969] ECR 193.
1420. Case C-111/89 *Staat der Nederlanden v P. Bakker Hillegom BV* [1990] ECR I-1735.
1421. Case 16/94 *Dubois et Fils SA and General Cargo Services v Garoner (GA) Exploitation SA* [1995] ECR I-2421.

Held:

The ECJ held that the "transit charge" was within the scope of Article 30 TFEU, i.e. it was a CEE even though it was not imposed by a Member State but resulted from an agreement concluded between a private undertaking (GE) and its customers (Dubois and General Cargo).

4. The designation and mode of application of a charge is irrelevant for the application of Article 30 TFEU. Thus, it is considered as a CEE whether it is called a special charge,[1422] or a "price supplement",[1423] or a fee levied in order to defray the costs of compiling statistical data,[1424] or otherwise.

5. Its beneficiaries or its destination are irrelevant. The leading authorities on this point are Joined Cases 2 and 3/69 *Sociaal Fonds*.[1425] In that case Belgium imposed a levy on imported diamonds which was not protectionist (Belgium is not a producer of diamonds), but was designed to provide social security benefits for workers in the Belgian diamond industry. The ECJ held that the levy was contrary to Article 30 TFEU. In Joined Cases C-441 and 442/98 *Michaïlidis*[1426] the imposition of a charge, the proceeds of which were to provide social benefits for workers in the tobacco industry, was condemned by the ECJ. Also, a charge made to protect the historical and artistic heritage of a Member State has been found unlawful.[1427]

In Case C-173/05 *Commission v Italy*,[1428] Sicily imposed a tax for environmental purposes.

THE FACTS WERE:

Sicily imposed an environmental tax on the ownership of a gas pipeline during the time when gas was actually in the pipeline. The pipeline was carrying gas from Algeria to Italy for distribution and consumption there, and for onward export to other Member States. The owners were described as those who carry on at least one of the activities of transportation, distribution, sales or purchasing of gas. The purpose of the tax was to fund investments to reduce and prevent environmental risks linked to the presence of the pipeline in Sicily. The gas was imported from Algeria to the EU on the basis of a Co-operation Agreement concluded between Algeria and the EU.

According to the Commission the real purpose of the fiscal imposition was to tax the transported product, namely gas, and not to tax the infrastructure itself (for environmental reasons) given that the tax was payable by owners who carried on one of the activities of

---

1422. Joined Cases 2 and 3/62 *Commission v Luxembourg* [1962] ECR 425.
1423. Case 77/76 *Fratelli Cucchi v Avez SpA* [1977] ECR 987.
1424. Case 24/68 *Commission v Italy (Re Statistical Levy)* [1969] ECR 193.
1425. Joined Cases 2 and 3/69 *Sociaal Fonds v Brachfeld and Chougol Diamond Co.* [1969] ECR 211.
1426. Joined Cases C-441/98 and C-442/98 *Kapniki Michaïlidis AE v Idryma Koinonikon Asfaliseon (IKA)* [2000] ECR I-7145.
1427. Case 7/68 *Commission v Italy* [1968] ECR 617; C-72/03 *Carbonati Apuani Srl v Comune di Carrara* [2004] ECR I-8027.
1428. [2007] ECR I-4917.

transportation, distribution, sale or purchasing of the gas only when gas was in the pipeline and that the basis of assessment for the tax was the volume of the gas contained in the pipeline.

Held:

The ECJ held that the Sicilian tax was in fact a CEE. The ECJ emphasised that the event giving rise to the tax was the actual presence of the gas in the infrastructure. Thus, the tax was charged on goods (the gas) and not on the ownership of infrastructure.

The purpose of the tax was irrelevant since a charge under Article 30 TFEU cannot be justified whatever its purpose or the destination of the revenue from it. The tax was not imposed at the frontier but at a later stage. It was called an "environmental tax" but was in fact a CEE.

6. It must be imposed by the reason of or on the occasion of the crossing of a frontier by goods, but the time and the place of imposition is not relevant. In Case 78/76 *Firma Steinike*[1429] the ECJ held that a charge need not be levied at a border in order to be a customs charge or CEE. Even a regional frontier is included. This was examined in Joined Cases C-363 and C-407–411/93 *Lancry*.[1430]

THE FACTS WERE:

A charge called "dock dues" was imposed on all goods imported, irrespective of their country of origin, including France itself, into French overseas territories. The purpose of "dock dues" was to raise revenue in order to encourage the local economy. Lancry, who imported flour into Martinique from France, challenged "dock dues" as contrary to Article 30 TFEU.

Held:

The ECJ held that a charge levied at a regional frontier is within the scope of Article 30 TFEU. This article expressly refers to intra-State trade because it is presumed that there are no internal obstacles to trade within Member States. The abolition of internal borders is a pre-condition of the creation of the customs union between Member States. The charge which had been imposed at a regional frontier constituted "at least as serious" an obstacle to the free movement of goods as a charge levied at national frontiers. Indeed, regional customs frontiers undermine the unity of the EU customs territory.

1429. Case 78/76 *Firma Steinike und Weinlig v Bundesamt für Ernährung und Forstwirtschaft* [1977] ECR 595.

1430. Joined Cases C-363 and C-407–411/93 *Lancry and Others v Direction Générale des Douanes and Others* [1994] ECR I-3957; see also Case C-163/90 *Administration des Douanes et Droits Indirects v Léopold Legros and Others* [1992] ECR I-4625; Case C-293/02 *Jersey Produce Marketing Organisation Ltd v States of Jersey and Jersey Potato Export Marketing Board* [2005] ECR I-9543. In Joined Cases C-485/93 and C-486/93 *Simitzi v Dimos Kos* [1995] ECR I-2655 the ECJ held that a charge imposed on goods dispatched from one region of a Member State to another region of that same State amounted to a CEE.

Comment:

This case raised controversy, mainly because Article 28(1) TFEU expressly refers to the prohibition of customs duties and CEEs "between Member States" and therefore its literal interpretation clearly excludes regional frontiers from its scope. Notwithstanding this, in Case C-72/03 Carbonati Apuani,[1431] the ECJ held that a charge imposed by the municipality of Carrara on marble quarried within the municipality when that marble was transported to other municipalities in Italy or to other Member States was a CEE. The Court stated that Article 28(1) TFEU must be read in conjunction with Article 26(2) TFEU which defines the internal market as "an area without internal frontiers in which the free movement of goods, persons, services and capital is ensured in accordance with the provisions of the Treaties" and therefore makes no distinction between intra-State borders and inter-State borders. According to the ECJ Article 28(1) TFEU makes "express reference only to trade between Member States . . . because the framers of the Treaty took it for granted that there were no charges exhibiting the features of a customs duty in existence within the Member States".[1432] Barnard[1433] rightly points out that Article 26(2) TFEU applies to all provisions of the Treaties relating to the internal market with the result that the reasoning of the ECJ in Carbonati Apuani should apply to other freedoms, i.e. the free movement of capital and the free movement of persons. However, the ECJ has always refused such extensive interpretation of Article 26(2) TFEU with regards to those freedoms.

7.   Article 30 TFEU encompasses charges imposed at any stage of production or marketing.[1434]

8.   Compensatory taxes are also CEEs. This was established in Cases 2 and 3/62 *Commission v Luxembourg (Re Gingerbread)*.[1435]

THE FACTS WERE:

The governments of Luxembourg and Belgium imposed a special import duty on imported gingerbread in order to compensate for the price difference between domestic gingerbread and imported gingerbread. Domestic gingerbread was more expensive as a result of high internal rates of taxation on rye, an ingredient of gingerbread.

Held:

The ECJ held that a special import duty levied on imported gingerbread was a CEE. Indeed, the objective of the tax was not to equalise the taxes on gingerbread but to equalise the price of it!

1431.   Case C-72/03 *Carbonati Apuani Srl v Comune di Carrara* [2004] ECR I-8027. For comments on this case see P. Oliver and S. Enchelmaier, "Free Movement of Goods: Recent Developments in the Case Law", (2007) 44 CMLRev., 649.
1432.   Ibid, para. 22.
1433.   C. Barnard, *The Substantive Law of the EU*, 2010, Oxford: OUP, 45–46.
1434.   Case 78/76 *Steinike und Weinlig v Germany* [1977] ECR 595.
1435.   [1962] ECR 425.

18.4 Categories of charges

There are two categories of charges: charges imposed solely on imported or exported good, and charges imposed on both domestic and imported goods. Each category must be examined in the light of Article 30 TFEU.

18.4.1 Charges imposed solely on imported or exported goods

If a charge is imposed only on imported products or exported products[1436] and does not fall within the permitted charges it is clearly in breach of Article 30 TFEU. It is a CEE and there are no justifications for it.

18.4.2 Charges imposed on both domestic and imported goods

It is important to establish whether such a charge is imposed in the same way on domestic products and on imported products and to assess its purpose.

In Case 29/72 *Marimex*,[1437] a charge imposed on both domestic and imported meat in respect of veterinary inspections carried out in Italy in order to verify whether meat satisfied health standards required by Italian legislation was held unlawful by the ECJ. This was on the ground that inspections of imported meat were conducted by a body different from that inspecting domestic meat and each body applied criteria different from those applied by the other. Accordingly, imported products were discriminated against as compared to domestic products.

Even if charges imposed on both domestic and imported products are applied in the same way and according to the same criteria, they may be CEEs if the proceeds of the charge are to benefit domestic products exclusively. This was decided in Case 77/72 *Capolongo*.[1438]

THE FACTS WERE:

Italy imposed a charge on all egg boxes, domestic and imported, in order to finance the production of paper and cardboard in Italy. The charge constituted a part of an overall charge on cellulose products.

Held:

The ECJ held that although the charge applied without discrimination to both domestically produced and imported egg boxes, it was to benefit domestic manufacturers alone and as such was discriminatory and constituted a CEE.

In Case 77/76 *Fratelli Cucchi*[1439] the ECJ set out the criteria which should be applied in order to assess whether a particular charge that is levied indiscriminately on both domestic and imported

---

1436. Joined Cases C-441/98 and C-442/98 *Kapniki Michaïlidis AE v IKA* [2000] ECR I-7145.
1437. 29/72 *Marimex SpA v Italian Minister of Finance* [1972] ECR 1309; See also Case 132/78 *Denkavit v France* [1979] ECR 1923.
1438. Case 77/72 *Capolongo v Azienda Agricola Maya* [1973] ECR 611; see also Cases C-78–83/90 *Compagnie Commerciale de l'Ouest and Others v Receveur Principal des Douanes de La Pallice Port* [1992] ECR I-1847.
1439. Case 77/76 *Fratelli Cucchi v Avez SpA* [1977] ECR 987.

products is contrary to Article 30 TFEU or is within the scope of other Articles of the Treaties. In this case the same charge was levied on domestic and imported sugar, but its proceeds were intended to finance "adaptation aids" to Italian beet producers and the Italian sugar-processing industry. The ECJ held that such a charge would be a CEE if all the following criteria were met:

- if it had the sole purpose of financing activities for the specific advantage of domestic products;

- if the domestic products on which a charge was imposed and the domestic products which were to benefit from it were the same; and,

- if the charge imposed on the domestic products was "made up" in full. That is, if, in fact, by way of a tax refund or otherwise domestic producers did not pay any charge at all. When applying the above-mentioned criteria due regard must be had to other provisions of the Treaties, in particular to Article 110 TFEU, which prohibits direct and indirect discriminatory internal taxation, and to Article 107 TFEU on State aid. If domestic products benefit only partially from the proceeds of the charge, that charge may constitute a discriminatory tax in breach of Article 110 TFEU. Also a charge may, in fact, be a form of State aid prohibited under the Treaties.

18.5 Permissible charges

In Case 18/87 *Commission v Germany*,[1440] the ECJ held that some charges may escape classification as CEEs. This occurs if a charge is levied for a service genuinely rendered to the trader; or a service required under EU law/international law; or, if it falls outside the scope of Article 30 TFEU because it is a tax.

18.5.1 A service rendered to the trader

Member States have tried to justify the imposition of charges on a number of grounds, the most popular being that a charge is in fact a fee paid for a service rendered to the trader. The first time this "justification" was invoked was in Joined Cases 52 and 55/65 *Commission v Germany*.[1441] The ECJ defined fees levied by Germany on importers for the provision of an import licence as a CCE on the ground that it did not bring any benefit to the importer.

The ECJ has gradually specified strict conditions which, if they apply cumulatively, allow a charge to escape the prohibition of Article 30 TFEU. A charge levied on goods by reason of the fact that they cross a frontier is not a CEE if it constitutes consideration for a specific service actually and individually rendered to the trader and the amount demanded is proportionate to the cost of supplying such a service. A charge will be lawful if it satisfies the three criteria examined below.

18.5.1.1 The service must be of genuine benefit to the trader

The condition that a service must provide a genuine benefit to the trader is very difficult to satisfy, taking into account the strict interpretation by the ECJ of a "genuine benefit". This is illustrated in Case 132/82 *Commission v Belgium (Re Storage Charges)*.[1442]

1440. [1988] ECR 5427, para. 6.
1441. [1966] ECR 159.
1442. [1983] ECR 1649.

THE FACTS WERE:

The Belgian authorities introduced a system whereby goods in transit could undergo customs clearance either at the border or in assigned warehouses within Belgium. If customs clearance in a warehouse was selected by the trader, the customs authorities imposed storage charges on the goods.

The Commission took exception to the levying of these costs, alleging that they were charges having an equivalent effect to customs duties. The Commission brought proceedings against Belgium before the ECJ.

Held:

The ECJ held that charges levied as part of the process of customs clearance on EU goods or goods in free circulation within the EU constitute CEEs, if they are imposed solely in connection with the completion of customs formalities. The ECJ accepted that the use of a public warehouse in the interior of the country offered certain advantages to importers. Nevertheless, given that such advantages were linked solely with the completion of customs formalities (which, whatever the place, were always compulsory) and that the storage charges were payable also when the goods were presented at the public warehouse solely for the completion of customs formalities, even though they had been exempted from storage and the importer had not requested that they be put in temporary storage, the ECJ ruled that they were in breach of Article 30 TFEU.

18.5.1.2 The service must provide a specific benefit to the trader

The service must be specific. This means that the trader must obtain a definite specific benefit, enhancing his personal interest, not the general interest of all traders operating in the particular sector of the economy. This criterion was explained, for the first time, in Case 63/74 *Cadsky*.[1443]

THE FACTS WERE:

Cadsky exported vegetables from Italy to Germany. The Italian Government imposed a mandatory quality control on products crossing the Italian frontier for which it charged exporters. Cadsky paid the relevant charge but later brought proceedings for recovery of the sums paid. The Italian Government argued that the challenged fees represented payment for a service rendered to the trader since quality control constituted recognition of the quality of its products abroad, and in addition contributed to the improvement of the reputation of Italian vegetables in external markets, and thus enhanced the competitiveness of Italian products.

Held:

The ECJ held that the charge did not constitute payment for a service rendered to the operator, because a general system of quality control imposed on all goods did not provide a

---

1443. *W. Cadsky SpA v ICE* [1975] ECR 281.

sufficiently direct and specific benefit to the trader. The benefit related to the general interest of all Italian vegetable exporters and, consequently, the individual interest of each of them was so ill-defined that a charge could not be regarded as consideration for a specific benefit actually and individually conferred.

Another leading case on this topic is Case 24/68 *Commission v Italy (Re Statistical Levy).*[1444]

THE FACTS WERE:

The Italian Government imposed a levy, designed to finance the gathering of statistics on all imports, and exports. It argued that the statistical service was for the benefit of importers and exporters.

Held:

The ECJ held that the advantage provided to importers was too general and uncertain to be considered as a service rendered to the trader.

Member States have often tried to justify charges in respect of health inspections, arguing that they provide a benefit to the trader consisting of recognising the quality of imported goods. This justification has been rejected by the ECJ.

In Case 39/73 *Rewe-Zentralfinanz*,[1445] charges imposed in relation to health inspections on apples were considered as CEEs on the grounds that the inspections were not carried out for the specific benefit of the trader but for public benefit as a whole.

In Case 87/75 *Bresciani*,[1446] the ECJ held that charges in respect of veterinary inspections carried out on imported raw cowhides were CEEs since the inspection was mandatory under Italian law, and thus did not provide a specific service to the importer and all importers were obliged to submit to the inspection. In addition they were conducted in the general interest and thus the inspection fees should be paid by the beneficiaries, that is, the general public, which benefits from the free movement of goods.

Another case on this topic is Case C-389/00 *Commission v Germany*.[1447]

THE FACTS WERE:

The German authorities imposed on exporters of waste a compulsory contribution to a solidarity fund set up under the 1989 Basle Convention on the Control of Transboundary Movements of Hazardous Wastes and their Disposals as implemented by the relevant EU legislation. The contribution was designated to guarantee the financing of the return of waste to Germany in the event of illegal or incomplete exports, in circumstances where the party

---

1444. [1969] ECR 193.
1445. Case 39/73 *Rewe-Zentralfinanz GmbH v Direktor der Landwirtschaftskammer Westfalen-Lippe* [1973] ECR 1039.
1446. Case 87/75 *Bresciani v Amministrazione Italiana delle Finanze* [1976] ECR 129.
1447. [2003] ECR I-2001.

responsible was not in a position to bear those costs or could not be identified. The German Government argued that this service conferred a real benefit on exporters, since the subsidiary guarantee taken on by the State allowed them to penetrate the markets of the other Member States and also of the other contracting parties to the Basle Convention.

Held:

The ECJ emphasised that the Basle Convention imposed the same obligations on all Member States in pursuit of the general interest, namely protection of health and the environment, and the compulsory contribution fund did not confer on exporters of waste established in Germany any specific or definite benefit. They had the same opportunities as their competitors established in other Member States. Thus, nothing had been given in return for their contribution. The charge was a CEE.

18.5.1.3 The sum charged must be proportionate to the cost of the service

The sum charged must be proportionate to the cost of the service. This criterion was explained by the ECJ in Case 170/88 *Ford España*.[1448]

THE FACTS WERE:

Ford España received a bill for clearing cars and goods through customs equal to 1.65 per cent of the declared value of the cars and other goods imported into Spain. The Spanish Government argued that the sum represented fees for services rendered to Ford España.

Held:

The ECJ accepted that in this case the service was genuine and the benefit was of the required specific nature. Nevertheless, the charge was in breach of Article 30 TFEU as it was based not on the cost of the service but on the value of the goods and as such was not commensurate with the service.[1449]

The position seems to be that only if a trader requests a service of his own volition will it be accepted as a benefit by the ECJ.

18.5.2 A mandatory service

If a service is required under EU law or under international law, that is, mainly on the basis of an agreement to which the EU is a contracting party, a Member State is allowed to charge for that service

---

1448. Case 170/88 *Ford España v Spain* [1989] ECR 2305.
1449. See also Cases 52 and 55/65 *Germany v Commission* [1966] ECR 159; Case 39/73 *Rewe-Zentralfinanz v Landwirtschaftskammer Westfalen-Lippe* [1973] ECR 1039.

provided the amount charged does not exceed the real cost of providing the service.[1450] This was examined by the ECJ in Case 18/87 *Commission v Germany (Re Animals Inspection Fees)*.[1451]

THE FACTS WERE:

Measures were brought into effect throughout the EU by Council Directive 81/389 which permitted Member States to carry out veterinary inspections on live animals transported into or through their national territories. Certain German provinces, known as Länder, charged fees for conducting those inspections. The fees imposed were justified, according to the German Government, to cover the actual costs incurred in maintaining the inspection facilities. The Commission argued that these charges amounted to CEEs and could not be justified under the Directive. Accordingly, the Commission brought an action against Germany before the ECJ.

Held:

The ECJ held that charges imposed in relation to health inspections required by EU law are not to be regarded as CEEs if the following conditions are satisfied:

1. *They do not exceed the actual costs of the inspections in connection with which they are charged;*

2. *The inspections are obligatory and uniform for the relevant products in the EU;*

3. *The inspections are prescribed by EU law in the general interests of the EU; and,*

4. *The inspections promote the free movement of goods, in particular by neutralising obstacles which could arise from unilateral measures of inspection adopted in accordance with Article 36 TFEU.*

The ECJ held that the charges imposed for health inspections were not CEEs as they satisfied the above-mentioned criteria.

Comment:

It may be argued that the fees for mandatory inspections, as opposed to permissible inspections including those authorised by the EU,[1452] should also be unlawful. After all, traders, by exercising their right to the free movement of goods, contribute to the advancement of the internal market. Accordingly, they should not be required to meet the costs of mandatory inspections. This is not the position of the ECJ although it accepted the negative effect that such a fee may have on intra-EU trade. The Court stated that this could be eliminated only by virtue of EU provisions providing for the harmonisation of fees, or by imposing the obligation on the Member States to bear the costs entailed in the inspections, or, finally, by establishing that the costs must be paid out of the EU budget. The best solution would be to fund mandatory inspections from the own resources of the EU but this is not likely to occur bearing in mind the limited funds of the EU.

1450. Case 46/76 *Bauhuis v Netherlands* [1977] ECR 5; Case 1/83 *IFG v Freistaat Bayern* [1984] ECR 349.

1451. [1988] ECR 5427.

1452. Case 314/82 *Commission v Belgium* [1984] ECR 1543. These kind of inspections are not mandatory under EU law, and thus a Member State cannot charge traders.

495

RECOMMENDED READING

Books

Barnard, C., *The Substantive Law of the EU. The Four Freedoms*, 3rd edn, 2010, Oxford: OUP.

Davies, G., *European Union Internal Market Law*, 2006, Abingdon: Routledge Cavendish.

Gormley, L. W., *EU Law of Free Movement of Goods and Customs Union*, 2009, Oxford: OUP.

Shuibhne, N. (ed.), *Regulating the Internal Market*, 2006, Cheltenham: Edward Elgar.

Snyder, F., *International Trade and Customs Law of the European Union*, 1998, London: Butterworths.

Articles

Barents, R., "Charges of Equivalent Effect to Customs Duties", (1978) 15 CMLRev., 415.

Oliver, P., and Enchelmaier, S., "Free Movement of Goods: Recent Developments in the Case Law", (2007) 44 CMLRev., 649.

Tryfonidou, A., "Carbonati Apuani Srl v Comune di Carrara: Should we Reverse 'Reverse Discrimination'?" (2005) 16 *King's College Law Journal*, 373.

PROBLEM QUESTION

Sugarex Ltd, a UK manufacturer of chocolate, has encountered the following problems:

A. When selling its products in Germany, it is required to pay €10 on each 1,000 chocolate bars sold. The German authorities state that this charge constitutes the counterpart of internal charges affecting German producers of chocolate who are required to pay a very high tax on cocoa butter, the main ingredient of chocolate.

Sugarex Ltd, feels that imposition of the €10 charge will mean that the total sale price of its products will be unattractive to potential customers.

B. Sugarex Ltd is required to pay €20 to a special fund created by the German government to be used by the German Children's Dentists Association with a view to undertaking a study on the relationship, if any, between the increased consumption of chocolate by children and the growth of tooth decay in children in Germany.

Advise Sugarex Ltd as to whether it is likely to successfully challenge the above pecuniary impositions.

ESSAY QUESTION

Critically discuss whether a CEE levied by a Member State in the course of trade conducted entirely within its territory should be within the scope of Article 30 TFEU.

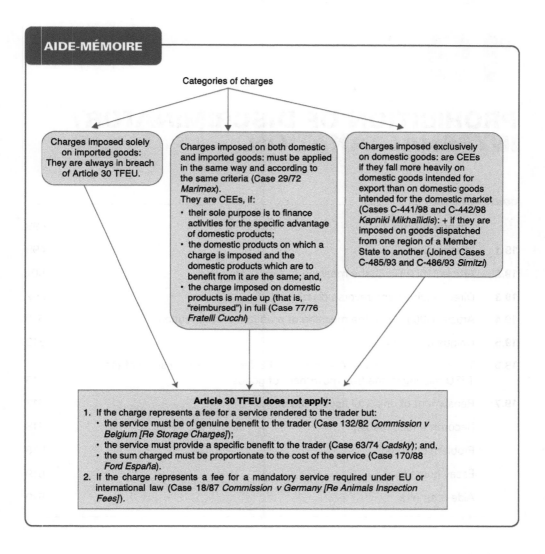

19

PROHIBITION OF DISCRIMINATORY INTERNAL TAXATION

CONTENTS

CHAPTER OUTLINE

1. Article 110 TFEU allows Member States to retain different internal tax regimes but prohibits the imposition of taxation which discriminates between domestic products and imported products, or which affords protection to domestic products.

2. Article 110 TFEU prohibits all discrimination, whether direct, indirect or reverse. Direct discrimination based on the origin of the product is plainly incompatible with the requirements of the internal market, and thus can only be justified under derogations set out in the Treaties. Indirect discrimination based on criteria other than the origin of the product, although generally prohibited, may be justifiable where it is based on objective criteria and is effected in order to achieve acceptable social, environmental or economic aims (but the Court tends not to accept purely economic justifications). The list of objective justifications is rather vague and open-ended but not inconsistent with allowed justifications in other areas of free movement. Reverse discrimination refers to a situation where domestic products intended for export are taxed more highly than the same or similar domestic products intended for a domestic market. This is prohibited under Article 110 TFEU.

3. Article 110 TFEU has two paragraphs, each of which contains a separate prohibition. Article 110(1) TFEU deals with imported products which are so similar to domestic products that they require the same tax treatment. It prohibits any taxation which directly or indirectly discriminates against imported products. Two criteria are used in order to assess similarity of domestic and imported products. The first refers to the objective characteristics of domestic and imported products, and the second takes into account consumers' views as to whether both products meet the same needs, i.e. whether they are substitutes for each other. If both criteria are answered in the affirmative, the products are similar. If not, Article 110(2) TFEU is likely to apply. If a Member State breaches Article 110(1) TFEU, the remedy consists of equalising taxes between similar domestic and imported products.

4. Article 110(2) TFEU deals with imported products, which although not similar to domestic products, are nevertheless in competition with domestic products. Article 110(2) TFEU prohibits taxation that affords protection to domestic products, and thus ensures that domestic products are not protected from competitive pressures by the internal system of taxation. In order to assess whether products are in competition in the same market, not only present but also future consumer habits are analysed. Even partial, indirect and potential competition is taken into account. If a Member State infringes Article 110(2) TFEU, it must remove the protectionist taxes. The result of this is likely to be that products in competition will continue to be taxed at different rates from each other but the difference will be less substantial than previously.

5. A situation where imported products are neither similar to nor in competition with domestic products is outside the scope of Article 110 TFEU. However, if tax levied on a unique product is so high as to constitute an obstacle to the free movement of goods, Article 34 TFEU may apply.

6. Proper classification of a fiscal imposition will determine whether such an imposition should be challenged under Article 110 TFEU in conjunction with other articles of the Treaties or whether it falls solely within the scope of Article 110 TFEU or Article 30 TFEU. Articles 110 and 30 TFEU are complementary as they both deal with fiscal charges, but are mutually exclusive in that the same fiscal charge cannot belong to both categories at the same time. However, to draw a demarcation line between Articles 110 and 30 TFEU is not an easy task.

19.1 Introduction

Each Member State has exclusive competence to determine its taxation policies with regard to direct taxation: i.e. in respect of taxes on personal income and company profits; and, indirect taxation, i.e. taxes imposed on products/services. However, when a Member State exercises its competence, it must comply with EU law, in particular with the principle of non-discrimination. When a Member State imposes discriminatory taxation on direct income it may be in breach of EU provisions on the free movement of persons[1453] (see Chapter 23.7.4). With regard to indirect taxation, a Member States is free to choose the tax systems it considers most appropriate and according to its preferences, but in doing so must conform with EU law, and is subject to EU rules on VAT, excise duties and other EU measures adopted with a view to ensuring that the internal market is not adversely affected by disparities in national tax systems. EU competences in matters of taxation are set out in Articles 110–13 TFEU.

1453. A. Cordewener, G. Kofler and S. van Thiel, "The Clash between European Freedoms and National Direct Tax Law: Public Interest Defences Available to the Member States", (2009) 46 CMLRev., 1951.

Article 110 TFEU deals with indirect taxation on products. It provides:

"No Member State shall impose, directly or indirectly, on the products of other Member States any internal taxation of any kind in excess of that imposed directly or indirectly on similar domestic products.

Furthermore, no Member State shall impose on the products of other Member States any internal taxation of such a nature as to afford indirect protection to other products."

Fiscal barriers to trade may result not only from customs duties and CEEs but also from the imposition on imported products of national taxes with which domestic products are not burdened. Article 110 TFEU guarantees that this will not happen. Its main objective is to ensure that the internal taxation system of a Member State makes no distinction between domestic and imported products. This was clearly stated by the ECJ in Case 252/86 *Bergandi*[1454] in which it was held that Article 110 TFEU "must guarantee the complete neutrality of internal taxation as regards competition between domestic products and imported products".

Article 110 TFEU does not provide any definition of a tax. However, in Case 90/79 *Commission v France [Re Levy on Reprographic Machines]*[1455] the ECJ held that a genuine tax is a measure relating to a system of internal dues applied systematically to categories of products in accordance with objective criteria irrespective of the origin of the products. Included in the concept of a tax are: tax refunds,[1456] stamp duties,[1457] countervailing charges[1458] and excise duties.[1459]

Article 110 TFEU applies only to products from Member States and to products originating in non-Member States which are in free circulation in the Member States[1460] and not to products imported directly from non-Member States.[1461] With regard to products in free circulation in the EU, Article 110 TFEU applies to imported and exported products (see Chapter 18.2) and to taxes imposed on the use of these products.[1462] Further, it also applies to a tax imposed on a specific activity of an undertaking connected with a product, e.g. the transportation of the relevant product, in so far as the tax produces direct[1463] or indirect[1464] discriminatory effect on products. In Case C-221/06 *Stadtgemeinde Frohnleiten*,[1465] the ECJ rejected the argument submitted by the Austrian authorities that a tax imposed on the deposit of waste at a waste disposal site concerned the supply of services by the operator of the waste depositing facilities and thus should be examined in the light of the provisions of the TFEU relating to the free movement of services rather than in the light of the prohibition of discriminatory taxation set out in Article 110 TFEU. It held that what is relevant for the application of Article 110 TFEU is the effect of the tax, whether direct or indirect, on the cost of national and imported

---

1454. Case 252/86 *Gabriel Bergandi v Directeur Général des Impôts* [1988] ECR 1343, para. 24.

1455. [1981] ECR 283.

1456. Case 148/77 *H. Hansen jun. & O. C. Balle GmbH & Co. v Hauptzollamt de Flensburg* [1978] ECR 1787.

1457. Case 77/69 *Commission v Belgium* [1970] ECR 237.

1458. Case C-167/05 *Commission v Sweden* [2008] ECR I-2127.

1459. Case 170/78 *Commission v UK* [1980] ECR 417; Case C-167/05 *Commission v Sweden* [2008] ECR I-2127.

1460. Joined Cases 37/73 and 38/73 *Sociaal Fonds voor de Diamantarbeiders v NV Indiamex and Feitelijke Vereniging De Belder* [1973] ECR 1609.

1461. Case C-130/92 *OTO SpA v Ministero delle Finanze* [1994] ECR I-3281; Case C-90/94 *Haahr Petroleum Ltd v Åbenrå Havn and Others* [1997] ECR I-4085.

1462. Case 252/86 *Gabriel Bergandi v Directeur Général des Impôts* [1988] ECR 1343, para. 27.

1463. Case 20/76 *Schöttle & Söhne OHG v Finanzamt Freudenstadt* [1977] ECR 247 and *Haahr Petroleum*, Ibid.

1464. Case C-221/06 *Stadtgemeinde Frohnleiten Gemeindebetriebe Frohnleiten GmbH v Bundesminister für Land- und Forstwirtschaft, Umwelt und Wasserwirtschaft* [2007] ECR I-9643.

1465. Ibid.

products. Accordingly, a charge imposed on an operator of a waste disposal site was a tax under Article 110 TFEU because it was imposed indirectly on deposited waste. Any discriminatory effect which undermines the equal treatment of domestic products and imported products is prohibited under Article 110 TFEU.

In order to reduce the risk of the application of discriminatory internal taxation in respect of products from other Member States, the ECJ, in one of its earliest judgments, recognised that Article 110 TFEU is directly effective. In Case 57/65 *Lütticke*[1466] the ECJ held that Article 110 TFEU is clear, unconditional and not qualified by any condition, or subject to the requirement of legislative intervention on the part of EU institutions. Consequently it is of direct effect in the relationship between a Member State and an individual.

Article 110 TFEU makes a distinction between similar products and products in competition. Under Article 110(1) TFEU any tax which discriminates directly or indirectly against an imported product which is similar to a domestic product is prohibited. If such discrimination occurs, a Member State must equalise the taxes. Article 110(2) TFEU condemns any fiscal protectionism on the part of a Member State in a situation where an imported product is in competition with a domestic product. If a breach of Article 110(2) occurs, a Member State is required to remove any protectionist element incorporated into the tax – this does not always lead to the imposition of the same amounts of tax on competing domestic and imported products.

19.2 Article 110(1) TFEU: the meaning of similar products

Article 110(1) TFEU prohibits the imposition of a higher rate of taxation on imported products than on similar domestic products. In this context it is necessary to define the concept of similarity. In Case 168/78 *Commission v France*,[1467] the ECJ emphasised that similarity should be assessed widely on the ground of analogy and comparability of uses rather than strict identity. Two criteria are applied in order to determine similarity:

- The first criterion refers to the objective characteristics of domestic and imported products. In Case 243/84 *John Walker*,[1468] the ECJ had to decide whether whisky and fruit liqueur wines were similar products. The ECJ specified the objective characteristics as relating to origin, production and organoleptic qualities, in particular the taste and alcohol content of these products. In both products the same raw material – alcohol – was found, but its content in whisky was twice that in liqueur wines. Further, the production and organoleptic qualities were very different. For these reasons the Court held that they were not similar products within the meaning of Article 110 TFEU.

- The second criterion is that if it is shown that domestic and imported products share the same objective characteristics, their similarity must be determined from the point of view of consumers. In Case 45/75 *Rewe-Zentrale*,[1469] the ECJ held that products are similar from the point of view of consumers if they are considered by them as having similar characteristics and meeting the same needs. The assessment of similarity is normally based on the Small but Significant and

---

1466. Case 57/65 *Lütticke GmbH v Hauptzollamt* [1966] ECR 205, see also Case 10/65 *Deutschmann v Germany* [1965] ECR 469.
1467. [1980] ECR 347.
1468. Case 243/84 *John Walker & Sons Ltd v Ministeriet for Skatter og Afgifter* [1986] ECR 875.
1469. Case 45/75 *Rewe-Zentrale des Lebensmittel-Großhandels GmbH v Hauptzollamt Landau/Pfalz* [1976] ECR 181.

Non-transitory Increase in Price test (the SSNIP test (see Chapter 28.3.1.1.1), according to which if a substantial number of consumers are likely to switch to an imported product if the price for the domestic product increases by 5 to 10 per cent (this is a small but significant increase) the imported product and domestic product are regarded as similar products, i.e. the imported product is a substitute of a domestic product from the point of view of consumers.

In Case 106/84 *Commission v Denmark*,[1470] the ECJ applied both criteria in respect of wine made from the grape and wine made from other fruits. They share the same objective characteristics as both are made from agricultural products, have the same alcohol content and are produced by means of the same process of fermentation. Also from the point of view of consumers they satisfy the same needs as they are highly substitutable. The ECJ held that wines made from the grape and wines made from other fruits were similar products.

19.3 Direct, indirect and reverse discrimination

Three types of discrimination can be identified. These are dealt with below.

19.3.1 Direct discrimination

Direct discrimination based on nationality of a product is easy to spot. For that reason there are only a limited number of cases in which the ECJ has dealt with direct discrimination against imported products. It happened, however, in Case 57/65 *Lütticke*,[1471] in which Lütticke imported whole milk powder from Luxembourg, on which German customs levied duty and a turnover tax. Lütticke challenged the claim for payment of turnover tax on the ground that domestic natural milk and whole milk powder were exempt from it. The ECJ condemned the German tax.

The ECJ insists on equal treatment of domestic and imported products, even though in some instances an internal tax may be beneficial to most importers and disadvantageous only to a few of them. This is illustrated in Case 127/75 *Bobie Getränkevertrieb*.[1472]

THE FACTS WERE:

German legislation on beer provided for a rate of taxation for domestic beer, which rate increased in proportion to the output of the various breweries (from DM12 to DM15 per hectolitre) and for a different rate of taxation for imported beer, which was taxed at a flat rate (DM14.40 per hectolitre). The objective of the variable domestic rate was to ensure the survival of small German breweries. A large brewer importing beer from another Member State was better off as compared to a large German brewer, as the former paid DM0.60 less per hectolitre of beer. However, a small brewer importing beer from another Member State was at a disadvantage as compared to a German brewer of a similar size, being taxed at DM14.40 rather than DM12 per hectolitre.

1470. [1986] ECR 833.
1471. Case 57/65 *Alfons Lütticke GmbH v Hauptzollamt Sarrelouis* [1966] ECR 205.
1472. Case 127/75 *Bobie Getränkevertrieb v Hauptzollamt Aachen-Nord* [1976] ECR 1079.

Held:

The ECJ held that the German legislation on the taxation of beer was in breach of Article 110 TFEU. The Court rejected the argument of Germany that the overall effect of a national taxation system should be taken into consideration. The ECJ emphasised that any discrimination is incompatible with Article 110 TFEU and thus two different systems of taxation, one which applies to domestic products and another which deals with similar imported products, cannot be justified. Despite the fact that the tax system applied to imported products ensured broad equivalence, it nevertheless, in some cases, placed importers at a comparative disadvantage. The Court stated that a Member State must choose a system, whichever it considers the most appropriate, in respect of all similar taxed products. In this case the German Bundesfinanzhof rejected the argument of the claimant that all imported beer should be taxed at a flat rate of DM12 per hectolitre. It stated that the variable rate should be upheld but applied indiscriminately to all domestic and imported beer.

Article 110 TFEU ensures that if treatment that would otherwise be preferential is given to domestic products, it must be extended to similar imported products. This issue was examined in Case 21/79 *Commission v Italy [Re Regenerated Oil].*[1473]

THE FACTS WERE:

Italy levied lower charges on regenerated oil than on ordinary oil on the grounds of protection of the environment, except that this advantage was not available to imported regenerated oil. Italy justified this on the basis that it was impossible to distinguish, by means of the then experimental testing methods, whether imported oil was of primary distillation or regenerated. Italy argued that taking into account the very high production costs of regenerated oils as compared to oils of primary distillation and the impossibility of distinguishing them, many importers would claim improperly the benefit of the lower tax rates and thus avoid paying the higher rates of tax imposed on ordinary oils. This would lead to tax evasion in respect of imported products.

Held:

The ECJ held that imported products should not, in any way, be prevented from obtaining the same tax advantages as products produced in Italy. It was for the importers who wished to enjoy the lower tax rate to prove that the oils imported were regenerated. Although the Italian authorities were entitled to require some evidence that removed the risk of tax evasion, they could not set standards of proof higher than necessary. The ECJ held that, for example, certificates issued by appropriate authorities of the exporting Member State should provide sufficient evidence.

1473. Case 21/79 [1980] ECR 1, see also Case 148/77 *Hansen v Hauptzollampt Flensburg* [1978] ECR 1787 and Case 26/80 *Schneider-Import* [1980] ECR 3469.

In Case 28/67 *Firma Molkerei*[1474] the ECJ held that the tax imposed on similar products must take into account the stage of development or construction at which the product is imported. Thus a Member State, when deciding upon the rate of taxation in respect of an imported product, must take into consideration all taxes levied on domestic products at earlier stages of their production, including taxes levied on raw materials and semi-finished products. However, the ECJ emphasised that the importance of these taxes diminishes proportionally as the previous stages of production and distribution become more remote.

Discriminatory conditions attached to the application of a tax are in breach of Article 110 TFEU. In Case 55/79 *Commission v Ireland*,[1475] the ECJ held that a tax which was applied without distinction to both imported and domestic products according to the same criteria, but which provided for several weeks' grace in paying the amount due for domestic producers while requiring importers to pay it immediately on importation, was directly discriminatory and thus in breach of Article 110 TFEU.

In Case 15/81 *Schul*,[1476] the ECJ condemned a Member State for imposing its VAT without taking into consideration the residual part of VAT which was incorporated in the value of the product at the time of importation and already paid in the exporting Member State.

In Case 299/86 *Drexl*,[1477] the ECJ condemned a national law that imposed more severe penalties on undertakings in breach of VAT regulations on imported products than on undertakings in breach of VAT regulations on domestic products.

19.3.2 Indirect discrimination

Direct discriminatory taxation is easy to detect in the light of the strict prohibition embodied in Article 110 TFEU. As a result, Member States have tended to try to conceal by subtle means discriminatory internal taxes imposed on imported products. This was examined in Case 112/84 *Humblot*.[1478]

THE FACTS WERE:

Under French law annual tax on cars differentiated between cars below 16 hp (horse power) (the tax rate was progressively increased up to a maximum of FF1,100) and above 16 hp (a flat rate tax of FF5,000 was applied). France did not manufacture cars above 16 hp. Consequently, all French-made cars were subject to a maximum tax of FF1,100 but all imported cars more powerful than 16 hp were subject to a higher tax. Humblot, who bought a Mercedes in France, challenged the French law.

Held:

The ECJ held that the French law was in breach of Article 110 TFEU as it was discriminatory in respect of cars imported from other Member States. It indirectly discriminated against imported cars, although there was no formal distinction between imported and domestic cars.

1474. Case 28/67 *Firma Molkerei-Zentrale Westfalen/Lippe GmbH v Hauptzollamt Paderborn* [1968] ECR 143.
1475. [1980] ECR 481.
1476. Case 15/81 *Gaston Schul Douane Expediteur BV v Inspecteur der Invoerrechten en Accijnzen, Roosendaal* [1982] ECR 1409 and 47/84 *Staatssecretaris van Financiën v Gaston Schul Douane-Expediteur BV* [1985] ECR 1491.
1477. Case 299/86 *Criminal Proceedings against Rainer Drexl* [1988] ECR 1213.
1478. Case 112/84 *Humblot v Directeur des Services Fiscaux* [1985] ECR 1367.

Both the rate of direct and indirect internal taxation on domestic and imported products and also the basis of assessment and rules regarding the imposition of the tax are important in determining whether there is a breach of Article 110 TFEU. This is exemplified by Case C-375/95 *Commission v Greece*.[1479]

THE FACTS WERE:

The Commission brought proceedings against Greece for introducing and maintaining in force the following national rules contrary to Article 110 TFEU:

Article 1 of Greek Law 363/1976 as amended by Law No 1676/1986 related to a special consumer tax applicable to imported used cars, under which in the assessment of their taxable value only 5 per cent reduction of the price of equivalent new cars was permitted for each year of age of the used cars and the maximum reduction was fixed at 20 per cent of the value of equivalent new cars;

Article 3(1) of Law No 363/1976, which was replaced by Article 2(7) of Law 2187/1994, concerning the determination of the taxable value of cars in order to levy the flat-rate tax, added a special duty which contained no reduction for used cars; and,

Article 1 of Law No 1858/1989 as amended many times regarding the reduction of a special consumer tax for anti-pollution technology cars applied only to new cars and not to imported used cars with the same technology.

The Commission stated that the Greek Government was in breach of Article 110 TFEU since the above-mentioned legislation created a system of internal taxation that indirectly discriminated against used cars imported from other Member States in comparison with used cars bought in Greece.

Held:

The ECJ held that the national rules for calculating special consumer tax and flat-rate added duty in order to determine the taxable value of imported used cars were in breach of Article 110 TFEU.

The special consumer tax applicable only to imported used cars was in breach of Article 110 TFEU. The ECJ rejected the argument submitted by Greece that the special consumer tax was also applied to domestic used cars when they were first purchased within the country, and that part of it remained incorporated in the value of those cars. The ECJ emphasised that the special consumer tax on imported used cars was usually higher than the proportion of the tax still incorporated in the value of used cars already registered and purchased on the Greek market, taking into account that the annual depreciation in the value of cars is considerably more than 5 per cent, that depreciation is not linear, especially in the first years when it is much more marked than subsequently, and, finally, that vehicles continue to depreciate more than four years after being put into circulation.

The ECJ condemned the special consumer tax for anti-pollution technology cars, which was applied only to new cars and not to imported used cars with the same technology, as being in breach of Article 110 TFEU.

1479. [1997] ECR I-5981.

Following the above case, the ECJ has dealt with many cases concerning discriminatory taxes imposed on second-hand cars imported from other Member States. Member States which joined the EU on and after 1 May 2004 have often faced this "old problem".[1480]

In Case C-387/01 *Weigel*,[1481] the ECJ confirmed that a national tax system that is liable to eliminate a competitive advantage held by imported products over domestic products would breach Article 110 TFEU.

THE FACTS WERE:

Mr and Mrs Weigel, both German nationals, changed their residence from Germany to Austria subsequent to the appointment of Mr Weigel as director of the Vorarlberger Landesbibliothek (Public Library) in Austria). Each spouse imported a car into Austria as personal property. In Austria they were required to register their cars and subsequently to pay the Austrian fuel consumption tax, which comprised the NoVA tax (the standard fuel consumption tax) and the NoVA surcharge tax (which represented a surchage equal to 20 per cent of the NoVA tax). Both were imposed at first-time registration of a motor vehicle in Austria, but in different circumstances: the NoVA tax was a standard fuel consumption tax; the NoVA surchage tax was applied to new and used imported cars and only exceptionally to domestic cars, e.g. when a car had been privately assembled by an enthusiast. Mr and Mrs Weigel jointly challenged the imposition of both.

Held:

The ECJ held that the NoVA tax was manifestly of a fiscal nature and as such should be assessed in the light of Article 110 TFEU. The Court, relying on its previous case law regarding the taxation of imported cars, found that the NoVA tax was imposed without making any distinction between imported used cars and used cars bought in Austria.[1482] Both were subjected to the same tax. Thus, the NoVA tax was not in breach of Article 110 TFEU.

The NoVA surchargeTax was in breach of Article 110 TFEU because it imposed a heavier tax burden on imported products than on domestic products. This tax was applied to imported used cars but never to second-hand domestic cars and only in exceptional circumstances to new domestic cars registered for the first time in Austria (for example, in respect of a car privately assembled by an enthusiast). The actual objective of the tax, as the ECJ pointed out, was to eliminate a competitive advantage held by imported products over domestic products rather than to prevent the distortion of competition as claimed by the Austrian government.

19.3.3 Reverse discrimination

It is extremely rare that a Member State imposes higher taxes on domestic goods intended for export than on identical or similar domestic goods. This may, for example, occur if a Member

---

1480. Joined Cases C-290/05 and C-333/05 *Nádasdi and Németh v Vám- és Pénzügyörség Dél-Alföldi Regionális Parancsnoksága* [2006] ECR I-10115; Case C-313/05 *Brzezinski v Dyrektor Izby Celnej w Warszawie* [2007] ECR I-513.
1481. Case C-387/01 *Harald Weigel and Ingrid Weigel v Finanzlandesdirektion für Vorarlberg* [2004] ECR I-4981.
1482. Case C-375/95 *Commission v Greece* [1997] ECR I-5981 and Case C-393/98 *Ministério Público and António Gomes Valente v Fazenda Pública* [2001] ECR I-1327.

State wishes to encourage retention of a rare natural national resource,[1483] and there are other possible circumstances.

In Case C-234/99 *Nygård*,[1484] the ECJ clearly stated, for the first time, that Article 110 TFEU applies to discriminatory taxes imposed on domestic goods for export.

THE FACTS WERE:

Under Danish law a production levy was charged for every pig bred and slaughtered in Denmark, irrespective of whether it was intended for the domestic market or for export. The same levy was also charged for every pig bred in Denmark and exported live. A part of the revenue generated by the levy was allocated to the financing of the production of pigs in Denmark and so benefited those exporting pigs. The remainder of the revenue generated by the levy was allocated to the financing of the slaughtering of pigs and of the processing of pig meat in Denmark and its sale on the domestic and export markets, and so did not bring any benefit to exporters of pigs. The levy scheme was, pursuant to Article 108(3) TFEU, notified and approved by the Commission as being lawful State aid.

Mr Nygård, a pig breeder established in Denmark, exported to Germany live pigs intended for slaughter between 1 August 1992 and 1 July 1993. Under German law he was required to pay a production levy in Germany for each pig supplied to the abattoirs. He paid the German production levy, but refused to pay the Danish production levy. The Danish Levy Fund commenced proceedings against Mr Nygård before the District Court in Skjern (Denmark). The Danish Court ordered Mr Nygård to pay the full amount of the Danish production levy in respect of the exported pigs, and interest. Mr Nygård appealed to the Vestre Landsret from the judgment of the District Court arguing, among other things, that the levy constituted discriminatory taxation prohibited under Article 110 TFEU. The Vestre Landsret referred the matter to the ECJ.

Held:

The ECJ held that the levy in question may be classified as discriminatory internal taxation prohibited by Article 110 TFEU if and to the extent to which the advantages deriving from the use made of its revenue compensate in part the charge imposed on pigs produced for slaughter in the Member State concerned, thereby placing at a disadvantage the production of pigs for live export to other Member State.

Comment:

The important aspect of this case is that the ECJ extended the application of Article 110 TFEU to discriminatory taxation imposed on exported products. This is despite the clear wording of Article 110 TFEU which states that Member States are prohibited from imposing discriminatory taxation "on the products of other Member States". The ECJ provided no justification for this broad interpretation of Article 110 TFEU. In paragraph 41 of the judgment the ECJ made a categorical statement on this matter. It said that Article 110 TFEU

1483. Case 142/77 *Statens Kontrol med ædle Metaller v Preben Larsen; Flemming Kjerulff v Statens Kontrol med ædle Metaller* [1978] ECR 1543.
1484. Case C-234/99 *Niels Nygård v Svineafgifsfonden, and Ministeriet for Fødevarer, Landbrug og Fiskeri* [2002] ECR I-3657, see also Case C-517/04 *Visserijbedrijf D.J.Koornstra & Zn vof v Productschap Vis* [2006] ECR I-5015.

> "must be interpreted as also prohibiting any tax discrimination against products intended for export to other Member States", and referred to Case 142/77 Larsen et Kjerulff,[1485] which contained a similar statement.
>
> One explanation of the broad interpretation of Article 110 TFEU may be that Article 110 TFEU should be interpreted as a complementary provision to Article 30 TFEU and therefore should seek to:
>
> > "fill in any breaches which a fiscal measure might open in the prohibitions laid down, by prohibiting the imposition on imported products of internal taxation in excess of that imposed on domestic products."[1486]
>
> Notwithstanding this, it remains that the ECJ's teleological interpretation of Article 110 TFEU, that is, based on the objective of the achievement of the internal market, is very far away from the literal interpretation of Article 110 TFEU.

The neutrality of the internal taxation system is not challenged when lower taxes are imposed on goods for export than on other domestic goods since it does not create an obstacle to the free movement of goods. Only domestic goods destined for the home market are affected.

19.3.4 Objective justification

Differential taxation of products, which may serve the same economic ends, is not prohibited under Article 110 TFEU in so far as it is justified on the basis of objective criteria. However, direct discrimination based on the nationality of the product can never be objectively justified. This kind of discrimination can only be justified on the grounds of a derogation set out in the Treaties.

In Case C-375/95 *Commission v Greece*[1487] (see Chapter 19.3.2), the ECJ held that national rules granting tax advantages (that is, reducing the special consumer tax) which applied only to new anti-pollution technology cars and not to imported second-hand cars with the same technology, could not be objectively justified under Article 110 TFEU. A Member State cannot confer tax advantages on low emission cars produced locally while refusing those advantages to cars satisfying the same criteria from other Member States without offending against the prohibition on discrimination laid down in Article 110 TFEU. Therefore, the imported used cars were discriminated against on the ground of nationality. This is always unlawful. Differential taxation where the criterion for charging a higher rate is the importation itself and where domestic goods are by definition excluded from the heavier taxation is always in breach of Article 110 TFEU.

Indirect discrimination, even if it results in discrimination against imported products, may be justified if it is based on objective criteria. The ECJ has taken a liberal approach in respect of these criteria. They may be based on the nature of the use of the raw materials, the processes employed in the production or manufacturing of goods, or they may refer to general objectives of economic and social policy of a Member State such as the protection of the environment or the development of regional

---

1485. Case 142/77 *Statens Kontrol med ædle Metaller v Preben Larsen; Flemming Kjerulff v Statens Kontrol med ædle Metaller* [1978] ECR 1543.

1486. Cases 2–3/69 *Sociaal Fonds v Brachfeld and Chougol Diamond Co* [1969] ECR 211.

1487. [1997] ECR I-5981.

policy, so far as those policies are compatible with EU law. The leading case on this topic is Case 196/85 *Commission v France*.[1488]

THE FACTS WERE:

France levied lower taxes on sweet wines produced in a traditional and customary fashion in certain regions of France than on imported liqueur wines (also sweet). The tax differentiation was not directly discriminatory as all similar wines, irrespective of the country of origin, could qualify for the lower rate of taxation. It was for France to justify the indirect discrimination. In this respect France showed that natural sweet wines were produced in areas of low rainfall and poor soil, whose economy depended on wine production. France argued that its regional policy was to encourage production in poor growing areas and thus develop those regions, and that this tax concession was open to all EU producers.

Held:

The ECJ accepted that a lower taxation levy on French sweet wines was objectively justified.

Comment:

The main reason why the ECJ accepted the justification submitted by the French government was that the concession offered to French producers of sweet wine was open to importers. Therefore there was no direct discrimination. If importers could show that they were in similar circumstances to French producers their sweet wine could qualify for the lower rate of taxation. The indirectly discriminatory effect of the French tax scheme was incidental and overridden by the scheme's lawful function.[1489]

In Case 132/88 *Commission v Greece*,[1490] the ECJ held that a Greek system of progressive taxation on cars, even though in practice it had discriminatory effect on imported cars, was not in breach of Article 110 TFEU. Greece justified its taxation scheme on the ground of poor road infrastructure and a problem with pollution. The ECJ held that although the scheme discouraged certain consumers from purchasing cars above 1880 cc which paid the highest tax and were of foreign manufacture, the next taxable category concerned cars between 1600 to 1800 cc which were of both foreign and Greek manufacture. The ECJ held that the Greek system did not have the effect of favouring the sale of cars of Greek manufacture. This was not the case in *Humblot*, in which the effect of the indirectly discriminatory tax was to discriminate against cars imported from other Member States.

The case law shows that what matters is the motive behind indirectly discriminatory tax. If the motive is accepted by the ECJ then a tax scheme, even though it indirectly favours domestic products, will be lawful.[1491] However, a Member State must not only submit a sound motive for an indirectly discriminatory tax scheme but also show that it has used appropriate means to achieve the objective

---

1488. [1987] ECR 1597.

1489. See J. Schwarze, "The Member States' Discretionary Powers under the Tax Provisions of the EEC Treaty", in J. Schwarze (ed.), *Discretionary Powers of the Member States in the Field of Economic Policies and Their Limits under the EEC Treaty*, 1988, Baden-Baden: Nomos, 147–48.

1490. [1990] ECR I-1567.

1491. M. Danusso and R. Dention, "Does the European Court of Justice Look for a Protectionist Motive under Article 95 [Article 110 TFEU]?", (1990) 1 LIEI, 67.

sought. Accordingly, an indirectly discriminatory tax scheme must satisfy the requirements of the principle of proportionality.

The list of objective justifications is rather vague and open-ended, but not inconsistent with justifications allowed in other areas of free movement.

19.4 Article 110(2) TFEU: the meaning of products in competition

The concept of "products in competition" is wider than the concept of "similar products". In Case 170/78 *Commission v UK (Re Tax on Beer and Wine)*,[1492] the ECJ explained the scope of the application of Article 110(2) TFEU in respect of "products in competition". It was one of many so-called "spirit cases".

THE FACTS WERE:

The UK maintained different levels of internal taxation for beer (£0.61 per gallon) and wine (£3.25 per gallon). Wine was mostly imported while beer was predominantly a domestic product. The Commission decided that this tax difference amounted to discrimination against imported wine and that by increasing the tax on wine, the British Government was encouraging consumers to buy beer. The UK argued that the two products were not interchangeable and therefore there was no breach of Article 110 TFEU.

Held:

The ECJ held that in order to determine the existence of a competitive relationship, it is necessary to take into account not only the present state of the market but also "possible developments regarding the free movement of goods within the Community and the further potential for substitution of products for one another which might be revealed by intensification of trade."[1493]

The ECJ stated that wine and beer were, to a certain extent, substitutable as they were capable of meeting the same needs of consumers. To measure the degree of substitutability, consumers' habits in a Member State, or in a particular region, should be taken into account, although these habits should not be regarded as immutable. Indeed, the tax policy of a Member State should not crystallise consumers' habits and thus consolidate an advantage gained by domestic producers. The Italian Government submitted that it was appropriate to compare beer with the most popular, lightest and cheapest wine because those products were in real competition. The ECJ agreed and held that the decisive competitive relationship between beer and wine must be established by reference to the lightest and cheapest wine. Those products were in competition. Consequently, the ECJ found the UK in breach of Article 110(2) TFEU.

Comment:

Following the decision of the ECJ the UK removed the unlawful element of protection by adjusting tax rates for beer upwards and for wine downwards, but different rates still applied.

1492. [1983] ECR 2265. On this topic see: A. Easson, "The Spirits, Wine and Beer Judgments: A Legal Mickey Finn?", (1980) 5 ELRev., 318, and "Cheaper Wine or Dearer Beer?" (1984) 9 ELRev., 57.
1493. Ibid, para. 6.

This case and many others show that often there is not only a potential market for an imported product competing with a domestic product, but also that while such a market may exist, it is often suppressed by an unfair tax system.

Case C-167/05 *Commission v Sweden*[1494] illustrates the stages which the ECJ follows in the application of Article 110(2) TFEU.

THE FACTS WERE:

The Commission brought proceedings against Sweden for breach of Article 110(2) TFEU on the basis that by applying a system of internal taxes under which strong beer (in excess of 3.5 per cent alcohol per volume), which was mainly produced in Sweden, was indirectly protected, as compared with the lightest, least expensive and the most popular wine (around 11 per cent alcohol per volume) mainly imported from other Member States. When Sweden acceded to the EU its excise duty on strong beer and light wine was almost identical. In 1997 Sweden reduced excise duty on beer by 40 per cent to respond to the substantial increase in cross-border trade in beer between Sweden and Denmark. Following the Commission's investigation, in 2001, Sweden reduced excise duty on wine by 18.8 per cent per volume. According to the Commission despite the reduction in excise duty on wine, it was subject to higher excise duty than beer by more than 20 per cent, and the Swedish tax system in respect of beer was therefore protectionist.

Held:

The ECJ held that the difference in the tax treatment of beer and wine was not such as to afford indirect protection to Swedish beer. This was because, first, the difference between the selling prices of a litre of strong beer and a litre of wine was virtually the same before and after taxation, and second, the Commission did not submit any statistical information showing that variations in the price of those products were likely to bring long-term changes in consumer habits in favour of wine and to the detriment of beer. The ECJ emphasised that certain sensitivity on the part of consumers to short-term changes in the prices of products in competition was not sufficient to evidence that the difference in the tax treatment of those products was liable to influence consumer behaviour.

Comment:

The ECJ followed three stages in order to establish whether Sweden was in breach of Article 110(2) TFEU. These were:

- *First, the ECJ had to establish a competitive relationship between an imported product and a domestic product. In conformity with the case law of the ECJ an imported product and a domestic product are in such a relationship if they are substitutable, i.e. they are capable of meeting the same needs of consumers. This is established on the basis of the SSNIP test. In this case, the ECJ agreed with the Commission and Sweden that lighter and less expensive wines (appox. 11 per cent alcohol per volume) were comparable to beer having alcohol strength of around 5 per cent per volume.*

1494. [2008] ECR I-2127.

■ Second, The ECJ examined the tax arrangements for each product in order to identify differences between the tax burden in terms of price, alcohol content and volume. In respect of products in competition this is not difficult given that they are dissimilar and therefore subject to different tax arrangements. In the commented case, the ECJ found that the alcohol strength by volume of the beverage, a factor used by the Swedish authorities for the basis of assessment of excise duty, was the most pertinent criterion. On this basis the ECJ decided that wine which was in competition with strong beer was subject to higher taxation than strong beer. In this respect the ECJ stated that: ".., it emerges from a comparison of the levels of taxation in relation to alcoholic strength that a wine with an alcoholic strength of 12.5% vol., which is in competition with strong beer, is subject to taxation per percentage of alcohol by volume which exceeds by approximately 20% per litre the taxation on strong beer (SEK 1.77 as against SEK 1.47), and that that difference increases to 36% in the case of a wine with an alcoholic strength of 11% vol. (SEK 2 as against SEK 1.47) and to 50% in the case of a wine with an alcoholic strength of 10% vol. (SEK 2.208 as against SEK 1.47)".[1495]

■ Third, once the ECJ found that there were differences in tax arrangements between light wine and strong beer, it examined the alleged protectionist consequences deriving from these differences. In accordance with the case law of the ECJ, not only the direct and actual, but also the indirect and potential protectionist effect is taken into account. In order to assess the alleged protectionist effect, the ECJ examined the impact of taxation by reference to the difference between the final selling prices of the products and the impact of that difference on consumers' choice, both at the level of an individual consumer and the collective tendencies of consumers. In respect of the impact of price difference on a choice of an individual consumer the ECJ considered the final selling prices of a litre of strong beer and a litre of wine which were in competition with each other, and compared the relationship between them with the relationship that would apply if the tax rates applied to beer were applied to wine. The ECJ found that the relationship between final selling prices of beer and wine was one, to two point one (1:2.1), and then found that this ratio was not high enough to change the attitude of an individual consumer. With regard to collective consumer tendencies the ECJ found that the Commission had failed to prove a long-term change in consumer habits in favour of beer. In this respect the Commission had submitted inconclusive evidence[1496] which according to the ECJ showed a certain sensitivity of Swedish consumers to prices, but not long-term changes in consumer habits.

1495. Ibid, para. 50.

1496. The Commission relied on statistical data produced by Systembolaget (a Swedish undertaking which has a monopoly on sales of alcoholic beverages in Sweden) showing that at the time of accession of Sweden to the EU the sales volumes of beer and wine in Sweden were relatively similar to each other and that, after the reduction by 40 per cent of the excise duty on beer, sales of wine dropped by 3.7 per cent, whilst sales of beer rose by 8.9 per cent. After the reduction in 2001, sales of wine increased by 11 per cent, which was the highest increase between 1995 and 2004. However, the data also showed that alongside that increase in wine sales, sales of beer increased by a much higher percentage.

19.5 Unique products

It may occur that an imported product is unique in the sense that there is neither a similar domestic product nor any domestic product in competition with the imported product.

In Case 193/79 *Cofruta*,[1497] Italy claimed that bananas were such unique products.

THE FACTS WERE:

Italy imposed a high tax on fresh bananas. Italy is not considered to be a producer of bananas (its production is so insignificant that it was not taken into consideration). Accordingly, the Italian Government argued that bananas were neither similar to nor in competition with any domestic product.

Held:

On the grounds that a consumption tax was imposed on other exotic products such as coffee, cacao, and so on, in order to raise revenue for the State, the ECJ decided that fresh bananas formed part of a broader Italian taxation system which was based on objective criteria unconnected with the origin of the product. The ECJ considered that fresh bananas were, nevertheless, in competition with other table fruits grown in Italy e.g. apples, oranges, peaches . Taking into account the high tax imposed on bananas as compared to other table fruits, the ECJ concluded that Italy indirectly protected domestic table fruits by setting such a high rate of taxation on fresh bananas. Consequently, Italy was held in breach of Article 110(2) TFEU.

Comment:

In contrast, in Case 184/85 Commission v Italy,[1498] Italy was not in breach of Article 110(2) TFEU in respect of a tax imposed on dried bananas and banana meals. The ECJ held that dried bananas and banana meals were not in competition with fresh table fruits.

Where there are no competing national products a tax imposed by a Member State on imported unique products is outside the scope of Article 110 TFEU, but may be caught by Article 34 TFEU,[1499] which prohibits quotas and equivalent restrictions on trade between Member States (see Chapter 20). This situation occurred in Case C-383/01 *De Danske*[1500] in which the ECJ, for the first time, had an opportunity to condemn a tax in the light of Article 34 TFEU, but declined to do so.

THE FACTS WERE:

De Danske, a Danish association of car importers, purchased a new Audi vehicle for a total price of €67,152, including €40,066 in registration duty. De Danske paid the duty but subsequently requested repayment from the Danish tax authorities. It argued that the

---

1497. Case 193/79 *Cooperativa Cofruta v Amministrazione delle Finanzo dello Stato* [1987] ECR 2085.

1498. [1987] ECR 2013.

1499. Case C-47/88 *Commission v Denmark* [1990] ECR I-4509.

1500. Case C-383/01 *De Danske Bilimportører v Skatteministeriet, Told-og Skattestyrelsen* [2003] ECR I-6065.

excessive level of the registration duty made it impossible to import motor vehicles to Denmark under normal commercial conditions, and that the duty was imposed to benefit domestic purchasers of previously registered used vehicles, which according to Danish law are regarded as Danish products and therefore exempt from registration duty.

The Danish tax authorities refused any repayment. They argued that as there is no production of motor vehicles in Denmark, they are allowed to impose any amount in respect of registration duty. Further, they stated that the registration duty was not obstructing the free movement of goods given that during the period from 1985 to 2000, the total number of registered vehicles in Denmark rose from 78,453 to 169,492.

Held:

The ECJ held that the Danish registration duty was of a fiscal nature and thus a part of a general system of internal dues on goods. The Court explained that Article 110 TFEU could not be used to censure the excessiveness of the level of taxation adopted by a Member State in circumstances where there were no similar or competing domestic products and the challenged tax had no discriminatory or protective effect. Accordingly, the Danish registration duty imposed on new cars was not caught by the prohibition set out in Article 110 TFEU. Further, based on the high and increasing number of registrations of new cars in Denmark, the ECJ found that the Danish tax was not impeding the free movement of goods and thus should not be classified as a measure having equivalent effect to a quantitative restriction within the meaning of Article 34 TFEU.

The above judgment confirms the ECJ's tendency to shy away from applying Article 34 TFEU to an apparently excessive tax imposed by a Member State in a situation where the product is unique.

Some commentators[1501] submit that the ECJ in Case C-313/05 *Brzezinski*[1502] ruled out the application of Article 34 TFEU to fiscal impositions by stating that: "the scope of that article [Article 34] does not extend to the obstacles to trade covered by other specific provisions and obstacles of a fiscal nature or having an effect equivalent to customs duties".[1503] If this is the case, then there is no way to condemn an excessive tax imposed on a unique product. Such a tax cannot be within the scope of Article 110 TFEU. Indeed, if a tax is neither discriminatory nor protectionist, as was the case in *De Danske*, how can a Member State breach Article 110 TFEU? On what grounds can such a tax be declared as unlawful? It is also submitted that the broad interpretation of Article 110(2) TFEU entails that even if there is no national production the concept of "product in competition" is broad enough to ensure that most products coming from other Member States will be in indirect or potential competition with national products.

1501.   C. Barnard, *The Substantive Law of the EU*, 3rd edn, 2010, Oxford: OUP, 66.

1502.   Case C-313/05 *Brzezinski v Dyrektor Izby Celnej w Warszawie* [2007] ECR I-513 [2007] ECR I-513.

1503.   Ibid, para. 50.

19.6 The relationship between Article 110 TFEU and other provisions of the TFEU relating to the free movement of goods

19.6.1 The relationship between Articles 110 and 30 TFEU

The connection between Article 110 TFEU and Article 30 TFEU is very close, given that Article 110 TFEU supplements the provisions of the Treaties on the abolition of customs duties and charges having equivalent effect. However, Articles 30 and 110 TFEU operate at different levels.

Article 30 TFEU aims at ensuring that fiscal impediments are eliminated when products of Member States cross each others' national borders, while the purpose of Article 110 TFEU is to make sure that, whatever the internal tax system of a Member State, it neither discriminates directly or indirectly against products from other Member States nor protects national products. A fiscal charge is either a customs duty or a CEE or part of a general system of internal taxation. For that reason Article 110 and Article 30 TFEU are complementary, yet mutually exclusive.[1504] So, an imposition cannot, at the same time, be contrary to both Article 30 and Article 110 TFEU. Although in many cases it is difficult to distinguish between CEEs and discriminatory internal taxation, there are some helpful clues which may render it less difficult. These are set out below:

- The determination of whether a charge is imposed only on imported products or on both domestic and imported products. If a fiscal charge is imposed exclusively on imported products, it is likely to be a CEE. If it is levied on both domestic and imported products, it is more likely to be part of internal taxation;

- Definitions provided by the ECJ of a CEE and of a tax:
  - The ECJ defined a charge having equivalent effect to a customs duty as encompassing any pecuniary charge, however small and whatever its designation and mode of application, that is imposed unilaterally on domestic or imported goods by reason of the fact that they cross a frontier;[1505]
  - In Case 90/79 *Commission v France (Re Levy on Reprographic Machines)*,[1506] the ECJ held that a genuine tax is a measure relating to a system of internal dues applied systematically to categories of products in accordance with objective criteria irrespective of the origin of the products. Therefore, if a charge is part of internal taxation and is based on criteria that are objectively justified by the nature of the products, their quality or their function, rather than the fact of crossing a national border, it will be considered under Article 110 TFEU;

- The destination of the proceeds of the charge. In Case 77/76 *Fratelli Cucchi*[1507] the ECJ stated that if a charge is imposed on both domestic and imported products but:
  - (i) has the sole purpose of providing financial support for the specific advantage of domestic products;

1504. Case 10/65 *Deutschmann v Germany* [1965] ECR 469; Case 57/65 *Alfons Lütticke GmbH v Hauptzollamt Sarrelouis* [1966] ECR 205; Case C-90/94 *Haahr Petroleum* [1977] ECR I-4085; Case C-234/99 *Nygård* [2002] ECR I-3657; Case C-387/01 *Weigel* [2004] ECR I-4981.

1505. Case 46/76 *Bauhuis v Netherlands* [1977] ECR 5; Case 132/78 *Denkavit v France* [1979] ECR 1923; Case 18/87 *Commission v Germany* [1988] ECR 5427; Case 340/87 *Commission v Italy* [1989] ECR 1483; Case C-130/93 *Lamaire NV v Nationale Dienst voor Afzet van Land- en Tuinbouwproducten* [1994] ECR I-3215.

1506. [1981] ECR 283.

1507. 77/76 *Fratelli Cucchi v Avez* [1977] ECR 987.

(ii) the domestic taxed products and the benefiting domestic products are the same; and,

(iii) the charge imposed on the domestic products is made good in full to domestic producers;

that charge is to be considered as a CEE under Article 30 TFEU. However, with regard to the third criterion, if the charge is only partially made good, it is not purely a customs duty or CEE and so the charge comes under Article 110 TFEU, and as such is prohibited in so far as it discriminates against the imported products or affords protection to domestic products. In Case C-266/91 *Celbi*,[1508] the ECJ held that if the revenue from such a charge is used only partially to provide advantages to domestic products, the charge will constitute discriminatory taxation contrary to Article 110 TFEU. The ECJ emphasised that "the criterion of the offsetting of the burden on domestic products is to be construed as requiring financial equivalence, to be verified over a reference period, between the total amount of the charge imposed on domestic products and the advantages exclusively benefiting those products;"[1509] and,

■ The event that has triggered the imposition. If the charge is imposed by reason of the product crossing the border of the Member State, that is, it is an import/export, it is an unlawful charge under Article 30 TFEU. Any other operative event indicates that the imposition should be regarded as part of a general system of internal dues on goods and hence should be examined in the light of Article 110 TFEU. For example, in Case C-387/01 *Weigel*,[1510] the referring court had doubts as to whether the tax imposed on Mr and Mrs Weigel constituted a customs duty or a CEE, or discriminatory internal taxation. The Court pointed out that the tax was imposed not just because the vehicle had crossed a border of a Member State, but because the vehicle was required to be registered for the first time in a host Member State. Therefore the tax was manifestly of a fiscal nature and as such should be assessed in the light of Article 110 TFEU.

If a charge is incompatible with Article 110 TFEU, it is prohibited only to the extent to which it discriminates against imported products,[1511] whereas a charge under Article 30 TFEU is unlawful in its entirety.

19.6.2 The relationship between Articles 110 TFEU and 107 TFEU

Article 107 TFEU concerns State aid. In Case 73/79 *Commission v Italy*,[1512] the ECJ held that Article 107 TFEU and Article 110 TFEU are complementary and may be applied cumulatively.

When a charge is applied without discrimination to domestic and imported products but the revenue from it is appropriated wholly to domestic products and thus fully offsets the burden of the charge imposed on them, this may constitute State aid in breach of Article 107 TFEU. It is for the Commission to decide whether that is the case.

1508. Case C-266/91 *Celulose Beira Industrial SA v Fazenda Pública* [1993] ECR I-4337.
1509. Ibid, para. 15.
1510. [2004] ECR I-4981.
1511. Case 68/79 *Hans Just I/S v Danish Ministry for Fiscal Affairs* [1980] ECR 501; Case C-72/92 *Herbert Scharbatke GmbH v Germany* [1993] ECR I-5509.
1512. [1980] ECR 1533.

19.6.3 The relationship between Articles 110 TFEU and 34 TFEU

Article 110 TFEU and Article 34 TFEU are mutually exclusive.[1513] However, subject to the judgment of the ECJ in Case C-313/05 *Brzezinski*,[1514] internal taxes, which are outside the scope of Article 110 TFEU, may be in breach of Article 34 TFEU if the charges levied on imported products are so excessively high as to constitute an obstacle to the free movement of goods.[1515]

19.7 Repayment of unlawful fiscal impositions

Unlawful fiscal impositions, whatever their name, that is, charges, levies, supplementary payments, must be repaid.[1516] Under the principle of autonomy of national procedural rules it is for the domestic legal system of each Member State to lay down procedural rules applicable to actions for recovery of sums unduly paid under Articles 30 and 110 TFEU. Such rules, however, are subject to the principle of equivalence and the principle of effectiveness (see Chapter 12.6).

In accordance with the principle that a person should not be unduly enriched at the expense of another, when a trader has paid an unlawful charge and subsequently passed the cost on to another person, he is not entitled to claim reimbursement from the relevant national authorities.[1517] However, if the charge has been transferred only in part to another party, the trader can still claim reimbursement of the amount not transferred. In Case C-192/95 *Comateb*,[1518] the ECJ made important clarifications in this area. It held:

- First, that even if under national law there is a legal obligation, enforceable by a penalty, to include a charge in the sale price of goods, that is, to pass the charge on to a purchaser, this does not give rise to a presumption that the entire charge has been passed on;

- Second, that the purchaser to whom an unlawful charge is passed on is entitled to claim reimbursement either from the trader or from the relevant national authority. In Case C-94/10 *Danfoss*,[1519] the ECJ provided some clarifications on this matter. It held that the purchaser's first recourse is against the person who has paid the charge to the exchequer, i.e. the taxable person. If the reimbursement by the taxable person were to be impossible or excessively difficult, the purchaser must be able to bring his claim against the tax authority directly. The ECJ gave one example of exceptional circumstances, i.e. a situation where the taxable person becomes insolvent. Also, the ECJ removed one legal impediment relating to a purchaser's claim against a Member State. The ECJ held that a Member State cannot claim that the purchaser has no right to reimbursement because of the lack of a causal connection in that it was the taxable person, not the purchaser, who paid the charge. The Court held that such a defence would be in breach of the principle of effectiveness. Further, it stated that a Member State must ensure that the necessary procedures are put in place to allow a purchaser to bring an action for reimbursement of a charge

---

1513. Case 74/76 *Iannelli & Volpi SpA v Ditta Paolo Meroni* [1977] ECR 557; Cases C-78 to 83/90 *Compagnie Commerciale de l'Ouest and others v Receveur Principal des Douanes de La Pallice Port* [1992] ECR I-1847.
1514. Case C-313/05 *Brzezinski* v *Dyrektor Izby Celnej w Warszawie* [2007] ECR I-513.
1515. Case 47/88 *Commission v Denmark* [1990] ECR I-4509; Case C-383/01 *De Danske Bilimportører v Skatteministeriet, Told- og Skattestyrelsen* [2003] ECR I-6065.
1516. Case 199/82 *Amministrazione delle Finanze dello Stato v SpA San Giorgio* [1983] ECR 3595; Case C-264/08 *Belgium v Direct Parcel Distribution Belgium NV* [2010] ECR I-731; and Case C-398/09 *Lady & Kid A/S and Others v Skatteministeriet* (judgment of 6/9/11(NYR)).
1517. Ibid, Case 199/82 *San Giorgio*.
1518. Case C-192/95 *Société Comateb v Directeur Général des Douanes et Droits Indirects* [1997] ECR I-165.
1519. Case C-94/10 *Danfoss A/S and Sauer-Danfoss ApS v Skatteministeriet* (judgment of 20/10/11 (NYR)).

unduly paid against the Member State. Notwithstanding the above, a potentially heavy evidential burden will be imposed on the purchaser. In addition to the conditions relating to State liability (see Chapter 12.3) he will have to prove that the charge was unlawful, that the taxable person has directly enforceable rights, and that he has not passed the burden of the charge down the supply chain; and,

■ Third, irrespective of whether a trader has passed a charge on to a purchaser, the trader is still entitled to claim damages caused by an unlawful charge. This is particularly so when, as a result of the unlawful charge, the trader's products are more expensive than other similar products so that purchasers are few. Consequently, when the increased price of imported goods results in a reduction of sales, and thus of profits, a Member State may be liable. If domestic law provides for such a remedy, the domestic court must give effect to the trader's claim; if not, the trader can rely on the principle of State liability (see Chapter 12).

RECOMMENDED READING

Books

Barnard, C., *The Substantive Law of the EU. The Four Freedoms*, 3rd edn, 2010, Oxford: OUP.

Davies, G., *European Union Internal Market Law*, 2006, Abingdon: Routledge Cavendish.

Davies, M., *Nationality Discrimination in the European Internal Market*, 2003, The Hague: KIL.

Shuibhne, N. (ed.), *Regulating the Internal Market*, 2006, Cheltenham: Edward Elgar.

Articles

Cordewener, A., Kofler, G., and van Thiel, S., "The Clash between European Freedoms and National Direct Tax Law: Public Interest Defences Available to the Member States", (2009) 46 CMLRev., 1951.

Danusso, M. and Dention, R., "Does the European Court of Justice Look for a Protectionist Motive under Article 95 [Article 90 EC]?", (1990) 1 LIEI, 67.

Easson, A., "Cheaper Wine or Dearer Beer?" (1984) 9 ELRev., 57.

Easson, A., "The Spirits, Wine and Beer Judgments: A Legal Mickey Finn?" (1980) 5 ELRev, 318.

Graetz, M. J., and Warren, Jr., A. C., "Income Tax Discrimination and the Political and Economic Integration of Europe", (2006) 115 Yale L.J., 1186.

Snell, J., "Non-Discriminatory Tax Obstacles in Community Law", (2007) 56 ICLQ, 339.

Schwarze, J., "The Member States' Discretionary Powers under the Tax Provisions of the EEC Treaty", in Schwarze, J. (ed.), *Discretionary Powers of the Member States in the Field of Economic Policies and Their Limits under the EEC Treaty*, 1988, Baden-Baden: Nomos, 147.

PROBLEM QUESTION

Copex GmbH ("Copex"), a German manufacturer of reprographic equipment, has been selling its products in France for two years. Recently it has encountered the following problems:

A.   Under French legislation a levy is charged at the rate of 3 per cent on sales of photocopiers (also known as copy machines) manufactured in France or imported to France. The sums raised by the levy are allocated to the French National Book Fund which uses them to subsidise the publication of quality books in France; the purchase of quality French and foreign books by libraries; and, the translation of quality foreign books into French. Copex states that French production of copy machines is very small compared to the number of such machines imported to France.

B.   Under French legislation a tax of €100 is imposed on every photocopier sold in France that makes colour copies of documents (a colour photocopier), and a tax of €5 is imposed on every photocopier sold in France that makes black and white copies of documents (a black and white photocopier). Colour photocopiers are not manufactured in France. Copex manufactures only colour photocopiers. Assume that the technology used to manufacture colour photocopiers and black and white photocopiers differs greatly.

C.   France imposes a charge of €10 on all imported and exported photocopiers for the purpose of financing statistical services for exporters of photocopiers.

Advise Copex as to its rights under EU law.

ESSAY QUESTION

Critically assess the contribution of the ECJ to the elimination of fiscal barriers to the free movement of goods within the internal market of the EU.

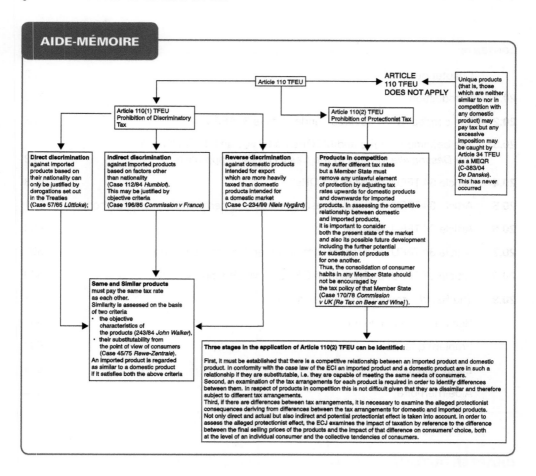

20

PROHIBITION OF QUANTITATIVE RESTRICTIONS (QRs) AND MEASURES HAVING EQUIVALENT EFFECT ON IMPORTS AND EXPORTS (MEQRs) – ARTICLES 34 AND 35 TFEU

CONTENTS

CHAPTER OUTLINE

1. Article 34 TFEU prohibits the imposition of quantitative restrictions (QRs) on imports, and measures having equivalent effect to them (MEQRs) between Member States. Article 35 TFEU extends the prohibitions to exports. These prohibitions are subject to Article 36 TFEU, which sets out derogations on which a Member State may justify national rules contrary to Articles 34 and 35 TFEU, and subject to exceptions developed by the case law of the ECJ, i.e. mandatory requirements (see Chapter 21.3).

2. Article 34 TFEU is addressed to Member States. It applies both to measures taken by a Member State and failures of a Member State to take appropriate measures.

3. The Treaties neither define QRs nor MEQRs. While QRs are easy to define as they refer to classical bans and quotas prohibiting or limiting importation by amount or by volume, MEQRs are more problematic. The ECJ first established the definition of MEQRs in Case 8/74 *Dassonville*. Known as the *Dassonville* formula, it describes MEQRs as any trading rules enacted by Member States which are capable of hindering directly or indirectly, actually or potentially, trade between Member States. With time this formula has been modified. It now refers to any national rules which are capable of hindering directly or indirectly, actually or potentially intra-EU trade. In Case C-110/05 *Commission v Italy (Italian Trailers Case)*, the ECJ held that MEQRs are: distinctly applicable measures; indistinctly applicable rules relating to product requirements; and, residual rules (see point 6 below).

4. In Case 120/78 *Rewe-Zentral* (otherwise and generally known as the *Cassis de Dijon* case) the ECJ focused on indistinctly applicable measures. Such measures, although non-discriminatory, i.e. making no distinction as to the origin of a product, can constitute a real hindrance to trade between Member States. This is because they impose a double burden on goods from other Member States in that such goods must satisfy regulatory requirements of a home Member State and a host Member State. In the *Cassis de Dijon* case the ECJ:

- introduced the principle of mutual recognition, that is, a presumption that goods which have been lawfully produced and marketed in one Member State can be sold without restrictions in any other Member State, even if they are produced to technical or quality specifications different from those applied in the Member State of importation. It is for the Member State of importation, and not for a trader, to rebut the presumption;

- introduced the concept of mandatory requirements under which a Member State is permitted to use measures which are reasonable (that is, "mandatory requirements") to protect its vital public interests in a manner which conforms with EU law, but only in the absence of common harmonising rules in the relevant area. The list of mandatory requirements is open-ended; and,

- assigned to the principle of proportionality a vital role in that indistinctly applicable measures must have effects which are proportionate to the aims they seek to achieve (see Chapter 21.4).

5. In Joined Cases C-267 and 268/91 *Keck and Mithouard* the ECJ made a dramatic about-turn and stated that "contrary to what has been previously decided", rules affecting certain "selling arrangements" are outside the scope of Article 34 TFEU provided that they satisfy the following conditions:

- they apply to all affected traders operating within the territory of a Member State; and,

- they affect in the same manner, in law and in fact, the marketing of both domestic and imported products even though they may have some impact on the overall volume of sales.

6. It emerges from Case C-110/05 *Commission v Italy* that national residual rules are subject to the access to the market test. Residual rules are those which cannot be classified as a distinctly applicable measure, or product requirements, or certain selling arrangements. The case law of the ECJ shows that rules such as bans/restrictions on the use of a product or restrictions on transportation of goods are to be regarded as residual rules. However, it is submitted that residual rules encompass all national rules which *inter alia* concern inspections, registrations, authorisation requirements, and obligations to provide statistical data. Residual rules which impede access to the market in a host Member State, are within the scope of Article 34 TFEU. Consequently, a Member State will be required to justify such rules either under Article 36 TFEU or as mandatory requirements set out in the *Cassis de Dijon* Case, and show that they are proportionate to the objective they seek to achieve. The application of the access to the market test poses many problems which can only be clarified by the ECJ.

7. In Case C-205/07 *Gysbrechts*, the ECJ broadened the scope of application of Article 35 TFEU. According to *Gysbrechts* it is no longer necessary to prove that a national measure has protective effects, i.e. provides a particular advantage for domestic products intended for a domestic market at the expense of domestic products intended for export. What is relevant is whether a national measure discriminates in fact against exported products and thus has a greater "actual effect" on the export of goods than on the marketing of the goods in the domestic market.

8. To deal speedily and efficiently with grave disruptions to the free movement of goods, which cause serious and continuing losses to the individuals affected, Regulation 2679/98 established a Rapid Intervention Mechanism (RIM). Under the Regulation, the Commission is required to act immediately when there is a threat or a major obstacle to the free movement of goods, and the Member State concerned is required to correct the situation within a very short time.

20.1 Introduction

The elimination of non-tariff barriers to the free movement of goods is governed by Articles 34 to 36 TFEU. Article 34 TFEU provides that:

> "Quantitative restrictions on imports and all measures having equivalent effect shall be prohibited between Member States."

Article 35 TFEU repeats the same prohibition in respect of exports. Article 36 TFEU contains derogations to the prohibitions laid down in Articles 34 and 35 TFEU (see Chapter 21). Articles 34 and 35 TFEU are vertically directly effective,[1520] but do not produce horizontal direct effect.

Article 34 TFEU has been used by the ECJ as the principal tool for the removal of all barriers to the free movement of goods. Its scope of application has been gradually extended in order to respond to the development of the EU and its changing economic objectives.

It is important to note that Articles 34 to 36 TFEU only apply when there are no harmonising measures in the relevant area at the EU level, i.e. when there is no secondary legislation adopted by EU institutions fully harmonising the relevant aspect of EU law (normally an EU regulation, or directive). When there is harmonising EU legislation any national measure must be assessed in the light of the relevant secondary legislation and not in the light of the Treaties,[1521] i.e. the principle of *lex specialis* applies.

Article 34 TFEU is very short. Nevertheless, it covers a number of concepts. These are examined below.

1520. In respect of Article 34 TFEU, see Case 74/76 *Iannelli and Volpi SpA v Ditta Paola Meroni* [1977] ECR 557; for Article 35 TFEU, see Case 83/78 *Pigs Marketing Board (Northern Ireland) v Redmond* [1978] ECR 2347.

1521. Case C-309/02 *Radlberger Getränkegesellschaft mbH & Co., S. Spitz KG v Land Baden-Württemberg* [2004] ECR I-11763.

20.2 The concept of "measures" under Article 34 TFEU

Article 34 TFEU is addressed to the Member States and concerns measures taken by a Member State as well as its failures to take appropriate measures. The ECJ has interpreted the concept of "a State" and the concept of "measures" broadly.

- The concept of a Member State includes not only any public body but also its emanations and private bodies controlled by it.

- The concept of "measures" covers not only binding rules, but also simple incentives[1522] and constant administrative practice generally based on an individual decision.[1523] It includes failures of a Member State to take measures when necessary. On this basis a Member State may be responsible for the conduct of its citizens who obstruct the free movement of goods, if it is in a position to prevent or terminate it. However, such conduct must be of a certain degree of consistency and generality in order to be caught by Article 34 TFEU.

It is important to note that Article 34 TFEU applies not only to national measures but also to measures adopted by EU institutions. In Case 15/83 *Denkavit*[1524] the ECJ held that measures adopted by EU institutions are capable of falling foul of Articles 34 and 35 TFEU. In Case C-114/96 *Kieffer*[1525] the ECJ held that EU acts of general application may hinder trade between Member States.

20.2.1 Measures taken by any public body, whether legislative, executive or judicial

Measures taken by any public authority of a Member State, whether legislative, executive or judicial are within the scope of Article 34 TFEU. Also measures taken by State's officials which are *ultra vires* are caught by Article 34 TFEU. In Case C-470/03 *Lehtinen*,[1526] an expert advising the Finish Ministry of Social Affairs and Health, during a television interview, stated that vehicle lifts made by an Italian company were not safe, although they conformed to standards laid down by the relevant EU directive. As a result, the Italian company lost sales in Finland[1527] (see Chapter 12.3). The ECJ held that personal statements made by officials of a Member State which give the persons to whom they are addressed the impression that they express an official position taken by the Member State may hinder trade between the Member States and thus fall within the scope of Article 34 TFEU.

20.2.2 Measures taken by semi-public bodies

In Case 266/87 *Royal Pharmaceutical Society of Great Britain*[1528] the ECJ had to decide whether a measure adopted by a professional body such as the Pharmaceutical Society of Great Britain may come within the scope of Article 34 TFEU.

1522. Case 249/81 *Commission v Ireland (Re Buy Irish Campaign)* [1982] ECR 4005.

1523. Case C-41/02 *Commission v The Netherlands* [2004] ECR I-11375.

1524. Case 15/83 *Denkavit Nederland BV v Hoofdproduktschap voor Akkerbouwprodukten* [1984] ECR 2171 and in Case C-51/93 *Meyhui NV v Schott Zwiesel Glaswerke AG* [1994] ECR I-3879.

1525. Case C-114/96 *René Kieffer and Romain Thill* [1997] ECR I-3629.

1526. C-470/03 *AGM COS.MET Srl v Suomen Valtio, Tarmo Lehtinen* [2007] ECR I-2749.

1527. The judgment in Case C-470/03 *Lehtinen* was criticised by N. Reich, "AGM–COS. MET or Who is Protected by EU Safety Regulation?", (2008) 33 ELRev., 85.

1528. Case 266/87 *R v Royal Pharmaceutical Society of Great Britain, ex parte Association of Pharmaceutical Importers and Others* [1989] ECR 1295. See also Case 222/82 *Apple and Pear Development Council v K J Lewis Ltd* [1983] ECR 4083.

THE FACTS WERE:

The Royal Pharmaceutical Society of Great Britain is a professional body established to enforce rules of ethics for pharmacists throughout the UK. This organisation convenes periodic meetings of a committee which has statutory authority to impose disciplinary measures on pharmacists found to have violated the rules of professional ethics. The Society enacted rules which prohibited a pharmacist from substituting one product for another that has the same therapeutic effect but bears a different trade mark when doctors prescribe a particular brand of medication. Pharmacists were therefore required to dispense particular brand name products when these were specified in prescriptions. This rule was challenged as being a MEQR.

Held:

The ECJ held that Article 34 TFEU applies not only to rules enacted by the Member States but also encompasses rules adopted by a professional body such as the Royal Pharmaceutical Society of Great Britain, which exercises regulatory and disciplinary powers conferred upon it by statutory instrument. The ECJ stated that professional and ethical rules adopted by the Society, which required pharmacists to supply under a prescription only a particular brand name drug, may constitute MEQRs in breach of Article 34 TFEU.

20.2.3 Measures taken by private companies supported financially or otherwise by a Member State when carrying out activities contrary to Article 34 TFEU

In Case 249/81 *Commission v Ireland (Buy Irish)*,[1529] the Irish Government launched a campaign "Buy Irish" in order to boost the sales of domestic products. First, it provided a free information service (the shoplink service) which informed consumers which goods were made in Ireland and where they could be purchased, and second, it organised exhibitions of Irish products only. When the Commission started its investigations these activities were abandoned by the Irish Government. However, activities organised by the Irish Goods Council, a limited company, consisting of organising a big publicity campaign in favour of Irish products and promoting the symbol "Guaranteed Irish" which was affixed on Irish products, were not. The Irish Government argued that the Irish Goods Council was not a public body. It was established that the members of the Council and its chairman were appointed by the Irish Ministry of Industry, its activities were mainly financed from grants and public subsidies and the aims and broad outlines of the campaign were defined by the Irish government. In those circumstances the ECJ held that the Irish Goods Council was a public body.

A more complex situation occurred in Case C-325/00 *Commission v Germany*.[1530]

THE FACTS WERE:

Germany argued that a German fund set up by the German Government to promote German agriculture and the German food industry, but which carried out its activity through the

---

1529. [1982] ECR 4005.
1530. [2002] ECR I-9977.

CMA – a private company whose organs were set up in accordance with private law rules and financed by compulsory contributions paid by undertakings in the German agriculture and food sector – was not a public body.

Held:

The ECJ held that CMA, although set up as a private body, established on the basis of law and bound by its Articles of Association, originally approved by the German public authorities, and financed by compulsory contributions, must be distinguished from bodies set up by producers on a voluntary basis. Accordingly the CMA was a public body as it did not enjoy the same freedom as regards the promotion of national products as would producers or their associations based on voluntary membership. The scheme established by the CMA consisting of awarding a quality label to national products satisfying certain requirements (the CMA label) and subsequently advertising such products by emphasising their German origin was condemned by the ECJ as encouraging consumers to buy products with the CMA label to the exclusion of imported products.

20.2.4 Failures of a Member State to take appropriate measures

Usually obstacles to the free movement of goods arise when a Member State takes an active measure. However inaction or passivity of a Member State may also breach Article 34 TFEU. Article 4(3) TFEU imposes on a Member State an obligation to take appropriate measures to fulfil its obligations arising out of the Treaties and EU acts and to ensure the full effectiveness of EU law. This obligation entails that if a Member State fails to take appropriate measures to control conduct of its citizens, which obstructs the free movement of goods, it may be in breach of Article 34 TFEU. This situation occurred in Case C-265/95 *Commission v France.*[1531]

THE FACTS WERE:

For a decade the Commission received complaints regarding the passivity of the French Government in the face of acts of violence and vandalism committed by French farmers, such as interception of lorries transporting agricultural products from other Member States and destruction of their loads, threats against French supermarkets, wholesalers and retailers dealing with those products, damage to such products when on display in shops, and so on. The Commission stated that on a number of occasions the French authorities showed unjustifiable leniency vis-à-vis the French farmers, for example, by not prosecuting the perpetrators of such acts when their identity was known to the police, since often the incidents were filmed by television cameras and the demonstrators' faces were not covered. Furthermore, the French police were often not present on the spot even though the French authorities had been warned of the imminence of demonstrations, or they did not interfere, as happened in June 1995 when Spanish lorries transporting strawberries were repeatedly attacked by French farmers at the same place over a period of two weeks and the police who

---

1531. [1997] ECR I-6959.

were present took no protective action. The government of France rejected the arguments submitted by the Commission as unjustified.

Held:

The ECJ held that France was in breach of its obligations under Article 34 TFEU, in conjunction with Article 4(3) TFEU, and under the common organisation of the markets in agricultural products, for failing to take all necessary and proportionate measures in order to prevent its citizens from interfering with the free movement of fruit and vegetables.

Comment:

This is one of the landmark decisions of the ECJ. It held that Article 34 TFEU is applicable where a Member State abstains from taking the measures required in order to deal with obstacles to the free movement of goods, which obstacles are not created by the Member State.

Abstention from taking appropriate measures thus constitutes a hindrance to the free movement of goods, and is just as likely to obstruct trade between Member States as is a positive act. However, Article 34 TFEU is not in itself sufficient to engage the responsibility of a Member State for acts committed by its citizens, but is so when read in the light of Article 4(3) TEU, which requires Member States not merely themselves to abstain from adopting measures or engaging in conduct liable to constitute an obstacle to trade, but also to take all necessary and appropriate measures to ensure that the fundamental freedom regarding the free movement of goods is respected on their territory.

Notwithstanding the fact that the ECJ recognises that a Member State has exclusive competences in relation to the maintenance of public order and the safeguard of internal security, it assesses the exercise of that competence by a Member State in the light of Article 34 TFEU. As a result, the ECJ stated that the French authorities failed to fulfil their obligations under the Treaty on two counts: first, they did not take necessary preventive and penal measures; second, the frequency and seriousness of the incidents, taking into account the passivity of the French authorities, not only made the importation of goods into France more difficult but also created a climate of insecurity that adversely affected the entire intra-EU trade.

The implications of the above case were highlighted in Case C-112/00 *Schmidberger*.[1532]

THE FACTS WERE:

Eugen Schmidberger, a German undertaking transporting timber and steel between Germany and Italy via the Brenner motorway, brought proceedings before the Austrian courts against the Republic of Austria, claiming that the Austrian authorities were in breach of Articles 34 and 35 TFEU as they failed to ban a demonstration organised by an Austrian environmental organisation, the Transitforum Austria Tirol (TAT), on the Brenner motorway that resulted in the complete closure of that motorway for almost 30 hours. TAT organised the demonstration

---

1532. C-112/00 *Eugen Schmidberger, Internationale Transporte und Planzüge v Austria* [2003] ECR I-5659.

in order to draw public attention to problems caused by the increase in traffic on the Brenner motorway and to call upon the Austrian authorities to take the necessary measures to deal with these problems; it had obtained authorisation from the local authorities to hold the demonstration on the Brenner motorway. Eugen Schmidberger sought compensation for losses suffered as a result of the closure of the Brenner motorway, claiming that Austria's failure to ban the demonstration constituted a sufficiently serious breach of EU law for which Austria should be liable. The Austrian government contended that the claim should be rejected on the grounds that the decision to authorise the demonstration was made after careful examination of the facts; that all known users and other parties likely to be affected by the closure of the motorway were informed in advance; that the demonstration was peaceful and did not result in traffic jams or other incidents; that the obstacle that it created was neither serious nor permanent; and, that the demonstrators were entitled to exercise their freedom of expression and freedom of assembly, rights which are fundamental in a democratic society and enshrined in the ECHR and the Austrian constitution.

Held:

The ECJ accepted that the fact that the authorities of a Member State did not ban a demonstration was not incompatible with Articles 34 and 35 TFEU read together with Article 4(3) TEU.[1533]

Comment:

The ECJ made a distinction between Case C-265/95 Commission v France and the Schmidberger case. The Court emphasised that although in both cases the free movement of goods was obstructed, there were important differences between the circumstances of the respective cases in terms of the geographic scale and the intrinsic seriousness of the disruptions caused by individuals, as well as the manner in which the national authorities had acted in order to deal with these disruptions. The ECJ pointed out that the demonstration in Austria took place after being duly authorised by the relevant national authorities; was limited to a single occasion; was of short duration; and, its objective was to allow citizens to exercise their fundamental right to express publicly their views on a matter which was of importance to them and to society. Furthermore, the Austrian authorities limited as far as possible the disruption to road traffic, taking into consideration that they had taken appropriate measures to ensure that the demonstration passed off peacefully and without any serious incidents; and, all parties likely to be affected were informed in advance and advised to take alternative routes specially designed for this occasion. In contrast, in Case C-265/95 Commission v France the French authorities did not take any measures when faced with serious and repeated disruptions of the free movement of goods by French nationals, which disruptions were of such seriousness as to create a general climate of insecurity undermining the free movement of goods.

The decisions of the ECJ in the above cases mean that a Member State may be liable under Article 34 TFEU linked with Article 4(3) TEU if it "manifestly and persistently abstained from adopting

---

1533. See paras 65–94 for examination of the justifications provided by the Austrian government.

appropriate and adequate measures"[1534] to deal with conduct of its economic operators which is capable of hindering the free movement of goods. It flows from Case C-112/00 *Schmidberger* that such conduct must be of a certain degree of consistency and generality to be caught by Article 34 TFEU.

20.3 The definition of QRs and MEQRs under Article 34 TFEU: from the *Dassonville* formula to the *Cassis de Dijon* approach

The Treaties neither define QRs nor MEQRs. There is no problem in defining QRs as these have been in use for centuries. They restrict importation and exportation by amount or by volume. The most common restrictions on the physical quantity of imports or exports are quotas and bans. In Case 2/73 *Geddo*[1535] the ECJ defined them as any measures which amount to a total or partial restraint on imports, exports or goods in transit. A total restraint refers to a ban. In Case 7/61 *Commission v Italy (Re Ban on Pork Imports)*,[1536] the ECJ condemned such a ban as contrary to Article 34 TFEU.

In respect of MEQRs, the ECJ provided the definition of MEQRs in Case 8/74 *Dassonville*.[1537]

THE FACTS WERE:

Traders imported a consignment of Scotch whisky into Belgium. The whisky had been purchased from a French distributor after having been in circulation in France. However, the Belgian authorities required a certificate of origin, which could only be obtained from British customs and which had to be made out in the name of the importers, before the goods could be legally imported into Belgium. As no certificate of origin could be obtained for the consignment, the traders forged the certificate and went ahead with the transaction. They were charged by the Belgian authorities with the criminal offence of importing goods without the requisite certificate of origin. The defendants claimed that the requirement of a certificate of origin in these circumstances was tantamount to a MEQR and therefore was prohibited by Article 34 TFEU. The Belgian court referred to the ECJ for a preliminary ruling on this question.

Held:

The ECJ held that the Belgian regulation constituted a MEQR because it potentially discriminated against parallel importers (that is, traders who are not authorised/approved dealers of a manufacturer of a product or the holders of intellectual property rights over it, but who lawfully purchase it in a Member State at one price and sell it in another Member State for a higher price) who would be unlikely to be in possession of the requisite documentation.

In *Dassonville*, the ECJ defined the concept of MEQRs as being all trading rules enacted by Member States which are capable of hindering directly or indirectly, actually or potentially, trade between

---

1534. Regulation 2679/98 on the Functioning of the Internal Market in Relation to the Free Movement of Goods among the Member States [2008] OJ L337/8, para. 65.
1535. *Risetia Luigi Geddo v Ente Nazionale Risi* [1973] ECR 865, para. 7.
1536. [1961] ECR 317.
1537. Case 8/74 *Procureur du Roi v Benoît and Gustave Dassonville* [1974] ECR 837.

Member States.[1538] This is known as the "*Dassonville* formula". The formula is very broad; the effect of national measures, including their potential effect,[1539] is decisive in determining whether they should be considered as MEQRs, regardless of the motive (discriminatory or not) for their introduction. Even if national measures have no significant effect on trade, they are still in breach of Article 34 TFEU. This is illustrated in Joined Cases 177 and 178/82 *Jan van der Haar*.[1540]

THE FACTS WERE:

Dutch excise law regulating the resale of tobacco products restricted imports of these products to a very small degree and provided for alternative ways of marketing them.

Held:

The ECJ held the Dutch rules breached Article 34 TFEU. The ECJ emphasised that Article 34 TFEU does not recognise the de minimis *rule as it:*

"does not distinguish between measures . . . according to the degree to which trade between Member States is affected. If a national measure is capable of hindering imports it must be regarded as having an effect equivalent to a quantitative restriction, even though the hindrance is slight and even though it is possible for imported products to be marketed in other ways."[1541]

It should be noted that although the ECJ has many times confirmed that the *de minimis* rule does not apply under Article 34 TFEU, it has in some cases held that a national rule was outside the scope of Article 34 TFEU because its restrictive effect on trade between Member States was too uncertain and indirect[1542] (see Chapter 20.6.2).

In *Dassonville* the ECJ focused on the restrictive effects of a measure rather than on its form. The Court encompassed within the formula both distinctly applicable measures, which affect imports only, and indistinctly applicable measures, which, without making a distinction between imported products and domestic products, may result in making imports more difficult or more expensive.

20.3.1 Refinement of the *Dassonville* formula by the ECJ

ECJ case law subsequent to *Dassonville* shows that in order to fall within the scope of the *Dassonville* formula, a measure need not be discriminatory. If it creates an obstacle to the free movement of goods it is a MEQR. This approach was confirmed by the ECJ in Case C-110/05 *Commission v Italy*[1543]

1538. Ibid, para. 5.
1539. Case 249/81 *Commission v Ireland (Re Buy Irish Campaign)* [1982] ECR 4005 and Case C-184/96 *Commission v France (Foie Gras)* [1998] ECR I-6197.
1540. Joined Cases 177 and 178/82 *Criminal Proceedings against Jan van de Haar and Kaveka de Meern BV* [1984] ECR 1797.
1541. Ibid, para.13.
1542. Case C-93/92 *CMC Motorradcenter GmbH v Pelin Baskiciogullari* [1993] ECR I-5009; Case C-379/92 *Criminal Proceedings against Matteo Peralta* [1994] ECR I-3453; Case C-44/98 *BASF AG v Präsident des Deutschen Patentamts* [1999] ECT I-6269.
1543. [2009] ECR I-519.

(see Chapter 20.6.1) in which the ECJ identified three categories of MEQR within the scope of the Dasonville formula. They are:

1. "Measures adopted by a Member State the object or effect of which is to treat products coming from other Member States less favourably."[1544] This refers to distinctly applicable measures which impose different burdens in law and in fact on imported products as compared to domestic products.

2. "Obstacles to the free movement of goods which are the consequence of applying to goods coming from other Member State where they are lawfully manufactured and marketed, rules that lay down requirements to be met by such goods . . . .even if those rules apply to all products alike."[1545] This refers to indistinctly applicable measures relating to product requirements (see Chapter 20.5.1.1) which impose a different burdens in fact on imported products although in law both imported and domestic products are treated in the same way. It is to be noted that the ECJ restricted the scope of the *Dassonville* formula in Joined Cases C-267 and 268/91 *Keck and Mithouard*,[1546] in which it excluded from the scope of application of Article 34 TFEU certain selling arrangements (see Chapter 20.5).

3. "Any other measure which hinders access of products originating in other Member States to the market of a Member State."[1547] This refers to measures which are not covered by 1 and 2 above, i.e. residual national measures. The case law of the ECJ so far shows that residual rules are those imposing bans on use of a product, restrictions on transportation of goods and obligations on retailers to obtain their supplies only from a State owned monopoly (see Chapter 20.6) and thus depriving them from procuring their supplies from wholesalers established in other Member States. It is submitted that residual rules encompass also national rules relating to, *inter alia*, inspections; registrations' authorisation requirements; and obligations to provide statistical data. Even if they are non-discriminatory they are within the scope of Article 34 TFEU when they hinder access to the market of imports.

In paragraph 6 of the *Dassonville* judgment the Court accepted that "reasonable" restrictions imposed by indistinctly applicable measures may be outside the scope of Article 34 TFEU. In this respect, the Court stated that in the absence of EU harmonising measures guaranteeing for consumers the authenticity of a product's designation of origin, a Member State is allowed to take measures to prevent unfair practices to protect consumers, subject to the condition that such measures are reasonable. This line of reasoning was further developed in Case 120/7 *Rewe-Zentral,* known as the *Cassis de Dijon* case.[1548]

20.3.2 Article 34 TFEU: national measures indistinctly applicable to domestic and imported goods – the *Cassis de Dijon* approach

In Case 120/78 *Cassis de Dijon*[1549] the ECJ decided on the extent to which national legislation restricting trade between the Member States is to be tolerated under EU law in the absence of harmonising measures.

1544. Ibid, para. 37.
1545. Ibid, para. 35.
1546. Joined Cases C-267 and 268/91 *Criminal Proceedings against Keck and Mithouard* [1993] ECR I-6097.
1547. Case C-110/05 *Commission v Italy* [2009] ECR I-519, para. 37.
1548. Case 120/78 *Rewe-Zentral v Bundesmonopolverwaltung für Branntwein* (the *Cassis de Dijon* case) [1979] ECR 649.
1549. Ibid.

THE FACTS WERE:

German legislation governing the marketing of alcoholic beverages set minimum alcohol strength of 25 per cent per litre for certain categories of alcoholic products. This regulation prohibited an importer from marketing Cassis de Dijon, a French liqueur with alcohol strength of between 15 and 20 per cent, in Germany. The German government invoked human health and consumer protection concerns as the justification for the prohibition. The importer challenged the German legislation in the German court, which then referred the matter to the ECJ for a preliminary ruling.

Held:

The ECJ held that the German government's argument that alcoholic beverages with a low alcohol content may more easily induce a tolerance towards alcohol than alcoholic beverages with a higher alcohol content could not be accepted, taking into account that in the German market consumers could buy an extremely wide range of weak or moderately alcoholic products, most of them in a diluted form.

The defence based on the protection of consumers against unfair practices on the part of producers and distributors of alcoholic beverages by means of fixing minimum alcohol content was also rejected. In this respect the ECJ emphasised that this objective could be ensured by requiring the importers to display an indication of origin and the alcohol content on the packaging of products. Accordingly the German government had not provided any valid reason why alcoholic beverages lawfully produced and marketed in France should not be introduced into Germany. As a result, the unilateral requirement imposed by Germany of minimum alcohol content for the purposes of the sale of alcoholic beverages constituted a MEQR.

In the *Cassis de Dijon* case, the ECJ laid down a number of fundamental principles in respect of indistinctly applicable measures as follows.

1. It confirmed that Article 34 TFEU applies to non-discriminatory national rules which hinder intra-EU trade. They do so because they are different from rules applicable in the Member State of origin of the relevant product.

2. It introduced the principle of mutual recognition, that is, a presumption that goods which have been lawfully produced or marketed in one Member State can be sold without restrictions in any other Member State, even if they are produced to technical or quality specifications different from those applied in the Member State of importation. It is for the Member State of importation, and not for a trader, to rebut the presumption. The implementation of this principle has been enhanced by Regulation 764/2008 laying down procedures relating to the application of certain national technical rules to products lawfully marketed in another Member State.[1550] Mutual recognition permits national differences to remain, and as such is seen as a way of maintaining diversity of products and services within the internal market without the need to harmonise Member States' national legislation. Harmonisation results in the adoption of identical rules throughout the EU and thus is very intrusive into the national regulatory autonomy of each Member State (see Chapter 17.1).

1550. [2008] OJ I218/21.

3.   It introduced the concept of "mandatory requirements"[1551] nowadays often referred by the ECJ as "overriding reasons (or requirements) in the public interest",[1552] or "legitimate public interest objectives"[1553] under which a Member State is permitted to use measures which, although within the *Dassonville* formula, will not infringe Article 34 TFEU if they are necessary to protect that State's vital public interests, This book uses the traditional terminology, i.e. "mandatory requirements". In the absence of EU rules in a particular area, a national measure that applies without discrimination to both domestic and imported products may escape the Article 34 TFEU prohibition if it is considered as being necessary in order to satisfy mandatory requirements. Unlike Article 36 TFEU, which contains an exhaustive list of possible justifications to the prohibition laid down in Article 34 TFEU, under *Cassis de Dijon* the list of mandatory requirements is not exhaustive (see Chapter 21.3).

4.   It stated that indistinctly applicable measures must have effects which are proportionate to the aims they seek to achieve. Accordingly, the principle of proportionality has become essential in excluding national measures when the objective they seek can be achieved by more suitable and less stringent means (see Chapter 21.4).

5.   It stated that the principles laid down in *Cassis de Dijon* were established in order to remedy the absence of EU rules in a particular area. When national laws of the Member States have been harmonised at EU level, the legality of additional requirements imposed by a Member State in the harmonised area depends upon whether or not the EU harmonisation is complete or partial. This question arose in Case 29/87 *Denkavit*.[1554]

THE FACTS WERE:

Directive 70/524 was enacted to harmonise all the national laws of the Member States with regard to both the presence of additives in, and the labelling requirements for, feed-stuffs. However, Danish importers of animal feed-stuff were required by Danish national law to obtain approval from the Danish authorities prior to import. In particular, foreign feed-stuffs were required to comply with certain procedural and labelling requirements which exceeded those specified in Directive 70/524.

Held:

The ECJ held that Directive 70/524 was intended to harmonise all the material conditions for marketing feed-stuffs, including the identification of additives and their purity. Consequently, a Member State was prohibited from imposing health inspections not provided for by the Directive itself.

Sometimes it is difficult to establish which aspects have been harmonised and which are still within the competence of a Member State. This is well illustrated in Case C-162/97 *Nilsson*.[1555]

1551. Ibid, para. 8.
1552. Case C-456/10 *Asociación Nacional de Expendedores de Tabaco y Timbre (ANETT) v Administración del Estado* (Judgment of 26/4/12 (NYR)), para. 53.
1553. Ibid, para. 52.
1554. Case 29/87 *Dansk Denkavit v Ministry of Agriculture* [1988] ECR 2965.
1555. Case C-162/97 *Gunnar Nilsson, Per Olov Hagelgren, Solweig Arrborn* [1998] ECR I-7477.

THE FACTS WERE:

The Swedish authorities brought criminal proceedings against a group of individuals who were selling bovine semen taken from Belgian bulls for insemination of Swedish cows. Swedish law prohibited the use of semen from bulls of breeds with specific genetic weaknesses, and Belgian bulls were considered as being of such a breed. The alleged offenders argued that Swedish law was contrary to Article 34 TFEU and that the product in question was subject to harmonised importation rules under EU law. The Swedish authorities claimed that the national law was justified on the ground of the protection of animal health and in particular the protection of animals from any breeding liable to entail suffering for animals or to affect their behaviour. The Swedish court referred two questions to the ECJ:

- Whether Article 34 TFEU or Directive 87/328 precludes national rules under which authorisation is required for insemination activities concerning bovine animals, in particular distribution of, and insemination, with semen?

- Whether Article 34 TFEU or Directive 87/328 precludes national rules prohibiting or subjecting to certain conditions the insemination and breeding of bovine animals where those activities are liable, in the opinion of the competent national authorities, to entail suffering for animals or affect their natural behaviour, or where the breed in question is regarded by those national authorities as carrying genetic defects?

Held:

The ECJ held that Directive 87/328 constituted a complete harmonisation of rules in this area and as such took into consideration the legitimate interests of Member States.

Comment:

In order to justify national rules preventing the use of semen from another Member State, a Member State could not invoke any of the arguments that the breed carried genetic defects, or that the use of semen would entail suffering for animals or that the use of semen would affect their natural behaviour. This was because the conditions of acceptance for the purpose of breeding of pure-bred breeding animals of bovine species and their semen had been harmonised under EU law.

The ECJ held that the Swedish law could be justified only if it was intended to regulate the qualifications and operations of inseminators, this being because neither Article 34 TFEU nor Directive 87/328 imposes any restrictions on a Member State in respect of the distribution of semen and on insemination activities.

20.4 Article 34 TFEU: types of MEQRs

There are various types of MEQRs. Some of them are identified below.

20.4.1 National measures encouraging discrimination

Discrimination based on the nationality of goods is considered to be the worst type of discrimination. National measures encouraging discrimination are the best example of distinctly applicable measures.

In Case 249/81 *Commission v Ireland [Re Buy Irish Campaign]*[1556] (for facts see Chapter 20.2.3) the Irish government conducted a campaign to promote Irish products called "Buy Irish". The ECJ held that the campaign was in breach of Article 34 TFEU as it sought to substitute domestic goods for imported goods in the Irish market and thus check the flow of imports from other Member States. This was so notwithstanding the fact that the campaign was a failure and that the Irish Government adopted non-binding measures in promoting Irish products. The ECJ stated that the campaign was capable of influencing the conduct of traders and consumers in Ireland.

In Case 207/83 *Commission v UK (Re Origin Marking of Retail Goods)*,[1557] the issue was whether origin-marking requirements imposed on all goods, whether imported or domestic, were a MEQR.

THE FACTS WERE:

Under UK legislation certain textiles, electrical and other goods offered for retail sale had to be marketed with or accompanied by an indication of their origin. The UK argued that for consumers it was necessary to have a clear indication of the country of origin of goods as it gave an indication of their quality.

Held:

The ECJ held that such a requirement merely enabled consumers to assert any prejudice they might have against foreign goods. UK legislation was contrary to Article 34 TFEU as it slowed down the economic interchange between Member States. The ECJ held that manufacturers were free to indicate the country of origin but should not be compelled to do so.

A national scheme under which quality labels are awarded and subsequently affixed only to national products, even though a national producer can choose whether or not to apply for that label, constitutes a MEQR if the label underlines the national origin of the relevant product and thus encourages consumers to buy national products to the exclusion of imported products. Such a scheme was condemned in Case C-325/00 *Commission v Germany*.[1558] On the same ground in Case C-255/03 *Commission v Belgium*,[1559] the ECJ condemned a scheme set up by the Walloon government instituting a "Walloon label of quality" attesting that any product on which it appeared was manufactured in Wallonia and possessed certain qualities and characteristics qualifying it for the award of the label. The Commission objected to any reference on the label to the geographical origin of the product. The ECJ agreed with the Commission.

20.4.2 National measures which give preference to domestic products or confer some advantages on domestic products

The ECJ considers national measures which give preference to domestic products or confer some advantages on domestic products as discriminatory and thus they amount to MEQRs. This is exemplified in Case 72/83 *Campus Oil*.[1560]

1556. [1982] ECR 4005.
1557. [1985] ECR 1201.
1558. [2002] ECR I-9977.
1559. Judgment of 17/06/2004 (unpublished).
1560. Case 72/83 *Campus Oil Limited and Others v Minister for Industry and Energy and Others* [1984] ECR 2727.

Case 192/84 *Commission v Greece*[1561] provides another example. In that case the Greek Government imposed on the Agricultural Bank of Greece an obligation not to finance any purchase of imported agricultural machinery unless there was proof that no similar machinery was manufactured in Greece. The ECJ ruled that this measure was a MEQR. Similarly, in Case 263/85 *Commission v Italy*,[1562] Italian legislation which made provision of State aid to Italian public bodies conditional upon the purchase of vehicles made in Italy was held in breach of Article 34 TFEU, since it modified the flow of vehicles from other Member States and thus constituted a hindrance to the free movement of goods.

20.4.3 Import licences and other similar procedures applicable to imported products

The ECJ held that import licences and other similar procedures, even if they are only formalities, constitute MEQRs in so far as they intend to limit or delay importations.[1563] This is exemplified in Case 40/82 *Commission v UK [Re Imports of Poultry Meat]*.[1564]

1561. [1985] ECR 3967.
1562. [1991] ECR 1991.
1563. Joined Cases 51–54/71 *International Fruit Company* [1971] ECR 1107; Case 68/76 *Commission v France* [1977] ECR 515; Case 41/76 *Suzanne Criel, née Donckerwolcke and Henri Schou v Procureur de la République* [1976] ECR 1921.
1564. [1982] ECR 2793.

> *imposed before Christmas (when consumers traditionally buy poultry); and, there had been no outbreak of Newcastle disease in France for five years! All these reasons convinced the ECJ that the UK introduced the licensing system to safeguard commercial interests, in particular in the light of massive State aid granted to French poultry breeders by the French Government.*

National measures which require that only persons established within a national territory may apply for a licence to sell products coming from other Member States are unlawful *per se*. In Case 155/82 *Commission v Belgium*,[1565] the ECJ condemned Belgian legislation restricting the right to apply for approval of pesticides for non-agricultural use and phytopharmaceutical products to persons established in Belgium. In Case 247/81 *Commission v Germany*,[1566] the ECJ condemned German law requiring that only undertakings having their headquarters in Germany were allowed to sell pharmaceutical products in Germany.

Prior authorisation procedures for importation of goods are not unlawful *per se* as they may be justified on the grounds of the protection of public health (see Chapter 21). However, such procedures must not impose unreasonable burdens on an applicant, must be readily accessible, capable of being brought to completion within a reasonable time, and if the procedure leads to a rejection of an application, that rejection must be open to challenge before national courts. This is exemplified in Case C-212/03 *Commission v France*.[1567]

THE FACTS WERE:

The French Government imposed a requirement of prior authorisations for the importation of homeopathic medicinal products for personal use, not effected by personal transport, in three types of situation as follows:

■ *The first situation: when such a product was authorised in France and in the Member State of purchase. The French Government argued that although the requirement was burdensome, in practice only 1 per cent of applications for authorisation were made annually by nationals of Member States.*

Held:

The ECJ held that the requirement created an obstacle to the free movement of goods and that the mere fact that it existed, not the number of authorisations, was decisive in establishing the infringement.

Comment:

Article 34 TFEU does not recognise the de minimis *rule and therefore the potential effect of the measure on the free movement of goods suffices to establish that it constitutes an unlawful restriction.*

1565. [1983] ECR 531.

1566. [1984] ECR 1111.

1567. [2005] ECR I-4213, see also Case C-244/06 *Dynamic Medien Vertriebs GmbH v Avides Media AG* [2008] ECR I-505.

■ *The second situation: when a product was registered in another Member State in accordance with Directive 92/73 on the approximation of provisions relating to medicinal products and laying down additional provisions on homeopathic products.*[1568] *The Commission argued that the product at issue was registered in accordance with the Directive and thus presented no risk to health. The French Government claimed that Directive 92/73 did not lay down a mutual recognition procedure, but a simple obligation for Member States to take due account of registrations or authorisations already issued by another Member State. For that reason the view could not be taken that the Directive had established a sufficient degree of harmonisation of EU law to release the Member State of importation from responsibility for the persons concerned.*

Held:

The ECJ upheld the argument of the Commission stating that since the product was registered in accordance with the Directive which guaranteed its safety, there was no necessity for further clinical tests, and that in any event the French Government had not demonstrated that grounds of health protection required a prior authorisation procedure in respect of that product.

■ *The third situation: when a product was not authorised in France but was authorised in the Member State of purchase.*

Held:

The ECJ held that national authorities were free to require authorisation for such a product but restated the requirements for the relevant procedures as mentioned above, and emphasised that those procedures must comply with the principle of proportionality (see Chapter 21.4). In this case the authorisation procedure applied by the French authorities was found to be disproportionate because the same procedure was applied to both imports for personal use and imports for commercial purposes.

It is well established in EU law that the requirement of prior authorisation in respect of products which are authorised in one Member State and which are identical to ones that have already been authorised in a Member State of importation is in breach of Article 34 TFEU.[1569]

As to similar products, in Case C-201/94 *Smith & Nephew*[1570] the ECJ held that a drug that was manufactured using the same formulation, the same active ingredient and having the same therapeutic effect as one that had already been authorised in the Member State of importation should be treated as being covered by the previous authorisation of the Member State of importation. The ECJ emphasised that the two drugs are not required to be "identical in all respects". This concept of similarity was further explained in Case C-74/03 *SmithKline Beecham plc*,[1571] in which the ECJ held that in order to assess similarity, emphasis should be placed on the therapeutic effect of the product rather than on the precise molecular structure of the active ingredients. Accordingly, an unauthorised product is not to be found similar to an authorised product if it shows significant difference from the authorised product as regards its safety or efficacy.

1568. [1992] OJ L297/8.
1569. Case C-368/96 *Generics (UK) and Others* [1998] ECR I-7967.
1570. Case C-201/94 *R v The Medicines Control Agency, ex parte Smith & Nephew Pharmaceutical* [1996] ECR I-5819.
1571. Case C-74/03 *SmithKline Beecham plc v Lægemiddelstyrelsen* [2005] ECR I-595.

It is important to note that in respect of authorisation procedures for medicinal products and homeopathic products there are harmonising measures at EU level which provide for simplified procedures or exemption of such products from any requirement of authorisation.[1572]

20.4.4 Phytosanitary inspections

Phytosanitary inspections constitute an effective way of excluding imported products from national markets, or at least of making imports or exports more difficult or more costly. Nevertheless, phytosanitary inspections may be justified under Article 36 TFEU. This occurred in Case 4/75 *Rewe-Zentralfinanz*,[1573] in which apples imported into Germany were subject to systematic sanitary inspections designed to control a pest called San José Scale that was not to be found in domestic apples. The ECJ held that such inspections constituted MEQRs, although in this case they were justified as there was a genuine risk of spreading the disease to domestic apples if no inspection was carried out on imported apples.

Provided there is no discrimination against imported products and thus inspections are not arbitrary, they may be justified under Article 36 TFEU. However, systematic inspections, whether performed inside the national territory or at the borders, are arbitrary and result in making imports more difficult or costly.[1574]

In Case C-293/94 *Brandsma*,[1575] the ECJ held that it was not necessary to carry out technical analyses or laboratory tests on imported goods if they had already been conducted by another Member State.

In respect of inspections of foodstuffs Directive 93/99 of 29 October 1993[1576] lays down general principles governing such inspections. It applies to inspection of foodstuffs, namely food additives; vitamins; mineral salts; trace elements; and, to materials coming into contact with foodstuffs. Its main objective is to ensure that foodstuffs present no risks to public health and that no double inspections are conducted.

20.4.5 National measures relating to the use of generic names

Abusive restrictions on the use of generic names are regarded as MEQRs. In Case 286/86 *Deserbais*,[1577] French law stated that only cheese containing a minimum 40 per cent fat could use the name "Edam". Deserbais imported Edam cheese from Germany which was lawfully produced there but contained only 35 per cent fat. When criminal proceedings were brought against Deserbais, he argued that French law was contrary to Article 34 TFEU. The ECJ held that Article 34 TFEU precluded a Member State from applying national legislation to products which have been lawfully manufactured and marketed under the name of "Edam" in another Member State provided that consumers are properly informed that imported "Edam" contains only 35 per cent fat.

A similar situation arose in Case 182/84 *Miro BV*.[1578]

1572. For example Directive 2001/83/EC on the Community Code relating to Medicinal Products for Human Use [2001] OJ L311/67]; Directive 65/65/EEC relating to Proprietary Medicinal Products (amended many times) ([1965–1966] OJ, English Special Edition: Series I Chapter 1965–1966, p. 24); Directive 92/73/EEC, examined above in Case C-212/03 *Commission v France* [2005] ECR I-4213.
1573. 4/75 *Rewe-Zentralfinanz eGmbH v Landwirtschaftskammer* [1975] ECR 843.
1574. Case C-272/95 *Dt. Milchkontor II* [1997] ECR I-1905 and Case 35/76 *Simmenthal v Italian Minister for Finance* [1976] ECR 1871.
1575. Case C-293/94 *Criminal Proceedings against Jacqueline Brandsma* [1996] ECR I-3159.
1576. [1993] OJ L290 14.
1577. Case 286/86 *Ministère Public v Deserbais* [1988] ECR 4907.
1578. Case 182/84 *Miro BV* [1985] ECR 3731.

In Case C-14/00 *Commission v Italy*,[1579] the generic name "chocolate" was at issue.

20.4.6 National measures imposing restrictions on use of certain ingredients in foodstuffs

The question of permissible ingredients in foods has arisen in a significant number of cases: for instance in respect of pain brioché,[1580] bread,[1581] alcoholic beverages,[1582] pasta,[1583] and so on.

1579. [2003] ECR I-513.
1580. Case 130/80 *Criminal Proceedings against Fabriek voor Hoogwaardige Voedingsprodukten Kelderman BV* [1981] ECR 527 dealing with a particular sort of French bread.
1581. Case C-17/93 *Criminal Proceedings against Van der Veldt* [1994] ECR I-3537; Case C-123/00 *Criminal Proceedings against Christina Bellamy and English Shop Wholesale SA* [2001] ECR I-2795. In both cases Belgian legislation prohibiting the marketing of bread and other bakery products whose salt content by reference to dry matter exceeded the maximum permitted level of 2 per cent was condemned by the ECJ as a MEQR.
1582. Case 27/80 *Criminal Proceedings against Anton Adriaan Fietje* [1980] ECR 3839.
1583. Case 407/85 *3 Glocken GmbH and Gertraud Kritzinger v USL Centro-Sud and Provincia Autonoma di Bolzano* [1988] ECR 4233.

The position of the ECJ on the matter is that in the absence of EU rules, a Member State is allowed to regulate these matters provided that its rules do not discriminate against imported products or hinder their importation. Thus, it is for the Member State concerned to produce scientific data supporting its claim that prohibited ingredients constitute danger to health. It is to be noted that there is an impressive amount of EU legislation concerning ingredients in foodstuffs.[1584] In December 2008, the "Package on Food Improvement Agents" was adopted. It comprises the following regulations: Regulation 1331/2008 establishing a common authorisation procedure for food additives, food enzymes and food flavourings;[1585] Regulation 1332/2008 on food enzymes;[1586] Regulation 1333/2008 on food additives;[1587] and, Regulation 1334/2008 on flavourings.[1588]

20.4.7 National measures imposing an obligation to use the national language

In Case C-33/97 *Colim*[1589] the ECJ restated its case law on linguistic requirements. A Member State cannot impose additional language requirements if an EU measure fully harmonises language requirements. However, in the absence of full harmonisation of language requirements applicable to information appearing on imported products, a Member State may adopt national measures requiring such information to be provided in the language of the area in which the products are sold, or in another language which can be readily understood by consumers in that area. In order to decide whether the language is easily understood by consumers account should be taken of such factors as "the possible similarity of words in different languages, the widespread knowledge amongst the population concerned of more than one language, or the existence of special circumstances such as a wideranging advertising campaign or widespread distribution of the product, provided that it can be established that the consumer is given sufficient information".[1590] In the light of those factors it was not surprising that in Case C-366/98 *Geffroy*,[1591] the ECJ held that an importer of Coca-Cola who bought it in the UK labelled in English and then sold it in France, contrary to the French law requiring all labels to be in French, did not need to make any changes to the English label given that the product was well known worldwide.

In Case C-33/97 *Colim*, the ECJ held that imposition of linguistic requirements in the pre-sale stage, i.e. on a producer in respect of importers, wholesalers and retailers, is in breach of Article 34 TFEU. They are not necessary given that persons involved in the distribution of goods are familiar with them or can always ask the producers for more information.

1584. Risk assessment regarding food and feed safety is the main task of the European Food Safety Authority (EFSA) which was created in 2002. For details see the official website of the EFSA at http://www.efsa.europa.eu/en/aboutefsa.htm (accessed 22/2/12).
1585. [2008] OJ L354/1.
1586. [2008] OJ L354/7.
1587. [2008] OJ L354/16.
1588. [2008] OJ L354/34.
1589. Case C-33/97 *Colim NV v Bigg's Continent Noord NV*, [1999] ECR I-3175, see Case C-85/94 *Piageme and Others v Peeters NV* [1995] ECR-I-2955; C-369/89 *Piageme and Others v BVBA Peeters* [1991] ECR I-2971 and Case C-51/93 *Meyhui NV v Schott Zwiesel Glaswerke AG* [1994] ECR I-3879.
1590. Case C-85/94 *Piageme and Others v Peeters NV* [1995] ECR I-2955, para. 30.
1591. Case C-366/98 *Geffroy and Casino France SNC* [2000] ECR I-6579.

20.4.8   National measures restricting advertisement

The judgment of the ECJ in Joined Cases C-267 and 268/91 *Keck and Mithouard*[1592] changed the way in which the compatibility of national rules relating to the advertising of products with Article 34 TFEU should be assessed (see Chapter 20.5.1).

One of the consequences of the *Keck* judgment is that a distinction must be made between advertisement on the label and other forms of advertisement. The ECJ regards advertisement on the label as being incorporated into the product and thus to concern product requirements.[1593] Other forms of advertisement, such as advertisement on TV, on the radio or in the press, are regarded by the Court as being selling arrangements. This was examined in Case C-368/95 *Familiapress*.[1594]

THE FACTS WERE:

Austrian legislation prohibited the sale of periodicals containing games or competitions for prizes. On the basis of this legislation an order was issued against Henrich Bauer Verlag, the German publisher of the weekly magazine "Laura," which was distributed in Germany and Austria and which contained a crossword puzzle offering readers sending the correct solution the opportunity to enter a draw for prizes of DM500, to cease to sell "Laura" in Austria. The publisher claimed that the Austrian law was a QR contrary to Article 34 TFEU. The Austrian Government argued that the prohibition concerned a method of promoting sales and as such was a selling arrangement outside the scope of Article 34 TFEU.

Held:

The ECJ held that: "even though the relevant national legislation is directed against a method of sales promotion, in this case it bears on the actual content of the products, in so far as the competitions in question form an integral part of the magazine in which they appear. As a result, the national legislation in question as applied to the facts of the case is not concerned with a selling arrangement within the meaning of the judgment in Keck and Mithouard.*"*[1595]

Similarly, in Case C-470/93 *Mars*,[1596] the ECJ held that an advertisement which was incorporated into the wrapping of the product, in this case ice-cream bars bearing the promotional marking "+ 10% ice cream", related to product requirements (for facts see Chapter 21.3.1).

The above case shows the difficulty of drawing a clear line between national rules relating to product requirements and those concerning some selling arrangements. This issue is examined below.

20.5   Article 34 TFEU: national measures relating to certain selling arrangements

The *Cassis de Dijon* case gave a new impetus to the exercise of the right to the free movement of goods within the EU. Following the judgment, any national rule indistinctly applicable, regardless of whether

---

1592.   Joined Cases C-267 and 268/91 *Criminal proceedings against Bernard Keck and Daniel Mithouard* [1993] ECR I-6097.
1593.   Case C-470/93 *Verein gegen Unwesen in Handel und Gewerbe Köln e.V. v Mars GmbH* [1995] ECR I-1923.
1594.   Case C-368/95 *Vereinigte Familiapress Zeitungsverlags- und Vertriebs GmbH v Henrich Bauer Verlag* [1997] ECR I-3689.
1595.   Ibid, para. 11.
1596.   Case C-470/93 *Verein gegen Unwesen in Handel und Gewerbe Köln e.V. v Mars GmbH* [1995] ECR I-1923.

it concerned the product itself or the way it was marketed was prohibited, save in the exceptional circumstances set out in Article 36 TFEU or justified by mandatory requirements. Further, the principle of mutual recognition, which requires a Member State to respect the manner in which a product was manufactured and commercialised in another Member State, created a presumption that once a product has been lawfully produced and marketed in one Member State, it is entitled to free circulation within the EU. Following the *Cassis de Dijon* case traders were vigorously enforcing their rights under Article 34 TFEU by challenging any national rule restricting their commercial freedom, even though the rule affected general conditions of trading in a Member State and had little effect on the integration of the internal market. The above is exemplified by the long-running saga of the cases dealing with the compatibility of the UK Sunday trading laws with Article 34 TFEU.

Section 47 of the Shops Act 1950 prohibited the opening of shops in England and Wales on Sundays except for the sale of certain "essential" items. Owners of shops were prosecuted by their local authorities for opening their shops on Sundays contrary to this statute. In their defence, they claimed that the prohibition was contrary to Article 34 TFEU because it entailed a restriction on trade which had a discriminatory effect on the sale of goods from other Member States, and they evidenced this by showing the reduction in their total weekly sales, including imported goods, resulting from the application of the Shops Act.

The ECJ's decisions in the Sunday Trading cases lacked clarity and direction.[1597] In Case 145/88 *Torfaen Borough*,[1598] the ECJ's judgment was so unclear that national courts used it both to justify[1599] and to reject[1600] the compatibility of the Shops Act with Article 34 TFEU. In Case C-169/91 *Stoke-on-Trent*,[1601] the ECJ delivered a very short judgment stating that the statute was compatible with Article 34 TFEU as it had a legitimate socio-economic function which was recognised under EU law. This case by case approach did not offer any guidelines to national courts. However, those judgments indicated that the ECJ was, on the one hand, reluctant to limit the scope of Article 34 TFEU, but on the other, was not immune to criticism suggesting that its case law should be reassessed given that it had gone beyond market integration into the realms of national laws that affected the volume of trade of all goods, whether domestic or imported, to an equal extent.

A reassessment of the pre-existing case law on Article 34 TFEU and a new strategy for regulating the internal market came from the ECJ in Joined Cases C-267 and 268/91 *Keck and Mithouard*,[1602] in which the ECJ moved away from the wide application of the *Dassonville* formula and thus set new limits on Article 34 TFEU.

THE FACTS WERE:

The French authorities commenced criminal proceedings against Keck and Mithouard for selling goods at a price lower than they had paid for them (resale at a loss), which, except regarding sales at a loss by manufacturers, was in breach of a French law. Both alleged offenders argued that the law in question was contrary to fundamental freedoms, that is, to

---

1597. See C. Bernard, "Sunday Trading: A Drama in Five Acts", (1994) 57 MLR, 449.

1598. Case 145/88 *Torfaen Borough Council v B & Q plc* [1989] ECR 3851.

1599. E.g. the *Torfean* case, ibid., and *Wellingborough Borough Council v Payless* [1990] 1 CMLR 773.

1600. *B & Q v Shrewsbury BC* [1990] 3 CMLR 535.

1601. Case C-169/91 *Council of the City of Stoke-on-Trent and Norwich City Council v B & Q plc* [1992] ECR I-6635.

1602. Joined Cases C-267 and 268/91 *Criminal Proceedings against Keck and Mithouard* [1993] ECR I-6097.

the free movement of goods, persons, services and capital, as well as being in breach of EU competition law. The French court referred to the ECJ.

Held:

The ECJ dismissed all the arguments except one based on the free movement of goods. The Court held that the Dassonville *formula did not apply to selling arrangements which:*

- *apply to all traders operating within the territory of a Member State; and*

- *affect in the same manner, in law and in fact, the marketing of both domestic and imported products.[1603]*

Once these two conditions are satisfied, national rules relating to selling arrangements fall outside the scope of Article 34 TFEU.

In *Keck,* the ECJ indicated how to deal with the so called market circumstances rules, i.e. rules concerning the time, place and manner of marketing products.[1604] They differ from MEQRs because they do not concern restrictions imposed on goods themselves, they are usually non-discriminatory as they impose the same restrictions on domestic goods as on imported goods and they apply to retailers rather than producers/manufacturers. Such rules are within the inherent regulatory competence of the Member States. However, the ECJ decided that they are within the scope of Article 34 TFEU if they fail to satisfy the two conditions set out in paragraph 16 of the judgment in *Keck.*

The first condition laid down in *Keck* according to which rules relating to selling arrangements must apply to all traders operating within the territory of a Member State was classified by A-G Stix-Hackl in Case C-322/01 *Deutscher Apothekerverband*[1605] as relating to the principle of universality. This condition has become almost redundant as the ECJ has always found it satisfied. However, the second condition, which according to the A-G embodies the principle of neutrality, is more challenging. To establish discrimination in law between national and domestic products, poses no difficulty. For example, in Case C-531/07 *LIBRO,*[1606] the ECJ found that Austrian legislation, under which an Austrian publisher or importer of German-language books was free to fix the retail price for such books whilst an importer of such books, established in another Member State, was obliged not to fix a price below the retail price fixed by the relevant Austrian Trade Association, was discriminatory in law. Accordingly, it constituted a MEQR.

The case law of the ECJ shows that in determining factual discrimination between domestic and imported products:

- A reduction in the volume of sales of a particular product after the introduction of a national measure is not decisive.[1607]

1603. Ibid, para. 16.

1604. See E. L. White, "In Search of The Limits To Article 30 of The EEC Treaty", (1989) 26 CMLRev., 235 and K. Mortelmans, "Article 30 of the EEC Treaty and Legislation relating to Market Circumstances: Time to Consider a New Definition", (1991) 28 CMLRev., 115.

1605. Case C-322/01 *Deutscher Apothekerverband eV v 0800 DocMorris NV and Jacques Waterval* [2003] ECR I-14887, para. 59.

1606. Case C-531/07 *Fachverband der Buch- und Medienwirtschaft v LIBRO Handelsgesellschaft mbH* [2009] ECR I-3717

1607. In Case C-441/04 *A-Punkt Schmuckhandels GmbH v Claudia Schmidt* [2006] ECR I-2093 the ECJ rejected the argument submitted by Mrs Schmidt that her method of sale (prohibited under Austrian legislation and consisting

■ A decisive criterion is whether or not other forms of marketing/advertising of the imported products are available to importers, and if so, to what extent, if any, these alternatives will make the marketing/advertisement of the product more onerous and more expensive for importers than if the restriction had not been imposed.

The above criterion for finding discrimination has been applied to many cases.[1608] In Case C-71/02 *Karner*,[1609] the ECJ had to determine whether Austrian legislation prohibiting any information which stated that goods on sale originated from an insolvent estate was outside the scope of Article 34 TFEU. The ECJ applied the two conditions set out in *Keck*. The first condition was met given that the Austrian legislation applied without any distinction to all the operators concerned who carried on their business on Austrian territory, regardless of whether they were Austrian nationals or foreigners.

The issue of whether the second condition was also satisfied was more controversial. In particular, the A-G grappled with the issue of the additional costs that an importer must bear in order to adjust its advertisements to the requirements imposed by the Austrian legislation. Indeed, bearing in mind the lack of familiarity of the public with them, advertising imported goods is more expensive than advertising domestic goods, but does the additional expenditure alone suffice to make access to the national market more difficult for foreign goods than for domestic goods? According to the A-G three factors demonstrated that the second condition set out in *Keck* was met.

■ First, the challenged legislation did not impose a total ban on advertisements but prohibited only advertisements which made reference to the fact that the goods advertised came from an insolvent estate;

■ Second, alternative means of advertising the marketed goods were available to importers; and,

■ Third, there was no evidence provided by the parties that the challenged legislation made it more difficult for goods from other Member States to gain access to the Austrian market.

The ECJ confirmed the conclusion reached by the A-G. The Court held that the prohibition on advertising contained in the Austrian law was outside the scope of Article 34 TFEU.

20.5.1 The scope of application of *Keck*: the distinction between measures relating to the product itself and to the selling arrangements

There is neither a definition of "measures relating to the product itself" (that is, the product requirements), nor of "measures relating to selling arrangements". However, some useful indications have been provided by the ECJ allowing a distinction to be made between them.

20.5.1.1 National measures relating to product requirements

In *Keck* the ECJ gave some examples of national measures relating to product requirements. Such measures concern name, designation, form, size, weight, composition, presentation, labelling and packaging of goods. Other measures can be identified from the post-*Keck* case law of the ECJ. They are:

---

of organising a "jewellery party" in private homes in order to sell silver jewellery of low value), being more efficient and profitable than sale in a fixed commercial structure, was likely to increase the volume of intra-EU trade. The Court stated that this was not "enough" to classify the Austrian legislation as a MEQR.

1608. Case C-322/01 *Deutscher Apothekerverband* [2003] ECR I-14887; Case C-20/03 *Criminal Proceedings against Marcel Burmanjer and Others* [2004] ECR I-4133.

1609. Case C-71/02 *Herbert Karner Industrie-Auktionen GmbH v Troostwijk GmbH* [2004] ECR I-3025.

■ requirements relating to formalities concerning the act of importation, such as the issue of a licence prior to the carrying-on of certain economic activity[1610] and licensing requirements relating to the characteristics of the products;[1611] and,

■ requirements relating to the manufacturing/growing of the product in question.

The last-mentioned requirements were examined in Case C-158 and 159/04 *Alfa Vita*.[1612] The case concerned requirements imposed by a Greek regulation on supermarkets, where "bake-off" products were only briefly thawed and reheated. The requirements were that such supermarkets must have "a flour store, an area for kneading equipment and a solid-fuel store", these being requirements normally imposed on traditional bakeries. The ECJ held that the requirements were related to the process of final production and baking of bread and therefore affected the nature of the product itself, and accordingly could not be regarded as a selling arrangement such as contemplated in *Keck*. Therefore, they were MEQRs.

The *Alfa Vita* case should be distinguished from Case C-416/00 *Morellato*,[1613] which also concerned "bake-off" products. In *Morellato*, Italian law required a trader or distributor to package bread baked from frozen or non-frozen part-baked bread before offering it for sale. Both the Commission and the AG in his opinion in this case argued that such a requirement related to the characteristics of the product (that is, the packaging). The ECJ disagreed. It held that the requirement was imposed after the production process had been completed including the final baking prior to offering for sale, which took place in the Member State of importation. Accordingly, the requirement for prior packaging related only to the marketing of the bread and as such was outside the scope of Article 34 TFEU. This was provided that the requirement did not, in reality, constitute discrimination against imported products, which matter was left to the referring court to assess.

Another example is provided in Case C-147/04 *De Groot*[1614] which concerned two different varieties of a type of onion known as shallots. One was produced by vegetative propagation in France, that is, by direct reproduction from the roots; the other was grown from seed in the Netherlands. The ECJ found French legislation permitting only shallots produced by vegetative propagation to be marketed as shallots in France, and thus preventing the marketing of Dutch shallots in France, to be in breach of Article 34 TFEU. It constituted a MEQR because it concerned the propagation of the product and thus related to its characteristics. The final product, irrespective of the way it was reproduced, was identical.

1610. Case C-120/95 *Nicolas Decker v Caisse de Maladie des Employés Privés* [1998] ECR I-1831; Case 124/81 *Commission v United Kingdom (UHT Milk)* [1983] ECR 203; Case C-304/88 *Commission v Belgium* [1990] ECR I-2801; Case C-212/03 *Commission v France* [2005] ECR I-4213; Case 434/04 *Criminal Proceedings against Jan-Erik Anders Ahokainen and Mati Leppik* [2006] ECR I-9171.

1611. For example, Case C-389/96 *Aher-Waggon GmbH v Germany* [1998] ECR I-4473; Case C-189/95 *Criminal Proceedings against Harry Franzén* [1997] ECR I-5909; C-390/99 *Canal Satélite Digital SL v Administración General del Estado and DIS* [2002] ECR I-607.

1612. Joined Cases C-158/04 and C-159/04 *Alfa Vita Vassilopoulos AE, formerly Trofo Super-Markets AE and Carrefour Marinopoulos AE v Elliniko Dimosio, Nomarchiaki Aftodioikisi Ioanninon* [2006] ECR I-8135.

1613. Case C-416/00 *Tommaso Morellato v Comune di Padova* [2003] ECR I-9343.

1614. [2006] ECR I-245. Case C-147/04 *De Groot en Slot Allium BV and Bejo Zaden BV v Ministre de l'Économie, des Finances et de l'Industrie and Ministre de l'Agriculture, de l'Alimentation, de la Pêche et des Affaires Rurales* [2006] ECR I-245.

20.5.1.2 National measures relating to selling arrangements

The concept of selling arrangements is difficult to define. On the basis of the case law of the ECJ subsequent to *Keck*, the national measures, examined below, were found to relate to selling arrangements.

A. **National rules relating to resale at a loss and national rules relating to the fixing of prices.** In Case C-63/94 *Belgapom*,[1615] the ECJ confirmed its ruling in *Keck*. In this case the scenario was very similar to *Keck* as it concerned the Belgian law on Commercial Practices and Consumer Protection (1991), which prohibited resale at a loss. In Case C-531/07 *LIBRO*,[1616] the ECJ held that national rules which fix prices are to be regarded as selling arrangements.

B. **National rules relating to advertising.** In Case C-292/92 *Hünermund*[1617] the ECJ held that advertisement as a method of sales promotion was a selling arrangement. The application of *Keck* to advertising was confirmed in Case C-412/93 *Leclerc-Siplec*,[1618] in which French legislation prohibiting the broadcasting of televised advertisements for the distribution sector (in this case advertisements concerning the "distribution of fuel" in Leclerc supermarkets) was held by the ECJ to relate to selling arrangements.

C. **National rules regarding business opening hours including closing of shops on Sundays and bank holidays.** In Joined Cases 69 and 258/93 *Punto Case*,[1619] an Italian law requiring a total closure of shops on Sundays and public holidays was regarded as relating to selling arrangements.

D. **National rules conferring a monopoly right to distribute certain products to a specific group of people.** In Case 391/92 *Commission v Greece (Re Processed Milk for Infants)*,[1620] Greek legislation reserved to pharmacists the distribution of pharmaceutical products. The ECJ stated that the Greek legislation related to a selling arrangement.

E. **National rules relating to distance selling, e.g. *via* the internet or by mail order.** In Case C-322/01 *Deutscher Apothekerverband*,[1621] German legislation restricted the sale of most medicinal products for human use, including not only prescription drugs but also non-prescription drugs, to pharmacies located in Germany, and thus prevented their importation by way of mail order through pharmacies approved in other Member States in response to individual orders placed by consumers over the internet. The ECJ held that the German legislation was a selling arrangement. However, it failed to satisfy the second condition in *Keck* because the prohibition had a greater impact on pharmacies established outside German territory and thus could impede access to the German market for foreign products more than

---

1615. Case C-63/94 *Belgapom v ITM Belgium SA and Vocarex SA* [1995] ECR I-2467.
1616. [2009] ECR I-3717.
1617. Case C-292/92 *Hünermund v Landesapothekerkammer Baden-Württemberg* [1993] ECR I-6787.
1618. Case C-412/93 *Société d'Importation Eduard Leclerc-Siplec v TFI Publicité SA and M6 Publicité SA* [1995] ECR I-179.
1619. Joined Cases 69 and 258/93 *Punto Case SpA v Sindaco del Commune di Capena* [1994] ECR I-2355. See also: Joined Cases 401–402/92 *Tankstation't Heuske and Boermans* [1994] ECR I-2199; Joined Cases 418–421/93, 460–462/93, 464/93 and 9–11/94, 14 and 15/94, 23 and 24/94, 332/94 *Semeraro* [1996] ECR I-2975.
1620. [1995] ECR I-1621.
1621. [2003] ECR I-14887.

it impeded access for domestic products. It was, therefore, within the scope of Article 34 TFEU. With regard to prescription drugs the prohibition was justified on the grounds of public health but not in respect of non-prescription drugs. This case has important implications for traders in that under EU law they can have access to a market in all Member States *via* the internet. Accordingly, the removal of the "bricks and mortar" requirement has opened up the internal market for web-based businesses.

F.   **National rules governing "itinerant" sales.** In Case C-254/98 *TK-Heimdienst*,[1622] the requirement imposed on traders, who were operating sales rounds of foodstuffs in a specific administrative district of Austria, to trade from permanent establishments in that district or in any municipality adjacent thereto was regarded as relating to selling arrangements. Door-to-door sales were categorised as selling arrangements in Case C-20/03 *Burmanjer*[1623] (sale of national periodicals) and in Case C-441/04 *Claudia Schmidt*[1624] (sale of silver jewellery).

20.5.1.3   Assessment

It is submitted that national measures fall within the category of a selling arrangement if they relate to any of the following:

- conditions and methods of marketing of goods;

- the times and places of the sale of goods; and,

- advertisement of goods.

20.5.2   *Keck*: Its legal consequences

The implications of *Keck* are examined below.

A.   **Obsolete judgments.** The most obvious consequence is that a number of previous judgments of the ECJ are obsolete, in particular in the areas examined above.

B.   **Difficulty in determining whether a particular national rule concerns the product requirements or the selling arrangements.** The question of how to determine whether a particular national rule concerns a product requirement or a certain selling arrangement poses considerable difficulty.[1625] The cases of *Morellato* and *Alfa Vita* (see Chapter 20.5.1.1) are some of many in which even A-Gs and the Commission, not mentioning the national courts, had doubts as to the correct categorisation of national measures at issue. This also occurred in Case C-244/06 *Dynamic Medien*.[1626]

1622. Case C-254/98 *Schutzverband gegen unlauteren Wettbewerb v TK-Heimdienst Sass GmbH* [2000] ECR I-151.
1623. [2005] ECR I-4133.
1624. Case C-441/04 *A-Punkt Schmuckhandels GmbH v Claudia Schmidt* [2006] ECR I-2093.
1625. Case C-368/95 *Vereinigte Familiapress Zeitungsverlags- und vertriebs GmbH v Heinrich Bauer Verlag* [1997] ECR I-3689.
1626. Case C-244/06 *Dynamic Medien Vertriebs GmbH v Avides Media AG* [2008] ECR I-505.

THE FACTS WERE:

Avides Media, a German company, imported from the UK to Germany Japanese cartoons called "Animes" in DVD or video cassette format. Prior to the importation the cartoons were classified by the British Board of Film Classification ("the BBFC") under the relevant provisions of British legislation relating to the protection of young persons as being "suitable only for 15 years and over". The image storage media bore a BBFC label stating that they may be viewed only by persons aged 15 years or older. Dynamic Medien, a competitor of Avides Media, asked the competent German court for an interim measure prohibiting Avides Media from selling such image storage media by mail order in Germany on the ground that German law on the protection of young persons prohibits the sale by mail order of image storage media which has not been examined in Germany in accordance with that law, and which does not bear an age-limit label corresponding to a classification decision from the competent German authority.

Held:

German law constituted a MEQR and could only be justified under Article 36 TFEU or under mandatory requirements (see Chapter 21).

Comment:

Advocate-General Mengozzi in his Opinion concluded that the national measure constituted a selling arrangement because the German law did not appear to impose an obligation for image storage media, whether imported or not, to be examined and classified by the competent German authority, and to be labelled accordingly. The ECJ disagreed. It held that under German law there was the need to adapt the products in question to the rules in force in the Member State. Therefore the German law was a MEQR because the importers needed to alter the labelling of their products.

It emerges from the case law of the ECJ that some rules, which at first glance relate to certain selling arrangements, in due course were found by the ECJ as relating to product requirements. Furthermore, in some cases, the ECJ did not apply the distinction between a product requirement and a selling arrangement and instead focused only on the effects of the challenged national rules.[1627]

C. **Difficulty in the application of Article 34 TFEU.** The *Keck* approach calls into question the simplicity and uniformity of the application of Article 34 TFEU. In *Keck* the ECJ explained that a new approach to Article 34 TFEU was necessary in order to clarify its case law and to curtail the growing tendency of traders to rely on Article 34 TFEU in order to challenge national rules restricting their commercial freedom, even though such rules were not aimed at producers from other Member States.

1627. See Case C-323/93 *Société Civile Agricole du Centre d'Insémination de la Crespelle v Coopérative d'Elevage et d'Insémination Artificielle du Département de la Mayenne* [1994] ECR I-5077, para. 29, concerning French rules requiring economic operators importing semen from another Member State to deliver it to a centre enjoying an exclusive concession, and Case C-189/95 *Criminal Proceedings against Harry Franzén* [1997] ECR I-5909, para. 71, concerning the Swedish rules on import and marketing of alcoholic beverages.

It is submitted that in the light of the post-*Keck* decisions emanating from the ECJ this explanation is less than convincing. Indeed, instead of clarifying the application of Article 34 TFEU, *Keck* has become a source of confusion and controversy. It is also submitted that the application of *Keck* is contrary to the philosophy of Article 34 TFEU which, in order to ensure unfettered access to national markets for goods coming from other Member States, requires the abolition of any measure which constitutes an obstacle to the free movement of goods.

D. **Exclusion, from the scope of Article 34 TFEU, of national rules relating to selling arrangements which do not discriminate against imported goods.** Another consequence of *Keck* in that it excludes from the scope of application of Article 34 TFEU non-discriminatory selling arrangements. However, in Case 405/98 *Gourmet*[1628] the ECJ applied the access to the market test to condemn a non-discriminatory selling arrangement.

THE FACTS WERE:

Swedish legislation totally banning the advertisement on radio, television and in periodicals and other publications of alcoholic beverages containing more than 2.25 per cent alcohol by volume, but allowing such advertisement in the specialist press (that is, the press addressed to manufacturers and restaurateurs, and publications distributed solely at the point of sale of such beverages), was challenged by Gourmet International Products AB (Gourmet), a Swedish publisher of a magazine entitled "Gourmet," as being in breach of EU law, inter alia, of Article 34 TFEU. Gourmet published in "Gourmet" three pages of advertisements for alcoholic beverages, one for red wine and two for whisky. These pages did not appear in the edition sold in shops but in the edition addressed to subscribers of the magazine, 90 per cent of whom were manufacturers and retailers and 10 per cent private individuals. The Swedish Consumer Ombudsman applied to the Stockholm District Court for an injunction restraining Gourmet from placing advertisements for alcoholic beverages in magazines and for the imposition of a fine in the event of failure to comply. The Stockholm District Court referred to the ECJ the question of whether or not national rules imposing an absolute prohibition on certain advertisements might be regarded as measures having equivalent effect to a quantitative restriction and if so, whether or not they might be justified under Article 36 TFEU.

Held:

The ECJ held that given the nature of the product, the consumption of which is linked to traditional social practices and to local habits and customs, a total prohibition of all advertising directed at consumers was liable to impede access to the market by products from other Member States more than it impedes access by domestic products with which consumers are instantly more familiar.

Comment:

The ECJ based its reasoning on the "market access" test. In paragraph 18 of the judgment the ECJ stated that in order to escape the application of Article 34 TFEU, national rules

---

1628. Case 405/98 *Konsumentombudsmannen (KO) v Gourmet International Products AB (GIP)* [2001] ECR I-1795.

> prohibiting certain selling arrangements *"must not be of such a kind as to prevent access to the market by products from another Member State or to impede access any more than they impede the access of domestic products".*

Although in *Gourmet* the ECJ embraced the market access test, in the subsequent cases it has clearly departed from its approach in *Gourmet*. Therefore, it seems that only in a situation where there is a total ban which prevents access to the market, there is no need to prove a discriminatory effect.

20.6 Article 34 TFEU: residual rules

The ECJ recently introduced a new category of MEQRs, i.e. residual rules, when deciding two cases relating to national measures which imposed a prohibition/restriction on the use of a product.

The first of these cases is Case C-110/05 *Commission v Italy (Italian Trailers Case)*.[1629]

THE FACTS WERE:

Under Italian legislation two-wheeled or three-wheeled vehicles (mainly motorcycles) were not permitted to tow a trailer. The Commission considered that the Italian legislation was a MEQR because Italian consumers knowing that they could not use trailers in Italy were not interested in buying them.

Held:

The ECJ held that Italian law prohibiting the use of trailers specifically designed for motorcycles constituted a MEQR because it prevented the existence of any demand. However, the Court found that the prohibition was justified because it aimed at ensuring road safety. It was necessary and proportionate to the objective that the Italian legislation sought to achieve taking into account that the circulation of a combination composed of a motorcycle and a trailer could be dangerous.

The second is Case C-142/05 *Åklagaren (The Swedish Jet-skis Case)*.[1630]

THE FACTS WERE:

The issue was whether a Swedish restriction on the use of jet-skis on generally navigable waterways (which in Sweden simply do not exist in much of the country, and those in existence are generally not suitable for the use of jet-skis on safety grounds) was within the scope of Article 34 TFEU. The restriction on use of jet-skis resulted in consumers being not

---

1629. [2009] ECR I-519.
1630. Case C-142/05 *Åklagaren v Percy Mickelsson and Joakim Roos (The Swedish Jet-skis Case)* [2009] ECR I-4273.

interested in buying jet-skis knowing that they could not use them. The restriction was justified by Sweden on the grounds of the protection of the environment and the protection of health and life of animals, humans and plants.

Held:

The ECJ held that the Swedish legislation was a MEQR. It might be justified by the objective of the protection of the environment and the protection of life of animals, humans and plants but was disproportionate given that a general prohibition on using jet-skis on waters other than general navigable waterways constituted a measure going beyond what was necessary to achieve the aim of protection in the light of the fact that in Sweden there were waterways other than general navigable waterways on which jet-skis could be used without giving rise to risks or pollution deemed unacceptable for the environment.

Comment:

In the above cases the ECJ had to decide whether national rules relating to arrangements for the use of products should be considered as product related restrictions, or selling arrangements. In Case C-110/05 Commission v Italy the Commission's position was that national rules imposing an absolute prohibition on the use of certain products constituted MEQRs on imports and that the criteria set out in Keck were not applicable, in particular, because this would lead to the creation of an additional category of measures to which Article 34 TFEU would not apply. Some Member States, e.g. Germany, considered that some national rules prohibiting the use of certain products may be regarded as selling arrangements and consequently the principles concerning selling arrangements should apply to them in so far as national rules were non-discriminatory, ensured fair competition between imported products and domestic products and did not hinder, completely, or almost completely, access to the market in the State of importation. A-G Bot in his Opinion in Case C-110/05 Commission v Italy argued that the Italian law was a MEQR[1631] whilst A-G Kokott in Åklagaren considered that it "appears logical to extend the Court's Keck case-law to arrangements for use" of the products[1632] because restrictions imposed on jet-skis did not require any modification of jet-skis themselves. The ECJ chose to follow the Opinion of A-G Bot.

20.6.1 Clarifications of the judgments of the ECJ relating to residual rules

The judgments in the *Italian Trailers Case* and the *Swedish Jet-skis Case*, which were subject to many interpretations, revived discussion on the application of the access to the market test under Article 34 TFEU.[1633] However, the subsequent case law of the ECJ has established that:

■ The ECJ has rejected the possibility that national rules which prohibit/restrict the use of a product can be classified as selling arrangements.

1631. Opinion [2009] ECR I-519, para. 159.

1632. Opinion, para. 55.

1633. See T. Horsley, "Anyone for Keck?" (2009) 46 CMLRev., 2001; E. Spavanta, "Leaving Keck Behind? The Free Movement of Goods after the Rulings in Commission v Italy and Mickelsson and Roos", (2009) 34 ELRev., 914; L.W. Gormley, "Free Movement of Goods and Their Use – What is the Use of It?" (2009) 33 Fordham Intl L J, 1589.

■ The ECJ has applied the usual *Keck* test to selling arrangements and has thus rejected the market access test as the overarching principle of Article 34 TFEU. In this respect in Case C-108/09 *Ker-Optika*[1634] the ECJ confirmed its case law on the application of *Keck* to certain selling arrangements.

THE FACTS WERE:

Hungarian legislation prohibiting the sale of contact lenses via the internet was challenged by Ker-Optika, a limited partnership governed by Hungarian law, which, among other activities, sells contact lenses via its internet site. The Hungarian legislation allows the sale of contact lenses only in specialist shops covering at least 18m² and by persons practising as optometrists or ophthalmologists. This precluded any sales on the internet.

The Hungarian government justified the strict rules which govern the conditions of sale of contact lenses on the ground of the protection of public health. It explained that contact lenses are particularly invasive medical devices, in direct contact with the membrane of the eye, and therefore it is imperative to avoid deregulation of the selling of such lenses to prevent impairments of sight and ophthalmic diseases caused by misuse of contact lenses.

Held:

The ECJ held that the Hungarian legislation was an unjustified MEQR as it failed to satisfy the requirement of proportionality.

Comment:

The examination of the Hungarian legislation by the ECJ confirms that the Court does not wish to depart from the distinction made in Keck between national measures relating to product requirements and selling arrangements. Thus, the ECJ, on the basis of its well established case law, e.g. Case C-322/01 Deutscher Apothekerverband[1635] classified the Hungarian legislation as relating to a selling arrangement and thus assessed its compatibility with Article 34 TFEU in the light of the two conditions set out in Keck. So far as the first condition was concerned the challenged legislation applied without distinction to all relevant traders operating within Hungarian territory. However, the second condition which requires that a national measure must affect in the same manner, in law and in fact, the marketing of domestic products and of those from other Member States was not satisfied given that in fact it had affected to a greater degree the selling of products from other Member States than domestic products, i.e. was in fact discriminatory. In this respect the ECJ held that: "It is clear that the prohibition on selling contact lenses by mail order deprives traders from other Member States of a particularly effective means of selling those products and thus significantly impedes access of those traders to the market of the Member State concerned."[1636] As a result, the Hungarian legislation constituted a MEQR. The ECJ accepted that the Hungarian legislation was appropriate for achieving the objective of protecting public health. However, it found that it went beyond what was necessary to attain that objective.

1634. Case C-108/09 *Ker-Optika bt v ÀNTSZ Dél-dunántúli Regionális Intézete* [2010] ECR I-12213.
1635. [2003] ECR I-14887.
1636. Supra note 1634, para. 54.

The case law of the ECJ has also established that MEQRs are to be divided into three categories, as laid down in the *Italian Trailers* case. These are:

1. "Measures adopted by a Member State the object or effect of which is to treat products coming from other Member States less favourably."[1637] This refers to distinctly applicable measures.

2. "Obstacles to the free movement of goods which are the consequence of applying to goods coming from other Member States where they are lawfully manufactured and marketed, rules that lay down requirements to be met by such goods . . . . even if those rules apply to all products alike."[1638] This refers to indistinctly applicable product requirements.

3. "Any other measure which hinders access of products originating in other Member States to the market of a Member State."[1639] The meaning of this third category of MEQRs is unclear. On the one hand they cover rules belonging to the first and second category because both affect market access, on the other, it may be said that they are intended to catch national rules which are not within the first and second category. However, it is clear from the subsequent case law of the ECJ that the Court has no intention of revising its approach to selling arrangements. Accordingly, the reference to "any other measures" means any measure which cannot easily be classified as a distinctly applicable measure or indistinctly applicable measure concerning product requirements or certain selling arrangements. For example, rules relating to the use of products, and bans on certain activities will be within the scope of this third category of MEQRs.

In Case C-28/09 *Commission v Austria*[1640] the ECJ held that the prohibition for an indefinite period of use of a section of a motorway in the Inn Valley in Austria imposed on lorries of over 7.5 tons carrying goods was a MEQR. The ban was neither a distinctly applicable measure, nor an indistinctly applicable measure concerning product requirements, nor a selling arrangement. Nevertheless, the prohibition hindered the access to the market of products coming from the south of Europe to the north of Europe and going from the north of Europe to the west of Europe, in the light of the fact that the section of the motorway concerned constituted the main Alpine corridor for transporting goods across Europe. As a result of the prohibition, goods had to be transported either by rail or *via* longer road routes. This created additional costs for manufacturers of the goods concerned who had to bear increased transportation costs, which affected competitiveness of their products. In this case, the ECJ rejected the justification submitted by Austria based on the protection of public health and the protection of the environment. It held that the prohibition was disproportionate on the ground that Austria did not sufficiently examine the possibility of having recourse to other less restrictive measures to achieve the objective of reducing the emission of nitrogen dioxide in the Inn Valley.

In Case C-456/10 *ANETT*[1641] Spanish legislation which prohibited Spanish tobacco retailers from importing manufactured tobacco products from other Member States was classified as a residual rule. In Spain the retail trade of manufactured tobacco product remains a monopoly owned by the State with

---

1637. Case C-110/05 *Commission v Italy* [2009] ECR I-519, para. 37.
1638. Ibid, para. 35.
1639. Ibid, para. 37.
1640. Judgment of 21/12/11 (NYR).
1641. In Case C-456/10 *Asociación Nacional de Expendedores de Tabaco y Timbre (ANETT) v Administración del Estado* (Judgment of 26/4/12 (NYR)).

the consequence that Spanish tobacco retailers are forced to obtain their supplies from the monopoly. They challenged the Spanish legislation. The Spanish legislation was neither a selling arrangement as it did not concern the marketing or advertising of tobacco products nor an indistinctly applicable measure relating to product requirements as it did not impose any requirements that such products must meet in Spain. However, the ECJ held that the Spanish legislation hindered the access of tobacco products to the Spanish market as it forced tobacco retailers to obtain their supplies from the monopoly. Accordingly, they suffered disadvantages. First, they could only sell the range of products offered by the monopoly and thus had no direct, flexible and quick means of responding to the demands of their customers who were interested in buying products not included in the range. Second, they were prevented from taking advantage of more advantageous procurement conditions, in particular if they were located in border areas. The ECJ concluded that: "All of these elements are capable of having a negative effect on the choice of products that the tobacco retailers include in their range of products and, ultimately, on the access of various products coming from other Member States to the Spanish market."[1642]

20.6.2 Conclusion

The following conclusions can be drawn from the case law of the ECJ relating to residual rules:

1. The access to the market test has not become a general criterion under Article 34 TFEU to be applied to all measures irrespective of whether they concern the product itself or relate to selling arrangements. Consequently, the vision of the internal market presented by A-G Jacobs in his Opinion in Case C-412/93 *Leclerc-Siplec*[1643] has not materialised. In that case he said: "the main concern of the Treaty provisions on the free movement of goods is to prevent unjustified obstacles to trade between Member States. If an obstacle to inter-State trade exists, it cannot cease to exist simply because an identical obstacle affects domestic trade ... Restrictions on trade should not be tested against local conditions which happen to prevail in each Member State, but against the aim of access to the entire Community market".[1644] Thus, according to him, Article 34 TFEU should ensure that not only unequal access to the market in the importing Member State, but also the unequal effect of "marketing rules" in that State, should be condemned. In *Leclerc-Siplec* A-G he proposed the application of the access to the market test to both product related measures and selling arrangements based on the significance of the hindrance to trade between Member States, i.e. in fact he proposed the introduction of the *de minimis* rule. In respect of product related measures he suggested that any national rule which requires the modification of imported products would amount to a substantial restriction on access to the market in the importing State. For selling arrangements, the assessment of whether a national rule constitutes a substantial impediment would depend on such factors as whether it "applies to certain goods ... or to most goods ... or to all goods, ... on the extent to which other selling arrangements remain available, and on whether the effect of the measure is direct or indirect, immediate or remote, or purely speculative and uncertain".[1645]

1642. Ibid, para. 42.
1643. Case C-412/93 *Société d'Importation Edouard Leclerc-Siplec v TF1 Publicité SA and M6 Publicité SA* [1995] ECR I-179, paras 39–40.
1644. Ibid.
1645. Ibid, para. 45.

2. Residual rules which neither concern product requirements nor selling arrangements are within the scope of Article 34 TFEU. To them the *Dassonville* formula applies and consequently they need to be justified. They are subject to the market access test which means that even if they are non-discriminatory, but affect the market access of imports, they will be caught by Article 34 TFEU. This is supported by Case C-142/05 *Åklagaren* in which the ECJ held that a non-discriminatory national rule may impose restrictions on the use of a product which may "depending on its scope, have a considerable influence on the behaviour of consumers, which may, in turn, affect the access of that product to the market of that Member State".[1646] This statement seems to suggest that the market access test should be based on the attitudes of consumers. If a national rule has a considerable influence on the behaviour of consumers it will impede access to the market with the consequence that such national rule will be in breach of Article 34 TFEU. However, if the access to the market test were to be linked to consumer behaviour, this would amount to the application of the *de minimis* rule which, the ECJ has refused to apply to the free movement of goods.[1647] In this respect, various interpretations as to the application of the *de minimus* rule are possible.

One is that the *de minimus* rule will apply only to residual rules. This interpretation provides a logical explanation of some cases decided prior to the *Italian Trailers* case and to the *Swedish Jet-skis* case, in which the ECJ held that a national rule was outside the scope of Article 34 TFEU because its restrictive effect on trade between Member States was too uncertain and indirect.[1648] For example, in Case C-69/88 *Krantz*,[1649] the ECJ decided that Dutch legislation under which national tax authorities were allowed, in order to recover a tax debt, to seize goods, other than stocks, found on the premises of a tax debtor, even if those goods had been received from a supplier established in another Member State who sold them on instalment terms with reservation of title, was outside the scope of Article 34 TFEU. The ECJ held:

> "the possibility that nationals of other Member States would hesitate to sell goods on instalment terms to purchasers in the Member State concerned because such goods would be liable to seizure by the collector of taxes if the purchasers failed to discharge their Netherlands tax debts is too uncertain and indirect to warrant the conclusion that a national provision authorising such seizure is liable to hinder trade between Member States."[1650]

Similarly, in Case C-93/92 *Motorradcenter*[1651] the ECJ held that the restrictive effects of national law which imposed an obligation on an unauthorised dealer of Yamaha motorcycles, which were the subject of parallel imports, to inform purchasers of such motorcycles that authorised Yamaha dealers often refuse to carry out repairs under the guarantee for motorcycles, were too uncertain and indirect to constitute a hindrance to the free movement of goods. In

---

1646. Case C-142/05 *Åklagaren v Percy Mickelsson and Joakim Roos (The Swedish Jet-skis Case)* [2009] ECR I-4273, para. 26.
1647. Joined Cases 177–178/82 *Criminal Proceedings against Jan Van de Haar* [1984] ECR 1797; Case C-461/01 *Commission v Germany* [2004] ECR I-11705.
1648. Case C-93/92 *CMC Motorradcenter GmbH v Pelin Baskiciogullari* [1993] ECR I-5009; see also Case C-379/92 *Criminal Proceedings against Matteo Peralta* [1994] ECR I-3453; Case C-44/98 *BASF AG v Präsident des Deutschen Patentamts* [1999] ECT I-6269.
1649. Case C-69/88 *Krantz GmbH & Co. v Ontvanger der Directe Belastingen and Netherlands State* [1990] ECR I-583.
1650. Ibid, para. 11.
1651. Case C-93/92 *CMC Motorradcenter GmbH v Pelin Baskiciogullari* [1993] ECR I-5009.

both the above cases, national rules can be clearly seen as fitting into the third category of MEQRs as set out in Case C-110/05 *Commission v Italy*.[1652]

Another interpretation is that suggested by A-G La Pergola in Case C-44/98 BASF.[1653] According to him, the ECJ does not apply the *de minimis* rule. However, when the ECJ finds that there is no causal link between the measure adopted and its restrictive effect on imports, Article 34 TFEU does not apply because the effect of the rule is "too uncertain and indirect".

Notwithstanding the above, the question arises how to apply the access to the market test in respect of residual national rules. What should be the threshold criteria triggering the application of Article 34 TFEU? This matter is unclear. Accordingly the following questions arise:

(i) Will the application of the access to the market test require a case-by-case assessment, based on an economic analysis of the actual or even potential impact on imports, of the relevant national measure? In the *Italian Trailers* case the ECJ neither engaged in any economic analysis of trade volumes nor required the parties to submit statistical information on the actual effect of the prohibition on imports. Similarly, in Case C-456/10 *ANETT*[1654] the ECJ did not assess the impact of Spanish law on imports. This suggests that the ECJ will focus on the content of the measure itself (e.g. whether it results in consumers having "practically no interest in buying" the product concerned or having only "a limited interest in buying" it, or as was the situation in *ANETT*, whether Spanish retailers of tobacco products were deprived of opportunity to import tobacco products from other Member States), rather than on an economic analysis of its impact on the volume of trade. As a result, only a national rule that has a substantial impact on imports will be caught by Article 34 TFEU;

(ii) Will the ECJ follow the suggestion of A-G Poiares Maduro in Joined Cases C-158/04 and C-159/04 *Alfa Vita*,[1655] in which the A-G defined a measure constituting a barrier to access to a national market as a measure which discriminates against the exercise of freedom of movement? According to the A-G a measure which constitutes a barrier to access to a national market is a measure which protects the acquired positions of certain economic operators on a national market or a measure which makes intra-EU trade more difficult than trade within a national market. As a result, it discriminates against the exercise of freedom of movement by foreign traders as opposed to discriminating against foreign products based on their nationality or other characteristics. If this approach is accepted then the difference between the access to the market test and the discrimination analysis carried out by the ECJ will not be significant;

(iii) Will the ECJ take account of the fact that a national rule generates additional costs for traders? In this respect in Case C-28/09 *Commission v Austria*,[1656] the Commission stated

---

1652. [2009] ECR I-519.

1653. Case C-44/98 *BASF AG v Präsident des Deutschen Patentamts* [1999] ECR I-6269, para. 18.

1654. In Case C-456/10 *Asociación Nacional de Expendedores de Tabaco y Timbre (ANETT) v Administración del Estado* (26/4/12 (NYR)).

1655. Joined Cases C-158/04 and C-159/04 *Alfa Vita Vassilopoulos AE, formerly Trofo Super-Markets AE v Iliniko Dimosio, Nomarkhiaki Aftodiikisi Ioanninon and Carrefour Marinopoulos AE v Elliniko Dimosio, Nomarkhiaki Aftodiikisi Ioanninon* [2006] ECR I-8135.

1656. Judgment of 21/12/11 (NYR) para. 58.

that "The sectoral traffic prohibition thus has substantial economic repercussions not only for the transport industry but also for manufacturers of the goods concerned by the regulation, who will have to bear higher transport costs, which will affect their competitiveness." However, the ECJ did not comment on the Commission's statement. Instead it held that the sectoral traffic prohibition was a MEQR because it had a substantial effect on the transit of goods between Northern Europe and Northern Italy (para. 116). The Court did not explain why it had reached this conclusion. However, it referred to its previous judgment in Case C-320/03 *Commission v Austria*[1657] in which it stated that the sectoral traffic restriction limited trading opportunities between Northern Europe and Italy. It is to be noted that in Case C-270/02 *Commission v Italy (Foodstuffs for Sportsmen and Women),*[1658] the ECJ condemned the prior-authorisation system for marketing high-energy foods and payments of ensuing administrative fees because those requirements rendered the marketing of such products more difficult and more expensive. Also, in Case C-189/95 *Franzén*[1659] a licence requirement imposed by Swedish law on individuals who wished to import alcoholic drinks was regarded by the ECJ as a MEQR because it imposed additional costs on beverages imported to Sweden. However, the imposition of additional costs is not always wrong. In this respect the A-G in Joined Cases C-158/04 and C-159/04 *Alfa Vita*[1660] stated that supplementary costs which arise from disparities in the national legislation of Member States are not restrictions on trade. They are within the scope of Article 34 TFEU only when they are imposed without taking account of "the particular situation of the imported products and, in particular, the fact that those products already had complied with the rules of their State of origin";[1661] and,

3. The access to the market test, which allows the application of Article 34 TFEU to non-discriminatory residual rules which substantially impede access to the market of imports, is firmly within the scope of Article 34 TFEU. However, its meaning is still elusive, and the threshold criteria for the application of Article 34 TFEU uncertain.

20.7 Article 34 TFEU: reverse discrimination and internal situations

Purely domestic situations are outside the scope of Article 34 TFEU because it is intended to protect only trade between Member States.[1662] However, in the light of the judgment of the ECJ in Joined Cases C-321/94, C-322/94, C-323/94 and C-324/94 *Pistre,*[1663] a national measure which creates and maintains a difference of treatment between imported goods and domestic goods will be within the scope of Article 34 TFEU not only when it directly and actually, but also indirectly or potentially, hinders intra-EU trade. The judgment in *Pistre* was further explained by the ECJ in Case C-448/98 *Guimont.*[1664]

1657. [2005] ECR I-9871, para. 68.
1658. [2004] ECR I-1559, para. 19.
1659. Case C-189/95 *Criminal Proceedings against Harry Franzén* [1997] ECR I-5909, para. 71.
1660. Supra note 1612.
1661. Ibid, para. 44.
1662. Case 98/86 *Ministère Public v Arthur Mathot* [1987] ECR 809.
1663. Joined Cases C-321/94, C-322/94, C-323/94 and C-324/94 *Criminal Proceedings against Jacques Pistre and Others* [1997] ECR I-2343.
1664. Case C-448/98 *Criminal Proceedings against Jean-Pierre Guimont* [2000] ECR I-10663.

THE FACTS WERE:

Mr Guimont, the technical manager of the Laiterie d'Argis located in Vaucluse in France, refused to pay a fine imposed by the Directorate for Competition, Consumer Affairs and Prevention of Fraud of the Department of Vaucluse. It was imposed on him for holding for sale, selling or offering Emmenthal cheese without rind contrary to the French law which expressly required that cheese bearing the designation "Emmenthal" must have, inter alia, "a hard, dry rind, of a colour between golden yellow and light brown." When Mr Guimont refused to pay the fine, criminal proceedings were brought against him before the Tribunal de Police (Local Criminal Court) of Belley. Mr Guimont argued that the French legislation was in breach of Article 34 TFEU. The Tribunal de Police asked the ECJ to answer whether or not this was the case.

Held:

The ECJ decided to accept the reference for a preliminary ruling, although the matter was purely internal. The acceptance was because its reply "might be useful" to the referring court "if its national law were to require, in proceedings such as those in this case, that a national producer be allowed to enjoy the same rights as those which a producer of another Member State would derive from Community law in the same situation,"[1665] i.e. if national law prohibits reverse discrimination.

Comment:

Surprisingly, the answer of the ECJ was based on the Dassonville *formula, that is, that Article 34 TFEU applies to any measure of a Member State which is capable, directly or indirectly, actually or potentially, of hindering trade between Member States, although the situation in this case was purely internal.*

The governments of Germany, the Netherlands and Austria, together with the Commission, supported Mr Guimont. Their argument was based on the decision of the ECJ in Joined Cases C-321–324/94 Pistre,[1666] *in which the Court held that Article 34 TFEU cannot be considered inapplicable simply because all facts of the specific case before the national court are confined to a single Member State. However, in* Guimont *the ECJ provided a justification for its solution in* Pistre. *The ECJ stated that "It should be noted that the Pistre judgment concerned a situation where the national rule in question was not applicable without distinction but created direct discrimination against goods imported from other Member States,"[1667] that is, the rule was distinctly applicable. However in* Guimont *the rule in question was indistinctly applicable. Accordingly, the ECJ explained in* Guimont *that in a situation where a national rule is indistinctly applicable, Article 34 TFEU applies "only in so far as it applies to situations that are linked to the importation of goods in intra-Community trade."[1668] In fact, there was no importation of goods in* Guimont *and accordingly the ECJ should have declined to answer the preliminary question. Nevertheless, the ECJ decided to answer the question referred to it by the Tribunal de Police (Local Criminal Court) of Belley because such*

1665. Ibid, para. 23.

1666. Joined Cases C-321/94, C-322/94, C-323/94 and C-324/94 *Criminal Proceedings against Jacques Pistre and Others* [1997] ECR I-2343.

1667. Ibid, para. 20.

1668. Ibid, para. 21.

a reply might be useful, in particular, in a situation where national law prohibits reverse discrimination. In such a situation national law must be interpreted in conformity with EU law. The outcome of this case was that if the relevant national law prohibits reverse discrimination (for example, Article 3 of the Italian Constitution as interpreted by the Italian Constitutional Court prohibits reverse discrimination[1669]), claimants such as Mr Guimont will be successful in their claim; otherwise they will not be able to challenge a national rule that is indistinctly applicable, if there is, under national law, no redress against reverse discrimination.

Two conclusions can be drawn from *Guimont*:

- First, the ECJ, without interfering in the internal competences of Member States, reminded national courts that if reverse discrimination is illegal under national law, the *Guimont* approach applies and the ECJ will accept a referral from a national court if its reply "might be useful". It is to be noted that the ECJ, by accepting referrals concerning purely internal situations, might deliver purely hypothetical preliminary rulings, wasting the time and money of the applicants, and both its own resources and those of the national courts (see Chapter 13.3.5).

- The second concerns the flexibility of the ECJ in interpreting the concept of a "purely domestic situation". This is exemplified in Case C-71/02 *Karner*,[1670] in which the only external element was that Troostwijk GmbH, an Austrian undertaking whose main activities consisted of purchasing the stock of insolvent companies and selling it by auction, advertised the auction in question on the internet among other means. Karner vigorously argued that the reference from an Austrian court should not be accepted by the ECJ given that the dispute before the referring court related to a purely internal situation, as both parties to the proceedings were established in Austria, the goods in question were acquired following a case of insolvency which took place in Austria and the relevant Austrian legislation concerned forms of advertising in Austria. This was not the view of the ECJ, which, for the first time, expressly recognised that an indistinctly applicable national measure applied within the context of a purely domestic dispute may still fall within the scope of Article 34 TFEU.

The disappointing aspect of the judgment in *Karner* is that the ECJ failed to explain its judgment. One can only speculate on this matter. Perhaps the ECJ, without any express reference in its judgment, considered that the existence of the internet and the opportunity to use it as a means of conveying information has already abolished the border between what should be regarded as a matter of purely domestic significance and what should be regarded as a matter which has an EU dimension.

1669. A. Tryfonidou, "Carbonati Apuani SRL v Comune di Carrera: Should we Reverse 'Reverse Discrimination'?", (2005) 16 King's College L.J, 373.

1670. Case C-71/02 *Herbert Karner Industrie-Auktionen GmbH v Troostwijk GmbH* [2004] ECR I-3025.

20.8   Article 35 TFEU: prohibition of QRs and MEQRs on exports

Article 35 TFEU prohibits quantitative restrictions and measures having equivalent effect on exports. The ECJ explained in Case 15/79 *Groenveld*[1671] that national measures are considered as MEQRs on exports if they "have as their specific object or effect the restriction of patterns of exports and thereby the establishment of a difference in treatment between the domestic trade of a Member State and its export trade in such a way as to provide a particular advantage for national production or for the domestic market of the State in question at the expense of the production or of trade of other Member States". However, the test, as just quoted from the *Groenveld* case, was abandoned by the ECJ in Case C-205/07 *Gysbrechts*.[1672]

THE FACTS WERE:

Belgian law on distance-selling contracts prohibited a seller from requiring a deposit, or form of payment from the consumer, or even a consumer's payment credit card number, before the expiry of the mandatory period of seven working days for withdrawal. The claimant argued that the Belgian legislation was in breach of Article 35 TFEU. The Belgian government submitted that the national law was justified on the ground of the protection of consumers. This was because the prohibition on requiring from the consumer an advance, or payment, or a consumer's payment credit card number before expiry of the period for withdrawal sought to ensure that the consumer could exercise his right of withdrawal effectively.

Held:

The ECJ held that:

1. *A national measure prohibiting a supplier in a distance sale from requiring an advance or any payment before expiry of the period for withdrawal constituted a MEQR but could be justified by the overriding requirements based on the protection of the consumer. The measure was also necessary and proportionate to the objective sought by the Belgian legislation;*

2. *A national measure prohibiting a supplier from requiring that consumers provide their payment card number, even if the supplier undertakes not to use it to collect payment before expiry of the period for withdrawals, was a MEQR, and could be justified by the necessity to protect consumers. However, it went beyond what was necessary to protect consumers. National law was disproportionate to the objective of protecting consumers because the uncertainty of the seller, who was not allowed to require the consumer to provide a credit card number, as to whether he would receive the payment might lead the seller to stop exporting goods sold over the internet or to reduce the volume of such exports.*

In this case the ECJ decided to harmonise, to some extent, the criteria for determining whether a national measure is a MEQR under Articles 34 and 35 TFEU.

1671.   [1979] ECR 3409; see also Case C-3/91 *Exportur SA v LOR SA and Confiserie du Tech SA* [1992] ECR I-5529.

1672.   Case C-205/07 *Criminal Proceedings against Lodewijk Gysbrechts and Santurel Inter BVBA* [2008] ECR I-9947.

Prior to the judgment, the definition of MEQR under Article 35 TFEU was more restrictive than the definition of a MEQR under Article 34 TFEU, i.e. the definition set out in the *Dassonville* formula.

A-G Trstenjak, in her Opinion in *Gysbrechts*, applied the criteria set out in *Groenveld* to the prohibition established under Belgian law. She concluded that there was no breach of Article 35 TFEU. However, it was obvious that the Belgian law had a greater effect on goods intended for export than on goods marketed domestically in so far as the imposition on a supplier of a prohibition on requiring that a consumer provide his payment credit card number in cross-border distance selling was concerned. This was one of the reasons why the A-G proposed a modification of the test for the determination of MEQRs under Article 35 TFEU. Among other reasons mentioned by the A-G, probably the most convincing was that if certain goods are only produced for export in a Member State the test in *Groenveld* is useless in that it will never be possible to determine whether there are differences in treatment between domestic trade and export trade because the goods in question are not traded on the domestic market. As a result, it will never be possible, either, to determine whether a certain measure confers an advantage on national production or on the domestic market of the Member State concerned.

The A-G proposed two ways to modify the *Groenveld* test:

- the first consisting of harmonising law on Articles 34 and 35 TFEU, i.e. applying all the definitions and case law relating to Article 34 TFEU to Article 35 TFEU; and,

- the second consisting of establishing a new definition of MEQRs under Article 35 TFEU which would be narrower than that contained in the *Dassonville* formula, and which might perhaps justify non-application of the criteria set out in *Keck* to exports. However, under a new definition there would be a possibility for justifying national measures by the imperative requirements set out in *Cassis de Dijon*.

The ECJ's response to the A-G's propositions was provided in para. 43 of the judgment which states: "even if a prohibition such as that at issue in the main proceedings is applicable to all traders active in the national territory, its actual effect is none the less greater on goods leaving the market of the exporting Member State than on the marketing of goods in the domestic market of that Member State".

In the above passage, the ECJ applied the factual discrimination test to define a MEQR under Article 35 TFEU. The Court stated that in order to determine whether a national measure constitutes a MEQR under Article 35 TFEU the basic criterion will be to determine its effect on the marketing of products leaving a Member State. Therefore, the Court focused on *de facto* discrimination, i.e. it found that the actual effect of national law on exports was greater than on the marketing of the goods in the domestic market. Further, the ECJ, for the first time, accepted that a Member State could rely on imperative requirements set out in *Cassis de Dijon* to justify a restriction imposed on exports.

20.9 The Rapid Intervention Mechanism (RIM)

In order to enable the Commission to intervene efficiently to restore the free movement of goods when normal procedures are not sufficient, Regulation 2679/98 of 7 December 1998 on the functioning of the internal market in relation to the free movement of goods among the Member States[1673] sets up a rapid intervention mechanism (RIM).

Under the Regulation, where there are "clear unmistakable and unjustified obstacles to the free movement of goods" within the meaning of Articles 34–36 TFEU, which may result in the serious

---

1673. [1998] OJ L337/1.

disruption of the free movement of goods and cause serious loss to natural or legal persons, the Commission may, by way of formal decision addressed to the Member State concerned, require that Member State to take all appropriate measures to remove the obstacle within a time limit fixed by the Commission.

The Regulation specifies that the Commission is obliged to act within five days following the day on which the Commission becomes aware of all the facts. The right to defence in respect of the Member State concerned is protected under the procedure. The Member State is given three to five working days from the date on which the Commission brings the matter to the attention of the Member State to submit its defence. Once the Commission adopts a formal decision, the Member State concerned must comply with it within the prescribed time limit. If it fails to comply, the Commission is required to notify the Member State concerned that it has three days to submit its observations, failing which the Commission will immediately issue a reasoned opinion requiring it to comply. If the Member State still refuses to comply, the Commission may bring proceedings before the ECJ. However, the RIM does not prejudice the Article 258 TFEU procedure and does not constitute a precondition for commencement of the pre-litigation procedure under that Article. It is up to the Commission to decide which of the two procedures is most appropriate to use in the light of the circumstances of the case.[1674]

The Regulation has important consequences in relation to the Member State which is in breach, since under the RIM that Member State can be promptly brought before the ECJ.

The clear beneficiaries from the RIM are natural or legal persons suffering damage resulting from obstacles to the free movement of goods:

- First, in the event of non-compliance an individual may immediately start proceedings under national law against the relevant Member State and the formal decision of the Commission will facilitate the proceedings;

- Second, an individual may seek remedy against the Commission under Article 340(2) TFEU in the event that the Commission fails to bring proceedings against a defaulting Member State; and,

- Third, the Regulation permits an individual to bring an action against the Commission under Article 265 TFEU in the case of Commission passivity in respect of serious breaches of Articles 34–36 TFEU by Member States.

RECOMMENDED READING

Books
Barnard, C., *The Substantive Law of the EU. The Four Freedoms*, 3rd edn, 2010, Oxford: OUP.
Davies, G., *European Union Internal Market Law*, 2006, London: Routledge Cavendish.
MacMaolain, C., *EU Food Law: Protecting Consumers and Health in a Common Market*, 2007, Oxford: Hart Publishing.
Shuibhne, N. (ed.), *Regulating the Internal Market*, 2006, Cheltenham: Edward Elgar.

Articles
Arnull, A., "What Shall we do on Sunday?", (1991) 16 ELRev., 112.
Barnard, C., "Trailing a New Approach to Free Movement of Goods", (2009) 68 CLJ, 288.
Connor, T., "Accentuating the Positive: the 'Selling Arrangement', the First Decade and Beyond", (2005) 54 ICLQ, 127.

1674. Case C-320/03 *Commission v Austria* [2005] ECR I-9871; Case C-394/02 *Commission v Greece* [2005] ECR I-4713.

Davies, G., "Can Selling Arrangements be Harmonised?", (2005) 30 ELRev., 37.

Garde, A., "EU Food Law – Protecting Consumers and Health in a Common Market", (2008) 14 EPL, 440.

Gormley, L. W., "Free Movement of Goods and Their Use – What is the Use of It?", (2009) 33 Fordham Intl L.J., 1589.

Horsley, T., "Anyone for Keck?", (2009) 46 CMLRev., 2001.

Maduro, M.P., "So Close and Yet so Far: The Paradoxes of Mutual Recognition", (2007) 14 JEPP, 814.

Pecho, P., "Good-Bye Keck? A Comment on the Remarkable Judgment in Commission v Italy, C-110/05", (2009) 36 LIEI, 257.

Roth, W-H., "Case C-205/07, *Lodewijk Gysbrechts, Santurel Inter BVBA*, Judgment of the Court of Justice (Grand Chamber) of 16 December 2008", (2010) 47 CMLRev., 509.

Snell, J., "The Notion of Market Access: A Concept or a Slogan?", (2010) 47 CMLRev., 437.

Spavanta, E., "Leaving Keck Behind? The Free Movement of Goods After the Rulings in Commission v Italy and Mickelsson and Roos", (2009) 34 ELRev., 914.

Szajkowska, A., "The Impact of the Definition of the Precautionary Principle in EU Food Law", (2010) 47 CMLRev., 173.

Tryfonidou, A., "Was Keck A Half-Baked Solution After All?", [2007] 34(2) LIEI, 167.

White, E.L. "In Search Of The Limits To Article 30 Of The EEC Treaty", (1989) 26 CMLRev., 235.

Wilsher, D., "Does Keck Discrimination Make any Sense? An Assessment of Non-discrimination Principle within the European Single Market", (2008) 33 ELRev., 3.

PROBLEM QUESTION

John, a French producer of sugar from cane, has been selling his products in Germany for two years. Recently he has encountered the following problems:

a) A year ago the German government created a central fund (CF) for the promotion of the German food sector. The CF carries out its task through a central body (CB), a private company whose organs were set up in accordance with private law. The CF is financed by compulsory contributions paid by undertakings in the German food industry. The CF's main task is to promote the distribution and exploitation of products of the German food sector, and it must not seek profit by the sale of goods. In order to promote German agricultural and food products, the CB has established quality requirements for a large number of different products. Producers of products which satisfy those requirements may, on application to the CB, be licensed to affix a quality label (the CB label) to their products. John's application for the CB quality label was rejected. He was told that the CB reserves the use of the label for products which are produced in Germany, from either German or imported raw materials;

b) Under new German law, in order to sell sugar from cane, John must obtain a prior authorisation from the German Health Authorities. He has discovered that the procedure for obtaining prior authorisation is lengthy; does not provide for any appeal against refusal of authorisation; and. the applicant must pay €800 for the application to be processed; and,

c) John has opened a shop in Germany which sells sweets made of sugar cane. Recently, he has been prosecuted for violation of a German law which prohibits shops from selling on Sundays. According to John the effect of the law is that his total turnover is about 10% less than would be the case if he could sell on Sundays.

Advise John as to the application, if any, of Article 34 TFEU to each of the above problems.

ESSAY QUESTION

Critically discuss the implications for the elimination of obstacles to the free movement of goods in the EU of the ECJ's judgment in the *Italian Trailers* case.

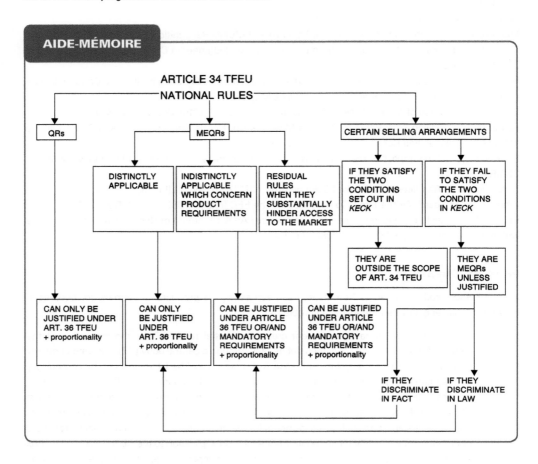

21

DEROGATIONS FROM ARTICLES 34 AND 35 TFEU LISTED IN ARTICLE 36 TFEU AND JUSTIFICATIONS BASED ON MANDATORY REQUIREMENTS

CONTENTS

CHAPTER OUTLINE

1. Article 36 TFEU contains an exhaustive list of derogations from the principle of the free movement of goods. It applies when there is no EU harmonising legislation. On the grounds set out in Article 36 TFEU Member States can justify national rules which are in breach of Articles 34 or 35 TFEU. However, such rules must not constitute a means of arbitrary discrimination or disguised restrictions on trade between Member States

2. An important feature of Article 36 TFEU is that distinctly applicable measures can only be justified on the grounds set out in that article (so they cannot be justified by the mandatory requirements). However, the ECJ has, on rare occasions, accepted justifications for distinctly applicable measures based on safety requirements and the protection of the environment, i.e. mandatory requirements. This has fuelled a debate on whether there should be a distinction between derogations based on Article 36 TFEU (Treaty based justifications) and those based on mandatory requirements (case law-based justifications).

3. The derogations set out in Article 36 TFEU relate to:

A.   Public morality. A Member State enjoys a margin of discretion to define the requirements of public morality in its territory but is prohibited from applying double standards of morality;

B.   Public policy. This refers to the protection of the fundamental interests of society. This is potentially a very broad derogation but has rarely been successful;

C.   Public security. This concerns the safeguarding of the institutions of a Member State, its essential public services and the survival of its population. This ground has rarely been relied upon by Member States;

D.   Protection of the health and life of humans, animals and plants. In order to successfully rely on this derogation a Member State must show that there is a genuine risk to health and life. Additionally, a Member State may invoke the precautionary principle (see point 6 below);

E.   Protection of national treasures which possess artistic, historic or archaeological value. So far this derogation has never been successfully relied upon; and,

F.   Protection of industrial and commercial property. Article 36 TFEU recognises that intellectual property rights (IPRs) may constitute MEQRs. The ECJ made a distinction between the existence of IPRs, which is protected under Article 345 TFEU, and their exercise, which is subject to the requirements set out in Articles 34 and 36 TFEU, depending upon the specific subject matter of the particular IPR. The benefit of the specific subject-matter was described in Case 15/74 *Centrafarm* as the exclusive right of a holder of IPRs to first marketing of the protected product, whether this marketing is direct or by means of the grant of licences to third parties, in more than one Member State of the EEA. Once a holder has had the benefit of the specific subject-matter of the IPR, his right is exhausted. Consequently, he cannot rely on the protection of IPRs provided for under the national law of a Member State to prevent parallel imports of the protected goods which have lawfully been marketed in any other Member State of the EEA by him or with his consent. However, the principle of exhaustion does not apply to parallel imports of protected products coming from outside the EEA.

4. In the *Cassis de Dijon* case, the ECJ accepted justifications for indistinctly applicable measures additional to those set out in Article 36 TFEU (see Chapter 20.3) and on the authority of the *Italian Trailers* case such justifications can also be relied upon by a Member State to justify national residual rules (see Chapter 20.6). These are called "mandatory requirements". They can be relied upon only in respect of non-harmonised areas of EU law. The list of mandatory requirements is non exhaustive as opposed to the list of derogations in Article 36 TFEU which is a closed list.

5. All derogations based on Article 36 TFEU, and justifications based on mandatory requirements, are subject to the principle of proportionality. This requires a Member State when it adopts restrictive measures to choose only measures which (1) are suitable to achieve the objective pursued and (2) are necessary, in that the objective sought could not have been achieved by a measure less restrictive of trade between Member States. If there are no less restrictive measures available to a Member State, a national measure may, nevertheless be struck down if it has excessive effect on intra-EU trade.

6. Under the precautionary principle a Member State is allowed to adopt a restrictive measure, without the necessity of waiting for scientific certainty, in order to prevent harm from the outset when the effects of a phenomenon, product or process raise threats to lives and health of humans, animals and plants, or to the environment. This entails a risk assessment by the relevant national authorities. Measures based on the precautionary principles must be non-discriminatory, proportionate to the level of protection which a Member State seeks to achieve, consistent with measures already taken in similar circumstances in which all scientific data are available, and are subject to review in the light of scientific progress in the relevant area.

21.1 Introduction

Article 36 TFEU states:

> "The provisions of Articles 34 and 35 shall not preclude prohibitions or restrictions on imports, exports or goods in transit justified on grounds of public morality, public policy or public security; the protection of health and life of humans, animals or plants; the protection of national treasures possessing artistic, historic or archaeological value; or the protection of industrial and commercial property. Such prohibitions or restrictions shall not, however, constitute a means of arbitrary discrimination or a disguised restriction on trade between Member States."

The Article 36 list is exhaustive. All exceptions must be interpreted strictly; otherwise they will undermine the general rule set out in Articles 34 and 35 TFEU.[1675] Distinctly applicable measures can only be justified under Article 36 TFEU. Indistinctly applicable measures can be justified under both derogations listed in Article 36 TFEU and mandatory requirements, i.e. justifications developed by the case law of the ECJ. However, the distinction between derogations and mandatory requirements has been, to some extent, blurred by the ECJ. On rare occasions, the ECJ has accepted justifications based on safety requirements, e.g. road safety,[1676] and on the protection of the environment[1677] to justify distinctly applicable measures. On the one hand, it can be argued that these justifications being closely connected with the derogation based on protection of the health and life of humans constitute its extension.[1678] On the other hand, they are a separate category from that relating to the protection of health and life of humans and thus should remain distinct from each other.

The majority of commentators consider that there should be a separate set of defences for discriminatory and for non-discriminatory national rules, i.e. they oppose a merger of Treaty-based justifications and case law-based justifications.[1679] However, some are in favour of the relaxation of the distinction.[1680] The main argument for the existence of the distinction is that distinctly applicable measures, being discriminatory, always constitute a hindrance to intra-EU trade and thus a Member State should not be allowed to justify such measures on grounds additional to those set out in Article 36

1675. E.g. Case 29/72 *S.p.A. Marimex v Italian Finance Administration* [1972] ECR 1309.

1676. Case C-297/05 *Commission v Netherlands* [2007] ECR I-7467.

1677. Case C-2/90 *Commission v Belgium* [1992] ECR I-4431.

1678. Case C-67/97 *Criminal proceedings against Ditlev (Brown Bees of Læsø)* [1998] ECR I-8033.

1679. See L.W. Gormley, "Free Movement of Goods and Their Use –What is the Use of It", (2011) 33 Fordham Int. L. J. 1592.

1680. P. Oliver, *Free Movement of Goods in the European Community*, 4th edn, 2003, London: Sweet & Maxwell, 216; see also A-G Jacobs in Case C-379/98 *PreussenElektra AG v Schleswag AG* [2001] ECR I-2099.

TFEU. The current position of the ECJ is unclear. In Case C-531/07 *LIBRO*,[1681] the Austrian government attempted to justify discriminatory national legislation on the ground of the protection of books as cultural objects. The ECJ held that "the protection of cultural diversity in general cannot be considered to come within the 'protection of national treasures possessing artistic, historic or archaeological value' within the meaning of [Article 36 TFEU]" as this justification is only available in respect of indistinctly applicable measures. However, it added that the protection of books as cultural objects could be considered as a mandatory requirement capable of justifying measures restricting the free movement of goods. It added that in this case Austrian law was in breach of the principle of proportionality as the objectives it pursued could have been achieved by less intrusive means. Was the message of the ECJ that there is no longer a distinction between derogations and mandatory requirements? Had the ECJ stated the protection of books as cultural objects should be added to the list of mandatory requirements? It is submitted that the ECJ should clarify its confusing case law bearing in mind that national judges who apply EU law on a daily basis should know whether to accept that both derogations and mandatory requirements can be relied upon as justifications for discriminatory measures; or whether the ECJ intends to add new derogations to the list set out in Article 36 TFEU; or, whether the distinction between derogations and mandatory requirements holds good.

The orthodox approach to the interpretation of Article 36 TFEU is illustrated in Case 113/80 *Commission v Ireland (Re Irish Souvenirs)*.[1682]

THE FACTS WERE:

Under Irish law souvenirs which were considered as typically Irish (for example, Irish round towels and shamrocks) but imported to Ireland from other Member States had to be stamped either with an indication of their place of origin or with the word "foreign". As a result, importers of Irish souvenirs were discriminated against, as compared to Irish producers of Irish souvenirs, as the former were burdened with an additional requirement imposed by Irish legislation, and suffered a reduction in sales, since tourists wanted to buy "original" souvenirs. Irish law was clearly discriminatory. The Irish Government argued that national measures were necessary to protect consumers and to ensure the fairness of commercial transactions.

Held:

The ECJ held that as the grounds argued by the Irish Government were not mentioned in Article 36 TFEU, it could not rely on that Article.

Article 36 TFEU applies only to non-harmonised areas of EU law on the free movement of goods. Accordingly it cannot be invoked to justify a national measure contrary to EU harmonised legislation.[1683] This is because all relevant interests and concerns of the Member States are duly taken account of when harmonising legislation is adopted. When there is only a partial harmonisation Member States are

---

1681. Case C-531/07 *Fachverband der Buch- und Medienwirtschaft v LIBRO Handelsgesellschaft mbH* [2009] ECR I-3717, paras 32 and 33.
1682. [1981] ECR 1626.
1683. Case C-5/94 *The Queen v Ministry of Agriculture, Fisheries and Food, ex parte Hedley Lomas (Ireland) Ltd* [1996] ECR I-2553 and Case C-473/98 *Kemikalieinspektionen v Toolex Alpha AB* [2000] ECR I-5681.

allowed to adopt national measures in non-harmonised areas and thus can rely on Article 36 TFEU to defend their national rules.

Examination of the case law regarding the application of Article 36 TFEU reveals the following points.

21.1.1 Justification of economic objectives

Purely economic objectives such as the necessity of ensuring the balance of payments, the reduction of public spending, or the survival of an undertaking, cannot be justified under Article 36 TFEU.[1684] In Case C-456/10 *ANETT*,[1685] the Spanish Government argued that the obligation imposed on tobacco retailers to obtain their supplies exclusively from a monopoly owned by the Spanish State, and thus preventing them from importing tobacco products from other Member States, was justified on the grounds that retailers would enjoy excessive competitive advantage had the possibility of importing tobacco products been available to them. The ECJ rejected this justification as being of a purely economic nature and thus unacceptable under EU law.

21.1.2 The principle of proportionality

The pursuit of the objectives set out in Article 36 TFEU is not in itself sufficient to justify national measures restricting trade between Member States. Such measures must also satisfy the requirements imposed by the principle of proportionality[1686] (see Chapter 21.4).

21.1.3 Arbitrary discrimination

Article 36 TFEU provides that national measures permitted under that article must not constitute a means of arbitrary discrimination or a disguised restriction on trade between Member States, i.e. they must not be protectionist. In Case 34/79 *Henn and Darby*,[1687] the ECJ emphasised that the purpose of this prohibition on arbitrary discrimination and disguised restriction is to:

> "prevent restrictions on trade based on the grounds mentioned in the first sentence of Article [Article 36 TFEU] from being diverted from their proper purpose and used in such a way as either to create discrimination in respect of goods originating in other Member States or indirectly to protect certain national products."

In order to determine whether a national measure is arbitrary or constitutes a disguised restriction aimed at protecting domestic goods, a comparison between the treatment of domestic goods and imported goods is necessary. The differentiation must be justified on objective grounds, that is, it must be genuine and must be proportionate (see Chapter 21.4).

1684. Case 7/61 *Commission v Italy* [1961] ECR 317; Case 104/75 *Adriaan de Peijper, Managing Director of Centrafarm BV* [1976] ECR 613; Case 95/81 *Commission v Italy* [1982] ECR 2189; Case 238/82 *Duphar BV and Others v The Netherlands* [1984] ECR 523; Case C-324/93 *The Queen v Secretary of State for Home Department, ex parte Evans Medical Ltd and Macfarlan Smith Ltd* [1995] ECR I-563.

1685. Judgment of 26/4/12 (NYR) see Chapter 20.6.1.

1686. See G. de Búrca, "The Principle of Proportionality and its Application in EC Law", (1993) 13 YBEL, 105.

1687. Case 34/79 *R v Maurice Donald Henn and John Frederick Ernest Darby* [1979] ECR 3795.

21.1.4 Burden of proof

It is for national authorities to prove that a national measure which restricts trade between Member States is justified under Article 36 TFEU. In Case 227/82 *Leendert van Bennekom*,[1688] the ECJ held that "it is for the national authorities to demonstrate in each case that their rules are necessary to give effective protection to the interests referred to in [Article 36 TFEU]". Consequently, a Member State is required to supply appropriate evidence; a mere statement that the measure is justified is not sufficient.[1689] However, in Case C-110/05 *Commission v Italy*,[1690] the ECJ held that the burden of proof "cannot be so extensive as to require the Member State to prove, positively, that no other conceivable measure could enable that objective to be attained under the same conditions". Notwithstanding this, in Case C-28/09 *Commission v Austria*[1691] (see Chapter 20.6.1) the ECJ held that a Member State, when adopting a measure as radical as a total traffic ban on a section of motorway vital for transporting goods between certain Member States, has a duty to carefully examine the possibility of using measures less restrictive of freedom of movement and, in particular, to examine alternative measures suggested by the Commission. The ECJ found the ban disproportionate on the ground that the Austrian government did not examine the possibility of having recourse to other less restrictive measures to achieve the objective of reducing the emissions of nitrogen dioxide in the Inn Valley.

21.2 Derogations listed in Article 36 TFEU

The following derogations are listed in Article 36 TFEU.

21.2.1 Derogation based on public morality

In principle, it is for each Member State to determine, in accordance with its own scale of values and in the form selected by it, the requirements of public morality in its territory. Thus, Article 36 TFEU permits a Member State to establish it own concept of "public morality". The use of the words "in principle" is important as it allows the EU to interfere, in particular in order to prevent a Member State from imposing double standards of morality, one applicable to domestic goods and another to imported goods, and thus discriminate against the latter on the ground of public morality.

In this respect it is interesting to contrast Case 34/79 *R v Henn and Darby*[1692] with Case 121/85 *Conegate.*[1693]

THE FACTS WERE:

In Henn and Darby the defendants imported a number of consignments of obscene films and publications into the UK from the Netherlands. They were caught by Customs officials and were charged with the criminal offence of being "knowingly concerned in the fraudulent

---

1688. Case 227/82 *Criminal Proceedings against Leendert van Bennekom* [1983] ECR 3883, para. 40.

1689. Case C-265/06 *Commission v Portugal* [2008] ECR I-2245.

1690. [2009] ECR I-519.

1691. Judgment of 21/12/11 (NYR).

1692. Case 34/79 *R v Maurice Donald Henn and John Frederick Ernest Darby* [1979] ECR 3795. See: J. H. H. Weiler, "Europornography: First Reference of the House of Lords to the European Court of Justice", (1981) MLR, 91.

1693. Case 121/85 *Conegate Limited v HM Customs & Excise* [1986] ECR 1007.

evasion of the prohibition of the importation of indecent or obscene articles." In their defence, the defendants claimed that the prohibition on the importation of pornographic material was contrary to Article 34 TFEU, as it constituted a MEQR.

Held:

The ECJ held that Article 34 TFEU is subject to a number of exceptions, one of which is contained in Article 36 TFEU and relates to restrictions intended to protect public morality. The British legislation fell within the scope of this exception and consequently the criminal charges were consistent with EU law.

Comment:

The interesting aspects of this case were that first, the mere possession of obscene articles for non-commercial purposes was not a criminal offence in the UK. Second there were some exceptions to the prohibition in that when such articles had scientific, literary or artistic or educational interest they were not prohibited. Third, there were some differences as to the treatment of such articles in different parts of the UK, i.e. Scotland, Northern Ireland, England and Wales. The referring court, the House of Lords, was of the view that the UK, as a whole, did have an internal ban on the type of material that had been confiscated, even though some of its constituent parts had more lenient laws than those imposed on imports to the UK. Accordingly, the matter arose whether the prohibition constituted an instrument of arbitrary discrimination. The ECJ stated that notwithstanding national diversity, "it is permissible to conclude, on a comprehensive view, that there is no lawful trade in such goods in the United Kingdom. A prohibition on imports which may in certain respects be more strict than some of the laws applied within the United Kingdom cannot therefore be regarded as amounting to a measure designed to give indirect protection to some national product or aimed at creating arbitrary discrimination between goods of this type depending on whether they are produced within the national territory or another Member State."[1694]

As a result, UK law was justified on the grounds of public morality.

The above situation is to be contrasted with that which occurred in Case 121/85 *Conegate*.[1695]

THE FACTS WERE:

A British company set up a business importing inflatable dolls from Germany into the UK. A number of consignments of the products were seized by Customs officials on the ground that the dolls were "indecent and obscene," and accordingly subject to the prohibition on imports contained in the UK Customs Consolidation Act 1876. Although national rules prohibited the importation of these dolls, no regulation prevented their manufacture and distribution in the UK.

The company brought an action for recovery of the dolls.

1694. Supra note 1692, para. 21.
1695. Case 121/85 *Conegate Limited v HM Customs & Excise* [1986] ECR 1007.

Held:

The ECJ held that the UK could not rely on Article 36 TFEU to prohibit the importation of products when no internal provisions had been enacted to prevent the manufacture and distribution of the offending products within the UK. To allow a Member State to prevent the importation of particular goods, while simultaneously allowing nationals to manufacture such products, would amount to arbitrary discrimination.

Comment:

The ECJ examined the internal law of the UK on trade of articles at issue. UK law was not uniform in that in some of its constituent parts there were restrictions on the sale of such goods, e.g restrictions on public display, and requirements that shops dealing with such goods were licensed to sell them only to persons aged 18 and over. The ECJ held that these restrictions did not amount to a prohibition on manufacturing and marketing of the type of goods at issue. The argument of the UK, based on the fact that no articles comparable to those imported by Conegate were manufactured in the UK territory, was rejected. The ECJ stressed that as long as UK does not adopt, "with respect of the same goods manufactured or marketed within its territory, penal measures or other serious and effective measures intended to prevent distribution of such goods in its own territory"[1696] importation from another Member State could not be prevented.

The difference between the judgments in Henn and Darby *and in* Conegate *is that in* Conegate *the prohibition amounted to arbitrary discrimination. No UK legislation prohibited the manufacture and marketing of obscene articles within its territory whilst importation of such goods was prohibited. There was no objective justification for arbitrary discrimination. Even if there was such a justification the UK would have been unable to show that the difference in treatment was proportionate.[1697] In* Henn and Darby *there was no unequal treatment.[1698] Different standards of morality may apply in different Member States, but no double standards are allowed under EU law. Accordingly, within a Member State imported and domestic goods must be treated in the same way.*

21.2.2   Derogation based on public policy and public security

Member States have rarely invoked derogations based on public policy and public security. The assessment of national measures necessary to ensure public security and public order is left to the Member States, which have to find the right balance between the extent of rights conferred on individuals and the requirements of public policy or public security.

Public policy refers to the fundamental interests of society. Public security concerns the safeguarding of the institutions of a Member State, its essential public services and the survival of its inhabitants.

1696.   Ibid, para. 15.

1697.   See Opinion of A-G Poiares Maduro in Case C-434/04 *Jan-Erik Anders Ahokainen and Mati Leppik v Virallinen Syyttäjä* [2006] ECR I-9171, para. 28.

1698.   L. Catchpole and A. Barav argued that there was discrimination against imported goods in *Henn and Darby*. See their article entitled "The Public Morality Exception and the Free Movement of Goods: Justification of a Dual Standard in National Legislation?", (1980) LIEI, 1.

Both derogations have been treated by the ECJ as exceptions of last resort. This is exemplified by the following cases.

Case 231/83 *Cullet*[1699]

THE FACTS WERE:

The French Government imposed minimum prices for fuel, arguing that the setting of those prices was necessary to avoid civil disorder, including the violent reactions which would have to be anticipated by retailers affected by unrestricted competition on the fuel market.

Held:

The ECJ rejected this argument on the ground that the French Government did not show that it would be unable to deal with potential disturbances.

Therefore, national measures may be justified on the ground of public policy only if a Member State shows that in their absence, civil unrest would be greater than the national authorities could be expected to control.

Case 154/85 *Commission v Italy*[1700]

THE FACTS WERE:

In this case an Italian Ministerial Decree concerning the registration of vehicles, which set out more stringent requirements for registration of used imported vehicles which had already been registered in the country of exportation than for new cars, was considered as a MEQR. The Italian government tried to justify the decree on the ground of public order, in particular the necessity to combat the trafficking of stolen vehicles.

Held:

The ECJ stated that under the decree the registration of imported used cars took longer, was more complex and was more expensive than that of new cars. This could not be justified on the ground of public order, taking into account that the multiplication of requirements relating to registration did not constitute an efficient manner of detecting and preventing the trafficking of stolen vehicles.

There are, however, a number of cases in which the requirements of public security were successfully invoked. Some of them are examined below.

1699. Case 231/83 *Henri Cullet and Chambre Syndicale des Réparateurs Automobiles et Détaillants de Produits Pétroliers v Centre Leclerc à Toulouse and Centre Leclerc à Saint-Orens-de-Gameville* [1985] ECR 305.
1700. [1987] ECR 2771.

Case 7/78 *Thompson*[1701]

> ## THE FACTS WERE:
>
> *The case concerned UK legislation prohibiting import of gold coins; export of silver UK coins minted before 1947, which were no longer in circulation; and, their destruction and melting. Export and import of coins was allowed only under a licence granted by the Board of Trade. Criminal proceedings were commenced against a number of British citizens who, despite the ban and without obtaining the required licence, imported gold coins into the UK from Germany and exported silver coins from the UK to Germany.*
>
> *Held:*
>
> *The ECJ held that the ban was a QR but was justified on the ground of public policy because it stemmed from the need to protect the right to mint coinage, which is traditionally regarded as involving the fundamental interests of the State.*

Case 72/83 *Campus Oil*[1702]

> ## THE FACTS WERE:
>
> *Irish law required that importers of petroleum products purchase up to 35 per cent of their requirements from the State-owned refinery at a fixed price. The measure was clearly discriminatory and protective. The Irish government argued that this measure was necessary to maintain the viability of the only petroleum refinery in Ireland, especially in the event of a national crisis.*
>
> *Held:*
>
> *The ECJ accepted that the need to avoid an interruption of supplies of petroleum products was a matter of public security and public policy.*

The public security exception has been successfully relied upon by Member States in respect of national legislation regulating transport of dangerous substances. In Case C-367/89 *Richardt*,[1703] the introduction of a requirement for special authorisation in respect of the transit of strategic material was justified on the ground of public security. However, it is not necessary for national legislation to provide for penal sanctions in order to be considered as being concerned with public policy within the meaning of Article 36 TFEU.[1704]

1701. Case 7/78 *R v Thompson, Johnson and Woodiwiss* [1978] ECR 2247.
1702. Case 72/83 *Campus Oil Ltd v Minister for Industry and Energy* [1984] ECR 2727.
1703. Case C-367/89 *Criminal Proceedings against Aimé Richardt and Les Accessoires Scientifiques SNC* [1991] ECR I-4621.
1704. Case 16/83 *Criminal Proceedings against Karl Prantl* [1984] ECR 1299.

21.2.3 Derogation based on the protection of the health and life of humans, animals and plants

The approach of the EU to the protection of the health of its citizens, animals and plants acquired a new dimension in the light of the epidemic of bovine spongiform encephalopathy (BSE), commonly known as mad-cow disease which in the 1990s affected cattle in the UK. On 27 March 1996 the Commission imposed a complete ban on exports of all kinds of bovine products from the UK to other Member States and third countries. This decision was adopted following the discovery of a probable link between a form of Creutzfeldt-Jakob disease in humans and BSE in cattle which, at that time, was quite widespread in the UK. Under the decision the Commission was monitoring the situation in the UK and in due course lifted the ban. The saga of the refusal of the French government to comply with the decision of the Commission to lift the ban is well known and had its epilogue before the ECJ, which, not surprisingly, found France in breach of Article 34 TFEU.[1705] What emerged from the case is that neither EU institutions nor the French Government reacted with proper consideration when facing BSE:

- At the EU level a scheme set up by virtue of Decision 98/692/EC based on animals' dates of birth (DBES) was inadequate.

- At the national level, the French Government's conduct was confusing and erratic. In particular, the French authorities did not prevent the import to France of beef and veal and other meat-based products from other Member States which did not bear the distinct mark of products subject to the DBES scheme, although there was a strong possibility that certain consignments of meat or meat products of UK origin could have been processed or rewrapped in other Member States.

However, both the EU and the Member States drew proper conclusions from the above situation. This is illustrated by the adoption of Regulation 178/2002,[1706] which laid down the General Principles and Requirements of Food Law, established the European Food Safety Authority and laid down Procedures in Matters of Food Safety. The Regulation constitutes a main tool for the EU and for the Member States to speedily react to any emergencies where human health, animal health or the environment is at risk. The Regulation:

- underlines the general principles of food law including the precautionary principle;

- sets up a new EU body, the European Food Safety Authority;

- establishes the rapid alert system, a network for exchange of information concerning a food-related risk; and,

- specifies measures available to the Commission and to Member States to deal with emergencies.

The basic principle underpinning the derogation based on the protection of health and life of humans, animals and plants is that a Member State must, in order to justify national measures on these grounds, demonstrate that there is a genuine risk to health and life.[1707] So, national measures must not serve as a pretext for introducing disguised discrimination against imported products. This happened in Case 124/81 *Commission v UK (Re UHT Milk)*.[1708]

1705. Case C-1/00 *Commission v France* [2001] ECR I-9989.
1706. The Regulation has been complemented by a number of items of secondary legislation, see the official website of the Commission at http://ec.europa.eu/food/food/foodlaw/principles/index_en.htm (accessed 28/2/12).
1707. Case 238/82 *Duphar BV v The Netherlands* [1984] ECR 523.
1708. [1983] ECR 203.

THE FACTS WERE:

The UK government imposed a requirement that UHT milk should be marketed only by approved dairies or distributors. This involved repackaging and retreatment of all imported milk. The UK government argued that the measure was necessary to ensure that the milk was free from bacterial or viral infections.

Held:

The ECJ held that there was evidence that milk in all Member States was of similar quality and subject to equivalent controls. For that reason the requirement, although it applied to both domestic and imported goods, was considered as disguised discrimination and therefore examined and rejected under Article 36 TFEU.

The derogation based on the protection of the health and life of humans, animals and plants has been successfully relied on in a number of cases. For example:

- In Case C-324/93 *Evans*,[1709] in which the refusal to grant an importation licence for diamorphine, a heroin substitute for medical purposes, was justified in order to ensure the reliability of supply of diamorphine in the UK and to avoid risk of unlawful traffic in diamorphine.

- In Case C-366/04 *Schwarz*[1710] the ECJ stated that Austrian legislation which prohibited the sale of unwrapped chewing-gum and other sugar confectionery products from vending machines was justified on the ground of the protection of public health given that non-packaged goods were capable of being impaired by moisture or insects, in particular ants, within vending machine containers.

21.2.4 Protection of national treasures possessing artistic, historic or archaeological value

This exception can be relied upon if a treasure or work of art is in the public domain, but not if such a work is on the market or the subject of a private sale.

Member States are free to determine their national treasures possessing artistic, historic or archaeological value. By virtue of Article 36 TFEU they may also impose restrictions on exports of such national treasures.

The scope of this derogation is uncertain as there is no case law concerning it. However, in Case 7/68 *Commission v Italy (Re Export Tax on Art Treasures)*,[1711] the ECJ held that the desire to protect national treasures could not justify charges under Article 30 TFEU. Therefore, the imposition of QRs seems to be the only way to protect national treasures. This was recognised by the French Conseil d'Etat (the highest administrative court in France), which held that French legislation prohibiting export of objects of art or objects of historic value was justified on the ground of Article 36 TFEU.[1712]

1709. Case C-324/93 *R v Secretary of State for Home Department, ex parte Evans Medical Ltd and Macfarlan Smith Ltd* [1995] ECR I-563.

1710. Case C-366/04 *Georg Schwarz v Bürgermeister der Landeshauptstadt Salzburg* [2005] ECR I-10139.

1711. [1968] ECR 423.

1712. CE 7 November 1987: Receuil Lebon 304; CE 25 March 1994, Syndicat National de la Librairie Ancienne et Moderne.

The completion of the internal market prompted the EU to adopt certain specific measures ensuring that the free movement of goods would not increase illegal exports of national treasures of a Member State. These measures are: Directive 93/7/EEC on the Return of Cultural Objects Unlawfully Removed from the Territory of a Member State;[1713] Regulation 3911/92/EEC on the Control of the Export of Cultural Goods;[1714] and, Regulation 116/2009 on the export of cultural goods from the EU.[1715]

21.2.5 Protection of industrial and commercial property

This topic is dealt with in Chapter 21.6.

21.3 Justifications based on mandatory requirements

In the *Cassis de Dijon* case the ECJ accepted justifications additional to those set out in Article 36 TFEU with regard to indistinctly applicable measures, and on the authority of the *Italian Trailers* case such justifications can also be relied upon by a Member State to justify national residual rules. In principle, mandatory requirements cannot be used to justify distinctly applicable measures and QRs, although on rare occasions the ECJ has deviated from this (see Chapter 21.1). The list of mandatory requirements is open-ended, i.e. it is always possible for a Member State to add new justifications. However, a Member State is not absolutely free to determine unilaterally the general interest it wishes to protect and the manner in which such protection should be achieved. In order to justify a national measure, it must:

▪ concern an area of law which is not harmonised;

▪ pursue an objective of general interest;

▪ be proportionate to the objective that the Member State wishes to achieve; and,

▪ take account of requirements imposed on an imported product in its home Member State.

The ECJ has narrowly interpreted justifications based on mandatory requirements. Only exceptionally have Member States been successful when relying on them.

21.3.1 Protection of consumers

The most popular justification invoked by Member States is based on the protection of consumers. In Case C-210/96 *Gut,*[1716] the ECJ defined a consumer as being "an average consumer who is reasonably well-informed and reasonably observant and circumspect". This definition entails that normally the ECJ, or national courts, will not be required to order "an expert's report or commissioning of a

---

1713. [1993] OJ L74/74.

1714. [1992] OJ L395/19.

1715. [2009] OJ L39/1 On this topic see: A. Biondi, "The Merchant, the Thief and the Citizen: The Circulation of Works of Art within the EU", (1997) 34 CMLRev., 1173.

1716. Case C-210/96 *Gut Springenheide GmbH and Rudolf Tusky v Oberkreisdirektor des Kreises Steinfurt - Amt für Lebensmittelüberwachung* [1998] ECR I-4657, para. 31. On this topic see: A. Johnston, "The Double-headed Approach of the ECJ concerning Consumer Protection", (2007) 44 CMLRev., 1237.

consumer research poll"[1717] to determine whether a national measure is appropriate to safeguard the interests of consumers.

The definition of a consumer provided by the ECJ in Case C-210/96 *Gut* was a direct consequence of two judgments of the ECJ relating to German law on the protection of consumers discussed below.

In Case C-315/92 *Clinique*,[1718] cosmetics manufactured by internationally known company Estée Lauder under the name "Clinique" were required to be sold in Germany under the name "Linique" in order to comply with German law against unfair competition, although in other Member States they were sold under the name of "Clinique". As a result of German law the company was required to use different labelling and advertisement in Germany than in other Member States. This had serious financial consequences for the company which, after many years of compliance with German law, decided to use the name "Clinique" instead of "Linique" in Germany. The German trade association brought proceedings against Estée Lauder. It argued that the name "Clinique" was likely to mislead German consumers into believing that "Clinique" products were pharmaceutical products rather than cosmetics. The ECJ stated that serious economic disadvantages such as additional packaging and advertisement for the manufacturer of Clinique products in Germany constituted a MEQR which could not be justified on the ground of the protection of consumers. The ECJ held that the products were normally sold in department stores, not in pharmacies, and that consumers in other Member States were apparently not misled by the name "Clinique", i.e. average reasonably well-informed consumers in Germany would have known that products sold under the name "Clinique" were cosmetic products due to their international popularity and reputation.

In Case C-470/93 *Mars*,[1719] the German consumer protection association submitted two arguments to challenge a Europe-wide promotional campaign organised by undertakings belonging to the US group Mars Inc, with regard to ice cream bars of the Mars, Snickers, Bounty and Milky Way brands, as contrary to German law. The promotional campaign included the sale of promotional ice cream bars which were 10 per cent larger than standard bars. The wrappers of those promotional bars were printed with the words "+10%". The area of the wrapping of the promotional bars covered by the words "+ 10%" was greater than 10 per cent of the actual wrapping, so potentially suggesting that the extra quantity was greater than 10 per cent, when in fact it was not.

The first argument submitted by the claimant was that the campaign would mislead consumers by indicating on the wrapping of the promotional ice cream bars "+10%", which covered more than a tenth of the total surface area of wrapping, that consumers were receiving more that 10 per cent extra quantity.

The second argument was that if the price for promotional bars was to be the same as that applied to standard bars, this would have amounted to a breach of German competition rules which prohibit fixing of prices by a manufacturer. If the price were to be increased by retailers this would mislead consumers into believing that the price of promotional bars was the same as standard bars. With regard to the first argument, the ECJ held that the "+ 10%" marking was not such as to mislead a reasonably circumspect consumer. With regard to the second argument the ECJ held that as there was no price increase in respect of the promoted products, the consumers benefited from the promotion, not the manufacturer. Accordingly, there was no breach of EU law.

The case law shows that the ECJ is willing to accept that a national measure may be justified by the need to protect consumers, i.e. that it is necessary to shield them from unfair trade practices, unfair contract terms, misleading and deceptive advertisement practices, etc. but often disagrees with Member

---

1717.   Ibid, para. 31.
1718.   Case C-315/92 *Verband Sozialer Wettbewerb eV v Clinique Laboratoires SNC and Estée Lauder Cosmetics GmbH* [1994] ECR I-317.
1719.   Case C-470/93 *Verein gegen Unwesen in Handel und Gewerbe Köln e.V. v Mars GmbH* [1995] ECR I-1923.

States as to the manner in which they seek to achieve the objective. Thus, "everything boils down" to the proportionality of the measure in question which is assessed in the light of the requirement of Article 34 TFEU, i.e. the necessity to ensure the free movement of goods. In most cases the ECJ has held that national measures intended to protect consumers were not proportionate in that objectives pursued by them could be achieved by means that would be less of a hindrance to trade between Member States, e.g. the *Cassis de Dijon* case itself.

Among cases in which the ECJ held that national measures may be appropriate to protect consumers, Case 6/81 *Beele*[1720] is of interest.

THE FACTS WERE:

Two Dutch undertakings were selling cable ducts; one imported them from Sweden and the other from Germany. The Swedish cable ducts were previously protected by a patent in Germany, the Netherlands and elsewhere; the German cable ducts were first imported into the Netherlands after the patent had expired. The undertaking selling Swedish ducts wanted to stop the other undertaking from selling the German cable ducts in the Netherlands on the ground that they were a precise imitation of the Swedish cable ducts.

Held:

The ECJ held that national legislation prohibiting slavish imitations of products of a third party was justified on the ground that such slavish imitations were likely to confuse the consumers as to which products were genuine and which were imitations.

In Case 16/83 *Prantl*[1721] the ECJ held that when there was a close resemblance between a German bottle known as a *bocksbeutel*, in which expensive wine from a particular region of Germany was sold, and an Italian bottle traditional to Italy, in which cheap imported Italian wine was sold, Germany could not rely on the protection of consumers to prohibit the sale of the Italian wine in Germany. The ECJ emphasised that as long as the Italian bottle was traditional to Italy and not an imitation of the German bottle, there was no reason to prohibit its sale in Germany.[1722] The above judgments were delivered before the EU adopted common rules on many aspects of the protection of intellectual property rights, in particular relating to the concept of confusion (see Chapter 21.6.2.2).

Another successful justification based on protection of consumers was invoked in Case 220/81 *Robertson*.[1723]

THE FACTS WERE:

Criminal proceedings were commenced against Mr Robertson in Belgium for selling silver-plated cutlery from other Member States whose hallmarks were in breach of Belgian legislation. Under that legislation the sale in Belgium of silver-plated articles not stamped

---

1720. *BV Industrie Diensten Groep v J.A. Beele Handelmaatschappij BV* Case 6/81 *Beele* [1982] ECR 707.
1721. Case 16/83 *Criminal Proceedings against Karl Prantl* [1984] ECR 1299.
1722. Contrast with Case C-317/91 *Deutsche Renault AG v Audi AG* [1993] ECR I-6227.
1723. Case 220/81 *Criminal Proceedings against Timothy Frederick Robertson and Others* [1982] ECR 2349.

either with a Belgian hallmark or a hallmark of the Member State of exportation containing information equivalent to that provided by Belgian hallmarks was prohibited.

Held:

The ECJ held that hallmarks must be intelligible to consumers of the Member State of importation and thus accepted the defence submitted by Belgium.

21.3.2 The protection of the environment

In Case 302/86 *Commission v Denmark (Re Returnable Containers)*,[1724] the ECJ held that the protection of the environment is a mandatory requirement which may restrict the scope of application of Article 34 TFEU.

THE FACTS WERE:

Under Danish law beer and soft drinks were required to be marketed only in containers that could be reused. Distributors of such products had to establish deposit-and-return schemes and recycle the containers. The containers had to be approved by the Danish National Agency for the Protection of Environment. The Danish government acknowledged that these requirements were unduly onerous to foreign manufacturers and for that reason permitted the use of non-approved containers for quantities not exceeding 3,000 hectolitres a year per foreign producer and for drinks sold by foreign producers to test the market. The Commission challenged these requirements as contrary to Article 34 TFEU.

Held:

The ECJ held that Danish law was in breach of Article 34 TFEU.

Comment:

The ECJ had extended the list of mandatory requirements laid down in Cassis de Dijon *to encompass the protection of the environment. However, with regard to this particular case the ECJ rejected the justification submitted by the Danish government based on the protection of the environment. The ECJ stated that the requirement for approval of the containers to be carried out solely by the Danish Agency was disproportionate and the concession for limited quantities was insufficient to remedy that violation of Article 34 TFEU.*

The ECJ reached similar conclusions:

- In Case C-463/01 *Commission v Germany*,[1725] in which the ECJ condemned a German deposit system for non-reusable packaging as failing to comply with the principle of proportionality.

- In Case C-320/03 *Commission v Austria*,[1726] in which the ECJ condemned a ban on heavy trucks (more than 7.5 tonnes) using a section of the A12 (a major artery for transport of goods between

---

1724. [1988] ECR 4607.
1725. [2004] ECR I-11705.
1726. [2005] ECR I-9871.

Germany and Italy) in order to improve air quality in the Inn Valley through which A12 passes, as disproportionate to the objective it sought to achieve (see Chapter 20.6.1).

21.3.3 The protection of the socio-cultural identity of a Member State

This justification was accepted by the ECJ in Cases 60 and 61/84 *Cinéthèque*.[1727]

THE FACTS WERE:

French legislation prohibited the marketing of videos of films during the first year of a film's release, irrespective of whether it was made in France or elsewhere, on the ground of the protection of the French film industry.

Held:

The ECJ held that the protection of cultural activities constitutes a mandatory requirement and that the French legislation was not in breach of Article 34 TFEU.

In Case 169/91 *Stoke-on-Trent*[1728] the ECJ recognised national and regional socio-cultural characteristics as a mandatory requirement.

21.3.4 The improvement of working conditions

In Case C-312/89 *Conforama*,[1729] the ECJ held that the improvement of the working conditions of workers may constitute a mandatory requirement.

21.3.5 The maintenance of press diversity

In Case C-368/95 *Familiapress*,[1730] the ECJ held that maintenance of press diversity may constitute a mandatory requirement justifying a restriction on the free movement of goods.

21.3.6 The prevention of fraud

In Case C-426/92 *Milch-Kontor*,[1731] the ECJ recognised that the prevention of fraud constituted a legitimate concern of a Member State and as such may constitute a mandatory requirement.

21.3.7 The protection of young persons, i.e. below the age of 15

In Case C-244/06 *Dynamic Medien*[1732] (for facts see Chapter 20.5.2.D), the ECJ held that the prohibition of e-mail order sales of image storage media containing games which may be dangerous to young

---

1727. Cases 60 and 61/84 *Cinéthèque SA v Fédération Nationale des Cinémas Français* [1985] ECR 2605.
1728. Case 169/91 *Stoke-on-Trent City Council v B & Q Plc* [1992] ECR I-6635.
1729. Case C-312/89 *Union Départmentale des Syndicats CGT de L'Aisne v SIDEF Conforama* [1991] ECR I-997.
1730. Case C-368/95 *Vereinigte Familiapress Zeitungsverlags- und vertriebs GmbH v Henrich Bauer Verlag* [1997] ECR I-3689.
1731. Case C-426/92 *Germany v Deutsches Milch-Kontor GmbH* [1994] ECR I-2757.
1732. Case C-244/06 *Dynamic Medien Vertriebs GmbH v Avides Media AG* [2008] ECR I-505.

persons, without prior examination by the relevant national authorities in the importing State, may be justified by mandatory requirements.

21.3.8 The protection of fundamental rights

In Case C-112/00 *Schmidberger*[1733] (for facts see Chapter 20.2.4), the ECJ accepted that the objective of safeguarding the protection of fundamental rights guaranteed under Articles 10 and 11 of the ECHR was a mandatory requirement.

In this case the task of the ECJ was not easy as the Court had to reconcile the requirements of the protection of fundamental rights, namely the right to freedom of expression and the right to freedom of assembly as guaranteed respectively by Articles 10 and 11 of the ECHR, with the requirements of one of the fundamental freedoms of EU law, the free movement of goods. The ECJ accomplished this task with great wisdom. It recognised that neither of the relevant rights was absolute. The principle of the free movement of goods is subject to derogations set out in Article 36 TFEU and to the mandatory requirements. Similarly Articles 10 and 11 of the ECHR may be subject to derogations justified by objectives in the public interest. In order to decide whether Member State interference with these rights can be justified, the ECtHR applies a four-tier test deciding:

■ First, whether there has been interference by Member State authorities with the rights guaranteed under Articles 10 and 11 of the ECHR;

■ Second, whether the interference has been "prescribed by law";

■ Third, whether the State concerned has pursued a legitimate aim when interfering with the exercise of the above rights; and,

■ Fourth, whether such interference is "necessary in a democratic society".

The ECJ applied the above test. In respect of the fourth tier, the ECJ assessed "what is necessary in a democratic society" in the light of the principle of proportionality and referred not only to its own case law but also to the judgments of the ECtHR.[1734]

It is to be noted that the entry into force of the Charter of Fundamental Rights will intensify the scrutiny by the ECJ of the compatibility of national measures with the protection of rights guaranteed under the Charter (see Chapter 8).

21.4 The principle of proportionality

Whether a national measure conforms with the requirements of the principle of proportionality is assessed by a two-stage inquiry:

1. A Member State must choose a measure which is suitable to attain the objective sought. In order to determine whether a national measure is suitable the ECJ will examine whether the means employed by the Member State are appropriate to achieve the objective

---

1733. Case C-112/00 *Eugen Schmidberger, Internationale Transporte und Planzüge v Austria* [2003] ECR I-5659.
1734. Case C-368/95 *Familiapress Vereinigte Familiapress Zeitungsverlags- und vertriebs GmbH v Heinrich Bauer Verlag* [1997] ECR I-3689; Case C-60/00 *Mary Carpenter v Secretary of State for the Home Department* [2002] ECR I-6279, and Eur. Court HR, *Steel and Others v UK* judgment of 23 September 1998, Reports of Judgments and Decisions 1998-VII, § 101.

sought.[1735] A national measure can be regarded as suitable for securing the attainment of the objective pursued only if it genuinely reflects a concern to attain that objective in a consistent and systematic manner.[1736]

2. A Member State must choose a measure which is necessary to achieve the objective pursued. When the ECJ assesses the necessity of a national measure it weighs the conflicting interests, on the one hand of a Member State which seeks to achieve a specific objective, and on the other, the requirements of the free movement of goods. The test of necessity involves the examination of whether the objective sought could not have been achieved by a measure less restrictive of trade between Member States, that is, if a Member State has a choice between different measures capable of attaining the same objective, it must choose the one which is of least hindrance to the free movement of goods.[1737] If there are no less restrictive measures available to a Member State, a national measure may, nevertheless, be struck down if it has excessive effect on intra-EU trade.[1738]

A-G Poiares Maduro pointed out in his Opinion in Case C-434/04 *Leppik*[1739] that the assessment of proportionality must satisfy the final requirement, i.e. a national measure must not constitute an instrument of arbitrary discrimination. He said that "This, again, requires an assessment of proportionality, but seen from a different perspective", i.e. from the perspective of distinguishing between justified discrimination and unjustified discrimination.

It is for the Member State concerned to demonstrate that a national measure which hinders the free movement of goods is suitable and necessary to attain the legitimate objective sought by it. However, in Case 110/05 *Commission v Italy* (*Italian Trailers* case),[1740] the ECJ stated that their "burden of proof cannot be so extensive as to require the Member State to prove, positively, that no other conceivable measure could enable that objective to be attained under the same conditions". This statement must be read in the light of the judgment of the ECJ in Case C-28/09 *Commission v Austria*,[1741] in which it held that a Member State has a duty to examine the possibility of using measures less restrictive of freedom of movement of goods. In this case, the Commission suggested some less restrictive measures that could have been used, but which the Austrian government had not examined. The ECJ found Austria in breach of Articles 34 and 35 TFEU on the ground that it had failed in its duty to examine alternative measures proposed by the Commission before adopting a measure as radical as a total traffic ban on a section of motorway constituting a vital route of communication between certain Member States. Thus, it seems that although a Member State is not required to envisage all possible alternative measures it must, nevertheless, carefully examine measures suggested by the Commission.

In the application of the principle of proportionality, the ECJ enjoys a wide margin of discretion and, on occasions, has disagreed with A-Gs as to the proportionality of a national measure. For example, in the

---

1735. T. Tridimas, "Proportionality in Community Law: Searching for the Appropriate Standard of Scrutiny", in E. Ellias (ed.), *The Principle of Proportionality in the Laws of Europe*, 1999, Oxford: Hart Publishing, 68.

1736. See, to that effect, Case C-169/07 *Hartlauer Handelsgesellschaft mbH v Wiener Landesregierung and Oberösterreichische Landesregierun* [2009] ECR I-1721, para. 55; Joined Cases C-171/07 and C-172/07 *Apothekerkammer des Saarlandes and Others* [2009] ECR I-4171, para. 42; and Case C-137/09 *Marc Michel Josemans v Burgemeester van Maastricht* [2010] ECR I-0000, para. 70

1737. For example, Case C-17/93 *Criminal Proceedings against J. J. J. Van der Veldt* [1994] ECR I-3537.

1738. Case C-170/04 *Rosengren and Others v Riksåklagaren* [2007] ECR I-4071.

1739. Case C-434/04 *Jan-Erik Anders Ahokainen and Mati Leppik v Virallinen Syyttäjä* [2006] ECR I-9171, para. 28.

1740. [2009] ECR I-5909, para. 66.

1741. Judgment of 21/12/11 (NYR).

Italian Trailers case,[1742] in which the issue was whether a general and absolute prohibition imposed in Italy on the use of trailers with motorcycles on Italian roads (for facts see Chapter 20.6) was proportionate to the objective of guaranteeing a certain level of road safety, A-G Léger's view was that the measure was disproportionate because it applied to the entire territory of Italy irrespective of the highway infrastructure and traffic conditions, and was not applicable to motorcycles towing trailers registered in other Member States. He suggested other less restrictive measures such as localised prohibitions, i.e. the prohibition could be applied to roads which were considered dangerous, or which were particularly congested. A-G Bot shared the view expressed by A-G Léger. However, the ECJ disagreed. It found that, first, the prohibition was suitable to achieve the objective of ensuring road safety given that "circulation of a combination composed of a motorcycle and an unapproved trailer could be dangerous both for the driver of the vehicle and for other vehicles on the road, because the stability of the combination and its braking capacity would be affected".[1743] Second, with regard to necessity of the prohibition, the ECJ acknowledged that there were other possible measures less restrictive on intra-EU trade but emphasised that "Member States cannot be denied the possibility of attaining an objective such as road safety by the introduction of general and simple rules which will be easily understood and applied by drivers and easily managed and supervised by the competent authorities".[1744] Accordingly, the ECJ found that the measure complied with the requirements of the principle of proportionality. The ECJ did not comment on the fact that motorcycles registered in other Member State were allowed to tow trailers on Italian roads, but this was probably because reverse discrimination does not breach EU law (see Chapter 20.7).

The ECJ normally leaves to a national court the task of assessing whether the contested national measure is proportionate. However, it often provides the national court with detailed instructions on how such an assessment should be carried out.[1745]

One of the leading cases on the application of the principle of proportionality is Case 261/81 *Walter Rau*.[1746]

THE FACTS WERE:

Under Belgian law margarine could only be sold in cube-shaped boxes in order to distinguish it from butter. A Belgian buyer refused to accept deliveries of margarine from a German seller on the ground that margarine was packed in tubes having the shape of a truncated cone and thus could not be marketed in Belgium. The seller sued the buyer for a breach of contract in a German court which referred the matter of compatibility of Belgian legislation with Article 34 TFEU to the ECJ.

Held:

The ECJ held that the requirement was disproportionate since consumers would be sufficiently protected by appropriate labelling of the product. The ECJ emphasised that appropriate labelling would achieve the same objective as national measures, with less hindrance to trade between Member States.

1742. Case C-110/05 *Commission v Italy* [2009] ECR I-519.

1743. Ibid, para. 63.

1744. Ibid, para. 67.

1745. See for example, C-368/95 *Vereinigte Familiapress Zeitungsverlags- und vertriebs GmbH v Henrich Bauer Verlag* [1997] ECR I-3689, para. 27.

1746. Case 261/81 *Walter Rau Lebensmittelwerke v De Smedt* [1982] ECR 3961.

In Case 178/84 *Commission v Germany (Re German Beer Purity Laws)*,[1747] Germany failed to convince the ECJ that its national law was proportionate to the objective it sought to achieve.

THE FACTS WERE:

Under German law enacted in the sixteenth century the use of additives in beer was banned and the marketing in Germany of beer containing additives was prohibited. In other Member States the use of additives was authorised. The Commission brought proceedings against Germany for breach of Article 34 TFEU. The German government argued that the prohibition was necessary, taking into account that beer was consumed in "considerable quantities" in Germany.

Held:

The ECJ held that there was no scientific evidence, in particular taking into account research conducted by the FAO (Food and Agriculture Organisation) and the WHO (World Health Organisation) and the EU's own Scientific Committee for foods, that additives constituted a danger to public health. Under Article 36 TFEU it was for a Member State to submit convincing evidence based on scientific research. However, the ECJ agreed that the drinking habits of the German population might have justified the prohibition of certain additives, but not all of them. As a result the German Beer Purity Laws were disproportionate as they went far beyond what was necessary to protect public health.

21.5 The precautionary principle

The precautionary principle applies to prevent harm to health of humans, animals and plants and to the environment (Article 191 TFEU). Its application was explained in a Commission Communication.[1748] According to the Communication, the precautionary principle may be invoked when the potentially dangerous effects of a phenomenon, product or process have been identified by a scientific and objective evaluation, and this evaluation does not allow the risk to be determined with sufficient certainty.

The application of the precautionary principle does not change dramatically the application of the derogation based on the protection of the health of humans, animals and plants, but certainly emphasises that any national measures must be based on the fullest possible scientific evaluation and the careful assessment of the potential consequences of action or inaction. Member States have relied on the precautionary principle in a number of cases.[1749] In Case C-236/01 *Monsanto*,[1750] the ECJ emphasised that the risk assessment must not be based on purely hypothetical considerations but on the most reliable scientific data and the most recent results of international research.

1747. [1987] ECR 1227.
1748. COM(2000) 1 final. See also, K. Lenaerts, "In the Union we Trust: Trust-Enhancing Principles of Community Law", (2004) 41 CMLRev., 317 and G. Majone, "The Precautionary Principle and its Policy Implications", (2000) JCMS, 89.
1749. Case C-236/01 *Monsanto Agricoltura Italia and Others* [2003] ECR I-8105; Case C-192/01 *Commission v Denmark* [2003] ECR I-9693; Case T-177/02 *Malagutti-Vezinhet v Commission* [2004] ECR II-827; Case C-132/03 *Ministero della Salute v Coordinamento delle Associazioni per la Difesa dell'ambiente e dei Diritti Degli Utenti e dei Consumatori* (Codacons) [2005] ECR I-4167.
1750. Case C-236/01 *Monsanto Agricoltura Italia and Others* [2003] ECR I-8105.

In Case C-333/08 *Commission v France*[1751] the ECJ provided guidance on the correct application of the precautionary principle; a Member State should identify all negative consequences deriving from the potentially dangerous effects of a phenomenon, product or process and then make a comprehensive assessment of the risk they represent based on the most reliable scientific data available and the most recent results of international research. When this assessment shows that it is "impossible to determine with certainty the existence or extent of the alleged risk because of the insufficiency, inconclusiveness or imprecision of the results of studies conducted, but the likelihood of real harm to public health persists should the risk materialise, the precautionary principle justifies the adoption of restrictive measures".[1752]

Measures based on the precautionary principles must be non-discriminatory, proportionate to the level of protection which a Member State seeks to achieve, consistent with measures already taken in similar circumstances in which all scientific data are available and are subject to review in the light of scientific progress in the relevant area. When a Member State evaluates costs and benefits of proposed action or inaction, it should take account of both economic and non-economic factors, such as the likely efficacy of possible actions and their acceptability by the public. Further, the decision-making procedure should be transparent and democratic in that it should involve, as early as possible and to the extent reasonably possible, all interested parties.

The burden of proof is normally on a Member State (or the EU) but the Communication states that in some circumstances the burden of proof may be placed on the economic operator. However, such reversal of the burden of proof must not be systematic but based on a case-by-case basis.[1753]

21.6 Derogation based on the protection of intellectual property rights (IPRs)

The essence of IPRs is that they create a form of monopoly for holders in order to either reward their creativity and investment in terms of time and money, or to protect their commercial reputation and goodwill. Intellectual property rights include patents, trade marks, copyrights, registered designs, and so on.

Under national law holders of intellectual property rights are protected against others copying or taking unfair advantage of their work or reputation. The period of protection varies depending on the national law of the Member State and the type of intellectual property.

The relationship between intellectual property rights and EU law is not easy. The fundamental objectives of EU law are in conflict with the very nature of IPRs. They might affect two areas of EU law in particular: the free movement of goods and the provisions of the Treaties regarding competition law, especially Articles 101 and 102 TFEU.

In respect of the free movement of goods Article 34 TFEU prohibits the imposition of any QRs and MEQRs. This provision clashes with the territorial protection granted to a holder of intellectual property rights who may use national law to partition the internal market alongside national lines in many ways. For example, he may charge different prices for the protected product in different Member States; he may restrict imports from one Member State to another; and, he may totally prevent any imports, since without his consent the protected product cannot be sold in another Member State. Thus, the exercise of a holder's rights may seriously hinder the free movement of goods. Article 36 TFEU recognises that IPRs may constitute MEQRs. It provides derogations from Article 34 TFEU subject to a very important

---

1751. [2010] ECR I-757.
1752. Ibid, para. 93.
1753. COM(2000) 1 final, para. 6.4.

limitation, which is that national measures based on IPRs must not constitute a means of arbitrary discrimination or a disguised restriction on trade between Member States.

The derogation from the free movement of goods contained in Article 36 TFEU applies to industrial and commercial property rights. The ECJ extended the scope of application of this derogation to copyrights and neighbouring rights[1754] in Case 78/70 *Deutsche Grammophon*.[1755]

21.6.1 Patents

In order to ensure, on the one hand, economic integration within the internal market and, on the other, that the protection afforded to IPRs under national laws of the Member States does not partition the internal market along national lines, the ECJ made a distinction between the existence of intellectual property rights and their exercise. Article 345 TFEU refers to the existence of such rights while Articles 34, 35 and 36 TFEU relate to their exercise.

Article 345 TFEU states: "The Treaties shall in no way prejudice the rules in Member States governing the system of property ownership."

Accordingly, under Article 345 TFEU EU law must not interfere with the existence of IPRs, but may restrict their exercise by virtue of Articles 34–36 TFEU. This means that the granting of IPRs and the content of such rights is governed by national law, while EU law supervises their exercise. The extent of protection granted by national laws which EU law is prepared to tolerate was defined by the ECJ in Case 15/74 *Centrafarm v Sterling Drug*.[1756]

THE FACTS WERE:

Sterling Drug Inc, a holder of the UK and Dutch patents for a drug called Negram, had marketed that drug itself or via its licensees in both the UK and the Netherlands. Centrafarm, a Dutch company, bought Negram in the UK and Germany, it being less expensive there, and resold it in the Netherlands. Sterling Drug Inc brought proceedings against Centrafarm before a Dutch court to prevent Centrafarm from marketing Negram in the Netherlands.

Held:

The ECJ held that: Article 36 TFEU justifies a derogation from the free movement of goods only "for the purposes of safeguarding rights which constitute the specific subject matter of this property" and the specific subject matter of the intellectual property in respect of patents is:

".. the guarantee that the patentee, to reward the creative effort of the inventor, has the exclusive right to use an invention with a view to manufacturing industrial products and putting them into circulation for the first time, either directly or by grant of licences to third parties, as well as the right to oppose infringements".

1754. Neighbouring rights are those which relate to stage productions and phonograms of radio broadcasting or cable TV organisations.

1755. Case 78/70 *Deutsche Grammophon GmbH v Metro-SB-Grössmarkte GmbH* [1971] ECR 487.

1756. Case 15/74 *Centrafarm BV et Adriaan de Peijper v Sterling Drug Inc* [1974] ECR 1147, paras 8 and 9.

> **Comment:**
>
> *The specific subject-matter is protected under EU law. Once a holder has had the benefit of the specific subject-matter, its rights are exhausted and consequently, it cannot rely on IPRs provided for under national law of a Member State to prevent parallel imports of the protected goods, which by the holder, or with its consent, have lawfully been marketed in any other Member State of the EEA.*
>
> *Bearing in mind that there is no full harmonisation of patent law and that slightly different patents for the same invention may be granted in different Member States to the patent holder, the ECJ decided that all patents that protect the same invention granted to the same holder are to be regarded as parallel patents.*

From the judgment of the ECJ in Case 15/74 *Centrafarm v Sterling Drug* a distinction can be made between three situations:

- Patentee A holds a patent in Member State A. It has manufactured and marketed the protected products in Member State A. B, who has manufactured products protected by A's patent in Member State B, without the consent of A, wants to export these products from Member State B to Member State A. Patentee A is entitled to prevent their importation into Member State A;

- Patentee A holds a patent in Member State A; patentee B holds a patent in Member State B. The patented products are similar in all respects. A and B are legally and economically independent of each other. Patentee A is entitled to prevent importation of B's products into Member State A and *vice versa*, in that patentee B can use its patent to keep A's products out of Member State B; and,

- Patentee A holds a patent in Member State A and has granted a licence to B to manufacture protected products in Member State B. C, a parallel importer (who has no economic or legal links with A or B), decides to export the protected products manufactured in Member State B by B to Member State A (C hopes to make a profit because in Member State A the protected products sell for higher prices than in Member State B). Patentee A cannot prevent importation by C of the protected products from Member State B to Member State A. Patentee A, by giving its consent (by granting a licence to B), has put the protected product into circulation for the first time. His rights are exhausted.

The first two situations concern the existence of intellectual property rights. In both situations the obstacle to the free movement of goods which arises from the existence of national legislation concerning IPRs is justified under EU law. However, the third situation concerns the exercise of IPRs. EU law will not tolerate any obstacle to the free flow of goods between Member States in that situation, and so in this way EU law has achieved a compromise between the competing interests at stake – national IPRs and EU free movement principles.

The doctrine of the exhaustion of rights applies even though the protected products have been put into circulation in a Member State where the invention is not patentable. This occurred in Case 187/80 *Merck and Co. Inc v Stephar BV*.[1757]

1757. [1981] ECR 2063.

THE FACTS WERE:

Merck held a Dutch patent relating to a drug used mainly in the treatment of high blood pressure. Merck was selling its drug in Italy. Under Italian law drugs were not patentable. Stephar bought the drug in Italy and imported it into the Netherlands where its price was much higher than in Italy. Merck brought proceedings against Stephar to prevent the latter from marketing the drug in the Netherlands. Merck argued that the impossibility of patenting its product in Italy deprived its creative effort from being rewarded.

Held:

The ECJ held that the right to reward for the patent holder was not guaranteed in all circumstances. It is for the holder of the patent to decide under what circumstances it will market its product including the possibility of marketing it in a Member State in which its product is not patentable. If the proprietor of the patent decides to market the product in a Member State where its product is not patentable, it must accept the consequences of its choice. In such circumstances its consent to put the product into circulation for the first time is presumed and it cannot rely on its patent to prevent parallel importation of its products.

Comment:

In Joined Cases C-267 and C-268/95 Merck and Beecham[1758] the ECJ qualified its judgment in Case 187/80 Merck. The ECJ held that consent is presumed unless the proprietor of the patent proves that it is subject to a real and actual duty to market its product (that is, a legal duty) in a Member State in which its product is not patentable. In this case the argument submitted by Merck that it was its moral duty as a manufacturer of drugs to market them even in countries where there was no patent protection, was rejected by the ECJ.

At the centre of the concept of the exhaustion of rights is the consent of the owner of IPRs. Consent is presumed when the protected product is put into the market by its owner, or through its subsidiary, or when the owner and the undertaking that has first put the protected product into circulation are under common control.

The concept of exhaustion of rights, does not apply in the following three situations:

- If the protected product has been put into circulation under compulsory licence. This was established in Case 19/84 *Pharmon BV v Hoechst AG*.[1759]

THE FACTS WERE:

Hoechst held a patent in Germany, the Netherlands and the UK for the process to manufacture a drug called Frusemide. In the UK Frusemide was manufactured under a compulsory licence by an undertaking named DDSA. Under UK law the consent of the holder of the patent to

---

1758. [1996] ECR I-6285.
1759. Case 19/84 *Pharmon BV v Hoechst AG* [1985] ECR 2281.

> *manufacturing, and so on, is not required under a compulsory licence although royalties on*
> *sales are paid to it. Pharmon, a Dutch undertaking, bought Frusemide in the UK and resold it*
> *in the Netherlands where Frusemide was more expensive. Hoechst brought proceedings*
> *against Pharmon to prevent the latter from marketing Frusemide in the Netherlands.*
>
> *Held:*
>
> *The ECJ held that Hoechst was entitled to rely on its patent to prevent Pharmon from*
> *marketing Frusemide. The ECJ emphasised that under a compulsory licence the patentee*
> *could not be deemed to have consented to the marketing of its product by a third party and*
> *thereby it is deprived of its rights to determine freely the conditions under which its product*
> *is marketed.*

- If the patent is not exploited in the territory of a Member State where it was granted but patented goods are manufactured in another country by the patentee, or on his behalf, and then imported into the patent-granting Member State.[1760]

- If patented goods are in transit in any Member State irrespective of their final destination.[1761] The case law confirms the view that transit (which consists of transporting goods lawfully manufactured in one Member State to another Member State or to a non-member country by passing through one or more Member States) does not involve any marketing of the goods in question and is therefore not liable to infringe the specific subject-matter of IPRs.

While the rules examined above in respect of patents apply to most types of intellectual property rights, some types of IPRs have peculiarities. These are examined below.

21.6.2 Trade mark rights

In Case 16/74 *Centrafarm v Winthrop*,[1762] the specific subject-matter of a trade mark was defined in terms similar to those regarding patents. The ECJ held that the specific subject-matter is the guarantee to the owner of the trade mark that he has the exclusive right to use that trade mark, for the purpose of putting products protected by the trade mark into circulation for the first time (either directly or by the grant of licences to third parties). Until he does this, he is protected against competitors wishing to take unfair advantage of the status and reputation of the trade mark by illegally selling products bearing it. However, once the owner has put the trade-marked products into circulation for the first time in more than one Member State his exclusive right is lost and consequently he cannot prevent import of protected goods from other Member States into his own Member State. He has exhausted his right.

Directive 2008/95/EC,[1763] which repealed Directive 89/104/EEC,[1764] is designed to approximate the laws of the Member States relating to trade marks. The procedure for obtaining EU trade marks is

---

1760. Case C-235/89 *Commission v Italy* [1992] ECR I-777; Case C-30/90 *Commission v UK* [1992] ECR I-829.
1761. Case C-23/99 *Commission v France* [2000] ECR I-7653); or outside the EU: C-115/02 *Administration des Douanes et Droits Indirect v Rioglass SA, and Transremar SL* [2003] ECR I-12705.
1762. [1974] ECR 1183.
1763. [2008] OJ L299/25.
1764. [1989] OJ L40/1.

governed by Regulation 207/2009 on the Community Trade Marks.[1765] Under the procedure, to be protected in all Member States, a trade mark must be registered with the Office for Harmonisation in the Internal Market (Trade Marks and Design (OHIM)) located in Alicante, Spain.

Under Directive 89/104/EE, now replaced by Directive 2008/95, the ECJ clarified the application of the principle of exhaustion to advertisement of the protected products; the meaning of the concept of confusion of consumers; the application of the doctrine of common origin of a trade mark; and, the circumstances in which repackaging and rebranding of protected goods is allowed. These topics are dealt with below.

21.6.2.1 *The exhaustion of rights with regard to advertisement of protected products*

For parallel importers who intend to sell protected products at lower prices than those fixed by the owner of the trade mark or his distributors, the vital issue is whether they can advertise the protected products. This was answered by the ECJ in Case C-337/95 *Parfums Christian Dior,*[1766] in which it decided that the principle of exhaustion applies to advertisement of the protected products.

The ECJ held that when trade-marked goods have been put into circulation in the EEA by or with the consent of the owner of the trade mark, a reseller is entitled not only to resell those goods but also to make use of the trade mark to bring to the public's attention their further commercialisation. In other words, an owner of a trade mark cannot prevent a reseller from advertising the protected goods and using the trade mark in so doing. However, the ECJ held that in some circumstances the owner of a trade mark may stop a reseller from advertising. The legitimate interests of the trade mark owner must be protected, especially when a reseller is using the trade mark for advertising in a manner which could damage its reputation.

Further clarification of the concept of exhaustion of trade mark rights in the context of advertisement of protected products was provided in Case C-63/97 *Deenik,*[1767] which concerned unauthorised use of the BMW trade mark in an advertisement for a garage business. In this case the ECJ distinguished between the sale of goods covered by that trade mark and their repair and maintenance. With regard to the sale of goods, the ECJ confirmed its decision in Case C-337/95 *Parfums Christian Dior,*[1768] that is, that a reseller is entitled to make use of a trade mark to bring to the public's attention the further commercialisation of the protected products. However, the owner of a trade mark may stop a reseller from using its trade mark if advertisements by the reseller damage the reputation of the trade mark. In respect of the advertisement for repair and maintenance of BMW cars, the ECJ held that the principle of the "exhaustion of rights" does not apply as there is no further commercialisation of goods. As a result, a garage owner is entitled to use a trade mark to inform the public about the intended purpose of products or services, and in particular with regard to items such as accessories or spare parts, unless the mark is used in a way that may create the impression that there is a commercial connection between the two undertakings, and in particular that the reseller's business is affiliated to the trade mark proprietor's distribution network or that there is a special relationship between the two undertakings. Accordingly, the use of a trade mark is lawful provided there is no risk that the public will be induced to believe that there is a commercial link between the two undertakings.

1765. [2009] OJ L78/1.

1766. Case C-337/95 *Parfums Christian Dior SA and Parfums Christian Dior BV v Evora BV* [1997] ECR I-6013.

1767. *Bayerische Motorenwerke AG (BMW) and BMW Netherlands BV v Ronald Karel Deenik* [1999] ECR I-905.

1768. Case C-337/95 *Parfums Christian Dior SA and Parfums Christian Dior BV v Evora BV* [1997] ECR I-6013.

21.6.2.2 The concept of confusion

Very often proprietors of trade marks try to prevent the import from other Member States of goods bearing a similar trade mark to their own and relating to similar products on the ground that this may give rise to confusion for consumers in the Member State of importation.

Under Directive 89/104, in particular its Article 4(1)(b), in Case C-251/95 *Sabel v Puma*[1769] the ECJ clarified the meaning of the concept of confusion. It held that the likelihood of confusion between two marks depends upon the distinctiveness of the earlier mark either *per se* or because of the reputation it enjoys with the public. The ECJ emphasised that in this case, because the earlier mark was not especially well known to the public and the idea conveyed by the pictorial element of the two trade marks was of little imaginative content, there was little risk that the public would confuse the two marks, although consumers may associate them in the sense that one would simply bring the other to mind without the likelihood of confusion about the origin of the goods. The ECJ held that the criterion of "likelihood of confusion which includes the likelihood of association with an earlier mark" means that the mere association which the consumers might make between two trade marks with analogous semantic content does not constitute in itself a sufficient ground for concluding that there is a likelihood of confusion. So, for the ECJ, likelihood of confusion is a narrower concept than likelihood of association. Association between two things in the public mind does not mean the public will necessarily confuse the two.

The case law of the ECJ on the concept of confusion can be summarised as follow:

■ The concept of likelihood of confusion includes the likelihood of association with the earlier trade mark, but the likelihood of association does not entail the likelihood of confusion;

■ The likelihood of confusion between two trade marks depends upon the distinctiveness of the earlier mark either *per se* or because of the reputation it enjoys with the public;

■ Visual, aural and conceptual similarity of allegedly conflicting trade marks is part of any global assessment;

■ When assessing the overall impression given by allegedly conflicting trade marks, their distinctive and dominant components must be taken into account;[1770]

■ Assessment is made from the perspective of an average consumer of the EU who is reasonably well-informed and reasonably observant and circumspect. He/she normally perceives a mark as a whole, not its details, and his/her level of attention is likely to depend on the category of goods or services in question; and,

■ The existence of a risk that an average consumer (referred to in the Directive as "the public") might believe that the goods or services under consideration come from the same undertakings, or from economically-linked undertakings, shows a likelihood of confusion.[1771]

1769. Case C-251/95 *Sabel BV v Puma AG, Rudolf Dassler Sport* [1997] ECR I-6191.
1770. Case T-292/01 *Phillips Van Heusen v OHIM – Pash Textilvertrieb und Einzelhandel (BASS)* [2003] ECR II-4335.
1771. Case T-6/01 *Matratzen Concord v OHIM – Hukla Germany* [2002] ECR II-4335 and Case T-129/01 *Alejandro v OHIM – Anheuser-Busch* [2003] ECR II-2251, para. 37.

21.6.2.3 The doctrine of common origin of a trade mark

It may occur that, for various reasons, the right to use the original trade mark has been split. As a result, undertakings independent from each other and operating in different countries are lawfully using the same trade mark. There is an issue as to whether under EU law undertakings using a trade mark of common origin may rely on their trade mark rights to prevent each other from importing protected goods into each other's territory. The ECJ's position on this matter is that irrespective of whether the splitting of the original trade mark was due to an act of a public authority or a contractual assignment a trade mark holder may rely on its trade mark to prevent importation of products made by a third party but bearing a trade mark with a common origin to its own.[1772]

21.6.2.4 Repackaging and rebranding of protected products

The term "repackaging" in EU law is used to refer to the practice of removing the original packaging of trade-marked products and displaying the original trade mark on new packaging.

"Rebranding" involves the replacement of the original packaging and trade mark, so that a new trade mark appears on the new packaging.

Repackaging and rebranding are often used by distributors of products such as pharmaceuticals in order to facilitate the selling of them at different prices in different Member States. Normally, a third party takes advantage of the price difference by buying such products in a Member State where they are cheaper, repackaging and/or rebranding them and then reselling them in a Member State where they are generally more expensive.

It emerges from the case law[1773] of the ECJ that a trade mark owner will not be able to oppose repackaging so long as the five conditions set out below are satisfied:

1. Repackaging is necessary to market the product in the Member State of importation (see below);

2. The repackaging does not adversely affect the original condition of the product;

3. The new packaging clearly states the name of the manufacturer and the person who has repackaged the product;

4. The repackaging is not such as to damage the trade mark's reputation; and,

5. The importer gives notice of its intention to repackage to the trade mark owner and supplies samples if requested.

With regard to the first condition, under EU law, a parallel importer is not allowed to repackage at will. Repackaging and rebranding is allowed only if such action is necessary for the product to be marketed in the Member State of importation. In Case C-443/99 *Merck, Sharp v Paranova*,[1774] the ECJ elucidated the concept of "necessity" of repackaging/rebranding. The Court stated that such necessity exists, for example, where:

- a parallel importer cannot place pharmaceutical products on the market in the Member State of importation because national law requires their repackaging;

1772. Case C-9/93 *IHT Internationale Heiztechnik GmbH v Ideal Standard GmbH* [1994] ECR I-2789 and Case C-10/89 *CNL Sucal v Hag (Hag II)* [1990] ECR I-3711.

1773. Case 102/77 *Hoffmann-la Roche v Centrafarm* [1978] ECR 1139; Case 3/78 *Centrafarm v American Home Product* [1978] ECR 1823; Cases C-427/93, C-429/93 and C-436/93 *Bristol-Myers Squibb and Others* [1996] ECR I-3457; Case C-379/97 *Pharmacia and Upjohn SA v Paranova* [1999] ECR I-6927.

1774. Case C-443/99 *Merck, Sharp & Dohme GmbH v Paranova Pharmazeutika Handels GmbH* [2002] ECR I-3703.

■ national sickness insurance rules make reimbursement of medical expenses conditional upon certain packaging; and,

■ well-established medical prescription practices are based, *inter alia*, on standard sizes recommended by professional bodies or by sickness insurance institutions.

The mere fact that a substantial proportion of consumers in the Member State of importation will refuse to buy relabelled foreign packs is not sufficient to be considered as making neccessary the repackaging/ rebranding of pharmaceutical products. In such circumstances a finding of necessity would depend on whether resistance to relabelled pharmaceutical products constitutes a real impediment to effective access to the market concerned. If so, the repackaging is necessary. It is a question of fact, so it is the task of a national court to ascertain whether strong resistance from a significant proportion of consumers in the Member State of importation constitutes an impediment to effective market access for the products concerned. The ECJ has emphasised that a trade mark owner will succeed in opposing repackaging/rebranding in a situation where a parallel importer, by repackaging, is seeking to secure a commercial advantage.

With regard to the third condition, in Joined Cases C-400/09 *Orifarm* and C-207/10 *Paranova Danmark*[1775] the ECJ recognised the commercial reality relating to the repacking of products in that the entity named on the packing and holding the marketing authorisation may not be the same as the entity performing the physical repacking. In those cases the trade mark owner opposed the repacking on the ground that the entity named on the packing was not the same as the entity which performed the physical repacking. The ECJ held that the entity named on the packing was solely responsible for the repacking and thus the opposition of the trade mark owner was not acceptable. It should be noted that in those cases the entity named on the packaging and the entity which performed the physical repacking belonged to the same group of companies, i.e. Paranova Group. The ECJ endorsed the Opinion of A-G Bot that when the entity which performs physical repacking is not closely connected with that named on the packing, opposition from the trade mark owner might be acceptable.

With regard to the fifth condition, in Case C-143/00 *Boehringer v Swingward*,[1776] the ECJ confirmed the requirement of prior notice in all circumstances. The parallel importer must give notice and provide a sample of the repackaged product to the trade mark owner. It is not sufficient that the owner is notified by other sources. If the parallel importer fails to give notice, the trade mark owner may oppose the marketing of the repackaged product. As to the period of notice given to the owner to react to the intended repackaging, the ECJ stated that the proprietor of the trade mark must have a reasonable time to react. What should be considered as a reasonable time depends upon all the relevant circumstances to be assessed by a national court in the event of a dispute. Due attention must be paid to the interests of the parallel importer who will want to put the product concerned on the market in the Member State of importation as soon as possible after completing the necessary formalities in that Member State.

It is for a parallel importer to prove that the five conditions set out above are satisfied.[1777] If one of them is not satisfied, the holder of a trade mark will be allowed to oppose the further commercialisation.

1775. Joined Cases C-400/09 and C-207/10 *Orifarm A/S and Others* (C-400/09) and *Paranova Danmark A/S and Paranova Pack A/S* (C-207/10) *v Merck Sharp & Dohme Corp. and Merck Sharp & Dohme BV and Merck Sharp & Dohme* (judgment of 29/7/11) (NYR)).

1776. Case C-143/00 *Boehringer Ingelheim KG and Others v Swingward Ltd and Downelhurst Ltd* [2002] ECR I-3759.

1777. Case C-405/03 *Class International BV v Colgate-Palmolive Company and Others* [2005] ECR I-8735.

21.6.3 Copyright

With regard to copyright a distinction is made between:

- non-performance copyrights such as those in literary and artistic works (for example, books, paintings, sound-recordings); and,

- performance copyrights concerning plays and films and their performance.

In respect of non-performance copyrights EU law has always distinguished between those rights which by their nature may be "exhausted", for instance the marketing of a book in another Member State with the consent of the owner,[1778] and those which cannot be "exhausted" such as rental rights. Rental rights cannot be exhausted by the marketing of the protected product in another Member State.[1779] In this respect Article 4(2) of Directive 2001/29/EC harmonising certain aspects of copyright and related rights in the information society[1780] provides that:

> "the distribution right shall not be exhausted within the Community [EU] in respect of the original or copies of the work, except where the first sale or other transfer of ownership in the Community [EU] of that object is made by the rightholder or with his consent."

Performance copyrights are to be viewed in the context of the provision of services rather than of the free movement of goods, as the exploitation of these works occurs through public exhibitions which can be repeated an indefinite number of times. In Case 62/79 *Coditels*,[1781] the ECJ held that Article 56 TFEU did not preclude "an assignee of the performing right in a cinematographic film in a Member State from relying upon his rights to prohibit the exhibition of that film in that State, without his authority, by means of cable diffusion if the film so exhibited is picked up and transmitted after being broadcast in another Member State by a third party with the consent of the original owner of the right".

The above position is restated in Article 3(3) of Directive 2001/29/EC which provides that the right of communicating to the public and the right to the making available to the public of protected works will not be exhausted by any act of communication to the public or of making available to the public. As a result, the Directive provides authors, during the protection period fixed under national law, with the exclusive right to authorise or prohibit any communication to the public of originals and copies of their works whether by wired or wireless means.[1782]

The specific subject matter of the right to rent, perform or show works in public allows the holder of such a right to control each and every use and thus to be paid fees for each and every use. The holder's right is not exhausted by the first showing, or the first performance or the lending of the relevant works in another Member State.

21.6.4 Design rights

The design of a product relates to its appearance, in particular, the shape, texture, colour, materials used, contours and/or ornamentation. Directive 98/71/EC on the legal protection of designs harmonises

---

1778. Joined Cases 55/80 and 57/80 *Musik-Vertrieb v GEMA* [1981] ECR 147.
1779. Case 158/86 *EMI Electrola, Warner Brothers Inc v Christiansen* [1988] ECR 2605.
1780. [2001] OJ L167/10.
1781. Case 62/79 *Coditel SA v Ciné Vog Films* [1980] ECR 881.
1782. The meaning of "communication to the public" was explained in Case C-306/05 *Sociedad General de Autores y Editores de España (SGAE) v Rafael Hoteles SA* [2006] ECR I-11519.

national laws relating to the legal protection of designs. Its Article 15 confirms the case law of the ECJ under which the principle of exhaustion of rights applies to design rights.[1783]

Directive 98/71/EC is complemented by Regulation 6/2002 which provides for unitary design right protection in the EU. It creates two distinct design rights, first the right obtained by registration with OHIM of a maximum duration of 25 years from the submission of an application in this respect to OHIM, and second, an unregistered right of a maximum duration of three years from the date on which the design was first made available to the public within the EU. Apart from the period of protection the difference between a registered and unregistered design right is that the former provides protection against any use of the protected design whilst the latter protects only against copying. The two distinct rights are explained by the fact that some sectors of industry produce a large number of designs for products which have relatively short market life, e.g. the fashion industry. For them the obligation of registration would have been excessively burdensome.

In order to obtain protection under either the registered or unregistered system a design must be new and must have individual character. EU harmonising legislation provides that designs may be protected under both EU law and national law and by different IPRs, e.g. under copyright law.

21.6.5 Parallel imports of goods from outside the European Economic Area (EEA)

The principle of the exhaustion of intellectual property rights does not apply to imports from outside the EEA. The holder of intellectual property rights is entitled to prevent parallel import of protected products coming from non-Member States to a Member State, even if the holder was first responsible for putting its goods into circulation. This was confirmed by the ECJ in Case C-355/96 *Silhouette*.[1784]

THE FACTS WERE:

Silhouette, a well-known manufacturer of top-quality fashion spectacles, used its trade mark "Silhouette" registered in Austria and most countries in the world to sell its product. In October 1995 Silhouette sold 21,000 out-of-fashion spectacle frames to a Bulgarian company. Silhouette instructed its representative to inform the purchaser that the frames were to be resold only in Bulgaria (at that time Bulgaria was not a member of the EU or the EEA) and the States of the former Soviet Union, and not in the territory of the EU. However, this restriction was not inserted into the contract, and it was not clear whether in fact the purchaser was aware of such a restriction. In December 1995 the frames were resold to Hartlauer, a retailer in Austria that sells spectacles and frames for low prices. Hartlauer offered frames bearing Silhouette's trade mark for sale in Austria. Silhouette had never supplied spectacles or frames to Hartlauer because Silhouette considered that distribution of its products by Hartlauer would be harmful to its image as a manufacturer of top-quality fashion spectacles. Silhouette brought an action for interim relief before the Landesgericht Steyr, seeking an injunction restraining Hartlauer from offering spectacles or spectacle frames for sale in Austria under Silhoutte's trade mark, as the sale of cut-price and outmoded spectacle frames would

---

1783. See Case 144/81 *Keurkoop BV v Nancy Kean Gifts BV* [1982] ECR 2853, and Case 53/87 *Consorzio Italiano della Componentistica di Ricambio per Autoveicoli and Maxicar v Régie Nationale des Usines Renault* [1988] ECR 6039 and Case 238/87 *AB Volvo v Eric Veng (UK) Ltd* [1988] ECR 6211.

1784. Case C-355/96 *Silhouette International Schmied GmbH & Co Kg v Hartlauer Handelsgesellschaft MbH* [1998] ECR I-4799.

damage its brand reputation within the EU. Silhouette argued that its trade mark rights were not exhausted within the meaning of Directive 89/104/EEC, as they are exhausted only when the goods have been put on the market in the EEA by the proprietor or with its consent. Hautlauer's answer was that Silhouette had not sold the frames subject to any prohibition of, or restriction on, reimportation and that the Austrian law implementing the Directive did not grant a right to seek prohibitory injunctions. Silhouette's action was dismissed by the Landesgericht Steyr and, on appeal, by the Oberlandesgericht Linz. Silhouette appealed to the Oberster Gerichtshof on a point of law.

The Austrian Oberster Gerichtshof (Supreme Court) referred to the ECJ for a preliminary ruling under Article 267 TFEU two questions concerning the interpretation of Article 7(1) of Directive 89/104. In particular, the Austrian court asked whether the holder of a trade mark who has consented to market the protected products in the EU and in the EEA can prevent a third party from using the trade mark outside the EEA, or whether it has exhausted its rights when the goods have been put in circulation, by or with its consent, in the EU and in the EEA.

At the time of the dispute Austria was a Member of the EEA only – not of the EU. Its national law prior to the implementation of Directive 89/104 recognised the principle of international exhaustion, according to which once goods have been marketed anywhere by, or with the consent of the owner, its rights are exhausted and therefore it has no control over the goods. Austrian rules implementing the Directive restricted the exhaustion principle to the time of first marketing within the EEA. For that reason Hautlauer argued that the Directive applied only to the EEA, and the question of international exhaustion was left to the national law of Member States.

Held:

The ECJ rejected the argument submitted by Hautlauer. The Court stated that Article 7 of the Directive had comprehensively resolved the question of exhaustion in the sense that it harmonised law in this area in all Member States. This solution ensures uniformity, and is in conformity with the objectives of the Directive. The ECJ emphasised that if some Member States recognised the principle of international exhaustion while others did not, the result might be the existence of barriers to the free movement of goods and services within the EEA.

Comment:

Silhouette had not exhausted its IPR and was able to stop Hautlauer from selling the protected products in the EEA. For consumers in the EEA the decision of the ECJ means that they are no longer able to buy branded goods imported from outside the EEA and obtained from unauthorised sources at a low price.

In Joined Cases C-414/99 to C-416/99 *Davidoff and Levi Strauss*[1785] the issue was whether the express consent of a trade mark holder is required for parallel importation of protected goods from outside the EEA into the EEA. The ECJ answered in the affirmative, adding that unequivocal consent

---

1785. Joined Cases C-414/99 to C-416/99 *Zino Davidoff SA v A & G Imports Ltd and Levi Strauss & Co. and Others v Tesco Stores Ltd and Others* [2001] ECR I-8691.

would equal express consent. The ECJ rejected the possibility that implied consent could be inferred from the mere silence of the trade mark proprietor; from the failure of the goods to carry any warning that their marketing in the EEA was prohibited; or, from the fact that the proprietor had not placed any express contractual restrictions on the resale of the goods in the EEA. The ECJ emphasised that preservation of the exclusive right of the proprietor of a trade mark "cannot depend on there being an express prohibition of marketing within the EEA, which the proprietor is not obliged to impose, nor, *a fortiori*, on a repetition of that prohibition in one or more of the contracts concluded in the distribution chain".[1786]

RECOMMENDED READING

Books

Barnard, C., *The Substantive Law of the EU. The Four Freedoms*, 3rd edn, 2010, Oxford: OUP.

Bently, L., and Sherman, B., *Intellectual Property Law*, 3rd edn, 2009, Oxford: OUP.

Oliver, P., assisted by M. Jarvis, *Free Movement of Goods in the European Community: Under Articles 28 and 30 of the EC Treaty*, 4th edn, 2003, London: Sweet & Maxwell.

Articles

de Bùrca, G., "The Principle of Proportionality and its Application in EC Law", (1993) 13 YEL, 105.

Harlander, L., "Exhaustion of Trademark Rights beyond the European Union in Light of Silhouette International Schmied v Hartlauer Handelsdesellschaft. Towards Stronger Protection of Trademark Rights and Eliminating the Grey Market", (2000) 28 Ga. J. Int'l & Comp L., 267.

Hays, T., "Paranova v Merck and Co-branding of Pharmaceuticals in the European Economic Area", (2004) 94 *Trademark Reporter,* 821.

Johnston, A., "The Double-headed Approach of the ECJ concerning Consumer Protection", (2007) 44 CMLRev., 1237.

Lenaerts, K., "'In the Union we Trust': Trust-Enhancing Principles of Community Law", (2004) 41 CMLRev., 317.

Scott, J., "Mandatory or Imperative Requirements in the EU and the WTO", in Barnard, C., and Scott, J. (eds), *The Law of the Single European Market, Unpacking the Premises*, 2002, Oxford: Hart Publishing, ch. 10.

Tridimas, T., "Proportionality in Community Law: Searching for the Appropriate Standard of Scrutiny", in Ellias, E. (ed.), *The Principle of Proportionality in the Laws of Europe*, 1999, Oxford: Hart Publishing, 68.

Weiler, J.H.H., "Europornography: First Reference of the House of Lords to the European Court of Justice", (1981) MLR, 91.

PROBLEM QUESTION

German Media GmbH ("German Media"), a company established in Germany, sells video tapes in many EU countries. It has recently encountered the following problems:

A.   An injunction prohibiting German Media from selling video tapes entitled "Violence is good" by mail order in Ireland has been issued by the Irish High Court. This is because Irish legislation on the protection of young persons prohibits the sale by mail order of video tapes which have not

---

1786.   Ibid, para. 64.

been examined in Ireland in accordance with that legislation and which do not bear an age-limit label corresponding to a classification decision from the competent Irish authority. Prior to importation to Ireland the video tapes were classified by the German Film Board (GFB) as being "suitable only for 15 years old persons and over". The video tapes bore a GFB label stating that they may be viewed only by persons aged 15 or older.

B.   The Estonian Customs Office has confiscated video tapes belonging to German Media on the ground that they are pornographic and therefore not allowed to be sold in Estonia. German Media submits that although the importation of pornographic video tapes is prohibited in Estonia, there is no legislation preventing the making of such tapes in Estonia.

Advise German Media as to whether the Irish and the Estonian authorities are in breach of Article 34 TFEU.

ESSAY QUESTION

Critically discuss whether the ECJ has found the right balance between the protection of IPRs and the requirements of the free movement of goods.

AIDE-MÉMOIRE

DEROGATIONS AND MANDATORY REQUIREMENTS

| DEROGATIONS | MANDATORY REQUIREMENTS |

ARTICLE 36 TFEU (TREATY-BASED JUSTIFICATIONS)
DISTINCTLY APPLICABLE MEASURES CAN ONLY BE JUSTIFIED UNDER ART. 36 TFEU.

Measures under Article 36 TFEU must not constitute a means of arbitrary discrimination or disguised restrictions on trade between Member States (Case 124/81 *Commission v UK [Re UHT Milk]*).
The list of derogations is exhaustive.
They are based on:

1. Public morality: Case 121/85 *Conegate Lt*;
2. Public policy: Case 154/85 *Commission v Italy*;
3. Public security: Case 72/83 *Campus Oil Ltd v Minister for Industry and Energy*;
4. Protection of the health and life of humans, animals and plants:
   Case 238/82 *Duphar BV*; Case C-366/04 *Schwarz*;
5. Protection of national treasures possessing artistic, historic or archaeological value: there is no case law on this point;
6. Protection of industrial and commercial property.

THE CASE-LAW BASED JUSTIFICATIONS (THE *CASSIS DE DIJON* CASE)

Indistinctly applicable measures and national residual rules can be justified under both: Art. 36 TFEU and mandatory requirements.
The list of mandatory requirements is not exhaustive. It includes:

1. The protection of consumers;
2. The protection of the environment;
3. The protection of fundamental rights;
4. The protection of road safety;
5. The protection of children

1. National measures must be proportionate, i.e. suitable and necessary to achieve the objective they seek
2. The burden of proof is on a Member State
3. The precautionary principle may be relied upon by a Member State to protect life and health of humans, animals, and plants and to protect the environment.

With regard to intellectual property rights EU law distinguishes between

Existence of IPRs
This is governed by national law and is not subject to any interference by EU law (Article 345 TFEU).

Exercise of IPRs
Exercise of IPRs falls within the derogation to free movement of goods in Article 36 TFEU in so far as such exercise relates to the **specific subject matter** of the relevant intellectual property.
The specific subject matter varies according to the type of IPR, but its bare essential is that it protects holders of IPRs until they put the protected product into circulation for the first time, in another Member State, themselves or by making appropriate arrangements with a third party.
The term **"putting into circulation"** means the marketing by IPR holders, or their consenting to the marketing of the protected product, in more than one Member State. Once IPR holders have marketed or have consented to the marketing of their product in another Member State of the EEA, their **intellectual property rights are exhausted**. They cannot invoke them subsequently to prevent parallel imports of the protected products but the principle of the exhaustion **does not apply** to imports from outside the EEA (Case C-355/96 *Silhouette*).

Patents

For patents the specific subject matter of IPRs protected under EU law is:

"... the guarantee that the patentee, to reward the creative effort of the inventor, has the exclusive right to use an invention with a view to manufacturing industrial products and putting them into circulation for the first time, either directly or by grant of licences to third parties, as well as the right to oppose infringements" (Case 15/74 *Centrafarm v Sterling Drug*).

To be noted:
The principle of exhaustion:
- **Applies** when the patent holder has put the protected product into circulation in a Member State where the product is of a class which is not patentable in that Member State (Case 187/80 *Merck*). However, the principle of exhaustion does not apply if that Member State imposes a legal obligation (not merely an ethical or a moral obligation) on the patent holder to market the product (Cases C-267 and C-268/95 *Merck and Beecham*).
- **Does not apply** in three circumstances:
  - When the protected product has been put into circulation under compulsory licence (19/84 *Pharmon*);
  - When a patent is not exploited in the territory of a Member State where it was granted but patented goods are manufactured in another country and then imported into the patent-granting Member State (Case C-235/89 *Commission v Italy*); and,
  - When patented goods are in transit in any Member State irrespective of their final destination (inside or outside the EU) (Case C-23/99 *Commission v France*).

Trade mark

For trade marks the specific subject matter is:

"... the guarantee that the owner of the trade mark has the exclusive right to use that trade mark, for the purpose of putting products protected by the trade mark into circulation for the first time, either directly, or by the grant of licences to third parties and thus to protect him against competitors wishing to take unfair advantage of the status and reputation of the trade mark by selling products illegally bearing his trade mark" (Case 16/74 *Centrafarm v Winthrop*).

The definition of the specific subject matter of a trade mark is largely the same as that for patents.

The principle of exhaustion of trade marks covers the advertisement of the protected products by parallel importers (Case C-337/95 *Parfums Christian Dior*).

The concept of confusion

The likelihood of confusion between two trade marks depends upon the distinctiveness of the earlier mark either per se or because of the reputation it enjoys with the public (Case C-251/95 *Sabel BV v Puma AG*).

The doctrine of common origin of a trade mark

A holder can rely on its trade mark to prevent the importation into its own Member State of products made by a third party but bearing a trade mark with a common origin to its own (Case C-10/89CNL *Sucal v Hag (Hag II)*).

Rebranding and repackaging of the protected product
Rebranding and repackaging, provided it is necessary, is allowed if:

- It does not adversely affect the original condition of the product;
- The new packaging clearly states the name of the manufacturer and the person who has repackaged the product;
- The repackaging is not such as to damage the trade mark's reputation;
- The repackager gives notice of its intention to the trade mark owner and supplies samples if requested (Case C-443/99 *Merck, Sharp & Dohme GmbH*).

Copyright

There is a distinction between non-performance copyrights and performance copyrights.
- Non-Performance copyrights (books, paintings, and so on). The subject matter is similar to patents except that there is an additional distinction between those rights which by their nature may be "exhausted" (for example, the marketing of a book in another Member State with the consent of the owner) and those which cannot be "exhausted" (for example, rental rights which cannot be exhausted by the sale of the protected product in another Member State).
- Performance copyrights (plays, films and their performance). This is related to the provision of services. The specific subject matter of the right to rent, perform and show the works in public allows the holder of such rights to control each and every use and thus to be paid fees for each and every use. Its right is not exhausted by first showing, performing or lending of the relevant works in another Member State (Case C-306/05 *SGAE v Rafael Hoteles SA*).

Design rights

The principle of exhaustion applies (Case 144/81 *Keurkoop BV v Nancy Kean Gifts BV*).

22

CITIZENSHIP OF THE EU

CONTENTS

CHAPTER OUTLINE

1. The concept of EU citizenship was established by the Treaty of Maastricht. The ToL emphasises the importance of creating closer ties between the EU and its citizens and that of ensuring that they fully participate in the democratic life of the Union. In particular, Part Two of the TFEU on "Non-discrimination and Citizenship of the Union" lists the most important rights attached to EU citizenship whilst Title II of the TEU on "Provisions on Democratic Principles" acknowledges that the participation of EU citizens in the decision making process in the EU is central to the creation of a democratic Union.

2. EU citizenship flows from national citizenship: every person holding the nationality of a Member State is an EU citizen. EU citizenship is thus derivative, rather than a right independent of, or autonomous from, national law. Although Member States have exclusive competence to determine who are to be considered their nationals, and such a determination cannot be challenged either by the EU or by other Member States, they must pay due regard to EU law, i.e. take it into account when nationality matters are within the scope of the Treaties.

3. In Case C-184/99 *Grzelczyk* the ECJ emphasised that EU citizenship "is destined to be the fundamental status of nationals of the Member States, enabling those who find themselves in the same situation [as nationals of a host Member State] to enjoy the same treatment in law irrespective of their nationality, subject to such exceptions as are expressly provided for".

The ECJ has greatly contributed to the development of the content of EU citizenship by requiring the Member States to remove all directly and indirectly discriminatory national measures as well as those which, whilst being non-discriminatory, restrict the exercise of rights deriving from EU citizenship. In Case C-34/09 *Zambrano* the ECJ introduced a new doctrine which may be called the doctrine of the "substance of rights", under which national measures are in breach of EU law if they deprive an EU citizen of enjoyment of the substance of the rights conferred on him by virtue of the status of EU citizen. The doctrine applies in situations where an EU citizen has not exercised his right to free movement and thus gives him an entitlement against his home Member State.

4. Part Two of the TFEU on "Non-discrimination and Citizenship of the Union" lists the most important rights attached to EU citizenship.

A.   Article 21(1) TFEU guarantees EU citizens and their families the right to move freely and reside within the territory of the Member States provided they are engaged in the internal market economic activity or are financially self-sufficient. Directive 2004/38 constitutes a response to problems encountered by EU citizens wishing to exercise the rights guaranteed under Article 21(1) TFEU.

B.   Article 22(1) TFEU confers on EU citizens the right to vote and stand for municipal elections in a host Member State, under the same conditions as nationals of that Member State. Directive 94/80/EC implements this Article.

C.   Article 22(2) TFEU confers on EU citizens voting rights in a host Member State for elections to the EP.

D.   Under Article 23 TFEU, EU citizens have the right to obtain diplomatic and consular protection in a third State, where their own Member State is not represented by a permanent consular or diplomatic mission, from any other EU Member State having a diplomatic establishment there, on the same conditions as nationals of that Member State. This right is confirmed in Article 46 of the Charter of Fundamental Rights.

E.   Article 24(1) TFEU sets out the procedure for implementing the right of EU citizens (i.e. at least one million citizens who are between them nationals of a significant number of Member States) to invite the European Commission to bring forward legislative proposals in areas where the Commission has the power to do so (see Chapter 5.2.2).

F.   Article 24(2) and (3) TFEU concerns the right to petition the EP and to complain to the EU Ombudsman. Anyone living within the territory of the EU or operating a business there can rely on this right. A petition to the EP must relate to a subject falling within the sphere of activity of the EU and concern the petitioner directly. A complaint to the Ombudsman must relate to a matter of "maladministration" by an EU institution, body, office or agency other than the EU courts, but it is not necessary that the complainant is personally affected by it.

G.   Article 24(4) TFEU provides that every citizen of the EU has the right to write to any EU institution, body, office or agency in one of the official languages of the EU and to receive an answer in the same language. It should be read in a broader perspective in that it gives EU citizens the right to information and thus enhances the principle of transparency.

5. Article 25 TFEU emphasises that EU citizenship is a dynamic concept. Indeed, since its establishment it has evolved from a not very coherent bundle of rights into a more cohesive and meaningful concept.

22.1 Introduction

Citizenship of the EU was established by the Treaty of Maastricht[1787] and has, since then, evolved considerably so that it has become "the fundamental status of nationals of the Member States".[1788] On the basis of this status alone, EU citizens, who reside lawfully in a host Member State, are able to claim important social, cultural and other rights (see Chapter 22.3) and citizens who have not exercised their right to free movement may challenge national measures which deprive them of enjoyment of the substance of the rights conferred on them by virtue of that status (see Chapter 22.3.1).

The ToL contains numerous provisions aimed at creating closer ties between the EU and its citizens and ensuring that they fully participate in the democratic life of the Union. Article 1 TEU, which contains the over-reaching objectives of the EU, states that "This Treaty marks a new stage in the process of creating an ever closer union among the peoples of Europe, in which decisions are taken as openly as possible and as closely as possible to the citizen". The new approach to EU citizenship is emphasised in the Preamble to the Charter of Fundamental Rights, which has the same binding force as the Treaties (see Chapter 8.4), and which states that "the individual is at the heart of" the Union. Further, the Treaties ensure that fundamental rights of EU citizens are respected and promoted (e.g. Articles 2 and 6 TEU). Probably, the most striking feature of the ToL is that many of its provisions are no longer addressed to the Member States but to citizens of the EU, e.g. Article 3(2) TEU offers to its citizens the AFSJ, and Article 9 TEU ensures equal treatment of its citizens, who shall receive equal attention from EU institutions, bodies, offices or agencies.

Part Two of the TFEU on "Non-discrimination and Citizenship of the Union" lists the most important rights attached to EU citizenship whilst Title II of the TEU on "Provisions on Democratic Principles" acknowledges that EU citizens' participation in the decision making process in the EU is central to the creation of a democratic Union.

1787. For the historical background see D. O'Keeffe, "Union Citizenship", in D. O'Keeffe and P. M. Twomey (eds), *Legal Issues of the Maastricht Treaty*, 1994, London: Chancery Law Publishing, 87–9.

1788. Case C-184/99 *Rudy Grzelczyk v Centre Public d'Aide Sociale d'Ottignies-Louvain-la-Neuve* [2001] ECR I-6193 and Case C-413/99 *Baumbast and R v Secretary of State for the Home Department* [2002] ECR I-7091.

With regard to Part Two of the TFEU on "Non-discrimination and Citizenship of the Union" it confirms a close relationship between EU citizenship and the prohibition of discrimination based not only on nationality (Article 18 TFEU) but also on other factors mentioned in Article 19 TFEU such as sex, racial or ethnic origin, religion, belief, disability, age or sexual orientation. It is important to note that rights of EU citizens are not limited to Articles 18–25 TFEU, but are also contained in other provisions of the Treaties and can have effect in situations where EU citizens are taxpayers, welfare recipients, consumers, workers, recipients of services, etc.

The issue of whether EU law imposes any duties on EU citizens, bearing in mind that Article 20(2) TFEU states that "Citizens of the Union shall enjoy the rights and be subject to the duties provided for in the Treaties", has to be answered in the negative. It seems that apart from an implied civic duty to vote in the elections to the EP, no duties are imposed on EU citizens, i.e. they are neither required to pay taxes to the EU nor to perform compulsory military service for the EU, nor do they have any duty of loyalty towards the Union. As Kadelbach stated:

"despite surrounding itself with attributes of statehood, such as a flag or an anthem, the Union does not expect personal duties of loyalty. The Union courts its citizens not because it expects them to perform duties but because it wishes to be accepted as a body politic for which everyone feels a sort of ethical responsibility."[1789]

With regard to "Provisions on Democratic Principles" they refer to the principle of equality (Article 9 TEU), the principle of representative democracy (Article 10 TEU) and the principle of participatory democracy (Article 11 TEU) which includes the right of "citizens' initiative", i.e. the possibility for at least one million citizens, who are between them nationals of a significant number of Member States, to ask the Commission to prepare a proposal for a legal act necessary to implement the Treaties (see Chapter 5.2.2). Further, Article 11 acknowledges the importance of a dialogue between EU citizens, civil society and the EU institutions, and ensures transparency in the working of EU institutions.

22.2 EU citizenship as a complement to citizenship of a Member State

EU citizenship is based on nationality[1790] of a Member State. Article 20(1) TFEU states that "Every person holding the nationality of a Member State shall be a citizen of the Union. Citizenship of the Union shall be additional to and not replace national citizenship." This point is enhanced in Declaration 2 on Nationality of a Member State attached to the Treaty of Maastricht, which provides that:

"wherever in the Treaty establishing the European Community reference is made to nationals of the Member State, the question whether an individual possesses the nationality of a Member State shall be settled solely by reference to the national law of the Member State concerned."

Consequently, matters relating to nationality are within the exclusive prerogative of a Member State. This was confirmed by the ECJ in Case C-369/90 *Micheletti*,[1791] where the ECJ held that the determination of conditions governing the acquisition and loss of nationality were, according to international law, matters which fell within the competence of each Member State, whose decision must be respected by

---

1789. P. S. Kadelbach, "Union Citizenship", in A. Von Bogdandy and J. Bast (eds), *Principles of European Constitutional Law*, 2nd edn, 2010, Oxford: Hart Publishing, 467.

1790. For a discussion on the difference between nationality and citizenship see S. Kadelbach, ibid., 449–51.

1791. [1992] ECR I-4239. See also: P. C. Jiménez Lobeira, "EU Citizenship and Political Identity: The Demos and Telos Problems", (2012) ELJ, 504.

other Member States. However, in *Micheletti*, the ECJ also stated that the Member States must, when exercising their powers in the sphere of nationality, have due regard to EU law. This statement was the subject of a preliminary reference in Case C-135/08 *Rottmann*[1792] in which the ECJ was asked whether Article 20 TFEU allows a Member State to withdraw from a citizen of the Union the nationality of that State acquired by naturalisation when that nationality was obtained by deception. In the referred case, the result of withdrawal would have been that the person concerned would become a stateless person, i.e. without nationality. The Austrian and German governments, supported by the Commission, argued that the situation was purely internal, i.e. it concerned a German national, living in Germany, who as a result of his deception (he did not mention in the naturalisation procedure that criminal investigations were commenced against him in his native country, Austria, on account of alleged serious fraud which caused him to move to Germany and subsequently apply for German nationality, the acquisition of which resulted in the automatic loss of his Austrian nationality) was facing the withdrawal of naturalisation. The ECJ found that the link between the situation of the person concerned and EU law was based on the citizenship of the EU and not on the fact that the person concerned had exercised his right to free movement when moving from Austria to Germany. The Court held that because the withdrawal of naturalisation would entail the loss of EU citizenship, and therefore the loss of important rights attached to the status of EU citizenship such withdrawal was within the scope of the Treaties and could only be effected if the requirements of the principle of proportionality were satisfied. In this respect the ECJ held:

> "it is necessary, therefore, to take into account the consequences that the decision entails for the person concerned and, if relevant, for the members of his family with regard to the loss of the rights enjoyed by every citizen of the Union. In this respect it is necessary to establish, in particular, whether that loss is justified in relation to the gravity of the offence committed by that person, to the lapse of time between the naturalisation decision and the withdrawal decision and to whether it is possible for that person to recover his original nationality."[1793]

It can be said that although a Member State has to accept as an EU national anyone who has nationality of another Member State regardless of the conditions of acquisition of that nationality,[1794] the fundamental importance that EU law attaches to the status of EU citizenship allows EU law to interfere in nationality laws of the Member States when a situation under consideration is within the scope of the Treaties.[1795]

The requirement of nationality of a Member State as a prerequisite of EU citizenship means that nationals of third countries, refugees and stateless persons legally residing in a Member State do not acquire any rights under Article 20 TFEU. To remedy this situation two directives were adopted:

■ Directive 2003/109/EC concerning the Status of Third-Country Nationals who are Long-term Residents in the EU.[1796] Under the Directive a Member State of residence of non-EU nationals and dependent members of their families is required to confer on such persons a set of rights which are as near as possible to those enjoyed by EU citizens. The status of a long-term resident

---

1792. Case C-135/08 *Janko Rottmann v Freistaat Bayern* [2010] ECR I-149.

1793. Ibid, para. 56.

1794. Case C-192/99 *The Queen v Secretary of State for the Home Department, ex parte: Manjit Kaur* [2001] ECR I-1237; Case C-200/02 *Kunqian Catherine Zhu and Man Lavette Chen v Secretary of State for the Home Department* [2004] ECR I-9925.

1795. See R. Morris, "European Citizenship: Cross-border Relevance, Deliberate Fraud and Proportionate Responses to Potential Statelessness, Case Note on Janko Rottman v Freistaat Bayern", (2011) 17 EPL, 417.

1796. [2004] L16/44.

can be claimed by those who have lawfully and continuously resided in the territory of the Member State concerned for a period of at least five years; are not a burden on that Member State's social assistance system; have appropriate medical insurance; and, represent no threat to its public policy, public security and public health. Students, asylum seekers, diplomats and other persons who have not been granted permanent leave to remain in a Member State are excluded. The status confers the entitlement to settle in another EU State in order to work. However, both a home Member State and a host Member State may impose some limitations, in particular in respect of access to social benefits or, in the case of a host Member State, of access to employment.

■ Directive 2003/86/EC on the Right to Family Reunification. By virtue of Article 3 of the Directive this right is conferred on any national of a third country who "is holding a residence permit issued by a Member State for a period of validity of one year or more who has reasonable prospects of obtaining the right of permanent residence" in that Member State. Under the Directive such a person is entitled to be reunited with members of his/her nuclear family if they are also third-country nationals – in other words, the Member State must allow the person's family members to join them in that Member State. However, this obligation is subject to derogations set out exhaustively in the Directive.[1797]

It should be noted that the UK, Ireland and Denmark are not bound by the above directives. Those Member States did not participate in their adoption as they had exercised their right to opt-out under the relevant Protocols attached to the Treaties (see Chapter 31.2).

22.3 Judicial developments of the concept of EU citizenship

Article 20 TFEU establishes EU citizenship. Its paragraph 2 lists the four rights granted to EU citizens, which are further elaborated in Articles 21–24 TFEU.

Article 21(1) TFEU states:

"Every citizen of the Union shall have the right to move and reside freely within the territory of the Member States, subject to the limitations and conditions laid down in the Treaties and by the measures adopted to give them effect."

The right to free movement of a member of an EU citizen's family is not an independent right but derives from the right conferred upon the EU citizen, unless the family member himself/herself has rights as a national of a Member State. A member of an EU citizen's family who is a national of a third country cannot exercise the right to free movement unless this is done in parallel with the EU citizen.[1798]

The ECJ has greatly contributed to the development of the concept of citizenship by interpreting Articles 20(1) and 21(1) TFEU broadly. The teleological interpretation of Articles 20(1) and 21(1) TFEU has been verging on judicial revision of the Treaties. As A-G Jacobs stated the ECJ has been able to "give the concept a more substantial content than the authors of the Treaties may have envisaged".[1799]

The case law shows that the concept of EU citizenship is most relevant to persons who are not economically active, and thus are not within the scope of more generous provisions of the Treaties

---

1797. Both directives are comprehensively examined by S. Peers in *EU Justice and Home Affairs Law*, 3rd edn, 2011, Oxford: OUP, 459–85. See also S. Peers, "Implementing Equality? The Directive on Long-term Resident Third Country Nationals", (2004) 29 ELRev., 437, at 437.

1798. Cases C-297/88 and 197/89 *Dzodzi v Belgium* [1990] ECR I-3763; Joined Cases C-64 and 65/96 *Land Nordrhein-Westfalen v Kari Uecker and Vera Jacquet v Land Nordrhein-Westfalen* [1997] ECR I-3171.

1799. F.G. Jacobs, "Citizenship of the European Union – A Legal Analysis", (2007) 13 ELJ, 591, at 592.

relating to the free movement of workers, self-employed persons and providers of services. It is well established that there is no need to examine the applicability of Articles 20(1) and 21(1) TFEU if other, more specific articles of the Treaties are applicable, e.g., Articles 49 or 45 TFEU, unless they only cover some aspects and not the whole matter under consideration.[1800] Consequently, Articles 20(1) and 21(1) TFEU have been used mainly to grant rights to EU citizens, who are not economically active, i.e. unemployed persons (see Chapter 23.7.3), students (see Chapter 22.3.4), children (see below and Chapter 23.5.1), carers of children (see below and Chapter 23.5.1), retired persons and those incapable of work due to illness.[1801] The ECJ held in Case C-413/99 *Baumbast*[1802] that Article 21(1) TFEU has direct effect so allowing EU citizens to rely on it before national courts.

THE FACTS WERE:

In 1990 Mrs Baumbast, a Colombian national, married Mr Baumbast, a German national, in the UK where they decided to establish a family home. They had two daughters; the elder was a daughter of Mrs Baumbast from a previous relationship and possessed Colombian nationality, and the younger had dual German and Colombian nationality. The British authority granted a residence permit to the Baumbast family in 1990 valid for five years.

From 1990 to 1993 Mr Baumbast worked in the UK, initially as an employed person and subsequently he worked as head of his own company. Following the failure of his company he tried to obtain employment in the UK to no avail. From 1993 onwards he was employed by German companies in China and Lesotho.

During the relevant period the Baumbast family owned a house in the UK and the daughters went to a UK school. The family did not receive any social benefits and was covered by comprehensive medical insurance in Germany, to which country they travelled for medical treatment when necessary.

In May 1995 Mrs Baumbast applied for indefinite leave to remain in the UK for her family. In January 1996 the Secretary of State refused to renew a residence permit for the Baumbast family. His decision was challenged by the Baumbast family before the UK Immigration Adjudicator, who decided that:

- *Mr Baumbast had no right to reside in the UK as he was neither a worker nor a person entitled to reside in the UK under Directive 2004/38[1803] (see Chapter 22.4);*

- *the daughters had independent rights of residence in the UK under Article 10 of Regulation 492/11 (see Chapter 23.5.1); and,*

- *Mrs Baumbast's right to reside in the UK derived from her children's rights and consequently she was allowed to stay in the UK for a period coterminous with that during which her daughters were benefiting from rights of residence under Article 10 of Regulation 492/11.*

Mr Baumbast appealed against the Adjudicator's decision to the Immigration Tribunal, which asked the ECJ for guidance under the preliminary ruling procedure, in particular on the

---

1800. Case C-193/94 *Criminal Proceedings against Skanavi and Chryssanthakopoulos* [1996] ECR I-929; Case C-470/04 *N v Inspecteur van de Belastingdienst Oost/kantoor Almelo* [2006] ECR I-7409.

1801. Case C-499/06 *Nerkowska v Zakład Ubezpiecze' Społecznych Oddział w Koszalinie* [2008] ECR I-3993.

1802. Case C-413/99 *Baumbast and R v Secretary of State for the Home Department* [2002] ECR I-7091.

1803. [2004] OJ 158/77.

question whether a citizen of the Union who has ceased to be a migrant worker in a host Member State is still entitled to reside there because of his citizenship of the EU, that is, on the basis of Article 21(1) TFEU.

Held:

The ECJ confirmed the decision of the UK Immigration Adjudicator in respect of Mrs Baumbast and the children and held that Mr Baumbast should not be refused a residence permit in the UK. The Court stated that Article 21(1) TFEU has direct effect in that

"the right to reside within the territory of the Member States under [Article 21(1) TFEU] . . . is conferred directly on every citizen of the Union by a clear and precise provision of the EC Treaty. Purely, as a national of a Member State, and consequently a citizen of the Union, Mr Baumbast therefore has the right to rely on [Article 21(1) TFEU]."[1804]

Comment:

Notwithstanding the confirmation by the ECJ that Article 21(1) TFEU has direct effect, it remains that in order to produce direct effect, a provision of EU law must not only be clear and precise but must also be unconditional in that it must not require the taking of any implementing measures by EU institutions or by Member States. On this point the ECJ did, however, acknowledge that the right granted under Article 21(1) TFEU was conditional on the limitations and conditions laid down by the Treaty and by measures adopted to give it effect. According to the ECJ Article 21(1) TFEU is directly effective, notwithstanding the fact that some implementing measures are still necessary, and therefore, in their absence, Article 21(1) TFEU can only be directly effective to some extent. The ECJ tackled this problem in the following manner:

"respect of the exercise of that right of residence is subject to judicial review. Consequently, any limitations and conditions imposed on that right do not prevent the provisions of [Article 21(1) TFEU from conferring on individuals rights which are enforceable by them and which the national courts must protect."[1805]

Consequently all limitations and conditions set out in Article 21(1) TFEU must be applied in compliance with EU law and in accordance with the general principles of law, in particular the principle of proportionality. The ECJ, when assessing the situation of Mr Baumbast in the light of the principle of proportionality, took into account the facts that:

- *he had sufficient resources;*

- *he had worked and resided for a number of years in the UK;*

- *his family resided with him during his stay in the UK as a worker and subsequently as a self-employed person;*

- *he had remained there even after his activities as an employed and self-employed person came to an end;*

- *neither Mr Baumbast nor his family had ever become burdens on the public finances of the host Member State; and,*

1804. Supra note 1804, para. 84.
1805. Ibid, para. 86.

> the Baumbast family including Mr Baumbast had comprehensive sickness insurance in Germany.
>
> In those circumstances the refusal of the UK to grant Mr Baumbast a residence permit was considered by the ECJ as being disproportionate.

In Case C-200/02 *Chen*,[1806] the claimant was allowed to rely on Article 21(1) in proceedings before a national court.

THE FACTS WERE:

Mr and Mrs Chen, both Chinese nationals, deliberately took advantage of Irish law which granted Irish citizenship to a child born in Ireland (including Northern Ireland) if such a child was not entitled to citizenship of any other country. Mr Chen often travelled to the UK for business purposes. His wife joined him in the UK when she was six months pregnant and two months later travelled to Northern Ireland to give birth to her daughter Catherine in order for her child to acquire Irish citizenship and, consequently, to secure for herself and her daughter the right to reside in the UK. When Catherine was eight months old Mrs Chen, who had resided in the UK, applied for a long-term residence permit in the UK. It was clear from the submission of Mrs Chen that she and her child had the necessary financial resources and the relevant health insurance so as not to be a burden on the social assistance system of the UK. The application was refused by the UK Secretary of State for the Home Department. Mrs Chen appealed to the Immigration Appellate Authority, which referred the matter to the ECJ.

Held:

The ECJ held that:

- *Children can exercise the right of free movement;*

- *It is not necessary that an EU citizen possesses personally sufficient resources to avoid being a burden on the social assistance system of the Member State of residence. What is required is that such a person has the necessary resources whatever their origin (but obviously not of criminal origin);*

- *There was no abuse of EU law when Mrs Chen deliberately went to Ireland in order to enable the child she expected to acquire Irish nationality, and consequently to enable her to acquire the right to reside with her child in the UK;*

- *Mrs Chen could not be regarded as a dependent relative within the meaning of EU law (see Chapter 22.4.1), bearing in mind that her child was dependent on her; and,*

- *Mrs Chen, as a primary carer for Catherine to whom EU law granted a right of residence in a host Member State, was entitled to reside with her child in the host Member State.[1807]*

1806. Case C-200/02 *Kunqian Catherine Zhu and Man Lavette Chen v Secretary of State for the Home Department* [2004] ECR I-9925.

1807. Subsequent to the judgment in *Chen*, Ireland changed its generous law on nationality to ensure that such cases could not happen again. See: B. Ryan, "The Celtic Cubs: The Controversy over Birthright Citizenship in Ireland", (2004) *European Journal of Migration and Law*, 173.

22.3.1 The doctrine of "substance of rights" and internal situations

Recent case law shows that the status of EU citizen can be relied upon in the citizen's home Member State, even though the citizen has not exercised his right to free movement. The ECJ emphasised that there is a difference between "purely internal" situations, which have no connection whatsoever with EU law, and situations which have factors linking them with EU law. Accordingly, a situation of an EU citizen who has not exercised his right to free movement, for that reason alone cannot be assimilated with a "purely internal situation".[1808] The citizenship is intended to be the fundamental status of EU citizens and thus of relevance when national measures deprive an EU citizen of enjoyment of the substance of the rights conferred on him by virtue of that status. This new approach, which can be called the doctrine of the "substance of rights", was introduced by the ECJ in Case C-34/09 *Zambrano*.[1809]

THE FACTS WERE:

Mr and Mrs Zambrano, both Colombian nationals, arrived in Belgium in 1999 and upon their arrival applied for political asylum there. Their application was rejected and an order was made requiring them to leave Belgium. However, the order contained a non-refoulement *clause, stating that Mr Zambrano and his family could stay in Belgium in view of the civil war in Colombia. Mr Zambrano applied many times to regularise his stay in Belgium but his applications were consistently rejected. In 2001, Mr Zambrano, despite the lack of a work permit, found full time employment. His work was declared to the relevant authorities and his pay was subject to statutory social deductions duly paid by his employer. However, as a result of Mr Zambrano applying for temporary unemployment benefit (which was rejected) when his contract was suspended in 2005 an inspection was carried out in his place of work revealing that Mr Zambrano had no work permit. As a result of this he was dismissed from work without compensation. He applied for full-time unemployment benefit which was refused. Mr Zambrano challenged this decision and the previous decision refusing temporary unemployment benefit which constituted the subject matter of the proceedings before the referring court,*

The link between EU law and the situation of Mr Zambrano had been that his wife had given birth to two children in Belgium. Mr Zambrano had failed to register their birth with the Colombian embassy in Belgium. As a result, his children were stateless persons (i.e. without any nationality). Under Belgian law aimed at reducing statelessness they had been granted Belgian nationality.

Mr Zambrano argued that as the father of minor children who were EU citizens, he was entitled to reside and work in Belgium.

Held:

The ECJ held that minor children who are nationals of a Member State but whose parents are citizens of third countries would be deprived of the genuine enjoyment of the substance

---

1808. See Case C-256/11 *Murat Dereci and Others v Bundesministerium für Inneres* (judgment of 15/11/11 (NYR)) paras 60–64.

1809. Case C-34/09 *Gerardo Ruiz Zambrano v Office National de l'Emploi (ONEM)* (judgment of 8/3/11 (NYR)). See A. Lansbergen and N. Miller, "European Citizenship Rights in Internal Situations: An ambiguous Revolution? Decision of 8 March 2011, Case C-34/09 Gerardo Ruiz Zambrano v Office National de l'Emploi (ONEM)" (2011) 7 *European Constitutional Law Review*, 287.

of the rights conferred on them by the status of EU citizenship if their parents were forced to leave the territory of the EU bearing in mind that the children would also have to leave the territory of the EU in order to accompany their parents. Similarly, if a work permit were not granted to the father, he would risk not having sufficient resources to provide for himself and his family, which would also result in the children, citizens of the Union, having to leave the territory of the Union. Accordingly, Mr Zambrano was entitled to stay and work in Belgium

Comment:

In paragraph 42 of the judgment the ECJ held that: "Article 20 TFEU precludes national measures which have the effect of depriving citizens of the Union of the genuine enjoyment of the substance of the rights conferred by virtue of their status as citizens of the Union". This new approach to the interpretation of the concept of EU citizenship entails that no cross-border element is required when national measures affect the "substance of the right" of an EU citizen. The situation in Zambrano must be distinguished from that in Chen. In Zambrano there was no cross-border movement. The children were Belgian nationals living in Belgium. In Chen the child was an Irish national living in the UK. Further in Chen the child and the dependent parent had independent means of support originating in China and appropriate medical insurance. Accordingly, the child had the right to reside in the host Member State only in such circumstances as would not place on the host Member State a financial burden arising out of her residence. The right of the child to remain in the host Member State did not entitle her parents to take up employment there. The Court of Appeal of England and Wales in W (China) and X (China)[1810] held that the judgment in Chen could not be used to "create" a right to work for a parent that did not previously exist independently. According to Lord Justice Sedley " Neither the child nor the parents can lawfully work here,[1811] i.e. in the UK." In Zambrano, the ECJ expressly stated that a parent of children who are EU citizens can claim a derivative right to work, i.e. the child's status makes it unlawful to deny the parent the right to work. This judgment also strongly implies that the Zambrano children were entitled to reside in Belgium even though the entire family was likely to become an unreasonable burden on Belgium's social security system. This is indeed a far-reaching judgment.

In Case C-434/09 *McCarthy*[1812] the ECJ provided some clarifications relating to the application of the doctrine of the "substance of rights".

THE FACTS WERE:

Mrs McCarthy, a holder of dual British and Irish citizenship, who was born and had always lived and worked in the UK, married a third State national, who under UK immigration law had no right to reside in the UK. In order to ensure that Mrs McCarthy's husband was entitled to reside with her in the UK, Mrs McCarthy applied for an Irish passport, which she obtained.

1810. *W (China) and X (China) v Secretary of State for the Home Department* [2006] EWCA Civ 1494; [2007] 1 WLR 1514.

1811. Para. 27.

1812. Case C-434/09 *Shirley McCarthy v Secretary of State for the Home Department* (judgment of 5/5/11 (NYR)).

> *Subsequently, she tried to assert her EU citizenship (based on her Irish citizenship) to bring her spouse into the UK to live with her.*
>
> *Held:*
>
> *The ECJ held that neither Directive 2004/36 nor Article 21 TFEU applied to the situation of Mrs McCarthy*
>
> *Comment:*
>
> *The ECJ held that Article 3(1) of Directive 2004/38 did not apply to Mrs McCarthy because she had never exercised her right of free movement and had always resided in a Member State of which she was a national. A literal, teleological and contextual interpretation of Article 3(1) of Directive 2004/38 supported the conclusion of the ECJ. The fact that Mrs McCarthy was a national of another Member State was irrelevant.*
>
> *With regard to Article 21 TFEU, the ECJ held that it applies to EU citizens who reside in their home Member State in a situation where a national measure has the effect of depriving them of the genuine enjoyment of the substance of that right or of impeding the right to move and reside freely within the territory of the Member State. Mrs McCarthy was not in such a situation bearing in mind that: "the failure by the authorities of the United Kingdom to take into account the Irish nationality of Mrs McCarthy for the purposes of granting her a right of residence in the United Kingdom in no way affects her in her right to move and reside freely within the territory of the Member States, or any other right conferred on her by virtue of her status as a Union citizen."[1813]*

The difficulty in application of the doctrine of "substance of rights" is well illustrated in Case C-256/11 *Dereci*,[1814] in which the issue was whether Article 20 TFEU prevents a Member State from refusing residence permits to non-EU citizens, who are members of a family of EU citizens, when those EU citizens are not dependent for subsistence on their family members who are third country nationals.

> **THE FACTS WERE:**
>
> *Five applicants were refused residence permits in Austria. They were:*
>
> ■ *Mr Dereci, a Turkish national who entered Austria illegally, married an Austrian national, lived with her there, and had with her three children who were minors and Austrian nationals;*
>
> ■ *Mr Maduike, a Nigerian national who entered Austria illegally, married an Austrian national, and resided with her in Austria;*
>
> ■ *Mrs Heiml, a national of Sri Lanka who entered Austria legally, married an Austrian national, and continued to live there, despite her residence permit having expired;*

1813. Ibid, para. 49.
1814. Case C-256/11 *Murat Dereci and Others v Bundesministerium für Inneres* (judgment of 15/11/11 (NYR)).

■ Mr Kokollari, who entered Austria legally at the age of two with his parents who were then Yugoslav nationals. At the time of proceedings he was 29; resided in Austria; and, claimed to be maintained by his mother who had acquired Austrian nationality; and,

■ Mrs Stevic, a Serbian national who resided with her husband and three adult children in Serbia. She sought residence in Austria in order to be reunited with her father, an Austrian national, who regularly provided financial support for her and her family.

Expulsion orders had been made against Mrs Heiml, Mr Dereci, Mr Kokollari and Mr Maduike.

Held:

The ECJ held that the principles in Zambrano apply only in very exceptional situations. It stated that the criterion relating to the denial of genuine enjoyment of the substance of the rights deriving from EU citizenship "refers to situations in which the Union citizen has, in fact, to leave not only the territory of the Member State of which he is a national but also the territory of the Union as a whole."[1815] The Court emphasised that only when the effectiveness of an EU citizen's rights derived from EU citizenship would be undermined would a refusal of a residence permit to a third country national, who is a family member of that EU citizen, be in breach of EU law. The Court added that "the mere fact that it might appear desirable to a national of a Member State, for economic reasons or in order to keep his family together in the territory of the Union, for the members of his family who do not have the nationality of a Member State to be able to reside with him in the territory of the Union, is not sufficient in itself to support the view that the Union citizen will be forced to leave Union territory if such a right is not granted."[1816]

Comment:

The ECJ identified two criteria for application of the "substance of rights" doctrine introduced in Zambrano. The first refers to the determination of whether an EU citizen will be forced to leave the territory of the EU in order to reside with a non-EU family member. Accordingly, a Member State will be in breach of EU law if an EU national would have to leave the territory of the EU in order to reside with a non-EU family member. If an EU citizen has an option to reside with a non-EU family member in another Member State, there will be no breach of EU law. This option was not available in Zambrano. With regard to adult EU citizens, the judgment in Metock (see Chapter 22.4.1.1) entails that a host Member State is required to admit to its territory an EU citizen and his/her non-EU spouse unless a refusal can be justified on the grounds of public policy, public security and public health. For Mr Kokollari the option to move to another Member State with his mother did not exist because he was an adult and a non-EU national. However, to him the second criterion based on the enjoyment of his human rights may apply. He was brought up in Austria and had lived there almost all his life. In Dereci, the ECJ left it to the referring court to decide whether the situation of the applicants was within the scope of Article 7 of the Charter of Fundamental Rights. If not, the ECHR will apply, bearing in mind that Austria is a Contracting Party to it. With regard to Mr Dereci, he was lucky in that the Association Agreement between the EU and Turkey applied to him.

1815. Ibid, para. 66.
1816. Ibid, para. 68.

> *On its basis he is entitled to establish himself in Austria by reason of his marriage to an Austrian national. It seems that Mrs Stevic will not be successful either under EU law or under the ECHR.*
>
> *It is submitted that in* Dereci *the ECJ has not only identified some criteria relevant to the application of the "substance of rights" doctrine, but also by applying them has limited the ambit of the principles set out in* Zambrano. *More clarifications of the "substance of rights" doctrine are expected in Joined Cases C-356 and 357/11* O *and* S[1817] *pending before the ECJ.*

It is to be noted that the doctrine of "substance of rights" applies not only to immigration cases but also to other matters. In Case C-148/02 *Garcia Avello*[1818] the effect of a national measure was that children had different surnames under Belgian law and under Spanish law. Children, holders of dual Belgian-Spanish nationality, whose father was a Spanish national and whose mother was a Belgian national, lived in Belgium with their parents. According to Belgian law a child could use only the surname of the father and was not able to have the patronymic surname changed to reflect well-established usage in Spanish law, according to which the surname of a child of a married couple consists of the first surname of the father followed by that of the mother. That situation was liable to cause serious inconvenience for children at both professional and private levels resulting from, *inter alia*, difficulties in benefiting, in one Member State of which they were nationals, from the legal effects of diplomas or documents drawn up in the surname recognised in the other Member State of which they were nationals. Accordingly, Belgian law was in breach of EU law on the ground of the "substance of rights" doctrine.

22.3.2   Application of Articles 20 and 21(1) TFEU to non-economically active EU citizens

Persons, who are not economically active, when they exercise their right to free movement, are subject to conditions and restrictions imposed by the Treaties and by secondary legislation. They must have sufficient financial resources to ensure that they will not become an unreasonable burden on the social security system of a host Member State (see Chapter 22.4.2.2). Further, they must have appropriate medical insurance cover. This raises the issue of whether such persons are entitled to social benefits in a host Member State. On the one hand, it can be said that as they have never made any contribution to the economic life of the host Member State, they should not be entitled to claim social benefits. On the other, Article 18 TFEU prohibits discrimination based on nationality. Before the adoption of Directive 2004/38 (see Chapter 22.3.4.2.2), the ECJ's answer to this conundrum was that a host Member State was required to show a "certain degree" of financial solidarity[1819] with regard to EU citizens who were not its own nationals, although when an EU citizen had become an unreasonable financial burden on its social assistance system, a Member State had the right to deport such a person. Under this approach a host Member State was required to extend social benefits to EU citizens, i.e. to show a certain degree of solidarity, in a situation where EU citizens had demonstrated a certain degree of integration into the society of a host Member State, i.e. had established "a real link" with the host Member State.

1817. See the official website of the ECJ (accessed 25/6/12).

1818. Case C-148/02 *Carlos Garcia Avello v Belgium* [2003] ECR I-11613.

1819. See Case C-184/99 *Rudy Grzelczyk v Centre Public d'Aide Sociale d'Ottignies-Louvain-la-Neuve* [2001] ECR I-6193, para. 44 and Case C-209/03 *The Queen, on the application of Dany Bidar v London Borough of Ealing and Secretary of State for Education and Skills* [2005] ECR I-2119, para. 56.

The decisive factor in establishing "a real link' was the length of residence in a host Member State, although depending upon circumstances other factors were also taken into consideration by the relevant national authorities.[1820] As Barnard stated: "The Court seems to be adopting a 'quantitative' approach to equality; the longer the migrants reside in the Member State, the more integrated they are in that state, and the greater the number of benefits they receive on equal terms with nationals."[1821] For example, in Case C-85/96 *Martínez Sala,*[1822] a Spanish national, who had resided in Germany for 25 years and who had two children there, without being a worker there within the meaning of Article 45 TFEU, obtained a child-raising allowance in Germany.

The concept of "a real link" has its disadvantages in that it introduces unpredictability, uncertainty and may be considered as unacceptable judicial activism.[1823] Directive 2004/38/EC (see below) responds to this concern by adopting a quantitative or incremental approach to the extension of social solidarity to migrant EU citizens.

Under the Directive all EU citizens, regardless of their length of stay in a host Member State are entitled to equal treatment but when they stay there less than three months, they are neither entitled to social benefits, nor to study finance unless a host Member State decides otherwise.

When the length of an EU citizen's residence in a host Member State is between three months and five years, the situation is more complex. Article 24(2) of Directive 2004/38 clearly states that a host Member State is not required to provide any maintenance aid to students in the form of grants and loans before the completion of a five-year residence period in a host Member State unless they can rely on their status as workers, self-employed persons or members of their families. The ECJ has interpreted this provision strictly. In Case C-158/07 *Förster,*[1824] the Court refused to consider the possibility of existence of a sufficient degree of integration into a host Member State's society based on any factors other than the completion of a five-year residence period in that State (see Chapter 22.3.4.2). However, the ECJ has maintained "a real link" approach in respect of jobseekers. In Joined Cases C-22/08 and C-23/08, *Vatsouras and Koupatantze,*[1825] the ECJ agreed with A-G Colomer's interpretation of Directive 2004/38 that jobseekers, as opposed to students, are entitled to social benefits without satisfying the condition of completion of five years residence in a host Member State (see Chapter 23.7.3).

EU citizens who have resided in a host Member State for more than five years are considered fully integrated and thus entitled to all social benefits and all study finance facilities in that State.

1820. See Case C-413/01 *Franca Ninni-Orasche v Bundesminister für Wissenschaft, Verkehr und Kunst* [2003] ECR I-13189, paras 90–91, and the Opinion of A-G Ruiz-Jarabo Colomer in Case C-138/02 *Brian Francis Collins v Secretary of State for Work and Pensions* [2003] ECR I-2703, paras 65–67.

1821. C. Barnard, *The Substantive Law of the EU,* 3rd edn, 2010, Oxford: OUP, 454. See also: C. Barnard, "EU Citizenship and the Principle of Solidarity", in M. Dougan and E. Spaventa (eds), *Social Welfare and EU Law,* 2005, Oxford: Hart Publishing.

1822. Case C-85/96 *María Martínez Sala v Freistaat Bayern* [1998] ECR I-2691.

1823. See: M. Dougan and E. Spaventa, "'Wish You Weren't Here . . .' New Models of Social Solidarity in the European Union" in M. Dougan and E. Spaventa (eds.), *Social Welfare and EU Law,* 2005, Oxford: Hart Publishing, 181, at 214; K. Haibronner, "Union Citizenship and Access to Social Benefits", (2005) 42 CMLRev., (2005), 1245, at 1251; M. Dougan, "The Spatial Restructuring of National Welfare States within the European Union: The Contribution of Union Citizenship and the Relevance of the Treaty of Lisbon", in U. Neergaard et al. (eds.), *Integrating Welfare Functions into EU Law. From Rome to Lisbon,* 2009, Copenhagen: DJØF Publishing, 171.

1824. Case C-158/07 *Jacqueline Förster v Hoofddirectie van de Informatie Beheer Groep* [2008] ECR I-8507.

1825. Joined Cases C-22/08 and C-23/08 *Athanasios Vatsouras (C-22/08) and Josif Koupatantze (C-23/08) v Arbeitsgemeinschaft (ARGE) Nürnberg 900* [2009] ECr I-4585.

22.3.3 The removal of discrimination, and beyond

Subject to Chapter 22.3.2 above, the ECJ, when applying the right of EU citizens to equal treatment, has condemned not only directly[1826] and indirectly discriminatory[1827] national measures, but also those which put EU citizens "at a disadvantage" because they have exercised the right to free movement.

With regard to national measures which are directly discriminatory, i.e. they discriminate on the ground of nationality, they can only be justified by express derogations provided for in the Treaties or secondary legislation, e.g. based on public policy, public security and public health, and must be proportionate to the objective that a Member State seeks to achieve.

Indirectly discriminatory measures and measures which are non-discriminatory, but prevent/hinder or create an obstacle to the exercise of the right provided for in Article 21 TFEU, may be justified either by express derogations as above, or by objective considerations of public interest, and must be proportionate to the objective that a Member State seeks to achieve. This is exemplified in Case C-224/02 *Pusa*.[1828]

THE FACTS WERE:

Mr Pusa, a Finnish national in receipt of a Finnish invalidity pension, lived in Spain where he paid his income tax. He owed a debt in Finland. To collect the debt an attachment order was made on his pension. Under Finnish legislation, the amount attached was calculated in such a manner as to leave him a minimum income. This calculation did not take account of his Spanish income tax. As a result, Mr Pusa was left with a monthly disposable sum which was less than would have been available to him had he continued residing in Finland.

Held:

The ECJ held:

"National legislation which places at a disadvantage certain of its nationals simply because they have exercised their freedom to move and reside in another Member State would give rise to inequality of treatment, contrary to the principles which underpin the status of citizen of the Union, that is, the guarantee of the same treatment in law in the exercise of the citizen's freedom to move."[1829] Accordingly, the Finnish legislation was in breach of Article 21(1) TFEU and could not be justified.

Comment:

In the above case, the ECJ followed the view of A-G Jacobs who stated that Article 21(1) TFEU should apply to remove any restriction, whether discriminatory or not, which imposes an unjustified burden on a person who seeks to exercise his rights to free movement.

This case shows that Article 21(1) TFEU may be relied upon by EU citizens against their home Member States.[1830]

1826. Case C-85/96 *María Martínez Sala v Freistaat Bayern* [1998] ECR I-2691.
1827. Case C-209/03 *The Queen, on the application of Dany Bidar v London Borough of Ealing and Secretary of State for Education and Skills* [2005] ECR I-2119.
1828. Case C-224/02 *Heikki Antero Pusa v Osuuspankkien Keskinäinen Vakuutusyhtiö* [2004] ECR I-5763.
1829. Ibid, para. 20.
1830. See, for example, Case C-148/02 *García Avello v Belgium* [2003] ECR I-11613; Case C-224/98 *Marie-Nathalie D'Hoop v Office National de l'Emploi* [2002] ECR I-6191.

The approach of the ECJ to non-discriminatory restrictions has been confirmed in subsequent cases. In Case C-192/05 *Tas-Hagen and Tas,*[1831] Dutch nationals, who lawfully resided in Spain, obtained a war pension, although Dutch legislation required applicants for the war pension to be actually resident in the Netherlands at the time when their application was submitted. In this case the ECJ provided clarifications as to the circumstances in which national measures which may restrict the free movement of EU citizens can be justified. Such measures must be based on objective considerations of public interest independent of the nationality of the person concerned, and must be proportionate to the objective that a Member State sought to achieve.

22.3.4 The rights of students

With regard to EU students, under the Treaties, as interpreted by the ECJ, EU students have access to educational institutions in a host Member State on the same terms as local students. However, their entitlement to study finance and social assistance during the first five years of their residence in a host Member State is subject to conditions set out in Directive 2004/38.

22.3.4.1 Access to education

In Case 293/83 *Gravier,*[1832] the ECJ created a right to non-discriminatory access to higher education institutions by including higher education within the term of "vocational training" and thus bringing it within the scope of the EC Treaty. It is to be noted that the conditions of access to vocational training were within the scope of the EEC Treaty but the EEC had no competence with regard to education as the EEC Treaty did not contain any provisions on education.

THE FACTS WERE:

Miss Gravier, a French national, was accepted by the Liège Académie des Beaux-Arts in Belgium for a four-year course in the art of strip cartoons. She was considered as a foreign student and charged a special fee, known as a "minerval," which neither Belgian nationals, irrespective of their place of residence, nor EU citizens and their families working in Belgium, were required to pay. She challenged the fee as discriminatory. She argued that the minerval constituted an obstacle to her freedom to receive services and that, as the ECJ recognised in Case 152/82 Forcheri,[1833] *vocational education was within the scope of the EC Treaty.*

Held:

The ECJ decided in favour of Miss Gravier. The minerval was discriminatory and was therefore in breach of Article 18 TFEU.

Comment:

This decision raised many controversies in Member States. One of them was the definition of vocational training, which the ECJ defined very broadly in Gravier *as including all forms of*

1831. Case C-192/05 *K. Tas-Hagen and R.A. Tas v Raadskamer WUBO van de Pensioen- en Uitkeringsraad* [2006] ECR I-10451.
1832. Case 293/83 *Gravier v City of Liège* [1985] ECR 593.
1833. Case 152/82 *Forcheri v Belgium* [1983] ECR 2323.

teaching that prepare for, and lead directly to, a particular profession, trade or employment. Furthermore, contrary to the Opinion of A-G Sir Gordon Slynn in this case, the ECJ refused to discuss the organisation and financing of such courses. Member States which financed university courses from public funds (in Belgium the minerval covered only 50 per cent of the cost of the course, the remaining 50 per cent coming from public funds) were deeply concerned about the implications of the judgment on their public finances.

In Case 24/86 *Blaizot*,[1834] the ECJ clarified the definition of vocational training. In this case Blaizot, following the decision of the ECJ in *Gravier*, sought reimbursement of the minerval charged for his university course in veterinary science. The ECJ held that university education constituted vocational training "not only where the final exam directly provides the required qualification but also insofar as the studies provide specific training (i.e. where the student needs the knowledge so acquired for the pursuit of his trade or profession), even if no legislative or administrative provisions make the acquisition of such knowledge a prerequisite".[1835]

Therefore all courses other than those which are intended to improve the general knowledge of students rather than prepare them for an occupation are considered as vocational courses. On the basis of the above case law of the ECJ, a host Member State may not charge non-local EU students tuition fees in excess of those imposed on local students, or refuse to grant them a tuition free loan/grant if these are available to local students.[1836]

The ECJ has not only dealt with tuition fees but also with other impediments to access to publicly financed educational institutions in a host Member State. In Case C-147/03 *Commission v Austria*,[1837] the ECJ condemned Austrian legislation which imposed on EU citizens, who wished to pursue study at an Austrian university, and who were not holders of an Austrian diploma certifying the completion of secondary education, a requirement that they show that they would have satisfied the entry requirements of the university in the Member State which had issued the secondary education diploma.

In Case C-40/05 *Lyyski*[1838] the ECJ condemned Swedish legislation which made access to a special teaching training programme, necessary to complete in order to become a teacher in Sweden, subject to the condition that applicants must be employed in a Swedish school during the training. In this case, the applicant, who had completed a course of higher education in Sweden, and found work in a Swedish language school in Finland, was refused admission to the special training programme.

The matter of whether a host Member State can restrict, by number, access to its university courses for non-resident EU students was examined in Case C-73/08 *Bressol*.[1839]

1834. Case 24/86 *Vincent Blaizot v University of Liège and Others* [1988] ECR 379.

1835. Ibid, para. 19.

1836. Case 197/86 *Steven Malcolm Brown v The Secretary of State for Scotland* [1988] ECR 3205.

1837. [2005] ECR I-5969.

1838. Case C-40/05 *Kaj Lyyski v Umeå Universitet* [2007] ECR I-99.

1839. C-73/08 *Nicolas Bressol and Others, Céline Chaverot and Others v Gouvernement de la Communauté Française* [2010] ECR I-2735.

THE FACTS WERE:

The French-speaking Community[1840] in Belgium adopted a decree which restricted the number of non-resident students permitted to enroll in medical and paramedical courses at its higher education institutions. The decree was adopted in order to deal with a significant increase in the number of students from Member States other than Belgium enrolling in higher education institutions of the French-speaking Community, in particular from France. The same language of instruction, and restrictions imposed on access to the courses concerned in France, were the factors which explained the influx of French students. Under the Decree a threshold was fixed on the admissibility of non-resident students. When the threshold was exceeded, the institution concerned organised the drawing of lots between the students concerned. A number of students challenged the compatibility of the decree with EU law, in particular with Article 18 TFEU which prohibits discrimination based on nationality, and Article 21 TFEU which ensures the freedom of movement of EU citizens in conjunction with Articles 165 and 166 TFEU which concern the mobility of students and trainees. The Belgian government provided three justifications:

- first, that an increased number of students attending the relevant courses had imposed excessive burden on the financing of the relevant courses as they had been financed from public funds;

- second, that non-resident students after completing their course of study, were returning to their home Member State with the result that the number of students residing in the Community who had remained after obtaining their diploma was not sufficient to ensure the quality of the public health system in the Community; and,

- third, based on the protection of the homogeneity of the higher education system.

Held:

The ECJ held that the decree was indirectly discriminatory with regard to non-resident students but nevertheless, could be objectively justified on the grounds of genuine risks to the protection of public health. It was for the referring court to decide whether and to what extent the decree could be so justified and whether it complied with the principle of proportionality.

Comment:

The following points are of interest.

First, the ECJ held that the decree in question created a difference in treatment between resident and non-resident students which difference constituted indirect discrimination. This was not the view of A-G Sharpston who considered that under EU law the distinction between direct discrimination and indirect discrimination was not clear and proposed the following definition of direct discrimination: "I take there to be direct discrimination when the category of those receiving a certain advantage and the category of those suffering a correlative disadvantage coincide exactly with the

---

1840. Belgium is a federal State comprising three Communities: the Flemish Community (Dutch-speaking), the French-speaking Community and the German-speaking Community.

respective categories of persons distinguished only by applying a prohibited classification."[1841]

The view of the A-G was that the Belgian decree was directly discriminatory so far as the requirement related to permanent residence was concerned because: "The difference in treatment [of resident and non-resident students] is clearly based on a criterion (the right to remain permanently in Belgium) which is necessarily linked to a characteristic indissociable from nationality."[1842]

Obviously, the classification of the decree as directly or indirectly discriminatory is vital in that direct discrimination based on nationality can only be justified on the explicit derogations set out in the Treaties whilst indirect discrimination can be justified on the grounds of objective criteria established by the ECJ. With regard to direct discrimination the Treaties do not provide for the possibility of any derogation from the prohibition on discrimination based on nationality enshrined in Article 18 TFEU with regard to access to education.

The ECJ did not comment on the A-G's definition of direct discrimination.

Second, in accordance with the ECJ's case law, as expected, the ECJ rejected the justification based on financial considerations, i.e. that the difference in treatment of resident and non-resident students was necessary to avoid excessive burdens on the financing of higher education in Belgium.

Third, with regard to the justification relating to the protection of the homogeneity of the higher education system and the justification relating to public health requirements, the ECJ decided that the national court should determine whether the decree was appropriate for the attainment of the objectives sought, and whether the decree satisfied the requirements of the principle of proportionality. In order to facilitate the task of the national court, the ECJ provided the national court with detailed guidance. In particular, the referring court was to verify whether the selection process for non-resident students was limited to the drawing of lots and, if this was the case, whether that method of selection based on chance, not on the aptitude of the candidates concerned, was necessary to attain the objective pursued by the decree.

22.3.4.2 Entitlement to financial assistance from a host Member State

Two situations should be distinguished, first, the entitlement of students to study finance and second, the entitlement of students to social assistance.

22.3.4.2.1 Entitlement to study finance

Article 24(2) of Directive 2004/38 limits the obligations of a host Member State to provide study finance consisting of student grants or student loans to persons other than workers and self-employed persons and their families during their residence up to five years. In Case C-158/07 *Förster,*[1843] the ECJ held that that the requirement of five years' uninterrupted residence set out in Article 24(2) of Directive

---

1841. C-73/08 *Nicolas Bressol and Others, Céline Chaverot and Others v Gouvernement de la Communauté Française* [2010] ECR I-2735, para. 56.
1842. Ibid, para. 67.
1843. Case C-209/03 *The Queen, on the application of Dany Bidar v London Borough of Ealing and Secretary of State for Education and Skills* [2008] ECR I-8507.

2004/38 constitutes an appropriate yardstick for finding that an applicant has indeed achieved the necessary level of integration into the society of a host Member State to be entitled to a maintenance grant. The position of the ECJ in *Förster* has been subject to differing interpretations,[1844] as it seems to suggest the judgment of the ECJ in Case C-209/03 *Bidar*[1845] is no longer good law.

THE FACTS WERE:

In 1998 young Mr Bidar, a French national, and his mother moved to the UK where she was to undergo medical treatment. Subsequently she died. Mr Bidar then lived in the UK with his grandmother as her dependant, and completed his last three years of secondary education without ever having recourse to social assistance. In September 2001 he enrolled at University College London and applied to the relevant English authority for financial assistance. He was granted assistance with tuition fees but was refused a maintenance loan on the ground that he was not "settled" in the UK.

Under the relevant legislation a person is considered as being "settled" in England or Wales if he/she will have been resident there for the three years prior to commencing their course, but it is impossible to become "settled" if one resides there, during any part of that three-year period, for the purpose of receiving full-time education.

Mr Bidar challenged the decision before the High Court of England and Wales on the basis that the requirement to be "settled" constituted discrimination based on nationality, in breach of the EU law. The High court referred the matter to the ECJ.

Held:

The ECJ held that Mr Bidar, having been a lawful resident in the UK during his secondary studies, had established a genuine link with the society of his host Member State and was, consequently, entitled to obtain study finance in the UK.

Comment:

The ECJ's starting point was that a citizen of the EU lawfully resident in another Member State could rely on the prohibition of discrimination on grounds of nationality in all situations within the scope of the EC Treaty. The ECJ held that the situation of Mr Bidar was within the scope of the Treaty as a result of developments in EU law. In this respect the ECJ held that since the judgments in Case 39/86 Lair[1846] and Case 197/86 Brown[1847] the EU had introduced the concept of EU citizenship and had made amendments to the EC Treaty consisting of including education and vocational training within its scope (see Chapter 23.8).

However, the ECJ then had to consider Article 3 of Directive 93/96 [now Article 7(1)(b)(c)] of Directive 2004/38] which states that students have the right of residence in a host Member State provided they have sufficient resources to avoid becoming a burden on that State's social assistance system and have appropriate sickness insurance cover. This Article excludes any right to receipt of maintenance grants by students, and therefore excludes students like

---

1844. See S. O'Leary, "Free Movement of Persons and Services", in P. Craig and G. de Búrca (eds), *The Evolution of EU Law*, 2nd edn, 2011, Oxford: OUP, 516–17.

1845. [2005] ECR I-2119.

1846. Case 39/86 *Lair v Universität Hannover* [1988] ECR 3161.

1847. Case 197/86 *Brown v Secretary of State for Scotland* [1988] ECR 3205.

Mr Bidar from receiving a maintenance loan. The ECJ solved this problem by stating the Directive did not preclude students like Mr Bidar, who are lawfully resident in a Member State in order to pursue their studies, from relying on the principle of non-discrimination enshrined in Article 18 TFEU. However, the application of this principle is limited given that the Member States remain competent to determine the conditions of granting assistance to cover students' maintenance costs. These conditions, however, must be based on objective criteria independent of nationality and proportionate to the objectives pursued by national legislation. In respect of the challenged legislation the ECJ found that it was indirectly discriminatory because it was placing nationals of other Member States at a disadvantage as compared to UK nationals. Indeed, the challenged legislation precluded any possibility of a national of another Member State obtaining settled status as a student in these circumstances. However, the justifications provided by the UK government were accepted by the ECJ. A Member State is allowed to ensure that the grant of assistance to cover the maintenance costs of students from other Member States does not become an unreasonable burden which could have consequences for the overall level of assistance which may be granted by that Member State. Thus, it is legitimate for a Member State to grant assistance to cover maintenance costs only to students who have demonstrated a certain degree of integration into the society of that Member State. Previously in Case C-138/02 Collins[1848] the ECJ accepted that a certain length of residence in the host Member State can be recognised as an appropriate factor in establishing the degree of integration between the student and the host Member State. In the case of Mr Bidar his lawful residence in the UK for a substantial part of his secondary studies showed that he had established a genuine link with the society of the host Member State. Consequently, the challenged legislation precluding him from obtaining the status of a settled person as a student was incompatible with EU law.

The ECJ in Case C-158/07 *Förster*, distinguished the situation of Miss Förster from that of Mr Bidar. It held that in the case of Mr Bidar the challenged legislation imposed not only the requirement of residence but also the requirement to be "settled' in the UK, with the consequences that it was impossible for students, regardless of their degree of integration, to ever qualify for a maintenance grant or loan in the UK. This was not the case in *Förster.*

It is submitted that it is possible to interpret the judgment of the ECJ in *Förster* in line with the previous case law of the ECJ on students' entitlement to study finance from a host Member State. In Case C-158/07 *Förster*, the ECJ clarified its previous case law in that it confirmed that it is acceptable for a Member State to have a five-year residence requirement when a person has entered a host Member State as a student. However, when a person enters a Member State in another capacity, as was the case of Mr Bidar, who entered the UK as a dependent child, the entitlement to study finance will depend on whether the person concerned has established a genuine link with the society of the host Member State. Accordingly, the requirement of five years' residence in a host Member State set out in Article 24(2) of Directive 2004/38 will not be the only factor in determining that person's entitlement to study finance.

1848. Case C-138/02 *Brian Francis Collins v Secretary of State for Work and Pensions* [2004] ECR I-2703.

22.3.4.2.2   Entitlement to social assistance

In Case C-184/99 *Grzelczyk*,[1849] the ECJ examined the matter of entitlement of EU students to social assistance from a host Member State.

THE FACTS WERE:

Mr Grzelczyk, a French national studying in Belgium supported himself for the first three years by working, but in his final year of study applied to the Belgian authorities for payment of the minimex, i.e. a non-contributory minimum subsistence allowance in Belgium. Initially, he was granted the minimex on the ground that he had worked hard to finance his studies and that during his final academic year, being more demanding than previous years, he would not be able to both work and study. Subsequently, his minimex allowance was stopped, on the ground that he was not a Belgian national, and he was asked to reimburse the sums received.

Held:

The ECJ held that Belgian legislation was directly discriminatory because Belgian nationals who found themselves in exactly the same circumstances as Mr Grzelczyk would satisfy the conditions for obtaining the minimex. Accordingly, he was allowed to rely on Article 18 TFEU to claim the minimex as long as he did not become an unreasonable burden on the Belgian social assistance system. Mr Grzelczyk appeared not to be an "unreasonable burden".

Comment:

The ECJ held that Mr Grzelczyk as an EU citizen was within the personal scope of the Treaties. His situation was also within the material scope of application of the Treaties because he had exercised his rights to free movement and residence in a host Member State. Accordingly, he could rely on Article 18 TFEU. However, the requirement relating to sufficient resources set out in Directive 93/96 was an obstacle to his claim for the minimex. In this respect, the ECJ held that on the one hand, Article 1 of Directive 93/96 required students to have sufficient resources to avoid becoming a burden on the social security system of a host Member State, but on the other, the Directive did not contain any provisions precluding students from receiving social benefits. In this respect Directive 2004/38, which repealed Directive 93/9, takes the same position. The ECJ stated that Articles 20 and 21 TFEU read in conjunction with Article 18 TFEU allowed Mr Grzelczyk to claim social assistance benefits as long as he did not become an unreasonable burden on the social assistance system of the host Member State. Even though a host Member State has the right to withdraw a residence permit, or not to renew it, in respect of students who have insufficient financial resources, and thus have to resort to the host Member State's social assistance system such measures should not be taken automatically. If financial difficulties are temporary, as was the case of Mr Grzelczyk, the host Member State must show a certain degree of financial solidarity towards such a student. Consequently, as long as an EU student is not considered as an "unreasonable" burden on the host Member State's social assistance system, he may be given social assistance from a host Member State.

1849. Case C-184/99 *Rudy Grzelczyk v Centre Public d'Aide Sociale d'Ottignies-Louvain-la-Neuve* [2001] ECR I-6193.

22.3.4.3 Entitlement to financial assistance from a home Member State

A student who wishes to pursue his/her education in a host Member State may be deterred from so doing by rules relating to financial assistance imposed by the home Member State. This is exemplified by Joined Cases C-11/06 *Morgan* and Case C-12/06 *Bucher*. [1850]

THE FACTS WERE:

In Case C-11/06 Ms Morgan, a German national, moved to the UK where she initially worked for one year as an au pair and subsequently commenced studies in applied genetics at the University of Bristol. When she applied to the relevant German authorities for a study grant, her application was refused on the ground that she had failed to satisfy the German law conditions relating to awards of education and training grants for studies outside Germany, requiring that the course of study outside Germany should constitute a continuation of education or training pursued for at least one year in a German establishment.

In Case C-12/06 Ms Bucher, a German national, moved from Bonn to Düren, a German town on the Netherlands border, in order to take a course of study in ergotherapy in the Netherlands town of Heerlen (located very close to the German border). When she applied to the German authorities for a study grant, her application was refused on the ground that she was not "permanently" resident near a border, as required by the German law, and thus did not satisfy the conditions of the German law relating to study grants outside Germany.

Both claimants submitted that the courses being taken in host Member States were not offered in Germany. Both challenged the decisions of the relevant German authorities. The referring courts asked the ECJ to rule on the compatibility of the German legislation with Articles 20 and 21 TFEU.

Held:

The ECJ held that the German legislation was in breach of Articles 20 and 21 TFEU as it constituted an unjustified restriction on the free movement of EU citizens.

Comment:

The Court stated that the challenged legislation was disproportionate. First, it forced the claimants to choose between abandoning the education they had planned to receive in a host Member State, and pursuing it, but losing their entitlement to an education grant. Second, the requirement that a student must first study for at least one year in a home Member State was too general and exclusive because: "It unduly favours an element which is not necessarily representative of the degree of integration into the society of that Member State at the time the application for assistance is made."[1851]

1850. Joined Cases C-11/06 *Rhiannon Morgan v Bezirksregierung Köln* and Case C-12/06 *Iris Bucher v Landrat des Kreises Düren* [2007] ECR I-9161. On this topic see: see M. Dougan, "Cross-border Educational Mobility and the Exportation of Student Financial Assistance", (2008) 33 ELR, 723.

1851. Ibid, para. 46.

22.3.4.4 Other rights conferred on non-resident EU students

The principle of equal treatment requires that non-resident students are entitled to reduced-cost public transport if such reductions are available to resident students, access to student accommodation on the same terms as local students, and entitlement to tax benefits. In Case C-76/05 *Schwarz*,[1852] the ECJ ruled that German tax law which precluded the granting of tax relief in respect of fees paid by German taxpayers to private schools in other Member States but granted relief where schools were situated in Germany, was in breach of Article 56 TFEU.

22.4 Directive 2004/38 on the right of EU citizens and their families to move freely and reside within the territory of the Member States

An important piece of legislation (which merged into one instrument all the legislation – consisting of two regulations and nine directives – on the right of entry and residence for EU citizens) is Directive 2004/38/EC of 29 April 2004 on the right of citizens and their family members to move and reside freely within the territory of the Member States.[1853] As the title indicates it applies to all EU citizens and their families, irrespective of whether they are economically active, e.g. workers, self-employed persons, providers of services, or not, e.g. students, retired persons, etc, when they exercise their right to free movement. The Directive brings together the piecemeal measures found in the complex body of legislation that had previously governed this matter, and reiterates the relevant case law. It simplifies and improves the rules in this area, in particular by:

- reducing administrative formalities to the bare essentials;

- providing a clear definition of the status of family members;

- limiting the scope for refusing entry and terminating the right of residence (see Chapter 25.5); and,

- introducing the right of permanent residence.

The main features of Directive 2004/38 are examined below and in Chapter 25.3, 25.4 and 25.5.

22.4.1 Persons covered by the Directive

The Directive applies to all EU citizens and their family members. Article 2(2) provides a definition of family members. They are the EU citizen's:

- spouse;

- partner with whom the citizen has contracted a registered partnership, on the basis of the legislation of a Member State if the legislation of a host Member State treats a registered partnership as equivalent to marriage;

- direct descendants who are under the age of 21 or are dependent and those of the spouse or partner; and,

---

1852. Case C-76/05 *Herbert Schwarz, Marga Gootjes-Schwarz v Finanzamt Bergisch Gladbach* [2007] ECR 1-6849. See also Case C-56/09 *Emiliano Zanotti v Agenzia delle Entrate-Ufficio Roma 2* [2010] ECR I-4517.
1853. [2004] OJ L 229/1.

- direct dependent ascendants and those of the spouse or partner, i.e parents and grand-parents of an EU citizen or his/her spouse/partner.

Article 3 concerns the right of entry and residence of members of the family who are not mentioned in Article 2(2). With regard to them a host Member State is required to examine the personal circumstances of such persons and must justify any denial of entry of residence. Three categories of persons are mentioned:

- those who were dependents, or members of a household, of an EU citizen in the country from which they have come;

- those who require personal care by an EU citizen on serious health grounds; and,

- a partner with whom an EU citizen has a durable relationship, duly attested.

It is well established in EU law that the status of dependency is not linked to the entitlement to maintenance because such a requirement would result in defining the status of dependency or otherwise on the basis of national law, which varies from one Member State to another. Further, the broad interpretation of provisions on the free movement of workers entails that neither the reason for recourse to financial support nor the assessment of whether the person concerned is able to support himself/herself by taking up employment are relevant in determining the status of dependency.[1854] However, the issue of how to prove the relationship of dependency is more controversial. In Case C-1/05 *Jia*,[1855] the ECJ provided some useful clarification. It held that:

- The same criteria apply when assessing the relationship of dependency, whether the EU national is a worker or a self-employed person;

- A host Member State is required to assess whether the person concerned is in a position to support himself/herself in the light of his/her financial and social conditions in the Member State of origin or the Member State from whence he/she came (or perhaps this should be expressed as the Member State where he/she was residing) at the time when the application to join the EU national was made. This clearly excludes the assessment of his/her financial and social conditions in the host Member State; and,

- Evidence of dependency may be adduced by any appropriate means. On the one hand, it is not necessary to require a document of the competent authority of the Member State of origin, or the Member State from which the applicant came, attesting the existence of a situation of dependency, although this kind of proof is particularly appropriate for that purpose. On the other hand, an undertaking from an EU national or his/her spouse to support a family member may not be sufficient.

22.4.1.1 Spouses

Article 2(2) of Directive 2004/38 expressly mentions a spouse of an EU national. In Case 267/83 *Diatta*,[1856] the ECJ held that it is not necessary for spouses to live under the same roof. This decision was delivered in the context of spouses living separately and intending to obtain a divorce (the wife was of Senegalese nationality, her husband was a French national working in Germany). However, in the

---

1854. Case 316/85 *Centre Public d'Aide Sociale (Public Social Welfare Centre), Courcelles v Marie-Christine Lebon* [1987] ECR 2811.
1855. Case C-1/05 *Yunying Jia v Migrationsverket* [2007] ECR I-1.
1856. Case 267/83 *Aissatou Diatta v Land Berlin* [1985] ECR 567.

light of Article 7(1)(d) of the Directive which states that a spouse must be accompanying or joining an EU citizen, and Article 16(2) of the Directive which states that a family member must reside with the EU citizen in order to acquire permanent residence in a host Member State, it seems that a separated spouse would not satisfy the requirements of Article 2(2) of the Directive.

The ECJ has interpreted the words "joining" broadly, to include not only a couple who met prior to their departure to a host Member State but also those who both met and subsequently got married in a host Member State. This is exemplified in Case C-127/08 *Metock*,[1857] in which the ECJ was asked to interpret Directive 2004/38 to assist the Irish High Court to decide whether Irish legislation implementing Directive 2004/38 was compatible with EU law. The Irish legislation provided that a national of a third country who is a family member of an EU citizen may reside with or join that citizen in Ireland only if that family member lawfully resided in another Member State immediately before residing with/joining the EU citizen in Ireland.

THE FACTS WERE:

The Irish High Court referred to the ECJ four cases. In each of the four cases, a non-EU national had entered Ireland and lodged an asylum application, which was refused. Subsequent to arrival in Ireland, each non-EU national married a national of another Member State who was living and working in Ireland. All marriages were genuine marriages, not marriages of convenience. After the marriage, the non-EU nationals applied for a residence card, which the Irish Minister for Justice refused. This refusal in three of the four cases was solely based on the fact that each applicant was not in a position to provide evidence that he had been lawfully resident in another Member State prior to arrival in Ireland. In the fourth case concerning Mr Igboanusi, a Nigerian national, who had married Ms Batkowska, a Polish national, subsequent to the final decision refusing his application for political asylum, a deportation order was made prior to his marriage. Therefore, when Mr Igboanusi married Ms Batkowska he was unlawfully residing in Ireland. In execution of the deportation order Mr Igboanusi was arrested on 16 November 2007, and deported to Nigeria in December 2007.

Held:

The ECJ:

Held that under Directive 2004/38 a host Member State is not allowed to impose a condition requiring a national of a non-member country, who is the spouse of an EU citizen residing in that Member State but not possessing its nationality, to have previously been lawfully resident in another Member State before arriving in the host Member State. The ECJ held that no such condition is provided for in Directive 2004/38 and that Article 2 of Directive 2004/38 makes no distinction between those family members who have already resided lawfully in another Member State prior to their arrival in a host Member State and those who joined an EU citizen in a host Member State without previously residing in any Member State, or whose residence in another Member State was unlawful prior to their arrival in a host Member State;

Confirmed that the EU has exclusive powers to regulate, as it did by Directive 2004/38, the entry (and subsequent residence there) of nationals of non-member

---

1857   C-127/08 *Blaise Baheten Metock and Others v Minister for Justice, Equality and Law Reform* [2008] ECR I-6241.

countries who are family members of an EU citizen into a Member State in which that citizen has exercised his right of freedom of movement, including a situation where the family members were not already lawfully resident in another Member State; and,

Held that non-EU nationals who are family members of an EU citizen benefit from the right to free movement irrespective of whether they have entered the host Member State before or after becoming family members of that EU citizen, and irrespective of when and where their marriage may have taken place, and of how they entered the host Member State. Obviously, in any event, under Article 27 of Directive 2004/38 a Member State is allowed to penalise a national of a non-Member State for, prior to becoming a family member of an EU citizen, entering into and/or residing in its territory in breach of the national rules on immigration. However, any punishment must be in conformity with EU law in that it must be proportionate.

Comment:

With regard to point 2, the ECJ made an important clarification bearing in mind that the Irish government and many other governments of the Member States, submitted that they retained exclusive competence, subject to Title IV of Part Three of the Treaty, to regulate the first access to EU territory of family members of an EU citizen who are nationals of non-member countries. Recognition of the exclusive competence of Member States in respect of the free movement of persons would have had very serious consequences on the effectiveness of the right to free movement of EU nationals and the uniformity of the application of EU law in this area. An argument in favour of the exclusive competences of Member States based on the necessity to control immigration at the external borders of the EU, which presupposes an individual examination of all the circumstances surrounding a first entry into EU territory, was rejected by the ECJ. The Court rightly stated first, that only non-EU nationals who are family members of EU nationals benefit from the right of entry into and residence in a Member State and second, that a Member State retains its power to refuse entry and residence to both EU citizens and non-EU family members of EU citizens on grounds of public policy, public security or public health.

In the light of the above judgment and the judgment of the ECJ in Case 291/05 *Eind*, the controversial judgment of the ECJ in Case C-109/01 *Akrich*[1858] has lost its importance. However, in *Akrich* the ECJ made two important clarifications:

1858. Case C-109/01 *Secretary of State for the Home Department v Hacene Akrich* [2003] ECR I-9607. In *Akrich* the issue was whether a national of a Member State, who is married to a third-country national who does not qualify under national legislation to enter and reside in that Member State, when he or she moves to another Member State with the non-national spouse with the intention of working there for only a limited period of time as an employee, can take advantage of EU law by securing the right of residence for the non-national spouse when returning to the Member State of nationality. The ECJ held that Mr Akrich could not rely on EU law to enter and remain in the home Member State of his spouse because he resided unlawfully there before he and his wife had moved to another Member State. The only remedy which might have been available to him is based on Article 8 of the ECHR. In this case the ECJ strongly emphasised the importance of the right to family life, referring to its own case law and the judgments of the ECtHR, but did not rule on the point. It is to be noted that in the light of the judgments of the ECJ in *Metock* and in *Eind*, Mr Akrich would have had no problem to return to his spouse's home Member State.

- that the marriage must be a genuine marriage and not a marriage of convenience. This is confirmed in Article 35 of Directive 2004/38; and,

- that the intention of EU migrant workers (including the intention to use rights conferred under EU law to evade the application of national rules which are unfavourable to them) when exercising their right to free movement has no impact on their entitlement under EU law.

22.4.1.2 Registered partners

Registered partners, irrespective of their sexual orientation and nationality, have the right to enter and reside in a host Member State when the partnership is recognised by both the home and host Member States. This means that, for example, a British national will be able to take his male Mexican partner, which whom he entered into civil partnership under the UK 2004 British Civil Partnership Act, to Sweden, where registered homosexual partnerships are recognised, but not to Greece, where no such recognition exists in law. However, Article 3(2)(b) of Directive 2004/38 imposes on a host Member State in which no registered partnerships, or partnerships, are recognised, an obligation to facilitate entry and residence of partners of EU nationals, irrespective of a partner's sexual orientation or nationality, in a situation where the partnership is durable and duly attested. Unfortunately, the Directive neither specifies the concept of "durable relationship" nor the manner in which an EU national may demonstrate its durability. Notwithstanding this, Case 59/85 *Reed*[1859] may be of assistance to EU nationals who are in durable relationships with partners. In this case, the ECJ held that by virtue of the principle of non-discrimination, a Member State cannot refuse a cohabitee of a worker who is an EU national the right to reside with the worker in so far as national law provides this possibility for its own nationals. As a result, Miss Reed, a British national, was allowed to remain in the Netherlands with her English cohabitee of five years.

Directive 2004/38 regulated, for the first time, the issue of the right of residence of a spouse/ registered partner who is not an EU national in the event of divorce, annulment of marriage or termination of registered partnership. Provided that such a person is a worker or a self-employed person (Article 7(a)); or has sufficient resources to avoid becoming a burden on the social security system of the host Member State and has appropriate sickness insurance cover (Article 7(b)); or is a student enrolled at an establishment accredited by the host Member State (Article 7(c)); or is a family member accompanying or joining an EU citizen who satisfies the conditions set out in Article 7 (a), (b) or (c), he/she retains the right of residence in a host Member State if:

- the relationship specified above has lasted at least three years, including one year in a host Member State; or

- by agreement or court order, he/she has custody of an EU citizen's children; or

- this is warranted by particularly difficult circumstances, such as having been a victim of domestic violence while the marriage or registered relationship was subsisting; or

- by agreement or by court order he/she has a right of access to a minor child, provided that the court has ruled that such access must be in the host Member State. In this case the right of residence is retained for as long as it is required.

The death of an EU citizen should not affect the right of residence of non-EU members of his/her family if they have resided in the host Member State as family members for at least one year before his/her death and can satisfy the conditions set out in Article 7(1)(a), (b), (c) or (d).

1859. Case 59/85 *The Netherlands v Ann Florence Reed* [1986] ECR 1283.

In the case of the death or departure of an EU citizen from a host Member State, Article 12(3) of Directive 2004/38 states that this should not entail loss of the right of residence by his/her children or by a parent who has actual custody of the children, regardless of their nationality, if the children reside in the host Member State and are enrolled at an educational establishment there. They, as well as the parent, retain the right to reside in the host Member State until the completion of their studies.

22.4.2 The right of residence

The right of nationals of a Member State to leave the territory of a home Member State, enter the territory of another Member State and reside there is conferred directly by the Treaties. This was decided by the ECJ in Case 48/75 *Royer*.[1860] Secondary legislation determines the scope of, and provides detailed rules for, the exercise of the right to move and reside in a host Member State which is conferred directly by the Treaties.

Directive 2004/38 reiterates the principle that failure to comply with formalities regarding entry and residence cannot justify a decision ordering expulsion from the territory of a host Member State[1861] or temporary imprisonment. In respect of sanctions that a Member State may impose on nationals from other Member States for failure to comply with administrative requirements regarding entry and residence, such sanctions are subject to the principle of proportionality. In Case 265/88 *Messner*,[1862] a requirement under Italian law imposing on all immigrants the obligation to register with the police within three days of their arrival, sanctioned by criminal penalties, was considered as disproportionate. Any national measures which are disproportionate to the objectives of the Treaties in the area of free movement of persons will be struck down by the ECJ as contrary to EU law.[1863]

Directive 2004/38 makes a distinction between residence of an EU national in a host Member State for up to three months and for more than three months.

22.4.2.1 *Right of residence for up to three months*

All EU citizens are entitled to enter another Member State on the basis of a valid identity document or passport. If they do not have these travel documents, the host Member State must afford them every facility in obtaining the requisite documents or having them sent. In Case C-215/03 *Salah Oulane*,[1864] the ECJ stated that a Member State may not refuse to recognise the right of residence on the sole ground that a person did not present one of these documents. Any document or evidence proving unequivocally that a person is an EU citizen should be accepted by a host Member State.

A Member State is prohibited from requiring either an entry or an exit visa. A family member who is a non-EU national accompanying an EU citizen may be required to have a short-stay visa as specified by Regulation 539/2001.

Under Article 8 of Directive 2004/38 EU citizens and members of their families may be required to register their presence in the territory of a host Member State within a reasonable and non-discriminatory period of time after their arrival, but any penalty for breach of the requirement must be proportionate and comparable to those which apply to similar national infringements.[1865]

1860. Case 48/75 *The State v Jean Noël Royer* [1976] ECR 497.

1861. See Case 118/75 *Lynne Watson and Alessandro Belmann* [1976] ECR 1185; Case 157/79 *R v Pieck* [1980] ECR 2171.

1862. Case 265/88 *Criminal Proceedings against Lothar Messner* [1989] ECR 4209.

1863. Case 30/77 *R v Pierre Bourchereau* [1977] ECR 1999.

1864. Case C-215/03 *Salah Oulane v Minister voor Vreemdelingenzaken en Integratie* [2005] ECR I-1215.

1865. Case C-378/97 *Criminal Proceedings against Florus Ariël Wijsenbeek* [1999] ECR I-6207; Article 8(2) of Directive 2004/38.

The question whether a host Member State may restrict the residence of an EU citizen to part of the national territory was examined by the ECJ in Case 36/75 *Rutili*.[1866]

THE FACTS WERE:

Rutili was an Italian national who resided in France, and between 1967 and 1968 he actively participated in political and trade union activities. The French authorities grew increasingly concerned with his activities, and issued a deportation order. This was subsequently altered to a restriction order requiring him to remain in certain provinces of France. In particular, the order prohibited him from residing in the province in which he was habitually resident and in which his family resided.

Rutili challenged the legality of these measures on the ground that they interfered with his right of freedom of movement. The matter was referred to the ECJ for a preliminary ruling.

Held:

The ECJ interpreted the right of a Member State to limit the free movement of workers on the ground of public policy and concluded that this right must be construed strictly. In particular, a Member State cannot, in the case of a national of another Member State, impose prohibitions on residence which are territorially limited except in circumstances where such prohibitions may be imposed on its own nationals. Consequently, if a Member State has no power to restrict the residence of its own nationals to a specific area, then it has only two options in relation to an EU migrant worker: either to refuse entry or to permit residence anywhere in the national territory.[1867] This solution has been incorporated into Article 22 of Directive 2004/38.

22.4.2.2 Right of residence for more than three months

The right of residence for a period exceeding three months is granted to three categories of persons:

- Workers or self-employed persons (Article 7(1)(a)), including those who are temporarily unable to work due to illness or accident, or are involuntarily unemployed and registered as job-seekers with the relevant employment office, or are embarking on vocational training;

- Economically inactive persons and their families (Article 7(1)(b)) where they have sufficient resources to avoid being a burden on the social assistance system of the host Member State. Further, they must have comprehensive sickness insurance cover in the host Member State; and,

- Students (Article 7(1)(c)). They must be enrolled at a private or public establishment accredited or financed by the host Member State and must have sufficient resources to avoid becoming a burden on the social security system of the host Member State. As a result they must have health insurance and adequate means of support. In addition only a spouse or a registered partner and dependent children are regarded as family members for the purposes of the Directive.

1866. Case 36/75 *Roland Rutili v Ministre de l'intérieur* [1975] ECR 1219.
1867. See Case C-100/01 *Ministre de l'Intérieur v Aitor Oteiza Olazabal* [2002] ECR I-10981.

The issue of what constitutes "sufficient resources" is of utmost importance for EU citizens exercising their right to free movement. In this respect Article 8(4) of the Directive specifies that in each case the personal situation of the person concerned should be assessed by a host Member State. It also states that a Member State is not allowed to set a fixed amount, and in any case the amount must not be higher than the threshold below which nationals of the host Member State become eligible for social assistance or, alternatively, the minimum social security pension paid by the host Member State.

In Case C-408/03 *Commission v Belgium*,[1868] the ECJ reiterated its case law on this topic. It held that the origin of resources, whether personal or belonging to third persons, including those with whom the EU citizen has no legal link (for example, an unregistered partner), are irrelevant. The ECJ found Belgium in breach of Article 21 TFEU and Directive 90/364 for refusing to take account of the income of a long-standing Belgian partner of a Portuguese woman, who went to Belgium with her three daughters to live with him, but without any agreement concluded before a notary and containing an assistance clause. According to the ECJ, an undertaking given by the Belgian partner in a not legally binding form was sufficient.

Directive 2004/38 abolished the requirement of residence permits for EU nationals but Member States are allowed to require them to register with the competent authorities within a period of no less than three months of their arrival. A registration certificate must be issued immediately on the presentation of:

- a valid identity card or valid passport;

- proof that the EU citizen meets the requirements set out by the Directive, e.g. a confirmation of engagement from the employer, a certificate of employment or any other relevant evidence.

Family members who are non-EU nationals, however, are required to obtain a residence permit, which must be delivered within six months of the application and be valid for five years from the date of issue.[1869]

The right of residence expires if the persons concerned break any of the conditions of their residence as prescribed by the Directives. Such persons may be deported on the grounds of public policy, public security and public health (see Chapter 25.3).

22.4.2.3 Permanent residence

Directive 2004/38 introduced the right of permanent residence. This is granted to EU nationals and members of their families, irrespective of their nationality, after a five-year period of uninterrupted and legal residence in a host Member State, provided that no expulsion decision has been enforced against them. In Case 162/09 *Lassal*[1870] the ECJ held that continuous periods of five years completed before the date fixed by the Directive for its implementation (30 April 2006) must be taken into account for the purposes of the acquisition of the right of permanent residence.

In Joined Cases C-424/10 and 425/10 *Ziolkowski and Szeja*[1871] the ECJ held that the concept of "legal residence" has an autonomous EU meaning. It refers to a period of residence which complies with the conditions set out in Directive 2004/38/EC, i.e. the person concerned must reside in a host Member State as a worker, or self-employed person, or have sufficient resources for himself/herself and

---

1868.   [2006] ECR I-2647.

1869.   Case C-157/03 *Commission v Spain* [2005] ECR I-2911.

1870.   Case 162/09 *Secretary of State for Work and Pensions v Taous Lassal* [2010] ECR I-9217.

1871.   Judgment of 21/12/11 (NYR).

his/her family not to become a burden on the social assistance system of a host Member State and have comprehensive sickness insurance cover in a host Member State. Accordingly, lawful residence in a host Member State according to national law of that State may not coincide with "legal residence" for the purpose of acquiring permanent residence in a host Member State if the conditions set out in the Directive are not satisfied. In the above cases, the applicants, Polish nationals, were unable to support themselves economically during their long stay in Germany. Their residence in Germany was lawful under German law, as they had been granted the right to reside there on humanitarian grounds in the 1980s. This right was terminated in 2006. The applicants had never satisfied the conditions set out in Directive 2004/38/EC and therefore Germany was entitled to deport them to Poland.

Article 16(3) specifies that continuity of residence is not affected by temporary absences not exceeding a total of six months a year, or by absence of a longer duration for compulsory military service, or by one absence of a maximum of 12 consecutive months for serious reasons such as illness, pregnancy, and study. In Case C-162/09 *Lassal*,[1872] Ms Lassal, who entered the UK in January 1999, left the UK in February 2005 and returned to the UK in December 2005. The UK Secretary of State argued that the absence of Ms Lassal from the UK from February 2005 to December 2005 resulted in her commencing to accrue a five-year period of residence either from 30 April 2006 (the date fixed by the directive for its implementation) or from December 2005 (the date she returned to the UK). The ECJ held that absences from the host Member State of less than two consecutive years, which took place before 30 April 2006 but following a continuous period of five years legal residence completed before that date do not affect the acquisition of the right of permanent residence.

In the circumstances described in Article 17 of the Directive some EU citizens and members of their families are entitled to become permanent residents of the host Member State before completion of a continuous period of five years of residence (for example, those who reach the age of retirement, or take early retirement or, become unable to work due to an accident at work or an occupational disease). The right of permanent residence once acquired, can be lost only in the event of an absence from the host Member State for more than two successive years.

22.4.3 Equal treatment

Article 24 of Directive 2004/38 provides that EU citizens and their family shall enjoy equal treatment with nationals of the host Member State. This is extended to family members who are non-EU nationals and who have the right of residence or permanent residence in the host Member State (see Chapter 22.4.2).

22.5 The right to participate in municipal elections and in elections to the EP

Article 22 TFEU confers both active rights (the right to stand as a candidate) and passive rights (the right to vote) in respect of municipal[1873] and EP[1874] elections on an EU citizen residing in a Member State of which he/she is not a national, under the same conditions as nationals of that Member State. Further measures (mentioned below) were necessary to implement those rights.

1872. Case C-162/09 *Lassal* [2010] ECR I-9217.
1873. Article 22(1) TFEU.
1874. Article 22(2) TFEU.

22.5.1 The right to participation in municipal elections

Participation in municipal elections for EU nationals residing in a Member State of which they are not nationals is important as it contributes to their integration into the society of a host Member State. It is also in line with the Council of Europe Convention of 5 February 1992 on the Participation of Foreigners in Public Life at Local Level provided they fulfil the requirement of residence.

The adoption of an EU measure in this area posed three problems:

- first, the matter of the determination of the local government unit;

- second, the matter of the determination of the public offices which nationals of other Member States may hold; and,

- third, the matter of the granting of local election rights in a Member State with a very high percentage of residents from other Member States.

All the above problems were addressed in Council Directive 94/80 of 19 December 1994, which conferred on citizens of the Union the right to vote and stand as candidates in local elections in their Member State of residence under the same conditions as nationals of that Member State.[1875]

The first matter was partially solved by Directive 94/80, which in Article 2(1) provides a definition of the basic local government unit, and partially by the Member States, which in the Annex to that Directive listed the relevant types of administrative entity. Article 2(1) defines the basic local governmental unit as "certain bodies elected by direct universal suffrage and . . . empowered to administer, at the basic level of political and administrative organisation, certain local affairs on their own responsibility". However, the reference to national law in determination of those bodies has resulted in wide diversity in the levels of local government accessible to EU citizens. For example, in the UK, non-national EU citizens are entitled to both passive and active voting rights in respect of all levels of government below national government, while in France they are limited to voting at the lowest level. The list of administrative entities provided by the UK encompasses "counties in England, counties, county boroughs and communities in Wales, regions and Islands in Scotland, districts in England, Scotland and Northern Ireland, London boroughs, parishes in England, the City of London in relation to ward elections for common councilmen".[1876]

The second matter relating to access to certain offices elected by direct universal suffrage, such as the post of mayor or alderman (a member of the local executive), is regulated in Article 5(3) of Directive 94/80 which states that "the office of elected head, deputy or member of the governing college of the executive of a basic local government unit if elected to hold office for the duration of his mandate" may be reserved to nationals of a Member State. This provision is contrary to European integration but in line with Articles 45(4) and Article 51 TFEU, which exclude nationals of Member States resident in other Member States from holding public office and from activities which involve the exercise of official authority. As a result, Directive 94/80 strengthens the limitations already existing under the Treaties instead of abolishing any difference in treatment between nationals and non-nationals being EU citizens residing in a host Member State.

The third matter was solved by allowing derogations from the Directive to accommodate Member States with a very high percentage of resident non-national EU citizens. If more than 20 per cent of foreign residents are nationals of the EU without being nationals of that Member State, the exercise of their electoral rights may be subject to the requirement of a certain period of residence in that Member

---

1875. [1994] OJ L368/38.
1876. Annex to Directive 94/80.

State. This derogation concerns mostly Luxembourg where approximately 30 per cent of the population are foreign residents and more than 90 per cent of them are EU nationals.

Other features of the Directive are:

■ It allows multiple voting. For example, a French national residing in England and in Belgium is entitled to exercise his/her voting rights in both countries;

■ It gives no definition of residence. It only provides that the owners of holiday homes are not considered as residents in a Member State where they have a holiday home unless they are allowed to participate in municipal elections on the basis of reciprocity.[1877] To illustrate reciprocity, an Englishman living in Southampton who owns a holiday home in Barcelona in Spain, will be allowed to vote and stand at municipal elections in Spain only if a Spanish national who owns a holiday home in Southampton in England has the same rights in England.

Directive 94/80 is very modest. It confers passive and active voting rights in municipal elections which are of little importance in the political life of any Member State.[1878] The grant of voting rights in national parliamentary elections, in direct presidential elections or in referenda would give real meaning to citizenship of the EU.

22.5.2 The right to participate in elections to the European Parliament

Article 22(2) TFEU confers on citizens of the EU the right to vote and to stand in elections to the European Parliament in the Member State of their residence under the same conditions as nationals of that Member State. The content of this right is examined in Chapter 3.6.1.

22.6 The right to diplomatic and consular protection

Article 23 TFEU states that an EU national is entitled to the diplomatic and consular protection of any Member State, under the same conditions as nationals of that Member State, in the territory of a third country in which the Member State of which he/she is a national is not represented.[1879] This right is confirmed in Article 46 of the Charter of Fundamental Rights of the EU.

Before the entry into force of the ToL, the procedure provided for enactment of further measures in the area of diplomatic and consular protection was based on inter-governmental co-operation. Pre-ToL measures included "Guidelines for the Protection of Unrepresented EC Nationals by EC Missions in Third Countries" on the basis of which the Council adopted the following binding measures, which remain in force:

■ Decision 95/553/EC[1880] on the protection of EU citizens in territories where their own Member State or the State which permanently represents their Member State maintains no accessible permanent mission or relevant consulate. Under the decision EU citizens can obtain assistance, relief and, if needed, repatriation, in most distressing circumstances, e.g. when they are victims of violent crimes; when they have serious accidents; when they are arrested; or, in detention.

1877. Article 4(2) of Directive 94/80.

1878. In the UK the Representation of the People Act (2000) enacted on 9 March 2000 governs the right to vote or to stand in both municipal and European Parliamentary elections.

1879. See A. I. Saliceti, "The Protection of EU Citizens Abroad: Accountability, Rule of Law, Role of Consular and Diplomatic Services", (2011) EPL, 91.

1880. [1995] OJ L314/73.

■ Decision 96/409/CFSP[1881] on the Emergency Travel Document, which provides for the issue by Member States of a common format emergency travel document to citizens of the EU in places where their Member State has no permanent diplomatic or consular representation or in other specific circumstances.

Under the ToL, measures relating to the protection of EU citizens outside the EU in the circumstances described in Article 23 TFEU are within the scope of the Treaties. Such measures may be adopted by the Council in accordance with a special legislative procedure and after consulting the EP. Measures adopted under Article 23 TFEU are under review by the Commission which considers that consular and diplomatic protection needs to be strengthened.[1882] In December 2011, the Commission following publication of a Green Paper, adopted a proposal for a directive on diplomatic and consular protection of Union citizens in third countries.[1883] The proposed directive refers to EU citizens who live in or travel in a third country where their Member State of nationality does not have an embassy or consulate as "unrepresented EU citizens". The proposed directive strengthens the protection by:

■ Extending the protection list to Union citizen's family members who are nationals of a third country;

■ Clarifying the concept of "accessibility of embassy or a consulate" in that it provides that they are accessible if they can effectively provide protection and can be reached safely within convenient travel distance and reasonable time (i.e. it should be possible for an EU citizen to return to the place of departure the same day, *via* means of transportation commonly used in the third country) (Article 3);

■ Identifying the types of assistance to be provided to unrepresented EU citizens (Article 6);

■ Requiring close co-operation and co-ordination between diplomatic and consular authorities of the Member States, including the establishment of a "lead State" in a given third country which will be in charge of co-ordinating and leading assistance in cases of crisis (Article 16);

■ Specifying financial procedures in the form of financial assistance advance or repatriation to unrepresented EU citizens (Article 3); and

■ Providing for monitoring and evaluation of the implementation of the directive by the Commission (Article 20).

Additionally, the Commission has prepared a dedicated website on consular protection.[1884]

22.7 The right of EU citizens' initiative

The right of EU citizens' initiative has been implemented by Regulation 211/2011[1885] (see Chapter 5.2.2).

1881. [1996] OJ L168/4.
1882. On 28 November 2006 the Commission published its Green Paper on Diplomatic and Consular Protection of Union Citizens in Third Countries, COM(2006)712 final.
1883. COM(2011) 881 final.
1884. See http://ec.europa.eu/consularprotection/index.action (accessed 3/3/12).
1885. [2011] OJ L65/1.

22.8 The right to petition the EP

Article 24(2) TFEU states that a citizen of the Union individually or in association with others may petition the EP in accordance with Article 227 TFEU. The right, however, is not limited to EU citizens. It has been granted to any natural or legal person residing or having its registered office in a Member State. There are certain limitations under Article 227 TFEU in that the submitted matter:

- must be within the fields of activity of the EU; and,

- must affect the petitioner directly.

The Committee on Petitions, set up to deal with petitions, decides on their admissibility. If a petition is admissible the Committee may ask the Commission or other body to provide information. Once there is enough information the petition is put on the agenda of the Committee. At its meeting a Commission representative is invited to make comments in respect of the matter raised in the petition. Depending on the case further action may be taken by the Committee:

- If the petition concerns the interests of an individual, the Commission will get in touch with relevant authorities or submit the case to the permanent representative of the Member State concerned. In some cases the Committee may ask the President of the EP to make representations to the national authorities in person;

- If the petition is of general interest, that is, a Member State is in breach of EU law, the Commission may start proceedings against the offending Member State; and,

- If the petition concerns a political matter, the EP or the Commission may use it as the basis for a political initiative, which may result in initiating or prompting an action at EU level.

In each case an applicant is informed of the action taken on the petition and of the result.

22.9 The right to submit complaints to the EU Ombudsman

Article 24(3) TFEU states that every EU citizen has the right to make a complaint to the EU Ombudsman who is also empowered to receive complaints from any natural or legal person residing or having its registered office in a Member State.[1886]

The Ombudsman is elected by the EP after its own elections, holds office for the duration of the term of the EP, and may be reappointed. The Ombudsman must be a citizen of the EU, chosen from persons whose independence is beyond doubt and who must possess the qualifications required for appointment to the highest judicial offices in their own Member State, or have the experience and the competences recognised as necessary for the exercise of the functions of Ombudsman.

The Ombudsman may be removed from office by the ECJ at the request of the EP if he/she no longer satisfies the conditions required for the performance of his/her duties or no longer meets the obligations resulting from his/her office, or is guilty of serious misconduct. The Ombudsman may not hold any office of an administrative or political nature, nor engage in any additional occupation or profession, paid or unpaid, during his/her term of office. The Ombudsman's role is to act independently, and thus the Ombudsman neither seeks nor takes instructions from anybody.

1886. See the EU Ombudsman website http://www.ombudsman.europa.eu/home/en/default.htm (accessed 18/4/12).

His general duties are set out in Article 228 TFEU and further specified in Council Decision 94/262 of 9 March 1994.[1887] The Ombudsman's competences *ratione materiae* are limited to maladministration in the activities of EU institutions, bodies, offices or agencies. The Ombudsman cannot investigate complaints of maladministration in the activities of the EU courts acting in their judicial role. The limitation of the Ombudsman's competences to investigation of maladministration of only EU institutions, bodies, offices or agencies is very disappointing since complaints regarding maladministration by national bodies pursuant to or in violation of EU law are extremely important and often vital for ordinary people. This limitation has been recognised by the EU Ombudsman. According to the Ombudsman in 2010, 50 per cent of complaints were outside the Ombudsman's mandate because they concerned the activities of national authorities.[1888] In order to assist EU citizens the EU Ombudsman works in close co-operation with national ombudsmen.

The Ombudsman may make investigations on his/her own initiative as well as in response to complaints from individuals, or submitted to him/her through members of the European Parliament, except if the alleged facts are, or have been, the subject of legal proceedings.

If the Ombudsman decides that a complaint is well founded, it is referred to the institution concerned, which has three months to express its views. After the expiry of that period, if the institution in question has not taken appropriate measures to resolve the matter, the Ombudsman must draft a report (which may include recommendations) and forward it to the EP and the institution concerned. However, the Ombudsman may then only inform the complainant of this process; the Ombudsman provides no legal remedy.

Even if the existence of the Ombudsman may seem superfluous taking into account that the competences of the EP Committee on Petitions and the Ombudsman overlap and that remedies for maladministration by EU institutions, bodies, offices or agencies are already provided by the Treaties, and are more adequate and more efficient than any resulting from the successful intervention of the Ombudsman, it is an important institution protecting rights of EU citizens and natural and legal persons residing in the EU. First, it helps them to find redress for maladministration by EU institutions. For example, in 2010, it was able to help complainants in almost 70 per cent of cases processed.[1889] Second, it has greatly contributed to the defining and development of ethical standards of good administration in EU institutions.[1890] Third, its existence certainly enhances the democratic nature of the EU.

22.10 The right to use one's own language in correspondence with EU institutions, bodies, offices and agencies

Article 24(4) TFEU provides that every citizen of the EU has the right to write to any EU institution, body, office or agency in one of the official languages of the EU (see Chapter 3.1.2) and to receive an answer in the same language. This provision seems to entail more than a simple right to use one's own language in correspondence with the EU institutions which, under Article 13 TEU, are required, *inter alia*, to serve a interests of EU citizens and therefore to communicate with them in a language that they

---

1887. [1994] OJ L113/15. This decision was amended by Decision 2008/587/EC ([2008] OJ L189/587) which increased the powers to the EU Ombudsman.

1888. See Annual Report on the Activities of the EU Ombudsman for the year 2010, http://www.ombudsman.europa.eu (accessed 3/3/12).

1889. See the 2010 European Ombudsman Report available at http://www.ombudsman.europa.eu/activities/annualreports.faces (accessed 3/3/12).

1890. See M. E. De Leeuw, "The European Ombudsman's Role as a Developer of Norms of Good Administration", (2011) 17 EPL, 349.

can understand. Indeed, Article 24(4) TFEU enhances the principle of transparency including the right of EU citizens to have access to information (see Chapter 5.2.3).

22.11 The evolving nature of EU citizenship

The most important aspect of Union citizenship is its dynamic character. So far, the rights of EU citizenship have mainly been developed by the ECJ, as evidenced by its broad interpretation of Articles 20 and 21(1) TFEU; by the Commission, which has taken many initiatives to strengthen and enhance the European identity and enable European citizens to participate in the EU integration process in an increasingly intense way;[1891] and, by the EP, which, being the democratic servant of EU citizens, has always promoted their interests.

It is submitted that the development of the rights of EU citizens has been stifled by the requirements set out in Article 25 TFEU, relating to the adoption of measures aimed at adding to or strengthening the rights of EU citizens. Article 25 TFEU states:

> "the Council, acting unanimously in accordance with a special legislative procedure and after obtaining the consent of the European Parliament, may adopt provisions to strengthen or to add to the rights listed in Article 20(2). These provisions shall enter into force after their approval by the Member States in accordance with their respective constitutional requirements."

As a result, any progress was, and remains, very slow. Under Article 25 TFEU the Council may only increase the list of rights granted to EU citizens and not reduce them.

It should be noted that under Article 21(3) TFEU specific legislative powers were granted to the Council with regard to the development of the social dimension of EU citizenship. This Article states that for the purposes of the removal of obstacles to the free movement of EU citizens:

> "if the Treaties have not provided the necessary powers, the Council, acting in accordance with a special legislative procedure, may adopt measures concerning social security or social protection. The Council shall act unanimously after consulting the European Parliament."

The importance of Article 21(3) TFEU is that the ToL brought social security and social protection matters within the scope of EU citizenship. So far, EU social law has been mainly concerned with co-ordinating social security schemes and social protection measures to ensure that migrant workers, self-employed persons and EU citizens in general are not discriminated against in a host Member State. Under Article 21(3) TFEU, Member States may, if they so decide, create a social dimension of EU citizenship beyond that which has been developed by the ECJ in its case law under Article 21(1) TFEU (see Chapter 22.3). However, Article 21(3) TFEU is not as revolutionary as it may appear. This is because any measure adopted under Article 21(3) TFEU requires a unanimous vote in the Council and therefore Member States have ensured that no social welfare rights will be granted to nationals of other Member States solely on the basis that they are EU citizens (as opposed to being EU workers, or self-employed persons) when any Member State expresses its opposition. This is an important safeguard for the Member States which, only when acting all together, are competent to decide whether they can afford to extend certain social benefits to EU nationals who are not their own citizens.

In the removal of barriers to the free movement of EU citizens the Commission's reports on the application of the provisions concerning citizenship of the EU are vital. Under Article 25(2) TFEU

1891. See the Commission's "Europe for Citizens Programme 2007–2013" available at http://ec.europa.eu/citizenship/index_en.html (accessed 3/3/12).

the Commission is obliged to prepare such a report every three years and to forward it to the EP; the Council; and, the Economic and Social Committee. The Commission 2010 Report[1892] recommending 25 actions has resulted in most of them being implemented.[1893] In order to make EU citizenship more relevant to citizens, the Commission launched a broad public consultation in 2012 on problems faced by EU citizens when exercising their rights. The consultation will serve as a basis for preparing an actions programme for the 2013 Report. The Commission also proposes to designate 2013 as "The European Year of Citizens" and to organise awareness events and promote citizen-related policies throughout the Year.

RECOMMENDED READING

Books

Dougan, M., and Spaventa, E. (eds), *Social Welfare and EU Law. Essays in European Law*, 2005, Oxford: Hart Publishing.

Goudappel, F., *The Effects of EU Citizenship*, 2010, The Netherlands: TMC Asser Press.

Hansen, P., and Hager, B. S., The *Politics of European Citizenship: Deepening Contradictions in Social Rights and Migration Policy*, 2010, Oxford: Berghahn Books.

Shaw, J., *The Transformation of Citizenship in the European Union: Electoral Rights and the Restructuring of Political Space*, 2007, Cambridge: CUP.

Articles

Besson, S., and Utzinger, A., "Introduction: Future Challenges of European Citizenship – Facing a Wide-Open Pandora's Box", (2007) 13 ELJ, 573.

Costello, C., "Metock: Free Movement and 'Normal Family Life' in the Union", (2009) 46 CMLRev., 587.

De Leeuw, M. E., "The European Ombudsman's Role as a Developer of Norms of Good Administration", (2011) 17 EPL, 349.

Dougan, M., "Cross-border Educational Mobility and the Exportation of Student Financial Assistance", (2008) 33 ELRev., 723.

Hailbronner, K., "Union Citizenship and Access to Social Benefits", (2005) 42 CMLRev., 1245.

Jacobs, F. G., "Citizenship of the European Union – A Legal Analysis", (2007) 13/5 ELJ, 1591.

Jacqueson, C., "Union Citizenship and the Court of Justice: Something New under the Sun? Towards Social 'Citizenship'", (2002) 27 ELRev., 260.

Kadelbach, P. S., "Union Citizenship", in A. Von Bogdandy and J. Bast (eds), *Principles of European Constitutional Law*, 2nd edn, 2010, Oxford: Hart Publishing, 467.

Lansbergen, A., and Miller, N., "European Citizenship Rights in Internal Situations: An ambiguous Revolution? Decision of 8 March 2011, Case C-34/09 Gerardo Ruiz Zambrano v Office national de l'emploi (ONEm)" (2011) 7 *European Constitutional Law Review*, 287.

Mather, J. D., "The Court of Justice and the Union Citizen", (2005) 11 ELJ, 722.

Morris, R., "European Citizenship: Cross-Border Relevance, Deliberate Fraud and Proportionate Responses to Potential Statelessness, Case Note on Janko Rottmann v Freistaat Bayern", (2011) 17 EPL, 417.

Peers, S., "Implementing Equality? The Directive on Long-term Resident Third Country Nationals", (2004) 29 ELRev., 437.

1892. The report is available at: http://ec.europa.eu/commission_2010-2014/reding/factsheets/index_en.htm (accessed 3/3/12).

1893. Progress in its implementation can be tracked at http://ec.europa.eu/commission_2010-2014/reding/factsheets/index_en.htm (accessed 27/7/12).

Reich, N., "The Constitutional Relevance of Citizenship and Free Movement in an Enlarged Union", (2005) 11 ELJ, 675.

Saliceti, A. I., "The Protection of EU Citizens Abroad: Accountability, Rule of Law, Role of Consular and Diplomatic Services", (2011) EPL, 91.

Shaw, J., "Citizenship: Contrasting Dynamics at the Interface of integration and Constitutionalism", in Craig, P., and De Búrca, G. (eds), *The Evolution of EU Law*, 2nd edn, 2011, Oxford: OUP, 575.

Shuibhne, N. N., "(Some Of) The Kids Are All Right: Comment on McCarthy and Dereci", (2012) 49 CMLRev., 349.

Slot, P. J. and Bulterman, M., "Harmonization of Legislation on Migrating EU Citizens and Third Country Nationals: Towards a Uniform Evaluation Framework", (2006) 29 Fordham Int'l L.J., 747.

Spaventa, E., "Seeing the Wood Despite the Trees? On the Scope of Union Citizenship and its Constitutional Effects", (2008) 45 CMLRev., 13.

Tryfonidou, A., "Redefining the Outer Boundaries of EU Law: The *Zambrano, McCarthy and Dereci* Trilogy", (2012) 18 EPL, 493.

PROBLEM QUESTION

John, and his son Jeremy, both Austrian nationals, moved from Austria to Germany 10 years ago. Recently, they have encountered the following problems:

A.   In January 2009 John acquired German nationality by naturalisation, the acquisition of which resulted in the automatic loss of his Austrian nationality. The German authorities have since discovered that when John applied for German citizenship he did not mention that he left Austria because criminal proceedings had been commenced against him on account of alleged serious fraud. As a result of their discovery, the German authorities intend to withdraw the naturalisation on the ground that it was acquired by deception. If this occurs, John will become a stateless person (i.e. he will be without any nationality).

B.   In November 2009, Jeremy, aged 22, met Nadia, a citizen of Barbaria (a fictitious country), who had arrived in Germany in June 2008 and immediately applied for political asylum. In February 2010, Nadia's application for political asylum was definitively refused and a deportation order was issued against her requiring her to leave Germany within seven days. In March 2010, Jeremy married Nadia. When in June 2010 Nadia applied for a residence permit in Germany as the spouse of an EU citizen working and residing in Germany, her application was refused, on the ground that, by reason of the deportation order, Nadia was staying in Germany illegally at the time of her marriage. In June 2012 a deportation order was made against Nadia. In July 2012 Nadia was deported to Barbaria.

C.   John wants his daughter Anna, aged 24, and her son James aged four, both Jamaican nationals residing in Jamaica, to join him in Germany. He has been supporting them financially for many years.

Advise John and Jeremy as to the application of EU law on EU citizenship on each aspect of the situations described above.

ESSAY QUESTION

Critically assess the contribution of the ECJ to the development of the concept of EU citizenship.

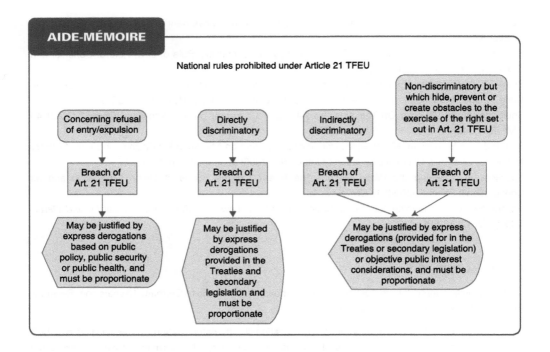

AIDE-MÉMOIRE

National rules prohibited under Article 21 TFEU

The right of family members of EU citizens to be admitted to the territory of a host Member State provided they do not fall under derogations based on public policy, public security, or public health.

MANDATORY ADMISSION (ARTS. 3(1) AND 2(2) OF DIRECTIVE 2004/38)	DISCRETIONARY ADMISSION (ART. 3(2) OF DIRECTIVE 2004/38)

1. Spouse, but marriage must not be of convenience.
2. Registered partner, irrespective of sexual orientation, when partnership was registered in a home Member State and when the host Member State treats registered partnerships as equivalent to marriages.
3. Direct descendants of an EU citizen, or an EU citizen's spouse (or a registered partner subject to point 2 above). They must be under 21 years of age or dependents.
4. Direct ascendants who are dependent on an EU citizen or his/her spouse, or his/her registered partner (subject to point 2 above).
	1. Family members, other than those whose admission is mandatory, if:
	  • They are dependent on either an EU citizen, or an EU citizen's spouse, or registered partner (this is subject to recognition by a host Member State of registered partnerships) in a country from which they wish to come;
	  • They are members of the household of an EU citizen in a home Member State;
	  • They have a serious health condition requiring personal care by an EU citizen.
	2. Partners, irrespective of their sexual orientation, who are in a durable relationship with an EU citizen. This must be duly attested.

23

FREE MOVEMENT
OF WORKERS

CONTENTS

CHAPTER OUTLINE

1. The free movement of workers and their families is governed by Article 45 TFEU, which has been implemented by secondary legislation, in particular:

- Directive 2004/38/EC of 29 April 2004 on the right of citizens of the European Union and their family members to move and reside freely within the territory of the Member States (see Chapter 22.4);

- Regulation 883/04 of 29 April 2004 on the coordination of social security systems; and,

- Regulation 492/2011 of 5 April 2011 on the free movement of workers within the Union, which governs access to, and conditions of, employment.

2. The right granted under Article 45 TFEU is not absolute. It suffers two exceptions, first, by virtue of Article 45(4) TFEU employment in the public service may be reserved to nationals of a host Member State; and, second, under Article 45(3) TFEU some limitations may be imposed on the grounds of public policy, public security and public health (see Chapter 25.3). Some further exceptions are provided for in secondary legislation.

3. Article 45 TFEU is vertically directly effective. It can also produce horizontal direct effect when an association or organisation, which is not governed by public law, adopts rules regulating "in a collective manner gainful employment". Further, an individual can rely on Article 45 TFEU against another private party when a contractual arrangement between them contains directly discriminatory conditions. However, in respect of indirectly discriminatory conditions, i.e. based on factors other than nationality, and in respect of measures which are non-discriminatory but prevent/hinder or create an obstacle to the exercise of the right set out in Article 45 TFEU, an individual cannot rely on Article 45 TFEU against another individual as this would constitute an unjustified interference in the freedom of contract of private parties.

4. The scope of application *ratione personae* of Article 45 TFEU is very broad, as not only workers and their families can rely on it, but so can employers and even, in certain circumstances, private sector recruitment agencies.

5. The concept of "worker" has been broadly interpreted by the ECJ and has an autonomous EU meaning. The essential feature of the concept of a worker is that a person must perform services of some economic value for and under the direction of another person, in return for which she/he receives remuneration. This definition has two elements. The first relates to the requirement that the activities performed by a worker must be real and genuine, to the exclusion of activities on such a small scale as to be regarded as purely marginal and ancillary. The second concerns the requirement that a worker must perform activities of an economic nature.

6. Some rights guaranteed to EU migrant workers survive the termination of an employment relationship, e.g. in the field of financial assistance for university education; or in respect of entitlement to social assistance; or when a worker returns to a home Member State, to be joined there by a family member being a third country national, who had not resided in the home Member State of the worker but had lived with the worker in a host Member State.

7. The rights of family members of a worker are parasitic on, or derivative from, those of the worker. Directive 2004/38/EC defines who are to be regarded as members of a worker's family. Regardless of their nationality, they are entitled to move with a worker, reside with him/her in a host Member State, take up employment as employees or self-employed persons, and be treated in the same way as nationals of a host Member State.

8. Article 45 TFEU prohibits all forms of discrimination, whether direct or indirect, and (as interpreted by the ECJ) any national provisions which prevent/hinder or create a barrier to the exercise of the right to the free movement of workers. Directly discriminatory national provisions can only be justified if permitted under the Treaties or secondary legislation. National provisions which are indirectly discriminatory or those which are not discriminatory but nevertheless substantially affect the exercise of the right to free movement, are not in breach of EU law if they pursue a legitimate aim compatible with the Treaties; are justified by overriding reasons of public interest; and, are proportionate to the objective that a Member State seeks to achieve.

9. Regulation 492/2011 provides a list of rights to which EU migrant workers and their families are entitled in a host Member State.

23.1 Introduction

Article 45 TFEU provides:

"1. Freedom of movement for workers shall be secured within the Union.

2. Such freedom of movement shall entail the abolition of any discrimination based on nationality between workers of the Member States as regards employment, remuneration and other conditions of work and employment.

3. It shall entail the right, subject to limitations justified on grounds of public policy, public security or public health:

   (a) to accept offers of employment actually made;

   (b) to move freely within the territory of Member States for this purpose;

   (c) to stay in a Member State for the purpose of employment in accordance with the provisions governing the employment of nationals of that State laid down by law, regulation or administrative action;

   (d) to remain in the territory of a Member State after having been employed in that State, subject to conditions which shall be embodied in regulations to be drawn up by the Commission.

4. The provisions of this Article shall not apply to employment in the public service."

Under Article 46 TFEU the Council and the EP in accordance with the ordinary legislative procedure, and after consulting the Economic and Social Committee, are empowered to adopt measures implementing Article 45 TFEU. Article 46 TFEU particularly refers to measures:

■ ensuring liberalisation of the movement of workers, e.g. the abolition of administrative procedures, practices and of qualifying periods in respect of eligibility for available employment whether resulting from national legislation or from agreements previously concluded between Member States;

■ restricting free choice of employment by EU workers other than restrictions imposed on national workers;

■ ensuring close co-operation between national employment services; and,

■ ensuring the harmonious development of the EU employment market.

Article 47 TFEU is addressed to the Member States which shall take measures encouraging the exchange of young workers.

Article 48 TFEU made an important change to the manner in which harmonising legislation in social security matters for migrant workers and their dependants is adopted. The changes being that the ordinary legislative procedure became applicable with the result that a unanimous vote in the Council has been replaced by QMV and the EP has become a co-legislator. However, as legislation in social security matters may have important financial implications for Member States an "emergency brake" procedure is provided for in Article 48 TFEU. Accordingly, any Member State may request that a proposed measure be referred to the European Council if that State considers that it would affect important aspects of its social security system. Such referral entails suspension of the ordinary legislative procedure and gives the European Council four months to decide whether to refer the proposal back to the Council (in which case the suspension of the ordinary procedure ends) or take no action, or request the Commission to prepare a new proposal. In the latter two cases, the proposed measure is deemed not to have been adopted.

The most important secondary legislation adopted to give effect to the principle of the free movement of workers is:

- Directive 2004/38/EC of 29 April 2004 on the right of citizens of the European Union and their family members to move and reside freely within the territory of the Member States.[1894] The Directive, which is examined in detail in Chapter 22.4, consolidates much secondary legislation and introduces new solutions;

- Regulation 883/04 on the coordination of social security systems.[1895] This regulation co-ordinates national legislation on social security rights of persons who move within the EEA and Switzerland in order to guarantee that all migrants have an adequate level of social protection and do not lose social security benefits when they move to another Member State; and,

- Regulation 492/2011 of 5 April 2011 on the free movement of workers within the Union, which governs access to and conditions of employment.[1896]

The right of free movement of workers is not absolute. It suffers two exceptions expressly provided for in Article 45 TFEU; exceptions introduced in secondary legislation implementing Article 45 TFEU; and, exceptions developed by the ECJ.

The exceptions provided for in Article 45 TFEU are:

- restrictions on the free movement of workers may be justified on the grounds of public policy, public security and public health (Article 45(3) TFEU) (see Chapter 25.3); and,

- employment in the public service may be reserved to nationals of a host Member State (Article 45(4) TFEU) (see Chapter 25.2).

Secondary legislation contains further exceptions: e.g. Article 3(1) of Regulation 492/2011 allows a Member State to impose genuine linguistic requirements on EU migrant workers. Further, workers need to be appropriately qualified to take up and pursue employment in a host Member State. Conditions for recognition of professional qualifications of workers in a host Member State are examined in Chapter 24.8.

The exceptions based on the case law of the ECJ concern national measures which are indirectly discriminatory or which constitute non-discriminatory obstacles to the free movement of workers but substantially affect the exercise of that right. These exceptions are based on overriding reasons of public interest, and are allowed if they pursue legitimate aims compatible with the Treaties and comply with the requirements of the principle of proportionality.

1894. [2004] OJ L158/77.
1895. [2004] OJ L166/1. Regulation 883/04 was amended by Regulation 988/2009 and implemented by Regulation 987/2009. Both entered into force on 1 May 2010.
1896. [2011] OJ L 141/1. It replaced Regulation 1612/68 [1968] OJ L257/1.

23.2 Vertical and horizontal direct effect of Article 45 TFEU

Article 45 TFEU has been directly effective since the entry into force of Regulation 1612/68 which has been replaced by Regulation 492/2011.[1897] In Case 36/74 *Walrave and Koch*,[1898] the ECJ held that Article 45 TFEU is also horizontally directly effective.

THE FACTS WERE:

The rules of the Union Cycliste Internationale, an international sporting association which was neither a public body nor part of the State, imposed nationality requirements in respect of "pacemakers" and "stayers" in the world cycling championships.

Held:

The ECJ ruled that a nationality requirement was contrary to Article 45 TFEU since the prohibition of discrimination "does not only apply to the action of public authorities but extends likewise to rules of any nature aimed at regulating in a collective manner gainful employment and the provision of services".[1899]

Since the judgment in *Walrave and Koch* it has been clear that an individual can rely on Article 45 TFEU against public bodies, and associations or organisations not governed by public law such as the Union Cycliste Internationale whose rules regulate "in a collective manner gainful employment". However, for many years, it was uncertain whether an individual could rely on Article 45 TFEU against private persons. The matter was decided in Case C-281/98 *Angonese*,[1900] in which the ECJ held that Article 45 TFEU is horizontally directly effective in circumstances where a contract of employment between individuals imposes directly discriminatory restrictions, i.e. based on nationality.

THE FACTS WERE:

Mr Angonese, an Italian national whose mother tongue was German and who was resident in the Italian province of Bolzano, when applying for a job in a private bank in Bolzano was required to submit a certificate of bilingualism issued by the local authorities. When Mr Angonese's application was rejected because he did not submit the particular certificate even though he was totally bilingual and had other relevant linguistic qualifications, he argued that the requirement to evidence his linguistic knowledge solely by means of one particular certificate issued in a single province of a Member State was contrary to Article 45 TFEU.

1897. Case 48/75 *The State v Jean Noël Royer* [1976] ECR 497; Case 167/73 *Commission v France (Re French Merchant Seamen)* 1974 ECR 359.
1898. Case 36/74 *B.N.O. Walrave and L.J.N. Koch v Association Union Cycliste International and Others* [1974] ECR 359.
1899. Ibid, para. 17.
1900. Case C-281/98 *Angonese v Casa di Risparmio di Bolzano SpA* [2000] ECR I-4139.

> *Held:*
>
> *The ECJ held that the requirement imposed by the private bank was in breach of Article 45 TFEU. The ECJ stated that: "Limiting application of the prohibition of discrimination based on nationality to acts of a public authority risks creating inequality in its application."[1901] Thus, the prohibition of direct discrimination applies to both agreements intended to regulate paid labour collectively and agreements between individuals.*

It should be noted, that in respect of indirectly discriminatory conditions, i.e. based on factors other than nationality, and in respect of conditions which are non-discriminatory but prevent/hinder or create an obstacle to the exercise of the right set out in Article 45 TFEU, an individual cannot rely on that Article against another private party[1902] as this would constitute an unjustified interference in contractual freedom of private parties.

23.3 The scope of application *ratione personae* of Article 45 TFEU

The ECJ has given a broad interpretation to the personal scope of Article 45 TFEU. It applies not only to EU migrant workers and their families but also to other natural and legal persons. In Case C-350/96 *Clean Car Autoservice*,[1903] the ECJ held that employers can rely on Article 45 TFEU to employ workers in accordance with the rules governing freedom of movement of workers.

In Case C-208/05 *ITC*[1904] the issue was whether a private sector recruitment agency could rely on Article 45 TFEU.

> **THE FACTS WERE:**
>
> *Under German legislation persons entitled to claim unemployment benefit who had not found a job after three months of receiving such benefit were entitled to a recruitment voucher, which constituted an undertaking made by the German government to pay a private sector recruitment agency the amount stated on the voucher in a situation where the agency found employment for the voucher holder. The voucher specified that the holder must be placed in employment subject to compulsory social security contributions for a minimum of 15 hours per week. Under this scheme Mr Halacz, a voucher holder, instructed a German private sector recruitment agency, ITC, which found him employment in the Netherlands subject to compulsory social security contributions in the Netherlands and for more than 15 hours a week. When ITC asked the relevant German authority for payment under the recruitment voucher, this was rejected on the ground that Mr Halacz had not been placed in employment subject to compulsory social security contributions in Germany. ITC challenged the refusal before the German Social Court in Berlin, which referred for a preliminary ruling*

1901. Ibid, para. 33.
1902. Case C-94/07 *Raccanelli v Max-Planck-Gesellschaft zur Förderung der Wissenschaften eV* [2008] ECR I-5939.
1903. [1998] ECR I-2521.
1904. Case C-208/05 *ITC Innovative Technology Center* [2007] ECR I-181.

to the ECJ the question of compatibility of the German legislation with Articles 45 and 56 TFEU. One of the main issues was whether a private sector recruitment agency could rely on Article 45 TFEU.

Held:

The ECJ held that a private sector recruitment agency may, in some circumstances, rely on Article 45 TFEU.

Comment:

The ECJ, first, gave consideration to the natural and ordinary meaning of Article 45 TFEU and stated that nothing in the wording of that article indicates that persons other than workers may not rely upon it. This was not very convincing, since there was equally no mention of the possibility of persons other than workers relying on it. Second, the Court turned to schematic and teleological interpretation. It stated that bearing in mind that ITC acted as a mediator and intermediary between work-seekers and employers, and thus represented the applicant and sought employment on his behalf, it is possible that it could, in certain circumstances, rely on Article 45 TFEU. Consequently, the ECJ did not extend the scope of Article 45 TFEU to all activities of private sector recruitment agencies, but stated that in some circumstances they may be able to rely on the rights granted directly to workers by Article 45 TFEU – exactly how far the principle goes will depend on future case law.

23.4 The concept of a worker

There is no definition of a "worker" in the Treaties. As a result, it became the task of the ECJ to provide such definition. The Court has interpreted the concept of a worker broadly[1905] and has given it an autonomous EU meaning.

23.4.1 The objective criteria characterising the employment relationship

In Case 66/85 *Lawrie-Blum*,[1906] the ECJ held that a "worker" is a person who performs services of some economic value for and under the direction of another person, in return for which she/he receives remuneration.

THE FACTS WERE:

Deborah Lawrie-Blum, a British national, after successfully passing her examination for the teaching profession, was refused admission to the period of probationary service which had to be completed in order to become a teacher in Germany. During the probationary period a trainee teacher is considered as a civil servant and receives remuneration for conducting classes. Under the German law of Land Baden-Württemberg only German nationals were admitted to probationary service. Deborah Lawrie-Blum challenged the decision of the German authorities on the basis of Articles 18 and 45(2) TFEU. In response, the Land

---

1905. Case 53/81 *D.M. Levin v Staatssecretaris van Justitie* [1982] ECR 1053.
1906. Case 66/85 *Lawrie-Blum v Land Baden-Württemberg* [1986] ECR 2121.

contended, inter alia, *that a trainee teacher was not a "worker" within the meaning of Article 45 TFEU.*

Held:

The ECJ held that a trainee teacher who, under the direction and supervision of the school authorities, is undergoing a period of service in preparation for the teaching profession, during which she/he provides services by conducting classes and receives remuneration, is regarded as a "worker" under Article 45 TFEU irrespective of whether her/his employer is a private entity or a public body.[1907]

In the context of the organisation of an undertaking, the personal and property relations between spouses resulting from marriage do not exclude the existence of a relationship of subordination which is characteristic of an employment relationship. The ECJ held in Case C-337/97 *Meeusen*[1908] that a person who is related by marriage to the director and sole shareholder of the company for which she pursues an effective and genuine activity is classified as a "worker" within the meaning of Article 45 TFEU.

23.4.2 Two elements of the definition of a "worker"

Two elements of the definition of a "worker" are provided by the ECJ:

23.4.2.1 *Genuine and effective activity*

The first relates to the requirement that the activity performed by a worker must be genuine and effective.

The ECJ stressed in a number of cases that provided the activities performed are effective and genuine, a person should be considered as a worker even though such a person is not employed full-time or receives pay at a rate lower than for full-time employment. This is illustrated in Case 139/85 *Kempf.*[1909]

THE FACTS WERE:

Mr Kempf, a German part-time music teacher working in the Netherlands from 1981 to 1982, whose income was below the national minimum salary, received supplementary benefit in the form of sickness benefit and general assistance. When he applied for a residence permit in the Netherlands, his application was refused on the ground that his income was insufficient to meet his needs and that he was not a worker.

1907. See Case C-71/93 *Guido Van Poucke v Rijksinstituut voor de Sociale Verzekeringen der Zelfstandigen* [1994] ECR I-1101.

1908. Case C-337/97 *C.P.M. Meeusen v Hoofddirectie van de Informatie Beheer Groep* [1999] ECR I-3289.

1909. Case 139/85 *R. H. Kempf v Staatssecretaris van Justitie* [1986] ECR 1741.

> **Held:**
>
> The ECJ held that Kempf should be regarded as a worker, irrespective of the fact that he was employed on a part time-basis. The ECJ held that if the activity performed is effective and genuine, a person is a worker even though his salary is insufficient to support him and he has to rely on some other means to bring his income to subsistence level.

It is also irrelevant whether the money used to supplement the income is obtained from the individual's private means or from public funds.[1910] Further, a person who works occasionally, according to the needs of the employer,[1911] or within the framework of an apprenticeship contract,[1912] or a training contract,[1913] should be considered as a worker for the purposes of Article 45 TFEU.

In Case 3/87 *Agegate*,[1914] the ECJ held that fishermen paid only when the caught fish were sold were considered as workers as they performed activities which were effective and genuine.

If a person's work is so limited as to be marginal or ancillary,[1915] she/he will not be regarded as a worker. In order to distinguish between genuine and effective and marginal or ancillary employment, a national court should take into account the duration and the regularity of the activity concerned[1916] and factors, such as those set out by the ECJ in Case C-188/00 *Kurz*,[1917] are irrelevant. In *Kurz* the ECJ held that: "neither the *sui generis* nature of the employment relationship under national law, nor the level of productivity of the person concerned, the origin of the funds for which the remuneration is paid or the limited amount of remuneration can have any consequence in regard to whether or not the person is a worker".

23.4.2.2 Economic nature of activity

The second element concerns the requirement that a worker must perform activities of an economic nature.

In Case 344/87 *Bettray*,[1918] the ECJ held that participation in a drug rehabilitation scheme for which its participants were paid did not involve performance of economic activities, and therefore was outside the scope of Article 45 TFEU. However, a plumber working for a religious community who did not receive any remuneration but worked for his keep and some pocket money qualified as a worker, since he performed an effective and genuine activity of an economic nature.[1919]

In Case C-456/02 *Trojani*,[1920] the ECJ provided some indications as to how to decide whether the activities in question are of an economic nature.

1910. Case C-188/00 *Bülent Kurz, né Yüce v Land Baden-Württemberg* [2002] ECR I-10691.
1911. Case C-357/89 *V. J. M. Raulin v Minister van Onderwijs en Wetenschappen* [1992] ECR I-1027.
1912. Case C-27/91 *URSSAF v Hostellerie Le Manoir Sàrl* [1991] ECR I-5531.
1913. Case 66/85 *Deborah Lawrie-Blum v Land Baden-Württemberg* [1986] ECR 2121; Case C-109/04 *Karl Robert Kranemann v Land Nordrhein-Westfalen* [2005] ECR I-2421; Case C-10/05 *Cynthia Mattern and Hajrudin Cikotic v Ministre du Travail et de l'Emploi* [2006] ECR I-3145.
1914. Case 3/87 *R v Ministry of Agriculture, Fisheries and Food, ex parte Agegate Ltd* [1989] ECR 4459.
1915. Case 197/86 *Steven Malcolm Brown v The Secretary of State for Scotland* [1988] ECR 3205.
1916. Case C-357/89 *V. J. M. Raulin v Minister van Onderwijs en Wetenschappen* [1992] ECR I-1027.
1917. Case C-188/00 *Bülent Kurz, né Yüce v Land Baden-Württemberg* [2002] ECR I-10691, para. 31.
1918. Case 344/87 *I. Bettray v Staatssecretaris van Justitie* [1989] ECR 1621.
1919. Case 196/87 *Udo Steymann v Staatssecretaris van Justitie* [1988] ECR 6159.
1920. Case C-456/02 *Michel Trojani v CPAS* [2004] ECR I-7573.

THE FACTS WERE:

A destitute French national was given accommodation in a Salvation Army Hostel in Brussels and performed for the Salvation Army (SA), and under its direction, various jobs for approximately 30 hours a week, as part of a personal reintegration programme run by the SA. In return for this he received benefits in kind and some pocket money.

Held:

The ECJ decided that the referring court was better placed to answer the question whether Mr Trojani was a worker. However, the ECJ identified a number of factors which a national court should take into account when ascertaining whether the services actually performed by Mr Trojani were capable of being regarded as forming part of the normal labour market, in particular:

- the status and practices of the hostel;

- the content of the social reintegration programme; and,

- the nature and details of performance of the services.

In respect of activities involving sport, only those which are of an economic nature are within the scope of Article 45 TFEU. As a result, a professional football player[1921] or a cyclist or a coach[1922] are regarded as workers, while the selecting of national representatives did not involve any economic activities.[1923]

23.4.3 Persons sentenced to prison

With regard to persons sentenced to prison in a host Member State, in particular those who had worked before their conviction, the fact that they are not employed during their detention does not necessarily mean that they lose their status of workers. Indeed, they should continue to be regarded as workers within the meaning of Article 45 TFEU provided they find employment within a reasonable time after the end of their detention.[1924] In Joined Cases C-482/01 and C-493/01 *Orfanopoulos and Oliveri*[1925] the ECJ applied the above reasoning to Mr Orfanopoulos. He had worked in Germany before serving his prison sentence and was a worker within the meaning of Article 45 TFEU when in prison.

1921. Case C-415/93 *Union Royale Belge des Sociétés de Football Association ASBL v Jean-Marc Bosman, Royal Club Liégeois SA v Jean-Marc Bosman and Others and Union des Associations Européennes de Football (UEFA) v Jean-Marc Bosman* [1995] ECR I-4921.

1922. Case 36/74 *B.N.O. Walrave and L.J.N. Koch v Association Union Cycliste International and Others* [1974] ECR 1405.

1923. Case 13/76 *Gaetano Donà v Mario Mantero* [1976] ECR 1333; Case 36/74 *Walrave* ibid.

1924. Case C-340/97 *Ömer Nazli, Caglar Nazli and Melike Nazli v Stadt Nürnberg* [2000] ECR I-957.

1925. Joined Cases C-482/01 and C-493/01 *Georgios Orfanopoulos and Others v Land Baden-Württemberg and Raffaele Oliveri v Land Baden-Württemberg* [2004] ECR I-5257.

23.4.4 Persons who work for international organisations

When an EU national works in a host Member State for an international organisation, he/she is regarded as a worker.[1926]

23.4.5 Persons who are within the scope of Article 7(3) of Directive 2004/38

Article 7(3) of Directive 2004/38 provides that in the following situations certain categories of persons retain their status as workers or as self-employed persons:

1. When they are temporarily unable to work due to illness or accident;

2. When they are involuntarily unemployed after having been employed for more than one year and have been registered as work-seekers with the relevant employment office;

3. When they are involuntarily unemployed either after having completed a fixed-term contract of less than a year duration, or during the first twelve months of employment, and after having registered as work-seekers with the relevant employment office. However, they retain the status of worker for no less than six months;

4. When they embark on vocational training. However, this applies only to workers who become involuntarily unemployed and whose training is related to the previous employment (see Chapter 23.8).

23.4.6 Persons who are workers in one Member State and reside in another Member State

Article 45 TFEU applies to persons who retain their residence in a home Member State but commute to another Member State to work[1927] (usually a neighbouring Member State, but many EU workers from Central and Eastern European Member States retain their residence in their home Member State but work in one of the "old" Member States) and to persons who are employed in their home Member State but have transferred their residence to a host Member State. In Case C-212/05 *Hartmann*,[1928] the ECJ held that a German national who, while continuing his employment in Germany had transferred his residence to Austria, from where he commuted to work in Germany could claim the status of "worker" under EU law[1929] (see Chapter 23.7.3).

23.4.7 Termination of relationship of employment

Persons specified in Article 7(3) of Directive 2004/39 retain the status of worker in accordance with conditions specified in that provision after termination of a relationship of employment. Even if a

---

1926. Joined Cases 389/87 and 390/87 *G. B. C. Echternach and A. Moritz v Minister van Onderwijs en Wetenschappen* [1989] ECR 723; Case C-209/01 *Theodor Schilling and Angelica Fleck-Schilling v Finanzamt Nürnberg-Süd* [2003] ECR I-13389; Case C-293/03 *My v ONP* [2004] ECRI-12013; Case C-185/04 *Ulf Öberg v Försäkringskassan, länskontoret Stockholm* [2006] ECR I-1453; Case C-392/05 *Georgios Alevizos v Ypourgos Oikonomikon* [2007] ECR I-3505.

1927. Case C-213/05 *Wendy Geven v Land Nordrhein-Westfalen* [2007] ECR I-6347.

1928. Case C-212/05 *Gertraud Hartmann v Freistaat Bayern* [2007] ECR I-6303.

1929. See also Case C-287/05 *D. P.W. Hendrix v Raad van Bestuur van het Uitvoeringsinstituut Werknemersverzekeringen* [2007] ECR I-6909.

person loses his/her status as a worker that former status may produce certain effects in that it may give a former worker and his/her family entitlement to claim certain rights for example, in the field of financial assistance for university education[1930] or in respect of other forms of social assistance.[1931]

In Case C-291/05 *Eind*,[1932] the ECJ held that a third country national who was a member of the family of an EU worker, and who had not resided in the home Member State of the worker but joined him in a host Member State had the right, in the event of the worker returning to the home Member State of which he was a national, to entry and residence in the home Member State of the EU worker. This is even when the former EU worker did not carry on effective and genuine economic activities in the home Member State and even if he/she was a recipient of social assistance in the home Member State. It should also be noted that children and non-EU spouses of EU workers who have settled in a host Member State, in circumstances where an EU worker dies or departs the host Member State or divorces a non-EU spouse, have been granted important rights under Article 10 of Regulation 492/2011 (see Chapter 23.5.1).

23.4.8 Unemployed persons

In Case 48/75 *Royer*,[1933] the ECJ held that Article 45(3) TFEU included the right to enter a host Member State in search of work, although it did not fix any time-limit for such a search.[1934] It seems that a six-month period can be considered as a reasonable time for the purpose of seeking employment. This was implied from the ECJ's decision in Case C-292/89 *Antonissen*,[1935] in which the ECJ accepted that if after a six-month stay in a host Member State for the purpose of seeking employment an EU migrant had failed to find employment, a deportation order could be issued unless the migrant provided evidence that he/she was actively seeking employment and had a genuine chance of being employed. The law as stated in the above case is enshrined in Article 14(4)(b) of Directive 2004/38.

It should be noted that Article 7(3) of Directive 2004/38 confers the status of worker on persons who become involuntarily unemployed and satisfy the conditions specified in that provision. It also provides that those who are temporarily unemployed because of illness or accident[1936] retain their status as workers.

Additionally, in Case C-43/99 *Lecrere*,[1937] the ECJ classified a person who had lost employment, but was genuinely seeking work, as a worker. Based on the judgment of the ECJ in Joined Cases C-22/08 and C-23/08 *Vatsouras and Koupatantze*[1938] all work-seekers, who genuinely seek employment in a host Member State are workers within the meaning of Article 45 TFEU. This is in line with the broad interpretation by the ECJ of the concept of "worker", but sits uncomfortably with the idea that someone who has never worked in a host Member State may be classified as a worker. In the *Vatsouras* case,

---

1930. Case 39/86 *Lair v Universität Hannover* [1988] ECR 3161, see Chapter 23.8.
1931. Case C-35/97 *Commission v France* [1998] ECR I-5325, in this case Belgian frontier workers who had been placed in early retirement were entitled to receive a similar supplementary retirement pension to that granted to French workers.
1932. Case C-291/05 *Minister voor Vreemdelingenzaken en Integratie v R.N.G. Eind* [2007] ECR I-10719.
1933. Case 48/75 *The State v Jean Noel Royer* [1976] ECR 497.
1934. In Case C-344/95 *Commission v Belgium* ([1997] ECR I-1035) deportation of an unemployed person who had been seeking a job for only three months was regarded as contrary to Article 45 TFEU.
1935. Case C-292/89 *R v Immigration Appeal Tribunal, ex parte Antonissen* [1991] ECR I-745.
1936. Case 75/63 *Hoekstra v BBDA* [1964] ECR 177.
1937. Case C-43/99 *Ghislain Leclere and Alina Deaconescu v Caisse Nationale des Prestations Familiales* [2001] ECR I-4265, para. 55.
1938. Joined Cases C-22/08 and C-23/08 *Athanasios Vatsouras and Josif Koupatantze v Arbeitsgemeinschaft (ARGE) Nürnberg 900* [2009] ECR I-4585.

unemployed persons had previously been engaged in gainful activities, For example, Mr Vatsouras, who had worked in a host Member State for a very short time was not classified as a worker by the referring court, but seemed to satisfy the definition of a worker according to the A-G and the ECJ. In any event, he had been engaged in gainful employment in a host Member State before becoming unemployed. Whilst in the *Vatsouras* case the application of Article 45 TFEU to persons who had lost their jobs in a host Member State, but were effectively seeking new employment there, seems justified as such persons are midway between being a worker and a work-seeker, the inclusion of "pure" work-seekers within the definition of workers seems to push the limits of Article 45 TFEU too far. However, the generous interpretation by the ECJ of the concept of a worker is balanced by the fact that the ECJ has taken account of the legitimate interest of the host Member State to prevent abuses of its social assistance system by "benefit tourists" (see Chapter 23.7.3).

23.5 The family of a worker

Directive 2004/38 defined in its Article 2(2) who is to be regarded as a family of an EU citizen for the purpose of the exercise of the right to free movement and thus applies to EU migrant workers.

The rights of family members of a worker are parasitic on those of the worker. Accordingly, a family member of an EU national cannot rely on Article 45 TFEU until that EU national exercises his/her right to work in another Member State,[1939] and then only in the Member State where that national is employed. This is exemplified in Case C-10/05 *Mattern*.[1940]

THE FACTS WERE:

Mrs Mattern, a national of Luxembourg, and her husband Mr Cikotic, a national of a third country, were residing in Belgium where Mrs Mattern was taking a professional course, which, according to the ECJ, might have conferred on her the status of worker (it was for a national court to decide whether in the course of her professional training she was pursuing a genuine and effective activity). When Mr Cikotic applied for a work permit in Luxembourg, his application was refused.

Held:

The ECJ held that a national of a third country married to an EU national may rely on Article 45 TFEU only in a Member State where that EU national pursues an activity as an employed or self-employed person. Thus, whilst Mr Cikotic would have been entitled to a work permit in Belgium, he was not entitled to obtain it in Luxembourg while his wife was working in Belgium.

The family members of an EU worker, as defined in Directive 2004/38, irrespective of their nationality, who have the right of residence or permanent residence in a host Member State (see Chapter 22.4.1) are entitled to take up and pursue activities as an employed or a self-employed person in the

---

1939. Cases C-297/88 and 197/89 *Massam Dzodziv v Belgium* [1990] ECR I-3763; Joined Cases C-64 and 65/96 *Land Nordrhein-Westfalen v Kari Uecker and Vera Jacquet v Land Nordrhein-Westfalen* [1997] ECR I-3171.
1940. Case C-10/05 *Mattern and Cikotic v Ministre du Travail et de l'Emploi* [2006] ECR I-3145.

territory of that host Member State under the same conditions as nationals of the host Member State (Article 23 of Directive 2004/38). If their profession is regulated within the meaning of EU secondary legislation (see Chapter 24.8.1), and they satisfy the conditions for taking up or pursuing a professional activity in a regulated profession, a host Member State must recognise their professional qualification.[1941] Under Article 24 of Directive 2204/38 members of a family of an EU worker have the right to equal treatment with nationals of a host Member State, subject to derogations set out in Article 24(2) (see Chapter 22.4.3).

Secondary legislation and the case law of the ECJ have expanded the catalogue of rights conferred on children of EU workers and carers of such children who are not EU citizens in a situation where a parent who is an EU national ceased to be a worker within the meaning of EU law. This topic is examined below.

23.5.1 Children of a worker

Under Article 2(2)(c) of Directive 2004/38 direct descendants of an EU worker and his/her spouse/ partner who are under the age of 21 or above that age but still dependent (see Chapter 22.4.1) are regarded as children for the purpose of EU law. They enjoy not only the rights driving from their status of EU citizens (see Chapter 22.3) but also those specifically granted to children of workers under Article 10 of Regulation 492/2011. Under the latter children are entitled to admission to general education, apprenticeship and vocational training courses under the same conditions as nationals of a host Member State. In Case 76/72 *Michel S*[1942] the ECJ ruled that the list of educational arrangements for such children was not exhaustive. In this case a mentally handicapped son of a deceased Italian worker, who was employed in Belgium before his death, was entitled to rehabilitation benefits from a fund set up to assist people whose employment prospects were seriously affected by handicap. The ECJ based its ruling on Articles 7 and 10 of Regulation 492/2011.

Children of workers are entitled to general measures of support such as grants and loans.[1943] This is exemplified in Case C-308/89 *Di Leo,*[1944] in which the ECJ held that Germany was in breach of the principle of non-discrimination in a situation where German authorities refused a daughter of an Italian worker employed in Germany financial support provided under German law on the ground that the daughter studied in Italy.

In Case 42/87 *Commission v Belgium,*[1945] the ECJ held that children of migrant workers (including workers who have retired or died) are to be treated on an equal footing with children of national workers in respect of access to all forms of State education.

In Case C-413/99 *Baumbast*[1946] the ECJ held that, on the ground of Article 10 of Regulation 492/2011, children of an EU migrant worker who have settled in a host Member State are entitled to reside there in order to attend general educational courses irrespective of the facts that their parents have meanwhile divorced, only one parent is a citizen of the Union, and that parent has ceased to be a migrant worker in the host Member State. Accordingly, children of EU migrant workers have an independent right to residence in a host Member State until they terminate their education there. This is

---

1941. Case 131/85 *Emir Gül v Regierungspräsident Düsseldorf* [1986] ECR 1573.

1942. Case 76/72 *Michel S. v Fonds National de Reclassement Social des Handicapés* [1973] ECR 457.

1943. Case 9/74 *Donato Casagrande v Landeshauptstadt München* [1974] ECR 773; Case 68/74 *M. Angelo Alaimo v Préfet du Rhône* [1975] ECR 109.

1944. Case C-308/89 *Di Leo v Land of Berlin* [1990] ECR I-4185.

1945. [1988] ECR 5445.

1946. Case C-413/99 *Baumbast and R v Secretary of State for the Home Department* [2002] ECR I-7091.

so even though a child interrupts his/her study in a host Member State and subsequently returns there because it is impossible to continue studying in the home Member State.[1947]

In Case C-7/94 *Gaal*,[1948] the ECJ held that Article 10 of Regulation 492/2011 applies to children who are over 21 years of age and independent. The ECJ emphasised that it would be contrary to the letter and to the spirit of Article 10 to construe it in such a manner as to render students already at an advanced stage in their education ineligible for the financial assistance available in a host Member State upon reaching 21 years or as soon as they ceased to be dependent on their parents.

In Case C-310/08 *Ibrahim*[1949] the issue was whether a parent, who is a non-EU national and the primary carer of children, and whose spouse ceased to be a worker in a host Member State and who, on the authority of the *Baumbast* case, is allowed to reside in a host Member State during the period of his/her children's education, is required under EU law to have sufficient resources to avoid being a burden on the social support system of the host Member State. The ECJ held that solely on the basis of Article 10 of Regulation 492/2011 a parent can claim a right of residence in the host Member State without such a right being conditional on him/her having sufficient resources and comprehensive sickness insurance cover in the host Member State.

In Case C-480/08 *Teixeira*[1950] the issue was whether a non-EU parent who is primary carer of a child of a migrant worker who derives her right to residence in a host Member State from Article 10 of Regulation 492/2011 retains that right upon the child reaching the age of 18, thus coming of age under the law of the host Member State. The ECJ held that there is no age limit for the rights conferred on a child under Article 10 of Regulation 492/2011. As to a parent who is the primary carer, he/she retains the right of residence until the child has completed his or her education provided that the child continues to need the parent's presence and care after attaining the age of majority.

The above two cases have important implications on social welfare systems of the Member States. In both cases the reference was made to the ECJ in a situation where the relevant national authorities refused to grant to non-EU nationals, who were primary carers, social welfare benefits. In Case C-310/08 *Ibrahim*, the parent, who had never worked and who, after the departure of her husband from the host Member State, had been entirely dependent on social assistance and had no comprehensive sickness insurance cover for herself and for her four children applied for housing assistance for herself and her children. In Case C-480/08 *Teixeira*, the parent applied for housing assistance for homeless persons. It is clear from the ECJ's judgments in *Ibrahim* and *Teixeira* that in both cases the parents, as primary carers for children, will be entitled to the social benefits they sought.

23.6 The principle of non-discrimination and beyond

The legal situation of EU nationals working in a host Member State results not only from Article 45 TFEU and secondary legislation implementing that article, but also from a broad interpretation by the ECJ of the principle of non-discrimination which is expressly mentioned in Article 45(2) TFEU and which increases the strength of the general prohibition of discrimination set out in Article 18 TFEU.

1947. Joined Cases 389 and 390/87 *G. B. C. Echternach and A. Moritz v Minister van Onderwijs en Wetenschappen* [1989] ECR 723. See also Case 63/76 *Vito Inzirillo v Caisse d'Allocations Familiales de l'Arrondissement de Lyon* [1976] ECR 2057.

1948. Case C-7/94 *Landesamt für Ausbildungsförderung Nordrhein-Westfalen v Lubor Gaal* [1996] ECR I-1031.

1949. C-310/08 *London Borough of Harrow v Nimco Hassan Ibrahim and Secretary of State for the Home Department* [2010] ECR I-1065.

1950. Case C-480/08 *Maria Teixeira v London Borough of Lambeth, and Secretary of State for the Home Department* [2010] ECR I-1107.

The main role of the principle of non-discrimination is to ensure equality in treatment between a national worker and a migrant worker as regards employment, remuneration and other conditions of work and employment.

23.6.1 The prohibition of direct and indirect discrimination

Not only direct discrimination based on nationality, but also indirect discrimination based on other factors, is prohibited. This was examined by the ECJ in Case 15/69 *Ugliola*.[1951]

THE FACTS WERE:

Ugliola, an Italian national employed in Germany, challenged German legislation which provided that military service in the Bundeswehr (German army) should be taken into account in calculating seniority in employment. Ugliola had performed military service in Italy some time before being employed in Germany. He argued that by not including similar provision for service in armies of other Member States, German legislation was in breach of the principle of non-discrimination. The German government submitted that its legislation was not discriminatory since it applied to any national of any Member State who served in the Bundeswehr and did not apply to any German national who performed his military service in other Member States.

Held:

The ECJ held that the likelihood of a national of other Member States serving in the Bundeswehr was more hypothetical than real. Consequently, German legislation indirectly discriminated against nationals from other Member States working in Germany.

The principle of non-discrimination requires not only that the same rules are applicable to similar situations but also, conversely, that different situations are treated differently. The case law of the ECJ shows that Article 45(2) TFEU prohibits all forms of indirect discrimination which, by applying distinguishing criteria other than nationality (such as residence), have in practice the same discriminatory result. However, in certain circumstances indirectly discriminatory rules may be justified as was the Case 152/73 *Sotgiu*.[1952]

THE FACTS WERE:

Indirect discrimination in respect of a separation allowance was claimed by an Italian worker whose family lived in Italy but who was employed by the German postal service in Germany. Under German law a separation allowance of DM10 per day was paid (if relevant) to workers residing within Germany at the time of their recruitment, while workers of German nationality as well as workers from other Member States received an allowance of DM7.50 per day if at the time of their recruitment they resided abroad. Sotgiu relied on Article 7(1) of Regulation

---

1951. Case 15/69 *Württembergische Milchverwertung-Südmilch v Ugliola* [1969] ECR 363.
1952. Case 152/73 *Sotgiu v Deutsche Bundespost* [1974] ECR 153.

492/2011 and the principle of non-discrimination to challenge the different amounts of the separation allowance. During the proceedings it became clear that workers residing in Germany at the time of their recruitment received the larger allowance under two conditions: the payment was conditional upon their willingness to move to their place of work and it was limited to the first two years of employment. Neither condition applied to workers who resided abroad at the time of their recruitment.

Held:

The ECJ held that the application of criteria other than nationality, in this case the place of residence at the time of recruitment, could in certain circumstances have a discriminatory result in practice. This would not be the case when the payment of a separation allowance was made on conditions which took into consideration objective differences in the situations of workers, which differences could concern the place of residence of workers at the time of their recruitment. The Court also stated that the difference in amount paid to both groups of workers could be objectively justified, taking into account that one group of workers received an allowance temporarily while for the other group it was of unlimited duration.

Rules of national law, which although indistinctly applicable to both national workers and migrant EU workers (that is, they make no distinction based on nationality) which essentially affect only migrant workers[1953] or the majority of them,[1954] are considered as indirectly discriminatory.

23.6.2 Beyond discrimination

In Case C-415/93 *Bosman*,[1955] the ECJ examined national rules which were not discriminatory directly or indirectly, but which constituted an obstacle to the free movement of workers.

THE FACTS WERE:

Belgian football player transfer rules, which were in conformity with the rules of international football organisations, provided that a club which sought to engage a player had to pay a specified sum of money to the player's existing club. The rules applied irrespective of the nationality of a player and irrespective of whether the transfer took place between clubs in the same country or between clubs located in different countries. Bosman, a Belgian player, wished to move from a Belgian club to a French club but was prevented from doing this because his Belgian club refused to accept a transfer fee from the French club.

1953. Case 41/84 *Pietro Pinna v Caisse d'allocations familiales de la Savoie* [1986] ECR 1; Case 33/88 *Pilar Allué and Carmel Mary Coonan and others v Università degli studi di Venezia and Università degli studi di Parma* [1989] ECR 1591.

1954. Case C-272/92 *Maria Chiara Spotti v Freistaat Bayern* [1993] ECR I-5185.

1955. Case C-415/93 *Union Royale Belge des Sociétés de Football Association ASBL v Jean-Marc Bosman, Royal Club Liégeois SA v Jean-Marc Bosman and Others and Union des Associations Européennes de Football (UEFA) v Jean-Marc Bosman* [1995] ECR I-4921.

> *Held:*
>
> The ECJ held that the Belgian rules:
>
> 1. *Constituted an obstacle to freedom of movement of workers;*
>
> 2. *Directly affected players' access to the labour market in other Member States and thus were capable of impeding freedom of movement of workers;*
>
> 3. *Could not be objectively justified.*

The ECJ confirmed the above approach in Case C-18/95 *Terhoeve*.[1956] It stated that it was not necessary to examine whether the challenged Dutch legislation (requiring higher social security contributions to be paid by workers who transferred their residence in the course of a year from one Member State to another in order to take up employment there, compared to contributions which would be payable by workers who continued to reside throughout the year in the same Member State) was indirectly discriminatory. It constituted an obstacle to the free movement of workers because it had deterred a national of a Member State from leaving his country of origin in order to exercise his right to freedom of movement in another country.

National rules which are not discriminatory but nevertheless substantially restrict access to the labour market of a Member State or the exercise of the right to free movement can be justified only if they are based on objective considerations, independent of nationality, and are proportionate to the aim legitimately pursued by the national law.[1957] It is to be noted that the concept of objective justification was developed by the ECJ itself, in the absence of any explicit provision in the Treaties.

The prohibition of all national provisions which hinder the free movement of workers, even if these provisions apply without discrimination, raised the question of whether there is a need to impose some limitations on the scope of application of Article 45 TFEU in order to avoid it becoming a "catch all" provision. This matter was clarified in Case C-190/98 *Graf*.[1958]

THE FACTS WERE:

Mr Graf, an Austrian national who had been employed by Filzmoser since 1992, terminated his contract of employment in 1996 in order to move to Germany to take up new employment. Filzmoser refused to pay Mr Graf compensation equal to two months' salary on termination of employment. Filzmoser relied on Article 23(7) of the Austrian Law on Employees (Angestelltengesetz) under which an employee is not entitled to compensation if he gives notice, leaves prematurely for no important reason or bears responsibility for premature dismissal. Mr Graf challenged this provision as contrary to Article 45(2) TFEU, which prohibits national rules precluding or deterring a worker from ending his contract of employment in order to take a job in another Member State, and invoked Article 23(1) of the above-mentioned

---

1956. Case C-18/95 *F.C. Terhoeve v Inspecteur van de Belastingdienst Particulieren/Ondernemingen buitenland* [1999] ECR I-345.

1957. Case C-15/96 *Schöning-Kougebetopoulou* [1998] ECR I-47; Case C-224/01 *Köbler v Austria* [2003] ECR I-10239; Case C-464/02 *Commission v Denmark* [2005] ECR I-7929; Case C-109/04 *Kranemann* [2005] ECR I-2421; Case C-208/05 *ITC Innovative Technology Center* [2007] ECR I-181.

1958. C-190/98 *Volker Graf and Filzmoser Maschinenbau GmbH* [2000] ECR I-493.

Austrian law which provided that: "If the employment relationship has continued uninterruptedly for three years, the employee shall be entitled to a compensation payment on termination of that relationship." The referring court was uncertain as to the implication of the decision of the ECJ in Bosman *on the above situation.*

Held:

The ECJ confirmed its decision in Bosman. *It held that Article 45 TFEU applies to national rules which impede the free movement of persons and are indistinctly applicable to both national workers and EU migrant workers. In this respect, the Austrian court had clearly established that Article 23(7) of the Austrian Law on Employees was not discriminatory as it neither restricted cross-border mobility to a greater extent than mobility within Austria, nor was the loss of compensation equal to two months' salary on termination of employment such as to result in a perceptible restriction on the freedom of movement for workers.*

Comment:

The ECJ assessed the effect of the contested Austrian legislation on access to the labour market. In Bosman *the impact of the rules of the Belgian Football Association on access to the labour market was considerable, taking into account the amount of penalty payment. In this case the situation was different. As the ECJ pointed out, not only the small amount of compensation, but also the fact that the entitlement to compensation was not dependent on the worker choosing whether or not to continue his employment, but on a future and hypothetical event led the ECJ to conclude that "such an event is too uncertain and indirect a possibility for legislation to be capable of being regarded as liable to hinder freedom of movement of workers where it does not attach to termination of a contract of employment by the worker himself the same consequences as it attaches to termination which was not at his initiative or is not attributable to him".*[1959]

This solution avoids all inconveniences deriving from the application of the Keck approach to the area of free movement of workers (see Chapter 20.5.2). Thus, non-discriminatory national rules are outside the scope of Article 45 TFEU when they do not substantially hinder access to the labour market, but they are within the scope of this provision when they do substantially hinder the free movement of workers, as evidenced by Case C-415/93 Bosman.

23.7 Rights granted to workers and their families under Regulation 492/2011

The principle of equal treatment laid down in Article 45 TFEU applies to all aspects of employment including eligibility, remuneration, and other conditions of employment. Regulation 492/2011 gives substance to the requirements of Article 45 TFEU. In accordance with the case law of the ECJ, Regulation 492/2011 prohibits not only direct and indirect discrimination, but also national measures which substantially prevent/restrict, or create an obstacle to, the free movement of workers. Thus, the term "discrimination" has a broad meaning.

1959. Ibid, para. 25.

23.7.1 Eligibility for employment

Articles 1 to 6 of Regulation 492/2011 prohibit any discrimination against EU migrant workers in respect of access to employment.

Article 1 guarantees to EU migrant workers the right to take up available employment, and pursue it, in the territory of a host Member State under the same conditions as nationals of that Member State.

Article 2 prohibits all discrimination against EU migrant workers with regard to the conclusion and performance of their employment contracts.

Article 3 provides that national provisions and practices, which limit the right to seek or to pursue employment, or which impose on migrant EU workers conditions not applicable to nationals, are inapplicable. However, Article 3(1) allows a Member State to impose conditions "relating to linguistic knowledge required by reason of the nature of the post to be filled". Article 3(1) was relied upon by the Irish government in Case 379/87 *Groener*.[1960]

THE FACTS WERE:

Irish legislation required that appointment to a permanent full-time post as a lecturer in public vocational schools in Ireland was conditional upon proficiency in Gaelic. On this basis Mrs Groener, a Dutch national, was refused a full-time post as an art teacher after she had failed a test intended to assess her knowledge of the Gaelic language.

Held:

The ECJ held that although knowledge of Gaelic was not required for the performance of the duties of teaching art in Ireland, the requirement was not in breach of Article 3(1) of Regulation 492/2011 as it was a part of a national policy for the promotion of the national language and therefore constituted a means of expressing national identity and language in the Irish Republic. It was also non-discriminatory, and not disproportionate to the objective pursued.

Under Article 4 of Regulation 492/2011 Member States must not restrict the employment of EU migrant workers by number or percentage. The leading case on this is Case 167/73 *Commission v France [Re French Merchant Seamen]*.[1961]

THE FACTS WERE:

The 1926 French Maritime Code set a ratio of three French to one non-French nationals for the employment of merchant seamen in the crew of French merchant ships. The justification submitted by the French Government was that the requirement was not used in practice, as oral instructions were given to appropriate national authorities not to apply it.

1960. Case 379/87 *Anita Groener v Minister for Education and the City of Dublin Vocational Educational Committee* [1989] ECR 3967.
1961. [1974] ECR 359.

> **Held:**
>
> *The ECJ condemned the French Maritime Code. It ruled that non-application of the requirement was a matter of grace, not of law, and thereby created uncertainty for all parties concerned.*

Under Article 5 of Regulation 492/2011 Member States must offer EU migrant workers the same assistance in seeking employment as is available to nationals.

Article 6 of the Regulation provides that the engagement or recruitment of a national of one Member State for a post in another Member State should not depend on medical, vocational or other criteria which are discriminatory as compared with those applied to national workers. However, when an employer actually offers a job to a national of another Member State, it may be on the express condition that the candidate undergoes a vocational test.

23.7.2   Employment and equality of treatment

Articles 7–9 of Regulation 492/2011 require a host Member State to ensure that EU migrant workers:

- ▪ are treated in the same way as national workers in respect of any condition of employment and work, in particular as regards remuneration, dismissal and, should they become unemployed, reinstatement or re-employment (Article 7(1));

- ▪ enjoy the same social and tax advantages (Article 7(2)) as its nationals. This provision has been broadly interpreted by the ECJ so as to become a source of important rights conferred on EU migrant workers, their families, and work-seekers;

- ▪ have the same access to vocational training as its nationals (Article 7(3));

- ▪ enjoy the same treatment as its nationals as regards membership of and participation in trade unions (Article 8); and,

- ▪ have the same access to all rights and benefits in matters of housing as its nationals (Article 9).

Article 7(4) provides that any provision in collective or individual employment agreements or in any other collective regulation concerning eligibility for employment, employment, remuneration and other conditions of work and dismissal which discriminates against EU migrant workers shall be null and void.[1962]

23.7.3   Social advantages

Article 7(2) of Regulation 492/2011 provides that a migrant worker "shall enjoy the same social and tax advantages as national workers".

The ECJ defined social advantages in Case 207/78 *Even*[1963] as covering all advantages:

> "which, whether or not linked to a contract of employment, are generally granted to national workers primarily because of their objective status as workers or by virtue of the mere fact of their residence in the national territory."

1962.   See Case C-400/02 *Gerard Merida v Germany* [2004] ECR I-8471.

1963.   Case 207/78 *Criminal Proceedings against Gilbert Even et Office National des Pensions pour Travailleurs Salariés (ONPTS)* [1979] ECR 2019, para. 22.

Social advantages are different from social security benefits.[1964] Entitlement to social security benefits is governed by Regulation 883/04. The ECJ has consistently held that Member States are competent to define the conditions for granting social security benefits, provided that the conditions are not directly or indirectly discriminatory against EU migrant workers.[1965]

Each Member State determines what benefits should be regarded as social advantages. For that reason they vary from one Member State to another. However, it is ultimately for the ECJ to determine the real nature of a particular benefit. The case law of the ECJ shows that Article 7(2) has bestowed a wide range of benefits upon workers and their families. Some examples are:

- In Case 65/81 *Reina*,[1966] an Italian couple residing in Germany obtained an interest-free discretionary loan on the birth of their child, which was payable only to German nationals living in Germany. These loans were an incentive to increase the birth rate in Germany and were granted by a credit institution set up under public law.

- In Case 137/84 *Mutsch*,[1967] the use of one's own language in national judicial proceedings was considered as being a social benefit.

- In Case 157/84 *Frascogna*,[1968] an Italian widow, living with her son in France, was entitled to an old-age pension falling outside the scope of the national social security rules.

- In Case C-237/94 *O'Flynn*, an Irish national working in the UK successfully claimed expenses incurred in connection with the costs of burying his son in Ireland. Under UK legislation the funeral payment was granted to workers and EU migrant workers alike if the burial or cremation took place within the UK. The ECJ held that this condition was indirectly discriminatory and could not be objectively justified. However, the Court agreed with the UK that the cost of transporting the coffin to Ireland had to be met by the applicant given that this benefit was not available to UK workers.[1969]

- In Case 32/75 *Cristini*,[1970] an Italian worker's widow living in France claimed the special fare reduction card issued by the French Railways to the parents of large families. The ECJ held that since the family was entitled to remain in France after the worker's death and that the card was available to the families of deceased French workers, it should not be denied to the families of deceased workers from other Member States.

- In Case 63/76 *Inzirillo*,[1971] an Italian national working in France obtained a disability allowance for his adult son.

- In Case 261/83 *Castelli*,[1972] an Italian widow living with her retired son in Belgium obtained a guaranteed income paid to old people in Belgium.

1964. Case 1/72 *Frilli v Belgium* [1972] ECR 457.

1965. Case C-12/93 *Bestuur van de Nieuwe Algemene Bedrijfsvereniging v V. A. Drake* [1994] ECR I-4337; Case C-320/95 *José Ferreiro Alvite v Inem and INSS* [1999] ECR I-951; Case C-306/03 *Cristalina Salgado Alonso v INSS and TGSS* [2005] ECR I-705.

1966. Case 65/81 *Francesco Reina and Letizia Reina v Landeskreditbank Baden-Württemberg* [1982] ECR 33.

1967. Case 137/84 *Criminal Proceedings against Robert Heinrich Maria Mutsch* [1985] ECR 2681.

1968. Case 157/84 *Maria Frascogna v Caisse des Dépôts et Consignations* [1985] ECR 1739.

1969. Case C-237/94 *John O'Flynn v Adjudication Officer* [1996] ECR I-2617.

1970. Case 32/75 *Anita Cristini v Société Nationale des Chemins de Fer Français* [1975] ECR 1085.

1971. Case 63/76 *Vito Inzirillo v Caisse d'Allocations Familiales de l'Arrondissement de Lyon* [1976] ECR 2057.

1972. Case 261/83 *Carmela Castelli v ONPTS* [1984] ECR 3199.

■ In Case 3/90 *Bernini*,[1973] the ECJ held that a study grant should be classified as a social benefit within the meaning of Article 7(2) of Regulation 492/2011. As a result, a dependent child of a migrant EU worker was entitled to obtain study finance under the same conditions as were applicable to children of national workers (see Chapter 23.5.1).

■ In Case 235/87 *Matteucci*,[1974] the ECJ ruled that a scholarship to study abroad, which was part of a reciprocal agreement between Belgium and Germany, should be granted to the son of an Italian worker, employed in Belgium, who wanted to study in Germany.

Entitlements to social benefits under Article 7(2) of Regulation 492/2011 of two categories of persons, i.e. work-seekers and those who are workers but resident in a Member State other than the Member State of employment, have raised difficulties. This matter is examined below.

A. **Work-seekers.** As to the entitlement of work-seekers to social advantages in a host Member State, Article 24(2) of Directive 2004/38 expressly states that a host Member State is not obliged to confer entitlement to social assistance during the first three months of residence of a work-seeker in that State, or where appropriate, the longer period of residence. This provision clashes with the case law of the ECJ prior to the entry into force of the Directive. In Case C-138/02 *Collins*,[1975] the ECJ held that in the light of the establishment of the concept of EU citizenship, it was no longer possible to exclude from the scope of Article 45(2) TFEU a benefit of a financial nature intended to facilitate access to employment in the labour market of a Member State in a situation where there is a genuine link between the person seeking work and the employment market of that Member State. A residence requirement is, in principle, appropriate for the purpose of ensuring such a link, if it is proportionate and does not go beyond what is necessary in order to attain that objective. In Joined Cases C-22/08 and C-23/08 *Vatsouras and Koupatantze*,[1976] the ECJ was asked to clarify its position on the entitlement of work-seekers to benefits of a financial nature intended to facilitate access to the labour market in a host Member State in the light of Article 24(2) of Directive 2004/38. The ECJ made the following findings:

■ First, nationals of a Member State seeking employment in another Member State are within the scope of Article 45 TFEU and therefore enjoy the right to equal treatment laid down in Article 45(2) TFEU;[1977]

■ Second, benefits of a financial nature, which are intended to facilitate access to the labour market in a host Member State cannot be regarded as constituting "social assistance" within the meaning of Article 24(2) of Directive 2004/38, but must be regarded as falling within the scope of Article 45(2) TFEU, i.e. they are social benefits; and,

■ Third, when an EU national can demonstrate a link with the labour market of a host Member State, he can rely on Article 45(2) TFEU and Article 7(2) of Regulation 492/2011 to receive a benefit of a financial nature intended to facilitate access to the labour market in that host Member State.

1973. Case 3/90 *M. J. E. Bernini v Minister van Onderwijs en Wetenschappen* [1992] ECR I-1071.

1974. Case 235/87 *Annunziata Matteucci v Communauté française of Belgium and Commissariat Général aux Relations Internationales of the Communauté Française of Belgium* [1988] ECR 5589.

1975. Case C-138/02 *Brian Francis Collins v Secretary of State for Work and Pensions* [2004] ECR I-2703.

1976. Joined Cases C-22/08 and C-23/08 *Athanasios Vatsouras and Josif Koupatantze v Arbeitsgemeinschaft (ARGE) Nürnberg 900* [2009] ECR I- 4585.

1977. Case C-258/04 *Office national de l'Emploi v Ioannis Ioannidis* [2005] ECR I-8275, para. 21.

On the basis of the above, it is submitted that when a work-seeker has never worked in a host Member State, such as was the situation of the applicant in Case C-292/89 *Antonissen*, [1978] no real and genuine link can be established between the applicant and the labour market of a host Member State. However, the situation is different where a person has lost his job in a host Member State and is effectively seeking new employment there. Such a person is likely to have established a genuine link with the labour market of the host Member State. In the *Vatsouras* Case, there was an issue of whether Mr Vatsouras and Mr Koupatantze were workers within the meaning of Article 45 TFEU. According to the referring court they were not workers because Mr Vatsouras had worked in a low-paid job for less than a year whilst Mr Koupatantze worked only for two months before he became involuntarily unemployed. A-G Ruiz-Jarabo Colomer disagreed with the assessment of the referring court. The ECJ strongly hinted that the applicants were workers. If so, under Article 7(3) of Directive 2004/38 they retained their status of workers and were therefore, entitled to protection under Article 45 TFEU. Irrespective of whether they were workers or not, as work-seekers, they were within the scope of Article 45 TFEU. Further, as both had been in gainful employment in the host Member State prior to their unemployment, and were genuinely seeking employment, which was demonstrated by both finding new jobs and no longer being in need of social assistance, they were likely to have established a genuine link with the host Member State labour market.

It is submitted that in the above case, the ECJ reached the right balance between, on the one hand, protecting a Member State from "benefit tourists" and on the other, encouraging integration of EU nationals into the labour market of a host Member State. The use of the criterion of a "genuine link" in a flexible manner, i.e. by taking account of factors such as the time of residence, previous employment, etc, in a host Member State, allows the ECJ to assist those who are not "benefit tourists".

B. **Entitlement to social benefits of EU workers who work in one Member State while residing in another Member State.** Persons who work in one Member State and return to a home Member State on a daily basis or at least once a week are usually defined as cross-border, or frontier, workers.[1979] There are also workers who work in one Member State but whose families live permanently in a home Member State, and the distance between the two Member States makes it economically difficult for such persons to return home every week. In this context, the question arises of how to reconcile the requirements of the free movement of workers with the traditional approach of the Member State to grant social advantages only to those residing within its territory. Should social advantages be exportable? In a number of cases the ECJ has stated its position on this matter. The ECJ used the concept of "a real link" to decide whether the degree of integration with the society of the paying Member State justifies the entitlement of a claimant to a particular social benefit. The case law of the ECJ indicates that "a real link" is not necessarily created by residence in a Member State in that other factors such as employment may create "a real link". However, the type and degree of social integration required by a paying Member State is assessed in the light of the principle of proportionality.

1978. Case C-292/89 *R v Immigration Appeal Tribunal, ex parte Antonissen* [1991] ECR I-745.

1979. According to the report of G. Nerb, there are some 780,000 cross- border workers in the EU/EEA. See G. Nerb, et al., "Scientific Report on the Mobility of Cross-Border Workers within the EU-27/EEA/EFTA Countries", p. VII, 16–27 available at: http://ec.europa.eu/social/BlobServlet?d ocId=3459&langId=en (accessed 2/8/12).

In Case C-212/05 *Hartmann*,[1980] the ECJ held that a person who works in one Member State whilst residing in another Member State is a worker within the meaning of Article 45 TFEU. In this case Mrs Hartmann, an Austrian national, married a German national who worked in Germany, but resided with her and their children in Austria. She claimed a child raising allowance from the German authorities. Her application was refused on the ground of her residence in Austria. The ECJ held that Mr Hartman was an EU worker despite the fact that he was working in his home Member State and that a family member of a worker could claim social benefits under Article 7(2) of Regulation 492/2011. The ECJ found that the child allowance was a social benefit and that Mrs Hartmann was entitled to it. Accordingly, the ECJ have interpreted broadly Article 7(2) of Regulation 492/2011. There was a real link between Mr Hartmann and his home Member State as he had made a substantial contribution to the German economy, being a full-time employee. This is to be contrasted with Case C0213/05 *Geven*,[1981] in which Mrs Geven, a Dutch national who lived in the Netherlands with her husband who worked there, after the birth of their son took part-time employment in Germany (3–14 hours per week). When she claimed a child raising allowance in Germany, her claim was refused on the ground of, *inter alia*, her residence in the Netherlands. The ECJ accepted that there was a link between Mrs Geven and a host Member State based on her employment, but decided that the link was not sufficient due to the marginal nature of her work. Accordingly, she was not entitled to the German child allowance benefit.

In Case C-287/05 *Hendrix*[1982] the ECJ created a presumption that when a Member State refuses to grant non-exportable social benefit such refusal is unlawful unless objectively justified and proportionate to the objective pursued. In this case a Dutch national, employed in a DIY store in the Netherlands, a recipient of a non-exportable incapacity benefit granted to disabled young people working in the Netherlands, was refused that benefit when he moved to Belgium, but continued working in the Netherlands. The ECJ found that Mr Hendrix was a worker within the meaning of Article 45 TFEU and the incapacity benefit was within the scope of Article 7(2) of Regulation 492/2011. The ECJ found that the criterion of residence was indirectly discriminatory and thus was allowed only if objectively justified and proportional to the objective pursue by the paying Member State. The ECJ left it to the referring court to decide whether the residence requirement was proportionate to achieve the legitimate objective pursued by the national legislation. However, the ECJ stated that the assessment must take account of the fact that Mr Hendrix had maintained all of his economic and social links with his Member State of origin.

In Case C-542/09 *Commission v the Netherlands*,[1983] the ECJ further clarified the entitlement to social benefits of families of EU cross-border workers and workers whose families permanently reside in another Member State.

1980. Case C-212/05 *Gertraud Hartmann v Freistaat Bayern* [2007] ECR I-6303.
1981. Case C-213/05 *Wendy Geven v Land Nordrhein-Westfalen* [2007] ECR I-6347.
1982. Case C-287/05 *D. P. W. Hendrix v Raad van Bestuur van het Uitvoeringsinstituut Werknemersverzekeringen* [2007] ECR I-6909.
1983. Judgment of 14/6/12 (NYR).

THE FACTS WERE:

Under Dutch law in order to qualify for funding (the so called "portable funding") to study outside the Netherlands EU citizens economically active in the Netherlands, and in fact, their families were required to reside there. This was because Dutch law stated that prospective students had to reside lawfully in the Netherlands during the last three out of six years preceding enrolment at an educational establishment abroad (hereafter referred to as the three out of six years rule). This requirement applied irrespective of the nationality of the prospective students. The Commission argued that the residency requirement amounted to indirect discrimination against EU migrant workers and was even more discriminatory for frontier workers and their children, who, by definition, reside in a Member State other than the Member State of employment and cannot possibly satisfy the "three out of six years" rule. Accordingly Dutch legislation was in breach of Article 7(2) of Regulation 492/2011 and/ or Article 45 TFEU.

Held:

The ECJ held that the portable funding constituted a social advantage within the meaning of Article 7(2) TFEU. The requirement of residency was indirectly discriminatory and as such could be objectively justified. However, even if objectively justified it must also be proportionate to the objective pursued by national legislation. The ECJ accepted the justification based on the objective of encouraging student mobility but found that the requirement of residency was disproportionate as it was too exclusive. In this respect the Court stated: "By requiring specific periods of residence in the territory of the Member State concerned, the 'three out of six years' rule prioritises an element which is not necessarily the sole element representative of the actual degree of attachment between the party concerned and that Member State."[1984]

Comment:

The government of the Netherlands submitted two justifications for the existence of the "three out of six years" rule. First, it argued that the residency requirement was appropriate in order to avoid unreasonable burden being imposed on State finances. The ECJ ruled that this justification could not constitute an overriding reason relating to the public interest because the residency requirement was inappropriate so far as EU migrant workers and their families were concerned. The link of sufficient integration with the society of the paying Member State was satisfied by EU migrant workers and cross-border workers by virtue of their employment in that Member State. They contribute to the financing of social policies of the Member State of their employment and therefore should benefit from those policies on the same terms as nationals of that State.

Second, the government of the Netherlands argued that the objective of encouraging student mobility constituted an overriding reason relating to the public interest justifying the imposition of the three out of six years rule. The rule aimed at encouraging the mobility of a particular group of students, i.e. students residing in the Netherlands who otherwise would pursue their education there and who were likely to return to the Netherlands after completing their studies abroad to work and reside there. The ECJ accepted that the residence

---

1984.   Ibid, para. 86.

requirement was appropriate to attain the objective of promoting student mobility. However, the Netherlands did not show that the requirement was proportionate, i.e did not show why it opted for the "three out of six years" rule. According to the ECJ, without proper justification, the requirement was too exclusive and thus disproportionate to the objective pursued by the Netherlands.

It is submitted that the concept of a "real link" reconciles the interest of a paying Member State to protect its welfare system by limiting its social solidarity obligation to those EU citizens who have sufficient connections with that Member State, with the necessity of ensuring the full effectiveness of the right to equal treatment for EU citizens who exercise their right to free movement. It avoids an "all or nothing" approach to entitlements to social benefits for EU citizens who have multiple horizontal relationships with several Member States. It is well suited to the lifestyle of many EU citizens in terms of their working, living and educational arrangements. It allows a flexible examination of the types and degree of social integration of EU citizens with the society of the paying Member State whilst ensuring that national restrictions satisfy the requirements of the principle of proportionality.[1985]

23.7.4 Tax advantages

Bearing in mind that there is no harmonisation of direct taxation at EU level, EU migrant workers may find themselves bearing an increased taxation burden as a result of moving to another Member State or may, depending upon circumstances, benefit from disparities in the tax legislation of the Member States.[1986]

In order to alleviate the disadvantages deriving from the lack of harmonisation of national taxation legislation the Member States have entered into bilateral double taxation conventions. Accordingly, EU citizens will not normally be subjected to double taxation. However, this matter is within the exclusive competence of a Member State and thus a Member State is not required under EU law to eliminate double taxation.[1987] Theoretically, double taxation would constitute a non-discriminatory barrier to the exercise of the right to free movement under Article 45 TFEU but, being an inevitable consequence of a Member State's tax sovereignty, can only be eliminated by harmonising measures. For that reason, the ECJ has a difficult task to reconcile, on the one hand, the requirements of the free movement of workers, and on the other, the need to take account of disparities of national taxation legislation and their legitimate objectives of combating tax evasion and tax avoidance by dishonest EU citizens.

In Case C-279/93 *Schumacker,*[1988] the ECJ emphasised that differences in treatment of taxpayers are allowed under EU law, provided that the situations of the taxpayers are not the same as each other. This

---

1985. On this topic see: C. O'Brian, "Real Link, Abstract Rights and False Alarms: The Relationship between the ECJ's "Real Link" Case Law and National Solidarity", (2008) 33 ELRev., 643 and R. White, "Free Movement, Equal Treatment and Citizenship of the Union", (2005) 54 ICLQ, 885.

1986. Case C-365/02 *Proceedings brought by Marie Lindfors* [2004] ECR I-7183 and Case C-403/03 *Egon Schempp v Finanzamt München V* [2005] ECR I-6421, para. 45; Case C-527/06 *R. H. H. Renneberg v Staatssecretaris van Financiën* [2008] ECR I-7735.

1987. See S. Kingston, "A Light in the Darkness: Recent Developments in the ECJ's Direct Tax Jurisprudence" [2007] 44 CMLRev. 1321, 1331 and J. Snell, "Non-Discriminatory Tax Obstacles in Community Law", (2007) 56 ICLQ, 339. See also Case C-194/06 *Staatssecretaris van Financiën v Orange European Smallcap Fund NV* [2008] ECR I-3747.

1988. C-279/93 *Finanzamt Köln-Altstadt v Roland Schumacker* [1995] ECR I-225.

means that if the situation of an EU migrant worker is objectively comparable to the situation of a national worker, an EU migrant worker should enjoy the same tax benefits as that national worker. In *Schumacker* the ECJ held that the situation of Mr Schumacker (a Belgian national who lived in Belgium but worked in Germany and who was denied certain tax benefits which were available to taxpayers resident in Germany) was comparable to the situation of a German resident taxpayer given that Mr Schumacker received all or almost all of his income in Germany. In this case, the ECJ held that the German tax rule which did not take account of personal and family circumstances of a non-resident employed person was indirectly discriminatory given that for resident employed persons such circumstances gave rise to tax reliefs and rebates. However, the ECJ emphasised that a Member State of employment is required to take personal and family circumstances into account only when non-resident tax payers obtain the major part of their income in the State of employment (i.e. approximately 90 per cent of income). Otherwise, a non-resident taxpayer would be privileged as he would be entitled to obtain those tax advantages twice, i.e. in the State of his residence and in the State of his employment.

If the situations of a national worker and an EU migrant worker as taxpayers are not comparable with regard to a particular tax benefit, the EU migrant worker is not entitled to that benefit. However, in some cases the ECJ went beyond the discrimination approach and condemned non-discriminatory measures which substantially prevent/hinder the exercise of the right to free movement of workers.[1989] Notwithstanding this, the ECJ is aware of the disparities of national tax legislations of the Member States and the inevitable consequences of such disparities, i.e. that a higher tax rate in a host Member State, as compared to a home Member State may discourage a worker from moving to that State, but this situation results from the tax sovereignty of the Member States and thus is outside the scope of EU law. This is probably the reason why in recent cases the ECJ has applied the discrimination approach rather than assessed a national tax rule, which it has found to be non-discriminatory, in the light of its deterrent effect on the exercise of the right to free movement guaranteed under Article 45 TFEU. This is exemplified by Case C-240/10 *Schulz-Delzers*.[1990]

THE FACTS WERE:

Mrs Schulz-Delzers, a French national, living in Germany, was employed by the French Government as a teacher in a German-French Primary school in Germany. She was married to a German national and had two children. In addition to her salary she received, inter alia, an expatriation allowance from the French government which was aimed at permitting her to maintain the same standard of living in Germany as if she were living in France. In Germany, the rate of income tax was fixed according to a progressive scale, i.e. the tax rate increased in accordance with the level of income. In order to mitigate the progressive application of the income tax in relation to spouses with different levels of income, the German legislation provided for the possibility of joint tax assessment i.e. the income of spouses being aggregated and attributed to them jointly. Mrs Schulz-Delzers chose to have her tax assessed jointly with her husband, as this was more advantageous to both spouses. Under the French-German Tax Convention, her expatriation allowance was exempted from tax but, like the rest of her salary, was included in the calculation of the rate of her income tax. Had her income been assessed separately, she would not have been subject to the progressive tax, because

---

1989. Case C-152/05 *Commission v Germany* [2008] ECR I-39.
1990. Case C-240/10 *Cathy Schulz-Delzers and Pascal Schulz v Finanzamt Stuttgart III* (judgment of 15/9/11 (NYR)).

under the German French Tax Convention, her income was not taxable in Germany as it was received from the French State.

Mrs Schulz-Delzers argued that the German legislation was discriminatory because expatriation allowances paid to German civil servants working abroad for the German government were not taken into account in the progressive application of the German tax.

Held:

The ECJ held that Mrs Schulz-Delzers' situation was not comparable to the situation of German civil servants working abroad. Accordingly, in the absence of discrimination German legislation was lawful.

Comment:

Mrs Schulz-Delzers' situation was not comparable to that of German civil servants working abroad for two reasons. First, she received her allowance from the French government, not from the German Government. Second, she was treated no less favourably than a German national would be treated in a purely internal situation.

The ECJ explained that the challenged legislation, which applied to German civil servants working abroad, was aimed at permitting them to maintain the same living conditions as those enjoyed by them in Germany, notwithstanding a higher cost of living abroad. Accordingly, the German tax allowance did not enhance the taxpayer's ability to pay tax. For that reason, the allowance was exempted from the determination of the progressive application of tax. By contrast, Mrs Schulz-Delzers' allowance was specifically intended to adjust her remuneration to the cost of living in Germany, and thus enhance her ability to pay tax and accordingly could be taken into account for the progressive application of the tax. Further, the possibility of Mr and Mrs Schulz-Delzers being jointly assessed for tax purposes granted Mr Schulz-Delzers a substantial advantage and was based on objective criteria. However, unlike A-G Mengozzi, the ECJ did not examine whether the challenged legislation constituted a non-discriminatory obstacle to the free movement of workers. According to the A-G, Mrs Schulz-Delzers did not suffer less favourable treatment than she would have received had she not exercised her right to free movement. Had she stayed in France she would not have received the French expatriation allowance. Further, her spouse, and consequently the entire family, had paid less tax in Germany as a result of her choice to have her own and her husband's income assessed together.

It is interesting to note that the effect of taking account of Mrs Schulz-Delzers' allowance would have increased the taxable income of the Schulz spouses by only € 10 per year.

A national taxation system which discriminates indirectly, or which deters a national of a Member State from leaving his country of origin to exercise his right to freedom of movement[1991] can be justified only if it pursues a legitimate aim compatible with the Treaties, is justified by overriding reasons in the public interest and does not go beyond what is necessary and appropriate to achieve that purpose.

1991. Case C-385/00 F.W.L. de Groot v Staatssecretaris van Financiën [2002] ECR I-11819.

In this connection Member States have submitted various justifications, most of which have been rejected by the ECJ. For example, the ECJ has consistently rejected purely economic justifications based on:

- reduction in tax revenue;[1992]

- practical difficulties in determining the tax actually paid in another Member State;[1993] and,

- necessity to prevent tax evasion.[1994]

The ECJ has accepted an argument based on the cohesion of the national tax system, but for this argument to succeed it is necessary to establish a direct link between the discriminatory tax rule and the compensatory tax advantage.[1995] In Case C-204/90 *Bachmann*[1996] such a link was established.

THE FACTS WERE:

Under the Belgian tax system a taxpayer could claim tax deductions in respect of sickness and invalidity insurance contributions paid to a Belgian insurance company, but not to an insurer established in any other Member State. Mr Bachmann, a German national, who worked in Belgium, but paid insurance premiums in Germany, challenged this.

Held:

The ECJ held that the Belgian legislation was justified by the need to preserve the cohesion of the Belgian tax system.

Comment:

Under the Belgian tax system, the Belgian State could offset the loss of income resulting from the tax deductions regarding insurance contributions in that when benefits were eventually claimed by the insured person those benefits were subject to tax. Conversely, when a person, like Mr Bachmann, could not claim tax deductions regarding his or her foreign insurance contributions, such a person was not liable to pay any tax in Belgium on the final benefits. Accordingly, the justification based on the cohesion of the Belgian tax system was accepted by the ECJ because "in the event of a State being obliged to allow the deduction of life assurances contributions paid in another Member State, it should be able to

---

1992. Case C-136/00 *Rolf Dieter Danner* [2002] ECR I-8147; Case C-436/00 *X and Y v Riksskatteverke* [2002] ECR I-10829.

1993. Case C-319/02 *Proceedings brought by Petri Manninen* [2004] ECR I-7477.

1994. Case C-464/02 *Commission v Denmark* [2005] ECR I-7929. However, in Joined Cases C-155/08 and C-157/08 *X and E.H.A. Passenheim-van Schoot v Staatssecretaris van Financiën* [2009] (ECR I-5093) in which taxpayers deliberately hid their bank accounts in other Member States and when found were subject to additional tax assessments and fines, the ECJ accepted justifications based on the effectiveness of fiscal supervision and the prevention of tax evasion.

1995. In most cases such a link has not been established by the Member State concerned; see Case C-107/94 *Asscher v Staatssecretaris van Financiën* [1996] ECR I-3089; Case C-55/98 *Skatteministeriet v Bent Vestergaard* [1999] ECR I-7641; Case C-436/00 *X and Y* [2002] ECR I-10829 but this occurred in Case C-157/07 *Finanzamt für Körperschaften III in Berlin v Krankenheim Ruhesitz am Wannsee-Seniorenheimstatt GmbH* [2008] ECR I-8061 in the context of the right to establishment.

1996. Case C-204/90 *Hanns-Martin Bachmann v Belgium* [1992] ECR I-249.

tax sums payable by insurers".[1997] This was not possible in the case of Mr Bachmann. Had he been allowed to deduct tax on premiums paid in Germany from his income earned in Belgium, the Belgian tax authorities would have been unable to tax the capital paid at the expiry of the insurance contract, which would be payable in Germany.

23.7.5 Trade union rights

Article 8 of Regulation 492/2011 regarding equality of treatment covers equal trade union rights. An EU migrant worker is entitled to equal treatment in respect of the exercise of trade union rights, including the right to vote and to be eligible for the administration and management posts of a trade union.

The ECJ ruled that Article 8 of the Regulation applies to organisations similar to trade unions, that is, whose objective is the protection of workers. Consequently, in a situation where EU migrant workers are mandatory members of professional associations and have to pay compulsory contributions, national legislation cannot deny them the right to vote in elections to choose members of their professional associations.[1998]

An EU migrant worker has the right of eligibility to serve on workers' representative bodies within the undertaking where he/she works.[1999]

23.7.6 Equal treatment in matters of housing and house ownership

Article 9 of Regulation 492/2011 ensures equal treatment of EU migrant workers in matters of housing and house ownership. This is exemplified in Case 305/87 *Commission v Greece*[2000] in which Greek legislation prohibiting foreign nationals from owning immovable property located in certain regions of Greece (namely, in areas close to Greece's external borders), which applied to approximately 55 per cent of Greek territory, was condemned by the ECJ.

23.8 Entitlement to study finance for EU migrant workers

By virtue of Article 7(3) of Regulation 492/2011 EU migrant workers are entitled to access to training in vocational schools and retraining centres under the same conditions as national workers.

The ECJ has interpreted this provision restrictively. In Case 39/86 *Lair*,[2001] the ECJ held that "the concept of vocational training is a more limited one and refers exclusively to institutions which provide only instruction either alternating with or closely linked to an occupational activity, particularly during apprenticeship. That is not true of universities".

Luckily for Lair the narrow construction of Article 7(3) was compensated for by the ECJ's generous approach to Article 7(2), causing the Court to rule in the above case that entitlement to study finance is to be regarded as a social benefit under Article 7(2) of the Regulation. Consequently, a person who has kept his/her status as a worker can rely on Article 7(2) to obtain means of financial support from a host

---

1997. Ibid, para. 23.
1998. Case C-213/90 *ASTI v Chambre des Employés Privés* [1991] ECR I-3507; Case C-118/92 *Commission v Luxembourg* [1994] ECR I-1891.
1999. Case C-465/01 *Commission v Austria* [2004] ECR I-8291.
2000. [1989] ECR 1461.
2001. Case 39/86 *Lair v University of Hanover* [1988] ECR 3161, para. 26.

Member State to take courses to improve his/her professional qualifications and social advancement. The ECJ also held that an EU worker must be able to export study finance entitlement when that opportunity is available to nationals of a host Member State.[2002] In this context it is irrelevant that a worker seeks to study in his home Member State.[2003]

The above rule is subject to limitations imposed by the ECJ in respect of workers who voluntarily become unemployed in order to undertake a course of study and workers who enter a host Member State and take up employment for a short period of time with a view to subsequently undertaking studies. These are two different situations.

The first situation occurred in the case of *Lair* mentioned above.

THE FACTS WERE:

Lair was a French national who had worked in Germany as a bank clerk for two and a half years. She was then made redundant and for the next two and half years was mainly working, but had spells of involuntary unemployment. She was considered as an EU worker and therefore entitled to retain that status when she decided to study languages and literature at the University of Hanover. However, when she applied for a maintenance grant, her application was refused on the ground that she did not satisfy the condition for the award of a maintenance grant in that she had not been engaged in occupational activity in Germany for at least five years. She challenged the refusal.

Held:

The ECJ ruled that although she was a worker "some continuity between the previous occupation and the course of study" was required in order to obtain a grant for university education. In her case there was no link between her previous job and her intended studies. She was entitled to payment of registration and tuition fees on the same basis as German nationals but not to assistance given in the form of maintenance grants. However, if a worker becomes involuntarily unemployed and is "obliged by conditions of the job market to undertake occupational training in another field of activity," he/she will be entitled to general measures of support such as grants and loans.

The second situation occurred in Case 197/86 *Brown*.[2004]

THE FACTS WERE:

Brown was a holder of dual nationality – French and British. He was employed as a trainee engineer with Ferranti Plc in Edinburgh for nine months with a view to studying engineering at the University of Cambridge. His work was a form of pre-university industrial training as it was a pre-requisite for his admission to university. He would not have been employed by his

---

2002. Case 235/87 *Annunziata Matteucci v Communauté Française of Belgium and Commissariat Général aux Relations internationales of the Communauté Française of Belgium* [1988] ECR I-5589, para. 16.

2003. Case C-3/90 *M. J. E. Bernini v Minister van Onderwijs en Wetenschappen* [1992] ECR I-1071, para. 20.

2004. Case 197/86 *Brown v Secretary of State for Scotland* [1988] ECR 1619.

employer if he had not already been accepted by the university. When he applied for a grant, his application was refused on the ground that he had not been a resident of the UK during the previous three years as required by UK legislation. He challenged this decision.

Held:

The ECJ held that Brown was a worker as he fulfilled the criteria laid down in the Lawrie-Blum *case. However, the ECJ decided that Brown was not entitled to a grant despite his status of a worker because he "acquired that status exclusively as a result of his being accepted for admission to undertake the studies in question. In such circumstances, the employment relationship which is the only basis for the rights deriving from regulation No 1612/68, is merely ancillary to the studies to be financed by the grant".*[2005]

Comment:

It can be seen that if employment is merely ancillary to studies, migrant workers are not entitled to financial assistance.

The rules established by the ECJ with regard to entitlements or otherwise of EU migrant workers to study finance in a host Member State are not easy to apply. This is exemplified in Case C-413/01 *Ninni-Orasche*.[2006]

THE FACTS WERE:

In 1993 Mrs Ninni-Orasche, an Italian national, married an Austrian national and moved with him to Austria. In September 1995 she found employment as a waitress/cashier in an Austrian catering company. The employment contract was, from the outset, for a fixed term. In October 1995 in Italy she successfully sat an examination, thus completing her secondary education in a form of evening classes in which her attendance was required only at examinations. Between October 1995 and March 1996 she was looking for a job in Austria. Being unsuccessful, she began studying Romance languages and literature at a university in Austria. When she applied for study finance, her application was refused. She challenged the refusal before an Austrian court, which referred a number of questions to the ECJ, in particular asking the ECJ whether she was a worker within the meaning of Article 45 TFEU bearing in mind her very short period of employment in Austria (two and a half months), and if so, whether her unemployment was voluntary or involuntary.

Held:

The ECJ held that the concept of a worker must be interpreted broadly and in accordance with objective criteria characterising the employment relationship. In determining whether Mrs Ninni-Orasche was a worker, neither the fact that her employment was of short duration, nor her conduct before and after the period of employment was relevant. What counted was

---

2005. Ibid, para. 27.

2006. Case C-413/01 *Franca Ninni-Orasche v Bundesminister für Wissenschaft, Verkehr und Kunst* [2003] ECR I-13187.

whether her work was genuine and effective or whether it was ancillary and marginal. It was for the referring court to decide this matter on the basis of objective criteria and the factual context of the case.

The ECJ held that the fact that an employment contract is concluded for a fixed period of time is, in itself, not conclusive when deciding whether unemployment is voluntary or involuntary. Such a contract should be assessed in the light of other factors such as:

- *practices in the relevant sector of economic activity;*

- *the chances of finding employment which is not fixed-term in that sector;*

- *whether there was an interest in entering into only a fixed-term employment relationship; and,*

- *whether there was a possibility of renewing the contract of employment.*

Comment:

The facts that Mrs Ninni-Orasche obtained a diploma entitling her to enrol at a university as soon as her employment contract had expired, that she was actively looking for employment, and of the kind of employment she was seeking, were not relevant in deciding whether her unemployment was voluntary or involuntary. However, the Court stated, those facts might be relevant when examining the question of whether she took up short-term employment with the sole aim of benefiting from the system of student finance in Austria. Although this matter was left to the referring court to decide, the ECJ emphasised that the facts were suggesting that she had not entered Austria with the sole aim of taking advantage of the Austrian study finance system, but to live there with her husband.

It is difficult to comment on this case without knowing all the facts known to the referring court. However, it seems that Mrs Ninni-Orasche was a worker as her employment was not ancillary or marginal. If she was voluntarily unemployed, she would not have been entitled to a study grant because there was no connection between her previous work and the studies pursued. If she was involuntarily unemployed, could not find another job and thus forced by the labour market conditions to undertake training in another field, then she would have been entitled to a study grant.

23.9 Workers and "purely internal" situations

Article 45 TFEU does not apply to purely internal situations. In Case 175/78 *R v Saunders*,[2007] the ECJ held that when there is no cross-border element, i.e. all facts are confined to one Member State, EU law does not apply. This is exemplified in Joined Cases 35 and 36/82 *Morson and Jhanjan (Re Surinam Mothers)*.[2008]

2007. Case 175/78 *R v Vera Ann Saunders* [1979] ECR 1129.
2008. Joined Cases 35 and 36/82 *Elestina Esselina Christina Morson v State of the Netherlands and Sweradjie Jhanjan v State of the Netherlands* [1982] ECR 3723.

THE FACTS WERE:

Two Dutch nationals working and residing in the Netherlands wanted to bring their mothers of Surinamese nationality to reside with them in the Netherlands. Under Dutch law they were not permitted to do so.

Held:

The ECJ held that EU law did not apply to cases which have no factor connecting them with any of the situations governed by EU law. Accordingly, as the matter was of a purely internal nature, EU law was not applicable.

Comment:

The development of the doctrine of "substantive rights" has changed the perspective of the determination of whether a situation is purely internal or whether it is within the scope of EU law. This topic is comprehensively analysed in Chapter 22.3.1.

RECOMMENDED READING

Books

Barnard, C., *The Substantive Law of the EU*, 3rd edn, 2010, Oxford: OUP.

Parrish, R., and Miettinen, S., *The Sporting Exception in European Union Law*, 2008, The Hague: TMC Asser Press.

Spaventa, E., *Free Movement of Persons in the EU: Barriers to Movement in their Constitutional Context*, 2007, The Hague: KLI.

White, R., *Workers, Establishment, and Services in the European Union*, 2004, Oxford: OUP.

Articles

Briggs, L. V., "UEFA v The European Community: Attempts of the Governing Body of European Soccer to Circumvent EU Freedom of Movement and Antidiscrimination Labor Law", (2005) 6 Chi.J.Int'l L. 439.

Castro Olivera, A. "Workers and Other Persons: Step-by-Step from Movement to Citizenship", (2002) 39 CMLRev., 77.

Dautricourt, C., and Thomas, S., "Reverse Discrimination and Free Movement of Persons under Community Law: All for Ulysses, Nothing for Penelope?" (2009) 34 ELRev., 433.

Golynker, O., "Jobseekers' Rights in the European Union", (2005) 30 ELRev., 111.

Kingston, S., "A Light in the Darkness: Recent Developments in the ECJ's Direct Tax Jurisprudence", (2007) 44 CMLRev., 1321.

O'Brian, C., "Real Link, Abstract Rights and False Alarms: The Relationship between the ECJ's 'Real Link' Case Law and National Solidarity," (2008) 33 ELRev., 643.

Trimikliniotis, N., "Exceptions, Soft Borders and Free Movement of Workers", in P. Minderhoud and N. Trimikliniotis (eds.), *Rethinking the Free Movement of Workers: The European Challenges Ahead*, 2009, Nijmegen: Wolf Legal Publishers, 135.

PROBLEM QUESTION

John, a British national, his wife Natasha, a Russian national, and John's cousin James, a German national, all moved their home from the UK to Spain three years ago. Recently, they have encountered the following problems:

A. John, shortly after arrival in Spain found part-time employment as a janitor in the Spanish Department for Home Affairs. Recently he has found that under Spanish legislation a public sector worker, on completion of four years' of employment in the Spanish public sector, is eligible for a special £1,000 per annum length-of-service increment. John applied for the special length-of-service increment explaining that, immediately prior to his employment in the Spanish Department for Home Affairs, he had been employed by the UK Ministry of Defence as a janitor for four years. His application was refused on the basis that the four years' service had to be completed exclusively in the Spanish public service and therefore his employment in the UK could not be taken into consideration.

B. Natasha has been working as a nurse in a private hospital. Recently, her employer told her that she could become a head nurse if she had a degree in nursing. Natasha decided to improve her knowledge and skills as a nurse and accordingly submitted two applications: one for admission to a nursing course at the local Medical College and another to the local Education Board for the award to her of a maintenance grant and payment of the fees for her nursing course. Spanish nationals do not pay any tuition fees and are entitled to maintenance grants. Natasha's applications were refused on the ground that she was not an EU national.

C. James has been working as an electrician on a part-time basis. His income is so low that it has been supplemented by Spanish social security benefits. A deportation order has been issued against James on the grounds, first, that he is not a worker within the meaning of EU law, and second, he is a burden on the Spanish social security system.

Advise John, Natasha and James as to the application of EU law to each aspect of the situations described above.

ESSAY QUESTION

Critically assess whether the concept of "worker" under EU law has been appropriately defined by the ECJ.

The definition of a worker

A person who performs services of some economic value for and under the direction of another person, in return for which she/he receives remuneration (Case 66/85 *Lawrie-Blum*).

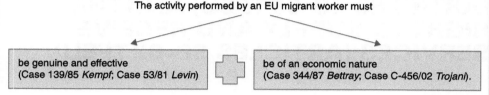

The activity performed by an EU migrant worker must

be genuine and effective (Case 139/85 *Kempf*; Case 53/81 *Levin*)

be of an economic nature (Case 344/87 *Bettray*; Case C-456/02 *Trojani*).

Prohibition of discrimination against EU migrant workers and beyond

Direct discrimination (based on nationality of the worker) **can only be justified under derogations set out in the Treaties**.

Indirectly discriminatory rules (based on factors other than nationality, for example, the place of recruitment (Case 152/73 *Sotgiu*)) and all national rules indistinctly applicable to both national workers and migrant EC workers, which **substantially** affect access to the labour market or exercise of the right of free movement of workers **can be justified** under principles developed by the ECJ, if based either on derogations set out in the Treaties or on **objective considerations that are independent of nationality** and **proportionate to the legitimate aim** pursued by the national provisions (Case C-415/93 *Bosman*).

Rights granted to workers and their families are set out in Directive 2004/38 (see Chapter 22), Regulation 1408/71 and Regulation 492/2011.

Under Regulation 492/2011 EU migrant workers are entitled to be treated in the same manner as workers who are nationals of the host Member State with regard to:

- Access to employment: any restriction by number or percentage is prohibited (Case 167/73 *Commission v France [Re French Merchant Seamen]*) but genuine linguistic requirements are allowed (Case 379/87 *Groener*);

- Conditions and terms of their employment;

- Entitlements to social advantages which are defined as all advantages "which, whether or not linked to a contract of employment, are generally granted to national workers primarily because of their objective status as workers or by virtue of the mere fact of their residence in the national territory" (Case 207/78 *Even*);

- Entitlements to tax advantages (Case C-279/93 *Schumacker*; Case C-204/90 *Bachmann*);

- Access to vocational training;

- The exercise of trade union rights;

- Housing and house ownership matters;

- Access to education and financial support relevant to education of their children

24

THE RIGHT OF ESTABLISHMENT (ARTICLES 49–55 TFEU) AND THE RIGHT TO SUPPLY AND RECEIVE SERVICES (ARTICLES 56–62 TFEU)

CONTENTS

CHAPTER OUTLINE

1. The freedom of establishment is guaranteed under Article 49 TFEU while the freedom to supply and receive services is enshrined in Article 56 TFEU. A Member State is prohibited from imposing any restriction on which of these freedoms an economic operator can choose.

2. EU rules on the right of establishment and the right to provide services have many common features, to a point where in some circumstances it is not easy to determine which provisions should apply to a situation at issue. However, each freedom is distinct. In order to decide whether Article 49 TFEU (establishment) or Article 56 TFEU (services) applies, account must be taken of the regularity, periodicity and continuity of the service provided in a host Member State. Generally, services are short-term while establishment is more long-term, but it results from the ECJ's judgment in *Schnitzer* that services may be provided over an extended period of time, even over several years. In such a situation, in order to determine whether an undertaking or a person has ceased to be a provider of services, and has become established in a host Member State, account must be taken of all available criteria and each case should be assessed individually.

3. Beginning with judgments of the ECJ in *Reyners*, in the context of the freedom of establishment, and *Van Binsbergen*, in the context of the provision of services, the ECJ has gradually condemned all discrimination, direct and indirect, as well as non-discriminatory measures which hinder the access to, or the exercise of, either freedom. For national rules which are directly discriminatory the only justifications are those allowed by the Treaties. With regards to indirectly discriminatory and non-discriminatory measures, the case law of the ECJ and Directive 2006/123 shows that they can be justified by both express derogations set out in the Treaties and imperative requirements in the general interest. In any event, such measures must be proportionate to the objective sought.

4. The beneficiaries of both freedoms are natural and legal persons. Natural persons are EU citizens. Legal persons are companies or firms created in accordance with the law of a Member State.

5. The beneficiaries of the right of establishment are entitled to leave their home Member State without any hindrance (although for companies, bearing in mind strict national rules relating to transfer of their seat, this is still problematic); establish themselves in a host Member State without any obstruction from either a host Member State or a home Member State, even if they set up a secondary establishment in order to circumvent incorporation requirements in a host Member State; and take up and pursue relevant economic activities and benefit from various general facilities which are of assistance in the pursuit of these activities.

6. Directive 98/5/EC governs the right of establishment for lawyers who have obtained professional qualifications in their home Member State and wish to practise their profession on a permanent basis in any other Member State.

7. A precondition for the application of Article 56 TFEU is that the activity in question must be of an economic nature, provided for remuneration, and be of a cross-border and temporary nature. Article 56 TFEU applies to both providers and recipients of services. In the context of the provision of services the principle of mutual recognition requires a host Member State to take into consideration rules of the home Member State of a provider of services in order to determine whether the public interest which a host Member State wants to protect is not already protected by rules applying to the service provider in the Member State where he/she is established. The freedom to receive services is an essential corollary to the freedom to provide services. Recipients of services must be treated in a host Member State on the same basis as nationals of that Member State.

8. With regard to publicly funded services, education is within the scope of Article 56 TFEU if provided by private establishments. However, when provided by public establishments, the ECJ has used the concept of EU citizenship to ensure access to education for non-resident EU students in a host Member State, and in some circumstances, entitlement to grants and scholarships and to non-contributory social advantages (see Chapter 22.3.4). With regard to health care services, they are within the scope of Article 56 TFEU. EU citizens and lawful residents of the EU insured under national sickness insurance schemes are entitled to obtain effective and speedy medical treatment from any other Member State, if this is not available in their own Member State. The case law of the ECJ on cross-border healthcare services was codified and expanded in Directive 2011/24/EU on the Application of Patients' Rights in Cross-border Healthcare.

9. Directive 2006/123/EC on Services in the Internal Market introduces novel solutions while confirming the existing case law of the ECJ on the freedom of establishment and the freedom to provide services.

10. Refusal by a host Member State to recognise qualifications acquired in another Member State prevents access to the relevant profession or economic activity and thereby devoids freedoms of any practical value. To remedy this, the Council adopted Directive 2005/36/EC on the Recognition of Professional Qualifications. It should be noted that this is expected to be substantially amended in the near future.

24.1 Introduction

The right of establishment is guaranteed under Article 49 TFEU, while the right to supply and receive services is enshrined in Article 56 TFEU. These rights are conferred on both natural persons who are nationals of Member States and legal persons established in Member States. Article 49 TFEU[2009] and Article 56 TFEU[2010] are vertically directly effective.[2011] In Case C-438/05 *Viking,*[2012] the ECJ held that Article 49 TFEU can be relied upon by a private party, e.g. a large ferry operator, against private bodies such as trade unions and international associations of trade unions in a situation where such bodies took collective action restricting the exercise of the right of establishment of the ferry operator (see Chapter 8.4.3.3). Thus, Article 49 TFEU can produce horizontal direct effect in some circumstances, i.e. where organisations, or associations, not emanating from public authorities impose substantial restrictions on the exercise of the right of establishment of private parties.[2013]

The interpretation of Articles 49 and 56 TFEU by the ECJ has evolved over time in that the ECJ has condemned not only directly and indirectly discriminatory national rules but also those which are non-discriminatory, but are liable to restrict or otherwise impede or make less attractive the exercise of the rights conferred under both freedoms. The relevant case law of the ECJ was, to a great extent, codified in Directive 2006/123[2014] on Services in the Internal Market which entered into force in December 2009 (see Chapter 24.7).

The provisions on the right of establishment and the right to provide and receive services when applied to natural persons must be read in the light of Directive 2004/38 on the right of citizens of the Union and their family members to move and reside freely within the territory of the Member States[2015] (see Chapter 22.4). Also, the concept of EU citizenship has significant impact on the exercise of both rights, in particular, the doctrine of "substantive rights" under which situations which have some connections with EU law may not be of a "purely internal" nature, and therefore within the scope of Articles 49 or 56 TFEU (see Chapter 22.3.1).

It is necessary to make a distinction between the freedom of establishment and the freedom to provide services because each imposes different legal requirements on its beneficiaries.

2009. Case 2/74 *Jean Reyners v the Belgian State* [1974] ECR 631.

2010. Case 33/74 *Johannes Henricus Maria van Binsbergen v Bestuur van de Bedrijfsvereniging voor de Metaalnijverheid* [1974] ECR 1299.

2011. Case 2/74 *Jean Reyners* [1974] ECR 631 and Case 33/74 *Van Binsbergen* [1974] ECR 1299.

2012. Case C-438/05 *International Transport Workers' Federation and Finnish Seamen's Union v Viking Line ABP and OÜ Viking Line Eesti* [2007] ECR I-10779.

2013. On this topic see: P. Chaumette, "Reflagging a Vessel in the European Market and Dealing with Transnational Collective Disputes: ITF & Finnish Seamen's Union v Viking Line" (2010) 15 *Ocean and Coastal Law Journal*, 1.

2014. [2006] OJ L376/36.

2015. [2004] OJ 158/77.

24.2 The distinction between the freedom of establishment and the freedom to provide services

The freedom of establishment and the freedom to provide services have much in common. First they are fundamental to the proper functioning of the internal market. Second, they have the same objective, i.e. the removal of obstacles to the establishment of the internal market for persons who wish to exercise economic activities. Third, they support each other in that the purpose of establishment in a Member State is to create a new base from which, in most cases, cross border services can be offered to EU citizens. Fourth, the beneficiaries of both freedoms are natural and legal persons. Fifth, some provisions of the Treaties relating to the right of establishment apply also to the provision of services (Article 62 TFEU).

Notwithstanding the above, the Treaties make a distinction between the freedom of establishment and the freedom to provide services. This is because:

- the provision of services is different in nature from migration from one Member State to another for the purpose of establishment; and,

- the freedom to provide services differs from the freedom of establishment, in that the former involves legislation by two Member States: the Member State of establishment of the provider of services and the Member State where the service is provided. It would inhibit free movement if short-term provision of services meant that the service provider had to comply with all the regulatory rules of the host Member State. For that reason a host Member State, on the basis of the principle of mutual recognition, is required to take account of national rules of a Member State of establishment of the provider of services. However, a host Member State may impose restrictions based on derogations set out in the Treaties, or justified by overriding reasons of general interest. When a natural or legal person is regarded as "established" in a host Member State it is burdened with complying with all rules relating to establishment in that Member State.

In law, the distinction between the right of establishment and the right to provide services is generally clear. However, in practice the distinction can be blurred, in particular because of the multiplicity of forms in which the person concerned may choose to exercise his economic activities. Further, a host Member State is, in respect of certain types of services, allowed to impose lawful restrictions on the exercise of the right to provide services which may obscure the distinction between the two freedoms. For example, in Case C-106/91 *Ramrath*,[2016] the ECJ accepted that, in principle, the exercise of the profession of auditor may require a permanent professional infrastructure and actual presence in a host Member State to ensure independence and integrity of auditors. However, in this case, the ECJ emphasised that such requirements will be unlawful if an auditor is already subject to rules of professional conduct aimed at ensuring independence and integrity of auditors in the Member State of his or her establishment. Consequently, the principle of mutual recognition, together with the principle of proportionality, will determine whether restrictions imposed by a host Member State are lawful.

In Case C-55/94 *Gebhard*,[2017] the ECJ emphasised that the regularity, periodicity and continuity of a service should be taken into consideration in order to decide whether Article 49 TFEU or Article 56 TFEU applies.

The provision of services normally involves temporary and occasional pursuit of economic activities in a host Member State and therefore does not require, as a matter of principle, a person to reside in the

---

2016. Case C-106/91 *Claus Ramrath v Ministre de la Justice, and l'Institut des Réviseurs d'Entreprises* [1992] ECR I-3351.

2017. Case C-55/94 *Reinhard Gebhard v Consiglio dell'Ordine degli Avvocati e Procuratori di Milano* [1995] ECR I-4165.

host Member State, even for the duration of the service.[2018] However, providers of services may equip themselves with some form of infrastructure in a host Member State in so far as such infrastructure is necessary for the purpose of performing the service in question. In particular with regard to the provision of professional services consumers may not trust and respect a provider who has no permanent infrastructure in a host Member State, e.g. a doctor in private practice. To be regarded as a "service", an activity has to be a self-employed activity, that is, it has to be provided by a natural or legal person outside the ties of a contract of employment.[2019]

In Case C-215/01 *Schnitzer*,[2020] one of the issues was whether services provided by an undertaking established in Portugal, consisting of carrying out large-scale plastering works in Germany from November 1994 to November 1997, should, given the long duration of the activity, be examined under Article 49 TFEU rather than Article 56 TFEU.

THE FACTS WERE:

Criminal proceedings were commenced against Mr Bruno Schnitzer for an alleged infringement of the German legislation against black-market work. Mr Schnitzer had engaged a Portuguese undertaking to carry out large-scale plastering work in Germany, which it did without being entered on the German Skilled Trades Register. The Portuguese undertaking was carrying out works in Germany from November 1994 to November 1997. The requirement of entry on the skilled trades register (including the requirement to pay subscriptions to the chamber of skilled trades) would apply without restriction had the Portuguese undertaking's activity ceased to be temporary, that is, had it ceased to provide services and in fact became established in Germany.

Held:

The ECJ held that:

- *With regard to providers of services, as previously held in Case C-58/98 Corsten,[2021] the requirement for entry on the trades register of the host Member State must neither delay nor complicate exercise of the rights of persons established in another Member State. Accordingly such an entry should be automatic and cannot constitute a condition precedent for the provision of services, result in administrative expense for the person providing them, or give rise to an obligation to pay subscriptions to the chamber of trades.*

- *The fact that a service was provided over several years did not necessarily, and certainly not on its own, mean that an undertaking was established in another Member State. The ECJ emphasised that no provision of the Treaties "affords a means of determining, in an abstract manner, the duration or frequency beyond which the supply of services, or of a certain type of service, in another Member State can no longer be regarded as the*

2018. However, in certain circumstances this may be required: see *Van Binsbergen* case 33/74 [1974] ECR 1299 and Case C- 106/91 *Ramrath* [1992] ECR I-3351

2019. Case 36/74 *B.N.O. Walrave and L.J.N. Koch v Association Union Cycliste Internationale, Koninklijke Nederlandsche Wielren Unie and Federación Española Ciclismo* [1974] ECR I-1405.

2020. Case C-215/01 *Proceedings against Bruno Schnitzer* [2003] ECR I-14847.

2021. Case C-58/98 *Josef Corsten* [2000] ECR I-7919.

provision of services within the meaning of the Treaty"[2022] and that, indeed, services covered by the Treaties may be provided over an extended period of time, even over several years.

Comment:

It results from the above judgment that each case should be assessed in the light of all the relevant factors, and that there is no decisive factor which will determine whether the case involves establishment or provision of services.

24.2.1 A choice between the right of establishment and the right to provide services

It is for economic operators to decide, depending on their business strategy, whether they wish to establish themselves in a Member State or whether they prefer to provide services. Consequently they should be able to choose between those two freedoms and their choice should be restricted neither by bureaucratic obstacles nor by legal barriers. Consequently, a Member State is prohibited from requiring that a service provider has its principal establishment[2023] or a registered office[2024] in that Member State, or in the case of vessels, that they are registered in that Member State.[2025] If an operator decides to establish himself (rather than merely provide services) in a host Member State, he can either create a new establishment or choose what type of secondary establishment, that is a branch, agency or other form, is the most appropriate for conducting its business activity in that Member State, and a host Member State is prohibited from giving more favourable treatment to one type of secondary establishment to the detriment of others.[2026]

24.3 Development by the ECJ of the right of establishment and of the right to provide services

In the course of the transitional period[2027] the Council was required to draw up a general programme for the abolition of existing restrictions on freedom of establishment and freedom to provide services. On 18 December 1961[2028] the Council adopted two general programmes for the abolition of restrictions, the first concerning the freedom of establishment and the second relating to the provision of services. Both programmes set out the general conditions necessary to achieve freedom of establishment and freedom to provide services in respect of each type of activity by progressive stages.

2022. Supra note 2020, para. 31.

2023. Case C-162/99 *Commission v Italy* [2001] ECR I-541; Case C-212/97 *Centros Ltd v Erhvervs- og Selskabsstyrelsen* [1999] ECR I-1459.

2024. Case C-101/94 *Commission v Italy* [1996] ECR I-2691.

2025. Case C-62/96 *Commission v Greece* [1997] ECR I-6725; Case C-334/94 *Commission v France* [1996] ECR I-1307; Case C-221/89 *The Queen v Secretary of State for Transport, ex parte Factortame Ltd and Others (Factortame (No. 1))* [1991] ECR I-3905.

2026. Case 270/83 *Commission v France* [1986] ECR 273; Case C-307/97 *Compagnie de Saint-Gobain, Zweigniederlassung Deutschland v Finanzamt Aachen-Innenstadt* [1999] ECR I-6161.

2027. Article 8 of the 1957 Treaty of Rome establishing the EEC provided for completion of an internal market over a transitional period of 12 years, in three stages ending on 31 December 1969.

2028. [1962] OJ 2.

A major consequence of the programmes was adoption by the Council of a number of directives covering various sectors of the economy, such as mining and quarrying, forestry, energy, coal, the film industry, food and beverage manufacturing industries, and so on. However, the task assigned to the Council by virtue of Articles 49 and 56 TFEU was far from being completed at the end of the transitional period. This was because the Member States were dragging their feet in implementing the programmes. In these circumstances two decisions delivered by the ECJ dramatically changed the approach of the Union towards the removal of the restrictions.

A.   The right of establishment: Case 2/74 *Reyners*.[2029]

THE FACTS WERE:

Jean Reyners, a Dutch national born and raised in Belgium, a holder of the Belgian doctorate in law (docteur en droit), sat the necessary examinations to become an advocate in Belgium. The Belgian legislation provided that only Belgian nationals could be called to the Belgian Bar. Reyners challenged the compatibility of this legislation with Article 49 TFEU. The Belgian Conseil d'Etat referred the matter to the ECJ under the preliminary ruling procedure. During these proceedings, the Belgian Bar and the government of Luxembourg submitted that the profession of advocate was excluded from Article 49 TFEU as its activities were connected with the exercise of official authority within the meaning of Article 51 TFEU. In Belgium an advocate may be called upon to sit as a judge in certain cases, and a judge exercises official authority.

Held:

The ECJ established three principles:

▪ *First, the ECJ held that the fact that Article 49 TFEU stated that the restrictions on the freedom of establishment "shall be abolished by progressive stages in the course of the transitional period" did not affect the right of nationals of one Member State wishing to establish themselves in another Member State to enjoy immediate protection. The ECJ held that Article 49 TFEU imposed an obligation to attain a precise result that was not conditional upon the implementation of a programme of progressive measures. Such a programme would only facilitate the attainment of the prescribed objectives. As a result, after the expiry of the transitional period Article 49 TFEU became directly effective despite the absence of implementing measures;*

▪ *Second, the ECJ held that Article 49 TFEU had to be interpreted in the light of the whole scheme of the Treaty, including Article 18 TFEU which prohibits any discrimination on the grounds of nationality; and,*

▪ *Third, the ECJ stated that the exception to freedom of establishment contained in Article 51 TFEU did not apply to the profession of advocate as it was restricted to activities which involved a direct and specific connection with the exercise of official authority (see Chapter 25.2.2).*

2029.   Case 2/74 *Jean Reyners v the Belgian State* [1974] ECR 631.

B.   The right to provide services: Case 33/74 *Van Binsbergen.*[2030]

THE FACTS WERE:

Mr Van Binsbergen was represented before the Dutch social security court by Kortmann, a Dutch national. During the proceedings Mr Kortmann, a legal adviser and representative in social security matters, moved from the Netherlands to Belgium and from there he corresponded with the Dutch court. He was informed by the court registrar that only persons established in the Netherlands were permitted to represent clients before the Dutch social security court, and as a permanent resident of Belgium he could no longer act for Mr Van Binsbergen. Mr Kortmann challenged this provision of the relevant Netherlands statute on procedure in social security matters as incompatible with Article 56 TFEU.

Held:

The ECJ established four principles in this case:

- *Articles 56 and 57 TFEU are directly effective;*

- *Both provisions are subject to the principle of non-discrimination based on the ground of nationality;*

- *National rules which are directly discriminatory can only be justified on the grounds set out in the Treaty. However, national rules indirectly discriminatory can be justified in some circumstances. In this respect the ECJ held that:*

  "taking into account the particular nature of the services to be provided, specific requirements imposed on the person providing the service cannot be considered incompatible with the Treaty where they have as their purpose the application of professional rules justified by the general good – in particular rules relating to organisation, qualifications, professional ethics, supervision and liability – which are binding upon any person established in the State in which the service is provided, where the person providing the service would escape from the ambit of those rules by being established in another Member State";[2031] and,

- *National rules imposing restrictions on the provision of services will be compatible with Articles 56 and 57 if they are objectively justified by the need to ensure observance of professional rules of conduct provided such rules are not directly discriminatory, are objectively justified and proportionate.*

Comment:

In this case the requirement of permanent residence applied without discrimination to nationals and non-nationals, and it was objectively justified by the general good, that is, by the need to ensure observance of professional rules of conduct, especially those connected with the administration of justice and those relating to professional ethics. Nevertheless the ECJ found the requirement of permanent residence disproportionate as the objective of the proper administration of justice could be achieved by less restrictive measures, such as the choosing of an address in the Member State in which the service is provided.

2030.   Case 33/74 *Van Binsbergen v Bestuur Van De Bedrijfsvereniging Voor De Mataalnijverheid* [1974] ECR 1299.
2031.   Ibid, para. 12.

24.3.1 Summary of the case law of the ECJ on the freedom of establishment and the provision of services

The judgments of the ECJ in *Reyners* and *Van Binsbergen*, as further developed in the case law of the ECJ, have important implications with regard to the application of the provisions of the Treaties relating to the freedom of establishment and the freedom to provide services. These implications are:

■ Articles 49 and 56 TFEU are directly effective and therefore they can be relied upon by individuals in proceedings before national courts. Further, in some circumstances Article 56 TFEU is horizontally directly effective (see Chapter 24.1);

■ The Treaties' provisions prohibiting discrimination, Article 18 TFEU (as well as Articles 49 and 56 TFEU), may be invoked to challenge a national rule, whether in the form of a nationality or other requirement, which is discriminatory. The principle of non-discrimination has been broadly interpreted in the context of the right of establishment and the right to provide services. Both direct and indirect discrimination is prohibited. Indirect discrimination is based on factors other than nationality, such as the place of birth, language, the place of residence, and so on;

■ The ECJ has gone beyond discrimination and has condemned non-discriminatory national measures which are liable to hinder or to make less attractive the exercise of either freedoms. In the context of the right to provide services, in Case C-76/90 *Säger*,[2032] the ECJ, for the first time, condemned a non-discriminatory national measure as contrary to Article 56 TFEU. Subsequently, the ECJ has treated indirectly discriminatory measures and non-discriminatory measures liable to prohibit or otherwise impede the provision of services as restrictions on the free movement of services. This approach has simplified the application of Article 56 TFEU in that it is no longer necessary to establish whether a measure is indirectly discriminatory or indistinctly applicable. If it constitutes a restriction on the freedom to provide services it is within the scope of Article 56 TFEU unless justified. In respect of the right of establishment, initially the ECJ refused to condemn national measures which were non-discriminatory.[2033] However, in *Gebhard*[2034] the ECJ followed its reasoning in *Säger* and held that any national measure which is indistinctly applicable and which is liable to hinder or to make less attractive the exercise of the freedom of establishment, as guaranteed by the Treaties, is a restriction within the meaning of Article 46 TFEU. Indirectly discriminatory measures and non-discriminatory measures can be justified on the basis of both express derogations set out in the Treaties and imperative reasons in the public interest. The list of imperative reasons in the public interest is non exhaustive (but see Directive 2006/123 Chapter 24.7.4). However, national measures must comply with the requirements of the principle of proportionality;

■ A distinction must be made between the application of the principle of non-discrimination in respect of the exercise of the freedom of establishment, and the exercise of the freedom to provide services. With regard to the freedom of establishment the principle of non-discrimination requires that nationals of other Member States are treated in a host Member State in the same manner as nationals of that Member State because they are in exactly the same situation. However, the application of "national treatment" to the providers of services from other Member States is unfair. They are not in the same situation as nationals established in the host Member

---

2032. Case C-76/90 *Manfred Säger v Dennemeyer & Co. Ltd* [1991] ECR I-4221.
2033. Case 221/85 *Commission v Belgium* [1987] ECR 719.
2034. Case 55/94 *Reinhard Gebhard v Consiglio dell'Ordine degli Avvocati e Procuratori di Milano* [1995] ECR I-4165.

State. They have already complied with all requirements relating to access to and the exercise of the relevant economic activity in their home Member State. They should not be subjected to the same requirements as are imposed on persons who are established in a host Member State and provide services there. Thus, the principle of non-discrimination seeks to eliminate discrimination which arises not only through the application of different rules to comparable situations, but also from the application of the same rule to different situations;[2035]

■ The prohibition of national measures imposing restrictions on both freedoms applies to the taking up of, and the pursuit of a particular activity, including rules relating to various general facilities which are of assistance in the pursuit of these activities. For example, in Case 63/86 *Commission v Italy [Re Housing Aid]*,[2036] the ECJ held that a cheap mortgage facility available only to Italian nationals should also have been available to all EU providers of services in Italy, so long as the nature of the service provided was such as to require a permanent dwelling in Italy;

■ The right of establishment and the right to provide services are not absolute. The exercise of both rights is subject to important limitations. The first is based on the Treaties: Article 51 TFEU provides that the chapter on the freedom of establishment does not apply to activities which are connected, even occasionally, with the exercise of official authority. The second is contained in Article 52(1) TFEU which states that limitations may be imposed on the grounds of public policy; public security; and, public health by a host Member State (see Chapter 25.3). By virtue of Article 62 TFEU, which states that the provisions on the right of establishment (Articles 51 to 54 TFEU) apply to the matters covered by Chapter 3 on services (Articles 56–62 TFEU), Articles 51 and 52(2) TFEU apply to providers of services; and,

■ The principle of mutual recognition plays a crucial role in the removal of obstacles to the exercise of both freedoms (see Chapter 17.2.3).

24.4 Beneficiaries of the right of establishment and of the right to provide services

Under the Treaties EU nationals and their families, and companies formed according to the law of any of the Member States, are beneficiaries of both freedoms.

24.4.1 Natural persons

Nationals of a Member State are entitled to exercise the right of establishment irrespective of whether or not they reside within the territory of the EU. However, nationals of a third country lawfully residing in a Member State cannot rely on Article 49 TFEU in order to establish themselves in another Member State,[2037] unless they are covered by Directive 2003/109/EC of 25 November 2003 concerning the status of third-country nationals who are long-term residents[2038] (see Chapter 22.2) or they come within the definition of a family member of an EU citizen exercising one of the four freedoms.

2035. C-279/93 *Finanzamt Köln-Altstadt v Roland Schumacker* [1995] ECR I-225; Case C-391/97 *Frans Gschwind v Finanzamt Aachen-Außensta* [1999] ECR I-5451.
2036. [1988] ECR 29.
2037. Case 65/77 *Jean Razanatsimba* [1977] ECR 2229.
2038. [2004] OJ L16/44.

With regard to the right of establishment a natural person may set up and maintain, subject to observance of the professional rules of conduct, more than one place of work within the EU.[2039] In Case C-106/91 *Ramrath*[2040] the ECJ held that a Member State was not allowed to prohibit a person from becoming established in its territory and practising there as an auditor because that person was established and authorised to practice in another Member State. Further, a person may be a worker in one Member State and work in a self-employed capacity in another Member State.[2041]

It should be noted that third-country nationals lawfully residing and working in a Member State can be temporarily sent by their employers to provide services in another Member State. This situation is covered by Directive 96/71/EC of 16 December 1996 concerning the Posting of Workers in the Framework of the Provision of Services.[2042]

The right to provide services is restricted to EU citizens who are established in a Member State.

If a national of a Member State has dual nationality, he or she can rely on that which is most favourable to the exercise of his/her right of establishment/provision of services.[2043]

24.4.2 Legal persons

The right of establishment and the right to provide services are granted to companies and firms. Article 54 TFEU contains a definition of "companies and firms". It covers companies and firms constituted under civil or commercial law including co-operative societies, and other legal persons governed by public or private law. Only companies and firms fulfilling the following conditions are entitled to exercise the right to freedom of establishment:

■ They must be formed in accordance with the law of a Member State;

■ They must have their registered office, central administration or principal place of business within the EU; and,

■ They must pursue activities which serve economic–profit making purposes. Under Article 54(2) TFEU non-profit making legal persons are expressly excluded from the scope of application of provisions of the freedom of establishment. However, this does not mean that other provisions of the Treaties are not applicable to non-profit making companies or firms.[2044]

Provisions of the Treaties relating to the freedom to provide services do not apply to non-profit making legal persons.

2039. Case 107/83 *Ordre des Avocats du Barreau de Paris v Klopp* [1984] ECR 2971, para. 19.

2040. Case C-106/91 *Claus Ramrath v Ministre de la Justice, and l'Institut des Réviseurs d'Entreprises* [1992] ECR I-3351.

2041. Case C-143/87 *Christopher Stanton and SA Belge d'Assurances "L'Étoile 1905" v Inast* [1988] ECR I-3351.

2042. [1997] OJ L18/1.

2043. Case 292/86 *Claude Gullung v Conseil de l'Ordre des Avocats du Barreau de Colmar et de Saverne* [1988] ECR 111.

2044. In Case C-386/04 *Stauffer* [2006] ECR I-8203 the ECJ applied provisions on the free movement of capital to an Italian non-profit making foundation so allowing it to claim a tax exemption on income obtained from the rental of its property in Germany. In Case C-172/98 *Commission v Belgium* [1999] ECR I-3999, the ECJ condemned Belgian law as contrary to Article 18 TFEU. The Belgian law required first, that at least one Belgian national had to be involved in the administration of a non-profit making association and second, that three-fifths of the members of such associations had to be of Belgian nationality for the associations to be recognised as having legal personality under Belgian law.

24.4.3 Reverse discrimination

Reverse discrimination is permitted under EU law relating to the freedom of establishment and the provision of services. In this respect two situations should be distinguished: "purely internal" situations to which national law is applicable[2045] and situations in which nationals of a Member State are denied the benefit of provisions of EU law because they are nationals of that Member State, even though their circumstances are ones to which EU law applies. However, sometimes it is not easy to distinguish a "purely internal" situation from one which is within the scope of EU law.

24.4.3.1 The difficult distinction between a "purely internal" situation and a situation within the scope of EU law

The concept of fundamentality of the status of Union citizenship has a significant impact on the determination of whether a situation is "purely internal" or is within the scope of EU law. In particular the doctrine of "substance of rights" entails that no cross-border element is necessary when a national measure affects the enjoyment of the substance of rights conferred on an EU citizen by virtue of his being an EU citizen (see Chapter 22.3.1). Accordingly, the situation that occurred in Case C-60/00 *Carpenter*[2046] which had a very tenuous link with EU law, if brought before the ECJ today would have had the same outcome but it is more likely that the ECJ would have based its reasoning on the doctrine of the "substance of rights" rather than on the protection of fundamental rights.

THE FACTS WERE:

Mary Carpenter, a Philippine national, overstayed her leave to enter the UK as a visitor. During this overstay she married Peter Carpenter, a British national. From 1995 onwards they lived together and she became the main carer for his children from a previous marriage.

Mr Carpenter owned and managed a company selling advertising space in medical and scientific periodicals, and offered the editors of those periodicals various administrative and publication services relating to advertisements. His company was established in the UK, but a significant proportion of his business was carried out with customers established in other Member States. Often Mr Carpenter travelled to those Member States for the purposes of his business.

When Mrs Carpenter applied for leave to remain in the UK as the spouse of a British national, her application was refused. She appealed on the basis that her deportation would hinder the provision of services by her husband because when her husband travelled to other Member States for the purposes of his business, she took care of his children.

Held:

The ECJ held that Mrs Carpenter could rely on Article 56 TFEU, read in the light of the fundamental right to respect for family life, to remain in the UK.

Comment:

The UK Government and the Commission argued that the situation of Mrs Carpenter must be classified as an internal situation within the meaning of the ECJ's judgment in Joined

---

2045. See for example, Case C-332/90 *Volker Steen v Deutsche Bundespost* [1992] ECR I-341; Joined Cases C-29–35/94 *Criminal Proceedings against Aubertin and Others* [1995] ECR I-301.

2046. Case C-60/00 *Mary Carpenter v Secretary of State for the Home Department* [2002] ECR I-6279.

Cases 35/82 and 36/82 Morson and Jhanjan [2047] (see Chapter 23.9). Accordingly, her right to reside in the UK, if it existed, depended exclusively on UK law. They submitted that since Mr Carpenter provided services from his home Member State, his non-national spouse could not derive from EU law a right of entry or residence in the UK.

The ECJ approached the issue in a different manner. The Court examined Directive 73/148/EEC on the Abolition of Restrictions on Movement and Residence within the Community for Nationals of Member States with regard to Establishment and the Provision of Services [2048] in order to decide whether it could be applied to the circumstances of the above case.

The ECJ concluded that the Directive granted rights of entry and residence to non-national spouses of EU nationals in a situation where EU nationals, accompanied by their spouses, had left their Member State of origin and moved to another Member State in order to establish themselves there, or to provide or to receive services in that Member State. However, the Directive did not govern the right of residence of members of the family of a provider of services in his/her Member State of origin. Thus the ECJ had discovered that there was a gap in the Directive, as it did not regulate a situation such as that in the main proceedings. In order to fill the gap the ECJ relied on the general principles of EU law, in particular the right to family life. The Court concluded that the separation of Mr and Mrs Carpenter would be detrimental to their family life and would constitute an obstacle to the provision of services by Mr Carpenter.

Although the ECJ recognised that a Member State may rely on reasons of public interest to justify national measures likely to hinder the exercise of the freedom to provide services, it pointed out that such measures must be compatible with fundamental rights protected by EU law. The ECJ referred to Article 8(1) of the ECHR and its interpretation by the ECtHR. The Court noted that although Article 8(1) of the ECHR does not confer on an alien the right to enter and reside in a particular country, the removal of such a person from a country where his/her close family lives may, in some circumstances, amount to an infringement of the right to respect for family life. In this context the decision of the UK authorities to deport Mrs Carpenter constituted an unjustified interference as it was disproportionate to the objective pursued by the UK of controlling immigration, taking into account that the marriage of Mr and Mrs Carpenter had been genuine, that since 1996 the spouses had led a true family life and that Mrs Carpenter's conduct since her arrival in the UK in September 1994 had not given any indication that she might in the future constitute a danger to public order or public safety.

24.4.3.2 Reverse discrimination and a "purely internal" situation

Reverse discrimination occurs when a national of a Member State is placed in a less advantageous position than a national of another Member State who has established himself/herself in that Member State. For example, under Directive 82/489/EEC laying down measures to facilitate the effective exercise of the right of establishment and freedom to provide services in hairdressing, six years' professional experience as a hairdresser is sufficient to exercise that profession in a host Member State.

2047. Joined Case 35/82 and 36/82 *Elestina Esselina Christina Morson v State of the Netherlands and Head of the Plaatselijke Politie within the meaning of the Vreemdelingenwet; Sweradjie Jhanjan v The Netherlands* [1982] ECR 3723.

2048. [1973] OJ 1973 L172/14.

However, for a French national to work in France as a hairdresser, a French diploma in hairdressing is required. A French hairdresser who fails an examination to become a hairdresser cannot rely on his/her six years' experience in France in order to practise the profession and is thereby reversely discriminated against. The explanation is that Directive 82/489/EEC did not harmonise the conditions of access to the profession of hairdressers in Member States. It merely established the conditions for the exercise of the right of establishment in a host Member State for members of that profession from another Member State.

24.4.3.3 A situation where a national of a Member State relies on EU law against his/her Member State in matters within the scope of the Treaties

In this situation there is some connection between the matter in issue and EU law. This is exemplified in Case 115/78 *Knoors*.[2049]

THE FACTS WERE:

Mr Knoors, a Dutch national who worked as a plumber in Belgium, was refused permission to work as a plumber in the Netherlands, even though Directive 64/427 governing certain trade skills was applicable to him as it covered the training and experience he had acquired in Belgium. The Dutch authorities argued that Knoors was trying to evade the application of national rules and that Directive 64/427 did not apply to nationals seeking to establish themselves in their own Member State.

Held:

The ECJ held that Mr Knoors was allowed to rely on Directive 64/427.[2050]

There are many cases in which a national of a Member State after obtaining professional qualifications in a host Member State returns to a home Member State where he wishes to practise the profession for which he has qualified in a host Member State. Such situations are either within the scope of Directive 2005/36 or Article 49 TFEU (see Chapter 24.8). When a situation is within the scope of the Treaties, it is irrelevant whether the nationality of the "home" Member State is by birth or has been acquired subsequently.[2051]

24.5 The right of establishment

Article 49 TFEU provides:

"Within the framework of the provisions set out below, restrictions on the freedom of establishment of nationals of a Member State in the territory of another Member State shall be prohibited. Such

---

2049. Case 115/78 *Knoors v Secretary of State for Economic Affairs* [1979] ECR 399; see also Case 136/78 *Criminal Proceedings against Vincent Auer I* [1979] ECR 437 and Case 271/82 *Auer II* [1983] ECR 2727.

2050. See also Case 246/80 *C. Broekmeulen v Huisarts Registratie Commissie* [1981] ECR 2311.

2051. See Case 271/82 *Auer II* [1983] ECR 2727 and Case C-369/90 *Mario Vicente Micheletti and others v Delegación del Gobierno en Cantabria* [1992] ECR I-4071.

prohibition shall also apply to restrictions on the setting-up of agencies, branches or subsidiaries by nationals of any Member State established in the territory of any Member State.

Freedom of establishment shall include the right to take up and pursue activities as self-employed persons and to set up and manage undertakings, in particular companies or firms within the meaning of the second paragraph of Article 54, under the conditions laid down for its own nationals by the law of the country where such establishment is effected, subject to the provisions of the Chapter relating to capital."

The case law of the ECJ shows that the ECJ defines the concept of establishment broadly. It has held that the exercise of the right of establishment involves the actual pursuit of an economic activity through a fixed establishment in another Member State for an indefinite period.[2052] In order to decide whether the activity is permanent, i.e. stable and continuous, all criteria characterising the activities carried on must be examined. In Case C-202/97 *Fitzwilliam*,[2053] the ECJ held that those criteria include:

"the place where the undertaking has its seat and administration, the number of administrative staff working in the Member State in which it is established and in the other Member State, the place where posted workers are recruited and the place where the majority of contracts with clients are concluded, the law applicable to contracts concluded . . . with its clients, and the turnover during an appropriately typical period in each Member State concerned. That list cannot be exhaustive; the choice of criteria must be adapted to each specific case."

Article 49 TFEU covers a wide range of activities. In Case C-268/99 *Jany*[2054] the ECJ regarded Polish and Czech women working as prostitutes in the Netherlands as being self-employed persons. They were entitled to establish themselves in the Netherlands on the basis of association agreements between the EU and Poland and the Czech Republic (at the relevant time Poland and the Czech Republic were not Member States), their activities were not contrary to the requirements of public morality of the Netherlands, given that prostitution is legalised there, and they were paying the relevant tax on their income.

Article 49 TFEU confers on EU citizens and EU companies a bundle of rights consisting of: the (implicit) right to leave a Member State of establishment; the right to establish themselves in a host Member State, the right to have a principal or secondary establishment there; the right to have access to the relevant economic activity; and, to exercise it under the same conditions as nationals or national companies of that Member State.

24.5.1 Legal persons

24.5.1.1 The right to leave a Member State of establishment: transfer of the seat of a company

It is unlikely that in reality somebody conducting a successful business in one Member State will want to move it to another Member State. For any organisation contemplating such a move

---

2052. Case C-221/89 *Factortame (No 1)* [1991] ECR I-3905.

2053. Case C-202/97 *Fitzwilliam Executive Search Ltd v Bestuur van het Landelijk Instituut Sociale Verzekeringen* [2000] ECR I-883, para. 43.

2054. Case C-268/99 *Jany and Others v Staatssecretaris van Justitie* [2001] ECR I-8615.

(perhaps believing it to be tax beneficial) the example of the *Daily Mail's* experience[2055] may be highly dissuasive.

THE FACTS WERE:

Daily Mail, an investment company incorporated in the UK, wanted to avoid paying UK tax when selling a significant part of its assets. Daily Mail decided to transfer its central management to the Netherlands but retain its legal status as a UK company. Before its relocation Daily Mail had to apply to the UK Treasury for permission to leave the UK. Nevertheless, Daily Mail went ahead with the relocation without waiting for the Treasury's consent. Subsequently, it argued that the requirement to obtain consent was unnecessary under Articles 49 and 56 TFEU.

Held:

The ECJ held that the right to freedom of establishment is not unconditional. Accordingly, a home Member State is allowed to impose restrictions on businesses wishing to move to another Member State.

In Case C-210/06 *Cartesio*[2056] the ECJ further clarified the scope of the right of a company to move its seat to a Member State other than that in which it was incorporated.

THE FACTS WERE:

Under Hungarian law a company incorporated under that law could not transfer its seat to another Member State and, at the same time, continue to operate under Hungarian law. Also, a change of a company's registered seat to a foreign country required a liquidation procedure in order to re-incorporate in another Member State. Cartesio, a Hungarian company, wanted to transfer its de facto head office to another Member State, i.e Italy, while continuing to operate under Hungarian law. The compatibility of the Hungarian law with Articles 49 and 56 TFEU was examined by the ECJ.

Held:

The ECJ held that as companies are creatures of national law, and bearing in mind that company law has not been harmonised at the EU level, the matter is within the competence of each Member State. That competence includes the possibility for that Member State not to permit a company governed by its law to retain that status if the company intends to reorganise itself in another Member State by moving its seat to the territory of the latter, thereby breaking the connecting factor required under the national law of the Member State of incorporation. Accordingly, the Hungarian law was not in breach of EU law.

2055. Case 81/87 *The Queen v H.M. Treasury and Commissioners of Inland Revenue, ex parte Daily Mail and General Trust plc* [1988] ECR 5483.

2056. C-210/06 *Cartesio Oktató és Szolgáltató bt* [2008] ECR I-9641.

Comment:

The ECJ distinguished between two situations:

- *the situation where the seat of a company incorporated under the law of one Member State is transferred to another Member State with no change regarding the law which governs that company. This was what Cartesio wanted, i.e. to transfer its real seat from Hungary to Italy whilst remaining a company governed by Hungarian law, i.e. without change in the application of national law to Cartesio. To this situation national law of incorporation is relevant and determines the conditions of incorporation and other relevant matters concerning the functioning of companies; and*

- *the situation where a company governed by the law of one Member State moves to another Member State with the consequence that the company has become a company which is governed by the law of the Member State to which it has moved, i.e. the case of reincorporation. To this situation EU law applies, and therefore, it would be an obstacle to the freedom of establishment to require the winding-up or liquidation of the company, which could only be justified by overriding requirements in the public interest.[2057] It is to be noted that whether reincorporation can take place depends on the law of a host Member State. In Cartesio, Hungary, the Member State of incorporation of the company could not prevent that company from converting itself into a company governed by Italian law, provided that this was permitted under Italian law.*

The loss of substantial value resulting from relocation expenses combined with increased taxation payments that a company or its shareholders, or both, are likely to have to make, shows that the relocation of businesses will not be a realistic option, unless harmonising measures at EU level are adopted allowing a company to retain its legal personality in a home Member State while transferring its seat to another Member State.[2058] Obviously, it makes more sense for a company to set up a secondary establishment in a host Member State or to take advantage of Regulation 2157/2001 on the Statute for a European Company.[2059]

24.5.1.2 Merger of companies

In Case C-411/03 *Sevic*,[2060] the issue was whether Article 49 TFEU applies to merger of companies.

THE FACTS WERE:

Sevic, a German company, and Security Vision, a company established in Luxembourg, concluded a merger contract providing for the dissolution without liquidation of the latter company and the transfer of the whole of its assets to Sevic, without any change in the

---

2057. Case C-442/02 *CaixaBank France v Ministère de l'Économie, des Finances et de l'Industrie* [2004] ECR I-8961.
2058. R. Drury, "Migrating Companies", (1999) 24 ELRev., 354.
2059. [2001] OJ L294/1.
2060. Case C-411/03 *Sevic System AG* [2005] ECR I-10805.

latter's company name. When Sevic applied for registration of the merger in the German commercial register, its application was rejected on the ground that the German law on company transformations provides only for mergers between companies established in Germany.

Held:

The ECJ held that:

- cross-border merger operations constitute particular methods of exercising the freedom of establishment;

- the German legislation was in breach of Articles 49 and 56 TFEU; and,

- whilst in some circumstances imperative reasons in the public interest, such as protection of the interests of creditors, minority shareholders and employees; the preservation of the effectiveness of fiscal supervision; and, the fairness of commercial transactions, may justify a measure restricting the freedom of establishment, this was not the situation in this case. The prohibition was too general and thus went beyond what was necessary to protect such interests.

24.5.1.3 Establishment of a branch, agency or subsidiary in another Member State

The establishment of a branch, agency or subsidiary in a host Member State may be hindered by laws and regulations not only of the host Member State but also of the home Member State of a parent company. Case C-446/03 *Marks & Spencer*[2061] provides a good example of this.

THE FACTS WERE:

UK tax law provided that a parent company established in the UK was charged corporation tax in respect of the profits attributable only to its branches or agencies established in the UK. Similarly, it allowed a parent company to deduct losses made by its subsidiaries established in the UK but precluded a parent company from deducting from its taxable profits any losses made by subsidiaries in other Member States. Marks and Spencer (M&S), a company established in the UK, challenged the decision of the UK tax authorities rejecting its claim for tax relief. M&S sought to deduct from its UK taxable profits losses incurred by its subsidiaries established in Belgium, Germany and France.

Held:

The ECJ held that: the UK tax law hindered the exercise by a parent company of its freedom of establishment by deterring it from setting up subsidiaries in other Member States.

2061. Case C-446/03 *Marks & Spencer plc v David Halsey (Her Majesty's Inspector of Taxes)* [2005] ECR I-10837. See also Case C-347/04 *Rewe Zentralfinanz* [2007] ECR I-2647 in which German tax law similar to the UK law was condemned by the ECJ.

The ECJ accepted that UK tax law was justified by overriding reasons of public interest such as:

- It ensured a balanced allocation of the power to impose taxes between Member States. The ECJ accepted the UK's argument that tax matters must be treated symmetrically in the same tax system, that is, in respect of profits and losses. Consequently, to allow a company to decide in which Member State to have its losses taken into account, that is, either in a Member State where a parent company is established or in a Member State where subsidiaries are established, could lead to a situation where the taxable base would be increased in the first Member State and reduced in the second to the extent of the losses transferred;

- It ensured that losses were not deducted twice, i.e. once in the Member State of establishment of a parent company and once in the Member State of establishment of its subsidiaries; and,

- It prevented tax avoidance. Indeed, the possibility of transferring losses incurred by a non-resident company to a resident company entails the risk that within a group of companies losses would be transferred to companies established in the Member States which apply the highest rates of taxation and in which the tax value of the losses is therefore the highest.

The UK tax law was, however, disproportionate because it precluded, in all circumstances, a parent company from deducting losses suffered by its subsidiaries. In this respect the ECJ stated that if a parent company provides evidence to the relevant tax authorities that its non-resident subsidiary has exhausted the possibilities available in its Member State of residence of having the losses taken into account for the present, previous and future tax periods, a parent company should be allowed to claim tax relief.

24.5.1.4 Setting up a company in one Member State and then exercising the right to set up a secondary establishment in another Member State in order to circumvent incorporation requirements in the host Member State of the secondary establishment

Under Article 49 TFEU a company is allowed to take advantage of more lenient rules of company law relating to its registration in a Member State other than the Member State where it intends to do business.[2062] This was examined in Case C-212/97 *Centros*.[2063]

2062. W.-H. Roth, "From Centros to Überseering: Free Movement of Companies, Private International Law and Community Law", (2003) 52 ICLQ 177.

2063. Case C-212/97 *Centros Ltd v Erhvervsog Selsstyrelsen* [1999] ECR I-1459.

THE FACTS WERE:

Mrs Bryde, a Danish national, registered her company Centros in the UK in May 1992, taking advantage of the UK law which did not impose any requirement on limited liability companies as to the paying-up of a minimum share capital.

During the summer of 1992 Mrs Bryde requested the Danish Trade and Companies Board to register a branch of Centros in Denmark. The Board refused on the grounds that Centros had never traded since its formation and that Mrs Bryde was, in fact, seeking to establish in Denmark not a branch but a principal establishment by circumventing Danish rules concerning the paying-up of a minimum share capital fixed at DKK200,000.

Centros challenged the decision of the Danish Trade and Companies Board.

Held:

The ECJ held that it was contrary to Articles 49 and 56 TFEU for a Member State to refuse, on the above-mentioned grounds, to register a branch of a company formed in accordance with the law of another Member State in which it had its registered office, but in which the company itself was not engaged in any business activities.

Comment:

The ECJ confirmed its liberal approach towards freedom of establishment by stating that national rules regarding the prevention of fraud cannot justify restrictions which impair the freedom of establishment of companies. This was not surprising given that the ECJ had, in previous cases, applied a restrictive approach to national measures intended to fight fraud, which measures imposed restrictions on the freedom of establishment.[2064]

The ECJ did not "look behind the veil" of a company; it applied the provisions relating to the right of establishment. Therefore, the fact that Mrs Bryde was taking advantage of more lenient company law in the UK that permitted her to avoid paying the capital required by Danish law for the establishment of a company and that the main purpose of establishing her company in the UK was to open a branch in Denmark, which actually was intended to be a principal establishment, did not constitute an abuse of the right of establishment.[2065]

24.5.1.5 Access to the market in a host Member State

Article 56 TFEU prohibits directly and indirectly discriminatory measures as well as those which are non-discriminatory but hinder or render less attractive access to the market of a host Member State.[2066]

National rules preventing access to the market of a host Member State may take various forms.

2064. Case 270/83 *Commission v France* ([1986] ECR 273), in which the right of establishment was exercised in order to benefit from tax advantages in another Member State and Case 79/85 *Segers v Bestuur van de Bedrijfsvereniging voor Bank- en Verzekeringswezen* [1986] ECR 2375 concerning social security benefits.

2065. On the concept of abuse in EU law see: R. de la Feria and S. Vogenauer (eds), *Prohibition of Abuse of Law: A New General Principle of EU Law*, 2011, Oxford: Hart Publishing. See also Case C-167/01 *Kamer van Koophandel en Fabrieken voor Amsterdam v Inspire Art Ltd* [2003] ECR I-10155 in which the ECJ confirmed the judgment in *Centros*.

2066. Case C-55/94 *Reinhard Gebhard v Consiglio dell'Ordine degli Avvocati e Procuratori di Milano* [1995] ECR I-4165.

They may impose a requirement that a company can only conduct its business through a primary establishment. This constitutes the negation of the right conferred on an economic operator to choose the type of establishment (i.e. primary or secondary) it wishes to establish in a host Member State.[2067]

They may impose on a company a requirement to obtain an authorisation in order to establish itself there, or set out criteria for obtaining authorisations which are, in fact, in breach of Article 56 TFEU. For example, in Joined Cases C-570/07 and C-571/07 *Pérez*,[2068] Spanish legislation which required prior authorisation for the opening of new pharmacies was at issue. An authorisation was given to candidates who scored the highest number of points. It favoured pharmacists who had pursued their activities on the relevant part of the national territory in that it increased by 20 per cent points to be given for professional qualifications if professional experience had been obtained within a specified part of the national territory. Further, in the event that several candidates scored an equal number of points, authorisations were to be granted in accordance with an order of priority in which preference was given to pharmacists who had pursued their professional activities within that part of the national territory. The ECJ held that the above criteria were indirectly discriminatory in that they could be more easily met by national pharmacists, who more often pursue their economic activities on the national territory, than by pharmacists who are nationals of other Member States, who more frequently pursue those activities in another Member State.[2069] The justification provided by the Spanish government that the difference in treatment was justified by the need to maintain a level of quality in the pharmaceutical service, which quality would be maintained if pharmacists were acquainted with the health programmes provided for by the regional administration and thus already providing pharmaceutical services in the relevant area, was rejected.

In some situations even national non-discriminatory measures may hinder access to the market in a host Member State. This occurred in Case C-518/06 *Commission v Italy (Re Motor Insurance)*,[2070] in which the ECJ held that Italian legislation which imposed:

■ an obligation to contract, under terms and rates published in advance, on all insurance companies (including those which had their head offices in another Member State but which pursued their business in Italy) offering third-party liability motor insurance to any potential customers;

■ limitations on the freedom of the companies to set their premiums; and,

■ heavy fines on companies which breached the above obligations,

interfered with the freedom to contract, and thus affected market access of companies from other Member States. The obligation to contract was non-discriminatory as it applied to all insurance companies wherever established which provided services in Italy. The ECJ agreed that restrictions relating to the obligations to cover any risks which were proposed to an insurance company and to moderate premium rates meant that many undertakings wishing to enter the Italian market "will be required to re-think their business policy and strategy, *inter alia,* by considerably expanding the range of insurance services offered".[2071] As a result, Italian legislation involved changes and costs, in particular for small companies, with the consequences that their access to the Italian market was less attractive

---

2067. See Case C-101/94 *Commission v Italy (Foreign Security Dealings)* [1996] ECR I-2691; Case C-514/03 *Commission v Spain* [2006] ECR I-963.

2068. C-571/07 *José Manuel Blanco Pérez, María del Pilar Chao Gómez v Consejería de Salud y Servicios Sanitarios* (C-570/07), *Principado de Asturias* (C-571/07) [2010] ECR I-4629.

2069. Case C-212/05 *Gertraud Hartmann v Freistaat Bayern* [2007] ECR I-6303, para. 31.

2070. [2009] ECR I-3491.

2071. Ibid, para. 69.

and once on the market, their competitiveness against companies traditionally established in Italy was greatly reduced. However, although the Italian legislation was in breach of Articles 49 and 56 TFEU it was justified by the social objective sought by the legislation, i.e. that victims of road accidents were fully compensated, and proportionate, in that it ensured that every owner of a vehicle was able to take out third-party insurance for a premium that was not excessive.

24.5.1.6 The exercise of the right of establishment

Most cases that have been decided by the ECJ in this area have concerned restrictions and disadvantages imposed on branches and subsidiaries established in a Member State as compared to companies and firms having their principal establishment in that Member State.[2072] The issue of direct or indirect discrimination as well as the application of non-discriminatory rules which hinder or make less attractive the exercise of the right of establishment often emerges in respect of a host Member State's direct taxation systems.

The main problem relating to the application of a non-discriminatory approach to national rules on direct taxation is that different tax treatment of a resident and non-resident company results from the fact that the Member States retain exclusive competence in this area and thus have different rules relating to tax basis, tax credits, taxation of dividends, deductibility of losses, etc. For that reason, A-G Geelhoed in Case C-374/04 *Test Claimants*[2073] suggested that a distinction should be made between "quasi" restrictions and "true" restrictions. According to him, quasi-restrictions are those that are an inevitable and direct consequence of co-existence of national tax systems and can only be eliminated by harmonising measures. Such restrictions should be outside the scope of Article 46 TFEU. True restrictions are those that are directly or indirectly discriminatory. They are within the scope of the Treaties. In other words, the A-G suggested that when a situation of a resident company and a non-resident company is comparable any discrimination, direct or indirect, should be prohibited. However, if the situations of a resident and a non-resident company are not comparable, i.e. there is no discrimination, Article 46 should not apply. The ECJ followed the A-G's suggestion in the above case and in Case C-446/04 *Test Claimants in the FII Group Litigation,*[2074] which was decided on the same day. It seems therefore that in the area of direct taxation, the ECJ has taken a more lenient approach to non-discriminatory restrictions than to discriminatory restrictions.

24.5.2 Natural persons

24.5.2.1 The right to leave a home Member State

EU citizens and their families are entitled to leave their home Member State and establish themselves in a host Member State. Their freedom should not be hindered. However, in Case C-9/02 *Lasteyrie du Saillant,*[2075] this freedom had been hindered by the French "exit tax".

2072. Case C-250/95 *Futura Participations SA and Singer v Administration des Contributions* [1997] ECR I-2471; Case C-324/00 *Lankhorst-Hohorst GmbH v Finanzamt Steinfurt* [2002] ECR I-11779; Case C-442/02 *CaixaBank France* [2004] ECR I-8961.

2073. Case C-374/04 *Test Claimants in Class IV of the ACT Group Litigation v Commissioners of Inland Revenue* [2006] ECR I-11673.

2074. Case C-446/04 *Test Claimants in the FII Group Litigation v Commissioners of Inland Revenue* [2006] ECR I-11753.

2075. Case C-9/22 *Hughes de Lasteyrie du Saillant v Ministère de l'Économie, des Finances et de l'Industrie* [2004] ECR I-2409.

THE FACTS WERE:

When Mr de Lasteyrie du Saillant left France in order to reside in Belgium, the French tax authorities charged him a tax on an unrealised increase in the value of securities, which was payable in the event of taxpayers transferring their residence outside France for tax purposes.

Held:

The ECJ held that a tax charged on an unrealised increase in the value of securities, which is due in the event of a taxpayer transferring his residence from France to another Member State for tax purposes, was in breach of Article 49 TFEU, given that the taxpayer who had transferred his establishment was subjected to disadvantageous treatment in comparison with a person who retained his residence in France. That is, had the taxpayer stayed in France, he would not have been liable to tax on values which had not yet been realised and which he did not have. Had he stayed in France the increases in value would have become taxable only when, and to the extent that, the securities were actually realised.

The ECJ held that the French legislation was likely to discourage a taxpayer from transferring his tax residence and could not be justified by imperative reasons including the prevention of fraud and tax avoidance. The ECJ emphasised that the transfer of a tax residence, in itself, does not imply tax avoidance and cannot justify fiscal measures which compromise the exercise of the freedom of establishment.[2076]

24.5.2.2 Right of access to an economic activity

National rules as well as rules of professional bodies, associations or organisations relating to access to a particular economic activity differ greatly. They may, in some cases, completely prevent access to the relevant economic activity. Obviously all directly and indirectly discriminatory rules are prohibited, as are indistinctly applicable rules which prohibit, hinder or render less attractive the exercise of the freedom of establishment. However, indirectly discriminatory rules and indistinctly applicable rules may be justified by overriding reasons of public interest. This entails that in some areas national barriers remain lawful and that in those areas the market can be integrated only through a legislative initiative. One of such areas concerns the recognition of diplomas and qualifications by a host Member State (see Chapter 24.8).

24.5.2.3 The exercise of the right of establishment

Directive 2004/38/EC on the Right of Citizens of the Union and their Family Members to Move and Reside Freely within the Territory of the Member States[2077] and Directive 2006/123 on Services in the Internal Market are the main secondary legislation applicable to the exercise of the right of establishment by self-employed persons. Unlike workers they are not carrying out their activities in the context of a relationship of subordination. They bear the risk of success or failure of their business and they are not paid directly and in full as is the case of workers.[2078] There is no secondary legislation similar in scope to Regulation 492/2011 (see Chapter 23.7). As a result, in many areas self-employed persons established

---

2076. Case C-478/98 *Commission v Belgium* [2000] ECR I-7587.

2077. See Chapter 22.4.

2078. Case C-268/99 *Aldona Malgorzata Jany and Others v Staatssecretaris van Justitie* [2001] ECR I-8615.

in a host Member State must rely on the principle of non-discrimination[2079] and the concept of EU citizenship to protect their rights deriving from the Treaties (see Chapter 22.2).

The prohibition of direct and indirect discrimination and of all indistinctly applicable national measures applies to access to and the pursuit of economic activities, including various general facilities which are of assistance in the pursuit of these activities. This was first decided by the ECJ in Case 197/84 *Steinhauser.*[2080]

THE FACTS WERE:

A German national, who was a professional artist and who resided in Biarritz, applied to the local authorities to rent a "crampotte" (a kind of a fisherman's hut used locally for the exhibition and sale of works of art). His application was refused on the grounds that only French nationals were allowed to rent a "crampotte". Steinhauser challenged this decision.

Held:

The ECJ held that the principle of non-discrimination applies not only to the taking up of activity as a self-employed person but also to the pursuit of that activity in the broadest sense.

In Case 63/86 *Commission v Italy*,[2081] the ECJ provided other examples of such facilities: the right to purchase, exploit and transfer real and personal property, and the right to obtain loans and to have access to various forms of credit.

24.5.3 Lawyers' rights of establishment

In 1998 the EP and the Council adopted Directive 98/5/EC on the right of establishment for lawyers who have obtained professional qualifications in their home Member State and wish to practise their profession on a permanent basis in any other Member State.[2082] The Directive applies to employed and self-employed lawyers and in the UK encompasses solicitors, barristers and advocates. The main features of Directive 98/5/EC are that:

- Lawyers establishing themselves in another Member State must use the professional title which they have obtained in their home Member State. This restriction was deemed necessary in order to avoid confusion between the lawyers' home Member State qualification and the qualification required in the host Member State. The professional title must be expressed in the official language of the home Member State;

- Lawyers who wish to establish themselves in another Member State must register with the competent authorities of the host Member State (see below);

2079. Case 197/84 *Steinhauser v City of Biarritz*; Case C-337/97 *C.P.M. Meeusen v Hoofddirectie van de Informatie Beheer Groep* [1999] ECR I-3289.

2080. Case 197/84 *P. Steinhauser v City of Biarritz* [1985] ECR 1819.

2081. [1988] ECR 29.

2082. [1998] OJ L77/36.

■ Lawyers are permitted to give legal advice on both the law of the host and home Member States as well as EU law and international law;

■ If a host Member State reserves some activities, such as the preparation of deeds, the administration of estates or the creation and transfer of interests in land for certain categories of lawyers, and in other Member States those activities are performed by persons other than lawyers, a host Member State is permitted to exclude lawyers practising under a home-country professional title obtained in a home Member State from carrying out those activities. This restriction is explained by the fact that the Directive does not encompass notaries who, in many EU countries, have exclusive rights in the above mentioned areas;

■ The directive requires lawyers to be accompanied in court by a local lawyer when representation by lawyer in legal proceedings is mandatory (see Chapter 24.6.2);

■ The rules of personal conduct and etiquette of both a home and a host Member State apply to lawyers wishing to practise in a host Member State;

■ The competent authorities of a host Member State are entitled to bring disciplinary proceedings against lawyers from another Member State registered in the host Member State who fail to meet the professional standards required by that Member State under the same conditions as apply to lawyers qualified in the host Member State; and,

■ The directive substantially revised the conditions under which lawyers from another Member State may qualify as lawyers in a host Member State. There are two ways:

● first, if they effectively and regularly pursue their practise in the law of the host Member State for three years; and

● second, even if they practise the law of their home Member State or EU law or international law, they may obtain the host Member State's qualification provided they carry out their professional activities in a host Member State for three years and satisfy the host Member State's authorities as to their competence with regard to that Member State's law.

The directive constitutes a complete harmonisation of conditions for the exercise of the right of establishment for lawyers. Consequently, a Member State is not allowed to impose further conditions in the area covered by the directive. This was clearly stated in Case C-506/04 *Wilson*,[2083] where lawyers from Member States other than Luxembourg were required to take a linguistic test as a precondition of registration. The ECJ was very clear on the point and stated that the only condition for registration is the presentation by the applicant to the competent authorities of the host Member State of a certificate attesting to registration with the competent authorities of the home Member State. In this case the ECJ further clarified that an appellate body against decisions refusing registration should be considered as a court or tribunal, within the meaning of Article 267 TFEU.

Obviously, Luxembourg was very unhappy with the directive, as it had already unsuccessfully challenged its legality[2084] and, in Case C-193/05 *Commission v Luxembourg*,[2085] was found in breach of EU law for imposing the following requirements on lawyers from other Member States wishing to practise in Luxembourg:

2083. Case C-506/04 *Graham J. Wilson v Ordre des Avocats du Barreau de Luxembourg* [2006] ECR I-8613.
2084. Case C-168/98 *Luxembourg v EP and Council* [2000] ECR I-9131.
2085. [2006] ECR I-8673.

■ requirements concerning language knowledge;

■ a prohibition on being a person authorised to accept service on behalf of companies; and,

■ the obligation to produce each year a certificate attesting to registration with the competent authority in the home Member State.

24.6 The right to provide and receive services

Article 56 TFEU provides:

"Within the framework of the provisions set out below, restrictions on freedom to provide services within the Union shall be prohibited in respect of nationals of Member States who are established in a Member State other than that of the person for whom the services are intended.

The European Parliament and the Council, acting in accordance with the ordinary legislative procedure, may extend the provisions of the Chapter to nationals of a third country who provide services and who are established within the Union."

Services are defined in Article 57 TFEU as being normally provided for remuneration and not covered by the provisions of the Treaties relating to the free movement of persons, capital and goods. In Case C-55/94 *Gebhard*,[2086] the ECJ stated that the provisions relating to the supply of services are applicable only if the provisions on the right of establishment are not applicable. Accordingly, the former will apply in so far as the latter are not applicable.

For the application of Article 56 TFEU it is necessary to establish that: the activity in question is of an economic nature; the service is offered for remuneration; there is a cross border element; and, the service provided is of temporary duration.

A. **An economic activity and its lawfulness.** An activity needs to be of an economic nature in order to fall within the scope of Article 56 TFEU. Some examples of what constitute services are provided in Article 57(1) TFEU which lists activities of craftsmen and the professions, and activities of an industrial and commercial character. The case law of the ECJ has expanded this list considerably by including within economic activities such activities as the transmission of a television signal,[2087] medical services (see Chapter 24.6.4), debt-collection work,[2088] sporting activities,[2089] and insurance services.[2090]

The ECJ in Case C-157/99 *Grogan*[2091] held that distribution in Ireland by Irish student associations of specific information relating to the identity and location of UK clinics where medical terminations of pregnancy were carried out lawfully under UK law was not an economic activity within the meaning of Article 56 TFEU. However, had the distribution of

---

2086. Case C-55/94 *Reinhard Gebhard v Consiglio dell'Ordine degli Avvocati e Procuratori di Milano* [1995] ECR I-4165.

2087. Case 155/73 *Giuseppe Sacchi* [1974] ECR 409.

2088. Case C-3/95 *Reisebüro Broede v Gerd Sandker* [1996] ECR I-6511.

2089. Joined Cases C-51/96 and C-191/97 *Christelle Deliège v Ligue Francophone de Judo et Disciplines Associées ASBL, Ligue Belge de judo ASBL, Union Européenne de Judo (C-51/96) and François Pacquée (C-191/97)* [2000] ECR I-2549.

2090. Case C-118/96 *Jessica Safir v Skattemyndigheten i Dalarnas Län, formerly Skattemyndigheten i Kopparbergs Län* [1998] ECR I-1897.

2091. Case C-159/90 *The Society for the Protection of Unborn Children Ireland Ltd v Stephen Grogan and Others* [1991] ECR I-4685.

information been carried out by, or on behalf of the UK clinics the activity would have been of an economic nature.

Case C-157/99 *Grogan* also raised the question whether an activity which is lawful in one Member State, but unlawful in another, is within the scope of Article 56 TFEU. In *Grogan*, abortion was prohibited by Irish law, but allowed under UK law. The Irish government submitted that the provision of abortion cannot be a service, on the ground that it is grossly immoral as it involves the destruction of the life of an unborn child. The ECJ answered that, irrespective of the merits of arguments on the moral plane "It is not for the Court to substitute its assessment for that of the legislature in those Member States where the activities in question are practised legally."[2092] The ECJ confirmed this approach in respect of gambling,[2093] prostitution,[2094] and transactions which were regarded as unlawful wagering contracts by a Member State where the recipient of services was established, but not by the Member State of the provider. However, in Case C-137/09 *Josemans*,[2095] the ECJ acknowledged that if some activity is prohibited in all Member States it will fall outside the scope of Article 56 TFEU. Accordingly, it seems that if the activity in question is lawful in at least one Member State it will be within the scope of Article 56 TFEU.

THE FACTS WERE:

The 1976 Dutch Law on Opium prohibited possession of, and dealing in narcotic drugs, including cannabis. However, for decades, the Netherlands has had a policy effectively decriminalising – though not legalising – the use of cannabis. This substance is sold mainly through coffee shops under certain conditions, e.g. no sales are allowed to underage customers. In some coffee shops non-alcoholic beverages and food are also sold. In order to reduce drug tourism affecting mainly Dutch border towns, the Municipal Council of Maastricht (the largest city in the far south of the Netherlands situated alongside the Belgian border and only a 30 minute drive from Germany), by decision of 20 December 2005, prohibited any coffee shop owner from admitting to his/her establishment persons who did not have their actual place of residence in the Netherlands.

In 2006, when Dutch authorities found two foreign nationals on the premises of a coffee shop "Easy Going" owned by Mr Josemans in the municipality of Maastricht, the Mayor of Maastricht adopted a decision temporarily closing that establishment. Mr Josemans lodged an objection against this decision. He argued that the decision forbidding the sale of cannabis to non-residents constituted unjustified unequal treatment of citizens of the EU and more specifically, contrary to EU law, denied EU citizens not resident in the Netherlands the possibility of buying legal products in coffee shops. This dispute came before the Raad van State (Council of State) which decided to stay the proceedings and to refer some questions to the ECJ for a preliminary ruling. The Dutch government justified the national measure on the ground of the maintenance of public order and public health.

2092. Ibid, para. 20. For a critique of the ECJ's judgment see: S. O'Leary, "Freedom of Establishment and Freedom to Provide Services: The Court of Justice as a Reluctant Constitutional Adjudicator: An Examination of the Abortion Information Case", (1992) 17 ELRev., 138.

2093. Case C-275/92 *Her Majesty's Customs and Excise v Gerhart Schindler and Jörg Schindler* [1994] ECR I-1039.

2094. Case 15/78 *Société Générale Alsacienne de Banque SA v Walter Koestler* [1978] ECR 1971.

2095. Case C-137/09 *Marc Michel Josemans v Burgemeester van Maastricht* [2010] ECR I-13019.

Held:

The ECJ held that: in the course of marketing narcotic drugs, which are not distributed through channels strictly controlled by the competent authorities with a view to use for medical or scientific purposes, a coffee shop proprietor may not rely on Articles 18 TFEU, 21 TFEU, 35 TFEU or 56 TFEU to object to municipal rules, which prohibit the admission of persons who are non-resident in the Netherlands to such establishments. As regards the activity of marketing non-alcoholic beverages and food in those establishments, Article 56 TFEU et seq. may be relied on by such a proprietor. The Dutch legislation, although a restriction on the freedom to provide services, is justified by the objective of combating drug tourism and the accompanying public nuisance.

Comment:

The approach of the ECJ to the issue of marketing cannabis in coffee shops was that drugs, apart from a situation where they are distributed through channels which are strictly controlled by the competent authorities to be used for medical and scientific purposes, are prohibited goods in all Member States and thus are not covered by the provisions of EU law. As a result, Mr. Josemans could not rely on the freedoms of movement, or the principle of non-discrimination, to object to municipal rules concerning the marketing of cannabis.

With regard to the sale of non-alcoholic beverages and food in Dutch coffee shops, the Court stated that Mr Josemans could rely on the provisions on the free movement of services to challenge the municipal rules. The Court held that the marketing of non-alcoholic beverages and food constituted a catering activity, as opposed to the supply of the product itself, and thus the provisions on the free movement of goods were secondary to those relating to the freedom to provide services. Hence, it was not necessary to examine the provisions on free movement of goods. Citizens of the EU, who do not reside in the Netherlands and wish to go into coffee shops in the municipality of Maastricht to consume, lawfully, goods there, are recipients of services within the meaning of Article 56 TFEU. This provision prohibits not only overt discrimination by reason of nationality but also covert forms of discrimination which, by application of other criteria of differentiation, lead, in fact, to the same result. Accordingly, under Article 56 TFEU a measure which distinguishes residents from non-residents, because it is liable to operate mainly to the detriment of nationals of other Member States, since non-residents are in the majority of cases foreigners, is prohibited. However, the ECJ decided that the restriction was justified by the objective of combating illegal drugs. The ECJ stated that the municipal rules were suitable and proportionate to attain this objective. They were suitable because they were capable of substantially limiting drug tourism, and consequently reducing the problems it causes, and proportionate because other measures implemented to combat drug tourism had proved insufficient and ineffective. In this regard, the ECJ pointed out that the possibility of granting non-residents access to coffee shops whilst refusing to sell cannabis to them, was not a feasible option given that "it is not easy to control and monitor with accuracy that that product is not served to or consumed by non-residents. Furthermore, there is a danger that such an approach would encourage the illegal trade in or the resale of cannabis by residents to non-residents inside coffee-shops."[2096]

2096. Ibid, para. 81.

Gambling services provide another example of economic activity which is very controversial and politically sensitive. Each Member State has unique national rules on gambling which it considers are appropriate to local conditions. Member States have regulated gambling in two ways. They have either created a monopoly run by a public company, or a private company controlled by the State, or have opened their markets to competition but restricted the number of operators by awarding a limited number of licences to operators who then provide gambling services within a strictly regulated framework. The position of the ECJ on gambling is that a Member State may impose restrictions, and even prohibit gambling, provided that such restrictions are justified by imperative requirements in the general interest (e.g. on the ground of the harmful effect of gambling, or of combating fraud and money laundering[2097]), are non-discriminatory and proportionate.[2098] In Case C-347/09 *Dickinger and Ömer* the ECJ held that "Member States have a wide discretion in relation to the objectives they wish to pursue and the level of protection they seek."[2099]

In some circumstances a Member State is required to impose restrictions in order to ensure that a public monopoly does not operate for personal and commercial profit but solely for charitable, sporting or cultural purposes[2100] and that advertisement is measured and strictly "limited to what was necessary to channel consumers towards controlled gaming networks".[2101] In Case C-176/11 *HIT LARIX*,[2102] the ECJ held that a Member State may impose a ban on advertising on a foreign operator of its casino located in another Member State if some conditions are met, i.e. when a host Member State has determined that the rules under which the foreign advertiser operates do not ensure equivalent levels of protection against the risks of gaming to its own rules. The principle of proportionality requires that a host Member State can neither impose requirements which are not directly related to the protection against the risk of gambling, nor require that the rules on the protection of consumers are identical to its own rules.

The ECJ accepted that a Member State may restrict access of foreign based gambling operators if the conditions set out by the case law are satisfied.[2103] However, when the gambling system established by a Member State is incompatible with Article 56 TFEU that Member State can neither impose criminal sanctions on gambling operators who are in breach of national rules, nor prohibit from its betting and gaming sector companies that are listed on Europe's stock markets.[2104] In Case C-42/07 *Liga*,[2105] the ECJ held that a gambling licence awarded in one

---

2097. On this topic see: B. Doukas and J. Anderson, "Commercial Gambling without Frontiers: When the ECJ Throws, the Dice is Loaded", (2008) 27 YEL 237.

2098. Case C-243/01 *Criminal Proceedings against Gambelli and Others* [2003] ECR I-13031 and Joined Cases C-338/04, C-359/04 and C-360/04 *Criminal Proceedings against Placanica and Others* [2007] ECR I-1891.

2099. Case C-347/09 *Criminal Proceedings against Jochen Dickinger and Franz Ömer* (judgment of 15/9/11 (NYR)), para. 99.

2100. Case C-275/92 *Her Majesty's Customs and Excise v Gerhart Schindler and Jörg Schindler* [1994] ECR I-1039; and Case C-124/97 *Läärä and Others v Finland* [1999] ECR I-6067.

2101. Case C-347/09 *Jochen Dickinger and Franz Ömer* (judgment of 15/9/11 (NYR)), para. 68; and, Joined Cases C-316/07, C-358/07 to C-360/07, C-409/07 and C-410/07 *Stoß and Others v Wetteraukreis and Kulpa Automatenservice Asperg GmbH and Others* [2010] ECR I-8069, para. 103.

2102. Case C-176/11 *HIT Hoteli, Igralnice, Turizem dd Nova Gorica and HIT LARIX, Prirejanje Posebnih Iger na Srečo in Turizem dd v Bundesminister für Finanzen* (judgment of 12/7/12 (NYR)).

2103. Case C-67/98 *Questore di Verona v Diego Zenatti* [1999] ECR I-7289.

2104. Joined Cases C-338/04, C-359/04 and C-360/04 *Placanica and Others* [2007] ECR I-1891.

2105. Case C-42/07 *Liga Portuguesa de Futebol Profissional and Bwin International v Departamento de Jogos da Santa Casa da Misericórdia de Lisboa* [2009] ECR I-7633.

Member State does not have to be recognised in another Member State and that a Member State was allowed to prohibit an operator who lawfully operated in another Member State, from providing gambling services *via* the internet.

In conclusion, it can be said that the ECJ has recognised, on the one hand, that gambling services are within the scope of Article 56 TFEU, and on the other, that Member States have wide discretion in protecting consumers from addiction to gambling. In the early cases on gambling, the ECJ did not assess a national restriction in the light of the principle of proportionality,[2106] but in more recent cases the principle of proportionality has been used as the main yardstick to decide whether a national restriction is justified. However, the ECJ normally leaves the assessment of proportionality to the referring court. The case law of the ECJ clearly shows that the ECJ does not encourage creation of an integrated market in gambling services.

The Commission prepared a Green Paper on "On-line Gambling in the Internet Market",[2107] in which it emphasised the need for the adoption of harmonising rules in this area. The Commission pointed out that differing national regulatory frameworks are no longer appropriate to deal with the increase in both legal and illegal on-line gambling. However, this matter is highly sensitive given that in some Member States gambling is unlawful and in most it constitutes an important source of income generated by national monopolies. Thus, the matter of how far, if at all, and in what direction, the harmonisation will go is unclear.

B. **Remuneration.** Article 57 TFEU refers to services as being "normally provided for remuneration".[2108] Thus, a gratuitous service, i.e. "provided for nothing",[2109] is excluded from the scope of Article 56 TFEU.

The case law of the ECJ indicates that the term "remuneration" has been interpreted broadly. Remuneration is not restricted to direct payments given by the beneficiary of the service to the provider but also encompasses payments that bear indirect relation to the service provided, and paid by a third party. This is exemplified in relation to payments for medical services covered by a social security scheme of a home Member State provided to a person insured under that scheme in a host Member State. In Case C-157/99 *Geraets-Smits and Peerbooms*,[2110] the ECJ held that:

> "Payments made by the sickness insurance funds . . . albeit set at a flat rate are indeed the consideration for the hospital services and unquestionably represent remuneration for the hospital which receives them and which is engaged in an activity of an economic character."

The term "normally" has not been defined by the ECJ as there is no case law on this matter. In this respect the issue arises whether "normality" should be assessed by the examination of the practice of an individual service provider, or the usual practice in the sector in which the provider operates, or more globally in the light of the practice in both the home and the host Member State.

2106. Case C-275/92 *Her Majesty's Customs and Excise v Gerhart Schindler and Jörg Schindler* [1994] ECR I-1039.
2107. COM(2011) 128 final.
2108. Case 263/86 *Belgian State v Humbel* [1988] ECR 5365.
2109. Case C-281/06 *Hans-Dieter Jundt and Hedwig Jundt v Finanzamt Offenburg* [2007] ECR I-12231, para. 32.
2110. [2001] ECR I-5473. Case C-157/99 *B.S.M. Geraets-Smits v Stichting Ziekenfonds VGZ and H.T.M. Peerbooms v Stichting CZ Groep Zorgverzekeringen* [2001] ECR I-5473, para. 58.

C. **The cross-border element.** A prerequisite for the application of Article 56 TFEU is the cross-border nature of the service. Based on the cross-border nature of the service Article 56 TFEU applies in the following situations:

● When a provider of services established in one Member State travels to another Member State to provide services in that Member State;

● When a recipient travels to another Member State to receive services there;[2111]

● When both a provider and a recipient are established in the same Member State but that provider travels to a host Member State to offer services there and the recipient seeks services from the provider in the host Member State;[2112] and,

● When neither a provider established in one Member State nor a recipient established in another Member State travel, as services are provided by post or by telecommunication (phone, fax, the internet[2113] or television[2114]).

It can be seen from the above that the cross-border element has been interpreted broadly by the ECJ. However, the ECJ has refused to extend the application of Article 56 to a situation where a provider of services is established in a Member State but is a national of a third country. Further, a service must be provided within the EU.[2115]

D. **The temporary nature of services.** In order to determine whether a person is established in a host Member State, or whether a person provides services there, such factors as the duration, regularity, periodicity and continuity of the service are of relevance.[2116] However, their application, as evidenced in Case C-215/01 *Schnitzer,*[2117] is not easy (see Chapter 24.2). Notwithstanding this, in Case C-456/02 *Trojani,*[2118] the ECJ held that when an activity is carried out on a permanent basis, or at least without a foreseeable limit to its duration, it would not fall within the services provisions.

24.6.1 Freedom to supply services

Article 58 TFEU provides that, without prejudice to the provisions on establishment, persons providing a service may, in order to do so, temporarily pursue their activity in the Member State where the service is provided under the same conditions as are imposed by the Member State on its own nationals.

However, national legislation is normally applicable to providers of services established in the national territory and not to providers of services established in another Member State. It would be unfair to providers of services established in another Member State to be treated in the same manner as providers of services established in the Member State where the service is to be provided. This is because providers have already complied with many regulatory rules in their home Member State. For that reason, the application of the principle of mutual recognition is vital for service providers. It requires a host Member State to take into consideration the rules of the home Member State of providers

---

2111. Joined Cases 286/82 and 26/83 *Graziana Luisi and Giuseppe Carbone v Ministero del Tesor* [1984] ECR 377.

2112. Case C-154/89 *Commission v France* [1991] ECR I-659.

2113. Case C-243/01 *Criminal Proceedings against Gambelli* [2003] ECR I-13031.

2114. Case 155/73 *Sacchi* [1974] ECR 409, Joined Cases 34–36/95 *Konsumentombudsmannen (KO) v De Agostini (Svenska) Förlag AB (C-34/95) and TV-Shop i Sverige AB (C-35/95 and C-36/95)* [1997] ECR I-3843.

2115. Case C-290/04 *FKP Scorpio Konzertproduktionen GmbH v Finanzamt Hamburg-Eimsbüttel* [2006] ECR I-9461.

2116. Case C-55/94 *Reinhard Gebhard v Consiglio dell'Ordine degli Avvocati e Procuratori di Milano* [1995] ECR I-4165.

2117. Case C-215/01 *Proceedings against Bruno Schnitzer* [2003] ECR I-14847.

2118. [2004] ECR I-7573, para. 28.

of services in order to determine whether the public interest which the host Member State wants to protect is not already protected by rules applying to the service providers in the Member State where they are established.[2119]

Article 56 TFEU, as interpreted by the ECJ prohibits, any direct discrimination and any restrictions, i.e. any national measures which are indirectly discriminatory,[2120] or which are non-discriminatory but are of such a nature as to prohibit or render more difficult the exercise of activities of a provider of services in a host Member State as compared to a person established in that Member State.[2121] This means that for a provider of services in a host Member State it should not be more difficult to reach potential customers than for a person established in that Member State and providing similar services.

Restrictions may take various forms, for example the requirement of authorisations; an obligation to register on a trade register in a host Member State;[2122] an obligation to have an establishment in the territory of a host Member State;[2123] more favourable rules on taxation in respect of providers of services established in a host Member State than for providers of services not established in a host Member State; or requirements of a host Member State relating to social protection of temporarily deployed workers for the purpose of providing services in a host Member State.[2124]

The case law of the ECJ indicates that the following imperative requirements in the general interest have been accepted:

- protection of the reputation of national markets;[2125]

- the requirements of the rules of professional conduct and the good administration of justice;[2126]

- the protection of: consumers,[2127] persons proposing for life assurance policies,[2128] workers,[2129] recipients of certain services,[2130] holders of intellectual property rights,[2131] the environment,[2132] a particular language or culture,[2133] and so on; and,

- the requirements of fundamental values laid down in a national constitution.[2134]

2119. Case 279/80 *Criminal Proceedings against Alfred John Webb* [1981] ECR 3305.

2120. Case C-360/89 *Commission v Italy* [1992] ECR I-3401.

2121. Case C-76/90 *Manfred Säger v Dennemeyer & Co. Ltd* [1991] ECR I-4221; as confirmed in subsequent cases: Case C-272/94 *Criminal Proceedings against Michel Guiot* [1996] ECR I-1905; Case C-3/95 *Reisebüro Broede v Sandker* [1996] ECR I-6511; Case C-222/95 *Parodi v Banque H. Albert de Bary* [1997] ECR I-3899.

2122. Case C-58/98 *Joseph Corsten* [2000] ECR I-7919; Case C-215/01 *Proceedings against Bruno Schnitzer* [2003] ECR I-14847.

2123. Case C-279/00 *Commission v Italy* [2002] ECR I-1425.

2124. Cases C-369/96 and C-376/96 *Criminal Proceedings against Arblade and Others* [1999] ECR I-8453.

2125. Case C-384/93 *Alpine Investments BV v Minister van Financiën* [1995] ECR I-1141.

2126. Case 33/74 *Van Binsbergen* [1974] ECR 1299; Case C-294/89 *Commission v France* [1991] ECR I-3591.

2127. Case 220/83 *France v Commission* [1986] ECR 3663; tourists: Case C-180/89 *Commission v Italy* [1991] ECR I-709; gamblers: Case C-275/92 *Schindler* [1994] ECR I-1039; customers of a bank: Case C-222/95 *Sci Parodi v Banque Albert de Bary* [1997] ECR I-3899.

2128. Case 205/84 *Commission v Germany* [1986] ECR 3755.

2129. Case 279/80 *Criminal Proceedings against Alfred John Webb* [1981] ECR 3305.

2130. Cases 110 and 111/78 *Ministère Public and "Chambre Syndicale des Agents Artistiques et Impresarii de Belgique" ASBL v Willy van Wesemael and Others* [1979] ECR 35.

2131. Case 62/79 *Coditel v Ciné Vog Films* [1980] ECR 881; Case 262/81 *Coditel II* [1982] ECR 3381.

2132. Case C-379/92 *Criminal Proceedings against Matteo Peralta* [1994] ECR I-3453.

2133. Case C-17/92 *Federación de Distributares Cinematográficas v Spain* [1993] ECR I-2239; Case C-473/93 *Commission v Luxembourg* [1996] ECR I-3207.

2134. Case C-36/02 *Omega Spielhallen- und Automatenaufstellungs-GmbH v Oberbürgermeisterin der Bundesstadt Bonn* [2004] ECR I-9609.

24.6.2 Provision of legal services by lawyers: Directive 77/249/EEC

Directive 77/249/EEC to Facilitate the Effective Exercise by Lawyers of Freedom to Provide Services[2135] assists lawyers in pursuing cross-border legal practice. Directive 77/249, as well as Directive 95/98 which concerns the right of establishment of lawyers (see Chapter 24.5.3), is based on the principle of mutual recognition of licences to practice. Directive 77/249/EEC has many similarities to Directive 95/98 in terms of areas of practice; the necessity of the use of the home professional title by a foreign lawyer; and, work in conjunction with a local lawyer admitted or authorised to practise in a host Member State if the host Member State requires it. The ECJ, in a number of cases, clarified the concept of "working in conjunction". The necessity for a foreign lawyer to be "shadowed" by a local lawyer concerns limited circumstances justified by public policy, i.e. when representation by a lawyer in legal proceedings before a court is mandatory.[2136] A foreign lawyer may undertake the same activities as a local lawyer and under the same conditions as a local lawyer, but is neither required to reside in a host Member State nor to register with the appropriate authorities of a host Member State. However, a Member State may require a foreign lawyer to be introduced to the presiding judge or the President of the relevant bar in a host Member State.

A foreign lawyer must observe the rules of professional conduct of the host Member State except to the extent that they would be disproportionate for activities other than those relating to legal proceedings. This is without prejudice to the rules of professional conduct of a home Member State relating in particular to confidentiality, advertising, conflicts of interest, relations with other lawyers and activities incompatible with the profession of law.

It should be noted that Directive 2006/123 on Services in the Internal Market (see Chapter 24.7) applies to the provision of cross-border legal services and thus a lawyer wishing to provide such services must be aware of, and comply with its provisions.

24.6.3 Freedom to receive services

In Joined Cases 286/82 and 26/83 *Luisi and Carbone*,[2137] the ECJ held that the freedom to provide services includes the freedom for the recipient of the services to go to another Member State in order to receive a service there without being obstructed by restrictions. In such a situation a national of a Member State should be treated in the same manner as nationals of the host Member State. This was established by the ECJ in Case 186/87 *Cowan*.[2138]

THE FACTS WERE:

A British national, Ian Cowan, was violently assaulted outside a Metro station in Paris. The perpetrators of the offence were never apprehended. Mr Cowan applied to the Commission d'Indemnisation des Victimes d'Infraction, the French equivalent of the UK Criminal Injuries Compensation Board, for compensation for his injuries. The French Code of Criminal Procedure allows compensation to be paid to victims of assaults if physical injury has been sustained and compensation cannot be sought from another source. However, the same

---

2135. [1977] OJ L78/17.

2136. Case 427/85 *Commission v Germany* [1988] ECR 1123 and Case 294/89 *Commission v France* [1991] ECR I-3591.

2137. Joined Cases 286/82 and 26/83 *Luisi and Carbone v Ministero del Tesoro* [1984] ECR 377.

2138. Case 186/87 *Cowan v Trésor Public* [1989] ECR 195.

> *Code of Criminal Procedure restricted the payment of compensation to French nationals and holders of French residence permits. On these grounds Mr Cowan's application for compensation was refused by the French Treasury. Mr Cowan challenged this decision, relying on Article 18 TFEU.*
>
> *Held:*
>
> *The ECJ held that since the right to receive services was embodied in the Treaty, it was subject to the prohibition of discrimination on the grounds of nationality as prescribed by Article 18 TFEU. Laws and regulations which prevent the exercise of this right were incompatible with EU law and, in the circumstances of this case, the requirement of French nationality or of a French residence permit in order to claim compensation for criminal injuries constituted unjustifiable discrimination. Tourists, among others, must be regarded as recipients of services.*

It should be noted that when a service is unlawful in one Member State but lawful in another, e.g. medical termination of pregnancy, it is unclear whether under EU law a home Member State is allowed to prohibit a person from travelling to a host Member State to receive the service in question. So far, no case on this matter has reached the ECJ. In the case of X, a 14-year-old victim of rape wanted to travel from Ireland to the UK for an abortion, and the Irish Supreme Court lifted a ban on her travel imposed by the Irish High Court, so allowing her to have an abortion in the UK.[2139] Similarly in the case of Diane Blood, a British national, the Court of Appeal of England and Wales allowed her to travel to Belgium with a sample of her husband's sperm in order to receive IVF treatment there despite the fact that her husband was in a coma, and thus unable to give written consent for use of his sperm as required by the UK 1990 Human Fertilisation and Embryology Act.[2140]

24.6.4 Publicly funded services

In the context of the freedom to receive services the most controversial matter is whether a national of another Member State is entitled to be treated in a host Member State, in respect of such services as education and health, in the same way as nationals of that Member State, given that these are not commercial activities but public services (the right to study finance for workers is examined in Chapter 23.8).

A. **Education.** The content of teaching curricula and the organisation of a Member State's educational system are within the exclusive competence of each Member State. However, as stated by the ECJ, this exclusive competence must be exercised in compliance with EU law, in particular with the right of EU citizens to move freely within the EU.[2141] In Case 263/86 *Humbel*,[2142] the ECJ held that Article 56 TFEU applies to privately funded education, but not to State-funded education. Nevertheless, the ECJ has used the concept of EU citizenship, in

---

2139. *Attorney General v X* [1992] CMLR 277, 290.
2140. *R v Human Fertilisation and Embryology Authority, ex parte Diane Blood* [1997] 2 CMLR 591.
2141. Case C-308/89 *Carmina di Leo v Land Berlin* [1990] ECR I-4185; Case C-337/97 *C.P.M. Meeusen v Hoofddirectie van de Informatie Beheer Groep* [1999] ECR I-3289; Case C-147/03 *Commission v Austria* [2005] ECR I-5969; and Case C-76/05 *Herbert Schwarz and Marga Gootjes-Schwarz v Finanzamt Bergisch Gladbach* [2007] ECR I-6849.
2142. Case 263/86 *Belgium v René Humbel and Marie-Thérèse Edel* [1988] ECR 5365.

particular the requirement of equal treatment, first, to ensure access to education of EU citizens in a host Member State, and second, in some circumstances to give them an entitlement to financial assistance for studies in a host Member State, either to be provided by a host Member State or a home Member State (see Chapter 22.3.4).

B. **Medical services.** The ECJ gradually developed a new right for all EU citizens and lawful residents of the EU, insured under national sickness insurance schemes, to obtain effective and speedy medical treatment from their own Member State, or if this is not available, from any other Member State. The ECJ achieved this by finding a "cross-border element" when persons who are insured under a national health care system, but are unable to obtain adequate medical treatment in their home Member State, have exercised their right under Article 56 TFEU[2143] or under Article 22 of Regulation 883/2004, and have sought such treatment in another Member State. As a result, an insured person, in the circumstances defined by the case law of the ECJ,[2144] is entitled to have the cost of medical treatment received in a host Member State reimbursed by the relevant institution of a home Member State.

The case law of the ECJ has been codified by Directive 2011/24/EU on the Application of Patients' Rights in Cross-border Healthcare.[2145] It is outside the scope of this book to examine the Directive in detail. However, it is important to note that the scope of the Directive exceeds the scope of the case law of the ECJ in that the Directive promotes co-operation between Member States in healthcare matters; imposes an obligation on each Member State to establish a national contact point with a view, *inter alia*, to provide assistance and information to patients; and, clarifies the relationship between Article 56 TFEU and Regulation 883/2004 in terms of reimbursement of cross-border healthcare services.

24.7 Directive 2006/123 on Services in the Internal Market[2146]

In order to create a genuine single market in services, on 13 January 2004 the Commission submitted a proposal for a Directive on Services in the Internal Market. This was fiercely attacked by some Member States and their trade unions. The proposed directive was called the "Frankenstein" Directive (previously it was often named as the Bolkestein Directive, after the former internal market commissioner Bolkestein, who originally proposed it) and played a major role in the French rejection of the proposed EU Constitution (see Chapter 1.18).

On 21 March 2005 nearly 100,000 people marched through the streets of Brussels to protest against the directive. Trade unions of Belgium, France, Germany, Italy and the Netherlands organised the protest. They described the directive as a declaration of war on working men and women and regarded it as destroying the achievements of two centuries of struggle of workers in social welfare, health care and educational matters. The main criticism concerned the establishment of the principle of origin

---

2143. Case C-158/96 *Raymond Kohll v Union des Caisses de Maladie* [1998] ECR I-1931.

2144. For example, see Case C-157/99 *B.S.M. Geraets-Smits v Stichting Ziekenfonds VGZ and H.T.M. Peerbooms v Stichting CZ Groep Zorgverzekeringen* [2001] ECR I-5473; C-372/04 *Yvonne Watts v Bedford Primary Care Trust and Secretary of State for Health* [2006] ECR I-4325; Case C-385/99 *V.G. Muller-Fauré v Onderlinge Waarborgmaatschappij OZ Zorgverzekeringen UA* [2003] ECR I-4509; Case C-466/04 *Manuel Acereda Herrera v Servicio Cántabro de Salud* [2006] ECR I-5341.

2145. [2011] OJ L88/45. See S. De La Rosa, "The Directive on Cross-border Healthcare or the Art of Codifying Complex Case Law", (2012) 49 CMLRev., 15.

2146. [2006] OJ L376/36.

under which a provider of services was to be subject only to the national provisions of its Member State of origin, that is, it would operate under the home Member State's rules as to, for example, working time; minimum wages; holidays; and, the right to strike. Any supervision of a provider of services could only be carried out by the authorities of the home Member State. Trade unions argued that the application of the principle of origin would lead to a "race to the bottom", with firms relocating to countries with lower wages and the weakest consumer and environmental protection, employment and health and safety rules. Resulting from this the opponents of the Directive argued that it would lead to competition between workers; reduction of wages; closure of many companies operating in Member States with high standards of social protection given that they could not compete with cheaper, foreign competitors; lower standards of social and environmental protection; and, an influx of foreign workers. Further, it was argued that a home Member State of a service provider would have no interest and often no resources to supervise businesses registered in that Member State but doing business in another Member State. The trade unions were successful in challenging the proposed directive. The European Council of March 2005 asked the Commission to redraft the directive. A watered-down version of the original directive was adopted by the Council on 12 December 2006 as Directive 2006/123/EC. The directive entered into force on 28 December 2009.

The main features of Directive 2006/123/EC are examined below.[2147]

24.7.1 Objective

The objective of the directive is to make progress towards the creation of a genuine internal market by removing obstacles to both the freedom of establishment and the freedom to provide services. This "big picture" approach is rare (in particular bearing in mind that the directive applies to numerous economic sectors), but not without precedent, as evidenced by secondary legislation adopted in respect of financial services. Does it suggest that, in the long run, the EU seeks to establish the same legal regime with regard to both freedoms? The "big picture" approach to fundamental freedoms is present in Case C-390/99 *Canal Satélite Digital*,[2148] in which the ECJ examined restrictions imposed by Spanish law simultaneously in the light of both Article 34 and Article 56 TFEU. However, the directive's contribution to the "big picture" approach to both freedoms is not a "wide screen" approach in that it clearly distinguishes between the right to establishment and the right to provide services, and provides definitions of the concept of "establishment" and the concept of "services" based on the case law of the ECJ.

24.7.2 Scope of application

The Directive applies to a wide range of commercial services, including legal and tax advice; management consultancy; real estate services; construction; trade services; tourism; and, leisure services. An incomplete list of included services in provided in recital 33 of the Preamble to the directive. Recital 33 specifies that provision of the included services may involve services requiring the proximity of provider and recipient, services requiring travel by the recipient or the provider and services which may be provided at a distance, including *via* the Internet.

2147. The Commission's detailed and helpful commentary on Directive 2006/123 is contained in its "Handbook on the Implementation of the Service Directive" [2006] OJ L376/36.

2148. Case C-390/99 *Canal Satélite Digital SL v Administración General del Estado and DTS* [2002] ECR I-607.

The list of the excluded services is set out in Article 2(2) of the directive and is long. Among the excluded services are the following:

- Non-economic services of general interest, that is, services which are not provided for remuneration, for example, services in the areas of primary and secondary education. Such services are not subject to EU competition law. However, services of general economic interest, such as those in the electricity, gas and waste treatment sectors, and the postal service are within the scope of the directive and EU competition law. Whether a particular service of general interest (SGI) is of an economic or non-economic nature is determined in the light of the case law of the ECJ. Under the ToL, SGIs are within the competences shared between the EU and the Member States. Article 14 TFEU emphasises the importance of SGIs and their contribution to achievement of social and territorial cohesion. Under that Article, the Council and the EP are empowered to adopt regulations in accordance with the ordinary legislative procedure to ensure that the SGIs "operate on the basis of principles and conditions, particularly economic and financial conditions, which enable them to fulfil their missions". However, Protocol 26 on SGIs attached to the Treaties emphasises that in the exercise of legislative powers the EU must recognise "the essential role and the wide discretion of national, regional and local authorities in providing, commissioning and organising services of general economic interest". Further Article 2 of Protocol 26 ensures that Member States retain exclusive competence in regulating the provision, commission and organisation of non-economic SGIs. It is submitted that the ToL did not make any great impact on SGIs. Further, the lack in the ToL of criteria which would make it possible to distinguish between SGIs of an economic nature and of a non-economic nature is regrettable. Indeed, the lack of any definition of SGIs entails that Member States will have some freedom to decide which services can be excluded from the scope of the directive. This may result is market fragmentation rather than integration;

- Services which are subject to harmonised rules, e.g. EU secondary legislation such as financial services covered by Directive 2006/48/EC relating to the taking-up and pursuit of the business of credit institutions;[2149] or electronic communication services and network and associated services to the extent that they are covered by other secondary legislation; or transport services. Urban transport, such as buses, taxis and ambulances, is however included, but excluded are driving school services, removal services and funeral services;

- Health care and pharmaceutical services, provided by health professionals, to patients consisting of assessing, maintaining or restoring those patients' state of health where those activities are reserved to a regulated health profession in the Member State where the services are provided. However, services provided to health professionals or related to enhancing wellness or to providing relaxation are covered by the directive;

- Activities connected with the exercise of official authority. This relates to the exclusion set out in Article 51 TFEU (see Chapter 25.2.2);

- Temporary work agencies concerning the service of hiring out workers, but other services carried out by them, such as placement or recruitment of workers, are covered by the directive;

- Private security services. However, the sale, delivery, installation and maintenance of technical security devices are covered by the directive;

2149. [2006] OJ L 177/1.

■ Gambling services (see Chapter 24.6);

■ Services provided by notaries and bailiffs who are appointed by an official act of government, irrespective of whether they are connected to the exercise of official authority as set out in Article 51 TFEU; and,

■ Tax matters.

Article 3(1) of the Directive provides that when there is a conflict between the directive and a particular aspect of the regulation of specific activities, or professions by other secondary legislation, the latter prevails with regard to that aspect. This means that the directive does not cease to apply, but merely gives priority to more specific secondary legislation with regard to a particular aspect. Article 3 provides an indicative list of more specific directives.

The directive states that it does not affect: criminal law; labour law and social security legislation; fundamental rights; private international law; or, the posting of workers in another Member State.

24.7.3 Principle of origin

The principle of origin was replaced by the "freedom to provide services" principle which embodies the well established case law of the ECJ on freedom to provide services (Article 16 of the Directive) (see Chapter 24.7).[2150] Drijber has explained the distinction between the two principles as follows:

"Under the Court's rulings, the law of the host state must be 'disapplied' to incoming services in so far as its application would give rise to an unjustified restriction of free trade. In other word, mutual recognition is a conditional obligation because the host state may always try to justify a restrictive means. By contrast, the country-of-origin principle works like a rule of conflict. It sets aside the law of the host state, including rules that are compatible with the Treaty. Mutual recognition becomes an unconditional obligation."[2151]

24.7.4 The approach to prohibited requirements

The directive approaches them in two ways: first it gives a broad general definition of prohibited requirements based on the case law of the ECJ, and second, it deals with particular requirements that are prohibited in respect of each freedom.

Requirements are defined as any obligation, prohibition, condition or any other limitation imposed on service providers or recipients of services which affect the access to, or the exercise of a service activity (Articles 14 and 16 of the directive). On this point the directive confirms the case law of the ECJ, which prohibits not only direct and indirect discrimination but also any measures which affect access to and exercise of a service activity. As to particular requirements, the directive sets out separate lists of prohibited requirements relating to each freedom. Both lists contain requirements previously condemned by the ECJ.

2150. On this topic see: B. de Witte, "Setting the Scene – How did Services Get to Bolkenstein and Why?" EUI Working papers, 20/2007.

2151. B. Drijber, "The Country of Origin Principle, Hearing before the Committee Internal Market and Consumer Protection on the proposed Directive on Services in the Internal Market, 11 November 2004", available at http://www.europarl.europa.eu/hearings/20041111/imco/ contributions_en.htm (accessed 4/8/12).

The list of prohibited requirements relating to the freedom to provide services is set out in Article 16(2) of the Directive. Member States are prohibited from imposing the following requirements on a provider:

- having an establishment in their territory;

- obtaining an authorisation from the competent authorities, including entry into a register or registration with a professional body or association in their territory, unless otherwise provided in the Directive or other EU measures;

- the setting-up of a certain form or type of infrastructure in their territory;

- the application of specific contractual arrangements between the provider and the recipient which prevent or restrict service provision by self-employed persons;

- possession of an identity document issued by a host Member State's authorities specific to the exercise of a service activity; and,

- conditions affecting the use of equipment and material which are an integral part of the service provided other than those necessary for health and safety at work.

Prohibited requirements in respect of recipients of services are listed in Article 19.

The prohibited requirements with regard to the freedom of establishment are listed in Article 14. Additionally, Article 15 lists requirements which constitute severe obstacles to the freedom of establishment but, nevertheless, in some circumstances may be justified. Those should be evaluated by Member States with a view to their possible replacement by less restrictive measures (see Chapter 24.7.4.2).

24.7.4.1   Prohibited requirements listed in Article 14

- Directly or indirectly discriminatory requirements based on nationality, or, in the case of companies, the location of the registered office;

- Prohibition on having an establishment in more than one Member State or on being entered in the registers or enrolled with professional bodies or associations of more than one Member State;

- Restrictions on the freedom of a provider to choose between a principal and secondary establishment, in particular an obligation imposed on it to have its principal establishment in the territory of a particular Member State, or to choose between establishment in the form of an agency, branch or subsidiary;

- Conditions of reciprocity with a Member State in which the provider already has an establishment;

- The case-by-case application of an economic test making the granting of authorisation subject to proof of the existence of an economic need or market demand, an assessment of the potential or current economic effects of the activity or an assessment of the appropriateness of the activity in relation to economic planning objectives set by the objective pursued;

- Direct or indirect involvement of competing operators in the granting of authorisations or in the adopting of other decisions of the competent authorities;

- An obligation to provide, or participate in, a financial guarantee or to take out insurance from a provider or body established in the territory of a Member State; and,

- An obligation to have been pre-registered, for a given period in the national registers, or to have previously exercised the activity for a given period in the same Member State.

24.7.4.2 *Requirements which should be evaluated*

Under Article 15 a Member State is required to evaluate existing requirements which constitute obstacles to the freedom of establishment in that State in the light of the criteria of non-discrimination, necessity and proportionality, to decide whether they can be replaced by less restrictive means. Member States are required to submit an evaluation report to that effect within the framework of a review and mutual evaluation procedure set out in Article 39 of the directive. Each report will be forwarded not only to the Commission but also to all Member States.

24.7.5 Justifications for prohibited requirements

The directive imposes stricter requirements as to justifications that a Member State may rely upon with regard to the provision of services than those relating to the freedom of establishment.

A. **Freedom of establishment.** By virtue of Article 15 of the Directive only requirements which are non-discriminatory, necessary (that is, based on an overriding reason relating to the public interest) and proportional, can be successfully invoked by a Member State. The list of overriding reasons relating to the public interest is not exhaustive. Listed reasons are to be interpreted in accordance with the case law of the ECJ.

B. **Freedom to provide services.** By virtue of Article 16(1) and (3) of the directive only require-ments which are indistinctly applicable, justified by reasons of public policy, public security, public health or the protection of the environment, and proportionate can be imposed on incom-ing service providers. Thus, the list of justifications is exhaustive. This strict approach taken to derogations relating to the freedom to provide cross-border services can be explained by the facts that first, the scope of the directive has been greatly narrowed as compared to its original version and second, additional justifications for specific sectors is provided for in Article 17.

24.7.6 Novel solutions introduced by the directive

These can be divided into two categories: those which relate to providers and recipients of services, and those aimed at enhancing co-operation between the Member States.

24.7.6.1 *Novel solutions relating to providers and recipients of services*

A. **The right to obtain information.** The directive creates a new right for providers and recipients of services, that is, the right to obtain information.

Member States are required to take necessary measures to ensure that information is easily accessible; provided in simple, unambiguous language; presented in a coherent and structured manner; and, available *via* the internet. Article 21 of the directive lists information which a Member State must make available to recipients of services. The list encompasses general information on requirements applicable to service providers in their home Member State; on the means of redress available in the event of a dispute between a provider and a recipient; and, the contact details of associations and organisations from which the recipient may obtain practical assistance.

It is for Member States to designate the bodies which will be in charge of providing information to consumers. With regard to the providers, "points of single contact" (see below) will be the places where they can obtain all necessary information.

B.   **Simplification of administrative procedures.** For providers of services the greatest innovation introduced by the directive relates to simplification of administrative procedures.

First, national authorisation procedures must be simplified and modernised. Member States are required to assess the existing procedures and formalities from the provider's perspective with a view to simplifying or abolishing them. The Commission proposes that many documents and forms should be harmonised at EU level, so relieving providers from supplying a multitude of different forms. Applications available in both non-electronic and electronic form are to be processed as quickly as possible, and, if within a reasonable time to be fixed by each Member State, no decision is notified to the applicant, the authorisation will be deemed to have been granted.

Second, each Member State must establish a "point of single contact" (PSC), i.e. set up a single body which will provide all relevant information to a provider and through which the provider can complete all procedures and formalities needed for access to, and exercise of, its service activity in that Member State. The PSC deals not only with providers established in another Member State but also with providers established in its territory.

In order to promote high quality services, the directive imposes on providers two important requirements:

▪   The first relates to transparency. Under Article 22(1) a provider is obliged to supply general information relating to its business and its services to recipients, who, under Article 22(3), at their request, are entitled to receive information additional to that specified in Article 22(1); and,

▪   The second concerns measures which a Member State may impose on a provider in order to protect recipients of services. Where services present a direct and particular risk to the health or safety of a recipient or a third person, or to the financial security of a recipient, a Member State may require the provider to subscribe to professional liability insurance or to make similar arrangements.

24.7.6.2   Novel solutions aimed at enhancing co-operation between Member States

The directive imposes a duty on the Member States to assist each other, in particular to reply to information requests and to conduct, if necessary, investigations and inspections (Articles 28 to 36). To ensure speedy and efficient exchange of information the Commission, in co-operation with the Member States, set up an electronic system – the Internal Market Information System (IMI). The obligation of assistance also encompasses an obligation on a Member State to alert other Member States if it becomes aware of acts of a service provider which could cause serious damage to health or safety of persons or to the environment.

24.7.7   Implementation of Directive 2006/123

Implementation of Directive 2006/123[2152] imposed a huge burden on the Member States, in that:

▪   First, they were required to review the legislative framework applicable to the services sector covered by the directive. The Member States notified almost 16,000 requirements imposed on

---

2152.   An Information Note issued by the Commission following the meeting of the Competitiveness Council on 1 and 2 March 2010, available at http://ec.europa.eu/internal_market/services/docs/services-dir/implementation/20100301_council_en.pdf (accessed 21/4/12). See also: M. Klamert, "Of Empty Glasses and Double Burdens: Approaches to Regulating the Services Market. A Propos the Implementation of the Service Directive", (2010) 37 *Legal Issues of Economic Integration*, 111.

establishment and 19,000 requirements imposed on cross-border provision of services. The information will serve as a basis of assessment of any future measures on removal of restrictions in respect of both freedoms;

■ Second, they had to adopt implementing measures. Almost all Member States adopted a "horizontal act", i.e. framework legislation dealing with all services covered by the directive. So far as amendments to specific legislation, i.e. regulating specific sectors of service, are concerned, about 6,000 legislative acts were modified in the Member States; and,

■ Third, they were required to establish the PSCs. In this respect, the Member States decided to develop a "common branding" and logo for their PSCs, and many provide information in languages other than their own. The Commission supported the efforts of the Member States by establishing an EU portal which identifies the PSCs in every Member State and provides direct links to all national PSCs' websites.

24.7.8 Conclusion

It is submitted that the Directive 2006/123 being a compromise, does not revolutionise EU law in respect of the two freedoms.[2153] It largely confirms the existing case law of the ECJ in both areas. However, it contains innovations, which, on the one hand, facilitate access to, and exercise of, both freedoms, and on the other, improve co-operation between Member States.[2154] It also introduced a new approach to harmonisation of EU law in that Member States, through review of existing administrative procedures, were required to take a proactive approach to the implementation of the directive. Finally, the directive responded to concerns of trade unions and does not erode the European social model. It is to be noted that the directive applies in addition to the existing EU law. Services not covered by it do, of course, remain subject to EU law.

24.8 Recognition of professional qualifications

The main limitations on the exercise of the right of establishment (as well as the right to provide services or to have access to employment in a host Member State as a worker) concern the conditions relating to admission to a particular profession. Indeed, whether an EU migrant works as a worker, as a self-employed person or as a provider of services, the exercise of his/her professional activities is conditional upon recognition by a host Member State of the fact that he/she is are adequately qualified to carry them out. In order to implement the free movement of economically active persons within the EU, the continuing harmonisation of rules on the recognition of diplomas and professional qualifications is of vital importance.

There are two approaches to harmonisation of the rules relating to the mutual recognition of diplomas and professional qualifications.

The first consists of the harmonisation of the rules in respect of individual professions or a particular sector of the economy by use of "sectorial" directives, one by one. The frequency of use of this approach has declined. It was initially applied under the general programme adopted in 1961 during the transitional period (see Chapter 24.3). Progress under the sectorial directives was slow and this approach

---

2153. On this topic see G. Davies, "The Service Directive: Extending the Country of Origin Principle and Reforming Public Administration", (2007) 32 ELRev., 232.

2154. See C. Barnard, "Unravelling the Service Directive", (2008) 45 CMLRev., 323.

was not appropriate to the requirements of the internal market, although it resulted in the adoption of a number of directives covering many professions, such as architects, dentists, doctors, midwives, nurses, veterinary surgeons, hairdressers, and so on, and a variety of economic sectors.

The second approach relates to Directive 89/48/EEC,[2155] which provided for a general system for the recognition of higher education diplomas awarded on completion of professional education and training of at least three years' duration. The directive covered all regulated professions for which university diplomas awarded for a course of at least three years' duration are required. This directive was supplemented by additional directives which created a system which was complex, rigid and lacked transparency. The Stockholm European Council (March 2001) requested the Commission to undertake a major reform of that system. This resulted in the adoption of Directive 2005/36/EC of 7 September 2005[2156] on the Recognition of Professional Qualifications which repealed and replaced three directives that had set up a general system for recognition (Directives 89/48/EEC; 92/51/EEC; and, 1999/42/EC) and 12 sectorial directives covering the seven professions of doctors, nurses, dentists, veterinary surgeons, midwives, pharmacists and architects. The Directive came into force in October 2007.

Directive 2005/36/EC sets out rules concerning recognition by any Member State of professional qualifications acquired in other Member States. They relate to the methodologies and procedures for evaluating credentials for work purposes and not for academic purposes such as the pursuit or continuation of higher education on the basis of qualifications obtained in a home Member State. The directive is neither concerned with the recognition of decisions adopted by other Member States pursuant to this directive, nor with the recognition of qualifications obtained outside the EU (but see Chapter 24.8.4).

Directive 2005/36/EC is very complex and has many shortcomings which have been identified by the Commission as creating obstacles to the mobility of qualified professionals in the EU. Accordingly, in December 2011, the Commission submitted a proposal for a new directive[2157] modernising Directive 2005/36/EC. The main features of Directive 2005/36/EC and the proposal for its amendment are examined below.

24.8.1 Recognition of professional qualifications under Directive 2005/36/EC

The main features of Directive 2005/36/EC are:

1. It applies to an EU citizen exercising his/her right to free movement and members of his/her family irrespective of whether they are EU citizens or nationals of third countries; nationals of the EEA and Switzerland; persons who have refugee status in a Member State when they move to another Member State; and persons, covered by Directive 2003/109/EC of 25 November 2003 Concerning the Status of Third-Country Nationals who are Long-term Residents in the EU[2158] (see Chapter 22.2).

2. The directive makes a distinction between a situation where a profession is regulated and one where it is not. Article 3(1)(a) of the directive defines the concept of "regulated profession". According to it a profession is regulated when national rules (whether legislation, regulations

---

2155.   [1989] OJ L19/16.
2156.   [2005] OJ L255/22.
2157.   COM(2011) 883 final.
2158.   [2004] L16/44.

or administrative provisions) which govern the conditions for taking up or pursuing a professional activity impose the possession of a diploma or other certificate of qualification as a precondition to the exercise of that profession. The directive only applies to regulated professions.

3. The directive makes a distinction between the provision of services and the freedom of establishment.

A Provision of services

When a professional service is provided on a temporary and occasional basis, a provider of services is not required to apply for recognition of his qualifications. Whether services are provided on a temporary and occasional basis is assessed on a case-by-case basis in the light of duration; frequency; continuity; and, regularity of the service provided. The provider must provide services under his original professional title, and is subject to certain conditions imposed with a view to protecting service users. In particular he may be required to comply with certain obligations to provide the recipients of the services and the national administration with information. With regards to health professionals, where public safety concerns are particularly important, those obligations include advance declarations to host Member State authorities and, in some cases, *pro forma* registration. If the profession in question is not regulated in a home Member State, the service provider must provide evidence of two years' professional experience during the ten years preceding the provision of services in a host Member State. This condition is not applicable if either the profession or the education and training leading to the profession is regulated in a host Member State.

B Establishment

The Directive provides for:

(i) Automatic recognition of training qualifications on the basis of the minimum training conditions in the cases previously covered by individual directives, that is, in respect of doctors, nurses responsible for general care, dental practitioners, veterinary surgeons, midwives, pharmacists and architects.

(ii) Automatic recognition of qualifications attested by professional experience in the case of the industrial, craft and commercial activities listed in the annexes to the directive. In respect of the recognition of professional qualifications on the basis of professional experience acquired in another Member State, the number of years and the capacity in which the applicant was employed, that is, as a manager, self-employed person or employee, are taken into consideration for each category of activities.

(iii) Application of the general system of recognition to all professions and to situations not covered by other harmonising measures, i.e. not covered by (i) and (ii) above.

The general system of recognition is based on the principle of mutual recognition, subject to the application of compensatory measures if there are substantial differences between the training acquired by the person concerned and the training required in the host Member State. The compensatory measure may take the form of an adaptation period or an aptitude test. The choice is left to the person concerned, unless specific derogations exist.

The directive refers to five levels of qualification as follows:

- Level 1 – an "attestation of competence" issued by a competent authority in a home Member State on the basis of a training course not forming part of a certificate or diploma, or three years' full time professional experience, or general primary or secondary education, attesting that the applicant has acquired "general knowledge" (Article 11(a));

- Level 2 – a "certificate" attesting to the successful completion of a secondary course which is either "general" or "technical or professional" in character, and which in either case is supplemented by a course of study or professional training (Article 11(b));

- Level 3 – a "diploma" certifying either successful completion of training at post-secondary level of at least one year's duration on a full time basis, or the equivalent part-time duration, or training with a "special structure" which provides a comparable professional standard and which prepares the trainee for a "comparable level of responsibilities and functions" (Article 11(c));

- Level 4 – a "diploma" certifying successful completion of training at post-secondary level of at least three and not more than four years' duration on a full time basis, or the equivalent part-time duration, at a university or equivalent establishment, as well as any additional professional training which may be required (Article 11(d)); and,

- Level 5 – a "diploma" certifying successful completion of a post-secondary course of at least four years' duration, or the equivalent part-time duration, at a university or equivalent establishment, and when appropriate attestation that the applicant has successfully completed any additional training required in addition to the post-secondary course.

The levels of qualification constitute a basis for recognition, or otherwise, of qualifications which is specified under Article 13. This article makes a distinction between a situation where a profession is regulated in both a home and a host Member State, and a situation where it is regulated in a host Member State but not in a home Member State.

In the first situation, the host Member State may not refuse to recognise a qualification obtained in a home Member State that attests to a level of qualification at least equivalent to the level immediately below that required in the host Member State. This means that if Poland requires Level 5 competence for a given profession, but the UK requires Level 4 competence, Poland must not reject the UK qualification, as it is required to accept qualification at least equivalent to the level immediately below that which is required in Poland. However, Poland may impose compensatory measures (see below).

In the second situation, i.e. where a profession is regulated in a host Member State but not in a home Member State, a host Member State must give access to the profession to applicants who provide evidence of having pursued that profession for at least two years on a full-time basis in the home Member State over the preceding ten years.

In both situations set out in Article 13 of the Directive, a host Member State may subject the recognition of a qualification to compensatory measures, i.e. an aptitude test or an adaptation period of up to three years if:

- the training is one year shorter than that required by a host Member State;

- the training covered substantially different matters from those covered by the evidence of formal training required in the host Member State; or

■ the profession as defined in the host Member State comprises one or more regulated professional activities that do not exist in the corresponding profession in the applicant's home Member State and requires specific training that covers substantially different matters from those covered by the applicant's training.

In general, an applicant is entitled to choose between an adaptation period and an aptitude test. A Member State may limit the choice when:

■ the practice of the profession requires precise knowledge of national law; and,

■ the provision of advice and/or assistance concerning national law is an essential and constant aspect of the professional activity.

The above limitation was explained in Case C-149/05 *Price*.[2159]

THE FACTS WERE:

Mr Price, a holder of a UK degree in Fine Arts Valuation, wished to pursue the profession of director of voluntary public auctions in France, which under French law required substantial knowledge of law. He was required to take an aptitude test. His preference was for an adaptation period (not surprisingly, as he had actually practised the profession for seven years in France).

Held:

The ECJ held that a Member State can limit the choice of an applicant in a situation where advice and/or assistance concerns a specialised area of law and constitutes an essential and constant element of the relevant activity. The ECJ left it to the referring court to decide which compensatory measure was appropriate in the applicant's case, but from the judgment it was quite clear that Mr Price's preference would not be accommodated.

---

4. In the context of recognition of professional qualifications under Directive 2005/36 and its predecessors, the meaning of "diploma" for the purposes of recognition was clarified by the ECJ. First in Case C-311/06 *Cavallera*:[2160]

THE FACTS WERE:

In this case an Italian national, who had been awarded a mechanical engineering qualification in Italy after three years' education and training, obtained homologation of his Italian qualification in Spain. As a result he could enrol in Spain in the Register of Engineers. When he applied to the Italian Ministry of Justice for the recognition of the Spanish homologation for the purpose of his enrolment in the register of engineers in Italy, his application was

---

2159. Case C-149/05 *Harold Price v Conseil des Ventes Volontaires de Meubles aux Enchères Publiques* [2006] ECR I-7691.

2160. C-311/06 *Consiglio Nazionale degli Ingegneri v Ministero della Giustizia and Marco Cavallera* [2009] ECR I-415.

successful. However, the Italian National Council of Engineers challenged the decision of the Ministry of Justice on the ground that the claimant had never worked professionally outside Italy and that he had not taken the State examination provided for under Italian legislation for the purpose of being entitled to pursue the profession of engineer in Italy. The matter went before the ECJ within the preliminary ruling proceedings.

Held:

The Court held that the concept of a diploma does not include a certificate issued by a Member State attesting professional qualifications obtained in another Member State. However, if qualifications were acquired, wholly or in part, under the education system of the Member State which issues the certificate in question then such a certificate will be regarded as a "diploma".

Comment:

The ECJ emphasised that the Spanish homologation did not provide evidence of any additional qualification as neither homologation nor enrolment in the register of engineers in Spain was based on an examination of the qualifications or professional experience acquired by the claimant. The ECJ held that in the light of the fact that there was no evidence that the claimant had obtained an additional qualification or professional experience in Spain it would be contrary to the principle enshrined by Directive 89/48, according to which Member States reserve the option of fixing the minimum level of qualification necessary to guarantee the quality of services provided in their territory, to consider the Spanish certificate of homologation as a "diploma".

Further important clarifications regarding the concept of "a diploma" were provided in Case C-151/07 *Khatzithanasis* [2161] and in Case C-84/07 *Commission v Greece*.[2162]

THE FACTS WERE:

Mr Khatzithanasis, a Greek national, after completing a two-year course in optical studies was awarded a diploma in optometry and optical studies by the Vinci Regional Institute for Optical Studies and Optometry (VRIOSO) located in Italy. That diploma authorised him to pursue the profession of optician in Italy. Subsequently, he took a one year course leading to an educational qualification in optometry awarded by the VRIOSO. Mr Khatzithanasis attended the above courses not at the seat of the VRIOSO in Italy, but in Greece, at an independent study centre for optometry. However, he also attended a 300-hour advanced course in optometry, and took the relevant examinations at the seat of the VRIOSO in Italy in order to acquire authorisation to pursue the profession of optician. The Greek study centre establishment was not recognised as an educational establishment by Greek legislation.

When Mr Khatzithanasis applied to the relevant Greek authorities for the recognition of his Italian diploma, they refused on the ground that he had received education, in whole or

---

2161. Case C-151/07 *Theologos-Grigorios Khatzithanasis v OEEK* [2008] ECR I-9013.
2162. [2008] ECR I-171.

in part, at an establishment located in Greece which, according to the Greek legislation, was not recognised as an educational establishment.

Both the Commission and Mr Khatzithanasis submitted that Greece was in breach of Council Directive 92/51/EEC as amended by Directive 2001/19/EC [now Directive 2005/36].

Held:

The ECJ held that Greece was in breach of the relevant directive and that subject to the application of Article 4 of that directive, was obliged to recognise a diploma awarded by a competent authority in another Member State.

Comment:

The ECJ provided the following clarifications concerning the recognition of diplomas:

- *It is for the institution which awards the diploma alone to decide whether education and training that a person received in another Member State is adequate for the purpose of awarding a diploma. Therefore, the claimant's diploma was within the scope of the Directive;*

- *Directive 89/48 [now Directive 2005/36] does not contain any limitation as regards the Member State in which an applicant must have acquired his professional qualifications; and,*

- *With regard to Article 4 of Directive 92/51/ECC [now Article 14 of Directive 2005/36], this article allows a Member State to take account of the fact that considerable differences may exist between the training and education required in that Member State and the Member State where the diploma was awarded for taking up the same regulated profession, and indeed it allows a Member State where the recognition is sought to require that the applicant either completes an adaptation period or takes an aptitude test. Greece did not give any choice to applicants. It imposed on them the requirement of completing an adaptation period. This was in breach of Article 4 (Case C-84/07 Commission v Greece).*

5. An application for recognition should be examined within the shortest possible time and must be completed within four months of its submission. The decision given by a competent national authority, or the absence of any decision, is subject to appeal.

6. The directive establishes a network of contact points (one being located in each Member State) which have the task of providing EU citizens with information and assistance in respect of recognition procedures and resolving any difficulties they might encounter in obtaining recognition of their professional qualifications. The network enhances co-operation between national administrations, and between them and the Commission.

7. The directive provides for the introduction of professional "cards" by professional associations and organisations with a view to monitoring the career of professionals. Under the proposed amendments the idea of professional cards has been further advanced and refined (see below).

24.8.2 Proposed amendments to Directive 2005/36/EC

The proposed amendments to Directive 2005/36/EC are aimed at increasing the mobility of professionals in the EU by simplifying the procedure for recognition of professional qualifications while ensuring the appropriate level of protection of consumers and patients. They are:

1. The establishment of a European Professional Card (EPC). This will be a new tool for the recognition of professional qualifications. All interested professions will have the choice of adopting an EPC. The EPC will certify that the person concerned has demonstrated the necessary credentials to exercise the relevant profession. The documentary burden will be imposed on a home Member State. In order to reduce expenses relating to the issuing of the card, the proposal provides for compulsory use of the Internal Market Information System (IMI) (see Chapter 24.7.6.2). This entails that when an application is made for an EPC, the relevant authorities of a home Member State will be required to create a professional file in IMI with all supporting documents. Further implementing measures will be adopted by the Commission relating to the technical specifications to be shown on the EPC and to measures ensuring integrity, confidentiality and accuracy of the information contained in the IMI file.

   It is important to note that the adoption of EPCs will be voluntary for both the relevant profession and for a member of that profession.

2. Better access to information on the recognition of professional qualification for EU citizens will be achieved by using PSCs created by the Directive on Services in the Internal Market (see Chapter 24.7.6.1), as a one-stop shop for providing such information, and dealing on line with applications for recognition.

3. In order to protect patients and consumers the proposal first, introduces an alert mechanism, and second allows a host Member State to check language knowledge of the applicant following recognition of the applicant's qualifications. An alert mechanism is of particular importance with respect to health professionals, who benefit from automatic recognition of their qualifications under Directive 2005/36/EC. Accordingly, when a health professional is prohibited by one Member State from exercising his profession by the relevant national bodies or courts, that Member State has an obligation to alert all other Member States. As to language requirements for health professionals, it is for the relevant national health authority to carry out language checks where strictly necessary.

4. With regard to the general system of recognition, the proposal provides that the system of qualification levels should be used as a benchmark and not as a means of excluding certain qualifications from the benefit of the Directive. Accordingly, in a situation where there are two or more levels of difference between the level of qualification obtained by an applicant and the requirements of a host Member State, the use of compensation measures will be appropriate. This is subject to an exception concerning persons whose qualifications are based on professional experience, but a university degree is required for access to the relevant profession in a host Member State. Further, the system of common platforms will be replaced by a common training frameworks and common training tests. Interested profession will be able to benefit from automatic recognition on the basis of a common set of knowledge, skills and competence, or a common test assessing the ability of professionals to pursue a profession.

5. With regard to automatic recognition of training qualifications in respect of doctors, nurses, etc, the proposal simplifies updates and clarifies training requirements.

6.   The proposal introduces the concept of partial access to a profession,[2163] i.e. a host Member State may "partially recognise" qualifications obtained by applicants. This will occur when:

• first, the difference between the professional activity exercised in the home Member State and the regulated profession in the host Member State is so large that the application of compensatory measures would amount to requiring the applicant to complete a full programme of education and training in a host Member State in order to have access to the full regulated profession; and,

• second, the professional activity can objectively be separated from other activities falling within the regulated profession in the host Member State. An activity is defined as separable if it is exercised as an autonomous activity in the home Member State.

A Member State may, however, refuse partial access on the grounds of an overriding reason of general interest, such as public health, but this is subject to the principle of proportionality.

7.   The proposal extends the scope of application of Directive 2005/36 to persons who hold a diploma but have yet to complete a remunerated traineeship required by a home Member State, and to notaries.

8.   The proposal enhances transparency by imposing on each Member State obligations to notify a list of regulated professions in that Member State and to assess its legislation on the access to regulated professions in the light of the principles of proportionality and non-discrimination. The outcome of this assessment must be notified to the Commission. It will also be subject to mutual evaluation by Member States in that they will be able to compare their regulatory approaches and simplify their legal frameworks for regulated professions when necessary.

24.8.3   Unregulated professions

An unregulated profession is one which is not covered by Directive 2005/36.[2164] The best way of verifying whether a profession is regulated in a particular Member State is to consult the EU regulated professions database or contact the national contact point for professional qualifications. If the relevant profession is not regulated, the person concerned is not required to apply for recognition, i.e. he/she can freely pursue his/her profession, but the principles established in Case C-340/89 *Vlassopoulou*[2165] apply, if relevant, i.e. a host Member State must examine the knowledge and qualifications already recognised or acquired by the applicant in another Member State, give reasons for non-recognition and ensure that the applicant has access to a judicial remedy.

The difference between the recognition of professional qualifications in regulated and unregulated professions is well illustrated in Case C-234/97 *Bobadilla*.[2166]

2163.   See Case C-330/*03 Colegio Ingenieros de Caminos, Canales y Puertos v Administración del Estado* [2006] ECR I-801.

2164.   Case C-285/*01 Isabel Burbaud v Ministère de l'Emploi et de la Solidarité* [2003] ECR I-8219; in Case C-586/08 *Angelo Rubino v Ministero dell'Università e della Ricerca* ([2009] ECR I-12013) the ECJ held that the profession of lecturer in Italy does not constitute a regulated profession given that no specific educational qualification is required to become a lecturer in Italy. In that country lecturers are recruited by means of a selection procedure.

2165.   Case C-340/89 *Irène Vlassopoulou v Ministerium für Justiz, Bundes- und Europaangelegenheiten Baden-Württemberg* [1991] ECR I-2357.

2166.   Case C-234/97 *Teresa Fernández De Bobadilla v Museo Nacional Del Prado, Comité De Empresa Del Museo Nacional Del Prado, Ministerio Fiscal* [1999] ECR I-4773.

THE FACTS WERE:

Ms Fernández de Bobadilla, a Spanish national residing in Madrid, after obtaining her Bachelor of Arts degree in History of Art at the University of Boston, US, obtained a Master of Arts degree in fine arts restoration at Newcastle upon Tyne Polytechnic in the UK in 1989. A grant from the Prado museum in Spain had helped her to study in the UK. From 1989 to 1992 she worked for the Prado in Spain under a temporary contract as a restorer of works of art on paper. Under the terms of a collective agreement concluded in 1988 by the Prado and staff representatives, the post of restorer was reserved to persons possessing qualifications awarded by the restoration department of the Faculty of Fine Arts or by the School of Arts in Spain, or any foreign qualification recognised by the competent authorities. In October 1992 Ms de Bobadilla applied to the relevant department of the Ministry of Education to have the degree obtained in the UK officially recognised as equivalent to a Spanish degree in the conservation and restoration of cultural assets. In response, she was given notice that in order for her English diploma to be recognised, she would have to demonstrate sufficient knowledge of 24 subjects which were listed in the notice, in an examination arranged in two parts. On 17 November 1992 the Prado organised a competition for a permanent post of a restorer of works of art on paper. The application/entry submitted by Ms de Bobadilla was rejected on the ground that she did not satisfy the requirements laid down in the collective agreement. Ms de Bobadilla brought an action for annulment of such requirements as contrary to the Spanish Constitution and Article 45 TFEU.

Held:

The ECJ focused on the issue of whether the collective agreement had a general scope of application, that is, whether in a general way it governed the right to take up or pursue a profession, or whether it governed relations only between the employer and the employees within a single public body. Then it stated that it was for the national court to determine the scope of the collective agreement.

Comment:

The ECJ held that if the collective agreement had a general scope of application, i.e. if the terms of a collective agreement "are common to other collective agreements entered into on an individual basis by other public bodies of the same kind and, furthermore, are the result of a single administrative policy laid down at national level, then those agreements may be sufficiently general in scope for their terms to be classified as rules regulating a professional activity for the purposes of Directives 89/48 and 92/51."[2167] Consequently, if one or other of Directives 89/48 or 92/51 was applicable, a public body could not require that a candidate's qualifications be granted official recognition by the competent national authorities other than according to the conditions set out in those two Directives. However, if neither directive applied, i.e. the collective agreement governed relations only between the employees and the employer and thus was not sufficiently general in scope for the relevant professional activities to be classified as a regulated profession for the purposes of Directives 89/48 and 92/51 the profession of restorer of cultural assets was not regulated within the meaning of Directives 89/48 and 92/51.

2167. Ibid, para. 22.

When a profession is not regulated, the procedure for granting official recognition must comply with the requirements set out by the ECJ in Cases C-340/89 Vlassopoulou[2168] *and C-164/94* Arantis.[2169] *In such a case the competent authorities of the Member State in which the recognition is sought must take into account the diplomas, certificates and other evidence of qualifications the applicant acquired in order to practise that profession in another Member State and compare them with the qualifications required by the host Member State. If the comparison reveals that the knowledge and qualifications certified by a foreign diploma correspond to those required by the national provisions, the diploma should be recognised by the host Member State. If there is partial equivalence, the host Member State is entitled to require the person concerned to demonstrate that he/she has acquired the additional knowledge and qualifications needed. However, where there is no general procedure for official recognition laid down by the Member State, or where that procedure does not comply with the requirements of EU law, it is for the public body advertising a particular post to investigate whether the diploma awarded in another Member State, together with practical experience where appropriate, is to be considered as equivalent to the qualification required. In this case, the Museum of Prado, as it advertised the post, was particularly well placed to assess the candidate's actual knowledge and abilities for two reasons: first, it had previously employed the candidate and second, it had made a grant to her to help her obtain a diploma in the UK.*

The above case shows that despite a profession being unregulated, i.e. when Directive 2005/36 is inapplicable, EU law remains relevant. The ECJ has consistently held that when the relevant national authorities of a host Member State receive a request to admit a person to an unregulated profession, access to which depends on the possession of diplomas and professional qualifications, they must: take due account of that person's professional qualifications and experience obtained in another Member State, by comparing them with the qualifications required by the national rules; give reasons for non-recognition; and, ensure that the person concerned has access to a judicial remedy.

It may occur that a person will not be able to practice an unregulated profession freely in a host Member State because it may not exist there as an independent profession in that it may involve activities which belong to another profession regulated by the host Member State. This occurred in case C-61/89 *Bouchoucha*[2170] in which a British national who was not qualified as a medical doctor in the UK but held British qualification in osteopathy, a profession which was not recognised in France and the practise of which was part of practice in France of medicine by qualified medical doctors, was fined by the French authorities for illegally practising medicine in France.

24.8.4 Recognition of qualifications obtained by EU citizens outside the EU

Initially, the ECJ refused to extend the application of the Treaties to a situation where EU citizens obtain their qualification in a non-Member State, exercise their right of establishment in a host Member State and subsequently seek to have their qualifications recognised in another Member State.[2171] However, in

---

2168. [1991] ECR I-2357.
2169. Case C-164/94 *Arantis v Land of Berlin* [1996] ECR I-135.
2170. Case C-61/89 *Criminal proceedings against Marc Gaston Bouchoucha* [1990] ECR I-3551.
2171. Case C-154/93 *Tawil-Albertini v Ministre des Affaires Sociales* [1994] ECR I-451.

Case C-319/92 *Haim*[2172] the ECJ changed its approach. In this case, Mr Haim, a German national, who had obtained his qualification as a dentist in a non-Member State and subsequently practised for eight years in Belgium (he was also admitted to private practice in Germany), was refused permission to work as a dentist in a social security scheme in Germany unless he completed a further two-year preparatory training course. He argued that his professional experience in Belgium should be taken into account by the German authorities. The ECJ held that "The competent national authority, in order to verify whether the training period requirement prescribed by the national rules is met, must take into account the professional experience of the plaintiff in the main proceedings, including that which he has acquired during his appointment as a dental practitioner of a social security scheme in another Member State."[2173]

The willingness of the ECJ to extend the scope of the Treaty to cover situations where a person has acquired some professional experience in a Member State was further extended in Case C-238/98 *Hocsman*.[2174]

THE FACTS WERE:

Doctor Hocsman, a national of Argentina, had acquired Spanish nationality before being naturalised in France in 1998. He obtained qualifications as a medical doctor in Argentina in 1976, which were recognised by a Spanish university as being equivalent to a Spanish qualification. On that basis he practised medicine in Spain, and was trained as a specialist in urology. In 1982 he was awarded the qualification of specialist in urology by the University of Barcelona. He then worked for some years as a specialist in urology in Spain. In 1990, he moved to France where he held posts of assistant or associate specialist in urology in a number of French hospitals. In 1997 the French authorities refused to grant Dr Hocsman authorisation to practise medicine in France on the ground that the Argentinian diploma did not entitle him to practise in France.

Held:

The ECJ held Article 47 TFEU requires that in a situation where harmonised EU rules are not applicable, all the diplomas, certificates and other evidence of formal qualifications of the person concerned and his relevant experience, must be taken into consideration by the relevant authorities when they compare experience, the specialised knowledge and the abilities certified by those diplomas with the knowledge and qualifications required by their national rules.

Comment:

In the above case the ECJ stated that Article 47 TFEU applies when harmonised rules are not applicable. The case law of the ECJ on the recognition of qualifications obtained outside the EU was codified in Article 3(3) of Directive 2005/38 which states that: "Evidence of formal qualifications issued by a third country shall be regarded as evidence of formal qualifications if the holder has three years' professional experience in the profession concerned on the territory of the Member State which recognised that evidence of formal qualifications in

---

2172. Case C-319/92 *Salomone Haim v Kassenzahnärztliche Vereinigung Nordrhein* [1994] ECR I-425.

2173. Ibid, para. 28.

2174. Case C-238/98 *Hugo Fernando Hocsman v Ministre de l'Emploi et de la Solidarité* [2000] ECR I-6623; see also Case C-110/01 *Malika Tennah-Durez v Conseil National de l'Ordre des Médecins* [2003] ECR I-6239.

accordance with Article 2(2), certified by that State." This means that the Directive applies to a person who has obtained all their qualifications outside the EU if:

- *his professional qualifications have been recognised in a Member State on the ground of national rules of that State (regarded as a home Member State for the purposes of the Directive);*

- *those qualifications permit practising of a regulated profession there;*

- *he has actually practised that profession for three years in a home Member State; and*

- *he has obtained a certificate issued by the home Member State attesting that period of practice.*

It is to be noted that non-EU citizens, apart from those specified Chapter 22.2, have no right to have their qualifications, obtained either abroad or within the EU, recognised under Article 47 TFEU or EU secondary legislation. Recognition of their qualifications will depend on the national law of the Member State concerned.

RECOMMENDED READING

Books
De la Feria, R., and Vogenauer, S. (eds.), *Prohibition of Abuse of Law: A New General Principle of EU Law*, 2011, Oxford: Hart Publishing.
Nascimbene, B., and Bergamini, E., *The Legal Profession in the European Union*, 2009, London: KLI.
Additionally, see recommended books on the internal market listed at the end of Chapter 17.

Articles
Acierno, S., "The Carpenter Judgment: Fundamental Rights and the Limits of the Community Legal Order", (2003) 28 ELRev., 398.
Barnard, C., "Unravelling the Services Directive", (2008) 45 CMLRev., 323.
Davis, A. C. L., "One Step Forward. Two Steps Back? The Viking and Laval Cases in the ECJ", (2008) 37 *Industrial Law Journal*, 126.
De La Rosa, S., "The Directive on Cross-border Healthcare or the Art of Codifying Complex Case Law", (2012) 49 CMLRev., 15.
Jørgensen, S., "The Right to Cross-Border Education in the European Union", (2009) 46 CMLRev., 1567.
Klamert, M., "Of Empty Glasses and Double Burdens: Approaches to Regulating the Services Market. A Propos the Implementation of the Service Directive", (2010) 37 *Legal Issues of Economic Integration*, 111.
Lee, R.G., "Liberalisation of Legal Services in Europe: Progress and Prospect", (2010) 30 *Legal Studies*, 186.
O'Leary, S., "Free Movement of Persons and Services", in Craig, P., and De Búrca, G. (eds), *The Evolution of EU Law*, 2nd edn, 2011, Oxford: OUP, 499.
Rich, R. F. and Merrick, K. R., "Cross Border Health Care in the European Union: Challenges and Opportunities", (2006) 23 J. Contemp. Health Law and Policy, 64.
Roth, W-H., "From Centros to Überseering: Free Movement of Companies, Private International Law and Community Law", (2003) 52 ICLQ, 177.
Sørensen, J., "Abuse of Rights in Community Law: A Principle of Substance or Merely Rhetoric?", (2006) 43 CMLRev., 423.

Spaventa, E., "From Gebhard to Carpenter: Towards a (non)-Economic European Constitution", (2004) 41 CMLRev., 743.

Vossestein, G., "Cross-border Transfer of Seat and Conversion of Companies under the EC Treaty provisions on Freedom of Establishment", (2009) 6 *European Company Law*, 115.

White, R., "Conflicting Competences: Free Movement Rules and Immigration Laws", (2004) 29 ELRev., 385.

PROBLEM QUESTION

A.   Anna, a French national, has been a member of the Paris Bar since 2005. She has recently moved to the UK. She wants to work as a solicitor in London. When she applied to the Law Society of England and Wales for a Practising Certificate for year 2012–2013, which would entitle her to practise as a solicitor in England and Wales, her application was refused on the grounds that she has no knowledge of English law and that she does not speak fluent English.

B.   James, a German national, has been a member of the Berlin Bar for many years. Recently, he has applied to the Paris Bar for registration as an *avocat*. He wishes to set up a law practice in Paris while retaining his law practice in Berlin. The Paris Bar Council has refused the application on the grounds that French rules require *avocats* to have only one place of establishment at a time, in order to maintain sufficient contact with their clients and the relevant judicial authorities, and to ensure that *avocats* respect the rules of professional conduct.

Advise Anna and James as to their rights under EU law.

ESSAY QUESTION

The rights of EU citizens to establish themselves, or to provide services, or to work anywhere in the EU are fundamental freedoms of the EU. However, national regulations, which require specific professional qualifications for certain professions, may restrict these fundamental freedoms. Critically assess whether such restrictions have been eliminated in the EU and, if not, suggest possible ways of eliminating them.

AIDE-MÉMOIRE

Distinction between the freedom of establishment and the freedom to provide services

Freedom of establishment
It involves actual pursuit of an economic activity through fixed establishment for an indefinite period in a host Member State

Freedom to provide services
To be considered as a service within the meaning of Art. 56 TFEU:
- an activity must of of an economic nature and lawful in at least one Member State;
- service must be provided for remuneration;
- there must be a cross-border element; and,
- service must be of a temporary nature.

Prohibition of discrimination and beyond

Directly discriminatory national rules	Indirectly discriminatory national rules	Non-discriminatory national rules which are liable to hinder or to make less attractive the exercise of both freedoms

Can be justified only under derogations contained in the Treaties (Case C/74 *Reyners* and Case 33/74 *Van Binsbergen*), and must be proportionate

Can be justified either under the derogations set out in the Treaties or by imperative requirements in the general interest, and must be proportionate

25

EXCEPTIONS TO THE FREE MOVEMENT OF PERSONS

CHAPTER OUTLINE

1. There are two main Treaties-based exceptions to the free movement of persons. The first allows a host Member State to impose restrictions on access of EU migrant workers to "employment in the public service" (Article 45(4) TFEU) and of self-employed persons to activities connected with the "exercise of official authority" (Article 51 TFEU). The second exception concerns all persons exercising their right to free movement within the EU and is based on the grounds of public policy, public security and public health.

2. The ECJ has applied a functional approach to the interpretation of the exception set out in Article 45(4) TFEU, i.e. it has focused on whether the tasks carried out by a holder of a post involve direct or indirect participation in the exercise of powers conferred by public law, designed to safeguard the interests of the State, rather than an institutional approach, i.e. focusing on whether a particular post is considered by a Member State as being within its "public sector".

Under Article 51 TFEU the activity in question must be directly and specifically connected with the exercise of official authority. As a result, activities which are merely auxiliary and preparatory; and activities which do not involve the exercise of decision-making powers, powers of constraint or powers of coercion, are outside the scope of Article 51 TFEU.

3. The second exception concerns derogations based on public policy, public security and public health. All have been interpreted restrictively by the ECJ so that Member States' discretion can only be exercised within the limits allowed by EU law in accordance with the requirements of the principle of proportionality. This restrictive approach embodied in the case law was confirmed by Directive 2004/38/EC on the Right of Citizens of the Union and their Family Members to Move and Reside Freely within the Territory of the Member States.

4. The concepts of public security and public policy are interrelated and often public security is invoked as an alternative to public policy, for example, terrorist or other criminal activities pose a threat to both public security and public policy. The concept of public policy is vague and bearing in mind that a wide range of activities may be found by a Member State as jeopardising its public policy (such as organising demonstrations, or walking nude in public places, or being a member of a particular religious sect), it is the most controversial. For that reason Member States are not allowed to determine the scope of either derogation unilaterally. Directive 2004/38/EC and the case law of the ECJ set the following limitations on the use of public policy and public security derogations:

- Measures taken on those grounds must be based on the personal conduct of the individual concerned. It does not have to be illegal, but, in order to rely on the derogations a Member State must provide evidence that it has taken repressive or other effective measures to combat such conduct;

- Previous criminal convictions are not in themselves sufficient grounds for relying on derogations, but past conduct may constitute a present threat to public policy where there is evidence that the individual concerned has a propensity to act in the same way in the future as he/she did in the past. Whilst an individual deterrence may be acceptable, a general deterrence is not, i.e., a Member State is not allowed to take measures against an individual for reasons of a general preventive nature;

- In order to justify any measure adopted on the grounds of public policy or public security., personal conduct of the individual concerned must represent a genuine, present and sufficiently serious threat affecting one of the fundamental interests of the host Member State;

- Derogations cannot be relied upon to serve economic ends; and,

- Non-compliance with administrative formalities in respect of entry and residence never justifies expulsion from the territory of a host Member State.

5. The derogation based on public health can only be relied upon in respect of diseases with epidemic potential and other infectious or contagious parasitic diseases, if they are the subject of protection provisions applying to nationals of the host Member State, and only during the first three months of residence in a host Member State.

6. Article 28 of Directive 2004/38/EC provides safeguards against expulsion from a host Member State for EU nationals who have resided in that Member State for a considerable length of time or are minors. Those who have obtained permanent residence in that Member State can only be deported on the grounds of serious requirements of public policy, while deportation of those who have resided in a Member State for more than 10 years or who are minors can only be justified on the grounds of imperative requirements of public policy.

7. Articles 31–33 of Directive 2004/38/EC set out important procedural rights for EU citizens who are refused entry and residence in a host Member State.

25.1 Introduction

The two exceptions to the fundamental principle of the Treaties guaranteeing the free movement of persons have been construed narrowly by the ECJ to ensure that the exceptions do not undermine the principle. They are examined below.

25.2 The concepts of "employment in the public service" and "the exercise of official authority"

Article 45(4) TFEU provides that Article 45 TFEU "shall not apply to employment in the public service" and Article 51 TFEU states that provisions relating to the freedom of establishment "shall not apply, so far as any given Member State is concerned, to activities which in that State are connected, even occasionally, with the exercise of official authority". Article 62 TFEU states that Articles 51 to 54 TFEU (provisions on the right of establishment) apply to provisions of the TFEU relating to the freedom to provide services (Articles 56–62 TFEU). As a result, Article 51 applies to providers of services.

25.2.1 The concept of "employment in the public service"

In Case 149/79 *Commission v Belgium (No 1)*[2175] the ECJ held that employment in the public service within the meaning of Article 45(4) TFEU concerned:

> "posts which involve direct or indirect participation in the exercise of powers conferred by public law and duties designed to safeguard the general interests of the State or other public authorities. Such posts in fact presume on the part of those occupying them the existence of a special relationship of allegiance to the State and reciprocity of rights and duties which form the foundation of the bond of nationality."

In the above case the ECJ made a distinction between tasks "belonging to the public service properly so called" and activities of "an economic and social nature which are typical of the public service yet which by their nature still come under the sphere of application of the Treaty".[2176] Only the first are within the scope of the derogation. Two elements are necessary in order to invoke the exception embodied in Article 45(4) TFEU, i.e. to justify that the post concerned must require a special relationship of allegiance to the Member State on the part of the person occupying it, which the bond of nationality seeks to safeguard:

- the post involves the exercise of rights under powers conferred by public law; and,

- the holder of the post is entrusted with responsibility for the general interest of the Member State.

The requirements are concurrent.

The above case shows that the ECJ has applied a functional approach to determine the scope of the exception, i.e. it focuses on whether the tasks carried out by its holders involve direct or indirect participation in the exercise of powers conferred by public law, designed to safeguard the interests of the State, rather than applying an institutional approach, i.e. focusing on whether a particular post is considered by a Member State as being within its "public sector". The functional approach ensures that

---

2175. [1982] ECR 1845, para. 9.
2176. Ibid, para. 11.

the concept of "employment in the public sector" has an autonomous EU meaning with the result that many posts, traditionally reserved for nationals, have been opened to EU citizens.

In respect of the exercise of powers conferred by public law reference to the case law of the ECJ on the interpretation of Article 51(1) TFEU is useful. In Case 2/74 *Reyners*[2177] the ECJ held that Article 51(1) TFEU must be restricted to those activities which in themselves involve a direct and specific connection with the exercise of official authority. This refers to authority emanating from the sovereignty of the Member State and involves the exercise of powers granted by the Member State to require compliance, by coercion if necessary.[2178]

In Case C-283/99 *Commission v Italy*,[2179] the ECJ held that the concept of employment in the public service does not encompass employment by a private natural or legal person, whatever the duties of the employee. In this case Italy argued that private security guards employed by private companies were within the exception because they exercised their duties in the public interest, such duties consisting of preventing and restraining the commission of criminal offences, and they were required to swear before the Italian judicial authority to be loyal to the Italian Republic. The ECJ disagreed. However, in Case C-47/02 *Anker*[2180] the ECJ qualified its judgment in Case C-283/99 *Commission v Italy*.

THE FACTS WERE:

Dutch nationals employed as seamen in private fishing vessels flying the German flag and engaged in small-scale deep-sea fishing, all holders of a Dutch diploma entitling them to captain the type of vessels on which they were serving, were denied permission to serve as masters on such vessels on the ground that the activity of a master in small-scale deep-sea fishing falls within the sphere of public service within the meaning of Article 45(4) TFEU.

Held:

The ECJ held that the activity of master of a small-scale deep-sea fishing vessel did not come within the scope of Article 45(4) TFEU, given that the public functions exercised are sporadic and represent a very minor part of the activity (the maintenance of safety, the exercise of police powers particularly in the case of danger on board and the registration of births, marriages and deaths). The core of a master's duty consists of the command of the vessel and the management of its crew.

Comment:

The ECJ held that the fact that a person is employed by a private natural or legal person is not, as such, sufficient to exclude the application of Article 45(4) TFEU. What is important is to establish whether a person acts as a representative of public authority in the service of the general interests of the Member State. In order to determine this, the ECJ examined powers which were conferred on holders of these posts by public law. According to the

---

2177. Case 2/74 *Jean Reyners v Belgium* [1974] ECR 631.
2178. The concept of "official authority" under Article 51 TFEU was defined by the A-G in his Advisory Opinion in Case 2/74 *Jean Reyners*, ibid. in the following terms: "Official authority is that which arises from the sovereignty of the State, for him who exercises it, it implies the power of enjoying the prerogatives outside the general law, privileges of official power and powers of coercion over citizens."
2179. [2001] ECR I-4363.
2180. Case C-47/02 *Anker and Others v Germany* [2003] ECR I-10447.

> judgment in Case C-4/91 Bleis,[2181] the exercise of rights under powers conferred by public
> law must constitute the core of the activity. Thus, when a holder of the post occasionally
> exercises rights under powers conferred by public law, such a post is outside the scope of
> Article 45(4) TFEU.

In the determination of posts which are within the scope of Article 45(4) TFEU, the 2002 Commission Notice on "Free Movement of Workers – Achieving the Full Benefits and Potential"[2182] is particularly helpful. According to the Notice the derogation in Article 45(4) TFEU applies to employment in the armed forces, the police, other forces for the maintenance of order, the judiciary, the tax authorities and the diplomatic corps provided that the posts in these fields do not consist of providing technical consultation and maintenance. With regard to posts in State ministries, regional governmental authorities and local authorities, the functional approach entails that if such posts involve only performance of administrative tasks, technical consultation or maintenance they are outside the scope of Article 45(4) TFEU.

In a number of cases[2183] the Member States have tried unsuccessfully to challenge the restrictive approach of the ECJ. In Case 307/84 Commission v France,[2184] the ECJ held that the post of a nurse in French public hospitals is not within the scope of Article 45(4) TFEU. Similarly neither a researcher employed by the Italian National Council of Research[2185] nor a teacher in a secondary school,[2186] nor a trainee teacher during probationary service[2187] should be regarded as employed in the public sector within the meaning of Article 45(4) TFEU. Furthermore the ECJ has, in a number of cases, condemned some Member States for reserving employment in the following sectors to their nationals: distribution of gas and electricity; health; education; all modes of transport including municipal and regional transport; civil research; telecommunications and postal services; radio and television; opera; and, municipal orchestras.[2188]

25.2.2 The concept of "exercise of official authority" under Article 51 TFEU

The concept of "exercise of official authority" under Article 51 TFEU has been construed by reference to Article 45(4) TFEU. This is not surprising given that a person who exercises rights under powers conferred by public law for the purposes of safeguarding the general interests of a Member State acts, in fact, as a representative of public authority. However, Article 51 TFEU has its own peculiarity in that the activity in question must be directly and specifically connected with the exercise of official authority[2189] with the consequence that merely auxiliary and preparatory functions are outside

---

2181. Case C-4/91 *Annegret Bleis v Ministère de l'Education Nationale* [1991] ECR I-5627.
2182. COM(2002) 694 final.
2183. Case 225/85 *Commission v Italy* [1987] ECR 2625; Case 149/79 *Commission v Belgium (No. 1) and (No. 2)* [1980] ECR 3881, [1982] ECR 1845.
2184. [1986] ECR 1725.
2185. Case 225/85 *Commission v Italy* [1987] ECR 2625.
2186. Case C-4/91 *Annegret Bleis v Ministère de l'Education Nationale* [1991] ECR I-5627.
2187. Case 66/85 *Deborah Lawrie-Blum v Land Baden-Württemberg* [1986] ECR 2121.
2188. Case C-473/93 *Commission v Luxembourg* [1996] ECR I-3207; Case C-173/94 *Commission v Belgium* [1996] ECR I-3265; Case C-290/94 *Commission v Greece* [1996] ECR I-3285.
2189. See Case 2/74 *Jean Reyners v Belgium* [1974] ECR 63; Case C-42/92 *Adrianus Thijssen v Controledienst voor de Verzekeringen* [1993] ECR I-4047 and Case C-283/99 *Commission v Italy* [2001] ECR I-4363.

the scope of application of Article 51 TFEU.[2190] This is well illustrated in Case C-438/08 *Commission v Portugal*.[2191]

THE FACTS WERE:

Portugal argued that the activity of the technical inspection of vehicles resulting in either certifying that a vehicle has passed a roadworthiness test, or conversely, refusing such certification, was directly linked to the exercise of public authority. The activity of vehicle inspection was organised in two stages. In the first stage technical inspections were carried out consisting of verifying whether the vehicles inspected complied with the relevant technical standards and drawing up a report of the inspection. The second stage related to the certification which resulted either in the taking of a decision to certify, or a refusal to certify, a vehicle's compliance with technical standards. In Portugal, both stages of the procedure, i.e. the technical inspection and the certification, were carried out by private bodies. The procedure was subject to the control of the public authority but the decisions regarding certification were taken without any intervention by the public administrative authority. Portugal submitted that these decisions, because of the effects they had on the legal rights of the owner of the vehicle, were connected with the exercise of public power.

Held:

The ECJ held that neither the first stage of the activity consisting of technical inspections nor the second stage of the activity, consisting of certification, was connected with the exercise of public power.

Comment:

With regard to the first activity, technical inspections, by their nature, have no link with the exercise of powers by a public authority.[2192]

The second activity, i.e. certification, however, contained some elements of the prerogatives of public authority in so far as legal consequences are drawn from technical inspections. Notwithstanding this, the second activity could not be considered as being "connected directly and specifically with the exercise of official authority" within the meaning of Article 51 TFEU because the private body to which the certification function had been delegated by the State:

- *had no decision-making powers as it essentially recorded the results of the roadworthiness test;*

- *lacked the decision-making independence inherent in the exercise of public authority powers as it acted under the direct control of a public authority; and,*

- *had no power of coercion as the right to impose penalties for failure to comply with the rules on vehicle inspection was exercised by the police and judicial authorities.*

2190. Case C-42/92 *Thijssen*, ibid.; Case C-393/05 *Commission v Austria* [2007] ECR I-10195.
2191. [2009] ECR I-10219.
2192. Case C-3/88 *Commission v Italy* [1989] ECR 4035.

In Joined Cases C-47/08, C-50/08, C-53/08, C-54/08, C-61/08 and C-52/08, *Commission v Belgium, France, Luxembourg, Austria, Germany and Portugal*[2193] the issue was whether the profession of notary[2194] is within the scope of the derogation set out in Article 51 TFEU.

THE FACTS WERE:

The national law of the six respondent Member States reserved access to the profession of notary to their own nationals. The Commission argued that these Member States were in breach of Articles 49 and 51 TFEU and, apart from France, in breach of Directive 2005/36/EC on the recognition of professional qualifications by not applying that directive to the profession of notary. The six Member States acknowledged that notaries generally provide their services as members of a liberal profession but submitted that the activities of notaries being connected with the exercise of official authority within the meaning of Article 51 TFEU were excluded from the provisions on freedom of establishment.

Held:

The ECJ held that Member States may not reserve access to the profession of notary to their own nationals as this constitutes discrimination on grounds of nationality prohibited by the Treaties.

Comment:

The ECJ held that the activity of authentication exercised by notaries does not involve a direct and specific connection with the exercise of official authority mainly because the documents which they authenticate are freely entered into by the parties who decide, within the limits laid down by law, on the extent of their rights and obligations and choose freely the conditions to which they wish to be subject. Furthermore a notary cannot alter the document at hand without first obtaining the consent of the parties. The ECJ pointed out that the fact that the activity of notaries pursues an objective in the public interest, namely to guarantee the lawfulness and legal certainty of documents entered into by individuals, is not in itself sufficient for that activity to be regarded as directly and specifically connected with the exercise of official authority.

Further arguments which supported the conclusion that activities of notaries are not connected with the exercise of official authority were:

- *The probative force of notarial acts derives from the rules of evidence of the Member States and therefore has no direct effect on the classification of the notarial activity of drawing up those acts;*

- *The enforceability of notarial acts does not derive from powers possessed by the notary, but from the intention of the parties to enter into a document or agreement, after its conformity with the law has been checked by the notary;*

2193. Judgment of 24/5/11 (NYR).
2194. The profession of notary in civil law countries is different from that of public notary in common law countries. In civil law countries notaries are lawyers practicing in non-contentious private civil law and vested by a State with powers to authenticate legal documents. They draft legal documents and provide legal advice. The deeds that a notary draws up, like judicial decisions, have a probative and binding force.

■ Notaries practise their profession in conditions of competition, which is not characteristic of the exercise of official authority; and,

■ Unlike public officials, notaries are directly and personally liable to their clients for loss arising from any default in the exercise of their activities.

On the basis of the case law of the ECJ the following activities were found as not being connected directly and specifically with the exercise of official authority:

Certain activities that are auxiliary or preparatory to the exercise of official authority as exemplified in Case C-438/08 Commission v Portugal[2195] above;

Certain activities whose exercise, although involving contacts, even regular and organic, with the administrative or judicial authorities, or indeed cooperation, even compulsory, in their functioning, leaves the discretionary and decision-making powers of public authorities intact. In this respect in Case 2/74 Reyners, the ECJ held that professional activities of avocat (a Belgian equivalence of a barrister) in Belgium, although they involve regular and organic contact with the courts, were not regarded as connected with the exercise of official authority because "the exercise of those activities leaves the discretion of judicial authority and the free exercise of judicial power intact".[2196] Under Belgian law avocats are sometimes called to exercise judicial functions. This occasional exercise of official authority, however, is not sufficient to exempt the entire profession of avocats from the scope of the Treaties. Nevertheless, a particular activity can be "severed" from the profession of avocat. In this respect the ECJ held that Article 51 TFEU could only be extended to the entire profession if the activities in questions "were linked with that profession in such a way that freedom of establishment would result in imposing on the Member State concerned the obligation to allow the exercise, even occasionally, by non-nationals of functions appertaining to official authority;"[2197] and,

Certain activities which do not involve the exercise of decision-making powers, powers of constraint or powers of coercion. For example, in Case C-160/08 Commission v Germany,[2198] the ECJ held that emergency ambulance services contributions to the protection of public health cannot be regarded as being connected with the exercise of official authority bearing in mind that any individual may be called upon to make such contribution when assisting a person whose life or health are in danger. With regard to the right of ambulance service providers to use the flashing blue lights or sirens, and their right of way with priority under the German Highway Code, the ECJ found that those rights reflect the importance that the German legislature attaches to public health as against general road traffic, but that such rights were not connected with the exercise of official authority bearing in mind that ambulance service providers have no official powers or powers of coercion to ensure that these rights are observed.

2195. [2009] ECR I-10219.
2196. [1974] ECR 631, paras 51 and 53.
2197. Ibid, para. 46.
2198. [2010] ECR I-3713.

25.2.3 Conclusion

Article 45(4) TFEU and Article 51 TFEU, being exceptions to the fundamental freedoms, have been interpreted strictly by the ECJ. Differing terms are used in Articles 45(4) and 51 TFEU although they have much in common and indeed, the ECJ has often referred to one of them when interpreting the other. [2199] They apply only to access to the employment/activity concerned in that once a migrant worker or a self-employed person is authorised to carry out employment/activity in a host Member State, such a person must be treated in the same manner as a national worker/self-employed person.[2200]

The main difference between Article 45(4) and Article 51 TFEU is that under Article 51 TFEU a Member State is allowed to rely on the exception when the holder of the post carries out activities connected with the exercise of official authority "even occasionally", an expression used in Article 51 TFEU, but not in Article 45(4) TFEU. This is not the case under Article 45(4) TFEU. In *Anker* the ECJ held that, regarding Article 45(4) TFEU: "It is . . . necessary that such rights are in fact exercised on a regular basis by those holders and do not represent a very minor part of their activities."[2201]

25.3 Derogations justified on the grounds of public policy, public security and public health

The right to freedom of movement is subject to limitations based on the grounds of public policy, public security and public health. The derogation in respect of workers is expressly provided for in Article 45(3) TFEU and that in respect of self-employed persons in Article 51(1) TFEU. They also apply to members of their families who have free movement rights under the Treaties.

Council Directive 2004/38/EC of 29 April 2004 on the Right of Citizens of the Union and their Family Members to Move and Reside Freely within the Territory of the Member States[2202] regulates the application of the three derogations from the right to freedom of movement conferred on EU nationals by EU law.

No definition is provided in respect of these three derogations in the Treaties or secondary legislation. However, in Case C-145/09 *Tsakouridis*,[2203] the ECJ defined the concept of "public security" as covering:

- both internal and external security of a Member State;[2204]

- "A threat to the functioning of the institutions and essential public services and the survival of the population, as well as the risk of a serious disturbance to foreign relations or to peaceful coexistence of nations, or a risk to military interests";[2205] and,

---

2199. Case 152/73 *Giovanni Maria Sotgiu v Deutsche Bundespost* [1974] ECR 153 at 156, and Cases 149/79 *Commission v Belgium (No.1) and (No. 2)* [1980] ECR 3881, [1982] ECR 1845.

2200. Case 152/73 *Sotgiu*, ibid.

2201. C-47/02 [2003] ECR I-10447, para. 69.

2202. [2004] OJ L229/35.

2203. Case C-145/09 *Land Baden-Württemberg v Panagiotis Tsakouridis* [2010] ECR I-11979.

2204. Ibid, para. 43, see also Case C-273/97 *Angela Maria Sirdar v The Army Board and Secretary of State for Defence* [1999] ECR I-7403; Case C-285/98 *Tanya Kreil v Germany* [2000] ECR I-69; Case C-423/98 *Alfredo Albore* [2000] ECR I-5965; and Case C-186/01 *Alexander Dory v Germany* [2003] ECR I-2479.

2205. Case C-145/09 *Tsakouridis*, supra note 2203, para. 44; see also Case 72/83 *Campus Oil and Others* [1984] ECR 2727; and Case C-398/98 *Commission v Greece* [2001] ECR I-7915.

■ Trafficking in narcotics as part of an organised group when it reaches "a level of intensity that might directly threaten the calm and physical security of the population as a whole or a large part of it".[2206]

The Directive permits a Member State some discretion in the application of these derogations, provided it exercises it within the limits of the Treaties. Furthermore, the directive provides procedural safeguards for EU citizens seeking to enforce their rights of entry and residence in a host Member State.

25.3.1 Public policy and public security

The ECJ has developed the following principles in respect of public policy, public security and public health exceptions:

■ All derogations from the free movement of persons must be interpreted strictly;[2207]

■ All national measures must be proportional to the objective pursued by them;[2208]

■ The concept of public policy and public security cannot be determined unilaterally by Member States. Although a Member State is free to determine the requirements of public policy and public security in the light of its national needs, the ECJ has jurisdiction to ensure, from the perspective of EU law, that a Member State exercises its discretion within the limits of the Treaties; and,

■ The majority of the provisions of Directive 2004/38 are directly effective.[2209]

Under Article 27(3) of Directive 2004/38/EC, a host Member State may, in order to decide whether a person concerned represents a danger to public policy or public security, request the home Member State of the person concerned, or any other Member State, to provide information concerning any police records of that person. This request may be made by a host Member State, when issuing the registration certificate or, in the absence of a registration system, not later than three months from the date of arrival of the person concerned on its territory or from the date of reporting his/her presence within the territory, or when issuing a residence permit. Such a request must not be a matter of routine. The Member State consulted shall give its reply within two months. A requesting Member State is obliged to give its decision within a very strict time limit: three months either from the date of arrival of the person concerned in its territory, from the date of him/her reporting his/her presence within the territory, or, from the submission of an application for registration, or for a residence card by that person with the relevant authority of that State.

Directive 2004/38/EC imposes limitations on a Member State in respect of the application of the public policy and public security exceptions. Its Article 27(2) provides that "measures taken on grounds of public policy or of public security must be based exclusively on the personal conduct of the individual concerned". For any of the exceptions to apply the personal conduct of the individual concerned must represent a genuine, present and sufficiently serious threat affecting one of the fundamental interests of the host Member State. These concepts require more detailed examination.

2206. Case C-145/09 *Tsakouridis*, supra note 2203, para. 46.
2207. Case 41/74 *Yvonne van Duyn v Home Office* [1974] ECR 1337; Case 36/75 *Roland Rutili v Ministre de l'Intérieur* [1975] ECR 1219; Case 30/77 *R v Pierre Bouchereau* [1977] ECR 1999.
2208. Case 352/85 *Bond Van Adverteerders and Others v Netherlands* [1988] ECR 2085.
2209. Case 41/74 *Yvonne Van Duyn v Home Office* [1974] ECR 1337; Case 131/79 *R v Secretary of State for Home Affairs, ex parte Mario Santillo* [1980] ECR 1585.

25.3.1.1 Personal conduct of the individual concerned

The ECJ emphasised that measures adopted on grounds of public policy, and for the maintenance of public security, against the nationals of Member States cannot be justified on grounds extraneous to the individual case. Only the "personal conduct" of those affected by the measures is to be regarded as determinative. This was explained by the ECJ in Case 67/74 *Bonsignore*.[2210]

THE FACTS WERE:

An Italian national permanently residing in Germany, Carmelo Bonsignore, shot his brother by accident. The weapon he used was a pistol he had illegally acquired. He was fined for this offence but no punishment was imposed for the accidental killing of his brother. The German authorities ordered his deportation for "reasons of a general preventive nature" based on "the deterrent effect which the deportation of an alien found in illegal possession of a firearm would have in immigration circles having regard to the resurgence of violence in the large urban cities." The German court referred to the ECJ a question whether Article 3(1) of Directive 64/221/EEC [now Article 27(2) of Directive 2004/38] prohibits deportation for reasons of a general preventive nature when it is clear that the individual concerned would not commit further offences.

Held:

The ECJ held that a Member State should base the decision on deportation exclusively on the personal conduct of the individual concerned. Future behaviour is only relevant in so far as there are clear indications that the individual would commit further offences. Article 3(1) of Directive 64/221/EEC prevents the deportation of a national of a Member State if such deportation is ordered for the purpose of deterring other aliens, that is, if it is based on reasons of a general preventive nature.

The concept of personal conduct was further clarified in Case 41/74 *Van Duyn*.[2211]

THE FACTS WERE:

Miss Van Duyn, a Dutch national, was a member of the Church of Scientology. She wanted to enter the UK to take up employment with the Church of Scientology in the UK but was refused entry. She brought an action against the UK Home Office. The High Court referred, inter alia, the following questions to the ECJ: whether membership of organisations should be considered as "personal conduct" within the meaning of Article 3(1) of Directive 64/221/EEC [Article 27(2) of Directive 2004/38] and if so, whether such conduct must be illegal in order to justify the application of the public policy exception.

2210. Case 67/74 *Bonsignore v Oberstadtdirektor der Stadt Köln* [1975] ECR 297.
2211. *Yvonne Van Duyn v Home Office* [1974] ECR 1337.

Held:

The ECJ answered that past association cannot count as personal conduct but present membership of an organisation, being a voluntary act of the person concerned, counts as "personal conduct". The activities of the Church of Scientology were not illegal in the UK. However, the UK Government considered them as socially harmful.

The ECJ held that it is not necessary that the conduct in question is illegal in order to justify exclusion of EU nationals from other Member States in so far as a Member State makes it clear that such activities are "socially harmful" and has taken some administrative measures to counteract the activities.

Van Duyn was a controversial judgment because it meant that a Member State was allowed to refuse entry to an EU national while allowing its own nationals, although with reluctance and disapproval, to be employed by the Church of Scientology. The justification provided by the UK government was not very convincing in the context of this case. It submitted that under international law a State has a duty to admit its nationals to the national territory and not to expel them from that territory. This aspect of the *Van Duyn* Case was further clarified in Joined Cases 115 and 116/81 *Andoui and Cornuaille.*[2212]

THE FACTS WERE:

Andoui and Cornuaille were French women who were refused a residence permit in Belgium on the grounds that they were "waitresses in a bar which was suspect from the point of view of morals" (that is, they were prostitutes).

Held:

The ECJ held that a Member State may only justify restrictions on the admission to or residence within its territory of nationals of another Member State if it has adopted, with respect to the same type of conduct on the part of its own nationals, repressive measures or other genuine and effective measures intended to combat such conduct.

25.3.1.2   Previous criminal convictions

Article 27(2) of Directive 2004/38/EC provides that "previous criminal convictions shall not in themselves constitute grounds for the taking of such measures".

The matter of previous convictions was examined by the ECJ in Case 30/77 *R v Bouchereau.*[2213]

THE FACTS WERE:

Mr Bouchereau, a French national, was convicted in the UK of possession of illegal drugs in January 1976 and again in June 1976. On the grounds of Article 45 TFEU and Article 3(2) of

---

2212.   Joined Cases 115 and 116/81 *Andoui and Cornuaille v Belgian State* [1982] ECR 1665.

2213.   Case 30/77 *R v Pierre Bouchereau* [1977] ECR 1999.

> *Directive 64/221 [Article 27(2) of Directive 2004/38] he challenged a deportation order made against him.*
>
> *Held:*
>
> *The ECJ held that a likelihood of reoffending may be found in past conduct although previous criminal convictions do not in themselves constitute grounds for taking measures on the basis of public policy or public security. The Court stated that it is possible that past conduct alone may constitute a threat to the requirements of public policy when the individual concerned has a "propensity to act in the same way in the future" as he did in the past.*

25.3.1.3 Present, genuine and sufficiently serious threat to requirements of public policy affecting one of the fundamental interests of society

In order to justify any measure adopted on the grounds of public policy or public security, personal conduct of the individual concerned must represent a genuine, present and sufficiently serious threat affecting one of the fundamental interests of the host Member State.

In Joined Cases C-482/01 and C-493/01 *Orfanopoulos and Oliveri*,[2214] the ECJ provided important clarifications in respect of the meaning of "present threat". The Court stated that "the requirement of the existence of a present threat must, as a general rule, be satisfied at the time of the expulsion". This judgment was confirmed and expanded in Article 32 of Directive 2004/38/EC, which provides that if an expulsion order is enforced more than two years after it was issued, the Member State must check whether or not the person concerned is currently and genuinely a threat to public policy or public security, and in order to do this it shall take into consideration whether there has been any material change in circumstances since the expulsion order was issued.

In the case of Mr Oliveri there were important changes in his personal circumstances since the issuing of the expulsion order by German authorities:

- First, he claimed that the risk of reoffending did not exist any more, as he had changed and had become a responsible adult as a result of difficulties he had to endure in prison; and,

- Second, he suffered from full-blown Aids and despite medical treatment received, he was dying from Aids.

25.3.2 Non-compliance with formalities regarding entry and residence in a host Member State

Non-compliance with administrative formalities imposed on EU migrant workers and their families in respect of entry and residence never justify an expulsion from the territory of a host Member State[2215] (see Chapter 22.4.2).

2214. *Georgios Orfanopoulos and Others (C-482/01) and Raffaele Oliveri (C-493/01) v Land Baden-Württemberg* [2004] ECR I-5257, para. 79.

2215. Case 48/75 *Jean Noël Royer* [1976] ECR 497.

25.3.3 Economic considerations

Article 27(1) of Directive 2004/38/EC provides that Member States are not allowed to invoke public policy derogations for economic purposes. The judgment of the ECJ in Case 139/85 *Kempf* [2216] confirms that a Member State cannot refuse entry and residence on economic grounds.

When EU migrant workers exercise effective and genuine activity of an economic nature in the territory of a host Member State, the fact that their remuneration is not sufficient to satisfy their needs, and that they receive social security benefits or social assistance from a host Member State, are not sufficient to deny them the right to reside in the territory of that Member State. This is subject to the principle that a migrant worker must not become an unreasonable burden on the social security system of a host Member State (Article 1 of Directive 2004/38/EC) – so it is a matter of interpretation of what is unreasonable (see Chapter 22.4.2.2).

25.3.4 Public health

Article 29 of Directive 2004/38/EC provides that only diseases with epidemic potential, as defined by the relevant instruments of the World Health Organisation, and other infectious or contagious parasitic diseases, if they are the subject of protection provisions applying to nationals of the host Member State, may justify restrictions on entry and residence.

The exception based on public health can only be relied upon by a host Member State at the time of the initial entry of the person concerned on its territory, and during the first three months of that person's residence there. Accordingly, diseases occurring after a three-month period from the date of arrival shall not constitute grounds for expulsion from the territory of the host Member State. However, under Article 29(3) a host Member State may, in exceptional circumstances, i.e. where "there are serious indications that it is necessary", require the person concerned to undergo free of charge medical examination in order to ensure that the person does not suffer from diseases mentioned in Article 29(1). However, such medical examination may only be required within three months of the date of arrival of the person on the territory of the host Member State and must not be required as a matter of routine.

25.4 Protection against expulsion for long-term residents and minors in a host Member State

Article 28 of Directive 2004/38/EC provides safeguards against expulsion on the grounds of public policy and public security. It incorporates and expands the judgment delivered by the ECJ in Case C-482/01 *Orfanopoulos*.[2217]

THE FACTS WERE:

Mr Orfanopoulos, a Greek national born in 1959 in Greece, joined his parents in Germany in 1972. Since then he had been living in Germany, apart from a two-year period during which he was completing his military service in Greece. In 1981 he married a German national. Three children had been born to the marriage.

2216. Case 139/85 *R. H. Kempf v Staatssecretaris van Justitie* [1986] ECR 1741.

2217. Case C-482/01 *Georgios Orfanopoulos and Others v Land Baden-Württemberg* [2004] ECR I-5257.

During his residence in Germany Mr Orfanopoulos had been given residence permits of limited duration. In November 1999 he submitted a request for renewal of his residence permit.

Mr Orfanopulos had no professional qualifications. Since 1981 he had had various jobs but periods of employment had been interrupted by extended periods of unemployment.

Mr Orfanopulos was a drug addict. He had been convicted nine times for various offences relating to possession and use of unlawful drugs and for violent assaults. In 1999 he was condemned to six months in prison. In January 2000 he had been admitted to a hospital for detoxification treatment and subsequently had tried to take detoxification cures in specialised institutions, but had been expelled from these institutions for disciplinary reasons. From September 2000 to March 2002 he was in prison serving terms of imprisonment imposed by earlier judgments. In March 2002 his remaining sentence was suspended as a result of his good behaviour while in prison and his willingness to accept detoxification treatment.

The German authorities warned Mr Orfanopoulos on a number of occasions about the serious consequences of his conduct on his residence status in Germany. In February 2001 the German authorities rejected his request for renewal of his residence permit and issued a deportation order against him. Mr Orfanopoulos was informed that he would be deported at the end of his prison sentence.

The German authorities justified the deportation order by the number and seriousness of offences committed by Mr Orfanopoulos and the high risk of his reoffending given his drug and alcohol addictions.

On 21 March 2002 Mr Orfanopoulos and his children appealed against the deportation order before the German court. Mr Orfanopoulos argued that the decision of expulsion was not based on his personal conduct but was taken as a general preventive measure and that this decision was disproportionate and in breach of Article 8 of the ECHR.

Held:

In respect of the issue of compatibility of the expulsion order with the principles of EU law, the ECJ stated that the situation of the individual concerned should be assessed in the light of the general principles of EU law, including the fundamental rights contained in the ECHR which are protected in the EU legal order.[2218] Both EU law and the ECHR recognise the right to respect for private and family life. Article 8(2) of the ECHR sets out the limits of permissible interference with the enjoyment of these rights by a Member State. Any interference in family life of the individual concerned must be necessary in a democratic society, in accordance with law, and proportionate to the legitimate aims pursued by a Member State. In connection with the proportionality test it is necessary to weigh up in each particular case the interests of the Member State taking the measure terminating residence of the person concerned and the interests of that individual. In respect of Mr Orfanopoulos the ECJ stated it was necessary for the referring court to take account of the following factors: the nature, seriousness and frequency of offences that he had committed; the period of time that had elapsed since his last conviction; the extent of his integration into the host Member State, socially, professionally and in terms of family relations; and, the seriousness of difficulties for · him and his wife to live together as a family should the expulsion order be carried out.

2218. C-260/89 *Elliniki Radiophonia Tiléorassi AE and Panellinia Omospondia Syllogon Prossopikou v Dimotiki Etairia Pliroforissis and Sotirios Kouvelas and Nicolaos Avdellas and others* [1991] ECR I-2925; C-368/95 *Familiapress* [1997] ECR I-3689; C-60/00 *Mary Carpenter v Secretary of State for the Home Department* [2002] ECR I-6279.

Article 28 of Directive 2004/38/EC adds a new gloss to the judgment in *Orfanopoulos*. It distinguishes between, on the one hand, serious requirements, and on the other hand, imperative requirements of public policy and public security of a Member State. As a matter of principle the host Member State is not allowed to make an expulsion order against EU citizens and members of their families who have acquired permanent residence in a host Member State, except on serious grounds of public policy or public security. In respect of persons who have resided in a host Member State for ten years or are minors, only imperative grounds of public security will justify an expulsion order.

In Case C-145/09 *Tsakouridis*,[2219] the ECJ elucidated the distinction between "imperative grounds of public security" and "serious grounds of public policy or public security" within the meaning of Directive 2004/38. The ECJ held that the concept of "imperative grounds of public security" "presupposes not only the existence of a threat to public security, but also that the threat is of a particularly high degree of seriousness, as is reflected by the use of the words 'imperative reasons'."[2220] The ECJ held that a host Member State may justify an expulsion measure on either "imperative grounds of public security" against an EU citizen who has resided in that State for ten years or longer or on "serious grounds of public security and public policy" with regard to an EU citizen who has not satisfied the residence requirement under Article 28(3) of the Directive in a situation where the EU citizen has been convicted in connection with dealing in narcotics as part of an organised group.

The meaning of "imperative grounds of public security" was further examined by the ECJ in Case C- 348/09 *P.I.*[2221]

THE FACTS WERE:

Mr I, an Italian national, arrived in Germany in 1987. During his residence there he was occasionally employed for simple unskilled work as he had no qualifications and no school-leaving certificate. He was unmarried and had no children but his mother and siblings lived either in Germany or in Italy.

In 2006, Mr I was sentenced to seven years and six months imprisonment for sexual abuses, sexual coercion and rape of a 14-year-old girl. Sexual abuses had started when the victim was eight years old. Mr I compelled the victim to have regular sexual intercourse with him and to perform other sex acts on an almost weekly basis by threatening to kill her mother or brother. Those acts took place over many years. The mother of the victim was a former partner of Mr I.

The German authorities decided to deport Mr I at the end of his sentence. They submitted that the possibility for reoffending was not excluded bearing in mind that he had regularly raped and sexually coerced the victim over a long period. According to the prison authorities Mr I considered himself as a victim and was unwilling to accept the enormity of his crime. Mr I, who resided in Germany for more than 20 years, brought proceedings against the deportation order arguing that there were no imperative grounds of public security justifying his expulsion. The referring court was uncertain whether sexual offences committed by Mr I were within the scope of "imperative grounds of public security."

2219. Supra note 2203.
2220. Ibid, para. 41.
2221. Case C-348/09 *P.I. v Oberbürgermeisterin der Stadt Remscheid* (judgment of 22/5/12 (NYR)).

Held:

The ECJ left to the referring court to decide whether the crimes committed by Mr I constituted a particularly serious threat to one of the fundamental interests of society, which might pose a direct threat to the calm and physical security of the population, and thus be covered by the concept of "imperative grounds of public security". However, even if the conduct of Mr I posed such a threat his deportation should not be automatic but subject to the requirements imposed by EU law.

Comment:

The referring court was uncertain as to the meaning of the ECJ's judgment in Tsakouridis *in that it was uncertain whether only dealing in narcotics as part of an organised group was within the scope of "imperative grounds of public security" or whether commission of other extremely serious offences could justify a measure expelling a Union citizen who had resided in the host Member State for the preceding ten years. Two points merit attention:*

First, the ECJ extended the list of criminal offences which may justify expulsion measures on "imperative grounds of public security" to encompass sexual abuses and sexual exploitation of children as defined in Directive 2011/93 and criminal offences defined in Article 83(1) TFEU (i.e. terrorism; trafficking in human beings and sexual exploitation of women and children; illicit drug trafficking; illicit arms trafficking; money laundering; corruption; counterfeiting of means of payment; computer crime; and, organised crime). According to the ECJ, they constitute a particularly serious threat to one of the fundamental interests of society and may pose a direct threat to the calm and physical structure of the population of a host Member State.

Second, the ECJ stated that even if the referring court were to find that Mr I posed a direct threat to the calm and physical security of the population, this should not necessarily lead to his expulsion. A referring court must take into account the requirements of EU law when deciding whether to deport an EU citizen, inter alia, the personal conduct of the individual concerned which must represent a genuine and present threat to the society; the length of his/her stay in a host Member State; his/her age; health; family and economic situation; social and cultural integration into that State; and, links with his country of origin. The position of the ECJ is not surprising. After considerably extending the list of extremely serious offences constituting a threat to one of the fundamental interests of society, and therefore capable of justifying expulsion of an EU citizen who had resided in a host Member State for more than ten years, the ECJ ensured that expulsion would not be automatic.

The position of the ECJ may be contrasted with that taken by A-G Bot in this case. According to the A-G the offences committed by Mr I were not within the scope of the concept of "imperative grounds of public security". He submitted that a threat to public security depends not only on the gravity of any relevant crime or crimes, but also on its or their nature. In the case of Mr I the nature of the crimes was different from that in Tsakouridis *which concerned dealing in narcotics as part of organised crime. Mr I's crimes were committed exclusively in the family context and thus could not be treated in the same way as that of a "sexual predator". The A-G stated that however repellent an act of incest may be, it did not involve the same threat to public security as the crime committed by Mr Tsakouridis and argued that "To decide otherwise would amount to acknowledging that only the objective seriousness of a criminal offence, determined by the penalties incurred or imposed for it,*

> may constitute justification of an expulsion measure on imperative grounds of public
> security."[2222] However, his opinion was that Mr I did not merit the benefit of enhanced
> protection under Article 28(3) of Directive 2004/38 because his conduct clearly showed that
> he was not integrated into the society of the host Member State. He concluded that Mr I
> should be deported on the grounds of public policy. To do this however, would have conflicted
> with the explicit wording of Article 28(3) of the Directive.

The relationship between the length of residence of an EU citizen in a host Member State and permitted grounds of expulsion is illustrated below.

Permitted grounds of expulsion	The length of residence in a host Member State of EU citizens and their families.
Public health	This ground can be relied upon by a host Member State at initial arrival and up to three months of residence in a host Member State.
Public policy and public security	This ground can be relied upon by a host Member State at initial arrival and up to the acquisition of permanent residence in a host Member State (five years residence in a host Member State, see Chapter 22.4.2).
Serious grounds of public policy and public security	This ground can be relied upon by a host Member State from the acquisition of permanent residence in a host Member State up to ten years of residence there.
Imperative reasons of public security	This ground can be relied upon by a host Member State with regard to those who have resided there for more than ten years and minors irrespective of the time of residence unless the expulsion is necessary for the best interest of the child.

25.5 Procedural safeguards under Directive 2004/38/EC

Directive 2004/38/EC provides procedural safeguards for EU nationals seeking to enforce their rights of entry and residence in a host Member State. Articles 31–33 set out important procedural rights for individuals who are refused entry and residence granted by the Treaties and by secondary legislation.

The procedural safeguards are as follows:

A. The persons concerned must be notified of any decision of expulsion in writing, in such a manner that they are able to comprehend its content and the implications for them. The notification must specify, precisely and in full, the relevant national authority which deals with appeals from such a decision, the time limit for the appeal, the grounds on which the decision was taken, unless this is contrary to the interests of state security, and the time allowed to leave the territory which, apart from duly substantiated cases of urgency, shall be no less than one month from the date of notification (Article 30).

2222.   Ibid, para. 44.

B.   The persons concerned are entitled to seek judicial review of the expulsion decision or, when appropriate, lodge an appeal against it before the administrative authorities of the host Member State. The case law of the ECJ has clarified many aspects of appeal proceedings before administrative bodies of the Member States.[2223] Such bodies must:

- be independent of the administrative authority which adopted the decision, or if no such body has been established, then an administrative court must deal with the appeal; and,

- examine all the facts and circumstances, including the expediency of the expulsion decision, before the final decision is taken by the appropriate administrative authority, save in cases of emergency.[2224]

When the applicant has, simultaneously, challenged the expulsion decision and applied for an interim order to suspend its enforcement, then, save in the cases specified in Article 31(2), he/she should not be removed from the territory of the host Member State until such time as the decision on an interim order has been taken. Pending the redress procedure Member States may exclude the applicant from their national territory but may not prevent him/her from submitting his/her defence in person, except when his/her appearance may cause a serious threat to the requirements of public policy or public security, or when the procedure concerns a denial of entry to the territory.

C.   Article 32 introduced the right for persons excluded on grounds of public policy or public security to lodge an application for the lifting of the exclusion order after a reasonable time, depending on the circumstances, and in any event after three years from enforcement of the final exclusion decision. It is for the applicant to submit evidence that there has been a material change in the circumstances that justifies the revision of the initial decision. The applicant is entitled to have an answer within six months of the submission of his/her application but has no right of entry to the territory of the host Member State while his/her application is being considered.[2225]

Article 32 provides that a Member State is not allowed to expel for life from its territory a national of another Member State. This issue was examined by the ECJ in Case C-348/96 *Calfa*.[2226]

THE FACTS WERE:

Donatella Calfa, an Italian national, went on holiday to Crete where she was convicted of the possession and use of prohibited drugs. She was sentenced by a Greek court to three months' imprisonment and expulsion for life from Greek territory. Under Greek penal law, foreign nationals convicted of certain drug offences were automatically subject to an expulsion order for life unless for some compelling reason, particularly family matters, their

---

2223. Joined Cases C-297/88 and C-197/89 *Massam Dzodzi v Belgium* [1990] ECR I-3763; Case C-357/98 *R v Secretary of State for the Home Department, ex parte Yiadom* [2000] ECR I-9265.

2224. Case 131/79 *Regina v Secretary of State for Home Affairs, ex parte Mario Santillo* [1980] ECR 1585; Joined Cases 115/81 and 116/81 *Adoui and Cornuaille v Belgium* [1982] ECR 1665; Joined Cases C-482/01 *Georgios Orfanopoulos and Others v Land Baden-Württemberg* (C-482/01) and C-493/01 *Raffaele Oliveri v Land Baden-Württemberg* [2004] ECR I-5257.

2225. Joined Cases C-65 and 111/95 *R v Secretary of State for the Home Department, ex parte Mann Singh Shingara, R v Secretary for the Home Department, ex parte Abbas Radiom* [1997] ECR I-3343.

2226. Case C-348/96 *Criminal Proceedings against Donatella Calfa* [1999] ECR I-11.

continued residence in Greece was allowed. Donatella Calfa challenged the expulsion order as contrary to a number of provisions of the Treaty, especially Articles 45, 49 and 56 TFEU and Directive 64/221/EEC [Directive 2004/38].

Held:

The ECJ held that Donatella Calfa, as a tourist, was a recipient of services in another Member State and as such within the scope of application of Article 56 TFEU. The ECJ emphasised that although national legislation in criminal matters is within the competence of a Member State, the requirements of EU law set limitations on Member States' powers. Such legislation should not limit the fundamental freedoms guaranteed by EU law. The ECJ held that expulsion for life from the territory of a Member State was an obstacle to the freedom to receive services under Article 56 TFEU as well as the freedom of establishment under Article 49 TFEU and the free movement of workers contained in Article 45 TFEU. It could not be justified on the ground of public policy since Greek legislation provided for an automatic expulsion for life following a criminal conviction without taking into account the personal conduct of the offender or whether that conduct created a genuine and sufficiently serious threat affecting one of the fundamental interests of society.

RECOMMENDED READING

Books

Barnard, C., *The Substantive Law of the EU*, 3rd edn, 2010, Oxford: OUP.

Spaventa, E., *Free Movement of Persons in the EU: Barriers to Movement in their Constitutional Context*, 2007, The Hague: KLI.

Articles

O'Keeffe, D., "Judicial Interpretation of the Public Exception to the Free Movement of Workers", in Curtin, D., and O'Keeffe, D. (eds), *Constitutional Adjudication in European Community and National Law*, 1992, Dublin: Butterworths Ireland, 89.

Pravita, M-I., "The Access of EU Citizens to the Public Service. A Comparative Study", (2010) 2/2 *Review of European Studies*, 18.

Shuibhne, N. N., "Derogating from the Free Movement of Persons: When Can EU Citizens be Deported?" (2006) 8 CYELS, 187.

Shuibhne, N. N., "The Third Age of EU Citizenship: Directive 2004/38 in the Case Law of the Court of Justice" in Stasinopoulos, P., "From *Van Duyn* to *Josemans*: How the Tide Might Affect EU's Freedoms", (2011) 17 ELRev., 277.

Syrpis, P. (ed.), *The Judiciary, The Legislature and The EU Internal Market*, 2012, Cambridge: CUP, 331.

PROBLEM QUESTION

Hans, a German national, who works in Belgium, consults you, an expert in EU law, on the following matters:

A.   Hans's wife, Anastasia, a Russian national, who is a piano teacher, applied for a job to work in the Belgian capital Brussels with the Belgian National Opera. She was told by the Belgian authorities first, that being a non-EU national she is not entitled to a work permit in Belgium and second, that employees of the Belgian National Opera are civil servants and thus are required to be Belgian nationals. Accordingly, her application has been rejected.

B.   A deportation order has been issued against Hans. The Belgian authorities explain that all non-Belgian nationals who are members of the Church of Demon, an organisation considered by the Belgian authorities as socially harmful and classified as an unlawful institution under Belgian law, have been required to leave Belgium. Hans tells you first, that he used to be a member of the Church of Demon, but is no longer a supporter of that Church, and second, that he has become a communist and profoundly dislikes any religion whatsoever.

C.   John, a brother of Hans, killed his friend Jeremy in Germany six years ago. At the time of Jeremy's death, both John and Jeremy were extremely drunk and were playing a game consisting of throwing a knife at each other. John was sentenced to five years' imprisonment for causing the accidental death of Jeremy. After completing his sentence John went to Belgium directly from Germany. The Belgian authorities state that, as a part of a new policy of "Zero tolerance for crimes", all foreigners who have ever been convicted of committing violent crimes must be deported. This, according to the Belgian authorities, will have a deterrent effect in immigration circles and will constitute an appropriate measure to fight an apparent resurgence of violence in Belgium.

Advise Hans regarding each of A, B, and C above.

ESSAY QUESTION

Critically assess the contribution of the ECJ to the removal of restrictions imposed on access of EU citizens to employment in the public services in a host Member State.

AIDE-MÉMOIRE

Exceptions to the free movement of persons set out in Articles 45(4) and 51 TFEU

Exception set out in Art. 45(4) TFEU	Exception set out in Art. 51 TFEU
A post in the public sector is within the scope of Art. 45(4) TFEU if its holder: ■ Exercises public functions on a regular basis and such functions constitute a major part of the holders' activities; and, ■ Is entrusted with responsibility for the general interest of the State.	An activity is within the scope of Art. 51 TFEU if it involves the exercise of official activity even occassionally. The activity must: ■ Not be merely auxilliary or preparatory; and, ■ Must involve the exercise of decision-making powers, or powers of constraint, or powers of coercion.

Exceptions based on the ground of public policy, public security and public health

Exception based on public policy and public security	Exception based on public health	Safeguards
Any national measure: ■ Must be based on personal conduct of the individual concerned. If relevant, this includes present membership of organisations but not past membership (Case 41/74 *Van Duyn*); ■ Must not be based on previous criminal convictions of the person concerned unless they show that the individual concerned has the propensity to act in the future as he/she did in the past (Case 30/77 *R v Bouchereau*); ■ Must not be a penalty or legal consequence of a custodial penalty unless it conforms with the requirements of Articles 27, 28, 29 of Directive 2004/38/EC; ■ Must show that the personal conduct of the individual concerned represents a genuine, present and sufficiently serious threat affecting one of the fundamental interests of society of the host Member State (Case 131/79 *Santillo*; C-493/01 *Oliveri*);	A national measure can be taken: ■ In respect of diseases with epidemic potential (as defined by the WHO); and ■ In respect of other infectious or contagious parasitic diseases if they are the subject of protection provisions applying to nationals of the host Member State but not if diseases occur after a three-month period from the date of arrival of the person concerned.	The person concerned: ■ Must be notified in writing of any decision taken on the grounds of public policy, public security and public health. Such notification must contain all information specified in Article 30; ■ Has the right of access to judicial or administrative redress procedures to appeal against the decision or to seek its judicial review under the conditions set out in Article 31; ■ Has the right to re-examination of the exclusion decision after a reasonable time has elapsed or, in any event, after three years from enforcement of the final exclusion decision if he/she can show that there has been a material change in circumstances since the adoption of the exclusion decision.

(Continued)

(Continued)

Exception based on public policy and public security	Exception based on public health	Safeguards
■ Must not be based on reasons of a general preventive nature (Case 67/74 *Bonsignore*); ■ Must not be based on economic considerations (Case 139/85 *Kempf*); ■ Must comply with the principle of proportionality (Case 352/85 *Bond Van Adverteerders*); ■ Must be supported by evidence that a Member State has taken repressive or other effective measures to combat conduct such as that of the individual concerned with regard to its own nationals (Joined Cases 115 and 116/81 *Andoui and Cornuaille*).		

26

INTRODUCTION TO EU COMPETITION LAW

CHAPTER OUTLINE

1. The main objectives of EU competition law are:

- to maintain the integrated internal market; and,

- to enhance consumer welfare and ensure efficient allocation of resources.

2. EU competition law applies to undertakings. Any natural or legal person is regarded as an undertaking if such a person is engaged in any economic activity and enjoys some autonomy in determining its course of action in the relevant market.

3. The concept of activity which "may affect trade between Member States" establishes a jurisdictional limitation on the scope of application of Articles 101 and 102 TFEU. According to this concept EU competition law applies only where anti-competitive conduct of an undertaking has an appreciable effect on trade between Member States.

4. EU competition law applies not only to undertakings established in the EU but also to those established outside the territory of the EU. The extraterritorial application of EU competition law is based: first on the doctrine of the single economic unit; second, on the "implementation doctrine", established by the ECJ in the *Wood Pulp Cartel case,* which has many similarities with the US effects doctrine; and, third, on the Merger Regulation which applies to undertakings satisfying the turnover threshold in the EU (see Chapter 29.2.2).

5. Generally, EU competition law applies to all sectors of the economy. However, the Treaties provide for some exceptions limiting or excluding the application of competition rules. They concern: undertakings which provide services of general interest; revenue-producing State monopolies; and, some sectors of economy, e.g. nuclear energy, military equipment and agriculture.

6. The relationship between EU competition law and the national competition laws of the Member States is regulated by Article 3 of Regulation 1/2003, which decentralised the enforcement of EU competition law and which emphasises the federal nature of EU competition law. Although competition laws of the Member States may differ from EU competition law, any conflict between the two is resolved in favour of EU competition law. Whatever the situation and circumstances may be, the EU law, being federal in nature, supersedes national competition laws.

26.1 Introduction

Since 1999, the Commission has undertaken a substantial programme of legislative reform of EU competition law.[2227] In the White Paper on Modernisation[2228] the Commission explained that modernisation of the enforcement of EU competition law was necessary, taking into account the globalisation of the economy, the enlargement of the EU and the existence of a single market and single currency. Overall the programme of reform dramatically altered EU competition law. Its main objective was to strengthen and decentralise the enforcement of EU competition law in an enlarged EU and, at the same time, focused on the importance of economic analyses in competition cases. The main features of the reform are analysed in detail in Chapter 30.

The key provisions of EU competition law examined in this book are:

- Article 101 TFEU which prohibits and renders null and void, subject to some exceptions, any agreements between undertakings, decisions by associations of undertakings, and concerted practices which may affect trade between Member States and which have as their object or effect the prevention, restriction or distortion of competition within the EU (see Chapter 27);

- Article 102 TFEU which prohibits any abuse, by one or more undertakings, of a dominant position within the internal market, or any substantial part of it, in so far as such abuse may affect trade within the EU (see Chapter 28);

- Merger Regulation 139/2004,[2229] which applies to concentrations which have an EU dimension (see Chapter 29); and,

- Regulation 1/2003 which provides the mechanisms for the enforcement of Articles 101 and 102 TFEU (see Chapter 30).

2227. On this topic see: I. Maher, *Competition Law Modernisation: An Evolutionary Tale,* in P. Craig and G. de Búrca, (eds), *The Evolution of EU Law,* 2nd edn, 2011, Oxford: OUP, 717.

2228. The White Paper on Modernisation of Rules Implementing Articles 81 and 82 of the EC Treaty [Articles 101 and 102 TFEU] [1999] OJ C132/1.

2229. [2004] OJ L 24/1.

26.2 Objectives of EU competition law

Competition policy can be defined as comprising measures and instruments used by governments (or regional integration organisations such as the EU) to influence conditions of competition that exist in a market. This may include well-motivated articulation of competition issues in industrial policy, trade policy, investment policy, service policy and consumer policy as well as enactment of competition law. Whish rightly points out that competition policy does not exist in a vacuum but "is an expression of the current values and aims of society and is susceptible to change as political thinking generally".[2230]

Competition law is a vital part of competition policy. Competition law has been defined by Jones and Sufrin as being "concerned with ensuring that firms . . . operating in the free market economy do not restrict or distort competition in a way that prevents the market from functioning optimally".[2231] More specifically competition law prohibits arrangements between firms which restrict competition, abuses of market power by dominant firms, and the creation of anti-competitive mergers. In the light of the above definition of competition policy it is clear that competition policy has a broader scope than competition law in that competition policy encompasses all aspects of government action (or of the actions of a supranational organisation such as the EU) that affect the conditions under which firms compete in a particular market, and that competition law is a servant of competition policy. Business conduct which competition law allows or prohibits will very much depend on the objectives pursued by competition law.[2232]

The objectives of EU competition law have changed over the years although the objective of ensuring an integrated internal market has remained constant. In Joined Cases 56 and 58/64 *Consten and Grundig* (for facts and comments see Chapter 27.2.2),[2233] the ECJ held the effectiveness of the prohibition of obstacles to the free movement of goods, people, labour and capital addressed to the Member States would have been devoid of any practical effect if firms were allowed to create private barriers to trade between Member States.

The Court stated:

"an agreement . . . which might tend to restore the national division in trade between member states might be such as to frustrate the most fundamental objectives of the Community. The Treaty, whose preamble and content aim at abolishing the barriers between states, and which in several provisions gives evidence of a stern attitude with regard to their reappearance, could not allow undertakings to reconstruct such barriers."[2234]

Since the judgment of the ECJ in the above case it has been accepted that the fundamental objective of EU competition law is to ensure that business conduct does not partition the EU along national borders. On many occasions the ECJ and the Commission have emphasised that the creation and maintenance of the internal market is the most important objective of EU competition law.[2235] Although,

---

2230. R. Whish, *Competition Law*, 5th edn, 2003, London: LexisNexis, 17.

2231. *EU Competition Law, Text, Cases and Materials*, 4th edn, 2011, Oxford, OUP, 1.

2232. On the importance of the objectives of competition law being clearly defined see: L. Parret, "Shouldn't We Know What We are Protecting? Yes We Should! A Plea for a Solid and Comprehensive Debate about the Objectives of EU Competition Law, and Policy", (2010) 6/2 EuroCJ, 339.

2233. Joined Cases 56 and 58/64 *Établissements Consten Sarl and Grundig-Verkaufs-GmbH v Commission* [1966] ECR 299.

2234. Ibid, paras 56 and 58–64.

2235. For example, see the IX Commission Annual Report on Competition Policy, which stated that the first objective of competition law is to maintain open and unified the internal market, the European Commission, Brussels, 1979.

with the reform of EU competition law new objectives have been set, i.e. the promotion of economic efficiency and consumer welfare,[2236] this does not, however, mean that market integration is no longer relevant. The objective of market integration has not been abandoned. The 2000 Commission Guidelines on Vertical Restraints provide that "the protection of competition is the primary objective of [EU] competition law, as this enhances consumer welfare and creates an efficient allocation of resources. In applying the EC competition rules, the Commission will adopt an economic approach which is based on the effects on the market. Market integration is an additional goal of [EU] competition law. Market integration enhances competition".[2237] Further, the 2009 Guidance on the Commission's Enforcement Priorities in Applying [Article 102 TFEU] to Abusive Exclusionary Conduct by Dominant Undertakings[2238] provides that the Commission may intervene with regard to "certain behaviour that undermines the efforts to achieve an integrated internal market".

Nowadays in the EU the objective of market integration runs in parallel with the objective of the promotion of consumer welfare and efficient allocation of resources. When these two objectives clash it seems that, despite the Commission's policy statements which appear to assign a secondary role to the objective of market integration, the ECJ will support the objective of market integration rather than the objective of the enhancement of efficiency and consumer welfare.[2239]

It is to be noted that the objective of enhancing consumer welfare and ensuring efficient allocation of resources emphasises the ever increasing role that economics play in the enforcement of EU competition law with the result that "Competition law is about economics, and anyone involved in this subject should endeavour to understand its underlying principles and policy objectives".[2240] It is outside the scope of this book to introduce students to the economics of EU competition law although some elements of economics are examined when necessary.

26.3 The personal scope of application of EU competition law – the definition of an undertaking

EU competition law applies only to undertakings. For that reason it is necessary to define this concept. Neither the Treaties nor secondary legislation provide a definition of an undertaking. However, the well-established case law indicates that under EU competition law any natural or legal person:

- engaged in any economic activity; and,

- enjoying some autonomy in determining its conduct on the relevant market;

should be regarded as an undertaking.

2236. See the White Paper on Modernisation of Rules Implementing Articles 81 and 82 of the EC Treaty [1999] OJ C132/1. See also the statement of the former European Commissioner for competition policy, Neelie Kroes, made in London in October 2005, in which she said: "Consumer welfare is now well established as the standard the Commission applies when assessing mergers and infringements of the Treaty rules on cartels and monopolies. Our aim is simple: to protect competition in the market as a means of enhancing consumer welfare and ensuring an efficient allocation of resources." SPEECH/05/512 available at http://www.ec/europea/eu/competition (accessed 4/4/12).

2237. [2000] OJ C291/1, para. 7.

2238. [2009] OJ C45/2, para. 7.

2239. See Joined Cases C-501/06 P, C-513/06 P, C-515/06 P and C-519/06 P *GlaxoSmithKline Services Unlimited v Commission* [2009] ECR I-9291.

2240. S. Bishop and M. Walker, *The Economics of EC Competition Law: Concepts, Application and Measurement*, 2010, London: Sweet and Maxwell, vii. This book provides an excellent introduction to the economics of EU law.

26.3.1 The meaning of "economic activity"

In Case C-41/90 *Höfner*,[2241] the ECJ stated that the concept of an "undertaking" covers any entity engaged in an economic activity, regardless of its legal status and the way in which it is financed, and any activity consisting of offering goods and services in a given market is an economic activity.

The case law indicates that the term "economic activity" refers to:

- an activity consisting of provision of goods and services on the market;[2242] and,

- an activity which can be carried out by private undertakings in order to make a profit and therefore if such an activity is carried out by a public body this does not change the nature of the activity, i.e. it remains an economic activity.[2243]

The second bullet point emphasises that the concept of an undertaking is a relative concept because an entity may be an undertaking under EU competition law with regard to some of its activities and a non-undertaking within the meaning of EU competition law with regard to the remaining activities. This is of crucial importance in respect of activities carried out by a public body in that its different activities must be examined separately in order to establish which, if any of them, are of an economic nature and thus within the scope of EU competition law, and which are of a non-economic nature and consequently outside the scope of EU competition law. In this respect the ECJ has excluded two types of activities from the scope of EU competition law:

- those based on the principle of national solidarity. The exclusion concerns bodies that fulfil an exclusively social function, i.e. provide social security, pensions, health insurance, etc. Solidarity was defined by A-G Fenelly in Case C-70/95 *Sodemare* as "the inherently uncommercial act of involuntary subsidisation of one social group by another";[2244] and,

- those which are connected with the exercise of powers which are typically those of a public authority.

26.3.1.1 Activities based on the principle of solidarity

It emerges from the ECJ's case law that a body managing a compulsory social protection scheme will not be classified as an undertaking under EU competition law if it satisfies three criteria:

- It is a non-profit-making entity which pursues purely social objectives;

- It provides social protection based on the principle of solidarity. This principle entails that benefits paid to the persons concerned are not strictly proportionate to the contributions paid by them; and,

- The essential elements of the scheme that the body in question manages are subject to State supervision.

2241. Case C-41/90 *Höfner and Elser v Macroton GmbH* [1991] ECR I-1979. The ECJ has confirmed this definition in numerous cases, for example see: Case C-218/00 *Cisal di Battistello Venezio and Co v Instituto Nazionale per Assicurazione Contro Gli Fortuni Sul Lavoro* (INAIL) [2002] ECR I-691.

2242. Case C-205/03P *FENIN v Commission* [2006] ECR I-6295.

2243. See Case C-113/07P *SELEX Sistemi Integrati SpA v Commission and European Organisation for the Safety of Air Navigation (Eurocontrol)* [2009] ECR I-2207.

2244. Case C-70/95 *Sodemare SA, Anni Azzurri Holding SpA and Anni Azzurri Rezzato Srl v Regione Lombardia* [1997] ECR I-3395, para. 29.

The application of the above criteria is not easy as exemplified by the following cases decided by the ECJ:

■ Case C-244/94 *Fédération Française des Sociétés d'Assurance.*[2245] The ECJ found that a body managing a supplementary old-age insurance scheme was engaged in economic activity because it was in competition with life assurance companies, given that its members could opt for other schemes which guaranteed better returns; the body applied the principle of capitalisation; and, the benefits depended solely on the amount of the contributions paid by the beneficiaries and on the financial results of the investments made by the managing organisation.

■ Case C-67/96 *Albany.*[2246] The ECJ found that a body in charge of managing a supplementary pension fund did not fulfil the criteria mentioned above as it could itself determine the amount of contributions of its members and their benefits and operate in accordance with the principle of capitalisation; thus it was engaged in competition with insurance companies and therefore was an undertaking within the meaning of EU competition law.

■ Joined Cases C-264, 306 and 355/01 *AOK.*[2247] The ECJ had to determine whether the latitude given to the German sickness funds to determine the fixed maximum amounts payable in respect of medicinal products constituted an activity of an economic nature unrelated to the sickness funds' functions. The ECJ held that the following factors indicated that the sickness insurance funds were not engaged in economic activities and therefore were not undertakings. The factors were:

(a) determination of the fixed maximum amounts constituted a task imposed upon them by statute;

(b) the procedure for determination was established by statute; and,

(c) the sickness funds discretion in this area was limited, that is, they could only determine the maximum amounts, but if they could not determine these amounts, the competent minister had to decide them.

■ Case C-350/07 *Kattner.*[2248] The ECJ found that a body which provided insurance against accidents at work and occupational diseases in Germany was not an undertaking. It satisfied the three criteria as:

● It pursued social objectives consisting of preventing, by all appropriate means, accidents at work and occupational diseases, and, on the occurrence of accidents or occupational diseases, restoring, by all appropriate means, the health and the capacity to work of insured persons and by providing financial compensation to insured persons or their dependants. Further, it was a non-profit-making body, governed by public law to which affiliation of undertakings established within a specific geographical area was mandatory;

● It was based on the principle of solidarity because, *inter alia*, amounts of benefits paid under the insurance scheme were not necessarily proportionate to the insured person's contributions; and,

● It was subject to State supervision. In this respect the ECJ held that although MMB had some

---

2245. Case C-244/94 *Fédération Française des Sociétés d'Assurance and Others v Ministère de l'Agriculture et de la Pêche* [1995] ECR I-4013.

2246. Case C-67/96 *Albany International BV v Stichting Bedrijfspensioenfonds Textielindustrie* [1999] ECR I-5751.

2247. [2004] ECR I-2493.

2248. Case C-350/07 *Kattner Stahlbau GmbH v Maschinenbau- und Metall-Berufsgenossenschaft (MMB)* [2009] ECR I-1513.

latitude, i.e. it could decide on factors to be taken into consideration when calculating amounts of contributions and benefits payable under the scheme, this latitude was established and strictly delimited by law.

26.3.1.2 Activities which are connected with the exercise of powers which are typically those of a public authority

The issue of how to determine which activities are connected with the exercise of public powers was examined, first by the General Court in Case T-155/04 *SELEX Sistemi*,[2249] and, second, on appeal by the ECJ in Case C-113/07P *SELEX Sistemi*.[2250]

THE FACTS WERE:

SELEX Sistemi Integrati SpA, an Italian undertaking operating in the sector of air traffic management systems, submitted a complaint to the Commission alleging that Eurocontrol, an international organisation developing a uniform system of air traffic management in Europe, was in breach of Article 102 TFEU when carrying out its standardisation tasks in relation to the creation of a uniform system of Air Traffic Management (ATM) equipment and systems. When the Commission rejected the complaint, SELEX Sistemi brought proceedings before the General Court for annulment of the Commission's decision. In particular three areas of activity of Eurocontrol were at issue:

- *The first area concerned the activity of regulation, standardisation and validation;*

- *The second area concerned research and development tasks, which involved, inter alia, the acquisition of and development of prototypes of ATM equipment and systems, for example radar control systems; and,*

- *The third activity concerned the assistance provided to the administrations of the Member States by Eurocontrol, when requested, particularly in the field of planning, specification and creation of ATM services and systems. In that context Eurocontrol could, inter alia, be called upon to assist national air traffic control authorities to establish tendering procedures for the supply of ATM equipment and systems.*

The main argument of the Commission was based on the ECJ's judgment in Case C-364/92 SAT Fluggesellschaft,[2251] in which the ECJ held that the activities of Eurocontrol were connected with the exercise of public functions and thus were not of an economic nature. Accordingly, the Commission argued that Eurocontrol was not an undertaking within the meaning of EU competition law.

Held:

The General Court held that:

- *Activities of an entity must be considered individually and the fact that some of them are connected to the exercise of public powers does not mean that the others are not*

2249. Case T-155/04 *SELEX Sistemi Integrati SpA v Commission* [2006] ECR II-4797.
2250. Case C-113/07P *SELEX Sistemi Integrati SpA v Commission and Eurocontrol* [2009] ECR I-2207.
2251. Case C-364/92 *SAT Fluggesellschaft mbH v Eurocontrol* [1994] ECR I-43.

economic in nature. Consequently, each activity, if it can be severed from those in which the entity engages as a public authority, must be assessed separately with a view to deciding whether or not it is of an economic nature.[2252]

The ECJ confirmed the General Court's reasoning on this point, but stated that each activity should be assessed in the light of the mission of Eurocontrol, i.e. its pursuit of public service objectives.

The first activity

The General Court held that the first activity consisting of technical standardisation was not of an economic nature because there was no market for technical standardisation services in the sector of ATM equipment, as the only purchasers of such services can be Member States in their capacity as air traffic control authorities. The purchase of prototypes necessary for producing technical standards did not change the nature of Eurocontrol's activity given that Eurocontrol purchased them for non-economic activities, that is, research. The General Court restated its judgment in T-319/99 FENIN,[2253] that being a purchaser in a particular market cannot, in itself, imply an economic activity. The decisive factor is the purpose for which goods are acquired, that is, for the purpose of offering goods and services as part of an economic activity or as part of some other activity such as social or research activity.

The ECJ agreed with the General Court on the above point but found that the General Court was incorrect when it made a distinction between the preparation or production of standards (a task which is undertaken by the Agency of Eurocontrol as the executive organ of that organisation), and their adoption by the Council of Eurocontrol. The ECJ held that the preparation of technical standards could not be dissociated from their adoption. Both activities were performed by Eurocontol as part of its integral task of technical standardisation and thus in the exercise of its public powers. However, as this error in law on the part of the General Court did not affect its final conclusion, i.e. the activity was considered as being of non-economic nature, the ECJ did not set aside the General Court's judgment.

The second activity

The second area of activity consisting of research and development, in particular the purchase of prototypes (which raised intellectual property rights issues) was not considered as being of an economic nature given that prototypes were acquired as a part of Eurocontrol's task as a public authority. They were offered to researchers for non-commercial purposes and licences were granted free of charge. The General Court once again emphasised that such activities were not economic in nature because they did not involve the offer of goods and services in a given market.

The ECJ agreed with the conclusion of the General Court.

The third activity

The General Court decided that the third activity consisting of providing assistance to national administrations in the implementation of tendering procedures for the acquisition of air traffic management systems or equipment was of an economic nature. It stated that this

---

2252. Case T-155/04 SELEX Sistemi, supra note 2249, para. 54. See also Case 107/84 Commission v Germany [1985] ECR 2655, paras 14 and 15 and Case T-128/98 Aéroports de Paris v Commission [2000] ECR II-3929, para. 108.
2253. Case T-319/99 FENIN v Commission [2003] ECR II-357.

activity, which is not indispensable to ensuring the safety of air navigation, can be carried out by private undertakings and the fact that such task was conferred upon a public body to be carried out free of charge did not change the nature of the activity. The General Court found that there was a market for advice in this area and that private undertakings specialised in this area could very well offer their services.

The ECJ held that the General Court made an error of law in classifying this activity as being of an economic nature. The ECJ emphasised that the provision of assistance constitutes one of the tasks of Eurocontrol as defined in Article 1 of the Convention on the Safety of Air Navigation under which Eurocontol was established. According to the ECJ, the provision of assistance plays "a direct role in the attainment of the objective of technical harmonisation and integration in the field of air traffic with a view to contributing to the maintenance of and improvement in the safety of air navigation".[2254] Therefore this activity was connected with the exercise of public powers by Eurocontrol and the fact that the assistance was provided only at the request of the national administration was irrelevant so far as the classification of this activity was concerned. What mattered was that the activity was connected with the maintenance and development of air navigation safety, i.e. connected with the exercise of public powers by Eurocontrol. However, the ECJ stated that the error in law made by the General Court did not justify the setting aside of the judgment given that the General Court did not annul the Commission's decision. Indeed, the General Court held that even if Eurocontrol's activity consisting of providing assistance to national administrations was to be considered as being of an economic nature Eurocontrol was not in breach of Article 102 TFEU.

Comment:

Both judgments emphasise that the existence of a competitive or potentially competitive market in the relevant area will be decisive in determining whether a specific activity can be classified as being of an economic nature and thus within the scope of EU competition law.

The definition of an "undertaking", being based on economic activity, means that for the application of EU competition law the following are immaterial.

26.3.1.3 The legal personality or form of the body in question

The definition of undertaking has included a Committee organising the World Cup,[2255] professional sports clubs,[2256] private individuals engaged in any form of business, commerce or profession, partnerships and co-operatives.[2257] In Case C-35/96 *Commission v Italy*,[2258] the ECJ confirmed the

---

2254. Case C-113/07P *SELEX Sistemi*, supra note 2250, para. 76.

2255. *The Distribution of Package Tours During the 1990 World Cup* [1992] OJ L326/31.

2256. *UEFA's Broadcasting Regulations*, OJ [2001] L171/12.

2257. E.g. *RAI/United* [1978] OJ L157/39 (opera singers); *Reuter/BASF* [1976] OJ L254/40 (an inventor); Case C-250/92 *Gøttrup-Klim Grovvareforening and Others v Dansk Landbrugs Grovvareselskab AmbA* [1994] ECR I-5641 (agricultural co-operatives).

2258. [1998] ECR I-3851, also see *CNSD* [1993] OJ L203/27 confirmed by the CFI in Case T-513/93 *CNSD v Commission* [2000] ECR II-1807.

Commission's decision that customs agents in Italy, who in exchange for fees were carrying out customs formalities in respect of export, import and goods in transit, were undertakings. Other examples are:

- In Case C-180–184/98 *Pavlov*[2259] the ECJ held that self-employed medical specialists who were contributing to their own individual supplementary pension schemes were undertakings.

- In Case C-309/99 *Wouters*, the ECJ held that individual members of the Dutch Bar carried out economic activities when they offered "for a fee, services in the form of legal assistance consisting of drafting of opinions, contracts and other documents and representing of clients in legal proceedings"[2260] and thus were undertakings under EU competition law.

26.3.1.4 The economic purpose of the body in question

The making of profit is not important. For that reason a non-profit-making organisation which is carrying out some economic activity is within the scope of EU competition law.[2261] It is apparent from the case law that the fact that a body is non-profit-making is a relevant factor for the purpose of determining whether or not an activity is of an economic nature but it is not in itself conclusive.[2262]

26.3.2 Autonomy in determining conduct on the market

In order to be regarded as an undertaking an entity must enjoy some autonomy in determining its course of action in the market irrespective of whether it has a separate legal personality. This is considered below.

26.3.2.1 A corporate body – the "single economic entity" doctrine

A subsidiary will not be regarded as a separate undertaking if both the parent undertaking and its subsidiary "form a single economic unit within which the subsidiary has no real freedom to determine its course of action on the market".[2263] This means that if a parent and its subsidiary, which is not capable of independent policy-making, enter into an agreement which would in other circumstances be prohibited under Article 101 TFEU, there will not be a breach of that provision since that agreement (or concerted practice) will reflect the allocation of functions within the corporate body. This is known under EU competition law as the "single economic entity" doctrine.[2264] On the basis of this doctrine when a subsidiary established within the EU abuses its dominant position, its behaviour is imputable to the parent company, irrespective of whether or not the parent company is established within the EU.[2265]

In Case C-97/08P *Akzo Nobel*[2266] the ECJ confirmed that where a parent company has a 100 per cent shareholding in its subsidiary there is a rebuttable presumption that the parent exercises a decisive influence over the conduct of its subsidiary and thus will be held responsible for the conduct of its subsidiary. When a parent company's shareholding in its subsidiary is less than 100 per cent the matter

---

2259. Case C-180–184/98 *Pavlov v Stichting Pensioen fonds Medische Specialisten* [2000] ECR I-6451.

2260. Case C-309/99 *Wouters v Algemene Raad van de Nederlandse Orde van Advocaten* [2002] ECR I-1577, para. 64.

2261. Joined Cases 209-15 and 218/78 *Heintz van Landewyck SARL and Others v Commission* [1980] ECR 3125.

2262. Case C-244/94 *Fédération Française des Sociétés d'Assurance and Others v Ministère de l'Agriculture et de la Pêche* [1995] ECR I-4013 and Case C-237/04 *Enirisorse SpA v Sotacarbo SpA* [2006] ECR I-2843.

2263. Case 22/71 *Béguelin Import Co. v S.A.G.L. Import Export* [1971] ECR 949. On this topic see: L. La Rocca, "The Controversial Issue of the Parent-company Liability for the Violation of EC Competition Rules by the Subsidiary", (2011) 32/2 ECLR, 68.

2264. Case C-73/95P *Viho Europe BV v Commission* [1996] ECR I-5457.

2265. Case 15/74 *Centrafarm BV and Adriaan de Peijper v Sterling Drug Inc* [1974] ECR 1147.

2266. Case C-97/08P *Akzo Nobel NV v Commission* [2009] ECR I-8237.

of "decisive influence" or otherwise is assessed according to the facts: e.g. whether the parent company appoints the board of directors, and whether it imposes its commercial policy on the subsidiary.[2267]

In Case C-407/08 P *Knauf*[2268] the ECJ further clarified the concept of "a single economic entity".

THE FACTS WERE:

The appellant, Knauf Gips KG, a world-leading manufacturer of building materials, challenged the conclusion of the Commission (approved by the General Court) that it formed a single economic entity with other companies owned by the Knauf family, and was thus liable for anti-competitive activities of those companies. Despite a complex legal structure, the capital of the Knauf group was owned by 21 members of the Knauf family and a company which held the shares of four other members. The Commission decided that Knauf Gips, a limited partnership managed by Mr B and Mr C, was the business organisation which was the most representative in the Knauf group and accordingly imputed to Knauf Gips liability for the activities of the entire Knauf group. Knauf Gips argued that Gebrüder Knauf Verwaltungsgesellschaft KG (GKV), a limited partnership and its subsidiaries (managed by the same partners), the function of which was to administer the other companies in the Knauf group did not form a single economic entity with Knauf Gips because Knauf Gips did not control GKV and that the fact that the same partners Mr B and Mr C managed GKV was irrelevant. Therefore, the Commission was wrong when it imputed liability for the infringement in question to Knauf and not to GKV.

Held:

The ECJ agreed with the Commission. It held that the fact that there is no single legal person at the apex of a group of companies, or legal entities, does not prevent the Commission from finding that one of those companies is solely responsible for the anti-competitive activities of the companies in that group, as a whole, as they constitute a single economic entity.

Comment:

Whether GKV formed part of a single economic entity or whether it was itself an undertaking within the meaning of EU law depended upon whether it could determine its conduct on the market independently. In this respect the ECJ referred to its case law which clearly establishes that all relevant factors should be taken into consideration (such as the economic, organisational and legal links which exist between it and the company in the same group) in order to decide whether a company determines its conduct on the market independently. The ECJ stated that a case by case assessment is required as there is no exhaustive list of factors to consider.[2269] The factors which convinced the ECJ that GKV formed part of a single economic entity with Knauf Gips were, inter alia, as follows:

- *GKV was a holding company. It had no staff. Its sole task was to manage the portfolio of companies which it held for the 22 shareholders who by virtue of their shareholding, in effect, owned it jointly;*

2267. Case T-102/92 *Viho Europe BV v Commission* [1995] ECR II-117.

2268. Case C-407/08 P, *Knauf Gips KG, formerly Gebr. Knauf Westdeutsche Gipswerke KG v Commission* [2010] ECR I-6371.

2269. This was previously stated by the ECJ in Case C-97/08 P *Akzo Nobel and Others v Commission* [2009] ECR I-8237, para. 74.

> *The two limited partnerships had exactly the same shareholding structure (the same individuals holding exactly the same shares in the company capital);*
>
> *GKV shared its staff and premises with Knauf Gips; and,*
>
> *Most of the Knauf Group's documents seized by the Commission during the inspections were printed on Knauf Gips's letterhead.*
>
> *The ECJ emphasised that "the fact that there is no single legal person at the apex of the Knauf Group is no obstacle to the appellant being held liable for the actions of that group"[2270] because in such a situation the legal structure of the group of companies is not decisive in so far as that structure does not reflect the effective functioning and actual organisation of the group. Accordingly, the ECJ decided that the lack of subordinating legal links between Knauf Gips and GKV was irrelevant in that Knauf Gips was liable for conduct of GKV as GKV was not an undertaking within the meaning of EU law.*

In the context of a corporate body two further matters arise relating to liability for infringement of EU competition law:

A. **Corporate reorganisation.** In Joined Cases 29 and 30/83 *CRAM*,[2271] the ECJ held that the successor to an undertaking being investigated may be considered to be the same undertaking for competition law purposes when the successor undertaking and the "old" undertaking are identical from an economic point of view. Thus, the change of legal form and name will not be sufficient to exempt a new undertaking from liabilities attributable to the "old" undertaking. The decisive factor in determining whether one undertaking can be liable for the past conduct of another is "whether there is functional and economic continuity between the original infringer and the undertaking into which it was merged".[2272]

B. **Acquisition by a third party of an undertaking which has committed an infringement of EU competition law.** With regard to a situation when an undertaking is acquired by a third party, the principle is that if a corporate body, i.e. the initial entity, which has sold its business and which is responsible for the infringement is still is existence, that initial entity will be liable for the offending conduct rather than the acquirer.[2273] However, if the initial entity does not exist in law after the infringement was committed; or it still legally exists but does not carry out economic activities, the acquirer will be liable if there are structural links between it and the initial entity.[2274]

2270. Case C-407/08 P, *Knauf*, supra note 2268, para. 107.

2271. Joined Cases 29 and 30/83 *Compagnie Royale Asturienne des Mines SA (CRAM) and Rheinzink GmbH v Commission* [1984] ECR 1679.

2272. *PVC Cartel*, [1990] 4 CMLR 345, para. 43.

2273. In Joined Cases T-109/02, T-118/02, T-122/02, T-125/02, T-126/02, T-128/02, T-129/02, T-132/02 and T-136/02 *Bolloré SA and others v Commission* [2007] ECR II-947. See also Case C-49/92P *Commission v Anic Partecipazioni* [1999] ECR I-4125; and Case C-297/98P *SCA Holding v Commission* [2000] ECR I-10101.

2274. Case C-204/00P *Aalborg Portland A/S v Commission* [2004] ECR I-123.

26.3.2.2 A commercial agent

The Commission in its 1962 Notice, as confirmed in its Guidelines on Vertical Restraints,[2275] considered that the true commercial agent who acts on behalf of a principal is not considered as an undertaking within the meaning of EU competition rules. However, the situation is different if the commercial agent acts not as an auxiliary but enjoys a degree of independence, permitting it to enter into agreements prohibited under Article 101 TFEU.

In Case 40/73 *Suiker Unie*,[2276] undertakings concerned acted in the sugar market both as agents for each other, and as principals on their own account. The ECJ held that taking into consideration the ambiguous relationships between them, they should be regarded as independent undertakings. It seems that in each case the Commission will assess the economic functions carried out by an agent in order to decide to what degree it acts as a genuine agent, that is, whether the activities the agent carries out are associated with a commercial risk. If an agent bears no risk or bears only a minimal risk on the contracts negotiated, it will be considered as a "genuine" agent[2277] and therefore not considered as an undertaking within the meaning of EU competition law.

26.3.2.3 An employee

In Case C-22/98 *Becu*,[2278] the ECJ held that employees, whether taken individually or collectively, cannot be regarded as undertakings given that they are incorporated into an undertaking which employs them and thus form an economic unit with it. However, an ex-employee who carries on an independent business would be considered as an undertaking.[2279]

In Case T-325/01 *DaimlerChrysler*,[2280] the General Court decided that commercial agents of DaimlerChrysler AG in Germany should be categorised as employees of DaimlerChrysler, given that they did not bear any commercial risk when acting for DaimlerChrysler either when soliciting orders for sales of new cars or providing other services such as repairs and after-sales services. Indeed, it appeared from the facts that they negotiated sales contracts for new vehicles in the name of DaimlerChrysler with a view to transmitting them to DaimlerChrysler, but they neither purchased new vehicles nor stocked them. In addition, they had neither the authority to fix their own prices for new vehicles nor to grant discounts on them. Further, the terms and conditions of their agency contracts were unilaterally determined by DaimlerChrysler. Consequently they could not be classified as independent undertakings.

26.3.2.4 A public body

Articles 101 and 102 TFEU apply to public bodies if they do not conduct commercial or economic activities in the exercise of "official authority"[2281] or when acting "as public authority" (see above the case of *Eurocontrol*).

2275. [2000] OJ C291/1, paras 12–21.
2276. Case 40/73 *Coöperatieve Vereniging "Suiker Unie" UA and Others v Commission* [1975] ECR 1663.
2277. Case 311/85 *ASBL Vereniging van Vlaamse Reisbureaus v ASBL Sociale Dienst van de Plaatselijke en Gewestelijke Overheidsdiensten* [1987] ECR 3801; Case C-266/93 *Bundeskartellamt v Volkswagen AG and VAG Leasing GmbH* [1995] ECR I-3477; Case C-217/05 *Confederación Española de Empresarios de Estaciones de Servicio v Compañía Española de Petróleos SA* [2006] ECR I-11987.
2278. Case C-22/98 *Criminal Proceedings against Jean Claude Becu and Others* [1999] ECR I-5665.
2279. *Reuter/BASF* [1976] OJ L 254/40.
2280. Case T-325/01 *DaimlerChrysler AG v Commission* [2005] ECR II-3319.
2281. Case 30/87 *Corinne Bodson v SA Pompes Funèbres des Régions Libérées* [1988] ECR 2479.

A private company acting in the capacity of a public authority cannot be regarded as an undertaking.[2282] Public bodies entrusted with the operation of services of general economic interest or having the character of a revenue-producing monopoly are subject to EU competition rules "in so far as the application of such rules does not obstruct the performance in law or in fact of the particular tasks assigned to them"[2283] and provided that their activities do not affect trade between Member States to such an extent as would be contrary to the interests of the EU.

26.3.2.5 The doctrine of "State compulsion"

EU competition law endorses the doctrine of "State compulsion". Under this doctrine when an undertaking is required by national legislation to act in breach of EU competition law or when the national legal framework is such as to eliminate any possibility of competitive activity on the part of an undertaking, EU competition law will not apply.[2284] The justification is that in these circumstances it cannot be said that the undertaking concerned has freely participated in anti-competitive conduct. However, for the doctrine to apply the legislation in question must have a "decisive influence" on the undertaking's conduct. This is not the case when a State simply encourages an undertaking to adopt anti-competitive conduct without compelling it.

26.4 The territorial scope of application of EU competition law

In the context of the territorial scope of application of EU law two aspects are examined.

- First, for the application of Articles 101 and 102 it is necessary that an agreement, decision, concerted practice or an abuse of a dominant position "may affect trade between Member States". The requirement that conduct prohibited under both Articles 101 and 102 TFEU must have effect on trade between Member States defines the boundaries between the application of EU competition law and the competition law of the Member States. It is often referred to as the inter-Member State clause[2285] as it establishes the jurisdictional limitation on the scope of application of Articles 101 and 102 TFEU, i.e. if the activity does not affect trade between Member States, it is outside the scope of EU competition law; and,

- Second, for the application of EU law it is irrelevant whether an undertaking is established within the EU or outside the EU. What matters is whether prohibited conduct "affects trade between Member States" in relation to the application of Articles 101 and 102 and whether an intended concentration has an EU dimension as defined under the Merger Regulation (see Chapter 29.2.2).

26.4.1 The meaning of "may affect trade between Member States"

The meaning of the requirement that prohibited conduct "may affect trade between Member States" was explained in Case 56/65 *STM* [2286] in which the ECJ held that:

"For this requirement to be fulfilled, it must be possible to foresee with a sufficient degree of probability on the basis of a set of objective factors of law or fact that the agreement in question may

---

2282. Case C-343/95 *Diego Cali v SEPG* [1997] ECR I-1547.
2283. Article 106(2) TFEU.
2284. Case T-4/96 *Commission v Bayer* [2000] ECR II-3383.
2285. R. Whish and D. Bailey, *Competition Law*, 7th edn, 2012, Oxford: OUP, 144 et seq.
2286. Case 56/65 *Société Technique Minière (STM) v Maschinenbau Ulm GmbH* [1966] ECR 235, 249.

have an influence, direct or indirect, actual or potential, on the pattern of trade between Member States."

The above interpretation shows that the ECJ has taken the same approach to EU competition law as to Article 34 TFEU, that is, it applies the *Dassonville* formula in the context of competition law (see Chapter 20.3). It is a broad test that brings within the scope of EU competition law even conduct that potentially may affect trade between Member States, although that effect must not be purely hypothetical (see below).

The reform of EU competition law prompted the Commission to publish its Guidelines on the Effect on Trade Concept Contained in Articles 101 and 102 TFEU.[2287] The Guidelines reiterate the previous case law. They provide that the requirement mentioned above constitutes "an autonomous Community [EU] law criterion, which must be assessed separately in each case" (paragraph 19). The taking into account of potential effect means that even if an undertaking concerned does not in fact carry out a prohibited agreement or a decision, its conduct will, nevertheless, fall under the prohibition of EU law. In Case T-77/92 *Parker Pen*,[2288] a clause prohibiting exports was ignored by a distributor but despite this, the potential effect of the clause on the pattern of trade was considered as sufficient to condemn the agreement.

The Commission Guidelines provide that to be in breach of the EU competition rules, any effect must have been sufficiently probable. This confirms the judgment of the CFI in Case T-374/94 *European Night Services*,[2289] in which the Court ruled that there must be "a real, concrete possibility" not just hypothesis and speculations unsupported by any evidence or any analysis of the structure of the relevant market.

The broad interpretation of the requirement entails that it is irrelevant whether the prohibited conduct will affect trade favourably, bearing in mind that the requirement establishes the jurisdictional limitation on the scope of application of Articles 101 and 102 TFEU, i.e. it only indicates whether the case should be examined under EU competition law or national competition law of a Member State.[2290]

The prohibition in Articles 101 and 102 applies when the effect on trade between Member States of unlawful conduct is appreciable. The Guidelines on the Effect on Trade Concept Contained in Articles 101 and 102 TFEU explain that the appreciability threshold is to be determined by reference to the position and importance of an undertaking in the relevant product market in the light of the circumstances of each individual case.[2291] In paragraph 52 of the Guidelines the Commission sets out quantitative criteria, which when applied cumulatively, may indicate in principle that agreements entered into by the parties do not affect trade. This is an equivalent concept to the *de minimis* principle developed in the case law of the ECJ (see below).

The criteria are as follows:

- the aggregate market share of the relevant parties does not exceed 5 per cent;

- for horizontal agreements, the aggregate community turnover of the parties does not exceed €40 million; and,

- for vertical agreements, the turnover of the supplier of the product does not exceed €40 million.

2287.   [2004] OJ C101/81.

2288.   Case T-77/92 *Parker Pen Ltd v Commission* [1994] ECR II-549.

2289.   Case T-374/94 *European Night Services v Commission* [1998] ECR II-3141, paras 139–47.

2290.   Joined Cases 56 and 58/64 *Établissements Consten S.à.R.L. and Grundig-Verkaufs-GmbH v Commission* [1966] ECR 299.

2291.   [2004] OJ C101/81.

Paragraph 52 of the Guidelines provides a short-term exemption for parties who have exceeded the above figures in terms of turnover by up to 10 per cent and of market share by up to 2 per cent in no more than two successive calendar years.

26.4.2 Agreements confined to one Member State

It should be noted that an agreement between undertakings in a single Member State may appreciably affect trade between Member States if it creates or reinforces partitioning of the internal market in accord with national borders[2292] or limits the capacity of production in a Member State by, for example, fixing prices to be charged in that Member State[2293] or by creating a common subsidiary there responsible for production and commercialisation of their products.[2294]

In Joined Cases T-259–264/02 and T-271/02 *Re: The Lombard Club*,[2295] the General Court held that in a situation where an agreement/concerted practice covers the whole of the territory of a Member State, there is a strong presumption that such an agreement/concerted practice by its very nature has the effect of reinforcing the compartmentalisation of national markets, and thus is capable of appreciably affecting trade between Member States. In this case Austrian credit establishments involved in a cartel did not rebut this presumption, given that almost all Austrian banks were involved and their agreement covered a wide range of banking products and services, in particular deposits and loans. Thus it was capable of affecting trade between Member States.

In the context of the requirement that to be in breach of Article 101(1) TFEU conduct of undertakings must appreciably affect trade between Member States, it is important to emphasise that the agreement as a whole must be taken into consideration, not just every clause restricting competition.[2296] If there is a network of agreements, the actual circumstances, both economic and legal, in which each agreement was made must be taken into consideration.[2297] In the case of abuse of a dominant position, it is necessary to take into account the entirety of the commercial activities of an undertaking, including those outside the internal market.[2298]

Obviously, if an agreement is confined to one Member State and it does not appreciably affect EU trade, such an agreement will be outside the scope of application of EU competition law.[2299]

2292. Case 8/72 *Vereeniging van Cementhandelaren v Commission* [1972] ECR 977; Case 246/86 *SC Belasco and Others v Commission* [1989] ECR 2117.

2293. *Flat Glass* [1989] OJ L33/44.

2294. *Fiat-Hitachi* [1993] OJ L20/10.

2295. Joined Cases T-259–264/02 and T-271/02 *Raiffeisen Zentralbank Österreich AG and Others v Commission (The Lombard Club)* [2006] ECR II-5169. This was confirmed by the ECJ in Joined Cases C-125/07P, C-133/07P and 135/07P *Erste Group Bank and Others v Commission* [2009] ECR I-8681.

2296. Case 193/83 *Windsurfing International Inc. v Commission* [1986] ECR 611.

2297. Case 23/67 *Brasserie de Haecht v Wilkin-Janssens (No. 1)* [1967] ECR 407.

2298. Joined Cases 6 & 7/73 *Istituto Chemioterapico Italiano S.p.A. and Commercial Solvents Corporation v Commission* [1974] ECR 223 and Case 22/79 *Greenwich Film Production v SACEM and Société des Editions Labrador* [1979] ECR 3275.

2299. See para. 60 of the Guidelines and Case C-215/96 *Carlo Bagnasco v BPN* [1999] ECR I-135, in which the ECJ held that an agreement concerning retail banking services had no appreciable effect on EU trade as the potential for trade in the sector concerned (being guarantees for current account credit facilities) was very limited, and undertakings from other Member States would not consider the restrictions imposed by the agreement as important factors in deciding to establish themselves in the relevant Member State.

26.4.3 The *de minimis* rule

Under the *de minimis* rule some agreements *prima facie* in breach of Article 101(1) TFEU are outside its scope of application where the market share of the parties is so minimal that their agreement has no effect on trade between Member States. The *de minimis* rule has developed as a logical complement to the concept of appreciable effect. It was first established in Case 5/69 *Völk*.[2300]

THE FACTS WERE:

Völk, a small undertaking manufacturing washing machines, concluded an exclusive distribution agreement with Vervaecke, a Dutch distributor. Völk's share of the market in washing machines was less than 1 per cent. When a dispute arose between the parties, a Dutch court referred to the ECJ a question whether Article 101(1) TFEU should apply, taking into account the small share of the market held by Völk.

Held:

The ECJ held that the exclusive distributorship agreement ensuring absolute territorial protection was outside the scope of Article 101(1) TFEU as the effects produced on trade between Member States were not appreciable (the agreement concerned only 600 units).

The *de minimis* rule applies also in the context of Article 102 TFEU.[2301]

26.4.4 Notice on Agreements of Minor Importance

In order to help businesses to assess whether the *de minimis* rule applies to their agreement, the Commission published its first Notice on Agreements of Minor Importance in 1970.[2302] The current version of the Notice was published in 2001.[2303]

The Notice is not binding on anyone, even on the Commission, but is very useful for undertakings since if their agreement falls below the fixed thresholds, they can reasonably assume that it is outside the scope of EU competition rules. The Notice states that no infringement proceedings will be commenced in respect of any such agreement.

The 2001 Notice refers to agreements between competitors (horizontal) and non-competitors (vertical). The Notice quantifies, by using market share thresholds, what constitutes an appreciable effect on trade between Member States within the meaning of Article 101(1) TFEU in the following manner:

- Agreements between competitors (actual or potential). In the case of undertakings operating at the same level of production or marketing, the threshold is fixed at 10 per cent, that is, the aggregate market share held by an undertaking participating in any of the relevant market must not exceed 10 per cent;

2300. *Franz Völk v S.P.R.L. Ets J. Vervaecke* [1969] ECR 295.
2301. Case 22/78 *Hugin Kassaregister AB and Hugin Cash Registers Ltd v Commission* [1979] ECR 1869.
2302. [1970] OJ C64/1.
2303. Commission Notice on Agreements of Minor Importance [2001] OJ C368/13.

▪ Agreements between non-competitors. Agreements between undertakings operating at different economic levels in the distribution process are within the scope of the Notice if the aggregate market share of participating undertakings does not exceed a threshold of 15 per cent in any of the relevant markets;

▪ Mixed agreements. For a mixed horizontal/vertical agreement (or in the event that the classification of an agreement is difficult) a threshold of 10 per cent is applicable; and,

▪ Networks of agreements. Paragraph 8 relates to networks of agreements. It provides that where competition in the relevant product market is restricted by the cumulative effect of agreements entered into by different suppliers and distributors, a reduced threshold of 5 per cent applies. The matter being addressed by paragraph 8 is that the cumulative effect of agreements may lead to foreclosure of the market. Paragraph 9 states that foreclosure is unlikely to occur if the cumulative effect of parallel networks of agreements affect less than 30 per cent of the relevant market.

The Commission will treat agreements as being within the scope of the Notice if they exceed the fixed threshold by no more that 2 per cent in relation to the market share over two successive financial years.

The Notice does not apply to agreements containing the so-called "hard-core restrictions", for example, those set out in Regulation 330/2010 (see Chapter 27.9.1). Thus, horizontal agreements which are within the scope of the *de minimis* rule but have as their object price fixing, restriction of production or sales or market sharing, being *per se* contrary to Article 101(1) TFEU, are excluded from the scope of the Notice (paragraph 11). However, the Commission will usually not commence proceedings in respect of such agreements unless the interests of the EU require it. This will be the case if an undertaking participates in a cartel.[2304] Similar treatment is applied to vertical agreements which fix resale prices, or confer absolute territorial protection upon participating undertakings or third undertakings.

The Notice acknowledges that agreements between small and medium sized undertakings, that is undertakings which have fewer than 250 employees, and have either an annual turnover not exceeding €40 million or an annual balance sheet total net worth not exceeding €27 million,[2305] are unlikely to have appreciable effect on trade between Member States.

26.4.5 The concept of "trade"

The concept of "trade" has been broadly interpreted by the EU institutions. It covers all economic activities including the provision of commercial services such as banking;[2306] insurance;[2307] and, financial services.[2308] It also encompasses other activities of a commercial nature such as the provision

---

2304. In Case T-56/99 *Marlines SA v Commission (Greek Ferries Cartel)* [2003] ECR II-5225 the General Court confirmed the Commission's decision that even if an undertaking is small and its market share is below the threshold of 10 per cent (in this case the ferry company operated between the Ports of Patras and Ancona, carrying a very small number of passengers and vehicles and had no ship of its own) but is a member of a cartel, it is not immune from application of Article 101 TFEU. Marlines argued, *inter alia*, that because of its limited size and very limited commercial influence it was not in a position to conclude price agreements with its competitors and thus did not participate in a cartel. The General Court replied that the fact that, despite its size, the other undertakings participating in the cartel perceived it as an undertaking whose opinion should be ascertained in order to establish a common position, constituted a factor indicating its participation in the cartel.

2305. Para. 3 of the Notice.

2306. Case 172/80 *Gerhard Züchner v Bayerische Vereinsbank AG* [1981] ECR 2021.

2307. Case 45/85 *Verband der Sachversicherer e.V. v Commission* [1987] ECR 405.

2308. [1985] *LSFM* OJ L369/25.

of exhibitions and trade fairs[2309] and the granting of aid to exporters by a professional body in order to finance promotion of their products abroad.[2310]

The concept includes not only import and export between Member States but also between Member States and non-Member States as, for example, the case of an agreement limiting export of Japanese cars to the UK.[2311]

The Commission published Guidelines on the Effect on Trade Concept Contained in [Articles 101 and 102 TFEU] which, relying on the case law of the EU courts, state that "the concept of trade is not limited to traditional exchanges of goods and services across borders. It is also a wider concept, covering all cross-border economic activity, including establishment. This interpretation is consistent with the fundamental objectives of the Treaty to promote free movement of goods, services, persons and capital".[2312]

26.4.6 The application of EU competition law to undertakings established outside the EU

EU competition law applies not only to undertakings established in the EU but also to those established outside it. The extraterritorial application of EU law is based, first on the single economic unit doctrine (see Chapter 26.3.2.1), second, on the "implementation doctrine" established by the ECJ in the *Wood Pulp Cases*)[2313] which has many similarities with the US effects doctrine and third, on the Merger Regulation which applies to undertakings satisfying the turnover threshold in the EU (see Chapter 29.2.2).

The application of competition law to foreign firms was initially developed in the US under the "effects" doctrine, which was first applied there in the *Aluminium* case.[2314] The question there was whether a Canadian company could be liable under US anti-trust legislation. The US court held that it had jurisdiction as the activities carried out by the Canadian company were intended and did indeed have effects within the US.

The effects doctrine was reformulated in 1982 in the Foreign Trade Anti-Trust Improvement Act which amended the Sherman Act (the main US legislation on competition: see Chapter 27.6) and provided for application of US anti-trust law in situations where the conduct of a foreign company has direct, substantial, and reasonably foreseeable effect on US commerce or US exports. In *Hartford Fire*[2315] the US Supreme Court held that conduct by foreign parties violates the Sherman Act if it satisfies both the intent and effects test. As to the intent the party must have intended to, and in fact, hurt competition in the US market. With regard to the effect, its conduct must have had direct, substantial and reasonably foreseeable effect on US commerce or US exports. The only defence available to the defendant is based on foreign legal compulsion. This means that comity will limit the assertion of jurisdiction of US courts only when a foreign State compels particular conduct which US antitrust law prohibits. The "intent and effect test" has also been applied in criminal proceedings against foreign companies and their officials.[2316] However, following from *Empagran*,[2317] the Sherman Act does not

---

2309. [1975] *UNIDI* OJ L228/17.

2310. [1985] *Milchförderungsfonds* OJ L35/35.

2311. Case T-37/92 *BEUC and National Consumer Council v Commission* [1994] ECR II-285.

2312. [2004] OJ C101/81, para. 19.

2313. Joined Cases 89, 104, 114, 116, 117 and 125–129/85 *Ahlström and Others v Commission (Re Wood Pulp Cartel)* [1988] ECR 5193.

2314. *US v Aluminium Co of America* (1945) 148 F 2d 416.

2315. *Hartford Fire Insurance Co. v California* 509 US 764,113 St.Ct.2891, 125 L.ED.2d 612 (1993).

2316. *United States v Nippon Paper Indus. Co* 109 F.3d 1 (1ˢᵗ Cir. 1997).

2317. *Hoffmann-La Roche Ltd v Empagran SA* 124 S.Cr 2359 (2004).

apply in a situation where foreign claimants seek damages in respect of conduct prohibited under the Act which has produced harmful effects outside the US.

The ECJ endorsed the extraterritorial application of EU competition law in the *Wood Pulp Cartel Cases*[2318] (for facts see Chapter 27.3.3.3) in which the Commission found 40 undertakings supplying wood pulp in violation of EU competition law despite the fact that they were not resident within the EU. The ECJ held:

> "It should be observed that an infringement of art [101 TFEU], such as the conclusion of an agreement which has had the effect of restricting competition within the Common Market, consists of conduct made up of two elements: the formation of the agreement, decision or concerted practice and the implementation thereof. If the applicability of prohibitions laid down under competition law were made to depend on the place where the agreement, decision or concerted practice was formed, the result would obviously be to give undertakings an easy means of evading these prohibitions. The decisive factor is therefore the place where it is implemented."[2319]

The above statement of the ECJ established the doctrine of "implementation". The doctrine is particularly relevant where a foreign undertaking has no subsidiaries, no agents, and no branches in the EU, i.e. the EU has no jurisdiction under the doctrine of the single economic unit. In the *Wood Pulp Cartel Cases*, the ECJ held that it had jurisdiction in a situation where a foreign undertaking sells directly to EU purchasers.

Under the "implementation doctrine" it is irrelevant for the application of EU law where an agreement, decision or a concerted practice, was formed, what counts is that it was implemented within the EU. However, this is only the first condition for the application of the doctrine. The second is that an agreement, decision or a concerted practice, must have appreciable effect on intra-EU trade.[2320] The implication of the "implementation" doctrine is that, when, for example, EU undertakings enter into a prohibited agreement on the territory of the EU but the agreement is implemented in a third country where it restricts competition, such an agreement is normally outside the scope of EU competition law.[2321] However, when such an agreement produces some "ricochet" effects in the EU it will be within the scope of EU law.[2322]

The "implementation" doctrine developed by the ECJ does not exactly match the US "effects" doctrine, i.e. the intent to harm intra-EU trade is irrelevant; what counts is the place of implementation of the relevant agreement decision, concerted practice or abusive practice and its appreciable impact on intra-EU trade. Further, some commentators argue that the "implementation" doctrine will not apply to a situation where undertakings conclude an agreement outside the EU, under which they agree not to sell within the EU or not to purchase from EU producers, whilst the US effects doctrine will apply if such an agreement is directed at the US market.[2323]

2318. Supra note 2313.

2319. Ibid, para. 16.

2320. Case T-329/01 *Archer Daniels Midland (Sodium Gluconate Cartel)* [2006] ECR II-3255.

2321. Case 30/78 *The Distillers Company* [1980] ECR I-2229; *Decision VVVF* [1969] OJ L168.22.

2322. Case C-306/96 *Javico International v YSL* [1998] ECR I-1983 in which the ECJ condemned a distribution agreement whereby a French undertaking Yves Saint Laurent imposed on its distributors in Russia, Ukraine and Slovenia (the latter was not an EU member at the relevant time) an obligation not to re-import the contract goods into the EU.

2323. J. Griffin, "Foreign Governmental Reactions to US Assertions of Extraterritorial Jurisdiction" (1998) 6 *George Mason Law Review*, 505.

26.5 The material scope of application of EU competition law

The Treaties provide certain exceptions which exclude either totally or partially certain activities or certain sectors from the application of competition law.

The first exception is contained in Article 106 (2) TFEU which states that undertakings entrusted with the operation of services of general interest, or having the character of a revenue-producing monopoly, are subject to competition rules "in so far as the application of such rules does not obstruct the performance, in law or in fact, of the particular tasks assigned to them. The development of trade must not be affected to such an extent as would be contrary to the interests of the Union".

The second exception concerns the agricultural sector. Under Article 42 TFEU EU competition law "shall apply to production and trade in agricultural products only to the extent determined by the EP and Council". This exception is justified on the ground that the full application of competition law to the agricultural sector would constitute an obstacle to the achievement of objectives of the Common Agricultural Policy set out in Article 33 TFEU. The extent to which competition law applies to the agricultural sector is defined in Council Regulation 1184/2006 Applying Certain Rules of Competition to the Production of, and Trade in, Agricultural Products[2324] (Codified version) and Council Regulation 1234/2007 establishing a Common Organisation of Agricultural Markets and on Specific Provisions for Certain Agricultural Products (Single CMO Regulation).[2325]

The third exception concerns the production of, and trade in, arms, ammunitions and war materials which, under Article 346(1)(b) TFEU are within the exclusive competence of the Member States. However, national measures relating to the production of, and trade in, military equipment must not adversely affect the conditions of competition in the internal market.

Finally, under the Euratom Treaty the nuclear energy sector is outside the scope of EU competition law although agreements regulating the supply and price of various nuclear materials are within the scope of Articles 101 and 102 TFEU.[2326]

26.6 The federal nature of EU competition law

EU competition law does not replace the national competition law of Member States. Undertakings are required to comply with both national and EU competition law.

Article 3 of Regulation 1/2003 sets out clear rules on the relationship between Articles 101 and 102 TFEU and national competition laws. They can be summarised as follows:

1. Under Article 3(1) NCAs and national courts, when applying national law to conduct which constitutes an agreement, decision or concerted practice within the meaning of Article 101 TFEU or an abusive conduct within the meaning of Article 102 TFEU which affects trade between Member States, are also obliged to apply Articles 101 and 102 TFEU;

2. Under Article 3(2) NCAs or national courts may apply national laws which are stricter than Article 102 TFEU. However, they are not allowed to do this in respect of an agreement that is permitted under Article 101 TFEU. This means that an agreement authorised under Article 101 TFEU cannot be prohibited under national law. The main reasons why Article 3(2) allows the application of stricter national law to Article 102 while excluding it in respect of Article 101 TFEU is that when an agreement is authorised under Article 101 TFEU (either because it

---

2324. [2006] OJ L214/7-9.
2325. [2007] OJ L299/1-149.
2326. See, for example, *United Reprocessors GmbH* [1976] OJ L51/7 and *GEC/Weir* [1977] OJ L327/26.

does not restrict competition or because it fulfils the criteria set out in Article 101(3) and therefore its pro-competitive effects prevail over its anti-competitive effects, or because it satisfies the conditions of a block exemption), its condemnation at national level would undermine the basic objectives of Article 101 TFEU, and such undermining would be entirely inappropriate.

The Regulation does not address the situation where conduct is unlawful under Article 101 or 102 TFEU, but lawful under national law. Perhaps this is because the solution is simple: the application of the principle of supremacy means that such conduct cannot be regarded as lawful under national law; and,

3. Article 3(3) precludes the application of paragraphs 1 and 2 of Article 3 to national merger control rules or national provisions that predominately pursue objectives which are not competition objectives, such as social objectives.

RECOMMENDED READING

Books recommended for Chapters 26–30

On economics of competition law

Bishop, S., and Walker, M., *The Economics of EC Competition Law: Concepts, Application and Measurement*, 3rd edn, 2010, London: Sweet & Maxwell.

Bork, R. H., *The Antitrust Paradox: A Policy at War with Itself*, 1978, Basic Books, reprinted with a new Introduction and Epilogue, 1993.

Geradin, D., Layne-Farrar, A., and Petit, N., *EU Competition Law and Economics*, 2012, Oxford: OUP.

Motta, M., *Competition Policy: Theory and Practice*, 2004, Cambridge: CUP.

Niles, G., Jenkin, H., and Kavanagh, J., *Economics for Competition Lawyers*, 2011, Oxford: OUP.

Posner, R. A., *Antitrust Law*, 2nd edn, 2001, Chicago: University of Chicago Press.

Posner, R. A., *A Failure of Capitalist Democracy*, 2010, Harvard: Harvard University Press.

Stiglitz, J., *Freefall: Free Markets and the Sinking of the Global Economy*, 2010, London: Penguin.

On EU competition law

Ezrachi, A., *EU Competition Law – An Analytical Guide to the Leading Cases*, 3rd edn, 2012, Oxford: Hart Publishing.

Furse, M., *Competition Law of the EC and UK*, 6th edn, 2008, Oxford: OUP.

Jones, A. and Sufrin, B., *EU Competition Law: Text, Cases and Materials*, 2011, 4th edn, Oxford: OUP.

Korah, V., *An Introductory Guide to EC Competition Law and Practice*, 2007, 9th edn, Oxford: Hart Publishing.

Lianos, I. and Kokkoris, I., *The Reform of EC Competition Law: New Challenges*, 2009, London: KLI.

Marco Colino, S., *Competition Law of the EU and UK*, 7th edn, 2011, Oxford: OUP.

Monti, G., *EC Competition Law*, 2007, Cambridge: CUP.

Prosser, T., *The Limits of Competition Law: Markets and Public Services*, 2005, Oxford: OUP.

Whish, R., and Bailey, D., *Competition Law*, 7th edn, 2012, Oxford: OUP.

Articles relating to Chapter 26

Crutchfield, G. B., "Increasing Extraterritorial Intrusion of European Union Authority into US Business Mergers and Competition Practices: US Multinational Businesses Underestimate the Strength of the European Commission From G.E.-Honeywell to Microsoft", (2004) 19 Conn. J. Int'l L., 571.

Howard, A., "Modernisation – a Brave New World?", (2007) 6/1 Comp. Law, 33.

Huffman, M., "Bridging the Divide? Theories for Integrating Competition Law and Consumer Protection", (2010) 6/1 EuroCJ, 7.

La Rocca, L., "The Controversial Issue of the Parent-company Liability for the Violation of EC Competition Rules by the Subsidiary", (2011) 32/2 ECLR, 68.

Lasok, K.P.E., "When Is an Undertaking Not an Undertaking", (2004) 25 ECLR, 383.

Maher, I., "Competition Law Modernisation: An Evolutionary Tale", in Craig, P., and de Búrca, G. (eds), *The Evolution of EU Law*, 2nd edn, 2011, Oxford: OUP, 717.

Nihoul, P., and Lübbig, T., "What Competition Policy after Lisbon?" (2010) *Journal of European Competition Law & Practice*, 91.

Nowag, J., "Selex Sistemi Integrati SpA v Commission of the European Communities (C-113/07P) [2009] ECR I-2207: Redefining the Boundaries between Undertaking and the Exercise of Public Authority" [2010] 12 ECLR, 483.

Parret, L., "Shouldn't We Know What We are Protecting? Yes We Should! A Plea for a Solid and Comprehensive Debate about the Objectives of EU Competition Law, and Policy", (2010) 6/2 EuroCJ, 339.

Weitbrecht, A., "From Freiburg to Chicago and Beyond – the First 50 years of European Competition Law", (2008) 29/2 ECLR, 81.

Wils, W.P.J., "The Undertakings as Subject of EC Competition Law and the Imputation of Infringements to Natural or Legal Persons", (2000) 25 ELRev., 99.

PROBLEM QUESTION

A Belgian entity named the Association of Medical Suppliers (AMS) is managed by the Belgian Minister of Health, and operates on the principle of national solidarity in that it is funded from social security contributions and other State funding. AMS provides medical services free of charge to Belgian nationals. It is the biggest purchaser of medical goods and equipment in Belgium and as such holds approximately 97 per cent of this market.

The managing director of one of the suppliers of AMS, MEDEQIP Inc, consults you, an expert in EU competition law. He tells you that AMS takes an average of 300 days beyond the contractual payment date to pay for purchased equipment and that AMS does, at least occasionally, charge patients, such as foreign visitors, who are not covered by the Belgian social security system, for the cost of medical care provided to them.

The managing director of MEDEQIP Inc wishes to know whether the above situation raises any EU competition law issues. Advise him.

ESSAY QUESTION

Critically discuss whether the application of the US effects doctrine is preferable to the approaches developed by the ECJ to deal with a situation where an undertaking is established outside the EU but its conduct restricts competition in the EU.

AIDE-MÉMOIRE

TO BE AN UNDERTAKING A NATURAL OR LEGAL PERSON

MUST

| BE ENGAGED IN ANY ECONOMIC ACTIVITY (CASE C-41/90 *HÖFNER*) THIS | **AND** | ENJOY SOME AUTONOMY IN ITS CONDUCT ON THE RELEVANT MARKET THIS |

INCLUDES
- ANY ACTIVITY CONSISTING OF PROVISION OF SERVICES AND GOODS
- ANY ACTIVITY WHICH CAN BE CARRIED OUT BY A PRIVATE UNDERTAKING IN ORDER TO MAKE PROFIT IF THIS ACTIVITY IS EXERCISED BY A PUBLIC BODY (CASE T-155/04 *SELEX SYSTEMI*)

EXCLUDES
- ANY ACTIVITY RELATING TO THE MANAGEMENT OF COMPULSORY SOCIAL SECURITY SCHEMES SUBJECT TO THE THREE CONDITIONS SPECIFIED IN CASES C-264, 306 AND 355/01 *AOK*
- ANY ACTIVITY CONNECTED WITH THE EXERCISE OF POWERS TYPICAL OF THOSE EXERCISED BY A PUBLIC AUTHORITY (CASE T-155/04 *SELEX SYSTEMI*)

EXCLUDES
- A SUBSIDIARY WHICH IS 100% OWNED BY THE PARENT COMPANY AS THE PRESUMPTION IS THAT THE PARENT COMPANY EXERCISES DECISIVE INFLUENCE. WHEN A PARENT COMPANY'S SHAREHOLDING IN ITS SUBSIDIARY IS LESS THAN 100% THE MATTER OF DECISIVE INFLUENCE IS ASSESSED ACCORDING TO THE FACTS (CASE C-97/08 *AKZO*)
- A COMMERCIAL AGENT WHO ACTS PURSUING THE INSTRUCTIONS OF A PRINCIPAL
- AN EMPLOYEE (CASE C-22/98 *BECU*)
- A PUBLIC BODY IN THE EXERCISE OF "OFFICIAL AUTHORITY" (CASE 30/87 *BODSON*)
- A PRIVATE UNDERTAKING WHEN COMPELLED BY A STATE

27

ARTICLE 101 TFEU

CHAPTER OUTLINE

1. Article 101(1) TFEU prohibits agreements between undertakings, decisions of associations of undertakings, and concerted practices which may have appreciable effect on trade between Member States and which have as their object or effect the prevention, restriction or distortion of competition. Article 101(1) TFEU provides a non-exhaustive list of prohibited arrangements. Under Article 101(2) TFEU any such agreement or decision is void. Concerted practices are not mentioned as they are informal arrangements and therefore cannot be rendered void. However, arrangements which fall within the scope of Article 101(1) may escape the prohibition if they meet the criteria set out in Article 101(3) TFEU, or in the relevant block exemption regulation.

2. Article 101(1) TFEU applies to both horizontal agreements, i.e. agreements between undertakings operating at the same level of production/distribution, and to vertical agreements, i.e. agreements between undertakings which do not compete with each other because they operate at different levels of the market, e.g. distribution agreements, franchising agreements, and purchasing agreements.

3. In Case T-41/96 *Bayer,* the General Court stated that the concept of an agreement "centres round the existence of a concurrence of wills between at least two parties, the form in which it is manifested being unimportant so long as it constitutes the faithful expression of the parties' intention". Accordingly, unilateral conduct of an undertaking falls outside the scope of Article 101(1) TFEU.

4. The concept of an association of undertakings and the concept of a decision of associations of undertakings have been broadly interpreted. They encompass not only a formal association of undertakings such as a trade association, but also an informal one such as a gathering of representatives of undertakings in a particular sector to deal with a particular situation or a particular competitor. The term decision refers to associations of undertakings' constitutions, bye-laws, decisions which can be formal (such as a code of conduct) or informal (such as recommendations, circular letters, and so on).

5. The concept of a concerted practice refers to collaboration between at least two undertakings which falls short of an agreement proper. Such co-ordination or co-operation must have been established as a result of direct or indirect contact between them for the purpose of eliminating uncertainties related to a competitor's behaviour in the relevant market. There must be conduct in the market pursuant to the relevant collusive practices, and a relationship of cause and effect between them. Tacit collusion is usually very difficult to prove, but the ECJ has adopted an approach whereby subtle forms of co-ordinated behaviour come within the concept (e.g. public announcements of price increases in advance of the actual increase, as a way of "tipping off" other players in the market who then follow suit, could amount to a concerted practice). It can, however, be the case that parallel behaviour may simply reflect the nature of the market rather than any attempt to restrict competition (e.g. in an oligopolistic market). Therefore, if the only plausible explanation for parallel conduct of undertakings is that they are engaged in a concerted practice, there will be a breach of Article 101(1) TFEU.

6. The Commission, supported by the ECJ, has developed two ways of alleviating the heavy burden of proof imposed upon it when dealing with complex cartels of long duration. First, it is not required to distinguish between agreements and concerted practices, i.e. it can apply a joint classification. Second, it has established the concept of a "single, overall agreement" for which all members of a cartel are responsible irrespective of the extent of their actual participation. However, for an undertaking to be held liable for the whole infringement, that is for conduct put into effect by other undertakings, even though it has participated only in some of its aspects, it must be established that the undertaking concerned was aware of the offending conduct of the other participating undertakings, that it could reasonably have foreseen it, and that it was ready to take the risk.

7. In Case 56/65 *Société Technique Minière (STM)*, the ECJ held that the words "object" and "effect" must be read disjunctively. Thus these concepts are not cumulative but alternative. If an agreement, decision, or a concerted practice restricts competition by its object, its effect is irrelevant. It is presumed that it has such a high potential for anti-competitive effect that it is not necessary to show any actual effect on the relevant market. If an agreement is not restrictive by object, it must be determined whether it has restrictive effect on competition. Not only actual and direct effect is taken into account but also potential and indirect effect on competition in the relevant market. An assessment takes account of the economic and legal setting of the relevant agreement, decision or concerted practice. Only those which have or are likely to have an appreciable adverse effect on competition in the relevant market are caught by Article 101(1) TFEU.

8. Article 101(1) contains a sweeping prohibition that, if interpreted literally, could render almost all commercial arrangements with European dimensions unlawful. For that reason, Article 101(3) TFEU provides for exemption of agreements/concerted practices which confer sufficient benefit to outweigh their anti-competitive effects. This occurs when the four cumulative conditions set out in Article 101(3) are satisfied.

9. Block exemptions have been issued in the form of EU regulations (which are thus legally binding). These make agreements, decisions and concerted practices, which are within their scope of application and which conform to their provisions, valid and enforceable even if they are restrictive of competition within the meaning of Article 101(1) TFEU. The best example is provided by Regulation 330/2010 on the application of Article 101(3) of the TFEU to categories of vertical agreements and concerted practices.

27.1 Introduction

Article 101 TFEU states:

"1.   The following shall be prohibited as incompatible with the internal market: all agreements between undertakings, decisions by associations of undertakings, and concerted practices which may affect trade between Member States and which have as their object or effect the prevention, restriction or distortion of competition within the common market, and in particular those which:

(a)   directly or indirectly fix purchase or selling prices or any other trading conditions;

(b)   limit or control production, markets, technical development, or investment;

(c)   share markets or sources of supply;

(d)   apply dissimilar conditions to equivalent transactions with other trading parties, thereby placing them at a competitive disadvantage;

(e)   make the conclusion of contracts subject to acceptance by the other parties of supplementary obligations which, by their nature or according to commercial usage, have no connection with the subject of such contracts.

2.   Any agreements or decisions prohibited pursuant to this Article shall be automatically void.

3.   The provisions of paragraph 1 may, however, be declared inapplicable in the case of:

–   any agreement or category of agreements between undertakings;

–   any decision or category of decisions by associations of undertakings;

–   any concerted practice or category of concerted practices,

which contributes to improving the production or distribution of goods or to promoting technical or economic progress, while allowing consumers a fair share of the resulting benefit, and which does not:

(a)   impose on the undertakings concerned restrictions which are not indispensable to the attainment of these objectives;

(b)   afford such undertakings the possibility of eliminating competition in respect of a substantial part of the products in question."

Breach of the prohibition embodied in Article 101(1) TFEU occurs when an entity identified as an undertaking (see Chapter 26.3) enters into an arrangement with another undertaking, which has as its object or effect the prevention, restriction or distortion of competition within the internal market, and which is capable of having, or has, an appreciable effect on trade between Member States.

In the circumstances set out in Article 101(3) TFEU arrangements which are *prima facie* in breach of Article 101(1) TFEU may fall outside the Article 101(1) TFEU prohibition. Also, arrangements which satisfy the conditions set out by the relevant block exemption regulation, or are within the *de minimis* rule (see Chapter 26.4.3), are outside the scope of Article 101(1) TFEU.

Agreements and decisions which infringe Article 101(1) TFEU and which are not eligible for exemption under either a block exemption regulation or Article 101(3) TFEU are, by virtue of Article 101(2) TFEU, automatically void from inception and as such unenforceable. The term "automatically" means that no decision to that effect is required from EU institutions or national courts.[2327] Concerted practices are not mentioned in Article 101(2) TFEU since they are informal arrangements and as such cannot be rendered void.

It is not necessary for the entire agreement or decision to be declared null and void if it is possible to sever offending clauses without destroying the substance of the agreement. Whether or not it is possible to do this is a matter for national courts to decide.[2328] Sometimes, EU institutions assist national courts in this task. For example, in Joined Cases 56 and 58/64 *Consten and Grundig*[2329] the ECJ severed the offending clauses of the agreement, which were those giving absolute territorial protection.

Since the entry into force of Regulation 1/2003 national courts have jurisdiction to apply Article 101(3) TFEU (see Chapter 30.1). Private enforcement of EU competition law is discussed in Chapter 30.4.

27.2 The application of Article 101 TFEU to horizontal and vertical agreements

Article 101 applies to both horizontal and vertical agreements. The difference between them is explained below.

27.2.1 A horizontal agreement

This is an agreement entered into by undertakings that compete with each other at the same level of the production/distribution chain, for example, agreements between producers, manufacturers or retailers.

Horizontal agreements which are in breach of Article 101 TFEU are the most harmful to competition because rival undertakings, instead of competing with each other, collude and therefore can act as one undertaking in the relevant market. An arrangement between rival undertakings is called a cartel. In a cartel participating undertakings considerably increase their market power and, in some cases, can monopolise the relevant market. As a result, they can reduce output to increase prices and are not subjected to pressure to improve the products they sell, to create new products or to find new ways of commercialisation of such products. Thus, cartels stifle creative innovation, impose higher prices for lower quality goods, and narrow the choice of products. Additionally, they harm consumers, who have to pay cartel prices. Further, they dampen opportunities for new undertakings to enter the relevant market. In short, the existence of cartels runs counter to the objectives of competition law and adversely affects the competitiveness of the economy as a whole.

2327. Case 22/71 *Béguelin Import Co. v S.A.G.L. Import Export* [1971] ECR 949, and Article 1 of Regulation 17/62 [1962] 13/204-211.

2328. Case 319/82 *Société de Vente de Ciments et Béton de L'Est v Kerpen and Kerpen GmbH and CO KG* [1983] ECR 4173.

2329. Joined Cases 56 and 58/64 *Établissements Consten Sarl and Grundig-Verkaufs-GmbH v Commission* [1966] ECR 299.

27.2.2 A vertical agreement

This occurs when two or more undertakings which operate at different levels of the production/distribution chain enter into an agreement, for example, agreements between producers and retailers. The undertakings involved do not in any event compete with each other because they operate at different levels of the market. The most popular vertical agreements are distribution agreements and franchising agreements.

Initially, there were some doubts as to whether Article 101 applies to vertical agreements, taking into consideration that the parties to such agreements are not on an equal footing. This question was examined by the ECJ in Joined Cases 56 and 58/64 *Consten and Grundig*.[2330]

THE FACTS WERE:

Grundig, a large German manufacturer of electrical equipment, entered into an exclusive distribution agreement with a French distributor, Consten, according to which Consten was appointed as Grundig's exclusive distributor in France, Corsica and the Saar region. Under the contract Consten agreed not to sell outside its territory. Grundig undertook not to compete itself, not to deliver to third parties, even indirectly, products intended for the territory assigned to Consten and to obtain assurances from its distributors in other Member States that they would not sell to buyers from outside their exclusive territories. This "airtight" exclusive distribution agreement was reinforced by a clause allowing Consten to use the Grundig trade mark "GINT" and emblem in its promotions. On the basis of this authority, Consten registered the Grundig trade mark in France.

A French competitor imported a number of Grundig products from Germany and attempted to sell these in the French market. Consten raised an action for trade mark infringement against this rival, relying on the earlier registration of the trade mark. The Commission objected to these proceedings and commenced an investigation into the functioning of the exclusive distribution agreement. The Commission found that the agreement was contrary to Article 101(1) TFEU, being an agreement which had the object of distorting competition within the EU by restricting trade. It found that the agreement could not be exempted under Article 101(3) TFEU as it failed to satisfy the condition that consumers should receive a fair share of benefits resulting from the agreement. Consten and Grundig brought an action before the ECJ contesting these findings.

Held:

The ECJ confirmed that vertical agreements are within the scope of Article 101 TFEU in the following words:

"Article [Article 101 TFEU] refers in a general way to all agreements which distort competition within the Common Market [Internal market] and does not lay down any distinction between those agreements based on whether they are made between competitors operating at the same level in the economic process or between non-competing persons operating at different levels. In principle, no distinction can be made where the Treaty does not make any distinction."[2331]

2330. Ibid,
2331. Ibid, p. 339.

> *The ECJ held that it is irrelevant that parties to such an agreement are not equal as regards their position and function in the economy. The Court upheld the Commission's decision that the agreement did not satisfy the criteria set out in Article 101(3) TFEU.*
>
> **Comment:**
>
> *The ECJ held that the agreement between Consten and Grundig would stifle parallel imports. Although the agreement did not explicitly exclude parallel imports, it discouraged them. The agreement was intended to isolate the national markets for Grundig products and therefore partition the internal market along national lines, which in itself distorted competition in the internal market. Thus, it restricted competition by object (see Chapter 27.4) and for that reason the Commission was not required to assess its effect on competition. In this respect, the ECJ agreed with the Commission that it was not necessary to show that in the absence of the agreement trade would have been greater as suggested by AG Roemer, i.e. it was not necessary to consider the concrete effect of the agreement.*
>
> *The judgment confirmed that the purpose of the requirement that an agreement must affect trade between Member States is to determine the jurisdictional competence of EU competition law. Consequently, the fact that an agreement increases the volume of trade between Member States was "not sufficient to exclude the possibility that the agreement may 'affect' such trade."[2332]*
>
> *With regard to Article 101(3) TFEU, the ECJ agreed with the Commission that it was for the undertakings concerned, not for the Commission to prove that the agreement brought benefits to consumers. The position of the Commission was that because the agreement conferred absolute territorial protection consumers could not receive any benefits.*
>
> *In relation to the trade mark, the ECJ held first, that the registration of the trade mark, which gave Consten additional protection based on the law of IPRs against the risk of parallel imports into France of Grundig products, constituted an abusive use of IPRs, because no third party could import Grundig products from other Member States for resale in France without running the serious risk of being liable for breach of trade mark rights, and second, that the use of the mark "GINT" was for the purpose of partitioning the internal market along national lines and as such in breach of Article 101(1) TFEU.[2333]*

Under EU competition law vertical agreements are treated less severely than horizontal agreements. They are in general less obviously anti-competitive than horizontal agreements. This is because each party to such an agreement exercises its power independently of any rivals. If any party is in a dominant position and abuses that position, the matter is dealt with under Article 102 TFEU. Usually, the only anti-competitive effect of such agreements is when there is insufficient inter-brand-competition.[2334] Many economists (in particular those allied to the Chicago School[2335]) emphasise that vertical agreements offer many pro-competitive benefits. This is also the current view of the Commission,

---

2332. Ibid, p. 341.

2333. However, in some exceptional situations absolute territorial protection may be permitted, see Case C-262/81 *Coditel SA, Compagnie Générale pour la Diffusion de la Télévision, and Others v Ciné-Vog Films SA and Others* [1982] ECR 3381; Case 258/78 *L.C. Nungesser KG and Kurt Eisele v Commission* [1982] ECR 2015.

2334. Inter-brand competition refers to competition between suppliers of competing brands. Intra-brand competition concerns competition between distributors of the same brand.

2335. W. S. Comanor, "Vertical Price-Fixing, Vertical Market Restrictions, and the New Antitrust Policy", (1985) 98 *Harvard Law Review*, 986.

which under Regulation 330/2010[2336] (see Chapter 27.9.1) introduced a rebuttable presumption of compatibility with Article 101(1) TFEU of vertical agreements where the parties to the vertical agreement have a share in the relevant product market of less than 30 per cent. This is subject to some exceptions, and subject to a limited number of "hard core" restrictions set out in the Regulation.

27.3 Agreements, decisions and concerted practices

Article 101(1) TFEU prohibits all arrangements between undertakings capable of distorting competition within the internal market. It lists three types of arrangement:

- agreements between undertakings;

- decisions by associations of undertakings; and,

- concerted practices.

Concerted practices are conceptually distinct from the other two types of arrangement. Nevertheless, in fact it is difficult to distinguish between the three types of arrangements mentioned because they are often interrelated. The ECJ, in Case C-8/08 *T-Mobile*,[2337] emphasised that "the definitions of 'agreement', 'decisions by associations of undertakings' and 'concerted practice' are intended, from a subjective point of view, to catch forms of collusion having the same nature which are distinguishable from each other only by their intensity and the forms in which they manifest themselves".

In Case C-49/92P *Anic*[2338] the ECJ held that although Article 101 TFEU distinguishes between "concerted practices", "agreements between undertakings" and "decisions by associations of undertakings", its objective is to catch different forms of co-ordination and collusion between undertakings, and therefore the General Court was correct in considering that "patterns of conduct by several undertakings were a manifestation of a single infringement, corresponding partly to an agreement and partly to a concerted practice". Therefore the two concepts are not incompatible and certain conduct may be qualified as being, in the first place a concerted practice and, in the second place an agreement, or as being at the same time an agreement and a decision of associations.[2339]

The joint classification is especially useful for the Commission as it eases the burden of proof imposed on it in respect of complex cartels of considerable duration involving many undertakings. As the Commission stated in *British Sugar*,[2340] in such circumstances it would be artificial and unrealistic to subdivide continuous conduct, having one and the same overall objective, into several distinct infringements. Further, the evidentiary task of the Commission in the context of complex cartels is also simplified by the establishment of the concept of a "single, overall agreement" (see below).

27.3.1 Agreements between undertakings

In Case T-41/96 *Bayer AG v Commission*,[2341] the General Court defined the concept of an agreement, which is relevant to both horizontal and vertical agreements, in the following terms:

2336. [2010] OJ L142/1.
2337. Case C-8/08 *T-Mobile Netherlands BV, and others v Commission* [2009] ECR I-4529, para. 23.
2338. Case C-49/92P *Commission v Anic Partecipazioni SpA* [1999] ECR I-4125, para. 3, also see Case T-62/98 *Volkswagen AG v Commission* [2000] ECR II-2707.
2339. *Visa International* [2002] OJ L318/17.
2340. *British Sugar plc, Tate and Lyle plc, Napier Brown and Co Ltd, James Budgett Sugars Ltd* [1999] OJ L76/1.
2341. [2000] ECR II-3383, para. 69.

"the concept of an agreement within the meaning of [Article 101(1) TFEU], as interpreted by the case-law, centres round the existence of a concurrence of wills between at least two parties, the form in which it is manifested being unimportant so long as it constitutes the faithful expression of the parties' intention."

The following were regarded as agreements within the scope of Article 101(1) TFEU: standard sale conditions;[2342] out-of-court settlements; correspondence between undertakings and conversations between representatives of those undertakings;[2343] and, rules adopted by a trade association which were binding on its members (such rules are considered as agreements with regard to the members and as a decision with regard to the association).[2344] An informal agreement such as a "gentlemen's agreement" also falls within the scope of Article 101(1) TFEU.[2345] Even if a contract is contrary to the economic interests of one of the parties,[2346] or was legally terminated but still produces unlawful effects,[2347] or was concluded subject to a condition,[2348] it is regarded as an agreement within the meaning of Article 101(1) TFEU. The legal nature of an agreement is determined by the EU institutions/national competition authorities in the light of factual considerations and not by the parties to it.[2349] There is no concurrence of wills between the parties at the stage of negotiations, preparatory discussions, and so on,[2350] as at that stage no agreement has been reached.

It should be noted that collective bargaining agreements between workers and employers are not regarded as agreements within the meaning of Article 101(1) TFEU in so far as their objective is to improve conditions of work and employment.[2351]

The General Court in Case T-99/04 *AC-Treuhand*[2352] interpreted the concept of "agreement" broadly. It classified conduct of a consultancy company, which was not active on the relevant market, but which contributed to the implementation and maintenance of a cartel by, *inter alia*, organising meetings for the three producers of organic peroxides which set it up and then by covering up evidence of its existence, as an agreement between undertakings within the meaning of Article 101 TFEU. The Court held that although the consultancy company was only an accessory and not a party to the cartel, the element of "joint intention" which is essential to the existence of an "agreement" does not require the relevant market, on which the undertaking which is the "perpetrator" of the restriction of competition is active, to be exactly the same as the one on which that restriction is deemed to materialise.

A.   **The concept of a "single, overall agreement".**The concept of a "single, overall agreement" was developed by the Commission and endorsed by the ECJ in Case C-49/92 P *Anic*.[2353] In this case, the Commission found that undertakings participating in a cartel were engaged in a single and continuous infringement, and thus it was not necessary to subdivide into distinct agreements

---

2342.   Case C-277/87 *Sandoz Prodotti Farmaceutici SpA v Commission* [1990] ECR I-45; Case T-168/01 *GlaxoSmithKline Services Unlimited v Commission* [2006] ECR II-2969.

2343.   Case T-7/89 *Hercules Chemicals NV v Commission* [1991] ECR II-1711.

2344.   *Nuovo Cegam* [1984] OJ L 99/29.

2345.   Case 41/69 *Chemiefarma NV v Commission* (*Quinine Cartel* cases) [1970] ECR 661.

2346.   *Johnson and Johnson* [1980] OJ L377/16; [1981] 2 CMLR 287, Case T-48/98 *Acerinox v Commission* [2001] ECR II-3859.

2347.   Case 51/75 *EMI Records Limited v CBS United Kingdom Limited* [1976] ECR 811.

2348.   *SAS/Maersk Air* [2001] OJ L265/15.

2349.   *Auditel and AGB Italia SpA* [1993] OJ L306/50.

2350.   Case T-60/02, *Deutsche Verkehrsbank AG v Commission* (NYR).

2351.   Case C-67/96 *Albany International BV v Stichting Bedrijfspensioenfonds Textielindustrie* [1999] ECR I-5751.

2352.   Case T-99/04 *AC-Treuhand AG v Commission* [2008] ECR II-1501.

2353.   [1999] ECR I-4125; see also Case T-334/94 *Sarrió SA v Commission* [1998] ECR II-1439.

and concerted practices conduct which formed part of an overall plan to restrict competition, and to identify in which each undertaking had participated. Anic submitted that when various actions amount to a single infringement, the Commission must show that the undertaking concerned had participated in all aspects of the infringement, that is, in all actions forming the infringement, in order to make it responsible for all aspects of the conduct of all the undertakings charged, during the relevant period. As Anic participated in only some concerted actions, but not all of them, it argued that it was wrongly held responsible for actions of other undertakings that participated in the infringement.

The ECJ emphasised that, taking into account the nature and degree of the ensuing penalties, responsibility for infringements of Article 101 TFEU is personal in nature. It added, however, that it flows from Article 101 TFEU that the anti-competitive conduct results from collaboration by several undertakings, and therefore each undertaking is a co-perpetrator of the infringement, even if it participates in different ways depending on a number of factors such as its position in the market; the characteristics of the market itself; the objectives pursued; and, the means of implementation of anti-competitive practices chosen or envisaged by it. The ECJ held that an undertaking may be held responsible for the conduct of other undertakings which participated in the same infringement:

> "where it is proved that the undertaking in question was aware of the unlawful conduct of the other participants, or could reasonably foresee such conduct, and was prepared to accept the risk. Such a conclusion is not at odds with the principle that responsibility for such infringements is personal in nature, nor does it neglect individual analysis of the evidence adduced, in disregard of the applicable rules of evidence, or infringe the rights of defence of the undertakings involved."[2354]

The concept of a "single, overall agreement" eases the evidentiary burden imposed on the Commission in that it is not required to show that every undertaking took part in every aspect of a cartel over a long period of time,[2355] a task which is very difficult, if not impossible bearing in mind how cartels operate in practice. Nevertheless, an alleged participant in a cartel may rebut the presumption. Further, its degree of participation in the infringement will be taken into consideration in the determination of the fine[2356] (see Chapter 30.2.7).

B. **The limit of the concept of an agreement: unilateral conduct of an undertaking.** One undertaking acting alone cannot be in breach of Article 101(1) TFEU. However, until the judgment of the General Court in Case T-41/96 *Bayer*,[2357] the concept of an agreement was being broadly interpreted so that even unilateral conduct could conceivably have come within it, for example, unilateral anti-competitive measures adopted by a manufacturer *vis-à-vis* its dealers, without account being taken of the actual conduct of the dealers with regard to those measures. The signature of the dealership contract was regarded as tacit acquiescence in subsequent anti-competitive initiatives of the manufacturer regardless of subsequent conduct adopted by the dealers.[2358]

2354. Case C-49/92P *Commission v Anic Partecipazioni SpA* [1999] ECR I-4125, para. 203.
2355. *PVC II*, (1994) OJ L239/14.
2356. The controversies surrounding the concept of a "single, overall agreement" are well explained by D. Bailey, in "Single, overall Agreement in EU Competition Law", (2010) 47 CMLRev., 473.
2357. Case T-41/96 *Bayer AG v Commission* [2000] ECR II-3383.
2358. Case C-277/87 *Sandoz Prodotti Farmaceutici SpA v Commission* [1983] ECR 3151.

The General Court in *Bayer*[2359] stated that unilateral behaviour of an undertaking would be considered as being an agreement only if a concurrence of wills of at least two parties could be established. The mere existence of an agreement and a measure imposed unilaterally does not suffice. The Commission must establish to the requisite legal standard that such a measure has the express or implicit acquiescence of the other party.

THE FACTS WERE:

Bayer AG, one of the most important chemical and pharmaceutical groups in Europe, which has subsidiaries in all the Member States, brought proceedings before the General Court challenging Decision 96/478/EC of the Commission in Adalat[2360] in which Bayer was found in breach of Article 101(1) TFEU.

Under the trade mark "Adalat" or "Adalate" Bayer AG had manufactured and marketed a range of medicinal preparations designed to treat cardio-vascular disease. In a number of Member States the price for "Adalat" was directly determined by the national health authorities. Between 1989 and 1993 in France and Spain the price was 40 per cent lower than the price in the UK. The price difference had encouraged parallel imports of "Adalat" from France and Spain to the UK. According to Bayer, sales of "Adalat" by its British subsidiary fell by almost half between 1989 and 1993. In order to recover the lost profit Bayer AG decided to cease fulfilling all of the increasingly large orders placed by wholesalers in Spain and France with its Spanish and French subsidiaries. Some French and Spanish wholesalers complained to the Commission. Following its investigations the Commission found that Bayer AG was in breach of Article 101(1) TFEU. The Commission decided that the prohibition of the export to other Member States of "Adalat" from France and Spain agreed between Bayer France and its wholesalers since 1991 and between Bayer Spain and its wholesalers since 1989 constituted a breach of Article 101(1) TFEU. Bayer AG argued that the Commission went too far in its interpretation of the concept of an agreement and that in fact Bayer's unilateral conduct was outside the scope of that Article.

Held:

The General Court ruled that in order to establish whether or not there was an agreement between the parties two elements should be considered:

- the intention of Bayer to impose an export ban; and,
- the intention of the wholesalers to adhere to Bayer's policy designed to reduce parallel imports.

In the light of the evidence submitted the General Court held that the Commission had failed to prove to the requisite legal standard that an agreement existed.

The Court emphasised that:

"The proof of an agreement between undertakings within the meaning of [Article 101(1) TFEU] must be founded upon the direct or indirect finding of the existence of the subjective element that characterises the very concept of an agreement, that is to say a concurrence of wills between economic operators on the implementation of a policy, the pursuit of an objective, or

---

2359. [2000] ECR II-3383. See also Case T-208/01 *Volkswagen AG v Commission* [2003] ECR II-5141.
2360. [1996] OJ L201/1.

the adoption of a given line of conduct on the market, irrespective of the manner in which the parties' intention to behave on the market in accordance with the terms of that agreement is expressed."[2361]

Comment:

It was clear from the facts that there was no "concurrence of wills" between the wholesalers and Bayer bearing in mind that the wholesalers had tried by all means to obtain extra supplies whilst Bayer was trying to restrict them.

27.3.2 Decisions by associations of undertakings

This concept refers to decisions of trade associations and of any economic interest grouping of undertakings irrespective of their legal form. As a result, it encompasses professional associations[2362] including a body set up by statute with public functions, members of which are appointed by the government,[2363] international organisations such as the International Railways Union,[2364] groupings such as the European Broadcasting Union[2365] which co-ordinates the Eurovision system, and even a maritime conference.[2366] In Case 123/83 *BNIC v Clair*,[2367] the ECJ held that an agreement concluded between two groups of traders must be regarded as "an agreement between undertakings or associations of undertakings". A decision adopted by a federal type association, that is, its members are themselves associations, is also within the Article 101(1) TFEU prohibition.[2368]

The distortion of competition may result from either a written constitution of an association which imposes certain rules of conduct on its members[2369] or decisions of its managing body which are binding and thus must be complied with by all its members.

The question of whether non-binding decisions of associations are within the scope of Article 101(1) TFEU was answered by the ECJ in Case 8/72 *Cementhandelaren*.[2370]

THE FACTS WERE:

A Dutch trade association, of which most Dutch cement dealers were members, recommended the prices at which cement should be sold in the Netherlands. The trade association actually controlled the Dutch cement industry given that it imposed detailed trading rules on its members (for example, the obligation to notify any change in

---

2361. Case T-41/96 *Bayer AG v Commission* [2000] ECR II-3383, para. 173.

2362. *COAPI* [1995] OJ L 122/37, including professional bodies such as the Bar of the Netherlands: Case C-309/99 *Wouters v Algemene Raad van de Nederlandse Orde van Advocaten* [2002] ECR I-577.

2363. E.g. the examination committee of the Italian Bar: Case C-250/03 *Mauri* (Ord) [2005] OJ C115/8.

2364. Case T-14/93 *UIC* [1995] ECR II-1503; or the International Olympic Committee, the supreme authority of the Olympic Movement, which brings together the various international sporting federations; Case C-519/04 P *Meca-Medina and Majcen v Commission* [2006] ECR I-6991.

2365. Joined Cases T-528, 542, 543/93 and 546/93 *Metropole Télévision SA and Reti Televisive Italiane SpA and Gestevisión Telecinco SA and Antena 3 de Televisión v Commission* [1996] ECR II-649.

2366. Joined Cases C-395 and 396/96P *Compagnie Maritime Belge Transport SA* [1996] ECR I-1365.

2367. [1985] ECR 391.

2368. *Milchförderungsfonds* [1985] OJ L35/35.

2369. *National Sulphuric Acid Association* [1980] OJ L 260/24; [1980] 3 CMLR 429.

2370. [1972] ECR 977.

> *management); supervised its members accounts; required that they sell to each other (and thus eliminated the possibility of the building-up of stocks of cement by third parties); and, was empowered to expel its members for non-compliance with these rules.*
>
> *Held:*
>
> *The ECJ held that a non-binding recommendation would amount to a decision in so far as its acceptance by undertakings actually influenced their conduct in the market. Cementhandelaren's decision recommending target prices had great impact on the level of prices: first, its members were actually complying with the recommendation and second, it removed to a great extent the uncertainty as to prices, as almost all dealers were charging the same as each other. Consequently, the recommendation was regarded as a decision within the meaning of Article 101(1) TFEU.*

27.3.2.1 The limit of the concept of an agreement or a decision – the "State compulsion doctrine"

By virtue of Article 4(3) TEU read in conjunction with Articles 101 and 102 TFEU, a Member State is prohibited from introducing or maintaining national rules which may render EU competition law ineffective.[2371]

If a trade association has been forced by a government through a mandatory act, whether legislative or administrative, to regulate industry in a manner contrary to Article 101(1) TFEU, the association will not be in breach of Article 101(1) TFEU.[2372] However, if a government merely encourages undertakings to impose anti-competitive restrictions, such encouragement will not constitute a defence for the association concerned.[2373]

27.3.3 Concerted practices

It derives from the very nature of a concerted practice that it does not have all the elements of a contract, but it constitutes a form of informal co-ordination between undertakings.

Concerted practices are difficult to evidence, taking into account that:

- ■ They are implicit, secret arrangements which the participating undertakings will try to hide from the public view at all costs. This is exemplified in *Graphite Electrodes Cartel*.[2374]

2371. Joined Cases 209–15 and 218/78 *Van Landewyck* [1980] ECR 3125.

2372. Case 123/83 *BNIC v Clair* [1985] ECR 391.

2373. Case C-35/99 *Arduino* [2002] ECR I-1529; Case C-198/01 *CIF* [2003] ECR I-8055; Case C-198/01 *Consorzio Industrie Fiammiferi (CIF) v Autorità Garante della Concorrenza e del Mercato* [2003] ECR I-8055; Joined Cases T-217/03 and T-245/03 *Fédération Nationale de la Coopération Bétail et Viande (FNCBV) and Others v Commission* [2006] ECR II-4987; Case C-280/08P *Deutsche Telecom* [2010] ECR I-9555.

2374. COMP/E-2/37.667. The General Court largely confirmed the Commission's decision but reduced the amount of fines for some participants: Joined Cases T-71, 74, 87 and T-91/03 *Tokai Carbon and Others v Commission* [2005] ECR II-10.

THE FACTS WERE:

The Graphite Electrodes Cartel was a worldwide cartel aimed at fixing prices and sharing markets for graphite electrodes. The participating undertakings from Europe, the USA and Japan, knowing that they were acting in breach of antitrust law, took great pains to conceal their meetings which were held in Switzerland. All expenses for hotel and travel were paid in cash with no explicit reference to those meetings being made in the expenses claims of those attending. The participants also took great care to avoid keeping any written evidence of meetings and agreements, and in such documents as did exist code names were used to refer to cartel participants (for example, "BMW" for Germany's SGL Carbon AG, "Pinot" for the USA-based UCAR and "Cold" for the group of Japanese companies).

Held:

When the cartel was discovered, the Commission imposed fines totalling €218 million on the participating undertakings.

■ When there is no direct evidence (e.g. meeting minutes, plans, etc), indirect evidence (e.g. parallel conduct) may indicate that an undertaking is engaged in a concerted practice. However, even in a case where the only logical explanation for parallel behaviour is concerted practice, this must be corroborated by evidence.[2375] Parallel behaviour of undertakings may be justified by factors such as a high degree of market transparency or the oligopolistic tendencies of the market, in which latter situation the market is dominated by a small number of large undertakings. In the context of an ologopolistic market it is extremely difficult to establish collusive practices as it is normal that when one producer changes its prices/policies, others will follow.

27.3.3.1 Meaning of a concerted practice

Three cases decided by the EU judicature have defined the meaning of a concerted practice. The findings are discussed below.

Case 48/69 ICI (Dyestuffs)[2376]

The ECJ held that a concerted practice refers to a form of co-operation between undertakings which, without having been taken to the stage where an agreement properly so-called has been concluded, knowingly substitutes for the risk of competition practical co-operation between them. Therefore, co-ordination and co-operation between undertakings constituted an essential feature in determining whether or not they had been engaged in a concerted practice.

Cases 40–48/73, 50/73, 54–56/73, 111/73, 113–114/73 Suiker Unie[2377]

The ECJ held:

■ That "the criteria of co-ordination and co-operation must be understood in the light of the concept inherent in the provision of the Treaty relating to competition that each economic operator must

---

2375. See Commission Decision IP/02/1603 dated 04/11/2002 *(Carlsberg-Heineken)*.

2376. Case 48/69 *Imperial Chemical Industries (ICI) Ltd v Commission (Dyestuffs)* [1972] ECR 619.

2377. Joined Cases 40 to 48, 50, 54 to 56, 111, 113 and 114-73 *Coöperatieve Vereniging "Suiker Unie" UA and Others v Commission* [1975] ECR 1663.

determine independently the policy which he intends to adopt on the Common Market".[2378] The ECJ emphasised that the autonomy of an undertaking must not be altered. This autonomy is called into question when competing undertakings intentionally exchange information, directly or indirectly, in order to influence the conduct of actual or potential competitors or to disclose to such a competitor an adopted or envisaged course of conduct.

■ That no actual plan is required, but for a concerted practice to exist it is necessary that undertakings have direct or indirect contact, the object or effect of which is to either influence the conduct of an actual or potential competitor or to disclose to such a competitor the course of action that the colluding undertakings have agreed to adopt or envisage adopting in the relevant market.

Joined Cases T-25 to 104/95 *Cimenteries CBR and Others v Commission* ([2000] ECR II-491)[2379]

The General Court:

■ First, made a distinction between passive reception of information and active reception of information. It stated that to amount to a concerted practice there must be an intention to communicate information to the other party and the latter must be aware that it is receiving such communication not accidentally, but on purpose. The exchange of information must go beyond mutual awareness of what the other party is doing based on normal sources of information such as the terms and conditions quoted to customers, which are easy to obtain and which will influence prices and policies adopted by competitors; and,

■ Second, stated that: "a concerted practice implies, besides undertakings concerting together, conduct on the market pursuant to those collusive practices, and a relationship of cause and effect between the two".[2380]

Summary

The above case law can be summarised as follows.

For there to be a concerted practice there must be direct or indirect contact between competing undertakings which influences the conduct on the market of an actual or potential competitor, the object or effect of such contact is "to create conditions of competition which would not correspond to the normal conditions of the market in question",[2381] and a relationship of cause and effect between the concertation and the market conduct.

A. **Direct or indirect contact.** Any direct or indirect contact between competitors which undermines the requirement of independence, i.e. the requirement according to which each economic operator must determine independently the policy which it intends to adopt on the relevant market, is prohibited.[2382] In this respect the issue of the participation of undertakings in meetings arises. Under EU law there is a presumption that when an undertaking participates

---

2378. Ibid, para. 4.
2379. Joined Cases T-25 to 104/95 *Cimenteries CBR and Others v Commission* [2000] ECR II-491.
2380. Ibid, para. 1852.
2381. Case T-208/06 *Quinn Barlo Ltd, Quinn Plastics NV, and Quinn Plastics GmbH v Commission* [judgement of 30/11/11 (NYR)] para. 37.
2382. See *Suiker Unie and Others v Commission*, para. 173; Case 172/80 *Züchner* [1981] ECR 2021, para. 13; Joined Cases 89/85, etc. *Ahlström Osakeyhtiö and Others v Commission* [1993] ECR I-1307, para. 63; and Case C-7/95P *Deere v Commission* [1998] ECR I-3111, para. 86.

in a meeting during which its competitor discloses its future policy regarding the relevant market, that undertaking takes account of such information for the purpose of determining its conduct on the market.

In *Cimenteries*, the General Court held that an undertaking could not argue that it was merely a passive recipient of information when it received information at a meeting about the future conduct of a competitor and failed to raise objections or express its reservations.[2383] The way for an undertaking, which finds itself participating in this type of meeting, to protect itself, is to prove by means of corroborated evidence[2384] that it participated in the meeting "in a spirit that was different" from the other participants,[2385] i.e. the undertaking concerned must publicly distance itself from what was discussed at the meeting.

In Case T-303/02 *Westfalen Gassen*,[2386] the General Court stated that the notion of public distancing must be interpreted narrowly in that the proper way for the undertaking concerned to dissociate itself from a collusive meeting was to write, after the meeting, to its competitors participating in the meeting and to the relevant professional association stating that it did not want to be considered as a member of a cartel or to participate in meetings of the association while it provides cover for an unlawful cartel. Obviously, the best way for an undertaking to dissociate itself from an anti-competitive meeting is to report it to the relevant administrative authority. The narrow interpretation of the notion of public distancing entails that:

- Non-implementation by an undertaking of any unlawful policy discussed at a meeting will not be sufficient to exclude it from liability under Article 101(1) TFEU. In Case T-334/94 *Sarrió*[2388] the General Court rejected the argument of Sarrió that despite its participation in an agreement which co-ordinated prices, it applied its own prices to each individual transaction. The General Court held that the agreement had an impact on transaction prices as it provided the basis for price negotiation in each transaction and that solely by participating in the agreement Sarrió had infringed Article 101(1) TFEU. The General Court rejected Sarrió's argument concerning no implementation of the agreement. It stated that a serious anti-competitive intent is contrary to Article 101(1) TFEU whether or not the agreement is in fact implemented;

- Subsequent conduct on the relevant market contrary to what was discussed at an anti-competitive meeting will not be enough to exclude the liability of an undertaking. In *Industrial and Medical Gases*,[2389] two undertakings which participated in anti-competitive meetings, Air Liquide and Westfalen, tried to convince the Commission that their conduct in the market subsequent to those meetings (which consisted of pursuing an "aggressive commercial policy" towards their competitors) provided sufficient evidence that they

---

2383. [2000] ECR II-491; Cases T-202/98 *Tate and Lyle Plc, British Sugar Plc and Napier Brown Plc v Commission* [2001] ECR II-2035.
2384. Case T-303/02 *Westfalen Gassen Nederland v Commission* [2006] II-4567, paras 103 and 124.
2385. Cases C-204/00, C-205/00, C-211/00, C-213/00, C-217/00, C-219/00 *Aalborg Portland AS v Commission* [2004] ECR I-123.
2386. Case T-208/06 *Quinn Barlo Ltd, Quinn Plastics NV, and Quinn Plastics GmbH v Commission* (judgement of 30/11/11 (NYR)) para. 37; see also Case T-303/02 *Westfalen Gassen Nederland v Commission* [2006] ECR II-4567, para. 124.
2387 [1998] ECR II-1439.
2388. [2003] OJ L84/1.
2389. In Case T-208/06 Quinn, supra note 2386, para. 50; and Case T-303/02 *Westfalen Gassen Nederland v Commission* [2006] II-4567, para. 124.

neither participated in the agreements nor implemented them. This argument was rejected by the Commission; and,

● Silence at an anti-competitive meeting will amount to tacit approval and thus render the participating undertaking liable under Article 101 TFEU.[2390]

In Case C-8/08 *T-Mobile*,[2391] the General Court held that the finding of a concerted practice does not require that competitors meet regularly over a period of time. A single meeting between competitors may constitute a sufficient basis for them to concert their market conduct. Accordingly, the number, frequency and form of meetings is irrelevant. What counts is whether a meeting or meetings allow the participating undertaking to take account of information exchanged with its competitors so as to influence its future conduct on the relevant market. Obviously, the presumption is stronger when undertakings are involved in a concerted practice on a regular basis over a long period of time.[2392]

B. **Conduct pursuant to direct or indirect contact and the relationship of cause and effect between the concertation and the market conduct.** In Case C-199/92 P *Hüls*,[2393] the ECJ set out a presumption according to which an undertaking which takes part in a concerted action and then remains active on the relevant market is presumed to have taken account of the information exchanged with its competitors for the purpose of determining its conduct on the relevant market. This presumption is almost impossible to rebut, unless the undertaking ceases to exist.

In Case C-8/08 *T-Mobile* the ECJ held that the presumption is substantive rather than procedural and thus must be applied by national courts when they apply Article 101 TFEU.

27.3.3.2 Exchange of information

Information may be exchanged directly by competitors, (e.g. during a meeting, by phone, etc.), or indirectly, through a common agency such as a trade association (see Chapter 27.3.2), or a third party such as market research organisations or suppliers or retailers.

The Commission's position on exchange of information between undertakings is stated in its Guidelines on the Applicability of Article 101 [TFEU] to Horizontal Co-operation Agreements.[2394] The Guidelines reiterate the case law[2395] on this matter. They state, on the one hand, that exchange of information may generate various types of efficiency gains, e.g. it may improve internal efficiency of undertakings through benchmarking against each other's best practices, and, on the other, that exchange of information may be harmful to competition as it may facilitate collusive behaviour and lead to anti-competitive foreclosure.

The Guidelines recognise that information may be exchanged in various contexts, e.g. in the context of R&D or specialisation agreements such exchange of information may be vital and necessary to the

---

2390. Case C-8/08 *T-Mobile Netherlands BV and Others v Raad van bestuur van de Nederlandse Mededingingsautoriteit* [2009] ECR I-4529.
2391. COMP/39.188 *Bananas*.
2392. Case C-199/92 P *Hüls AG v Commission* [1999] ECR I-4287.
2393. [2011] OJ C11/1.
2394. Case C-7/95 P *John Deere v Commission* [1998] ECR I-3111; Case C-238/05, *Asnef-Equifax, Servicios de Información sobre Solvencia y Crédito, SL v Asociación de Usuarios de Servicios Bancarios (Ausbanc)* [2006] ECR I-11125; and Case C-8/08, *T-Mobile Netherlands* [2009] ECR I-4529.
2395. See Joined T-117/07 and T-121/07 *Areva v Commission* [2011] ECR II-633.

implementation of agreements and thus benefit from the relevant block exemption regulation. However, it may also support an unlawful cartel in which case it will be unlawful.[2396]

The Guidelines set out two factors which will be decisive in deciding whether an exchange of information can produce anti-competitive outcome:

- First, the characteristics of the relevant market, i.e. whether the market is highly concentrated, stable, transparent, complex, symmetric, etc.; and,

- Second, the types of information that is exchanged. In this respect exchange of strategic data, i.e. concerning prices, actual or future; discounts; customer lists; production costs; quantities; turnovers; sales; capacities; qualities; marketing plans; risks; investments; technologies; and, R&D programmes and their results. The Commission considers that information related to prices and quantities is the most strategic, followed by information about costs and demand. However, if companies compete with regard to R&D it is the technology data that may be the most strategic for competition. The strategic usefulness of data depends on its aggregation (i.e. if it is individualised it is more likely to have anti-competitive outcome than aggregated data, which normally makes the recognition of data of an individual undertaking difficult); the age of information (i.e. exchange of historic data is unlikely to have a collusive outcome) the market context; frequency of the exchange; and, whether information is public or non-public.

Exchange of information may restrict competition by object or effect (see Chapter 27.4). It restricts competition by object when strategic information is exchanged between competitors. Paragraph 74 of the Guidelines states that exchanges of information relating to intended future prices or quantities should be considered a restriction of competition by object unlikely to be exempted under Article 101(3) TFEU. With regard to restriction of competition by effect, the Guidelines provide that the economic conditions of the relevant market and the nature of information exchanged will determine whether "pure exchange" of information between competitors in itself infringes Article 101(1) TFEU.

27.3.3.3 Parallel behaviour

When there is no direct evidence of any contact, direct or indirect, between undertakings but they exhibit parallel conduct over a period of time, the question arises whether their conduct constitutes sufficient evidence of a concerted practice. This is of particular relevance in a situation where the relevant market is oligopolistic. This issue was examined in Joined Cases 89, 104, 114, 116, 117 and 125–129/85 *Ahlström (Re Wood Pulp Cartel)*.[2397]

THE FACTS WERE:

The Commission found more than 40 suppliers of wood pulp in the EU in violation of Article 101(1) TFEU and imposed fines on 36 of them. A number of companies challenged the Commission's finding that they breached Article 101(1) TFEU through concertation of prices for their products by means of a system of quarterly price announcements. The factors that the Commission took into account, inter alia, were the system of early announcements of

---

2396. Joined Cases 89, 104, 114, 116, 117 and 125–129/85 *A. Ahlström Osakeyhtiö and Others (Re Wood Pulp Cartel) v Commission* [1993] ECR I-1307.

2397. Ibid, para. 126.

prices which made prices transparent, the uniform fluctuation of prices and the uniform approach to prices which could be explained in a narrow oligopolistic situation where undertakings had to follow a market leader. However, at that time there were more than 50 producers of wood pulp. On this basis the Commission had concluded that the market was not oligopolistic and that the uniform market behaviour could be explained only by concerted practice.

Held:

The ECJ annulled the decision of the Commission on the ground that the Commission had not provided a firm, precise and consistent body of evidence of infringement.

The ECJ held that parallel conduct could not be regarded as furnishing proof of concertation unless concertation constituted the only plausible explanation.

Comment:

The ECJ appointed its own experts to analyse the market. Their findings convinced the ECJ that there may be explanations of parallel behaviour other than concertation, such as the natural structure of the market. In the present case the market was cyclical. In respect of transparency of prices, the early announcements were requested by customers; taking into account the cyclical nature of the market, they wanted to know the price for wood pulp as soon as possible. The ECJ held that: "it must be stated that, in this case, concertation is not the only plausible explanation for the parallel conduct. To begin with, the system of price announcements may be regarded as constituting a rational response to the fact that the pulp market constituted a long-term market and to the need felt by both buyers and sellers to limit commercial risks. Further, the similarity in the dates of price announcements may be regarded as a direct result of the high degree of market transparency, which does not have to be described as artificial. Finally, the parallelism of prices and the price trends may be satisfactorily explained by the oligopolistic tendencies of the market and by the specific circumstances prevailing in certain periods. Accordingly, the parallel conduct established by the Commission does not constitute evidence of concertation."[2398] Accordingly, a heavy burden of proof is imposed on the Commission which must exclude one by one any alternative potential justification which might otherwise justify the parallel conduct in order to show that concerted action is the only plausible explanation for such conduct.

27.3.3.4   The burden of proof

The Commission is always required to prove the infringement. It must demonstrate to the requisite legal standard the existence of circumstances constituting an infringement.[2399] The test is based on the balance of probabilities.[2400]

In respect of the burden of proof, in Case C-199/92P *Hüls*[2401] (one of the *Cartonboard Cartel* cases) the ECJ held that it was the task of the Commission to establish that Hüls participated in the meetings at which price initiatives were decided, organised and monitored. However, it was incumbent on Hüls

---

2398.   Case C-185/95P *Baustahlgewebe GmbH v Commission* [1998] ECR I-8417, para. 58.

2399.   See Article 2 of Regulation 1/2003.

2400.   Case C-199/92P *Hüls AG v Commission* [1999] ECR I-4287.

2401.   Joined Cases T-67/00, T-68/00, T-71/00 and T-78/00 *JFE Engineering v Commission* [2004] ECR II-2501.

to prove that it had not subscribed to those initiatives, if that was the case. Consequently, there was no reversal of the burden of proof. The ECJ emphasised that the principle of the presumption of innocence constitutes one of the fundamental principles of the EU legal order and as such applies to competition procedures. However, in the above case the Commission was not in breach of that principle.

It is well established that statements made by an undertaking alleged to be participating in a cartel, which run counter to its interests, are regarded as particularly reliable evidence.[2402] However, if an undertaking makes self-incriminating statements that are contested by several other participants in a cartel, such statements are not regarded as constituting adequate proof of a breach committed by that undertaking unless corroborated by other evidence.[2403]

27.4 Object or effect of an agreement, decision or concerted practice

Article 101(1) TFEU is intended to catch all anti-competitive agreements between undertakings that have as their object or effect the prevention, restriction or distortion of competition.

In Case 56/65 *STM*[2404] the ECJ stated that the terms "object" and "effect" are to be read disjunctively. As a result, the Commission must:

■ In the first place, establish whether or not an agreement, decision or concerted practice has as its object the restriction of competition. The restriction of competition by object entails a rebuttable presumption that the collusive conduct has anti-competitive market effects. Not only actual but also potential effects are sufficient to trigger the application of the presumption. In Case 8/08 *T-Mobile*,[2405] the ECJ clarified the meaning of the concept of an anti-competitive object. It set out the criteria to be applied to decide whether a concerted practice (this also applies to agreements and decisions) has as its object restriction of competition. These criteria are: the content and the objective of the concerted practice, which should be assessed in the light of the circumstances of the case, i.e. its legal and economic context. Further, the intent of the parties is relevant although not an essential factor in determining whether a concerted practice is restrictive. The ECJ stated that "the distinction between 'infringement by object' and 'infringement by effect' arises from the fact that certain forms of collusion between undertakings can be regarded, by their very nature, as being injurious to the proper functioning of normal competition."[2406] As a result, when the restriction of competition is an inevitable consequence of an agreement, decision or concerted practice, it will be regarded as having an anti-competitive object irrespective of whether it has actually restricted competition or whether it has only the potential to have restrictive effect on competition. Examples of restriction by object in respect of horizontal agreements are: price fixing; exchange of information which reduces uncertainty about future conduct of competitors in the relevant market; market-sharing agreements; and, collective exclusive dealing.[2407] With regard to vertical agreements, examples of restrictions by object are: the imposition of

---

2402. *JFE Engineering v Commission*, ibid. See also: Case T-337/94 *Enso-Gutzeit v Commission* [1998] ECR II-1571; Joined Cases T-109/02, T-118/02, T-122/02, T-125/02, T-126/02, T-128/02, T-129/02, T-132/02 and T-136/02 *Bolloré SA and Others (Carbonless Paper Cartel) v Commission* [2007] ECR II-947.

2403. Case 56/65 *Société Technique Minière v Maschinenbau Ulm GmbH* [1966] ECR 235.

2404. Case C-8/08 *T-Mobile Netherlands BV and Others v Raad van bestuur van de Nederlandse Mededingingsautoriteit* [2009] ECR I-4529.

2405. Ibid, para. 29.

2406. See Case T-5/00 and T- 6/00 *Nederlandse Federatieve Vereniging voor de Groothandel op Elektrotechnisch Gebied and Technische Unie BV v Commission* [2003] ECR- II-5761.

2407. E.g. Joined Cases C-501/06 P, C-513/06 P, C-515/06 P and C-519/06 P *GlaxoSmithKline Services Unlimited, formerly Glaxo Wellcome plc v Commission* [2009] ECR I-9291.

export bans[2408] and the hard-core restrictions specified in Article 4 of Regulation 330/2010 (see Chapter 27.9.1) such as fixing prices, or prohibiting cross-supply by authorised distributors.

▨ In the second place, if an agreement is not intended to restrict competition by object, e.g. a standard distribution agreement, the Commission must assess whether an agreement, decision or concerted practice has restrictive effects on competition. In Case 7/95P *John Deere*, the ECJ held: "in order to determine whether an agreement is to be considered to be prohibited by reason of the distortion of competition which is its effect, the competition in question should be assessed within the actual context in which it would occur in the absence of the agreement in dispute".[2409] However, not only the actual and direct effect but also the potential and indirect effects of the restriction are taken into account.[2410] Anti-competitive effects of an agreement must be established with reasonable probability. Further, it is necessary that an agreement has appreciable or potentially appreciable effects on trade between Member States (see Chapter 26.4.1).

There are a number of factors which should be taken into consideration in order to assess the effect of an agreement on the particular market. These are:

▨ The parties' combined share of the relevant market. The combined market share may be assessed in percentage terms or on a quantitative basis.[2411] However, in Case 19/77 *Miller*[2412] the ECJ considered that an agreement in which the parties' combined share of the relevant market was only 5 per cent had an appreciable effect on trade between Member States;

▨ The type of agreement. Some agreements are capable of having appreciable effect even where the combined market share is not significant. These are mainly agreements which directly or indirectly fix prices, share markets, impose bans on export, or are one of a network of similar agreements which have a cumulative effect in the relevant market;

▨ The position of the undertaking concerned in the relevant market and the size of the parties concerned;

▨ The nature and the quantity of the product concerned;

▨ The number of undertakings competing within the relevant geographical and product market; and,

▨ The general economic and legal context of the agreement.

The Commission's Guidelines on the Interpretation of [Article 101(3) TFEU] explain the factors to be taken into account when assessing whether or not an agreement restricts competition by effect.

The issue of whether an agreement is restrictive of competition by its effect is the most controversial in competition law. This is because eventually everything boils down to economic matters, that is, how, why and in the light of what general objectives an economic assessment is carried out. Thus expert economic evidence plays a very important role in the fact-finding part of proceedings.

2408. 7/95P *John Deere v Commission* [1998] ECR I-3111.

2409. Case 56/65 Case 56/65 *Société Technique Minière v Maschinenbau Ulm GmbH* [1966] ECR 235 and Case 31/80 *L'Oréal v De Nieuwe AMCK* [1980] ECR 3775.

2410. *Kawasaki* [1979] OJ L16/9.

2411. Case 19/77 *Miller International Schallplatten GmbH v Commission* [1978] ECR 131.

2412. [2004] OJ C101/97, para. 24.

27.5 Prevention, distortion and restriction of competition

Each of the words "prevention", "distortion" and "restriction" imply a manipulation of the market in a manner which is improper or unlawful and each refers to a situation in which a restraint is imposed on competition.

Article 101(1) TFEU provides a non-exhaustive list of types of agreements which will generally fall within a prohibition but subject to the *de minimis* rule (see Chapter 26.4.1); subject to exemptions provided in block exemption regulations (see Chapter 27.9); and, subject to the legal exception in Article 101(3) TFEU. The list sets out the most common types of anti-competitive agreement. As it is open-ended, there will be other types of agreements not listed which are prohibited because of their particular conditions or restrictions.

27.6 The evolution of the interpretation of Article 101(1) TFEU: the *per se* rule v the rule of reason?

The US antitrust law,[2413] first enacted in 1890, has served as a model for competition law in many countries, including some of the Member States of the EU. It has also influenced interpretation of competition law around the world.

US antitrust law uses two methods to analyse conduct under Section 1 of the Sherman Act, which prohibits contracts, combinations and conspiracies in restraint of trade. They are:

- The *per se* rule, under which certain conduct of companies, such as price fixing and other hard core horizontal restraints, is inherently illegal, that is, if a company has been found engaging in illegal conduct, it will automatically be deemed to have breached competition law. The *per se* rule creates an unrebuttable presumption of unlawfulness of certain conduct. Illegality follows as a matter of law. No market analysis is carried out.

- The rule of reason. Under Section 1 of the Sherman Act there is no possibility for exemption. All contracts, combinations and conspiracies in restraint of trade are prohibited. The concept of "restraint of trade", if interpreted broadly, could outlaw many useful business arrangements bearing in mind that any commercial contract somehow restricts trade. For that reason, the US courts developed the rule of reason as the main tool for adjusting Section 1 of the Sherman Act to changing economic conditions. Under the rule of reason, US courts are required to consider the overall impact of an agreement on competition within the relevant market. In order to do so, they have to identify and weigh the anti-competitive and pro-competitive effects it produces. If pro-competitive effects prevail, the agreement is regarded as not being restrictive of competition.

Since the 1970s, US courts have restricted the scope of the *per se* rule, and expanded the scope of the rule of reason with the result that the rule of reason has become the default standard in the enforcement of US antitrust law. This is exemplified in *Leegin*,[2414] in which the US Supreme Court overruled its 1911 precedent under which the imposition of minimum resale price in horizontal

---

2413. It comprises the 1890 Sherman Act which prohibits "every contract, combination, or conspiracy in restraint of trade", and any "monopolization, attempted monopolization, or conspiracy or combination to monopolize"; the 1914 Federal Trade Commission Act, which created the US Federal Trade Commission, which enforces US antitrust law, and the 1914 Clayton Act which prohibits anti-competitive mergers and interlocking directorates. With some revisions, these are the three core US antitrust laws.

2414. *Leegin Leather Products Inc v PSKS* 551 US 877 (2007).

agreements was *per se* illegal. It held that the practice should be examined on a case-by-case basis under the rule of reason.

In order to understand the debate on whether EU competition law needs the rule of reason, and indeed whether it has endorsed the US style rule of reason, it is important to note:

1. Under Section 1 of the Sherman Act there is no possibility for exemption. All contracts, combinations and conspiracies in restraint of trade are prohibited. Under EU competition law Article 101(3) TFEU provides a mechanism under which an agreement is scrutinised from the point of view of its effect on competition consisting of weighing its pro and anti-competitive aspects. So the economic assessment of conduct is carried out under Article 101(3) TFEU (see Chapter 27.8).

2. In the EU, prior to the entry into force of Regulation 1/2003 (see Chapter 30.1) only the Commission was allowed to grant exemptions under Article 101(3). This entailed that based on Article 101(1) TFEU, which was and remains directly effective, national courts had jurisdiction under Article 101(1) TFEU, but were unable to apply Article 101(3) TFEU. As a result, undertakings had no possibility of obtaining exemptions under national law. The application of the rule of reason would have alleviated this problem in that if the balancing of anti- and pro-competitive effects of an agreement could be carried out under Article 101(1) TFEU, many agreements would not need to be notified to the Commission. With the entry into force of Regulation 1/2003, which abolished the system of notification, and makes Article 101(3) directly effective, businesses have to make their own assessment of an intended agreement and national courts and national competition authorities, on the basis of the existing case law, have to determine whether the agreement is in conformity with EU competition rules.

3. From the perspective of the Commission, the application of the rule of reason would mean that it would have to assess anti-competitive effects and pro-competitive effects of an agreement under Article 101(1) TFEU. This would impose on the Commission a heavy burden of proof bearing in mind that under Article 101(3) TFEU, the defendant has to prove the existence of pro-competitive effects of an agreement.

4. The case law of the ECJ indicates that when an agreement has as its object the restriction of competition no economic examination is necessary under Article 101(1) TFEU. Such agreements must be assessed in the light of Article 101(3) TFEU in order to decide whether they are lawful. Accordingly, the debate on the application of the rule of reason to Article 101(1) TFEU is of relevance to agreements which restrict competition by "effect".

The debate on the existence of the rule of reason under EU competition law was initiated by the ECJ judgment in Case 56/65 *STM*.[2415]

THE FACTS WERE:

STM, a French undertaking supplying equipment for public works, and Maschinenbau, a German producer of heavy grading machinery, entered into an exclusive distribution agreement under which Maschinenbau agreed not to supply to any other distributor in France, and not to sell there itself, any large earth levellers of the type in which STM dealt.

2415. Case 56/65 *Société Technique Minière (STM) v Maschinenbau Ulm GmbH* [1966] ECR 235.

STM agreed to buy a large number of machines from Maschinenbau over a period of two years but could not then find a sufficient number of purchasers for them. When Maschinenbau did not receive payment, it sued STM in France. STM argued that the agreement, or at least some clauses in it, were in breach of Article 101(1) TFEU.

Held:

The ECJ held that exclusivity was essential to the setting-up of a distribution system in the context of the high commercial risks taken by STM when entering into the agreement, as the product was highly specialised and expensive.

The ECJ emphasised that:

"The competition in question must be understood within the actual context in which it would occur in the absence of the agreement in dispute. In particular it may be doubted whether there is an interference with competition if the said agreement seems really necessary for the penetration of a new area by an undertaking."[2416]

The ECJ identified a number of factors which should be taken into consideration in assessing whether or not an exclusive distribution agreement is within the scope of Article 101(1) TFEU. They are:

- *the nature of the product and its volume, that is whether the supply was limited or unlimited in amount;*
- *the importance of both the supplier and the distributor with respect to the relevant market;*
- *whether the agreement was one of or a part of a network of agreements covering at least a substantial area or region of a Member State; and,*
- *the degree of territorial protection afforded by the agreement, in particular whether it provides for absolute territorial protection and whether it allows parallel imports.*

This case has been followed by numerous cases in which the ECJ has applied the analytical framework set out above to vertical agreements (see Chapter 27.6.3).

27.6.1 The rejection of the US style rule of reason by the EU judicature

In Case T-112/99 *Métropole Télévision*[2417] the General Court expressly rejected the application of the rule of reason to Article 101(1) TFEU. The Court held that:

"the existence of such a rule has not, as such, been confirmed by the Community courts. Quite to the contrary, in various judgments the Court of Justice and the [General Court] have been at pains to indicate that the existence of a rule of reason in [EU] competition law is doubtful."[2418]

The General Court emphasised that the pro and anti-competitive effects of an agreement should be assessed in the light of Article 101(3) TFEU, which Article "would lose much of its effectiveness if

---

2416.   Ibid, p. 250.
2417.   Case T-112/99 *Métropole Télévision (M6) and Others v Commission* [2001] ECR II-2459. See also Case T-65/98 *Van den Bergh Foods Ltd v Commission* [2003] ECR II-4653.
2418.   Case T-112/99 *Métropole Télévision (M6)* [2001] ECR II-2459, para. 72.

such an examination had to be carried out under Article 101(1) of the Treaty".[2419] However, the Court acknowledged that Article 101(1) TFEU had, for some time, been interpreted in a more flexible manner by the EU institutions but this did not mean that the rule of reason had become recognised under EU law. The General Court in Case T-328/03 *O2 (Germany)*,[2420] confirmed its position. It held that the examination of an agreement under Article 101(1) TFEU consists of taking account of the impact of the agreement on existing and potential competition and of what the competition situation would be in the absence of the agreement on the relevant market. This examination does not, however, involve "an assessment of the pro and anti-competitive effects of an agreement and thus the application of the rule of reason which the [EU] judicature has not deemed to have place under Article 101(1) TFEU".[2421] Notwithstanding this, in Case T-328/03 *O2 (Germany)*, the General Court weighed the pro and anti-competitive effects of the agreement in question when it analysed the conditions of actual and potential competition in the absence of the agreement.[2422]

It is clear from the case law of the ECJ that under Article 101(1) TFEU it is necessary to examine what would be the state of competition, actual and potential, in the relevant market if the agreement with its alleged restrictions did not exist (see Chapter 27.6.2). Accordingly, it is necessary to carry out some economic analysis under Article 101(1) TFEU. Some commentators[2423] suggest that in accordance with the statement of the General Court in Case T-112/99 *Métropole Télévision*[2424] not all the economic analysis should be carried out under Article 101(1) TFEU, some pro-competitive effects should be examined under Article 101(1) TFEU, and some under Article 101(3) TFEU. However, there is no consensus, or indeed, case law, as to how to determine which pro-competitive effects should be analysed under Article 101(1) and which under Article 101(3) TFEU. In economics pro-competitive effects can be divided into two categories, those which enhance consumer welfare and have an impact on price, output (i.e. on interbrand competition), and market power, and those which are agreement specific, i.e. those concerning reduction of the cost of production and incentive to innovate.[2425] Some commentators suggest that the first category of pro-competitive effects should be examined under Article 101(1) TFEU whilst the second category should be assessed under Article 101(3) TFEU.[2426] Bearing in mind that the case law shows that weighing of pro-competitive effects of an agreement, in fact, takes place under Article 101(1) TFEU,[2427] it would be useful to have some clarifications from the Commission and the ECJ as to which pro-competitive effects are relevant to each paragraph of Article 101 TFEU.

2419. Ibid, para. 74.
2420. Case T-328/03 *O2 (Germany) GmbH & Co. OHG v Commission* [2006] ECR II-1231.
2421. Ibid, para. 69.
2422. See M. Marquis, "O2 (Germany) v Commission and the Exotic Mysteries of Article 81(1) EC", (2007) ELRev., 29.
2423. Ibid.
2424. Supra note 2418.
2425. R. Nazzini, "Article 81 EC between Time Present and Time Past: A Normative Critique of 'Restriction of Competition in EU Law'", (2006) 43 CMLRev., 519.
2426. O. Odudu, "A New Economic Approach to Article 81(1) [Article 101(1) TFEU]?", (2002) 27 ELRev., 104 and M. Marquis, "O2 (Germany) v Commission and the Exotic Mysteries of Article 81(1)", (2007) ELRev., 46.
2427. See for example, Case 56/65 *Société Technique Minière (STM)* [1966] ECR 235; Joined Cases T-374, 375, 384 and 388/94 *European Night Services Ltd and Others v Commission [1998]* ECR II-3141; and Case C-519/04P *David Meca-Medina and Igor Majcen v Commission* [2006] ECR I-6991.

27.6.2 Conclusion

In conclusion it can be said that application of a more economic approach to the interpretation of Article 101(1) TFEU, amounts to the establishment of a European style rule of reason. This rule has two aspects.

First, the case law shows that the Commission is required to determine, at the least, what would be the state of competition, actual and potential, in the relevant market if the agreement, with its alleged restrictions, did not exist. This is known as a "Counterfactual standard" or "But for" analysis. It entails a three step approach: first, the Commission must establish the hypothetical degree of competition in the relevant market if the agreement did not exist; second, it must determine the degree of competition in the light of the existing agreement; third, it must compare the two. If the degree of competition has been reduced there will be an infringement of Article 101(1) TFEU. The introduction of the "counterfactual standard" represents an important development in EU law given that the comparison between the potential and the actual degree of competition in the relevant market entails that "the specific factors or conditions that differ between the two must be identified and how those factors or conditions lead (or potentially will lead) to consumer harm must be explained. This alone provides some rigour to the analysis."[2428]

Second, it allows the ECJ to include non-economic considerations in the assessment of an agreement under Article 101(1) TFEU. This second aspect is evident in Case C-309/99 *Wouters*,[2429] in which Mr Wouters challenged a rule adopted by the Dutch Bar prohibiting lawyers in the Netherlands from entering into partnership with non-lawyers. The ECJ held that the challenged rule was liable to limit production and technical development within the meaning of Article 101(1) TFEU, but held that it did not infringe Article 101(1) TFEU. The ECJ balanced the anti-competitive effects of collusive behaviour against both pro-competitive effects and non-economic objectives, the latter being the mandatory requirements of Dutch public policy.

In Case C-519/04P *Meca-Medina*[2430] regarding the implementation of anti-doping rules of the International Swimming Federation the ECJ held that those rules were within the scope of EU competition law, but were justified as they pursued legitimate non-competition objectives. These objectives being: combating drugs in order for competitive sport to be conducted fairly; maintaining the integrity and objectivity of competitive sport; and, maintaining ethical values in sport.

Monti has explained that in respect of non-economic objectives the European-style rule of reason is similar to, and indeed based on, the *Cassis de Dijon* rule (see Chapter 20.3.2), under which a national measure which is indistinctly applicable to both domestic and imported goods will not breach the prohibition of Article 34 TFEU if it is necessary to satisfy mandatory requirements. This transposition of the *Cassis de Dijon* rule to competition cases means that "an anti-competitive agreement necessary to preserve a domestic mandatory requirement of public policy is allowed to escape the application of Article 81 [Article 101 TFEU]."[2431] However, the Commission in its Guidelines firmly rejects the taking into account of non-economic considerations in the application of both Article 101(1) and Article 101(3) TFEU (see Chapter 27.8).

2428. D. Geradin, A Layne-Farrar, and N. Petit, *EU Competition Law and Economics*, 2012, Oxford: OUP, p. 128.
2429. Case C-309/99 *Wouters v Algemene Raad van de Nederlandse Orde van Advocaten* [2002] ECR I-1577.
2430. [2006] ECR I-6991.
2431. G. Monti, "Article 81 EC and Public Policy", (2002) CMLRev., 1057, in particular p. 1088. See also, C. Townley, *Article 81 EC and Public Policy*, 2009, Oxford: Hart Publishing.

27.6.3 Ancillary restraints

One implication of the adoption of the European style rule of reason is that the ECJ has applied the concept of ancillary restraints, to the interpretation of Article 101(1) TFEU.

Under US antitrust law a distinction is made between "naked restraints" and "ancillary restraints":

- "Naked restraints" refer to those restraints which are always anti-competitive and unlawful, for example, fixing prices by means of a cartel (even if the prices fixed are reasonable).

- In *US v Addyston Pipe and Steel Co.*[2432] Judge Taft described ancillary restraints as being restrictions necessary to some transactions in order to make them viable. Ancillary restraints which would otherwise be unlawful can become acceptable if used to support pro-competitive transactions. The example given by Judge Taft concerned non-competition clauses normally contained in a business sale agreement and in particular in respect of partners who retire.

Ancillary restraints under EU competition law have been defined as covering "any alleged restriction of competition which is directly related and necessary for the implementation of a main non-restrictive transaction and proportionate to it".[2433]

In order to decide whether a particular restraint is ancillary or not, the Commission Notice on Ancillary Restraints in the context of concentrations may be of assistance (see Chapter 29.4.5).

With regard to vertical agreements the ECJ has found the following restraints as being ancillary:

- In Case 42/84 *Remia BV*,[2434] a non-compete clause inserted into a contract of sale of a business, provided such restriction was necessary for the successful transfer of an undertaking;

- In Case C-250/92 *Gøttrup-Klim*,[2435] a clause in a statute of a Danish co-operative association, which distributed farm supplies, prohibiting its members from participating in other forms of organised co-operation in direct competition with that association. The Court held that "dual membership" would jeopardise both the proper functioning of the co-operative and its contractual power in relation to producers; and,

- In Case 161/84 *Pronuptia*,[2436] the ECJ found that the protection of the franchisor's know-how was necessary for the successful operation of a franchising agreement (see Chapter 27.7.3).

However, in Case T-112/99 *Métropole Télévision (M6)*[2437] the ECJ refused to classify the exclusivity clause under which the appellant would be allowed the exclusive broadcasting of general-interest channels for an initial period of 10 years as being ancillary to the creation of TPS-Télévision par Satellite (i.e. television by satellite).

27.7 Assessment of vertical agreements under Article 101(1) TFEU

Economic-based interpretation of Article 101(1) TFEU has been carried out mainly in respect of vertical agreements. The concept of vertical agreements has been defined by the Commission in its Guidelines on Vertical Restraints (hereafter referred as Vertical Guidelines),[2438] as "agreements or

---

2432. 85 F.271 (6th Cir.1897), aff'd, 175 U.S. 211, 20 S.Ct.96, 44 L.Ed.136 (1899).
2433. Guidelines on Application of Article 81(3) EC [Article 101(3) TFEU], para. 29.
2434. Case 42/84 *Remia BV and Others v Commission* [1985] ECR 2545.
2435. C-250/92 *Gøttrup-Klim e.a. Grovvareforeninger v Dansk Landbrugs Grovvareselskab AmbA* [1994] ECR I-5641.
2436. Case 161/84 *Pronuptia de Paris GmbH v Pronuptia de Paris Irmgard Schillgallis* [1986] ECR 353.
2437. Case T-112/99 *Métropole Télévision (M6) and Others v Commission* [2001] ECR II-2459.
2438. [2010] OJ C 130/1, para. 24.

concerted practices entered into between two or more companies each of which operates, for the purposes of the agreement, at a different level of the production or distribution chain, and relating to the conditions under which the parties may purchase, sell or resell certain goods or services".

It is to be noted that only vertical agreements which have appreciable effect on trade between Member States are within the scope of Article 101 TFEU (see Chapter 26.4.1). Further, the ECJ in Case C-260/07 *Perdo IV*[2439] held that it is not necessary to assess vertical agreements under Article 101(1) TFEU when they satisfy the requirements of Regulation 330/2010 (see Chapter 27.9.1) or are within the scope of the *de minimis* rule (see Chapter 26.4.3).

The Commission's Vertical Guidelines provide the methodology for assessment of whether a vertical agreement infringes Article 101(1) TFEU and if so, whether it may be justified under Article 101(3) TFEU.[2440] Paragraph 110 of the Vertical Guidelines sets out nine factors relevant to the assessment carried out under Article 101(1) TFEU. They are:

- the nature of the agreement;

- the market position of the parties;

- the market position of competitors;

- the position of the buyers of the contract products;

- entry barriers;

- the maturity of the market;

- the level of trade affected by the agreement;

- the nature of the product; and,

- other factors, examples of which are given in paragraph 121 of the Vertical Guidelines, e.g. whether there is a "cumulative effect" within the market of similar vertical agreements, whether a restriction under the agreement was imposed by one party on the other rather than agreed by them, and the regulatory environment.

The Vertical Guidelines confirm the case law of the ECJ in that, apart from a situation where an agreement infringes competition by object, it must be assessed in the light of its legal and economic contexts.

The Vertical Guidelines provide clarifications as to the application of Article 101(1) TFEU to ten types of vertical agreement, i.e. single branding; exclusive distribution; exclusive customer allocation; selective distribution; franchising; exclusive supply; up-front access payment; category management; agreements; tying; and, resale restrictions. It is outside the scope of this book to analyse them all. However, the most popular types of vertical agreements, i.e. selective distribution agreements, franchising agreements and exclusive purchasing agreements as well as the position of the ECJ on export bans, are discussed below.

2439. C-260/07 *Perdo IV Servicios SL v Total España SA* [2009] ECR I-2437.
2440. Supra note 2438, paras. 110–27.

27.7.1 Direct and indirect exports bans

Only in the exceptional circumstances specified in paragraphs 60–64 of the Vertical Guidelines, will a direct or indirect ban[2441] on export imposed on distributors be lawful under Article 101(1) TFEU or benefit from exception set out in Article 101(3) TFEU. The imposition of bans restricts competition by object and thus is contrary to the objective of an integrated market as it prevents parallel imports and partitions the internal market.

27.7.2 Selective distribution agreements

In selective distribution agreements the supplier sells the goods or services either directly or indirectly only to distributors selected on the basis of specific criteria, and the distributors undertake not to sell such goods or services to unauthorised distributors.

Selective distribution agreements are normally used by producers of branded high technology or luxury products. The very nature of distribution agreements entails that such agreements may adversely affect the competitive conditions of the market by facilitating collusive behaviour between suppliers and distributors, by reducing or eliminating intra-brand competition (this refers to competition among the distributors of a given brand, for example, between distributors of Rolex watches), by foreclosing access to the market, and by increasing the price of the goods/services to the detriment of consumers. However, selective distribution agreements can also have pro-competitive effects, for example, they may ensure greater efficiency in distribution and thus provide benefits to all parties concerned including consumers.

The application of Article 101(1) TFEU to selective distribution agreements was examined by the ECJ in Case 26/76 *Metro*.[2442]

THE FACTS WERE:

Saba, a producer of electrical and electronic equipment, refused Metro's request for access to its selective distribution network in Germany. Outside Germany Saba's products were sold directly to sole distributors dealing exclusively with approved specialist dealers who were serving the public. The German selective distribution system was open to wholesalers who were reselling goods purchased from Saba to approved specialist dealers, whose turnover had to be obtained from the sale of electric and electronic products. Metro, as a cash and carry self-service business established in Germany, served retailers and the public. This was the main reason for Saba's refusal, although Metro did not fulfil other requirements of Saba's in that neither its trading premises nor its turnover nor the technical qualifications of its staff were appropriate to handle highly sophisticated electronic goods. Metro complained to the Commission, which decided that in general the Saba system of selective distribution did not breach Article 101(1) TFEU. Saba was allowed to prohibit direct supplies

---

2441. An example of an indirect ban is a withdrawal, by a French producer of cognac, of discounts previously granted to its French distributor, when the latter exported the product to Italy. Prices for cognac charged to distributors in Italy were 25 per cent higher than those charged to similar distributors in France. Thus the producer's aim was to discourage parallel export, *Gosme/Martell-DMP* [1991] OJ L185/23. In *DaimlerChrysler* [2002] OJ L257/1 the requirement that foreign customers should pay a 15 per cent deposit for a new vehicle while no such requirement was imposed on locals was considered as an indirect ban.

2442. Case 26/76 *Metro SB-Großmärkte GmbH & Co. KG v Commission* [1977] ECR 1875.

by wholesalers or sole distributors to consumers although particular clauses, for example prohibiting its wholesalers, sole distributors and specialised dealers from exporting to other EU countries or prohibiting "cross-supplies" (wholesaler to wholesaler or retailer to retailer), were condemned. Metro sought to annul the Commission's decision.

Held:

The ECJ held that a selective distribution system such as that put in place by Saba was justified in so far as resellers were selected "on the basis of objective criteria of a qualitative nature relating to the technical qualifications of the reseller and his staff and the suitability of his trading premises and that such conditions are laid down uniformly for all potential resellers and are not applied in a discriminatory fashion."[2443] This is known as the Metro test.

The Vertical Guidelines restate the *Metro* test. The Guidelines make a distinction between purely qualitative and quantitative selective agreements. Purely qualitative selective agreements are outside the prohibition of Article 101(1) TFEU provided three conditions are satisfied:

- The nature of the product in question necessitates a selective distribution system (but this is no longer required under Regulation 330/2010);

- Resellers must be chosen on the basis of objective criteria of a qualitative nature; and,

- The objective criteria laid down must not go beyond what is necessary.

With regard to the first condition the ECJ stated in *Metro* that selective distribution agreements were justified in "the sector covering the production of high quality and technically advanced consumer durables".[2444] The ECJ in subsequent cases confirmed that, apart from technically sophisticated products,[2445] other types of products such as luxury or branded products[2446] and newspapers (given their extremely short life)[2447] justified selective distribution. It is important to note that Regulation 330/2010 abolished the requirement to establish that the product concerned merits a selective distribution system (see Chapter 27.9.1).

In respect of the second condition, it requires that dealers are selected on the basis of objective criteria of a qualitative nature, which are laid down uniformly for all potential dealers and applied in a non-discriminatory manner. When a potential dealer satisfies the qualitative criteria he should be able to become a dealer. The distinction between qualitative and quantitative criteria is not always easy. Nevertheless, quantitative restrictions "more directly limit the potential number of dealers by, for instance, requiring minimum or maximum sales, by fixing the number of dealers, etc."[2448]

In *Metro* the ECJ found that restrictions relating to technical qualifications of the reseller and its staff and to the suitability of the reseller's premises were of a qualitative nature.

2443. Ibid, para. 20.
2444. Ibid.
2445. Personal computers: *IBM* [1984] OJ L 118/24; cameras: *Hasselblad* [1982] OJ L 161/18.
2446. Perfumes: *(Parfums Givenchy)* [1992] OJ L236/11; high quality gold and silver products: *Murat* [1983] OJ L348/20.
2447. Case 126/80 *Maria Salonia v Giorgio Poidomani* [1981] ECR 1563; Case 243/83 *Binion v Agence et Messageries de la Presse* [1985] ECR 2015.
2448. Guidelines on Vertical Restraints [2000] OJ C291/1, para. 185.

With regard to quantitative restrictions the following clauses were considered as such and accordingly were in breach of Article 101(1) TFEU: in *Metro* a clause requiring dealers to maintain specific amounts of stock, to promote the manufacturer's product and to stock an entire range of products; in Case 31/80 *L'Oréal*[2449] and in *Givenchy*[2450] a requirement that the distributor should guarantee a minimum turnover; in *Hasselblad*[2451] a clause prohibiting distributors from selling to each other; and, in *Kodak*[2452] a clause prohibiting distributors from selling to customers in other Member States.

With regard to the third condition, in *Metro* the ECJ made it clear that "qualitative criteria" should not go beyond what is necessary to maintain the quality of the goods or to ensure they are sold under proper conditions. What is necessary depends on the nature of the product. This is illustrated in Case T-19/91 *Vichy*,[2453] where the requirement that Vichy's cosmetics should be sold in retail pharmacies in which a qualified pharmacist was present in all EU countries but France (where this was not required), was considered as being disproportionate, taking into account that the objectives which Vichy wanted to achieve outside France (that is, improving the quality both of its product and the service, as well as enhanced competition with other cosmetic manufacturers) could be achieved by less restrictive measures. In *Ideal-Standard*,[2454] requirements imposed on wholesalers that they specialised in the sale of plumbing fittings and sanitary ware, and had a specialised department for their sale, was considered as unjustified on the ground of the nature of the product, that is, plumbing fitting devices were not sufficiently technically advanced. In Case C-439/09 *Pierre Fabre*,[2455] the ECJ held that the *de facto* prohibition of online sales imposed by a producer of dermo-cosmetic products, in the context of the selective distribution for its cosmetic and personal care products, could not be justified by the need to provide individual advice to customers, or by the protection of brand image. Indeed, the producer required physical presence of a qualified pharmacist for the sale of its products and thus, *de facto*, prohibited internet selling.

Selective distribution agreements which fail the *Metro* test, i.e. they are not purely qualitative, may be exempted under Regulation 330/2010 if they satisfy its criteria relating to the market share, and neither contain "hard-core restrictions" specified in Article 4, nor restrictions set out in Article 5. Regulation 330/2010 applies to such agreements regardless of the nature of the products and regardless of the selection criteria (see Chapter 27.9.1). Further, a selective distribution agreement which is not purely qualitative and which does not fall within the scope of Regulation 330/2010 may be justified under Article 101(3) TFEU.

27.7.3 Franchising agreements

The nature of franchising agreements is that they contain licences of intellectual property rights relating to trade marks or signs or know-how for the use and distribution of goods and services, and that the franchisor provides technical and commercial assistance to the franchisee during the life of the agreement. The franchisee gets to exercise the rights in question and, in exchange, the franchisee pays a franchise fee for the use of the particular business method. Franchising agreements usually contain a

---

2449. [1980] ECR 3775.

2450. [1992] OJ L236/11.

2451. [1982] OJ L161/18.

2452. [1970] OJ L142/24.

2453. [1992] ECR II-415.

2454. [1985] OJ L20/38.

2455. Case C-439/09 *Pierre Fabre Dermo-Cosmétique SAS v Président de l'Autorité de la concurrence and Ministre de l'Économie, de l'Industrie et de l'Emploi* (judgment of 13/10/11 (NYR)).

combination of different vertical restraints relating to the manner in which the products must be distributed.

In respect of franchising agreements the leading case is Case 161/84 *Pronuptia*.[2456]

THE FACTS WERE:

Pronuptia de Paris, which specialised in selling wedding dresses and other wedding accessories, entered into a franchise agreement with Mrs Schillgalis. In exchange for the exclusive right to use the trade mark "Pronuptia de Paris" in three areas in Germany – Hamburg, Oldenburg and Hanover – Mrs Schillgalis was required: to purchase 80 per cent of dresses intended to be sold by her directly from Pronuptia and a certain percentage of other dresses from suppliers approved by the franchisor; to make the sale of wedding dresses her main business activity; to advertise in a manner approved by the franchisor; to sell in shops decorated and equipped according to the franchisor's requirements; to fix prices in conformity to recommendations of the franchisor; to pay "entry" fees of DM15,000 for the know-how and thereafter a "royalty" of 10 per cent on her initial sales of Pronuptia products; to refrain from transferring her shop to another location without the approval of the franchisor; and, to refrain (both during the agreement and for one year afterwards) from competing in whatever way with Pronuptia outside the territory assigned in the franchise agreement. Pronuptia promised to refrain from opening any other Pronuptia shop in the territory covered by the agreement and to offer its assistance in all aspects of the business from staff training to marketing.

When Pronuptia sued Mrs Schillgalis for non-payment of "royalties", she argued that the franchise agreement was void as contrary to Article 101(1) TFEU. The German Supreme Court referred to the ECJ a preliminary question concerning the application of Article 101(1) TFEU to franchise agreements.

Held:

The ECJ held that restrictions imposed by the franchisor are outside the scope of Article 101(1) TFEU if they satisfy two conditions:

- *First, the legitimate interests of the franchisor should be protected under EU law, that is, the franchisor should be protected from a risk that the know-how and assistance provided by it to the franchisees would be used to benefit its competitors. As a result, a clause preventing the franchisee, during and after termination of the agreement, from opening a shop selling the same or similar items outside her territory and the requirement for the franchisor's approval of a proposed transfer of the shop to another party were not in breach of Article 101(1) TFEU; and,*

- *Second, the franchisor is entitled to protect the reputation and the identity of its network and therefore to retain some measure of control in this respect. In particular the requirements concerning the location of the shop, the lay-out and decoration of the shop, the percentage of dresses purchased and sources of supplies were legitimate.*

Price recommendations were not in breach of Article 101(1) TFEU if the franchisee was able to fix her own prices and thus there was not a concerted practice between the parties on prices.

2456. Case 161/84 *Pronuptia de Paris GmbH v Pronuptia de Paris Irmgard Schillgallis* [1986] ECR 353.

A clause restricting the franchisee from opening a second shop within her exclusive territory without the consent of the franchisor was in breach of Article 101(1) TFEU, taking into account that it might lead to the division of a Member State's territory into a number of closed territories. In addition this restriction would prevent the franchisee from benefiting from her investment, taking into account that "a prospective franchisee would not take the risk of becoming part of a chain, investing its own money, paying a relatively high entry fee and undertaking to pay a substantial annual royalty, unless he could hope, thanks to a degree of protection against competition on the part of the franchisor and other franchisees, that his business would be profitable."[2457] Consequently, such a clause should be examined under Article 101(3) TFEU.

The EU institutions have taken a liberal approach to restrictions imposed by franchising agreements by considering their overall beneficial effect on trade and the advantages they offer to both the franchisor and the franchisee. Even a clause condemned in *Consten and Grundig* ensuring absolute territorial protection may fall outside the Article 101(1) TFEU prohibition if it is considered as necessary to induce the franchisee to enter into the agreement.[2458]

27.7.4 The cumulative effect of exclusive purchasing agreements

Exclusive purchasing agreements in many ways closely resemble exclusive distribution agreements. Under exclusive purchasing agreements the buyer is required to purchase goods from the manufacturer. Both parties potentially benefit from that arrangement. Manufacturers are able to calculate the demand for their product for the duration of the agreement, and adjust their production accordingly; buyers, in exchange for their commitment, receive advantageous prices, technical assistance, preference in supply, and so on. In dealing with exclusive purchasing agreements the Commission takes into consideration whether the agreement in question forms part of a network of similar agreements. If so, the cumulative effect of such agreements on trade between Member States is assessed. This was illustrated in Case 23/67 *Brasserie de Haecht (No.1)*.[2459]

THE FACTS WERE:

The proprietors of a café in Esneux, Belgium, promised, in exchange for a loan made by a brewery in Belgium, to buy all their requirements for beer, lemonade and other drinks from that brewery for the duration of the loan and two further years. When the café proprietors were sued by the brewery for breach of the contract, they argued that the agreement infringed Article 101(1) TFEU as it restricted trade between Member States by limiting the outlets in Belgium for breweries from other Member States.

2457. Ibid, para. 24.

2458. See: Commission's decision in *Computerland Europe SA* [1987] OJ L222/12, [1989] 4 CMLR 259.

2459. Case 23/67 *Brasserie de Haecht v Wilkin-Janssens (No.1)* [1967] ECR 407.

Held:

The ECJ held that the agreement should be assessed in its economic and legal context, in particular whether there was only one agreement or whether the agreement was part of a network of similar agreements. If it was a separate agreement, its effect on trade between Member States was insignificant. However, if it formed part of a network of agreements, its overall impact might result in making it difficult or even impossible for new undertakings to enter the market through the opening of new outlets.

Comment:

Exclusive purchasing agreements will not fall within the scope of Article 101(1) TFEU if the effect of such an agreement, either individually or as part of a network of several similar agreements, does not have a "blocking" effect on potential competitors.[2460]

27.8 From exemption to legal exception: Article 101(3) TFEU

Agreements in breach of Article 101(1) TFEU may be eligible for exemption under the conditions laid down in Article 101(3) TFEU. With the coming into force of Regulation 1/2003, Article 101(3) exemptions became legal exceptions.[2461] Regulation 1/2003 rendered Article 101(3) directly effective, whereas previously it was not directly effective and thus could not be relied on by individuals in national courts. It also abolished the system of notification of envisaged agreements to the Commission which alone had the power to grant exemptions under Article 101(3) TFEU.

Under Article 101(3) an agreement, decision or concerted practice will qualify for exemption provided the benefit from it outweighs the disadvantage resulting from the restriction that it imposes on competition and provided it fulfils two positive and two negative criteria.

The positive criteria are:

- it must contribute to improving the production or distribution of goods or the promotion of technical or economic progress; and,

- it must allow consumers a fair share of the resulting benefit.

The negative criteria are:

- it must not impose on the undertakings concerned restrictions which are not indispensable to the attainment of the objectives set out in the agreement; and,

- it must not afford an undertaking the possibility of eliminating competition in respect of a substantial proportion of the products in question.

The principles which guide the Commission in deciding whether or not an agreement might qualify for exemption are embodied in Guidelines on the Application of [Article 101(3) TFEU].[2462] The guidelines indicate, *inter alia*, that:

2460. This line of reasoning has been continued in Case C-234/89 *Delimitis v Henninger Bräu* [1991] ECR 1935; Joined Cases T-374, 375, 384 and 388/94 *European Night Services and Others v Commission* [1998] ECR II-3141.
2461. However, commentators, including the author, continue to refer to them as exemptions.
2462. [2004] OJ C101/1.

■ No agreement, even if it seriously restricts competition, can be *a priori* excluded from the benefit of exemption. In Case T-17/93 *Matra Hachette*,[2463] the General Court held that as a matter of principle there is no anti-competitive practice which cannot qualify for exemption provided that the criteria laid down in Article 101(3) TFEU are satisfied;

■ An economic assessment of the agreement should be carried out in each case. Under Article 101(3) the analysis of the pro and anti-competitive aspects of an agreement is carried out.[2464] There is an ongoing debate whether aspects other than economic efficiency, such as wider socio-political considerations, should play any role in the assessment of an agreement. While the Commission takes the position that only economic factors should be taken into consideration,[2465] the case law provides examples where account has been taken of non-competition factors, such as the creation of employment in one of the poorest regions of the EU[2466] or the protection of environment,[2467] as being relevant to the exemption decisions; and,

■ All four criteria laid down in Article 101(3) TFEU must be satisfied. The burden of proof is on the applicant.[2468] If one of them is not fulfilled, the agreement will not be exempted.[2469] The exemption ceases to apply if any of the criteria ceases to be satisfied, but in some circumstances the assessment will be made on the basis of the facts existing at the time of implementation of an agreement.[2470]

The criteria set out in Article 101(3) TFEU are examined below.

27.8.1   First criterion: efficiency gains

The first positive criterion requires that agreements, decisions or concerted practices must contribute "to improving the production or distribution of goods or to promoting technical or economic progress". The criterion does not require that all four possibilities are present; it is sufficient if only one of them occurs. In applying the first criterion, advantages flowing from the agreement must be compared with disadvantages resulting from the restriction that it imposes on competition. The advantages must prevail over the disadvantages. The advantages are objectively assessed and refer to the general interest, and not to the benefit which the parties to the agreement may derive for themselves in production or distribution.[2471]

2463. Case T-17/93 *Matra Hachette SA v Commission* [1994] ECR II-595.

2464. Case T-65/98 *Van den Berg Foods v Commission* [2003] ECR II-4653. See also the Guidelines on the Application of [Article 101(3) TFEU], supra note 2462, para. 33.

2465. In the Guidelines the Commission stated that the objective of [Article 101(3) TFEU] is "to provide a legal framework for the economic assessment of restrictive practices and not to allow the application of the competition rules to be set aside because of political considerations", supra note 2462, para. 33.

2466. *Ford/Volkswagen* [1993] OJ L20/14.

2467. *European Council of Manufacturers of Domestic Appliances (CECED)* [2000] OJ L 187/47, *DSD* [2001] OJ L319/1.

2468. Case 71/74 *Nederlandse Vereniging voor de fruit- en groentenimporthandel, Nederlandse Bond van Grossiers in Zuidvruchten en Ander Geimporteerd Fruit "Frubo" v Commission* [1975] ECR 563; and Case 42/84 *Remia BV and Others v Commission* [1985] ECR 2545.

2469. Joined Cases T-528, 542, 543 and 546/93 *Métropole Télévision and Others v Commission* [1996] ECR II-649; Case T-395/94 *Atlantic Container Line AB v Commission* [2002] ECR II-875.

2470. Guidelines on the Application of [Article 101(3) TFEU], para. 45.

2471. Cases 56 and 58/64 *Établissements Consten S.à.R.L. and Grundig-Verkaufs-GmbH v Commission* [1966] ECR 299.

According to the Commission's Guidelines on the Application of [Article 101(3) TFEU] all types of objective economic efficiencies can be claimed by undertakings. The Guidelines, as an example, examine two types of efficiencies: cost efficiencies; and qualitative efficiencies. They state that each efficiency must be substantiated by the undertaking claiming the benefit of the exception so the following can be verified:

"(a)   The nature of the claimed efficiencies;

(b)   The link between the agreement and the efficiencies;

(c)   The likelihood and magnitude of each claimed efficiency; and,

(d)   How and when each claimed efficiency would be achieved."[2472]

27.8.2 Second criterion: benefit to consumers

The second positive criterion requires that an agreement, decision or concerted practice must not only contribute to improving the production or distribution of goods or to promoting technical or economic progress, but must also allow consumers a fair share of the resulting benefits.

The term "consumers" applies not only to final consumers, but also to wholesalers and retailers, who purchase products in the course of their trade and business.[2473] The Commission takes into consideration the interests of the majority of consumers. In *VBBB/VBVB*,[2474] the Commission refused to grant exemption to an agreement between associations of booksellers and publishers in the Netherlands and Belgium imposing collective prices on books in the Dutch language to be sold in Belgium and in the Netherlands. Under this agreement less popular books on specific subjects published in a limited number of copies were to be subsidised by more popular books. The Commission condemned the agreement on the ground that it would be unfair to the majority of consumers, taking into account that they prefer popular books rather than specialised books which have a limited number of readers.

The "fair share" concept entails that "the pass-on of benefits must at least compensate consumers for any actual or likely negative impact caused to them by the restriction of competition found under Article 101(3) TFEU".[2475] As a result, the net effect of an agreement on the affected consumers must at least be neutral. If they are worse off, the second condition will not be fulfilled.

As to the term "benefit" it covers not only reduction of purchase prices but also improvements in the quality of product; improvement of after-sales service; the possibility of a greater range of products; an increase in the number or quality of outlets from which the products may be purchased; and, quicker delivery.[2476]

27.8.3 Third criterion: indispensable restrictions

This first negative criterion requires that an agreement, decision or concerted practice must not impose on the undertakings concerned restrictions which are not indispensable to the attainment of the objectives of the agreement.[2477] This requires that the agreement must not go beyond what is absolutely necessary to achieve the objectives regarded as beneficial. This condition involves a two-fold test. First, the restrictive agreement must be reasonably necessary in order to achieve the efficiencies. Second, the

---

2472. Para. 51 of the Guidelines.

2473. *Kabel und Metallwerke Neumeyer/Luchaire* [1975] OJ L222/34, [1975] 2 CMLR D40.

2474. [1982] OJ L54/36; [1982] 2 CMLR 344.

2475. Para. 85 of the Guidelines.

2476. Ibid, para. 88 et seq.

2477. Ibid, paras 73 and 74.

individual restrictions of competition that flow from the agreement must also be reasonably necessary for the attainment of the efficiencies.[2478]

27.8.4 Fourth criterion: no possibility of eliminating competition

The second negative criterion requires that an agreement, decision or restrictive practice must not result in eliminating competition in respect of a substantial part of the relevant product market.[2479] In order to apply this criterion, the Commission must determine the relevant geographic and product markets.[2480] However, an agreement for joint research may qualify for exemption even if the undertakings concerned have a substantial share of the relevant product market.[2481]

In assessing the fourth criterion, competition between similar competing products (inter-brand competition) rather than competition between rival distributors of the same brand of products (intra-brand competition) is taken into account. The major factor in deciding whether to exempt an agreement under the fourth criterion will be the retention of reasonable competition between the different brands and the absence or otherwise of any restriction on parallel import of these brands.

27.9 Block exemption regulations

Article 101 TFEU does not specify the body which is empowered to grant or refuse individual exemption under Article 101(3) TFEU. However, this task was assigned to the Commission under Article 9 of Council Regulation 17/62.[2482] It was decided that the exclusive competence of the Commission to grant individual exemptions would ensure uniformity in the application and interpretation of Article 101(1) TFEU.

Soon after Regulation 17/62 was adopted, the Commission received about 30,000 notifications of exclusive distribution agreements alone. In order to ease the Commission's workload, the Council under Regulation 19/65 empowered it to adopt block exemption regulations exempting classes of agreements (that is why they are called "block" exemption regulations) such as exclusive distribution agreements, purchasing agreements and agreements licensing IPRs so long as the agreements conform to any exemption regulations so adopted. The first regulation adopted by the Commission under the said powers concerned exclusive distribution agreements and was embodied in Regulation 67/67.

Before the reform of the application of Article 101 TFEU (see Chapter 30.1) block exemption regulations provided important advantages to undertakings. They were not required to notify to the Commission an agreement which conformed to the terms of a block exemption regulation. Thus, they could avoid the delays and uncertainty of the procedure for individual exemption. The result of the reform is that the usefulness of block exemption regulations remains, but now the parties themselves are required to determine (rather than having the option of obtaining exemption from the Commission) whether their agreement conforms to any relevant block exemption regulation and, if necessary, defend their position before national competition authorities or national courts.

Each block exemption is contained in a separate regulation and is, of course, legally binding. If an agreement strictly complies with every condition and term of a block exemption regulation, it is outside

---

2478. Ibid, para. 73 of the Guidelines.
2479. Ibid, paras 105–16.
2480. *Lightweight Paper* [1972] OJ L182; Joined Cases 19 and 20/74 *Kali und Salz v Commission* [1975] ECR 499. See Chapter 28.3.1.
2481. *Michelin* [1981] OJ L353/33.
2482. OJ (1959–62) Spec.ED.87.

the scope of Article 101(1) TFEU,[2483] i.e. there is no need to examine the agreement under Article 101(3) TFEU.

The number of block exemption regulations adopted either by the Council or by the Commission, under delegated authority from the Council, increased considerably over the years. This was highly criticised. This, and factors, discussed in see Chapter 30.1, resulted in the adoption of a new style to block exemption regulations. The first was Regulation 2790/99 on the Application of [Article 101(3) TFEU] to Categories of Vertical Agreements and Concerted Practices,[2484] which entered into force on 1 June 2000 and which has been replaced by Regulation 330/2010[2485] (see below).

The main features of the new style block exemption regulations are first, that they abolish the presumption that a restrictive agreement is contrary to Article 101(1); and, second, that small and medium-sized undertakings are largely excluded from the scope of Article 101(1) as the regulations set out market share thresholds which range from 30 per cent for vertical agreements to 20 per cent for specialisation and transfer of technology agreements. The Commission has also published a number of guidelines and explanatory notes which clarify the application of the block exemption regulations.[2486]

Regulation 330/2010 applies to all vertical agreements, and therefore merits special attention.

27.9.1 Commission Regulation 330/2010 of 20 April 2010 on the application of Article 101(3) of the Treaty on the Functioning of the European Union to categories of vertical agreements and concerted practices[2487]

Regulation 330/2010 entered into force on 1 June 2010 and is expected to expire on 31 May 2022.[2488] It is accompanied by Commission's Vertical Guidelines.[2489]

It applies in the following agreements:

1. All vertical agreements between non-competitors where the supplier of goods or services under the agreement has a share in the relevant product market of less than 30 per cent and the market share of the buyer does not exceed 30 per cent of the relevant market.

2. Vertical agreements entered into between an association of undertakings and its members, or between such an association and its suppliers if:

   (i) all the members of the association are retailers of goods (not services); and,

   (ii) each member has a turnover not exceeding €50 million.

2483. Case C-260/07 *Perdo IV Servicios SL v Total España SA* [2009] ECR I-2437.

2484. [1999] OJ L336/21.

2485. [2010] OJ L142/1.

2486. Among them are: the Guidelines on Vertical Restraints (2010) OJ C130/1; Guidelines on the Applicability of Article 101 to Horizontal Agreements (2010) OJ C11/1; Guidelines on the Application of Article [101 TFEU] to Technology Transfer Agreements (2004) OJ C101/2. All these documents are available on the Commission's official website: http://ec.europa.eu/competition/antitrust/legislation/legislation.html (accessed 21/6/12).

2487. [2010] OJ L142/1.

2488. On Regulation 330/2010 see R. Whish and D. Bailey, "Regulation 330/2010: The Commission's New Block Exemption for Vertical Agreements", (2010) 47 CMLRev., 1757.

2489. [2010] OJ C130/1.

3.   Vertical non-reciprocal agreements between competitors[2490] within the market share thresholds specified in point 1 above but only if:

   (i)   the supplier is a manufacturer and a distributor of goods while the buyer is only a distributor and not a competing undertaking at the manufacturing level; or,

   (ii)   the supplier supplies services at several levels of trade while the buyer does not provide competing services at the same level at which it purchases the contract services.

4.   To vertical agreements containing provisions relating to the assignment/use of IPRs and which are within the market share threshold specified in point 1 where five conditions are satisfied:

   (i)   The IPRs provisions must be part of a vertical agreement;

   (ii)   The IPRs must be assigned to, or licensed for use by, the buyer;

   (iii)   The IPRs provisions must not be the primary object of the agreement;

   (iv)   The IPRs provisions must be directly related to the use, sale or resale of goods by the buyer or its customer; and,

   (v)   The IPRs provisions concerning goods or services must not contain restrictions of competition having the same object as vertical restraints which are not exempted under the Regulation.

The Commission considers that, in principle, vertical agreements do not have an adverse effect on competition. However, the market share test was introduced to make sure that when the parties to a vertical agreement have market power, the agreement will not produce anti-competitive effects.

Para. 23 of the Vertical Guidelines states that "hard-core restrictions' set out in Article 4 of the Regulation restrict competition by "object". As a result, they can only be justified under Article 101(3) TFEU. Under Regulation 330/2010 the hardcore restrictions are as follows:

- Article 4(a): the restriction of the buyer's ability to determine its sale price (i.e. resale price maintenance), except the setting of maximum resale prices or of recommended resale prices provided that they do not, in practice, amount to fixed or minimum resale prices.

- Article 4(b): Restrictions of the territory into which, or of the customers to whom, a buyer may sell. In four situations restrictions on territory or customer exclusivity are permitted:

   (i)   Restrictions on active sales into the exclusive territory or to an exclusive group reserved to the supplier or allocated by the supplier to another buyer, where such a restriction does not limit sales by the customers of the buyer. The distinction between "active" and "passive" sales is vital to the application of the exception. Paragraph 51 of the Vertical Guidelines defines both. It states that "active" sales mean: "actively approaching individual customers by for instance direct mail, including the sending of unsolicited e-mails, or visits; or actively approaching a specific customer group or customers in a specific territory through advertisement in media, on the internet or other promotions specifically targeted at that customer group or targeted customers in that territory".

Passive sales mean "responding to unsolicited requests from individual customers, including delivery of goods or services to such customers". General advertisement or promotion is regarded as passive selling. Article 51 states that advertising that reaches customers in other territories or customer groups reserved to another buyer is considered as general advertisement

---

2490. A competitor is defined in Article 1(1)(c) of the Regulation as "an actual or potential competitor on the same relevant market, irrespective of whether or not they operate in the same geographic market".

if it would be attractive for the buyer to invest in that advertising/promotion even if it would only reach customers in the buyer's own territory or customer group there.

The Vertical Guidelines provide important clarifications concerning online sales on the Internet. They state that in general the use of a website to sell products is considered as passive selling. However, in some circumstances, e.g. advertising specifically addressed to customers of another distributor, or paying a search engine or online advertisement provider to have advertisements displayed specifically to users in an exclusive territory of another distributor, is to be regarded as active selling. Paragraph 54 of the Vertical Guidelines states that the supplier is allowed to impose quality standards on the use of the website by its distributors. Further, the supplier may require that distributors have one or more bricks and mortar shop or showroom as a condition for becoming a member of the distribution system. In Case C-439/09 *Pierre Fabre*,[2491] the ECJ held that a total ban on online selling imposed on distributors within a selective distribution system was a "hardcore restriction" under Article 4(c) of Regulation 330/2010 as it restricted competition "by object". Thus, it could only be justified under Article 101(3) TFEU;

(ii) Restrictions on both active and passive sales to end users by a buyer operating at the wholesale level. Paragraph 55 of the Vertical Guidelines explain that this exception allows the supplier to keep the wholesale and retail levels of the market separate. However, the supplier may allow wholesalers to sell to some end users, for example large customers, though not to others;

(iii) Restrictions on sales, both active and passive, and at any level of trade, by members of a selective distribution system to unauthorised distributors in the territory where that system is currently in operation and also in the territory where the supplier does not yet sell the contract product; and,

(iv) restrictions on sales, active and passive, of goods or services which are supplied for the purpose of incorporation into other products which would compete with those of the supplier.

■ Article 4(c) prohibits restrictions of active or passive sales to users, whether professional end users or final customers, by members of a selective distribution system operating at the retail level of trade.

■ Article 4(d) prohibits restriction of cross-supplies between distributors within a selective distribution system, including between distributors at different levels of trade.

■ Article 4(e) prohibits restrictions which prevent end-users, i.e. repairers and service providers, from obtaining spare parts directly from the manufacturers of those parts, in a situation where repairers and service providers are not entrusted by the buyer with the repair or servicing of its goods.

The above hardcore restrictions are contained in Article 4 of Regulation 2790/99. The insertion of any of them will result in the entire agreement being excluded from the benefit of block exemption.

Article 5 of the Regulation concerns non-compete clauses which, although prohibited, are severable from the agreement. This means that such clauses will be invalid while the remainder of the agreement can benefit from the block exemption. The following are prohibited:

■ Any direct or indirect obligation imposed on members of a selective distribution scheme to sell or not to sell "specified brands" of competing suppliers;

2491. [2011] ECR I-000.

■ A non-competition obligation on the buyer exceeding five years in duration, unless the goods to which the agreement relates are intended to be resold by the buyer from premises owned or leased by the supplier, provided that the duration of the non-competition obligation does not exceed the period of occupancy of the premises by the buyer; and,

■ Post-term non-compete obligations. Article 5(1)(b) states that "any direct or indirect obligation causing the buyer, after termination of the agreement, not to manufacture, purchase, sell or resell goods or service" is prohibited. This is unless the obligations: relate to goods or services competing with contract goods or services; are limited to the premises and land from which the buyer has operated during the agreement; are indispensable to protect know-how transferred by the supplier under the agreement; and, are limited to a period of one year.

RECOMMENDED READING

Books
Those recommended in Chapter 26 and the following:

Goyder, J., *EU Distribution Law*, 5th edn, 2011, Oxford: Hart Publishing.

Odudu, O., *The Boundaries of EC Competition Law: The Scope of Article 81*, 2006, Oxford: OUP.

Townley, C., *Article 81EC and Public Policy*, 2009, Oxford: Hart Publishing.

Wijckmans, F., Tuytschaever, F. and Vanderelst, A., *Vertical Agreements and the EC Competition Rules*, 2006, Oxford: OUP.

Articles

Albors-Llorens, A., "A Horizontal Agreement and Concerted Practices in EC Competition Law: Unlawful and Legitimate Contacts between Competitors", (2006) 51 *Antitrust Bulletin*, 837.

Bailey, D., "Single, Overall Agreement in EU Competition Law", (2010) 47 CMLRev., 473.

Bailey, D., "'Publicly Distancing' Oneself from a Cartel", (2008) 31 *World Competition*, 177.

Black, O., "Agreement: Concurrence of Wills or Offer and Acceptance", (2008) 4/1 EuroCJ, 103.

Dethmers, F., and Posthuma de Boer, P., "Ten Years On: Vertical Agreements under Article 81", (2009) ECLR, 42.

Jones, A., "The Journey Towards an Effect-Based Approach under Article 101(1) TFEU – The Case of 'Hardcore' Restraints", (2010) *Antitrust Bulletin*, 55.

Jones, A., "Resale Price Maintenance: A Debate about Competition Policy in Europe?" (2009) 5 EuroCJ, 479.

Jones, A., "Left Behind by Modernisation? Restrictions by Object under Article 101(1)", (2010) 6 EuroCJ, 649.

King, S., "The Object Box: Law, Policy or Myth?" (2011) 7/2 EuroCJ, 269.

Lianos, I., "Collusion in Vertical Relations under Article 81 EC", (2008) 45 CMLRev., 1027.

Lidgard, H. H., "Unilateral Refusal to Supply: an Agreement in Disguise?", (1997) 18 ECLR, 352.

Mahtani, M. R., "Thinking Outside the Object Box: An EU and UK Perspective", (2012) 8/1 EuroCJ, 1.

Marquis, M., "O2 (Germany) v Commission and the Exotic Mysteries of Article 81(1) EC", (2007) ELRev., 29.

Meyring, B., "T-Mobile: Further Confusion on Information Exchanges between Competitors: Case C-8/08 T-Mobile Netherlands and others [2009] ECR 0000", *Journal of European Competition Law & Practice Advance*, 2009, 30.

Nazzini, R., "Article 81 EC between Time Present and Time Past: A Normative Critique of 'Restriction of Competition in EU Law'", (2006) 43 CMLRev., 497.

Odudu, O., "Indirect Information Exchange: The Constituent Elements of Hub and Spoke Collusion", (2011) 7 EuroCJ, 205.

Whish, R., and Bailey, D., "Regulation 330/2010: The Commission's New Block Exemption for Vertical Agreements", (2010) 47 CMLRev., 1757.

Wickihalder, U., "The Distinction between an 'Agreement' within the Meaning of Article 81(1) of the EC Treaty and Unilateral Conduct", (2006) 2 EuroCJ, 87.

PROBLEM QUESTION

There are seven undertakings active on the EU plasterboard market. On 7 March 2010, the European Association of Producers of Plasterboard (EAPP) held a meeting attended by the managing directors of the seven enterprises with a view to discussing the EAPP's participation in the world fair of plasterboard producers. During the meeting the participants agreed that it would be good for all European producers of plasterboard to set up an information exchange system and that the EAPP should prepare a detailed proposal on how such a system should operate.

After the meeting the managing directors of the three largest producers of plasterboard in the EU, that is BPB Ltd ("BPB"), an English undertaking, Buildex GmbH ("Buildex"), a German undertaking and Gypex Sarl ("Gypex"), a French undertaking, held an informal meeting during which they expressed a common desire to rationalise the EU plasterboard market, in particular, to deal with the problem of how to respond to a growing demand for plasterboard in Italy.

In April 2010 BPB and Buildex set up a system for exchanging information between themselves relating to their sales volumes on the EU plasterboard market. Gypex subsequently acceded to this system.

Plastex Ltd ("Plastex"), a Spanish undertaking, is one of the seven undertakings operating on the EU plasterboard market. John, the managing director of Plastex, has recently been invited to a meeting of the managing directors of BPB, Buildex and Gypex. Plastex holds a 20% share in the EU plasterboard market.

John consults you, a lawyer specialised in EU competition law, with regard to the following issues:

A. He wants to know whether he should accept the invitation to the meeting of the managing directors of BPB, Buildex and Gypex. He tells you that the managing directors of these undertakings have told him that they have no intention of injuring competition in the EU plasterboard market, any competitors on that market or the welfare of consumers. To the contrary, their meetings have the purpose of rationalising the EU plasterboard market.

B. He is uncertain as to whether to accept an invitation to participate in the exchange of information system proposed by the EAPP.

C. He tells you that whatever measures, if any, have been agreed by BPB, Buildex and Gypex they have had no impact on the EU plasterboard market.

D. He has instructed Plastex's agents in Poland to sell plasterboard at a fixed price of US $20 per square foot.

E. He has instructed Plastex's exclusive distributors in Poland and Estonia to terminate transactions, concluded *via* their websites, with customers whose credit card data reveals an address that is not within the distributor's exclusive territory.

Set out your advice to John on all the above.

ESSAY QUESTION

Critically discuss whether Regulation 330/2010 adequately responds to competition concerns raised by vertical agreements.

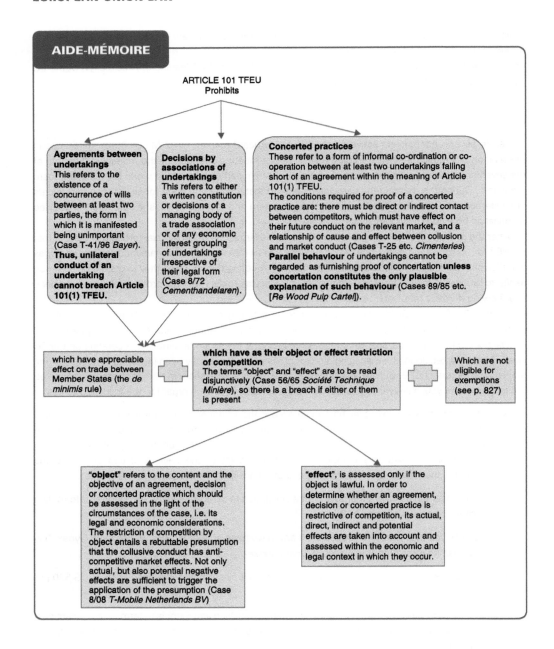

AIDE-MÉMOIRE

ARTICLE 101 TFEU
Prohibits

Agreements between undertakings
This refers to the existence of a concurrence of wills between at least two parties, the form in which it is manifested being unimportant (Case T-41/96 *Bayer*). **Thus, unilateral conduct of an undertaking cannot breach Article 101(1) TFEU.**

Decisions by associations of undertakings
This refers to either a written constitution or decisions of a managing body of a trade association or of any economic interest grouping of undertakings irrespective of their legal form (Case 8/72 *Cementhandelaren*).

Concerted practices
These refer to a form of informal co-ordination or co-operation between at least two undertakings falling short of an agreement within the meaning of Article 101(1) TFEU.
The conditions required for proof of a concerted practice are: there must be direct or indirect contact between competitors, which must have effect on their future conduct on the relevant market, and a relationship of cause and effect between collusion and market conduct (Cases T-25 etc. *Cimenteries*)
Parallel behaviour of undertakings cannot be regarded as furnishing proof of concertation **unless concertation constitutes the only plausible explanation of such behaviour** (Cases 89/85 etc. [*Re Wood Pulp Cartel*]).

which have appreciable effect on trade between Member States (the *de minimis* rule)

which have as their object or effect restriction of competition
The terms "object" and "effect" are to be read disjunctively (Case 56/65 *Société Technique Minière*), so there is a breach if either of them is present

Which are not eligible for exemptions (see p. 827)

"object" refers to the content and the objective of an agreement, decision or concerted practice which should be assessed in the light of the circumstances of the case, i.e. its legal and economic considerations. The restriction of competition by object entails a rebuttable presumption that the collusive conduct has anti-competitive market effects. Not only actual, but also potential negative effects are sufficient to trigger the application of the presumption (Case 8/08 *T-Mobile Netherlands BV*)

"effect", is assessed only if the object is lawful. In order to determine whether an agreement, decision or concerted practice is restrictive of competition, its actual, direct, indirect and potential effects are taken into account and assessed within the economic and legal context in which they occur.

Article 101 TFEU applies to

Horizontal agreements: agreements entered into by undertakings that compete with each other at the same level of the production/distribution chain (for example, agreements between producers, or between manufacturers or between retailers)

Vertical agreements: agreements entered into by undertakings that operate at different levels of the production/distribution chain and do not compete with each other (for example, franchising and distribution agreements) (Cases 56 and 58/64 *Consten and Grundig*)

Exemptions from Article 101(1) TFEU

Under block exemption regulations (BER)

If an agreement/concerted practice satisfies the conditions of the relevant BER, it is outside the scope of Article 101(1) TFEU

If an agreement/concerted practice does not satisfy the conditions of the relevant BER, it is to be assessed under Article 101(3) TFEU

Under Article 101(3) TFEU
In order to qualify for an exemption, an agreement/ decision/concerted practice must satisfy four criteria set out in Article 101(3) TFEU.

The positive criteria are:
- it must contribute to improving the production or distribution of goods or the promotion of technical or economic progress; and,
- it must allow consumers a fair share of the resulting benefit.

The negative criteria are:
- it must not impose on the undertakings concerned restrictions which are not indispensable to attainment of the objectives pursued by it; and,
- it must not afford undertakings concerned the possibility of eliminating competition in respect of a substantial proportion of the products in question.

Consequence of a breach of Article 101(1) TFEU specified in ARTICLE 101(2) TFEU

Agreements and decisions in breach of Article 101(1) TFEU which neither qualify for exemption under the relevant BER nor under Article 101(3) TFEU are automatically void from their inception. The term "automatically" means that they are prohibited *per se* and no decision to that effect is required from EU institutions or national courts. Concerted practices are not included in Article 101(2) TFEU since they are informal arrangements and as such cannot be rendered void.

28

ARTICLE 102 TFEU

CHAPTER OUTLINE

1. Article 102 TFEU prohibits the abuse of a dominant position by a single undertaking or by a number of undertakings, which abuse affects trade between Member States and cannot be objectively justified.
2. The concept of dominance was defined by the ECJ in Case 85/76 *Hoffmann-La Roche* as referring to such a position of market power being held by an undertaking as to enable it to act independently from its competitors and consumers and thus not subjecting it to normal competitive forces.
3. In order to establish dominance it is vital to determine whether an undertaking has market power. This concept has been defined as the seller's ability to raise and sustain a price increase without losing so many sales that it must rescind the increase. The first step in assessing whether an undertaking has market power is to define the relevant market. This has three components: the relevant product market

(RPM); the relevant geographical market (RGM); and, if appropriate, the relevant temporal market (RTM). Once the relevant market has been defined, the Commission will use three main factors to assess the market power of the undertaking concerned, i.e.

■ constraints imposed by the existing supplies firms, and the position on the market of the actual competitors (i.e. the position of the undertaking concerned and its rivals);

■ constraints imposed by credible threats of future expansion by actual competitors or entry by potential competitors to the relevant market (i.e. expansion and entry barriers); and,

■ constraints imposed by the bargaining power of the dominant undertaking's customers (countervailing buyer power).

4. The concept of "collective dominance" concerns the situation where the relevant market is oligopolistic and undertakings, through tacit parallel conduct, can act in a similar way to a cartel or a monopoly. To prove collective dominance three conditions must be met. These are:

■ transparency, that is, each member of the dominant oligopoly must have the ability to know how the other members are behaving in order to monitor whether or not they are adopting the common policy;

■ sustainability, that is, there must be a retaliatory mechanism in place which secures unity within an oligopoly and thus dissuades its members from deviating from their common policy adopted in the relevant market; and,

■ an absence of competitive constraints, so allowing undertakings within a dominant oligopoly to act independently of their customers and consumers, actual or potential.

5. The concept of abuse is an objective concept. It has been interpreted broadly to encompass not only conduct by which a dominant undertaking exploits its position, that is, conduct which may cause damage to purchasers or consumers directly, but also conduct which affects the structure of the market, that is, conduct which excludes competitors, strengthens the dominant position of the undertaking concerned and weakens competition in the market, and thus is detrimental to purchasers and consumers through its impact on an effective competition structure of the relevant market.

6. Article 102(a)–(d) TFEU sets out a non-exhaustive list of abusive practices. On its basis abuses can be classified as follows:

■ Exclusionary abuses – these are aimed at foreclosing the relevant market. They are especially harmful to competition;

■ Exploitative abuses – these occur when an undertaking is, at the expense of customers or consumers, using its economic power to obtain benefits, or to impose burdens, which are unobtainable or imposable within normal competition on the merits. An example of this type of abuse is the imposition of excessively high prices; and,

■ Discriminatory prices – these occur when a dominant undertaking treats its customers in a dissimilar manner without costs based or legally acceptable justification.

7. A dominant undertaking may justify its abusive conduct by demonstrating that:

■ it is objectively necessary, e.g. justified by imperative considerations such as health and safety reasons related to the nature of the product concerned; or

■ it produces substantial efficiencies which outweigh any anti-competitive effects on consumers. The test here is similar to that set out in Article 101(1) TFEU.

28.1 Introduction

Article 102 TFEU states:

"Any abuse by one or more undertakings of a dominant position within the internal market or in a substantial part of it shall be prohibited as incompatible with the internal market in so far as it may affect trade between Member States.

Such abuse may, in particular, consist in:

(a) directly or indirectly imposing unfair purchase or selling prices or other unfair trading conditions;

(b) limiting production, markets or technical development to the prejudice of consumers;

(c) applying dissimilar conditions to equivalent transactions with other trading parties, thereby placing them at a competitive disadvantage;

(d) making the conclusion of contracts subject to acceptance by the other parties of supplementary obligations which, by their nature or according to commercial usage, have no connection with the subject of such contracts."

The concept of an undertaking has the same meaning under Article 102 as under Article 101 TFEU (see Chapter 26.3). Further, as indicated in Chapter 26.4.1, abusive conduct of a dominant undertaking must have appreciable effect on trade between Member States in order to be caught by Article 102 TFEU, i.e. must affect the "competitive structure"[2492] of the relevant market. Indeed, the structure of the relevant market is already weakened by the mere existence of a dominant undertaking and thus any conduct by a dominant undertaking which alters the competitive structure of the relevant market will have effect on trade between Member States.[2493]

Within the framework of modernisation of EU competition law, and in line with the reform that is taking place regarding Article 101 TFEU (see Chapter 30.1) and the Merger Regulation (see Chapter 29.1.1) the Commission has commenced revising its approach to the enforcement of Article 102 TFEU. The main objective is to develop a more economic-based approach, often referred to as the effects-based approach, to the enforcement of EU law on the abuse of a dominant position, focusing on the promotion of economic efficiency and consumer welfare. The Guidance on the Commission Enforcement Priorities in Applying [Article 102 TFEU] to Abusive Exclusionary Conduct by Dominant Undertakings[2494] (hereafter referred to as the Guidance) confirms the applicability of the effects-based approach to the establishment of exclusionary abuses under Article 102 TFEU. It makes clear that under Article 102 TFEU there are no *per se* abuses. Additionally, the Guidance establishes a generalised system of justifications for abusive practices.

It is important to note that the Guidance has no binding force, and that the ultimate interpretation of Article 102 rests with the ECJ.[2495] Indeed, in Case C-52/09 *TeliaSonera*[2496] the ECJ held that, contrary to the position of the Commission in the Guidance, a margin squeeze is a separate category of abuse, not merely a particular instance of refusal to deal (see Chapter 28.6.1.3).

Under Article 102 TFEU neither a dominant position nor its creation[2497] is prohibited. However, once an undertaking is in a dominant position on the relevant market EU competition law imposes on

---

2492. See para. 20 of the Commission's Guidelines on the Effect on Trade Concept Contained in Articles [101 and 102 TFEU], [2004] C101/81.

2493. See Joined Case 6/73 and 7/73 *Istituto Chemioterapico Italiano S.p.A. v Commercial Solvents Corporation v Commission* [1974] ECR 223 and Case T-57/01 *Solvay SA v Commission* [2009] ECR II-4621.

2494. [2009] OJ C45/7–20.

2495. See the Commission's decision in *Intel* COMP/37/990.

2496. Case C-52/09 *Konkurrensverket v TeliaSonera Sverige AB* [2011] ECR I-527.

2497. Case 6/72 *Europemballage Corp. and Continental Can Co. Inc. v Commission* [1973] ECR 215.

it a standard of conduct different from that of an undertaking which is not in a dominant position. In this respect, the ECJ emphasised that an undertaking in a dominant position "has a special responsibility not to allow its conduct to impair genuine undistorted competition on the [internal] market".[2498] This means that an undertaking in a dominant position may breach Article 102 TFEU by engaging in conduct which, if carried out by its competitors rather than by it, would be lawful. The imposition of a different standard of conduct on an undertaking in a dominant position which entails that it "has special responsibility" is explained by the fact that such an undertaking has greater capacity to distort competition on the relevant market than an undertaking which is not in a dominant position. Under Article 102 TFEU an undertaking in a dominant position is prohibited from abusing its dominant position. In order to show a breach of the prohibition set out in Article 102 TFEU, it is necessary to establish that:

- one or more undertakings (for a definition of an undertaking, see Chapter 26.3);

- in a dominant position within the internal market or in a substantial part of it;

- has abused that position;

- the abuse has appreciably affected trade between Member States (see Chapter 26.4.1); and,

- there are no objective or efficiency justifications for the abuse.

The TFEU does not define any of the above terms. Their meanings have gradually been clarified by the EU courts and the Commission.

28.2 The concept of dominance

The ECJ defined the concept of dominance in Case 27/76 *United Brands v Commission*[2499] as being

> "a position of economic strength enjoyed by an undertaking which enables it to prevent effective competition being maintained on the relevant market by giving it the power to behave to an appreciable extent independently of its competitors, customers, and ultimately of its consumers."

This definition was further explained in Case 85/76 *Hoffmann-La Roche*,[2500] in which the ECJ restated the above-mentioned definition and added that:

> "such a position does not preclude some competition which it does where there is a monopoly or quasi-monopoly but enables the undertakings which profit by it, if not to determine, at least to have an appreciable influence on the conditions under which that competition will develop, and in any case to act largely in disregard of it so long as such conduct does not operate to its detriment."

Accordingly, an undertaking is in a dominant position when it can act independently from its competitors and consumers and thus is not subject to normal competitive forces. In Case T-219/99 *British Airways plc v Commission*,[2501] the General Court confirmed that a dominant position may exist

---

2498. Case 322/81 *Nederlandische Banden-Industie Michelin NV v Commission (Michelin 1)* [1983] ECR 3461, para. 57.

2499. Case 27/76 *United Brands v Commission* [1978] ECR 207, para. 65.

2500. Case 85/76 *Hoffmann-La Roche & Co. AG v Commission* [1979] ECR 461, para. 4.

2501. T-219/99 *British Airways (BA) plc v Commission* [2003] ECR II-5917. Upheld by the ECJ in Case C-95/04P *BA v Commission* [2007] ECR I-2331.

not only in the supplier market but also in the buyer market. In this case British Airways was found to be in a dominant position as a purchaser of services in the UK from travel agents.

The Commission's Guidance adopts an economic approach to the definition of dominance. The Commission considers that "an undertaking which is capable of profitably increasing prices above the competitive level for a significant period of time does not face sufficiently effective competitive constraints and can thus generally be regarded as dominant".[2502]

28.3 Establishing dominance: market power, market definition, assessing the existence of market power

Determination that an undertaking has market power is vital for the enforcement of any competition law. This is because only undertakings which have market power can distort the competitive process. Market power is usually linked to the elasticity of supply and demand.[2503]

Market power can be exercised by a seller or by a buyer. However, economists generally refer to the position of a seller rather than a buyer to define market power.[2504] In a perfectly competitive market, no undertaking has market power because no undertaking has the ability to individually affect either the total quantity of goods on the market or the prevailing prices in the market. As there is no such market an undertaking has market power when it has those abilities. Usually economists refer to "market power" to describe the ability of a seller to profitably impose prices above competitive prices for a sustainable period of time. The crucial issue is how to assess whether an undertaking has market power. Competition enforcement authorities, including the Commission, usually determine whether market power exists by first, defining the relevant market, second, determining the market share which the relevant undertaking holds on the market and third, considering other relevant factors. In this respect the Commission's Guidance confirms the effects-based approach. The Commission intends to abandon the mechanical calculation of dominance based on a market shares threshold and instead take into account the competitive structure of the market. In particular, the Commission identifies three main factors as essential to the assessment of market power:

- constraints imposed by the existing supplies firms, and the position on the market of the actual competitors (i.e. the position of the undertaking concerned and its rivals);

- constraints imposed by credible threats of future expansion by actual competitors or entry by potential competitors (i.e. expansion and entry); and,

- constraints imposed by the bargaining power of the undertaking's customers (i.e. countervailing buyer power).

28.3.1 Market definition

Only in the context of the relevant market can dominance or otherwise be ascertained. Thus, identification of the relevant market is of crucial importance and is the first step for the application of Article 102 TFEU and the Merger Regulation. It is also relevant for the application of Article 101 TFEU

2502. Supra note 2494, para. 11.

2503. On the economic aspects of competition law, see: S. Bishop and M. Walker, *The Economics of EC Competition Law: Concepts, Application and Measurement*, 3rd edn, 2010, London: Sweet & Maxwell.

2504. W. Landes and R. Posner, "Market Power in Antitrust Cases", (1981) 94 *Harvard Law Review*, 939.

given that undertakings with low market shares, that is, below 30 per cent, are within the scope of Regulation 330/2010 (see Chapter 27.9.1).

The main purpose of market definition was explained by the Commission in its Discussion Paper on the Application of [Article 102 TFEU] to Exclusionary Abuses[2505] in the following words: "The objective of defining a market in both its product and geographic dimension is to identify all actual competitors of the undertaking concerned that are capable of constraining its behaviour."

The relevant market has three components:

■ The relevant product market (RPM). The determination of the RPM is the most important and the most common issue in every case which raises competition concerns but poses a great challenge because of the interchangeability of many products (see below);

■ The relevant geographic market (RGM). The definition of the RGM is necessary as Article 102 TFEU only applies if an undertaking abuses its dominant position "within the internal market or in a substantial part of it"; and,

■ The relevant temporal market (RTM).

The Notice on the Definition of the Relevant Market for the Purposes of Community Competition Law[2506] issued by the Commission in 1997 is very helpful in understanding the concept of the relevant market. The Notice sets out the means (which are based on the practices of both the Commission and the EU courts) of assessing the relevant product and geographical market.

The Commission identifies three main factors of competitive constraints to which undertakings are subject and which are used to identify the three relevant markets: RPM, RGM and RTM. They are:

■ demand substitutability;

■ supply substitutability; and,

■ potential competition.

With regard to potential competition, it should be noted that this factor, although of relevance when supply substitutability is assessed, is essentially taken into consideration by the Commission subsequent to definition of the relevant market, when it examines other factors relevant to the assessment of the market power of the undertaking concerned.

28.3.1.1 The relevant product market (RPM)

The 1997 Commission Notice provides the following definition of the RPM: "a relevant product market comprises all those products and/or services which are regarded as interchangeable or substitutable by the consumers, by reason of the products' characteristics, their prices and their intended uses."[2507]

The identification of the RPM depends on the determination of which products are substitutable one for another. In order to determine whether products are or can be substituted for one another, and thus to identify the RPM, two main factors of competitive constraints are taken into consideration:

■ demand substitutability; and,

■ supply substitutability.

2505. Available at http://ec.europa.eu/comm/competition/antitrust/art82/discpaper2005.pdf, para. 12 (accessed 20/4/12).
2506. [1997] OJ C372/5.
2507. Ibid, para. 7.

The above definition, however, focuses on demand substitutability because, according to the Commission: "from an economic point of view, for the definition of the relevant market, demand substitutability constitutes the most immediate and effective disciplinary force on the suppliers of a given product, in particular in relation to their pricing decision."[2508] The Commission explained in its Notice that an undertaking cannot hold a dominant position in the relevant market, and consequently cannot have market power, if consumers can easily switch to available substitute products or to suppliers offering the same product located within the same geographical market. The focus on demand substitutability has been subject to criticism given that the consequence of ignoring other constraints, such as supply substitutability and potential competition, is that the relevant market will be too narrowly defined, and consequently, an undertaking's apparent position on the relevant market will not reflect its actual position, that is, it may be found to be in a dominant position by the Commission but, in fact, may have no market power.[2509]

Divergences between the Commission and the undertaking under investigation in the determination of the RPM usually follow a similar pattern, bearing in mind that undertakings always seek a broad definition and the Commission always seeks the opposite. The narrower the definition of a product market, the greater the market power of any one undertaking and thus the more likely it is that the undertaking will have to bear the extra responsibilities that go with being in a dominant position.

28.3.1.1.1   Demand substitutability

To assess demand substitutability the test is based on the question of whether consumers of the relevant product would switch to substitute products if prices for the relevant product were raised by a small but significant amount (between 5 and 10 per cent) above the competitive levels (this is known as the SSNIP test – a Small but Significant Non-transitory Increase in Price). If so, the relevant product market should include the substitutes. It would be unrealistic to expect that all or even the majority of customers would switch. The decisive factor is whether, if prices were raised as mentioned above, a sufficiently large number of consumers would be likely to switch to substitutes and so dissuade an undertaking in a dominant position from charging prices above competitive levels.

The identification of the RPM was at issue in Case 27/76 *United Brands*.[2510]

THE FACTS WERE:

United Brands, a multinational corporation registered in New Jersey (USA), was the main supplier of bananas to many Member States. Identification of the relevant product market was crucial to the outcome of the case. United Brands argued that bananas were interchangeable with other fruits such as apples and oranges from the perspective of the consumer, and thus it did not enjoy a dominant position as it was not free from competitive pressures, taking into account that any producers of other fruits were able to challenge its performance. Further, United Brands argued that the banana market was seasonal and thus affected by the availability of other fresh fruits in the summer. The Commission decided that bananas were not part of a wider product market encompassing other fruits because of their unique characteristics. The effect of this decision was that the percentage share in the

---

2508. Ibid, para. 13.
2509. S. Bishop and M. Walker, *The Economics of EC Competition Law: Concepts, Application and Measurement*, 3rd edn, 2010, London: Sweet & Maxwell, 112.
2510. Case 27/76 *United Brands v Commission* [1978] ECR 207.

relevant market held by United Brands was much greater than it would have been if the relevant product had included many other fruits.

Held:

The ECJ upheld the Commission's decision. It ruled that bananas were not substitutable by other fruits because a "banana has certain characteristics, appearance, taste, softness, seedlessness, easy handling, and a constant level of production which enable it to satisfy the constant needs of an important section of the population consisting of the very young, the old and the sick." [2511] *In addition, the seasonal arrival on the market of fruits such as apples did not have any impact on the consumption of bananas and there was almost never any fluctuation of prices for bananas. Therefore, there was no substitutability as the consumers of bananas were not likely to switch to other fruits in order to satisfy their needs, even if an increase in the price of bananas was substantial.*

28.3.1.1.2 The cellophane fallacy

The SSNIP test does not work in a situation where current prices are above competitive prices. Indeed, if current prices are monopoly prices, that is, above competitive prices, it would be unprofitable for a monopoly to increase prices further since its product would probably be replaced by its closest substitutes as there is a limit to what consumers are likely to pay. Therefore, if current prices are above competitive prices, a small increase of 5 per cent will force a switch to a product outside the relevant market. For example, if prices for railway tickets rise to that point, a significant number of consumers will drive their own vehicle or take a coach. Thus it may appear that there are many substitutes (e.g. private cars and coaches) but they are not in the same product market as the monopolist product (i.e. trains). This problem is known as the cellophane fallacy after a US case involving cellophane products.[2512] In this case the US Supreme Court accepted erroneously that cellophane was not a separate relevant market but formed part of a market for flexible packaging materials such as aluminium foil, polythene and wax paper. As a result, the Court failed to recognise that the price charged for cellophane was already a monopoly price.

The 1997 Notice recognises that the application of the SSNIP test may be inappropriate where the price of the relevant product has been determined in the absence of competition. Bearing in mind that the SSNIP test may not be reliable in a situation where the current price is already a monopoly price, in order to identify the relevant product market, the EU institutions have to take into account other factors such as excessive profit made by an undertaking and past price fluctuations, together with other evidence of market power and of the undertaking's conduct. As the UK's Guideline on Market Definition published by the Office of Fair Trading emphasised, the market definition is only a tool for assessing whether undertakings possess market power, not an end in itself.[2513]

28.3.1.1.3 Supply substitutability

Supply substitutability (the supply-side substitution) refers to substitutability of products or otherwise as assessed from the point of view of suppliers. The question to be asked is whether suppliers, who do

---

2511. Ibid, para. 31.

2512. *US v El Du Pont de Nemours & Co* [1956] 351 US 377. This problem was acknowledged by the UK Office of Fair Trading in Case CA98/14/2002 *Aberdeen Journals Ltd v Office of Fair Trading* [2002] UKCLR 740 and in Case CA98/20/2002 *BSkyB Investigation: Alleged Infringement of the Chapter II Prohibition* [2003] UKCLR 240.

2513. Para. 2.14. Available at http://www.oft.gov.uk/shared_oft/business_leaflets /ca98_guidelines/oft403.pdf (accessed 6/7/12).

not currently supply the relevant products, would be able to switch production to the relevant products and market them in the short term without incurring significant additional costs or risk in response to small and permanent changes in prices in respect of the relevant product. If this occurs, according to the 1997 Notice, "the additional production that is put on the market will have a disciplinary effect on the competitive behaviour of the companies involved" and will be taken into consideration when defining the relevant product market, given that its effect in terms of effectiveness and immediacy is equivalent to the demand substitution effect.[2514]

The important factor in assessing supply substitutability is time. If supply-side substitution would take place within a short time (usually one year, but it depends on the product), the supply-side substitution will be relevant to the definition of the RPM. Further, if a substantial investment would be needed, or undertakings which might be involved in substitution had no spare capacity, or there would be substantial costs involving the advertisement or distribution of a substitute product, that product would not normally be included in the relevant product market.

Supply substitutability was examined by the Commission in *Torras/Sarrió*.[2515]

THE FACTS WERE:

The case concerned the supply of paper for use in publishing. Only the coating used for paper determines the grade of the paper and, consequently, it is very simple to switch production from one grade to another as the same raw materials and the same plant can be used. Following from this there was, in this case, a great measure of supply substitutability given that if an undertaking increased prices for a particular grade of paper above competitive levels, other undertakings could easily and quickly change their production in order to produce that grade.

Held:

The Commission decided that the existence of supply substitutability would undermine any potential market power in that particular grade of paper. Therefore, the relevant product market was that in publishing paper generally and not that in any particular grade of publishing paper.

The assessment of supply-side substitutability was at issue in Case 6/72 *Continental Can*.[2516]

THE FACTS WERE:

Continental Can, a multinational corporation engaged in packing operations worldwide, acquired 86 per cent of the shares in Schmalbach-Lubeca-Werke AG (SLW), a maker in Germany of light metal containers for meat and fish and of bottle-sealing machines. A year

---

2514. The Notice on the Definition of the Relevant Market for the Purposes of Community Competition Law [1997] OJ C372/5, para. 20.
2515. [1992] 4 CMLR 341.
2516. Case 6/72 *Europemballage Corporation and Continental Can Company Inc. [Continental Can] v Commission* [1973] ECR 215.

later, Continental Can set up a new corporation in Delaware, Europemballage, which opened an office in Brussels and subsequently acquired 91.7 per cent of the shares of a Dutch company, TDV, which was a leading manufacturer of packaging material in the Benelux countries. Continental Can wanted to transfer the ownership of its shares in SLW to Europemballage and thus indirectly control large market shares. The Commission decided that Continental Can, through its shares in SLW, was in a dominant position in three product markets, i.e:

- *for light containers for canned meat products;*

- *for light containers for canned seafood; and,*

- *for metal closures for glass containers.*

Held:

The ECJ annulled the Commission's decision on the ground that the Commission had not assessed supply-side substitutability. It held that in order to ascertain the relevant product market, the products in question must be individualised "not only by the mere fact that they are used for packing certain products, but by particular characteristics of production which make them specially suitable for this purpose. Consequently, a dominant position in the market for light metal containers for meat and fish cannot be decisive, as long as it has not been proved that competitors from other sectors of the market for light metal containers are not in a position to enter this market, by a simple adoption, with sufficient strength to create a serious counterweight." [2517]

28.3.1.1.4   Small undertakings and narrow product markets

An undertaking can fall foul of Article 102 TFEU without being a powerful multinational and without the relevant product market being very large.

In *British Brass*,[2518] the RPM was defined very narrowly as it concerned instruments for British-style brass bands in which Boosey & Hawkes held a 90 per cent share. In this case the Commission found that the important factor was whether the market, or in this case the sub-market, "was sufficiently distinct in commercial reality". In making this finding the Commission was influenced, *inter alia*, by advertising material published by Boosey & Hawkes claiming that the market for brass band instruments for British-style brass bands was distinct from that for brass instruments generally. However, in Case T-5/02 *Tetra*,[2519] the General Court held that statements made by undertakings as to how they perceived the RPM, not supported by any other evidence, have no probative value.

The fact that some activities of an undertaking are insignificant in terms of quantity does not necessarily stop them from being caught by Article 102 TFEU. This can be seen in Case 26/75 *General Motors Continental (GMC)*,[2520] in which under Belgian law, GMC was the only undertaking allowed to provide test certificates for imports of second-hand Opel cars and was held to be in a dominant position in relation to issuing such certificates, even though it delivered merely five of them in 1973!

2517.   Ibid, para. 33.
2518.   *British Brass Band Instruments v Boosey & Hawkes* [1987] OJ L286/36.
2519.   Case T-5/02 *Tetra Laval v Commission* [2002] ECR II-4381.
2520.   Case 26/75 *General Motors Continental (GMC)* [1975] ECR 1367.

28.3.1.1.5 Power in aftermarkets

For many products a customer will need to purchase spare parts or repair/maintenance services or other supplementary (for example, cartridges for a laser printer) or complementary products (for example, nails for use with nails guns) at a later date. The market for those products/services is referred to as an aftermarket. The issue here is that an undertaking may not be in a dominant position with regard to its original product, but may, nevertheless, be regarded as being in a dominant position in respect of aftermarket products/services. Accordingly, if the RPM is defined as being confined to aftermarket products/services rather than the original products, the RPM may be very narrow and the undertaking concerned will be found to be in a dominant position in that market. This was at issue in Case 22/78 *Hugin*.[2521]

> **THE FACTS WERE:**
>
> *Hugin, a Swedish manufacturer of cash machines, supplied spare parts to Liptons Cash Registers and Business Equipment Ltd (a British undertaking specialising in reconditioning and repairing used Hugin cash registers) in the UK through its British subsidiary. Hugin held only 12 per cent of the cash registers market within the EU. However, it had a monopoly with regard to supply of its own spare parts for its cash machines. Hugin refused to continue the supply of spare parts to Liptons. The reason was that Hugin intended to enter the downstream market for servicing. Hugin argued that spare parts and maintenance services were not a separate market but formed part of the market for cash registers as a whole. The Commission decided that Hugin was in a dominant position in respect of its own spare parts as they were not interchangeable with those of other cash machines, and that Hugin abused its dominant position in the spare parts market by refusing to supply them to Liptons.*
>
> *Held:*
>
> *The ECJ upheld the Commission's finding with regard to the definition of the RPM, although it annulled the decision on the ground that the Commission had failed to show that Hugin's conduct was capable of affecting trade between Member States.*

The ruling of the ECJ in *Hugin* was followed in subsequent judgments. In Case 238/87 *Volvo*[2522] and Case 53/87 *CICRA*[2523] the ECJ confirmed that spare parts can form a market separate from that relating to the original product. Also complementary products, such as nails for use with nail guns[2524] and cartons for use with filling machines[2525] were defined as forming a separate market from that of the original product. It is important to note that the RPM in aftermarkets can only be determined after a factual inquiry into all circumstances of the case. A consumer may have already taken account of high prices of products/services in the aftermarkets when purchasing the original products. Accordingly, the high prices charged for spare parts or other supplementary or complementary products/services may constitute competitive restraints with regard to the original product market. In such a situation there is

---

2521. Case 22/78 *Hugin Kassaregister AB v Commission* [1979] ECR 1869.

2522. Case 238/87 *AB Volvo v Erik Veng (UK) Ltd* [1988] ECR 6211.

2523. Case 53/87 *CICRA v Régie Nationale des Usines Renault* [1988] ECR 6039.

2524. Case T-30/89 *Hilti AG v Commission* [1990] ECR II-163.

2525. Case T-83/91 *Tetra Pak International SA v Commission* [1994] ECR II-755.

only one RPM, not two separate product markets. This was recognised in paragraph 56 of the Commission's Notice on Market Definition.[2526] In Case T-427/08 *CEAHR*[2527] the General Court held that for there to be a distinct secondary market, it must be shown that a price increase in secondary products/services won't be able to affect the volume of sales in the primary market in such way as to render such increase unprofitable.

28.3.1.2 The Relevant Geographic Market (RGM)

In order to establish dominance it is necessary to determine the RGM, given that Article 102 TFEU requires that an undertaking must hold the alleged dominant position "within the internal market or in a substantial part of it".

The main purpose of the requirement that an undertaking must hold a dominant position "within the internal market or in a substantial part of it" is to determine whether the matter is of relevance to the EU, that is, within the scope of Article 102 TFEU, or whether it is of a local/national interest, that is, subject to national competition rules. Only conduct of undertakings which has appreciable effect on competition within the internal market can threaten the EU objectives (see Chapter 26.4.1).

Geographic markets are defined using the same criteria as those used to define the RPM. The demand side and the supply side are the main factors in determining the RGM. If customers will or can travel in order to obtain a different product in response to a 5 per cent increase in price, a hypothetical monopolist would not initiate a price increase as this would lead to a large reduction in its sales, and consequently its profit would fall.

According to the Notice a major factor in determining the geographic market is that within that market the cost and feasibility of transporting products are similar for all traders. Accordingly, when the cost of the product is low as compared with its transportation cost, for example, potatoes, the RGM is likely to be narrow, and when the cost of the product is high as compared to its transportation cost, for example, cameras, the RGM is likely to be wide. This was taken into consideration in Case T-30/89 *Hilti*,[2528] in which the General Court upheld the Commission's decision that the RGM for Hilti's nails was the entire EU for two reasons: first, there were large differences in the price of Hilti products between the Member States and, second, transport costs for nails were low. The General Court held that:

> "Those two factors make parallel trading highly likely between the national markets of [the EU]. It must therefore be concluded that the Commission was right in taking the view that the relevant geographic market in this case is [the EU] as a whole."

In Case 27/76 *United Brands*,[2529] the ECJ held that the geographic market is an area in which "the conditions of competition are sufficiently homogeneous for the effect of the economic power of the undertaking to be able to be evaluated". In this case the ECJ stated, in particular, that the RGM encompassed all Member States except France, Italy and the UK. The reason for this finding was that in all Member States except those three countries the conditions of competition were homogeneous, taking into account that in those markets there was free competition in respect of

---

2526. [1997] OJ C372/5, see also *Kyocera/Pelikan*, XXVth Report of Competition Policy (1995), point 87.

2527. Case T-427/08 *Confédération Européenne des Associations d'Horlogers-réparateurs (CEAHR) v Commission* [2010] ECR II-5865.

2528. Case T-30/89 *Hilti AG v Commission* [1990] ECR II-163, para. 81.

2529. Case 27/76 *United Brands Company and United Brands Continentaal BV v Commission* [1978] ECR 207, para. 39.

banana imports while residents of the UK, France and Italy preferred bananas coming from their former colonies.

In Case T-229/94 *Deutsche Bahn*,[2530] the General Court held that it is not necessary for the purposes of defining the RGM that the conditions of competition are homogeneous. It is sufficient that they are "similar" or "sufficiently homogeneous". This is a question of fact to be decided in each case.

In respect of the meaning of a substantial part of the internal market under Article 102 TFEU, the emphasis is put not on an area by measurement but on the economic importance of the market located in a particular part of the internal market. In Joined Cases 40–48, 50, 54–56, 111, 113 and 114/73 *Suiker Unie*[2531] the ECJ held that: "For the purpose of determining whether a specific territory is large enough to amount to 'a substantial part of [the internal market] within the meaning of Article [102 TFEU] the pattern of volume of the production and consumption of the said product as well as the habits and economic opportunities of vendors and purchasers must be considered". Following from this, it should be noted that even if the internal market in the relevant product is small in absolute terms, it may, nevertheless, be within the scope of Article 102 TFEU.

In Case 322/81 *Michelin I*[2532] the RGM was confined to the territory of the Netherlands, whereas in *Sealink Harbours*[2533] the Commission decided that the RGM was the port of Holyhead, which although confined to a small geographical area was, nevertheless, found to be a substantial part of the internal market as it was an important corridor for ferry services between Ireland and the UK.

It can be seen that in order to determine whether the RGM constitutes a substantial part of the internal market, every case will be assessed on the basis of the facts. Furthermore, the 1997 Commission Notice is very useful in providing the following definition of relevant geographic markets:

> "the area in which the undertakings concerned are involved in the supply and demand of products or services, in which the conditions of competition are sufficiently homogeneous and which can be distinguished from neighbouring areas because the conditions of competition are appreciably different in those areas."

In order to identify the RGM, criteria very similar to those used to define the RPM will be applied, although not all of them will be relevant in any one case. The criteria are:

- past evidence of diversion of orders to other areas;

- basic demand characteristics, that is whether there are local preferences based on brand, language, culture and the need for a local presence;

- views of customers and retailers;

- the current geographic pattern of purchases;

- the trade flow/pattern of shipment when ascertaining the actual geographical pattern in the context of a large number of customers; and,

- barriers and costs associated with switching orders to companies situated in other areas.

2530. Case T-229/94 *Deutsche Bahn v Commission* [1997] ECR II-1689.
2531. Joined Cases 40–48, 50, 54–56, 111, 113 and 114/73 *Suiker Unie and Others v Commission* [1975] ECR 1663.
2532. Case 322/81 *NV Nederlandsche Banden Industrie Michelin (Michelin I) v Commission* [1983] ECR 3461.
2533. *B & I Line v Sealink Harbours* [1992] 5 CMLR 255.

28.3.1.3 The Relevant Temporal Market (RTM)

The third dimension of the relevant market is that of the RTM. The existence of a temporal market affects the position of an undertaking in the market because in order to be considered as being in a dominant position, an undertaking must be capable of sustaining such position for a considerable time.

Temporal markets may refer to seasonal variations, such as summer months and winter months. *United Brands* argued that the banana market was seasonal as it was affected by the availability of other fresh fruits in the summer. Both the Commission and the ECJ disagreed.

The risk of customers changing their preferences according to seasons or the time of the day, for example in relation to peak and off-peak services (different charges being made for consumption of electricity or water or gas or telephone services during the day as against during the night), must be taken into consideration when identifying the relevant product market as it may concern, for example, off-peak supply of electricity only.[2534]

The temporal market should be assessed both from the point of view of consumers, for example, they may not consider bananas and apples as substitutes for each other, and from the point of view of suppliers' capacity, for example, they may not be able to supply fresh strawberries in winter.

28.3.2 Assessment of market power

There are different economic methods for measuring market power. The most common, and used by the Commission, was through determining the market share in the RPM of the undertaking under consideration. Although holding a high percentage of the market is likely to indicate that an undertaking has market power, the opposite may also be true. Some undertakings with high market shares may have relatively little market power if, for example, entry barriers are low. Similarly in an oligopolistic market, an undertaking may have market power while having a relatively low market share as a result of high brand differentiation. For these reasons using the size of the market share for measuring market power is a highly contested issue, full treatment of which is outside the scope of this book. In accordance with the effects-based approach to the enforcement of Article 102 TFEU, the Commission's Guidance identifies three factors which the Commission will take into consideration when assessing the market power of an undertaking:

- constraints imposed by the existing supplies from, and the position on the market of, actual competitors;

- expansion and entry constraints; and,

- constraints imposed by the bargaining power of the undertaking's customers.

28.3.2.1 Market shares and structure

The reform of EU competition rules, from 1999 onwards, entailing the application of the effects-based approach to the enforcement of Article 102, created a debate with regard to what weight should be given to the existence of a very large market share in the determination of dominance.[2535] On the one hand, it can be said that even if an undertaking holds an 80 per cent share of the relevant market, it is still in competition with the undertakings holding the remaining 20 per cent, and therefore to focus on the

---

2534. On this topic see: S. Pype, "Dominance in Peak-term Electricity Markets", (2011) 32/2 ECLR, 99.

2535. For a discussion on this topic see: A. Jones and B. Sufrin, *EU Competition Law*, 4th edn, 2011, Oxford: OUP, 325–26.

holding of a very large market share in establishing dominance is to fail to take account of the degree to which competitors can constrain the conduct of the allegedly dominant undertaking. On the other hand, the existing case law clearly indicates that high market shares have been regarded as conclusive in proving dominance.[2536]

Relying on the Guidance and the statements of the Commission in the Intel Case,[2537] its position on the relevance of market shares to finding dominance is that:

- Market shares of over 50 per cent are considered in themselves as evidence of a dominant position unless exceptional circumstances indicate otherwise.[2538]

- Market shares between 70 and 80 per cent are in themselves clear indication of a dominant position. The position of the EU courts is that a presumption of dominance arises where an undertaking has a market share of 50 per cent or more,[2539] with the result that it will be for an allegedly dominant undertaking to rebut it. However, the Commission stated that even market shares of between 70 and 80 per cent are not conclusive but subject to further verifications by other factors such as barriers to entry and expansion and buyer power (see below). This confirms the Commission's view that market shares are an important indicator of the market structure, but a high market share, alone, is not conclusive in establishing a dominant position.[2540]

- Market shares below 40 per cent are unlikely to give rise to dominance. However, market structure is also of relevance. For example, in Case C-95/04 *British Airways (BA)*,[2541] BA which held a steadily falling 39.7 per cent of the market was regarded as being in a dominant position given that its largest competitor had only 5.5 per cent of the relevant market. This shows that under Article 102 TFEU there is no safe harbour below which an undertaking may not be found as being in a dominant position. This is particularly important for undertakings which are far from being monopolies. Indeed, once an undertaking is aware of its dominant position it will adjust its conduct to that position. If it is unaware, it may breach Article 102 TFEU by conduct which is normal so far as non-dominant undertakings are concerned but prohibited with regard to dominant undertakings.

28.3.2.2 Barriers to entry and expansion

Market shares indicate the current situation in the market. An undertaking may not have market power if existing competitors could easily expand or potential competitors could easily enter the relevant market. The Commission's Guidance confirms this view. As a result, the Commission will take account of whether there are barriers to expansion or entry into the market.

The definition of barriers to entry has been debated at length by lawyers and economists. There is no definition under EU competition law. Relying on the UK Office of Fair Trading's guidelines on the

---

2536. In Case T-30/89 *Hilti v Commission* [1990] ECR II-163, the General Court held that a very large share of the relevant market is in itself evidence of a dominant position. In this case it was established that Hilti had a share of between 70 and 80 per cent of the relevant market. According to the General Court, this constituted in itself a clear indication of the existence of a dominant position.

2537. COMP/37.990 para. 852.

2538. In Case C-62/86 *AKZO v Commission* [1991] ECR I-3359.

2539. Ibid, para. 60. See also Case T-57/01 *Solvay SA v European Commission* [2009] ECR II-4621, paras 277–305 and Case T-321/05 *AstraZeneca AB and AstraZeneca plc v Commission* [2010] 5 CMLR 1585, paras 242–254.

2540. See para. 15 of the Guidance.

2541. Case C-95/04 *British Airways (BA) plc v Commission* [2007] ECR I-2331.

Assessment of Market Power[2542] three types of barrier to entry can be identified. The Guidelines describe the barriers in terms of advantages of an "existing" undertaking over new entrants. The three are:

- ■ "Absolute advantage" which refers to a situation in which a new undertaking does not have equal access to important assets (for example, raw materials or intellectual property rights).

- ■ "Strategic advantage" which refers to a situation in which a new entrant will have to incur "sunk costs", that is, those which are necessary to enter the market but cannot be recovered on exit. If a new entrant expects to recover the entry costs, it will be tempted to enter a new market. However, if an undertaking already active in a market would fiercely compete with a new entrant, sunk costs may be irrecoverable and therefore prohibitive for a new entrant.

- ■ "Exclusionary behaviour". This refers to the exclusionary behaviour of an undertaking already active in a market such as predatory pricing and refusals to supply, and the extent to which that undertaking is "tying up" its distributors or retailers.

An additional important consideration in connection with barriers to entry into the market is the rate of innovation which exists in the particular market under consideration. If that rate is very high, it will be relatively easy for an undertaking to enter into a new market.[2543]

The question of barriers to entry into a market was examined in Case 85/76 *Hoffmann-La Roche*.[2544] Hoffmann-La Roche (a Swiss pharmaceutical giant) had no potential competitors in the vitamins market. Barriers to entry to that market were very high principally because of the considerable amount of capital investment necessary. Further, in assessing the barriers to entry to the vitamins market, the Commission took into consideration any unused manufacturing capacity capable of creating potential competition between manufacturers established in that market. This factor reinforced the conclusion of the Commission as to Hoffmann-La Roche's dominant position. Hoffmann-La Roche admitted that during the period covered by the contested decision, its manufacturing capacity was sufficient to meet world demand without surplus capacity placing the company in a difficult economic or financial situation.

In *Eridania/ISI*,[2545] the Commission took into consideration the potential competition when deciding that the merger between Italian undertakings operating in the industrial sugar market did not create a risk of the merged undertaking occupying a dominant position in the market. It took into account the likelihood of imports of sugar at a lower price from neighbouring areas, and the low cost of transport.

In contrast, in Case T-228/97 *Irish Sugar*,[2546] Irish Sugar argued that the Commission had failed to take into account potential competition in the industrial sugar market in Ireland. It claimed that due to the overproduction of sugar in the EU, there were many potential competitors that could supply the Irish market many times over without suffering any economic or financial difficulties. The General Court rejected this argument. The Court held that the Commission had identified the applicant's residual and potential competitors in the industrial sugar market. The Commission had determined that residual

---

2542. OFT 415, paras 5.1–5.29.
2543. See C. Ahlborn, D. Evans and A. Padilla, "Competition Policy in the New Economy: Is Competition Law Up to the Challenge", (2001) ECLR, 156.
2544. Case 85/76 *Hoffmann-La Roche v Commission* [1979] ECR 461.
2545. [1991] OJ C204.
2546. Case T-228/97 *Irish Sugar plc v Commission* [1999] ECR II-2969.

competition was very weak as only one undertaking had actually tried to import industrial sugar to Ireland and had demonstrated that potential competition was unlikely to develop, taking into account the impact of the cost of transport on imports of industrial sugar to Ireland "particularly in the absence of a load travelling in the opposite direction".

28.3.2.3 Countervailing buyer power

The Commission's Guidance provides that the Commission will take account of the bargaining power of customers of a dominant undertaking, including a situation where such an undertaking holds a high market share. This development should be welcome given that when a buyer can easily switch to competing suppliers, to promote new entry or to vertically integrate its power, important constraints are imposed on the market power of a dominant undertaking.

28.4 The concept of collective dominance

The question whether in an oligopolistic market (i.e. when a few undertakings independent from each other operate in the relevant market) Article 102 TFEU applies was examined, for the first time, by the General Court in Joined Cases T-68/89, 77/89 and 78/89 *Societá Italiana Vetro [Re Italian Flat Glass]*.[2547]

THE FACTS WERE:

Three Italian producers of flat glass, who held between them a 79 per cent to 95 per cent share of the Italian market in flat glass, agreed to share the market by allocating quotas to each other and to fix prices for flat glass. The Commission held that the undertakings had breached both Articles 101(1) and 102 TFEU.[2548] The undertakings concerned challenged the Commission's decision before the General Court.

Held:

The General Court partially annulled the Commission's decision on the ground that the Commission did not provide sufficient evidence as to dominance. However, the cumulative application of Articles 101 and 102 TFEU was not called into question. The Court emphasised that the Commission should, when dealing with Article 102 TFEU, not merely recycle the evidence used in respect of the breach of Article 101(1) TFEU, that is, deduce from the fact that the undertakings concerned held a substantial part of the market and by virtue of that fact, combined with their unlawful behaviour, claim that they collectively abused their dominant position. The Commission must clearly distinguish between the scope of application of each article and thus must carry out an independent assessment of the factual situation in the light of the requirements laid down in both Articles.

2547. Cases T-68/89, 77/89 and 78/89 *Societá Italiana Vetro [Re Italian Flat Glass] v Commission* [1992] ECR II-1403.
2548. [1989] OJ L33/44.

The Commission followed the General Court's above advice and in Cases T-24–26, 28/93 *Compagnie Maritime Belge*[2549] addressed separately breaches of Article 101(1) TFEU and infringements of Article 102 TFEU. The General Court confirmed the cumulative application of Articles 101(1) and 102 TFEU. It held that a joint dominant position consists of a number of undertakings being able together, in particular because of factors giving rise to a connection between them, to adopt a common policy in the market and to act to a considerable extent independently of their competitors, their customers and ultimately consumers.

In Case T-228/97 *Irish Sugar*,[2550] the General Court confirmed that a collective dominant position could apply to vertical relationships. At the time of the decision in that case, this concept was rather confusing; no definition was contained in the relevant legislation. It was also unclear what kind of structural or economic links between undertakings were necessary to establish collective dominance. It was clear, however, that introduction of the concept of joint dominance was to assist the Commission in tackling the problem of oligopolistic markets in which undertakings, without entering into prohibited agreements or concerted practices, adjust their conduct with their competitors in a manner advantageous to both parties but disadvantageous to their customers and to consumers generally.

The uncertainty was partially resolved when it became apparent that the concept of collective dominance has the same meaning under Article 102 TFEU as it has under the Merger Regulation[2551] (see Chapter 29.3). It is important to note, however, that under Article 102 TFEU collective dominance is assessed retrospectively while under the Merger Regulation a prospective analysis of the relevant market is required in order to decide whether the envisaged merger will lead to the creation, or strengthening of, a collective dominance.

The most important judgment on collective dominance is that delivered by the General Court in Case T-342/99 *Airtours/First Choice*.[2552] In paragraph 62 of the judgment the Court agreed with the applicants that three conditions are necessary for a finding of collective dominance:

- Mutual awareness of the colluding parties concerning the adoption and execution of the common policy;

- Sustainability, which means that there must be a retaliatory mechanism put in place which secures unity within an oligopoly and thus dissuades its members from deviating from their common policy adopted in the relevant market; and,

- An absence of competitive constraints, so allowing undertakings within a dominant oligopoly to act independently of their customers and consumers, actual or potential.

Collective dominance thus defined is based on tacit co-ordination between the undertakings concerned and not on any structural[2553] or economic links[2554] between them, although when such links exist they facilitate a finding of collective dominance.

2549. Cases T-24–26, 28/93 *Compagnie Maritime Belge and Others v Commission* [1996] ECR II-1201, upheld by the ECJ in Joined Cases C-395/96P and C-396/96P *Compagnie Maritime Belge Transports SA v Commission* [2000] ECR I-1365. See also Cases C-68/94 and C-30/95 *France and Others v Commission (Kali and Salz)* [1998] ECR I-1375.

2550. [1999] ECR II-2969; Case T-374/00 *Verband der Freien Rohrwerke and Others v Commission* [2003] ECR II-2275, para. 121.

2551. See: Joined Cases C-68/94 and C-30/95 *France and Others v Commission (Kali & Salz)* [1998] ECR I-1375 and Case T-102/96 *Gencor Ltd v Commission* [1999] ECR II-753.

2552. [2002] ECR II-2585.

2553. Supra note 2547.

2554. Supra note 2550.

On the basis of the case law, it can be said that the conditions set out in *Airtours/First Choice* will rarely be met. In *Airtours/First Choice* the General Court annulled the Commission's Decision on the ground that the Commission failed to provide convincing evidence supporting its conclusion that a proposed hostile acquisition by Airtours of First Choice would create a collective dominance of three undertakings (Airtours/First Choice, Thompson Travel Group and Thomas Cook) in the market for short-haul package holidays from the UK. In subsequent cases the Commission, after its serious reprimand by the General Court in *Airtours/First Choice*, has cautiously applied the definition of collective dominance set out in that case.[2555]

In Case T-193/02 *Piau*,[2556] the General Court found that the Commission was wrong in deciding that the Fédération Internationale de Football Association (FIFA), a Swiss-based association whose members are national associations of professional and amateur football clubs, did not hold a collective dominant position in the market for players' agents' services. Although the General Court decided that the three conditions set out in *Airtours/First Choice* were satisfied,[2557] it did not find that FIFA had abused its position of collective dominance.

It appears from the case law that the General Court has set the requisite standard of proof in respect of both a finding of a position of collective dominance and the abuse of that position, at a very high level.

It is to be noted that undertakings in an oligopolistic market are, at the same time independent from each other and interdependent. If one of them increases prices, it will lose the clear benefit it enjoys from the mirroring conduct of its competitors. It is also aware that any action to increase its share of the relevant market by, for example, dramatically reducing prices would result in a similar action taken by its competitors. Accordingly, oligopolists know that they would derive no benefit from such an action because they will all be affected by the collective reduction in price levels. In order to ensure high profits, they maintain a tacit understanding that they will take no action changing the existing situation in the relevant market. However, this will not be sufficient to breach Article 102 TFEU as there are further requirements set out the *Airtours/First Choice* test.[2558]

28.5 The concept of abuse

In the early years of the EU the issue of whether the concept of abuse covered only exploitative abuses or whether it also applied to conduct which had structural effects on the competition conditions in the relevant market was controversial.[2559] This was settled by the ECJ in Case 6/72 *Continental Can*,[2560] in which, in the context of a merger, the Court rejected the narrow interpretation of Article 102 TFEU under which only exploitative behaviour was caught by Article 102 TFEU. The ECJ interpreted

---

2555. E.g. in *UPM-Kymmenne/Haindl* COMP/M2498 [2002] OJ L233/38 and *Ernst and Young France/Anderson France* COMP/M 2816 the Commission refrained from an adverse finding, that is, that there was or would be the possibility of tacit co-ordination.

2556. Case T-193/02 *Laurent Piau v Commission* [2005] ECR II-209.

2557. [2002] ECR II-2585, paras 111–16.

2558. P. Massey, and M. McDowell, "Joint Dominance and Tacit Collusion: Some Implications for Competition and Regulatory Policy", (2010) 6/3 EuroCJ, 427 and F. E. Mezzanotte, "Using Abuse of Collective Dominance in Article 102 TFEU to Fight Tacit Collusion: The Problem of Proof and Inferential Error", (2010) 33 *World Competition*, 77.

2559. R. Joliet, *Monopolisation and Abuse of Dominant Position*, 1970, Dordrecht: Nijhof, 250–52.

2560. Case 6/72 *Europemballage Corp and Continental Can Inc v Commission* [1973] ECR 215.

Article 102 TFEU teleologically and concluded that it prohibits not only practices which may cause damage to consumers directly, but also those:

"which are detrimental to them through their impact on an effective competition structure. . . . Abuse may therefore occur if an undertaking in a dominant position strengthens such position in such a way that the degree of dominance reached substantially fetters competition."[2561]

The ECJ ruled that in the circumstances of the case, where there was no monopolistic exploitation of the market, an undertaking in a dominant position, by merging with its rival and thus strengthening its position to the possible extent of eliminating any competition in that market, was in breach of Article 102 TFEU, i.e. its conduct indirectly prejudiced consumers by impairing the competitive structure of the relevant market.

The ECJ's definition of an abuse under Article 102 TFEU was provided in Case 85/76 *Hoffmann-La Roche*,[2562] where the ECJ held that the concept of abuse is:

"an objective concept relating to the behaviour of an undertaking in a dominant position which is such as to influence the structure of a market where, as the result of the very presence of the undertaking in question, the degree of competition is weakened and which, through recourse to methods different from those which condition normal competition in products or services on the basis of the transactions of commercial operators, has the effect of hindering the maintenance of the degree of competition still existing in the market or the growth of that competition."

The case law of the ECJ on the concept of abuse can be summarised as follows.

First, in *Hoffmann-La Roche* the ECJ held that the concept of abuse is an objective concept. This means that, in general, a subjective intent, or bad faith, of a dominant undertaking to distort competition is irrelevant for the application of Article 102 TFEU,[2563] although in some circumstances intent can be used as evidence of an abuse (see Chapter 28.6.1.1). Further, conduct of an undertaking in a dominant position may be found abusive even when such conduct did not bring any financial or competitive advantage to the undertaking concerned. For example, in the *1998 World Cup* Decision,[2564] the Commission found a French body in charge of organising the 1998 World Cup in breach of Article 102 TFEU for distributing tickets in a manner which discriminated against fans who were not French. This practice did not bring any commercial or other advantages to that body.

Second, under Article 102 TFEU a dominant undertaking is allowed to compete on the merits, but is not allowed to use methods which are different from those governing normal competition in products and services based on traders' performance.[2565] This means that only "abnormal" conduct of a dominant undertaking is prohibited. The difficulty here is how to define what constitutes "normal" conduct, i.e. to establish an appropriate benchmark to decide whether a dominant undertaking competes on the merits. In this respect economists have proposed a number of tests,[2566] such as the "as efficient competitor" test; the "profit sacrifice" test; the "consumer welfare balancing" test; and the "no economic sense" test. These tests are endorsed by the Commission's Guidance.

2561. Ibid, para. 76.
2562. Case 85/76 *Hoffmann-La Roche & Co. AG v Commission* [1979] ECR 461.
2563. Case T-321/05 *AstraZeneca AB and AstraZeneca plc (AZ) v Commission* [2010] ECR II-5 CMLR 1585.
2564. [2000] OJ I5/55.
2565. Ibid, See also Case 322/81 *NV Nederlandsche Banden Industrie Michelin (Michelin I) v Commission* [1983] ECR 3461.
2566. See A. Jones and B. Sufrin, *EU Competition Law*, 4th edn, 2011, Oxford: OUP, 371.

Third, the ECJ in Case 322/81 *Michelin (No. 1)*[2567] held that an undertaking in a dominant position has a "special responsibility" towards the competitive process. It stated that:

"A finding that an undertaking has a dominant position is not in itself a recrimination but simply means that, irrespective of the reason for which it has such a dominant position, the undertaking concerned has a special responsibility not to allow its conduct to impair genuine undistorted competition on the common market."

One obvious implication of the above statement is that an undertaking in a dominant position may be in breach of Article 102 TFEU by engaging in conduct which, if carried out by a non-dominant undertaking would be lawful. Accordingly, EU competition law attaches special duties to an undertaking in a dominant position.

It has been a matter of debate whether the special responsibility imposed on a dominant undertaking increases depending upon the degree of dominance. This debate was initiated by A-G Fennelly in Joined Cases C-395 and 396/96P *Compagnie Maritime Belge*[2568] in which he introduced the concept of "super-dominance", and explained that where an undertaking enjoys a position of overwhelming dominance, "it would be consonant with the particularly onerous special obligation affecting such a dominant undertaking not to impair further the structure of the feeble existing competition". The concept of "super dominance" was, however, rejected by the ECJ in Case C-52/09 *TeliaSonera*.[2569] In this case the ECJ endorsed the view of A-G Mazák who stated that:

"the degree of market power of the dominant undertaking should not be decisive for the existence of the abuse. Indeed, the concept of a dominant position arguably already implies a high threshold so that it is not necessary to grade market power on the basis of its degree."[2570]

The ECJ confirmed that it is the nature of the abuse and not the nature of the undertaking (i.e. whether it is "merely" dominant or "super" dominant), which is relevant to the establishment of an infringement of Article 102 TFEU. This is in line with the "effects-based" approach, which requires that in order to establish whether there is an abuse the Commission will have to determine the effect of a dominant undertaking's conduct on the relevant market. The degree of the market power of a dominant undertaking is irrelevant for finding abuse as this would amount to the presumption that large market shares are anti-competitive in themselves.[2571] Further, under EU competition law, all undertakings in a dominant position, irrespective of "how dominant" they are, have a special responsibility, but EU law does not impose upon them different obligations according to the degree of their dominance.

Fourth, with the reform of enforcement of Article 102 TFEU, the Commission and the ECJ have emphasised that the purpose of Article 102 TFEU is to protect the competitive process for the benefit of consumers rather than competitors. This entails that competitors which are not as efficient as a dominant undertaking are not protected by Article 102 TFEU.

Fifth, in order to establish an abuse it is sufficient to show that the practice has a potential anti-competitive effect. It is not necessary to show that the practice has actual anti-competitive effect.[2572]

2567. Case 322/81 *NV Nederlandsche Banden Industrie Michelin (Michelin I) v Commission* [1983] ECR 3461, para. 57.

2568. Joined Cases C-395 and 396/96P *Compagnie Maritime Belge and Others v Commission* [2000] ECR I-1365.

2569. Case C-52/09 *Konkurrensverket v TeliaSonera Sverige AB* [2011] ECR I-527.

2570. See Opinion of A-G Mazák, para. 41.

2571. See E. Szyszczak, "Controlling Dominance in European Markets", (2011) 33 Fordham Intl L.J., 1738, 1758. Many commentators submit that from an economic perspective the concept of "super dominance" is flawed and introduces uncertainty in the application of Article 102 TFEU: R. O'Donoghue and A. J. Padila, *The Law and Economics of Article 82*, 2006, Oxford: Hart Publishing, 167–68.

2572. Case C-280/08 P *Deutsche Telekom v Commission* [2010] ECR I-9555.

Sixth, Article 102 TFEU applies only when an abuse committed by a dominant undertaking has an appreciable effect on trade between Member States (see Chapter 26.4.1).

Seventh, Article 102 TFEU, unlike Article 101(3) TFEU, makes no provision for exemptions. However, the Commission and the EU judicature accept that conduct that would otherwise constitute an abuse may be outside the scope of Article 102 TFEU if an undertaking in a dominant position has objective justification for its conduct and if it has behaved in a proportionate way. Additionally, the Commission in its Guidance stated that a dominant undertaking may justify its conduct by demonstrating that it has produced substantial efficiencies which outweigh any anti-competitive effects on consumers. The test set out in para. 30 of the Commission's Guidance is similar to that contained in Article 101(3) TFEU (see Chapter 27.8). The burden of proof is on the dominant undertaking alleging objective justifications and/or the existence of efficiencies.

Eighth, Article 102 TFEU applies to a situation where an undertaking is in a dominant position in one market but commits an abuse in a different market in which it is not dominant, e.g. Chapter 28.6.1.3.

28.5.1 Categories of abuses

Article 102 (a)–(d) TFEU sets out a non-exhaustive list of various types of prohibited behaviour. It is always possible to add to that list. For example in Case T-321/05 *AstraZeneca (AZ)*,[2573] the General Court held that AZ, the Anglo-Swedish pharmaceutical group active worldwide in the sector of inventing, developing and marketing innovative pharmaceutical products, committed two abuses of its dominant position:

■ The first consisting of making misleading representations to the patent offices and national courts of several Member States in order to obtain extended patent protection for Losec (the ulcer drug developed by AZ), which would allow AZ to block or delay its competitors' market entry for generic versions of Losec.

■ The second consisting of the submission of requests for deregistration of the marketing authorisations for Losec capsules in Denmark, Norway and Sweden combined with the withdrawal from the market of Losec capsules and the launch of Losec MUPS tablets in those three countries. The purpose of deregistration was to delay the marketing of generic versions of Losec by AZ's competitors.[2574]

Most commentators divide abuses as follows:

■ exclusionary abuses: these are aimed at foreclosing the relevant market;

■ exploitative abuses: these occur when an undertaking is, at the expense of customers or consumers, using its economic power to obtain benefits or to impose burdens which are not obtainable, or imposable, within normal competition on the merits; and,

■ discriminatory prices: these occur when a dominant undertaking treats its customers in a dissimilar manner without costs based or legally acceptable justification.

Additionally, reprisal abuses are within the scope of Article 102 TFEU. They occur when the conduct of an undertaking in a dominant position is directed at injuring another undertaking in order to punish

---

2573. Case T-321/05 *AstraZeneca AB and AstraZeneca plc (AZ) v Commission* [2010] ECR II-2805.

2574. The deregistration of marketing authorisations for Losec capsules had the effect of preventing the use by AZ's competitors of a simplified authorisation procedure and thus created obstacles to the market entry of generic products and to parallel imports. As a result, the use of deregistration procedures by AZ was outside the scope of competition on the merits and constituted an abuse under Article 102 TFEU.

it, usually for what the undertaking in a dominant position considers as "disloyal" conduct towards it. The best example is provided in Case 27/76 *United Brands*,[2575] in which United Brands decided to punish its Danish distributor Olesen, who promoted a competitive brand of banana, by refusing to supply Olesen with its "Chiquita" banana. The ECJ held that the punitive action of United Brands was out of proportion to the alleged "disloyal" conduct of Olesen and decided that an undertaking in a dominant position was not allowed to refuse to supply a long-standing distributor, so long as the distributor's orders placed with the supplier remained within the normal range.

An abuse may be, at the same time, exploitative; exclusionary; and, reprisal.

28.6 Exclusionary abuses

The Commission's Guidance defines anti-competitive foreclosure as a situation "where effective access of actual or potential competitors to supplies or markets is hampered or eliminated as a result of the conduct of the dominant undertaking whereby the dominant undertaking is likely to be in a position to profitably increase prices to the detriment of consumers".[2576]

This definition encompasses two elements:

- ▪ Foreclosure. The concept of foreclosure is understood as a situation where "access of actual or potential competitors to supplies or markets is hampered or eliminated". To prove anti-competitive foreclosure the Commission must establish that foreclosure has actually occurred or is likely to occur. Paragraph 20 of the Guidance states that in deciding whether the allegedly abusive conduct is likely to lead to anti-competitive foreclosure the Commission must submit cogent and convincing evidence. Paragraph 20 lists factors which will be taken into account in the determination of a credible risk of foreclosure. Those factors are:

  - the position, on the relevant market, of the dominant undertaking;
  - the conditions on the relevant market;
  - the position of the dominant undertaking's competitors;
  - the position of the customers or input suppliers, i.e. those with which the dominant undertaking has concluded exclusive supplies arrangements;
  - the extent of the alleged abusive conduct;
  - possible evidence of actual foreclosure; and,
  - direct evidence of any exclusionary strategy.

  However in some situations, i.e. where anti-competitive conduct may be inferred, the Commission will not carry out a detailed assessment of the likely consumer harm caused by anti-competitive conduct based on the factors mentioned in para. 20. This occurs in particular, "if it appears that the conduct can only raise obstacles to competition and that it creates no efficiencies". The Guidance provides two examples of conduct that it considers to be within this category. First, when a dominant undertaking prevents its customers from testing the products of competitors (either by making this a condition of sale or by offering payment not to test competitors' products). Second, when a dominant undertaking pays a distributor or a customer to delay the introduction of a competitor's product.

- ▪ Consumer harm. This occurs when conduct of the dominant undertaking "is likely to be in position to profitably increase prices, to the detriment of consumers" once its competitors are

---

2575. Case 27/76 *United Brands v Commission* [1978] ECR 207.
2576. Supra note 2494, para. 19.

eliminated. The concept of "consumer harm" is the main factor distinguishing anti-competitive foreclosure from foreclosure arising from competition "on the merits". The exclusion of competitors, being a preliminary step, to the exploitation of consumers, is therefore a key element in the assessment of adverse impact on consumer welfare.

The Guidance distinguishes between "price-based" and "non-price-based" exclusionary conduct (see below) of a dominant undertaking.

28.6.1 Price-based exclusionary conduct and the "as efficient competitor" test

The Guidance states that the Commission will intervene "where the conduct concerned has already been or is capable of hampering competition from competitors which are considered to be as efficient as the dominant undertaking".[2577] This indicates that the Commission will use the test of hypothetical rivals that are "as efficient" (the AEC test) as the dominant undertaking in order to determine whether the "price-based" conduct of a dominant undertaking leads to foreclosure. If a rival is less efficient the Commission will normally assume that foreclosure results from mere competition on merits and thus is not anti-competitive. However, this is subject to an exception. In some circumstances the Commission will depart from the AEC test, i.e. when the relevant market is one in which network and/or learning effects are important. In such a situation the Commission will use the hypothetical prospective entrant standard. Departures from the AEC test have been criticised as introducing uncertainty in that a dominant undertaking will not be able to assess whether its conduct is potentially exclusionary and this may lead to its overly cautious response to competition. This could result in higher prices to consumers. Further, some authors have criticised the use of the AEC test on the basis that a failure to protect a less efficient rival may have negative effects on consumers, in particular the presence of a less efficient rival on the market may constitute a competitive constraint on the market power of a dominant undertaking and thus prevent it from raising prices and reducing consumer surplus.[2578]

In order to determine whether a hypothetical rival is "as efficient" as the dominant undertaking the Commission will examine economic data relating to cost, and sales prices. This will require detailed analyses of sufficiently reliable data. Paragraph 25 of the Guidance states that "where available, the Commission will use information on the costs of the dominant undertaking itself".

The Guidance identifies two cost benchmarks in order to determine whether a dominant undertaking's pricing should be regarded as exclusionary. These are:

- average avoidable cost (AAC);[2579] and,

- long-run average incremental cost (LRAIC).[2580]

Paragraph 26 of the Guidance explains that failure to cover AAC indicates that the dominant undertaking is sacrificing profits in the short term (the undertaking is not recovering its fixed and variable costs) and

---

2577. Ibid, para. 23.

2578. I. Lianos, "The EU Commission's Guidance on Exclusionary Abuses: A Step Forward or a Missed Opportunity", available at http:/ssm.com/Abstract=1398943 (accessed 27/02/11).

2579. AAC is the average of the costs that could have been avoided if the undertaking had not produced a discrete amount of (extra) output which is allegedly the subject of abusive conduct. In most cases AAC and the average variable cost (AVC) are the same. AVC refers to a firm's variable costs such as the costs of input or energy used in the production process divided by the quantity of output produced. Average fixed costs refer to the fixed costs of production such as property taxes and rents, divided by the quantity of output produced.

2580. In footnote 18 of the Guidance the Commission gives the following definition of LRAIC: "the average of all the (variable and fixed) costs that a company incurs to produce a particular product".

that an equally efficient rival could not serve the targeted customers without incurring a loss. LRAIC is usually above AAC. This is because in contrast to AAC (which only includes fixed costs incurred during the period under examination), LRAIC includes product specific fixed costs incurred before the period in which allegedly abusive conduct took place. Failure to cover LRAIC indicates that the dominant undertaking is not recovering all the (attributable) fixed costs of producing the goods or services in question and that an equally efficient competitor could be eliminated from the market.

28.6.1.1 Predatory prices

Predatory pricing refers to a situation where a dominant undertaking sets prices below costs over a long enough period of time in order to drive competitors out of the market or obstruct potential competitors from entering the market, with the objective of solidifying its market position and obtaining long-term profit. The practice is profitable because a dominant undertaking after predation can recoup its short-term lost profits (referred to as "sacrifice") and obtain a long-term profit by raising and maintaining anti-competitive prices, thereby causing consumer harm.

The leading case on predatory prices is Case C-62/86 *AKZO v Commission*[2581] in which the ECJ established the following test in order to discover whether an abuse in the form of predatory pricing existed:

■ If average variable costs (AVC) (i.e. costs that vary depending on the quantities produced), are not covered by the selling price, an abuse is "automatically" presumed;

■ If AVC are covered, but average total costs (ATC) are not, the pricing is deemed to constitute an abuse if it forms part of a plan to eliminate rivals from the relevant market.

A good example of the application of the test set out in *AKZO* is provided in the *Wanadoo* case.[2582]

THE FACTS WERE:

Wanadoo Interactive, a subsidiary of France Telecom, was charging retail prices below cost for its ADSL-based Internet access service from the end of 1999 to August 2002 in order to pre-empt the highly profitable market for high-speed Internet access. Wanadoo had every intention of eliminating rivals and was aware of the level of losses it was suffering. After the initial period of selling its services at a loss, during which the main competitors were eliminated and any potential new competitors were dissuaded from entering the market (given the level of losses they could expect to suffer in order to compete with Wanadoo), Wanadoo's market share rose spectacularly. From January 2001 to September 2002 it increased from 46 per cent to 72 per cent of the market, which market multiplied five times during that period.

Held:

The Commission found that Wanadoo charged predatory prices. They were below variable costs until August 2001 and subsequently, although AVC were covered in full, Wanadoo's pricing policy formed part of a plan to pre-empt the market in high-speed Internet access during a key phase in its development. The Commission imposed a fine of €10.35 million on Wanadoo.[2583]

2581. Case C-62/86 *AKZO Chemie BV v Commission* [1991] ECR I-3359.
2582. COMP/38.223 of 16/07/2003, [2005] 5 CMLR 120.
2583. The General Court upheld the Commission's decision in Case T-340/03 *France Télécom SA v Commission* [2007] ECR II-107.

In Case C-209/10 *Post Danmark*,[2584] the ECJ seemed to accept that in respect of an undertaking entrusted with a task of general economic interest (in this case the provision of postal services), which has already an infrastructure in place for the provision of a public/universal service, the appropriate cost criterion is the average incremental cost (AIC) rather than AVC. The A-G explained that:

> "to take the variable costs of the dominant undertaking as the only criterion could ... lead to an overestimate of its costs if it operates with high fixed costs (for example, the costs of utilisation of its network) and small variable costs". [2585]

The Guidance provides that the Commission will take AAC,[2586] as a starting point in the assessment of whether the dominant undertaking incurred or is incurring losses. Charging prices below AAC will be indicative of sacrifice and therefore such prices will be predatory. The Guidance uses LRAIC instead of ATC.[2587] If prices are above AAC but below LRAIC, the Commission will assess, on a case-by-case basis, whether there is evidence of predatory strategy on the part of the undertaking concerned. Prices above LRAIC will normally not amount to predatory prices capable of foreclosing competition.

The contentious matter relating to predation is that of recoupment, i.e. the ability of a dominant undertaking to obtain additional profits that more than offset profit sacrifices stemming from predatory pricing. It is accepted by economists that predation only makes sense if the alleged predator expects to recoup short-term losses which it has incurred by the long-term profits to be earned once its rivals are destroyed.[2588] Despite the views of economists, under Article 102 TFEU recoupment is not required for establishing predatory conduct.[2589] This is different from the position of US antitrust law which requires recoupment for a finding of predatory pricing.[2590]

28.6.1.2 Rebates

Rebates granted by a dominant undertaking are not in themselves in breach of Article 102 TFEU. They constitute a form of price competition and encourage a customer to do business with a supplier on a long-term basis. A rebates system which seeks to tie dealers to an undertaking in a dominant position by granting advantages which are not based on a countervailing economic advantage, and to prevent those dealers from obtaining their supplies from the undertaking's competitors infringes Article 102 TFEU. Such rebates are loyalty-inducing rebates and have exclusionary effect. Under Article 102 TFEU the grant of a discount must be based on economic considerations.[2591]

Article 102 TFEU is breached by the giving of rebates only if they are anti-competitive, that is, if they tend to remove or restrict the buyers' freedom to choose their sources of supply, or to bar

---

2584. Case C-209/10 *Post Danmark A/S v Konkurrencerådet* (judgment of 29/3/12 (NYR)).

2585. Ibid, para. 34.

2586. AAC is normally identical to AVC, but in some situations, AAC will capture costs that are fixed. The following example illustrates this point. If a firm decides to expand its production and purchases a licence for using a patent this will not be part of AVC because the cost of purchase does not vary with output. Accordingly, the increase in fixed costs attributable to acquisition of the licence is avoidable and thus will be part of AAC.

2587. ATC and LRAIC are identical for an undertaking producing only one product. In respect of a multi-product undertaking with economies of scope LRAIC will be lower than ATC for each product.

2588. See S. Bishop and M. Walker, *The Economics of EC Competition Law: Concepts, Application and Measurement*, 2010, 3rd edn., London: Sweet and Maxwell, 308–10.

2589. See Case C-202/07 *France Telecom SA v Commission* (judgment of 2/4/09 (NYR)), para. 113; and the Commission's decision in *Wanadoo Interactive*, COMP/38.233, at 335.

2590. *Pacific Bell Telephone v LinkLine Communications Inc* 555 US (2009).

2591. Case 322/81 *NV Nederlandsche Banden Industrie Michelin v Commission* (*Michelin I*) [1983] ECR 3461.

competitors from access to the market, or to apply dissimilar conditions to equivalent transactions with other trading partners, or to strengthen a dominant position by distorting competition.[2592] Any discount system must also be non-discriminatory. This was explained in Case C-163/99 *Portugal v Commission (Landing Fees at Portuguese Airports)*.[2593]

THE FACTS WERE:

Portugal set up a scheme for granting discounts on landing fees to airlines depending on the number of planes they landed. In fact only two airlines, both Portuguese, qualified for the highest rate discount.

Held:

The ECJ held that a non-abusive rebates system must be non-discriminatory in fact. The Court emphasised that while it was inherent in any quantity rebates system that the largest buyers obtained the highest price reduction, nevertheless the system could be discriminatory if it set out thresholds that only a few very large users could reach and which gave them disproportionate rewards.

The very strict approach to the treatment of discounts and rebates under Article 102 TFEU, which has been widely criticised as not taking account of economic reality, was confirmed and expanded by the General Court in *Michelin II*[2594] and in *British Airways*.[2595] In *Michelin II* the General Court found Michelin in breach of Article 102 TFEU by applying to its dealers a complex system of rebates, discounts and various financial benefits whose main objective was to tie resellers to it and to entrench its dominant position.

The Commission's Guidance responds to the above-mentioned criticism. The Commission makes clear that it will intervene if rebates are likely to lead to anti-competitive foreclosure of actual or potential competitors "as efficient" as the dominant undertaking. The Commission lists factors which it will take into account when analysing potential anti-competitive foreclosure.[2596] The Guidance makes a distinction between single-product rebates and multi-product or bundle rebates. Bundle rebates are discussed in the Guidance in respect of tying, but it seems more logical to examine them in this section.

With regard to single-product rebates, the Commission will use the effective-price test, a variant of the AEC test, to determine what "effective price" a competitor would have to offer in order to compensate a customer for the loss of rebates if the customer would switch part of its demand (referred to in the Guidance as the "relevant range") in the relevant time period to a competitor of the dominant undertaking. Paragraph 41 of the Guidance states that "The effective price that the competitor will have to match is not the average price of the dominant undertaking, but the normal (list) price less the rebate the customer loses by switching, calculated over the relevant range of sales and in the relevant period of time".

2592. Ibid.
2593. Case C-163/99 *Portugal v Commission (Landing Fees at Portuguese Airports)* [2001] ECR I-2613.
2594. Case T-203/01 *Manufacture Française des Pneumatiques Michelin v Commission (Michelin II)* [2003] ECR II-4071.
2595. Case T-219/99 *British Airways v Commission* [2003] ECR II-5917.
2596. Supra note 2494, paras. 38 et seq.

The Guidance makes a distinction between a "non-contestable portion" and "contestable portion" of the demand of each customer. The non-contestable portion of the demand refers to the amount that a customer would in any event purchase from the dominant undertaking because there is no proper substitute whilst a contestable portion refers to the portion of the customer's demand for which substitutes are available elsewhere.

The determination of the relevant range depends on the facts of each case, and whether the conditional rebate is incremental (i.e. given on purchases made in excess of those required to achieve the threshold) or retroactive (i.e. given retrospectively on all purchases made in the reference period after the threshold is reached). For incremental rebates, the relevant range is normally the incremental purchases which the customer is considering to make from an undertaking that competes with the dominant undertaking. For retroactive rebates, it will generally be relevant to assess in the specific market context how much of a customer's purchase requirements can realistically be switched to a competitor (the "contestable portion").

The Commission will not intervene if the "effective price", i.e. the price charged by a competitor for the relevant range, is higher or equal to the dominant undertaking's LRAIC for the relevant range. If the effective price is below LRAIC of the dominant undertaking the rebate scheme is likely to foreclose an equally efficient competitor. If the effective price is between AAC and LRAIC, the Commission will examine additional factors to establish whether the rebates scheme will affect entry and expansion of an as efficient competitor. In this respect, paragraph 44 of the Guidance states: "the Commission will investigate whether and to what extent competitors have realistic and effective counterstrategies at their disposal, for instance their capacity to also use a 'non contestable' portion of their buyers' demand as leverage to decrease the price for the relevant range. Where competitors do not have such counterstrategies at their disposal, the Commission will consider that the rebate scheme is capable of foreclosing equally efficient competitors".

With regard to bundle rebates, paragraph 60 of the Guidance states that the Commission will not intervene if the incremental price that customers pay for each of the dominant undertaking's products in the bundle, including the bundled product, remains above LRAIC of the dominant undertaking.

28.6.1.3 *Margin or price-squeeze*

A "margin-squeeze" leads to anti-competitive foreclosure when a dominant undertaking in an upstream market which supplies goods or services to its rivals, who use them to compete with that dominant undertaking in one or more downstream market, squeezes its downstream rivals by charging prices which do not allow as efficient rivals as the dominant undertaking to make a living profit. As a result of the upstream price (which is set by the dominant undertaking) the prevailing price in the downstream market is such that a rival or potential rival is forced out of the downstream market.

The Guidance treats margin squeezes and refusals to supply as one and the same thing. However, the ECJ in Case C-280/08P *Deutsche Telecom*[2597] and in Case C-52/09 *TeliaSonera*[2598] confirmed that a margin squeeze is an entirely separate abuse, i.e. independent from that of refusal to supply. In Case C-52/09 *TeliaSonera*,[2599] the ECJ provided a test for determining the circumstances in which a price squeeze will constitute an abuse. The ECJ used the "as efficient competitor test" to determine the level of margin squeeze of competitors. It accepted the proposition that unlawful margin squeeze takes place where competitors would need to offer goods/services either at a loss, or "at artificially reduced levels

---

2597. Case C-280/08P *Deutsche Telekom AG v Commission* [2010] ECR I-9555.
2598. Case C-52/09 *Konkurrensverket v TeliaSonera Sverige AB* [2011] ECR I-527.
2599. Ibid.

of profitability". The Court also established that it is necessary to demonstrate anti-competitive effect, or at least potential anti-competitive effect, of the practice on the relevant market. The Court found that when establishing whether a margin squeeze infringes Article 102 TFEU:

- it is irrelevant whether the dominant undertaking is dominant in the downstream market;

- it is irrelevant whether the dominant undertaking has a legal obligation to supply its downstream competitors;

- it is irrelevant whether customers to whom the margin squeeze is applied are new or existing customers of the dominant undertaking;

- the degree of dominance is irrelevant;

- the inability to recoup losses by a dominant undertaking is irrelevant; and,

- the fact that the relevant market concerns new technology as opposed to established technology is irrelevant.

28.6.2 Non-price-based exclusionary conduct

Examples of non-price-based exclusionary conduct are examined below.

28.6.2.1 Tying and bundling

In tying arrangements an undertaking makes customers purchase not only one product/service which they want to purchase but obliges them to buy an additional item, or items, or service whether they want to do this or not. Thus, the purchase of the main product/service (the tying product) is conditional upon the purchase of another product/service (the tied product). In bundling the additional product is already incorporated in the main product. In both tying and bundling the customer has no choice other than to buy both products/services or not to buy at all.

Tying, in the context of Article 102 TFEU, was examined in depth in Case C-333/94P *Tetra Pak II*.[2600] In this case the ECJ held that when an undertaking in a dominant position makes the purchase of one product (the tying product) conditional on the purchase of a second product (the tied product), this may amount to an abuse, even though such sales are in conformity with commercial usages and even though the two products are closely associated, unless the "natural link" between them can be objectively justified. Tetra Pak argued that both products (that is, the carton-filling machinery and the requisite cartons for milk products) constituted an "integrated service". The ECJ rejected this argument. It held that it would be justified to consider the manufacturing equipment and the cartons as forming a natural link, and thus being treated as an integrated service only if there was no other independent manufacturer specialising in the production of non-aseptic cartons or if it was impossible for other manufacturers to start producing non-aseptic cartons for reasons relating to intellectual property rights.

The above was confirmed in Case T-30/89 *Hilti*,[2601] in which the General Court held that Hilti abused its dominant position by requiring the end users or distributors of its patented cartridge strips to buy nails, thus "tying" cartridge strips and nails. The argument submitted by Hilti that its tying arrangement was necessary for the protection of users against injury was rejected by the General Court as not

---

2600. Case C-333/94P *Tetra Pak International SA v Commission* [1996] ECR I-5951.

2601. Case T-30/89 *Hilti AG v Commission* [1990] ECR II-163 and upheld by the ECJ in Case C-53/92P *Hilti AG v Commission* [1995] ECR I-667.

sufficient to objectively justify the tie. In many tying arrangements the owner of the "tying" product refuses to supply a customer who wishes to buy the tying product but not the "tied" product.

In the *Microsoft* case,[2602] the Commission clarified its approach to the matter of tying. The Commission found that Microsoft by tying Windows Media Player (WMP) to desktop operating systems (OS) was in breach of Article 102(d) TFEU. This was an example of technical tying, which occurs where the tied product is physically integrated into the tying product, so that it is impossible to buy one product without the other. In *Microsoft*, the Commission set out the criteria (which criteria apply to both tying and bundling) which have to be satisfied for an abuse under Article 102(d) TFEU to be established. These criteria are:

(i) The tying and tied goods must not be within the same product market. In *Microsoft* the Commission found that there were two separate product markets, one for OS and one for WMP;

(ii) The undertaking concerned must be in a dominant position in the tying product market. In this respect Microsoft was in a position of "super-dominance" in the OS market.

(iii) The undertaking concerned does not give customers a choice to obtain the tying product without the tied product. WMP was sold as a package with OS. Users could not get OS without WMP. Therefore, as the Commission stated, the issue was not whether users were forced to use WMP, but whether they had the choice to get OS without WMP. As WMP was a built-in feature of OS, obviously consumers had no choice. The argument of Microsoft that the customers were not required to pay separately for WMP was rejected; and,

(iv) The tying must foreclose competition. The Commission stated that:

> "tying WMP with the dominant Windows makes WMP the platform of choice for complementary content and applications which in turn risks foreclosing competition in the market for media players. This has spillover effects on competition in related products such as media encoding and management software (often server-side), but also in client PC operating systems for which media players compatible with quality content are an important application. Microsoft's tying practice creates a serious risk of foreclosing competition and stifling innovation."[2603]

The Commission established that the above criteria were met in *Microsoft*. It was left to Microsoft to attempt to show that the efficiencies of tying prevailed over the harm to competition. The argument of Microsoft was that the pro-competitive effects of tying, that is, distribution efficiency, platform efficiency, the desirability of one unique media player worldwide, and so on, outweighed the harm to competition. The Commission stated that these argued benefits of tying could be achieved in the absence of Microsoft tying WMP with OS. The major benefit, according to the Commission was "Microsoft's own profitability" which, being disproportionate to the anti-competitive effect of tying, could not be accepted as an objective justification. It is to be remembered that the burden of proof to establish an objective, proportional justification is on the undertaking concerned.

Finally, the Commission (relying on the judgments in *Michelin II*[2604] and *British Airways*[2605]) assessed the potential effect of tying in the light of the probability of, and the possible magnitude of, harm to competition and established that there was a reasonable likelihood that tying WMP with OS would lead

---

2602. COMP/C3/37.792 [2005] 4 CMLR, p. 965.

2603. Ibid, para. 842.

2604. Case T-203/01 *Manufacture Française des Pneumatiques Michelin [Michelin II] v Commission* [2003] ECR II-4071.

2605. Case T-219/99 *BA v Commission* [2003] ECR II-5917.

to a lessening of competition, so that if the tying were to continue, the maintenance of an effective competition structure in the relevant product market would not be ensured in the foreseeable future.

Microsoft was ordered:

- To prepare and market a version of its OS without WMP, although it was allowed to continue selling OS bundled with WMP.

- To reveal to server software rivals complete interface information that would allow the interconnection of server terminals with a central computer using Microsoft's OS. Accordingly this would allow rivals to design compatible products.

- To pay a record fine of €500 million.

The Commission's decision was upheld by the General Court.[2606]

The Commission's Guidance confirms the criteria used in *Microsoft* as decisive in the determination of anti-competitive foreclosure. The Guidance sets out the distinct products test as follows: "Two products are distinct if, in the absence of tying or bundling, a substantial number of customers would purchase or would have purchased the tying product without also buying the tied product from the same supplier, thereby allowing stand-alone production for both the tying and the tied product".[2607]

In order to show that products are distinct the Commission will use direct evidence, i.e. based on the choice of customers in that when they have a choice to purchase the tying and the tied product from different sources of supply they will choose to do this, and indirect evidence such as the presence on the market of undertakings which manufacture and sell the tied product without the tying product, or the fact that undertakings with little market power, particularly in a competitive market, tend not to tie or not to bundle such products.

28.6.2.2   Exclusive dealing

Exclusive sales or exclusive purchasing agreements aim at creating an obligation or an incentive as a result of which the buyer makes all of its purchases on the relevant market from one dealer alone. This is exemplified in Case 85/76 *Hoffmann-La Roche*.[2608]

THE FACTS WERE:

Under an exclusive purchasing agreement 22 of Hoffmann-La Roche's largest buyers of vitamins had agreed to acquire all or most of their vitamin requirements from that company.

Held:

The ECJ held that:

"an undertaking which is in a dominant position on a market and ties purchasers – even if it does so at their request – by an obligation or promise on their part to obtain all or most of their

---

2606.   Case T-201/04 *Microsoft Corp. v Commission* [2007] ECR II-3601.
2607.   Supra note 2494, para. 51.
2608.   [1979] ECR 461. Similar conclusions were reached by the Commission in *Soda-Ash-ICI* [2003] OJ L10/33, para. 142, in which the obligation or promise by customers to obtain the whole or substantially the whole of their requirements from Soda-Ash-ICI constituted an abuse.

> requirements exclusively from the said undertaking abuses its dominant position within the meaning of [Article 102 TFEU], whether the obligation in question is stipulated without further qualification or whether it is undertaken in consideration of the grant of a rebate."

Indeed, exclusive purchasing or dealing agreements may lead to the foreclosure of a market if purchasers are tied to an undertaking enjoying a dominant position. In such circumstances the ability of new competitors to enter the market is restricted as well as the ability of the existing competitors to expand their market share.[2609]

The Guidance states that the Commission will concentrate on cases where consumers, as a whole, do not benefit as a result of an exclusive purchasing obligation. This will, in particular, occur where there are many customers and the exclusive purchasing obligations imposed by a dominant undertaking, taken together, will have the effect of preventing the entry or expansion of competitors. Other factors (mentioned in para. 20 of the Guidance) will also be taken into account. In general, the likelihood of anti-competitive foreclosure will increase the longer the duration of the exclusive purchasing agreement. However, in a situation where the dominant undertaking is an unavoidable trading partner for all or most customers, even an exclusive purchasing obligation of short duration can lead to anti-competitive foreclosure.

28.6.2.3 "Freezer exclusivity"

This relates to a practice whereby frozen goods suppliers provide retail outlets with freezers free of charge, but require that no other supplier's brand can be stored in the freezers so provided. This practice leads to the same effect as an exclusive purchasing obligation (see above).

The leading case on this topic is Case T-65/98 *Masterfoods*.[2610]

THE FACTS WERE:

HB (a wholly-owned subsidiary of the Unilever group), which was a leading manufacturer of ice cream in Ireland, for a number of years supplied its ice cream retailers free of charge with freezer cabinets on the proviso that they were used exclusively for HB products. Further, a condition was imposed that no other freezer cabinets could be used in the retailers' premises. In 1989 Masterfoods, a subsidiary of the US corporation Mars Inc, entered the Irish ice cream market. From that time a number of HB's retailers began to stock and display Masterfoods products in the freezer cabinets belonging to HB. HB insisted that its retailers comply with the exclusivity clause contained in the agreements for the supply of its freezer cabinets. Masterfoods commenced proceedings against HB before the High Court in Ireland, challenging the validity of the exclusivity clause on the grounds of Articles 101 and 102 TFEU. HB answered by bringing proceedings for an injunction to restrain Masterfoods from inducing retailers to breach the exclusivity clause. Both parties sought damages.

2609. See: D. Ridyard, "Exclusive Contracts and Article 82 Enforcement: An Effects-Based Perspective", (2008) 4 EuroCJ, 579.

2610. Case T-65/98 *Masterfoods Ltd v HB Ice Cream Ltd and HB Ice Cream Ltd v Masterfoods Ltd* [2003] ECR II-4653.

On 28 May 1992 the High Court dismissed the action brought by Masterfoods and granted HB a permanent injunction, but dismissed HB's claim for damages.

On 4 September 1992 Masterfoods appealed against that decision to the Irish Supreme Court. In parallel with these proceedings Masterfoods lodged a complaint against HB with the Commission. On 29 July 1993 the Commission in its statement of objections found HB in breach of Articles 101 and 102 TFEU. In response HB submitted a proposal to alter the distribution agreements (which proposal was never implemented).

On 11 March 1998 the Commission adopted Decision 98/531/EC (OJ (1998) L 246), which found HB in breach of Article 101(1) TFEU for imposing the exclusivity clause requiring that its retailers must have one or more freezer cabinets supplied by HB in their retail outlets and must not have freezer cabinets procured by themselves or provided by another ice-cream manufacturer, and in breach of Article 102 TFEU for inducing its retailers to enter into the above freezer cabinet agreements.

HB, which in the meantime had changed its name to Van Den Berg Foods Ltd, brought an action under Article 263 TFEU for annulment of that decision (Case T-65/98 van den Berg v Commission) and an action for the suspension of the application of Decision 98/531 until the General Court had given a ruling on the substance.

Held:

The General Court upheld the Commission's decision.

Comment:

In respect of Article 101 TFEU the General Court ruled that the effect of the agreement as a whole was to restrict competition in the market given the specific conditions of the market, the popularity of HB ice creams, HB's dominant position in the market, and the fact that retailers were unlikely to stock ice creams from various manufacturers if they were not allowed to do so in one and the same freezer. In addition, the exclusivity clause constituted a barrier to entry for new suppliers given that retailers were not inclined to accept freezers that were not free, and thus the supplier had to acquire a stock of cabinets, which represented a large investment and could dissuade it from entering the market.

With regard to Article 102 TFEU the General Court found that in the context of a competitive market the provision of freezer cabinets on a condition of exclusivity constitutes a standard practice and does not restrict competition, but the situation is different in respect of a market dominated by one trader where competition is already restricted. In a market dominated by one undertaking the exclusivity clause "has the effect of preventing the retailers concerned from selling other brands of ice cream, even though there is a demand for such brands, and of preventing competing manufacturers from gaining access to the relevant market". Therefore, by inducing retailers by those means to obtain supplies exclusively from HB, HB abused its dominant position in the market.

28.6.2.4 Refusal to deal or continue to deal with existing and potential customers and the doctrine of essential facility

It is important to make a distinction between the situation when a dominant undertaking refuses to deal with existing customers and the situation when such an undertaking decides to deny access to an essential facility, that is, when a dominant undertaking is in possession of a scarce resource or facility which cannot be duplicated, for example, access to a port, or a railway station, or other facility protected by intellectual property rights.

28.6.2.4.1 Refusal to deal or to continue to deal on a non-discriminatory basis with existing or potential customers

The principle of the freedom of contract entails that an undertaking, whether dominant or not, should be free to decide with whom it wants to do business. The importance of preserving the freedom of contract was recognised by the General Court in *Bayer*[2611] when the Court held that "refusal to supply, even where it is total, is prohibited only if it constitutes an abuse". Based on the case law it seems that a refusal will constitute an abuse if a dominant undertaking refuses to supply either its existing or new customers without some objective justification.[2612] This occurred in Joined Cases 6 and 7/73 *Commercial Solvents*.[2613]

THE FACTS WERE:

Commercial Solvents, the world's only large-scale producer of raw materials from which the drug ethambutol could be made (and as such holding a dominant position in that sector), refused to supply raw materials to Zoja, one of the three makers of ethambutol in the EU. The circumstances of the case were that Commercial Solvents' refusal to supply Zoja was intended to eliminate Zoja from the secondary market for Commercial Solvents (i.e. the downstream market for Commercial Solvents) where ICI, a subsidiary of Commercial Solvents, was emerging as a competitor to Zoja. The main market, that is, the upstream market of Commercial Solvents was the market for the raw materials. The secondary or downstream market was the market for the manufacture of drugs for the treatment of tuberculosis, in which market Zoja was the main competitor of Commercial Solvents' subsidiary, ICI.

Held:

The ECJ held that Commercial Solvents was in breach of Article 102 TFEU as its refusal to supply a competitor in a downstream market would result in the elimination of all competition in the downstream market.

Comment:

From the above case the so-called doctrine of essential facilities has gradually emerged, which is concerned not with refusal to supply but with access to some kind of facility or resources controlled by a dominant undertaking.

In Case 22/78 *Hugin*,[2614] Hugin refused to supply spare parts for Hugin's cash register machines to Liptons, a UK-based undertaking that services cash registers. The reason was that Hugin intended to

---

2611. Case T-41/96 *Bayer AG v Commission* [2000] ECR II-3383.
2612. *BP v Commission* [1978] ECR 1513, in this case the refusal to supply occasional customers while nevertheless supplying regular customers was objectively justified in the time of oil shortage resulting from the OPEC oil boycott in 1973.
2613. Joined Cases 6 and 7/73 *Commercial Solvents v Commission* [1974] ECR 223.
2614. Case 22/78 *Hugin Kassaregister AB and Hugin Cash Registers Ltd v Commission* [1979] ECR 1869.

enter the downstream market for servicing. The Commission found Hugin in breach of Article 102 TFEU. The ECJ did not depart from the Commission's finding that the refusal to supply was abusive, but annulled the decision on the ground that the Commission failed to show that Hugin's conduct was capable of affecting trade in the EU.

It the light of the above cases it is clear that refusals to supply an existing or a new customer,[2615] unless objectively justified, will constitute an abuse where the refusal would result in eliminating or weakening competition in the downstream market.[2616]

In *BBI/Boosey and Hawkes*[2617] and in Case 27/76 *United Brands*[2618] the refusal to supply was a retaliatory measure against an existing customer, in the first case because a distributor wanted to start a rival business, and in the second, because the distributor's conduct was considered as disloyal with regard to United Brands. Such refusals constitute abuses.

In Case T-65/89 *British Gypsum*[2619] the ECJ condemned BPB for giving priority, in a time of shortage, to "loyal" customers, i.e. those who were almost exclusively buying BPB's products over those who were normally buying plasterboard from BPB's competitors. In Case 7/82 *GVL*[2620] the refusal of GVL (the only undertaking in Germany entitled to manage services relating to secondary rights vested in performing artists and manufacturers) to conclude management agreements, with undertakings and persons residing outside Germany, constituted an abuse. The above cases confirm that a dominant undertaking has a duty to deal with customers on a non-discriminatory basis unless such action is objectively justified.

28.6.2.4.2 Refusal to deal in the pharmaceutical sector

Competition in the pharmaceutical market is of great importance to EU citizens. This is because, first, the pharmaceutical sector is a vital part of national health care systems in the Member States, and second, the market's potential for growth is increasing as EU citizens consume ever greater volumes of pharmaceutical products at a time when the average life span of these citizens is increasing in parallel with demand for a wider choice of those products at affordable prices. The market, however, has two characteristics which differentiate it from other sectors of the economy:

- The price of patented and new drugs tends to be regulated by the Member States. Often governments are the only buyers. This means that pharmaceutical companies cannot freely set prices; and,

- The structure of the market is peculiar in that the ultimate consumer (the patient) differs from the decision maker (the doctor) and often from the payer (the national insurance service or private health insurer). The decision of a doctor is not based on the price but on the therapeutic effect of the relevant drug.

In the light of the above, the issue of whether the refusal by a dominant undertaking to supply its wholesalers, in circumstances where those wholesalers could benefit from parallel trading, raised many

---

2615. *London-European-Sabena* [1988] OJ L317/47.
2616. *Napier Brown v British Sugar* [1990] 4 CMLR 196. In this case British Sugar refused to supply Napier and used other unlawful practices to weaken Napier's position in the market for consumer retail one-kilogram sugar bags, in which market Napier was a rival of British Sugar.
2617. In *BBI/Boosey and Hawkes: Interim Measures* [1987] OJ L286/36.
2618. Supra note 2575.
2619. Case T-65/89 *BPB Industries Plc and British Gypsum Ltd v Commission* [1993] ECR II-389.
2620. Case 7/82 *GVL v Commission* [1983] ECR 483.

concerns and controversies. The ECJ in Joined Cases C-468 to C-478/06 *GlaxoSmithKline*[2621] stated the position of EU competition law on the matter.

THE FACTS WERE:

GlaxoSmithKline plc, a pharmaceutical research and manufacturing company established in the UK, both warehoused products in Greece and distributed them there through its subsidiary GSK AEVE ("GSK"). Until November 2000 GSK met in full orders from Greek pharmacists and wholesalers for three drugs (Imigran, for migraine, Lamictal, for epilepsy, and Serevent, for asthma). The wholesalers had, for a number of years, supplied these products both to the Greek and other markets, particularly Germany and the UK where prices were higher than in Greece. After November 2000 GSK alleged that, as a result of a shortage in Greece of the three products due to their export by Greek wholesalers, it was forced to change its system of distribution in Greece. Under the new system GSK refused to supply the products to its wholesalers in Greece and decided to supply the products itself to hospitals and pharmacies in Greece. In February 2001 GSK resumed its supplies to wholesalers but limited them in terms of quantity. Greek wholesalers and pharmacists started proceedings against GSK for abuse of its dominant position on the Greek market. During the proceedings the Greek Court of Appeal decided that it needed an answer from the ECJ on the compatibility of the practices of GSK with Article 102 TFEU.

Held:

The ECJ held that an undertaking in a dominant position is entitled to protect its own commercial interests and if it is confronted with orders that are out of the ordinary in terms of quantity, it may refuse to meet such orders but if the orders are ordinary, any refusal to meet them will constitute an abuse prohibited by Article 102 TFEU.

Comment:

The ECJ held that Article 102 TFEU applies in the same manner to the pharmaceutical sector as to other sectors of the economy. As a result, it confirmed that there is no justification under EU competition law for various anti-competitive practices used by the pharmaceutical industry, such as supply quotas, dual-pricing and direct-to-pharmacy distribution schemes.

The Court found that parallel trade in medical products is pro-competitive, benefits the final consumers, constitutes an important factor in market integration, and that in cases where it would result in a shortage of medical products on a given national market, it would not be for an undertaking in a dominant position, but for the relevant national authorities to resolve the situation by taking appropriate and proportionate steps. However, the ECJ accepted that an undertaking in a dominant position is allowed to refuse to meet orders which are out of ordinary but not those which are ordinary. To decide whether orders are ordinary, factors such as the previous relations between the pharmaceutical company and the wholesalers concerned, and the size of the orders in relation to the requirements of the market in the Member State concerned must be taken into account. The ECJ held that it was the task of the referring court to decide whether, in the light of the above mentioned factors, a restriction of supply by GSK was abusive.

2621. Joined Cases C-468 to C-478/06 *Sot. Lelos Kai Sia EE (C-468/06) and Others v GlaxoSmithKline AEVE Farmakeftikon Proionton* [2008] ECR I-7139.

28.6.2.5   The doctrine of essential facility

To understand the doctrine of essential facility it is necessary to determine what facilities should be considered as essential. This is done on a case-by-case basis. A-G Jacobs, in his opinion in Case C-7/97 *Oscar Bronner*[2622] stated that a facility is considered as essential if access to it is indispensable in order to compete in a related market, and duplication of that facility is impossible or extremely difficult owing to physical, geographic or legal constraints, or is highly undesirable for reasons of public policy.

Examples of essential facilities are ports,[2623] bus stations, and intellectual property rights. One of the most commented cases was the *Magill* case,[2624] which concerned intellectual property rights. In *Magill* the Irish television companies refused to supply information, which was protected by copyright under Irish law, regarding the weekly schedules of certain television channels to Magill. The ECJ held that in the "exceptional circumstances" the refusal to supply was in breach of Article 102 TFEU. These "exceptional circumstances" were that the refusal prevented the introduction of a new product, that is, a general television guide, for which there was potential consumer demand, the refusal was not based on any objective justification, and was likely to have the effect of excluding all competition in the market for television guides. Further clarifications were provided by the ECJ in Case C-7/97 *Oscar Bronner*.

THE FACTS WERE:

A dispute had arisen between two Austrian undertakings. They were: Oscar Bronner, editor, publisher, manufacturer and distributor of the daily newspaper Der Standard, which in 1994 held 3.6 per cent of the Austrian daily newspaper market in terms of circulation and 6 per cent in terms of advertising revenues, and Mediaprint Zeitungs, publisher of two daily newspapers which in 1994 held 46.8 per cent of the Austrian daily newspaper market in terms of circulation and 42 per cent in terms of advertising revenues. Mediaprint Zeitungs' two newspapers reached 53.3 per cent of the population above the age of 14 in private households and 71 per cent of all newspaper readers. Mediaprint set up a nationwide delivery system consisting of delivering the newspapers directly to subscribers in the early hours of the morning. Oscar Bronner (for financial reasons) was not able to set up a similar system of delivery on its own and had to use a postal service for delivery of its newspaper, which occurred late in the morning. Bronner sought an order requiring Mediaprint to cease its alleged abuses by including Bronner's newspaper, Der Standard, in its home-delivery service against payment of reasonable remuneration. Mediaprint refused to do this voluntarily.

Held:

The ECJ specified four conditions (which must all pertain simultaneously) under which the refusal of the dominant undertaking (Mediaprint) could not be justified:

2622.   Case C-7/97 *Oscar Bronner GmbH & Co. KG v Mediaprint Zeitungs- und Zeitschriftenverlag GmbH & Co. KG* [1998] ECR I-7791.

2623.   E.g. the port of Holyhead in *B&I Line v Sealink Harbours* [1992] 5 CMLR 255.

2624.   Cases C-241 and C-242/91P *RTE and ITP v Commission* [1995] ECR I-743 on appeal from Cases T-69–70/89 *RTE, ITP, BBC v Commission* [1991] ECR II-485, on appeal from *Magill TV Guide* [1989] OJ L78/43.

> First, if the refusal would be likely to eliminate all competition in the downstream market;
>
> Second, if such a refusal was incapable of being objectively justified;
>
> Third, if access was indispensable to carrying on business by the person requesting access; and,
>
> Fourth, if there was no actual or potential substitute for the facility to which the person requested access.
>
> **Comment:**
>
> These four conditions were not satisfied in this case and, therefore, the ECJ held that there was no abuse of a dominant position by Mediaprint. The Court emphasised that in all normal circumstances undertakings are free to decide who is to have access to their facilities and assets. Only in exceptional cases can an undertaking rely on EU competition law to gain access to such facilities. The burden of proof lies with the alleged victim.

The Commission's Guidance states that the Commission is likely to intervene in the following circumstances:

- the refusal relates to a product or service that is objectively necessary to be able to compete effectively on a downstream market;

- the refusal is likely to lead to the elimination of effective competition on the downstream market; and,

- the refusal is likely to lead to consumer harm.

28.7 Exploitative abuses

Article 102(a) TFEU prohibits the imposition of unfair purchase or selling prices or other unfair trading conditions by a dominant undertaking in order to exploit consumers. Exploitative abuses may take two forms, the charging of excessive prices and the imposition of unfair contractual terms and conditions. This section examines an abuse consisting of charging excessively high prices to customers.

28.7.1 Excessively high prices

The meaning of "unfair" price has usually been understood as referring to "excessive" prices. Prices may be considered as excessive if they allow an undertaking to sustain profits higher than it could expect to earn in a competitive market.

The definition of excessively high prices was provided by the ECJ in Case 26/75 *General Motors Continental*.[2625] In this case the ECJ held that "charging a price which is excessive because it has no reasonable relation to the economic value of the product supplied is . . . an abuse".

2625.   In Case 26/75 *General Motors Continental NV v Commission* [1975] ECR 1367.

This definition was also applied by the ECJ in Case 27/76 *United Brands*,[2626] although the Commission's finding of excessive prices was rejected by the ECJ. In *United Brands* the ECJ set out a test to be applied in order to determine whether the price was excessive. It states:

"... the questions therefore to be determined are whether the difference between the costs actually incurred and the price actually charged is excessive, and if the answer to this question is in the affirmative, whether a price has been imposed which is either unfair in itself or when compared to competing products".[2627]

Accordingly, the first limb of the test will seek to establish the profit margin achieved by the dominant undertaking, if it is found to be excessive, the second limb will be applied. The Court insisted that evidence of excessive price must be obtained objectively by means of an analysis of the relevant factors such as the cost structure and the profit margin,

The *United Brands* test was explained by the Commission in *Sundbusserne*.[2628]

THE FACTS WERE:

A Danish company, Sundbusserne, which provided ferry services for passengers between Helsingborg (Sweden) and Elsinore (Denmark), complained to the Commission that HHAB, a Swedish company owned by the City of Helsingborg, responsible for the provision of facilities and services to vessels using the port and for the determination of the fees for users, was, inter alia, charging excessive prices to ferry operators. This conclusion was based on the answer to the first question in the United Brands *test. The Commission, contrary to the submission of Sundbusserne, stated that both questions set out in the* United Brands *test must be answered and therefore even if it appeared that the difference between the revenue derived from the ferry operations through the port charge and the costs incurred by HHAB was "excessive,"*[2629] *this was not conclusive as regards the existence of an abuse. The second question also had to be answered, that is, the Commission had to decide whether or not the prices charged to the ferry operators were unfair, either when compared to other ports or in themselves. The comparison was very difficult given that HHAB held a monopoly position in the port of Helsingborg. Nevertheless, the Commission referred to various points of comparison.*

First, based on Case 30/87 Bodson,[2630] *the Commission tried to compare the prices charged by HHAB with prices charged in other ports. This approach failed because the Commission could not find a substitute product or service provided by competitors on the same relevant market. In each port conditions were different from those in the Port of Helsingborg in terms of services provided, activities and the repartition between the ship fee and the goods fee.*

Second, the Commission made a comparison between the port fees charged by HHAB to the ferry operators and those charged to cargo vessel operators. This failed as the services

---

2626.   Case 27/76 *United Brands Company and United Brands Continental BV v Commission* [1978] ECR 207.
2627.   Ibid, para. 252.
2628.   *Sundbusserne v Port of Helsingborg* COMP/A.37.792/DS of 23 July 2004; [2005] 4 CMLR 965.
2629.   It is interesting to note that according to the assessment of cost allocation submitted by HHAB to the Commission, the ferry operations were not profitable! This assessment was rejected by the Commission as being unrealistic.
2630.   Case 30/87 *Bodson v Pompes Funèbres des Regions Liberées* [1988] ECR 2479.

provided to the ferry operators market and to the cargo vessel operators market were not equivalent. Therefore it was impossible to compare the level of the charges to ferry operators with those to cargo vessel operators.

Third, the Commission compared the Port of Elsinore with the Port of Helsingborg in terms of fees charged to ferry operators. Sundbusserne argued that this was an ideal point of comparison while the Commission disagreed on the ground that the infrastructure in Elsinore, being much less developed than that in Helsingborg, explained the differing cost structures of those ports.

Fourth, the Commission returned to the first point of comparison. It decided to compare the fees charged by HHAB with the fees charged by other European ports to ferry operators. The Commission admitted that any meaningful comparison was difficult, but nevertheless this was the best it could achieve in terms of comparison. The Commission's comparison was based on the official tariff published by several European ports relating to their port charges to ferry operators.

Held:

The conclusion drawn by the Commission, on the above shaky basis, was that the difference between the costs actually incurred by HHAB and the price charged by it was not excessive. Subsequently, the Commission proceeded to the assessment of whether the port charges were unfair in themselves. The Commission took account of the relevant economic factors in the determination of the economic value of the services and facilities provided to ferry operators by HHAB. The conclusion reached by the Commission was that there was insufficient evidence to establish that the port charges had no reasonable relation to the economic values of the services provided by HHAB and, consequently, the Commission did not find the prices charged by HHAB as being unfair in themselves.

It can be said that in some circumstances prices may, at first glance, seem excessive but in fact may be justified by objective considerations.[2631] Such objective considerations include a temporary increase of demand, greater efficiency of an undertaking than that of its competitors in the relevant market, the introduction of an innovation where the profits earned are necessary in order to provide a fair return on the cost of the development of the innovation and a fair reward for the risks taken by an undertaking in developing and introducing the innovation to the market. For these reasons, normally, it is very difficult to assess whether high prices are excessive and thus amount to an abuse. For example, in 1999 the Commission started an inquiry into excessive "roaming"[2632] charges imposed by mobile phone operators in the EU. The inquiry was dropped in 2007 without any mobile operator being found guilty of charging excessive prices. Although the Commission established that on average roaming charges were four times higher than national mobile calls and that this difference could not be explained by the cost incurred by the network operator, it was unable to show analytically the

---

2631. On this topic see: L. Hou, "Excessive Prices within EU Competition Law", (2011) 7 EuroCJ, 47.

2632. Roaming relates to the use of a mobile phone when abroad. As a home network operator cannot provide a service in another country, when a person travels to another country, and in that country, receives or makes calls, the person is using the network of an operator in that country, i.e. "roaming" on a foreign network. For this, the foreign network operator charges the home network operator a wholesale rate. The home operator then charges its customer a retail price for using a mobile phone abroad.

existence of an abuse. As a result, the Commission decided to regulate roaming charges *via* secondary legislation.[2633]

Case law on excessive pricing is scarce. This paucity can be explained by three factors:

1. It is assumed that competitive forces within the relevant market can readjust excessive pricing in particular in the absence of entry and expansion barriers. New entrants will be attracted to enter the relevant market and compete with the dominant undertaking.

2. Standards for assessment of the exploitative nature of high-prices are notoriously difficult to find and to apply;[2634] and,

3. If prices are found to be excessive the issue is of how to establish the right price. In this respect competition authorities should not act as price regulators as this task should be left to specialised authorities.

Charging excessive prices will constitute an exclusionary abuse when a dominant undertaking charges excessive prices for access to an essential facility (see Chapter 28.6.2.5) or, when in the context of aftermarkets, it levies excessive prices for spare parts or complementary products.[2635]

28.8 Price discrimination

Article 102(c) TFEU states that it is an abuse for a dominant undertaking to apply "dissimilar conditions to equivalent transactions with other trading parties, thereby placing them at a competitive disadvantage".

The interpretation of this provision raises the following difficulties.

First, the concept of price discrimination applies to many practices such as rebates; tying; selective price cutting; imposition of discriminatory prices by vertically integrated undertakings on its downstream competitors; and, geographical discrimination (see below). Each practice has a different objective and thus it is impossible to establish one analytical framework that can deal with all of them appropriately.

Second, according to economists price discrimination can have beneficial effects on consumer welfare in some circumstances. To condemn all of them would be contra-productive.[2636]

Third, economists divide discriminatory practices into three categories depending on whether they create primary line injury, which injures rivals of a dominant undertaking, secondary line injury, which harms consumers and geographic discrimination, which consists of applying different prices depending on the geographical location of the customer without objective justifications, with the consequence that the internal market is divided alongside national lines. Some commentators argue that Article 102(c) should only apply to "the limited circumstances where a non-vertically integrated dominant firm price discriminates between customers with the effect of placing one or several of them at a competitive disadvantage vis-à-vis other customers (secondary line price discrimination)".[2637] Accordingly primary

---

2633. Regulation 717/2007 on Roaming in Public Mobile Communications Networks within the Community [2004] OJ L171/32.
2634. See D. Evans and J. Padilla, "Excessive Prices: Using Economics to Define Administrable Legal Rules", (2005) 1 *Competition Law and Economics*, 97.
2635. Case 238/87 *AB Volvo v Eric Veng* [1988] ECR 6211.
2636. S. Bishop and M. Walker, *The Economics of EC Competition Law: Concepts, Application and Measurement*, 3rd edn, 2010, London: Sweet & Maxwell, 252–56.
2637. D. Geradin, A Layne-Farrar, N, Petit, *EU Competition Law and Economics*, 2012, Oxford: OUP, 293.

line price discrimination and geographic discrimination should be dealt with under other provisions of the TFEU.

With regard to primary line price discrimination, the ECJ used Article 102 (c) TFEU to condemn rebate schemes in *Hoffman-La-Roche*,[2638] *Michelin (I)*[2639] and *Irish Sugar*,[2640] because they were weakening competition on the producer's market.

With regard to secondary line price discrimination, in most cases the ECJ has held a dominant undertaking in breach of Article 102(c) TFEU when it discriminated against its customers on the ground of nationality.[2641] That Article has also been applied to vertically integrated undertakings when they charged lower prices to their downstream subsidiaries than to rivals of their subsidiaries.[2642]

Case 27/76 *United Brands*,[2643] although decided a long time ago, is still one of the leading cases on Article 102 TFEU, and one which exemplifies many aspects of Article 102 TFEU. In this case the matter of geographic price discrimination was also at issue.

THE FACTS WERE:

United Brands (UB), a multinational US corporation, shipped bananas from its own plantations in South America to Rotterdam and Bremerhaven using its own ships. In both ports unloading costs were almost identical. The bananas were sold, at those ports, at prices which differed substantially to distributors from different Member States. The distributors then transported the bananas at their own cost to ripening rooms in their Member States. UB explained that it fixed the prices taking into account what the market in a particular Member State would bear. Further, under contractual arrangements between UB and its distributors, the latter were prevented from exporting green, unripened bananas. As a result, any parallel import from one Member State to another was prevented.

Held:

First, the ECJ held that United Brands' prices were discriminatory because "bananas unloaded in two [EU] ports on practically identical terms as regards costs, quality and quantity were sold to the customers at prices which differed considerably – by between 30 and 50 per cent – from one Member State to another, although the services offered were identical in each case". The ECJ rejected the explanation submitted by UB and stated that differences in prices can only be justified on the basis of objective criteria such as differences in transport costs, taxation, customs duties, labour wages, and so on.

Second, the ECJ held that the clause seeking to prevent parallel imports constituted an abuse since it limited markets to the prejudice of consumers and affected trade between Member States, in particular by partitioning national markets.

2638. Case 85/76 *Hoffmann-La Roche & Co AG V Commission* [1979] ECR 461.
2639. Case 322/81 *NV Nederlandsche Banden Industrie Michelin v Commission* [1083] ECR 3461.
2640. Case C-497/99P *Irish Sugar plc v Commission* [2001] ECR I-5333.
2641. Joined Cases C-147/97 and C-148/97 *Deutsche Post AG v Gesellschaft für Zahlungssysteme mbH GZS and Citicorp Kartenservice GmbH* [2000] ECR I-825.
2642. Case T-229/94 *Deutsche Bahn AG v Commission* [1997] ECR II-1689.
2643. [1978] ECR 207.

> **Comment:**
>
> This judgment was criticised [2644] for the following reasons:
>
> 1. Only the clause prohibiting parallel import should be condemned bearing in mind that the consequence of this clause was that the internal market was partitioned and that UB could charge discriminatory prices.
> 2. Distributors were not placed at a comparative disadvantage bearing in mind that when the market for the resale of bananas was partitioned, they were not in competition with each other.
> 3. It suggests that a dominant undertaking should charge uniform prices throughout the EU. In this respect economists submit that "price discrimination unambiguously reduces welfare only when it does not raise total output, whereas the sign of welfare change is ambiguous in all other cases". [2645] Accordingly, discrimination should not be condemned merely because some consumers are deemed to be "exploited" by having to pay higher prices than other consumers as this may have negative effects on consumer welfare. For example, if price discrimination increases sales to customers who would have been left out of the market if uniform prices had been charged and there is no decrease or likely decrease in consumer welfare, there should be no abuse under Article 102 TFEU.

Notwithstanding the above criticism, geographic price discrimination constitutes an abuse under EU law as confirmed in *Tetra Pak II*. [2646]

RECOMMENDED READING

Books
Those recommended in Chapter 26 and the following:

Etro, F. and Kokkoris, I. (eds), *Competition Law and the Enforcement of Article 102*, 2010, Oxford: OUP.

Lovdahl Gormsen, L., *A Principled Approach to Abuse of Dominance in European Competition Law*, 2010, Cambridge: CUP.

O'Donoghue, R. and Padilla, J. A., *The Law and Economics of Article 82 EC*, 2006, Oxford: Hart Publishing.

Rousseva, E., *Rethinking Exclusionary Abuses in EU Law*, 2010, Oxford: Hart Publishing.

Articles

Azevedo, J.P. and Walker, M., "Dominance: Meaning and Measurement", (2002) ECLR, 363.

Ezrachi, A. and David Gilo, D., "Are Excessive Prices Really Self-Correcting?" (2009) *Journal of Competition Law & Economics*, 1.

Faella, G. and Pardolesi, R., "Squeezing Price Squeeze Under EC Antitrust Law", (2010) 6 EuroCJ, 255.

2644. W. Bishop, "Price Discrimination under Article 86: Political Economy in the European Court", (1981) 44 MLR, 282 and L. Zanon, "Price Discrimination under Article 86 of the EEC Treaty: The United Brands Case", (1982) 31 ICLQ, 36.

2645. M. Motta, *Competition Policy: Theory and Practice*, 2004, Cambridge: CUP, 496.

2646. [1992] OJ L 72/1, paras 154, 155 and 160 and upheld by the General Court in Case T-83/91 *Tetra Pak International SA v Commission* [1994] ECR II-755 and on appeal by the ECJ in Case C-333/94P *Tetra Pak International SA v Commission* [1996] ECR I-5951.

Gohari, R.S., "Margin Squeeze in the Telecommunications Sector: A More Economics-based Approach", (2012) 35 *World Competition*, 205.

Harbord, D., and Hoehn, T., "Barriers to Entry and Exit in European Competition Policy", (1994) 14 *International Review of Law and Economics*, 411.

Hou, L., "Excessive Prices within EU Competition Law", (2011) 7 EuroCJ, 47.

Massey, P., and McDowell, M., "Joint Dominance and Tacit Collusion: Some Implications for Competition and Regulatory Policy", (2010) 6 EuroCJ, 427.

Mateus, A.M., "Predatory Pricing: A Proposed Structured Rule of Reason", (2011) 7 EuroCJ, 243.

Mezzanotte, F.E., "Using Abuse of Collective Dominance in Article 102 TFEU to Fight Tacit Collusion: The Problem of Proof and Inferential Error", (2010) 33 *World Competition*, 77.

Monti, G., "Article 82 EC: What Future for the Effects-Based Approach?", (2010) *Journal of European Competition Law & Practice*, 2.

Petit, N., "From Formalism to Effects? The Commission's Communication on Enforcement Priorities in Applying Article 82 EC", (2009) 32 *World Competition*, 485.

Pozdnakova, A., "Excessive Pricing and the Prohibition of the Abuse of a Dominant Position", (2010) 33 *World Competition*, 121.

Pype, S., "Dominance in Peak-term Electricity Markets", (2011) 32 ECLR, 99.

Ridyard, D., "Exclusive Contracts and Article 82 Enforcement: An Effects-Based Perspective", (2008) 4 EuroCJ, 579.

Vickers, J., "Market Power in Competition Cases", (2006) 2 ELJ, 3.

PROBLEM QUESTION

Smiling Fish GmbH, a German undertaking, is the largest producer of both frozen fish and vegetables in the EU. Its retailers in Ireland have been provided with free of charge freezer cabinets on the condition that no competing products are to be placed in them. Although those retailers are not contractually prevented from having other freezer cabinets in their premises, in fact, Smiling Fish's cabinets are so big that only 2 per cent of its retailers could find space to fit additional freezer cabinets into their shops.

Smiling Fish has recently introduced the following marketing strategies in order to boost its business:

A.   It pays a huge bonus to any retailer who contractually commits itself to buy all its requirements of frozen fish and vegetables from Smiling Fish for a period of one year;

B.   It has opened a club for customers of its retailers. Upon the purchase of five products of a minimum value within any calendar month, the customer will receive one product free during the next month;

C.   It has offered huge discounts to customers of its competitor, Flying Fish Ltd, a French undertaking, if they agree to switch their custom to Smiling Fish during the next 12 months; and,

D.   It has charged retailers who are established in wealthier States, such as Germany and France, higher prices for its products than it has charged retailers established in less wealthy States, such as Greece and Slovenia.

The financial director of Smiling Fish has complained that, as a result of the above new strategies, sales have failed to cover the cost of producing products manufactured by Smiling Fish.

Relying upon your knowledge of EU competition law discuss whether the situations described above raise any EU competition law issues.

ESSAY QUESTION

Critically examine the approach that the Commission adopted to price-based exclusionary conduct in its Guidance on its enforcement priorities in applying Article 102 TFEU to abusive exclusionary conduct by dominant undertakings.

DOMINANCE

An undertaking is in a dominant position when it can act independently from its competitors and consumers and thus is not subject to normal competitive forces.

Establishing dominance

The determination of whether an undertaking has market power involves two stages:

Stage one: the definition of the relevant product market (RPM); geographic market (RGM); and temporal market (RTP). All three are defined by reference to demand substitutability; supply substitutability; and, potential competition, although the last mentioned is normally examined in stage two below.

> The RMP comprises all those products and/or services which are regarded as interchangeable or substitutable by the consumer, by reason of the products' characteristics, their prices and their intended use

> The RGM comprises the area in which the undertakings concerned are involved in the supply and demand of products or services, in which the conditions of competition are sufficiently homogeneous and which can be distingulished from neighbouring areas because the conditions of compettion are appreciably different in those areas

> The RTM is rarely of relevance hence it is not mentioned in the 1977 Commision's Notice on the Definition of the Relevant Market. Usually, the Commission considers the factors indirectly when defining the RPM.

Stage two: consists of the determination of the market power of the allegedly dominant undertaking. The Commission in its Guidance identifies three main factors as essential to the assessment of market power:

- Constraints imposed by the existing supplies firms, and the position on the market of the actual competitors (i.e. the position of the undertaking concerned and its rivals);

- Constraints imposed by credible threats of future expansion by actual competitors or entry by potential competitors (i.e. expansion and entry); and,

- Constraints imposed by the bargaining power of the undertaking's customers (i.e. countervailing buyer power).

The concept of abuse is an objective concept. It refers to conduct of an undertaking in a dominant position "which is such as to influence the structure of a market where, as the result of the very presence of the undertaking in question, the degree of competition is weakened and which, through recourse to methods different from those which condition normal competition in products or services on the basis of the transactions of commercial operators, has the effect of hindering the maintenance of the degree of competition still existing in the market or the growth of that competition" (Case 85/76 *Hoffmann-La Roche*).

Categories of abuses:

To Note: categories of abuses are not mutually exclusive!

Exclusionary abuses: these are aimed at foreclosing the relevant market	• *Price-based exclusionary conduct. Some examples are: imposition of predatory prices, unlawful rebates; and margin squeeze.* • *Non price-based exclusionary conduct. Some examples are: tying and bundling; exclusive dealing agreements and refusal to deal*
Exploitative abuses: these refer to conduct of an undertaking in a dominant position which is prejudicial to the interests of its customers or consumers.	• Imposition of unfairly high or low prices is an example of exploitative abuses
Price discrimination: this occurs when a dominant undertaking treats its customers in a dissimilar manner without costs or legally acceptable justifications	• Price discrimination causing primary line injuries • Price discrimination causing secondary line injuries • Geographic discrimination

A dominant undertaking may justify its abusive conduct by demonstrating that:

- It is objectively necessary, e.g. justified by imperative considerations such as health and safety reasons related to the nature of the product concerned; or,

- It produces substantial efficiencies which outweigh any anti-competitive effects on consumers. The test here is similar to that set out in Article 101(1) TFEU.

29

MERGER CONTROL

CHAPTER OUTLINE

1. The 1957 Treaty of Rome did not include merger control provisions. This omission had serious consequences for competition conditions in the EU given that undertakings could circumvent the prohibitions set out in Articles 101 and 102 TFEU by merging. The first Merger Regulation (Regulation 4064/89) was adopted in 1989 and subsequently replaced by Regulation 139/2004 (MR), which entered into force on 1 May 2004.

2. The MR uses the term "concentration" to describe mergers and acquisitions. Concentrations are classified as horizontal when they occur between direct competitors, vertical when they involve undertakings in a customer–supplier relationship, and conglomerate when they neither involve direct competitors nor customer–supplier relationships, that is, they are neither horizontal nor vertical in nature.

3. Article 3(1) of the MR identifies two types of concentration:

- those which occur when previously independent undertakings merge; and

- those arising from an acquisition of control.

A third type, being a full-function joint venture, is defined in Article 3(4) as a joint venture performing on a lasting basis all the functions of an autonomous economic entity. A joint venture which satisfies this definition is within the scope of the MR, otherwise it is dealt with under Article 101 TFEU.

4. Only concentrations which have an EU dimension are within the scope of the MR. Article 1 of the MR sets out two sets of thresholds, expressed in terms of turnover of the undertakings concerned worldwide, and within the EU, to establish whether the relevant operation has an EU dimension. The thresholds also determine the jurisdiction of the Commission or of national competition authorities to deal with the intended concentration.

5. Article 2(2) of the MR contains the substantive test for assessment of compatibility of the intended concentration with the requirements of the internal market. According to this test a concentration may be prohibited first, if it strengthens or creates a dominant position, and second, when it takes place in the context of a non-collusive oligopoly and does not lead to a single or joint dominance but produces effects which significantly impede effective competition in the internal market or a substantial part of it.

6. All concentrations which are within the scope of the MR must be notified to the Commission. If a concentration is implemented either before notification or before it is cleared by the Commission, the parties concerned may be fined by the Commission. Further, Article 7(1) of the MR provides that no concentration may come into legal effect until the Commission has delivered a compatibility decision or failed to make such a decision. The Commission (in what is known as the Phase I Investigation) is required to take an initial decision within 25 working days of receipt of complete notification (however, this period may be extended to 35 working days in the circumstances described in Article 9 of the MR). At the end of this procedure the Commission may decide that the concentration under consideration:

- is compatible with the internal market subject to some conditions which it attaches to the decision, or without any conditions;

- falls outside the scope of the MR, in which case national laws may apply to the concentration; or

- requires more investigation as it raises serious doubts about its compatibility with the internal market. In that case the Phase II Investigation commences.

If the Commission takes no decision, the concentration is deemed to be compatible with the internal market.

The Phase II Investigation must be concluded in principle within 90 working days of commencement (there are some exceptions). At the end of this phase the Commission may declare the concentration:

- compatible with the internal market, with or without conditions. Such a decision also covers ancillary restraints; or

- incompatible with the internal market.

7. Under the MR the Commission has important enforcement powers: to revoke approved concentrations, to request information and to search and to fine for breaches of the MR.

8. The Commission's exclusive jurisdiction with regard to concentrations with an EU dimension is subject to some exceptions as set out in the MR.

29.1 Introduction

The Treaty of Rome was silent on the topic of mergers. This omission had serious consequences for competition conditions within the EU. Undertakings were able to circumvent the application of Articles 101(1) and 102 TFEU. Instead of entering into agreements prohibited by virtue of Article 101(1) TFEU, they could achieve the same objectives by merging with other undertakings. In respect of Article 102 TFEU, an undertaking in a dominant position (the existence of which *per se* weakens competition within the relevant market) could lawfully increase its market power by acquiring or merging with its competitors and thus further reduce competition to the detriment of its customers/consumers, although the merged entity might then be subject to Article 102. The Commission was powerless to prevent such mergers between, and acquisitions by, undertakings having market power, and could only act afterwards under Article 102 or Article 101 TFEU. However, it made attempts to bring mergers within the scope of EU competition law.

First, under Article 102 TFEU. In Case 6/72 *Continental Can*,[2647] the Commission failed to prove that Continental Can held a dominant position in the German market,[2648] but the ECJ recognised, for the first time, that Article 102 TFEU was, in principle, applicable to mergers. The main drawback was that the Commission could not prevent mergers from taking place but could only act after a merger had occurred.

Second, under Article 101 TFEU in Joined Cases 142 and 156/84 *Reynolds*.[2649] The Commission was successful but the judgment showed that Article 101 TFEU was not an appropriate tool to deal with mergers, taking into account the nullity sanction under Article 101(2); the possibility of the revocability of exemption under Article 101(3); and, the lack of thresholds triggering its application to mergers. Further, the judgment gave a clear signal to Member States reluctant to deal with mergers at EU level that in order to avoid further judicial developments by the ECJ on the control of mergers and the uncertainty of whether or not the Commission would exercise its discretion, a wise option for the Member States would be to adopt legislation on merger control, especially in the light of the then forthcoming completion of the internal market. It should be noted that in *Reynolds* the ECJ, by interpreting Article 101 TFEU broadly, had in effect extended the scope of the Treaty and thus judicially revised it. In the light of the above the Member States decided to deal with merger control at EU level.

29.1.1 Adoption of Regulation 4064/89 and its replacement by Regulation 139/2004 (MR)

In March 1988 a draft Regulation was submitted to the Council which, after a number of amendments, was adopted on 21 December 1989 as Merger Regulation 4064/89 and came into force on 21 September 1990.[2650] However, the reform of EU competition law (see Chapter 30.1) encompassed Regulation 4064/89 which resulted in the adoption of Regulation 139/2004[2651] (MR). It entered into force on 1 May 2004.

2647. Case 6/72 *Europemballage and Continental Can v Commission* [1973] ECR 215 (for facts and further comments see Chapter 28.3.1.1.3).
2648. The Commission failed to assess the supply-substitutability of the relevant product market.
2649. Joined Cases 142 and 156/84 *British-American Tobacco Company Ltd (BAT) and R. J. Reynolds Industries Inc. v Commission and Philip Morris* [1987] ECR 4487.
2650. [1989] OJ L395/1.
2651. [2004] OJ L24/1.

The MR is accompanied by an implementing Regulation,[2652] Notices (including the Notice on the Appraisal of Horizontal Mergers) and guidelines (including Best Practice Guidelines on the Conduct of EU Merger Regulation Proceedings).[2653]

In order to strengthen the economic approach to the assessment of intended concentrations and to respond to criticism expressed by the General Court regarding the failure of the Commission to provide good quality evidence to satisfy the requisite standard of proof,[2654] the Commission appointed a chief competition economist, working with a team of economists, and set up, within the Phase II investigation of concentrations (see Chapter 29.4.3), arrangements for a peer review panel to scrutinise the conclusions reached in that Phase by an investigating team.

Particularly helpful in the interpretation of the MR is the Commission's Consolidated Jurisdictional Notice.[2655] The Notice is user-friendly, takes account of the existing case law in the area, and of the practices of the Commission, and reflects the changes that the MR introduced in respect of jurisdictional matters in merger control.

29.2 The scope of application of the Merger Regulation (MR)

The MR does not prohibit concentrations. Unlike Articles 101 and 102 TFEU the repressive element is absent. The emphasis is on the structure of the relevant market, not on the anti-competitive conduct of an undertaking. On the one hand, many concentrations are necessary in order to reinforce the competitiveness of EU undertakings, but on the other, concentrations may have damaging effects on the competitive structure of the market. Concentrations can be classified as horizontal, vertical and conglomerate.

■ Horizontal. This occurs when a concentration takes place between undertakings which are competing in the same product and geographic market and at the same level of production/distribution. Such concentrations have great impact on the market, given that after the concentration the number of undertakings in the relevant market is reduced, at least by one, and ordinarily the new, merged undertaking has a larger market share than either undertaking had previously. Horizontal mergers are the most likely to adversely affect the structure of the relevant market in terms of its competitiveness. The Commission's Guidelines on the Assessment of Horizontal Mergers[2656] are of great help to parties who are actual or potential competitors in the same relevant market when they intend to merge.

■ Vertical. This refers to a concentration between undertakings operating at different levels of the economy (for example, between a manufacturer and its supplier of raw material). It does not increase concentration of the relevant product market but "can give rise to a number of competition issues, including the possibility of foreclosure or of creating a more favourable environment for collusive behaviour. As with vertical restraints, anti-competitive

---

2652. Regulation 802/2004 [2004] OJ L133/1.
2653. [2004] OJ C31/5.
2654. The General Court overturned the Commission's decisions in many important cases, e.g. Case T-342/99 *Airtours plc v Commission* [2002] ECR II-2585; Case T-310/01 *Schneider Electric SA v Commission* [2002] ECR II-4071; and Case T-5/02 *Tetra Laval BV v Commission* [2002] ECR II-4381, confirmed by the ECJ in Case C-12/03P *Commission v Tetra Laval BV* [2005] I-1113.
2655. [2008] C95/1.
2656. [2004] OJ C31/5.

effects are likely to occur only if there is horizontal market power at one or more of the vertical levels".[2657]

■ Conglomerate. This refers to a concentration between undertakings that are not competing with each other in any product market and which does not result in any vertical integration. Three types of conglomerate concentration can be identified:

● product line extension, where one undertaking adds a new product to its existing products by merging with another;

● market extension, where prior to their merger undertakings operated in the same product market but in different geographical markets; and,

● pure conglomerate, where there is no functional connection between the merged undertakings, i.e. they involve neither a market extension concentration nor a product-line extension concentration.

Ordinarily conglomerate concentrations are neutral, or even beneficial for competition.[2658]

The MR applies to all sectors of the economy, to both public and private undertakings, and to undertakings which are established within and outside the EU.

Concentrations are within the scope of the MR if they satisfy two conditions:

■ they are "concentrations" as defined by the MR; and,

■ they have "an EU dimension" within the meaning of the MR.

Concentrations with an EU dimension must be notified to the Commission in conformity with the requirements laid down in Form "CO". The Commission is required to deal with notifications as soon as they are received and must adopt relevant decisions within a very strict, legally binding timetable. Business operators greatly appreciate this feature of the MR. Unlike cases examined under Articles 101 and 102 TFEU (where there are no binding deadlines for the Commission), in concentration cases they have certitude that whatever the decision of the Commission, at least it will be adopted within a well-defined time frame.

An appeal from the decision of the Commission can be lodged with the General Court.

The concept of concentration and the concept of EU dimension are essential for the application of the MR. They are examined below.

29.2.1 The concept of concentration

Article 3(1) of the MR states that the MR applies only to concentrations which permanently modify the structure of the undertakings concerned. The concept of concentration is defined in Article 3 of the Regulation and covers two types of concentration:

■ first, the case where two or more previously independent undertakings merge; and,

■ second, the case where one or more undertakings already controlling at least one or more undertakings, acquire direct or indirect control of the whole or parts of one or

---

2657. S. Bishop and M. Walker, *The Economics of EC Competition Law: Concepts, Application and Measurement*, 2002, 2nd edn., London: Sweet and Maxwell, para. 7.61.

2658. In Case C-12/03P *Commission v Tetra Laval BV* [2005] I-1113 the ECJ stated that the General Court was correct in requiring the same standard of proof in respect of conglomerate concentrations as in cases of vertical and horizontal concentrations (para. 40). US antitrust law is not interested in conglomerate concentrations, considering them as being, at the worst, neutral for competition. See R. Whish and D. Bailey, *Competition Law*, 2012, 7th edn., Oxford; OUP, 811.

more other undertakings, whether by purchase of securities or assets, by contract or by any other means.

A third type of concentration is a full-function joint venture (JV) defined in Article 3(4) of the MR as a joint venture performing on a lasting basis all the functions of an autonomous economic entity. A joint venture which satisfies the above definition is within the scope of the MR, otherwise it is dealt with under Article 101 TFEU.

29.2.1.1 Merger

This first type of concentration is not very complex. There is no definition of a "merger". Merger may occur in two ways:

- Legal merger where two or more undertakings cease to be legally distinct and independent from each other and form a single separate legal entity; or,

- *De facto* merger where two or more undertakings create a permanent economic management while continuing to exist as separate legal entities. In fact, they act on the relevant market as a single economic unit.

29.2.1.2 Acquisition

The second type of concentration refers to acquisition, by whatever means, of control over the whole or part of other undertakings. The situation of "acquisition of control" is more complex than that of merger. Further, a distinction is made between:

- sole control, a situation where one undertaking alone can exercise *de facto* or *de jure* decisive influence on another undertaking;[2659] and,

- joint control, which exists where two or more undertakings are able to exercise decisive influence over another undertaking. As Article 62 of the Jurisdictional Notice explains: "Decisive influence normally means the power to block actions which determine the strategic commercial behaviour of an undertaking." As in the case of sole control, the acquisition of joint control may be established on a *de facto* or on a *de jure* basis.

The MR also covers situations where the acquisition of sole or joint control leads to a change in the quality of control. Article 83 of the Notice explains that changes in the quality of control occur:

- when there is a change from sole to joint control and *vice versa*; and,

- with regard to a change in joint control, if there is a reduction in the number or a change in the identity of the controlling shareholders.

Acquisition of control is defined in Article 3(1)(b) of the MR in the following terms:

"Control shall be constituted by rights, contracts or any other means which, either separately or in combination, and having regard to the considerations of fact or law involved, confer the possibility of exercising decisive influence on an undertaking, in particular by:

(a) ownership or the right to use all the assets of an undertaking;

2659. See the Consolidated Jurisdictional Notice para. 54 et seq.

(b)   rights or contracts which confer decisive influence on the composition, voting or decisions of the organs of an undertaking."

The definition of control is broad. In many cases the existence of control is easy to determine, for example, on the basis of ownership. In other cases an economic analysis will be necessary to establish the existence of control. For example, minority shareholders may have sole control on a *de facto* basis in a situation where at a shareholders' meeting they are highly likely to achieve a majority vote for any proposal put forward by them because the remaining shares are widely dispersed. In such cases the Commission has consistently based its assessment on the actual participation in shareholders' meetings in previous years.[2660]

In Joined Cases 142 and 156/84 *Reynolds*,[2661] it was established that control was exercised by a minority shareholding, as in fact no other shareholder or group of shareholders could combine to oppose that minority shareholder. Even a shareholding of 25 per cent may amount to control. In *CCIE/GTE*, by acquiring 19 per cent of the voting rights in EDIL, CCIE had acquired control over EDIL given that the remaining shares were held by independent banks whose approval of important business decisions was not necessary.[2662]

In Case *RTL/M6*,[2663] RTL, a Luxembourg TV channel (which already owned a 48.4 per cent shareholding), acquired sole control of M6, a French TV channel, without acquiring any additional shares in M6. This occurred when Suez Lyonnaise des Eau (Suez) sold its shares in M6. Before the divestment Suez held 37.6 per cent and RTL held 48.4 per cent of shares in M6. Under a decision of the French Conseil Supérieur de l'Audiovisuel, which supervises ownership of French TV channels, the voting rights held by any shareholder or group of shareholders in this sector were limited to 34 per cent. Although RTL held 48.4 per cent of M6 shares, its voting rights were limited to 34 per cent. The divestment of Suez's shares led to passive acquisition of sole control by RTL because the remaining shares, other than the 48.4 per cent owned by RTL, with their maximum 34 per cent voting power became widely dispersed among a large number of small shareholders who were unlikely to coalesce to reach a majority in future shareholders' meetings.

There may be acquisition of control even if this is not the declared intention of the parties.[2664]

By virtue of Article 3(3)(b) indirect control, that is, the situation where title to the assets or contracts conferring control is "divorced" from the ability to benefit from such rights, is within the scope of the MR. This can be illustrated by the following example: when undertaking A acquires a controlling interest in undertaking B that has subsidiaries C and D, undertaking A will have direct control over B and indirect control over C and D. A is not a holder of the rights to shares in C and D but as a result of its control over B, it exercises indirect control over C and D. In order to decide whether a change of control has amounted to a concentration, all relevant factual and legal considerations are taken into account.[2665]

An acquisition of control must result in a lasting change in the control of the undertaking concerned. Agreements which provide for a definite end-date are within the scope of the MR if the period envisaged

---

2660.   Cases No. IV/M 343 *Société Generale de Belgique/Generale de Banque* of 3/08/1993; No. IV/M/754 *Anglo American Corporation/Lonrho* of 23/04/1997 and No. IV/M.1157 *Skanska/Scancam* of 11/11/1998; Case COM/M 2574 *Pirrelli/Edizione/Olivetti/Telecom Italia* of 20/09/2001.

2661.   Joined Cases 142 and 156/84 *British-American Tobacco Company Ltd (BAT) and R. J. Reynolds Industries Inc. v Commission and Philip Morris* [1987] ECR 4487.

2662.   No. IV/M 258.

2663.   COMP/M3330.

2664.   Case No. IV/M/157 *Air France/Sabena* [1994] 5 CMLR M1.

2665.   Case T-102/96 *Gencor Ltd v Commission* [1999] ECR II-753.

is sufficiently long to result in a lasting change. The Commission considers that 10–15 years constitutes a sufficient period but not a period of three years.[2666]

29.2.1.3 Joint ventures (JVs)

JVs can be described as commercial arrangements between two or more undertakings to create a new entity by contributing equity and then sharing the profit/losses, expenses and control of the new entity. JVs are created in order to achieve a particular commercial goal. The term JV covers a wide variety of business arrangements, ranging from merger-like operations to co-operation for a particular function such as R&D, production, distribution, and so on. The difference between mergers and JVs is that in a JV there is no transfer of ownership. Some JVs are within the scope of the MR, others are dealt with under Article 101 TFEU. This is because generally competition law, including EU competition law, treats concentrations differently from agreements between undertakings. The difference rests on the theory that concentrations affect the structure of the relevant market while agreements between undertakings relate to behaviour of undertakings in the relevant market. As a JV can have both behavioural and structural aspects, either the MR or Article 101 TFEU may apply depending upon whether it is a full-function or a non-full-function joint venture.

Only a full-function JV having an EU dimension is within the scope of the MR. Such a JV should be notified by the parties to the Commission. Article 3(4) of the MR defines a full-function JV as a concentration where a joint venture performing on a lasting basis all the functions of an autonomous economic entity is created. The Commission's Consolidated Jurisdictional Notice explains in Chapter IV the definition set out in Article 3(4) of the MR. Three requirements must be satisfied for a JV to be within the scope of Article 3(4) of the MR:

- The first requirement is that there must be joint control by two or more entities over another entity. The concept of joint control is defined in Article 3 of the MR (see Chapter 29.2.1.2);

- The second requirement refers to full-functionality.[2667] In this respect paragraph 93 of the Notice states that:

  "Full function character essentially means that a joint venture must operate on a market, performing the functions normally carried out by undertakings operating on the same market. In order to do so the joint venture must have a management dedicated to its day-to-day operations and access to sufficient resources including finance, staff, and assets (tangible and intangible) in order to conduct on a lasting basis its business activities within the area provided for in the joint-venture agreement."

As can be seen, it is essential for a JV to operate as an autonomous economic entity. Substantial dependency on parent companies will disqualify it from being "full-function". However, during the first three years of its existence support from parent companies is allowed, for example, during that period a JV may rely almost entirely on sales to or purchases from its parent companies; and,

- The third requirement is that a JV must be intended to operate on a lasting basis. The period for which it has been created must be sufficiently long to bring about a lasting change in the structure of the parent undertakings. Accordingly, if a JV is created for a short finite period, it will

---

2666. See para. 28 of the Consolidated Jurisdictional Notice.
2667. See para. 92 of the Consolidated Jurisdictional Notice.

not be considered as operating on a lasting basis. An example of this is provided in paragraph 104 of the Notice in relation to a JV established in order to construct a power plant, which excludes any involvement of the JV in the operation of the plant once the construction has been completed.

If a joint venture falls within the definition set out in Article 2(4) of the MR but has as its object or effect the co-ordination of the competitive behaviour of undertakings that remain independent, such co-ordination is assessed in the light of Article 101(1) TFEU.

The MR excludes from its scope of application joint ventures between a parent and its subsidiary when the former uses the latter in order to co-ordinate its business practices to the detriment of fair competition in the particular market. These kinds of situation are within the realm of Articles 101 and 102 TFEU.

29.2.2 The EU dimension

The MR applies to all concentrations having an EU dimension. This occurs when they exceed either of the following thresholds (known as the quantitative jurisdictional tests):

■ The combined aggregate worldwide turnover of all participating undertakings is over €5 billion and the aggregate EU-wide turnover of each of at least two of the undertakings concerned is more than €250 million, unless each of the undertakings concerned achieves more than two-thirds of its aggregate EU-wide turnover within one and the same Member State (Article 1(2) of the MR).

This is the primary test. If the requirement for the turnover set out in Article 1(2) of the MR is satisfied but each of the undertakings concerned achieves more than two-thirds of its aggregate EU-wide turnover within one and the same Member State, the concentration has no EU dimension and thus it should be dealt with by the relevant NCA.

■ When the primary test is not satisfied, there is a secondary test contained in Article 1(3) of the MR which may bring the intended concentration within the scope of the MR. The test is as follows.

The combined aggregate worldwide turnover of all the undertakings concerned is more than €2.5 billion and an aggregate EU-wide turnover of €100 million or more is spread between not fewer than three Member States, and:

(i) each of at least two of the undertakings concerned generates at least €25 million turnover in each of the Member States over which the above-mentioned €100 million or more turnover is spread; and,

(ii) the aggregate EU-wide turnover of each of at least two of the undertakings concerned is more than €100 million.

However, if each of the undertakings concerned achieves more than two-thirds of its aggregate EU-wide turnover within one and the same Member State, the MR will not apply (Article 1(3) of the MR).

Article 1(3) provides for a "one-stop-shop" EU notification procedure for cross-border merger agreements which in any way involve at least three Member States and meet a slightly lower turnover threshold than that set out in Article 1(2) of the MR. The lower threshold was set out in Article 1(3) of the MR in order to bring more concentrations within the scope of the MR. It offers a substantial advantage to undertakings involved in merger agreements stretching across at least three Member States and falling short of having an EU dimension as defined in Article 1(2) of the MR. Instead of notifying their intended concentration to the competent authorities in the three or more Member States concerned and being subject to investigations in all those Member States (which would impose considerable hardship on them and be very time-consuming), such undertakings can obtain a decision from the Commission within a time limit specified in the Regulation.

Article 5 of the MR provides detailed rules on how the turnover of the relevant parties is to be calculated. The Commission's Consolidated Jurisdictional Notice[2668] provides further assistance in this respect.

The thresholds in the MR are much higher than those the Commission expected. The Commission's attempts to lower the thresholds failed. Nevertheless, the MR provides that the Commission is required to report on the operation of thresholds by 1 July 2009 and may present proposals to have the thresholds amended (Article 1(4) and (5) of the MR). The Commission submitted a Report on 30 June 2009[2669] in which it concluded that the threshold criteria in Articles 1(2) and 1(3) had, in the light of corrective mechanisms, i.e. the referral mechanism, operated during the relevant period overall, in a satisfactory way in allocating jurisdiction between the Commission and NCAs (see Chapter 29.6). However, the Report noted that the efficiency of the merger control system across the EU could be enhanced by, *inter alia*, improving the pre-notification referral mechanism (see Chapter 29.4.1) and by increasing the coming together of the national and EU rules on merger control.

29.2.3   Extraterritorial application of the MR

The MR has an extraterritorial scope of application.[2670] The EU institutions have jurisdiction "when it is foreseeable that a proposed concentration will have an immediate and substantial effect in the [EU]".

While the Commission enjoys a large measure of discretion in relation to the enforcement of Articles 101 and 102 TFEU and has used it to avoid international disputes, this is not the case in relation to the control of concentrations. Once an envisaged concentration satisfies the threshold requirements, the Commission must act, or at least assess the proposed concentration from the point of view of the interests of the EU.

29.3   Substantial appraisal of concentration

If an intended concentration has an EU dimension within the meaning of the MR, the Commission has to assess whether it is compatible with the internal market. The substantive test for the assessment of a concentration is set out in Article 2(3) of the MR. It states that:

"a concentration which would significantly impede effective competition in the common market or in a substantial part of it, in particular as a result of strengthening of a dominant position, shall be declared incompatible with the common market."

The test has two objectives: first, to prohibit a concentration which strengthens or creates a dominant position; and, second, to block a concentration which takes place in the context of a non-collusive oligopoly, and does not lead to a single or joint dominance, but, nevertheless, produces effects which significantly impede effective competition in the internal market or a substantial part of it.[2671]

2668. Paras. 157–220.

2669. The Staff Working Paper Accompanying the Communication from the Commission to the Council, Report on the Functioning of Regulation No. 139/2004 [COM (2009) 281 final].

2670. See recital 10 of the preamble to the MR.

2671. For example, in *Linde/BOC* (COMP/M4141), the Commission applied the above test to an intended concentration between two undertakings active in the helium market. The Commission prohibited the concentration on the

Under Article 2(1) of the MR the Commission, in assessing whether a concentration is compatible with the internal market, should take into consideration:

- the necessity to maintain and develop effective competition within the internal market in the light, *inter alia*, of the structure of all the markets concerned and the actual or potential competition from undertakings located either within or outside the EU; and,

- the market position of the undertakings concerned, and their economic and financial power based on the following factors:

  - market share;
  - the alternatives available to suppliers and users and their access to supplies and markets;
  - any legal barriers to entry to the relevant market;
  - supply and demand trends for the relevant product market;
  - the interests of intermediate and ultimate consumers; and
  - the development of technical and economic progress which must bring advantages to consumers but must not constitute an obstacle to competition.

The Commission, before assessing the compatibility of an intended concentration with the internal market, must identify the relevant product market and the relevant geographic market.[2672] It will use the "counterfactual" standard to assess the effects of the intended concentration, i.e. the Commission will compare the conditions of competition that would result from the intended concentration with the conditions that would have existed in its absence. If the intended concentration would create or strengthen a dominant position or significantly impede effective competition in the relevant market, it will be declared incompatible with the internal market.

29.3.1 The concept of collective dominance

The concept of collective dominance has the same meaning under Article 102 TFEU as under the MR. This topic is examined in Chapter 28.4. It is important to note that the assessment of collective dominance under the MR is prospective. In Case C-12/03P *Tetra Laval*[2673] the ECJ emphasised that a prospective analysis "does not entail the examination of past events – for which often many items of evidence are available which make it possible to understand the causes – or of current events, but rather a prediction of events which are more or less likely to occur in future if a decision prohibiting the planned concentration or laying down the conditions for it is not adopted."[2674]

29.4 Procedure under the MR

The basic rule is that any intended concentration satisfying the criteria laid down by the MR should be notified to the Commission after the conclusion of the agreement, announcement of the public bid, or the acquisition of a controlling interest. A concentration can neither be implemented before its

---

ground that the effect of the concentration would be to significantly impede effective competition on the relevant market, although the merged entity would not become the market leader.

2672. Both concepts are examined in Chapter 28.3.1.

2673. Case C-12/03P *Commission v Tetra Laval BV* [2005] ECR I-987.

2674. Ibid, para. 42. On the standard of proof in merger control see G. Drauz, "Conglomerate and Vertical Mergers in the Light of the Tetra Judgment", (2005) *Competition Policy Newsletter*, No. 2, 35–9.

notification[2675] nor until it has been cleared by the Commission as compatible with the internal market, otherwise the Commission may impose fines on the undertakings concerned.

Further, Article 7(1) of the MR provides that no concentration may come into legal effect until the Commission has delivered a compatibility decision or has failed to do this. However, this is qualified by the other provisions of Article 7.

In practice, it is unlikely that parties will fail to notify, given the adverse consequences which may result from such a situation. First, if a concentration is implemented without being notified to the Commission, the Commission may declare it incompatible with the internal market and consequently require undertakings or assets brought together to be separated, or the cessation of joint control.[2676] Second, the Commission may impose fines not exceeding 10 per cent of the aggregate turnover of the undertakings concerned for intentional or negligent failure to notify a concentration in accordance with Articles 4 and 22(3) prior to its implementation.

Under Article 4(1) of the MR notification may be made where the undertakings demonstrate to the Commission a good faith intention to enter into an agreement or, in the case of a public bid, where they have publicly announced an intention to make such a bid, in a situation where their intended agreement or bid would result in a concentration with an EU dimension.

29.4.1   Pre-notification reasoned submissions

The MR introduced a pre-notification system whereby parties to an intended concentration are allowed to make pre-notification reasoned submissions to the Commission or the relevant NCA. This is to settle jurisdictional issues in a situation where the application of numerical turnover thresholds set out in Regulation 139/2004 may result, in a limited number of cases, in jurisdiction being assigned wrongly either to the Commission or to an NCA. A request for referral of an intended concentration to an NCA is dealt with under Article 4(4) of the MR and a request for referral to the Commission under Article 4(5) of the MR.

- Under Article 4(4) parties to a concentration with an EU dimension may ask the Commission to refer it, or some aspects of it, to an NCA of the Member State where the intended concentration may significantly affect competition in a distinct market of that Member State.

- Article 4(5) concerns a situation where a concentration does not have an EU dimension but is likely to affect at least three Member States and thus the parties are required to make multiple notifications. In this situation, the parties may ask the Commission to assess the concentration, but this request will be rejected if any of the Member States concerned disagree with the giving of jurisdiction to the Commission.

29.4.2   The Phase I Investigation

The Commission takes an initial decision (i.e. as to whether the Commission has serious doubts regarding the compatibility of the concentration with the internal market) within 25 working days following receipt of complete notification. This period is extended to 35 working days when a Member State, relying on Article 9 of the MR, informs the Commission that the proposed concentration would have an undesirable impact on competition within that Member State or in cases where commitments

---

2675. There are some exceptions to this rule: see Art. 7 (2) and (3) of the MR.
2676. Para. 114 of the Notice states that the parties must re-establish the *status quo ante*.

are made by the parties aimed at making a proposed concentration compatible with the internal market. At the end of that period the Commission may take any of the following decisions:

- declare the concentration as being outside the scope of the MR;

- declare the concentration compatible with the internal market;

- declare the concentration as compatible with the internal market subject to acceptance of commitments by the parties; or,

- declare that the Commission has serious doubts as to the compatibility of the concentration with the internal market.

If no decision is taken within the prescribed time limit, the concentration is deemed to be compatible with the internal market.

The Commission gives clearance to between 90 and 95 per cent of concentrations by the end of Phase I, but usually makes this subject to conditions.

29.4.3 The Phase II Investigation

If the Commission considers that the intended concentration raises serious concern, it must open the Phase II Investigation, which must be concluded within 90 working days and which involves consultation with third parties. The time limit may be extended by the Commission by 15 working days where commitments (that is, adjustments to the concentration) are offered by the parties in order to satisfy the Commission's reservations on competition grounds. Further, this period may be extended to 20 working days at the request of either party, or of the Commission with the consent of the parties. In complex cases the time limit may be extended up to a maximum of 125 working days. The Commission may also "stop the clock" if it has obtained insufficient information from the undertakings concerned.[2677] If no decision is taken within the prescribed time limit, the concentration is deemed to be compatible with the internal market.

At the end of the Phase II proceedings the Commission may take any of the following decisions:

- declare the concentration compatible with the internal market;

- declare the concentration compatible with the internal market but impose conditions to ensure that the parties comply with commitments they have offered. if the parties breach the commitments, the decision of compatibility can be revoked; or,

- declare that the concentration is incompatible with the internal market.

The Advisory Committee on Concentrations, made up of representatives of NCAs, must be consulted before a final decision is taken and when the Commission intends to impose pecuniary sanctions on an undertaking. Under the MR the Commission's powers to fine undertakings are similar to those under Regulation 1/2003 (see Chapter 29.5).

The MR contains provisions for oral hearings and for informal and confidential discussions of proposals. The undertakings concerned are permitted to comment on any objections to the proposals by the Commission.

In order to guarantee the right of the parties, and of third parties whose interests are likely to be affected by an intended concentration, to be heard and to have access to the files of the Commission, the

---

2677. See Case COMP/M.2282 *Schneider/Legrand.*

post of Hearing Officer was created in 1984. He/she is an independent person experienced in competition matters whose task is to ensure that the right to be heard is respected in all competition proceedings including proceedings under Articles 101 and 102 TFEU (see Chapter 30.2.4).

29.4.4 Commitments

During the examination of a notification parties are free to propose adjustments to the concentration so as to avoid a negative decision. The Commission codified its practices regarding the assessment, acceptance and implementation of commitments in Phases I and II of merger investigations in its 2001 Notice.[2678] It refers to them as "remedies".

The Commission is very clear that promises not to abuse dominance are not sufficient. It insists upon commitments which will ensure a specific, lasting and appropriate solution to any problems created by the envisaged concentration.

Implementation of commitments must occur within a short period of time and be speedy and effective. The notice sets out deadlines for the submission of commitments in Phase I (20 working days from the submission of the notification) and in Phase II (within 65 working days of the date of commencement of the Phase II investigation).[2679]

29.4.5 Ancillary restraints

The concept of restraints is explained in Article 10 of the Commission's 2005 Notice on Restrictions Directly Related and Necessary to Concentrations[2680] in the following terms: "In addition to these arrangements and agreements [which carry out the main object of the concentration, such as the sale of shares or assets of an undertaking] the parties to the concentration may enter into other agreements which do not form an integral part of the concentration but can restrict the parties' freedom of action in the market." Examples of restraints are non-competition clauses and restrictions imposed in licence agreements.

Restraints are part of the concentration and therefore they are not separately assessed in the context of Article 101 TFEU, which is the case where restraints occur outside the context of a related concentration. The Notice makes a distinction between restraints "directly related" (meaning subordinate in importance to the main object of concentration) and "necessary" (meaning that in the absence of such restraints the proposed concentration could not be implemented or could only be implemented under less unsatisfactory conditions, for example at higher cost).

The 2005 Notice provides very useful guidance on the interpretation of the notion of restraints given that it is for the parties to assess whether any proposed agreement between them can be regarded as ancillary to a proposed concentration. The Notice states that if there is genuine uncertainty as to the assessment of a restraint, that is, the case presents "novel or unresolved questions", the parties may ask the Commission to provide clarifications.[2681]

2678. The Remedies Notice [2001] OJ C6/3.
2679. When commitments are offered in the Phase I Investigation, the time period for examination of a concentration is extended by 10 days. If offered in the Phase II Investigation, the time period may be extended by 15 working days. Also in the Phase II Investigation, in respect of complex cases, a further extension of up to 20 days may be agreed.
2680. [2005] OJ C56/3.
2681. Article 3 of the 2005 Notice.

29.4.6 Simplified procedure

Reliance on the quantitative jurisdictional tests (see Chapter 29.2.2) means that many under-takings must notify their intended concentration even though it does not significantly impede effective competition in the internal market. This involves costs and inconvenience for the undertakings.

In order to alleviate this problem, the Commission issued a Notice on Simplified Procedures in 2005.[2682] According to the Notice the parties to a concentration, which is eligible for the simplified procedure, do not have to submit a full-form notification. On receipt of notification the Commission will, if appropriate, publish a notice in the Official Journal that the concentration is eligible for the simplified procedure. The purpose of the notice is to give interested parties the opportunity to make representations to the Commission, in particular on circumstances which may require an investigation. If the Commission is satisfied that the concentration meets the criteria for the simplified procedure, it will normally, within 25 working days from the date of notification, adopt a short-form clearance decision declaring the concentration compatible with the internal market, which decision will be published in the Official Journal.

29.5 Enforcement and investigating powers of the Commission under the MR

The MR contains its own rules on investigations and on the enforcement powers of the Commission, which are broadly similar to those under Regulation 1/2003 (see Chapter 30.2). The Commission is entitled to request information (Article 11) and to carry out on-the-spot investigations (Article 13). The Commission may also interview any natural or legal person, but only with that person's consent (Article 11(7)) but has no power to conduct "dawn raids" or any other sort of raids on the homes of directors of undertakings concerned.

Under the MR the Commission is empowered to impose fines and pecuniary sanctions in the event of failure to notify or to co-operate.

The Commission is empowered to impose fines if undertakings concerned fail to supply relevant information, or supply incorrect or misleading information. In *Sanofi/Synthélabo*, the Commission imposed a fine of €50,000 on each of two undertakings for being grossly negligent and for supplying incorrect information when notifying their intended merger.[2683] In *Mitsubishi*,[2684] for the first time, the Commission imposed a fine on a third party, not involved in a concentration, for failure to provide required information. In respect of procedural infringements a fine of up to 1 per cent of turnover of the undertaking or undertakings concerned may be imposed. In respect of substantial infringements a maximum fine of 10 per cent of the total worldwide turnover of the undertakings concerned achieved in the preceding business year may be imposed.

29.6 The role of the Member States in the enforcement of the MR

Under the MR the Commission has exclusive power to deal with concentrations which have an EU dimension, subject to the exception mentioned below. The Commission and NCAs have a duty to co-operate with each other and indeed there are situations where cases are referred from the Commission

---

2682. [2005] OJ C56/4.
2683. [2000] OJ L95/34.
2684. [2001] OJ L4/31.

to NCAs and *vice versa*. The MR specifies exceptions to the principle of exclusive competence of the Commission to deal with concentrations with an EU dimension. These are set out below:

■ First, Article 9 (known as the German clause) provides for a referral, at the initiative of either a particular Member State or the Commission, of a concentration (this is known as a total referral) or of aspects of a concentration (this is known as a partial referral) to a NCA of a Member State where a concentration threatens to significantly affect competition in a distinct market in that Member State. Article 9 therefore provides a safeguard in that the interests of a Member State will be taken into consideration in the assessment of a concentration either by the requesting Member State itself, when the Commission agrees to refer to the relevant NCA, or the Commission when it deals with the case;

■ Second, by virtue of Article 21(4) the Commission may refer a concentration with an EU dimension to a Member State if the Commission perceives that there may be a need for a Member State to protect "legitimate interests" which are not protected by the MR. "Legitimate interests" refer to public security, plurality of media and prudential rules of a Member State. This provision is rarely used;

■ Third, under Article 22 (known as the Dutch clause) a Member State may, on its own initiative or at the invitation of the Commission, refer to the Commission a concentration which does not have an EU dimension, but "affects trade between Member States and threatens to significantly affect competition within the territory of the Member State or Member States making the request". This provision is rarely used; and,

■ Fourth, under Article 346 TFEU, when essential interests of security of a Member State are at stake, that Member State may instruct the parties to a concentration not to notify the military aspects of a concentration to the Commission.[2685] Article 346 TFEU is distinct from Article 21(4) of the MR and as a Treaty provision is hierarchically superior to the MR (see Chapter 4.1). When Article 346 TFEU is relied upon by a Member State, the Commission will normally assess only the non-military aspects of a concentration.

In order to rationalise the system of referral, the Commission published a Notice on Case Allocation under the Referral rules of the Merger Regulations.[2686]

RECOMMENDED READING

Books
Those recommended in Chapter 26 and the following:

Cumming, G., *Merger Decisions and the Rules of Procedure of the European Community Courts*, 2012, The Hague: KLI.

Furse, M., *The Law of Merger Control in the EC and the UK*, 2007, Oxford: Hart Publishing.

Ilzkovitz, F. and Meiklejohn, R. (eds.), *European Merger Control: Do We Need an Efficiency Defence?*, 2006, Cheltenham: Edward Elgar.

Kekelekis, M., *EC Merger Control Regulation: Rights of Defence*, 2006, The Hague: KLI.

2685. See Case IV/M 1438 *British Aerospace/GEC Marconi* [1999] OJ C241/8.
2686. [2005] OJ C56/2.

Articles

Budzinski, O., "An Institutional Analysis of the Enforcement Problems in Merger Control", (2010) 6 EuroCJ, 445.

Gerard, D., "Protectionist Threats against Cross-border Mergers: Unexplored Avenues to Strengthen the Effectiveness of Article 21 ECMR", (2008) 45 CMLRev., 987.

Howarth, D., "The Court of First Instance in GE/Honeywell", (2006) ECLR, 485.

Reeves, T., and Dodoo, N., "Standards of Proof and Standards of Judicial Review in European Commission Merger Law", (2006), 29 Fordham Int'l L.J., 1034.

Riesenkampff, A., "The New EC Merger Control Test under Article 2 of the Merger Control Regulation", (2004) 24 Nw. J. Int'l L. & Bus., 715.

Wang, W., "Structural Remedies in EU Antitrust and Merger Control", (2011) 34/4 *World Competition*, 571.

Werden, G.J., "Economic Reasoning in Merger Cases and How Courts should Evaluate", (2009) 5 EuroCJ, 701.

Witt, A.C., "From *Airtours* to *Ryanair*. Is the More Economic Approach to EU Merger Law Really about More Economics?" (2012) 49 CMLRev., 217.

PROBLEM QUESTION

A and B are undertakings operating in the rolled zinc market. The managing directors of A and B have agreed that A and B will jointly acquire C, an undertaking active in the rolled zinc market which would have had to close down within five months had it not found a buyer. C operates mainly in the EU. Its turnover in the last financial year was €600 million. The managing directors of A and B have decided that immediately after the acquisition of C its assets will be divided between A and B in that A will acquire two-thirds of them and B will acquire one-third. The managing director of A expects that after the acquisition and division of C's assets, A's world-wide annual turnover will quickly increase from €6,000 million to €6,300 million and its EU-wide turnover will increase from €300 million to €600 million. The managing director of B expects that after the acquisition and division of C's assets, B's world-wide turnover will quickly reach €500 million and its EU-wide turnover will be €300 million.

The managing directors of A and B are uncertain whether they should notify to the Commission the joint acquisition of C, the division of C's assets thereafter, or both or neither.

Advise the managing directors of A and B how they should proceed, if at all, with regard to notification to the Commission.

ESSAY QUESTION

Critically discuss the situations where the Commission and NCAs may refer to each other the assessment of compatibility of an intended concentration with the internal market.

MERGER CONTROL
Types of concentration

Merger
Where two or more previously independent undertakings merge *de facto* or *de jure*

Acquisition of control
Where one or more persons already controlling at least one or more undertakings, acquire, whether by purchase of securities or assets, by contract or by any other means, direct or indirect control of the whole or parts of one or more other undertakings

Full-function joint ventures
Must perform on a lasting basis all the functions of an autonomous economic entity

The concept of an EU dimension
A concentration has an EU dimension when it exceeds either of the following thresholds

Primary test

Secondary test

The combined aggregate worldwide turnover of all participating undertakings is over €5 billion and the aggregate EU-wide turnover of each of at least two of the undertakings concerned is more than €250 million, unless each of the undertakings concerned achieves more than two-thirds of its aggregate EU-wide turnover within one and the same Member State (Article 1(2) of the MR).

The combined aggregate worldwide turnover of all the undertakings concerned is more than €2.5 billion and an aggregate EU-wide turnover of €100 million or more is spread between not fewer than three Member States, and

(i) Each of at least two of the undertakings concerned generates at least €25 million turnover in each of the Member States over which the above-mentioned €100 million or more turnover is spread; and
(ii) The aggregate EU-wide turnover of each of at least two of the undertakings concerned is more than €100 million.

However, if each of the undertakings concerned achieves more than two-thirds of its aggregate EU-wide turnover within one and the same Member State, the MR will not apply (Article 1(3) of the MR).

Substantial appraisal of concentration

The substantive test for the assessment of concentrations provides that:

"a concentration which would significantly impede effective competition in the common market or in a substantial part of it, in particular as a result of strengthening of a dominant position, shall be declared incompatible with the common market."

The test has two objectives:

to prohibit a concentration which strengthens or creates a dominant position;

to block a concentration which takes place in the context of a non-collusive oligopoly, and does not lead to a single or joint dominance, but still produces effects which significantly impede effective competition in the internal market or a substantial part of it.

The procedure under the MR

Any intended concentration with an EU dimension must be notified to the Commission after the conclusion of the agreement, announcement of the public bid, or the acquisition of a controlling interest.

Phase I Investigation

- The Commission takes an initial decision (that is, whether the Commission has serious doubts as to the compatibility of the concentration with the internal market) within 25 working days following receipt of complete notification (but the time limit may be extended).

Phase II Investigation

- If the Commission considers that the intended concentration raises serious concern, the Commission must open a Phase II investigation, which must be concluded within 90 working days (but the time limit may be extended).

30

ENFORCEMENT OF ARTICLES 101 AND 102 TFEU

CHAPTER OUTLINE

1. This chapter examines the enforcement of Articles 101 and 102 TFEU by the Commission, by national courts and by NCAs and the manner in which all competition law enforcement bodies within the EU are required to co-operate in order to ensure the uniform application of EU competition law.

2. There is an on-going process of modernisation and simplification of EU competition law, part of which has resulted in a major overhaul of the enforcement of Articles 101 and 102 TFEU. The previous system of notification under Article 101(3) TFEU was abolished; Article 101(3) has become directly effective; and, the enforcement system has been decentralised, i.e. when the jurisdictional threshold concerning effect on trade between Member States is met, the relevant NCA is required to apply Articles 101 and 102 TFEU alone, or together with relevant national competition rules.

3. The Commission may become aware of an infringement of EU competition law by many means, one being a complaint lodged by a Member State or any natural or legal person. The Commission is under a duty to reply to a formal complaint by a natural or legal person, i.e. a complaint written on the official form ("Form C") by a person who can show a legitimate interest. A complaint may be rejected if it does not raise sufficient EU interest. Failure to reply may result in an action under Article 265 TFEU. Informal complaints may lead the Commission to open a case, but confer no rights on the complainant.

4. The Commission may adopt final decisions and procedural decisions during investigations. It can also impose the following fines on undertakings (but not on individuals):

■ Substantive fines for:

● Infringements of Articles 101 and 102;
● Failure to comply with an interim measures decision; and,
● Failure to comply with a binding commitment made under Article 9 of Regulation 1/2003.

These can be as high as 10 per cent of the undertaking's global turnover in the preceding business year.

■ Procedural fines up to 1 per cent of an undertaking's global turnover in the preceding business year when the undertaking has committed offences in relation to requests for information or inspections.

■ Periodic penalty payments for defiance of the Commission of up 5 per cent of the average daily turnover in the preceding business year at a daily rate.

5. The Commission runs a leniency programme aimed at combating cartels. It offers undertakings participating in a cartel immunity or reduction of fines which would have been imposed, had the Commission discovered the cartel, in exchange for self-reporting and co-operation in the Commission's investigation.

6. In order to ensure consistency and uniformity in the parallel enforcement of Articles 101 and 102 TFEU (by NCAs and by the Commission), Regulation 1/2003 sets out basic rules on co-operation between the Commission and the NCAs and between NCAs themselves. These rules mainly concern matters relating to allocation of cases, exchange of information and consultation. To foster co-operation between NCAs, there is an informal "European Competition Network" (ECN), consisting of all NCAs and the Commission. It has no legal status. It provides a forum for discussions and exchange of information on best practices.

7. National courts have an important role to play in the enforcement of EU competition law having been empowered to apply Article 101 TFEU in its entirety since the entry into force of Regulation 1/2003. The basic rules on co-operation between the Commission and national courts are defined in the Commission's 2004 Notice on Co-operation between the Commission and the Courts of the EU Member States.

8. Private enforcement of EU competition law before national courts has been regarded by the Commission as vital. In 2008 the Commission published a White Paper on antitrust damages actions by private claimants, a follow-up to its 2005 Green Paper.

30.1 Introduction

Under Article 103 TFEU the Council is empowered to adopt any appropriate measures in order to give effect to Articles 101 and 102 TFEU. The first and the most important implementing measure was Council Regulation 17/62[2687] adopted by the Council in 1962 which set out detailed rules for the application of Articles 101 and 102 TFEU. Regulation 17/62 provided for a centralised enforcement system which put the Commission in charge of the notification procedure under Article 101(3) TFEU.

When Regulation 17/62 was adopted the Community had only six Member States and the internal market was at the nascent stage. With the development and expansion of the EU a new approach was

---

2687. [1959–61] OJ Spec. Ed, 87.

needed. The Commission recognised this and in May 1999 published a White Paper which proposed a profound reform of the rules implementing Articles 101 and 102 TFEU.[2688] The Commission explained that there was a need for modernisation of EU competition law taking into account the following external factors:

- ▪ the enlargement of the EU;

- ▪ the existence of a single market and single currency; and,

- ▪ the globalisation of economy;

and the following internal factors:

- ▪ the limited resources available to the Commission;

- ▪ the requirements of the principle of subsidiarity; and,

- ▪ the need for coherent application of competition rules at national and at EU levels entailing the avoidance of parallel proceedings before the Commission and national authorities.

With regard to the enforcement of Articles 101 and 102 TFEU, the reform culminated with the adoption of Regulation 1/2003,[2689] which entered into force on 1 May 2004. The Regulation is accompanied by Regulation 773/2004[2690] on the Conduct of Proceedings by the Commission Pursuant to Articles [101 and 102 TFEU] (which gives "flesh to the bare bones" of Regulation 1/2003 – the implementing regulation) and a number of notices and guidelines which form the so-called "Modernisation Package".[2691] In 2008 the Commission introduced a system under which some cartel cases can be settled.[2692] In 2011, the Commission adopted a Notice on Best Practices for the Conduct of Proceedings Concerning Articles 101 and 102 TFEU[2693] which seeks to increase the efficiency, transparency and predictability of those proceedings. The application of the effects-based approach prompted the Commission to adopt a Notice on Best Practices for the Submission of Economic Evidence and Data Collection in Cases concerning the Application of Articles 101, 102 TFEU and in Merger cases.[2694]

The two main themes of the modernisation were simplification and decentralisation. This was achieved by the following:

A. **The replacement of the notification and authorisation system by a "legal exception" system.** Under the legal exception system, agreements, decisions and concerted practices are lawful from the outset if they do not breach Article 101(1) TFEU or if they meet the conditions set out block exemption regulations or in Article 101(3) TFEU (see Chapter 27.8 and 27.9). According to Article 1 of Regulation 1/2003, commercial arrangements within the meaning of Article 101(1) TFEU need no longer be notified to the Commission in order to obtain

---

2688. [1999] OJ C132/1.

2689. [2003] OJ L1/1. It replaced Regulation 1/17.

2690. [2004] OJ L123/18.

2691. Detailed examination of the modernisation "package" is provided in this chapter.

2692. Regulation 622/2008 which amended Regulation 773/2004 ([2008] OJ L171/3) by inserting a new Article 10a entitled "Settlement Procedure in Cartel Cases". The Commission explains the procedure in its "Notice on the Conduct of Settlement Procedures in View of the Adoption of Decisions Pursuant to Article 7 and Article 23 of Council Regulation 1/2003 in Cartel Cases" [2008] OJ C167/1.

2693. [2011] OJ C308/6-32.

2694. Available at http://ec.europa.eu/competition/antitrust/legislation/best_practices_submission_en.pdf (accessed 25/4/12).

exemption. Undertakings themselves must assess whether their agreements, decisions or concerted practices meet the criteria set out in Article 101(3) TFEU and be ready to defend their assessment before national courts and NCAs.

B. **Direct applicability of Article 101(3) TFEU.** Article 101 TFEU became directly applicable in its entirety, whereas previously only the first two paragraphs were directly applicable. This means that national courts and NCAs are empowered to apply directly not only Articles 101(1) and (2) TFEU and 102 TFEU but also Article 101(3) TFEU.

C. **Decentralisation of enforcement.** Under Regulation 1/2003 the Commission shares its enforcement powers with NCAs and national courts. The decentralisation of the enforcement of Articles 101 and 102 TFEU means that when the jurisdictional threshold concerning effect on trade between Member States is met (see Chapter 26.4.1), the relevant NCA is required to apply Articles 101 and 102 TFEU alone or together with relevant national competition rules. The Commission supervises the system and will intervene whenever necessary to ensure that EU competition law is applied consistently and uniformly in the Member States. This system allows the Commission to concentrate its limited resources on important matters, and the most serious infringements of EU law, leaving less important tasks to NCAs and national courts. The Commission alone is empowered to initiate legislation at EU level in competition matters as well as to draw up further notices and guidelines to assist national authorities in the application of EU competition rules and policies. In order to make the system work properly, a mechanism entitled the European Competition Network (ECN) was set up to increase co-operation between the Commission and NCAs.

D. **Increase of the Commission's investigatory powers.** The Commission's investigatory powers were increased, particularly with regard to obtaining information from undertakings under investigation. Regulation 1/2003 also provides for additional fines for failure to co-operate with the Commission.

E. **Confirmation of the application of EU law over national law.** In order to ensure uniformity in the application of EU competition law Article 3 of Regulation 1/2003 sets out the relationship between Articles 101 and 102 TFEU and national competition law. Under Article 3(1) national courts and NCAs are required to apply EU competition law alongside national law whenever a case falls within the scope of Articles 101 and 102 TFEU. They may also apply Articles 101 and 102 TFEU exclusively. Further, in order to ensure the supremacy and the effectiveness of EU competition law Article 3(2) provides that any commercial arrangement which is lawful under Article 101 EC is also lawful under national competition law. However, Member States are not precluded from adopting and applying on their territory stricter national laws which prohibit or sanction abuses of a dominant position, that is, national competition rules which are stricter than Article 102 TFEU.

30.2 Enforcement of Articles 101 and 102 TFEU by the Commission

Within the Commission the Directorate General for Competition (DG Competition) is in charge of competition policy and enforcement of EU competition law. DG Competition comprises 10 directorates covering management, antitrust and merger policy, cartel enforcement, sectoral expertise (four directorates) and state aid (three directorates). A Director General, who is a career manager, is responsible for DG Competition and reports directly to the Commissioner for Competition.

DG Competition employs a chief economist, who works with a team to provide independent advice on economic issues in the application of EU competition law, in general and in respect of particular cases, and who co-ordinates the activities of the Economic Advisory Group on Competition Policy. The post of chief economist is of great importance given that enforcement of competition law is inextricably linked with economics, in particular with its branch called industrial organisation. Its creation was the Commission's response to criticism that it neglected the importance of economic analyses to the application of competition law.

There are two hearing officers who are independent of DG Competition and who report directly to the Commissioner for Competition (see Chapter 30.2.4).

The procedures and powers of the Commission in competition matters are dealt with below.

30.2.1 The initiation of proceedings: complaints to the Commission in respect of infringements of Articles 101 and 102 TFEU

The Commission may become aware of the infringement of EU competition law through any source, for example, the press, TV, complaints from competitors and the general public. It may act *ex officio*, or upon an application from a Member State. With regard to natural or legal persons, a distinction must be made between an informal and formal complaint. The Commission is under a duty to reply to a formal complaint, i.e. a complaint written on the official form ("Form C")[2695] by a person who can show a legitimate interest.[2696] It is not difficult to show such an interest. Complainants must demonstrate that their interest is, or is likely to be, adversely affected by the anti-competitive conduct of an undertaking.[2697]

Under Regulation 1/2003 a complaint may be made to both the Commission and the relevant NCA. The Commission's 2004 Notice on the Handling of Complaints by the Commission under Articles 101 and 102 TFEU[2698] provides guidance to a potential complainant. According to the Notice a complaint should be lodged with the authority which is best placed to deal with it. In this respect the Commission's Notice on Co-operation (see Chapter 30.3.1) is helpful as it sets out criteria for identifying the best placed authority in respect of allocation of cases between the Commission and the Member States. Article 23 of the 2004 Notice on the Handling of Complaints provides that the members of the ECN will endeavour to determine within the time limit of two months which NCA is best placed to deal with the complaint, and that complainants must be informed of the location at which their complaint is being dealt with and of any change in that location. Under Article 25 of the 2004 Notice the Commission may reject a complaint on the ground that a NCA is dealing with, or has dealt with the case. The Commission must inform the complainant without delay of the NCA which is dealing with or has dealt with the case.

A complainant should take into consideration many factors when choosing whether to bring an action based on Article 101 or Article 102 before national authorities, national courts or before the Commission. The factors include:

- The inability of the Commission to award damages to an aggrieved party or to provide the remedy of restitution;

- The powers of the Commission to investigate the alleged infringement, which are more extensive than those of national authorities;

2695. Case 210/81 *Oswald Schmidt, trading as Demo-Studio Schmidt v Commission* [1983] ECR 3045.
2696. Article 7 of Regulation 1/2003.
2697. See Case T-144/92 *BEMIM v Commission* [1995] ECR II-147, where it was accepted that a trade association had standing in a situation where its members were likely to be adversely affected by the conduct complained of.
2698. [2004] OJ C101/65.

- The cost of proceedings before national courts whereas proceedings before the Commission are free;

- The possibility for the Commission to impose substantial fines; and,

- The length of time likely to be taken to achieve the desired result.

In Case T-24/90 *Automec (II)*[2699] the General Court stated that the procedure concerning individual complaints before the Commission could be divided into three stages:

- First stage: the submission of the complaint, which is followed by the gathering of information by the Commission and involves informal contact with the parties;

- Second stage (if appropriate): notification by the Commission of its intention not to pursue the complaint, specifying the reasons for the Commission's decision and inviting complainants to submit their observations within a fixed time limit; and,

- Third stage: following receipt of observations from the complainants, if any (or in the absence of the second stage), the Commission has a duty[2700] either to initiate a procedure against the subject of the complaint or to adopt a definitive decision rejecting the complaint.

In Case C-282/95P *Guérin*,[2701] the ECJ specified that at the end of the third stage the Commission is required to take a definitive position as to whether to proceed with the complaint within a reasonable time.[2702] If the Commission adopts a final decision on rejection or acceptance of a complaint, the complainant has *locus standi* to seek judicial review of that decision under Article 263 TFEU.[2703]

30.2.1.1 The meaning of "EU interest"

The Commission may reject a complaint on the ground that it does not raise sufficient EU interest. The concept of "EU interest" was clarified by the General Court in Case T-24/90 *Automec II*.[2704] In that case the General Court stated that the Commission is entitled to prioritise cases and assess on a factual and legal basis whether a case raises significant EU interest, in particular as regards the functioning of the internal market, the probability of establishing the existence of an infringement and the required scope of the investigation. Thus, the Commission is not required to start an investigation in each case, although it is obliged to reply to the complainant.

Some helpful guidelines as to the criteria to be applied in order to assess whether a particular case has an EU interest are provided by Article 44 of the 2004 Notice on Handling Complaints. These are:

- whether or not complainants can bring action to enforce their rights before a national court;

- the seriousness, duration, and effect within the EU of the alleged infringement on competition;

2699. Case T-24/90 *Automec Srl v Commission* [1992] ECR II-2223.
2700. Case C-282/95P *Guérin Automobiles v Commission* [1997] ECR I-1503.
2701. Ibid.
2702. Case T-127/98 *UPS Europe SA v Commission* [1999] ECR II-2633.
2703. Case 26/76 *Metro v Commission* [1977] ECR 1875.
2704. [1992] ECR II-2223. The definition of "EU interest" provided in *Automec* rather than that provided in Article 44 of the 2004 Notice was applied by the General Court in Case T-458/04 *Au Lys de France SA v Commission* [2007] ECR II-71.

- the significance of the alleged infringement as regards the functioning of the internal market, the probability of establishing the existence of the infringement and the scope of the investigation to be carried out;

- the stage of investigation if the investigation has already commenced;

- whether or not the infringement has ceased and if so whether its anti-competitive effects are serious and persistent; and,

- whether the undertaking concerned, as a result of the complaint, has agreed to change its conduct in such a way that it can be considered that there is no longer a sufficient EU interest to intervene.

30.2.2 The first stage of the procedure: obtaining information

Under Article 18 of Regulation 1/2003 the Commission has power to compel undertakings to provide "all necessary information". In Case 374/87 *Orkem*,[2705] the ECJ held first, that it is up to the Commission to decide what information is "necessary", and second, that "necessary information" relates to anything which is connected to or has some relationship to the information requested and the infringement under investigation.

In Case C-36/92P *SEP*,[2706] the ECJ further explained that information should be regarded as necessary if it has some connection with the alleged infringement, assists detection of, or confirmation of, the alleged infringement or confirms evidence already gathered by the Commission.

The request for information may take two forms. Under Regulation 1/2003 the Commission can choose which is the most appropriate in the light of the circumstances of the case.

- A simple request. The Commission may ask the competent authorities of the Member States, their officials and other servants, undertakings and associations of undertakings for information. There is no duty to comply with a simple request. However, if incorrect or misleading information is supplied, the Commission may impose a fine up to 1 per cent of the undertaking's turnover in the preceding business year (Article 18(2) of Regulation 1/2003).

- A formal decision requesting the information to be provided. If the Commission adopts a decision requesting information and the undertaking concerned fails to comply within a time limit specified in that decision, the Commission may impose periodic penalties under Article 24 (up to 5 per cent of the average daily turnover). The Commission has a duty to send a copy of the decision to the NCA in the place of the seat of the undertaking and to the Member States which are affected. Often when an addressee of a simple request for information fails to provide it within a fixed time limit or supplies incomplete or inexact information, the Commission adopts a formal decision requiring the supply of information (Article 18(3) of Regulation 1/2003).

Each of the above requests for information must specify the legal basis and the reason for the request, the information requested, the consequences of an incorrect or misleading response and a deadline for response.

2705. Case 374/87 *Orkem v Commission* [1989] ECR 3283.
2706. Case C-36/92P *Samenwerkende Elektriciteits Produktiebedrijven (SEP) NV v Commission* [1994] ECR I-1911.

30.2.2.1   Self-incriminating information

In Case 27/88 *Solvay*[2707] and in Case 374/87 *Orkem*[2708] the issue was whether an undertaking under investigation could refuse to supply the relevant information by relying on the right not to incriminate oneself. The ECJ held that it is the task of the Commission to evidence the infringement of Articles 101(1) or 102 TFEU and that an undertaking cannot be compelled to admit an infringement, as this would undermine its rights to defence, but added that an undertaking is obliged to co-operate with the Commission and thus to supply documents required by the Commission even though these might serve to establish the infringement.[2709]

It follows from the above that the ECJ, on the one hand, recognises the right not to self-incriminate by admitting the infringement but, on the other, refuses the right not to provide evidence against oneself. This position is contrary to the case law of the European Court of Human Rights (ECtHR), which has developed subsequent to the judgment of the ECJ in *Orkem*. The ECtHR in, *inter alia*, *Funke v France*,[2710] *Saunders v UK*[2711] and *J.B. v Switzerland*[2712] ruled that the right to remain silent and not to contribute to incriminating oneself applies to undertakings and is therefore covered by Article 6 of the ECHR.

In *PVC Cartel II*,[2713] the undertakings concerned argued that EU competition law should adjust to the case law of the ECtHR. The ECJ held that the developments in the ECtHR jurisprudence since *Orkem* did not change the position of EU law on these matters. The ECJ in *PVC Cartel II* stated that the right of undertakings not to be compelled by the Commission to admit an infringement of EU competition law is to be understood as meaning that: "in the event of a dispute as to the scope of a question, it must be determined whether an answer from the undertaking to which the question is addressed is in fact equivalent to the admission of an infringement, such as to undermine the rights of the defence."[2714] In this judgment the ECJ emphasised that the case law of the ECtHR requires, first, the exercise of coercion against the suspect in order to obtain information from him or her; and second, establishment of an actual interference with the protected right in order for there to be a violation of Article 6 of the ECHR (see Chapter 30.2.8).

In conclusion, it can be said that the privilege against self-incrimination applies:

- First, when a request for information makes provision of the information compulsory, i.e. made under Article 18(3) of Regulation 1/2003 (thus the privilege does not apply to information provided in response to a simple request for information under Article 18(2) of Regulation 1/2003).

- Second, when it is addressed to an undertaking under investigation.

- Third, only in respect of questions addressed by the Commission to the undertaking under investigation and not in respect of documents in its possession which must be forwarded to the Commission even if those documents may incriminate the undertaking concerned. The Notice on

---

2707.   Case 27/88 *Solvay & Cie v Commission* [1989] ECR 3355.

2708.   Case 374/87 *Orkem v Commission* [1989] ECR 3283.

2709.   This was confirmed in Case C-301/04P *Commission v SGL Carbon* [2006] ECR I-5915.

2710.   (1993) 16 EHRR 297. The ECtHR held that anyone charged with a criminal offence has the right to remain silent and not to contribute to incriminating himself. This includes the right not to supply incriminating documents.

2711.   (1997) 23 EHRR 313.

2712.   [2001] 12/5–6 Human Rights Case Digest p 281.

2713.   Cases C-238, 244–245, 247, 250–252 and 254/99P *Limburgse Vinyl Maatschappij NV and Others v Commission* [2002] ECR I-8375.

2714.   Ibid, para. 273.

Best Practices in the Conduct of Proceedings Concerning Articles 101 and 102 specifies that when there is a disagreement between the undertaking concerned and the Commission on whether the answer to questions asked by the Commission is covered by the privilege, the undertaking concerned may, after raising this matter with the Directorate-General for Competition of the Commission, refer it to the Hearing Officer, who will make a reasoned recommendation as to whether the privilege against self-incrimination applies. The recommendation will be taken into account when the Commission adopts any decision under Article 18(3) of Regulation 1/2003.

30.2.2.2   Legal professional privilege (LPP)

The principle of lawyer–client confidentiality is recognised under EU law, but a distinction is made between communications between a client and its in-house lawyer and a client and its independent lawyer.[2715]

Only communications between a client and an independent lawyer, which are made for the purpose and in the interests of the client's rights of defence, are privileged. The explanation is that an in-house lawyer is bound to his client by an employment relationship and that in some Member States there are differing rules of ethics with regard to independent lawyers and in-house lawyers.

It was expected that this position might change as a result of the order in Case T-125/03 and T-253/03 *Akzo Nobel*, in which the president of the General Court stated in his Order[2716] of 30 October 2003 that the arguments presented by *Akzo Nobel* regarding the extension of professional privilege to cover communications with in-house lawyers were not unfounded, in particular (as was the situation in this case) when an in-house-lawyer is subject to professional rules equivalent to those imposed on an independent lawyer. However, on 17 September 2007 the General Court[2717] rendered a judgment maintaining the pre-existing position. The Court held that there was no valid reason to reconsider that position given that comparative examination of national laws of the Member States shows that a large number of them exclude in-house lawyers from the benefit of LPP, and that the principle of equal treatment in the context of the right of establishment and the right to provide services has not been infringed. The Court stated that the situation of an independent lawyer and an in-house lawyer are different due to the functional, structural and hierarchical integration of in-house lawyers within the undertakings that employ them.

In the above case the General Court made important statements regarding privileged documents:

- It held that during investigations the Commission is not allowed to take even a cursory look at documents which are claimed by the undertaking concerned as being privileged.

- The Commission is not entitled to read such documents before it adopts a decision refusing to classify such documents as privileged, and before a challenge, if any, to that decision by the undertaking concerned has been rejected by the General Court.

- Documents which were drafted exclusively for the purpose of seeking legal advice from an independent lawyer in the exercise of the rights of defence, even if they have not been communicated with a lawyer, may be classified as privileged.

2715.   Case 155/79 *AM and S Ltd v Commission* [1982] ECR 1575.

2716.   Case T-125/03 and T-253/03 *Akzo Nobel Chemicals Ltd and Akcros Chemicals Ltd v Commission* [2003] ECR II-4771.

2717.   [2007] ECR II-3523.

■ Documents which were discussed with an independent lawyer are not necessarily covered by LPP. This depends on whether they were prepared for the purpose of seeking legal advice.

In Case C-550/07 P *Akzo Nobel*,[2718] the ECJ upheld the above judgment of the General Court. The ECJ held that communications of lawyers are covered by LPP if two cumulative conditions are satisfied: first, the communication must be connected to the client's rights of defence; and second, it must be from an independent lawyer, i.e. a lawyer which is not in a relationship of employment with her or his client. The Court specified that the second condition is not satisfied so far as exchanges of communications within a company or group of companies with their in-house lawyers are concerned because the requirement of independence is absent even when an in-house lawyer is a member of a Bar or Law Society and thus bound to follow rules of the professional ethical obligations. In this respect the ECJ emphasised that the ability of in-house lawyers to exercise professional independence are affected by the facts that they, being employees, cannot ignore the commercial strategies pursued by their employers and that depending upon the terms of their employment contracts in-house lawyers may be required to perform tasks which are not confined to providing legal advice. Accordingly, the ECJ held that in-house lawyers do not enjoy a level of professional independence comparable to that of external lawyers on the grounds of their economic dependence on and close ties with their employers. This case confirmed that where there is a disagreement between an undertaking and the Commission as to whether relevant documents are covered by LPP, it is the task of the General Court to decide the matter. Accordingly, officials of the Commission have no right to see those relevant documents, or even to take a cursory look at them until the disagreement has been resolved as this may influence their final decision. The proper procedure for the Commission is to adopt a decision requiring the relevant documents to be forwarded to it, which decision may then be appealed by the undertaking concerned to the General Court, which will make a final decision on whether the relevant documents are covered by LPP.

30.2.2.3 Power to take statements

Article 19 of Regulation 1/2003 gives the Commission power to interview any natural or legal persons, with their consent, in order to collect information relating to the investigation. An NCA in whose territory the interview will be held must be informed and is entitled to be present during interviews. There are no penalties for providing incorrect or misleading information at an interview.

30.2.2.4 Sector enquiries

The objective of sector enquiries is to study the functioning of the relevant sector and to decide what measures, if any, should be taken to improve conditions of competition in that sector. Since the entry into force of Regulation 1/2003 this provision has been used often. The Commission has launched enquiries into, *inter alia*, the retail banking sector, the energy sector, the pharmaceutical industry and the financial services sector. Accordingly, the reform of the enforcement of EU competition law allows the Commission to be more proactive in the enforcement of that law, and sector enquiries, which were very rarely carried out under the old regulation, are the best example of this.

30.2.3 Inspections

Article 20 of Regulation 1/2003 defines the Commission's powers of investigation.

2718. C-550/07 P *Akzo Nobel Chemicals Ltd, and Akcros Chemicals Ltd v Commission* [2010] ECR I-18301.

Article 20(2) authorises the Commission to undertake all necessary investigations into undertakings and associations of undertakings including:

- examination of books and other business records;

- taking copies of or extracts from the books and business records;

- asking for oral explanations on the spot;

- entering any premises, land and means of transport belonging to undertakings; and,

- sealing any business premises and books or records for the period and to the extent necessary for the inspection. If seals are broken, the Commission may impose a fine on the undertaking of up to 1 per cent of its total turnover in the preceding year.

Investigations may be carried out under a "simple" written authorisation given by the Commission or under a formal decision adopted by the Commission, and with or without prior notification to the undertaking concerned.

In Case 136/79 *Panasonic*,[2719] the ECJ held that the Commission may choose between a simple written authorisation and a formal decision in the light of the special features of each case. Both the written authorisation and the formal decision must specify the subject-matter and purpose of the investigation.

An undertaking is not obliged to submit to investigation under a "simple authorisation". Due notice of its refusal is, however, taken by the Commission's officials. In such a situation the Commission may adopt a formal decision to inspect. Also, when the Commission fears that vital evidence may be destroyed, it adopts a formal decision. Refusal of an undertaking to submit to an investigation ordered by way of a decision was examined in Joined Cases 46/87 and 227/88 *Hoechst*.[2720]

THE FACTS WERE:

The plaintiff objected to the conduct of the search on the ground that this had infringed general principles of EU law and the need to respect due process of law as enshrined in the ECHR.

Held:

The ECJ held that certain rights of defence, such as the right to legal representation and the privileged nature of correspondence between an independent lawyer and his client, must be respected as from the preliminary inquiry stage. Other usual rights of defence which relate to the contentious proceedings which follow the delivery of the statement of objections could be overridden during the investigations stage, taking into account that inspections may be decisive in providing evidence of the unlawful nature of conduct engaged in by undertakings.[2721]

2719. Case 136/79 *National Panasonic v EC Commission* [1980] ECR 2033.

2720. Joined Cases 46/87 and 227/88 *Hoechst AG v Commission* [1989] ECR 2859.

2721. See also Case 322/81 *NV Nederlandsche Banden Industrie Michelin (Michelin I) v Commission* [1983] ECR 361.

Commission officials may decide to carry out a so-called "dawn raid" – that is, arrive at the undertaking's premises without warning (at any time of day!). In such event, the relevant NCA must be consulted before the inspection is carried out but there is no special procedure to be followed. A phone call from the Commission will suffice.[2722] The undertaking under investigation is legally obliged to submit to an investigation ordered by a Commission decision under Article 20(4) of Regulation 1/2003. However, if it refuses to admit the Commission staff, under EU law alone the Commission's officials are not entitled to enter the premises of the undertaking under investigation. They have to respect the relevant procedural guarantees laid down in the national law of the undertaking under investigation.

Under Article 20(5), at the request of the Commission, officials of the relevant NCA shall actively assist the Commission with inspections. Article 20(6) provides that when an undertaking refuses to submit to investigations, NCAs are required to provide necessary assistance to enable the Commission to make its investigation. Article 20(7) states that if judicial authorisation is required, such authorisation should be applied for. Article 20(8) incorporates the principle emanating from Case C-94/00 *Roquette Frères*,[2723] in which the ECJ held that when judicial authorisation is required, a national court is neither entitled to call into question the need for the investigations (since only the ECJ can review the acts of the Commission) nor demand to be supplied with all the information in the Commission's possession. A national court is empowered to verify whether the Commission's decision is authentic and whether the coercive measures sought are arbitrary or excessive. If in doubt, a national court may ask the Commission to provide further clarification.

A refusal to co-operate with the Commission during an inspection is considered by the Commission as an aggravating factor to be taken into account when, if relevant, it determines the amounts of fine for the substantive infringement (see Chapter 30.2.7). For example, in the case of *Professional Videotapes*[2724] the Commission increased the fine imposed on Sony by 30 per cent when an employee refused to answer questions and another shredded documents during the inspection.

It is clear that the Commission is not permitted to carry out "fishing expeditions". The subject of the investigations must be specified in an authorisation or decision, that is, the suspicion which the Commission is seeking to verify must be clearly indicated, but, as the ECJ held in *Hoechst*, the Commission is not obliged to provide the addressee with all the information at its disposal in relation to the alleged infringement.

30.2.3.1   Inspections in premises other than those of an undertaking under investigation

Incriminating documents may be kept at non-business premises including private homes.[2725] Article 21 of Regulation 1/2003 gives the Commission power, subject to prior judicial authorisation, to search private homes if such documents are likely to be kept there.

30.2.4   The second stage of the procedure: hearings

Under both Article 27 of Regulation 1/2003 and Article 10(1) of Regulation 773/2004 the Commission is required to give undertakings concerned the opportunity to be heard before adopting any decision finding an infringement, taking interim measures, or imposing fines or periodic payments.

2722.   Case 5/85 *AKZO Chemie BV and AKZO Chemie UK Ltd v Commission* [1986] ECR 2585, para. 24.

2723.   Case C-94/00 *Roquette Frères SA v Commission* [2002] ECR I-9011.

2724.   See Commission press release IP/07/1724 of 20/11/07.

2725.   In *SAS/Maersk Air* [2001] OJ L265/15 the Commission discovered incriminating documents relating to a market sharing agreement in individuals' homes.

The first step of the contentious procedure starts when the Commission sends a letter to the undertaking concerned specifying the objections raised against it. This "statement of objections" (SO) must set forth clearly all the essential facts upon which the Commission relies against the undertaking. In the final decision the Commission must repeat only objections set out in the SO and cannot add any new matters. This is to ensure that the undertaking concerned is aware of the allegations to which it will wish to respond and to protect the undertaking's right to be heard.[2726] The Commission specifies a time limit for a written submission which an undertaking concerned may submit in response to the SO. An undertaking is not obliged to reply,[2727] although this is necessary if the undertaking wishes to have the opportunity to submit its arguments orally at an oral hearing.

The Commission will offer the parties the opportunity to attend an oral hearing. In order to ensure that the rights of the parties are respected, hearings are conducted by persons appointed by the Commission and referred to as "hearing officers". This post was created in 1982[2728] to respond to criticism that the Commission acts as prosecutor, jury and judge and uses biased evidence against the defendant. The powers of hearing officers were greatly extended by Commission Decision 2001/462[2729] and Decision 2011/695.[2730] The hearing officer, an independent person (although appointed by the Commission and attached to the commissioner in charge of competition) experienced in competition matters and of high moral standing, is familiar with the file, and ensures that the hearing is properly conducted and that the requirements of due process are respected.[2731]

30.2.5 The right of access to the file

Access to documents relevant to the case is of vital importance to the parties concerned. The extent to which a party can have access to documents has been specified in a number of cases decided by the EU judicature, and further explained by the Commission in its Notice on the internal rules of procedure for processing requests for access to the file in merger and antitrust procedures.[2732] Access to a file is granted only to addressees of a SO. However, the Notice recognises a separate right, granting limited access to specific documents on the file to complainants in antitrust cases (see Chapter 30.4) and in merger cases to persons other than those directly involved in an intended concentration. The "Commission file" contains all documents that are part of the specific procedure on which the SO has been based. The Notice distinguishes between documents which are accessible and those which are not. Non-accessible documents are:[2733]

- ▪ Documents which the Commission considers to be confidential. Article 245 TFEU imposes a duty of confidentiality on the members of the Commission. This general duty of confidentiality is reinforced by Article 28 of Regulation 1/2003 which provides that information collected for

---

2726. Joined Cases C-89/85, C-114/85, C-116/85, C-117/85 and C-125/85 to C-129/85 *Ahlström and Others v Commission [Re Wood Pulp Cartel]* [1993] ECR I-1307.

2727. Case T-30/89 *Hilti AG v Commission* [1991] ECR II-1439.

2728. [1982] OJ C251/2 and the Commission Decision 94/810 [1994] OJ L330/67.

2729. [2001] OJ L162/21.

2730. [2011] OJ L275/29.

2731. On the role of the Hearing Officer see Durante and Williams, "The Practical Impact of the Exercise of the Right to be Heard: A Special Focus on the Effect of Oral Hearings and the Role of the Hearing Officer", (2005) *Competition Policy Newsletter*, 22.

2732. [2005] OJ C325/7-15.

2733. Case T-7/89 *SA Hercules Chemicals NV v Commission* [1991] ECR II-1711; Case C-185/95P *Baustahlgewebe GmbH v Commission* [1999] ECR I-8417; Cases C-204–205/00P, C-211/00P, C-231/00P, C-217/00P and C-219/00P *Aalborg Portland A/S and Others v Commission* [2004] ECR I-123.

the purposes of investigations in competition matters must only be used for the purposes for which it was acquired. Two kinds of documents may be identified: those concerning business secrets and those relating to other confidential documents:

- Documents which relate to business secrets. In Case 53/85 *AKZO*,[2734] the ECJ emphasised that undertakings have a legitimate interest in protecting their business secrets, taking into account the extremely serious damage which could result from improper communication of documents to a competitor. It then held that it is for the Commission to judge whether or not a particular document contains business secrets. If there is a request from a third party to consult a particular document, the Commission must inform the undertaking from which a document was taken. If the undertaking concerned identifies that this document is of a confidential nature, the Commission has two options. First, it may agree with the undertaking concerned, whereupon a document will not be communicated to a third party. Second, the Commission may disagree, in which case it must give the undertaking an opportunity to state its views. If the Commission still disagrees, it is required to adopt a decision in that connection which contains an adequate statement of the reasons on which it is based and which must be notified to the undertaking concerned. The Commission must, before implementing its decision, give the undertaking an opportunity to bring an action before the General Court with a view to having the decision reviewed by it, and to prevent disclosure of the document in question. The right of an undertaking to protect documents containing business secrets is contained in Article 27(2) of Regulation 1/2003 and Article 15(2) of Regulation 773/2004 (for exchange of information between the Commission and NCAs and between NCAs themselves see Chapter 30.3).

- Other confidential documents. The Commission will refuse access to some other documents in order to protect the identity of an informer, or if documents were supplied to the Commission subject to a condition of non-disclosure, or if documents relate to military secrets.

■ Documents which do not form part of the investigation. These are internal documents of the Commission and the NCAs (for example, draft notices, projects, correspondence within the ECN, and so on). These documents are not binding but their disclosure may prejudice the confidentiality of the deliberations of the Commission in respect of the case in hand. Access to them is not permitted. In order to make them truly inaccessible they are not placed in the main file, although in Case T-134/94 *Stahlwerke*[2735] the General Court held that a list of those documents together with a short description of their content should be attached to the main file in order to allow the parties to decide whether those documents were of any relevance to them and if so, to apply for their disclosure. This exception was codified in Article 27(2) of Regulation 1/2003 and Article 15(2) of Regulation 773/2004.

By way of the above exceptions the Commission tries to reconcile the opposing obligations of safeguarding the right of defence and of protecting confidential information.[2736]

2734. Case 53/85 *AKZO Chemie BV and AKZO Chemie UK Ltd v Commission* [1986] ECR 1965.

2735. Case T-134/94 *NMH Stahlwerke GmbH v Commission* [1999] ECR II-239.

2736. On this topic see: R. L. J. Carlton and M. McElwee, "Confidentiality and Disclosure in European Commission Antitrust Proceedings – The Case for Clarity", (2008) 4/2 EuroCJ, 401 and A. E. Beumer and A. Karpetas, "The Disclosure of Files and Documents in EU Cartel Cases: Fairytale or Reality?" (2012) 8 EuroCJ, 123.

If the Commission refuses access to documents in its possession without sufficient reasons, its final decision may be annulled by the EU courts.[2737] In Case C-51/92P *Hercules*,[2738] the appellant, an undertaking which had participated in a cartel, challenged the Commission's refusal to allow access to the replies of the other undertakings to the SO. The ECJ held that a refusal to grant access would have led to annulment of the contested decision only if the relevant documents were capable of having some influence on the procedural or substantive outcome of the case, that is, only if the defence of the undertaking concerned had actually been prejudiced. This was not the case, taking into account that although Hercules was granted access at a later stage following joinder of the case, it did not draw from those replies any exonerating evidence and therefore was not in fact prejudiced.

However, in Case C-109/10P and Case C-110/10P *Solvay*,[2739] which took 21 years to come to conclusion, the ECJ emphasised that the rights of defence guaranteed under Article 41(2)(a) and (b) of the Charter of Fundamental Rights constitute fundamental rights forming part of the general principles of EU law, which EU courts must protect. It also held that an undertaking must have access to documents which are considered as accessible in administrative proceedings, i.e. in this case proceedings before the Commission, and that the fact that Solvay had access, for the first time, to some documents (but not all of them as the Commission had lost five binders of documents), during the proceedings before the General Court could not remedy the procedural failure of the Commission.

With regard to access to documents at the stage of proceedings before the General Court, the ECJ pointed out the difference between the procedure before the Commission, prior to the adoption of a decision, and the procedure before the General Court. In this respect, a review of the Commission's decision before the General Court is limited to the plea of law put forward and thus does not re-enact the Commission investigation. Contrary to the judgment of the General Court, the ECJ held that when access to documents is granted, for the first time, during proceedings before the General Court, the party alleging breach of its rights of defence has to show "not that if it had had access to the non-disclosed documents, the Commission decision would have been different in content, but only that those documents could have been useful for its defence".[2740]

With regard to lost documents, the ECJ pointed out that because a whole sub-file had been lost, not just a few documents, "it cannot be excluded that Solvay could have found in the sub-files evidence originating from other undertakings which would have enabled it to offer an interpretation of the facts different from the interpretation adopted by the Commission, which could have been of use for its defence".[2741]

Resulting from the above, the ECJ annulled the judgments of the General Court and thus demonstrated that it will not tolerate procedural flaws on the part of the Commission, which resulted in the infringement of the fundamental rights of defence of Solvay.

The matter of access to the EU courts' documents relating to proceedings was examined in Case' C-185/95P *Baustahlgewebe*.[2742] On appeal from the General Court the appellant argued that it was entitled to consult documents. The ECJ held that although the right of access to documents constitutes a fundamental principle of EU law, "contrary to the appellant's assertion, the general principles of [EU law] governing the right of access to the Commission's file do not apply, as such, to court proceedings, the latter being governed by the [EU] Statute of the Court of Justice and by the Rules of Procedure of

2737. Cases T-10 to 12 and 15/92 *Cimenteries CBR SA and Others v Commission* [1992] ECR II-2667.
2738. Case C-51/92P *Hercules Chemicals NV v Commission* [1998] ECR I-8417.
2739. Case C-109/10 P and 110/10 P *Solvay SA v Commission* (judgments of 25/10/11 (NYR)).
2740. Ibid, para. 57.
2741. Ibid, para. 62
2742. Case C-185/95P *Baustahlgewebe GmbH v Commission* [1999] ECR I-4235.

the [General Court]."[2743] However, the appellant was entitled to ask the General Court to order the Commission to produce certain documents in its possession. In this respect it was for the General Court to determine whether it was necessary to order the production of those documents. Further, the party requesting production had to identify the documents which it wished to inspect, and provide the General Court with at least minimum information indicating the utility of those documents for the purposes of the proceedings. In this case the appellant did not sufficiently identify the documents which it wanted produced and therefore the General Court was right to reject its request for the production of documents.

30.2.6 Decisions of the Commission

Under Regulation 1/2003 the Commission is empowered to adopt the following decisions:

1. A finding and termination of infringement. When the Commission, acting on a complaint or on its own initiative under Article 7, finds an infringement of Articles 101 or 102 TFEU, it may adopt a decision requiring the undertaking concerned to end the infringement and the Commission may impose on undertakings behavioural or structural remedies proportionate to the infringement and necessary to bring the infringement to an end;

2. Interim measures. Under Article 8 the Commission is empowered to order interim measures. In Case 792/79R *Camera*,[2744] the ECJ held that the Commission may grant interim relief in urgent cases where there is immediate danger of irreparable damage to the complainant, or where there is a situation which is intolerable for the public interest;

3. Commitments. Under Article 9 of Regulation 1/2003 when the Commission intends to adopt a decision requiring the parties to terminate infringements, the parties may offer commitments to meet the concerns expressed to them by the Commission. In such a situation the Commission may adopt a decision making these commitments binding on the undertakings. Commitment decisions may be reopened by the Commission if there has been a material change in facts, or if the undertakings breach their commitments, or if the decision was based on incomplete, incorrect or misleading information provided by the parties. Recital 13 of Regulation 1/2003 states that commitment decisions are not appropriate when the Commission intends to impose a fine. Further, Recital 13 says that commitment decisions are without prejudice to the powers of NCAs and national courts to decide a case. Perhaps this is because, as Recital 13 specifies, commitment decisions are not conclusive as to whether or not there has been, or still is, an infringement;

4. A finding of inapplicability. Under Article 10, where the public interest of the EU requires, the Commission, acting on its own, may find that Article 101 TFEU is not applicable to agreements, decisions or concerted practices, either because these commercial arrangements are outside the scope of Article 101(1), or because they satisfy the conditions of Article 101(3). The Commission may likewise make such a finding with reference to Article 102 TFEU. Recital 14 states that such a finding should only be adopted in "exceptional circumstances", that is, to clarify the law and ensure its consistent application in the EU "in particular with regard to new types of agreements or practices that have not been settled in the existing case-law and administrative practice". Findings of inapplicability are not intended to

---

2743. Ibid, para. 90.
2744. Case 792/79R *Camera Care Ltd v Commission* [1980] ECR 119.

be for the benefit of the parties and are of a declaratory nature. The Commission has never adopted any decision under Article 10.

If parties are confronted by issues raising genuine uncertainty because they present novel or unresolved questions, they may ask the Commission for informal guidance. If appropriate, the Commission will provide such guidance in a written statement called a guidance letter.[2745] These letters are not binding on national courts or NCAs but their value will certainly depend on the procedure the Commission follows in adopting such decisions. If a decision is adopted subsequent to an investigation carried out by the Commission, the status of such "informal guidance letter" should be similar to that of a qualified comfort letter[2746] and therefore unlikely to be overruled by national courts and NCAs. The Commission's Notice on Informal Guidance relating to Novel Questions Arising under Articles [101 and 102 TFEU][2747] specifies the conditions under which the Commission will issue a guidance letter.[2748] No such letters have been issued; and,

5. A settlement decision in cartel cases. In 2008 the Commission introduced a procedure under which some cartel cases can be settled.[2749] The application of the procedure is entirely at the discretion of the Commission. It may be applied when undertakings involved in a cartel acknowledge their participation in a cartel, and their liability, and co-operate with the Commission. In order to reward their co-operation the Commission may reduce by 10 per cent the amount of fine to be imposed on participating undertakings. When settled cases also involve leniency applicants (see Chapter 30.2.9) the amount of the reduction of the fine granted to them for settlement will be added to their leniency reward. However, a settlement cannot be imposed on the participating undertakings. The main advantages of the settlement procedure are that cases are concluded quickly and are unlikely to be appealed to the EU courts.

Under Article 14 of Regulation 1/2003 the role and powers of the Advisory Committee on Restrictive Practices and Dominant Positions (AC), which was first established under Regulation 17/62, were reinforced. The AC is made up of representatives of the NCAs. The 2004 Commission Notice on Co-operation within the Network of Competition Authorities[2750] states that the AC provides a forum "where experts from various national authorities discuss individual cases and general issues of [EU competition law]". Under Article 14 of Regulation 1/2003, the AC must be consulted before the Commission adopts any important decision of a type mentioned above. Further, an NCA may, when the

---

2745. The Commission issued a Notice on Informal Guidance Relating to Novel Questions Concerning [Articles 101 and 102 TFEU] that Arise in Individual Cases [2004] OJ C101/78.
2746. Prior to the entry into force of Regulation 1/2003 the Commission had often sent a comfort letter in response to an application for individual exemption under Article 101(3) TFEU. In such a letter the Commission stated that it had no intention of pursuing the matter and was closing the file because the notified agreement was not in breach of Article 101(1) TFEU, either because it was outside its scope, or because it was covered by a block exemption regulation, or would merit an individual exemption under Article 101(3) TFEU. Comfort letters had no binding force, but in fact national courts never disputed their content.
2747. [2004] OJ C101/78.
2748. Ibid, para. 8.
2749. Regulation 622/2008 amended Regulation 773/2004 ([2008] OJ L171/3) by inserting a new Article 10a entitled "Settlement Procedure in Cartel Cases". The Commission explains the procedure in its Notice on the Conduct of Settlement Procedures in View of the Adoption of Decisions Pursuant to Article 7 and Article 23 of the Council Regulation 1/2003 in Cartel Cases [2008] OJ C167/1.
2750. [2004] OJ L123/18.

Commission decides to relieve it from taking a case under Article 11(6) of Regulation 1/2003, request that the AC be consulted.

30.2.7 Fines that can be imposed by the Commission

In order to enforce EU competition law the Commission is empowered to impose pecuniary sanctions on undertakings. Financial penalties can be imposed for infringements that have already ceased (subject to the limitation period) as well as for ongoing infringements. There are three kinds of penalty:

- Procedural fines up to 1 per cent of the undertaking's total turnover in the preceding business year. These may be imposed on an undertaking which refuses to supply information, or when it provides incorrect or misleading information intentionally or negligently, or in other circumstances set out in Article 23(1) of Regulation 1/2003;

- Periodic penalty payments not exceeding 5 per cent of the undertaking's average daily turnover in the preceding business year and calculated from the date fixed by the Commission decision. These may be imposed at a daily rate during continued defiance of the Commission decision. Article 24 provides a list of circumstances in which the Commission may impose periodic penalty payments, for example, when an undertaking has not terminated an infringement despite a decision adopted by the Commission to that effect, or has not complied with a decision ordering interim measures; and,

- "Substantive" fines. Under Article 23(2) of Regulation 1/2003 the Commission is empowered to impose fines for substantive infringements (either intentional or negligent) of Articles 101 or 102 TFEU, of a decision ordering interim measures under Article 8, or for failure to comply with a commitment made binding by a decision pursuant to Article 9. To find intention or negligence it is not necessary that the partners or principal managers of an undertaking have themselves acted negligently or with intent, or have even been aware of an infringement. It suffices that the prohibited action was performed by a person authorised to act on behalf of the undertaking.[2751] Intentional infringement has been defined by the ECJ as an act deliberately committed with the intention of achieving some object prohibited by the Treaties.[2752] A negligent infringement occurs when an undertaking knew or ought to have known that its action would result in infringement of the prohibition.[2753] An undertaking may be regarded as having acted intentionally or negligently even though it participated in an infringement under pressure.[2754] This factor will be considered when fixing the fine. The amount of the fine is:

- up to 10 per cent of the undertaking's total turnover in the preceding business year for each undertaking and association of the undertaking participating in the infringement; or,
- where an infringement by an association of undertakings relates to the activities of its members, the fine should not exceed 10 per cent of the sum of the total turnover of each member active in the market affected by the association's infringement.

2751. Joined Cases 100–103/80 *SA Musique Diffusion Française and Others v Commission* [1983] ECR 1825.
2752. Case 172/80 *Gerard Züchner v Bayerische Vereinsbank AG* [1981] ECR 2021.
2753. Case 27/76 *United Brands v Commission* [1977] ECR 207.
2754. *Tipp-ex* [1987] OJ L2221.

The fining policy of the Commission has changed over the years. Initially, the Commission imposed relatively low fines. However, in *Pioneer Hi-Fi Equipment*[2755] the Commission indicated a change in its policy. It stated that fines should be a real deterrent and should be of sufficiently greater amounts in cases of serious infringements.[2756]

In Case C-185/95P *Baustahlgewebe*,[2757] the ECJ held that the General Court has unlimited jurisdiction to determine the amount of fines imposed on undertakings for infringements of EU competition law and that if the ECJ becomes involved by virtue of its appellate capacity, it can only rule on questions of law and therefore has no jurisdiction, even on grounds of fairness, to substitute its assessment of the amount of fines for that of the General Court. Obviously, the relevant Guidelines for setting fines in competition cases adopted by the Commission contain limitations as to the setting of maximum fines. In practice, on appeal the General Court quite often reduces the amount of fines imposed by the Commission.

In 1998, with a view to ensuring the transparency and impartiality of its decisions, the Commission published a Notice regarding its fining policy under [Articles 101 and 102 TFEU].[2758] Its 2006 Guidelines on the Method of Setting Fines imposed pursuant to Article 23(2)(a) of Regulation No 1/2003 replaced that Notice.[2759] The Guidelines set a basic amount of fines at a much higher level than previously, although fines must not exceed the limits specified in the Regulation, that is, 10 per cent of the undertaking's total turnover in the preceding business year, and thus makes them a real deterrent.

The Notice is not binding. The Commission enjoys a wide discretion in the determination of the amount of fine in each case.

The Guidelines provide that the Commission's first task in assessing the amount of fine is to determine the basic amount. This is based on up to 30 per cent of the undertaking's annual sales, multiplied by the number of years of participation in the infringement. Irrespective of the duration of infringement, a so-called "entry fee" may be imposed to punish the undertaking's participation in a cartel – from 15 to 25 per cent of its annual sales in the relevant sector. An entry fee may also be imposed in other types of infringements.

The second task consists of adjusting the basic amount in the light of two sets of circumstances, that is, it is increased by reference to aggravating circumstances or reduced by reference to attenuating circumstances.

Aggravating circumstances refer to a situation where:

- An undertaking is either a first-time repeat offender or a multiple repeat offender. The basic amount may be increased by up to 100 per cent for each previous infringement established. The Commission will take into account not only its own previous decisions but also those of the relevant NCA.

- An undertaking refused to co-operate with the Commission during investigations.

- An undertaking was a leader in, or instigator of the infringement, or coerced other undertakings to participate in the infringement, or took retaliatory measures against other undertakings in order to enforce its own anti-competitive conduct.

The above list is not exhaustive.

2755. [1980] OJ L60/1.
2756. On this topic see: G. J. Werden, "Sanctioning Cartel Activity: Let the Punishment Fit the Crime" (2009) 5 ECJ, 19.
2757. Case C-185/95P *Baustahlgewebe GmbH v Commission* [1998] ECR I-8417.
2758. [1998] 3 CMLR 472.
2759. [2006] OJ C210/2.

The list of extenuating circumstances (also not exhaustive) refers to a situation where:

- An undertaking terminated its infringement as soon as the Commission intervened, except when it participated in secret agreements and practices, in particular, cartels.

- An undertaking's infringement was unintentional or negligent.

- An undertaking did not implement an anti-competitive agreement or practice.

- An undertaking terminated an infringement as soon as the Commission so requested.

- An undertaking actively co-operated with the Commission and beyond its legal obligation to do so.

- An undertaking's anti-competitive conduct was authorised or encouraged by public authorities or by legislation.

The Commission will take into consideration the economic context of the infringement and the ability of an undertaking to actually pay the fine. It is important to note that under Article 25 of Regulation 1/2003 there are limitation periods in respect of infringements of EU competition law. With regard to infringements concerning requests for information or the conduct of inspections the period is three years from a request or inspection, for all other infringements five years. The burden of proving the duration of infringement is on the Commission, i.e. it must establish whether the limitation period has expired.

30.2.8 Enforcement of EU competition law in the light of fundamental rights

The conformity of the system for enforcement of EU competition law with the Charter of Fundamental Rights and the ECHR, to which the EU is in the process of acceding (see Chapter 8.5) is controversial and highly debated.[2760] The main controversies are:[2761]

A. **First**, the determination of whether an infringement of EU competition law constitutes a criminal offence. This determination is vital given that under Article 6(2) and (3) of the ECHR defendants in criminal proceedings enjoy rights additional to those specified in Article 6(1) of the ECHR which sets out general requirements for "fair trial" in criminal and civil proceedings. Among rights relating only to criminal trials, Article 6(2) of the ECHR guarantees the rights to be presumed innocent until proven guilty, remain silent, and not to incriminate oneself. So far as EU law is concerned, Article 23(5) Regulation 1/2003 states that decisions imposing fines "shall not be of a criminal law nature". However, in the *Engel* case[2762] the ECtHR held that for the purpose of applying Article 6 of the ECHR: "If the Contracting States were able at their discretion to classify an offence as disciplinary instead of criminal, or to prosecute the author

---

2760. See: J. Flattery, "Balancing Efficiency and Justice in EU Competition Law: Elements of Procedural Fairness and their Impact on the Right to a Fair Hearing", (2010) 7/1 CLR, 53; A. Scordamaglia, "Cartel Proof, Imputation and Sanctioning in European Competition Law: Reconciling Effective Enforcement and Adequate Protection of Procedural Guarantees", (2010) 7 CLR, 5; and I.S. Forrester, "Due Process in EC Competition Cases: A Distinguished Institution with Flawed Procedures", (2009) 34 ELRev., 817.

2761. See "Towards a More Judicial Approach? EU Antitrust Fines under the Scrutiny of Fundamental Rights", Editorial Comments, (2011) 48 CMLRev., 1405.

2762. *Engel v The Netherlands*, Series A, No. 22 (1979–80) 1 EHRR 647.

of a 'mixed' offence on the disciplinary rather than on the criminal plane, the operation of the fundamental clauses of Articles 6 and 7 would be subordinated to their sovereign will. A latitude extending this far might lead to results incompatible with the purpose and object of the Convention."[2763] In the *Menarini* case[2764] the ECtHR stated that three criteria are to be applied to decide whether a procedure is of a criminal nature within the meaning of Article 6 of the ECHR. However, it noted that they are not cumulative. The criteria are:

1. the classification of the offence by national legislation;

2. the nature of the offence; and,

3. the nature and severity of the applied penalty.

In *Menarini,* an Italian pharmaceutical company was found by the Italian Competition Authority in breach of national competition law by price fixing and market sharing in the national diabetes test market. A fine of €6 million was imposed on Menarini. The ECtHR held that the fact that under Italian law the offence was classified as having an administrative nature was not determinative. With regard to the nature of the offence, the ECtHR confirmed its previous judgment in *Stenuit*[2765] in which it held that the application of competition law by a competition authority affecting general interests of society was of criminal nature within the meaning of Article 6 of the ECHR. As to the nature and severity of the fine, its amount and deterrent effect led the ECtHR to conclude that the fine was a criminal sanction.

In the *Jussila* case[2766] the ECtHR made a distinction between the "hard core of criminal law" and "cases not strictly belonging to the traditional categories of criminal law, for example . . . competition law" to which "the criminal head guarantees will not necessarily apply with their full stringency".[2767] What are the implications of this distinction? In this respect, the ECtHR in the *Menarini* case was not entirely clear. However, the EFTA Court in Case E-15/10 *Posten Norge*[2768] held that guarantees provided by the criminal head of Article 6 of the ECHR apply in a differentiated manner depending upon the nature of the case and "the degree of stigma carried by certain criminal cases".[2769] In this case the EFTA Surveillance Authority (ESA) found Norway Post, a Norwegian postal service owned by the Norwegian State, in breach of Article 54 of the EEA Agreement (which is identical to Article 102 TFEU) by abusing its dominant position in the business-to-consumer parcel market in Norway between 2000 and 2006. A fine of €12.89 million was imposed on Norway Post. On appeal, the EFTA Court held that bearing in mind the gravity and severity of the offence, and the considerable stigma attached to the finding that Norway Post had abused its dominant position the guarantees provided by the criminal head of Article 6 of the ECHR apply with their full stringency. Although judgments of the EFTA court are not binding on EU courts the fact that EEA

2763. Ibid, para. 81.
2764. *A. Menarini Diagnostics SRL v Italy*, No. 43509/08 judgment of 27/9/11. Can be found on the official website of the ECtHR http://www.echr.coe.int/echr/homepage_EN (accessed 13/5/12).
2765. *Société Stenuit v France* [1992] ECHR 34.
2766. *Jussila v Finland*, No. 73053/01 judgment of 23/11/06.
2767. Ibid, para. 43.
2768. Case E-15/10 *Posten Norge AS v EFTA Surveillance Authority* (judgment of 18/4/12 (NYR)) available at http://www.eftacourt.int/images/uploads/15_10_JUDGMENT.pdf (accessed 27/4/12).
2769. Ibid, para. 89.

competition law mirrors EU competition law and that often A-Gs refer to the case law of the EFTA Court[2770] may not be completely ignored by the ECJ.

B. **Second**, the fining policy of the Commission in that fines are uncertain as to their amounts, their addressees and the infringements for which they are imposed. In this respect, the first criticism is that the Commission's Notices and Guidelines are not formal sources of law, and accordingly the proper way of defining the EU's fining policy is to adopt secondary legislation on this topic. The second criticism is that the concept of a "single, overall agreement" (see Chapter 27.3.1) and the "single economic entity" doctrine (see Chapter 26.3.2.1) entail that addressees of fines are not always involved in the infringement, or are involved only in some aspect of the infringement. So far as the concept of a "single, overall agreement" is concerned it seems unreasonable to ask the Commission to determine in detail the degree of involvement of each party in a complex cartel of long duration, bearing in mind the way in which a cartel operates in practice.[2771] EU competition law cannot impose on the Commission a burden of proof which would make the task of the Commission impossible. However, with regard to the concept of a single economic entity, in Joined Cases T-122-124/07 *Siemens*,[2772] the General Court rightly stated that penalties must be specific to the offender and to the offence concerned, and rejected the argument submitted by the Commission that those held liable jointly and severally are completely free to distribute the total amount of the fine among themselves. According to the General Court:

> ". . . each company must be able to discern from the decision imposing a fine on it to be paid jointly and severally with one or more other companies the amount which it is required to bear in relation to the other joint and several debtors, once payment has been made to the Commission. To that end, the Commission must, inter alia, specify the periods during which the companies concerned were jointly liable for the unlawful conduct of the undertakings which participated in the cartel and, where necessary, the degree of liability of those companies for that conduct."[2773]

As can been seen, the General Court rejected the idea that the Commission has the discretion to determine the addressees of fines and the amounts to be paid by them jointly and severally.

With regard to the definition of infringements, the application of the effects-based approach (see Chapter 28.1) makes it difficult for undertakings to determine whether their conduct is prohibited or allowed. This is a consequence of the rejection of the *per se* rule, for which economists and undertakings criticised the Commission. Unfortunately, in many cases economists are not always clear on whether, and in what circumstances, a particular practice harms consumers, directly or indirectly. As a result, the establishment of an infringement is not easy, in particular under Article 102 TFEU. In this respect, the Guidance on the Commission's Enforcement Priorities in Applying [Article 102 TFEU] to Abusive Exclusionary Conduct by Dominant Undertakings[2774] constitutes an important source of information as to how the Commission applies the "effects-based approach" to cases under Article 102 TFEU.

2770. See e.g., the opinion of Advocate Mengozzi in Case C-49/11 *Content Services* (pending), para. 39.
2771. On this topic see: J. Joshua, "Single Continuous Infringement of Article 81 EC: Has the Commission Stretched the Concept Beyond the Limit of Its Logic?" (2009) 5 EuroCJ, 451.
2772. Joined Cases T-122-124/07 *Siemens AG Österreich and Others v Commission* [2011] ECR II-793.
2773. Ibid, paras 153–54.
2774. [2009] OJ C45/7–20.

Notwithstanding this, the criticism is valid bearing in mind that the fundamental principle of criminal law *nullum crimen, nulla poena sine lege* enshrined in Article 7(1) of the ECHR requires that an offender must know for what conduct it may be punished.[2775]

C. **Third**, there is no effective judicial review of the Commission's decisions in competition matters because the EU courts defer, to an excessive and unreasonable extent, to the Commission's discretion regarding assessment of complex economic or technical matters. As a result, it is alleged that the EU courts perform only limited review of these matters which is incompatible with the right to a fair trial guaranteed under Article 6 of the ECHR.[2776] This Article requires that review courts should have full jurisdiction, i.e. should review all aspects of a case, factual and legal including complex economic assessments. The criticism is that in the EU the review is limited to procedural rules, factual errors, law errors and manifest errors of appraisal. The position of the ECJ was stated in the *Plain Copper Plumbing Tubes Cartel Cases*[2777] in which it found that the rules of judicial review in the EU are in conformity with the principle of effective judicial protection enshrined in Article 47 of the Charter of Fundamental Rights. In this case the ECJ made a distinction between a review of the legality of decisions of the Commission and a review of penalties for infringements of EU competition law.

With regard to the review of legality, in the *Plain Copper Plumbing Tubes Cartel Cases*, the ECJ held that the fact that the Commission enjoys a margin of discretion in respect of complex economic assessments does not mean that EU courts must refrain from reviewing the Commission's interpretation of information of an economic nature. This is demonstrated in particular in respect of assessment of concentrations.[2778]

With regard to the imposition of fines, the ECJ stated that under Article 23 of Regulation 1/2003 the Commission has a duty to carry out a thorough examination of the circumstances of an infringement in order to determine the amount of the fine. In the interests of transparency the Commission's Guidelines on this topic indicate the basis on which such determination is effected (see Chapter 30.2.7). In particular the Guidelines reinforce the Commission's duty to state reasons for its decisions and to explain any departure from the Guidelines. The ECJ emphasised that the EU courts must review *ex officio* the statement of reasons. However, the fact that EU courts have unlimited jurisdiction to review all facts and the law of any particular case does not mean that they have to review them *ex officio*. With the exception of pleas involving matters of public policy, e.g, an *ex officio* review of a statement of reasons, it is the task of the party concerned to raise pleas against the decision in question and to adduce evidence in support of these pleas. The ECJ concluded that:

2775. On this topic see, W. H. Roth, "The 'More Economic Approach' and the Rule of Law", in Schmidtchen, Albert and Voight (eds), *The More Economic Approach to the European Competition Law*, Mohr Siebeck, 2007, 37.

2776. On this topic see: R. Nazzini, "Administrative Enforcement, Judicial Review and Fundamental Rights in EU Competition Law: A Comparative Contextual-functionalist Perspective", (2012) 49 CMLRev., 971.

2777. Case C-272/09 P *KME Germany AG, KME France SAS, KME Italy SpA, v Commission* (judgment of 8/12/11 (NYR)); Case C-386/10P *Chalkor v Commission* (judgment of 8/12/11 (NYR)); and Case C-389/10P *KME Germany v Commission* (judgment of 8/12/11 (NYR)).

2778. Joined Cases C-204/00 P, C-205/00 P, C-211/00 P, C-213/00 P, C-217/00 P and C-219/00 P *Aalborg Portland and Others v Commission* [2004] ECR I-123, para. 91.

"The review provided for by the Treaties thus involves review by the Courts of the European Union of both the law and the facts, and means that they have the power to assess the evidence, to annul the contested decision and to alter the amount of a fine. The review of legality provided for under Article 263 TFEU, supplemented by the unlimited jurisdiction in respect of the amount of the fine, provided for under Article 31 of Regulation No 1/2003, is not therefore contrary to the requirements of the principle of effective judicial protection in Article 47 of the Charter."[2779]

In the above case the ECJ has clearly established its position on the conformity of judicial review of Commission decisions in competition matters with the Charter of Fundamental Rights. In Case C-389/10P *KME Germany*,[2780] the ECJ stated that the EU courts cannot use the Commission's margin of discretion as a basis for dispensing with the conduct of an in-depth review of the law and of the facts. Notwithstanding this, there is a lack of guidance as to the applicable standard of review in the EU, i.e. as to the requisite level of its intensity. In this respect in Case E-15/10 *Posten Norge*, the EFTA Court was very clear. It held that "the submission that the Court may intervene only if it considers a complex economic assessment to be manifestly wrong must be rejected".[2781] It held that the presumption of innocence entails that the Court must be convinced that the assessment of complex economic evidence submitted by the ESA is supported by facts. However, the Court stated that it will not replace the ESA's assessment of economic evidence by its own if it merely disagrees with the weighing of individual factors made by the ESA.[2782]

D. **Fourth,** that the Commission combines investigating and judicial functions and this may be in breach of Article 6(1) of the ECHR which requires that a court, tribunal, etc. determining civil rights and obligations or a criminal charge must be and must appear to be "independent and impartial". In the *Menarini* case[2783] (see above), the ECtHR held that an administrative authority can lawfully impose a criminal sanction within the meaning of Article 6(1) of the ECHR as long as the decision imposing that criminal sanction is subject to review by a court having "full jurisdiction". It is important to note that the enforcement of Italian competition law is modelled on EU competition law in that the Italian Competition Authority has similar powers to the Commission. Accordingly, the fact that the Commission acts as prosecutor, jury and judge in competition matters raises no issues under the ECHR provided that the EU courts effectively exercise "full jurisdiction" (see point C above).

30.2.9 The EU Leniency Programme

The main objective of the leniency programmes is to provide an incentive to an undertaking participating in an unlawful cartel to come forward and expose the cartel. The incentive being the obtaining of immunity from, or a reduction of, the fines that would have been applicable to the undertaking had the cartel been discovered by the relevant competition enforcement authorities without the undertaking's assistance. However, the immunity/reduction is only available if the undertaking crosses certain thresholds in respect of evidence provided by it.

2779. Case C-272/09 P *KME Germany* AG, para. 106.
2780. Judgment of 8/12/11 (NYR).
2781. Supra note 2768, para. 102.
2782. Ibid, para. 101.
2783. Supra note 2764.

The Commission established the first Leniency Programme in 1996.[2784] Although effective, it had many flaws. These were, to a large extent, remedied by the 2002[2785] and 2006 Leniency Programmes.[2786]

The 2006 Leniency Programme, which is outlined in the 2006 Notice on Immunity from Fines and Reduction of Fines in Cartels Cases, improved the transparency and certainty of the conditions on which the immunity and the reduction of fines is granted.

The evidential thresholds for immunity were clarified by the 2006 Notice. In order to obtain immunity the undertaking has to provide sufficient evidence for the Commission to commence an investigation, or must be the first to enable the Commission to establish an infringement of Article 101 TFEU.[2787] Article 12 specifies the extent of the duties imposed on an applicant for immunity, *inter alia*, it must promptly supply the Commission with any evidence in its possession or available to it, remain at the Commission's disposal to answer any relevant questions, not have destroyed, falsified or concealed any evidence before or after making an application, and subsequently, not disclose the fact of, or any of the content of, its application, before the Commission has issued a statement of objections, unless otherwise agreed. It must also terminate its participation in the cartel unless otherwise agreed between the Commission and the applicant.

The 2006 Notice introduced a marker system, whereby an applicant can, first, know where it stands with respect to any other applicants in the queue for immunity, and second, when it is first in the queue, keep its place while it gathers necessary information and evidence in order to meet the evidential threshold requirements. The Notice specifies the kind of information the applicant is required to provide, including the identity of the applicant and some details of the cartel. These details distinguish the application from a hypothetical one, whereby an application can be made in such a way as to preserve the anonymity of the applicant who wishes to know whether evidence in its possession meets the relevant evidential immunity threshold.

The Notice states that an undertaking which has coerced any other undertaking into participating in the infringement, or remains in it, does not qualify for immunity, although it may qualify for a reduction of fines.

When an applicant does not qualify for immunity, it may nevertheless be eligible for a reduction of fines. The first applicant who provides the Commission with evidence that represents significant added value with respect to the evidence already in the Commission's possession will receive a reduction in fines between 30 per cent and 50 per cent. The next, a reduction between 20 per cent and 30 per cent, and any subsequent applicant a reduction of up to 20 per cent.

Article 25 of the Notice specifies that evidence which needs little or no corroboration is considered as significantly adding value. In addition, this kind of evidence will be rewarded outside the normal bands for reduction of fines when its assists the Commission in establishing any additional facts increasing the gravity or duration of the infringement. The extent of the duty of co-operation for applicants for a reduction of fines is similar to that imposed on applicants for immunity from fines.

The Programme does not protect an undertaking that has come forward from civil claims. Therefore there is nothing to prevent parties who have suffered damage as a result of the cartel operation starting separate proceedings in national courts. The 2006 Leniency Notice introduces a procedure aimed at protecting corporate statements given by an undertaking to the Commission from discovery in civil damage proceedings. In this respect the Commission can take oral corporate statements at its premises. The Commission will record and transcribe the statements and no one else will have a copy. Such

---

2784. [1996] OJ C207/4.
2785. [2002] OJ C45/3.
2786. [2006] OJ C298/17.
2787. Articles 8, 9 and 10 of the Notice.

statements will form part of the Commission's file, access to which is limited to the addressees of a statement of objections in the same case and under strict conditions specified in paragraph 34 of the Notice.

The leniency programme has been very successful in detection of cartels. From 2008 to March 2012, the Commission adopted 26 cartel decisions and imposed fines totalling (as adjusted by Court judgments) €7,541,918,732.[2788]

30.3 Enforcement of Articles 101 and 102 TFEU by national competition authorities (NCAs), co-operation between the Commission and NCAs, and co-operation between NCAs within the European Competition Network (ECN)

Article 5 of Regulation 1/2003 provides that NCAs are empowered, and (in situations described in Article 3 of Regulation 1/2003) obliged to apply both Article 101 TFEU in its entirety and Article 102 TFEU. Under Article 3 of Regulation 1/2003 NCAs may make the following decisions:

- order an infringement to be brought to an end;

- order interim measures;

- accept commitments from the parties concerned; and,

- impose fines or other penalties provided for in their national laws.

The basic rules on co-operation between the Commission and the NCAs are contained in Chapter IV of Regulation 1/2003 and further explained in a Joint Statement of the Council and the European Commission on the Functioning of the Network of Competition Authorities[2789] and in the 2004 Commission's Notice on Co-operation within the network of competition authorities.[2790]

30.3.1 Co-operation between the Commission and the NCAs

The main features of the co-operation relate to:

1. Allocation of cases. This is a very important issue given an infringement of EU competition law may involve a single NCA, several NCAs acting in parallel, or the Commission. The principles upon which cases are allocated are set out in the 2004 Notice. The determination of the competition authority which is best placed to deal with a case is based on the following three criteria:

    - the agreement or practice has substantial direct and actual or foreseeable effects on competition within that NCA's territory, is implemented in, or originates from its territory;

    - the authority is able to effectively bring to an end the entire infringement; and,

    - it can gather, possibly with the assistance of other authorities, the evidence to prove the infringement.

2788. See the official website of the Commission at http://ec.europa.eu/competition/cartels/statistics/statistics.pdf (accessed 28/4/12).

2789. Available at http://ec.europa.eu/competition/ecn/joint_statement_en.pdf (accessed 12/7/12).

2790. [2004] OJ C101/43.

The allocation of cases should be determined speedily, normally within a period of two months.[2791]

2. Exchange of information. Under Article 11(3) of Regulation 1/2003 an NCA is required to inform the Commission and other NCAs "before, or without delay after, commencing the first formal investigative measures". Further the Commission is obliged to send to the relevant NCA copies of documents in its possession relating to the case. The relocation of a case should be avoided but this may occur when the circumstances of the case change materially during the proceedings (paragraph 19 of the 2004 Notice).

The Commission and the NCAs keep each other informed when acting under Articles 101 and 102 TFEU. An NCA is obliged to inform the Commission at least 30 days before adopting any of the following decisions:

■ requiring that an infringement be terminated;

■ accepting commitments; and,

■ withdrawing the benefit of a block exemption regulation.

The NCA is required to provide to the Commission a summary of the case and of the intended decision, or (in the absence of any decision) of any other relevant document indicating the proposed course of action, or at the request of the Commission, any other relevant document necessary for the assessment of the case. The information may also be made available to other NCAs.[2792]

3. Consultations. Under Article 11(5) of Regulation 1/2003 an NCA may consult the Commission on any case involving the application of EU competition law.

An NCA may ask the Commission to place any case or cases that are being dealt with by it on the agenda of the Advisory Committee. The Commission may also do this on its own initiative. In particular, such request or placing on the agenda is likely to occur in a situation where the Commission intends to take over a case which has already been started by the requesting NCA, either because the case presents "EU interest" or because the Commission, in the light of a draft decision submitted under Article 11(6) Regulation 1/2003, disapproves of the manner in which the NCA intends to deal with the case.

30.3.2 Co-operation between NCAs

Regulation 1/2003 provides for co-operation between NCAs in respect of:

1. Allocation of cases. By virtue of Article 13 the fact that two or more NCAs are dealing with the same case or complaint constitutes a sufficient ground for all but one to suspend their proceedings or to reject the complaint. The purpose of this provision is to avoid a number of decisions emanating from various NCAs in the same case, which decisions may contradict each other.

2. Exchange of information. Under Article 11(3) and (4) the NCAs are required to inform each other of the commencement of proceedings and in respect of decisions they intend to adopt

---

2791. See para. 18 of the 2004 Notice.
2792. Article 11(4) of Regulation 1/2003.

(see below). In a situation where an NCA suspends national proceedings or rejects a complaint because another NCA is better placed to deal with the case, the first NCA is permitted to transfer information, including confidential information, to the other NCA.

In this context it is very important that individuals and undertakings are protected against the misuse of exchanged information. Accordingly, Articles 12 and 28 of the 2004 Notice provide for the following safeguards:

- the competition authorities are bound by the obligation of professional secrecy;

- the information exchanged can only be used for the purposes of Articles 101 and 102 TFEU and in respect of the subject-matter for which it was collected; and,

- the information can only be used to impose sanctions on natural persons in two sets of circumstances:

  - First, where the law of the receiving NCA provides for sanctions of a similar kind to the law of the transmitting NCA. This means, for example, that if the law of both the transmitting and receiving NCAs provides for criminal sanctions, such as imprisonment, for a breach of Article 101 or 102 TFEU, information exchanged can be used as evidence in criminal cases leading to imprisonment; and,
  - Second, where the rights of defence as regards the collection of evidence have been respected by the transmitting authority to the same standard as is guaranteed by the receiving authority. This means that when differing sanctions are imposed under national law of the transmitting and receiving NCAs, information exchanged can only be used in evidence to impose sanctions on natural persons if the exchanged information has been collected by the transmitting NCA in a manner which protects the individual's right to defence to the same standard as is protected under the rules of the receiving NCA. However, information cannot be used as evidence in proceedings leading to custodial sanctions but can be used to impose non-custodial sanctions such as fines.

30.3.3 The European Competition Network (ECN)

The NCAs and the Commission form a network of public authorities, which co-operate in order to protect competition within the internal market. The network, which was established in 2002, is called the European Competition Network (ECN). It is made up of representatives of all NCAs. It constitutes a forum for discussion, *inter alia*, on issues that arise in the enforcement of competition law and on the improvement of the existing enforcement system. Additionally, it provides a flexible mechanism for increasing co-operation between NCAs.

The ECN does not take decisions and cannot compel an NCA to act in a particular way or to expel its members. One of the biggest achievements of the ECN was the adoption of a Model Leniency Programme in 2006. It has no binding force but it is perceived as a first step in the harmonisation of national leniency programmes and contains substantial procedural rules that the NCAs consider should be incorporated into any leniency programme. The heads of Member States' national competition authorities have agreed to use their best efforts to align their leniency programmes with the Model Programme within the shortest possible time. Twenty-six Member States have implemented national leniency programmes.

30.4 Private enforcement of Articles 101 and 102 TFEU before national courts and co-operation between the Commission and national courts

This section examines, first, the enforcement of Articles 101 and 102 TFEU before national courts by natural or legal persons, and second, the manner in which the Commission and national courts co-operate in order to ensure the proper enforcement of EU competition law.

30.4.1 Private enforcement of EU competition law before national courts

In Case 127/73 *BRT v SABAM*,[2793] the ECJ held that Articles 101(1) and 102 TFEU are directly effective. They are both horizontally and vertically directly effective. As a result of entry into force of Regulation 1/2003 Article 101(3) TFEU is also directly effective, both horizontally and vertically.

In Case C-453/99 *Crehan*,[2794] the ECJ confirmed the existence of the right to damages based on Articles 101 and 102 TFEU. The decision of the ECJ in *Crehan* has far-reaching consequences regarding private enforcement of EU competition law. In this case the ECJ held that even parties to a contract that is liable to restrict or distort competition within the meaning of Article 101(1) TFEU are entitled to rely on breach of that provision before a national court. Their participation in an unlawful contract does not deprive them of the right to bring an action unless they bear significant responsibility for the distortion of competition. In order to determine whether a party bears significant responsibility for the distortion of competition, and therefore to assess the merits of a claim for damages, a national court must take into account the economic and legal context in which the parties found themselves and their respective bargaining power and conduct.

30.4.2 Factors encouraging private enforcement of Articles 101 and 102 TFEU before national courts

Among factors which encourage private enforcement of Articles 101 and 102 before national courts, the following are relevant:

1. The right to claim damages based on Article 101 or 102 TFEU as set out in the *Crehan* judgment. This was confirmed in Joined Cases C-295/04 and C-298/04 *Manfredi*,[2795] in which the ECJ held that:

   - any individual is entitled to rely on the invalidity of an agreement or practice prohibited under Article 101 TFEU in order to seek damages for the harm suffered where there is a causal link between that agreement or practice and the harm;
   - the right to seek compensation includes not only compensation for actual loss (*damnum emergens*) but also for loss of profit (*lucrum cessans*) plus interest.

2. Only national courts can:

   - award damages to individuals or undertakings for loss suffered as a result of the infringement of Articles 101 and 102 TFEU;
   - rule on claims for payment or fulfilment of contractual obligations based on an agreement under Article 101 TFEU;

2793. Case 127/73 *BRT v SABAM* [1974] ECR 313.
2794. Case C-453/99 *Courage Ltd v Crehan* [2001] ECR I-6297.
2795. Joined Cases C-295/04 and C-298/04 *Vincenzo Manfredi v Lloyd Adriatico Assicurazioni SpA* [2006] ECR I-6619.

- apply the civil sanction of nullity of contracts based on Article 101(2) TFEU; and,
- award legal costs to a successful claimant.[2796]

3. With the entry into force of Regulation 1/2003, Article 101 TFEU became, in its entirety, both vertically and horizontally directly effective and thus major problems previously encountered by national courts in its application (see Chapter 30.1) were solved.

   The rationale for this solution seems to be that EU competition law has become well established. Consequently, decentralisation is less likely to undermine uniformity of enforcement than it would have been in the early days of the European Community.

4. The Commission's policy is to encourage private enforcement of EU competition law. On 2 April 2008, the Commission adopted a White Paper on Damages Actions for Breach of EU Antitrust Rules.[2797] This is a follow-up to a Green Paper on damages actions for breach of EU competition rules, which stirred a debate across Europe on the need for legal reform that would encourage private plaintiffs to claim compensation for losses suffered as a result of the anti-competitive conduct of undertakings.

A new approach to enforcement is necessary because:

- First, for reasons next mentioned the number of damages claims for infringement of EU competition law has been few; and,

- Second, in the absence of EU rules governing private enforcement of EU competition law, the principle of national procedural autonomy, although subject to the requirements of equivalence, effectiveness and proportionality (see Chapter 12.6), has a great impact on private enforcement. National procedural rules (which govern, for example, matters relating to *locus standi*, methods of proof of damage, types of damage for which compensation is recoverable, the principles of damage calculation), which differ greatly from one Member State to another, often not only determine the outcome of the case but also encourage or discourage private enforcement. For example, in *Manfredi* the ECJ held that it is for a Member State to decide whether to recognise the award of punitive damages as this matter falls within the scope of the procedural autonomy of each Member State. Obviously, the possibility for a claimant to be awarded punitive damages would constitute an important incentive to start proceedings before a national court.

Private enforcement of competition law requires that the right balance should be struck between the rights of alleged victims and the needs of undertakings. It should not create a US-style private litigation culture, in particular if punitive damages are accepted as an important part of private enforcement, and class actions are allowed. Such incentives may lead to a situation where undertakings choose to forgo legitimate competitive initiatives and this may, in the long run, be harmful to the economy and to consumers.[2798]

2796. Para. 14 of the 2004 Notice on the Handling of Complaints by the Commission ([2004] OJ L101/65) specifies the advantages resulting from bringing claims before national courts.

2797. COM(2008) 165.2.4.2008. This should be read together with the Commission's Staff Working Paper SEC(2008) 404.2.4.3008.

2798. W. Breit and K. G. Elzinga, "Antitrust Enforcement and Economic Efficiency: The Uneasy Case for Treble Damages", (1974) 17 J.L.& Econ., p 329.

The 2008 White Paper states that its recommendations take account of the need to overcome the existing over-deterrence in private enforcement of competition law and the necessity to avoid excessive litigation. The recommendations concern:

- The possibility of class action.[2799] This recommendation is that redress should be available *via* representative actions, e.g. by recognised consumer protection groups.

- The necessity to ensure equal access to the evidence by both parties to the proceedings. The Commission proposes to achieve this by a "form of judge-controlled" pre-trial disclosure of relevant evidence rather than by recommending an automatic right to wide pre-trial discovery which may lead to procedural abuses.

- The granting of *locus standi* not only to direct customers of an undertaking, but also to indirect customers.

- The possibility for an alleged infringer to rely on the "passing-on" defence whilst facilitating the proof of the passing-on by the eventual victims.

- The probative value of NCAs' final infringement decisions. In actions for damages they should constitute sufficient proof of the infringement in question.

On the basis of the 2008 White Paper, the Commission prepared a Draft Guidance Paper entitled "Quantifying Harm in Actions for Damages based on Breaches of Article 101 or 102 TFEU",[2800] which was submitted for public consultation in 2011.[2801] The intention of the Commission is to publish a non-binding guidance to assist private parties and national courts in the difficult task of quantifying damages in competition cases. Further, a legislative act based on the White Paper is expected to be proposed by the Commission.[2802]

30.4.3 Co-operation between the Commission and national courts

The 2004 Commission Notice on Co-operation between the Commission and the Courts of the EU Member States in the Application of [Articles 101 and 102 TFEU][2803] sets out general rules aimed at ensuring that EU competition law is applied uniformly. The Notice expands and clarifies the principles of co-operation set out in Articles 15 and 16 of Regulation 1/2003.

Under Article 15(1) of Regulation 1/2003 national courts are entitled to obtain from the Commission information in its possession with a view to applying Articles 101 and 102 TFEU. They may also ask for the Commission's opinion in this area.

Article 15(3) introduces the right for the Commission to make written and oral submissions to national courts acting in the interest of the EU (as *amicus curiae*), but not in favour of one of the parties. Such submissions will not be binding on the national court. The main objective of submissions is to draw the attention of national courts to certain issues of considerable importance for the uniform

---

2799. See Commission's Consultation Paper SEC(2011) 173 final and the EP's Report on "Collective Redress in Antitrust" available at: http://www.europarl.europa.eu/committees/en/studiesdownload.html?languageDocumen t=EN&file=74351 (accessed 8/8/12).

2800. Available at the official website of the Commission (accessed 8/8/12).

2801. See: SEC(2011) 173 final and R. Noble, "How to Quantify Damages? A Brief Overview of Economic Concepts and Techniques", (2008) 28 *World Competition*, 3.

2802. See the Commission's work programme for 2012 available at http://ec.europa.eu/competition/antitrust/ actionsdamages/documents.html (accessed 14/8/12).

2803. [2004] OJ C101/54.

application of EU competition rules. Additionally, national courts will, at the specific request of the Commission, be obliged to supply information concerning national proceedings. This will allow the Commission to decide whether it should make a submission in a particular case.

Article 16 of Regulation 1/2003 deals with the uniform application of EU competition law. It sets out general rules aimed at avoiding the taking of conflicting decisions in the same case at national and EU level. It emphasises that national courts must use every effort to avoid such conflict; in particular they should, if appropriate, refer a case to the ECJ for a preliminary ruling and if a decision adopted by the Commission is pending before the EU courts, national courts should suspend their own proceedings. This was endorsed in Case C-344/98 *Masterfoods*.[2804]

RECOMMENDED READING

Books
Those recommended in Chapter 26 and the following:
Andreangeli, A., *EU Competition Enforcement and Human Rights*, 2008, Cheltenham: Edward Elgar Publishing.

Basedow, J. (ed.), *Private Enforcement of EC Competition Law*, 2007, The Hague: KLI.

Brammer, S., *Co-operation between National Competition Agencies in the Enforcement of EC Competition Law*, 2009, Oxford: Hart Publishing.

Möllers, T. M., and Heinemann, A. (eds), *The Enforcement of Competition Law in Europe*, 2008, Oxford: OUP.

Rodger, B. J. (ed.), *Ten Years of UK Competition Law Reform*, 2010, Dundee: Dundee University Press.

Articles
Berghe, P. and Dawes, A., "'Little Pig, Little Pig, Let Me Come In': An Evaluation of the European Commission's Powers of Inspection in Competition Cases", (2009) 30/9 ECLR, 407.

Beumer, A. E. and Karpetas, A., "The Disclosure of Files and Documents in EU Cartel Cases: Fairytale or Reality?" (2012) 8 EuroCJ, 123.

Boylan, P., "Privilege and In-house Lawyers", (2007) 6 Comp L, 15.

Carlton, R. L. J., and McElwee, M., "Confidentiality and Disclosure in European Commission Antitrust Proceedings – the Case for Clarity", (2008) 4/2 EuroCJ, 401.

De Broca, H., "The Commission Revises its Guidelines for Setting Fines in Antitrust Cases", (2006) 3 *EC Competition Policy Newsletter*, 1.

Fritzsche, A., "Discretion, Scope of Judicial Review and Institutional Balance in European Law", (2010) 47 CMLRev., 361.

Kortman, J. S., and Swaak, Ch. R. A., "The EC White Paper on Antitrust Damage Actions: Why the Member States are (Right to be) Less Than Enthusiastic", (2009) 30 ECLR, 340.

Nazzini, R., "Administrative Enforcement, Judicial Review and Fundamental Rights in EU Competition Law: A Comparative Contextual-functionalist Perspective", (2012) 49 CMLRev., 971.

Noble, R., "How to Quantify Damages? A Brief Overview of Economic Concepts and Techniques", (2008) 28 *World Competition* , 3.

Nowag, J., "Due Process: The Exchange of Information and Risk of Hindering Effective Cross-border Co-operation in Competition Cases", (2010) 7 Comp. L, 105.

2804.   Case C-344/98 *Masterfoods Ltd v HB Ice Cream Ltd* [2000] ECR I-11369.

Parlak, S., "Passing-on Defence and Indirect Purchaser Standing: Should the Passing-on Defence Be Rejected Now the Indirect Purchaser Has Standing after *Manfredi* and the White Paper of the European Commission?", (2010) 33 *World Competition*, 31.

Slater, D. T. S., and Waelbroeck, D., "Competition Law Proceedings before the European Commission and the Right to a Fair Trial: No Need for Reform?" (2009) 5 EuroCJ, 97.

Werden, G. J., "Sanctioning Cartel Activity: Let the Punishment Fit the Crime", (2009) 5/1 EuroCJ, 19.

Wouter, P., and Wils, J., "The Increased Level of EU Antitrust Fines, Judicial Review and the ECHR", (2010) 33 *World Competition*, 5.

PROBLEM QUESTION

John, the managing director of Relax Ltd ("Relax"), a company established in England, when entering his office this morning, was approached by two men who introduced themselves as officers of the European Commission and provided proof of their positions with the Commission. They showed John a formal decision of the Commission requiring John to permit the officers to search the premises of Relax and asked him to let them in for that purpose. John refused the request. One of the officers told John that his refusal may have important financial consequences if the Commission finds Relax in breach of EU competition law. He also asked John some questions concerning recent meetings between John and George, the managing director of Easy Life Ltd, the main competitor of Relax. John refused to answer as he felt that the answers may incriminate Relax.

In the afternoon, John received a letter from the Commission asking him to send specific documents to the Commission. Some of these documents were prepared by an in-house lawyer of Relax, and some were prepared by John's personal solicitor for the purpose of seeking expert legal advice about the possible legal implications of John's meetings with George. John feels that the requested documents, if forwarded to the Commission, would provide sufficient evidence that Relax was engaged in a concerted practice prohibited under Article 101(1) TFEU. John keeps some of the requested documents at home. Now, at 9 pm, John phones you, a lawyer specialising in EU competition law. He desperately needs to know whether he was right to refuse the request by the officers from the Commission to search the premises of Relax, and whether he should now send to the Commission the documents requested by it.

Advise John.

ESSAY QUESTION

"The leniency policy of the Commission proves very successful in fighting cartels".
Critically discuss the above statement.

AIDE-MÉMOIRE

Reform of the enforcement of Articles 101 and 102 TFEU

The main themes of the reform were simplification and decentralisation. This has been achieved by the following

The replacement of the notification and authorisation system under Article 81(3) EC [Article 101(3) TFEU] by a "legal exception" system	Direct applicability of Article 101(3) TFEU	Decentralisation of enforcement of Articles 101 and 102 TFEU

Increase of the Commission's investigatory powers	Confirmation by national courts and national competition authorities of the application of EU competition law over national law

ENFORCEMENT OF ARTICLES 101 AND 102 TFEU BY THE COMMISSION
Under Regulation 1/2003 the Commission is empowered to adopt the following decisions

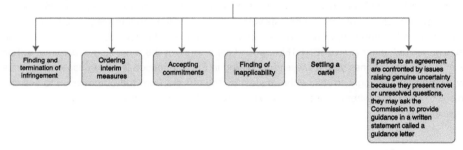

Finding and termination of infringement	Ordering interim measures	Accepting commitments	Finding of inapplicability	Settling a cartel	If parties to an agreement are confronted by issues raising genuine uncertainty because they present novel or unresolved questions, they may ask the Commission to provide guidance in a written statement called a guidance letter

Complaints to the Commission in respect of infringements of Articles 101 and 102 TFEU

The Commission may act *ex officio* or upon an application from a Member State, or from "any natural or legal person who can show a legitimate interest" (Case T-144/92 *BEMIM*). A complaint may be rejected if it does not raise sufficient EU interest (Case T-24/90 *Automec*). The Commission is not obliged to start investigations but is obliged to reply to the complainant within a reasonable time (Case C-282/95P *Guérin*).

The request for information may take two forms

A simple request. There is no duty to comply, but if inexact or misleading information is supplied, the Commission may impose a fine up to 1 per cent of the undertaking's turnover in the preceding business year.	A formal binding decision requiring the information to be provided. For failure to comply the Commission may impose periodic penalties of up to 5 per cent of the undertaking's average daily turnover.

BUT NOTE

Incriminating information

The ECJ, on the one hand, recognised the right not to self-incriminate by admitting the infringement but, on the other, refused the right not to provide evidence against oneself (Case 27/88 *Solvay*; Case C-301/04P *Commission v SGL Carbon*).

Legal professional privilege (LPP)

The principle of lawyer–client confidentiality is recognised under EU law, but only communications between a client and an independent lawyer (permitted to practise in at least one Member State) are privileged (not those between a client and an in-house lawyer) (T-125/03 and T-253/03 *AKZO*).

Power to take statements (Article 19 of Regulation 1/2003)

The Commission may interview any natural or legal person, with their consent, in order to collect information relating to the investigation.

Inspections (Article 20 of Regulation 1/2003)

The Commission is authorised to undertake all necessary investigations into undertakings and associations of undertakings including:

▪ Examination of books and other business records;

▪ Taking copies of or extracts from the books and business records;

▪ Asking for oral explanations on the spot;

▪ Entering any premises, land and means of transport owned by undertakings; and,

(Continued)

■ Sealing any business premises and books or records for the period of, and to the extent necessary for the inspection. If seals are broken, the Commission may impose a fine on the undertaking of up to 1 per cent of its total turnover in the preceding year.

An undertaking is obliged to submit to an investigation ordered by way of a decision (Cases 46/87 and 227/88 *Hoechst AG v Commission*) but co-operation of the relevant NCA is required and, if necessary, judicial authorisation must be obtained (Case C-94/00 *Roquette Frères*).

Inspections at premises other than those of an undertaking under investigation (Article 21 of Regulation 1/2003)

If incriminating documents are likely to be kept in private homes, the Commission is empowered to search those homes, subject to prior judicial authorisation.

Hearing (Article 27(1) of Regulation 1/2003 and Article 10(1) of Regulation 773/2004)

The Commission is required to give undertakings the opportunity to be heard before adopting any decision finding an infringement, taking interim measures or imposing fines or periodic payments. Hearings are conducted by a hearing officer.

Access to documents (Article 27(2) of Regulation 1/2003 and Articles 15 and 16 of Regulation 773/2004) (C-51/92 Hercules)

The principle that interested parties should have access to all files held by the Commission is subject to three exceptions concerning:

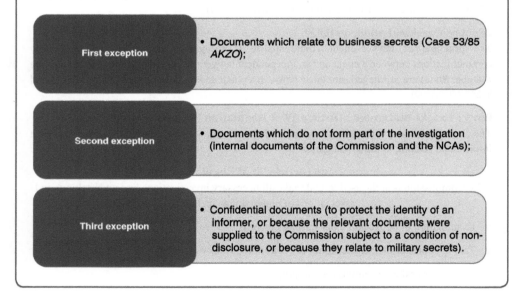

First exception	• Documents which relate to business secrets (Case 53/85 *AKZO*);
Second exception	• Documents which do not form part of the investigation (internal documents of the Commission and the NCAs);
Third exception	• Confidential documents (to protect the identity of an informer, or because the relevant documents were supplied to the Commission subject to a condition of non-disclosure, or because they relate to military secrets).

Fines that the Commission may impose on undertakings

Procedural fines	Periodic penalty payments	"Substantive" fines
Up to 1 per cent of the undertaking's total turnover in the preceding business year. These may be imposed on an undertaking which refuses to supply information, or when it provides incorrect or misleading information intentionally or negligently, or in other circumstances set out in Article 23(1) of Regulation 1/2003	Not exceeding 5 per cent of the average daily turnover in the preceding business year and calculated from the date fixed by the Commission decision. These may be imposed at a daily rate during continued defiance of the Commission decision. Article 24 provides a list of circumstances in which the Commission may impose the periodic penalty payments	Under Article 23(2) of Regulation 1/2003 the Commission is empowered to impose fines for substantive infringements (either intentional or negligent) of Articles 101 or 102 TFEU, of a decision ordering interim measures under Article 8, or for failure to comply with a commitment made binding by a decision pursuant to Article 9

2006 EU Leniency Programme

The main objective of the Programme is to provide an incentive to an undertaking participating in an unlawful cartel to come forward and to expose the cartel. The incentive is to offer immunity from, or a reduction in, the fine that would be applicable to the undertaking had the cartel been discovered without the undertaking's assistance.

Co-operation in enforcement of Articles 101 and 102 TFEU

Co-operation between NCAs and the Commission
This concerns:
- Allocation of cases;
- Exchange of information;
- Consultations.

Co-operation between NCAs
This is in respect of:
- Allocation of cases;
- Exchange of information, but there are safeguards aimed at protecting individuals and undertakings against the misuse of exchanged information.

Co-operation between the Commission and national courts
This is provided for in Articles 15 and 16 of Regulation 1/2003 and in the 2004 Commission Notice on Co-operation between the Commission and the Courts of the EU Member States in the Application of Articles [101 and 102 TFEU].

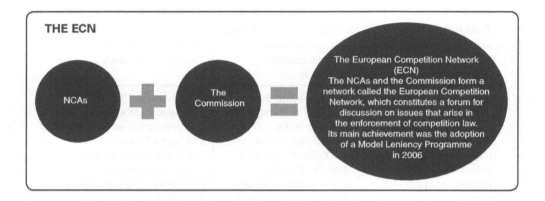

THE ECN

NCAs + The Commission =

The European Competition Network (ECN)
The NCAs and the Commission form a network called the European Competition Network, which constitutes a forum for discussion on issues that arise in the enforcement of competition law. Its main achievement was the adoption of a Model Leniency Programme in 2006

31

THE AREA OF FREEDOM, SECURITY AND JUSTICE (AFSJ)

CHAPTER OUTLINE

1. The European Tampere Council of 1999 launched one of the most ambitious projects of the EU, i.e. the creation of an AFSJ throughout the EU. The ToL greatly advanced the development of the AFSJ by incorporating provisions of Pillar 3 of the TEU into the TFEU, including the Schengen acquis, and thus ensuring that the "EU method" applies to the adoption of measures relating to the AFSJ. Such measures concern the following policies: asylum; immigration; visas; border controls; judicial co-operation in civil matters; and, judicial and police co-operation in criminal matters.

2 The ToL confirmed and expanded the differing participation of Denmark, Ireland and the UK in measures relating to the AFSJ in that those Member States are allowed to opt-out of participation in the adoption of intended measures or amendments to the existing measures, previously accepted by them as binding.

3. The Schengen system in which not only the Member States of the EU (apart from the UK and Ireland) participate, but also non-EU European States, creates a territory without internal borders between participating States whilst establishing common rules relating to the crossing of the external border. In order to ensure that the Schengen system works properly, the participating States have established a common visa policy for non-EU nationals and common rules for asylum seekers; enhanced police and customs co-operation; reinforced judicial co-operation in criminal matters; and, established the Schengen Information System (SIS).

4. The creation of the AFSJ entails a great deal of co-operation between the Member States in civil and criminal matters. This is based either on the principle of mutual recognition or the establishment of common rules in civil and criminal matters.

5. Judicial co-operation in criminal matters is effected *via* the European Judicial Network (EJN), and Eurojust. It may be further enhanced by the creation of a European Prosecutor's Office as envisaged in Article 86 TFEU.

6. Police co-operation involves operational co-operation (Article 89 TFEU); exchange of information: joint training; and, so on. The European Police Office (Europol) is in charge of improving and developing co-operation between national police forces.

31.1 Introduction

The creation of an AFSJ constitutes one of the objectives of the EU set out in Article 3(2) TEU, and certainly it is as ambitious as was the creation of the internal market. By setting the objective of the creation of the AFSJ, the ToL confirmed that the safety and well-being of EU citizens are at the centre of EU concerns.

The creation of the AFSJ was initiated by the European Tampere Council (October 1999), which adopted a five-year programme, called the Tampere Programme, defining the priority areas, specific objectives and a timetable for implementing these objectives. The Tampere Programme expired in June 2004.[2805] In 2010 the Hague Programme, which had been agreed by the European Hague Council in November 2004, expired and was replaced by the Stockholm Programme, adopted by the European Council in December 2009. The Stockholm Programme contains 170 initiatives to be translated into concrete proposals, which if adopted, should be implemented by the end of 2014. The Commission has prepared 10 proposals which cover many aspects of the AFSJ, i.e. from proposals on fighting cybercrime, border control, and asylum, to proposals concerning the choice of law in divorce proceedings for a couple with differing nationalities.[2806]

To achieve the objective of the creation of the AFSJ, the ToL incorporated the provisions of Pillar 3 created by the Treaty of Maastricht (including the Schengen system) into the TFEU and thus the "EU method" applies to them. As a result, the ordinary legislative procedure under which the Commission has the exclusive right to initiate legislative proposals, and legislation is adopted jointly by the EP and the Council voting by QMV, has become the general rule in respect of the adoption of measures in the AFSJ. There are, however, exceptions to this rule:

- In respect of measures concerning police and judicial co-operation, the Commission shares the right to initiate legislative proposals with Member States. Under Article 76 TFEU, at least a quarter of Member States acting together can initiate a proposal.

2805. For the assessment of the Tampere Programme by the Commission see: COM(2004) 4002 final.
2806. See MEMO/10/139.

- ▪ A unanimous vote in the Council is required in respect of measures concerning:
  - passports, residence permits, and any other such documents (Article 77(3) TFEU);
  - family law matters with cross-border implications (Article 81(3) TFEU);
  - the establishment of minimum rules concerning "other" (i.e. not expressly mentioned in the article) aspects of criminal procedure (Article 82(2)(d) TFEU);
  - the identification of areas (these are areas which are not expressly mentioned in Article 83(1) TFEU) of serious crime for which the establishment of minimum rules is needed;
  - the establishment of a European Public Prosecutor's Office (Article 86(1) TFEU); and,
  - operational co-operation between national law enforcement authorities (Article 87(3) TFEU) and the limitations under which such authorities may operate in the territory of another Member State (Article 89 TFEU).

Unanimity is required in the European Council in respect of any extension of the mandate of the European Public Prosecutor's Office (Article 86(4) TFEU).

In the areas where unanimity is required the EP is either consulted or must give its consent.

The ECJ has jurisdiction over all measures relating to the creation of the AFSJ. Pre-ToL jurisdictional restrictions have been removed. Additionally, under Article 263 TFEU, the ECJ has jurisdiction to review the legality of Council decisions adopted under the CFSP which impose sanctions on natural or legal persons. However, in the area of police and judicial co-operation in criminal matters, the pre-ToL legislation remains in force until 1 December 2014 unless repealed, amended or annulled meanwhile.[2807] In parallel, until that date the Commission will have no power to bring proceedings against a Member State under Article 258 TFEU in respect of breaches of such legislation. Further, Article 276 TFEU excludes jurisdiction of the ECJ to review the validity or proportionality of operations carried out by the police or other law enforcement agencies of a Member State, or the exercise of responsibilities incumbent of law and order and the safeguarding of internal security. This seems obvious given that the ECJ has never had jurisdiction to review internal situations. This restriction, however, does not prevent the ECJ from ruling on the validity of certain acts of national authorities in the light of EU law and on the interpretation of the relevant EU acts.

The extension of judicial control over the whole of the AFSJ, in particular in respect of police and judicial co-operation in criminal matters (subject to the above mentioned exceptions), is essential to ensure adequate protection of the fundamental rights of alleged offenders and alleged victims. It is to be noted that the urgent preliminary ruling procedure applies to extremely urgent cases relating to the AFSJ (see Chapter 13.4.1). One type of these is expressly mentioned in Article 267(4) TFEU which requires that the ECJ acts with the minimum of delay in a situation where a case pending before a referring court or tribunal concerns a person in custody or deprived of liberty and the answer to the question raised in the referral will be decisive as to the assessment of that person's legal situation (see Chapter 13.4.1).

Under the ToL, national parliaments have been assigned an important role in the AFSJ. Under Article 7(2) of Protocol 2 attached to the ToL they may use the "yellow card" procedure to ensure that a legislative proposal concerning the AFSJ respects the principle of subsidiarity (see Chapter 6.8.2). Under Article 70 TFEU national parliaments are to be informed of the results of evaluations of the implementation of measures adopted in the AFSJ, in particular, of results of evaluation of the implementation of measures aimed at facilitating full application of the principle of mutual recognition in respect of judicial decisions and in respect of the activities of the Standing Committee on Internal Security established under Article 71 TFEU (see Chapter 31.7). National parliaments also have their input in the control (Article 88(2) TFEU) and evaluation of activities of Europol (Article 85(1) TFEU).

2807. Article 10 of Protocol 36 on "Transitional Provisions" attached to the Treaties.

It is submitted that the application of the "EU method" to the AFSJ will result in an increase of efficiency, legal certainty, accountability and democratic control by the EP and national parliaments.

31.2 Opt-out possibilities and other special arrangements applicable to the AFSJ

The ToL did not eliminate the differing participation of the Member States in measures relating to the AFSJ. On the one hand, the ToL allows opt-out possibilities and, on the other, facilitates "enhanced co-operation" (see Chapter 6.9).

The pre-ToL opt-outs are respected and new ones have been granted to the UK, Ireland and Denmark. Under Protocol No. 21 attached to the Treaties "On the Position of the United Kingdom and Ireland in respect of the Area of Freedom, Security and Justice", the opt-out possibilities apply to the entire AFSJ. Protocol No. 22 gives the same right to Denmark. As a result, each of the UK, Ireland and Denmark is entitled to decide, on a case-by-case basis, which pieces of legislation relating to the AFSJ it wishes to adopt. Those three Member States may decide to opt-in during the decision-making stage or later after a measure has already been adopted. Protocol 21 details the consequences of non-participation of the UK and Ireland (the same applies to Denmark under Protocol No. 22) in the amendment of measures in the adoption of which any of the UK, Ireland and Denmark have decided to participate, and by which they are therefore bound. Under Article 4a of Protocol No. 21 if the Council determines that non-participation by the UK and Ireland (this also applies to Denmark) makes the existing measure "inoperable", it may, by QMV, urge those Member States to indicate their desire to participate within two months. If the invitation to participate is not accepted, after the expiry of that period or at the entry into force of the amending measure, whichever is later, the measure will cease to be binding for a non-participating Member State. Under Article 4a(3) of Protocol No. 21 the Council may, by QMV, decide that a non-participating Member State, bears the "direct financial consequences . . . necessarily and unavoidably incurred" resulting from the cessation of its participation in the existing measure. This solution, on the one hand, puts pressure on a non-participating State to participate in a measure, although that State cannot be forced to participate, but on the other, ensures that participating Member States can move forward by ejecting a non-participating Member State from the existing measure. Additionally, a non-participating Member State may be required to pay costs which are necessarily and unavoidably incurred as a direct consequence of its cessation of participation.

The opt-out possibilities from the Schengen system for the UK, Ireland and Denmark have been amended to match those contained in Protocol No. 21 for the UK and Ireland and Protocol No. 22 for Denmark. As a result, these Member States have complete freedom to decide whether to participate in the adoption of a new Schengen measure and in the amendment of any Schengen measure in which they have participated. The consequences of non-participation in the amendment of an existing measure are the same as under Protocol No. 21 for the UK and Ireland and Protocol No. 22 for Denmark.

Protocol No. 19 "On the Schengen Acquis Integrated into the Framework of the EU" also deals with the position of States which participate in the Schengen acquis but which are not Member States of the EU (see Chapter 31.4.2). Those countries are: Iceland, Lichtenstein, Norway and Switzerland. They can participate in Council meetings when it deals with Schengen items and express their views on them but have no voting rights. They are, nevertheless, bound by measures adopted by the Council.

31.3 The definition of the AFSJ

The term "AFSJ" is flexible enough to encompass the following policies: asylum; immigration; visas; border controls; judicial co-operation in civil matters; and, judicial and police co-operation in criminal matters.

There is no definition of the concepts of "freedom", "security" and "justice". With regard to "freedom", Article 3(2) TEU makes reference to freedom of movement of persons thus ensuring that EU citizens are able to move across borders within the area without being subject to border controls. Further, paragraph 6 of the 1998 Vienna Action Plan, which was the first programme document adopted by the Council with a view to creating the AFSJ, specifies that "freedom" means more than freedom of movement, it includes "freedom to live in a law-abiding environment in the knowledge that public authorities are using everything in their individual and collective power (nationally, at the level of the Union and beyond), to combat and contain those who seek to deny or abuse that freedom".[2808] Accordingly, the concept of freedom is linked to the concept of "security", in that it includes freedom from threats posed by criminals. It can be argued that the term "freedom" implicitly includes all freedoms which have been conferred on EU citizens, e.g. the freedom to work in a host Member State, the freedom to provide and receive services, and the freedom to establish a business in a host Member State.

The concept of "security" has a similar meaning as under national law. It means that the EU shall ensure that EU citizens enjoy a high level of internal security, i.e. freedom from crime. However, Article 72 TFEU states that Member States have the main responsibility for the maintenance of law and order and safeguarding of internal security and specifies that "national security remains the sole responsibility of each Member State". As a result, any action at EU level will be complementary and subject to the principle of subsidiarity.

The concept of "justice" was referred to in the Conclusions of the Tampere Presidency as aiming at ensuring that EU citizens "are not discouraged or prevented from exercising their rights"[2809] by divergences and differences between national justice systems. The "justice" dimension of the AFSJ is based on judicial co-operation between Member States. In order to remove obstacles resulting from differences in national justice systems, the EU must ensure that either on the basis of the principle of mutual recognition, or by means of harmonising legislation, judgments and other similar decisions in civil and criminal matters given in one Member State are recognised in another Member State, and that EU citizens have access to justice in respect of matters with a cross-border dimension.

31.4 The Schengen *acquis*

A Protocol attached to the ToA (now Protocol No. 19 attached to the Treaties) incorporated the Schengen *acquis* into the framework of the EU. Apart from opt-out possibilities granted to the UK, Ireland and Denmark and special arrangements for non-EU States participating in the Schengen system, the Schengen *acquis* applies to all Member States. There are no possibilities for opt-outs by candidate States when they join the EU.

31.4.1 A brief history of the Schengen system

An agreement between France and Germany in July 1984 in Saarbrücken on the elimination of frontier controls between the two countries, which was intended as a way of strengthening Franco-German relations, gave birth to the Schengen system. The Benelux countries had already abolished border checks for their nationals. They decided to join the Franco-German project. It resulted in the adoption of the Schengen I Agreement on the gradual abolition of checks at common borders, which was signed on 14 June 1985, between the Benelux countries and France and Germany in Schengen, a small town

---

2808. [1999] OJ C19/1.
2809. Bull. EU, 10-1999, para. 28.

in Luxembourg. It provided that border controls should be abolished on 1 January 1990 between territories of the contracting parties. In order to achieve this objective, working groups were established to draw up necessary measures on the relaxation of border controls and co-ordination of measures strengthening the control of external borders to keep out undesirables by harmonising visa controls, asylum and deportation policies. Issues relevant to internal security such as harmonisation of firearms and ammunition laws, police co-operation in combating illegal trading in drugs and serious international crimes were also addressed. The above work culminated in the adoption of the Schengen Implementing Convention on 19 June 1990 (Schengen II) between the same five contracting States. This Convention entered into force on 26 March 1995.

In the relationship between the Schengen group and the EC, the Commission had the status of observer at the Schengen meetings. The Schengen system was subordinated to EC law by means of the compatibility requirement established in Article 134 of Schengen II, which stated that the Schengen provisions should apply only if they were compatible with EC law. For that reason it was quite easy to incorporate the Schengen system into the EC Treaty. The protocol attached to the ToA provided for the incorporation of the Schengen II agreement into the EU's legal framework. In order to do this, the Council of the European Union, which took over from the Executive Committee set up under the Schengen Agreement, adopted a number of decisions. On 1 May 1999 it established a procedure incorporating the Schengen Secretariat into the General Secretariat of the Council.[2810] The elements of Schengen II which needed to be incorporated into the EC Treaty (the Schengen *acquis*) were defined by a Council decision adopted on 20 May 1999.[2811]

Member States that joined the EU after 1 May 2004 are bound by the Schengen *acquis*, but certain provisions will apply to them only after abolition of border controls at their borders adjacent to States participating in the Schengen system. Such border controls will be abolished when a Member State has passed the preparedness test in respect of four areas: air borders; visas; police co-operation; and, personal data protection. Experts from the EU will assess the level of preparedness by means of questionnaires and visits to selected institutions and places of the country of assessment.

The incorporation of the Schengen system into the framework of the EU means that all principles of EU law are applicable to the Schengen *acquis* and that EU institutions are supervising its proper implementation.

31.4.2 Membership of the Schengen area

As of mid-2012, 26 States fully apply the Schengen *acquis*: 22 EU countries (Austria; Belgium; the Czech Republic; Denmark; Estonia; Finland; France; Germany; Greece; Hungary; Italy; Latvia; Lithuania; Luxembourg; Malta; the Netherlands; Poland; Portugal; Slovakia; Slovenia; Spain; and, Sweden), and four non-EU countries: Norway; Iceland; Switzerland; and, Lichtenstein. Bulgaria and Romania are in the process of joining, whilst Cyprus will join after various political problems have been resolved. The UK and Ireland maintain border controls with other EU countries and are therefore outside the Schengen area. In March 1999 the UK asked to participate in some aspects of Schengen, namely police and legal co-operation in criminal matters; the fight against drugs; and, the Schengen Information System (see below). The Commission gave a favourable opinion on 21 July 1999 and the Council approved on 29 May 2000.[2812] Ireland, because of the existence of a Common Travel Area with no border controls between Ireland and the UK, was unable to implement the Schengen Agreement

---

2810.   [1999] OJ L119/49.
2811.   [1999] OJ L176/1.
2812.   [2000] OJ L131/43.

without terminating the existing agreement with the UK. Ireland asked in June 2000 to participate in the same aspects of Schengen as the UK. The request was approved by the Council in 2002.[2813]

31.4.3 The main features of the Schengen II agreement

The main features of the Schengen II agreement are:

- It creates a territory without internal borders. Between participating countries internal border posts have been closed (and often demolished). Inside the Schengen territory there are no road or rail identity checks. However, when travelling by air, passports or national ID cards must usually be shown. This is not required under the Schengen system but constitutes an international air security measure. There are passport checks between two EU Member States when one of them is a non-Schengen Member State, for example, between the UK and France. As to customs checks between Members of the EU, there are none, but between two Schengen Member States, one of which is not a Member State of the EU, customs controls remain;

- It introduces tight controls on non-EU nationals entering the Schengen territory. These are aimed at eliminating illegal immigration and combating crime. In this respect common rules for crossing external borders and uniform rules and procedures for controls have been adopted by the participating Member States, including harmonisation of rules regarding the conditions of entry and visas for non-EU nationals. A Community Code on the rules governing the movement of persons across borders has been adopted. Its latest version, at the time of writing, is contained in Regulation 810/2009[2814] which provides an opportunity for a third country national to challenge the refusal of a visa, and which establishes common fees for a visa. Its Articles 13, 14 and 15 set out numerous conditions to be satisfied by non-EU nationals when they are entering the Schengen area. A Schengen visa covers all Schengen territory. If non-EU nationals are considered to be unlawfully in one Schengen country, they are deemed to be illegally in all and will be expelled from Schengen territory;

- It strengthens the co-operation between police (including the rights of cross-border surveillance and hot pursuit), immigration, customs and judicial authorities of the participating Member States;

- It provides for common rules for asylum-seekers;[2815]

- It provides for separation in air terminals and ports of people travelling within the Schengen area from those arriving from elsewhere; and,

---

2813. [2002] OJ L 64/20.

2814. [2009] OJ L243/1. The regulation entered into force in April 2010.

2815. The most important provisions relating to asylum are, *inter alia*, contained in Regulation 343/2003 (also known as the Dublin II regulation) establishing the criteria and mechanisms for determining the Member State responsible for examining an asylum application lodged in one of the Member States by a third-country national ([2003] L222/3–23); Directive 2003/9 setting minimum reception conditions for asylum seekers ([2003] L31/18–25); Directive 2004/83 giving the definition of a refugee or person who may obtain subsidiary protection ([2004] L304/12–23); Directive 2005/85 on minimum standards of procedure for granting and withdrawing refugee status ([2005] L326/3–33); Regulation 2725/2000 on Eurodac, a Europe-wide fingerprint database for asylum-seekers ([2000] L316/1–10), Regulation 407/2002 implementing Eurodac ([2002] OJ L62/1–5) and Regulation 439/2010 [2010] OJ L123/11 which established the Asylum Support Office in Valetta, Malta.

■ It sets up a system, known as the Schengen Information System. This is referred to as SIS II. The previous system SIS I was replaced by SIS II by Regulation 1987/2006[2816] because SIS I was designed to accommodate a maximum of 18 Member States and with the enlargement of the EU it needed a major overhaul. SIS II, which is expected to become fully operational in early 2013,[2817] provides for a computerised exchange of information. SIS II allows the placing of alerts concerning persons (wanted, missing, foreign nationals banned from entering the EU and persons to be discreetly monitored by the relevant national authorities) together with a request that a specific action be taken if the person is found. Alerts concerning lost and stolen property can also be placed. The Schengen Member States supply/receive information through national networks (N-SIS II) which are connected online with a central system (C-SIS II), located in Strasbourg. C-SIS II is a hub which provides technical support for the system, that is, it works as an intermediary in the exchange of information.

Although the system is European, the information is national as each participating Member State decides what information it wishes to enter into the alert database.

Within SIS II, any N-SIS II can exchange information directly with another N-SIS II without having to go through C-SIS II and can obtain information additional or supplementary to that provided by C-SIS II *via* the SIRENE (Supplementary Information Request at the National Entries) system. The SIRENE system is the human interface of SIS II. This service is available 24 hours a day, seven days a week. In each Schengen Member State there is a SIRENE Bureau operated by staff who receive and transmit additional data, enforce "alerts" and assist SIS II users. The SIRENE offices are connected with each other *via* SISNET, a sophisticated telecommunication system which ensures that the exchanged information is adequately protected.

Requests for information through SIS II are verified and legally validated.

The electronic data exchange system is the most controversial aspect of the Schengen system as it raises issues relating to data protection and correctness of information. To answer these concerns safeguards have been put in place. First, the Schengen Implementing Convention contains very strict rules as to the categories of alerts that can be entered; the categories of persons who can access SIS II; the purpose for which personal data may be collected; and, the categories of data. Second, monitoring of the proper application of the Convention's rules has been entrusted to an independent body, the Joint Supervisory Authority for the Schengen Information System (JSA), made up of two representatives of each Schengen Member State who are members of national bodies that are in charge of the protection of personal data. Members of JSA may visit sites and have access to all relevant documents.[2818]

In respect of immigration, visas, asylum and checks at external borders many legislative acts have been adopted at EU level. It is outside the scope of this book to examine each of them. However, it should be noted that under the ToL the Member States have all necessary legal tools to develop a common asylum (Article 78(2) TFEU) and immigration policy (Article 79 TFEU) in accordance with the principle of solidarity (Article 89 TFEU).

2816. [2006] OJ L381/4.

2817. See Commission's Report, SEC(2010) 1138 final (accessed 4/11/11).

2818. See: Schengen Information System SIS, http://www.europarl.europa.eu/comparl/libe/elsj/zoom_in/25_en.htm (accessed 10/5/12).

31.5 Mutual recognition and harmonisation in civil and criminal matters

The Tampere European Council (October 1999) endorsed the principle of the mutual recognition of judicial decisions as the foundation of judicial co-operation in both civil and criminal matters. The principle involves a great amount of trust on the part of one Member State in the judicial system of another. Under this principle, courts/relevant authorities in one Member State will recognise a judgment or other similar decision delivered in another Member State in conformity with the legislation of that other Member State.

The difference between mutual recognition and harmonisation is that:

■ Mutual recognition is a regulatory technique aimed at achieving an objective sought at EU level without the need to harmonise Member States' legislation, and thus national law and its peculiarities are maintained. It entails that a Member State will recognise a judgment, or other similar instrument delivered by the relevant authorities of another Member State, in accordance with the laws and regulations of the Member State where the recognition is sought.

■ Harmonisation occurs when the same laws are adopted in all Member States. EU harmonising measures are regulations, directives and decisions. With regard to a regulation, it becomes part of national law at the date specified in that regulation. Consequently pre-existing national legislation which is incompatible with the regulation must be repealed. As to a directive, a Member State is required to achieve the objective it seeks to achieve within the time limit specified in the directive. If this objective has already been achieved, there is no need to legislate; otherwise a Member State must take all necessary measures, for example, it must enact national legislation, to comply with the relevant directive. Decisions enter into effect on the date specified by them. Usually, they require changes in national law.

31.5.1 Judicial co-operation in civil matters having cross-border implications

Judicial co-operation in civil matters having cross-border implications is based on the principle of mutual recognition. The areas in which the EU has competence to act are listed in Article 81(2) TFEU. They are:

■ The mutual recognition and enforcement between Member States of judgments and of decisions in extrajudicial cases. The most important secondary legislation in this area is:
  ● Regulation 44/2001 (the Brussels I Regulation) which ensures the free movement of judgments in civil and commercial matters and regulates jurisdictional rules regarding those judgments;[2819]
  ● Brussels II Regulation,[2820] which ensures the free movement of orders on parental responsibility including orders concerning the return of the child in cases of child abduction within the EU; and,
  ● Regulation 1346/2000[2821] which ensures the free movement of insolvency orders.

In March 2011 the Commission presented two proposals. One on jurisdiction, applicable law and the recognition and enforcement of decisions in matters of matrimonial property regimes,[2822] and the other

---

2819. Regulation 44/2001 [2001] OJ L12/1.
2820. Regulation 2201/2003 [2003] OJ L338/1.
2821. [2000] OJ L160/1.
2822. COM(2011) 126.

on jurisdiction, applicable law and the recognition and enforcement of decisions regarding the property consequences of registered partnerships:[2823]

- The cross-border service of judicial and extrajudicial documents. Regulation 1393/2007 provides rules for the service of documents in civil and commercial cases;[2824]

- The compatibility of the rules applicable in the Member States concerning conflict of laws and of jurisdiction. Two regulations harmonise conflict of law rules: the Rome I Regulation[2825] which replaces the 1980 Rome Convention on the Law Applicable to Contractual Obligations, and which applies to all contracts concluded after 17/12/09, and the Rome II Regulation[2826] which unifies conflict of law rules relating to non-contractual obligations;

- Co-operation in the taking of evidence. This was addressed by Regulation 1206/2001[2827] which applies to civil and commercial matters;

- Effective access to justice. Effective access to justice was improved under Directive 2003/8/EC[2828] which established minimum common rules relating to legal aid for cross-border disputes concerning civil and commercial matters;

- The elimination of obstacles to the proper functioning of civil proceedings, if necessary by promoting the compatibility of the rules on civil procedure applicable in the Member States. Apart from secondary legislation mentioned in the first above bullet point, EU legislation aimed at simplifying the recognition of judgments is: Regulation 805/2004[2829] establishing a European Enforcement Order for Uncontested Claims, Regulation 1896/2006[2830] establishing a European Payment Order, and Regulation 861/2007[2831] establishing a European Small Claims Procedure. All three regulations apply to civil and commercial matters;

- The development of alternative methods of dispute settlement. Directive 2008/52[2832] on mediation concerning disputes relating to civil and commercial matters constitutes the main instruments in this area; and,

- Support for the training of the judiciary and judicial staff. This is facilitated within the framework of the "Civil Justice".[2833]

Direct co-operation between judicial authorities of the Member States in civil and commercial matters was established under Decision 2001/470/EC[2834] as amended by Decision No 568/2009/EC[2835] which created the European judicial network (EJN). It consists of contact points established in each Member State through which judicial authorities of Member States are in direct contact with each other. These

---

2823. COM(2011) 127.
2824. [2007] OJ L324/79.
2825. Reg. 593/2008 [2008] OJ L177/6.
2826. Reg. 864/2007 [2007] OJ L199/40.
2827. [2001] OJ L174/1.
2828. [2003] OJ L26/41–47.
2829. [2004] OJ L143/15.
2830. [2006] OJ L399/1.
2831. [2007] OJ L199/1.
2832. [2008] OJ L136/3.
2833. COM/2011/0551/final.
2834. [2001] OJ L174/25.
2835. [2009] OJ L168/35.

contact points also provide the legal or practical information necessary to help authorities concerned to prepare an effective request for judicial co-operation.

Under the ToL the ordinary legislative procedure is used in the adoption of measures relating to civil and commercial matters with cross-border implications. There is an exception to this regarding the adoption of measures relating to family law. Such measures can only be adopted by the Council acting by unanimity after consulting the EP (Article 81(3) TFEU). However, a *passerelle* clause under Article 81(3) TFEU allows the Council to switch to the ordinary legislative procedure for adoption of measures in aspects of family law to be determined by the Council. A decision by the Council to make a switch must be notified to national parliaments. If none oppose it within 6 months of the date of notification, the Council may adopt the decision. With regard to family law the most important EU legislation is: the Brussels II Regulation and Regulation 4/2009[2836] on jurisdiction, mutual recognition and co-operation as regards maintenance proceedings.

31.5.2 Mutual recognition and harmonisation in criminal matters

31.5.2.1 The application of the principle of mutual recognition to criminal procedure

In respect of criminal law, taking account of the differences between the legal traditions and systems of the Member States, they are prepared to accept harmonising measures consisting of establishing common minimum standards. Thus, they do not wish to harmonise substantive/procedural criminal law beyond the degree required for successful mutual recognition of judgments and decisions delivered by the relevant authorities of other Member States. Article 82 TFEU reflects this reality. It deals with harmonisation of procedural criminal law. It states that any harmonising measure will be adopted "to the extent necessary to facilitate mutual recognition of judgments and judicial decisions and judicial co-operation in criminal matters having a cross-border dimension" and must take account of differences between legal traditions and criminal justice systems of the Member States. Such measures are adopted in accordance with the ordinary legislative procedure in respect of the following aspects of criminal procedure:

- mutual admissibility of evidence;

- the rights of individuals in criminal procedure;

- the rights of victims of crime; and,

- other aspects of criminal procedure which the Council may identify by a decision adopted by unanimity after obtaining consent from the EP.

An emergency brake procedure is provided in Article 82(3) TFEU in that if a Member State considers that a draft measure would affect fundamental aspects of its criminal justice system it may request that the draft measure be referred to the European Council. If this occurs, the ordinary legislative procedure is suspended and the European Council, within four months of the suspension, acting by consensus, may either refer the draft back to the Council, in which case the suspension is terminated and the Council may proceed with the adoption of the measure, or do nothing, or refer the draft back to the Commission, in which cases the draft is deemed not to be adopted. When a draft proposal is referred to the European Council, States other than the State that applied the brake, at least nine of them, may establish enhanced co-operation on the basis of the draft directive concerned during the suspension

---

2836. [2009] OJ L7/1.

period or subsequently if the draft measure is not adopted by the Council. They may proceed after notifying the EP, the Council and the Commission. It is important to note that Article 82(2) TFEU states that the adoption of the minimum rules should not prevent Member States from maintaining or introducing a higher level of protection for individuals than that provided by the minimum rules.

The principle of mutual recognition of decisions in criminal matters has been implemented, *inter alia*, through:

- The adoption of a Framework Decision on the European Arrest Warrant and the Surrender Procedures between Member States[2837] aimed at shortening extradition procedures;

- The adoption of a Framework Decision on the Execution in the European Union of Orders Freezing Property or Evidence;[2838]

- The adoption of Framework Decision 2008/978/JHA[2839] on the European evidence warrant for the purpose of obtaining objects, documents and data for use in proceedings in criminal matters. The warrant allows prosecutors in EU Member States to collect and transfer evidence in cross-border cases;

- The adoption of Framework Decision 2009/315/JHA on the exchange of information on EU citizens' criminal records and its implementing Decision establishing the European Criminal Records Information System;[2840]

- The adoption of Framework Decision 2009/829/JHA on the application, between Member States of the European Union, of the principle of mutual recognition to decisions on supervision measures as an alternative to provisional detention;[2841] and,

- The adoption of Framework Decision 2008/909/JHA on the application of the principle of mutual recognition to judgments in criminal matters imposing custodial sentences or measures depriving of liberty for the purpose of their enforcement in the European Union.[2842]

It is to be noted that two important proposals are under consideration. First, a proposal for a directive on a European Investigation Order, which if adopted in its current form, would replace the Framework Decision on the European Evidence Warrant and those provisions of Framework Decision 2008/978/ JHA which concern the freezing of evidence. Second, a proposal to create a European Protection Order with a view to protecting victims of violence when they move to another Member State. Under the proposal national authorities of a host Member State would be required to recognise protection orders issued on the basis of domestic criminal law in any Member State.

The protection of rights of suspects and accused persons, on the one hand, and of victims of crime, on the other, has been addressed by the EU. With regard to the procedural rights of suspects and accused persons, the 2004 Commission's proposal for a framework Decision on certain procedural rights aimed at improving the procedural safeguards of suspects and accused persons, i.e. at going beyond the basic standards set out in the ECHR, was rejected by the Member States. As a result, the Commission and the Council changed the approach in that each particular aspect of procedural rights, which in the

---

2837. [2002] OJ L190/1.
2838. [2003] OJ L196/45.
2839. [2008] L350/72–92. The Decision entered into force on 19 January 2011.
2840. [2009] OJ L93/23 and 33.
2841. [2009] OJ L294/20.
2842. [2008] OJ L327/27

Commission's view needs to be addressed, has been dealt with in a separate proposal. Under this approach a Framework decision on the right to interpretation and translation for criminal suspects was agreed[2843] in 2010, and further proposals have been made (e.g. relating to legal aid and assistance) and are to be made (e.g. on the presumption of innocence and the burden of proof).

The main measures concerning the protection of victims of crime are: Directive 2004/80 relating to Compensation for Crime Victims, and Framework Decision 2001/220/JHA on the Standing of the Victim in Criminal Proceedings.[2844] Indeed, for victims of crime it is vital that not only the offender is punished but also that the victims can obtain compensation for their suffering. The basic rule is that a victim should sue the offender for compensation. The minimum standard in exercising this right is provided for in the Decision on the Standing of the Victim in Criminal Proceedings.[2845] This decision imposes an obligation on a Member State to ensure that victims of crime can obtain a decision on compensation in the course of criminal proceedings and that the offender provides adequate compensation. However, it may occur that the offender has not been identified, or the offender has no assets or income. In such circumstances the Directive Relating to Compensation for Crime Victims[2846] is of assistance. It sets up a system of co-operation among Member States to facilitate access to compensation. Under the directive a Member State is obliged to set up a national scheme under which victims can obtain fair, easily accessible and appropriate compensation. A victim of crime in a cross-border situation will be compensated in accordance with the national rules of the Member State where compensation is sought.

31.5.2.2   Harmonisation of substantive criminal law

Article 83 TFEU deals with harmonisation of substantive criminal law. Article 83(1) TFEU provides that the EP and the Council may, by means of directives adopted in accordance with the ordinary legislative procedure, establish minimum rules concerning the definition of criminal offences and the sanctions to be imposed for such offences. Only the most serious crimes which have a cross-border dimension will be subject to EU legislation. These are listed in Article 83 TFEU as follows:

- terrorism;

- trafficking in human beings and sexual exploitation of women and children;

- illicit drug trafficking;

- illicit arms trafficking;

- money laundering;

- corruption;

- counterfeiting of means of payment;

- computer crime; and,

- organised crime.

2843. COM(2010) 82.
2844. [2001] OJ L82/1.
2845. [2001] OJ L82/1.
2846. [2004] OJ L261/15.

The Council may, on the basis of a decision adopted by unanimity after obtaining consent from the EP, add to the list of crimes in the light of developments in crime.

Article 83(2) TFEU provides for a legal basis alternative to the above for the adoption of harmonising measures, which define criminal offences and sanctions where this is necessary to "ensure the effective implementation of Union policy in an area which has been subject to harmonising measures". The procedure to be used will be the same as that used for the adoption of the harmonising measure in question, i.e. if a harmonising measure was adopted under the ordinary legislative procedure, then a measure adopted under Article 83(2) TFEU, i.e. defining a criminal offence and sanctions, must also be adopted in accordance with the ordinary legislative procedure. Article 83(2) raises a question as to whether it constitutes the *lex specialis* on the basis of which the EU will be allowed to establish minimum rules relating to criminal offences in areas outside Title IV, or whether that article applies only to Title IV. This matter is important for Member States which have secured for themselves opt-out possibilities from measures relating to the AFSJ. So far the EU has established its competence to adopt rules relating to criminal offences in respect of environmental matters.[2847]

An emergency brake is provided for in Article 83(3) TFEU in respect of measures adopted under Article 82(1) and 82(2) TFEU. However, when a Member State operates the emergency brake the other Member States, at least nine of them, may establish enhanced co-operation in respect of that measure under the same conditions as those specified in Article 82(3) TFEU.

The Council has adopted a number of framework decisions, joint actions and directives in order to approximate the definitions of certain serious offences such as terrorism; drug trafficking; counterfeiting the euro; money laundering; human trafficking; sexual exploitation of children; and, corruption in the private sector.

31.6   Judicial co-operation in criminal matters

Judicial co-operation in criminal matters is facilitated through the European Judicial Network (EJN) and Eurojust. The possibility of creating a European Prosecutor's Office, of which Eurojust is the embryonic form, is provided for in Article 86 TFEU.

31.6.1   The European Judicial Network (EJN)

This network was created in 1998 to improve judicial assistance, in particular in respect of serious crime. It is a decentralised network of contact points that advises and assists judicial authorities in criminal matters. The network comprises:

- the central authorities in each Member State responsible for international judicial co-operation; and,

- one or more contact points, that is, persons appointed by the central authorities to facilitate judicial co-operation between Member States. The contact points are intermediaries providing legal and practical information, first to central authorities in their own Member State, second, to contact points in other Member States and third, to local judicial authorities to help them to prepare a request for judicial co-operation in respect of serious crime or in respect of improving co-operation in general. The Commission is also a contact point for areas within its competence.

2847.   See Case C-176/03 *Commission v Council* [2005] ECR I-7879 and Case C-440/05 *Commission v Council* [2007] ECR I-9097.

31.6.2 The European Prosecutors Co-operation (Eurojust)

This is a permanent body created in 2002 in order to reinforce the fight against serious crime. Eurojust is made up of 27 members (one from each Member State) who are experienced prosecutors, judges or police officers (The College of Eurojust). The objective of Eurojust is to facilitate the optimal co-ordination of actions for investigations and prosecutions regarding serious cross-border and organised crime, in particular by facilitating the execution of international mutual assistance requests, and the implementation of extradition requests. Eurojust organises meetings between investigators and prosecutors from different Member States dealing with a particular crime, or with a specific type of criminality. It may also ask a Member State to start investigation, or prosecution, in respect of specific events. Eurojust actively co-operates with Europol and the European Judicial Network. Article 85 TFEU strengthens the role of Eurojust and assigns to it specific tasks such as:

"(a) the initiation of criminal investigations, as well as proposing the initiation of prosecutions conducted by competent national authorities, particularly those relating to offences against the financial interests of the Union;

(b) the coordination of investigations and prosecutions referred to in point (a);

(c) the strengthening of judicial cooperation, including by resolution of conflicts of jurisdiction and by close cooperation with the European Judicial Network".

However, Eurojust has no power to carry out acts of judicial procedure when it initiates criminal investigations. Article 85(2) specifies that those acts should be carried out by the competent national officials.

31.6.3 European Public Prosecutor's Office

Article 86 TFEU provides for the possibility of the establishment of a European Public Prosecutor (EPP) responsible for investigating and prosecuting perpetrators of, and accomplices in, offences against the financial interests of the EU. It remains to be seen whether the Council will consider it necessary to establish an EPP. The Commission intends to issue a communication on this matter in 2013.[2848]

31.7 The Standing Committee on Internal Security (COSI)

Article 71 TFEU provides for the establishment of a standing committee on internal security. Council Decision 2010/131/EU on setting up the Standing Committee on Operational Co-operation on Internal Security implemented Article 71 TFEU.[2849] The abbreviation chosen for this committee is COSI. It is made up of representatives of the Member States, normally, directors of police and heads of security forces of the Member States. Its main task is to facilitate, promote and strengthen the co-ordination of operational actions between Member States concerning internal security. For that purpose it:

■ prepares joint strategies on how to deal with global threats;

■ evaluates the efficiency of operational co-operation in order to identify any shortcomings and adopts recommendations to deal with them;

2848. [2010] OJ C 115, point 3.1.1 COM(2010) 171.
2849. [2010] OJ L52/50.

- ensures that actions taken by other EU agencies and bodies, e.g. Eurojust, Europol and Frontex, do not overlap; and,

- together with the Political and Security Committee (PSC), assists the Council in the implementation of the "solidarity clause" contained in Article 222 TFEU (see Chapter 2.2), i.e. to provide help and assistance if a Member State is the object of a terrorist attack or a victim of natural or man-made disaster.

COSI is required to regularly report to the Council which, in turn, must inform the EP and national parliaments of the reported activities. COSI is neither empowered to conduct operations nor to prepare legislative acts.

31.8 Police co-operation

Article 87 TFEU provides that common action in the field of police co-operation should include operational co-operation between police, customs and other specialised law enforcement authorities of the Member States to prevent, detect and investigate criminal offences, and to provide for exchange of information, joint training of police forces, and so on.

Police co-operation may take place between national police authorities and through the European Police Office (Europol), which was established in 1992 to deal with Europe-wide criminal investigations. It became fully operational on 1 July 1999. Europol has its headquarters in The Hague and its staff includes representatives of national law enforcement agencies (police, customs, immigration services, and so on). It has no executive powers and thus its officials are not entitled to conduct investigations or to arrest suspects. On 1 January 2010 Europol became an agency of the EU by virtue of Decision 2009/371/JHA of 6 April 2009.[2850] Europol is in charge of improving and developing co-operation between police forces in the following ways:

- by facilitating the exchange of information between national police forces;

- by providing expertise and technical support for investigations and operations carried out within the EU; and,

- by preparing intelligence analysis on the basis of information and intelligence provided by the Member States.

Europol's priorities are to co-ordinate Member States' actions against international money laundering; drug smuggling; illegal imports of nuclear materials; imports of stolen vehicles; illegal immigration networks; trafficking of human beings; sexual exploitation of children; money counterfeiting; and, terrorism. Europol's computer system (TECS) facilitates exchanges of information on persons suspected of criminal activities.

Article 89 TFEU provides for the possibility of police forces of one Member State operating in the territory of another Member State. Under Article 89 TFEU the conditions and limitation of the exercise of this possibility will be established by the Council, acting by unanimity after consulting the EP.

In the context of police co-operation the European Police College (CEPOL) must be mentioned. It is a police academy training senior and middle-rank police officers from the Member States. The emphasis is on the fight against cross-border and organised crime. CEPOL was set up in 2001 and is based at Bramshill, United Kingdom.

2850. [2009] OJ L121/37.

In respect of illegal drugs the European Monitoring Centre for Drugs and Drug Addiction (EMCDDA) was set up in February 1993. It collects, examines and compares data in this area and co-operates with European and international bodies. It has its own computer network, the European Information Network on Drugs and Drug Addiction (REITOX).

RECOMMENDED READING

Books

Baldaccini, A., Guild, E., and Toner, H. (eds.), *Whose Freedom, Security and Justice? EU Immigration and Asylum Law and Policy*, 2007, Oxford: Hart Publishing.

Battjes, H., *European Asylum Law and International Law*, 2006, Leiden: Martinus Nijhoff.

Eckes, C., *EU Counter-Terrorist Policies and Fundamental Rights: The Case of Individual Sanctions*, 2009, Oxford: OUP.

Eckes, C., and Konstadinides, T., *Crime within the Area of Freedom, Security and Justice, A European Public Order*, 2011, Cambridge: CUP.

Peers, S., *EU Justice and Home Affairs Law*, 3rd edn, 2011, Oxford: OUP.

Surhone, L. M., Timpledon, M. T., and Marseke, S. F. (eds.), *Schengen Area*, 2010, Saarbrücken: VDM Verlag Dr. Mueller e.K.

Williams, A., *The Ethos of Europe*, 2010, Cambridge: CUP.

Articles

Acosta, D., "The Good, the Bad, and the Ugly in EU Migration Law", (2009) 11 EJML, 19.

Baldaccini, A., "The Return and Removal of Irregular Migrants under EU Law: An Analysis of the Returns Directive", (2009) 11 EJML, 1.

Marin, L., "A Spectre Is Haunting Europe: European Citizenship in the Area of Freedom, Security, and Justice", (2011) 17 EPL, 70.

Murphy, C., "Fundamental Rights and Security: The Difficult Position of the European Judiciary", (2010) 16 EPL, 289.

Peers, S., "Mission accomplished? EU Justice and Home Affairs Law after the Treaty of Lisbon", (2011) 48 CMLRev., 661.

ESSAY QUESTIONS

1. "Application of the principle of mutual recognition to criminal law might result in the harmonisation of substantive criminal law and criminal procedure of the Member States 'through the back door'." Critically discuss this statement.

2. Explain and critically assess the main features of the Schengen system.

AIDE-MÉMOIRE

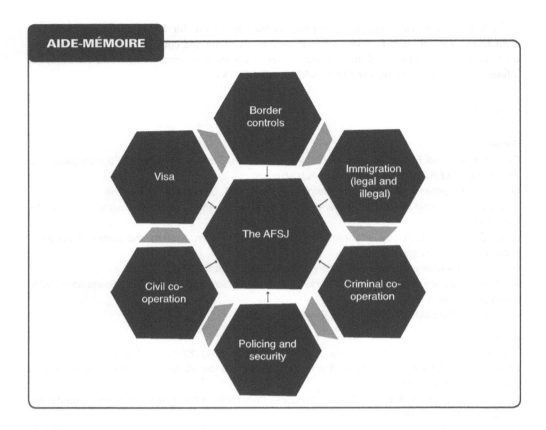

INDEX